HOW TO USE THIS BOOK

CONTENTS

This book contains actual questions that have been asked on the essay portion of the Illinois Bar Exam since 1995. This book also includes practice questions covering the Multistate Bar Exam ("MBE") subjects that were added to the list of testable subjects on the essay exam beginning in July 2007: Constitutional Law, Contracts, Criminal Law and Procedure, Evidence, Real Property, and Torts.

START AT THE END OF EACH SUBJECT SECTION

The Illinois Bar Exam has changed somewhat over time; topics have been tested more heavily or less heavily according to the state bar examiners' determination of which topics are most important for Illinois lawyers to know. Thus, the *most recent questions in this book are the most important* ones for you to study—they are most like the types of questions and topics you will see on your exam. Therefore, we strongly recommend that you start working through questions at the end of each subject section rather than at the beginning.

A NOTE ABOUT OUR ANSWERS

Note that the answers in this book were not written under exam conditions. They generally are better written and more complete than the answers that you will be able to write in the half-hour that you may allot for each question on the exam. Thus, they serve as a guide to what you could or should include in your answer and they are excellent study tools. But when you write practice answers to selected questions in this book (*which you will need to do to prepare for the exam*), do not be discouraged if your answer does not include every issue in the model answer. In many cases, examinees received "5s" (the highest score possible for that question) with a less complete answer, and sometimes with an alternative analysis.

FORMAT OF THE ILLINOIS ESSAY EXAM

A.   MORNING SESSION

The morning session of the exam lasts three hours and includes three essay questions that must be answered in 90 minutes (30 minutes each) and a 90-minute Multistate Performance Test ("MPT"). (Refer to your MPT Workbook for guidance on that part of the exam.) As to the three morning session essays, *all of the MEE topics* (*see* below) plus Equity, Civil Practice, Personal Property, and Sales are testable.

Note: The Illinois Supreme Court Rules also list Administrative Law, Illinois Constitutional Law, Suretyship, and Taxation as possible exam subjects, but questions on these topics have not been asked in decades, and it seems unlikely that the Bar Examiners will stray from this pattern.

B.   AFTERNOON SESSION

The Multistate Essay Exam ("MEE") is given during the afternoon of the Illinois essay day. The MEE consists of six questions, to be answered in three hours (about 30 minutes per question). The MEE can cover any of the following topics, possibly asking about more than one topic per question, but you will not see all of these topics on any one exam:

Agency and Partnership
Commercial Paper
Conflict of Laws*
Constitutional Law
Contracts
Corporations
Criminal Law/Procedure
Evidence

Family Law
Federal Jurisdiction and Procedure
Real Property
Secured Transactions
Torts
Trusts and Future Interests
Wills

*   Conflict of Laws concepts are tested only as a subissue in questions on the other subjects.

barbri®

Illinois Essay Testing

Table of Contents

To be used in conjunction with the Summer 2009 and Winter 2010 BAR/BRI Bar Review Courses

ILT

QUESTION 1

Smith, Jones, and Baker were partners in a consulting business. Approximately 60% of the partnership's work was performed for two major corporations, ABC Inc. and XYZ Inc. The partners did not have a written partnership agreement. They never decided how the management responsibility for the affairs of the partnership was to be allocated or how long the partnership would continue to exist. They always shared the profits and losses of the business equally and did not receive salaries for working in the partnership business.

Although the partnership was very profitable, Smith often disagreed with the other two partners regarding partnership business. When the partnership received a proposal from Newco Inc. to enter into a substantial consulting contract on terms that appeared to be favorable to the partnership, Jones and Baker favored entering into the proposed contract. Smith was opposed and wrote a letter to the other two partners stating that Smith would not agree to any contract with Newco. In spite of Smith's objections, Jones and Baker entered into the contract, purporting to act on behalf of the partnership.

Smith was very upset that Jones and Baker had entered into the contract with Newco. Smith contacted ABC and XYZ and entered into contracts in his own name to do consulting work for them. The work to be done under the contracts was of the same kind the partnership had done for these corporations in the past.

The contract with Newco turned out to be very unprofitable. In contrast, Smith's contracts with ABC and XYZ were very profitable. Smith refused to share the losses under the Newco contract, arguing that those losses were not partnership obligations. In addition, Smith refused to share the profits from the ABC and XYZ contracts with Jones and Baker, arguing that the profits were not partnership profits.

Jones and Baker now plan to enter into a second contract with Newco, on behalf of the partnership, to do additional consulting work. The rate of compensation to the partnership would be greater than in the original contract. Smith wants to prevent them from taking on any new business on behalf of the partnership, and he tells them that, as far as he is concerned, the partnership is at an end.

1. Did Jones and Baker have the right to enter into the original contract with Newco on behalf of the partnership? Explain.

2. May the partnership recover the profits earned by Smith in performing the contracts with ABC and XYZ? Explain.

3. Did Smith terminate the right of Jones and Baker to enter into new contracts with Newco on behalf of the partnership? Explain.

ANSWER TO QUESTION 1

1.   Jones and Baker had the right to enter into the original contract with Newco on behalf of the Smith, Jones, and Baker partnership. At issue is the authority of a partner or partners to bind the partnership in dealings with third parties in the absence of an express agreement defining such authority.

2. AGENCY AND PARTNERSHIP

Partners have an equal right to manage the business of the partnership, absent an agreement to the contrary. [U.P.A. §18] The Smith, Jones, and Baker partnership had no such agreement. A particular act within the ordinary course of partnership business must be approved by **majority vote** of the partners, while unanimous consent is required to authorize certain other acts (*e.g.,* submission to arbitration, assignment for benefit of creditors, confession of judgment, disposition of goodwill of the business, interference with ordinary partnership business). [U.P.A. §9]

Here, Jones and Baker constituted a majority of partners. Their approval of the original Newco contract was sufficient to authorize their entering into it on behalf of the partnership, despite the fact that Smith communicated his objections to Newco, because the contract was within the ordinary course of the business of the partnership. Smith's argument, that the losses under the original Newco contract are not partnership obligations, is erroneous, and he may be held liable for his share of those losses.

2.   The partnership may recover the profits earned by Smith from his individual contracts with ABC and XYZ. The issue is whether Smith owes a duty to the partnership that would require him to account for the benefits he received through these contracts.

Each partner owes a fiduciary duty to the partnership, and one partner will not be allowed to gain for himself at the expense of the partnership. Every partner holds, as trustee for the partnership, any profit made by him without the consent of the other partners from any transaction connected with the conduct of the partnership. [U.P.A. §21]

By entering into the consulting contracts with ABC and XYZ in his own name, Smith took business away from the Smith, Jones, and Baker partnership. In gaining profit at the expense of the partnership, by acts within the scope of the partnership's business and without the other partners' consent, Smith breached his fiduciary duty of loyalty to the partnership. Jones and Baker are entitled to an accounting under these circumstances, and may recover from Smith the profits from his individual contracts with ABC and XYZ.

3.   Smith terminated the right of Jones and Baker to enter into new contracts with Newco because he effectively dissolved the partnership. At issue is whether the other partners may take on new business for a partnership once one partner has declared that the partnership is at an end.

A partner may cause a dissolution by his express will, without violation of any agreement between the parties, when no definite term or particular undertaking is specified. [U.P.A. §31(1)(b)] Absent an agreement to the contrary, the dissolution of a partnership terminates the authority of any partner to act as an agent for the partnership except for the purpose of winding up the affairs of the partnership. [U.P.A. §33] Entering into a new contract is considered new business which is beyond the scope of the partners' authority once a dissolution has occurred. A partner who acts for the partnership after dissolution, other than for the purpose of winding up, is not entitled to copartner contribution for a liability arising from that act, if the acting partner had notice of the dissolution at the time of the act. [U.P.A. §34]

Here, there was no agreement as to the term of the partnership; therefore, it was a partnership at will. Smith was entitled to, and did, cause a dissolution when he informed Jones and Baker that the partnership was at an end. Because the partners had no agreement allowing the continuation of business after dissolution, Jones and Baker no longer have the authority to bind the partnership in a new contract with Newco.

Note, however, that the partnership *may be bound* to any new contract regardless of the dissolution, if Newco did not receive proper notice of the dissolution as required by U.P.A. section 35. Having done business with the partnership in the past, Newco was entitled at least to notice printed in a general circulation newspaper; if Newco was a creditor prior to dissolution, it would be entitled to personal notice of the dissolution. If Jones and Baker did bind the partnership after dissolution, Smith would be liable *to Newco* for his share of any liability, but would *not* be liable *to Jones and Baker.* This is because Jones and Baker already knew of Smith's act of dissolution, yet went beyond their limited authority to wind up, and thus, they had no right to contribution from Smith under U.P.A. section 34

QUESTION 2

For several years, Susan had owned and operated "Susan's Super Service," a combination gasoline station and convenience store. Last year, Susan sold the business to Bart. The contract of sale allowed Bart to continue to use the name "Susan's Super Service" and provided that Susan would continue to manage the business, as Bart's employee, for two years, and would receive a salary plus a commission based on a percentage of the business's gross sales.

Although Susan had always sold cigarettes and other tobacco products when she owned the business, Bart opposed smoking, and therefore instructed Susan to stop carrying any tobacco products. Nonetheless, Susan believed that discontinuing tobacco sales would seriously impair the station's business (and therefore her commission). She felt that she could persuade Bart to change his mind by showing him how profitable such sales were. Thus, Susan continued to place her regular monthly order for tobacco products from Acme Wholesalers. Susan never informed Acme that she no longer owned the station and was purchasing the merchandise on behalf of Bart.

Bart has now learned of Susan's tobacco purchases and refuses to pay Acme's bill. Susan likewise refuses to pay the bill on the ground that it is Bart's store.

1. **Is Susan personally liable for the Acme bill? Explain.**

2. **Is Bart personally liable for the Acme bill? Explain.**

ANSWER TO QUESTION 2

1. *Susan's Liability:* Yes, Susan is liable for the Acme bill. At issue is the liability of an agent for contracts entered into by the agent on behalf of an ***undisclosed principal***.

An agent generally is not personally liable for contracts entered into on behalf of the principal if the principal's existence and identity are known to the third party with whom the agent deals (*i.e.,* a "disclosed principal" situation). However, the agent is liable if the existence and identity of the principal are unknown to the third party (*i.e.,* an "undisclosed principal" situation), because in an undisclosed principal situation, the third party is dealing with the agent as if she were actually a party to the contract.

4.   AGENCY AND PARTNERSHIP

As to Acme, Bart is an undisclosed principal. After Bart bought the station, Susan continued to use the name "Susan's Super Service" and dealt with Acme just as she had in the past when she owned the business. Acme had no reason to know that Susan was not in fact the owner of the station. Acme believed that Susan was making the purchases on her own behalf. Thus, this is an undisclosed principal situation and Susan can be held personally liable for the unpaid bill.

2.   *Bart's Liability:* Yes, Bart is liable for the Acme bill. At issue is a principal's liability on a contract entered into by an agent.

The general rule is that a principal is bound by transactions that (i) an agent enters into on the principal's behalf if the agent had authority or (ii) the principal later ratifies. Authority can be actual or apparent. Actual authority includes the authority expressly granted by the principal to the agent and any authority that the agent reasonably can imply from the express grant. Apparent authority, on the other hand, arises when the principal holds out the agent as having certain authority and a third party enters into a contract with the agent reasonably believing the agent has such authority based on the holding out. Ratification is authority expressly granted after the fact.

In this case, Susan did not have actual authority to make the tobacco purchases because Bart expressly instructed her not to do so. Neither do the facts indicate that Bart ratified the purchases. However, Susan did have apparent authority. Bart has affirmatively held out Susan as the manager of the station, and has continued to use the name "Susan's Super Service" for the business. It is arguable that Bart's failure to take steps to notify persons previously dealing with Susan of the change in ownership even amounts to a holding out of Susan as the owner of the station. A third party dealing with Susan could reasonably believe she had whatever authority a manager or owner would have. Because Susan ordered tobacco products from Acme on previous occasions, it was reasonable for Acme to believe she continued to have authority to make the purchases, notwithstanding Bart's secret limiting instruction to Susan. Thus, Bart is liable on the contract because Susan had apparent authority

Note that Acme may file suit against both the principal and the agent but must elect prior to judgment one person from whom recovery will be sought. Also note that, even though the principal may be liable, he does have a remedy against the agent for damages for her breach of the duty to follow reasonable instructions.

QUESTION 3

Able is in the business of buying and selling rare coins. She buys coins for her inventory mostly at sales conducted by auction houses. Able uses the services of "purchasers," who attend the sales and bid for coins to be added to her inventory. Each of the purchasers signs an agreement, the form of which is reproduced below:

PURCHASER AGREEMENT

The undersigned ("Purchaser") agrees to act on behalf of Able ("Able") as an independent contractor purchaser of rare coins. Purchaser shall attend sales specified by Able and bid on coins from a confidential listing supplied by Able (the "Buy List"), at a price not to exceed the amount shown on the Buy List. Purchaser shall not submit any bid until Able has given telephonic approval for the specific bid.

Purchaser shall contract in the name of Purchaser for such coins, without disclosing the identity of Able. Funds for authorized purchases shall be supplied by wire transfer upon Purchaser's request.

Purchaser shall be compensated for travel expenses at the lesser of (i) Purchaser's actual costs in attending such sales or (ii) a per diem of $150. Purchaser shall also receive a quarterly bonus equal to 25% of the savings effected by Purchaser on coins purchased during each quarter for less than the authorized prices set forth on the Buy List.

This arrangement may be terminated upon notice by either Purchaser or Able.

Baker signed a purchaser agreement. Baker thereafter attended several sales on Able's behalf. At the first sale, Baker located coins on the Buy List. After calling Able for authorization, Baker contracted to buy the coins in his name at prices less than the Buy List prices. Able wired funds allowing Baker to consummate that transaction.

Baker subsequently learned from the other purchasers that, although they have all been informed of the standard policy requiring them to get prior approval, they never call Able for authorization. If a coin is on the Buy List, they buy it if they can get it at or under the Buy List price. None of the other purchasers has ever had a problem getting the funds from Able to complete a purchase. Able has refused to forward the money only when the sale price has exceeded the Buy List price. After learning this information, Baker began purchasing coins at prices below the Buy List prices without Able's prior authorization. Able always supplied Baker with funds to cover these purchases, despite the lack of Able's prior approval.

Last Saturday, Baker attended an auction and found a U.S. 1913 Leaping Liberty quarter in mint, uncirculated condition. The price shown on the current Buy List for a 1913 Leaping Liberty quarter is $50,000. Without calling Able, Baker contracted to buy the coin for $30,000, and now claims a bonus of $5,000 (25% of the difference between the $50,000 Buy List price and the $30,000 contract price).

It turns out that the Buy List was in error. The entry should have read "1913 Leaping Liberty Quarter, mint, uncirculated condition: $20,000."

Able refused to wire the funds to close the transaction.

What is the legal relationship between Able and Baker, and, in light of that relationship, what are the liabilities of Able and Baker to the third-party seller and to one another? Explain.

ANSWER TO QUESTION 3

1. ***Legal Relationship Between Able and Baker:*** Baker is the agent of Able. An agency is a consensual relationship that arises when one person (the "principal") manifests an intention that another person (the "agent") shall act on the principal's behalf.

In order to form an agency, both the principal and the agent must ***consent*** to the relationship. Furthermore, both must have ***capacity***; the principal needs contractual capacity, while the agent must have only minimal mental capacity. In most cases, a writing is not required, although a writing does exist in this case. No other formalities are required.

Under the facts, Able and Baker appear to have consented to an agency relationship by virtue of the signed purchaser agreement—Able did not agree to purchase coins ***from Baker*** (*i.e.*, the agreement did not make Baker a supplier); rather, Able asked Baker to purchase coins from others ***on Able's behalf***. Since nothing indicates that either party was incompetent, an agency relationship was created.

According to the purchaser agreement, Baker is an independent contractor rather than an employee, but the parties' determination is not necessarily binding. The single most important factor in determining whether Baker is an employee or an independent contractor is whether Able, as principal, has the right to control the manner and method in which Baker does his job. An employee is subject to the supervision of the principal in the details of the employee's work, whereas an independent contractor follows his own discretion.

The purchaser agreement requires Baker to attend sales specified by Able, to bid on coins from a listing supplied by Able, to not exceed the price given by Able, and to not submit a bid without Able's approval. The lack of discretion allowed to Baker in purchasing the coins for Able indicates that Baker is subject to Able's supervision and therefore is Able's employee. The right to control overrides even the purchaser agreement's characterization of Baker as an independent contractor. However, the independent contractor/employee distinction does not affect Able's liability here; the distinction is important only in cases of ***tort*** liability, and the issue here is one of ***contractual*** liability.

2.   ***Liability of Able and Baker to Third-Party Seller:*** Able and Baker both are liable to the seller on the contract to purchase the Leaping Liberty quarter. At issue is whether the agent had authority to enter the transaction and under what circumstances an agent and undisclosed principal are liable for such transaction.

First, it is necessary to determine whether Baker was authorized to enter into the contract to purchase the coin. There are three types of authority on which Baker could attempt to rely: ***actual, apparent, and ratification***. Actual authority is that which the agent reasonably believes he has based on the dealings between himself and the principal. Apparent authority arises when the principal "holds out" another as having certain authority, causing the third party to believe that authority exists. Ratification is authority given by the principal by acceptance of a transaction after the transaction has taken place. Because Baker had actual authority, it is unnecessary to discuss the other two types.

There are two types of actual authority: express and implied. Express authority is that specifically contained in the communication from the principal to the agent that grants authority. Implied authority is that which the agent reasonably believes he has based on the actions of the principal.

Baker certainly has actual express authority, pursuant to the purchaser agreement, to enter into contracts to purchase coins on behalf of Able. That authority is subject to certain ***limiting instructions***, *e.g.*, that Baker receive approval of a bid before submitting it, and that Baker not exceed the price on the Buy List. However, because Able has failed to object to a series of prior transactions in which Baker made bids without calling Able, Baker has *implied authority* by acquiescence to submit the bid on the quarter without Able's approval.

The next question is whether Able, Baker, or both are liable on the contract. Generally, both the principal and the agent are liable on a contract entered into by an authorized agent on behalf of an undisclosed principal (*i.e.*, a principal whose existence and identity are unknown to the third party).

Because Baker was authorized, as discussed above, and Able was unknown to the third-party seller as required by the purchaser agreement, both would be liable to the seller. Able would be liable as the principal, and Baker would be liable as if he were actually a party to the contract, because the third party dealt with Baker as if Baker were purchasing the coin on his own behalf, rather than as an agent for someone else.

3.   *Able's and Baker's Liability to Each Other:* Baker is entitled to recover his commission and the expenses he incurred in purchasing the quarter for Able. At issue is the principal's duty to compensate and reimburse an agent for expenses or losses incurred in discharging the agent's duties.

The principal owes the agent a duty to indemnify him for any legal liability *reasonably* incurred by the agent in acting for the principal, unless the liability was due to the agent's own fault. As discussed above, Baker had authority to purchase the quarter despite his failure to telephone Able for approval. Able would argue that Baker was not authorized to bid in excess of the value of the quarter; however, the agency agreement specifically provided that the price could not exceed that "*shown* on the Buy List." Baker acted within these instructions. Furthermore, Able could hardly escape her obligation to indemnify Baker based on an error in a list that Able herself provided. Therefore, Able must reimburse Baker for the entire amount of the purchase price.

Able also has a duty to compensate Baker for the 25% quarterly bonus, pursuant to the purchaser agreement. A principal owes the agent a duty to compensate the agent reasonably for his services unless the agent has agreed to act gratuitously. Where the agent has breached his fiduciary duty, the principal may refuse to pay the agent for compensation attributable to the particular transaction in question. For the reasons discussed above, however, Baker is not in breach. As a result, Able is liable to Baker for the $5,000 Baker is claiming under the purchaser agreement.

QUESTION 4

Painter, an internationally renowned artist, lived as a recluse in his secluded villa. His paintings were sold only by a select group of dealers. Agent was Painter's authorized dealer in Lawburg, a large U.S. city. On August 1, when Collector decided to purchase an original work by Painter, she went to Agent's gallery. Prominently displayed on the gallery wall was an elegant certificate, signed by Painter, designating Agent as his exclusive agent in Lawburg, with full authority to enter into any contracts on Painter's behalf for the sale of his paintings.

Painter insisted on retaining possession of all his paintings until they were sold. Therefore, he prepared for use by his dealers an elaborate catalog containing pricing information and photographic reproductions of the paintings. In keeping with standard practice in the art

world, on the front page of the catalog was a statement signed by Painter certifying the catalog's authenticity and declaring that its use was restricted to his authorized agents. Agent allowed Collector to take the catalog home to make her selection.

Unknown to Collector, a bitter dispute over unpaid commissions had been brewing between Agent and Painter, who had grown quite ill. On August 15, Agent received a notice from Painter revoking Agent's authority to act on Painter's behalf. That week, Painter took out a quarter-page advertisement in the *Lawburg Times*, stating that Agent was no longer his authorized agent. Collector never saw, or knew of, the ad. Throughout these developments, Painter's certificate remained displayed on Agent's gallery wall.

On September 1, when Collector returned to Agent's gallery, Painter's certificate was still on display. Collector signed a contract with Agent for the purchase of one of the Painter paintings displayed in the catalog.

1.   Is Collector's September 1 contract binding against Painter? Explain.

2.   If Painter had died two days before the contract was signed, but neither of the parties knew of his death and no public announcement was made of it until September 5, would the contract be binding against Painter's estate? Explain.

ANSWER TO QUESTION 4

1.   Collector's September 1 contract is binding against Painter. The issue in this case is whether Painter validly terminated Agent's authority to act on behalf of Painter. A principal will be bound by the acts of his agent if the agent acted with authority. The facts in this case involve two types of authority—actual and apparent. Actual authority is that authority the agent reasonably believes he possesses based on the principal's dealings with him. Apparent authority is that authority third parties reasonably believe an agent possesses based on the principal's holding out the agent as having such authority. A principal can unilaterally terminate his agent's actual authority by communicating to the agent that the agency is at an end. However, mere communication to the agent is not sufficient to terminate an agent's apparent authority. To terminate an agent's apparent authority, the principal must personally notify third parties he knew had dealings with the agent and must publish notice for all others. Even these steps are not sufficient to terminate apparent authority where a principal has given his agent a writing manifesting the agent's authority. To terminate apparent authority in such cases, the principal must collect the writing from the agent.

In this case, Painter terminated Agent's actual authority in the notice received by Agent on August 15. Even though Painter was unaware of Agent's dealings with Collector, Painter's public notice was not sufficient to terminate Agent's apparent authority because Painter had given Agent writings (the certificate of authority and the catalog) manifesting Agent's authority. Under such circumstances, Painter would have had to recover the writings to prevent Agent from having apparent authority as to people who saw the writings. Since Painter did not collect these writings and Collector was unaware of the public notice, Agent possessed apparent authority to enter into the contract with Collector and Painter is bound by the contract.

2.   The contract would not be binding against Painter's estate. At issue is whether an agent may bind a principal after the principal's death. The general rule is that death or incompetency of the

principal immediately terminates *all* authority of the agent even if the agent and/or third party with whom the agent deals is unaware of the principal's condition. In this case, Painter died two days before the contract was executed. All of Agent's powers terminated as of Painter's death. Agent could not legally bind Painter's estate once Painter died. It is irrelevant that Agent and Collector were unaware of Painter's death. Notice is not required to terminate an agent's powers upon the death of the principal. Therefore, Painter's estate would not be bound by the contract executed two days after Painter's death between Agent and Collector.

QUESTION 5

Wareco is a corporation that operates a small commercial storage warehouse. Pres is the president of Wareco and Sec is the secretary of Wareco. Both Pres and Sec regularly attend board meetings, although neither of them is a director or shareholder of Wareco. At a January 1 board meeting, the Wareco board of directors passed a resolution stating that the president of the corporation may not enter into any contract for over $1 million without the express prior approval of the board of directors.

On February 1, Pres signed a contract as president of Wareco providing that Wareco would purchase a fleet of 50 trucks from Able, Wareco's usual supplier of trucks. The purchase price specified in the contract was $20 million. Able was unaware that the board of directors of Wareco had never approved this transaction, but he did know that Wareco had never owned more than five trucks at any one time. On February 2, the board learned of the contract with Able and immediately repudiated it.

On March 1, Pres proposed to the board of directors of Wareco that the corporation purchase a forklift from Beta. Forklifts are essential to Wareco's business and it owns several of them. Because the board did not believe Wareco needed an additional forklift, it passed a resolution disapproving the proposed purchase. Nevertheless, without the board's knowledge, on March 5, Pres signed a contract as president of Wareco to purchase a forklift from Beta for $2,000. Beta had no knowledge of the board's disapproval. On March 6, the board learned of the contract with Beta and immediately repudiated it.

On April 1, Pres signed a contract as president of Wareco providing that Wareco would purchase a herd of cattle from Rancher for $2 million. Sec, as secretary of Wareco, signed and delivered a document certifying to Rancher that the Wareco board of directors had earlier approved the execution of this contract by Pres in a resolution validly passed at a duly called meeting of the board. Sec attached a copy of the text of the resolution to the certificate. Sec frequently signed such certificates as part of Sec's duties as secretary. In fact, the execution of this contract had not been approved at a board meeting, but instead was previously approved without a meeting by a consent resolution signed by four of the five members of the Wareco board of directors. Rancher was unaware that Sec's certificate was incorrect. On April 2, the board learned of the contract with Rancher and immediately repudiated it.

1.   Can Able recover damages from Wareco? From Pres? Explain.

2.   Can Beta recover damages from Wareco, and, if so, does Wareco have a cause of action against Pres? Explain.

3.   Can Rancher recover damages from Wareco? Explain.

ANSWER TO QUESTION 5

1.   Able cannot recover damages from Wareco, but it can recover damages from Pres. At issue is whether Pres, the president of Wareco, had the power to bind Wareco on a contract to purchase a fleet of trucks for over $1 million.

As a general rule, the authority of a corporate officer is governed by the regular rules of agency. Thus, whether an officer has the power to bind his corporation on a contract depends on whether the officer acted with actual or apparent authority. If the officer acted without authority, the corporation will not be bound unless it ratifies the transaction. If the corporation is not bound, however, the officer can be held liable to the other party to the contract for breach of the implied warranty that the officer acted with authority.

Here, it is clear that Pres lacked actual authority to purchase the fleet of trucks. Actual authority arises from the communications between an agent and a principal. The agent will have whatever actual authority the principal grants the agent plus any authority that reasonably can be implied from the express grant. Here, the corporation expressly prohibited Pres from entering into contracts for $1 million or more without board approval. Thus, Pres lacked actual authority. Neither has the board done anything to ratify the purchase. Thus, Wareco will be bound only if Pres had apparent authority to purchase the trucks.

Pres did not have apparent authority to purchase the fleet of trucks. Apparent authority arises from the communications between third parties and a principal. An agent will have apparent authority to do anything the third party reasonably believes the agent has authority to do based on the principal's communications with the third party. A third party may reasonably assume that a person held out as a corporation's president has authority to enter into ordinary contracts (*i.e.*, those within the ordinary course of the corporation's business operations), secret limiting instructions by the corporation to the president notwithstanding. Here, however, the contract was not an ordinary contract; it was rather extraordinary, and Able knew this. Able entered into the contract to sell Wareco 50 trucks knowing that Wareco had never owned more than five trucks. Under these circumstances, it was not reasonable for Able to assume that Pres had the authority to enter into the contract. Thus, Wareco is not bound, and Able can hold Pres liable for its damages since Pres breached his warranty of authority.

2.   Beta can recover from Wareco and Wareco does have a cause of action against Pres. At issue is whether Pres acted with authority and whether he breached any duty owed to his principal.

As discussed above, a corporation can be bound on a contract entered into by its president if the president had actual authority or apparent authority, or if the corporation ratifies the transaction. Here, Pres did not have actual authority to purchase the forklift because the board specifically prohibited the purchase, but Pres did have apparent authority: Beta could reasonably assume that the president of a warehouse company with several forklifts would have the authority to purchase another forklift for $2,000. Since Beta did not know of the board's prohibition of the purchase, the corporation will be bound because a secret limiting instruction on an agent's actual authority has no effect on the agent's apparent authority.

Pres will be liable to Wareco for any damages it suffers as a result of Pres's contract to purchase the forklift. An agent owes his principal a number of duties, including the duty to follow reasonable instructions. A compensated agent, such as a corporation's president, can be held liable for breaching this duty. Thus, because Pres purchased the forklift when he was told not to, he may be liable to the corporation for damages.

3.   Rancher can recover from Wareco under an apparent authority theory. At issue is whether Pres had the power to bind Wareco on a contract outside the corporation's ordinary course of business where the corporation's secretary incorrectly certified that the contract was authorized by the board.

As discussed above, a principal can be held liable on a contract entered into by an agent if the agent had actual or apparent authority to enter into the contract, or if the principal ratifies the contract. Here, Pres did not have actual authority to enter into the contract because under the law of corporations, officers get their power to act from the board and the board can act only at duly held meetings or through unanimous written consents. Here, there was no meeting, and only four of the five directors signed written consents; thus, Pres lacked actual authority. Neither did the corporation seek to ratify the contract.

Nevertheless, Wareco can be held liable under an apparent authority theory. In a strict sense, the corporation did not hold out Pres as having the authority to enter into the cattle purchase contract since the corporation did not authorize Sec to make such a representation and the purchase of cattle is certainly outside the ordinary course of Wareco's business. However, courts hold principals liable for an agent's misrepresentations if the agent had any type of authority to make the representation. Here, Sec had apparent authority to certify the board's action since that is precisely the duty that corporate secretaries are held out to perform. Thus, Wareco can be held liable for Sec's misrepresentation. This will likely result in the corporation being estopped from denying that Pres lacked the authority to enter into the contract.

QUESTION 6

Peachscrub Circle Limited Partnership ("Peachscrub") is a limited partnership. Peachscrub was formed 10 years ago, and its principal asset is a tract of land that Peachscrub is holding for development. At formation, Peachscrub had one general partner, Termand, Inc. ("Termand"), and eight limited partners.

Two years ago, Termand decided to sell its interest in Peachscrub. One of the limited partners, Jainhinz, Inc. ("Jainhinz"), expressed an interest in taking over for Termand, and eventually Termand and Jainhinz worked out a deal. The contract reflecting that deal provided that:

- **Jainhinz would acquire all of Termand's interest in Peachscrub in return for $3 million in cash, a $2 million nonnegotiable promissory note, and Jainhinz's promise to indemnify Termand from any claims arising out of Termand's role as a general partner;**

- **Jainhinz would become the general partner of Peachscrub; and**

- **Termand would withdraw as a general partner.**

The contract was subject to the approval of the other limited partners and was submitted to them at a properly scheduled partnership meeting. The partners unanimously approved the contract, and the contract took effect 14 months ago.

Six months ago, Jainhinz discovered a serious toxic waste problem in one parcel of the land owned by Peachscrub. The wastes are at a long-abandoned dump site. Peachscrub never

operated the dump, but under applicable federal and state environmental statutes, Peachscrub is nonetheless liable as an "owner" for clean-up costs. Those costs may well bankrupt Peachscrub.

Jainhinz has learned that Termand knew of the waste problem when the Termand-Jainhinz deal was being negotiated. Termand had discovered the problem long after Peachscrub had acquired the land, but had taken no action to address the situation. There is no indication, however, that Termand's inaction made the problem worse.

Termand had never informed Peachscrub's limited partners of the waste problem and had never updated Peachscrub's books and records to reflect the problem. During the Termand-Jainhinz negotiations, Jainhinz never asked any environmental questions, and Termand never volunteered any information. The written contract made no representations in any way connected to the problem.

1. What claim(s), if any, does Jainhinz have against Termand based on the nondisclosure? *Do not consider securities law claims.* Explain.

2. Peachscrub is liable for clean-up costs as an "owner" of the contaminated site, and a government agency asserts that Termand is liable for those costs as a partner of Peachscrub. Termand argues that it has no liability because: (a) there is no "flow through" liability to a partner in a limited partnership; and (b) even if Termand had been liable, its withdrawal as a general partner caused dissolution of the limited partnership, which—coupled with Jainhinz's agreement to indemnify Termand—released Termand from any liabilities it might have had in its capacity as a partner.

Are Termand's arguments valid? *Do not consider federal and state environmental law.* Explain.

ANSWER TO QUESTION 6

1. Jainhinz has a claim against Termand for breach of fiduciary duty. As a general partner, Termand owed the partnership and all partners a fiduciary duty which prohibited it from acting unfairly toward the partnership and the other partners. Termand breached its duty by failing to notify Jainhinz or any other member of the partnership about the toxic waste problem before seeking the limited partners' approval of the Termand-Jainhinz contract.

Termand's failure to disclose also constitutes a fraud. While generally a party to a contract has no duty to disclose material facts, an exception applies if a fiduciary relationship exists between the parties. Where a fiduciary actively conceals a material fact it is under a duty to disclose, failure to do so constitutes a misrepresentation. Here, as a general partner of Peachscrub, Termand owed fiduciary duties to the limited partners. These duties include the duty to disclose "inside information" before selling out to a limited partner who is without knowledge of the inside information. This is analogous to a corporate director's duty to disclose under the "special facts doctrine." Because Termand failed to disclose the toxic waste problem, its actions constituted a fraud against Jainhinz.

2. Termand's arguments that it has no liability for the clean-up costs are not valid.

(a) Termand's first argument—that it is not liable for the clean-up costs because there is no "flow through" liability to a partner in a limited partnership—is not valid. As a general rule, a limited partner is not personally liable for partnership obligations, but a general partner in a limited partnership is personally liable for all partnership obligations. Termand was a general partner of Peachscrub when the liability first arose and thus was liable for the clean-up costs at that time. Relinquishing its general partner status does nothing to change this because a general partner remains liable for partnership obligations incurred while it was a general partner even after leaving the partnership. Consequently, Termand is personally liable for the partnership's clean-up costs of the toxic waste.

(b) Termand's second argument—that it was released from liability for the clean-up costs because its withdrawal as a partner caused a dissolution of the partnership and Jainhinz agreed to indemnify it—is also incorrect. First, there was no dissolution of the limited partnership. A limited partnership will be dissolved upon the withdrawal of a general partner unless all the partners agree in writing to the appointment of any necessary general partners within 90 days of the withdrawal. Here, the partners unanimously approved the contract between Termand and Jainhinz substituting Jainhinz for Termand as general partner (we will assume that the partners approved the contract in writing because the facts do not indicate if such was the case). Thus, the partnership was not dissolved. Even if the partnership were dissolved, Termand would still be liable because, as discussed above, a general partner remains liable for all obligations incurred by the partnership while it was a member of the partnership. The facts indicate that the partnership incurred liability for the toxic waste problem while Termand was a general partner; therefore, Termand remains liable for the clean-up costs.

The second part of Termand's argument that it was released from liability because Jainhinz agreed to indemnify it is invalid because an agreement to indemnify does not release a party from the payment of an obligation. As discussed above, an outgoing partner remains liable on partnership obligations incurred while he was a member of the partnership. The contract agreement between Termand and Jainhinz does not affect Termand's partnership obligations to third parties. Instead, Termand would have to pay for the clean-up costs and then bring an action against Jainhinz for indemnification. Such an action would probably fail because, as discussed above, Termand breached its fiduciary duty.

QUESTION 7

Laura, Tammy, and Sam agreed to open Central Subs, a fast food delicatessen. They each invested $10,000 in Central Subs for its initial expenses, and they agreed that Sam would manage the business and purchase supplies, although the approval of Laura and Tammy would be required for all expenditures over $500. Finally, they agreed that Central Subs' profits and losses would be shared equally among them.

As part of Central Subs' grand opening, promotional flyers were distributed that pictured Sam, Laura, and Tammy and identified them as the owners of the business.

Sam worked hard managing the store. However, one day when Sam was cleaning the bathroom, he negligently left water on the floor, and Karly, a customer, slipped and fell, severely injuring herself. Karly sued Central Subs and the three investors individually, claiming they were responsible for the injuries she had incurred. She demanded $100,000 in damages.

Several weeks later, the store ran out of luncheon meats. Without consulting anyone, Sam walked into Meatco, a nearby butcher shop, and ordered $600 worth of meat. Although Meatco was not the shop where Central Subs usually did business, Meatco agreed to sell Sam the meat on credit when Meatco's owner recognized Sam from the Central Subs promotional flyer.

After several months of operation, Central Subs' business was not profitable, and Laura and Tammy blamed it on Sam's poor management of the store. At the next meeting of the investors, Laura and Tammy told Sam that they were closing down the business and that his job at the store was terminated. They also told him to return to the store after the meeting to drop off all of Central Subs' property. They also refused to pay Meatco's bill, claiming that Sam had exceeded his authority by making the purchase without their approval.

Immediately after the meeting, while he was driving back to the store to drop off Central Subs' property, Sam negligently ran over Pat, a pedestrian, causing Pat serious physical harm. Pat filed suit against Central Subs and the three investors individually for tort damages. Meatco also filed suit against Central Subs and the three investors individually for the amount of its unpaid bill.

Can Karly, Meatco, and Pat each recover from Central Subs? Explain. From the investors individually? Explain.

ANSWER TO QUESTION 7

Karly, Meatco, and Pat can each recover. At issue is the liability of partners for obligations of a partnership.

Although each potential plaintiff here presents a slightly different issue, there are a few general liability rules applicable to all three plaintiffs. It should first be noted that Central Subs is a partnership. Although the facts do not indicate whether Laura, Tammy, and Sam formally called their business a partnership, such an express statement is not necessary. Under the Uniform Partnership Act ("U.P.A."), an association of two or more persons to carry on as co-owners a business for profit is a partnership. Here, Laura, Tammy, and Sam agreed to contribute money to start a fast food deli. It could be argued that Laura and Tammy merely loaned Sam money to start a deli, since day-to-day management was vested in Sam, but this is unlikely. Laura and Tammy retained management power by requiring Sam to consult them before making expenditures over $500. Thus, they look more like partners than creditors. Moreover, the three agreed to share profits and losses. Under the U.P.A., such an agreement is prima facie evidence of partnership.

In a partnership each partner is personally and individually liable for the entire amount of any obligation of the partnership, whether arising from tort or contract. In most states, partners are jointly liable for contract obligations (which means that each partner must be served individually), but liability in tort is joint and several (i.e., an action for the full obligation can be brought against one or more partners or the partnership, but a judgment is not binding on a partner unless he is personally served). The rules are a little different in states following the Revised Uniform Partnership Act ("R.U.P.A."). In those states, partners are not personally liable for partnership obligations unless the partnership fails to satisfy a judgment or is bankrupt.

In determining what claims are claims against a partnership, ordinary agency rules apply: Every partner is an agent of the partnership for the purpose of carrying on its business. The act of any partner carrying on in the usual way the business of the partnership will bind the partnership, and this is true with regard to both contract and tort.

Karly: The partnership and each partner can be held liable for Karly's injuries arising from Sam's alleged negligence. As discussed above, agency rules govern the liability of a partnership for torts occurring within the course of the partnership's business. Karly was injured while inside the partnership's restaurant. The injury allegedly arose from Sam's negligent act of leaving water on the floor. Since Sam's negligence occurred while performing duties within the scope of the partnership's business, the partnership and each individual partner can be held liable for Karly's injuries.

Meatco: Meatco can hold the partnership and the partners liable on the contract even though Sam exceeded his actual authority.

As discussed above, a partnership will be bound by the acts of a partner carrying on the business of the partnership. Here, Sam purchased meat from Meatco for the deli. The partnership's business is to operate a fast food deli. Purchasing meat appears to be an act needed to carry on the business of the partnership. While Meatco had not previously done business with the partnership, Sam was held out publicly as a partner, and thus had apparent authority to buy meat for the partnership. The fact that the purchase exceeded Sam's actual authority is unavailing. Under agency principles, apparent authority cannot be limited by secret limiting instructions from a principal to an agent.

Pat: Pat can also hold the partnership and the partners individually liable. At issue is the liability of a partnership for negligent acts of a partner occurring after dissolution but before the winding up of the partnership's business.

The general rules discussed above apply here: The partners are liable for torts committed within the scope of the partnership's business. The main issue with regard to Pat is whether Sam was acting for the partnership when he injured Pat. The answer is yes. Although the partners had just dissolved the partnership, a partnership does not cease to exist at dissolution, but rather at the conclusion of winding up the partnership's affairs. Immediately after the dissolution, Sam was instructed to drive to the partnership's place of business to return partnership property there. It was on this trip that he injured Pat. Thus, Sam injured Pat while acting for the partnership, and the partnership can be held liable.

QUESTION 8

Ashley, Bill, and Diane are equal partners in ABD Partnership, which manufactures computer components, including keyboards. Ashley supervises the factory, Bill supervises the sales force, and Diane is responsible for the financial management of the business.

Ashley and Diane are concerned about Bill's dealings with XYZ Computer Components, the partnership's most direct competitor. Two years ago, ABD Partnership wanted to sell some used manufacturing equipment valued at $250,000. ABD had an established policy of not selling used equipment to its competitors. Without the knowledge or consent of Ashley and Diane, Bill sold the equipment to XYZ for $275,000. Acquisition of the ABD equipment

enabled XYZ to bid successfully against ABD for a profitable government contract. When Ashley and Diane learned of the sale, they became very angry and confronted Bill. Bill claimed he believed that the premium price paid by XYZ justified the sale.

Several months later, Bill developed an improved keyboard configuration for disabled computer users who suffer from limited hand and arm mobility. Bill had developed the configuration to accommodate his disabled child. He worked on the keyboard at home in his spare time, without using any of ABD's facilities. Bill obtained a patent on the special keyboard in his own name, and then he entered into a partnership with XYZ, called B-XYZ Partnership, to manufacture it.

Ashley and Diane recently learned of Bill's patent for the special keyboard. They criticize him for obtaining the patent in his own name and for forming the partnership with XYZ. Bill correctly points out that he developed the keyboard on his own time and that XYZ is in the business of manufacturing computers to accommodate people with disabilities, while ABD is not in that line of business.

1.   Did Bill violate any duties to ABD Partnership by selling the surplus equipment to XYZ? Explain.

2.   What rights, if any, does ABD Partnership have in the patent for the special keyboard obtained by Bill? Explain.

3.   Did Bill breach any duties to ABD Partnership by entering into B-XYZ Partnership, and, if so, must he account to ABD Partnership for any portion of the profits received by B-XYZ Partnership derived from the sale of the computer keyboards designed to accommodate the disabled? Explain.

ANSWER TO QUESTION 8

1.   Bill violated his fiduciary duty owed to the partnership by selling the surplus equipment to XYZ. Each partner owes a fiduciary duty to the partnership. Bill violated the duties of care and obedience by not consulting with his partners before selling the property, especially because the partnership policy was not to sell property to competitors. By not discussing the sale with Ashley and Diane, Bill breached his fiduciary duty.

2.   ABD does not have any rights in Bill's patent of the special keyboard. At issue is whether the patent is partnership property or Bill's personal property. Generally this is determined by intent of the parties. The court will look at a number of factors to determine intent, such as whether the property was acquired or improved with partnership funds or other partnership resources, and whether the property is closely related to the business of the partnership. Here, Bill developed the keyboard on his own time and with his own resources. Furthermore, his job with the partnership was not to develop products, but rather to supervise the sales staff. Furthermore, ABD was in the business of *manufacturing* computer components and not designing them. In sum, it seems that the patent is Bill's personal property and does not belong to the partnership.

3.   Bill breached his fiduciary duty by entering into the partnership with XYZ. The fiduciary duty is one of utmost good faith and fair dealing. Here, because the keyboard Bill patented was

so closely related to the products offered by ABD, Bill owed a duty to ABD to offer the patent to ABD before offering it to others. His failure to do so results in a breach. Where a partner personally profits at the expense of his partnership, he must account to the partnership for those profits. Because Bill breached his fiduciary duty, his profits from the keyboard can be seen as coming at the expense of the partnership, and, therefore, he must account to ABD for those profits.

QUESTION 9

Sam, Jake, and Bill are partners in a dry cleaning business. At the time the partnership was created, the three executed a written partnership agreement. The agreement recites that the partnership is being formed for the purpose of operating a dry cleaning business. The partnership agreement also states that each partner has an equal voice in the partnership's operations, will receive an equal share of any partnership profits, and will bear an equal share of any partnership losses. The agreement does not contain any provisions relating to the dissolution of the partnership and is silent on the duration of the partnership.

Lately the partnership has been losing money, and relations among Sam, Jake, and Bill have deteriorated. Bill believes that the business judgment of Sam and Jake is poor.

On April 15, the partnership contracted with Hotel to dry clean drapes from Hotel's guest rooms under a phased delivery schedule that would last until June 30. The partnership expects to make a profit on this contract, payment for which is to be made by Hotel on July 15. In the meantime, the partnership has to pay the cost of performing the contract out of current operating capital.

On May 1, Bill sent separate letters to Sam and Jake stating that Bill was "ending" the partnership. The letters stated that Bill would no longer be bound by any actions of Sam and Jake, demanded that Sam and Jake immediately cease transacting any business whatsoever on behalf of the partnership, and stated that Bill would not be responsible for any expenses incurred or losses suffered by the business after May 5.

1. **What is the effect of Bill's May 1 letters on the ability of the partnership to continue to conduct business, on the allocation of its future profits, and on Bill's continuing liability for expenses or losses? Explain.**

2. **Is Bill liable to Sam and Jake for wrongful dissolution of the partnership? Explain.**

ANSWER TO QUESTION 9

1.   The effect of Bill's letters was to dissolve the partnership. Under the Uniform Partnership Act ("U.P.A."), a partner may dissolve a partnership at will at any time. A partnership will be considered to be a partnership at will unless the partnership agreement states that the partnership will last for a specified time or until a particular undertaking is completed. Here, the partnership agreement did not specify the time that the partnership was to last; it merely stated that the partnership was to carry on a dry cleaning business. Since this is not a particular undertaking, the partnership is a partnership at will and Bill had the power and the right to dissolve it. However, dissolution is not the end of the partnership.

Under the U.P.A., dissolution does not end the partnership, it merely changes the relationship of the parties. After dissolution the partners must wind up the business of the partnership. They are not allowed to take on any new business, but they may fulfill the contractual obligations that have already been made. Thus, the letters have no effect on Sam and Jake's ability to complete the contracts already made. Future profits that the partnership will make on the Hotel dry cleaning contract are also unaffected by the letters, and Bill will be liable for his share of any losses that arise from the existing contracts. However, if Sam and Jake enter into any new business, Bill would not be liable for those debts provided Bill gives proper notice of his withdrawal (personal notice to creditors of their partnership and public notice to others).

2.   Bill is not liable for wrongful dissolution. In a partnership at will, a partner has the right to dissolve at any time. No reason need be given for the dissolution, and the partner is not liable to the other partners since dissolution of a partnership at will is not wrongful. As discussed above, the partnership here was a partnership at will. Thus, Bill had the power and the right to dissolve the partnership and is not liable for wrongful dissolution. It should be noted that had the partnership been for a particular time or for the completion of a particular project, Bill would still have the power to dissolve the relationship at any time, but dissolution would be wrongful if it occurred before the time stated or completion of the project. In that case, Bill would be liable for wrongful dissolution, but that is not the case here.

QUESTION 10

In 1992, XYZ limited partnership was formed in Central State by the proper filing of all necessary documents. XYZ's limited partnership agreement provided that it would engage in the purchase and sale of rare uncut blue diamonds. The partnership agreement further provided that the agreement could be amended only by the affirmative vote of 60% of the limited partnership interests.

XYZ has one general partner, GemCorp (a properly organized corporation), and three limited partners, individuals named Bill, David, and Emily. The three limited partners hold equal percentages of XYZ limited partnership interests. GemCorp is wholly owned by Bill, who is GemCorp's only officer and director. Bill's ownership of GemCorp has been disclosed to David and Emily. All corporate formalities have been complied with in the operation of GemCorp.

In addition to being the general partner of XYZ, GemCorp operates a number of other businesses including one that purchases and sells rare gemstones. XYZ's limited partnership agreement includes a provision permitting GemCorp to engage in its other businesses without offering any business opportunities to XYZ. However, it is silent about whether GemCorp can enter into business transactions with XYZ.

From 1992 until January 1996, XYZ built a successful diamond business and was a profitable and harmonious enterprise for all of the partners.

In 1992, GemCorp purchased three virtually identical lots of uncut rare blue diamonds for $1 million per lot from a well-known international dealer. In 1993, GemCorp sold one of the lots to an unrelated third party for $2 million. In 1994, GemCorp sold the second lot for $3 million to another unrelated third party. During 1995, vast quantities of uncut blue diamonds began to flood the market. **By January 1996, the diamond market was in chaos and the price of uncut blue diamonds had dropped by 90%.**

Shortly thereafter, GemCorp sold the third lot of uncut blue diamonds to XYZ for $5 million.

Central State has adopted the Revised Uniform Limited Partnership Act (1976) with the 1985 amendments (the "RULPA") and the Uniform Partnership Act ("UPA").

1. **On what basis, if any, could the XYZ limited partners challenge the actions of GemCorp in selling the blue diamonds to XYZ? Explain.**

2. **Are the claims of the XYZ limited partners against GemCorp derivative or direct, and what procedural steps, if any, must they take prior to bringing a claim? Explain.**

3. **What actions, if any, could GemCorp have taken before the sale to eliminate any potential liability it might have to the XYZ limited partners? Explain.**

4. **On what basis, if any, could Bill be found individually liable to the other limited partners for the sale of the blue diamonds to the partnership? Explain.**

ANSWER TO QUESTION 10

1.   The XYZ limited partners can challenge GemCorp's sale of the blue diamonds to XYZ on the basis of breach of fiduciary duty. Each partner owes a fiduciary duty to the partnership. That is, each partner must exercise partnership powers for the benefit of the partnership and not for the partner alone. In this case, GemCorp was a general partner of XYZ. It sold the blue diamonds to XYZ for $5 million when the price of blue diamonds had dropped by 90%. Thus, GemCorp breached its fiduciary duty by entering into a transaction with XYZ that benefited GemCorp and was unfair to XYZ.

2.   The claim of the XYZ limited partners against GemCorp is derivative. GemCorp breached a fiduciary duty owed to XYZ by selling XYZ the blue diamonds at an inflated price; thus the partnership was damaged. Any loss suffered by the limited partners is derived from the loss suffered by the partnership. Therefore, the claim of the limited partners is derivative.

A limited partner may bring an action in the right of the limited partnership to recover a judgment in its favor if the general partner refuses to do so, or if an effort to cause the general partner to do so is not likely to succeed. Here, the limited partners may bring the action against GemCorp because GemCorp, as the general partner, will not bring the action against itself, and an effort to cause GemCorp to do so will likely not succeed.

3.   To have eliminated any potential liability after the sale of the blue diamonds to XYZ, GemCorp should have disclosed the terms of the sale and the market conditions, including the 90% drop in the price of blue diamonds to David and Emily *before* the sale. At that point, David and Emily could have made an informed decision whether to buy the diamonds and at what price.

In addition, GemCorp could have eliminated any liability by amending the partnership agreement prior to the sale to provide that GemCorp can enter into transactions with XYZ on terms more favorable to GemCorp. Such an amendment would have required the vote of 60% of the limited partnership interests. In this case, Bill, as the owner of GemCorp, should have abstained from voting and allowed David and Emily to approve the amendment. To have eliminated any later charges by the limited partners that they were tricked into voting for the amendment, GemCorp should have disclosed the terms of the blue diamond sale to the limited partners prior to their amendment vote.

4.   Bill most likely will not be personally liable to the limited partners solely because of his role as the owner of GemCorp, the general partner of XYZ. The limited partnership act provides that a limited partner is not liable beyond his contribution for obligations of the limited partnership to third parties. The act does not address whether a limited partner can be held liable beyond his contribution if a claim is made by the limited partners. However, in this case the limited partners were aware that Bill was the owner of GemCorp. As such, Bill should not be held personally liable to the limited partners because of his status as the owner of GemCorp.

An argument can be made that Bill will be personally liable not as a limited partner, but as an officer of GemCorp. An officer of a corporation who commits a tort is personally liable to injured third parties. Here, Bill is the only officer of GemCorp and GemCorp breached its fiduciary duty to XYZ by selling the diamonds to it at an inflated price. Therefore, Bill can be held personally liable to the limited partners as the officer of GemCorp.

QUESTION 11

Susan is a talented furniture restorer. Benjamin is a wealthy furniture collector who enjoys buying and selling furniture. Benjamin and Susan agreed to form what they called a "limited partnership." Benjamin would be the limited partner, would contribute $50,000 for working capital, and would contribute an additional $100,000 if needed. Susan would be the general partner, with full authority to buy, restore, and sell furniture, using her own well-equipped workshop and custom tools. They would split the profits as follows: 70% to Benjamin and 30% to Susan until Benjamin received an amount equal to his $50,000 capital contribution plus interest at 11%. Thereafter, the profits would be split 50%-50%.

Benjamin and Susan did not put their agreement in writing or take any other action to formalize it. Benjamin gave Susan $50,000 for the business, and Susan purchased, restored, and sold furniture. After six months of allocating distributions under the 70%-30% formula, Benjamin was repaid his total $50,000 capital contribution and accrued interest. Thereafter, profits were split 50%-50%.

The business has now become so successful that Susan will not need any additional capital from Benjamin. The business has $8,500 in its bank account and has no outstanding debts.

Susan has told Benjamin that she wants to end their business relationship. Benjamin claims that Susan has no right to dissolve the business just as it begins to produce profits. He further claims that if Susan does end the relationship, she must pay him 50% of the cash in the bank account, his share of the goodwill, and an amount equal to 50% of the value of her tools. The tools, which were Susan's before she entered into the agreement with Benjamin, are worth $50,000, and Benjamin asserts that they are assets of the business. Susan denies that Benjamin is entitled to a share of the goodwill, if any, or to 50% of the value of the tools.

1. **Was Benjamin and Susan's business relationship a general partnership, a limited partnership, or neither? Explain.**

2. **Does Susan have the right to end her business relationship with Benjamin? Explain.**

3. **Assuming Susan has the right to end the business relationship, how should Benjamin's claims be resolved? Explain.**

ANSWER TO QUESTION 11

1. The business relationship between Benjamin and Susan was a general partnership. Although Benjamin and Susan agreed to form a limited partnership, a limited partnership was not created because a limited partnership may only be created under specific statutory authority. The Revised Uniform Limited Partnership Act requires, among other things, that a certificate of limited partnership be filed with the secretary of state. Here, the facts indicate that Benjamin and Susan did not put their agreement in writing or take any other action to formalize it. Thus, Benjamin and Susan's relationship was not a limited partnership.

Notwithstanding the fact that Benjamin and Susan did not create a limited partnership, they did create a general partnership. A partnership is an association of two or more persons to carry on as co-owners a business for profit. No formal agreement is required to create a partnership, and it is generally not necessary for a partnership agreement to be in writing. In this case, it is clear that Benjamin and Susan created a partnership although they did not evidence such a relationship in writing. Benjamin and Susan agreed to operate a furniture business with Benjamin providing the working capital and Susan having full authority to operate the business. They further agreed that they would split the profits of the business. The Uniform Partnership Act provides that the receipt by a person of a share of the profits is prima facie evidence that he is a partner in the business (and under the Revised Uniform Partnership Act, a person who receives a share of the profits is presumed to be a partner). Here, the profits would initially be split 70% to Benjamin and 30% to Susan until Benjamin was repaid his capital contribution, and later they would be split 50%-50%. Consequently, a partnership was established between Benjamin and Susan.

2. Susan has the right to end the business relationship with Benjamin. As noted above, the relationship between Benjamin and Susan was a partnership. When no definite term or particular undertaking is specified for a partnership, a partnership at will is created. A partnership at will may be dissolved by the express will of any partner at any time without penalty to the partner dissolving the partnership. Because Benjamin and Susan did not specify a term or particular undertaking for their partnership, Susan has the right to end the business relationship.

3. Benjamin is entitled to 50% of the cash in the bank account and may be entitled to his share of the goodwill of the business, but he is not entitled to 50% of the value of Susan's tools. Dissolution gives to each partner the right to have the business wound up and her share of the surplus paid in cash. Here, Susan has rightfully terminated the partnership and is entitled to have the business liquidated. Because there are no partnership liabilities and Benjamin has been repaid his capital contribution, Benjamin and Susan will split the partnership assets equally per their agreement.

Benjamin is not, however, entitled to receive 50% of the value of Susan's tools because the tools are not partnership property. The controlling factor in determining if property is partnership property is the intent of the partners. Although Susan and Benjamin agreed that Susan would use her tools in conducting partnership business, they did not agree that Susan would make a contribution of the tools to the partnership. If Benjamin and Susan had intended for the tools to become partnership property, why was Susan not repaid the value of her contribution by way of a greater share of the profits as was Benjamin for his capital contribution? Even if the tools are partnership property, Susan contributed the tools to the partnership and is entitled to a return of her capital contribution on dissolution. Thus, whether the tools are partnership property or the separate property of Susan, Benjamin is not entitled to 50% of the value of the tools.

Benjamin may be entitled to his share of the goodwill of the business. "Goodwill" is that value of the business above the value of the business's tangible assets. Benjamin is arguing that the goodwill of the partnership is an asset of the partnership and, as such, he is entitled to one-half of its value. However, Susan may argue that there is no "business" goodwill, but instead the goodwill is attributable to her own reputation and skills as a professional. Assuming that a court finds that there is "business" goodwill, Benjamin will be entitled to one-half of its value.

Benjamin is also entitled to 50% of the partnership bank account because the $8,500 in the account is a profit, which Benjamin and Susan agreed to split equally. Therefore, Benjamin will receive $4,250 from the bank account and he may receive one-half of the value of the goodwill of the business.

QUESTION 12

Dwight L.P. is a properly formed limited partnership created to purchase, renovate, and sell the historic Dwight Building in the downtown preservation district. The sole general partner of Dwight L.P. is Able, Inc. The Dwight L.P. partnership agreement provides that it will continue its operations until such time as the Dwight Building is renovated and sold.

Initially, Able estimated that it would cost $10 million to purchase and renovate the Dwight Building in a way that would maintain its unique architectural elements. Able's financial plan for the limited partnership was to admit limited partners who would contribute a total of $1 million to the partnership and then to obtain an additional $9 million in financing from a bank. Able found 10 local investors who contributed $100,000 each to join the partnership as limited partners. Bank made a loan to Dwight L.P. of $9 million, and Dwight L.P. bought the historic building and began work to renovate it.

Now, one year after formation of Dwight L.P., the Dwight Building renovation project has run into financial difficulty. Able failed to take into account the special requirements that the city imposed on materials and workmanship in the historic district and therefore seriously, but not fraudulently, underestimated the renovation costs of the Dwight Building. As a result, the $10 million financing has been spent, and the renovation is only three-fourths complete. The limited partners have retained a reputable independent architectural consultant who has informed them that the project can be completed for an additional $2.5 million and, upon completion, the building will probably be worth $13.5 million.

In the two weeks since the limited partners and Bank were informed of the financial situation, Bank, Able, and the limited partners have had a series of meetings. Able wants to complete the project but has no capital to contribute. Bank is unwilling to grant another loan to the partnership. Able is pressuring the limited partners to make additional capital contributions to cover the costs of completion. None of the limited partners wants to contribute any additional funds, and they are not obligated to do so under the limited partnership agreement. Able has threatened to dissolve the limited partnership unless the limited partners can come up with the additional funds required within the next 10 days.

Last week, Historical Society contacted Able and offered $10 million to Dwight L.P. to purchase the Dwight Building in its present uncompleted state. Historical Society has full information about the project, and its offer is firm. Because Able does not want to sell the building until it has been fully restored as originally intended, Able has rejected the offer without notifying the limited partners either of the offer or of Able's rejection.

Recently, the limited partners found out about Historical Society's offer and Able's failure to inform them of the offer. The limited partners believe they can no longer trust Able to run the partnership. They are now united in their desire to take one or more of the following actions: (1) dissolve the limited partnership; (2) push for the sale of the Dwight Building to Historical Society; (3) remove Able as general partner and elect a new general partner; or (4) allow Able to continue as general partner but require approval by the limited partners for every action Able takes.

1. Did Able have an obligation to inform the limited partners of Historical Society's offer? Explain.

2. Can Able carry out its threat to dissolve the limited partnership, and, if so, what options, if any, do the limited partners have as a result? Explain.

3. Can the limited partners take each of the four actions listed above without exposing themselves to unlimited liability? Explain.

ANSWER TO QUESTION 12

1.   Able had an obligation to inform the limited partners of Historical Society's offer. The Revised Uniform Limited Partnership Act ("R.U.L.P.A.") does not specifically address whether a general partner has an obligation to inform the limited partners of certain matters before undertaking action, but it does provide that a general partner has all the rights and powers and is subject to all the restrictions and liabilities of a partner in a regular partnership. Under general partnership law, a partner owes the partnership and the other partners a fiduciary duty to exercise its partnership powers for the benefit of the partnership and not for itself alone. This duty would include a duty of a general partner to disclose to the other partners relevant matters that would affect the partnership and the other partners. Here, Able violated its fiduciary duty when it rejected the offer by Historical Society without discussing the offer with the limited partners. In rejecting the offer without discussing it with the limited partners, Able was acting for its own benefit because it did not want to sell the Dwight Building before renovation, even though the sale to Historical Society would have been in Dwight L.P.'s best interest since it had no money to finish the renovations.

2.   Able can carry out its threat to dissolve the limited partnership. A limited partnership will be dissolved by the withdrawal of a general partner unless within 90 days after withdrawal, all

partners agree in writing to continue the partnership and appoint any necessary general partners. A general partner may withdraw at any time by providing written notice to the other partners. However, if the withdrawal is in violation of the partnership agreement, the partner will be liable to the partnership for damages caused by its breach of the partnership agreement. Here, Able has the power to withdraw, but its withdrawal would be in violation of the partnership agreement because the partnership agreement states that the partnership is to continue until the Dwight Building is renovated and sold. Therefore, if Able withdraws, it would be liable to the partnership for damages caused by its wrongful withdrawal.

If Able withdraws from the partnership, the limited partners may agree, within 90 days from Able's withdrawal, to continue the partnership and appoint a general partner. Based on the fact that the limited partners do not wish to contribute more capital to complete the renovation project and the bank is unwilling to lend the necessary capital, it is unlikely that the limited partners would agree to continue the partnership. Consequently, if the limited partners do not agree to continue the partnership, the limited partners would have the right to wind up the partnership. In winding up the partnership, the limited partners would have the right to sell the Dwight Building, pay off creditors, pay back contributions, and divide any profits.

3.   The limited partners can dissolve the partnership, push for the sale of the Dwight Building, or remove Able as a general partner and elect a new general partner without exposure to unlimited liability; however, the limited partners may not allow Able to continue as a general partner and vote on every action it takes without exposing themselves to unlimited liability. Generally, a limited partner is not liable beyond her contribution for the obligations of the limited partnership. However, a limited partner may be liable beyond her contribution if she participates in control of the business. [*Editor's note:* In states that have adopted the 2001 revisions to the U.L.P.A., this is no longer true.] The R.U.L.P.A. does allow a limited partner to take part in extraordinary partnership affairs without being found to have participated in control of the business. Dissolving the partnership, voting for a sale of the partnership assets, and removing a general partner and appointing a new general partner are all extraordinary partnership affairs that the limited partners may participate in without exposure to unlimited liability. On the other hand, the limited partners may not allow Able to continue as a general partner and vote on every action it takes without exposing themselves to general-partner liability. The general partner controls the day-to-day business of the partnership. If the limited partners have to approve every action of the general partner, they will be participating in the control of the business and will expose themselves to unlimited liability as general partners. Note, however, that if the limited partners are participating in control of the business, they are liable as general partners only to those persons who transact business with the limited partnership reasonably believing, based on the limited partners' conduct, that the limited partners are general partners.

QUESTION 13

Three siblings, Andrew, Brenda, and Charles, are equal partners in ABC Partnership, a general partnership, which owns and operates a 2,000-acre farm. ABC does not have a written partnership agreement. The three partners meet periodically to discuss ABC's business but do not hold formal partnership meetings.

Andrew lives on the farm and manages its day-to-day operations. Neither Brenda nor Charles lives on the farm. Brenda owns an accounting business in town and helps keep

ABC's books and records. Charles has an irrigation business in town and helps maintain ABC's irrigation system.

Andrew spent $10,000 to purchase a disease-resistant hybrid seed for the farm. Ordinary seed would have cost $6,000. Andrew purchased the seed in ABC's name, but the $7,000 down payment for the seed was made using his own funds. Charles believes Andrew wasted money on this expensive seed because disease has never been a problem for ABC's farm. Charles is particularly concerned because the balance of the purchase price ($3,000) is due in a month, and ABC does not have sufficient funds to pay the bill. Brenda and Charles never authorized Andrew to buy the more expensive seed and did not ask him to advance his own money for the down payment.

Andrew spends about twice as much time as his siblings conducting ABC business. Andrew has demanded that ABC pay him for the value of his services, although there is no express agreement that any of the partners should be compensated for their services.

Andrew entered into a written agreement with XYZ Farms to swap 500 acres of ABC crop land for 1,000 acres of woodland owned by XYZ that Andrew thinks ABC could divide and develop for a residential subdivision. Charles disagrees with Andrew's plan and is upset that any land would be sold since, in the 50 years that the farm has been operated by the partners' family, no land has ever been transferred. Andrew defends the swap saying, truthfully, that he and Brenda had agreed to the transaction after all three partners had discussed it.

1.   Is Charles liable for any part of the unpaid balance on the seed? Explain.

2.   Is Andrew entitled to reimbursement from the partnership or the partners for the down payment he made on the seed? Explain.

3.   Is Andrew entitled to be paid for the value of all or part of his services to ABC? Explain.

4.   Is the land swap agreement with XYZ Farms binding on ABC? Explain.

ANSWER TO QUESTION 13

1.   Charles is liable for the unpaid balance on the seed. Every partner is an agent of the partnership, and the act of a partner for apparently carrying on in the usual way the business of the partnership will bind the partnership. Here, Andrew managed the day-to-day operations of the farm and appears to have been responsible for purchasing seed. The seller of the seed could reasonably believe that Andrew's purchase of the seed in the partnership name was for carrying on the partnership business and that Andrew, as manager of the farm, had authority to purchase the seed. Thus, even though Andrew's purchase of the disease-resistant seed was not agreed to by all partners, it was within the scope of partnership business and therefore bound the partnership.

If, as indicated in the facts, the partnership does not have sufficient funds to pay the unpaid balance on the seed, then Charles can be held liable for the unpaid balance ($3,000). Each partner is personally and individually liable for contracts made by a partner in the scope of partnership business. Here, Andrew's purchase of the seed was within the scope of partnership business and as such Charles is personally and individually liable therefor. However, under the Uniform Partnership Act, partners are *jointly* liable for *contract* obligations of the partnership; *i.e.*, an action cannot be maintained unless all partners are served. (Note that under the Revised Uniform Partnership Act ("R.U.P.A."), partners are *jointly and severally* liable for *all* partnership obligations; *i.e.*, an action may be maintained against any one or more partners.) Because this is a contract action, Charles is jointly (and severally under the R.U.P.A.) liable with Andrew and Brenda for the unpaid balance. If Charles is required to pay the whole of the partnership debt, he may require Andrew and Brenda to contribute their pro rata shares.

2.   Andrew is entitled to reimbursement for the down payment he made on the seed. A partnership must indemnify a partner with respect to payments made by the partner in the ordinary and proper conduct of the partnership's business. Andrew's payment of the $7,000 was within the ordinary and proper conduct of the partnership business because to operate the farm, seed had to be purchased, and as managing partner Andrew was responsible for purchasing the seed. Andrew was not specifically prohibited from purchasing the disease-resistant seed and may have believed that the disease-resistant seed was necessary. Therefore, Andrew may seek reimbursement from the partnership for the $7,000. However, because the partnership is lacking funds to reimburse Andrew, Andrew may require Brenda and Charles to contribute their pro rata shares of the $7,000.

3.   Andrew is not entitled to be paid for the value of all or part of his services to ABC. Absent an agreement to the contrary, a partner is not entitled to remuneration for services rendered to the partnership, except for reasonable compensation for services rendered in winding up the partnership business. Here, Andrew was not winding up the partnership business. Furthermore, the facts specifically state that there was no express agreement that the partners should be compensated for their work. There also are no facts to indicate that there was an implied agreement to compensate Andrew for his services. Thus, Andrew is not entitled to be paid for his services to the partnership.

4.   The land swap agreement with XYZ Farms is not binding on ABC. As stated above, a partner's act will bind the partnership if it was apparently within the scope of partnership business. Andrew's purchase of the 1,000 acres of woodland was not within the scope of partnership business because it was not the business of the farm to buy and sell land, and the land purchased by Andrew was woodland which would be difficult to farm. Also, XYZ could not reasonably believe that Andrew had the authority to purchase the land because the act was not apparently within the scope of the partnership business, which was farming. The fact that Andrew and Brenda agreed to buy the land does not make the agreement binding on ABC because unanimous consent of the partners is needed to engage in business other than that contemplated by the partnership agreement. Here, Andrew's swapping land to develop a residential subdivision is not related to the operation of the farm, and Charles did not consent to the swap; therefore, ABC is not bound by the agreement with XYZ Farms.

QUESTION 14

Principal is an antiques dealer. As is common in the antiques business, Principal acquires inventory by using a group of buyers to purchase antiques on his behalf. Principal pays the buyers a percentage commission on the items they buy for Principal. Principal trains the buyers to be able to evaluate potential purchases and sends them into the field with specific instructions as to the items Principal wants them to buy. The buyers are given credentials

identifying them as buyers for Principal, and they use these credentials to introduce themselves to potential sellers. The buyers, using Principal's contract forms, enter into contracts with sellers.

Agent, one of Principal's buyers, was sent out to purchase antiques for Principal. During the next several months, the following three transactions took place:

Using Principal's credentials, Agent bought an antique church bell for $3,500 from Bellseller, who believed that Agent was acting on behalf of Principal. The church bell was on Principal's acquisition list and the price was within the range authorized by Principal. However, Agent did not intend to purchase the bell for Principal. Instead, Agent bought the bell for Greta, a competing antiques dealer, who had agreed to pay Agent $250 to find such a bell. Agent's intention was to use Greta's money to pay for the bell. Greta rejected the bell. Principal, who has received a demand from Bellseller, has decided he does not want the bell and has refused to pay Bellseller.

Agent had a written authorization from Principal to buy several books, including *Looking Backward* by Edward Bellamy. Agent showed this authorization to Tomeseller, who had a first edition of *Looking Backward.* However, Agent did not tell Tomeseller that Principal had given Agent an oral instruction, not to be disclosed to anyone, that Agent should not pay more than $8,000 for the book. Agent bought the book on Principal's behalf for $12,500. Principal now refuses to pay Tomeseller.

When Principal learned of Agent's transactions with Bellseller and Tomeseller, he decided to stop using Agent as his buyer. Principal sent Agent a letter terminating his agency and asking Agent to return the credentials that Principal had provided to Agent.

Several days after Agent received the letter from Principal, Agent purchased for his own account a whale oil lamp for $5,000 from Lampseller. Agent told Lampseller that the purchase was for Principal's account, showed Lampseller his credentials from Principal, and purchased the lamp using the contract forms provided to him by Principal. Agent did not disclose to Lampseller that Principal had terminated Agent as his buyer. Principal now refuses to pay Lampseller because, at the time of the purchase, Principal had terminated Agent and Agent was no longer Principal's buyer.

Is Principal liable to:

1. Bellseller for the purchase of the church bell? Explain.

2. Tomeseller for the purchase of the book? Explain.

3. Lampseller for the purchase of the whale oil lamp? Explain.

ANSWER TO QUESTION 14

1.   Principal is liable to Bellseller for Agent's purchase of the church bell. A principal is liable to a third party for contracts entered into by an authorized agent. An agent is authorized to act on behalf of a principal if he has actual or apparent authority. Actual authority is that authority which an agent reasonably believes he possesses based on the principal's dealings with him. Apparent authority is that authority which a third party reasonably believes an agent possesses

based on the principal's holding out the agent as having such authority. In this case, Agent had the actual authority to purchase the bell *for Principal*. Agent had an acquisition list prepared by Principal that contained the bell, and the price Agent paid for the bell was within the range actually authorized by Principal. However, Agent did *not* purchase the bell for Principal. Even though Agent purported to purchase the bell for Principal, he in fact purchased it for Greta. Thus, Principal is not liable to Bellseller based on Agent having actual authority because Principal did not give Agent the authority to purchase the bell for Greta.

Notwithstanding Agent's lack of actual authority to purchase the bell, Principal is liable to Bellseller because Agent had the apparent authority to purchase the bell for Principal. Agent purported to act on Principal's behalf in purchasing the bell. Agent had credentials issued by Principal, and he showed those credentials to Bellseller before he purchased the bell. Thus, Bellseller could reasonably believe, based on the credentials shown to Bellseller that were supplied by Principal to Agent, that Agent had the authority to purchase the bell for Principal. Therefore, Principal is liable to Bellseller for Agent's purchase of the bell.

2. Principal is liable to Tomeseller for Agent's purchase of the book. Although Agent did not have the actual authority to purchase the book for $12,500, he had the apparent authority to do so. Agent did not have the actual authority to purchase the book for $12,500 because Principal specifically told him that he should pay no more than $8,000. Agent, however, did have apparent authority to buy the book for $12,500 because Principal gave Agent a written authorization to buy the book; the written authorization contained no limit as to how much Agent could pay for the book; and Agent showed the authorization to Tomeseller. Thus, Tomeseller could reasonably believe, based on the written authorization from Principal, that Agent had the authority to purchase the book for $12,500. Therefore, Principal is liable to Tomeseller for Agent's purchase of the book in the amount of $12,500.

3. Principal is liable to Lampseller for Agent's purchase of the whale oil lamp. Even though Agent had no actual authority to act for Principal, he had the apparent authority to do so. Principal terminated Agent's actual authority when he sent him a letter so indicating. However, Principal did not provide Lampseller with notice of Principal's termination of Agent's authority. Thus, Agent still had the apparent authority to act for Principal because Agent possessed the credentials and form contracts supplied by Principal. Principal did request Agent to return the credentials to him, but Agent never returned the credentials. Agent instead showed the credentials to Lampseller to purchase the lamp; consequently, Lampseller could reasonably believe, based on the credentials and lack of notice of termination of Agent's authority, that Agent had the authority to buy the lamp for Principal. Therefore, Principal is liable to Lampseller for Agent's purchase of the lamp.

QUESTION 15

Several years ago, Bill, Carl, Donna, and several other participants formed a limited partnership named Transitions L.P., which operated a career counseling business. The limited partnership was properly formed, a written limited partnership agreement was properly executed, and all required filings were made in the proper state offices. The certificate of limited partnership and the limited partnership agreement did not modify any default provisions of the Revised Uniform Limited Partnership Act.

Bill is the sole general partner in Transitions. Carl, Donna, and the remaining partners are limited partners. Although the career counseling industry has experienced a rapid boom in the past few years, Transitions's business has not been financially successful and no distributions of profits have been made to the limited partners. As a result, several of the limited partners, including Carl and Donna, are unhappy with Bill's management of Transitions.

Carl decided that the limited partners should reach a consensus on how Transitions's day-to-day business should be conducted and then force Bill to follow their instructions. Carl went to Bill, asking questions about the business operations of the limited partnership and asking to see Transitions's limited partnership records, including a list of the names and addresses of the other partners. Bill refused to answer any of Carl's questions, to allow Carl to examine any limited partnership records, and to provide him with information about the other partners. Bill claims that even if the limited partners all agree to change the way Transitions's business is run, Bill has no obligation to listen to them.

Donna does not believe that Transitions will be able to succeed in business if Bill remains in control. When Carl tells Donna that Bill does not intend to give up management of Transitions, Donna sells her interest in the limited partnership to Edward. Donna informs Bill that she has sold her interest to Edward and that Edward is now a limited partner in Transitions. Bill tells Donna that he does not approve of the sale and that Edward has no rights in the limited partnership and is not a partner.

1. Can Carl and the other limited partners decide how the day-to-day business of Transitions is to be conducted? Explain.

2. What rights, if any, does Carl have to obtain information from Bill about the business operations and records of Transitions? Explain.

3. What rights, if any, did Edward acquire as a purchaser of Donna's interest in Transitions? Explain.

ANSWER TO QUESTION 15

1. Carl and the other limited partners cannot decide how the day-to-day business of Transitions is to be conducted. The issue is whether limited partners have the right to manage the affairs of the limited partnership. A limited partnership is a partnership composed of one or more general partners and one or more limited partners. Generally, the general partners of a limited partnership have the rights of partners in a regular partnership, including the right to manage the limited partnership. General partners also have the liabilities of partners in a regular partnership, including personal liability for the limited partnership's obligations. Limited partners, on the other hand, have limited rights—limited partners do not have the right to manage the partnership but they may vote on specific partnership matters, bring derivative suits, obtain information from the partnership, etc.; consequently, their liability also is generally limited to their partnership contributions. Here, Carl and the other limited partners want to decide how the daily business of Transitions is to be conducted; however, they have no right to do so.

2. Carl has the right to obtain information from Bill about the business operations of Transitions, and he has the right to inspect and copy partnership records. The issue is whether a limited

partner has the right to demand information from a general partner regarding the limited partnership, and whether a limited partner is entitled to access partnership records. Every limited partner has the right to obtain from a general partner, upon reasonable demand, full information respecting the business and financial condition of the limited partnership and other information concerning the limited partnership's affairs. In addition, every limited partner has the right to inspect and copy partnership records that the partnership is required to maintain. A limited partnership must maintain a records office with such records as the certificate of limited partnership, partnership agreement, tax returns for the three most current years, and the names and addresses of the general and limited partners. Here, when Carl asked Bill questions regarding the business operations of Transitions, Bill should have responded to those questions because Carl has the right to obtain information from Bill concerning the business operations of the limited partnership. Also, when Carl asked Bill to see the limited partnership records, including a list of the names and addresses of the other partners, Bill should have allowed him to do so because Carl has the right to inspect and copy partnership records.

3.   The only right Edward acquired as a purchaser of Donna's interest in Transitions is the right to receive distributions to which Donna is entitled. The issue is whether an assignee of a limited partner's interest becomes a limited partner upon assignment and may exercise the rights of a limited partner. A limited partner has an interest in the partnership that may be assigned. A limited partner's assignment of her partnership interest does not entitle the assignee to exercise the rights of a limited partner. An assignee is entitled to receive only the distributions to which the assignor is entitled. An assignee may become a limited partner only if: (i) the partnership agreement gives the assignor authority to convey that right; or (ii) all partners consent. Here, Donna sold/assigned her partnership interest to Edward, but the facts do not indicate that the partnership agreement gave Donna the right to bring in a new limited partner. Moreover, there is no indication that all partners consented to Edward becoming a limited partner—in fact, the facts state that Bill is opposed to the assignment. Therefore, Edward is entitled to receive distributions to which Donna is entitled, but he is not entitled to exercise the rights of a limited partner.

QUESTION 16

Sunrise Lodge is a corporation that develops and operates luxury resort hotels. Sunrise recently began constructing a hotel in East Beach, a beach town on the Atlantic coast of the United States. Sunrise hoped to give the East Beach hotel a local flavor by using local sources for materials.

Sunrise hired Adam to be its interior design agent on the East Beach project. The contract between them, which was for a one-year term, included the following language:

> **Adam has the discretion to make selections for interior floor and wall coverings, works of art, furniture, plumbing fixtures, and lighting fixtures for East Beach hotel, provided that (i) the cost of such purchases does not exceed the budgeted amounts listed in Exhibit A, (ii) all purchases will be made from local vendors, and (iii) the items selected are within the quantity and style guidelines described in Exhibit B. Adam shall inform vendors that purchases are for Sunrise East Beach and should arrange for Sunrise to be billed on a 30-day net basis.**

The style guidelines in Exhibit B include a comprehensive list of themes and styles typical of an Atlantic fishing village like East Beach, including lighthouses, whitewashed wood, lobster traps, wicker furniture, and sailboats.

After hiring Adam, Sunrise sent a letter to prospective local suppliers on Sunrise stationery signed by the Sunrise president, announcing Adam's appointment as follows:

> Sunrise Lodge is delighted to announce the appointment of Adam, a well-known local interior designer, to act on its behalf in the selection of interior floor and wall coverings, works of art, furniture, and plumbing and lighting fixtures for the Sunrise East Beach hotel. We are confident that—working only with local suppliers—Adam will exercise a wonderful creative flair in coming up with just the right look for this exciting project. Know that you deal with Sunrise when you deal with Adam on this project.

During the first months of Adam's one-year term, Adam entered into the following transactions with suppliers who had received Sunrise's letter.

First, Adam contracted with Tahini for the main lobby area of the hotel to be decorated entirely in a Tahitian theme. The items for the Tahitian décor are within the budget and are from a local supplier. However, they are not within the Exhibit B style guidelines.

Second, Adam contracted with Moby for the guest rooms to be decorated using authentic themes from the Atlantic seaboard region as required by Exhibit B. The décor selections are within budget and are from local suppliers, but the Sunrise officials do not like the design.

Sunrise has refused to pay either vendor and has terminated Adam's contract.

1. On what agency principles, if any, is Sunrise liable to Tahini and Moby on their respective contracts? Explain.

2. Is Adam liable to Sunrise as a result of the contracts with Tahini and Moby? Explain.

3. May Sunrise terminate Adam's agency before the end of their one-year contract term without incurring liability to Adam? Explain.

ANSWER TO QUESTION 16

1. Sunrise is liable to Tahini and Moby. The issue is whether Adam had actual or apparent authority to bind Sunrise on the contracts with Tahini and Moby.

A principal will be liable on a contract entered into by his agent with actual or apparent authority. Actual authority is authority that an agent reasonably believes he possesses based on his dealings with the principal. Apparent authority is authority that a third party reasonably believes an agent has based on the principal's holding out the agent as having such authority.

Here, Adam did not have actual authority to contract with Tahini, but he did have apparent authority. The contract between Sunrise and Adam provided that Adam would have authority to purchase items of a certain quantity and style (*i.e.*, those contained in Exhibit B) from local vendors within a budgeted amount. The items Adam purchased from Tahini were from a local vendor and within the budgeted amount, but they were not within the Exhibit B guidelines—they were of a Tahitian theme and not an Atlantic seaboard theme. Thus, Adam did not have actual authority to purchase the items from Tahini. However, Adam did have apparent authority to purchase the items from Tahini because Sunrise held Adam out as having such authority. Sunrise sent local suppliers, including Tahini, a letter indicating that Adam had authority to purchase flooring, wall coverings, etc., for Sunrise, and Sunrise did not place any limitations on this authority. Sunrise did not include Exhibit B in its letter. Consequently, Tahini could reasonably believe, based on Sunrise's letter, that Adam had authority to purchase the items from Tahini, and thus Sunrise is liable to Tahini for Adam's purchases.

In regard to Adam's contract with Moby, Adam had actual authority to purchase the items from Moby because the purchase was within the provisions of the contract between Sunrise and Adam. The items Adam purchased from Moby were from a local vendor, within the budgeted amount, and complied with the Exhibit B guidelines (they were of an Atlantic seaboard theme). Because Adam had actual authority to contract with Moby for the purchased items, Sunrise is liable to Moby for Adam's purchases. Note that Adam also had the apparent authority to purchase the items from Moby because of the letter Sunrise sent to the suppliers (including Moby) granting Adam authority to purchase decorations for its hotel without any limitations.

2.   Adam is liable to Sunrise only for damages Sunrise sustains as a result of Adam's contract with Tahini. At issue are a principal's remedies when an agent breaches an agency agreement.

An agent has a duty to obey all reasonable directions of his principal. If an agent acts contrary to the principal's directions, the agent is liable to the principal for damages that result from the disobedience. In this case, the agency agreement stated that Adam was to purchase hotel decorations only as provided in Exhibit B. Adam complied with the Exhibit B guidelines when he purchased the items from Moby; however, he did not do so when he purchased the items from Tahini. Therefore, Adam breached his duty to obey directions as to the Tahini contract and is liable to Sunrise for any damages that it suffers because of his breach.

3.   Sunrise may terminate Adam's agency before the end of their one-year contract term without incurring any liability to Adam. At issue is whether a principal may terminate an agency before the end of the agreed-upon term.

Generally, if an agency term is specified, the agency terminates at the end of the term. Either the principal or agent may unilaterally terminate the agency before the end of the term, but the breaching party may be liable for damages. However, where an agent breaches his duties, the principal may terminate the agency before the end of the agreed-upon term without incurring any liability for breach. Here, as discussed above, Adam breached his agency contract by buying items from Tahini that were not within the style guidelines specified in Exhibit B. Thus, Sunrise may terminate its agency with Adam before the end of the term without incurring any liability to Adam for breach. However, even if a court found that Adam's breach did not justify his early termination, Sunrise probably still would not incur liability to Adam for his early termination because Sunrise could set off against Adam's claim the damages Adam caused by breaching his contract with Sunrise.

QUESTION 17

Lessor owns and manages apartment buildings in the town of Utopia.

Handy is the sole proprietor and only employee of a small business called "Rapid Repairs." Most of the income from this business is generated by making small household repairs for homeowners and apartment dwellers in Utopia. Handy has a good reputation for performing quality work and charging reasonable rates.

One year ago, Lessor contracted for an indefinite period with Handy to perform repair work at several apartment units that Lessor owns in Utopia. The tenants of these units are told to make requests for repairs by calling a telephone number listed as "Lessor's Repair Line."

Under the Lessor/Handy contract, any call to "Lessor's Repair Line" actually rings directly through to Rapid Repairs. Handy is obligated to investigate any tenant's request for repair within 24 hours. Before actually making any repair, however, Handy is required to contact Lessor, describe the nature of the repair, and seek authorization to proceed. Once authorized to make the repair, Handy must make it within 24 hours. Lessor is obligated to pay Handy $50 per hour for any work done pursuant to the contract (including investigating repair requests) and, in addition, to reimburse Handy's out-of-pocket expenses.

The Lessor/Handy contract further provides that Handy:

- May perform similar work on other apartment buildings, but may not perform work "on the side" for Lessor's tenants in Lessor's buildings;

- Must provide his own tools;

- May not perform any electrical work, but must subcontract it to a licensed electrician, approved by Lessor, who will work under Handy's supervision.

Last month, Tenant called "Lessor's Repair Line." Handy answered. Tenant said that he had a cracked sink drainpipe. Handy immediately investigated. After obtaining permission from Lessor to repair the sink, Handy returned to make the repair. While Handy was making the repair, Tenant asked Handy to install an electrical outlet in the apartment for Tenant's computer. Despite his contract with Lessor, Handy agreed to do so, but told Tenant there would be a charge of $200 as it was an improvement to the apartment, not a repair covered under the lease. Tenant agreed to pay $200 for a new outlet. Tenant assumed that the money would go to Lessor, but Handy intended to keep it for himself.

Handy was negligent in installing the electrical outlet. The outlet caused a fire, which destroyed Tenant's personal property. Tenant never paid for the installation work.

On what alternative theories should Tenant argue that Lessor is liable for Handy's negligence, and what is the likely outcome on each theory? Explain.

ANSWER TO QUESTION 17

Tenant can argue that Lessor is liable for Handy's negligence under the doctrine of respondeat superior. The issue is whether Handy is an employee and whether his negligence occurred within the scope of his employment.

Under respondeat superior, an employer is liable for the negligence of his employee committed within the scope of the employee's employment. To hold Lessor liable for Handy's negligence under respondeat superior, the first determination to be made is whether Handy was an employee as opposed to an independent contractor. Generally, an employer is not liable for the torts of an independent contractor. The overriding factor in determining whether a person is an employee is whether the employer has the right to control the manner and method by which the person performs his tasks. In determining right to control, the following factors should be considered: the characterization by the parties of their relationship, whether the person hired is engaged in a distinct business of his own, the customs of the locality regarding supervision of the type of work to be performed, the degree of skill required, whether the employer provided the tools to perform the job, the length of the employment period, the basis of compensation, and whether the person was hired to perform an act in furtherance of the employer's business.

An argument can be made that Handy was an independent contractor and not an employce because Lessor did not have the right to control Handy. Handy was engaged in his own business of providing repair services, Handy's work required skill to perform, Handy provided his own tools, and Lessor did not supervise Handy's work. If Handy was not an employee, Lessor is not liable to Tenant under the doctrine of respondeat superior.

However, an equally plausible argument can be made that Handy was an employee. Handy was hired for an indefinite period of time, Handy was paid on an hourly basis, Handy was hired to provide repair services in furtherance of Lessor's business, which was owning and managing apartment buildings, and Handy was required to obtain authorization from Lessor before he undertook any repairs. Thus, Handy could be considered an employee.

If Handy is considered an employee, Lessor will not be liable for Handy's negligence unless Handy's negligence occurred within the scope of his employment. Three tests are used to determine if an employee's conduct was within the scope of employment: (i) whether the conduct was of the same general nature as, or incident to, that which the employee was employed to perform; (ii) whether the conduct was substantially removed from the authorized time and space limits of the employment; and (iii) whether the conduct was actuated, at least in part, by a purpose to serve the employer.

Here, an argument can be made that Handy's negligence occurred within the scope of his employment because his installing the electrical outlet for Tenant was incident to his repair services and it was not substantially removed from the authorized time and space limitations—he installed the outlet after providing the repair services authorized by Lessor. If Handy's negligent installation of the electrical outlet was within the scope of his employment, Lessor will be liable to Tenant for Handy's negligence.

However, an argument can be made that Handy's installation of the electrical outlet was not within the scope of his employment because Handy's conduct was not incident to that which he was employed to perform, and Handy's conduct was not actuated by a purpose to serve Lessor. Handy was not authorized by Lessor to install the outlet, and in fact his contract with Lessor prohibited him from doing electrical work and from doing side jobs for tenants. Also, Handy charged $200 for the installation work and had no intention of giving this money to Lessor. Thus, it can be concluded that Handy's negligent installation of the electrical outlet was outside the scope of his employment; consequently, Lessor would not be liable to Tenant under the doctrine of respondeat superior for Handy's negligence.

If Lessor is not liable to Tenant under the doctrine of respondeat superior—either because Handy was not an employee or because Handy's negligence was not within the scope of his employment—Lessor may still be liable to Tenant based on the theory that Handy had apparent authority to install the outlet. Apparent authority is authority that a third person reasonably believes an agent has based on the principal's holding out the agent as having such authority. In this case, it can be argued that Lessor held Handy out as being able to install the electrical outlet. Lessor told tenants to call the Lessor's Repair Line to request repairs. That line rang directly through to Handy, and Handy investigated the requests and made general repairs. Here, when Tenant requested Handy to install the outlet, Handy was already at Tenant's apartment making a repair (fixing Tenant's drainpipe) on behalf of Lessor. The facts do not indicate that Tenant was aware that Lessor prohibited Handy from doing electrical work. Moreover, Tenant believed that the $200 Handy charged him for the installation of the outlet was going to Lessor. Therefore, it was reasonable for Tenant to believe that Handy had authority to act on Lessor's behalf in installing the electrical outlet, and thus Lessor would be liable for Handy's negligent installation.

However, an argument can be made that Handy did not have the apparent authority to install the outlet. Handy specifically told Tenant that the installation of the outlet was an improvement and not a repair. In addition, Handy actually charged Tenant $200 for his services. Thus, a conclusion can be made that Handy did not have apparent authority to install the outlet and thus Lessor is not liable to Tenant for Handy's negligence.

QUESTION 18

Adam, Barbara, and Carl are partners in a beverage distribution business. They have no written partnership agreement. The partnership distributes alcoholic and nonalcoholic beverages to bars and restaurants throughout State A. Jane owns one of these bars. She also owns a number of pinball and video game machines, which are located in many of the same bars and restaurants served by the partnership. In past dealings with the partnership, Jane has dealt exclusively with Carl.

A number of beverage distribution businesses have expanded into the pinball and video game machine business. To capitalize on this trend, Jane decided to sell her pinball and video game machines. At about the same time, Adam, Barbara, and Carl decided that their partnership should consider expanding into the pinball and video game machine business. The partners agreed that Carl would approach Jane to obtain information about the number of machines she had for sale, their locations and condition, and the associated revenues and expenses. However, because the opportunity represented a new line of business, Adam and Barbara instructed Carl not to finalize a deal with Jane without first discussing the terms with them.

When Carl met with Jane, she said that she owned 127 machines located in 72 bars and restaurants. After they visited 50 bars and saw 98 machines, Carl decided he had seen enough. Carl told Jane he would go back to the office to "run some numbers" and would call her soon.

Based on Jane's representations and his observations of 98 machines, Carl decided to offer $225,000 for all of Jane's 127 machines. Jane accepted the offer and signed the contract Carl had drafted. Carl signed the contract on behalf of the partnership. At no time, however, did Carl consult with Adam or Barbara before finalizing the deal. Adam and Barbara

later discovered that the revenue generated by the machines was insufficient to justify the contract price.

1.   Is the partnership bound by the contract that Carl signed? Explain.

2.   Can the partnership recover from Carl any loss on the contract with Jane? Explain.

ANSWER TO QUESTION 18

1.   The partnership may be bound by the contract that Carl signed. The issue is whether Carl had authority to enter into the contract. A partnership can be bound by a contract entered into by a partner with actual or apparent authority.

Carl did not have actual authority to make the contract here. Actual authority is authority that a partner reasonably believes he has based on the communications between the partner and the partnership. Authority to enter into transactions regarding matters within the ordinary course of business requires a majority vote of the partners, and authority to enter into matters outside the ordinary course of business requires unanimous consent of all partners. Here, Carl did not have actual authority to enter into the contract with Jane because Adam and Barbara specifically instructed Carl not to finalize a deal with Jane without first discussing it with them. Thus, even if the purchase of pinball and video game machines is considered to be within the ordinary course of the partnership's business, Carl did not have the necessary consent, because a majority of the partners did not consent.

Even though Carl lacked actual authority to enter into the contract with Jane, the partnership may be bound if he had apparent authority. The act of any partner apparently carrying on in the ordinary course of the partnership business, or business of the kind carried out by the partnership, will bind the partnership unless the partner had no authority to act for the partnership and the third party with whom the partner dealt knew that the partner lacked authority. In this case, Carl had no authority to act for the partnership; however, Jane did not know this. In the past, Jane had dealt exclusively with Carl, and she was not aware that he could not enter into a contract for the purchase of the machines. Therefore, the partnership will be bound if Carl's purchase of the machines was an act for apparently carrying on partnership business or business of the kind carried out by the partnership. Here, the partnership business was beverage distribution. The purchase of the pinball and video game machines generally would not seem to be an act for carrying on a beverage distribution business. However, an argument can be made that the purchase was apparently for carrying on that type of business, because the facts indicate that a number of beverage distribution businesses in the area had expanded into the pinball and video game machine business, and Jane was aware of this fact. Thus, Jane could reasonably believe that the partnership was expanding its business and Carl had the authority to purchase the machines. Consequently, the partnership could be bound by the contract Carl signed with Jane.

2.   Yes, the partnership can recover from Carl any loss on the contract with Jane. At issue is whether Carl breached any duties owed to the partnership when he signed the contract with Jane that would make him liable to the partnership. Under agency principles, a partner is an agent of the partnership and has a duty to obey all reasonable directions of the partnership. Here, the partnership instructed Carl not to purchase the machines from Jane until Carl discussed the terms with Adam and Barbara. Thus, Carl breached his duty of obedience and is consequently liable to the partnership therefor.

A partner also owes a duty of care to the partnership that requires the partner to refrain from engaging in grossly negligent or reckless conduct, intentional misconduct, or knowing violation of the law. It can be argued that Carl's purchase of the machines without discussing the purchase with Adam and Barbara was an act of intentional misconduct, and consequently Carl breached his duty of care owed to the partnership and is responsible for any losses resulting therefrom. Another argument can be made that Carl's purchase of the machines without seeing all of the machines and fully investigating the purchase price was a violation of Carl's duty of care. However, this argument is weak because although the revenue from the machines was insufficient to justify the purchase price, there is nothing in the facts to indicate that Carl's offer of $225,000 was grossly negligent or reckless.

Finally, a partner must provide complete and accurate information concerning the partnership. Here, Carl was supposed to discuss the purchase of the pinball machines with Adam and Barbara, but he did not do so. Therefore, Carl breached his duty to provide the partnership with all information concerning the purchase of the machines and is liable to the partnership for any resultant losses.

QUESTION 19

One year ago, Randy and Sandy formed a partnership to manufacture widgets. They did not enter into a written partnership agreement. Randy contributed $10,000, and Sandy contributed $5,000 to the partnership. They participated equally in the management of the partnership and shared the profits equally.

The widget market has since declined, and business has been slow. Last Monday, Randy told Sandy, "I don't want to do this anymore. I am quitting this partnership." Randy then left town on an extended vacation. At that time, the partnership still had some short-term widget contracts to fulfill and owed trade creditors $30,000.

The next day, Barney, a widget broker, met with Sandy at the widget factory. Barney knew about Randy and Sandy's partnership but had not previously done business with the partnership. For over a month, Sandy had been soliciting a long-term contract to produce widgets for Barney. Without telling Barney about Randy's statement the previous day, Sandy, on behalf of the partnership, entered into a contract with Barney to produce 500,000 widgets a year for three years.

After Randy's departure, Sandy, using her own funds, paid the $30,000 owed to trade creditors.

1. What is the effect of Randy's statement, "I don't want to do this anymore. I am quitting this partnership"? Explain.

2. Is the partnership bound by the contract with Barney? Explain.

3. What contribution, if any, can Sandy claim from Randy for Sandy's $30,000 payment to trade creditors? Explain.

ANSWER TO QUESTION 19

1.   Randy's statement that he "does not want to do this anymore" and that he is "quitting this partnership" caused his dissociation from the partnership, and it also caused the dissolution of the partnership. A partner is dissociated from the partnership upon notice of the partner's express will to withdraw as a partner. Dissociation is a change in the relationship of the partners caused by any partner ceasing to be associated in the carrying on of the business. Here, Randy gave notice of his express will to withdraw as a partner when he told Sandy that he did not want to participate in the widget business anymore and that he was quitting the partnership. Thus, Randy was dissociated from the partnership at that time.

Randy's statement to Sandy also caused a dissolution of the partnership. A partnership is dissolved and its business must be wound up when a partner in a partnership at will notifies the partnership of his intent to withdraw. In this case, the partnership between Randy and Sandy was an at-will partnership because the partners did not agree that the partnership was to continue for any specific amount of time. Therefore, Randy's statement to Sandy that he is quitting the partnership caused the dissolution of the partnership. Its business, therefore, must be wound up.

2.   The partnership is bound by the contract with Barney. A partnership will be bound by a partner's act after dissolution if the act is appropriate for winding up the partnership business. A partnership also will be bound by a partner's postdissolution act—even an act that is not appropriate for winding up the partnership, such as entering into a contract to carry out new business—where the party with whom the partner dealt did not have notice of the dissolution. Here, Sandy's entering into a three-year contract to produce widgets for Barney is not an act appropriate for winding up partnership business. However, Barney was not aware that the partnership had been dissolved; Barney had been dealing with Sandy regarding a long-term widget contract for over a month. Thus, because Barney was unaware that Randy dissolved the partnership, the partnership is bound on the contract Sandy entered into with Barney. As a result, because partners are personally liable on partnership obligations, Randy can be held liable on the contract along with Sandy if Sandy breaches the contract in the future.

3.   Sandy can claim a contribution of $15,000 from Randy for her payment of the $30,000 to the trade creditors. Each partner is jointly and severally liable for obligations of the partnership. Where one partner pays the whole of a partnership debt, she may require the other partner to contribute his pro rata share of the payment. In this case, the $30,000 owed to trade creditors was a partnership debt, and Randy and Sandy shared profits and losses equally. Thus, Sandy can claim a $15,000 contribution from Randy as his share of the partnership debt.

QUESTION 20

Best Care Hospital, one of five hospitals in City, operates the largest emergency room in City. Best Care advertises extensively about the quality of care provided in its emergency room. It has billboards strategically placed throughout City urging local citizens to come to Best Care "because Best Care's emergency room doctors are the absolute *best* and will really *care* for you." In fact, Best Care employs no doctors; instead, it contracts with seven doctors in City to staff the emergency room on a 7-day, 24-hour basis. These contracts provide:

1. Each doctor is an "independent contractor," not an "agent/employee," and may conduct a private practice but may not work in any other emergency room;

2. Each doctor is responsible for the manner in which he or she provides medical care and for the purchase of malpractice insurance;

3. Each doctor is authorized to purchase supplies and equipment for Best Care's emergency room from a list of approved vendors located in City and within Best Care's price guidelines;

4. Each doctor is periodically reviewed by Best Care's governing board to assure that each doctor provides quality care;

5. Each doctor independently bills patients for services provided; and

6. All emergency services are performed in the Best Care emergency room using supplies and equipment provided by Best Care.

Three months ago, Owen, a local orthopedist and one of the doctors with whom Best Care contracts, ordered a portable X-ray machine costing $25,000 from Vision, a company located in a town 450 miles from City. Vision is not on Best Care's approved vendor list and Owen did not consult with anyone at Best Care before he placed the order. When Owen ordered the machine, which was to be custom-designed for Best Care, he truthfully told Vision that he was one of the seven emergency room doctors at Best Care and needed the machine for the emergency room. Owen also stated that he was acting on behalf of Best Care. Vision had had no previous dealings with Owen or Best Care and agreed to make the machine according to the custom specifications provided by Owen. When Vision shipped the X-ray machine, Best Care refused to accept delivery, even though the price for the machine was within its price guidelines. Best Care claimed that Owen had no authority to purchase the machine on its behalf. Vision filed an action for breach of contract against Best Care.

Last month, Anita was hit by a bus. When the ambulance arrived, Anita asked the ambulance driver to take her to Best Care, quoting the billboard claim that "Best Care's emergency room doctors are the absolute *best*." When Anita arrived at the emergency room, she was treated by Owen. Owen correctly told Anita that she needed immediate surgery. During the operation, Owen negligently severed one of Anita's arteries, and she bled to death. Anita's estate has filed a wrongful death action against Owen and Best Care for damages resulting from Owen's negligence.

1. Is Owen an independent contractor or servant (employee) of Best Care? Explain.

2. Is Best Care liable to Vision for breach of contract? Explain.

3. Assuming Owen is an independent contractor, is Best Care liable to Anita's estate for Owen's negligence? Explain.

ANSWER TO QUESTION 20

1.   Owen is most likely an independent contractor for Best Care. The primary factor in determining whether an individual is an employee or an independent contractor is whether the principal has the right to control the individual's method and manner of work. Several factors demonstrate that Best Care did not control Owen's work, thus making him an independent contractor. Specifically, doctors are highly skilled professionals, and Best Care doctors may maintain their own practices. Furthermore, the doctors are responsible for the manner in which they provide medical care, they must provide their own malpractice insurance, and they bill independently for their services. Also, although not dispositive on the issue, the contract provides that the doctors are independent contractors.

However, some factors suggest an employer/employee relationship. The doctors use facilities and equipment supplied by Best Care, they provide continuous service on behalf of Best Care, and they may not work in any other emergency room. Additionally, their work is reviewed by the Best Care board, and while they are authorized to purchase supplies and equipment, both the vendor and the price must be approved by Best Care.

In light of the foregoing factors, Best Care has no significant right to control the manner and the method by which Owen performs his tasks. Thus, Owen is an independent contractor rather than an employee.

2.   Regardless of Owen's status as an independent contractor or employee, Best Care is not liable to Vision for breach of contract. In order for a principal to be liable in contract to a third party, the agent must have had the authority to enter into the disputed contract or the principal must ratify the agent's act. Owen had neither actual nor apparent authority to order the X-ray machine.

Owen lacked actual authority to order the X-ray machine. Actual authority is authority that an agent reasonably believes he possesses based on his dealings with the principal. Owen had express authority to order equipment within a specified price range, but it must have been purchased from certain vendors within City. Owen exceeded his authority by purchasing the machine from Vision, a company not approved by Best Care. Thus, he acted without actual authority.

Additionally, Owen did not have apparent authority to purchase the X-ray machine from Vision. Apparent authority is authority that a third party reasonably believes the agent has based on the principal's holding out the agent as having such authority. Here, Owen informed Vision that he was acting on behalf of Best Care and Vision relied on his assertion of authority. Best Care did nothing to indicate to Vision that Owen had authority to purchase the machine from Vision. Owen's assertion alone is insufficient to bind Best Care; Best Care must have acted or failed to act in a manner that caused Vision's belief. Because there was no such action on Best Care's part, Owen lacked apparent authority.

Finally, Best Care did not ratify Owen's unauthorized purchase, as it refused to accept delivery. Thus, Best Care cannot be bound on the contract.

3.   Even assuming that Owen is an independent contractor, Best Care is likely liable to Anita's estate for his negligence. Ordinarily, a principal is not liable for the torts of an independent contractor. However, in this case, Best Care can probably be held liable under an estoppel theory. Estoppel can be raised when the principal creates the appearance that an employer/employee relationship exists, and a third party relies on that relationship. Here, Best Care advertises that its

doctors are "the absolute best," creating the impression that the Best Care doctors are actually employed by Best Care. Anita relied on this impression when she directed the ambulance to take her to Best Care. Therefore, Best Care will be estopped from denying the existence of an employer/employee relationship and can be held liable by Anita's estate via respondeat superior.

QUESTION 21

For many years, Ruth owned and operated a restaurant as a sole proprietorship doing business as (d/b/a) Ruth's Family Restaurant. In 2001, Ruth sold the assets of the restaurant to Scott. Ruth and Scott agreed that: (1) the restaurant would operate under the name "Ruth's Family Restaurant"; (2) Ruth would manage the restaurant for Scott but would have no ownership interest in the restaurant; (3) all necessary licenses would remain in Ruth's name; and (4) Ruth would hire all employees, but only on an at-will basis (as is customary in the restaurant business). No one other than Ruth and Scott was aware that Scott had bought the restaurant.

Prior to Scott's purchase of the restaurant, Ruth had purchased supplies from Wholesale Restaurant Supply Co. (Wholesale), always signing the contracts as "Ruth, d/b/a Ruth's Family Restaurant." Following Scott's purchase of the restaurant, Scott instructed Ruth in very clear terms not to make any purchases of restaurant supplies from Wholesale in the future. Ruth complied with this instruction for the next several months.

In 2003, Ruth hired Nora, her niece, as assistant manager of the restaurant under a written employment contract for a 20-year term. Ruth signed the contract as "Ruth, d/b/a Ruth's Family Restaurant."

Soon after Nora was hired, she pointed out to Ruth that Wholesale's prices were generally less than those of the other local supply company. Despite Scott's clear prohibition, Ruth resumed buying supplies from Wholesale, again signing all contracts as "Ruth, d/b/a Ruth's Family Restaurant."

When Scott discovered what Ruth had done, Scott took over management of the restaurant, discharged Nora and Ruth, and refused to pay thousands of dollars of invoices from Wholesale for restaurant supplies delivered to the restaurant.

Wholesale has sued Scott to recover on the outstanding invoices. Nora has sued Scott for breach of the employment contract.

Under agency law:

1. Is Scott liable to Wholesale? Explain.

2. Is Scott liable to Nora? Explain.

ANSWER TO QUESTION 21

1. Scott is liable on the contract with Wholesale. The issue is whether Ruth acted with authority.

Ruth is clearly Scott's agent. For an individual to be an agent of a principal, the parties must assent to the relationship, the agent must act for the principal's benefit, and the principal must have the right to control the agent. Here, Ruth and Scott assented to the relationship, as evidenced by their sales agreement. Furthermore, because Ruth is managing the restaurant on Scott's behalf, the agency benefits Scott. Finally, Scott has the authority to control Ruth's actions, as he owns the restaurant and Ruth is the manager.

A principal is liable on a contract entered into by an agent only if the agent had authority to enter into the contract on the principal's behalf. An agent may have actual authority—either express or implied—or apparent authority to act on behalf of her principal. Here, Ruth clearly did not have actual authority to contract with Wholesale, as Scott specifically prohibited her from doing so. However, Ruth had apparent authority to enter into the contract. An agent has apparent authority to act on behalf of her principal where the principal holds the agent out as having that authority and a third party reasonably relies on the holding out. Here, Scott held Ruth out as having authority to contract on his behalf by allowing Ruth to manage the restaurant and run it under the name "Ruth's Family Restaurant." Wholesale reasonably relied on Scott's holding out—it is reasonable for a supplier to believe that a restaurant's manager has authority to order restaurant supplies. Thus, Ruth acted with apparent authority and Scott will be bound on the contract. [*Note:* Alternatively, it can be argued that Ruth had inherent agency power or that Scott would be estopped from denying that Ruth was his agent under these circumstances.]

Some courts would also find apparent authority here through the doctrine of lingering apparent authority. An agent may have lingering apparent authority where she previously had actual authority and had a pattern of dealing with a third party in that capacity. In such a case, the principal is liable if he knows of his agent's past dealings with the third party and fails to give notice to the third party that the agent no longer has authority. Here, Ruth previously had authority to contract with Wholesale, as she was the owner and operator of the restaurant. Scott did not give notice of the termination of Ruth's authority to contract with it, nor did Wholesale have reason to know of the termination. Thus, Ruth had lingering apparent authority to contract with Wholesale.

Finally, it should be noted that Scott's instruction to Ruth—that she should not order supplies from Wholesale—does not affect Ruth's apparent authority because Wholesale was not told of the limitation. Such a secret limiting instruction does not affect apparent authority.

2.   Scott probably is not liable to Nora on the employment contract. Again the issue is whether Ruth had authority to enter into the contract.

Here, as with the contract with Wholesale, Ruth did not have actual authority to hire Nora for 20 years—Scott gave Ruth authority only to hire at-will employees. Thus, Scott could be bound only if Ruth had apparent authority to hire Nora for 20 years, and Ruth had no such apparent authority. While here again Scott held Ruth out as his manager, it was not reasonable for Nora to believe that a restaurant manager had authority to hire her under a 20-year contract because the facts say it is customary in the industry to hire restaurant employees on an at-will basis. Thus, Scott will not be bound on the contract with Nora.

QUESTION 22

See Corporations Question 16 for Agency issue.

QUESTION 23

Rich, who lives in Smalltown, recently bought a sports utility vehicle ("SUV") from Dealer in Capital City, which is located approximately 60 miles from Smalltown. Rich asked if Dealer would have the SUV delivered to him in Smalltown. Rich offered to pay the driver $75. Dealer does not ordinarily deliver SUVs to its customers. Nonetheless, Dealer agreed to have Sales, a full-time salesperson employed by Dealer, deliver the SUV to Rich's house because Dealer was eager to please Rich. At the end of the normal workday, Dealer gave Sales directions to Rich's house in Smalltown. As Sales prepared to drive off in the SUV, Dealer told him, "Drive straight to Rich's house; no detours. Drive carefully and no speeding. I don't want any dents in that SUV."

On his way to Rich's house, Sales stopped to visit Friend, who was in the process of moving. Friend was distraught because the movers had not shown up. Friend asked Sales if he would like to earn $200 by transporting "a few loads" in the SUV. Sales agreed and transported many of Friend's belongings in the SUV. Friend paid Sales $200.

Helping Friend took several hours, so Sales was running late. In his rush to Rich's house Sales negligently ran over Ped, who was trying to cross the street. Ped was seriously injured.

Dealer learned that Sales had used the SUV to help Friend move and demanded the $200 Friend had paid Sales.

1.   Can Ped recover from Dealer for Sales's negligence? Explain.

2.   Must Sales give Dealer the $200 he earned helping Friend move? Explain.

ANSWER TO QUESTION 23

1.   Ped can recover from Dealer for Sales's negligence. At issue is whether Sales was acting within the scope of his employment when he ran over Ped.

As a general rule, an employer can be held liable for an employee's negligent acts that occur within the scope of the employment. Thus, Dealer will be liable to Ped for his injuries if: (i) Sales was Dealer's employee, and (ii) the accident occurred within the scope of Sales's employment.

Here, the facts provide that Sales is a full-time employee of Dealer. This is probably enough to establish an employer-employee relationship between Dealer and Sales. Where it is unclear whether an employer-employee relationship exists, courts will first look to whether the parties have created an agency relationship. An agency relationship is created where the agent consents to act for the principal's benefit and subject to his control. If such a relationship existed and the principal had the right to control the physical conduct of the agent's performance, an employer-employee relationship existed. Here, Sales worked full-time for dealer selling vehicles for the benefit of Dealer. Moreover, Sales's performance appears to have been subject to Dealer's control (*e.g.,* Dealer was able to instruct Sales to drive carefully and to go directly to Rich's house). Thus, an employer-employee relationship existed.

Sales probably was acting within the scope of his employment when he ran over Ped, but this is a close question. Three tests generally are used to determine whether the conduct in question was within the scope of the employment. A court will first look to see whether the conduct was of the same type authorized by the employer. Here, Sales was employed as a salesperson and did not ordinarily deliver vehicles for Dealer. Indeed, Dealer did not usually deliver vehicles at all. Moreover, the delivery was to be made 60 miles away from the dealership and Rich offered to pay the delivery person $75 to deliver the SUV. Nevertheless, delivery of vehicles is strongly related to the job of selling vehicles and servicing customers, so a court will likely hold that the delivery was still part of Sales's employment. [*Editor's note:* An opposite conclusion is equally valid.]

A court will also determine whether the conduct occurred within the time and space authorized by the employer. A minor detour from the employer's tasks will not relieve the employer from liability, but a substantial deviation from the employer's tasks (sometimes called a "frolic") will release the employer from liability. Once an employee abandons the employer's tasks, there must be proof of a return to the task before a court will hold the employer liable. Here again, we have the issue of whether delivery of a vehicle after hours was within the scope of Sales's employment. The same arguments can be made as were made above. Assuming that delivery of vehicles was within the scope of Sales's employment, it can be argued that Sales made a substantial departure from his assigned task of delivering the SUV. He spent several hours moving furniture for Friend instead of delivering the SUV as instructed. Had Sales run over Ped while moving the furniture, Dealer surely would not be liable. However, by the time Sales ran into Ped, he had finished moving his friend's furniture and had returned to his assigned task of delivering the SUV to Rich. Thus, Sales was within the scope of his employment from this standpoint.

Finally, a court will look to whether the negligent conduct was motivated, at least in part, by a desire to serve the employer. Here, it seems clear that Sales was speeding in order to deliver the SUV to Rich, which was his assigned task. Thus, a court would likely find that Sales was within the scope of his employment when he hit Ped. Therefore, Dealer will be liable to Ped.

2.   Sales must turn over the money he earned from helping Friend move. At issue is an agent's duty to his principal.

Generally, an agent owes a duty of loyalty to his principal and a duty to obey the principal's instructions. Where an employee breaches these duties, the principal can hold the agent liable for damages, including the recovery of any profits that the agent made as a result of the breach. Here, Dealer told Sales to avoid speeding and negligent driving, and Sales ignored both instructions. Sales also used the SUV for his personal purposes (moving Friend). Thus, Dealer can recover any damages he suffered as a result of the breach and the $200 profit that Sales made as a result of his disobedience.

QUESTION 24

Two years ago Nephew asked Uncle for a loan to purchase a tire dealership. Uncle agreed. Nephew decided to name the new business "Monster Tires" and to focus on selling oversized tires made by Big Rubber, Inc. Uncle agreed to accept 50% of the profits generated by Monster Tires, instead of a fixed payment, until the loan was fully repaid.

One year after Monster Tires was established, Nephew approached Friend, who had a knack for sales and marketing and was well-connected in the trucking business. Friend agreed to join Monster Tires in exchange for a one-third share of all of its profits. Friend and Nephew approached Uncle to renegotiate the repayment of the loan. Uncle was excited by Friend's ideas to expand the business and agreed to forgive the loan and instead accept a one-third share of all of the profits of Monster Tires. Uncle also offered to let Monster Tires use one of his properties rent-free so that Monster Tires could open a second location.

Nephew and Friend both worked full-time at Monster Tires. Friend began an aggressive sales campaign and spent a significant amount of time entertaining potential customers. Uncle was not involved in the day-to-day operations of Monster Tires.

Nephew, Uncle, and Friend were all present when Monster Tires opened its second store. The store was packed with potential customers, but Uncle was dismayed by the sparse inventory. When a representative of TireCo asked Uncle about placing its line of tires in the stores, Uncle agreed and signed a large purchase order for TireCo tires without consulting either Nephew or Friend.

After the store opening, Uncle, Nephew, and Friend went out to celebrate. Friend suggested that Monster Tires should buy a yacht for entertaining. Nephew agreed because he wanted to expand to a third location near the beach. Uncle vehemently protested and said: "We can't afford a yacht. I forbid you to purchase one." Two weeks later, Friend signed a contract with Custom Yachts to purchase a yacht for Monster Tires.

Monster Tires is now refusing to pay both TireCo and Custom Yachts.

1.   Is Monster Tires liable to TireCo for the tires Uncle ordered? Explain.

2.   Is Monster Tires liable to Custom Yachts for the yacht Friend ordered? Explain.

3.   Are Uncle, Nephew, and Friend personally liable on either of the contracts? Explain.

ANSWER TO QUESTION 24

1.   Yes, Monster Tires is liable to TireCo for the tires that Uncle ordered. At issue is whether Uncle is a partner of Monster Tires. A partnership is formed when two or more people associate to carry on as co-owners of a business for profit. A person who receives a share of the profits from a business is presumed to be a partner. Uncle and Nephew did not form a partnership when Uncle loaned money to Nephew to buy the tire dealership, since Uncle was not a co-owner. It is immaterial that Nephew was to repay the loan with profits from the store. Uncle became a partner, however, when he agreed to accept one-third of the Monster Tires profits. Additionally, Uncle agreed to let Monster Tires use one of his properties rent free, which is something a co-owner of a business would likely do. Therefore, Uncle is a partner of Monster Tires.

As a partner, Uncle is an agent of the partnership and therefore can bind the partnership to the contract to buy tires. At issue is whether Uncle can bind the partnership to the contract with TireCo. Each partner is an agent of the partnership for the purpose of its business. A partnership can be bound on a contract entered into by a partner with actual or apparent authority. Actual authority is authority that a partner reasonably believes he has based on his communications with the partnership. Uncle did not have actual authority to enter the contract since he ordered the TireCo tires without consulting either Nephew or Friend. Uncle did, however, have apparent authority to enter the contract. The act of any partner apparently carrying on in the ordinary course of the partnership business or business of the kind carried out by the partnership will bind the partnership unless the partner had no authority to act for the partnership and the third party with whom the partner dealt knew that the partner lacked authority. Ordering tires is an activity that is in the ordinary course of business for a tire dealership. So unless the TireCo representative had reason to know that Uncle lacked authority to order the tires, Monster Tires is liable to TireCo.

2.   No, Monster Tires is not liable to Custom Yachts for the yacht. At issue is whether Friend had the authority to bind the partnership to the yacht contract. A partnership can be bound by a contract entered into by a partner with actual or apparent authority. Authority to enter into trans-actions regarding matters within the ordinary course of business requires a majority vote of the partners, and authority to enter into matters outside the ordinary course of business requires unanimous consent of all partners. Buying a yacht is not in the ordinary course of business of a tire dealership, despite the fact that Friend often entertains potential customers. Therefore, the unanimous consent of all of the partners is required for Friend to have the actual authority to purchase the yacht. Since Uncle told Friend he was opposed to buying the yacht, there was not unanimous consent, and Friend did not have actual authority. Friend also did not have apparent authority to enter the contract since Custom Yachts could not reasonably believe that purchasing a yacht was in the ordinary course of business of a tire dealership. Since Friend did not have the authority to enter the contract on behalf of Monster Tires, Monster Tires is not liable on the contract and will not have to pay Custom Yachts.

3.   Uncle, Nephew, and Friend are jointly and severally liable on the TireCo contract; only Friend is liable on the Custom Yachts contract. At issue is whether individual partners are liable on contracts entered into on behalf of the partnership. All partners are jointly and severally liable for all obligations of the partnership, which means that each partner is personally liable for the entire amount of such obligations. [*Editor's note:* In a jurisdiction that follows the Uniform Partnership Act, partners are jointly liable for debts of the partnership.] As discussed above, the contract to TireCo occurred in the ordinary course of business and Monster Tires is liable to TireCo. Thus, Uncle, Friend, and Nephew are each personally liable to TireCo for the entire amount of the contract. To recover from the partners individually, TireCo must secure a judgment against both Monster Tires and the individual partners. TireCo also must first go after the partnership's assets before it can try to recover from the individual partners.

Only Friend is liable on the Custom Yachts contract. When a partner enters a contract he had no authority to enter on behalf of the partnership, the partnership is not bound by the contract. Friend had no authority to buy the yacht for the partnership. Therefore, he alone is personally liable on the Custom Yachts contract.

QUESTION 25

Astoria Limited Partnership ("Astoria") is a properly formed limited partnership. The general partner of Astoria is Baker, an individual. The limited partners are Tim, Uma, and Vivian, who are also individuals. Under the limited partnership agreement, distributions and voting rights in the limited partnership are allocated to Baker (10%), Tim (30%), Uma (30%), and Vivian (30%).

The limited partnership agreement of Astoria gives the limited partners the right to remove Baker as the general partner—with or without cause—if the holders of 60% of the voting rights concur.

Three weeks ago, articles appeared in the business press raising questions about Baker's management of Caldonia Limited Partnership ("Caldonia"). While the articles did not specifically mention Astoria, the misconduct documented in the articles—contracts between Caldonia and a janitorial company owned by Baker that charged greatly inflated fees for its services—raised concerns on the part of Astoria's limited partners. Tim wrote Baker requesting that Baker, in his capacity as the general partner of Astoria, provide: (i) copies of any contracts between Astoria and any entities related to or controlled by Baker, (ii) copies of any contracts for janitorial services between Astoria and any entity, (iii) copies of Astoria's federal and state tax returns for the past three years, and (iv) copies of all correspondence between Astoria and any other parties for the past five years. Alternatively, Tim requested access to Astoria's records in order to secure copies of the documents himself.

Baker responded by refusing all four of Tim's requests. Thereupon, Tim contacted Uma and Vivian to request their votes that Baker be removed as the general partner. Tim also proposed that the three limited partners, Tim, Uma, and Vivian, agree in writing to jointly run Astoria until a suitable replacement for Baker could be found.

1.   Did Baker act wrongfully in refusing to provide Tim the information and documents he requested? Explain.

2.   If the limited partners do no more than remove Baker as general partner of Astoria, will they be liable to persons who transact business with Astoria? Explain.

3.   If the limited partners remove Baker and run Astoria until a replacement general partner can be found, under what circumstances will they be liable to persons who transact business with Astoria? Explain.

ANSWER TO QUESTION 25

1.   Baker acted wrongfully in refusing to provide copies of the tax returns. He probably also acted wrongfully in refusing to provide copies of the contracts. However, he was likely justified in refusing to provide copies of the correspondence. At issue is whether a limited partner has the right to demand information from a general partner regarding the limited partnership, and whether a limited partner is entitled to access partnership records. Every limited partner has the right to obtain from a general partner, upon reasonable demand, full information respecting the business and financial condition of the limited partnership and other information concerning the limited partnership's affairs. In addition, every limited partner has the right to inspect and copy partnership records that the partnership is required to maintain.

Copies of contracts between Astoria and entities related to or controlled by Baker: Baker probably acted wrongfully in refusing to provide Tim with copies of contracts between Astoria and entities related to or controlled by Baker. Any such contracts likely constitute information relating to the business and financial condition of the limited partnership. Furthermore, there are allegations that Baker may have engaged in self-dealing. These contracts would likely help to confirm or deny these allegations. Therefore, Baker should have provided Tim with the requested copies.

Copies of contracts for janitorial services: Baker probably acted wrongfully in refusing to provide copies of any contracts for janitorial services between Astoria and any entity. Again, these contracts are likely relevant to the business and financial condition of Astoria and to the allegations that Baker has engaged in self-dealing. Therefore, Baker should have provided copies of any such contracts to Tim.

Copies of tax returns: Baker acted wrongfully in refusing to provide Tim with copies of Astoria's federal and state tax returns. Tax returns are documents that a limited partnership is required to keep. A limited partner may inspect and copy them at any time. Therefore, Baker acted wrongfully when he refused Tim's request for copies.

Copies of Astoria's correspondence: Baker was likely justified in refusing to provide copies of all correspondence between Astoria and any other parties for the past five years. Under the Revised Uniform Limited Partnership Act ("R.U.L.P.A."), information that does not relate to the state of the business or financial condition of the limited partnership need only be provided if it is reasonable. Here, Tim has requested all of Astoria's correspondence for the past five years. Tim will argue that this demand is reasonable and the information will help him determine whether Baker was properly managing the business. Baker will argue that Tim's request is unreasonable and it would be cumbersome to provide Tim with this information. It seems that Tim's request is essentially a fishing expedition for evidence of Baker's possible misconduct. Therefore, it is likely that Baker was justified in refusing this request.

2.   No, the limited partners will not be liable to persons who transact business with Astoria. At issue is whether limited partners are liable as general partners for removing a general partner. Generally, a limited partner is not personally liable beyond her contribution for the obligations of the limited partnership. However, a limited partner may be liable beyond her contribution if she participates in the control of the business. [*Editor's note:* In states that have adopted the Uniform Limited Partnership Act of 2001 ("U.L.P.A."), this is no longer true.] However, the R.U.L.P.A. allows a limited partner to take part in extraordinary partnership affairs without being found to have participated in control of the business. Removing a general partner is an extraordinary partnership affair that a limited partner may participate in without exposure to unlimited liability. Here, the limited partners want to remove Baker as general partner of Astoria. Because removing a general partner is not considered participating in the control of the business, the limited partners will not be liable to those who transact business with Astoria.

3.   The limited partners will be liable to people who transact business with Astoria if those people reasonably believe that the limited partner is a general partner. At issue is whether limited partners can be held liable as general partners if they participate in the control of the partnership. A limited partner is liable as a general partner if she participates in the control of the business and the person dealing with the limited partnership reasonably believes, based on the limited partner's conduct, that the limited partner is a general partner. [*Editor's note:* In states that have adopted the U.L.P.A. of 2001, this is no longer true.] Here, Tim wants Uma and Vivian to join him in running Astoria until a new general partner can be found. This would constitute participating in the control of the business. As such, the limited partners would be liable as general partners if anyone they do business with reasonably believes that the limited partners are general partners. Therefore, unless they give notice to those they do business with that they are in fact not general partners, the limited partners will be liable as general partners.

QUESTION 26

Talker is a persuasive salesperson, Fixer is a talented carpenter, and Manager is an experienced small business manager. The three are friends and often discussed going into business together. Two months ago they orally agreed to form a cabinet restoration business and to share profits equally.

The three friends began doing business under the name TFM Restored Cabinets ("TFM"). Manager collected accounts receivable, paid all bills, and distributed the profits equally among the three. Fixer restored the cabinets, and Talker marketed them. The three friends operated independently in performing their respective duties, but they met periodically to discuss and decide other business matters.

Everything went smoothly until Fixer announced that he intended to hire Crafty to help with the restoration work because there was more work than one carpenter could handle. Talker and Manager opposed hiring Crafty. They believed that most of TFM's customers were attracted by Fixer's reputation and that the business would be harmed if Crafty performed restoration work. Despite their objections, Fixer hired Crafty.

One month later, Crafty quit after Manager refused to pay for the work that Crafty had performed.

1. What is the legal relationship of Talker, Fixer, and Manager? Explain.

2. Did Fixer have authority to hire Crafty on behalf of TFM? Explain.

3. Under what circumstances, if any, could Crafty collect from Talker the wages TFM owes Crafty? Explain.

ANSWER TO QUESTION 26

1. Talker, Fixer, and Manager are general partners of TFM. The issue is the characterization of the legal relationship between Talker, Fixer, and Manager. A partnership is formed when two or more people associate to carry on as co-owners a business for profit. There is no requirement that the parties subjectively intend to form a partnership, only that they intend to run a business as co-owners. Generally, neither a formal agreement nor writing is required; in fact, the intent of the parties to carry on as co-owners of a business can even be implied from their conduct. Additionally, the sharing of profits raises a presumption that a partnership was formed. Here, Talker, Fixer, and Manager orally agreed to form a business for profit and to share any profits equally. Each partner played an active role in the partnership's business and they met periodically to discuss business matters. This conduct supports the presumption that a partnership was formed. Therefore, the relationship between Talker, Fixer, and Manager is that of general partners of TFM.

2. Fixer had apparent authority to hire Crafty. The issue is whether Fixer had actual or apparent authority to hire Crafty on behalf of the partnership. Generally, the acts of a partner will bind the partnership if the partner acted within the ordinary course of the partnership's business and with actual or apparent authority. TFM was in the business of restoring cabinets, and Fixer hired Crafty because he needed assistance with the restoration work. Hiring an employee to perform partnership business is within the ordinary course of the partnership's business. Thus, TFM will be bound if Fixer had actual or apparent authority to hire Crafty.

Actual authority is the authority a partner reasonably believes he has based on the communications between the partnership and the partner. It can be granted either in the partnership agreement or by the consent of the partners. Here, Fixer had no actual authority to hire Crafty. Talker and Manager both opposed the hiring of Crafty; therefore, Fixer lacked actual authority to hire Crafty because a majority of the partners opposed the action.

Apparent authority is the authority that a third party would reasonably believe a partner has based on his being held out by the partnership as a partner. Generally, the act of a partner in the ordinary course of the partnership business will bind the partnership unless the partner had no actual authority to act for the partnership in the particular matter and the third person with whom the partner was dealing knew or received notice that the partner lacked authority. Here, the partnership is bound by Fixer's act because: (i) he acted within the ordinary course of the partnership's business, as discussed above; (ii) he had no actual authority to hire Crafty; and (iii) there is nothing in the facts to indicate that Crafty knew that Fixer lacked the authority to hire him. Thus, Fixer had apparent authority to hire Crafty.

3.   Yes, Crafty can collect his wages from Talker. The issue is whether a partner is personally liable for the obligations of the partnership. Partners are jointly and severally liable on contracts made by a partner in the scope of the partnership business and on any other contracts expressly authorized by the partners. Each partner is personally and individually liable for the entire amount of all partnership obligations; thus, if one partner satisfies the whole of a partnership obligation, he is entitled to indemnification from the partnership. A judgment is not personally binding on a partner unless he has been served. Here, all the partners are jointly and severally liable for the wages earned by Crafty, as he was hired by Fixer in the ordinary course of the partnership's business. Crafty may seek payment from one or all of the partners, and if served, they will be liable for the amount of the obligation. Crafty is attempting to collect his wages from Talker, and if Talker has been served, he is liable for the entire amount of the obligation, though he can seek indemnification from the partnership.

QUESTION 27

Fifteen years ago, Amy, Beck, and Curt formed a partnership, "Amy, Beck, and Curt Co.," to engage in a retail shoe store business. The partnership is for a 25-year term. All real estate owned by the partnership is titled to "Amy, Beck, and Curt Co., a partnership."

While the partnership has done well, the three partners have not managed their respective personal finances successfully. In order to deal with personal financial problems, Amy borrowed $25,000 from Green, Beck borrowed $50,000 from Red, and Curt borrowed $75,000 from White. The three partners each have defaulted on their respective loans.

Green, Red, and White are pursuing various avenues to recover what is owed to each of them.

Green has obtained a judgment against Amy, who is judgment-proof, and is considering attaching the partnership real estate.

Red has taken no legal action against Beck but wants to collect the amount of his loan to Beck from Beck's interest in the partnership.

Curt has assigned all of his interest in the partnership to White. After the assignment, White asked to inspect the partnership books and records and demanded the right to participate in the management and affairs of the partnership. White is also considering the possibility of collecting Curt's debt by forcing a dissolution and winding up of the partnership.

1. **Can Green, as a judgment creditor of Amy, attach and execute upon the partnership real estate? Explain.**

2. **What steps should Red take to collect the amount of his loan to Beck from Beck's interest in the partnership? Explain.**

3. **Does White have a right to inspect partnership books and records and to participate in the management of the partnership? Explain.**

4. **Can White force a dissolution and winding up of the partnership? Explain.**

ANSWER TO QUESTION 27

1.　Green cannot attach and execute upon the partnership real estate to satisfy Amy's debt. The issue is whether a creditor of a partner can satisfy its judgment through partnership property. Generally, property that is titled in the partnership name is deemed to be partnership property; a partner has no interest in partnership property. Therefore, the creditor of a partner cannot reach partnership property in satisfaction of a partner's personal debts. In this case, the real estate owned by the partnership is titled in the name of the partnership. As such, Amy has no personal interest in the real estate and Green cannot reach it in satisfaction of Amy's debt.

2.　Red should seek a judgment against Beck and ask the court to grant a charging order against Beck's transferable (*i.e.*, financial) interest in the partnership. The issue is the manner in which the creditor of a partner can collect its debt. Once a judgment is issued against a partner, the creditor can charge (*i.e.*, attach) the transferable interest of the partner to satisfy the judgment. The charging order then becomes a lien on the partner's transferable interest in the partnership. Red should seek a judgment against Beck and then ask the court to grant him a charging order, which will attach Beck's transferable interest in the partnership (consisting of his rights to profits, losses, and distributions).

3.　White has neither the right to inspect partnership books and records nor the right to participate in the management of the partnership. The issue is the rights of an assignee of a partner's transferable interest in the partnership. A partner has a transferable interest in the partnership, which consists of his share of the profits and losses and the right to receive distributions. He cannot transfer his interest in management and other rights. The transferable interest can be assigned to a third party, and upon transfer of such rights, the assignee is entitled to receive distributions to which the assigning partner would have been entitled. The transferee does not, however, become a partner by virtue of the transfer, and therefore has no right to interfere in the management of the partnership or to inspect the partnership books and records. Here, it was permissible for Curt to assign his transferable interest in the partnership to White, but that entitles White only to distributions that Curt would have received. He has no right to inspect partnership books or to participate in the management of the partnership.

4.   White cannot force a dissolution and winding up of the partnership. The issue is whether the assignee of a partner can force the winding up of the partnership. The assignee of a partner's transferable interest can ask the court for a judicial decree that it is equitable to wind up the partnership only if: (i) the term specified in the partnership agreement has expired, or (ii) it is a partnership at will. The partnership established by Amy, Beck, and Curt was not a partnership at will. It was for a term of 25 years, and currently only 15 years have passed. Thus, the partnership cannot be dissolved by White because the 25-year term has not expired.

QUESTION 1

On September 13, Uncle wrote a check in the amount of $15 to Niece's order and gave it to her as a birthday gift. Niece immediately indorsed the check by signing her name on the back. She wrote nothing else on the check. Before Niece deposited the check, Thief stole it. Because of Uncle's negligence in filling in the amount payable, it was easy for Thief to raise the amount of the check by changing "$15" to "$1,500" and the written sum "Fifteen" to "Fifteen Hundred."

Thief, without signing her name on the check, delivered it to Garageco in payment for $1,500 worth of work Garageco had done on Thief's car. Thief told Garageco that she had received the check from a relative. Garageco had no reason to doubt Thief's veracity or to suspect the alteration. In return for the check, Thief was permitted to take possession of her car, which Garageco had been holding until Thief paid for the work.

On September 15, Garageco indorsed and delivered the check to Supplier in payment for a compressor that Supplier was to deliver no later than October 1. Supplier presented the check to the drawee bank. The bank dishonored the check on September 17 because of a stop payment order placed by Uncle at Niece's request.

On September 19, Supplier learned the check had been altered and dishonored. In order to preserve its business relationship with Garageco, Supplier nevertheless delivered the compressor to Garageco on September 20. On September 21, Supplier, still in possession of the check, concluded that it would not be practical to attempt to recover from Thief. Supplier would prefer not to sue Garageco.

What rights, if any, does Supplier have against Niece and Uncle? Explain.

ANSWER TO QUESTION 1

Supplier can sue Niece for $15 and Uncle for $1,500. At issue is the liability of an indorser and a drawer on an altered, negligently drawn check.

When an indorser signs her name to an instrument, she enters into a contract that if the instrument is presented for payment and is dishonored, and the indorser is given notice of dishonor, she will pay on the instrument according to its terms at the time of the indorsement. Here, the check was presented for payment and it was dishonored. Thus, if Supplier gives Niece notice of dishonor, it can hold her liable for $15—the amount of the check at the time that she indorsed.

Since Supplier's loss is substantially more than $15, it should seek to recover the full $1,500 from Uncle on his drawer's contract. The drawer of a draft (including the drawer of a check) also enters into a contract that he will pay the draft according to its terms when signed. Thus, Supplier can hold Uncle liable for $15 under the general rule. However, under the facts, Supplier can argue that under the holder in due course ("HDC") rule, it should be able to recover the full $1,500 from Uncle because of his negligence in drafting the check.

Under the HDC rule, if a negotiable instrument, which includes a check, is negotiated to an HDC, he takes free of personal defenses and claims and is subject only to real defenses. Here, Supplier is not an HDC but has the rights of an HDC under the "shelter doctrine," and while the alteration defense is available to Niece, Uncle is precluded from asserting it.

The instrument here was properly negotiated to Supplier because it contained all necessary signatures. When it was given to Niece, it was order paper, requiring both delivery and her signature for negotiation. When Niece indorsed the check without naming a new payee, she converted the check to bearer paper, which could be negotiated by delivery alone. Thief delivered the check to Garageco, and Garageco indorsed the check (which was not necessary for negotiation) and delivered the check to Supplier. Thus, there was proper negotiation.

Although Supplier is not an HDC, under the shelter doctrine it succeeds to Garageco's rights, and Garageco is an HDC. To be an HDC, a holder (*i.e.*, one to whom an instrument was properly negotiated) must take the instrument for value, in good faith, and without notice of any defenses on the instrument. Whether a holder has notice is measured at the later of the time the instrument is taken or when value is given. Here, Supplier took the check in good faith, but it had notice of Uncle's defense—alteration of the instrument—when it gave value (*i.e.*, when it delivered the compressor). Thus, Supplier is not an HDC. However, Supplier has the rights of an HDC because under the shelter doctrine, most subsequent holders of a negotiable instrument succeed to the rights of prior holders, and here Garageco was an HDC. It took the check for value (*i.e.*, release of Thief's car), in good faith, and without notice of any defenses on the check. Thus, Supplier is free from personal defenses and is subject only to real defenses.

Alteration of an instrument is a real defense except as against persons precluded from raising the defense. A person is precluded from raising alteration as a defense when the person's negligence substantially contributes to the alteration. Here, Niece might have been negligent in signing the check and allowing it to be stolen, but such negligence is not the type of negligence that precludes assertion of the alteration defense. Uncle, on the other hand, negligently drew the check. This is the type of substantial negligence that precludes assertion of the alteration defense. Thus, Niece can assert alteration as a defense and is liable only for $15—the amount of the instrument when she signed—but Uncle is liable for the full $1,500.

QUESTION 2

See Secured Transactions Question 3 for Commercial Paper issue.

QUESTION 3

On January 4, Maker agreed to purchase a snowmobile for $1,500 from Smith and Wright, each of whom was a 50% owner of the snowmobile. Smith and Wright agreed to deliver the snowmobile to Maker on January 5. They also agreed to allow Maker to delay payment until March 5, provided that Maker signed a negotiable noninterest-bearing promissory note payable on March 5.

On January 5, Smith delivered the snowmobile to Maker, along with a bill of sale signed by Smith and Wright. Maker, in turn, delivered to Smith the negotiable promissory note signed by Maker, in the amount of $1,500, payable on March 5. The note was payable to the order of "Smith and Wright."

Without Wright's permission and without even informing Wright, Smith delivered the note to Rogers on January 7. Before delivering the note to Rogers, Smith wrote on the back of

the note, "This instrument is given in satisfaction of all amounts due and owing to Rogers." Below this legend, Smith simply signed "Smith." Prior to the delivery of this note, Smith and Rogers had disagreed on the amount Smith owed Rogers. Smith claimed it was only $1,300, and Rogers claimed it was $1,700.

On March 5, Rogers presented the instrument to Maker for payment.

1. If Maker pays the $1,500 to Rogers on March 5, what rights, if any, does Wright have against Maker? Explain.

2. If Maker refuses to pay Rogers the $1,500, on what theories, if any, might Rogers recover against Smith? Explain.

ANSWER TO QUESTION 3

1. If Maker pays the $1,500 to Rogers, Wright will have a right to recover $750 from Maker, either on the underlying obligation or on a conversion theory. At issue are the rights of a co-payee of a promissory note when the note has been transferred by the other co-payee without the first co-payee's indorsement or permission.

Ordinarily, payment by a maker to a person entitled to enforce an instrument (generally the holder or a transferee with the rights of a holder) discharges the maker's liability on the instrument. However, payment to one not entitled to enforce the instrument does not discharge the maker. As will be discussed below, Rogers was not entitled to enforce the note here. Thus, Maker was not discharged by his payment to Rogers.

Wright may bring an action against Maker on the underlying obligation or for conversion. Generally, taking an instrument for an obligation suspends the duty on the obligation. The person who took the instrument may enforce only the instrument until it is discharged or dishonored. [U.C.C. §3-310] This rule does not apply to Wright, however, because Wright never received possession of the note. Maker gave the note to Smith, who stole it. Thus, Maker's obligation to Wright to pay for the snowmobile was not suspended, and Wright is free to sue on the underlying obligation.

In the alternative, Wright may bring an action for conversion. Article 3 provides that the law applicable to conversion of personal property applies to instruments, and also provides that an instrument is converted if it is taken by transfer from a person not entitled to enforce the instrument. [U.C.C. §3-420(a)] There is one limitation, however: a payee may not bring a conversion action unless the payee has received delivery of the instrument directly or through delivery to an agent or a co-payee.

Maker converted the note here because he took it from Rogers. Rogers was not entitled to enforce the note. Generally, only a holder of a note has a right to enforce it. [See U.C.C. §3-301] One may become a holder only through negotiation. What is necessary for negotiation depends on whether the paper is bearer paper or order paper. Bearer paper may be negotiated by mere delivery; negotiation of order paper requires the indorsement of the named payees plus delivery. [U.C.C. §3-201]

The note here was payable to the order of Smith and Wright. Thus, the note was order paper. [*See* U.C.C. §3-109(b)] Negotiation of order paper payable to two persons jointly requires the indorsement of both. [U.C.C. §3-110(d)] Here, Smith indorsed the note before delivering it to Rogers, but Wright did not indorse. Hence, the note was not negotiated to Rogers, and he did not become a holder through the transfer of the note to him by Smith. Neither did he gain the rights of a holder through the transfer. While a transferee generally receives whatever rights his transferor had, Smith could not alone qualify as a holder because the note was payable to Smith and Wright jointly. Thus, Maker converted the note when he took it from Rogers. Since the note was originally delivered to Smith and delivery to a co-payee constitutes delivery to all co-payees for conversion purposes, Wright is entitled to bring an action for conversion.

Wright's recovery will be limited to $750. The measure of liability for conversion is presumed to be the amount payable under the instrument, up to the plaintiff's interest in the instrument. Here, Wright had a half-interest in the $1,500 note; thus his recovery is limited to $750.

2.   If Maker refuses to pay the note, Rogers can sue Smith either for breach of transfer warranty or on the original obligation, but probably cannot sue Smith as an indorser.

When a person transfers an instrument for value, he warrants, among other things, that he is entitled to enforce the instrument. Thus, when Smith transferred the note here to Rogers, Smith warranted that he was entitled to enforce the note. This warranty was broken, because, as discussed above, Smith was not entitled to enforce the note alone; he was a joint payee and only together do joint payees have the right to enforce an instrument. Thus, Rogers can sue Smith for the $1,500 due under the instrument.

Alternatively, Rogers could sue Smith on the original underlying obligation. When an instrument is given to satisfy an obligation, the obligation is suspended to the same extent as it would be discharged if cash were given. [U.C.C. §3-310(b)] An instrument that conspicuously states that it is given in full satisfaction of an unliquidated or disputed debt, therefore, can suspend the obligation for the full debt just as any other accord agreement would. [*See* U.C.C. §3-311] If the instrument is paid, it generally will discharge the entire debt. However, if the instrument is dishonored, the underlying obligation is not discharged. The Code provides that when an instrument is dishonored and in the hands of the obligee, he may enforce the underlying obligation.

Here, Smith gave Rogers the note in full satisfaction of the obligation Smith owed Rogers. The note conspicuously stated that it was in full satisfaction of all amounts owing to Rogers. However, the note was dishonored. Thus, the obligation has not been discharged. Since the note is still in the hands of Rogers—the obligee for which the note was given—he may bring an action to enforce the underlying obligation as he could in any other case when there is no satisfaction of an accord agreement.

Note that Rogers probably cannot sue Smith on his indorsement. As a general rule, if an instrument is dishonored, an indorser is liable on the instrument according to its terms at the time of the indorsement. However, the indorser's liability extends only to one entitled to enforce the instrument. As discussed above, Rogers is not entitled to enforce the note here because it was not properly negotiated to him.

QUESTION 4

Able and Baker decided to sell a rental house they owned jointly. Because the house was in

poor condition, they hired Contractor to perform necessary repairs. Contractor agreed to perform the work for $15,000. After finishing the work in March, Contractor accepted the following document, signed by Able and Baker, in payment of the contract price:

PROMISE TO PAY

We, the undersigned, ABLE and BAKER, promise to pay to the order of cash the sum of $15,000 on December 31, or upon the sale of our house at 340 George Street, whichever occurs first. This promise is made with the expectation that payment will be made with proceeds from the sale of said house.

Dated: March 5.

/s/ _Able_
/s/ _Baker_
Co-makers

In April, Contractor agreed to discharge Able's "Promise to Pay" (but not Baker's) if Able hired Contractor to do repair work on other property Able owned. Able hired Contractor. Contractor crossed out Able's signature on the document and said, "Your liability as co-maker is hereby discharged."

In June, Contractor sold the document for $14,000 to Doe, a good-faith purchaser. Doe knew nothing about the underlying transactions among Contractor, Baker, and Able. Contractor did not sign the document, but simply transferred it to Doe in its original form (with Able's signature crossed out).

Able and Baker's house was sold in November. Because of Contractor's shoddy workman-ship, the house sold for $30,000 less than the asking price. Thereafter, Doe presented the "Promise To Pay" to Baker, and Baker refused to honor it on the ground that Contractor's shoddy workmanship discharged his obligation to pay the contract price. Under local contract law, poor workmanship is a breach of contract and a defense to payment of the contract price.

1. Is the "Promise to Pay" a negotiable instrument? Explain.

2. Can Baker successfully raise Contractor's shoddy workmanship as a defense against paying Doe on the "Promise to Pay"? Explain.

3. If Baker is forced to pay Doe, does Baker have any rights of recovery from Able? Explain.

ANSWER TO QUESTION 4

1.   The promise to pay is a negotiable instrument. Article 3 of the Uniform Commercial Code ("U.C.C.") governs commercial paper, including promissory notes. To be negotiable, under Article 3, an instrument must be (i) signed by the maker (note) or drawer (draft) and (ii) be unconditional, (iii) contain a promise to pay (note) or order to pay (draft) (iv) a fixed amount of money (with or without interest), (v) to bearer or to order, (vi) on demand or at a definite time, and (vii) without any undertaking or instruction not authorized by law.

The instrument here is in writing, and it is signed by Able and Baker. It also is unconditional. The statement that payment is expected to be made from the proceeds of the sale of the house does not make the instrument conditional since the statement does not say that payment will be made only if the sale proceeds are sufficient, and even if it did, Article 3 allows instruments to state that they are to be paid from a particular fund or source. The instrument contains a promise to pay (and thus is a note) a fixed amount of money ($15,000) "to the order of cash." Under Article 3, a note payable to the order of cash is payable to bearer because the note indicates that it is not payable to an identified person. The note here also is payable at a definite time. To be payable at a definite time, the latest date on which payment may be made must be known. Here, the statement that the note was to be paid on December 31 or upon the sale of the house, whichever occurs first, establishes December 31 as the latest date on which the note could be paid. The provision regarding the sale of the house operates as an acceleration clause (*i.e.*, it allows payment to be made earlier than the latest date for payment), which is permitted under Article 3. Finally, the note does not contain any other promise or undertaking. Thus, it meets the Article 3 requirements for negotiability.

2.   Baker cannot successfully raise the Contractor's shoddy workmanship as a defense against paying Doe. Under Article 3, the defenses that a maker can raise against payment of a note depend on whether the note has been negotiated to a holder in due course ("HDC"). If the note has been negotiated to an HDC, only so-called real defenses are available; personal defenses are not available. If the note has not been negotiated to an HDC, all defenses available in a regular contract action may be raised. The defense here—shoddy workmanship—is a personal defense. Thus, it cannot be raised if the note was negotiated to Doe and Doe is an HDC. And, under the facts, the note was negotiated to Doe and Doe is an HDC.

The steps necessary to negotiate a note depend on whether the note is a bearer instrument or an order instrument. As discussed above, the note here is a bearer instrument because it is payable to cash and, thus, does not purport to be payable to an identified person. All that is necessary to negotiate a bearer instrument is delivery. Here, Contractor delivered the note to Doe; thus, the note was negotiated.

Doe also qualifies as an HDC. To be an HDC one must take a note for value, in good faith, and without notice of any defenses on or claims to the note. Doe qualifies. He took the note for value ($14,000). The facts say that Doe took the note in good faith. And the fact that the note was sold at a discount and that one co-maker's signature had been crossed out does not give notice of any defense. Thus, Baker cannot raise the shoddy workmanship as a defense since that is a personal defense.

3.   If Baker is forced to pay Doe, Baker may recover from Able. At issue is whether a co-maker can recover from a fellow co-maker after the first co-maker pays on the instrument and a holder discharged the second co-maker. Unless co-makers provide otherwise, they are jointly and severally liable on the instrument they sign. Under Article 3, if one co-maker pays the entire instrument, he has a right of contribution from the other co-maker. Discharge of one co-maker by a person entitled to enforce the instrument does not affect the right of contribution. Here, Able and Baker signed as co-makers and so were jointly and severally liable in that capacity. Thus, although Contractor, a person entitled to enforce the note, released Able, Able remains liable to Baker, who paid the full amount of the note.

QUESTION 5

Software, Inc., applied to Bank for a $250,000 loan to finance an expansion of its business. Bank was unwilling to make the loan unless Investor, an independently wealthy businessman

with a substantial stock interest in Software, agreed to co-sign the loan. Despite the fact that he held stock in Software, Investor played no role in managing the company and did not serve on its board of directors.

Software's chief executive officer ("CEO") asked Investor to co-sign the loan. After studying Software's expansion plans, Investor urged CEO to seek a $500,000 loan, arguing that $250,000 was not enough to finance fully the proposed expansion. CEO, however, was adamantly opposed to incurring any debt beyond $250,000 and refused to consider seeking a larger loan. Nonetheless, Investor agreed to talk further with Bank about co-signing the loan.

In separate negotiations with Bank, to which neither CEO nor Software was party, Investor explained his belief that a $500,000 loan was necessary to finance the proposed expansion and indicated his unwillingness to co-sign a loan for $250,000, which he felt would prove inadequate. Investor agreed to co-sign the $250,000 loan on condition that Bank agree to lend Software an additional $250,000 within six months, if necessary to complete the project. Bank agreed and wrote a letter to Investor to that effect. This agreement and letter were not disclosed to Software or CEO.

On January 15, Bank made Software a $250,000 loan with a due date of November 1. A negotiable promissory note was signed both by CEO on behalf of Software and by Investor personally. Software and Investor were designated co-makers on the note.

Within three months, Software had spent the full $250,000 and had still not completed the expansion project. Software approached Bank about a second loan for $250,000. Bank, fearful that Software was in a shaky financial situation, refused the second loan. As a result, Software was unable to complete the expansion project.

When the $250,000 loan came due on November 1, Investor told Software of the secret agreement between Investor and Bank. Both Software and Investor refused to pay Bank. After several requests for payment, Bank sold the overdue note to Collection Agency for $150,000. Bank endorsed the note and transferred it to Collection Agency on December 15.

Collection Agency has now sued both Software and Investor seeking payment of the note. State law permits the introduction of evidence of contemporaneous or previous agreements in suits for breach of contract.

What are the rights and liabilities of Investor, Software, and Collection Agency on the note? Explain.

ANSWER TO QUESTION 5

Collection Agency has a right to enforce the note against Investor and Software, but is subject to their breach of contract defense. At issue are the rights of a holder of a negotiable promissory note against the note's maker and an accommodation maker, both of whom have personal defenses with regard to the transaction out of which the note arose. Since a negotiable promissory note is involved, Article 3 of the Uniform Commercial Code will govern.

Collection Agency has a right to enforce the note against its makers, Software and Investor, since Collection Agency qualifies as a holder. Article 3 grants a number of persons the right to enforce a negotiable promissory note, but the primary person to enforce is a holder. A holder is a person in possession of a note payable to bearer or to the person in possession. Here, the note presumably was originally payable to Bank, but Bank indorsed the note over to Collection Agency and transferred it to Collection Agency. This was a proper negotiation which would make Collection Agency a holder of the note.

The holder of a note may hold liable the makers of the note or any indorsers on the note. Thus, Collection Agency could sue Bank (under its indorsement) or any maker(s). The facts state that Collection Agency has chosen to sue Investor and Software. Software is clearly liable as a maker of the note, since the note was signed by Software's CEO on behalf of Software. Investor is also a maker of the note even though he signed only as an accommodation party (*i.e.,* as a surety), because an accommodation party is liable on an instrument in the capacity in which he signed, and here Investor signed as co-maker. Nevertheless, Software and Investor might not be liable for the entire $250,000 due under the note because they can raise Bank's breach of contract as a defense.

Breach of contract is a personal defense, and under Article 3's holder in due course ("HDC") rule, is available to Software and Investor only if Collection Agency is not an HDC. Article 3 provides that when a negotiable instrument is negotiated to a holder in due course, he takes free of personal defenses and is subject only to the so-called real defenses. The facts tell us that the note here was negotiable; thus, Software and Investor can raise their defense only if Collection Agency is not an HDC.

Collection Agency is not an HDC. To qualify as an HDC, a holder must have taken the instrument for value, in good faith, and without notice of any defenses on or claims to the instrument. Collection Agency took the note here for value (the $100,000 discount does not negate the value element) and in good faith, but it will be deemed to have had notice of a defense since the note was overdue. Thus, Collection Agency does not qualify as an HDC and is subject to any defense that could be raised on a simple contract.

Here, Investor will raise Bank's breach of contract as a defense. Bank promised Investor that if Investor would co-sign the $250,000 loan, Bank would loan Software up to $250,000 more if necessary to complete the expansion. Bank failed to make the additional loan; thus, Investor could raise this breach as a defense.

Software could also raise Bank's failure to make the loan as a defense, even though Software did not know of the agreement between Bank and Investor. Generally, a party to a negotiable instrument can raise only its own defenses in an action on an instrument. While at first blush it appears that Bank's breach is a defense only for Investor, it is also a defense for Software because Software was an intended third-party beneficiary of the contract between Investor and Bank, and intended third-party beneficiaries have a right to sue on the contract benefiting them.

Finally, it should be noted that while Investor was a co-maker, as between Software and Investor, Software has primary responsibility for the entire $250,000 note because a principal is liable to an accommodation party if an accommodation party is forced to pay on account of the accommodation. Of course, this right would be useless if, as it appears, Software is insolvent.

QUESTION 6

On August 1, Alice sold her piano to Bart. In addition to a down payment, Bart gave Alice a

negotiable note for $2,000 payable on demand to the order of Alice. On August 5, Alice asked to borrow $2,500 from Cathy. Cathy agreed, but she insisted as a condition of the loan that the loan be secured by Bart's $2,000 note. Alice signed an agreement that granted Cathy a security interest in Bart's note and promised to deliver the note to Cathy in the next week or so. Cathy delivered the $2,500 to Alice that same day but did nothing further to perfect Cathy's interest in Bart's note.

On August 9, through no fault of Alice, Dan stole the note. Alice had already signed her name, and nothing more, on the back of the note. Dan wrote his own signature beneath Alice's. Dan then sold the note for $1,900 to Edwin, who had no way of knowing how Dan had acquired the note. On August 15, Edwin brought the note to Bart and presented it to him for payment. Bart refused to pay Edwin because the piano Alice had sold him turned out to be worthless. Also on August 15, Cathy learned that Edwin had the note and demanded that Edwin turn it over to her.

1.   Can Edwin successfully enforce the note against Bart? Explain.

2.   Is Cathy's claim to the note superior to Edwin's claim? Explain.

ANSWER TO QUESTION 6

1.   Edwin can successfully enforce the note against Bart. At issue is whether Edwin has the rights of a holder in due course ("HDC").

The maker of a note undertakes to pay the note when it is properly presented for payment by a holder, unless the maker has a valid defense. Bart has refused to pay on his note because of failure of the underlying consideration for the note (*i.e.*, the piano was worthless). Failure of consideration is a so-called personal defense. An HDC is not subject to personal defenses. Thus, if Edwin is an HDC, he is not subject to Bart's defense and Bart must pay on the note.

An HDC is a holder who takes a note for value, in good faith, and without notice of any claims to the note or defenses on the note. Here, Edwin purchased the note from Dan for value ($1,900), apparently in good faith, and without notice of either Dan's thievery or the condition of the piano. Thus, all that remains is to determine whether Edwin qualifies as a holder.

Edwin qualifies as a holder of the note. A holder is a person in possession of a note to whom the note has been properly negotiated. What is required to properly negotiate a note depends on whether the note is a bearer note or an order note. Bearer notes are negotiated by delivery alone; order notes require a proper indorsement plus delivery. Here, the note originally was order paper, since it was made payable to the order of Alice. Alice converted it to bearer paper by signing her name on the note "in blank" (*i.e.*, with "nothing more"). Thus, it could be further negotiated by delivery alone. Dan stole the note and delivered it to Edwin. This was a proper negotiation. Thus, Edwin is a holder, and since Edwin also qualifies as an HDC, he may successfully enforce the note against Bart despite Bart's defense.

2.   Cathy's claim is not superior to Edwin's claim. At issue is whether a perfected security interest in a negotiable instrument has priority over the claim of an HDC.

Cathy has a perfected security interest in the note. A security interest can attach to a negotiable instrument in the same way a security interest can attach to other property: (i) the parties must agree to create a security interest, as evidenced by a written security agreement signed by the debtor or by the secured party's taking possession of the collateral; (ii) the debtor must have rights in the collateral; and (iii) the secured party must give value in exchange for the security interest. Moreover, a security interest in a negotiable instrument is temporarily perfected on attachment for 20 days if new value is given for the security interest.

Here, Alice signed a security agreement giving Cathy a security interest in the note, Alice was the holder of the note when she gave the security interest, and Cathy gave new value for the security interest in the note (a $2,500 loan). Thus, Cathy's security interest attached to the note and was temporarily perfected for 21 days.

Although it has been only 15 days since Cathy's security interest attached to the note, and her interest is still perfected, she nevertheless does not have priority over Edwin. Article 9 of the Uniform Commercial Code provides that an HDC of a negotiable instrument has priority over a prior perfected security interest in the note. Thus, Edwin's claim to the note is superior.

QUESTION 7

Ted is the treasurer of Acme Corporation. As treasurer, he is authorized to sign checks and issue them on behalf of Acme.

Ted and his brother-in-law Fred devised a plan to defraud Acme. Ted would issue checks to a fictitious sole proprietorship, SupplyCo, purportedly in payment of invoices for goods supplied to Acme by SupplyCo. To accomplish the fraud, Fred had phony invoices prepared on forms bearing the letterhead "SupplyCo" and opened an account at Small Bank in the name of SupplyCo. Ted and Fred made checks payable to the order of SupplyCo from their own personal accounts to establish a "track record" with Small Bank of checks payable to SupplyCo being honored by drawees.

After a month during which such checks cleared in amounts ranging from $100 to $10,000, Ted prepared a check as treasurer of Acme drawn on Acme's bank, Big Bank, in the amount of $9,000 payable to the order of SupplyCo. Ted signed the Acme check as treasurer and then gave the check to Fred. Fred indorsed the check as follows: "For Deposit Only—SupplyCo" and deposited the check in the SupplyCo account at Small Bank. The check was presented by Small Bank to Big Bank, and Big Bank honored the check.

After Big Bank honored the SupplyCo check, a routine audit of Acme was made. The audit uncovered the fraudulent payment to SupplyCo. However, by the time Acme discovered the fraud, Fred had withdrawn the $9,000 from the SupplyCo account in a transaction in which Small Bank was acting in good faith. Fred and Ted have disappeared.

Under Article 3 of the Uniform Commercial Code, which, among Small Bank, Big Bank, and Acme, must bear the $9,000 loss? Explain.

ANSWER TO QUESTION 7

Acme will bear the loss. At issue is who bears the loss when a corporate employee draws a corporate check payable to a fictitious payee and the check is cashed: the drawer corporation, the depositary bank, or the drawee bank. Because this question involves a check, Uniform Commercial Code ("U.C.C.") Articles 3 and 4 govern.

It should first be noted that the check here contained a forgery: It was made payable to "SupplyCo," and SupplyCo did not exist; rather Fred signed the name SupplyCo on the check. The general rule is that a forgery is ineffective as the name signed and effective only as the signature of the forger. If SupplyCo's signature is invalid, Big Bank would have to recredit Acme's account because a bank may not charge its customer's account for a check that is not properly payable. The check here was not properly payable because it was payable only to SupplyCo and SupplyCo—being nonexistent—was not paid; instead payment was made to Fred. Big Bank, in turn, could recover from Small Bank. Although the general rule is that payment is final on a negotiable instrument if it is made to a holder in due course or someone who changes position in reliance on the payment, an exception exists if the person paid breaches a warranty. Small Bank breached a presentment warranty. A person presenting a check for payment warrants, among other things, that he is entitled to enforce the check. A holder is entitled to enforce a check only if the indorsements of the payee and any special indorsee are genuine. Since the payee's signature was forged here, Small Bank breached the warranty, thus enabling Big Bank to recover from Small Bank.

However, the general rule will not apply here because the U.C.C. provides that if the drawer, or other person whose intent determines to whom an instrument is payable, draws the instrument payable to a fictitious payee, any person in possession of the instrument is a holder and any indorsement in a name substantially similar to the name of the fictitious payee is effective as an indorsement of the named payee as to anyone who takes the instrument in good faith and for value. The person paying or taking the instrument must nevertheless use ordinary care in taking the instrument or it will become liable to the extent its failure contributed to any loss.

Here, Ted, the treasurer of Acme, drew the check payable to SupplyCo, which he knew to be a fictitious sole proprietorship, and gave the check to Fred. Under the fictitious payee rules discussed above, Fred was a holder of the check and his indorsement in the name of SupplyCo was effective. Since the forgery was effective, the check was properly payable by Big Bank, and Big Bank does not have to recredit Acme's account. Moreover, Acme will not be able to recover from Small Bank. Nothing in the facts indicates that Small Bank did not act in good faith, and it certainly gave value for the check, since it allowed the proceeds to be removed from the account. Small Bank also exercised ordinary care: Ted and Fred wrote checks to SupplyCo in amounts similar to the Acme check for several months to make it appear that SupplyCo genuinely existed, and those checks cleared without incident. Thus, Small Bank had no reason to doubt SupplyCo's validity. Therefore, Acme will bear the loss.

QUESTION 8

Trucker owned a truck insured by Insurance Co. ("Insco") against loss by theft.

On January 2, Trucker reported the truck stolen and filed a claim for its value with Insco. The police were not able to recover the truck and, on February 2, Insco issued a draft in the amount of $10,000 in settlement of the loss. The draft is a negotiable instrument, payable to the order of Trucker, and is drawn by Insco on itself, payable through Bank.

On February 3, Trucker negotiated the draft to Acme Motors in partial payment for a new truck. Trucker signed on the reverse side of the draft, "Pay to Acme Motors, Trucker."

On February 4, Acme Motors stamped on the reverse side of the draft "Pay to State Savings, Acme Motors." Later that day, Acme Motors and Trucker had a disagreement about the purchase of the new truck. They rescinded their sales contract, and Acme Motors returned the Insco draft to Trucker. Trucker immediately drew lines through both Trucker's February 3 indorsement and the language stamped on the draft by Acme Motors.

On February 5, Trucker again endorsed the draft by signing "Trucker" on the reverse side. He delivered it to Bank with instructions to apply it to a loan on which Trucker owed Bank $20,000. Bank immediately applied the full amount of the $10,000 draft to the indebtedness Trucker owed to Bank.

On February 6, Insco learned from the police that Trucker had received $2,000 from Rob as part of a prearranged scheme between Rob and Trucker, in which Rob "stole" Trucker's truck and disposed of it.

On February 7, Bank presented the draft to Insco for payment, and the draft was dishonored. The draft is in the possession of Bank, which has timely given all necessary notices of dishonor.

Trucker is insolvent.

Are Acme Motors and Insco liable to Bank on the draft? Explain.

ANSWER TO QUESTION 8

Acme is not liable on the draft, but Insco is. Since this question involves a negotiable instrument, Article 3 of the Uniform Commercial Code governs.

Acme: Acme is not liable on the note because Acme was discharged by Trucker's drawing lines through Acme's indorsement. At issue is the liability of an indorser after a prior indorser reacquires the instrument and strikes out the later indorser's indorsement.

Generally, a person who indorses a negotiable instrument enters into a contract that if the instrument is presented for payment and is dishonored (*i.e.*, is not paid), the indorser will pay if timely notified of the dishonor. However, the indorser's contract can be discharged in a number of ways. Relevant here, if a former holder reacquires an instrument and strikes out the indorsements that were made between the time he formerly held the instrument and the present, the cancellation will discharge the stricken indorsers against all subsequent holders, including holders in due course ("HDCs") who have notice of the discharge. This is exactly what happened here. Trucker was a holder when Insco issued the draft to Trucker. Trucker indorsed the draft and gave it to Acme Motors, which also indorsed the draft. Acme then returned the draft to Trucker, who then drew lines through Acme's indorsement. This should be sufficient to discharge Acme, even against an HDC, because the HDC would have notice of the discharge because the indorsement was physically lined through on the draft itself.

It might be argued that Trucker did not properly reacquire the draft because Acme had indorsed the draft "Pay to State Savings," so the draft could not be further negotiated without State Savings's indorsement. However, Article 3 does not require a reacquisition to be by negotiation. The reacquisition here was proper because the draft was never transferred from Acme to State Savings; thus, State Savings Bank never became a holder and nothing in Article 3 prohibits a holder from "changing his mind" before an instrument is transferred to a new holder.

Insco: Insco is liable on the draft since it was the draft's drawer. At issue is whether fraud in the inducement is a valid defense against Bank. Article 3's HDC rule will govern here.

The drawer of a draft can be held liable on the draft unless the drawer has a defense to payment. Under the HDC rule, if a negotiable instrument is negotiated to an HDC, the HDC takes free of personal defenses; the drawer may successfully assert only real defenses. An HDC is a holder who takes a negotiable instrument for value (which includes antecedent debts), in good faith, and without notice of defenses on or claims to the instrument. Real defenses are limited to the defenses provided in Article 3, such as fraud in the execution (but not fraud in the inducement), insanity, duress, etc.

Here, the facts state that the draft is negotiable. It was properly negotiated to Bank by Trucker. As discussed above, Trucker reacquired the draft and then struck out the intervening indorsements. Therefore, Trucker was free to negotiate the draft again. Proper negotiation requires the signature of the named payee (originally Trucker) and delivery, and here Trucker indorsed and delivered the draft to Bank. Bank also gave value: It applied the proceeds to reduce a debt owed by Trucker. While satisfaction of an antecedent debt is not consideration, it is value for purposes of Article 3. Moreover, the fact that the draft only partially satisfied the antecedent debt does not negate the value element. Bank gave full value by applying the full face amount of the draft to the antecedent debt. Bank also apparently took the draft in good faith and without notice of any defenses or claims. The mere fact that Trucker had reacquired the draft would not be sufficient to give notice of a defense. The fact that the draft at one time was payable to State Savings and that State Savings never indorsed might be sufficient to give notice of a claim by State Savings, but under the facts, State Savings has no claim to the draft, so this argument probably would not prevail. Finally, Insco's defense is not one of the real defenses in Article 3. Essentially, Insco is claiming that it was defrauded into issuing the draft, but fraud in the inducement is not a real defense. Thus, Bank is not subject to the defense, and Insco will be required to pay the draft.

QUESTION 9

Andy wanted to install siding on his house. Barbara agreed to do the work for $10,000 and to accept as payment a $10,000 note that would come due on October 1. Andy issued the note to Barbara on August 1 using a form note that he bought at a stationery store. Assuming that Barbara would complete the form in accordance with their agreement, Andy did not fill in two parts of the form: the due date and the amount to be paid. He did, however, sign the note and insert Barbara's name in the space following the words "I promise to pay to the order of."

After Barbara took the note, she typed $20,000 in the blank space reserved for the amount instead of the $10,000 to which she and Andy had agreed. Barbara did not bother filling in the empty space for the due date. On August 15, Barbara properly indorsed the note and sold it to Carl for $19,000. When Carl took the note, he was unaware of the alteration and had no notice of any other claims or defenses to the note.

On August 20, Carl presented the note to Andy and demanded that Andy pay him $20,000. Andy explained to Carl that he had agreed to pay Barbara only $10,000 and that, in any event, he and Barbara agreed that the note would not be due until October 1.

1.   Can Carl enforce the note against Andy for $20,000? Explain.

2.   Can Carl enforce the note against Andy before October 1? Explain.

ANSWER TO QUESTION 9

1.   Carl can enforce the note against Andy for $20,000. At issue is the holder in due course ("HDC") rule. Because this question involves a promissory note, it is governed by Article 3 of the Uniform Commercial Code ("U.C.C."), which governs all commercial paper.

A central theme of Article 3 is the HDC rule: If a negotiable instrument is negotiated to an HDC, the HDC takes the instrument free of personal defenses and is subject only to the so-called real defenses enumerated in Article 3.

The note here appears to have been negotiable. To be negotiable, a note must be in writing and signed by its maker; it must contain an unconditional promise to pay a fixed amount of money, to order or to bearer, on demand or at a definite time, without any undertakings or instructions not authorized by Article 3. The note here was in writing and signed by the maker (Andy). We were not told of any conditions on payment or undertakings or instructions listed on the note; presumably there were none. When Andy signed the note, he made it payable to the order of Barbara. Thus, all of the requisites for negotiability, except the amount and the time of payment requirements, were met. These latter two elements require more discussion.

When the note here was issued by Andy, it did not state when it was payable or the amount that was payable. Under Article 3, if an instrument does not state the date that it is payable, it is payable on demand. The U.C.C. also provides that if the amount is left blank and is later completed by an unauthorized person or in an unauthorized manner, the note is enforceable against the maker according to the completed terms if held by an HDC. Thus, the note here qualifies as a negotiable instrument.

The note was also negotiated. What is required for negotiation depends on whether the note was order paper or bearer paper. Here the note was payable *to the order of* Barbara. Order paper requires the indorsement of the named payee and delivery. Barbara indorsed and gave the note to Carl. Thus, there was a proper negotiation.

Finally, Carl meets the requirements for HDC status. To be an HDC, one must be a holder (*i.e.*, one to whom the instrument was issued or negotiated) who took the instrument for value, in good faith (both subjective good faith and within the objective bounds of what is commercially reasonable), and without notice of any defenses or adverse claims to the instrument. Carl qualifies as a holder because the note was negotiated to him, as discussed above. He also took for value ($19,000), in good faith (nothing in the facts indicates bad faith; the $1,000 discount is not so big as to call into question the bona fides of the transaction; neither does the fact that the due date was not filled in), and without notice of defenses.

Carl can enforce the note against Andy for the full $20,000. As discussed above, Carl is an HDC, and an HDC is subject only to the real defenses provided in Article 3, which do not apply here. Unauthorized completion is not one of the real defenses. An HDC takes free of this defense. Thus, Carl can enforce the note against Andy.

2.   Carl can enforce the note immediately. The fact that the note did not have the due date filled in, as discussed above, did not affect its negotiability because it will be treated as a note payable on demand. If the note is treated as one payable on demand, Carl will not have to wait until October 1 to be paid and can demand payment at any time.

QUESTION 10

Aaron agreed to paint Bob and Cathy's house for $2,000. After finishing the paint job, Aaron took as full payment from Bob and Cathy a $2,000 negotiable note that Bob and Cathy signed as co-makers. The note was due in one month and provided for 10% interest to accrue after the due date. A week after receiving the note from Bob and Cathy, Aaron sold the note for $1,500 to Debra, a good faith purchaser for value. Aaron properly indorsed the back of the note.

Debra held the note for about two weeks and then sold it for $1,700 to Edward, another good faith purchaser for value. Debra also properly indorsed the note on the back, directly beneath Aaron's signature. When Edward came into possession of the note, he crossed out Aaron's signature as indorser as a gesture of friendship to Aaron. Edward then indorsed the note and sold it to Frieda for $1,900.

Upon learning that Frieda was now in possession of the note, Bob approached Frieda on the note's due date and properly tendered $2,000 in payment of the note. Frieda did not need the cash at that time and assumed the note would continue to accrue interest, so she arbitrarily refused to accept payment. Six months later, Frieda decided to collect $2,000 in principal and $100 in accrued interest for the note.

What are Frieda's rights to recover the principal, interest, or both from:

(a)   Bob? Explain.

(b)   Cathy? Explain.

(c)   Debra? Explain.

(d)   Aaron? Explain.

ANSWER TO QUESTION 10

Frieda may recover the principal, but no interest, from Bob and/or Cathy; she may not recover anything from Debra or Aaron. At issue are the rights of a holder of a note to collect from its co-makers and indorsers after one co-maker has tendered payment and the holder refused to accept the tender. Because this question involves a promissory note, Article 3 of the Uniform Commercial Code will control the parties' rights.

Under Article 3, a maker or co-maker of a note is primarily liable to pay the note according to its terms at the time the note was written. Co-makers have joint and several liability, and so a holder can seek payment of the entire amount due under a note from either co-maker. An indorser, on the other hand, is liable to pay on a note only if the note is presented to the maker for payment, is dishonored, and the holder gives the indorser notice of dishonor. If a maker of a note tenders payment to the holder when the note is due, the tender discharges the maker(s) from the duty to pay interest after the due date, but does not discharge the duty to pay the principal. The tender also discharges any person who has a right of recourse against the party making tender. Based on these rules, Frieda will have the following rights against the parties:

(a)   Frieda will have a right to recover the principal from Bob, but not the interest. Bob signed the note as a co-maker and thus is liable for the full amount due. However, Bob tendered payment on the date the note was due. The note provided that it would not accrue any interest until after the due date. Thus, Bob will not be liable for any interest on the note.

(b)   Frieda will have a right to recover the principal from Cathy, but not the interest for the same reasons as discussed with regard to Bob. Cathy signed as co-maker.

(c)   Frieda will not be entitled to recover anything from Debra. Debra signed the note as an indorser. As noted above, an indorser is liable on a note only if the note is presented to its maker for payment, is dishonored, and notice of dishonor is given. Here, none of these prerequisites to indorser liability were met. Moreover, if an indorser is forced to pay a note, the indorser has a right of recourse against the note's maker. That is, an indorser who is forced to pay on a note can recover the payment from the maker. Thus, as discussed above, Bob's tender of payment has the effect of discharging Debra. For either of these two reasons, Debra has no liability on the note.

(d)   Frieda will not be entitled to recover anything from Aaron because Aaron's indorsement was stricken by Edward. A person entitled to enforce an instrument may, even without consideration, discharge any party from the instrument by a voluntary act, such as striking out the party's signature. Here, Edward was a holder of the note before Frieda, and while he held the note, he struck out Aaron's name. Thus, Aaron was released from liability on the note. It should be noted that if Edward had not crossed out Aaron's name, Aaron would still not be liable for the same reasons that Debra is not liable—Aaron signed the note as an indorser, and Frieda's refusing Bob's tender of payment has the effect of releasing all indorsers.

QUESTION 11

On February 1, Roofer and Brother agreed that Roofer would install a new roof on Brother's house for $8,000. They also agreed that Roofer would accept as payment a non-interest-bearing promissory note from Brother that would come due six months after Roofer finished the job.

Because Roofer had some concerns about Brother's creditworthiness, Roofer convinced Brother to have Sister, who lived in her own house, also sign the note. In addition, Brother

agreed to secure his obligation on the note with a perfected security interest in Brother's three computers, each of which was worth $2,000.

On March 1, Roofer finished installing the roof on Brother's house. On that same day, Brother issued and signed as maker an $8,000 negotiable note payable "to the order of Roofer" and due on September 1 of the same year. Sister put her signature on the back of the note. There were no notations or descriptive words accompanying Sister's signature. At the same time, Roofer obtained and properly perfected a security interest in Brother's three computers.

On May 1, Roofer sold the note to Lender, who purchased the note in good faith for $7,500. Before transferring the note to Lender, Roofer signed the note on the back, beneath Sister's signature. Roofer also properly transferred his security interest in the computers to Lender.

On June 1, Brother convinced Lender to release Lender's rights to one of the three computers that secured the note, and Brother sold that computer. Sister had no knowledge of this release by Lender.

On July 1, it became clear that Roofer had done such a poor roofing job that Brother would need to spend $3,000 to fix the roof. On September 1, Lender still held the note. When Lender demanded payment, Brother refused because "the roof job was shabby."

(A) Can Lender enforce the note to its full extent against Brother? Explain.

(B) Can Lender enforce the note to its full extent against Sister? Explain.

(C) If Sister has to pay all or part of the note, what rights, if any, does she have against Brother? Explain.

ANSWER TO QUESTION 11

(A) Lender can enforce the note to its full extent against Brother. At issue is the holder in due course ("HDC") rule. Because this question involves a promissory note, it is governed by Article 3 of the Uniform Commercial Code, which governs all commercial paper.

Generally, the maker of a note is obligated to pay the note according to its terms to any holder who presents the note for payment. While this liability is not absolute, if the HDC rule is applicable, the maker's defenses against payment are very limited. Under the HDC rule, if a negotiable instrument is negotiated to an HDC, the HDC takes the instrument free of personal defenses and is subject only to the so-called real defenses enumerated in Article 3. The rule applies here. The facts say that the note was negotiable. The note was also negotiated. What is required for negotiation depends on whether the note was order paper or bearer paper. Here the note was payable to the order of Lender and so was order paper. Order paper requires the indorsement of the named payee and delivery. Brother indorsed the note and gave it to Lender. Thus, there was a proper negotiation.

Finally, Lender meets the requirements for HDC status. To be an HDC, one must be a holder (*i.e.*, one to whom the instrument was issued or negotiated) who took the instrument for value, in good faith (both subjective good faith and within the objective bounds of what is commercially reasonable), and without notice of any defenses or adverse claims to the instrument. Lender qualifies as a holder because the note was negotiated to it, as discussed above. Lender also took for value ($7,500), in good faith (as per the facts), and without notice of any defenses.

Because Lender is an HDC, Brother does not have a valid defense against payment. As noted above, an HDC is subject only to the real defenses provided in Article 3. Brother's defense—that the roofing job was shabby—is not one of the real defenses and so cannot be used against Lender. Thus, Lender can enforce the note to the extent of its full $8,000 face value against Brother.

(B) Lender cannot enforce the note to its full extent against Sister. At issue is the effect of Lender's releasing the computer that served as collateral.

Sister signed the note as an accommodation indorser. An accommodation indorser is a person who indorses an instrument for the purpose of lending her name and credit to another party to the instrument. Generally, a person who indorses a negotiable instrument enters into a contract that if the instrument is presented for payment and is dishonored (*i.e.*, is not paid), the indorser will pay if timely notified of the dishonor. However, the indorser's contract can be discharged in a number of ways. Relevant here, if the person entitled to enforce an instrument impairs collateral securing the instrument, and an accommodation party had a right of recourse against the collateral, the accommodation party will be discharged to the extent of the impairment if the person entitled to enforce the instrument knew of the accommodation. A party entitled to enforce an instrument will be deemed to know of an accommodation if the accommodating party's signature is anomalous (made by a person who was not a holder) or that otherwise indicates that the party signed as a surety.

Here, Sister's indorsement was anomalous: The note was payable to the order of Roofer, and Roofer was the holder who transferred the note to Lender, yet Sister had indorsed. Thus, it should have been obvious to Lender that Sister was serving as surety. Therefore, she will be discharged to the extent of the collateral released by Lender. Since the collateral released was worth $2,000, Sister will be liable only for $6,000 of the note's $8,000 face value.

(C) If Sister has to pay on the note, she can recover whatever she pays from Brother. At issue are the duties owed to an accommodation party.

If an accommodation party pays on an instrument, she will have an action on the instrument against the party accommodated, irrespective of her formal positions on the note. Thus, since Sister was an accommodation party, if she has to pay on the note, she can recover from Brother. Moreover, Sister would be able to recover from Brother even if she were not an accommodation party, since generally the maker of a note is liable to an indorser who pays out on the instrument.

QUESTION 12

Maker and Neighbor own adjacent properties. For several years, Maker deposited leaves and grass clippings in a compost pile located in Neighbor's yard without Neighbor's permission. After a number of unsuccessful efforts to convince Maker to remove the compost pile, Neighbor sued Maker for trespass.

In settlement of the suit, Maker agreed to remove the compost pile and to give Neighbor a promissory note for $1,000, payable on demand. Neighbor dismissed the lawsuit and, at the same time, Maker prepared, signed, and delivered to Neighbor a document that contained the following and nothing more:

> I promise to pay $ 1,000 to the order of Neighbor.
> /s/Maker

Neighbor, who owed Bank an overdue debt of $900, got Bank to agree to accept Maker's note in full satisfaction of the overdue debt. Without notice to Maker, Neighbor wrote on the back of the note, "Pay to the order of Bank," signed it, and delivered it to Bank. Bank thereupon canceled the debt owed to it by Neighbor.

The following week, Maker removed the compost pile. At that time, Neighbor approached Maker and without presenting the note said, "I'm here to collect my $1,000." Maker, unaware of the transaction between Neighbor and Bank, paid Neighbor $1,000.

A few days later, Bank presented the note to Maker and demanded that Maker pay Bank $1,000. Maker refused to pay Bank, telling Bank that he had already paid Neighbor the $1,000.

1. Was Maker obligated to pay Neighbor when Neighbor demanded payment? Explain.

2. Was Maker obligated to pay Bank when Bank demanded payment? Explain.

ANSWER TO QUESTION 12

1.   Maker was not obligated to pay Neighbor when Neighbor demanded payment. At issue is the effect of giving a negotiable instrument to satisfy an obligation. Because this question involves commercial paper (a promissory note), Article 3 of the Uniform Commercial Code governs.

Maker had no obligation to pay Neighbor on the instrument. Generally, a maker is obligated only to pay the holder of a negotiable instrument. To qualify as a holder, one generally must have possession of the instrument. Here, at the time Neighbor sought payment, he had already transferred possession of the note to Bank. Thus, at the time of Neighbor's request, Bank was a holder and Neighbor was not. Therefore, Maker had no obligation to pay Neighbor on the note when Neighbor asked for payment.

Neither did Maker have an obligation to pay Neighbor on the obligation underlying the note. If an instrument is given to satisfy an obligation, unless the parties agree otherwise, the obligation is suspended until the instrument is paid or is dishonored. Thus, having given Neighbor a promissory note to satisfy the $1,000 obligation, Maker had no obligation to pay Neighbor other than as provided in the note.

2.   Maker was obligated to pay Bank. At issue is the holder in due course ("HDC") rule.

Generally, the maker of a note is obligated to pay the note according to its terms to any holder who presents the note for payment. While this liability is not absolute, if the HDC rule is applicable, the maker's defenses against payment are very limited. Under the HDC rule, if a negotiable instrument is negotiated to an HDC, the HDC takes the instrument free of personal defenses and is subject only to the so-called real defenses enumerated in Article 3.

The note here is negotiable. To be negotiable, a note must be in writing and signed by its maker; it must contain an unconditional promise to pay a fixed amount of money, to order or to bearer, on demand or at a definite time, without any undertakings or instructions not authorized by Article 3. The note here was in writing and signed by the maker (Maker). It did not contain any conditions on payment. It was for a fixed amount ($1,000) payable to the order of Neighbor. It was payable on demand because it did not state a date for payment. Finally, it did not contain any other undertakings or instructions. Thus, all of the requisites for negotiability were met.

The note here was also negotiated. What is required for negotiation depends on whether the note was order paper or bearer paper. Here the note was payable to the order of Neighbor when it was issued. Negotiation of order paper requires the indorsement of the named payee and delivery. Neighbor indorsed the note and gave it to Bank. Thus, there was a proper negotiation.

Finally, Bank meets the requirements for HDC status. To be an HDC, one must be a holder (*i.e.*, one to whom the instrument was issued or negotiated) who took the instrument for value, in good faith (both subjective good faith and within the objective bounds of what is commercially reasonable), and without notice of any defenses or adverse claims to the instrument. Bank qualifies as a holder because the note was negotiated to Bank, as discussed above. It also took for value (an antecedent debt is value), in good faith (nothing in the facts indicates bad faith), and without notice of defenses.

Since Bank was an HDC, Maker was obligated to pay when Bank demanded payment unless Maker had a real defense. Maker's only defense here is that Maker already paid the obligation. But payment is a personal defense that cannot be asserted against an HDC. So Maker was obligated to pay Bank.

QUESTION 13

Singer was a famous musician. Agent was authorized to collect payment for all of Singer's performances. Agent had no rights in any of the payments due Singer.

In payment for a completed performance by Singer, Concert issued a $20,000 check drawn on Bank One. As instructed by Singer, Concert made the check payable to the order of "Agent, as agent for Singer," and delivered the check to Agent. On the memo line on the face of the check, Concert had written, "For Singer's June 19th performance."

Agent visited Bank Two, where both she and Singer maintained separate checking accounts. Agent's personal account, #12345, was overdrawn. Agent spoke with Bank Two's manager, Manager, and apologized for being overdrawn in her personal account. Agent told Manager that, as a "temporary arrangement to cover the overdrafts," she wanted to deposit the $20,000 check from Concert into her own personal account at Bank Two. Agent indorsed the check as follows: "For Deposit To Account #12345 s/Agent."

Manager made the deposit as indicated by Agent, although he knew that on all prior occasions Agent had deposited checks for Singer's performances into account #56789, which was Singer's checking account with Bank Two. The check was credited to Agent's personal account With Bank Two, clearing Agent's overdrafts, and the check was then timely presented to and paid by Bank One. Within the next few days, Agent withdrew the remaining balance from account #12345 and closed the account.

Subsequently, Agent and Singer had a falling out. Singer discovered the above facts and demanded that Bank Two pay him $20,000. Bank Two refused. Agent cannot be located.

Under the Uniform Commercial Code:

1. Can Singer successfully sue Bank Two for conversion and recover the $20,000? Explain.

2. What rights, if any, does Singer have to recover from Bank One? Explain.

3. What rights, if any, does Singer have to recover from Concert? Explain.

ANSWER TO QUESTION 13

1. Singer can successfully sue Bank for conversion. At issue is whether Singer will be treated as having received the check.

A person entitled to possession of an instrument may bring an action for conversion of the instrument under circumstances that would give rise to an action for conversion of other property. However, an action for conversion cannot be maintained unless the person bringing the action received possession of the instrument. Receipt of the instrument by an agent will be treated as receipt by the principal.

Here, the check will be treated as having been converted. It was made out to Agent, as agent for Singer. Thus, Singer was entitled to beneficial ownership of the check and Agent had bare legal title. Bank Two paid the funds under the check over to Agent, some for Agent's existing personal debt and the rest was drawn out otherwise. This constitutes conversion. Singer will be treated as having received possession of the check even though it was never in his hands, because receipt of the check by his agent will be treated as possession of the check by Singer. Thus, Singer may bring an action for conversion.

It should be noted that Bank Two cannot claim that it is a holder in due course and is free of Singer's claim. A holder in due course must take an instrument without notice of defenses or claims. Here, because Bank Two knew that the check was made out to Agent only in his fiduciary capacity, as agent for Singer, and Bank Two knew that the check was being deposited into Agent's personal account to clear Agent's personal debt, Bank Two had notice that Agent was breaching his fiduciary duty, at least to the extent that the check was applied to Agent's personal debts. It might be argued that Bank Two did not have notice that the remainder of the $20,000 was improperly applied (since the question does not explain the circumstances surrounding withdrawal of the remainder), but this seems unlikely. Since Bank Two knew that such checks normally were deposited into Singer's account rather than Agent's account, it could be argued that Bank Two was negligent in paying out the rest of the funds to Agent, no matter what the circumstances were surrounding the subsequent withdrawals.

2.   Singer cannot recover anything from Bank One. Where an instrument is payable to a person in trust, as explained above, the depositary bank can be held liable for paying the instrument inconsistent with the trust. However, a subsequent transferee is not liable in conversion unless it has notice that the fiduciary breached his duty. Here, Bank One had no such notice, so it is not liable in conversion or otherwise.

3.   Singer has no right to recover from Concert. When a obligor gives an instrument, such as a check, for payment on an obligation, the obligation is suspended to the same extent as if cash were given. If the instrument is lost or stolen, the original obligation is permanently suspended, and the obligee's rights are limited to enforcement of the instrument. Thus, because the check here was converted, Concert's obligation is treated as having been paid in cash and Singer's only remedy is an action for conversion against Bank Two.

QUESTION 14

On March 1, Lender lent $10,000 to Borrower in exchange for a promissory note from Borrower. The promissory note was a form note Borrower had obtained from a stationery store. Borrower signed the note as maker and filled in the "date due" line to provide that payment was due September 1 of the same year.

Borrower and Lender had agreed that the amount due on the note would be $10,500, representing both principal and interest on the loan. However, Borrower neglected to fill in the blank space on the form note for the amount due and also neglected to fill in the name of the payee in the blank space following the "pay to the order of" language. Despite these two omissions, the language of the form note did contain an unconditional promise to pay and did not contain any other promise or undertaking by Borrower.

A week after Lender accepted the note in exchange for the loan proceeds, Lender realized that both the amount and the payee lines had been left blank. Lender filled in his own name as payee and wrote $ "10,500" as the amount due.

On August 25 of that same year, Lender's home was burglarized by Robber, who stole the note. Lender did not realize at that time that the note was missing. Robber then forged Lender's indorsement on the note and sold the note on August 26 to Innocent, a good-faith purchaser for value, who paid $10,350 for the note.

On September 1, Lender realized for the first time that the note was missing.

On September 2, Innocent presented the note for payment to Borrower, who paid $10,500 in good faith to Innocent without knowledge of the forged signature or the theft of the note from Lender's home.

1.   After Lender filled in the blank amount and payee lines on the note, was the note enforceable against Borrower as completed? Explain.

2.   Assume the note was enforceable and that Lender, unable to produce the note, demanded payment from Borrower on September 1 *before* Borrower had paid Innocent. What would be the rights and obligations of Lender and Borrower on the note? Explain.

3. **Assuming the note was enforceable, did Borrower's payment to Innocent discharge Borrower's obligation to Lender on the note? Explain.**

4. **After Borrower paid Innocent, did Borrower have any rights of recovery against Innocent? Explain.**

ANSWER TO QUESTION 14

1. The note was enforceable against Borrower after Lender filled in the blank amount and payee lines on the note. At issue is the enforceability of an incomplete instrument. Because this question involves a promissory note, it is governed by Article 3 of the Uniform Commercial Code.

Under Article 3, an incomplete instrument may be enforced according to its incomplete terms or as augmented by an authorized completion. This is true even if the instrument would not qualify as an instrument but for the completion. The burden of establishing that an instrument was completed without authority is on the person asserting lack of authority.

Here, the note was incomplete. To be a note, an instrument must be a written and signed unconditional promise to pay a fixed amount of money, to order or to bearer, on demand or at a definite time, without any unauthorized undertakings or instructions. The note here was incomplete because it did not name a payee or specify the amount payable. Lack of a named payee did not prevent the note from being a negotiable instrument; it merely made the note payable to bearer. Lack of fixed amount payable would have prevented the instrument from being a negotiable instrument, but this problem was alleviated when Lender filled in the amount payable and payee name. Moreover, because Lender merely filled in the terms that the parties had agreed to, Borrower will be unable to prove that the completion was unauthorized. Therefore, the note was enforceable against Borrower as completed.

2. If Lender had sought payment on the note before Borrower had paid Innocent, Lender probably could have obtained payment. At issue are the rights of parties when an instrument is stolen.

If a person entitled to enforce an instrument cannot produce it because it has been stolen, he nevertheless is entitled to maintain an action on the instrument as if it were in his possession, as long as he can prove ownership, the terms of the instrument, and the facts that prevent him from producing it. The court may then order the maker of the note to pay, but the court may also require the payee to indemnify the maker against losses from additional claims on the note.

Here, Lender can show that he was entitled to enforce the note because it was made payable to him and he had not further negotiated the note nor signed it in blank (which would make the current holder the person entitled to enforce it). Lender can also show the terms that the parties had agreed to and testify that he did not have the note because it was stolen. Therefore, the court would order Borrower to pay Lender, although it might make Lender post a bond to protect Borrower from other claims on the note.

3. Borrower's payment to Innocent did not discharge Borrower's obligation to Lender on the note. At issue is whether Innocent qualified as a holder of the note.

If a maker of a note pays a holder, the maker is discharged from liability; but if the maker pays someone who is not a holder, the maker will have to pay on the note again when the true holder comes along. Innocent was not a holder of the note; therefore payment to Innocent did not discharge Borrower from his obligation to pay. As discussed above, the note here as completed was payable to the order of Lender. When a note is payable to a specific payee, a later transferee cannot become a holder of the note unless the specific payee has indorsed the note by signing his name on the back of the instrument. Here, Innocent did not qualify as a holder because Lender did not indorse the note; instead, Robber forged Lender's signature, and a forgery generally is valid only as the signature of the forger. Therefore, Innocent was not a holder, and payment to Innocent did not discharge Borrower's obligation to Lender, the true holder.

4. Borrower does have a right to recover the money Borrower paid Innocent. At issue is the finality of payment rule.

Generally, when a maker pays out on a note, payment is final and the maker cannot recover money paid out on the instrument. However, there is an exception to this finality of payment rule. A person who presents a note for payment makes a warranty that he is entitled to enforce the note, and if this warranty is breached, the maker can recover money paid to the presenter under a breach of warranty theory. As discussed above, Innocent was not entitled to enforce the note here because he was not a holder, Lender's indorsement having been forged. Therefore, Borrower can recover the money paid to Innocent.

QUESTION 15

On May 10, Driver contracted to buy a sports car from Motors for $25,000. The car was a popular model in high demand, and there was a four-month waiting period. Motors promised to deliver the car in September, and Driver promised to pay for the car at delivery using a cashier's check.

To make sure he had the money to pay for the car in September, Driver immediately bought the necessary $25,000 cashier's check, payable to Motors, from First Bank. The cashier's check was dated May 11. Driver paid for the cashier's check by negotiating to First Bank a $25,000 check that Driver had obtained from a lender called Auto-Loans.

On September 15, Motors delivered the sports car to Driver and took in exchange the $25,000 cashier's check. Motors immediately presented the cashier's check to First Bank for payment.

First Bank refused to pay the cashier's check because the Auto-Loans check that Driver had negotiated to First Bank was dishonored. First Bank's refusal to pay the cashier's check surprised both Motors and Driver because neither of them knew of any problem with the Auto-Loans check. Driver has retained the sports car and has refused to make good on the cashier's check, claiming that his transfer of the cashier's check to Motors discharged his obligation under the contract.

What rights, if any, does Motors have against First Bank and Driver under Article 3 of the Uniform Commercial Code? Explain.

ANSWER TO QUESTION 15

Motors v. First Bank: Motors may not enforce the cashier's check against First Bank. At issue are the rights of a holder of a cashier's check against its issuer. Because this question involves a check, it is governed by Article 3 of the Uniform Commercial Code.

A cashier's check is a check drawn by a bank on itself. The issuer of a cashier's check is like the maker of a note and is obligated to pay the instrument according to its terms at the time it was issued. The holder of a cashier's check may enforce it against the issuer, but like other holders is subject to any defenses that the issuer may have unless the holder qualifies as a holder in due course ("HDC"), in which case the HDC is subject only to the so-called real defenses. Here, First Bank is asserting as a defense that the check that it received for issuing its cashier's check was dishonored. This is a "failure of consideration" claim. Failure of consideration is a personal defense. Thus, First Bank may not raise this defense against Motors if Motors qualifies as an HDC.

Motors qualifies as a holder but does not qualify as an HDC. The definition of a holder includes a person in possession of a check made payable to the person. Here, Motors is in possession of the cashier's check and it is payable to Motors. Thus, Motors is a holder.

Motors does not qualify as an HDC because Motors took the check with notice that it was overdue. An HDC is a holder who takes an instrument for value, in good faith, and without notice that it is overdue, has been dishonored, or is subject to some other claim or defense. Here, Motors took the check for value (the car), and it apparently acted in good faith in taking the cashier's check. However, when Motors took the check it either knew or should have known that the check was overdue. Checks are due within 90 days after their date of issue. Here, the check was dated May 11 and Motors took the check on September 15, more than four months after its date of issue. Therefore, Motors is not an HDC, First Bank can raise its defense against Motors, and, as a result, Motors will not be able to recover from First Bank.

Motors v. Driver: Driver has no liability to Motors on the original obligation but is liable to Motors for breach of a transfer warranty. The first issue here is the effect of giving a cashier's check as payment for an obligation.

If a cashier's check is given in satisfaction of an obligation, the obligation is discharged to the same extent that it would be discharged if cash were given. Thus, because Driver gave a cashier's check to Motors in exchange for the car, his obligation to pay for the car was discharged, and Motors cannot recover from him on the underlying obligation.

Motors can recover from Driver for breach of warranty. At issue is the effect of transferring an overdue check.

Driver is liable for breach of warranty because the cashier's check was overdue when Driver transferred it to Motors. A person who transfers an instrument for consideration makes five transfer warranties, including a warranty that no defense of any party is good against the transferor. Here, Driver transferred the check for consideration (the car) when the check was subject to the defense that it was overdue (see discussion above). Thus, Driver breached this transfer warranty. Note that the fact that Driver did not sign the check does not affect his liability here—if a transferor transfers a check without indorsing, he makes the transfer warranties only to his immediate transferee, but here, Motors was Driver's immediate transferee.

QUESTION 16

Mariner owned several large fishing nets that required repairs. In January 2002, he took the nets to Chandler, who sells and repairs all kinds of new and used fishing equipment, including nets. Chandler agreed to repair and return the nets for $4,000 payable in 45 days. Mariner issued a valid, negotiable promissory note to Chandler, promising to pay $4,000 to the order of Chandler on March 1, 2002.

Chandler repaired the nets but did not return them to Mariner. Instead, on February 27, 2002, without Mariner's knowledge or permission, Chandler sold the nets as used goods to Trawler. At the time of the sale, Trawler was shopping for nets in Chandler's store and believed the nets belonged to Chandler.

When Mariner's note became due on March 1, 2002, he refused to pay Chandler because Chandler had not returned the nets.

On March 10, 2002, Chandler indorsed the note and sold it to Financier for $3,500. However, Chandler did not tell Financier anything about his dealings with Mariner and Trawler. In negotiating the note to Financier, Chandler wrote the words "without recourse" above his indorsement. When Financier later presented the note to Mariner and demanded payment, Mariner refused to pay.

Despite repeated requests, Trawler has refused to return the fishing nets to Chandler or to Mariner.

1.   What rights, if any, does Financier have on the note against Mariner? Explain.

2.   What rights, if any, does Financier have on the note against Chandler? Explain.

3.   What rights, if any, does Mariner have against Trawler for recovery of the nets? Explain.

ANSWER TO QUESTION 16

1.   Financier does not have any rights on the note against Mariner. At issue is whether Financier is a holder in due course ("HDC"). Because this question involves a negotiable instrument, it is governed by Article 3 of the Uniform Commercial Code ("U.C.C.").

Under U.C.C. Article 3, the holder of a promissory note generally has a right to enforce the note against its maker according to its terms. However, the holder is subject to any contract defense that the maker might have against enforcement unless the holder is an HDC; an HDC takes free of most personal defenses and is subject only to the so-called real defenses set forth in Article 3. Mariner's defense—that he did not receive the consideration for which he exchanged the promissory note—is a personal defense. Thus, Mariner can raise this defense against Financier only if Financier is not an HDC.

Although Financier is a holder of the note, he is not an HDC. A holder is any person in possession of an instrument if the instrument is payable to bearer. An HDC is a holder who takes an instrument for value, in good faith, and without notice of any defenses or claims to the instrument or that the instrument is overdue. Here, the note originally was payable to Chandler, but

Chandler indorsed the note in blank (*i.e.*, he did not name a new payee), making the note payable to bearer. Thus, because Financier is in possession of the note, he qualifies as a holder. Financier also took the note for value ($3,500), and he apparently acted in good faith (he did not know about Chandler's dealings with Mariner, and the $500 discount from the face value of the note would not be sufficient to give him notice of any problem). However, when Financier took the note, he had notice that the note was overdue. The note was payable on March 1, 2002, and Financier purchased the note on March 10, 2002. Thus, Financier was not an HDC and is subject to Mariner's defense that he did not receive the consideration for which the note was given. Therefore, Financier cannot enforce the note against Mariner.

2.   Financier has a right to enforce the note against Chandler under a warranty theory. At issue is the effect of a person transferring a note "without recourse." Again, because this question involves liability on a negotiable instrument, U.C.C. Article 3 governs.

Under Article 3, the holder of a negotiable instrument generally has a contract right to enforce the instrument against any prior indorser. However, such contract liability is negated if an indorser indorses with the words "without recourse." However, in addition to his contract liability, an indorser who transfers an instrument for consideration also incurs warranty liability. Among other things, such a transferor warrants that no defense of any party is good against him. This warranty can be negated by language disclaiming it, but the words "without recourse" are not sufficient to negate warranty liability.

Here, Chandler breached the warranty that no defense of any party is good against him because Mariner's defense can be raised against Chandler. Thus, Financier can hold Chandler liable for his damages under a breach of warranty theory. Note that Chandler cannot avoid his warranty liability by raising Mariner's failure of consideration defense, because that defense belongs to Mariner, and a party on a negotiable instrument can raise only his own defenses.

3.   Mariner has no right to recover the nets from Trawler. At issue is whether a merchant has power to transfer title to goods that do not belong to the merchant. Because this question involves the sale of goods, it is governed by U.C.C. Article 2.

Under Article 2, generally, a person cannot transfer better title to goods than he has. However, there is an exception to this rule: If the owner of goods entrusts the goods to a merchant (*i.e.*, one who regularly deals in goods of the kind sold), the merchant has the power to transfer all the rights of the entruster to a buyer in the ordinary course of the merchant's business. Here, title to the fishing nets in question originally was vested in Mariner. Mariner took the nets to Chandler to be repaired. Chandler is a fishing net merchant because he sells both new and used fishing nets in addition to repairing them. After repairing Mariner's nets, Chandler sold them to Trawler in the regular course of Chandler's business. Thus, Trawler now is the rightful owner of the nets and Mariner is not, and Mariner cannot compel Trawler to return them. Mariner's only remedy is against Chandler for breach of his duties as a bailee.

QUESTION 17

Garden Shop borrowed $10,000 from Finance Co. to finance its current operations. The parties agreed that Garden Shop would repay the loan in 90 days by making a single payment of $10,450. The additional $450 represented interest at a lawful rate.

Finance Co. issued a $10,000 check to Garden Shop. In exchange, Garden Shop delivered to Finance Co. a signed and dated promissory note stating: "In 90 days, Garden Shop promises to pay to the order of Finance Co. $10,000.00 (*Ten thousand four hundred fifty and 00/100 dollars*)." Neither party noticed the inconsistency between the numerically expressed amount as "$10,000.00" and the written "*Ten thousand four hundred fifty and 00/100 dollars.*"

On the 90th day, Finance Co. demanded payment from Garden Shop but could not produce the note, which, despite a diligent search, Finance Co. could not find. Finance Co. could not remember whether it had indorsed the note.

1. **If Finance Co. later finds the note, can Finance Co. enforce it and, if so, in what amount? Explain.**

2. **If Finance Co. does not produce the note and Garden Shop nonetheless pays Finance Co., would Garden Shop's obligation on the note be discharged as against all persons? Explain.**

3. **If Garden Shop refuses to pay because Finance Co. cannot produce the note, what must Finance Co. prove and what conditions must it satisfy in order to obtain a judgment against Garden Shop? Explain.**

ANSWER TO QUESTION 17

1.   If Finance Co. later finds the note, it may enforce it for $10,450. At issue is the effect of a discrepancy between the written amount of a note and the numeric amount of a note.

The maker of a negotiable instrument has a duty to pay the instrument according to its terms when it is presented for payment. The note here was negotiable. To be negotiable, an instrument must be written and signed and contain an unconditional promise to pay a fixed amount of money, to order or to bearer, on demand or at a definite time, without any unauthorized undertakings or instructions. The note here meets these requirements. It was in writing and signed, and it contained an unconditional promise to pay $10,450 to the order of Finance Co. after 90 days. The fact that there was a discrepancy between the written amount and the numerical amount does not make the note nonnegotiable, because the written amount will control over the numerical amount. Neither is the time for payment (in 90 days) uncertain, because the facts say that the note was dated. Therefore Finance Co. would be able to enforce the note against Garden Shop for the full $10,450 owed.

2.   If Finance Co. does not produce the note and Garden Shop pays Finance Co. anyway, it is uncertain whether Garden Shop's obligation on the note would be discharged. At issue is whether payment of the obligation underlying a note discharges parties from their obligation on the note.

If a maker of a note pays a person entitled to enforce the note, the maker's obligation on the note generally is discharged. Thus if Finance Co. was entitled to enforce the note, Garden Shop's obligation would be discharged by its payment to Finance Co. However, the maker's obligation is not discharged against a person who acquired the rights of a holder in due course (*i.e.,* a person to whom the note was properly negotiated and who took the note for value, in good faith, and without notice of any defenses on or claims to the note).

If Finance Co. did not indorse the note before losing it, Garden Shop's payment would discharge its obligations on the note. This is because the note was order paper when it was delivered to Finance Co., which means it required Finance Co.'s indorsement for further transfer. Absent such an indorsement, no one after Finance Co. could qualify as a holder in due course. However, if Finance Co. indorsed the note and then lost it, the note would have been converted to bearer paper by Finance Co.'s indorsement. Bearer paper is freely transferable, so a third party could subsequently become a holder in due course of the note. Garden Shop would not be discharged against such a holder.

3.   If Garden Shop refuses to pay Finance Co., and Finance Co. cannot produce the note, Garden Shop can be forced to pay if it proves that it is entitled to enforce the note, the terms of the note, and the facts that prevent production of it. To prove that it is entitled to enforce the note, Finance Co. would have to prove that it was the holder of the note and then lost it. Because Finance Co. is not sure whether or not it indorsed the note, the court can also require Finance Co. to post security to indemnify Garden Shop, in case a person with the rights of a holder in due course subsequently comes forward with the note and demands payment from Garden Shop.

QUESTION 18

Bill purchased a used car from Sally and paid her $15,000 with a check drawn on his account at Local Bank. The check was payable to the order of Sally and was certified by Local Bank. Sally accepted the certified check and gave Bill the car and its paper title.

Before Sally had a chance to deposit the check, it was stolen by Thief. Thief forged Sally's indorsement on the check, then indorsed the check with his own signature underneath Sally's forged signature and deposited the check into his own bank account at Depositary Bank.

Depositary Bank provisionally credited Thief's account for $15,000 and forwarded the check for payment to Local Bank, which made final payment. Thief then withdrew $15,000 from his checking account at Depositary Bank and disappeared.

In the meantime, Sally contacted Bill and asked him to stop payment on the certified check. Before Bill could contact Local Bank, however, it had already made final payment on the check.

Sally now demands payment from Bill, who refuses on the ground that he has already paid her. Sally is also demanding $15,000 from both banks.

1.   What rights of recovery, if any, does Sally have against Bill? Explain.

2.   What rights of recovery, if any, does Sally have against Depositary Bank and/or Local Bank as a result of the payment made to Thief for the amount of the certified check? Explain.

3.   If Local Bank paid Sally the amount of the certified check, what rights would Local Bank have against Depositary Bank? Explain.

ANSWER TO QUESTION 18

1.   Sally has no rights of recovery against Bill. At issue is whether Bill's liability has been discharged. Because this question involves a check, Uniform Commercial Code Articles 3 and 4, which govern negotiable instruments, will control. Bill's obligations to Sally were discharged because he gave her a certified check for payment for the car. If a certified check is given in satisfaction of an obligation, the obligation of the drawer is discharged to the same extent that it would be discharged if cash were given. Here, Bill gave Sally a certified check as payment for the car. The certified check discharged Bill's obligation to Sally, and therefore Sally has no right of recovery against Bill.

2.   Sally has a right of recovery against Local Bank and Depositary Bank because she is still entitled to possession of the check; she may maintain an action for conversion against both Local Bank and Depositary Bank. Sally may sue both banks for converting the check because she never transferred the right to possess the check. A transfer of the right to possess the check requires proper negotiation. An order instrument (*i.e.,* an instrument that is payable to an identified person) is negotiated by transferring possession of the instrument along with the indorsement of the identified person. For a proper negotiation, the payee's indorsement must be valid and authorized. Forging the payee's name breaks the chain of title, and no subsequent possessors of the instrument can qualify as holders. Here, the check was an order instrument—payable to the order of Sally. Neither Depositary Bank nor Local Bank is a holder because there was never a proper negotiation. Before Sally could indorse the check, Thief stole it and forged Sally's signature. Title to the check stops with Sally, and it is still her property. No one taking the check after the forgery has the right to enforce it, and therefore Sally can get her check back.

3.   Local Bank can recover $15,000 from Depositary Bank for a breach of a presentment warranty. When a drawee pays on a negotiable instrument, payment generally is final, but the payor can pursue those who breach a presentment warranty. Among other things, a party presenting an instrument for payment warrants that he has a right to enforce the instrument or is authorized to act on behalf of someone who does. This is known as a warranty of good title; the presenter warrants that there are no unauthorized or missing indorsements. The warranty is breached when there is a forgery of a necessary indorsement. Here, the check was payable to the order of Sally. Thus, Sally's indorsement was necessary. Sally did not indorse; instead Thief forged Sally's indorsement, which is not effective. Thus, Thief breached the warranty of title when he presented the check to Depositary Bank, and Depositary Bank breached when it presented the check to Local Bank. Thus, Local Bank may recover the $15,000 it paid on the check from Depositary Bank based on a breach of warranty theory.

QUESTION 19

Kit wanted to purchase a car that cost $4,800. Dealer agreed to loan Kit the money if she got someone to co-sign the loan.

Art agreed to co-sign the loan but only if Kit agreed to paint his house. On November 2, 2002, Kit signed a separate agreement with Art in which she promised to paint Art's house within 90 days.

On November 3, 2002, to cover the cost of the car and accumulated interest, Kit signed a promissory note that stated "On November 4, 2003, I promise to pay to the order of Dealer, $5,000." Art signed his name directly beneath Kit's signature.

Kit never painted Art's house. On November 4, 2003, without consulting Art, Kit went to see Dealer. Kit told Dealer that she currently had the money to repay the loan, but she had a rare opportunity to take a trip to the Far East and needed the money to pay for the trip. Kit offered Dealer a check for $2,000 and requested an extension of time to pay the remaining $3,000 on the loan. Dealer, sympathetic to Kit's situation, refused to accept the check and agreed to extend the entire loan until January 2, 2004. The next day Kit left on her trip. As of January 3, 2004, she had not returned, and neither Art nor Dealer can find her.

Dealer sues Art on the note for $5,000. Art defends on the following grounds: (1) The note is not a valid negotiable instrument because it was subject to the condition that Kit paint Art's house; (2) Dealer did not first try to collect from Kit; (3) Art was discharged when Dealer refused Kit's tender of $2,000; and (4) Art was discharged when Dealer extended the loan date without Art's consent.

Does each of Art's grounds of defense relieve him partly or completely of any obligation to pay Dealer? Explain.

ANSWER TO QUESTION 19

(1) Art's first defense is without merit. At issue is whether a negotiable instrument becomes nonnegotiable if it is subject to a condition, but the instrument does not expressly mention the condition.

To be negotiable, an instrument must be a written and signed unconditional promise (note) or order (draft) to pay a fixed amount of money to order or to bearer, on demand or at a definite time, without any additional undertaking or instruction not authorized by Article 3 of the Uniform Commercial Code. An instrument will be considered to be conditional only if it expressly states that it is conditional or that it is subject to or governed by another writing. Here, the note is negotiable. It was in writing and signed by Kit and Art. It did not contain any express conditions or state that it was governed by some other writing. The fact that Art and Kit entered a separate agreement making Art's promise conditional did not affect negotiability because the other agreement was not mentioned in the note. The note also contained a promise to pay a fixed amount of money ($5,000) to the order of Dealer at a definite time (November 4, 2003), without any other promise or undertaking. Thus, Art's argument that the note was not negotiable because it was subject to a separate condition is unavailing.

(2) Art's second defense also is without merit. At issue is whether an accommodation maker has a right to compel a holder to collect from the principal debtor before attempting to collect from the accommodation maker.

As a general rule, an accommodation party (*i.e.*, a person who signs an instrument to lend his name and credit to another) is bound on the instrument in the capacity in which he signs. Here, Art signed the note to provide extra credit for Kit and thus signed as an accommodation party. Art signed his name on the front of the note, under the maker's (Kit's) name. Thus, Art was an accommodation maker. A maker is primarily liable on an instrument. A holder may demand full payment from any co-maker without asking for payment from any other co-maker. Dealer is a holder because the note was issued to him and he is in possession of the note. A holder is entitled to enforce a note. Thus, Dealer can collect from Art and Art's second defense—that Dealer should have tried collecting from Kit first—will not succeed.

(3)   Art's third defense will be partially successful. At issue is whether an accommodation party is discharged when a holder refuses a tender of payment by the principal debtor.

If payment of an obligation on an instrument is tendered and refused, the tender discharges any duty to pay interest on the instrument after the tender and discharges, to the extent of the tender, any person who may have had a right of recourse against the party making the tender. Here, Kit tendered a $2,000 payment to dealer on the day the note was due. Dealer refused the tender. Thus, Art is not liable for any interest that accrued on account of the $2,000 after the tender. Moreover, as an accommodation party, Art had a right of recourse against Kit—the principal debtor. An accommodation party has a right to recover from the principal debtor any sum that the accommodation party is forced to pay on behalf of the principal debtor. Thus, Dealer's refusal of the tendered $2,000 also discharges Art to the extent of the $2,000 tender.

(4)   Art's fourth defense also will be successful. At issue is whether extending the due date on a note will discharge an accommodation party.

The extension of an instrument's due date discharges an accommodation party to the extent of the loss caused by the extension. The accommodation party has the burden of proving any loss. Here, Kit had the money needed to pay the note on its due date. Had Dealer not extended the note's due date and demanded timely payment, it seems likely either that Kit would have paid or Art would have been able to collect from Kit had Art been forced to pay. Now Kit is out of the country. Thus, Art has no one to collect from because Dealer extended the note's due date. Therefore, the extension is a good defense for Art and he will not be required to pay the remaining $3,000 of the $5,000 note (*i.e.,* the part of the note that was not discharged by the $2,000 tender).

QUESTION 20

Vendor recently decided to dispose of some unneeded commercial printing equipment. Two local printers, named Ben and Frank, entered into a written contract to buy the equipment on credit from Vendor for its appraised value or $10,000, whichever was less.

Vendor transferred title to the equipment to Ben and Frank. In exchange, Ben and Frank gave Vendor a negotiable promissory note. The note, which they both signed, said: "We promise to pay to the order of Vendor $10,000." Notwithstanding the terms of the note, but consistent with the contract, Vendor understood that Ben and Frank would pay only the appraised value of the equipment if the appraised value was less than $10,000. An independent appraiser promptly determined that the equipment was worth $7,000, a value that everyone accepts as reasonable.

Ben paid Vendor $4,000. Vendor then gave the note as a gift to Cousin, who was having financial troubles. Vendor did not indorse the note. Cousin had no knowledge of the contractual provision relating to the appraised value.

1.   **What is the amount still due on the note and from whom, if anyone, may Cousin recover it? Explain.**

2.   **May Ben recover from Frank any part of the $4,000 already paid to Vendor? Explain.**

ANSWER TO QUESTION 20

1.   The outstanding liability on the note is $3,000 that remains due, and Cousin may seek to recover that amount from Ben and/or Frank.

Cousin may pursue Ben and Frank to recover on the note. At issue is the apportionment of liability when there is more than one maker of a note. The maker of a note, merely by signing his name, becomes obligated to pay the instrument according to its terms. Ben and Frank are co-makers of the note because they each signed it. As a result, they are jointly and severally liable on the note. Joint and several liability means that each party can be sued for the entire outstanding balance of the note. Therefore, Cousin may enforce the note against either Ben or Frank, or both.

Cousin has a right to recover on the note, but the amount he will be entitled to depends on whether Cousin is a holder in due course ("HDC"). To be an HDC, Cousin must be a holder (*i.e.*, have possession of the instrument and the instrument must be payable to either the bearer or to the person in possession) who has taken the note (i) for value, (ii) in good faith, and (iii) without notice of any defenses to the note. Under these facts, Cousin is not an HDC. Although Cousin has possession of the note, Cousin is not a holder because Vendor never indorsed the note. Without his indorsement, the note remains payable to Vendor, and Cousin may not be deemed a holder. Additionally, Cousin did not take the note for value—it was a gift from Vendor.

Cousin may still enforce the note against Ben and Frank, even though he is not an HDC, but is subject to the same defenses that Vendor would have been subject to. At issue is the application of the shelter rule. The shelter rule provides that a transferee acquires whatever rights his transferor had—the transferee is said to take "shelter" in the status of his transferor. Under these facts, Cousin steps into the shoes of Vendor and may assert the same rights as Vendor had to enforce the note. Cousin is also subject to the same defenses that Vendor would have been subject to, and those defenses will limit the amount of his recovery, as discussed below.

Only $3,000 may be collected on the note, even though the original amount was $10,000. At issue is whether there are any defenses to enforcement. Vendor took the note subject to any defenses of the parties with whom Vendor dealt. The sales contract between Vendor and Ben and Frank provides one defense. Article 3 permits defenses based upon separate agreements. One such separate agreement existed here—the contract that limited Ben and Frank's total liability to the appraised value of the equipment if that appraised value was less than $10,000. Under the facts, the appraised value was only $7,000, which is obviously less than the $10,000 amount of the note. Therefore, the contract will limit Ben and Frank's liability for payment to $7,000.

Ben and Frank may also assert "the payment rule" as a defense. The liability of any party obligated to pay on an instrument is discharged by payment to a person entitled to enforce the instrument. Vendor was, before gifting the note to Cousin, entitled to enforce the note at the time of payment. Such a payment to a person entitled to enforce a note discharges liability on the note to the extent of payment. Therefore, Ben's $4,000 payment on the note reduced both Ben and Frank's liability on the note from $7,000 to $3,000.

2.   Ben has a right to contribution from Frank and may recover $500 from him, but Frank has no right to contribution from Ben. At issue is whether one co-maker may recover from another co-maker. As discussed above, co-makers have joint and several liability on the instrument. As such, if one party pays more than his share, he generally has a right of contribution against the other jointly liable party. Here, Ben and Frank's total liability on the note before payment was

$7,000. Therefore, the proportionate share of liability was $3,500 each. Ben has paid $4,000, or $500 more than his proportionate share. Ben may therefore recover a maximum of $500 from Frank, unless Ben makes additional payments to Cousin in the future, in which case Ben could recover any amount he paid Cousin in excess of $3,500. Frank has no such right to contribution from Ben because Ben has already paid more than Ben's proportionate share.

QUESTION 21

Consumer bought a sofa from Department Store for $2,000 with her Department Store charge card. Shortly after purchasing the sofa, Consumer lost her job and could no longer afford the monthly payments on the sofa. Unwilling to lose the sofa but unable to pay the $1,800 she knew she still owed, Consumer sent a check for $100 to Department Store's charge card operations, conspicuously writing "Payment in Full for All Amounts Owed" on both the memo line on the front of the check and on the back of the check. Department Store received the check and deposited it. The check cleared Consumer's checking account a week later.

When her next statement from Department Store arrived, it showed a $100 credit for the payment Consumer had made and a balance of $1,700 still owed for the sofa. Consumer promptly wrote a letter to Department Store claiming that she no longer owed any money for the sofa. She mailed the letter at the post office and then stopped for lunch at a local restaurant. Consumer left her handbag unattended on a table in the restaurant while she visited the restroom. Consumer's handbag was stolen by Thief, a woman who closely resembles Consumer. Consumer's checkbook and driver's license were in the handbag.

As soon as she realized her handbag was missing, Consumer reported to her bank, Bank, that her checkbook had been stolen. Meanwhile, using one of Consumer's checks, Thief wrote a check for $150 to Grocer. The signature appeared to be Consumer's but had actually been forged by Thief. Grocer gave Thief $150 in groceries for the check in the reasonable but mistaken assumption that the check and identification Thief had shown him really belonged to Thief.

One day after Consumer notified Bank of the theft, Grocer stopped in at Bank to cash the check Grocer had received from Thief. Bank refused to cash the check. Following Bank's refusal, Grocer contacted Consumer and demanded that she pay the $150 face amount of the check.

1.   Does Consumer still owe $1,700 to Department Store? Explain.

2.   Must Consumer pay Grocer $150? Explain.

ANSWER TO QUESTION 21

1.   Consumer does still owe Department Store $1,700. At issue is a "payment in full" check. Because this question deals with a check, which is a type of negotiable instrument, Article 3 of the Uniform Commercial Code applies, as Article 3 governs negotiable instruments.

Article 3 has some very specific rules regarding payment in full instruments. It provides that a negotiable instrument (including a check) can accomplish an accord and satisfaction (*i.e., can satisfy an obligation in full*) if: (i) the claim or obligation is disputed or unliquidated, (ii) the person against whom the claim is asserted in good faith tenders an instrument, (iii) that conspicuously states that it is tendered in full payment of the obligation, and (iv) the claimant obtains payment of the instrument.

Not all of the elements required for an effective accord and satisfaction under Article 3 are present here. The check did include a conspicuous statement on the memo line on the face of the check that it was "Payment in Full for All Amounts Owed." Department Store also cashed the check. However, the claim here was not unliquidated or in dispute. Nothing in the facts indicates that Consumer had any reason to believe that she owed anything other than $1,800 on the sofa. Moreover, given that Consumer knew this, it cannot be said that she tendered the check in good faith. Indeed, she tendered it hoping that she could get out of her obligation to pay $1,800 by paying $100. Thus, no accord and satisfaction will be found here and Consumer still owes the remaining $1,700 on the sofa.

2. Consumer probably will not have to pay Grocer $150. At issue is liability on an instrument that contains a forged drawer's signature. Again, because we are dealing with a check, Article 3 governs.

Generally under Article 3, a person is not liable on an instrument unless she has signed the instrument, and a forgery generally is not effective as the name signed and is effective only as the signature of the forger. Thus, a drawer generally is not liable on a check when someone forges the drawer's signature. Here, Thief signed Consumer's name on her check, which constitutes a forgery. Thus, under the general rules, Consumer is not liable on the check; only Thief is liable.

Article 3 includes a few exceptions to the general rules, but none is applicable here. The exception that comes closest to being applicable provides that a person whose failure to exercise ordinary care substantially contributes to a forged signature on the instrument will be precluded from asserting the forgery against a person who gave value for the instrument in good faith. Here, it appears that Grocer acted in good faith, as the facts specifically provide that grocer took the check under the reasonable belief that the signature and identification that Thief showed were genuine. Moreover, Grocer took the check for value, in that he gave groceries in exchange for the check. Nevertheless, the exception is not applicable because Consumer's carelessness in leaving her purse unattended at the restaurant is not the type of negligence that the Code contemplates as substantially contributing to a forgery. Leaving blank spaces on an instrument, mailing an instrument to a person having the same name as the payee, and keeping a signature stamp and check together in an unlocked place are the types of negligence the Code contemplates. Thus, Consumer likely will not be found liable for the $150.

In the unlikely event that Consumer's carelessness is considered to have substantially contributed to the forgery here, she would be liable for the $150. In that case, she would not be able to raise the forgery as a defense. Thus, the forgery would be considered her signature. A drawer of a check is liable on the check to a person entitled to enforce the check if the person presents the check for payment and it is dishonored. Grocer was entitled to enforce the check here, as it was payable to him and in his possession. The check also was dishonored by Consumer's bank. Thus, she would be liable to Grocer for $150 in the unlikely event that her carelessness is found to be sufficiently negligent.

QUESTION 22

Uncle owns a chain of sandwich shops. Nephew has worked for Uncle for several years, first as a line cook in various sandwich shops and then as a sandwich shop manager. Uncle recently sold Nephew the sandwich shop that Nephew had been managing.

Nephew paid for the shop with $10,000 cash and a $10,000 negotiable demand note made payable to the order of Uncle. Nephew signed the note as a maker. To show her faith in her son, Nephew's mother, Mom, signed the note with the words "Mom, as guarantor." Her signature appears on the front of the note, immediately below Nephew's signature and under the additional word "Guaranteed."

The note provided that all parties to it waived presentment and notice of dishonor. When they signed the note, Uncle, Nephew, and Mom orally agreed that Uncle would not seek payment of the note until the shop was making a good profit and that he would negotiate the note only with Nephew's and Mom's consent.

Three months after the note was signed and before any payment had been made, Uncle indorsed the note and sold it to Acme Finance Co. for $9,000 cash. Uncle did not obtain Nephew's or Mom's consent to this sale. Acme had no knowledge of the oral agreement among, Uncle, Nephew, and Mom.

When Acme sought payment from Nephew, Nephew persuaded Acme that any effort to collect full payment from him would be futile. Acme therefore gave Nephew a written release from his obligations under the note in exchange for a payment of $1,000.

Acme has sued Mom for payment of the $9,000 still due on the note.

What rights, if any, does Acme have against Mom under Article 3 of the Uniform Commercial Code? Explain.

ANSWER TO QUESTION 22

Acme may recover the $9,000 still due on the note from Mom because she is liable as an accommodation party and has no good defense against Acme.

This question raises several issues. First, to what extent is Mom, as guarantor on the note, liable to the holder of the note? A guarantor, or accommodation party, is one who signs an instrument for the purpose of lending her name and credit to another party to the instrument. An accommodation party is liable on the instrument in the capacity in which she signs, even where the taker is aware of the accommodation. If the person seeking to enforce the instrument is aware of the accommodation status, it merely allows the accommodation party to raise her special suretyship defenses and does not release the accommodation party from her liability. Here, Mom signed the note on the front, as the person undertaking to pay, and thus signed in the capacity of a maker. As a maker, she is obliged to pay the instrument to the holder. Acme is the holder of the note because Uncle indorsed the note to Acme, which took possession of it. As a holder, Acme has a right to enforce the note against any party who signed it. Therefore, Mom has an obligation to pay Acme unless she can assert a valid defense to payment that is good against Acme.

Mom has a defense based on Uncle's breach of his agreement not to enforce or negotiate the note. However, this defense may not be successfully used against Acme. The problem for Mom is that Acme appears to be a holder in due course ("HDC"). An HDC is a holder who takes the instrument: (i) for value; (ii) in good faith; and (iii) without notice that the instrument is overdue of has been dishonored, contains an unauthorized signature or has been altered, that there is a claim to the instrument or that any party has a defense of claim in recoupment on the instrument. An HDC takes an instrument free from personal defenses and claims and is subject to only real defenses. As discussed above, Acme is the holder of the note. Under the facts given, Acme also seems to be an HDC. Acme gave value for the note ($9,000). It also took the note in good faith. The discount was not steep enough to put Acme on guard that there might be a problem with the instrument and nothing in the facts otherwise indicates a lack of good faith. Finally, Acme took the note without notice. The agreement restricting Uncle's right to negotiate the note does not appear on the face of the note and there is nothing to indicate that Acme had any notice of the oral agreement. Thus, Acme is an HDC and took the note free of personal defenses. Personal defenses include every defense available in simple contract actions, including unauthorized negotiation. Therefore, Acme will not be subject to Mom's personal defense of unauthorized negotiation due to its status as an HDC.

Mom may attempt to assert another defense, that her liability on the note was discharged by Acme's release of Nephew's liability. At issue is whether an accommodation party may raise a defense against the maker based upon the discharge of the principal obligor on the instrument. Under the U.C.C., a discharge of an obligated party does not discharge the obligation of an indorser or accommodation party having right of recourse against the obligated party. Here, Mom is an accommodation party and is liable to Acme even upon Nephew's discharge. Therefore, Mom will be liable to Acme for $9,000, the amount of the note that remains unpaid. However, Mom will still have a right of recourse against Nephew and may seek reimbursement to the extent she is obligated to pay on the note.

[*Editor's note: Under the most recent revisions to the U.C.C. (adopted in a few states), Mom—as an accommodation party—qualifies as a "secondary obligor" on the instrument signed by Nephew. As a secondary obligor, Mom will have additional defenses contained in the revised U.C.C., including one pertinent to this scenario: When a person entitled to enforce an instrument releases the obligation of the principal obligor to pay the instrument, the secondary obligor is discharged to the same extent as the principal obligor from any unperformed portion of its obligation on the instrument, unless the person enforcing the instrument explicitly retains the right to enforce the instrument against the secondary obligor. [Revised U.C.C. §3-605(a)(2)] Thus, when Acme accepted $1,000 and released Nephew from his obligation to pay the remaining balance due on the note, Mom was also discharged, as nothing in the facts indicates that Acme expressly retained its rights against Mom.*]

QUESTION 23

Sam worked as an administrative assistant to the president of Corporation. In this capacity, Sam had responsibility for opening all of Corporation's mail. If the mail contained any checks, Sam was supposed to secure the indorsement of the president in the name of Corporation and deposit the checks in Corporation's bank account.

One day, Corporation received a $3,000 check. When the check arrived at Corporation's offices, Sam secretly took it from the mail, concealed it in his coat pocket, and took it home. That night, Sam fraudulently indorsed the check in the name of Corporation. Sam then mailed the check to Lender with instructions to cover a $3,000 mortgage payment on Sam's home.

Acting in good faith, Lender applied the amount of the check to reduce Sam's indebtedness on his mortgage by $3,000. Before Lender could deposit the check, Corporation learned of Sam's actions. Corporation told Lender that it owned the check and demanded that Lender return it.

Must Lender return the check to Corporation? Explain.

ANSWER TO QUESTION 23

Lender will not be obligated to return the check to Corporation. At issue is whether a holder in due course ("HDC") is subject to the ownership claim of the payee on an instrument.

A check is a negotiable instrument. In most cases, Corporation would be entitled to assert its rights and recover a negotiable instrument from a thief (*e.g.*, Sam) or from a person who took the instrument from the thief (*e.g.*, Lender). However, a claim of a personal or property right in the instrument may not be successfully asserted against an HDC. If Lender is an HDC on the check, Lender will not be subject to Corporation's claim to the check, even though Corporation was the original payee of the check and has both a possessory and property right in the check. In order to be an HDC, the party must be a holder who takes the instrument for value, in good faith, and without notice of certain claims or defenses.

To be deemed a holder, the transferee must have possession and the instrument must be payable either to bearer or to the person in possession. The instrument must be free of forgeries of those names necessary to the chain of title (*i.e.*, the payee and any special indorsees). In this case, the check was payable to Corporation, and possession was transferred to Lender. Therefore, if the check was indorsed by Corporation, Lender would become a holder of the instrument through negotiation. Here, the check was not indorsed by Corporation, but instead by Sam, who made an unauthorized indorsement in the name of Corporation. Under most circumstances, an unauthorized signature would not be sufficient to negotiate a check. However, if an employer entrusts an employee with responsibility with respect to an instrument, and the employee makes a fraudulent indorsement on the instrument, the indorsement is effective (although the person who takes the instrument and fails to exercise ordinary care may be held liable to the extent of loss caused by the failure).

In this case, Corporation entrusted Sam, as administrative assistant to the president, with responsibility for the check because he was authorized to deposit checks in Corporation's bank account. Sam made a fraudulent indorsement in the name of Corporation. This fraudulent indorsement therefore was effective as the indorsement of Corporation. Accordingly, when the check was negotiated to Lender, Lender became the holder of the check

To achieve HDC status, Lender must have taken the check for value. Any one of the following five things constitutes value: (i) performance of the agreed consideration; (ii) acquisition by the holder of a lien or security interest in the instrument other than a lien obtained by judicial proceeding; (iii) taking the instrument as payment of or security for an antecedent debt; (iv) trading a negotiable instrument for another instrument; or (v) giving the instrument in exchange for the incurring of an irrevocable obligation to a third person by the person taking the instrument. Here, Lender took the $3,000 check in payment of an antecedent debt—Sam's mortgage. Therefore, even though Sam did not receive any tangible thing from Lender, Lender still took the check for value.

Finally, to be an HDC, Lender must take the check without notice of any claim to or defense on the check. An HDC cannot have notice that the instrument is overdue or has been dishonored, the instrument contains an unauthorized signature or has been altered, or that any party has a defense or claim in recoupment on the instrument. The instrument must not bear apparent evidence of forgery or alteration, or be so irregular as to call into question its authenticity. Under the facts given, Lender had no notice of Sam's fiduciary status and, as a result, cannot be charged with knowledge of Sam's breach of his fiduciary duties. There was nothing inherently suspicious in Sam's transferring an indorsed check that was not originally payable to him.

Therefore, Lender is an HDC. It is a holder, took the instrument in good faith and for value, and had no notice of Corporation's claim to the instrument. Because Lender is an HDC, it is not subject to Corporation's claim on the check and need not return the check to Corporation.

QUESTION 24

Two months ago, Finisher, an individual who refinishes antique furniture, entered into a contract with Law Firm to refinish a bookcase for $3,000.

Two weeks ago, Finisher entered into a contract with Restaurant to refinish a table for $1,000.

Ten days ago, Finisher hired Administrator to help Finisher manage the business. Finisher put Administrator in charge of opening the mail, recording incoming payments from customers, indorsing checks on behalf of Finisher, and depositing checks to Finisher's account at Bank. Finisher also put Administrator in charge of answering and resolving customer complaints.

Five days ago, Administrator opened Finisher's mail and found two checks.

The first check was from Law Firm and was drawn on Law Firm's account at Bank. The check was payable to the order of Finisher in the amount of $1,500. The words "Payment in full for bookcase work" appeared in handwriting on the bottom left-hand corner of the face of the check. The Law Firm check was stapled to a letter addressed to Finisher in which Law Firm reminded Finisher that when Finisher's employees were installing the refinished bookcase, one of them ripped a hole in an expensive carpet. Law Firm claims that the damage was $1,500, while Finisher claims that the damage to the carpet was only $500.

The second check was from Restaurant and was drawn on Restaurant's account at Bank. It was payable to the order of Finisher in the amount of $1,000.

The day the checks arrived, Administrator indorsed both checks in the name of Finisher. Administrator deposited the Law Firm check in Finisher's account at Bank. Administrator

cashed the Restaurant check at CheckNow, a check cashing business. CheckNow gave Administrator $1,000 for the check. CheckNow then deposited the Restaurant check in its account at Bank.

The following day, Bank paid the Law Firm and Restaurant checks, and Administrator disappeared.

Two days ago, Finisher discovered that the Restaurant check was cashed by CheckNow and demanded that CheckNow repay the $1,000 to Finisher.

Yesterday, Finisher discovered the "full satisfaction" letter in Administrator's files. Finisher immediately contacted Law Firm, tendered back $1,500, the amount of the Law Firm check, and demanded payment of the full amount owed. Law Firm refused to accept the tender and insisted that it was no longer liable for the additional $1,500 that Finisher claimed was still owed.

1. May Finisher recover the balance of $1,500 from Law Firm for the refinishing work on the bookcase? Explain.

2. May Finisher recover from CheckNow the amount of the Restaurant check? Explain.

ANSWER TO QUESTION 24

1. Finisher most likely will not recover the balance of $1,500 from Law Firm for his refinishing work on the bookcase. At issue is whether Law Firm's check and accompanying letter constitute an accord and satisfaction of Finisher's claims against Law Firm, and if so, whether Finisher may avoid the accord and satisfaction.

An accord and satisfaction is the acceptance of a proposed settlement of a debt. Under the Uniform Commercial Code ("U.C.C."), when a claim is subject to dispute, the claim can be discharged in full if the person against whom the claim is asserted in good faith tenders an instrument that conspicuously states that it is tendered in full satisfaction of the claim (e.g., if the memo line says "payment in full") and the claimant obtains payment of the instrument. Under the facts given, Law Firm has met the requirements of an accord and satisfaction. There was a claim subject to dispute, i.e., the amount of money to be deducted from Law Firm's payment to Finisher as compensation for the damage inflicted by Finisher's employees during the installation of the bookcase. The claim was still in dispute—the parties had not yet reached an agreement, as the facts state that Law Firm claimed the damages totaled $1,500 and Finisher claimed only $500 worth of the damages. Nothing in the facts suggests that Law Firm did not act in good faith. The check tendered is an instrument, and it was marked with the words "payment in full for bookcase work" on the bottom left corner of the face of the check. When Finisher (through Administrator) deposited the check into his bank account, he obtained payment of the instrument, fulfilling the final requirement for an accord and satisfaction.

An accord and satisfaction may be avoided under certain circumstances, provided that the claimant returns the payment within 90 days. A claimant may require in advance that the notice of an accord and satisfaction be tendered to a designated person, office, or place to be effective. Additionally, a claimant may avoid an accord and satisfaction that is inadvertent. Here, although

Finisher is still within the 90-day window, he will not be able to avoid the accord and satisfaction. There is no indication that Finisher ever restricted the tender or that Administrator, his agent, was not authorized to accept on his behalf. Additionally, there is no inadvertency—the check was clearly marked as "payment in full" and was accompanied by a letter expressing the same sentiment. Finisher therefore may not avoid the accord and satisfaction.

2.   Finisher will not be able to recover $1,000 from CheckNow. At issue is whether Administrator had authority to indorse the Restaurant check on Finisher's behalf. If an employer entrusts an employee with responsibility with respect to an instrument and the employee makes a fraudulent indorsement on the instrument, the indorsement is effective (although a person who takes the instrument and fails to exercise ordinary care may be held liable to the extent of the loss caused by the failure). Under the facts given, Administrator was Finisher's agent and had his express authority to indorse and deposit checks—it was a clear part of Administrator's job description. Even though Administrator did not have permission to cash the check and keep the proceeds, his signature on the check from Restaurant was authorized. As such, Administrator was a person entitled to enforce the instrument. There is nothing in the facts to suggest that CheckNow failed to exercise ordinary care in cashing the check presented by Administrator. CheckNow gave value, in good faith, to a person entitled to enforce the instrument and, therefore, will not be held liable for Finisher's loss.

QUESTION 1

Gray and Ray formed X Corp. to act as agent for athletes and to promote sporting events. X Corp. was incorporated in State Orange but had its principal place of business in State Blue. At the time of the formation of X Corp. in 1975, Gray and Ray entered into a voting agreement with respect to the election of directors. The agreement provided that it would remain in effect as long as Gray and Ray each owned at least 50% of the common stock of X Corp.

In 1980, X Corp. entered into a contract with Punjab to manage his boxing matches. The contract was signed in State Red where Punjab resided. Punjab was also to receive his share of any receipts from boxing events in State Red. At the request of Punjab's lawyer, the contract also provided that State Red law would be used to interpret the contract.

In January 1986, Gray refused to vote for the election of directors as called for in the voting agreement. Ray sued in State Blue to have the agreement enforced. Under the laws of State Orange, the voting agreement was only enforceable for a period of 10 years. Under the laws of State Blue, voting agreements were enforceable in accordance with their provisions without any time limit.

In February, 1986, X Corp. and Punjab had a dispute over Punjab's obligations to fight in State Blue under the management contract. X Corp. sued Punjab in State Red. Under the laws of State Red, all management contracts pertaining to professional boxers were to be interpreted under State Red law. Under the laws of State Blue, disputes pertaining to boxing events to be held in State Blue were to be governed by State Blue law.

Discuss:

1. What state law should be applied in Ray's suit regarding the enforceability of the voting agreement?

2. What state law should be applied to interpret the management contract?

Give reasons.

ANSWER TO QUESTION 1

1. State Blue law applies. At issue is the enforceability of an 11-year-old voting agreement.

Under the First Restatement, contractual rights regarding performance issues are governed by the law of the place of performance, and formation issues are governed by the law of the place of formation. Here, the issue in question regards the boundaries of the duty of performance (*i.e.*, whether the parties are bound to perform under an 11-year-old voting agreement). Such issues generally are governed by the law of the place of formation, but there is some overlap in this area, so a court might apply the law of the place of performance. In either case, State Blue law will be applied because State Blue, as the principal place of business, is probably the place of formation as well as the place of performance (even though this is not specifically stated in the facts).

The Second Restatement focuses on the state having the most significant relationship to the transaction, considering factors such as the place of (i) contracting, (ii) negotiation, (iii) performance,

2. CONFLICT OF LAWS

(iv) location of the subject matter, (v) incorporation, and (vi) principal location of business. Here, State Orange is the place of incorporation. State Blue appears to be the place of performance and the location of the principal place of business of the parties, and may have been the place of contracting and negotiation (although not specified in the facts). Given these facts, State Blue also has a reasonable interest in the outcome of the litigation. Thus, State Blue is most significantly related to the litigation, and its law will be applied.

Under the governmental interest approach, if the forum determines that it has a legitimate interest in applying its own law, it generally will do so. Here, State Blue has a legitimate interest in applying its law to an agreement concerning a corporation that has its principal place of business in the state. Thus, State Blue will apply its own law.

2.   State Red law will be applied. At issue is which state's law to apply where the parties have included a choice of law provision in their contract.

Generally, an express choice of governing law in a contract will be followed, regardless of which choice of law approach a court applies. There are a few exceptions, but none applies here. Since the parties chose State Red law to apply to their boxing contracts and State Red has a statute requiring that its law be applied to such contracts, a State Red court will probably apply State Red law, despite the State Blue statute requiring that State Blue law be applied.

QUESTION 2

1.   **Robert James, a resident of State X, bought a homecooker at Mike's Appliance Store in 1983. Robert bought the cooker as a Christmas present for his wife. The cooker was manufactured by S Corp., a Delaware corporation, with its principal place of business in State Y. In July 1984, while the cooker was filled with hot oil, it tipped over and severely burned two of the Jameses' children.**

   In August 1986, James sued the manufacturer in State Y for breach of warranty. S Corp. moved to dismiss on the ground that the two-year statute of limitations in State X applied. Under the State X statute of limitations, suits for breach of warranty must be brought within two years from the date of the sale. Under the law of State Y, such suits must be brought within four years from the date of sale.

   Which state law should apply? Give reasons.

2.   **Robert James was hired by Abba Services, Inc. in State Y as corporate controller. He left the company in July 1985. In 1984, prior to leaving the company, Abba had become a target for acquisition by another major corporation. Prior to the merger with this corporation, Abba directors approved new employment contracts for its senior executives which provided specified benefits if their employment was terminated or their duties reduced as a result of the merger. James received such a contract. The contract provided that State Y law would apply.**

   Subsequent to the merger, James was informed that the new company would be hiring a new controller, but he could remain as chief financial officer. Feeling that the restructuring constituted an involuntary termination under his employment agreement, James left the company.

James sued Abba in State Y, asserting that its actions constituted a breach of an implied covenant of good faith and fair dealing. The law of State X, where James resided, provided more liberal remedies to terminated employees than did the law of State Y.

Which state law should apply? Give reasons.

ANSWER TO QUESTION 2

1. If, like most states, State Y has enacted a borrowing statute, it will apply the State X statute of limitations.

Although a forum may apply a foreign substantive rule of law, it will always apply its own procedural laws. Statutes of limitations are generally treated as procedural; thus, a forum will apply its own statute of limitations, unless an exception to the general rule applies. One such exception is found in borrowing statutes, under which the forum, in deciding a cause of action that arose in a foreign state, will apply the shorter of its own or the foreign state's limitation period.

Here, the cause of action arose in State X because the injuries occurred there. Under the general rule, State Y (the forum state) would apply its own four-year statute of limitations. However, if State Y has enacted a borrowing statute, the shorter two-year State X statute will be applied.

2. State Y law will apply. At issue is which state's law to apply where the parties have contractually made a choice of law decision.

Generally, an express choice of governing law in a contract will be followed regardless of which choice of law approach a court applies. The one exception that might be relevant under the facts here applies when one of the parties does not truly consent to the provision, *e.g.,* in adhesion contracts. This exception will fail here, however, because the parties were not in greatly unequal bargaining positions—James was free to seek employment on other terms elsewhere. Thus, the contractual choice of law, State Y law, will apply.

QUESTION 3

PowerCorp, a public utility incorporated and with its principal place of business in State A, embarked on a program of nuclear power generation. First reading of these plans in the *Wall Street Journal*, the Westingbridge Corp. of State C, which designs and fabricates nuclear reactors, responded to PowerCorp's formal request for bids. It was ultimately chosen, being the lowest responsible bidder, as the main contractor on the reactor. Thereafter, a contract was negotiated between PowerCorp and Westingbridge and signed in State A. The reactor was to be manufactured in State C and shipped to State A for the installation.

As the design and fabrication process for the reactor proceeded in State C, various disputes arose between PowerCorp and Westingbridge for services performed prior to final completion of the project. As a result, Westingbridge stopped work on the contract and sued PowerCorp in a state court of State C. Jurisdiction there was based on a long arm statute of

State C, which provided for personal jurisdiction over "foreign corporations doing substantial business in this state." PowerCorp was doing substantial business in State C.

PowerCorp entered no appearance and a default judgment was entered against it for $1.2 million plus costs in State C. Westingbridge then sued PowerCorp on the judgment in state court in State A.

The standards for awarding damages in contract actions differ substantially in States A and C, with State A applying a very restrictive approach. Under that approach the damages awardable in this case would be no more than $500,000. The courts of State A have said (in cases not involving multistate elements) on numerous occasions that damage limitations in contract actions are a matter of "grave public importance to public policy as to which there should be no exceptions." State A follows the Second Restatement of Conflicts of Law approach to choice of law problems in the contract area. State C follows "governmental interest" analysis.

How should the court in State A rule on the enforcement of the judgment? Discuss fully and give reasons.

ANSWER TO QUESTION 3

The State A court should fully enforce the State C judgment.

Under the Full Faith and Credit Clause of the United States Constitution, judgments rendered by a court in one state are to be recognized and enforced in another state as a matter of right. There are three requirements before full faith and credit will be granted: (i) the rendering court must have had proper jurisdiction; (ii) the judgment must be final; and (iii) the judgment must be on the merits.

The State C judgment in favor of Westingbridge meets all three requirements. Jurisdiction was properly based on the long arm statute because PowerCorp does substantial business in State C. The judgment was final because no further action by the rendering court is necessary to resolve the action. The judgment was on the merits, even though obtained by default, as default judgments, which give rise to the res judicata effects of merger and bar, are regarded as being on the merits for the full faith and credit purposes of recognition of the judgment.

The State A court must also consider whether PowerCorp has any defenses to full faith and credit. It is well-settled that the fact that the underlying cause of action or relief granted by the rendering state is contrary to the established public policy of the recognizing state is not a defense to the constitutional mandate of full faith and credit. Also, the judgment is not penal since it redresses a private party injury.

Because no other defenses apply and because the requirements of full faith and credit have been met, State A should enforce the full $1.2 million State C judgment.

QUESTION 4

After being born in State A, baby Joe was separated from his sister, Julie, and moved away. When he was 21, he visited State A, where Julie had always lived. They met, fell in love, and decided to wed. Before they did, they discovered that they were siblings and that incest was illegal in State A.

Because they wanted to be husband and wife but live and work in State A, they went to State B to get married. State B permits incestuous relationships under Joe and Julie's circumstances. Another advantage was that State A required a certificate of a blood test whereas State B did not. After the wedding ceremony, the couple returned to State A to live.

1.   Is the marriage valid in State A? Give reasons.

2.   Is the marriage valid in State B? Give reasons.

3.   If Joe and Julie were to move to State C, would State C be required to recognize the marriage of State B?

Give reasons.

ANSWER TO QUESTION 4

1.   Joe and Julie's marriage is not valid in State A.

As a general rule, a marriage that is valid where celebrated is valid everywhere. An exception exists, however, where the out-of-state marriage violates a prohibitory rule of the domicile of one or both of the parties, and the parties immediately return to that domicile after the marriage is performed. A **prohibitory** rule is one expressing a strong public policy of the state, as opposed to a **directory** rule, which is more administrative in nature. With respect to Joe and Julie's marriage, the State A law forbidding incestuous relationships is a prohibitory rule; the State A law requiring a blood test is a directory rule. Thus, the invalidity of Joe and Julie's marriage in State A rests on State A's incest law, not on its blood test law.

2.   Joe and Julie's marriage is valid in State B. The marriage violates no law or public policy of State B, and State B thus has no reason not to use its own law and recognize the validity of a legal marriage performed there.

3.   As discussed in (a) above, the general rule is that a marriage valid where celebrated is valid everywhere. Under this rule, State C would recognize the marriage because it is valid in State B, where it was celebrated.

(State C, however, is not **required** to recognize a marriage that violates a prohibitory rule, as Joe and Julie's marriage does. Under the Second Restatement, a marriage should not be recognized even if valid where celebrated if it violates the strong public policy of the state with the most significant relationship to the spouses and the marriage. Since State C would have the most significant relationship to the marriage after the couple moved there, the result under the Second Restatement would depend on State C's own public policy with respect to incestuous marriages.)

QUESTION 5

Walter Whunker is a permanent resident of State Blue. In late April 1992, Whunker left State Blue for a two-week fishing trip to State Gray. Whunker planned to return to State Blue at the end of this trip.

On May 2, 1992, Whunker became involved in an automobile accident in State Gray. Whunker was injured when his automobile was hit by another car, driven by Clifford Clune. Some evidence suggested that negligence by both Whunker and Clune contributed to this accident. Clune and Whunker had not met each other before this accident.

Clune is a permanent resident of State Gray. Clune works in State Gray, servicing and repairing air conditioning equipment. At the time of the May 2 accident, Clune was commuting from his State Gray business office to his home in State Gray.

On July 11, 1992, Whunker filed a suit in a Blue state court. Assume personal jurisdiction was obtained over Clune in State Blue. Whunker's complaint named Clune as the only defendant. The suit stated a single cause of action for negligence. According to Whunker's complaint: "Defendant Clune's negligence proximately caused the May 2, 1992, auto accident between Plaintiff Whunker and Defendant Clune. Whunker suffered serious injuries in this accident." Whunker sought damages of $50,000.

The courts of State Gray have adopted a contributory negligence rule. Under this rule, if a plaintiff's injury was caused in part by the plaintiff's own negligence, the plaintiff cannot recover any damages from other parties. Defendant Clune argues that the contributory negligence law of State Gray applies to Whunker's suit.

On the other hand, Whunker argues that the law of State Blue applies to his suit. The courts of State Blue have developed a comparative negligence rule. Under this rule, a plaintiff's negligence does not completely prevent the plaintiff's recovery of damages from other parties. Instead, a plaintiff's negligence merely reduces the amount of damages that the plaintiff may recover from other tortfeasors.

Assume that the May 2, 1992, automobile accident resulted from the negligence of both Plaintiff Whunker and Defendant Clune. Should Plaintiff Whunker be able to recover damages from Defendant Clune under the State Blue comparative negligence doctrine? Or should the State Gray contributory negligence doctrine bar Whunker's recovery? Explain.

ANSWER TO QUESTION 5

Whunker will probably prevail. The result depends on which choice of law approach State Blue follows and whether the matter is characterized as substantive or procedural.

Vested rights approach of the First Restatement: The court would first note that the substantive area of law is torts. For an action in tort, the place of the injury will determine what law is applied. Under this basic rule, the State Blue court would apply the contributory negligence law of State Gray, and Whunker would not be able to recover anything since he was partly at fault. Whunker, however, might argue that the State Gray law should not apply since it is procedural. In a given case, a forum state may apply the substantive law of another state, but it will always apply its own procedural law. The issue is thus whether contributory negligence is a matter of substance or procedure. Because of the important effect this choice has on the outcome, the court should probably characterize contributory negligence as substantive. This characterization, however, would mean that Whunker, a State Blue domiciliary, would be unable to collect for his injuries. The court might thus choose to avoid this result by characterizing contributory negligence as procedural.

Most significant relationship approach of the Second Restatement: The court will first consider the connecting facts, which are the specific contacts with each jurisdiction. These are evaluated according to their relative importance with respect to the particular issue. The court will then consider policy-oriented principles as set forth in the Second Restatement. The principles in this group address the interest the forum and any other factually connected state will have in the outcome. The connecting facts point to State Gray, since it was the place of injury, the place of the conduct causing the injury, and the domicile of the defendant. The main State Blue fact is that the plaintiff is domiciled there. In considering the policy principles, the court will have to balance the interest each state has in the outcome since each state has a party as a domiciliary. However, there is a trend away from contributory negligence (the State Gray law), which often leads to harsh results, and toward comparative negligence (the State Blue law), which is fairer to plaintiffs who have been only slightly negligent. This consideration would lead State Blue to apply its own comparative negligence doctrine in spite of State Gray's greater factual contacts. (As discussed above, however, the court could have reached this same result by characterizing this issue as a procedural rather than a substantive matter.)

Governmental interest approach: The forum will generally apply its own law unless requested to apply another state's law, in which case the court will look to see if a true conflict or a false conflict exists. A true conflict exists if the forum and another state have an interest in having their laws applied; a false conflict exists when only one state has such an interest. If there is a true conflict, the forum will first reconsider its own policies. If after reconsideration it finds that it has a legitimate interest in applying its own law, it will do so. If it does not have a legitimate interest in applying its own law, it may use the foreign jurisdiction's law or a compromise. In Whunker's case, Clune would no doubt request that the State Blue court apply State Gray's contributory negligence law. The State Blue court would find that a true conflict exists, since both it and State Gray have an interest in having their laws applied. Because State Blue's own interest is significant—a state domiciliary will go uncompensated for his injuries, possibly at state expense, if State Blue's law is not used—State Blue will apply its own comparative negligence law.

QUESTION 6

Petrol, a company incorporated in State X, purchased an insurance policy by mail from Insurer Inc. Insurer is incorporated and headquartered in State Y. The policy protected oil fields located in States X and Y against out-of-control oil wells and other risks. In early 1991, two wells, one in State X and one in State Y, went out of control, causing more than $75,000 damage to Petrol's fields. Petrol did not notify Insurer about these losses until 1993.

Insurer promptly rejected Petrol's two claims. Insurer relied on a clause in its policy with Petrol that denied coverage of any loss unless Petrol gave "written notice to Insurer in State Y of the loss as soon as practicable." This denial of coverage is valid under the law of State X. The denial of coverage, however, is not valid under the law of State Y, because Insurer cannot

show prejudice caused by Petrol's delay in notifying it of a loss. There is no federal law on the subject and no choice of law clause in the insurance contract. State X courts apply First Restatement rules to resolve choice of law issues. State Y courts proceed first under governmental interest analysis; in the event of a true conflict, they also apply the First Restatement.

Petrol properly filed a diversity action against Insurer in the federal district court in State Y. After the court had determined the appropriate choice of law, Insurer successfully moved for a change of venue to the federal district court for State X. The case therefore is pending before the federal district court of State X.

Should the law of State X or the law of State Y be applied to determine the validity of the denial-of-coverage clause in the insurance contract? Explain.

ANSWER TO QUESTION 6

State Y law will be applied to determine the validity of the denial-of-coverage clause in the insurance contract. The issues are: (i) which state's **choice of law rule** will apply, and (ii) which state's **substantive law** will be determinative based on the resolution of the choice of law question.

Choice of law: Under the doctrine of *Erie Railroad v. Tompkins* and other cases, a federal court in a diversity action generally will apply the law of the state in which it is located. This includes the choice of law rules that the state would apply. An exception to this general rule applies when one federal court of proper venue transfers a case under 28 U.S.C. section 1404(a) to another federal court of proper venuc for the convenience of the parties. In that situation, the transferee court will apply the law that the transferor court would have used.

The facts do not explicitly state that the transfer in *Petrol v. Insurer* was pursuant to section 1404(a). However, the other statutory basis for a transfer, that for improper venue under 28 U.S.C. section 1406(a), would not apply because (i) the action originally was brought in the state of the defendant's domicile and venue was therefore proper, and (ii) even if venue had been improper, the facts indicate that the district court in State Y had already taken some action in the case (*i.e.*, by making a determination of the law to be used), rendering any objection to venue untimely.

Because the transfer was for the convenience of the parties, the federal court in State X should apply the choice of law rule of State Y—*i.e.*, governmental interest approach first, and in the event of a "true conflict," First Restatement approach.

Substantive law to be applied: Under the governmental interest approach of State Y, the forum generally will apply its own law (or in this case, the law of the state in which the court sits) if the state has a legitimate interest in the outcome of the litigation. However, if a true conflict exists, the First Restatement or "vested rights" approach will be applied. A true conflict occurs when the forum determines that both it and another jurisdiction have a **legitimate** interest in having their own law govern. Ordinarily, therefore, the forum court should first decide whether it alone has an interest in the outcome or whether both states involved have conflicting interests.

State X's interests are (i) seeing that companies domiciled in State X are paid for insurance claims they have made, and (ii) protecting oil fields located in State X from out-of-control oil wells. However, neither of these interests would be served by an application of State X law, which would lead to the denial of coverage under Petrol's policy and would protect only the interests of a nondomiciliary insurance company, Insurer. State Y's interests are: (i) the timely notification of State Y insurance companies of policy claims, and (ii) the protection of oil fields in State Y. Of these two interests, (ii) **would be served** by the application of State Y law, while (i) would not be served. Because only one state has a legitimate interest in the application of its own law, a "classic false conflict" situation exists.

Once it is determined that no true conflict exists, no further analysis would be necessary under State Y choice of law rules, and the court in State X should apply State Y law.

Alternatively, it is arguable that the policies underlying each state's law do not support the application of *either* law; therefore, neither state would have a legitimate interest in seeing its own law applied to the case. This is the "unprovided-for" case. The purpose of State X's law upholding the denial clause is to *protect State X insurance companies*, and the purpose of the State Y law is to *protect State Y insureds*. However, because Insurer is a *State Y* company, and Petrol is a *State X* insured, it could be said that neither state's policy will be furthered if its own law is applied.

The proper treatment of an unprovided-for case is unsettled. What is perhaps the most widely accepted solution is simply to apply the law of the forum, because there is no justification for applying the law of any other jurisdiction and because application of the forum law promotes judicial economy by avoiding the need to determine foreign law. [*See, e.g.*, Erwin v. Thomas, 264 Or. 454 (1973)] Again, because of the transfer of venue, it would be proper to apply State Y law as the law of the forum.

It is also possible, given this unique fact pattern, that the court might apply the "tie breaker" First Restatement approach. The issue here would probably be viewed as a performance issue, and the law of the place where Petrol's performance was to be completed would apply. Petrol's performance— providing notification of loss to Insurer—was to be completed in State Y. Thus, State Y law will apply.

QUESTION 7

See Family Law Question 3 for Conflict of Laws issue.

QUESTION 8

See Federal Civil Procedure Question 8 for Conflict of Laws issue.

QUESTION 9

See Wills Question 12 for Conflict of Laws issue.

QUESTION 10

See Federal Civil Procedure Question 11 for Conflict of Laws issue.

QUESTION 11

See Family Law Question 10 for Conflict of Laws issue.

QUESTION 12

See Family Law Question 12 for Conflict of Laws issue.

QUESTION 13

See Family Law Question 15 for Conflict of Laws issue.

QUESTION 14

See Federal Civil Procedure Question 23 for Conflict of Laws issue.

QUESTION 15

See Family Law Question 25 for Conflict of Laws issue.

QUESTION 16

See Family Law Question 26 for Conflict of Laws issue.

QUESTION 17

See Family Law Question 29 for Conflict of Laws issue.

QUESTION 1

Student is a junior at Westwood High School, a public high school located in a Midwestern state. Both of Student's parents are architects. Student plans to go to college, major in architecture, and join his parents' firm. He would like to attend Northern Central College of Architecture ("Northern Central"), a state-sponsored architectural school located in Student's home town. Attending Northern Central would allow Student to both go to school and work at his parents' firm. He would thus be able to gain valuable work experience while still in college.

Student's college entrance exam score and high school record exceed the academic qualifications to be admitted into Northern Central. Nevertheless, Student fears that he will not be admitted to Northern Central because of his sex—Northern Central admits only female applicants. Northern Central's catalogue explains that its all-female policy is intended to compensate for past discrimination against women in the field of architecture.

Yesterday, Student came to the law firm at which you are employed and related the above facts to a partner. He went on to explain that his sister, who is currently taking a constitutional law class in college, has suggested that Northern Central's female-only policy probably violates the Due Process and Equal Protection Clauses of the United States Constitution.

Student would like to settle matters now. The partner with whom Student met comes to you and asks you to look into Student's claims. Please write a memo explaining the following:

1. Regardless of whether Student can bring his suit now, does Student have a viable due process claim?

2. Regardless of your answer to the first question, does Student have a viable equal protection claim?

ANSWER TO QUESTION 1

1. Student does not have a viable due process claim. The main issues here are whether Student is being deprived of a life, liberty, or property interest without adequate procedures and whether the school's female-only policy is rational.

The Fourteenth Amendment to the United States Constitution provides that a state may not deprive a person of life, liberty, or property without due process of law. Due process actually has two components: procedural due process and substantive due process. Procedural due process guarantees that a person's life, liberty, or property shall not be taken without adequate procedures. Substantive due process requires that the government's deprivation of a person's life, liberty, or property be justified by a sufficient purpose.

Student has no viable procedural due process claim here, because he has no life, liberty, or property interest in attending Northern Central. The loss of freedom involved in not being able to choose Northern Central as a college is too insignificant a restraint to amount to a deprivation of liberty. Neither is the mere expectancy of attending Northern Central enough to create a property interest—there must be some state-created right to attend to amount to a property interest, and the facts do not mention such a right. Finally, there is no threat to Student's life. Thus, Student's procedural due process guarantees have not been violated.

Neither does Student have a viable substantive due process claim. The main issue here is whether the female-only policy is rationally related to a legitimate governmental interest. Under the Due Process Clause, if a government rule affects a fundamental right (the rights of travel, privacy, and voting and First Amendment rights), due process requires that the rule be necessary to promote a compelling interest. Rules affecting other interests are valid under the substantive Due Process Clause as long as they are rationally related to a legitimate government interest. The rule here does not affect a fundamental right and it is rationally related to the legitimate government interest of remedying past discrimination against women. Thus, there is no substantive due process violation here.

2.   It is uncertain whether Student will prevail on his equal protection claim. The main issue here is whether the female-only policy is substantially related to an important governmental interest.

In addition to providing due process rights, the Fourteenth Amendment to the United States Constitution provides that a state may not deprive a person of the equal protection of the laws. The standard for determining whether government action that classifies people violates equal protection depends on the nature of the right involved and the basis of the classification. If a fundamental right or a suspect classification (*e.g.,* race, national origin) is involved, the action will be upheld only if it is necessary to achieve a compelling interest. If a quasi-suspect class (*e.g.,* gender) is involved, the action will be upheld if it is substantially related to an important government interest. The government bears the burden of showing an exceedingly persuasive justification. In all other cases, the action will be upheld as long as it is rationally related to a legitimate government interest.

Here, gender, a quasi-suspect classification, is involved. Northern Central has adopted a female-only policy "to compensate for past discrimination against women in the field of architecture." In essence, Northern Central has adopted an affirmative action program. The Supreme Court has not resolved a case involving the same facts at issue here. The Court has struck down a female-only admission policy at a state nursing school because it found that there was no discrimination against women in the field of nursing. However, it has upheld a Navy rule granting females longer tenure than males before mandatory discharge for nonpromotion to make up for past discrimination against females in the Navy. It can be argued that unlike the nursing school case, there is past discrimination to remedy in the case at bar. However, it is uncertain whether the Court would find a total prohibition against admitting men to the state architectural school to be sufficiently justified by the past discrimination against women.

[*Editor's note:* Your conclusion here can go either way, as long as you support your conclusion with a relevant legal argument.]

QUESTION 2

Plains College is a small state-sponsored community college offering only two-year associate degree programs. More than half of the students attend part time, taking classes only in the evenings. Its faculty is made up mostly of adjunct professors who are hired on a need basis. If at least 10 students do not sign up for a class, the class is not held and the professor who was scheduled to teach the class receives no compensation for it.

The college usually offers a journalism class. As part of the curriculum in the journalism class, students publish a student newspaper four times a year. The class instructor serves as

the faculty advisor and must approve all articles and ads before publication. Publication expenses are paid from student activity fees and from advertisements purchased by local businesses.

A few days ago, the most recent edition of the paper came out. It included editorials that were very critical of the college president. After the faculty advisor approved the proof of the paper, the student editor made several changes that were not approved by the faculty advisor. The changes included a scathing editorial accusing the college president of illegal conduct, a condom ad, and an ad soliciting student participation in a citizen's militia group.

The college president fired the faculty advisor immediately upon seeing the paper, replaced the advisor with another professor, and forbade the class from publishing another paper.

1.   If the faculty advisor who was terminated brings suit in a court of proper jurisdiction claiming that his termination violated his due process rights, how will the court likely rule?

2.   If the student editor who made the changes in the paper brings a suit in a court of proper jurisdiction claiming that cancellation of the paper violates his First Amendment rights, how will the court likely rule?

ANSWER TO QUESTION 2

1.   The court would likely rule that there was no due process violation here. At issue is whether the faculty advisor had a property interest in continued employment at the college. While it is not a First Amendment violation to terminate a government employee for speech made while on the job, if the employee has a property interest in his job, he has a right to due process with regard to termination. A property right in continued employment will exist if the employee had a contractual right to continued employment or there is some clear policy that the employee may be terminated only for cause. If a government employee has such a property interest in continued employment, generally he cannot be terminated unless he is given notice of the charges against him and a pretermination opportunity to respond. There must also be an evidentiary hearing to determine whether just cause exists for the termination, but this hearing can be after the termination.

Here, the advisor was terminated immediately after publication of the offending issue of the newspaper. Nothing in the facts indicates that the faculty advisor received any kind of pretermination notice nor that a hearing was held regarding the matter. However, the facts seem to indicate that the faculty advisor did not have a property interest in continued employment, because professors are hired at Plains College on a need basis and they are not retained absent sufficient interest in their class. Unless the advisor can show that there was some understanding that as long as there was sufficient enrollment, the professor would be retained absent good cause, he had merely an expectancy in continued employment. Thus, despite the fact that he might have been fired rashly and for something that was not his fault, it does not appear that the firing violated any of the professor's due process rights.

2.   The court would likely rule that there was no First Amendment violation. At issue is whether the newspaper constituted a public forum.

Under the First Amendment, the government generally cannot prevent speech (*i.e.*, impose a prior restraint) or regulate the content of speech unless the prior restraint or regulation is necessary to serve a compelling interest. However, the government can place restrictions on the conduct aspects of speech. As to public forums (*i.e.*, places historically associated with, or otherwise open for, the exercise of First Amendment rights), the government may impose content neutral time, place, and manner restrictions that are narrowly tailored to serve a significant government interest. As to nonpublic forums, the government may impose time, place, and manner restrictions that are viewpoint neutral and reasonably related to a legitimate government interest (*i.e.*, something other than the suppression of speech). In any case, the government has no duty to fund speech.

Here, we are concerned with a college newspaper that was printed as part of a journalism class curriculum. Since it was part of the class curriculum, it will probably be held to be a nonpublic forum, despite the fact that it was supported by student activity fees and advertisements sold to local businesses. The facts state that the faculty advisor had to approve all articles and ads before publication and that the paper has now been canceled. Both of these actions could constitute a form of prior restraint that is generally prohibited by the First Amendment. However, because the newspaper is not a public forum and cancellation of the paper is a viewpoint-neutral act (*i.e.*, the college is not allowing a newspaper that includes one view vs. another; rather it has cancelled all newspapers regardless of content or view), the court would likely find that there has been no First Amendment violation.

QUESTION 3

The governor of the state of Acme has signed legislation passed by the Acme state legislature, which creates the state Marketing of Domestic Milk/Fairness in Milk Sales Act (the "Act"). The Act provides as follows:

1. **The state of Acme does hereby create a state office called the "Acme State Office of Milk Marketing" that shall have as its purpose the marketing of milk and milk products produced in the state of Acme. Such office shall utilize general advertising and other marketing tools to promote the sale of milk and milk products produced in the state of Acme. In order to finance the activities of the Acme State Office of Milk Marketing, there is hereby imposed a surcharge equal to 10% of the wholesale cost on all out-of-state milk and milk products sold in the state of Acme. "Out-of-state milk and milk products" shall be defined as milk and milk products produced outside of the territorial boundaries of the state of Acme.**

2. **It shall be unlawful for any wholesaler, with the intent to damage or lessen competition, to sell or offer to sell, at wholesale, milk or milk products at less than the cost to such wholesaler.**

3. **The invalidity of any part or portion of this Act shall not affect the remaining valid portions thereof.**

The preamble to the Act states:

> **An Act creating a state agency for the purpose of marketing milk and milk products produced in the state of Acme; imposing a surcharge on**

sales of milk and milk products produced outside of the state of Acme; determining that the offering for sale of milk or milk products below cost by wholesale distributors with the intent of injuring competitors or destroying or lessening competition is an unfair and destructive business practice; determining that it is the policy of the state of Acme to promote the public welfare by prohibiting below cost sales of milk or milk products made with predatory intent by which fair and honest competition is destroyed or prohibited; and providing a severability clause.

Monopoly Dairy, Inc. ("MDI"), the largest wholesale distributor of milk and milk products in the United States, has filed suit in United States district court to have the Act declared unconstitutional in its entirety. In its complaint, MDI argues that the Act infringes on its property interests without due process of law and is an invalid state regulation of commerce, and it asserts that MDI and like wholesalers should be allowed to sell their milk products at any price (above or below cost) and should not be required to pay to the state of Acme a surcharge on out-of-state milk that they sell in the state of Acme. In its complaint, MDI challenges the Act's constitutionality *only* under the United States Constitution.

You have been contacted by the state of Acme Independent Milk Producers' Association (the "Association"), a group comprised of 10 local, small wholesale distributors of milk and milk products, and asked to represent the Association in defending the Act against this constitutional challenge. First and foremost, the members of the Association fear that if the Act is declared unconstitutional, MDI will sell milk and milk products below cost until all of the Association's members have been run out of business. In addition, the Association would like to receive the obvious benefits associated with the marketing activities of the Acme State Office of Milk Marketing.

You have completed your research. Jane Spencer, the Association's Executive Director, having scheduled an appointment with you, is now in your office. You must now discuss with Ms. Spencer whether you believe the Act can withstand challenge under the United States Constitution. You must advise her by stating what you predict the outcome of the lawsuit will be and why. You should discuss your answer thoroughly.

ANSWER TO QUESTION 3

I would first advise Ms. Spencer that the first paragraph of the Act is unconstitutional. At issue is whether that paragraph violates the Commerce Clause.

The Commerce Clause gives Congress the power to regulate interstate commerce. While this power is not exclusive—states can regulate local aspects of interstate commerce—it is so pervasive that it includes some negative implications (sometimes called the "Dormant Commerce Clause"—"DCC") that are binding on the states. The DCC is the principle that state or local laws are unconstitutional if they place an excessive burden on interstate commerce. A law that discriminates against interstate commerce clearly violates this standard unless it is necessary to achieve an important, or even a compelling, government interest. If a law is not discriminatory, it violates the DCC if the burdens it places on interstate commerce outweigh its benefits.

Here, the first paragraph of the Act clearly discriminates against interstate commerce. It imposes a 10% tax on out-of-state milk and milk products that are sold within the state of Acme while milk and milk products produced within the state of Acme incur no such tax. This is impermissible under the Commerce Clause unless it is necessary to an important or compelling government interest. The creation of a milk marketing office probably would not be found to be a sufficiently important interest to justify the discrimination here, but even if it were, a tax only on out-of-state milk producers is not necessary to achieve this interest. Thus, the tax will be stricken.

I would advise Ms. Spencer that the constitutionality of the second paragraph is a close question, but there is a good chance that the second paragraph would be found to be constitutional. Once again the issue is whether the paragraph violates the DCC. There is also a question whether it violates the Due Process Clause of the Fourteenth Amendment.

The second paragraph of the statute prohibits wholesalers from selling their products at prices below the wholesalers' cost with the intent to damage or lessen competition. This paragraph does not directly discriminate against out-of-state producers—it treats all producers the same. Nevertheless, it could still violate the DCC. A law that does not discriminate against interstate commerce can be found to violate the DCC if it unreasonably interferes with interstate commerce when compared to its legitimate local benefits. The Supreme Court balances the burden the law places on interstate commerce against the local interest being promoted.

Here, the law is aimed at preventing monopolies that would lessen competition. This is a legitimate state goal. On the other hand, the law seems to only slightly burden interstate commerce. It might prevent a wholesaler who purchased milk products at a high price outside the state of Acme from selling those products at a competitive price within Acme. However, it is doubtful that many wholesalers would want to sell their products for less than cost. Moreover, the statute applies only if the wholesaler's intent in doing so is to damage or lessen competition. Thus, the balance would seem to strongly favor finding that this paragraph passes constitutional muster under the DCC.

I would also advise Ms. Spencer that the second paragraph would be constitutional under the Due Process Clause of the Fourteenth Amendment. The issue here is what standard of review the Court would apply.

The Due Process Clause of the Fourteenth Amendment requires laws to be reasonable and not arbitrary. What is reasonable depends on the nature of the law and interests involved. If the law involves economic regulation and does not affect a fundamental right, the Supreme Court tests reasonableness using a rational basis standard—the challenger must prove that the law is not rationally related to a legitimate state interest. MDI would not be able to make such a showing here for the reasons stated above—the state has a legitimate interest in preventing monopolies, and a law that prohibits a wholesaler from selling products below its costs with the intent to damage or lessen competition appears to be rationally related to that interest. Thus, the second paragraph would pass constitutional muster under the Due Process Clause as well.

QUESTION 4

The legislature of the state of Red recently passed legislation known as the "Red Patriot Act," which is set out below in its entirety:

The Red Patriot Act

Section 1. This enactment shall be known as the "Red Patriot Act."

Section 2. The recitation of the Pledge of Allegiance shall be a regular part of the morning activities of every school in this state. Every school in this state shall include in its curriculum instruction as to the proper protocols for the display, protection, and honoring of the flags of Red and of the United States. At the beginning of the fourth grade, every child attending a public or private school in the state of Red shall demonstrate knowledge of the words of the Pledge of Allegiance as then defined in the United States Code.

Section 3. Red citizens who register for the draft shall receive upon their registration for the draft or upon their presentation to the Office of the Red Secretary of State proof of their registration, a tuition credit check in the amount of $500, which may be used only to offset the tuition or fees charged by any university, college, or technical school operated by the state of Red.

The governor has indicated that he will sign the legislation so long as there exist reasonable arguments in favor of the Act's constitutionality under the United States Constitution. As counsel for the governor, you have been asked to provide a memorandum discussing whether the legislation could withstand a constitutional attack.

Note that under federal law, females are neither required *nor permitted* to register for the draft.

Please:

1. Describe the challenge that might be made to the Patriot Act under the Free Speech Clause of the First Amendment to the United States Constitution.

2. Describe the challenge that might be made to the Pledge of Allegiance under the Establishment Clause of the First Amendment to the United States Constitution.

3. Describe the challenge that might be made to the Patriot Act under the Equal Protection Clause of the Fourteenth Amendment to the United States Constitution.

For each of the issues above, be sure to explain the test or standard that a court will apply in resolving the question, and describe the strongest argument that you think can reasonably be made in favor of the constitutionality of the legislation.

ANSWER TO QUESTION 4

1. The challenge that could be made under the Free Speech Clause of the First Amendment is that the Patriot Act unconstitutionally compels speech. The issue is whether the Patriot Act's provisions impinge on the freedom of speech.

The First Amendment, which is applicable to the states through the Due Process Clause of the Fourteenth Amendment, provides that the government shall not abridge the freedom of speech. The freedom of speech includes the freedom to refrain from speaking; the government may not compel people to profess views with which they disagree. The freedom of speech is a fundamental right. Government action that interferes with the freedom of speech will be upheld only if it is necessary to a compelling government interest.

Here, it can be argued that the Patriot Act requires students to recite the Pledge of Allegiance every morning. Nothing in the Patriot Act provides for an exemption for students who object to participating. The Supreme Court has held that the government does not have compelling interest in forcing students to say the Pledge.

The strongest argument that can be made in favor of the constitutionality of the Patriot Act is that it does not compel any speech. The first part of Section 2 provides only that recitation of the Pledge shall be part of the morning activities of every school. It does not require individual students to recite the Pledge or provide a penalty for failure to do so. Similarly, the second part of Section 2 does not require students to profess that they agree with the Pledge; it merely requires them to demonstrate their knowledge of it as they would with any other historic document, and such a requirement is not repugnant to the Constitution.

If the preceding argument fails, it could be argued that the state has a compelling interest in promoting the ideals of freedom, liberty, and the indivisibility of our nation and that requiring students to say the Pledge fosters such beliefs. However, this argument would probably fail because while the state may have a compelling interest in promoting freedom and liberty, the Supreme Court has held that recitation of the Pledge is not a necessary precondition to achieving that interest.

2.   The challenge that could be made to the Pledge under the Establishment Clause is that inclusion of the words "under God" respects an establishment of religion. The main issues here are whether inclusion of the words "under God" has a secular purpose and a primary effect that neither advances nor inhibits religion.

The Establishment Clause prohibits government from passing any law respecting an establishment of religion. The clause is applicable to the states through the Due Process Clause of the Fourteenth Amendment. Under current Establishment Clause precedents, a law or government action preferring one religious sect over another is invalid unless it is narrowly tailored to promote a compelling interest. If government action does not involve a preference of one religious sect over another, the Supreme Court will uphold the action only if it: (i) has a secular purpose, (ii) has a primary effect that neither advances nor inhibits religion, and (iii) does not produce excessive government entanglement with religion.

The Pledge will probably be considered government action that does not involve a sect preference and so will be tested under the more lenient three-part test. Including the words "under God" in the Pledge does not seem likely to cause any excessive government entanglement with religion. Thus, the specific argument against its unconstitutionality would be that the purpose of including the words "under God" is not secular, but rather is to recognize the hand of God as part of the fabric of the United States. Consequently, the primary effect of the words appears to be to advance a religious belief in God. [*Editor's note: This argument is best understood in historical context—the words "under God" were added to the pledge in 1954, motivated by a desire to fight "godless communism."*]

The best argument in favor of the constitutionality of the Pledge is that the words "under God" have a secular purpose—to recognize the long history of religious ideals to which many United States citizens adhere. The Supreme Court has recognized a similar argument in upholding inclusion of religious items in Christmastime displays.

3. The argument that might be made under the Equal Protection Clause of the United States Constitution is that the Patriot Act discriminates against women. At issue is whether the $500 tuition assistance constitutes sex discrimination.

The Equal Protection Clause of the Fourteenth Amendment prohibits states from unreasonably discriminating against a group of persons. What is reasonable depends on the basis of the discrimination and justification for it. Sex discrimination is subject to an intermediate level of scrutiny: Government action that discriminates on the basis of sex will not be upheld unless it is substantially related to an important government interest. The government bears the burden of showing an exceedingly persuasive justification for the discrimination. Here, it can be argued that the Patriot Act discriminates against women in that it provides $500 in tuition assistance to men who register for the draft while women are neither required nor permitted to register for the draft.

The strongest argument that can be made in favor of the constitutionality of the Patriot Act here is that the law does not include any sex classification—it is a sex-neutral law. The purpose of enacting the law is to encourage draft registration, and it was not enacted with an intent to discriminate against women. Such a law is tested using a rational basis test—*i.e.,* it will be upheld unless the challenger can show that it is not rationally related to a legitimate government interest.

Here, the Patriot Act was enacted to ensure a ready source of recruits for the military. Surely, the government has a legitimate interest in ensuring a source of military recruits. Indeed, the tuition benefit would probably pass muster even if it were considered to be an instance of sex discrimination. Ensuring a ready source of recruits for the military is an important, if not compelling, government interest, and providing a tuition benefit for men who register for the draft is substantially related to achieving that interest. Thus, the Act is valid.

QUESTION 5

Oscar is the owner of a 150-unit apartment building in City. City passed an ordinance requiring security cameras in the common areas of all apartment buildings with more than 100 units. The ordinance was passed in response to a rash of burglaries in large apartment complexes in City. The ordinance provided that:

    a.   Security cameras would be installed by a company approved by City;

    b.   The installation cost and a monthly service charge would be billed to the building owner;

    c.   The building owner must provide sufficient space for a monitoring station on the premises; and

    d.   The building owner may not pass the costs on to the residents.

Oscar would have to use one of his rental units to house the monitoring station required by the ordinance.

Several of Oscar's apartments are rented by members of the religious group, Astra. The Astras use one of the apartments to conduct religious services. It is a central tenet of Astra that its members may not be photographed. The Astras are politically active and have protested the passage of the camera ordinance and other ordinances. City's Council, after publicly expressing frustration and annoyance with the Astras, passes the following ordinance: "Due to public health and safety concerns, no religious organizations may hold services in apartment buildings."

1.   **Applying federal constitutional law, discuss whether City may be required to compensate Oscar for the effects of the camera ordinance.**

2.   **Applying only the Free Exercise Clause of the United States Constitution, discuss whether the members of Astra can successfully challenge:**

   a.   **The camera ordinance; and**

   b.   **The religious services ordinance.**

ANSWER TO QUESTION 5

1.   City can be required to compensate Oscar for the effects of the camera ordinance. At issue is whether the ordinance amounts to a taking under the Fifth Amendment.

The Fifth Amendment to the United States Constitution prohibits the government from taking private property for public use without just compensation ("the Takings Clause"). The Fifth Amendment is applicable to local governments through the Due Process Clause of the Fourteenth Amendment.

Under the Fifth Amendment, a taking can arise from any physical invasion or appropriation of property, or from a regulation. A physical invasion or appropriation generally constitutes a per se taking, no matter how small the area appropriated or occupied. For example, the Supreme Court found a taking where an ordinance required apartment owners to allow cable companies to install cables.

However, there is an exception to the general rule for emergency situations—no compensation is due when property is appropriated or physically invaded to combat an emergency. In the past, the Supreme Court has applied this exception to destruction of diseased trees to prevent the spread of the disease and the destruction of oil wells during war to prevent them from falling into enemy hands.

Here, Oscar will argue that the ordinance effectively appropriates not only the space in his building in which the cameras must be placed, but also an entire apartment for the monitoring equipment. Thus, a taking has occurred and he must be paid compensation.

The City might argue that no compensation is due under the emergency exception, as the ordinance was adopted in response to a rash of burglaries in large apartment buildings. However, nothing in the facts indicates that the rash of burglaries amounted to an emergency. Neither does a rash of burglaries seem like the kind of threat that has justified application of the exception in the past.

As a final point, it should be noted that under the Fifth Amendment, a taking is proper only if it is for a public use. The Supreme Court has defined the term "public use" very broadly. For example, taking private property to turn over to a private developer in order to stimulate the local economy has been found to be a "public use." Here, the ordinance was enacted to promote safety and prevent burglaries. This would certainly qualify as a public use.

Thus, because City has caused an appropriation of Oscar's private property for public use through its ordinance, it will be required to compensate Oscar.

2.a.   The members of Astra cannot successfully challenge the camera ordinance under the Free Exercise Clause. At issue is whether the ordinance impermissibly punishes religious practices under the First Amendment.

The Free Exercise Clause of the First Amendment applies to the states and their political subdivisions through the Due Process Clause of the Fourteenth Amendment. The Clause generally prevents government entities from imposing burdens on individuals on the basis of their religious beliefs. However, a neutral law of general applicability will not be struck down merely because it has an incidental effect on a religious practice. Such a law, like any other law, will be upheld if it has a rational basis. The Free Exercise Clause does not relieve individuals from their obligations to comply with valid and neutral laws of general applicability on the ground that the law proscribes (or prescribes) conduct that the religion prescribes (or proscribes).

Here, the camera ordinance is facially neutral toward religion and is a law of general applicability that does not in any way target religion. It may have the effect of burdening the Astras' religion because members would need to pass cameras to reach the apartment in which their services are held, and their religion prohibits them from being photographed. Nevertheless, because the ordinance here does not appear to target the Astras and is generally applicable, it does not violate the Free Exercise Clause.

b.   A challenge to the religious services ordinance is likely to succeed. A law is not neutral if its object is to infringe on or restrict religious practices. A law is not of general applicability if it specifically targets only religious services. The ordinance here would probably not qualify as neutral because the circumstances of its passage suggest that it was intended to infringe on the Astras' religious practices. In any event, it is not of general applicability because it targets religious services. A law that is not a neutral law of general applicability must pass strict scrutiny: it must be narrowly tailored to meet a compelling state interest. This ordinance will not survive strict scrutiny for a number of reasons: (i) the asserted "health and safety concerns" would not be considered a compelling interest if they were demonstrated to be a sham; (ii) the ordinance is not narrowly tailored because no connection is drawn between religious services in apartments and health and safety concerns; and (iii) even if some connection between religious services in apartments and health and safety concerns could be discerned, banning services would not be the least restrictive means of addressing the health and safety concerns.

QUESTION 6

Lex, a nationally prominent criminal defense attorney, has a weekly television show on LNN, a national cable television station devoted to legal news. Lex's show deals with a variety of legal topics. Lex often uses his show as a platform to argue that adultery should be criminalized. Lex and his wife are both 60 years old.

Scoop is a reporter for *News*, a nationally distributed newspaper. Scoop received an accurate tip that Lex was engaging in an adulterous affair at a hotel in State X. Scoop then broke into the hotel through a back door, an act constituting trespass under generally applicable tort law, and attempted to get into Lex's hotel room. Before he could get into the room, however, he was discovered by a hotel employee and escorted out of the hotel. Later

that day, while waiting on a public street outside the hotel, Scoop saw Lex get into a car with a young woman who was clearly not Lex's wife. Scoop took a photograph of Lex and the young woman, who were kissing passionately. Scoop mistakenly thought the woman was Star, a world-famous actress.

Scoop hurried back to the newspaper and wrote a news story that was published with the photograph in *News* the next day. The story stated that Lex was having an affair with Star and that Lex's adultery was contrary to the beliefs he advocated on his television show. By coincidence, the next page of the same edition of *News* featured a separate story about the premiere of Star's new movie, correctly stating that Star had been in State Y for the entirety of the previous day. Scoop honestly believed that the woman in the photograph was Star, even though most people would have been able to tell from the photograph that this was not the case.

Would the First Amendment preclude liability if:

1. Star sued *News* for libel on the ground that the news story falsely stated that she was having an affair with Lex? Explain.

2. The hotel sued Scoop for trespass? Explain.

3. Lex sued *News* for invasion of privacy, claiming that the publication of the news story and photograph disclosed the truthful but highly offensive fact that he had engaged in an extramarital affair? Explain.

ANSWER TO QUESTION 6

1. The First Amendment would probably preclude a suit by Star against *News* for libel, but this is a close question. At issue is whether the story was published with malice.

At common law, a plaintiff may bring a defamation action against a defendant who makes a false statement about the plaintiff. However, the First Amendment limits common law suits brought by public figures. Such persons cannot recover for defamation unless they can show that the statement was made with malice. Malice will be found where the statement is made with knowledge that it is false or with reckless disregard of its truth or falsity.

Star, a world-famous actress, is a public figure, and it is uncertain whether malice can be shown here. Nothing in the facts indicates that Scoop or the paper knew that the woman in the picture was not Star. Indeed, the facts state that Scoop honestly thought it was Star. Thus, the statement was not made with knowledge of its falsity. It is a closer question whether the statement was made with reckless disregard for its truth. On the one hand, the facts say that most people would have known that the picture was not of Star. Moreover, there was a story about Star one page away in the same edition of the paper indicating that the picture could not have been of Star because she was out of state when the picture was taken. On the other hand, the reporter honestly believed that the woman in his picture was Star, and nothing indicates that anyone at the paper had any reason to doubt his story (*e.g.*, nothing indicates that the same editor read both stories). Without more information, we probably cannot find malice here. Thus, Star would not be able to recover from *News*.

2.   The hotel can sue Scoop for trespass. Trespass is an intentional physical invasion of a plaintiff's real property caused by the defendant. Here, Scoop intentionally broke into the hotel without permission. It does not matter that he was caught and expelled; the tort was committed upon his breaking in. Moreover, the First Amendment does not provide the press with any special right to trespass—even if the trespass was done in order to investigate a story about a public figure or a matter of public concern. Thus, the hotel can hold Scoop liable for his trespass.

3.   Lex cannot successfully sue *News* for invasion of privacy. Generally, it is a tort to publish private information about a person—even if it is true—if a reasonable person would object to having the information made public. However, if the matter is one of legitimate public interest, its publication is privileged if it is made without malice, especially if the information was obtained legitimately, such as a picture taken in public. Thus, it is clear that Lex cannot successfully complain about the picture itself, as it was taken in public. Neither would he be able to complain about the allegation that he was having an extramarital affair. Whether Lex, a public figure who advocates criminalizing adultery, is having an extramarital affair would constitute a matter of public concern, because it impacts the strength and conviction of Lex's position. And Lex will not be able to show malice because (i) the picture of him passionately kissing a woman who was not his wife was taken in public and legitimately, and (ii) it is true that he was having an extramarital affair. Thus, Lex cannot recover from *News*.

See also the Sales Questions section of this book.

QUESTION 1

Bridget Shea ran for the Metropolis city council on an environmental platform. Save Our Springs ("SOS"), a nonprofit environmental group, usually distributes recorded telephone messages beginning two months before an election to mobilize support for environmental candidates like Bridget. Analysts think the messages are critical in stopping developers from taking over Metropolis politics. The election was scheduled for May 3.

On January 9, SOS and TAMU Technology formed an enforceable written contract providing that TAMU would send out 50,000 messages between March 1 and March 15, and SOS would pay TAMU $25,000. SOS felt this was just enough time for the messages to have the desired effect. Because of equipment failure, on March 1, TAMU notified SOS that it would be unable to deliver any of the agreed-upon messages. Frantically, SOS searched around for another phone message provider; SOS spent $250 on telephone calls and faxes in its quest. As it turned out, the only provider with available capacity was LBI, Inc. Given the time crunch, LBI demanded that SOS pay 20% more than LBI's usual price for message delivery. On March 19, LBI agreed to distribute 20,000 messages by April 3; in return, SOS agreed to pay LBI $12,000.

By early April, the Daily Planet reported that Bridget's 12-point lead in the polls had "evaporated," and tagged SOS's failure to distribute phone messages as a primary cause. Ultimately, the LBI messages were "too little, too late." Bridget lost the election by a handful of votes. As a result, SOS is no longer the leading force in Metropolis environmental politics. Donations to SOS are down, and support for environmental causes in Metropolis appears to be waning.

1.   What rights, if any, does SOS have against TAMU under contract law?

2.   Would it matter if TAMU failed to timely deliver because TAMU's president was an opponent of SOS? Again, limit your answer to remedies under the law of Contracts.

ANSWER TO QUESTION 1

1.   *SOS's rights against TAMU:* SOS has the right to recover damages from TAMU for its breach of their January 9 contract. At issue is what kind of damages are available when a contract for services has been breached.

SOS should be able to recover its expectation interest, which would put it in the same position as full performance. Additionally, SOS will be able to recover incidental damages, and possibly consequential damages.

Expectation damages are based on the contract price, with the purpose of putting the nonbreaching party in the position he would have been in if the contract had been performed. SOS was to have paid 50¢/message ($25,000/50,000 messages) to TAMU; instead it paid 60¢/message ($12,000/

20,000 messages) to LBI. Thus, it paid 10¢ more per message for 20,000 messages than it would have paid had the contract been fully performed. Under an expectation theory, SOS should be able to recover in damages the extra 10¢/message in order to make SOS whole.

However, one must inquire as to why SOS paid more. Was this a reasonable mitigation of damages? It does not appear that SOS paid more to take advantage of TAMU's breach, but rather because of the time crunch created by TAMU's failure to make timely delivery. Moreover, SOS called around to find another provider; LBI was the only one available. SOS was "stuck" with LBI, and should be able to recover the difference from TAMU.

SOS also spent an additional $250 in phone calls and faxes trying to arrange a substitute, which it may seek to recover from TAMU. "Incidental damages" comprised of the expenses incurred by the nonbreaching party in responding to the breach are recoverable. Incidental damages are normally added to expectation damages. Here, SOS should not have to bear the expense of coordinating acquisition of the substitute provider after TAMU's breach. Because SOS was acting reasonably in trying to find someone else to distribute the messages that it needed immediately, SOS should recover the $250 in incidental damages as well.

SOS may also claim that it should be entitled to damages for the messages that were not sent. At common law, it may be hard for SOS to justify this, because it did not spend any extra money for them.

SOS may also claim that it suffered consequential damages, including harm to its reputation, a decline in donations, and the loss of the election. Its success on the argument will be contingent upon whether TAMU could have foreseen the damages, as discussed below. However, SOS clearly has the right to recover expectation and incidental damages from TAMU.

2.   ***Impact of intentional breach by TAMU for political reasons:*** If TAMU's president was an opponent of SOS, and knew that the breach could hurt SOS politically, there is a chance SOS may be able to recover more, although it is uncertain. At issue is whether consequential damages may be awarded to SOS.

Consequential damages are special damages, above and beyond general damages, that flow from a breach as a result of the buyer's particular circumstances. Consequential damages generally consist of lost profits resulting from the breach. Consequential damages are recoverable only if (i) they were foreseeable by the breaching party at the time of the contract; (ii) they could not have been avoided through reasonable efforts; and (iii) they can be proved with reasonable certainty.

Here, the facts do not state whether SOS told TAMU why it needed the messages by March 1. However, if TAMU's president was an opponent of SOS, it is reasonable to assume that he was familiar enough with the Metropolis political scene to understand the impact of SOS being unable to distribute its messages as planned. Thus, the damages were foreseeable. Moreover, SOS appears to have made reasonable efforts to avoid any losses; it looked for a replacement provider and did everything it could to remedy the situation, but to no avail. However, it is questionable whether SOS can prove damages flowing from its loss of reputation or loss of the election; such losses are quite speculative. Thus, it is uncertain whether it would matter that TAMU's president was an opponent of SOS.

SOS might also claim that if TAMU's president intentionally caused the breach, TAMU should be liable for punitive damages, but SOS will not prevail on this argument. As a general rule, punitive damages are not available for breach of a commercial contract. The purpose of contract damages is to compensate the injured party, not to punish the breaching party. Thus, as long as SOS is given the benefit of the bargain, there is no additional reason to punish TAMU. Therefore, even if the breach was intentionally caused by TAMU's president, SOS's damages could not be increased by punitive damages under contract law, although there is a possibility that its damages award could be increased due to the addition of consequential damages.

QUESTION 2

Delta is the owner of an equipment installation company. In May, Pratt, a meat market owner, called Delta and asked whether Delta could install six used coolers that Pratt had recently purchased. The coolers were to be installed in a new meat market that Pratt was opening. Pratt emphasized the need to complete the installation by July 1, in time for the new market's grand opening on that day for the Fourth of July holiday.

On May 31, Delta met with Pratt, and after a brief discussion Pratt signed a form entitled "Authorization Agreement." The document provided that:

> **In consideration of $12,000 to be paid on completion of the work, Delta will install in Pratt's meat market six used coolers, including pressurizing all cooling lines and calibrating the equipment for proper temperature within 30 days from the making of this contract.**

Delta told Pratt that he would sign the Agreement and send it back to Pratt as soon as Delta had verified that he had the necessary compatible fittings for the valves on the used coolers. On June 4, having verified that the compatible equipment was on hand, Delta dated, signed, and sent back to Pratt the Authorization Agreement.

Delta's crew began installing the equipment on Monday, June 25, and by Friday, June 29, had installed five of the six coolers with pressurization and calibration complete. The crew chief informed Pratt that he and his crew would be back on Monday, July 2, to finish up the installation. Pratt became enraged and told the crew chief that she specifically told Delta that installation would have to be completed by July 1 and that Delta would be in breach of contract if the chief and his crew waited until Monday to finish up the job. The crew chief phoned Delta and informed him of the situation. Delta, in turn, phoned you, his lawyer, informed you of all of the above facts, and asked whether he is contractually obligated to complete the installation by July 1 (which means that he will have to pay his crew overtime pay), or can they complete the installation on Monday. What do you tell Delta? Please explain the reasons for your advice.

ANSWER TO QUESTION 2

I would tell Delta that he is not contractually obligated to finish by July 1; he can wait until Monday. The main issue here is the application of the parol evidence rule.

Under the parol evidence rule, if a contract is reflected in a fully integrated writing, evidence of an earlier oral agreement will not be permitted to vary, add to, or contradict the terms of the writing. A written contract will be considered fully integrated if the parties intended the writing to be the final and complete expression of their agreement. There are a couple tests for determining whether a writing is a complete integration. The traditional view looks to the face of the writing. If it appears to completely express the parties' agreement, it is an integrated document. Many courts, however, try to discern the parties' actual intent, considering any relevant evidence. In any case, even if a document is only a partial integration of the parties' agreement, courts will not admit parol evidence on subjects covered by a writing.

Here, the parties' contract is reflected in a writing called the "Authorization Agreement," and that document will likely be found to be a complete integration of the parties' agreement under either test. It looks like a complete integration on its face—it sets out the performance due from each party and the time for performance, and it is signed by each party. Given the fact that Delta told Pratt that he would not sign the agreement until he verified that he had the necessary valves, the parties must have viewed the document as the embodiment of their full agreement. However, even if the Agreement is only considered a partial integration of the contract, it covers the time that performance is due and will control that issue. The Authorization Agreement provides that installation must be completed "within 30 days from the making of the contract."

Pratt is asserting that installation must be completed by July 1. This assertion must be based on the notion either that the July 1 completion date that Pratt stated in his initial phone conversation is part of the parties' contract, or that July 1 is 30 days from the making of the parties' contract. However, each of these assertions is incorrect.

Because, as discussed above, the contract here was reduced to at least a partially integrated writing covering the time performance is due, Pratt cannot contradict the terms of the writing with an earlier oral statement such as the one here. Pratt might argue that she is not offering the conversation to contradict the terms in the Authorization Agreement, but rather is seeking to explain what the contract term "within 30 days" meant. The parol evidence rule does not bar admission of extrinsic evidence to show what the parties meant by the words used in their written agreement. However, in common law contracts—such as the one here for installation services—such an argument generally can be used only if the term in question is ambiguous, and "30 days from the making of this contract" is not ambiguous. Thus, this argument likely will fail.

Neither is July 1 within 30 days from the making of the contract here. Formation of a contract requires mutual assent—an offer and an acceptance. An offer is an expression of present willingness to enter into a bargain, made in such a way that the offeree would believe that he could reasonably conclude a bargain merely by giving assent in the manner required by the expression. Here, the Authorization Agreement will be deemed an offer by Pratt. By signing the Agreement on May 31, Pratt showed a willingness to be bound by the terms in the Agreement. However, Delta did not assent to the terms of the Agreement on that date; on May 31, Delta indicated that he would not sign—that he did not want to bind himself—until he could verify the availability of necessary supplies. Delta finally signed the Agreement on June 4, and that was the day on which the contract was made. Thirty days from June 4 is July 4, so that is the day by which the installation must be completed. Therefore, I would tell Pratt that he need not send his crew in on Saturday, June 30, and can complete the work on Monday, July 2.

QUESTION 3

In May, Betty, eager to start law school in the fall, offers to buy Abe's law school texts for

$450. Abe tells Betty that the books will not be available until July at the earliest. Overhearing the negotiations, Clyde reminds Abe that he still owes Clyde $450 for bar review materials. Abe then tells Betty she can have the books in July if she promises to pay Clyde the $450 when she picks them up. Betty agrees.

1. Assume that Abe and Betty have entered into an enforceable contract. What is Clyde's status under the contract? Explain.

Immediately after the conversation described above, Clyde buys a stereo on credit, planning to use the money from Betty for his final payment. A month later, Betty decides to go to medical school rather than law school. She calls Abe and tells him that she will no longer need his books, and he tells her that that's fine, because he found someone willing to pay him $600 for the books.

In July, Clyde asks Betty for the $450. She tells him to see Abe because she no longer has any need for the books.

2. What are Clyde's rights against Betty?

3. What are Clyde's rights against Abe?

ANSWER TO QUESTION 3

1. Clyde is an intended, or creditor, third-party beneficiary of the contract between Abe and Betty. At issue is whether Clyde has any rights under the original contract.

A third-party beneficiary is a person who was not a party to the bargain and gave no consideration, but benefits by the contract's performance. Third-party beneficiaries are divided into three classes: (i) creditor beneficiaries, (ii) donee beneficiaries, and (iii) incidental beneficiaries. If the promisee's primary intent was to discharge an obligation he owed to a third party, the third party is then a "creditor beneficiary."

Here, Clyde was not a party to the bargain between Abe and Betty, nor did he give consideration, but he stands to benefit from the contract, as he will be paid $450. Furthermore, Clyde is an intended beneficiary and not merely an incidental beneficiary. There are several factors that support this conclusion: First, Clyde was expressly named in the contract between Abe and Betty. Second, Betty is to make payments to Clyde directly, indicating that both parties intended that Clyde would benefit from the contract. Finally, Abe owed money to Clyde, which supports an inference that Abe would be willing to sell his books and have the proceeds go to Clyde. Because one of the purposes of the contract was to satisfy the debt owed by Abe to Clyde, Clyde is also a creditor beneficiary.

2. Clyde may sue Betty and recover the $450. At issue is whether Clyde's rights had vested before Abe and Betty modified their contract.

Generally, a third-party beneficiary of a contract can enforce the contract directly against the promisor. However, a third-party beneficiary generally is subject to any defense that the promisor could have asserted against the promisee concerning formation or performance of the contract. Moreover, the promisor and original promisee are free to modify or terminate the contract before the rights of the third-party beneficiary have vested. Under the Restatement (Second) of Contracts, the rights of an intended beneficiary vest only when the beneficiary either: (i) manifests assent to the promise in a manner invited or requested by the parties; (ii) brings suit to enforce the promise; or (iii) materially changes position in justifiable reliance thereon.

Here, after Abe and Betty made the contract benefiting Clyde, they agreed to cancel their contract. However, the cancellation came too late. Clyde justifiably changed his position in reliance on the contract—thinking that he would be repaid in July pursuant to the contract, he purchased a stereo, intending to use the $450 he was to receive under the contract as his final payment. Thus, Abe and Betty were prohibited from modifying the contract without Clyde's consent. Therefore, Clyde may seek payment of the contract price—$450—from Betty.

It should also be noted that while Clyde is subject to any defense that Betty could raise against Abe based on formation of the contract, Betty will be held to have waived any defense based on Abe's nonperformance, because she told Abe that she no longer wanted the books.

3.   Clyde may sue Abe on the underlying contract for the sale of bar review materials. At issue is whether a third-party beneficiary may recover from the promisee.

If a third-party beneficiary is a creditor beneficiary, then by definition the promisee owed the third party a preexisting obligation. Therefore, if the promisor fails to pay the beneficiary, the beneficiary can sue the promisee on the original, preexisting obligation.

Here, Abe—the promisee—still owes Clyde, the third-party beneficiary, $450 for bar review materials. The contract between Abe and Betty with Clyde as a beneficiary did not relieve Abe of his obligation to Clyde. Thus, Clyde can sue Abe on this contract. However, while Clyde may sue Abe or Betty, or both, he can recover only once. Therefore, if he recovers the $450 from Betty, as discussed above, he cannot additionally recover from Abe.

QUESTION 4

Adam grew up in a poor neighborhood with the dream of opening his own "rib joint." After graduating from culinary school, Adam met Bill, who was looking for new ventures in which to invest. Bill was impressed with Adam's drive, and the two entered into an oral agreement whereby Bill agreed to open a rib joint called "Adam's Ribs" if Adam won a gold medal at a rib cook-off to be held the following month. Bill also agreed that he would sell the restaurant to Adam in three years for $20,000 cash, as long as Adam managed the restaurant in a manner that produced reasonable profits during the three years. Adam asked Bill to sign a written agreement, but Bill declined, telling Adam that his "word is his bond."

Adam was a little disappointed after the rib cook-off because he won only a silver medal instead of a gold medal. Nevertheless, Bill opened "Adam's Ribs" anyway, and without further discussion, Adam began operating the restaurant. The restaurant was quite popular with the locals, and one month before the three-year period was to expire, Adam approached Bill about the $20,000 payment. Bill acknowledged his earlier agreement, but refused to accept the proffered $20,000, claiming that the restaurant was producing too great a profit.

Discuss whether Adam can enforce the oral agreement.

ANSWER TO QUESTION 4

Adam is entitled to enforce the oral agreement. There are two main issues here: whether Adam can enforce the contract despite the Statute of Frauds and whether Bill will be held to have waived the gold medal condition.

Statute of Frauds: Bill's primary argument will be that the Statute of Frauds precludes enforcement of the oral agreement against him. At issue is whether a three-year contract is enforceable absent a writing.

Contracts falling within the Statute of Frauds must be evidenced by a writing signed by the party to be charged. A contract which, by its terms, cannot be performed with one year is within the Statute. Failure to satisfy the Statute of Frauds precludes enforcement of the agreement against the party from whom performance is due. However, there are a number of exceptions to the general rule, including an exception that applies when one of the parties has fully performed— once the contract has been fully performed on one side, it will be enforceable even though oral.

Here, the agreement between Adam and Bill required Adam to run a restaurant for three years and is thus subject to the provisions of the Statute of Frauds. Adam may argue that because Bill had the power to terminate performance within one year (for failure to produce reasonable profits), the agreement was not within the Statute. However, Adam is unlikely to succeed on this argument, because the Statute requires that performance be ***completed*** within one year—if the contract is terminated prematurely, performance has not been completed.

Adam will be more successful in his attempt to defeat the Statute of Frauds defense if he argues that the contract has been removed from the Statute by performance. Here, the contract provided that Bill would sell the restaurant to Adam for $20,000 if Adam operated the restaurant for three years and produced reasonable profits. Adam has operated the restaurant for the required three years and has produced more than reasonable profits (Bill described profits as "great"). Thus, the contract may be taken out of the Statute by Adam's performance.

Waiver of condition: Bill will also argue that the agreement is unenforceable because Adam's failure to win a gold medal constituted a failure to satisfy an express condition of the contract. The main issue here is whether Bill can retract his waiver.

A condition is an event, not certain to occur, which must occur or fail to occur, unless excused, before performance becomes due (*i.e.,* a condition "precedent") or that will release a party from an existing duty to perform (a condition subsequent). Conditions may also be due concurrently.

The nonoccurrence of a condition precedent entitles the obligor to suspend his performance. However, the party who is entitled to fulfillment of a condition precedent may waive the condition (*i.e.,* knowingly relinquish the right to demand fulfillment of the condition). Such a waiver will be enforceable and cannot be retracted if consideration is given for the waiver or the other party changed his position in reliance on the waiver.

Here, one of the conditions precedent to Bill's opening the restaurant was that Adam had to win a gold medal in the rib cook-off. Adam did not win a gold medal, and so Bill was not obligated to open the restaurant. However, Bill did open the restaurant and allowed Adam to run it for three years. Bill's opening the restaurant appears to be a waiver of the gold-medal condition, and Adam's running the restaurant for three years would constitute a change in position in reliance on the waiver. Thus, Bill would not now be allowed to retract the waiver. Therefore, failure of the condition would not be a defense to enforcement of the contract.

QUESTION 5

You have been appointed a judicial extern to Judge Elaine Williston of the Contract Law Division of the Circuit Court of Commerce County. The following facts have been established in a consolidated bench trial before Judge Williston:

Edward Shears was the sole owner and proprietor of a decorative landscaping business. That is, Edward maintains the lawns and gardens of his clients, occasionally trimming shrubbery and trees into fanciful shapes. At 9:00 a.m. on October 1, Edward faxed a signed offer to Val Orange, a citrus tree specialist. The offer read as follows:

> Val, I offer to pay you $10,000 if you trim the orange trees at Mr. Burton's estate into the shape of diamonds by 3:00 p.m. tomorrow (October 2). I promise that this offer will be left open until then.

An hour later (at 10:00 a.m.), Edward telephoned Mac Apple, who was renowned for apple tree care and maintenance. During the course of the conversation, Edward orally made Mac the following offer:

> Mac, I offer to pay you $10,000 if you prune and trim the apple trees at Mr. Burton's estate by 3:00 p.m. tomorrow (October 2). I promise that this offer will be left open until then if you give me a bushel of apples right away.

After hanging up the phone, Mac stopped by Edward's office and gave him a bushel of apples to hold the offer open while Mac checked on his availability to work on the Burton apple trees.

At noon on October 1 (unknown to Val and Mac), Edward suffered a heart attack that immediately took his life. As of that time, neither Val nor Mac had taken any steps toward performing the services requested by Edward. However, by 6:00 p.m. that evening, both Val and Mac had begun to tend to the trees as requested by Edward.

At 2:00 p.m. on October 2, Val and Mac had both completed their respective gardening tasks. But Edward's daughter, Edwina, acting as executor of Edward's estate, refused to pay for the services that Val and Mac performed. (Upon Edward's death, his estate succeeded to the ownership of his business.) Shortly afterwards, Val and Mac filed separate lawsuits, each seeking to recover $10,000 from Edward's estate.

Is Edward's estate liable to either Val or Mac, as the case may be, for breaching a contract? If so, would it be appropriate to award either Val or Mac, as the case may be, the $10,000 in damages each seeks?

ANSWER TO QUESTION 5

Breach of contract: Edward's estate will be liable to Mac for breach of a bargain contract, but no contract was formed with Val. At issue is whether Edward's offers were terminated by his death. Because the transactions involve services rather than the sale of goods, the common law of contracts controls here rather than Article 2 of the Uniform Commercial Code.

At common law, formation of a contract requires an offer, an acceptance, and consideration on both sides of the contract. Edward made an offer to each party. An offer is an expression of present willingness to enter into a contract, made in such a way that a reasonable person in the shoes of the person to whom the expression is addressed would believe that he could enter into a contract with the offeror merely by giving assent in the manner required by the expression. Moreover, if by the terms of the offer it can be accepted only through performance, it is an offer to enter into a unilateral contract.

Here, Edward's fax to Val and his call to Mac constituted offers to have each party trim trees in exchange for $10,000, and because these offers could be accepted only through performance by 3:00 p.m. on October 2, each was an offer to form a unilateral contract.

There was consideration here. Consideration exists if there is a "bargained-for exchange," *i.e.,* an exchange of promises, acts, or forbearance in which each party views what he gives as the price for what he gets. Each party's performance here (trimming the trees) would be valid consideration to support Edward's promise to pay because the tree trimming was the performance that Edward bargained for.

However, the tree trimming was not a valid acceptance for both parties. For an acceptance to be valid at common law, it must come before the offer has terminated. An offer will terminate at the time specified in the offer. It can also terminate sooner, by operation of law, on the offeror's death. This is true even if the offeree does not know of the offeror's death. However, the offeror's death will not terminate the offer if the offeror has made a legally enforceable promise not to revoke the offer (*i.e.,* an option contract, or, in a unilateral contract situation, performance has begun).

Here, each offer specified that it would not terminate until 3:00 p.m. on October 2, and each party fully performed before that time. Thus, each party's performance would constitute a valid acceptance unless the offer had terminated earlier.

Edward's offer to Val terminated upon Edward's death, but his offer to Mac continued. As stated above, an offer will terminate on the offeror's death unless: (i) in a unilateral contract situation, performance has begun; or (ii) the offeree has an option contract. Here, although we have a unilateral contract situation, neither Val nor Mac had begun performance before Edward's death. However, Edward promised each party that he would keep his offer open until 3:00 p.m. on October 2, and the promise made to Mac was a legally enforceable promise (*i.e.,* an option contract was created) because Edward offered to keep the promise open if Mac gave Edward a bushel of apples. Mac accepted this offer, and gave consideration to keep the offer open, by giving Edward the apples that he requested. Thus, Edward and Mac formed an option contract to keep the offer open. Therefore, the underlying offer was not terminated by Edward's death.

On the other hand, no consideration was given in exchange for Edward's promise to keep his offer to Val open. Thus, no option contract was created and the underlying offer terminated on Edward's death.

Damages: Mac is entitled to $10,000 and Val is entitled to the reasonable value of his services. When a party fully performs under a contract and the other party breaches, the nonbreaching party is entitled to expectation damages. The purpose of expectation damages is to put the victim of a breach in the position he would have been in if the contract had been performed.

Here, the only performance due from Edward is payment of the contract price, $10,000. Thus, that is what Mac should receive.

Val is entitled to the reasonable value of his services under a quasi-contract theory. Quasi-contractual relief is available when, as here, parties attempt to enter into a contract but the contract fails and one of the parties performed or partially performed under the purported contract and thereby bestowed a benefit on the other party, who has not given anything in return for the benefit. The amount of damages typically is based on the value of the benefit conferred to prevent unjust enrichment.

Here, Val performed services for Edward (trimming trees at the Burton estate), thinking that he and Edward had a contract, but the contract failed because of Edward's death. Thus, quasi-contractual damages based on the reasonable value conferred on Edward's estate would be appropriate.

QUESTION 6

Baker is a renowned pastry chef. Café, a sole proprietorship, is a well-known restaurant in need of hiring a pastry chef. Baker and Café's Owner had extensive conversations regarding Baker coming to work at Café. On May 1, a week after those conversations occurred, Baker sent Café a signed letter dated May 1 stating: "I will work for Café as head pastry chef for two years for an annual salary of $100,000."

On the morning of May 7, Café's Owner telephoned Baker and said: "The $100,000 is pretty stiff. Could you possibly consider working for less?" Baker replied: "I am a renowned pastry chef. I will not work for any less!"

Later that morning, Café's Owner sent Baker a signed letter by regular mail stating: "You obviously think you are too good for my restaurant. I am no longer interested in hiring you to work at Café."

Later that afternoon, Café's Owner had a change of heart and sent Baker a registered, express-mail signed letter stating: "Okay, if you really won't work for less, I agree to pay you the $100,000 a year you demand to work as head pastry chef at Café for two years."

On May 10, the registered, express-mail letter was delivered to Baker's office. The regular-mail letter containing the rejection was still on its way. Baker accepted delivery of the registered, express-mail letter from the postal carrier and placed it on his desk without opening it.

On May 11, before Baker read the registered, express-mail letter on his desk, he accepted an offer to work for Restaurant. As a courtesy, Baker called Café's Owner and said, "Sorry, I just took a job at Restaurant. Too bad you couldn't afford me." Café's Owner responded, "You can't work for Restaurant, I already accepted your offer to work at Café for $100,000 a year."

Does Café have an enforceable contract with Baker? Explain.

ANSWER TO QUESTION 6

Café has an enforceable contract with Baker. At issue is whether Café accepted an offer from Baker and, if so, whether the Statute of Frauds is available to Baker as a defense.

A contract requires mutual assent (offer and acceptance), consideration, and the absence of any formation defenses. An offer is an expression of promise, undertaking, or commitment to enter into a contract. It contains terms that are definite and certain and is communicated to the offeree. Once an offer is made, it may be accepted or rejected until and unless it is terminated. At common law, which governs contracts for services (the U.C.C. governs contracts for the sale of goods), an offeree may accept an offer expressly or by other means not relevant here, or reject the offer. An acceptance is a manifestation of assent to the terms of an offer in the manner prescribed or authorized by the offer. Under the "mailbox rule," an acceptance is effective at the moment of dispatch. Rejection of an offer may be made expressly or by making a counteroffer, *i.e.*, an offer that contains the same subject matter as the original offer but that differs in its terms. A counteroffer is both a rejection of the original offer, which terminates the offer, and a new offer. A mere inquiry is not a counteroffer. A rejection is effective upon receipt. Note that the mailbox rule does not apply if an offeree sends a rejection and then sends an acceptance—in that case, whichever is received first is effective.

The deal here is governed by common law because it involves a contract for services, *i.e.*, an employment contract. Baker's letter to Café on May 1, stating that he will work for Café as head pastry chef, was a valid offer because its terms were definite and certain (the letter included the job title, term of employment, and salary) and it was communicated to Café via mail. Thus, it was a valid offer.

Café's first response to Baker's offer on May 7, telling Baker that the salary amount contained in the offer was "pretty stiff," and asking Baker if he would "possibly consider working for less" was mere inquiry. The response did not flatly reject the offer; it merely raised the question of whether Baker would consider working for less money. Thus, it was not a rejection and counteroffer and did not terminate Café's power to accept (or reject) Baker's offer.

Café's second communication regarding Baker's offer—made later that same morning—constituted a rejection. In plain terms, Café rejected Baker's offer in a signed letter sent by regular mail. However, such a rejection would not be effective—*i.e.,* would not terminate the offer and Café's power of acceptance—until it was received by Baker.

Café's third communication regarding Baker's offer was made later on the same day—he sent a letter accepting Baker's offer by registered, express mail. Because Café had sent a rejection letter first, the mailbox rule did not apply to the acceptance and it was not effective upon dispatch. Instead, whichever letter was received first was effective. In this case, the acceptance letter was received first. Baker's act of accepting delivery of the letter from the postal carrier is all that matters; the fact that he did not open the letter or know its contents is irrelevant. Therefore, because the facts do not reveal any formation defenses, such as lack of capacity, fraud, or duress, Baker's receipt of Café's acceptance before his receipt of Café's rejection was sufficient to form a contract.

Moreover, the contract is enforceable, as no defense to enforcement is apparent on the facts. The only defense even remotely raised by the facts is the Statute of Frauds. Under the Statute, contracts that cannot by their terms be performed within a year are unenforceable unless they are evidenced by a writing or writings signed by the party to be bound and containing the contract's essential terms, including the identity of the party to be charged and a description of the contract's subject matter. Here, the subject matter of the contract is employment for two years. Thus, the contract must be evidenced by a writing signed by the party sought to be bound.

Here, Café is seeking to hold Baker to the contract, so we must look for a sufficient writing signed by Baker. In this case, Baker's letter constitutes a sufficient writing. It identifies himself as the person to be hired, describes the employment position at issue (head pastry chef), states the term of employment (two years), and includes the salary ($100,000/year). Thus, the Statute of Frauds has been satisfied and the contract is enforceable against Baker. However, as this is a contract for services, the court will not enforce it through an order for specific performance. A court will not order specific performance of a contract for services, both because of difficulties in enforcing such an order and because it may constitute involuntary servitude. Instead, the court would likely award damages against Baker or prohibit him from working for anyone else during the two year term of the contract.

QUESTION 7

Barry Builder and Harry Homebody made a contract reciting Barry to build a custom designed house for Harry for a total sum of $300,000. There were complex provisions stating a schedule of performance to be completed and payments to be made. This schedule was designed so that $35,000 would remain unpaid at the end of Barry's performance to ensure the job was done well. Harry had dictated this contract design during the negotiations because he had been "shorted" by contractors in the past who walked out with their money before completing the touch-up, clean-up, and other detail work called for in the contract. The contract also contained a "guaranteed damages" provision that read as follows:

> **For, and in consideration of their mutual understandings contained herein, Builder and Homebody agree that the last payment to be made under this contract will be made only if Builder completes each and every part of this contract to exact specifications and to Homebody's satisfaction. They further agree that the last payment constitutes a penalty which may be withheld by Homebody in the event Builder fails to complete each and every part of the undertaking defined herein, however small.**

After Barry had finished the construction and Harry had moved in, Harry discovered that the interior wiring was not in compliance with the contract specifications. Barry had, inadvertently, used a heavier gauge of wiring, suitable for commercial use, and far more durable than that specified in the contract. Nonetheless, the wiring clearly was not in accordance with the specifications. Experts will testify that replacing the wiring will cost $25,000 - $30,000, though none will testify that he would actually replace a higher quality wiring with a lower quality.

When Barry demanded the final $35,000 under the contract, Harry invoked the foregoing contract provision. He stated that the wiring was not in accord with the specifications and that Harry was not, in any event, satisfied with the job. On that basis, Harry refused to make any payment of the last installment.

1. **Is the foregoing provision of the contract enforceable? Explain.**

2. **Apart from the provision quoted above, and assuming that the house was, in all other respects, built in accordance with the contract, to what extent will Barry be able to recover the last installment under the contract? Explain.**

ANSWER TO QUESTION 7

1.   The contract provision is not enforceable. The main issue here is whether a liquidated damages provision is valid if it constitutes a penalty.

Parties to a contract may stipulate in a liquidated damages clause what damages are to be paid in the event of a breach, and the clause will generally be enforced if two requirements are met: (i) damages for contractual breach were difficult to ascertain or estimate at the time the contract was formed; and (ii) the amount agreed upon was a reasonable forecast of compensatory damages in the case of breach. Courts will not enforce a liquidated provision if it is construed to be a penalty rather than a reasonable forecast of compensatory damages.

In this case, the liquidated damages provision explicitly states that "the last payment *constitutes a penalty*." Because courts do not enforce liquidated damages clauses that are penalties, this provision will not be enforced by the court. Even if the provision did not explicitly state that the last payment could be withheld as a penalty, it would still be unenforceable because both of the above requirements have not been met. While it is arguable that damages in a contract to build a house might be difficult to ascertain in advance, the $35,000 amount agreed to here—regardless of how big or how small the breach was—was not a reasonable forecast of compensatory damages. The fact that the $35,000 figure is close to the $25,000 - $30,000 estimated amount it would cost to replace the nonconforming wiring here is not dispositive. Thus, the provision is unenforceable.

It should be noted that the provision is not unenforceable merely because it contained language conditioning Homebody's duty to pay on Builder's meeting the exact specifications of the contract and Homebody's satisfaction. While at common law, a contract to build generally is enforceable as long as there is substantial performance (*i.e.*, the buyer gets the substantial benefit of his bargain and any breach is minor), the parties are free to change the common law rule and require strict compliance with the contract's specifications. Moreover, while at common law, a court generally will not enforce a condition that is solely within the control of the promisor—because such a promise is deemed illusory—a court will enforce a provision conditioning payment on a promisor's satisfaction, because the court will imply a duty of good faith (*i.e.*, the promisor may reject the performance only if he is truly dissatisfied with the performance). Thus, the provision here is not unenforceable merely because it includes the "exact specifications" and "satisfaction" requirements.

2.   With the above provision aside, there is no language of condition in the contract, and the courts are reluctant to imply conditions. Therefore, Builder should be able to recover the $35,000, less damages to Homebody, if any. The issue is whether a builder has a right to recover under a contract to build when he has committed an immaterial breach.

A breach of contract occurs when (i) the obligor is under an absolute duty to perform, and (ii) this absolute duty of performance has not been discharged. As discussed above, a breach of contract is minor when the obligee gains the substantial benefit of his bargain despite the obligor's defective performance; *e.g.*, there are small deficiencies in the quality of performance where precision is not critical. At common law, if a breach is substantial, the aggrieved party is discharged from his obligations under the contract; if a breach is minor, the aggrieved party is ***not*** relieved of his duty to perform but may receive money damages to compensate for the defective performance. The purpose of contract damages is to put the nonbreaching party in the same position he would have been in had the promise been performed.

Here, we have a contract to build, which is governed by the common law. Builder breached the contract by installing wiring of a higher grade than that called for in the contract. Clearly, Homebody obtained the substantial benefit of his bargain—Builder built the home called for in the contract. Thus, Builder will be allowed to enforce the contract to recover the $35,000 left owing to him. Moreover, while Builder technically breached by using wiring of a better grade than that called for in the contract, because such a breach did not harm Homebody, Homebody will not be able to set off the $25,000 - $30,000 cost of replacing the wiring with the grade called for in the contract, and neither will he be able to set off anything else from the $35,000 left owing to Builder because the breach here does not appear to have caused any harm to Homebody.

QUESTION 8

Rancher conducts cattle roping clinics in various locations around the country. Rancher thought it would be more profitable to buy his own land and conduct the clinics there.

In March, Rancher bought the Bar-X Ranch ("Ranch") with a large pasture on which Rancher could hold the roping clinics.

In April, before Rancher had offered any roping clinics on the property, Rancher agreed to allow Gasco, an oil and natural gas company, to explore for gas reserves on Ranch. Before the parties signed a contract, Gasco executives drove around Ranch, and Rancher pointed out to them the pasture where he planned to hold his roping clinics. Rancher told the Gasco executives, "I can't wait to start holding my clinics here so that I won't have to go on the road anymore. Every summer that I travel with my clinics costs me $50,000. It will cost me only $10,000 to work from Ranch."

In July, Rancher and Gasco signed a contract in which Gasco agreed to complete its gas exploration and restore Ranch to its pre-exploration condition by March 31 of the following year. Gasco immediately began exploring for gas on Ranch.

By March 31 of the following year, Gasco had completed its exploration but chose not to restore Ranch to its pre-exploration condition. Because of Gasco's failure to restore Ranch, the pasture was not usable, and Rancher had to cancel his plans to conduct roping clinics on Ranch that summer.

Rancher sued Gasco for breach of contract. At trial, an expert for Rancher testified that because of Gasco's failure to promptly restore Ranch to its pre-exploration condition, it would cost $500,000 and take three years to restore Ranch. Furthermore, during that time Ranch could not be used for roping clinics.

An expert for Gasco testified that Ranch was worth only $20,000 less in its unrestored condition than if it had been restored to its pre-exploration condition. There was no other expert testimony.

Rancher testified that Ranch could not be used for roping clinics for the next three summers. Rancher estimated that 50 people would have attended the roping clinics each year, and each person would have paid a fee of $2,000, for a total of $100,000 per year. Therefore, Rancher seeks $300,000 for his losses.

The trial court found that there was an enforceable contract between the parties and that Gasco had breached the contract by failing to restore Ranch. The court awarded Rancher $500,000 for the cost of restoring Ranch to its pre-exploration condition and $300,000 for his losses.

1.   Did the court err in awarding Rancher the cost of restoring Ranch to its pre-exploration condition? Explain.

2.   Did the court err in awarding Rancher $300,000 for damages resulting from Rancher's inability to conduct roping clinics on Ranch for three years? Explain.

ANSWER TO QUESTION 8

1.   The court probably did not err in awarding Rancher the cost of restoring Ranch to its pre-exploration condition. The issue is whether Rancher's damages for harm to Ranch should be measured by the cost to restore the ranch to its pre-exploration condition ($500,000) or by the difference in the value of Ranch in its restored versus unrestored state, given the fact that the former would greatly exceed the latter.

For breach of contract, the injured party may be entitled to expectation damages. These damages are intended to put the injured party in the same position as if the contract had been performed. Because Gasco did not restore Ranch to its pre-exploration condition, as it agreed to do under the contract, Gasco has breached the contract and Rancher is entitled to damages. One measure of damages is the cost of restoration—here, $500,000. Often, where the cost to restore is many times greater than the difference in value of a property in its unrestored condition, damages are measured by the difference in value. However, in a case of willful breach, where only the completion of the contract will enable the nonbreaching party to use the land for its intended purposes, the cost of completion will be considered the appropriate damage award. Here, the cost to restore ($500,000) is many times greater than the difference in value of Ranch in its unrestored state ($20,000). But Gasco's breach in failing to restore the land to its pre-exploration condition appears to be willful. Therefore, the court probably did not err in awarding Rancher the cost of returning Ranch to its pre-exploration condition.

2.   The court erred in awarding Rancher $300,000 for damages resulting from Rancher's inability to conduct roping clinics on Ranch for three years. The issue is whether Rancher's losses from the roping clinics were foreseeable as well as ascertainable with reasonable certainty and, if they were, whether the court should have reduced the award by any amount (i) that was saved by not conducting the clinics, and (ii) that could have been avoided through mitigation.

Contract damages must be foreseeable to be recoverable. Damages are foreseeable if a reasonable person in the position of the breaching party would have known at the time the contract was made that the damages were likely to occur as a result of the breach. Here, it is likely that Gasco would have known that if it did not restore Ranch, Rancher would not be able to hold his roping clinics. In fact, Rancher specifically told Gasco of his plans to hold the clinics on Ranch. Because of this direct communication, the damages caused by Rancher's inability to conduct the roping clinics were foreseeable.

Contract damages must also be ascertainable with reasonable certainty to be recoverable. Here, Rancher faces the problem of a "new business." Although Rancher had conducted clinics on the road in the past, Rancher had not conducted clinics on Ranch. While most states no longer apply a per se rule denying recovery to all new businesses, courts still are reluctant to award lost profits to new businesses, because such profits are regarded as being "too remote, contingent, and speculative to meet the standard of reasonable certainty." In this case, it is a close call whether there is sufficient certainty to award Rancher his lost profits from the roping clinics. On one hand, there is no reasonable certainty that the clinics would have been a success, or that 50 people would have attended each year. On the other hand, Rancher has run roping clinics in the past and so has some track record on which to base a damage award.

[*Note:* An applicant could reasonably reach either conclusion on this point.]

If Rancher's losses from the roping clinics meet the tests of being foreseeable as well as ascertainable with reasonable certainty, the next question is whether Rancher's award should have been reduced by the expenses Rancher saved by not conducting the roping clinics. Contract damage awards must take into account costs avoided because of the breach. Here, even if Rancher's claimed damages of $300,000 were foreseeable and certain, that amount represents the gross amount that Rancher would have received. In order to receive that amount, Rancher would have incurred expenses. Gasco's breach saved him those expenses. Therefore, damages should be reduced to the net amount Rancher would have earned after expenses.

The last question is whether Rancher's award should have been reduced by the amount of loss that Rancher could have avoided by going on the road with his roping clinics. The $300,000 award of damages may be reduced by the amount that Rancher would have earned by mitigating his loss. The nonbreaching party has a duty to mitigate damages. Here, Rancher offered clinics on the road before he bought Ranch. After the breach, Rancher could have resumed these activities as mitigation, because that alternative may not be viewed as substantially different from or inferior to the clinics Rancher planned to offer on the ranch. However, the need to travel might make this alternative inferior. Thus, the court will probably not reduce Rancher's award by the amount he could have earned by offering the roping clinics on the road.

QUESTION 9

Le Petite Bovine is a well-known restaurant, located in Jersey County, Illinois. Owen owns Le Petite Bovine.

Prior to February 2007, Fred was the long-time head chef at Le Petite Bovine. In February 2007, Fred quit the restaurant. After Fred quit, Owen sought a temporary head chef, while looking for a more permanent replacement.

When he quit the restaurant, Fred earned a salary of $7,000 per month. Head chefs in Jersey County earn an average salary of about $7,000 per month. When a restaurant hires a new head chef, training the chef to become familiar with the restaurant and the menu usually costs about $500.

Cindy is a chef who lives in Jersey County. In March 2007, Owen talks with Cindy about the temporary head chef position at the Le Petite Bovine restaurant. All of the negotiations between Cindy and Owen occur in four phone calls, summarized below:

Phone Call 1. Owen says: "Cindy, I would like you to work for us as our head chef. The job would last for three months. Your salary would be $5,500 per month."

Phone Call 2. Cindy says: "Owen, I would be happy to work for you for six months, at $7,000 per month. I accept."

Phone Call 3. Owen says: "Cindy, I can hire you for six months, at $6,000 per month. However, if you quit work before the end of six months, you would owe me $50,000 for violating our agreement. I accept those terms."

Phone Call 4. Cindy says: "Owen, I accept your offer."

(a)   Have Cindy and Owen formed a contract? If so, what is Cindy's salary? Explain.

(b)   For the purpose of this part only, assume that in March 2007, Owen and Cindy have entered into a contract. Now assume that Fred regrets quitting his job as the head chef at Le Petite Bovine. Fred wants to return to the restaurant. After talking with Fred, Owen contacts Cindy. Owen contends that his contract with Cindy is unenforceable, because the agreement was oral and not a signed writing.

Can Cindy enforce her employment contract with Owen? Explain.

(c)   For the purpose of this part only, assume that Owen and Cindy have entered into an enforceable contract. The contract requires that Cindy work at Le Petite Bovine for six months. Further, assume that the contract includes Owen's statement to Cindy in Phone Call 3: "If you quit work before the end of six months, you would owe me $50,000 for violating our agreement."

As Owen had feared, Cindy leaves the job earlier. After working at Le Petite Bovine for five months, Cindy quits to work at a higher-paying restaurant in Jersey County.

Can Owen enforce the contract provision, and require that Cindy pay $50,000 for leaving the restaurant one month before the end of her employment contract? Explain.

ANSWER TO QUESTION 9

(a)   Cindy and Owen have formed a contract under which Owen is to pay Cindy $6,000 per month. At issue is whether the requirements for a contract have been met in the round of phone calls between Cindy and Owen.

To form a contract, there must be mutual assent (offer and acceptance), consideration, and the absence of any formation defenses. An offer is an expression of promise, undertaking, or commitment to enter into a contract. It contains terms that are definite and certain and is communicated to the offeree. Once made, an offer may be accepted or rejected until and unless it is terminated. Under the common law, which governs contracts for services, an offeree may accept an offer expressly or by other means not relevant here, or reject the offer. An acceptance is a manifestation of assent to the terms of an offer. Rejection of an offer may be made expressly or by making a counteroffer, *i.e.*, an offer that contains the same subject matter as the original offer but different terms. A counteroffer is both a rejection of the original offer, which terminates the offer, and a new offer.

The common law applies here because this is a contract for services, *i.e.*, an employment contract. Here, Owen made an offer in the first phone call—he would hire Cindy for three months at $5,500 per month. Although Cindy said she "accepted" Owen's offer in the second phone call, there was no valid acceptance because Cindy changed the terms—she said she would work for six months at $7,000 per month. This constitutes a counteroffer—a rejection of Owen's offer and a new offer to Owen, giving him the power to accept. Likewise, although Owen purported to "accept" Cindy's offer in the third phone call, he too made a counteroffer, because he changed the terms of Cindy's offer. In effect, Owen rejected Cindy's offer to work six months at $7,000 per month and made an offer to hire Cindy for six months at $6,000 per month if Cindy promised to pay him $50,000 if she left early. In the fourth phone call, Cindy accepted the terms Owen made in the third phone call. Thus, there was mutual assent.

Consideration is present on both sides. For there to be consideration there must be a bargained-for exchange between the parties. Also, under the majority rule, that which is bargained for must constitute a legal detriment to the promisee (*i.e.*, the promisee must do something she is under no legal obligation to do or refrain from doing something she has a legal right to do). Here, Owen's promise to pay Cindy $6,000 for six months supports Cindy's promise to work for six months and vice versa. Thus, there is a bargained-for exchange between the parties. Cindy's working for Owen is a legal detriment to her, and Owen's promise to pay $6,000 per month is a legal detriment to him, so there is adequate consideration. Whether Owen can raise the Statute of Frauds as a valid defense will be discussed in (b), below.

(b) Cindy can enforce her employment contract with Owen even though the agreement was oral and not memorialized by a signed writing. At issue is whether the Statute of Frauds is a valid defense for Owen.

Oral contracts that are properly formed (*see* (a), above) are valid in most instances. However, the Statute of Frauds requires that certain contracts be evidenced by a writing signed by the party sought to be bound. Contracts that fall under the Statute of Frauds include those that cannot by their terms be performed within a year and those for the sale of goods of $500 or more.

Here, the subject matter of the contract is employment for six months. Thus, the contract by its own terms can (and would) be performed within a year and need not be evidenced by a writing signed by the party sought to be bound. Moreover, although the contract provides for a total payment to Cindy of $36,000 (*i.e.*, more than $500), this is a services contract and not a contract for the sale of goods, so the $500-or-more requirement is inapplicable here. Therefore, Cindy can enforce her employment contract with Owen even though it is oral.

(c) Owen cannot enforce the contract provision requiring Cindy to pay him $50,000 for leaving the restaurant one month before the end of her employment contract. The issue is whether the $50,000 is a valid liquidated damages provision.

Parties may stipulate what damages are to be paid in the event of a breach of contract, and these liquidated damages clauses are enforceable if: (i) damages for the breach were difficult to ascertain or estimate at the time the contract was formed, and (ii) the amount is a reasonable forecast of compensatory damages. If the liquidated damages amount is unreasonable, the court will treat it as a penalty and not enforce the provision.

Here, Cindy could argue that Owen's damages would be at most $1,500: Owen would have to pay Cindy's replacement the average salary of a head chef in the area, which at $7,000 per month is $1,000 more than Owen would have had to pay Cindy had she worked the last month, and it would cost $500 to train a replacement. No other facts are given. While it might be argued that other damages would arise if Owen is without a chef for a month, nothing in the facts indicates that the $50,000 is tied to any realistic estimate of damages. Indeed, because the liquidated amount of $50,000 does not change whether Cindy left with five months remaining on her contract or one week, the amount seems to be nothing more than a penalty. Thus, it is unenforceable.

QUESTION 1

Two events at Shoes International Corporation ("SIC") have caused legal concern:

First, SIC's board decided to develop a suburban office complex in which SIC's new head-quarters is to be the centerpiece building. SIC has never engaged in a real estate develop-ment project before, and several experts have questioned whether or not this project can be profitable. Moreover, the planned SIC headquarters building will be expensive and have substantially more space than SIC needs. Despite these negatives, which were fully dis-closed to SIC's board, the board unanimously approved the project. Thereafter, the price of SIC's stock fell 5%.

Second, after an extensive search covering several states and 10 locations, SIC bought a tract of land for a new factory. The price was consistent with the appraised value of the land. It has now been revealed that a trust for the benefit of SIC's CEO and her family owned this land. The CEO had not participated in the selection of the site or in presenting a recommendation to the board. She did vote in favor of the project, and she made no disclo-sure to the board of her interest in the land.

Several shareholders are considering suits challenging these two transactions.

1.   Are the shareholders likely to prevail? Explain.

2.   Would it affect the outcome if the board were to reconsider either action and reaffirm its decision? Explain.

ANSWER TO QUESTION 1

1.   ***Decision to develop office complex:*** It is unclear whether the shareholders would prevail in challenging SIC's board's decision to build the office complex. At issue is the directors' duty of care.

By statute, directors owe their corporation a duty to operate the corporation in a manner the directors reasonably believe to be in the best interests of the corporation, with at least the care that an ordinarily prudent person would exercise in a like position. Directors are not insurers of the corporation's success; as long as they make their decisions within the statutory guidelines, they will not be liable for decisions that turn out poorly.

The facts here are insufficient to determine whether the directors met the statutory standard. The facts indicate that the corporation had never before engaged in real estate development, that several experts questioned the project's profitability, and that the new building would have more space than the corporation really needed. No advantages in building the new office complex are mentioned, but presumably there are some. If there are, the court would not likely substitute its judgment for the judgment of the board. If there are no advantages in building the new office complex, no reasonable person would have taken the risks that the directors here took, and so the directors could be held liable.

Purchase of CEO's land: The shareholders would probably be unsuccessful in challenging the purchase of the CEO's land.

CORPORATIONS AND LLCs

Although the facts do not explicitly so state, the CEO appears to be a director. A director owes her corporation a duty of loyalty and will not be allowed to profit at the corporation's expense. However, a transaction between a corporation and an interested director will not be set aside if the transaction was fair to the corporation at the time it was entered into.

Here, it can be argued that the CEO breached her fiduciary duty by failing to disclose her interest in the land transaction. Nevertheless, the transaction probably cannot be set aside, despite the CEO's failure to disclose her interest, since the CEO did nothing to influence the board's decision to purchase the property and the facts indicate that the price that the corporation paid for the land was fair.

2. *Decision to develop office complex:* The result would not be any different if the board were to reconsider and affirm its prior decision to build the office complex. If the board had no rational reason for building the office complex before, confirming the prior decision without additional reasons would do nothing to alleviate the breach of duty. If the board had a rational reason to approve construction of the office complex originally, reapproving now also would have no effect—because under such circumstances, the project already was validly approved.

Purchase of CEO's land: The result would not be any different if the board were to reconsider and reaffirm its prior decision to buy the CEO's land, since, as indicated above, the initial decision probably cannot be successfully challenged, but reaffirmation would provide an additional reason for upholding the transaction—a director's conflicting interest transaction cannot be set aside if all material facts of the transaction are known by the board and a disinterested majority of the board approves the transaction.

QUESTION 2

Crothers Power Tool, Inc. ("CPT") is an Illinois corporation. CPT, a publicly held corporation, maintains its principal place of business in Manzanita County, Illinois, and manufactures and sells a variety of industrial machinery.

For the past five years, Jack Eisen has served as the president of CPT. CPT has employed Eisen under a series of one-year employment contracts expiring on January 28 of each year. The CPT board of directors regularly has renewed Eisen's employment contract. Eisen has enjoyed a successful tenure as the president of CPT. Each year that Eisen has served as president, the company's profits have increased. Over the past five years, the price of CPT stock has risen from $10 per share to $30 per share.

During 1993, Eisen publicly invites other companies and investors to acquire CPT. In 1993, the price of CPT stock jumps from $20 per share to $30 per share. Some of this price increase reflects takeover speculation. Despite the increase in the price of CPT stock, some members of the CPT board of directors disapprove of Eisen's efforts aimed at encouraging an outsider to acquire CPT.

On January 27 and January 28, 1994, CPT holds its annual meeting. The meeting takes place in Manzanita County, Illinois. The following events occur at the 1994 annual meeting.

1. *Voting trust.* Don Winkler, Lori Mitchell, and Tracy Schwartz are three of the largest holders of CPT stock. Winkler is 34 years old. Mitchell is 33 years old. Schwartz is 30 years

old. Winkler, Mitchell, and Schwartz anticipate that several different companies will seek to acquire CPT. Winkler, Mitchell, and Schwartz wish to assure that they each will receive the highest possible price for their CPT stock.

On January 27, 1994, Winkler, Mitchell, and Schwartz execute a voting trust. Under this written agreement, attorney Karen Glaze is appointed as the trustee. The agreement empowers Glaze to vote the CPT stock as the trustee for Winkler, Mitchell, and Schwartz. According to the trust agreement, Glaze must vote all of this stock for a single slate of board of directors candidates. Glaze must receive the unanimous approval of Winkler, Mitchell, and Schwartz before Glaze votes the shares. The voting trust will remain in effect "as long as Winkler, Mitchell, and Schwartz continue living."

On January 27, 1994, Winkler, Mitchell, and Schwartz transfer their CPT stock certificates to Karen Glaze. Also on January 27, Glaze delivers a copy of the voting trust agreement to the registered office of CPT in Manzanita County.

2.   *Acquisition of the Weaver patent.* Janet Weaver holds a patent, which covers a new and less expensive method for manufacturing drill bits. In December 1993, Weaver bought this patent from Dan Hariton for $30,000. Hariton had invented the new drill bit manufacturing technology and subsequently received the patent that protects his invention.

Nine members serve on the CPT board of directors. On January 28, 1994, the board of directors votes 9-0 to acquire the patent from Weaver. In exchange for the patent rights, CPT provides Weaver with stock valued at $40,000. Prior to this transaction, no member of the CPT board of directors had met Weaver. Also, no member of the board of directors had entered into any dealings with Weaver.

3.   *Refusal to declare a dividend.* For the past 10 years prior to 1994, CPT has paid a $1 dividend for each share of stock that the company has issued. On January 28, 1994, the CPT board of directors determines by a 9-0 vote that the company will not pay a dividend in 1994. In a statement released after the board of directors meeting, the board explained its reasons for not paying a dividend. According to the statement, the board "decided to defer any dividend and may use this cash either to replace aging equipment, or to expand the corporation's production facilities."

4.   *Removal of Eisen.* On January 28, 1994, the CPT board of directors removes Eisen as the company's president. The decision is approved by a 9-0 vote. The board replaces Eisen with a new president, Linda Campbell. In a prepared statement, the board explains only that the decision to remove Eisen "was in the best interests of the corporation."

Is each of the actions taken at the January 1994 annual meeting of CPT valid? Explain.

ANSWER TO QUESTION 2

Most of the events that took place at CPT's annual meeting are valid.

The voting trust. Shareholders have a statutory right to enter into voting trusts. To establish a voting trust, shareholders must do almost exactly what Winkler, Mitchell, and Schwartz did here: Enter into a written agreement granting legal ownership of their shares to a trustee and retaining beneficial ownership of their shares in themselves. The agreement must also be filed with the corporation, as Glaze did here. A voting trust may provide that the trustee is to vote a certain way, so there is no problem with the trust provision here that the trustee must vote as the beneficial owners unanimously agree. There is a problem, however, with the duration of the trust here. A voting trust can be valid only for up to 10 years. Here, the trust purports to be for so long as the beneficial owners live and thus is invalid.

Purchase of Weaver patent. The purchase of Weaver's patent was a valid exercise of board discretion. A corporation's board of directors has the power to authorize extraordinary purchases by the corporation. When the board purchases property in exchange for stock, such as the board did with the patent here, the board must determine that the value of the property is sufficient to pay for the stock. The board's good faith valuation of the property is conclusive. Here the board determined that the patent was worth $40,000. While it might be argued that the board overpaid for the patent (because Weaver bought it for $30,000 a month before the sale here), there is nothing in the facts that indicates a bad faith valuation, especially since no one on CPT's board had ever met or dealt with Weaver before. Thus, the purchase was proper.

Refusal to declare dividend. CPT's board's refusal to declare a dividend was proper. A corporation's board of directors has discretion to declare a dividend, and a court will seldom interfere with that discretion. The fact that CPT is profitable and has always declared a dividend in the past is irrelevant. Moreover, while it was unnecessary for the board to do so, at the meeting the board stated a valid business reason for withholding the dividend—to replace aging equipment or expand production facilities. A court would not interfere with such a decision.

Removal of Eisen. The removal of Eisen, the company's president, by the board was proper. Officers of a corporation are appointed by the board of directors, and the board has the power to fire officers as well, even without cause. If termination breaches the officer's contract, the corporation may be liable for damages, but the board nevertheless has the power to terminate the officer's service. Thus, the board could terminate Eisen's employment here even though Eisen has made the company profitable. Moreover, the corporation is not liable to Eisen for damages, because the term of his employment contract was at an end.

QUESTION 3

ZuderCo is a corporation that has owned and operated the historic Palms Hotel and two smaller hotels since 1914. The Palms Hotel constitutes approximately 50% of the fair market value of the total assets of ZuderCo.

ZuderCo has 15 shareholders. Thirteen of them are descendants of the founder, and the remaining two are Able and Baker. No shareholder owns more than 10% of the outstanding shares. ZuderCo has a three-person board of directors, consisting of Able, Baker, and Chase (a Zuder family member).

Able and Baker believe that the property on which the Palms Hotel is located has great potential for development as an office park. They value it at $18 million based on their own close study of public documents relating to the development pattern in that area. The other ZuderCo shareholders disagree because they believe that the Palms property has greater economic potential as a hotel. They arrive at a more modest valuation of about $13 million for the property's use as an office park. Able and Baker have obtained three independent

appraisals placing the value of the Palms property as an office park at between $14 million and $18 million.

Able and Baker decide to offer ZuderCo $14.5 million to buy the Palms property, and then to vote as directors at the next board meeting to accept the offer. They do not plan to approach the third director, Chase, before the meeting. They expect that Chase will go along with their plan without asking any questions or causing delay because Able and Baker will have their two votes in favor of the sale and because the $14 million appraisal will support the amount of their offer. They do intend to disclose the $14 million appraisal to Chase, but they do not intend to disclose the other two higher appraisals.

The relevant corporate documents for ZuderCo contain no special or extraordinary provisions directly on point as to the following questions:

1. Can the board of directors of ZuderCo authorize the sale by its unilateral action? Explain.

2. What disclosures, if any, must Able and Baker make at the board meeting? Explain.

3. Will the votes of Able and Baker be sufficient to approve the transaction? Explain.

4. What duty, if any, does Chase have as a director, in light of the sale proposal presented by Able and Baker? Explain.

ANSWER TO QUESTION 3

1. The board can unilaterally authorize the sale of the hotel here. At issue is whether a sale of half a corporation's assets to two of its three directors can be authorized by the board of directors without shareholder approval.

Unless the articles of incorporation provide otherwise, directors ordinarily have sole discretion to manage the normal affairs of their corporation; shareholders generally have a direct voice in management decisions only with respect to fundamental corporate changes. Most states consider a sale of all or substantially all of a corporation's assets outside the regular course of the corporation's business to be a fundamental corporate change that requires shareholder approval. Here, however, the sale is not of all or substantially all of ZuderCo's assets; rather, the hotel to be sold represents only half of ZuderCo's assets. Thus, the sale would ***not*** be considered a fundamental corporate change and can be approved by the board of directors unilaterally. (Note, however, that as will be discussed below, because two of the three directors have conflicting personal interests in the sale, shareholder approval should be obtained to give the directors the best chance of preventing the sale from being overturned.)

2. Able and Baker must disclose all material facts of the transaction, including their interest, all three appraisals, and their belief that the hotel is worth $18 million based on careful study. At issue is what must be disclosed when a director seeks to enter into a transaction with his corporation.

In most states, when a corporation is to enter into a transaction in which a director has a conflicting personal interest, the transaction can be set aside unless the director can prove that the transaction was fair or that it was approved by a disinterested majority of the board (but not less than two directors) or the disinterested shareholders after disclosure to the board or shareholders of all material facts regarding the interest and the transaction. Here, the material facts include Able and Baker's intent to purchase the hotel, all three appraisals of the hotel, and Able and Baker's valuation.

3.   The votes of Able and Baker would not be sufficient to approve the transaction, at least if they want the best chance of preventing the sale from being set aside. At issue is whether directors with conflicting personal interests in a corporate transaction can vote to approve the transaction.

The Revised Model Business Corporation Act, followed by a number of states, provides that a transaction shall not be set aside merely because a director has a conflicting personal interest in the transaction if: (i) the interested director discloses all material facts regarding the transaction to the disinterested members and a majority of them (but more than one) approve the transaction, (ii) the interested director discloses all material facts regarding the transaction to the disinterested shareholders and a majority of them approve the transaction, or (iii) the transaction is fair to the corporation. Here, since Able and Baker both have conflicting interests in the transaction, if they want the best chance of preventing the sale from being set aside, they should not vote regarding the transaction. Only the disinterested director—Chase—should vote. However, most states do not permit a conflicting interest transaction to be approved by only one director. In such states, it would be best to submit the transaction to a shareholder vote. Otherwise, the transaction will be upheld only if Able and Baker can prove that the transaction was fair.

Note also that Able and Baker would be breaching their fiduciary duty if they voted in favor of selling the hotel to themselves for $14.5 million. As noted below, a director has a duty to act in the best interests of his corporation. A director who believes that the value of a corporate asset is $18 million would breach this duty by approving a sale of the asset to himself for $14.5 million.

4.   If Chase is to approve the transaction, he owes his normal, fiduciary duty to act in good faith, in the best interest of the corporation, using the same degree of care that an ordinarily prudent person would exercise under like circumstances. In making the decision, Chase is entitled to rely on opinions of experts, such as the expert appraisals obtained by Able and Baker. If Chase complies with these guidelines, he will not be held personally liable for his decision.

QUESTION 4

Triton Steel is a State X corporation that manufactures high quality steel at its steel mill located in State X. Five years ago, Triton was the subject of an employee buyout. As a result, the corporation has two classes of stock: Class A and Class B. Triton Class A shares are publicly owned, although ownership is concentrated in fewer than 100 sophisticated investors and the stock is not traded on any established market. There are 7 million shares of Class A authorized, issued, and outstanding. Triton Class B shares are held by an employee stock ownership plan of the Triton employees, which votes all of the Class B shares as a block. There are 3 million shares of Class B authorized, issued, and outstanding.

Triton's articles of incorporation contain two special provisions negotiated as part of the employee buyout. The first requires an affirmative vote of each class of stock before Triton can invest in steel production facilities located outside of State X. The second special provision adopts class voting for directors, with Class A shareholders electing seven directors and the Class B shareholder electing three directors.

The investors and the employees disagree over the future of Triton. Triton has posted modest profits over the past two years. However, the Class A investors believe that for Triton to be profitable in the long term, production costs have to be cut substantially. They want Triton to construct a steel mill in State Z where costs are lower and, over time, to shift all production to the new facility. However, the employees believe that Triton can increase its profitability through other measures that do not require relocating its steel production facilities.

The board of directors recently voted 7 to 3 to approve the proposal to construct a new steel mill in State Z, with all seven Class A directors voting in favor and all three Class B directors voting against. However, when the proposal was brought to the Triton shareholders for a vote, the Class B shareholder voted all of the Class B shares against it, and the proposal was defeated. The Class A shareholders are frustrated because, although they have a 7 to 3 majority on the board of directors and a 70% to 30% majority of the total outstanding stock, they have been unable to cut Triton's production costs by moving the steel mill to State Z.

The Class A shareholders are considering the following three alternatives:

- <u>First</u>, attempt to change Triton's articles of incorporation to allow the out-of-state production facility. Have the Class A directors, acting either alone or with the 70% Class A shareholder majority, amend the articles of incorporation to delete the provision that requires special voting in order to move the steel mill.

- <u>Second</u>, if the suggested change to the articles of incorporation does not work, realize Triton's value as a going concern. Have the corporation sell all of its assets to an independent third party for a mixture of cash and stock. Even if the Class B shareholder dissents, it will have no option but to go along with the Class A vote.

- <u>Third</u>, if a going-concern sale cannot be accomplished, have the Class A shareholders dissolve the corporation.

Discuss whether each of the three alternatives can be successfully implemented. For each alternative that can be implemented, what rights will the Class B shareholder have? Explain.

ANSWER TO QUESTION 4

Amendment of Articles: The Class A directors will not be successful in an attempt to amend the articles, either alone or with the 70% majority of shareholders.

As a general rule, most amendments to a corporation's articles of incorporation are considered fundamental corporate changes that require approval by both the directors and the shareholders. Amendment to eliminate the restriction in Triton's articles requiring class voting regarding purchases of production facilities outside the state would certainly fall within the general rule. Thus, the Class A directors acting alone cannot approve the amendment.

Neither will the Class A directors be successful in adopting the amendment with the 70% Class A majority. While generally an amendment to a corporation's articles can be approved by the affirmative vote of the directors and a majority vote of the shareholders, an amendment that affects the rights of a particular class of shares must be approved separately by a majority of that class. The amendment here would certainly affect the rights of the Class B shareholder since it would remove its veto power over purchase decisions regarding out-of-state production facilities. Because it is doubtful that the Class B shareholder would approve this amendment, the Class A directors will not be successful in amending the articles.

Sale to third party: The Class A directors could successfully arrange a sale of the corporation to a third party with the approval of the Class A shareholders.

A sale of all or substantially all of a corporation's assets outside the corporation's regular course of business is a fundamental corporate change requiring the approval of both a majority of the board and a majority of the outstanding shares. Class voting is not required unless the articles so provide. Here the sale of all of Triton's production facilities appears to be a sale of all its assets outside its regular course of business, and nothing in Triton's articles requires class voting with regard to sales of assets. Therefore the Class A directors with their majority on the board, combined with the Class A shareholders' 70% majority of outstanding stock, can approve the sale.

It should be noted, however, that the sale of all or substantially all of a corporation's assets can trigger dissenters' rights. The Class B shareholder can vote against the sale and demand fair payment for its shares. If the parties cannot agree on what is fair payment, the issue ultimately will have to be decided by a court, thus complicating the sale and, perhaps, depleting the amount the Class A shareholders will retain from the sale.

Dissolution: The Class A directors could successfully vote to dissolve the corporation with the approval of the Class A shareholders.

Dissolution, like the sale of assets above, is a fundamental corporate change that can be approved by a majority of the board and a majority of the outstanding shares. There is no requirement of class voting unless the articles so provide. Here, the articles are silent with regard to class voting for dissolution. Thus, the Class A directors, with their majority on the board, and the Class A shareholders, with their 70% majority in outstanding shares, can successfully approve the dissolution over the Class B directors' and shareholder's objections. Since in a dissolution, all shareholders receive cash, there are no dissenters' rights with regard to dissolution, as there was with the sale of assets, above. Thus, dissolution would be the simplest alternative.

QUESTION 5

See Agency Question 5 for Corporations issue.

QUESTION 6

Chempro is a closely held chemical company incorporated in State F. In addition to a number of smaller shareholders, Chempro has five principal shareholders, each of whom owns 15% of the shares: Paula, who is Chempro's Chief Executive Officer and Chairwoman of the Board; and Lawrence, Alan, Bruce, and Charles, who are also officers and directors of Chempro. Although each is an officer of Chempro, none of the five principal shareholders has an employment contract with the company.

The five shareholders signed a valid, enforceable shareholders' agreement requiring all of them to vote to elect each other as directors of Chempro.

For many years, Chempro's business prospered, and its value increased substantially. However, Lawrence recently became aware that Paula was diverting corporate funds into her personal bank account. Shortly after his discovery, Lawrence took Paula aside, confronted her with evidence of her wrongdoing from the company's files, and demanded that she repay the funds to Chempro. Paula responded by calling a board of directors' meeting to discuss dismissing Lawrence from the board of directors and firing Lawrence from his position as an officer of Chempro. Paula also immediately removed all of the incriminating files from Lawrence's office.

At the board meeting, Paula claimed that Lawrence had been taking corporate funds and using them for personal reasons. Lawrence responded that Paula was lying and that, in fact, Paula was the responsible party. Lawrence also told the board that he had documents to prove his story but that they had recently been stolen from his office. Without further investigation, Paula and the remaining board members, Alan, Bruce, and Charles, all of whom never really liked Lawrence, voted to remove Lawrence as both an officer and a director of Chempro. Lawrence dissented.

The State F corporate code and Chempro's articles of incorporation and bylaws permit directors and officers to be removed by the board without cause.

1.   What claims, if any, does Lawrence have against Chempro, Paula, Alan, Bruce, and/or Charles in Lawrence's capacity as:

   a.   A director? Explain.

   b.   An officer? Explain.

   c.   A shareholder? Explain.

2.   Are Lawrence's claims derivative or direct, and, as to any derivative claims, are there any procedural prerequisites he must satisfy before filing the derivative claims in court? Explain.

ANSWER TO QUESTION 6

1.a. As a director, Lawrence has a claim against Paula, Alan, Bruce, and Charles for breach of the shareholders' agreement. At issue are the rights of a director who was dismissed by his fellow directors despite a shareholders' agreement among them that they would elect each other.

According to the facts, Chempro is incorporated in a state that allows directors to remove other directors without cause, and nothing in Chempro's articles or bylaws negates this. Thus, under the general law, Lawrence could have been removed with or without cause by the directors, and he would have no rights arising from his dismissal even though the apparent reason for his dismissal was erroneous. However, the general rule will not apply here because of the shareholders' agreement.

The facts indicate that all of the directors have entered into a valid and enforceable shareholders' agreement to elect each other as directors. Such an agreement would be useless if it were construed to allow the directors to remove each other without cause after electing each other. Here, Lawrence appears to have been removed without cause—the directors did not investigate Paula's accusations or Lawrence's claims, so it cannot be said that he was dismissed for cause. Thus, Lawrence's removal breached the shareholders' agreement, and Lawrence can force the directors to reinstate him.

b.   Lawrence has no right to reinstatement as an officer. At issue are the rights of an officer who has been removed on erroneous grounds.

As a general rule, officers serve at the discretion of the board of directors. In most states, the board is free to fire officers with or without cause, even if the firing constitutes a breach of the officer's contract, although in such a case the officer may sue for damages. Here, the facts state that the officers did not have employment contracts with the corporation, so this is not even an issue. Thus, Lawrence has no valid claim with regard to being dismissed as an officer.

c.   Lawrence has two claims he may bring as a shareholder: First, against Paula for breach of her duty of loyalty and second against the entire board for breach of their duty of care.

Lawrence can claim that Paula breached her duty of loyalty to the corporation. A director must act in the best interests of her corporation and is not allowed to siphon off corporate funds for her own use. Such actions breach the directors' duty of loyalty to the corporation, and where the corporation does not act to alleviate the harm, a shareholder may bring an action on behalf of the corporation (*see* 2., below).

Lawrence can also claim that the entire board breached its fiduciary duty of care. A director must act in good faith and in a manner the director reasonably believes to be in the best interest of the corporation, using the care an ordinarily prudent person in a like position would exercise. Paula clearly breached this duty since she voted to remove Lawrence knowing that the allegations against him were untrue. The rest of the board also breached this duty because a reasonably prudent person would have undertaken some investigation before choosing which of the two directors' claims of thievery to believe.

2.   Lawrence's claim to be reinstated is direct, but his claim regarding Paula's theft is derivative.

A claim is direct if there is a breach of duty owed to the shareholder individually and is derivative if there is a breach of duty owed to the corporation. Here, the duty to reinstate Lawrence as a director really is a claim to vindicate his personal rights, whether it is based on the breach of the shareholders' agreement or on the breach of the duty of care. Under either theory, Lawrence just wants *his* directorship reinstated. The claim against Paula to return the money she diverted, however, is derivative. Lawrence is not asking for Paula to return the money to him, but rather to the corporation. Thus, Lawrence is seeking to enforce the corporation's rights and not his own. Such an action is a derivative action.

Before Lawrence may bring a derivative action, most states require that he have owned stock in the corporation when the alleged wrong occurred and require him to maintain ownership of the stock throughout the litigation. Most states also require the shareholder to first demand that the board bring an action against the alleged wrongdoer. Many states waive this demand requirement, however, where it would be futile. Here, since the entire board voted to oust Lawrence and did not investigate or believe his claim against Paula, it would be futile to make a demand on the board now, so this requirement would probably be excused.

QUESTION 7

Several years ago, Able, Baker, and Campbell properly incorporated Transport, Inc., a highway freight hauling business. Able and Baker each own 45% of Transport stock, and Campbell owns 10%. Since its incorporation, Transport has been quite profitable. However, most of its earnings have been retained to help the business grow, and only small dividends have been paid to the three shareholders.

Able, the president of Transport, is in charge of finance and sales for the business. Baker, the vice president, is in charge of operations. Able and Baker make all major decisions by consensus. Campbell is an artist and does not participate in the business operations. No shareholder or director meetings have ever been called or held. Able, who has expensive tastes and lives beyond his means, often uses corporate funds of Transport to pay his personal bills, telling Baker that once he gets his personal finances in order he will repay the company.

Last year, Able and Baker decided to expand Transport's hauling business to start hauling hazardous waste from local factories to a newly constructed hazardous waste disposal facility. Recognizing that hauling hazardous waste would be a risky business, Able and Baker wanted to keep the hazardous waste hauling activities separate from the rest of Transport's business. They formed a new corporation called HotTrucks, Inc., which was properly incorporated as a wholly owned subsidiary of Transport. Transport contributed the use (but not ownership) of a fleet of 10 trucks to HotTrucks. HotTrucks's only asset was its right to use the trucks. In order to save money, Able and Baker did not obtain general business liability insurance for HotTrucks.

Able and Baker thought it wise not to be directors or officers of HotTrucks, so they asked Campbell to serve as the sole director and officer of HotTrucks. Campbell did not want to spend time on business matters when he could be working on his paintings. However, he agreed to serve as director and officer on the understanding that Able and Baker would handle all day-to-day management and operation of the business and that Campbell would not have to attend any directors' meetings or make business decisions.

A month ago, one of the trucks operated by HotTrucks crashed through the front of a video store. Baker, who was the driver of the truck, had negligently fallen asleep at the wheel. The regularly scheduled driver had called in sick, and Baker had taken his place, not having slept for 20 hours. The accident seriously injured five people.

1. On what basis, if any, can the injured persons hold Transport liable for tort claims resulting from the HotTrucks accident? Explain.

2. On what basis, if any, can the injured persons hold Able, Baker, and Campbell personally liable for such claims? Explain.

ANSWER TO QUESTION 7

1. The injured people may be able to hold Transport liable either because HotTrucks is merely an alter ego of Transport or because Transport did not adequately capitalize HotTrucks. At issue

is whether there are grounds to pierce the corporate veil in order to hold the parent corporation liable for its subsidiary corporation's obligations.

Generally, a shareholder is not liable for corporate obligations; only the corporation is liable. This general rule applies even when the shareholder is a corporation: A parent corporation generally is not liable for the obligations for its subsidiaries. However, in certain circumstances, the corporate veil will be pierced and a shareholder will be held liable for corporate obligations. Two possible grounds for piercing are present here: First, a court will pierce the corporate veil if the parent corporation does not adequately fund its subsidiary, *i.e.,* contribute enough money at formation to enable the subsidiary to pay prospective liabilities. The court might also look to whether the subsidiary can expect to achieve independent financial stability. Second, a court also will pierce the corporate veil if the subsidiary is merely an alter ego of the parent (*e.g.,* the officers and directors are the same, assets are shared, separate books are not kept, etc.).

Here, it could be argued that HotTrucks was both undercapitalized and a mere alter ego of Transport. HotTrucks's only asset was the right to use Transport's trucks. Given that the nature of HotTrucks's business (hauling hazardous wastes) involved great risks, it could be argued that to adequately capitalize HotTrucks, Transport had to contribute at least enough money to purchase liability insurance. Having failed to do so, Transport should now be held liable for liabilities arising from HotTrucks's operations. The fact that the tort claims here do not arise from the hazardous nature of HotTrucks's loads is inconsequential; it is foreseeable that any kind of trucking company will have liabilities arising from accidents in which its vehicles are involved.

The corporate veil can also be pierced on alter ego grounds. Although the two corporations technically had separate boards and officers, in fact, that was a sham. Able and Baker operated both corporations. Moreover, the two corporations shared assets. We are not told whether separate books were kept, whether profits were siphoned off to Transport, etc. But the facts we do know probably are a sufficient basis for piercing.

2.   If the tort victims are allowed to reach Transport's assets, as discussed above, and Transport does not have sufficient funds to cover HotTrucks's liabilities, the victims may be able to pierce the corporate veil to reach Able's assets under an alter ego theory. A court will allow a tort victim to reach a shareholder's personal assets if the shareholder has ignored the separateness of the corporation and some injustice results. Able did not recognize the separateness of Transport since he used corporate funds to pay personal debts. Because this may be the very reason that Transport does not have enough money to pay the tort victims, it would be a sufficient ground on which to pierce.

The tort victims could hold Baker liable for his own negligence. While generally a shareholder, officer, and/or director is not personally liable for his corporation's obligations, a person is always liable for his own torts. Here, Baker was negligent in that he was driving the truck having not slept in 20 hours, fell asleep, and drove into the video store.

The victims probably could not reach Campbell's personal assets. Although he was a director of both corporations, as discussed above, shareholders, directors, and officers generally are not liable for the obligations of their corporation. No grounds for piercing apply to Campbell: His failure to hold or attend directors' and shareholders' meetings constitute sloppy corporate administration, but sloppy administration alone is not a ground for piercing; it must be coupled with some other injustice. Since Campell's nonfeasance did not really contribute to the tort victim's losses, the court will probably not pierce on these grounds.

QUESTION 8

Acquiror, Inc., a publicly held corporation, entered into negotiations to buy the stock of XYZ Corporation through a merger. Although the companies were close to a final agreement on September 1, Acquiror insisted on delaying consummation and public announcement of the deal until September 15. XYZ agreed to the delay.

Usually, a corporation such as Acquiror that makes a merger offer for another corporation can expect that its stock price will decline after the announcement of the merger.

During the first week of September, while the merger was being delayed, XYZ's stock price increased and Acquiror's stock price remained unchanged at $10 per share. Several press reports suggested that Acquiror might be planning a merger with XYZ. On September 5, in response to specific inquiries from financial reporters and from the stock exchange where Acquiror's stock was listed for trading, Acquiror denied that it had "any agreement to enter into a merger agreement" with XYZ. Investors believed the statement, and the price of Acquiror's stock did not decline but remained at $10 per share.

On September 15, Acquiror announced its merger with XYZ. As expected, Acquiror's stock declined to $8 per share.

1. Do investors who purchased Acquiror's stock after Acquiror's denial on September 5 and before the disclosure of the merger have a claim for damages under federal law? Explain.

2. Do continuing shareholders in Acquiror have any basis under federal law to make a claim against Acquiror or its officers and directors if, because of Acquiror's statements, Acquiror is liable to other investors of Acquiror's shares? Explain.

ANSWER TO QUESTION 8

1.   Investors who purchased Acquiror's stock after Acquiror's denial on September 5 and before the disclosure of the merger have a federal cause of action under rule 10b-5 under the Securities Exchange Act of 1934.

Rule 10b-5 makes it unlawful to commit fraud in connection with securities. A person injured by such unlawful conduct may bring a private cause of action for damages. To make out a private cause of action under rule 10b-5, a plaintiff must show: (i) that the defendant made an untrue statement of material fact or omitted to state a material fact necessary to make the statements made not misleading, (ii) that the misstatement/omission was made with scienter (*i.e.,* an intent to deceive), (iii) that the statements are somehow connected to the purchase or sale of securities by the plaintiff, (iv) use of some means of interstate commerce, (v) reliance by the plaintiff, and (vi) damages.

All of the elements were met here. Acquiror's statement to the press and the stock exchange that there was no merger agreement, while literally true, was misleading and therefore fraudulent because making that statement without disclosing that the parties were close to a final agreement makes the statement that was made misleading. The misstatement/omission was also material. A misstatement or omission will be considered material if there is a substantial likelihood that a reasonable investor would consider the information important in making an investment decision. Since the facts state that mergers usually affect the price of the stock involved, the information here clearly was material.

The misstatement/omission was also made with scienter. The corporation's misstatement/omission here was clearly intended to give the public the wrong impression—that a merger was not being considered. Thus, this element is present.

The misstatement/omission was also connected to the purchase of the plaintiff's securities. There is no requirement that the defendant have purchased or sold shares; a corporate defendant that intentionally publishes misleading information can be liable to a person who purchased or sold securities on the market on the basis of the misleading information.

The misstatement/omission here was also made through means of interstate commerce. Both the press and the stock exchange were given the misinformation.

Reliance is also present here. Where the basis of a cause of action is the omission of information, it is difficult to show reliance (how can one rely on information one does not possess); thus, reliance generally is presumed if the plaintiff shows the omission was material.

Finally, the investors can show that the defendant's fraud caused damages. While the misinformation was circulating, the investors purchased their stock at $10 per share and immediately after the truth was disseminated, the stock dropped to $8 per share. Thus, the investors' damages are $2 per share. Therefore, the investors can successfully bring a cause of action under rule 10b-5.

2.   The continuing shareholders have no cause of action under federal law, but they do have a state law claim. Under rule 10b-5, as discussed above, a private plaintiff must have been damaged by the purchase or sale of a security. Continuing shareholders neither purchased nor sold shares on the basis of the false information and therefore have no federal cause of action. However, such shareholders may be able to bring a derivative action against the officers or directors who disseminated the false information. By acting unlawfully, the officers and/or directors breached their fiduciary duty owed to the corporation. Shareholders who owned stock at the time of the breach and who continue to own stock may make a demand on the board to bring an action against the officers or directors responsible for the breach. If the board refuses to bring the action, the shareholder may be able to file a derivative action on the corporation's behalf, seeking damages that resulted from the unlawful conduct.

QUESTION 9

FurnitureCo has manufactured quality furniture for 20 years. It was incorporated under the Revised Model Business Corporation Act and its articles of incorporation and bylaws contain no provisions overriding the statutory provisions. FurnitureCo's articles of incorporation provide that the corporation can engage in any lawful business.

Adam owns 70% of the stock of FurnitureCo, and Diane and Edward each own 15%. The board of directors has five members: Adam; Adam's loyal children, Beth and Charles; and the two outsiders, Diane and Edward. Adam is the president of FurnitureCo, Beth is vice president, and Charles is secretary. Their duties are not specified in the bylaws. Neither Diane nor Edward is an officer.

Over the past few years, FurnitureCo's business has been flat, but marginally profitable. At its last regular board meeting, attended by Adam, Beth, Charles, and Edward, Adam presented a plan to diversify FurnitureCo's business, which included entering the tennis club business. Diane had been called out of town suddenly and was unable to attend the board meeting. After hearing Adam's presentation on the expanding opportunities in the sports field, the board voted 3 to 1 to direct Adam as president to "study and implement at his discretion a program for restructuring and/or reorienting the business operations of the company." It was Edward who voted against authorizing Adam to restructure the business.

After studying the matter, Adam decided that FurnitureCo's profits would be maximized by getting out of the furniture business altogether, selling all of its current assets, and using the sale proceeds and the cash on hand to buy a tennis club. On his own initiative and without anyone else's approval, he then scheduled an auction for next month to sell all of FurnitureCo's existing assets.

Diane and Edward were sure that Adam's plan would ruin the business, so they visited Adam in his office to tell him that they disagreed with his plan and to demand that he cancel the auction. Adam told them that he did not need their approval to implement his plan and ordered them to leave his office.

1.   Does Adam have sufficient authority as president to change FurnitureCo's business and to sell its existing assets? Explain.

2.   Could Adam, Beth, and Charles lawfully act together to approve and implement the change in the business and the sale of assets without the participation of Diane and Edward? Explain.

3.   Assuming that Diane and Edward cannot block the sale, do they have any other remedies? Explain.

ANSWER TO QUESTION 9

1.   Adam probably has sufficient authority as president to change FurnitureCo's business but not to sell its assets. At issue is the authority of a corporation's president.

A corporate president is an agent of the corporation and has whatever power the corporation grants him. As a general rule, unless specifically excluded by the corporation, a president will have the power to enter into ordinary contracts involving the day-to-day operation of the corporation. A corporate president can have power to enter into extraordinary transactions if authorized by the board of directors. However, the board cannot give the president power that the board itself does not have.

Here, the board voted to give Adam the authority to "study and implement at his discretion a program for restructuring the business operations of the company." Whether this was sufficient to give Adam authority to take such action depends on two things: whether the board's meeting and vote were proper and whether the board could delegate such authority.

The directors' meeting and their vote appears to have been proper. If the articles are silent, as they are here, a meeting can take place if there is a quorum consisting of a majority of the directors.

Resolutions can be passed at the meeting by the vote of the majority of the quorum. Here, four of the five directors were present at the meeting and three of the four voted to grant Adam such authority. Thus, the meeting and vote were proper. However, the board appears to have granted Adam more authority than it had.

The board certainly has the power to study business options and could delegate that power to its agent. Also, because the articles state that the purpose of the corporation is to conduct "any lawful business," the board probably has authority to restructure the business to head in a new direction, such as the tennis club, and could authorize the president to do so. However, Adam's decision to sell all of the corporation's assets is a fundamental change, and the board does not have the power to authorize fundamental corporate changes without shareholder approval. Therefore, it could not validly delegate this authority to Adam. Thus, Adam does not have sufficient authority as president to implement the sale of assets.

2.   Adam, Beth, and Charles can lawfully act together to implement the plan, but Diane and Edward do have a right to participate in the decision. As indicated above, the sale of all of a corporation's assets outside the scope of ordinary business is a fundamental corporate change. Such a change can be implemented only if the directors first pass a resolution to implement the plan and the plan is then approved by the holders of a majority of the shares entitled to vote on the matter.

Here, Adam, Beth, and Charles make up a majority of the board. Thus they can call a board meeting and pass a resolution recommending the sale. Note that the fact that Adam is the one who wants to implement the plan and that Beth and Charles are his loyal children does not prevent them from voting in favor of the plan; this is not a conflict of interest situation (*i.e.*, there is no self-dealing here). After approving the action, the three would then call a shareholders' meeting, giving notice to Adam, Diane, and Edward. The shareholders would then vote on the plan. Since Adam owns 70% of the shares, his vote in favor of the plan would be sufficient to approve it.

3.   Since Diane and Edward cannot block the sale, their only remedy is appraisal. Shareholders who dissent from a fundamental corporate change can force the corporation to purchase their shares at a fair price. To use the appraisal remedy, the shareholders must file an objection to the transfer before or at the shareholders' meeting at which the vote is taken; they must not vote in favor of the plan; and then they must send the corporation a written demand for the fair value of their shares. If the corporation and the shareholders cannot agree on fair value, the shareholders may bring a suit to have the court determine fair value.

QUESTION 10

Carl decided to form a corporation to provide various support services to small businesses on a contract basis. After several months of searching, Carl found suitable office space in an office park that he thought was ideal for his future corporation. Leaseco was willing to rent the office space at a very favorable rate but only if the lease could be signed immediately. Although Carl had not taken any steps to incorporate, he began negotiations with Leaseco for the lease. Carl told Leaseco that the lease was on behalf of a corporation that would be formed, to be called Small Service Corporation ("SSC"), and that Carl would be president of SSC. Carl signed a two-year lease with Leaseco for the office space at the favorable rate. The parties named in the lease were Leaseco and SSC. Carl signed the lease

as "Small Service Corporation, a corporation to be formed, by Carl, President." The following week, Carl moved his equipment and supplies into the office space and began business operations.

Two weeks after the lease was signed, Carl properly incorporated SSC. The articles of incorporation named Carl and two other individuals, David and Ellen, as the initial directors of the corporation, and the directors properly elected Carl as president.

At the first meeting of the board of directors, Carl provided David and Ellen with copies of the Leaseco office lease. SSC printed corporate letterhead with the address of the leased office space and began making monthly lease payments to Leaseco. SSC's business was an immediate success and after nine months of operations it began to show a profit. Because of the initial success of the business, Carl, David, and Ellen needed to hire additional personnel. However, the office space leased from Leaseco was too small for any expansion. The directors unanimously voted to terminate the Leaseco lease before the end of its term. Then they entered into a lease with Rental, Inc. for a larger space, vacated the Leaseco premises, and refused to pay any further rent to Leaseco.

Several months after SSC began operations, at a regularly scheduled meeting of the board of directors for which all proper notice was given, Carl proposed that SSC contribute 4% of SSC's profits earned since incorporation to a local charity that operates a nonprofit job training program. Carl and David voted to approve the resolution; Ellen voted against it. The SSC articles of incorporation have no provisions dealing with the power of the corporation to make charitable contributions.

1.   Is Carl personally liable on the Leaseco office lease? Explain.

2.   Is SSC liable on the Leaseco office lease? Explain.

3.   Does SSC have the power to make the charitable contribution? Explain.

ANSWER TO QUESTION 10

1.   Carl is liable on the Leaseco office lease. At issue is the liability of a promoter who enters into a contract on behalf of a corporation to be formed.

The general rule is that when a promoter enters into a contract on behalf of a corporation to be formed, the promoter becomes personally liable on the contract unless the promoter can show that the parties had a contrary intention. Where a promoter signs as an agent for the nonexistent corporation, and both parties know that the corporation has not yet been formed, the courts usually assume that the parties intended the promoter to be held liable. The rationale is that a nonexistent corporation cannot be bound on a contract. Thus, if the parties intended to form a contract, they must have intended the promoter to be bound; otherwise, the "contract" would not have two parties and would only be an offer.

Here, Carl signed as an agent for the corporation to be formed, and both parties clearly knew that the corporation was not yet formed. Carl informed Leaseco of this fact and his signature on the lease stated that the corporation was *to be* formed. Moreover, Leaseco's insistence that the lease be signed immediately, and its refusal to wait for the formation of SSC, indicate that Leaseco wanted someone to be bound on the lease immediately. Since SSC was not yet formed and could not be bound, the parties must have intended Carl to be bound.

2.   SSC is liable on the Leaseco office lease. At issue is the liability of a corporation on contracts made by its promoters before the corporation was formed.

The general rule is that a corporation is not bound on a contract made by a promoter unless and until the corporation adopts the contract after the corporation is formed. Adoption may be express, such as by a resolution of the board of directors. Adoption may also be implied from the action of the board. Here, the SSC directors were presented with copies of the lease agreement at the first meeting of the directors. The corporation had already moved into the office space, and the directors started making lease payments. This is sufficient evidence that the directors impliedly adopted the lease. Thus, the corporation is liable on the lease. Note that the corporation's becoming liable on the lease does not end Carl's liability. Both parties are liable unless all parties agree that the corporation will be substituted for the promoter (a novation contract).

3.   SSC has the power to make charitable contributions. At common law, charitable contributions by a corporation were viewed with suspicion by some courts, on the theory that they were a waste of corporate assets. However, other courts upheld such contributions either on public policy grounds or because they recognized that corporations get some good out of making charitable donations (*e.g.,* increased goodwill in the community). Most states now allow corporations to make charitable donations as long as the donations are reasonable. Modern corporations codes either specifically provide for charitable donations or courts read authorization for donations into the broad statutory language—contained in most corporations codes—allowing corporations to do whatever is necessary or convenient to carrying on their business. Here, the donation was only 4% of corporate profits. This seems to be a reasonable amount. Thus, SSC has the power to make the contributions.

QUESTION 11

PrattCo is a corporation. It has been developing a new textile inspection system that promises to revolutionize the market if it can be made to work. PrattCo has one class of stock, Class A Common, of which three million shares are authorized. All three million shares of the Class A Common are currently issued and outstanding. The Class A Common shares are currently trading at $25 a share on a recognized market.

PrattCo has two immediate problems. First, it needs a new chief executive officer with the expertise and drive to get the new system working and to expand PrattCo's operations. Second, PrattCo needs at least $75 million to finance the development of the new system and the expansion of its operations.

The PrattCo board has offered Leslie the job of PrattCo's president and chief executive officer. Leslie's salary requirements are modest, but as part of her compensation Leslie wants to receive options for 100,000 shares of Class A Common at $25 a share, with the right to exercise the options phased over a three-year period.

Brenda has offered to invest $75 million in PrattCo in return for three million shares of Class A Common at $25 per share, but she wants her Class A Common shares to be different from the existing Class A Common. Brenda wants her shares to have a preference such

that any dividends would be allocated first to Brenda's Class A Common shares up to $2 per share per annum, then to the other Class A Common shares up to $2 per share per annum, and then to all Class A Common shares equally.

William currently owns 30% of the Class A Common stock. William was an inside candidate for the position of president and chief executive officer and is bitter that Leslie was offered the job. William also disagrees with the $75 million capital infusion from Brenda. William wants to license the new system to third-party manufacturers rather than have PrattCo expand its own operations.

William objects that: (a) the grant of the proposed stock options to Leslie is illegal; (b) the sale to Brenda of the Class A Common shares with preferential rights is illegal; (c) if the sale to Brenda can be legally accomplished, it requires William's consent; and (d) even if the grant to Leslie and the sale to Brenda can be made, William would have the right to purchase shares equal to 30% of the stock issued to both Leslie and Brenda.

PrattCo's articles of incorporation state that "the corporation elects to have preemptive rights." Assume the board and the stockholders of the remaining 70% of Class A Common will vote to hire Leslie, to grant her the options requested, and to accept Brenda's financing proposal. Also assume William has sufficient financial resources to exercise any stock purchase rights he may have.

Are each of William's four objections to PrattCo's plans valid and, if so, what steps could PrattCo take to avoid the objections? Explain.

ANSWER TO QUESTION 11

(a)   William's first objection is not valid. At issue is a corporation's right to issue options. Generally, the board of directors has a right to issue options to purchase shares on whatever terms the board chooses. Here, the board has chosen to issue options in exchange for Leslie's promise to work as CEO of PrattCo. Options are merely the right to purchase shares and do not themselves constitute shares that have been issued. Thus, the restrictions that will be discussed below on the sale of shares are not applicable to the issuance of options. Therefore, there is nothing illegal about the grant of stock options to Leslie. On the other hand, it might be argued that issuance of the options is an illusory promise and would make the corporation liable for damages because, as discussed below, the corporation currently is not authorized to issue any more shares to honor the options. However, this problem can be eliminated by amending the articles, as discussed below.

(b)   William's second objection is valid for two reasons. First, a corporation may not issue more stock than is authorized in its articles of incorporation. Second, a corporation may not issue shares that have a preference unless the articles of incorporation so provide. Here, the articles authorize the issuance of 3 million shares and all 3 million shares have been issued and are outstanding. Thus, PrattCo will not be allowed to issue the additional 3 million shares to Brenda as things stand now. Similarly, PrattCo's articles do not authorize the issuance of shares with a preference. However, PrattCo can easily remedy both of these problems by amending its articles of incorporation to authorize the sale of 3 million more preferred shares.

A corporation can amend its articles with any provision that would be valid in original articles. To amend, the board of directors must first adopt a resolution to amend the articles. It must then send notice to the shareholders that a shareholders' meeting will be held to vote on the proposed amendment. The notice must be sent at least 10 days before the meeting. The amendment must be approved by a majority of the shares entitled to be voted at the meeting. Articles of amendment must then be filed with the secretary of state.

Here, to obviate William's objections, the board should adopt a resolution authorizing the issuance of: (i) at least 100,000 more Class A common shares, so that the corporation can honor the options it will grant to Leslie, and (ii) at least 3 million Class A preferred shares, with the preference described, so it may issue shares to Brenda. The board should then call a shareholders' meeting. The facts state that 70% of the outstanding shares will be voted in favor of the proposal, which is sufficient to approve the amendment in most states.

(c)   The sale to Brenda does not require William's consent. Generally, shareholders do not have a right to make decisions regarding operation of the corporation. Shareholders can protect their interests by electing candidates to the board of directors, and they may vote when fundamental changes are made in the corporation. While the amendment of the articles described above is a fundamental change requiring shareholder approval, the corporation does not have to get William's approval because, as discussed above, more than a majority of the outstanding shares will be voted in favor of the sale.

(d)   William would not have the right to purchase any of the shares to be issued to Leslie, but would have a right to purchase 30% of the shares to be issued to Brenda. At issue are preemptive rights.

Generally, unless the articles of incorporation provide otherwise, shareholders do not have any preemptive rights (*i.e.*, the right to buy a sufficient number of newly issued shares in order to maintain current voting strength). Here, however, the articles provide that the shareholders will have preemptive rights. Where the articles provide for preemptive rights, the rights generally extend only to shares that are newly authorized and issued for cash; they do not extend to shares issued as part of an employee's or officer's compensation or in exchange for options issued as part of an employee's compensation. Thus, William will not have preemptive rights in the 100,000 shares that will be issued under the options granted to Leslie. However, William will have preemptive rights in 30% of the 3 million shares to be issued to Brenda as things stand now. Thus, 900,000 of the new shares must be offered to William at the same price and terms as they are being offered to Brenda.

PrattCo can avoid having to sell the 900,000 shares to William if it makes the preferred shares nonvoting. Holders of voting shares without preferential rights in distributions do not have preemptive rights in shares issued with a distribution preference but without voting rights. Here, William holds Class A common stock with no distribution preference. Thus, if PrattCo issues shares to Brenda that include the distribution preference she desires, but that do not have voting rights, William will not have any preemptive rights in the shares.

QUESTION 12

In 1950, John Smith founded Store, Inc., and he was its sole shareholder. Since 1970, Store has been a profitable business with eight large stores. In 1975, Smith took several steps to

try to ensure that control of the business would stay in his family. One such step was properly to amend Store's Articles of Incorporation to provide that no Store shareholder could transfer any Store stock unless the shareholders unanimously consented to the transfer and approved the transferee.

In 1990, observing the formalities required by the amended Articles, Smith gave all of his Store stock in equal shares to his four children: Anne, Bob, Clyde, and Dave. Smith died in 1992, and his four children continued Store's business. After Smith's death, Anne, Bob, and Clyde served as the officers and directors of Store, and each was also employed by the corporation. Dave was a full-time dentist and was not interested in being an officer or a director of Store.

During the years following Smith's death, Anne, Bob, and Clyde followed a policy of reinvesting Store's earnings in order to expand the number of stores. Dave consistently opposed this policy and believed that the majority of the earnings should be distributed as dividends to Store's shareholders.

After Smith's death, Store's board of directors also substantially increased the compensation paid to Anne, Bob, and Clyde as directors and doubled their salaries as employees, increasing them to levels well above market salaries. During the same period, however, the board voted to eliminate the quarterly dividends that Store had historically paid out, even though Store had sufficient profits to pay those dividends. At every shareholders' meeting, Dave objected to the way Store was being run, but he was ignored each time. Eventually, Dave advised the three other shareholders, Anne, Bob, and Clyde, that he wanted to become a member of the board of directors or, in the alternative, that he wanted them to buy his shares. They refused both requests.

Last year, Dave pledged one-half of his Store stock to Bank as collateral for a personal loan, and Dave and Bank executed a pledge agreement covering those shares. Recently, the loan came due, and Dave was unable to repay it. Consequently, Bank properly foreclosed and became the owner of the shares under the pledge agreement.

Bank has told Anne, Bob, and Clyde that it is now the owner of one-half of Dave's shares of Store stock, and Bank requests that the shares be transferred on Store's books. Anne, Bob, and Clyde have told Bank that it is not the owner of any shares of Store stock because they have not approved the transfer as required by Store's Articles of Incorporation. Therefore, Store will not record the transfer of the shares to Bank.

Dave believes he is being "frozen out" of the corporation and wants to have Store dissolved.

1.   Is the stock transfer restriction enforceable against Dave? Explain.

2.   Can Bank compel Store to record the stock transfer? Explain.

3.   Can Dave force a dissolution of Store? Explain.

ANSWER TO QUESTION 12

1.   The stock transfer restriction probably is not enforceable against Dave. At issue is whether a corporation can prohibit the transfer of shares absent unanimous shareholder approval.

Generally, a corporation can restrict the transfer of shares for any reasonable purpose. The RMBCA includes examples of permissible restrictions. For example, a restriction can require a shareholder to offer the shares to the corporation first or require the corporation or other persons to purchase offered shares. A prohibition on transfer to a designated person or class of persons is also permissible as long as the prohibition is not manifestly unreasonable. Here, the prohibition will probably be found to be manifestly unreasonable because it is so absolute. It prohibits the sale of any shares to anybody unless the shareholders unanimously agree to the transfer. Such a restriction could effectively lock minority shareholders into the corporation, because the majority can disapprove of any attempted sale. Thus, the restriction is unenforceable. [*Note:* The opposite could also be argued: It is not manifestly unreasonable for shareholders in a family owned business to require unanimous approval for transfers of shares.]

2.   Bank can compel Store to record the stock transfer. At issue is the enforceability of a stock transfer restriction against a third party.

A corporation generally must record transfers of shares in its corporate records. Since the share transfer restriction here is invalid, as discussed above, the corporation has no justification for its refusal. Moreover, even if the share transfer restriction were valid, the corporation might still be required to record the transfer unless Bank knew about the restriction. A share transfer restriction is unenforceable against a third party who purchases the restricted shares unless existence of the restriction is conspicuously noted on the share certificates or the purchaser otherwise knows of the restriction. The facts here are not clear, but presumably Bank would not have taken the shares as collateral if it knew of the severe transfer restriction or if the certificates indicated that their transfer was severely limited. Thus, Bank can compel the transfer.

3.   Dave can force a dissolution of Store. At issue is whether there are grounds for judicial dissolution of the corporation.

A shareholder may seek a judicial dissolution under a number of circumstances, including cases where the directors have acted in an oppressive manner or where corporate assets are being wasted. Both grounds are present here. Anne, Bob, and Clyde have acted oppressively in denying Dave any dividends. Generally, directors have sole discretion to decide whether to declare a dividend, and it would take a very strong case in equity for a court to interfere with the directors' decision, but the facts seem sufficient here. Store has a history of paying quarterly dividends and it has sufficient money to continue to do so. It appears that the directors voted to stop paying dividends and to take the corporation's profits out in the form of increased salary instead, leaving Dave without an opportunity to realize any profits on his shares. Moreover, the directors have refused to allow Dave to join the board to have a vote in such decisions. These acts seem oppressive under the circumstances.

The directors also are committing waste by overpaying themselves. Directors have the power to set their own compensation as well as the compensation for employees. Nevertheless, directors are restricted by their fiduciary duty to act in the best interest of the corporation. If the directors set unreasonably high salaries, especially for themselves, they breach their fiduciary duty and commit a waste of corporate assets. Here, Anne, Bob, and Clyde have breached their duty and committed waste by voting themselves raises so that their compensation is well above market salaries. Thus, the court should grant a dissolution here.

QUESTION 13

Acme Corp. has 100 shares of common stock authorized, issued, and outstanding. Each share is entitled to one vote. The corporate records show that these shares are owned equally by five shareholders: Brenda, Candace, David, Eric, and Fran.

Acme held its annual meeting of shareholders on March 25. The record date for the meeting was 20 days before the meeting, as permitted by applicable law. Acme gave proper notice of the meeting to all five shareholders.

Of the five shareholders of record, only Candace and Fran were present at the meeting. However, two other individuals, George and Henry, were also present. George handed to the corporate secretary a proxy signed by Brenda and dated the day before the meeting, authorizing George to vote Brenda's shares at the meeting. Henry had purchased Eric's shares the day before the meeting and produced evidence of a sale.

The Chair of the meeting declared that a quorum was present and that Candace, Fran, and George were entitled to vote at the meeting. However, the Chair declared that Henry was not entitled to vote at the meeting.

One of the items on the agenda was the election of directors. According to Acme's bylaws, three directors have to be elected at Acme's annual shareholders' meeting.

At the meeting, the votes for director were cast as follows:

Candace cast 20 votes for Candace, 20 votes for Fran, and 20 votes for David. Fran cast 20 votes for Candace, 20 votes for Fran, and 20 votes for David. George cast 20 votes for George, 20 votes for Brenda, and 20 votes for Henry.

Henry attempted to cast a ballot of 20 votes for George, 20 votes for Brenda, and 20 votes for Henry. However, the Chair refused to accept Henry's ballot. The Chair then declared that Candace, Fran, and David were elected as directors.

There are no provisions in the articles of incorporation or the bylaws of Acme that are relevant to the following questions.

1. Was Henry entitled to vote at the annual meeting and, if not, what could he have done to acquire the right to vote? Explain.

2. Was there a quorum present for shareholder action at the annual meeting? Explain.

3. Did Candace, Fran, and David receive sufficient votes to be elected as directors of Acme? Explain.

ANSWER TO QUESTION 13

1. Henry was not entitled to vote at the meeting. At issue is the record date.

When a corporate meeting is to be held, generally only shareholders of record on the record date are allowed to vote at the meeting. Here, the facts state the record date was 20 days before the meeting. Thus, only persons who were shareholders as indicated in the corporation's records on the date 20 days before the meeting would be allowed to vote at the meeting. Here, Henry did not become a shareholder until the day before the meeting. Thus, he was not a shareholder of record on the record date and was not entitled to vote at the meeting.

There is an exception to the record date requirement under which Henry would have been allowed to vote. A shareholder may give a proxy to allow another to vote his shares for him. Indeed, although proxies generally are revocable, if Henry would have obtained a written proxy from Eric stating that Eric was irrevocably appointing Henry as Eric's proxy, the proxy would have been irrevocable because it was coupled with an interest (the sale of the shares to Henry).

2.   There was a quorum present for shareholder action at the meeting. At issue are quorum requirements when the articles and bylaws are silent.

To validly conduct a shareholders' meeting, a quorum must be present. If the articles and bylaws are silent, a quorum requires the presence, in person or by proxy, of a majority of the outstanding shares entitled to vote at the meeting. Here, Acme Corp. had 100 shares outstanding, and the articles and bylaws were silent as to quorum requirements. Thus, a quorum required the presence of more than 50 shares. Candace and Fran were present at the meeting, representing 20 shares each. George was also present. He presented the chair a written proxy from Brenda allowing George to vote Brenda's shares. The chair determined the proxy to be valid and allowed George to vote. This was proper because, as discussed above, the record date requirement does not apply to proxies—as long as the shareholder who gave the proxy was a shareholder of record on the record date, and the proxy is valid, the proxy holder will be allowed to vote the shareholder's shares and the shares are counted as being present for quorum and other voting purposes. Thus, Brenda's 20 shares were also represented at the meeting, bringing the total shares represented at the meeting to 60, which is more than a simple majority of the outstanding voting shares. Therefore, a quorum was present.

3.   Candace, Fran, and David received sufficient votes to be elected. At issue is the vote required to elect directors.

Unless the articles or bylaws provide otherwise, directors are elected by a plurality of the votes cast; that is, the directors receiving the most votes win, even if they do not receive a majority. Here, as discussed above, it was proper to not allow Henry to vote. Thus, Candace, Fran, and David each received 40 votes (20 each from Fran and 20 each from Candace) and George, Brenda, and Henry each received only 20 votes (from George). Since a quorum was present and Candace, Fran, and David received a plurality of the votes cast, they were properly elected to the board.

QUESTION 14

The articles of incorporation of Ergo, Inc. authorize the issuance of 400,000 Class A Common Shares and 1,000,000 Class B Common Shares, all of which are issued and outstanding. Dart owns all of the Class A shares and none of the Class B shares. Ergo's articles provide that Ergo has seven directors elected by straight voting, with Class A shares to elect four directors and Class B shares to elect three directors.

Several months ago, Ergo's board of directors properly approved an expansion plan for the business that would require $5 million of additional capital. At their regular February 1

meeting, the directors discussed possible sources to fund the expansion plan. One Class B director suggested that Ergo borrow the funds from a bank.

Dart, who had elected herself as one of the Class A directors, suggested that Ergo issue a new class of shares that Dart would purchase for $5 million. The new class of shares (Class C Preferred) would be entitled to a cumulative preferred dividend. In support of this alternative, Dart presented an opinion from an independent investment bank that stated:

    (1) $5 million would be a fair value for the Class C Preferred; and

    (2)   In the long run, payment of the proposed preferred dividend would be less costly to Ergo than interest payments on a loan.

After one hour of spirited discussion of these alternatives, all seven directors voted to recommend to the shareholders that Ergo's articles be amended to authorize the issuance of the Class C Preferred as proposed by Dart. A special meeting of the shareholders was properly called for the purpose of voting on the proposed amendment to the articles.

Prior to that meeting, a proxy statement was issued to all shareholders disclosing all relevant information about the plan to issue the Class C Preferred to Dart. However, the proxy statement did not disclose the alternative funding method the Class B director initially proposed. At the shareholders' meeting a quorum was present, and the amendment to the articles was adopted by the following vote:

	In Favor	Opposed
Class A Shares	400,000	0
Class B Shares	720,000	100,000

Following shareholder approval, the Ergo board of directors met to consider the issuance of the newly authorized Class C Preferred. All seven directors voted to issue the Class C Preferred to Dart for $5 million in cash.

A Class B shareholder filed a derivative action against the directors to enjoin the issuance of the Class C Preferred to Dart. The Class B shareholder alleged (a) that the directors erred in deciding to issue the Class C Preferred rather than borrow the money from the bank; (b) that the directors had breached their duty of care to Ergo; and (c) that Dart had breached her duty of loyalty to Ergo.

Considering the Class B shareholder's allegations and all possible defenses, who is likely to prevail? Explain.

ANSWER TO QUESTION 14

The corporation is likely to prevail in the derivative action on all counts. At issue is the approval of a director's conflicting interest transaction.

As a preliminary matter, the first issue to consider is whether the shareholder may bring a derivative action at all. Generally, to bring a derivative action, a shareholder must have been a shareholder at the time of the act or omission complained of or must have become a shareholder through operation of law (*e.g.*, through inheritance). The shareholder must also fairly and adequately represent the interests of the corporation and must make written demand on the corporation that it take suitable action. If the corporation finds, after making a good faith, reasonable inquiry, that an action would not be in the corporation's best interests, its decision generally will be upheld.

Here, the shareholder presumably was a shareholder at the time of the act complained of, and nothing indicates that the shareholder would not fairly and adequately represent the corporation's interests. However, neither does anything indicate that the shareholder made a demand on the corporation that it take suitable action. Some courts will excuse demand if it would be futile, but others will not. The shareholder might claim that demand would be futile here because all of the directors are charged with wrongdoing, and a court might be inclined to agree. Nevertheless, in many states, that would not be a sufficient excuse.

(a)   The Class B shareholder cannot prevail on a claim that the directors erred in deciding to issue Class C preferred rather than borrow funds from a bank. At issue is the business judgment rule.

Directors generally are vested with the power to manage the business and affairs of the corporation. They may act on this power by a majority vote at a meeting at which a quorum of directors are present. If they manage the corporation to the best of their ability in good faith, with the care that an ordinarily prudent person in a like position would exercise, and in a manner that they reasonably believe is in the best interests of the corporation, a court will not second-guess their decisions. A person challenging director action has the burden of proving that the above standard was not met.

Here, all of the directors voted to issue preferred stock rather than to borrow funds from a bank. This decision will be upheld unless the Class B shareholder can show that the directors breached their duty of care. As will be discussed in (b), below, the shareholder will probably be unable to make such a showing. Therefore, the shareholder will be unable to prevail on this claim.

(b)   The Class B shareholder will also be unable to show that the directors breached their duty of care. The standard of care that the directors must meet is discussed in part (a), above. In discharging his duties, a director is allowed to rely on reports from (i) corporate officers whom the director reasonably believes to be reliable and competent, and (ii) corporate outsiders as to matters that the director reasonably believes to be within the outsider's professional competence.

Here, the Class B shareholder will argue that it was unreasonable to rely on Dart's opinion as to what was best for the corporation because Dart had a conflicting personal interest in the transaction (she was to buy the Class C stock). Such an argument probably would prevail. However, it is a closer question whether the other directors breached a duty in relying on the independent banker's opinion. On the one hand, the opinion was provided by Dart; on the other hand, the opinion was of an independent investment bank. Given the independence of the opinion, the fact that the directors had a one-hour "spirited discussion" regarding the issue, and that the decision did not involve a major change to the corporation (it was about how to fund a change rather than about the change itself), a court would probably determine that the directors met their burden and that the Class B shareholder's claim that the directors breached their duty of care is without merit.

(c)   Finally, the shareholder's claim that Dart breached her duty of loyalty is without merit. While directors owe their corporation a duty of loyalty that prohibits the directors from profiting at the expense of the corporation, not every deal between a director and the corporation is prohibited. Indeed, a transaction in which a director has a conflicting personal interest will not be set aside because of that interest if the director discloses all of the material facts of the transaction and the deal is approved by a disinterested majority of the directors or the shareholders or the deal is fair. Here, it appears that all of the material facts of the transaction were disclosed to the directors, who voted to approve the transaction. While Dart's personal interest in the transaction prevents her vote from counting and might also invalidate the votes of the directors she controls (because if they voted against her, she could replace them), every other director in the corporation voted in favor of the transaction. Thus, the transaction was approved by a disinterested majority of the directors.

The transaction was also approved by a majority of the shareholders. The shareholder bringing the derivative suit would probably argue that not all of the material facts were disclosed to the shareholders and therefore their vote should not count; the directors did not disclose the possibility of obtaining bank financing. However, because the directors had not approved that option, it does not seem relevant to the decision whether to approve issuance of the new Class C shares.

Finally, it also appears that the deal was fair, at least according to the independent investment bank (*see* discussion above). Therefore, the court should probably find against the shareholder on this count as well.

QUESTION 15

Zeta, Inc., is a corporation with 80,000 shares outstanding. Its articles of incorporation provide for a nine-person board of directors, with staggered three-year terms. Three directors are elected each year. Zeta's articles require cumulative voting. Therefore, when electing the three directors, each share is entitled to three votes, meaning that there are 240,000 votes eligible to be cast. Accordingly, a person who receives at least 60,001 votes would be elected a director. Neither the articles nor Zeta's bylaws contain any other provisions concerning elections, voting, or removal of directors.

Diane is one of Zeta's directors. Although Diane's term does not expire for another two years, at the request of a group of shareholders, Zeta has scheduled a special shareholders' meeting on September 1 to consider removing Diane from office. Proper notice of that meeting has been given to all of Zeta's shareholders.

Sam owns 16,000 of the 80,000 outstanding Zeta shares. On August 1, Sam gave Arnie a proxy to vote Sam's shares at the special meeting. The proxy signed by Sam stated that it was "irrevocable."

On August 15, Betty, another Zeta shareholder, convinced Sam that giving a proxy to Arnie was a mistake. Sam then signed another proxy, dated August 15, which revoked the proxy to Arnie and gave Betty the right to vote Sam's 16,000 shares.

At the special shareholders' meeting on September 1, the shareholders in favor of Diane's removal argued that Diane was too critical of the company's management at board meetings and was "rocking the boat." No one alleged any breach of duty or other wrongdoing by

Diane. Both Arnie and Betty attempted to vote Sam's shares by proxy. Counting Arnie's vote of Sam's shares, the result was 117,000 votes to remove Diane and 123,000 votes not to remove her. Counting Betty's vote of Sam's shares, the result was 165,000 votes to remove Diane and 75,000 votes not to remove her.

Zeta's corporate secretary ruled that Diane was not removed as a director because: (1) no valid cause was shown for removing Diane and showing cause was required to remove her; (2) Arnie was entitled to vote Sam's shares and removal therefore failed by a vote of 117,000 votes to remove Diane and 123,000 votes not to remove her; and (3) even if Betty had the right to vote Sam's shares, the resulting vote of 165,000 votes to remove Diane and 75,000 votes not to remove her was insufficient to remove Diane.

Was each of these three rulings correct? Explain.

ANSWER TO QUESTION 15

Ruling (1) was incorrect. At issue is whether cause must be shown to remove a director. Generally, the shareholders may remove a director, with or without cause, at a specially called shareholders' meeting, unless the articles of incorporation provide otherwise. Here, the articles are silent on the topic of removal. Thus, ruling (1) is incorrect; no cause was needed to remove Diane as a director.

Ruling (2) was incorrect. At issue is whether Sam could and did revoke the proxy that he gave to Arnie.

The proxy that Sam gave to Arnie was revocable. Generally, a shareholder may give someone else a form of proxy, which gives that person the right to vote the shareholder's shares. Proxies are revocable unless they say that they are irrevocable and are coupled with an interest (*e.g.*, the shares have been pledged or sold to the proxy holder). Here, Sam gave Arnie a form of proxy that said that it was irrevocable, but nothing in the facts indicates that Arnie had an interest in Sam's shares. Therefore, the proxy was revocable.

Sam revoked his proxy by later appointing Betty as his proxy. A shareholder can revoke a proxy in a number of ways (*e.g.*, by retrieving the form of proxy from the proxy holder, by showing up at the shareholders' meeting to vote his shares himself, by later appointing another person to be a proxy holder of the same shares). Here, Sam appointed Betty as his proxy after he appointed Arnie to be his proxy, which is effective to revoke the proxy to Arnie.

Therefore, Sam had the power to revoke his proxy to Arnie and actually did so by appointing Betty as his proxy. Thus, ruling (2)—that Arnie was entitled to vote Sam's shares and that Betty was not entitled to vote the shares—was incorrect.

Ruling (3) was correct. At issue is the vote required to remove a director when cumulative voting was used to elect the director. Generally, when a director is elected through cumulative voting, the director cannot be removed if the votes cast against removal would be sufficient to elect the director if cumulatively voted at an election of the directors. Here, if Betty's votes were counted, 75,000 votes were cast against Diane's removal and the facts explain that a director could be elected through cumulative voting with 60,001 votes. Thus, the ruling was correct that even if Betty had the right to vote Sam's shares, there were not enough votes to remove Diane.

QUESTION 16

Corp, a corporation validly incorporated in State A, manufactures computer desks and sells them to furniture stores in State A and several nearby states. The board of directors of Corp consists of three members. The board of directors appointed Presley as the president of Corp. The bylaws of Corp provide that "the president, as the chief executive officer of the corporation, shall manage the business of the corporation and perform such other duties as the board of directors may from time to time direct."

Furniture Store ("FS") owes Corp $11,000 for computer desks that it purchased last year. Presley learned that FS was on the verge of bankruptcy and retained an attorney to file suit against FS to collect payment. The attorney filed suit as directed.

Presley believes that Corp should pay a dividend to its shareholders. Consequently, Presley sent a letter to all shareholders declaring a dividend of 10 cents per share to be paid at the end of the month.

Large Corp ("Large"), a large national furniture chain, contacted Presley and offered to sell its local manufacturing plant to Corp for what Presley considers a very reasonable price. Further, Large is willing to accept payment of the purchase price over 10 years. Acquiring this plant would triple Corp's manufacturing capacity. Presley signed a purchase agreement for the plant on behalf of Corp without consulting the board.

1. Did Presley, as president, have the authority to retain an attorney to file suit against FS on behalf of Corp? Explain.

2. Did Presley, as president, have the authority to declare a dividend payable to Corp's shareholders? Explain.

3. Did Presley, as president, have the authority to enter into a purchase agreement with Large to acquire its local manufacturing plant on behalf of Corp? Explain.

ANSWER TO QUESTION 16

Each of the three questions posed raises an issue regarding the authority of a corporate president to enter into a particular transaction. As a general rule, the authority of a corporate president to enter into transactions on behalf of his corporation is governed by the principles of agency. Under agency principles, authority may be actual or apparent, or an agent's previously unauthorized act may be later ratified by the corporation if it is, *e.g.,* approved by the board of directors. Actual authority includes authority expressly given to the agent and implied authority that the agent reasonably believes he has based on the express grant. Under the doctrine of apparent authority, an agent has whatever power a third party reasonably believes the agent has based on the principal's holding the agent out. Here, the facts do not discuss any ratification by the corporation, so our discussion will focus on actual and apparent authority.

1. As president, Presley did have authority to retain an attorney to file suit against FS on behalf of Corp. A corporate president has express actual authority to do any act specified in the corporation's articles or bylaws or that is specifically approved by the directors. Here, the only express grant of authority mentioned is a bylaw provision stating that the president "shall manage the business of the corporation." This is a broad grant of authority and would probably be held to include the

power to hire an attorney to sue on the corporation's behalf in order to collect on a debt owed to the corporation.

Even if a court were to find that Presley did not have express authority to hire an attorney to aid in collecting on the debt from FS, Presley would probably be held to have had implied authority to hire the attorney. An agent's actual authority includes not only the authority expressly granted to the agent, but also any authority that the agent reasonably believes he would have based on the express grant. Here, it would be reasonable for a corporate president to assume that if he is given the power to mange the corporation, that power would include the power to hire an attorney to aid in collecting on a debt owed to the corporation. Thus, Presley did have authority to hire the attorney.

Even if the above two arguments failed, Presley would be found to have had apparent authority to hire the attorney. Corp held Presley out as its president, and a corporation's president usually has the power to hire help and to collect on debts owed to the corporation. Thus, it was reasonable for a third party (*e.g.,* the attorney who was retained by Presley) to believe that Presley had authority to hire an attorney on behalf of the corporation.

2.   Presley did not have authority to declare a dividend. Ordinarily, by statute only the board of directors has authority to declare a dividend. A corporation's president does not have authority to do so. Here, even though the bylaws provide that the corporation's president shall have the power to manage the corporation, the provision will not be read so broadly as to include the power to declare a dividend; the president's power would be limited to that reasonably related to actually running the operations of the corporation. Moreover, it would not be reasonable for the president to assume that this express grant of authority included the power to declare dividends, because that ordinarily is not a power a corporation's president has. Thus, Presley did not have either express or implied authority to declare the dividend. Additionally, because corporate presidents generally do not have authority to declare dividends, neither did Presley have apparent authority to declare the dividend.

3.   Presley probably did not have authority to enter into the purchase agreement with Large to acquire its local manufacturing plant. It could be argued that Presley had actual authority to enter into the transaction, because the bylaws gave him express power to manage the corporation's business, and maintaining the corporation's production capacity is part of managing the corporation's business. However, a president's actual authority usually is limited to ordinary business transactions, and purchasing a new manufacturing plant appears to be an extraordinary transaction here (*e.g.,* nothing in the facts indicates that Corp routinely purchased new facilities). Thus, most likely, Presley will be found to have acted without express or implied actual authority. Similarly, because the transaction is extraordinary, a third party such as Large could not reasonably assume that based on Corp's holding Presley out as its president he had the power to make such a purchase. Thus, Presley probably will be found to have acted without authority. It should be noted, however, that the mere fact that payments for the purchase were to be made over a period of 10 years would not destroy Presley's authority if he had authority; a corporation's president can enter into contracts that are binding beyond the president's term.

QUESTION 17

Peg, an entrepreneur, decided to develop a widget manufacturing business. Widget production requires the use of a chemical called chromite. Because the market price for chromite

has fluctuated between $150 and $200 per ton over the past year, the first thing Peg did was contact numerous chemical companies to find a long-term supplier for chromite.

On May 20, Peg received a quote from Chem Corp. stating that it could supply Peg's corporation with all of its chromite at $145 per ton for the next three years. Chem Corp. indicated that the quote would expire at the end of the week. Peg informed Chem Corp. that her corporation, to be called "Acme, Inc.," would not be formed by that time. Peg further indicated that, "The deal should be between Acme, Inc. and Chem Corp. If Chem Corp. does not care if I sign for a nonexistent corporation, you have a deal." Chem Corp. responded: "No problem. We know with whom we are dealing and what the chromite's for. Do not waste our time. If you are serious, lock in the deal."

On May 26, Peg and Chem Corp. signed a three-year requirements contract for Chem Corp. to supply her soon-to-be-formed corporation with all of its chromite at a price of $145 per ton. Peg signed the contract "Peg, as agent for Acme, Inc., a corporation to be formed." The requirements contract was valid under state law. It contained a valid and substantial liquidated damages clause in the event Acme purchased chromite from any other supplier.

On August 1, Peg formed Acme, Inc. Peg was a shareholder, but not an officer or a director. Neither the board of directors nor the officers of Acme, Inc. formally reviewed or approved the contract with Chem Corp.

On August 15, Chem Corp. made its first delivery of chromite to Acme, Inc. at the contract price of $145 per ton. Vic, an Acme employee, acting pursuant to the direction of Acme's board of directors, accepted delivery and approved payment of the invoice after checking the contract and determining that the invoice agreed with the contract price. Acme, Inc. immediately began widget production.

In September and October, Chem Corp. made deliveries of chromite to Acme and charged Acme according to the contract. Acme promptly paid each invoice.

During the fall, the market price for chromite fell. By November, the market price for chromite was $100 per ton. The Acme board of directors, seeking a cheaper supply of chromite, entered into an agreement with Supply, Inc. to provide Acme with its monthly requirements of chromite at $95 per ton.

Acme immediately contacted Chem Corp. and instructed it not to ship Acme any more chromite. When Chem Corp. demanded payment under the liquidated damages clause, Acme refused.

1. Is Peg personally liable to Chem Corp. under the contract? Explain.

2. Is Acme, Inc. liable to Chem Corp. under the contract? Explain.

ANSWER TO QUESTION 17

1.   Peg can be held personally liable on the contract. At issue is the liability of a promoter on a contract that she enters on behalf of a corporation to be formed.

Peg is a promoter. A promoter is a person who procures commitments for capital and instrumentalities on behalf of a corporation that will be formed in the future. As a general rule, promoters are personally liable on all such contracts, and this liability continues even after the corporation is formed and even if the corporation also becomes liable on the contract by adopting it (*see* below). However, there is an exception to the general rule: A promoter will not be liable on a preincorporation contract if the agreement between the parties expressly indicates that the promoter is not to be bound. In such a case, the "contract" is considered to be an offer to the proposed corporation.

Here, the contract does not expressly provide that Peg will not be liable on the contract. While Peg asked whether Chem Corp. minded that she was signing on behalf of a nonexistent corporation, Chem Corp.'s response was at best ambiguous. It replied, "No problem. We know with whom we are dealing." This statement could be taken to mean that Chem Corp. knew that it was dealing with Peg, or that it was dealing with a nonexistent corporation. In any case, the response does not expressly provide that Chem Corp. would look only to the corporation to be formed for payment. Therefore, Peg is personally liable.

[*Note:* An equally plausible argument could be made that the parties' dealings did make it clear that Chem Corp. would look only to Acme for payment. This is a question of fact and the facts may be interpreted either way.]

The fact that Peg signed the contract, "Peg, as agent for Acme Inc., a corporation to be formed," does nothing to resolve the issue. While under Agency law such a signature would release an agent from liability on a contract that the agent entered into on behalf of a principal, Peg was not acting as Acme Inc.'s agent because one may not be an agent of a nonexistent principal.

2. Acme Inc. is liable to Chem Corp. on the contract. At issue is the liability of a corporation on a promoter's contract.

As a general rule, a corporation is not liable on a contract entered into by a promoter. However, the corporation can become liable if it adopts a promoter's contract. Adoption can be express (*e.g.,* by resolution by the board of directors) or implied (*e.g.,* by acquiescence or conduct normally constituting estoppel). Here, there was no express adoption—the contract was never reviewed by the board of directors or any of Acme Inc.'s officers. However, there was an implied acceptance—Vic, an employee of Acme acting pursuant to the direction of Acme's board of directors, accepted several shipments of chromite and approved payment of the invoices for the shipments. Thus, Acme Inc. is bound on the contract through adoption.

QUESTION 18

Green Corporation ("Green") was properly incorporated in State A. Green's articles of incorporation authorize 100 shares of common stock ("Common") and 300 shares of Class A nonvoting cumulative preferred stock ("Class A Preferred"). Each Class A Preferred share is entitled to a quarterly dividend of $1. Green's articles provide that, if Green fails to pay this dividend for four consecutive quarters, each Class A Preferred share becomes entitled to one vote on all matters voted on at shareholders' meetings until all arrearages have been paid.

Deb owns all 100 shares of the Common and 100 shares of the Class A Preferred. Ed owns the remaining 200 shares of the Class A Preferred. Neither Deb nor Ed is a director or officer of Green.

Green has been experiencing financial difficulties for some time and has not paid the Class A Preferred dividends for more than four consecutive quarters. On September 2, Green's board unanimously adopted a proposal to dissolve the corporation. The board then called a special meeting of the shareholders to vote on this proposal. The notice of the special meeting indicated that a special meeting would be held at the corporation's principal office on October 15. The notice did not state the purpose of the meeting. The notice was sent to Deb. She received it on September 10.

On October 13, two days before the special meeting, Deb and Ed met for dinner. At dinner, Deb asked Ed to serve as her proxy at the special meeting because she could not attend. Ed was surprised because he had not received any notice of the special meeting from Green. Nonetheless, Ed told Deb that he would attend the meeting and vote her shares.

On October 15, at breakfast before the meeting began, Ed first learned of the proposed dissolution of Green. Ed immediately called Deb to inform her of the proposal. Deb directed Ed to vote all of her shares in favor of the proposal. Ed went to the meeting and voted Deb's shares in favor and his own shares against the proposal to dissolve Green.

1.   Was the special shareholders' meeting called to dissolve Green properly held? Explain.

2.   Was the proposal to dissolve Green properly adopted by its shareholders? Explain.

ANSWER TO QUESTION 18

1.   The special shareholders' meeting was not properly held. At issue is whether proper notice of the meeting was given or validly waived.

Generally, the directors of a corporation have the power to run its affairs. However, before undertaking a fundamental change in the corporation, directors must seek approval from the shareholders. Dissolution of a corporation is a fundamental corporate change. Each shareholder—even those not entitled to vote—must be given at least 10 days' written notice of the meeting at which a vote will be taken on the fundamental corporate change. The notice must state the date, time, place, and purpose of the meeting. However, defects in notice may be waived if a shareholder attends a meeting and votes, despite the defective notice, unless he attends solely for the purpose of objecting to the improper notice.

Here, Ed was not given any notice of the meeting, but he waived any objection that he had to the notice by attending and voting his shares in person. While Deb did receive notice, the notice was defective as to her because it did not state the purpose of the meeting. It might be argued that she, too, waived the defects in the notice because she made Ed her proxy and he voted her shares at the meeting. However, Deb's appointment of Ed as her proxy was invalid. A proxy can be appointed only by a writing or an authorized electronic transmission. Here, nothing indicates that Deb gave Ed any sort of written appointment; rather, she asked him at dinner to be her proxy. Therefore, Ed could not validly vote Deb's shares or waive the defects in the notice. As a result, the notice was defective and the meeting was not properly called.

2.   The proposal was not properly adopted by the shareholders. At issue is the vote required to approve a fundamental corporate change.

Generally, approval of a fundamental corporate change requires approval at a properly called meeting at which a quorum is present of a majority of all of the shares entitled to be voted on the matter, or at least that the votes cast in favor of the proposal exceed the votes cast against the proposal. Unless the articles provide otherwise, a quorum requires at least a majority of the shares entitled to be voted on the matter.

Here, the proposal was not properly approved for a number of reasons: First, as established above, the notice of the meeting was improper, and the impropriety was not waived by Deb. Any action taken at a defectively noticed meeting is voidable by a person who received improper notice and did not waive the defect. Of course, because Deb favors dissolution, it is doubtful that she would seek to avoid the action here.

Second, none of Deb's shares were properly voted in favor of dissolution because she did not give Ed a written proxy. Thus, effectively, no shares were voted in favor of dissolution.

Third, also because of the improper proxy, a quorum was not present at the meeting. Although Ed held shares that originally were nonvoting, the shares provided that they would include the right to vote if dividends were not paid for at least four quarters, and that was the case here. Thus, the corporation had outstanding 100 Common voting shares and 300 Class A Preferred voting shares, for a total of 400 voting shares. More than 200 shares had to be represented at the meeting in order for there to be a quorum, and only Ed's 200 shares were represented because of the improper proxy appointment. Thus, a quorum was lacking and no vote could be taken.

Finally, even if Ed had properly been appointed as Deb's proxy, a majority of the outstanding shares were not voted in favor of dissolution, and neither was the alternative test met (*i.e.*, the votes cast in favor of dissolution did not exceed the votes cast against dissolution). If Ed had validly been appointed Deb's proxy, 200 shares would have been voted in favor of dissolution and 200 shares would have been voted against dissolution—a tie. Thus, the proposal to dissolve Green was not properly adopted by the shareholders.

QUESTION 19

Until early this year, Parensco, Inc. ("Parensco") owned 75% of the outstanding shares of Subco Corp. ("Subco"). The remaining 25% of the outstanding shares of Subco were held by numerous other shareholders. The president of Parensco is Carr, who is also a director of Parensco.

Several months ago, the president of Aster, Inc. ("Aster") approached Carr, expressed an interest in acquiring control of Subco, and stated that Aster would consider a purchase price in the range of $200 per Subco share. After Carr's conversation with Aster, the board of directors of Parensco decided to merge Subco into Parensco. The purchase price for the 25% of the outstanding shares of Subco not owned by Parensco was set at $120 per share.

After its board duly authorized this transaction, Parensco issued the following press release:

> **The board of Parensco announced today that it seeks to acquire the 25% of Subco that it does not own. Subject to the approval of the Subco board, Parensco will pay $120 for each share of Subco in a cash-out merger, for a total cost to Parensco of $200 million.**

Shortly after this press release was issued, the board of directors of Subco ("Subco board"), consisting solely of officers and directors of Parensco, but not including Carr, met to consider the merger offer. At the meeting, the Subco board heard a brief presentation from Carr and reviewed a report from Banker, an investment banker. Banker's report advised that, after undertaking a review of Subco, a fair valuation of Subco was $800 million and the price of $120 per share was generous for a minority interest in the corporation. Neither the Subco board nor Banker was aware of the discussion between Carr and Aster. After hearing Carr's presentation and reviewing Banker's report, the Subco board voted to approve the merger after a brief discussion and without any further investigation.

Parensco and Subco then issued a proxy statement to the Subco shareholders, which was complete and accurate except for its failure to mention the Aster proposal.

The merger was approved by a vote of 90% of the outstanding Subco shares, consisting of the 75% of the outstanding shares held by Parensco and 15% of the outstanding shares held by minority shareholders. The merger was then consummated and Parensco sent checks to the Subco shareholders in payment for their stock. A few months later, Parensco announced the sale for $3 billion of the division of its business consisting almost exclusively of assets acquired in the Subco merger.

1. **Did Parensco breach any of its fiduciary duties by failing to disclose the Aster proposal to the minority shareholders of Subco? Explain.**

2. **Did the Subco board breach its duty of care in approving the merger? Explain.**

3. **Did Parensco breach any duty to the minority shareholders of Subco by offering them only $120 per share? Explain.**

ANSWER TO QUESTION 19

1.   Parensco probably did breach a fiduciary duty by failing to disclose the Aster proposal to the minority shareholders of Subco. At issue are the duties that a majority shareholder owes to a minority shareholder.

Although generally shareholders are free to act for their own benefit and do not owe any fiduciary duties to their fellow shareholders, there is an exception for controlling shareholders. A controlling shareholder must refrain from using his control to obtain a special advantage or to cause the corporation to take action that unfairly prejudices the minority shareholders. This would include a duty to disclose material information to the minority shareholders.

Here, Parensco breached its duty as a controlling shareholder. Parensco, through its president, Carr, learned that Aster was willing to pay $200 per share for Subco shares. As a controlling shareholder, Parensco had a duty to disclose this information to the Subco shareholders because this information would be material for Subco to determine the true value of its shares. Instead, Carr kept the information confidential in order to more easily convince the Subco board to approve Parensco's proposed cash-out merger. Thus, Parensco breached its duty.

Parensco might argue that the minority shareholders were not harmed in that they received a "generous" price for their shares as determined by an independent expert. However, because

Parensco did not tell the expert about Aster's offer, he could not properly evaluate Subco's shares, either. Moreover, given Parensco's subsequent sale of Subco's assets a few months later for $3 billion, far above the $800 million valuation of the expert, it would seem that the Subco minority shareholders were, indeed, harmed.

2.   The Subco board probably breached its duty of care in approving the merger, but this is a close question. At issue are the fiduciary duties of directors.

A director is a fiduciary of his corporation and owes the corporation a duty: (i) to act in good faith, (ii) with the care that an ordinarily prudent person in a like position would exercise under similar circumstances, and (iii) in a manner the director believes is in the best interest of the corporation. A director who meets this standard of conduct is protected from personal liability for decisions regarding the corporation, and anyone who challenges a decision of the board has the burden of proving that the statutory standard was not met. At common law, this is known as the business judgment rule. It should be noted that in making business judgments, directors generally are entitled to rely on the reports of professional persons within their areas of expertise and corporate officers and employees whom the director reasonably believes to be reliable and competent.

Here, the Subco board decided to approve a cash-out merger after hearing only from Carr and an expert provided by Carr. While they generally would be entitled to rely on the opinion of an expert and probably even of Carr, it can be argued that because Carr had an interest in the trans-action as a director of the purchasing corporation, a reasonable person would not rely on his opinion and would get another expert (specifically, one not provided by Carr) to investigate the proposed cash-out merger. Moreover, the facts state that the Subco directors approved the merger after only a "brief discussion." Given the money at stake ($200 million), a reasonable person would probably have more than a "brief discussion." Thus, it could be argued that the Subco directors breached their duty of care.

3.   Parensco did breach a duty to the minority shareholders of Subco by offering them only $120 per share. Again, the issue is the duty of a controlling shareholder to the minority share-holders.

As discussed above, a controlling shareholder must refrain from using his control to obtain a special advantage or to cause the corporation to take action that unfairly prejudices the minority shareholders. Here, Parensco used its majority position to acquire the minority shareholders' Subco stock for $120 per share when it knew that Aster would pay the shareholders $200 per share. Parensco then sold Subco's assets to Aster at a substantial premium over the $120 price that the Subco shareholders received. Thus, Parensco used its control to obtain a profit at the expense of the minority Subco shareholders, which is a breach of fiduciary duty.

QUESTION 20

Last July Art, Brett, and Chad formed LeaseAll, Limited Liability Company ("LLC"), to lease personal property to individuals and businesses. Art, Brett, and Chad had equal ownership interests in LLC and entered into a written operating agreement ("OA"). Under the OA, only Art had authority to manage the business, to hire and fire employees, and to buy and sell real and personal property. Art contributed a business plan and his expertise to the leasing business, and Brett and Chad each contributed $50,000 to the capital of LLC.

Over the next year, Brett and Chad did not participate in the business. No meetings were held, and Art did not provide Brett or Chad with any information about LLC. In accordance with the business plan, Art purchased, in the name of LLC, a building and inventory for the leasing business.

Things have not gone well for LLC. Its initial capital is exhausted, and the cash generated by operations is inadequate to allow it to pay its debts as they come due. Additionally, one of LLC's customers, Peter, was badly injured when a chainsaw he rented from LLC malfunctioned. Peter sued LLC and obtained a judgment of $500,000. LLC does not have liability insurance because Art forgot to sign the check when he sent the premium payment to the insurance company and, as a result, the company did not issue the policy. LLC cannot pay Peter's judgment from its current capital.

1. **If Brett and Chad bring an action against Art to recover damages, claiming that Art mismanaged LLC, should that action be direct or derivative and what corporate law requirements must they meet before bringing an action? Explain.**

2. **Did Art breach his fiduciary duty in managing LLC? Explain.**

3. **Can Peter recover the $500,000 judgment against LLC from Art, Brett, and/or Chad personally? Explain.**

ANSWER TO QUESTION 20

1.   If Brett and Chad bring an action against Art to recover damages, claiming that Art mismanaged LLC, the action should be a derivative action. At issue is whether a claim for mismanagement of an LLC is a claim of injury to the individual members or the LLC as a whole.

Direct actions may be filed when the harm done is personal to the plaintiff. Derivative actions are used when a member is attempting to recover for a wrong done to the LLC. Here, a claim of mismanagement—based on either the failure of the business or Art's failure to obtain insurance—is a claim of breach of duty owed to the LLC. Because the cause of action seeks to vindicate rights of the LLC, it is derivative in nature.

Before bringing the derivative action, Brett and Chad might be required to first make a demand on Art that he resolve the issue. However, states often dispense with the demand requirement if the demand would seem futile. Here, in essence the demand would be asking Art to admit wrongdoing and to pay personally for LLC's losses. Such a demand seems futile, so a court likely would dispense with the demand requirement here.

2.   Art probably did not breach his fiduciary duty in managing the LLC but probably did breach his fiduciary duty in failing to obtain insurance. At issue is whether Art breached the standard of care imposed on managers of LLCs.

A manager of an LLC is a fiduciary of the LLC. Some states require a manager of an LLC to act in good faith, with the care of a reasonably prudent person acting under similar conditions, in a manner reasonably believed to be in the best interests of the LLC. In such states, managers have the benefit of the business judgment rule—if they meet the above standard, they cannot be held personally liable for business decisions that turn out poorly. Other states are even more lenient and require only that an LLC manager refrain from acting with gross negligence, recklessly, with intent to harm the LLC, or in knowing violation of the law.

Here, it is doubtful that Art breached his duty merely because he did not operate the LLC profitably. Nothing in the facts suggests that he acted in bad faith or without reasonable care, let alone with gross negligence, recklessly, or intentionally to cause the business to fail. However, it is a much closer question with regard to his failure to sign the check for the insurance premium. It can be argued that a reasonably prudent manager would be careful in assuring that his company maintains insurance. The failure to maintain insurance could even be argued to amount to gross negligence. Thus, a claim of breach of fiduciary duty for Art's failure to sign the insurance premium check may be successful.

3.   Peter probably cannot recover the $500,000 judgment from Art, Brett, and/or Chad. At issue is whether the members of an LLC are personally liable for the obligations of the LLC.

Generally, members of an LLC are not personally liable for the obligations of an LLC. However, like shareholders of a corporation, personal liability may be imposed on the members if there are grounds for piercing the LLC veil of limited liability. Grounds for piercing an LLC are similar to the grounds for piercing a corporation (*e.g.,* piercing may be proper where the LLC is the alter ego of one or more shareholders, where the LLC was undercapitalized at its inception, or where the LLC was formed to commit a fraud), but a court generally will not pierce an LLC for lack of formality (*e.g.,* failure to hold meetings, etc.), because the statutes require less formalities in an LLC than in a corporation.

Here, there is little ground to claim that the LLC was the alter ego of any of the parties. While Art was the sole manager of the LLC, nothing indicates that he was using LLC funds as his own, commingling assets, etc. Clearly the LLC was not the alter ego of either Brett or Chad, as neither took part in the management of the LLC. Similarly, while the LLC now does not have sufficient funds to pay its obligations, it was initially capitalized with $100,000 ($50,000 from Brett and $50,000 from Chad). Nothing in the facts indicates that $100,000 was insufficient start-up capital. Finally, nothing in the facts indicates that the LLC was formed to perpetrate a fraud. Therefore, it is unlikely that a court would pierce the LLC veil here to reach the personal assets of either Art, Brett, or Chad.

QUESTION 21

Cal is the CEO and chairman of the 12-member board of directors of Prime, Inc. ("Prime"). Three other members of Prime's board of directors (the Board) are also senior officers of Prime. The remaining eight members of the Board are wholly independent directors.

Recently, the Board decided to hire a consulting firm to help Prime market a new product. The Board met to consider whether to hire Wiseman Consulting ("Wiseman") or Smart Group ("Smart"). The Board first heard from a representative of Wiseman. The Wiseman representative described some of the projects Wiseman had completed for other clients and outlined the work it proposed to do for Prime for $500,000. The Board then heard from a representative of Smart, another consulting firm. The Smart representative described a similar work plan and stated that Smart's proposed fee was $650,000. Either of these amounts would be a significant outlay for Prime.

After the Board heard both presentations, Cal disclosed to the Board that he had a 25% partnership interest in Smart. Cal stated that he would not be involved in any work to be performed by Smart for Prime. He knew but did not disclose to the Board that Smart's proposed fee for this consulting assignment was substantially higher than it normally charged for comparable work. The Board did not ask about the basis for Smart's proposed fee.

After receiving all of this information, and no other information, the Board discussed the relative merits of the two proposals for 10 minutes. The Board then voted unanimously (Cal abstaining) to hire Smart, even though hiring Smart would cost Prime approximately 30% more than hiring Wiseman. Cal was present throughout the meeting but did not participate except to the extent indicated above.

1. Did Cal violate his duty of loyalty to Prime? Explain.

2. Assuming Cal breached his duty of loyalty to Prime, does he have any defense to liability? Explain.

3. Did the directors of Prime, other than Cal, violate their duty of care? Explain.

ANSWER TO QUESTION 21

1. Cal did violate his duty of loyalty to Prime. At issue is whether Cal disclosed all relevant facts of the transaction to the board of directors.

Directors of a corporation owe the corporation a duty of loyalty which generally prevents the directors from profiting at the expense of the corporation. Here, Cal is a partner in Smart. Partners generally share profits of a partnership. Thus, because Smart was awarded the consulting contract, Cal will profit from it even though he himself performs none of the work. This potentially is a breach of the duty of loyalty.

2. Cal does not have any viable defenses. At issue are the defenses available to prevent a claim based on conflict of interest.

Generally, the law provides three defenses against a conflict of interest claim. The director cannot be held liable if his corporation enters into a transaction in which the director has personal interests if: (i) the director discloses all material facts to the board and a majority of the independent directors approve the transaction; (ii) the director discloses all material facts to the shareholders who then approve the transaction; or (iii) the transaction is fair to the corporation. Here, there was no shareholder involvement, and the transaction does not appear to be fair to the corporation because Wiseman was willing to do similar work for the corporation for 30% less remuneration. Thus, the question is whether Cal made sufficient disclosure and obtained proper approval from the board.

Cal's disclosure to the board was insufficient. Although he did disclose his interest in Smart and did not participate in the decisionmaking process regarding the transaction, Cal failed to disclose that Smart was charging more than it usually would charge for its services. That fact would be considered material to the transaction. Thus, Cal did not disclose all material facts. But for this failure, the approval would have been sufficient. The facts say that Cal did not participate. And while three of the remaining members of the board might not be considered to be independent (because they are officers and would report to Cal as CEO), the other eight members of the board were independent and all approved the transaction.

3.   The other members of Prime's board probably did breach their duty of care. At issue is whether the directors are protected by the business judgment rule.

Generally, directors are not insurers of a corporation's success. They cannot be held liable for business decisions if they act in good faith and like a reasonably prudent person in a like position. Here, as mentioned above, eight directors were independent of the transaction, and nothing in the facts indicates that they acted in bad faith. Nevertheless, they did breach their duty of care. The facts indicate that the transaction constituted a significant transaction for the corporation. The board considered it for only 10 minutes and knew that Smart was charging $150,000 more for services similar to those offered by Wiseman. Given these facts, a reasonable person would have investigated further.

QUESTION 1

Marge decided to kill her husband, Homer. First, she put a lethal dose of poison in Homer's hamburger. However, she burned the burger, and Homer refused to eat it. Next, she asked her 18-year-old daughter, Lisa, to help her cut the brake line to Homer's car, figuring that Homer would be killed when he raced around dead man's curve on his way to work the next morning. However, while Lisa thought that Homer was a poor excuse for a father, she told her mother that she wanted no part of her evil scheme. Marge then approached Bart, Lisa's ne'er-do-well twin brother, and asked him to help her in her scheme. Bart agreed to show Marge how to cut the brake line and went to the store to purchase a hacksaw to accomplish the task. However, on returning from the store, Bart had a change of heart and told Marge that he would not go through with the plan.

A few weeks later, Marge ran into Crusty, who was Marge's boyfriend when they were in high school together. Marge told Crusty that she would like to rekindle their relationship, but that he would have to get Homer out of the way first. Crusty agreed to kill Homer and immediately set off to accomplish this task. When Crusty arrived at Homer's house, he peered through a few windows and spotted Homer, in bed with Patty, Marge's sister. Assuming that Marge would be furious with her sister for sleeping with her husband, and not wanting to leave any witnesses who could testify against him, Crusty shot and killed both Homer and Patty. He then fled the scene, returned to where he had left Marge, and told her about both killings. To Crusty's surprise, Marge cried out, "I always wished those two would get along better!" Filled with remorse, Marge went to the nearest police station and confessed all of the above facts after she had been given full *Miranda* warnings.

Discuss the criminal charges that prosecutors may bring against Marge, Lisa, and Bart. Your answer should consider each crime independently and should include a discussion of any possible defenses that may be raised.

ANSWER TO QUESTION 1

Marge: Marge could be charged with attempted murder, murder, solicitation, and conspiracy.

The first crime with which Marge could be charged is attempted murder. All attempt crimes require the specific intent to commit the target crime; thus, attempted murder requires the specific intent to commit murder. For all attempt crimes, most states also require that the defendant take some substantial step beyond mere preparation toward the completion of the target crime. Here, Marge put a lethal dose of poison into Homer's hamburger, and intended him to eat it. That clearly (i) shows a specific intent to murder Homer and (ii) constitutes a substantial step toward the commission of the crime of murder. Marge has no defense to this crime.

Marge could also be charged with three counts of solicitation to commit murder. Solicitation consists of inciting another to commit a crime with the specific intent that the person solicited commit the crime. If the person who is solicited agrees to commit the crime or actually attempts or completes the crime, the solicitation merges with the conspiracy, attempt, or completed crime. The crime is complete the moment the question is asked. Here, Marge asked Lisa to show her how to cut the brake line to Homer's car. She also explained why she wanted to cut the brake line—to cause Homer to be killed when he rounded dead man's curve on his way to work. She did the same with Bart, which accounts for the second count of solicitation. Finally, she asked

Crusty to kill Homer. This is the third charge of solicitation. However, assuming she is charged with the greater crimes, Marge could not be convicted of soliciting Bart or Crusty to commit murder because the solicitation merges with the conspiracy (Bart agreed to commit the crime) and the completed crime (Crusty actually killed Homer).

Marge could also be charged with two counts of conspiracy. Conspiracy is agreement between two or more people to pursue some unlawful objective. Conspiracy requires an agreement, an intent to agree, an intent to pursue the unlawful objective, and an overt act in furtherance of the conspiracy. In many states, unlike solicitation, conspiracy does not merge with the completed crime. Here, Marge solicited Bart to help her murder Homer, explaining what she wanted done and why, and Bart agreed. In turn, Bart performed an overt act in furtherance of the act by buying a hacksaw. Thus, there is a conspiracy to commit murder between Marge and Bart. Furthermore, Marge asked Crusty to murder Homer, and Crusty agreed to do so. Given that Crusty actually completed the crime, he clearly performed an overt act in furtherance of the conspiracy. As a result, Marge could be charged with two counts of conspiracy.

Furthermore, Marge could be charged with the murder of Homer, either as Crusty's accomplice or under a conspiracy theory. An accomplice (*i.e.*, one who, with the intent that a crime be committed, aids, counsels, or encourages another—the principal—before or during the commission of a crime) can be held liable for a criminal act committed by the principal. Here, Marge told Crusty that she would rekindle their relationship if Crusty killed Homer, and Crusty did so. Crusty's killing of Homer qualifies as a murder. Murder generally is defined as the unlawful killing of another human being with malice aforethought. The element of malice aforethought can be satisfied by an intent to kill. Here, Crusty went to Homer's house with the intent to kill him and did kill him. Therefore, Crusty committed murder, and even though Marge was not there and did not actually pull the trigger, she can also be held liable for Homer's murder as an accomplice.

Similarly, Marge could be held liable for Homer's murder under a conspiracy theory. A conspirator is liable for criminal acts of a co-conspirator that reasonably result from the conspiracy and are committed in furtherance of the conspiracy. Here, the purpose of the conspiracy was to kill Homer, and Homer was killed. Thus, Marge could be held liable for Homer's death under a conspiracy theory.

Finally, Marge could be charged with the murder of Patty even though Marge did not intend for Crusty to kill Patty. As explained above, co-conspirators are criminally liable for all crimes that reasonably result from the conspiracy and are committed in furtherance of the conspiracy. Here, Crusty killed Patty, at least in part, to keep her from possibly testifying against him. This murder was a reasonably foreseeable result of the conspiracy and was committed in furtherance of the conspiracy. Thus, Marge is criminally liable for Patty's murder too.

Lisa: Lisa cannot be charged with any crime, even though she knew that Marge wanted to kill Homer. A person cannot be held liable for failing to report another's planned criminal activity absent a duty to act. A parent has a duty to act to protect his child, but there is no well-defined reciprocal duty on a child to protect a parent. Thus, Lisa had no legal duty to contact the police and cannot be held liable for any crime.

Bart: As indicated above, Bart may be charged with conspiracy to commit murder. He agreed to cut the brake line of Homer's car and bought a hacksaw for that purpose. His subsequent withdrawal is not a defense to the conspiracy charge because the conspiracy was already completed.

However, because he did not go through with the agreement, he cannot be charged with Marge's later acts that eventually led to Homer's death.

QUESTION 2

On April 29, Vera was working behind the counter at a fast food restaurant in Anytown. A woman, whom Vera later identified as Carolyn, entered the restaurant and asked for a glass of water. Vera went to get the water and when she returned to the counter to give Carolyn the glass, Carolyn was still standing at the counter, but she now had a white paper bag over her hand. Carolyn pointed the paper bag at Vera and said, "Empty the cash register into a bag or I'll fill you full of holes." Vera told Carolyn to "stay cool" and not to shoot, but that she did not know how to open the register. Carolyn responded, "Damn! I give up. Did you ever have one of those days when nothing goes right?" Carolyn then threw down the bag which had covered her hand, revealing that her hand held nothing but air under the bag. She had never had a weapon of any sort and had merely pointed her finger at Vera.

Vera called the police, who quickly arrived and arrested Carolyn about two blocks from the restaurant. Carolyn has been charged with attempted robbery. Discuss the likelihood of conviction.

ANSWER TO QUESTION 2

Carolyn likely will be convicted of attempted robbery. The first issue is whether Carolyn had the required intent to commit robbery and whether she progressed sufficiently toward completion of the crime to be convicted of attempt.

At common law, attempt consists of a specific intent to commit a crime and an act in furtherance of that intent. More specifically, the mens rea of attempt has two components: (i) the intent to commit the acts or cause the result constituting the target crime; and (ii) the intent necessary for the target crime. There are a number of approaches for describing the actus reus of attempt (*e.g.,* an act of "perpetration" rather than "preparation," control over indispensable elements of the crime, an act physically proximate to the intended crime, etc.). The Model Penal Code is gaining increasing acceptance. It requires (i) an act constituting a "substantial step" in the course of conduct intended to result in the crime, and (ii) that the act be of strong corroboration of the defendant's criminal purpose, although it need not establish purpose by itself.

Carolyn had the intent to commit robbery and the intent necessary for robbery. Robbery generally is defined as (i) a trespassory (ii) taking and (iii) carrying away of (iv) the personal property (v) of another (vi) with the intent to permanently deprive the owner of possession of the property, (vii) by means of violence or threats. The threat must be of serious bodily injury. Here, Carolyn demanded that Vera empty money into a bag and threatened to shoot Vera if she did not comply. Her conduct evinces both an intent to wrongfully take and carry away another's property by means of threats of serious bodily injury and the intent to permanently deprive the owner of possession. It is irrelevant that she actually did not have a gun, as she made the threat and appeared to be holding a gun under the bag. Thus, she had the mens rea for attempted robbery.

Carolyn also committed sufficient acts toward completion of the crime. She went to the restaurant, pretended to have a concealed gun, and demanded that Vera hand over money; all that was left to complete the crime was for Vera to hand over the money and Carolyn to begin to move away with it. Such acts go beyond preparation to perpetration; gave her control of the indispensable elements of robbery; put her in the physical proximity of committing the robbery; and constitute a substantial step toward the completion of the crime that is strongly corroborative of her criminal purpose. Thus, regardless of the test the jurisdiction uses, Carolyn committed a sufficient act.

Carolyn will likely raise the defense of abandonment, but will be unsuccessful. The main issue is whether her abandonment of the crime was voluntary and complete.

Traditionally, abandonment is not a defense to attempt. However, the Model Penal Code and modern statutes permit a defendant to avoid liability for attempt if she can prove that: (i) the abandonment was entirely voluntary, which means it must not have been motivated in any way by circumstances not present or apparent earlier which increase the difficulty of committing the crime; and (ii) the abandonment was complete, which means that it must not have been simply a decision to postpone the crime until a better time or until a different victim or opportunity is found. If the crime was simply becoming more complicated than envisioned, the decision to abandon is not voluntary and perhaps not complete.

Here, Carolyn's abandonment was not entirely voluntary, as she gave up only after Vera said that she could not open the register, hindering Carolyn from completing the crime. It also may not have been complete, as her reference to having a day when nothing goes right suggests that she may simply be postponing the crime until a better time or easier victim or opportunity. Thus, she will not succeed on a defense of abandonment.

Carolyn might also attempt to assert the defense of impossibility because Vera could not actually give Carolyn money, but this defense will fail. Generally, the fact that a crime is factually impossible to complete is not a defense to an attempt charge. If the act that the defendant sets out to do is criminal, the defendant may be guilty of attempt (assuming all other elements have been established) despite the fact that the crime was factually impossible to complete. Here, Carolyn's mistake was as to a matter of fact (that Vera could open the cash drawer). Had the facts been as Carolyn believed them to be (that Vera could access the cash), Carolyn would have been guilty of attempted robbery. Thus, the defense of impossibility fails here.

QUESTION 3

Defendant was charged, tried, and convicted in the trial court with two counts. Count one charged defendant with attempt to commit the crime of indecent liberties with a child of under the age of 14 by attempting to engage in lewd fondling or touching with the child (Kim), with the intent to arouse or satisfy the sexual desires of the child or the defendant, but that he was intercepted and prevented in executing the completed crime by arrest.

At trial the facts established defendant traveled to State A to meet with Kim, a person whom defendant had met on the Internet. Their e-mail exchanges, which initially occurred on a website that was targeted at teenagers, developed that Kim claimed to be under 14 years of age and that she wanted to enter into a sexual relationship with someone who would tickle her with feathers and other devices until she obtained sexual satisfaction. A fairly long-term exchange of e-mails was carried on between Defendant and Kim, discussing in graphic detail the thrills of such conduct. In one exchange, Defendant asked Kim whether she was going to act on her desire. Kim suggested that Defendant come to State A,

meet with her, and carry out her fantasy. When Defendant showed up at the hotel, he brought with him a variety of feathers and other paraphernalia designed to meet the needs of Kim.

When Defendant arrived at the hotel, he was met by a 30-year-old policewoman posing as Kim. The policewoman had conducted the e-mail correspondence with Defendant. When Defendant pulled out a turkey feather and took off his pants, Kim displayed her shield and attempted to arrest Defendant. Defendant did not go quietly. He grabbed Kim by the throat and attempted to choke her. In the melee, a lamp overturned, causing the feathers to catch fire, burning Kim seriously. Other officers rushed into the room, and Defendant was subdued. This conduct caused Defendant to be charged with a second count. It was alleged that Defendant committed the crime of attempted involuntary manslaughter, by unintentionally, but recklessly, under circumstances manifesting indifference to the value of human life, attempting to kill Kim, but that he was prevented and failed in the perpetration thereof.

Defendant was convicted in the trial court on both counts, but argued there, and now on appeal, that he could not be guilty of either crime.

Defendant claims that the facts show that the crime of attempted indecent liberties with a child was a factual and legal impossibility, that the conviction of attempted involuntary manslaughter is for an offense that is not a crime, and that to the extent any of his conduct was criminal, he was entrapped.

You are the appellate judge assigned the task of writing the opinion on this appeal. How should the court rule in regard to Defendant's claims?

ANSWER TO QUESTION 3

Attempted indecent liberties with a child: The conviction for attempted indecent liberties with a child should stand. At issue is whether a conviction based on a charge of attempted indecent liberties with a child is precluded based on the defenses of factual or legal impossibility.

Generally, it is no defense to an attempt charge that it would have been factually impossible for the defendant to complete his plan. In the instant case, it was factually impossible for the defendant to commit indecent liberties with a child, in that the "child" was in reality a 30-year-old undercover police officer. However, had the attendant circumstances been as the defendant believed them to be (*i.e.*, that he would engage in sexual activity with a 14-year-old victim), he would have been guilty of indecent liberties with a child. Thus, factual impossibility is not a defense to the attempt of indecent liberties with a child.

Next, legal impossibility arises only when the defendant does or intends to do an act that would not in fact be criminal. Here, what the defendant intended to do—engage in sexual activity with a minor—*is* a crime. Thus, legal impossibility is not a defense under the facts of the case. As a result, the conviction for attempted indecent liberties with a child should stand.

Attempted involuntary manslaughter: The defendant is correct that a conviction based on a charge of attempted involuntary manslaughter is precluded because there is no such crime.

To convict on a charge of attempt to commit a particular crime, the state must prove that the defendant had the specific intent to commit the crime. A person commits involuntary manslaughter by unintentionally, but with criminal negligence, causing the death of another. Thus, to prove an attempted involuntary manslaughter, the state would have to prove that the defendant had the specific intent to commit a criminally negligent act, and that is logically impossible. (In contrast, attempted voluntary manslaughter could be committed, as that crime requires an intentional killing.) As a result, the defendant is correct—there is no crime of attempted involuntary manslaughter.

If the defendant acted with specific intent to kill Kim, he should have been charged with attempted murder. If he did not act with the specific intent to murder Kim, other lesser charges (*e.g.*, battery) may have been appropriate.

Entrapment: The defense of entrapment will likely fail. At issue is whether the criminal plan originated with the law enforcement officers.

To succeed with an entrapment defense, it must be shown that: (i) the criminal design originated with the law enforcement officers; and (ii) in most states, the defendant was not predisposed to commit the crime prior to the initial contact by the government. Merely providing an opportunity to commit the crime is not entrapment. In the instant case, the facts state that the initial contact occurred on a website that targeted teenagers. Additionally, it appears that Defendant may have led Kim into asking him to come to State A by asking if she intended to fulfill her desire to be tickled with feathers. Furthermore, nothing in the facts indicates that the correspondence included any encouragement from Kim urging defendant to continue on with the criminal plan. Thus, on the whole, it does not appear that an entrapment defense would be successful.

QUESTION 4

Bob physically abused Amber throughout their six-year marriage. Amber was reluctant to contact the police. However, Amber recently reported the abuse to her neighbor, Charlie.

The following day, Charlie heard Amber screaming from her apartment. Charlie broke through Amber's door. Charlie saw Bob hitting Amber. Charlie pulled out his handgun and ordered Bob to stop. Instead, Bob ignored Charlie and raised his hand to hit Amber again. Charlie shot Bob in the leg to disable him.

Bob writhed in pain and begged Amber to call for an ambulance. Charlie set the gun on the mantel and grabbed the phone. Amber picked up the gun and shot Bob in the head, killing him.

Amber told Charlie not to call the police. She asked for help in disposing of Bob's body. Charlie placed Bob's body in the trunk of his car. Charlie disposed of the body in a nearby lake.

The police found Bob's body and went to Amber's home to investigate. After waiving her *Miranda* rights, Amber confessed to killing Bob. Amber told the police that Charlie also shot Bob and helped her dispose of the body.

The police applied for and received a warrant for Charlie's arrest. The police arrested Charlie while he was driving his car to work. The police searched his car and found a gun in the glove box and blood in the trunk of his car. DNA tests matched Bob's blood with the

blood in the trunk. Ballistic tests showed that the gun found in the glove box fired the bullets that killed Bob.

1.   **Discuss the crimes Amber could be charged with and any defenses she may raise.**

2.   **Discuss the crimes Charlie could be charged with and any defenses he may raise.**

3.   **Discuss the constitutional issues that arise as a result of the search of Charlie's car.**

ANSWER TO QUESTION 4

1.   Amber could be charged with voluntary manslaughter. At issue is whether a recent serious battery is adequate provocation to reduce what otherwise would be murder to voluntary manslaughter.

At common law, murder is the unlawful killing of a human being with malice aforethought. Malice can be shown by: (i) the intent to kill; (ii) the intent to inflict great bodily injury; (iii) a reckless indifference to an unjustifiably high risk to human life; or (iv) the intent to commit a felony. However, if the defendant acts with adequate provocation—provocation that would arouse a sudden and intense passion in the mind of an ordinary person such as to cause him to lose self-control—the killing is reduced to voluntary manslaughter. Being subjected to a serious battery is generally considered to be adequate provocation.

Here, Amber's acts probably show the intent to kill, in that she shot Bob in the head; if Amber were to claim the act was unintentional, pointing a loaded gun and firing it at another show a reckless indifference to human life. In either case, the definition of malice was met. However, the facts state that Amber shot Bob shortly after Bob beat her, and that Bob had abused Amber throughout their six-year marriage. Considering this abuse, Amber likely will be deemed to have acted in the "heat of sudden passion." As a result, Amber's criminal liability is reduced to voluntary manslaughter.

If Amber were to attempt to claim self-defense, she would be unsuccessful. At issue is whether a defendant may claim self-defense (and use deadly force) when the threat had already passed. Generally, deadly force may be used when the defendant is (i) without fault; (ii) confronted with unlawful force; and (iii) threatened with imminent death or great bodily harm. The threat must be a present one—there is no right to use deadly force when the attacker has no present ability to carry out the threat. In the instant case, Amber would have been justified in using deadly force had Bob been beating her. However, Bob had already been shot, and he was lying on the floor moaning when Amber killed him. Clearly, he was no longer able to carry out the threat; thus, the claim of self-defense must fail.

Amber may also attempt to raise some sort of diminished capacity defense based on her six years of abuse. Some states recognize the defense of "diminished capacity," under which the defendant may assert that, as a result of a mental defect (*e.g.,* a personality disorder) short of insanity, the defendant could not form the intent required for the crime. Here, Amber would argue that the years of abuse affected her ability to correctly perceive the threat that Bob posed. However, this would not affect the crimes with which she could be charged, as such a defense would have to be raised at trial by Amber, and most jurisdictions would place the burden of proof on her at trial.

2.   Charlie's crimes could include battery, accessory after the fact, and obstruction of justice. The issue is a factual one—whether Charlie was justified in shooting Bob in the leg.

Charlie could not be successfully charged with battery. Battery is an intentional, unlawful application of force to the victim's person. Charlie would successfully overcome a battery charge by raising the defense of a third person. A defendant may use deadly physical force if necessary to defend a third person who is in immediate danger of an unlawful deadly attack. Charlie's use of force was justified based on his observation that Amber was injured and continued to be in a dangerous situation. Moreover, Charlie had been given information relating to Bob's violent nature prior to witnessing the assault. It is both objectively and subjectively reasonable to believe that Charlie thought that Bob was engaging in an unlawful deadly attack. Thus, it appears that application of force by Charlie was not unlawful, and he should not be charged with battery.

However, Charlie could be charged as an accessory after the fact, and he does not have a defense to that crime. The elements of accessory after the fact include: A person, knowing another has committed a completed felony, renders aid to the felon personally to prevent apprehension, prosecution, or conviction. Charlie is responsible for the crime of accessory after the fact for disposing of Bob's corpse.

3.   The search of Charlie's car was lawful because the arrest of Charlie is lawful, given that an arrest warrant had been issued. At issue is how intrusive a search, if any, is allowed for a search incident to arrest.

When a suspect is lawfully arrested, the police may search his person without first obtaining a warrant. This search is known as a search incident to an arrest. Such a search must be limited to searching the person or areas within the person's wingspan. The police are allowed to conduct such searches to remove any weapons that the arrestee might use to resist or escape and to seize any evidence on the arrestee's person in order to prevent its concealment or destruction.

When an arrestee is seized in a car, the search incident to arrest may include the entire passenger area, including the glove compartment and any containers found within the car. Therefore, the gun located in the glove compartment will be admissible in Charlie's trial.

The automobile exception to the warrant requirement would also operate to allow the officers to legally search and seize any evidence found within the trunk of the vehicle. If the police have probable cause to believe that the vehicle contains contraband or the fruits, instrumentalities, or evidence of crime, they may search the vehicle without a warrant.

The automobile exception to the warrant requirement relates to any vehicle moving or temporarily stopped. As a general rule, a warrantless search of a vehicle may properly extend to any portion of the entire vehicle where the items for which there is probable cause to search may reasonably be found. Here, Amber's statements, coupled with the gun found during the search incident to arrest, provide the probable cause necessary to make the warrantless entry into the motor vehicle trunk. Therefore, the blood located in the trunk is admissible.

The blood may also be admissible were the officers to testify that they searched the trunk pursuant to an inventory policy. Generally, the police may conduct a warrantless inventory search of any property taken into their custody. Such a search must be executed in good faith and pursuant to an established policy. The search may not be a pretext to investigate for evidence of a crime. The reasonableness of such a search arises from the important governmental interests of protecting the owner's property, protecting the state against claims for damaging or losing such property, and guarding the police from danger (from articles such as weapons in the vehicle).

QUESTION 5

Throughout the spring, a number of convenience stores in Any County had been the victims of armed robberies, many of which appeared to be related. With the fall election only six months away, detectives were under a great deal of pressure to identify and arrest the perpetrators of these armed robberies. Thus they were not particularly pleased to discover that Jason, a 17-year-old high school senior, would be "interning" at their offices as part of his school's spring job-interest program for seniors. Pursuant to the agreement between the school and the detectives' unit, Jason was to ride along with detectives and participate in their daily activities, as long as he was well away from any foreseeable danger.

One Tuesday morning, Jason was assigned to ride shotgun with Detective Katz as he went on patrol. Detective Katz, like all other detectives in the department, wore street clothes rather than a uniform and drove an unmarked car. As Detective Katz was cruising through a rough area of town, looking for anything amiss, he spotted a late model sedan parked in the lot of a seedy motel. When he ran a routine license check on the vehicle, it came up belonging to an SUV rather than a sedan; thus he called for backup, got out of his car to get a better look, and instructed Jason to remain in the vehicle.

As Detective Katz approached the sedan, an enormous man burst out of one of the motel units shouting, "Keep away from my car, you [expletive]." Detective Katz identified himself as a police officer, which drew more angry comments from the large man (whose name was later determined to be Stephen, a/k/a "The Moose," Meyers). Backup arrived almost immediately and, with two additional detectives helping Detective Katz, Jason ignored Detective Katz's instructions and left the police car to check out the sedan. While the three detectives were distracted, Jason noted that the sedan's trunk was unlocked, opened it, and was stunned to see a number of guns, ski masks, and a variety of clothing. A shout to the detectives brought them running to see what he had found. When he saw what was in the trunk, Detective Katz instructed the other two detectives to take possession of the items in the trunk, then he arrested Meyers for the armed robberies of seven convenience stores. As he was being led to the patrol car, Meyers shouted to the detectives to "leave my stuff alone; it's mine, and you can't touch it." The detectives subsequently confirmed that the sedan was titled in Meyers's name.

1.(a) Discuss the validity of Meyers's arrest for the robberies based on the facts above. (Do not consider pretrial motions or evidentiary matters).

(b) To ensure the admissibility of any statements which Meyers might make, what action, if any, must the detectives take before questioning Meyers?

(c) Would your answer to (b) change if the detectives had elected to question Meyers on the street, before taking him into custody?

2.   Assume that you have been appointed to represent Meyers. The state has indicated that at trial it intends to introduce (a) the items found in the trunk of Meyers's car; and (b) Meyers's statements at the scene regarding ownership of the vehicle and ownership of the items in the trunk.

What pretrial motions would you file on behalf of Meyers? For any motions that you would file, discuss: (i) the basis for the motion; (ii) the state's anticipated arguments against the motion; and (iii) the state's burden as to each issue raised. (In answering this question, do not consider impeachment evidence.)

ANSWER TO QUESTION 5

1.(a)   Meyers's arrest for the robberies probably was invalid. At issue is whether the police had probable cause to arrest Meyers. Under the Fourth Amendment to the United States Constitution, which is applicable to the states through the Due Process Clause of the Fourteenth Amendment, to be valid, a search or seizure must be reasonable. An arrest is a seizure of the person. For an arrest made in a public place to be reasonable, the arresting officer must have reasonable cause to believe that a felony has been committed and that the person before him has committed the felony. Here, the police probably did not have reasonable cause to suspect that Meyers committed the armed robberies. Although they knew that there had been a string of armed robberies and that Meyers's sedan had an improper plate, nothing in the sedan's trunk—the clothes, ski masks, and guns—linked Meyers to the robberies. The items are highly suspicious and warranted further investigation (*e.g.,* there are few legitimate uses for ski masks in springtime), but because nothing in the facts indicates that the robbers wore ski masks or used the type of guns found in Meyers's trunk, there is nothing here giving reasonable cause for Meyers's arrest.

(b)   To ensure that Meyers's statements are admissible, the police must give Meyers *Miranda* warnings and must obtain a valid waiver of Meyers's Fifth Amendment rights. The Fifth Amendment, which is applicable to the states through the Due Process Clause of the Fourteenth Amendment, guarantees a freedom against compelled self-incrimination. To protect this right, the Supreme Court requires police to inform detainees of their rights—via *Miranda* warnings—before conducting a custodial interrogation. The warnings are that the detainee has a right to remain silent, that anything he says can be used against him in court, that he has a right to an attorney, and that if he cannot afford an attorney, one will be appointed for him if he so desires. Statements obtained as a result of a custodial interrogation conducted without giving the warnings generally are inadmissable. Thus, the police must give Meyers *Miranda* warnings.

(c)   If the police questioned Meyers on the street without taking him into custody, the answer would change. The Supreme Court requires *Miranda* warnings only before custodial interrogations. Such warnings are not necessary when the interrogation is not custodial. Thus, if the detectives had questioned Meyers before taking him into custody, they need not have given him any warnings.

2.(a)   I would make a pretrial motion to have the items found in the trunk suppressed. At issue is whether there was a valid search of the car's trunk. If the government conducts a warrantless search and the search is not within one of the recognized exceptions to the warrant requirement, any evidence found during the search will be suppressed under the Supreme Court's exclusionary rule.

We would first argue that opening the sedan's trunk constituted a warrantless, illegal search. The state would likely counter, arguing that the Fourth Amendment proscribes only government conduct and here the trunk was opened by Jason, a private citizen. We could argue that because Jason was riding around with the police as an "intern," his actions should be attributed to the police. However, the government can counterargue that Jason's actions did not constitute government action because Jason is a high school student and not a police officer, the agreement with the school was that Jason was to stay well away from foreseeable danger, and Detective Katz specifically told Jason to stay in the car; he did not direct Jason to open the trunk. The state would have the burden of showing that the search was proper.

If we prevail in showing that Jason's conduct should be attributed to the police, the state will argue that the search of the trunk was valid under the automobile exception to the warrant requirement. Under the automobile exception, the police may search a vehicle without a warrant if they have probable cause to believe that the automobile contains fruits, instrumentalities, or evidence of a crime. The police would argue that because the car had an improper license plate, they had probable cause to search the car for evidence that it was stolen.

If the state is successful in either argument above, it will then have to argue that once the trunk was legitimately opened, the items within the trunk were seizable under the plain view exception. Police may seize evidence under this exception if they are legitimately on the premises where the evidence is found, the evidence is in plain view, and the police have probable cause to believe that the evidence is seizable (*i.e.,* that it is evidence, contraband, or the fruit or instrumentality of a crime).

(b)   I would move to have the statements made at the scene suppressed on the ground that they were obtained without *Miranda* warnings. The state will probably argue that no *Miranda* warnings were needed because Meyers's statements were not made in response to police interrogation (*see* above) and were not otherwise coerced. The state would have to show that at the time Meyers made his statement, a reasonable person under the circumstances would feel free to leave.

QUESTION 6

Defendant and Friend were on a hunting trip together. One evening, while watching television in their hunting cabin, Defendant decided to scare Friend, who had fallen asleep in his chair. Defendant loaded his rifle and aimed it at a lamp that was on a table just behind the chair in which Friend was sleeping. Just as Defendant pulled the trigger to shoot the lamp, Friend suddenly sat up and moved into the line of fire. Defendant's bullet hit Friend in the shoulder and seriously wounded him.

Defendant loaded Friend into his car and sped off toward the nearest hospital, which was 15 minutes away. En route, Defendant hit a pothole, lost control of his car, and collided with a telephone pole. Defendant was seriously injured and Friend suffered further injuries. The accident occurred on a lightly traveled country road, and no other vehicle passed by for 45 minutes.

By the time help arrived, Friend was dead. An autopsy established that Friend bled to death as a result of the combined impact of the gunshot wound and the injuries suffered in the car crash. The coroner concluded that the gunshot wound alone would not have been fatal had Friend received medical treatment within a half hour of the shooting.

Murder is defined as "a killing with malice aforethought." In this jurisdiction, second-degree murder is "all murder that is not deliberate or premeditated." Defendant has been charged with second-degree murder on account of his shooting Friend and Friend's subsequent death.

Is Defendant guilty of second-degree murder? Explain.

July 2007

ANSWER TO QUESTION 6

Defendant is guilty of second-degree murder. At issue is the mens rea for second-degree murder and when an intervening event will relieve a defendant from criminal liability.

Murder is defined in the jurisdiction as a "killing with malice aforethought," with second-degree murder being defined as "all murder that is not deliberate or premeditated." Thus, in this jurisdiction, second-degree murder is a killing done with a reckless indifference to an unjustifiably high risk to human life (or with the intent to commit a felony or to inflict great bodily injury, not relevant here). In the instant case, Defendant shot a rifle in the close proximity of Friend in order to scare him (by attempting to hit a lamp that was "just behind" the chair in which Friend was sleeping). Defendant exhibited a reckless indifference to an unjustifiably high risk to human life by pointing and shooting a rifle at a target behind Friend, given the high risk that Friend would be killed by such an act.

Next, the defendant's act must be the proximate cause of the victim's death; a "but for" test is applied (but for the defendant's conduct, the victim would not have died). An intervening act will shield the defendant from criminal liability when the intervening act is mere coincidence or unforeseeable. The intervening act will then be deemed to be the actual, proximate cause of the victim's death. In the instant case, but for Defendant's unlawful act of shooting Friend, there would have been no need to attempt to rush Friend to the hospital, during which attempt Friend was further injured in a car accident. It is also foreseeable that one would get into an accident while rushing another to the hospital for life-saving care. Furthermore, the accident does not appear to have occurred in any unusual manner. Finally, there is testimony that both the accident and the gunshot wound contributed to Friend's death. Thus, Defendant was a proximate cause of Friend's death.

Given that Defendant had a sufficient mens rea for second-degree murder and that Defendant was the proximate cause of Friend's death, Defendant may be convicted of second-degree murder.

QUESTION 7

On April 10, a convenience store was robbed by someone carrying a gun. The store's video camera caught the robbery on tape. The tape was shown on the evening news.

On April 11, an anonymous caller contacted the police saying, "I saw that tape of the robbery. The robber kind of looks like Student. He's an 18-year-old student at the high school."

On April 12, two police officers took the tape to the high school and showed it to the principal, who said, "It could be Student. It's hard to tell because the tape is not clear." The tape was also shown to Student's homeroom teacher, who said, "It might be him, but I couldn't say for sure."

Later that day, the police officers went to the store where Student works after school. They asked the manager if they could talk with Student, who was called to the manager's office. The police introduced themselves to Student and said, "We'd like to talk to you." They walked with Student into the manager's office and shut the door. One police officer sat behind the manager's desk; the other, in full uniform with his revolver visible, sat near the door. Student sat between them. The manager's office measures eight feet by ten feet.

The police officers told Student they wanted to ask him some questions about the convenience store robbery on April 10. Student said he knew nothing about a robbery. He continued to deny that he had any knowledge of the robbery for about 20 minutes. Student did not ask to leave, and neither police officer told Student he was free to leave.

After about 20 minutes, the police officers told Student that they had a videotape of the robbery and that they had shown it to three people, all of whom positively identified Student as the robber.

Student said nothing for a few minutes. One of the police officers then said, "You know, if we can tell the prosecutor that you cooperated, she might go a lot easier on you. I'd hate to see you end up doing a long stretch in prison. Let's just say it's not a nice place." Student then blurted out, "I did the robbery. I used a little air gun."

Immediately after Student made that statement, the police officers informed Student that he was under arrest for the robbery of the convenience store. They read him his *Miranda* rights. Student stated he understood his *Miranda* rights and told the police officers that he was not going to say anything more to them. The police officers placed Student in handcuffs and took him to the police station where he was booked for armed robbery.

Student had had two earlier brushes with the law. When he was 16, he had been found delinquent in juvenile court for auto theft and had been placed on supervision for one year. When he was 17, he had received a ticket for underage drinking and had paid a fine of $150. He is a "C" student, but his teachers believe he is an "underachiever."

Student's defense attorney has filed a motion to suppress Student's statements on three grounds:

(1) Student's statements were obtained in violation of Student's Fourth Amendment rights.

(2) Student's statements were obtained in violation of his *Miranda* rights.

(3) Student's confession was not voluntary.

How should the trial court rule on each of the grounds in the motion to suppress? Explain.

ANSWER TO QUESTION 7

(1) The trial court should deny the motion to suppress based on the Fourth Amendment. At issue is whether Student was unreasonably seized.

The Fourth Amendment, which is applicable to the states through the Due Process Clause of the Fourteenth Amendment, prohibits unreasonable searches and seizures. Generally, a seizure must be pursuant to a warrant or at least be based on probable cause. Here, Student probably was seized. The officers asked him to go into his manager's office to talk with them. Moreover, the police did not have a warrant to make the seizure, nor did they have probable cause. However, the police may make an investigatory stop without a warrant and without probable cause if they have reasonable suspicion, based on articulable facts of criminal activity. Here, three people said that the person seen committing the robbery on the videotape could be Student. While the identifications probably were not positive enough to amount to probable cause, they were likely sufficient to give rise to reasonable suspicion to investigate. Thus, the seizure was reasonable under the Fourth Amendment.

(2)   The motion to suppress based on *Miranda* presents a very close question, with no certain result. At issue is whether Student was in custody when he was being interrogated.

To offset the coercive effects of police interrogation, the Supreme Court requires police to give detainees certain warnings (*e.g.*, that they have a right to remain silent and to an attorney) before conducting any custodial interrogation. That Student was interrogated is not in doubt—the officers asked him questions about the robbery. The only question here is whether Student was in custody. Whether a person is in custody is determined by whether a reasonable person would feel free to leave in the situation. Here, we have facts that go both ways. On the one hand, the officers brought Student into a small office, and a uniformed officer with a gun was stationed between Student and the door. Moreover, the officers did not tell Student that he was free to go at any time. On the other hand, the officers did not place Student under arrest; they merely told him that they wanted to talk to him. They did not restrain Student with handcuffs or take him to the police station. The result here remains very much an open question with there being no clear result.

(3)   The motion to suppress Student's confession based on voluntariness should also be denied. An involuntary confession will be suppressed as a violation of the Due Process Clause of the Fourteenth Amendment. Whether a confession is involuntary is determined under the totality of the circumstances. Here, two police officers questioned Student in a small room, and one was armed and between Student and the door. Moreover, the officers lied to Student about the strength of their evidence (telling him that three people had positively identified him when in fact no one was sure if it was Student). They also told him that prison would not be good for him.

On the other hand, Student seems to have possessed at least average intelligence (he was a C student), he had experience with the criminal justice system, he was an adult, and the interview was relatively brief (30 minutes). Given the latter facts, a court would probably find the confession voluntary. Thus, the motion should be denied.

QUESTION 1

Pat was remodeling his restaurant, which featured a display case from which customers could select their steaks. On October 1, 1994, Pat signed a contract with Darwin Meat-keepers for installation, by June 1995, of a Darwin A-34 meat display case. The price was $15,000 and the contract contained a liquidated damages clause which specified payment of $2,000 if Darwin failed to perform. The specifications were incorporated, by Pat's architect, in the remodeling plans.

On October 30, 1994, Darwin sent Pat a letter saying they had stopped making the components of the A-34; the letter asked Pat to promptly specify another model. Pat, who was in the middle of a dispute with a business partner, did not respond until December 1. On that date he wrote Darwin, expressing anger that he had not been told in September of the discontinuance of the A-34, and said he planned to consult his attorney.

Pat consulted your firm and asked whether he is entitled to require Darwin to install an A-34. You have discovered that it would cost $4,500 to redesign the restaurant to accommodate another display case. Plumbing would also need to be redone. Darwin has asserted that if Pat had responded promptly, they could have set the components for a Model A-34 aside for him, but that by December 1 they had promised all of their inventory of A-34 parts to other customers, and that it is impractical for them to specially manufacture parts for an additional unit at this late date.

Discuss the arguments and defenses which Darwin is likely to raise in opposing a suit for specific performance, including their assertion that Pat's own delay is the source of his problem. You can assume the validity of the contract, that Darwin has repudiated it, and that Pat has chosen to treat the repudiation as a breach. You can also assume that the contract is one primarily for installation services, and not for the sale of goods, even though the unavailability of parts was a reason for repudiation.

ANSWER TO QUESTION 1

Darwin is likely to raise not only Pat's delay as a defense to specific performance, but also the adequacy of a remedy at law and that enforcement is not feasible.

A plaintiff seeking specific performance of a contract must prove six things: (i) that a contract exists, (ii) all contractual conditions have been fulfilled, (iii) the legal remedy is inadequate, (iv) mutuality of remedy exists, (v) enforcement is feasible, and (vi) no defenses are available to the defendant.

Here, the facts specify that there is an enforceable contract between Darwin and Pat and that there has been a breach (indicating that Pat has fulfilled all conditions precedent to Darwin's performance). Mutuality also is present, because the court could ensure Pat's performance by ordering him to pay for the case as agreed. However, Pat may have trouble proving the other three elements of his case.

If damages provide an adequate remedy, specific performance will not be granted. Here, Pat will argue that damages at law cannot make him whole because no one besides Darwin can install and provide the parts for a Darwin A-34 meat display case. Darwin, however, will likely argue that there is an adequate remedy at law, either because the contract contains a liquidated damages clause or because for $4,500 and the cost of replumbing Pat can redesign his restaurant to accept Darwin's new meat display case. The liquidated damages clause argument, however, will probably fail because absent language in the clause clearly making the clause the nonbreaching party's only remedy, the courts typically treat a liquidated damages clause only as an alternative remedy, not necessarily making the remedy at law adequate. It seems likely, though, that Darwin would prevail on the argument that ordinary damages is an adequate remedy at law, provided the delay does not cause further damages that cannot adequately be assessed.

Darwin will also argue that enforcement is not feasible. The facts state that this contract is to be considered one primarily for installation services. As a rule, courts will not grant specific performance of a contract for services, both because forced service is prohibited by the Constitution and because of problems the courts would have in supervising the performance. Darwin could probably successfully defend against Pat's suit on this ground alone.

Finally, Darwin will claim that the defense of laches prevents a grant of specific performance here. Laches is an equitable defense available when one party delays in enforcing his rights and the delay causes prejudice to the other party. Here, Darwin claims that had Pat responded to Darwin's October 30 letter, Darwin could have set aside components for Pat's A-34 model, but having not heard from Pat, Darwin sold the components to other customers. Darwin would further claim that Pat's dispute with a business partner does not justify his failure to respond to Darwin; a letter or phone call by Pat asserting his contractual right to an A-34 case would have taken but a moment.

QUESTION 2

Paul owned two items which had once belonged to Theodore Roosevelt: a ceremonial sword and a book of poetry in which Roosevelt had written his name and made marginal notes. In 1994, Paul was induced by fraud to sell the sword and book to Denise. (He only recently discovered the fraud; the details of the fraud are unimportant to this question, but that there was fraud is certain, and easily proved. Until Paul discovered the fraud, no one had reason to doubt Denise's integrity.) In August 1994, Denise gave the book of poetry (worth $4,000) to the Community Museum, hoping to increase her standing in the community. In the same month she sold the sword to Collector for $25,000, receiving a certified check. She indorsed the check to Builder as a final payment on construction of a cottage on her lakeside lot. The lot was worth $25,000 and the modest cottage cost $50,000. Improvements to county roads in the area have led to an increase in values of properties, and the property, improved by the cottage, is now worth $125,000. Denise is unlikely to be able to enjoy the increase in value. She has been implicated in a series of frauds and is almost certainly broke—owing much more than she has.

Paul has come to you and has asked whether he has any claims:

1. **Against Museum to recover the book of poetry? Explain.**

2. **Against Collector to recover the sword? Explain.**

3. **Against Builder to get the money Denise got for the sword and paid to Builder? Explain.**

4. **Against Denise? Explain.**

ANSWER TO QUESTION 2

1. ***Paul v. Museum***. Paul may recover the book of poetry from the museum under a constructive trust theory. At issue is whether a seller of goods sold pursuant to fraud can recover the goods from a donee of the defrauder.

A constructive trust is an equitable remedy imposed by courts to prevent unjust enrichment when a wrongdoer has gained title to property through misappropriation. The person holding the ill-gotten property is declared a trustee with the sole duty of conveying the property to the plaintiff. A constructive trust will be imposed when a defendant has title to property and retention of the property will unjustly enrich the defendant. A number of courts also require that the remedy at law be inadequate. There is no requirement that the defendant/trustee be the wrongdoer—the trust can be imposed not only on property in the hands of the wrongdoer, but also on property traceable to ill-gotten property in the hands of third parties who would be unjustly enriched by retention of the property.

Imposition of a constructive trust is appropriate here. Denise gained title to the book of poetry through fraud. The museum now has the ill-gotten book and would be unjustly enriched if allowed to keep it, since the museum was a donee (*i.e.*, it gave nothing in exchange for the book). The remedy at law would also be inadequate because the book is unique, having Roosevelt's autograph and notes in it. Thus, the book may be recovered from the museum.

2. ***Paul v. Collector***. Paul may not recover the sword from Collector. At issue is whether a defrauded seller of goods may recover them from a bona fide purchaser.

While Denise obtained the sword from Paul through fraud, a constructive trust may not be imposed against Collector—the third party holding the sword—because Collector is a bona fide purchaser who purchased without notice of the fraud. Bona fide purchasers cut off equitable rights in property. When there is a bona fide purchaser, a constructive trust may not be imposed because the bona fide purchaser has not been unjustly enriched, having paid for the property. However, Paul is not without a remedy as to the sword; as will be discussed below, Paul can seek damages from Denise.

3. ***Paul v. Builder***. Paul may not recover from Builder for much the same reason that Paul cannot recover from Collector. The issue here is similar to the issue in Paul's case against Collector, but here Paul is trying to reach proceeds of the ill-gotten property rather than the property itself.

A constructive trust is not limited to the exact property that was misappropriated; through tracing, it may be imposed on proceeds of the misappropriated property. Here, the proceeds of the misappropriated property—the $25,000 certified check—may be traced to Builder, since Denise sold the misappropriated sword to Collector in exchange for Collector's $25,000 check and then transferred the check to Builder. However, like Collector, Builder is a good faith transferee and will not be unjustly enriched if allowed to retain the check (or its proceeds, if it has been cashed), because Builder gave value for the check: the improvements made to Denise's cottage. Thus, a constructive trust may not be imposed on the check or its proceeds.

4. ***Paul v. Denise***. Paul can recover the value of the sword from Denise through imposition of an equitable lien on Denise's cottage. At issue is whether a defrauded seller can impose a lien on property improved with the proceeds of ill-gotten property.

Since Denise defrauded Paul into selling the sword, Paul may recover damages from Denise. However, because Denise is insolvent, an action for damages at law would not adequately protect Paul. Neither may a constructive trust be imposed here, because a constructive trust is not available when proceeds of ill-gotten property are used to improve property of the defendant; rather, an equitable lien is the appropriate remedy under these circumstances.

An equitable lien is an equitable charge on property imposed to prevent unjust enrichment. It is available when a plaintiff can show: (i) a wrongdoer has misappropriated the plaintiff's money or property; (ii) the plaintiff's money or property can be traced to property owned by the defendant; (iii) retention of the property by the defendant would result in unjust enrichment; and (iv) (in some courts) the remedy at law is inadequate. The equitable lienholder is treated as other lienholders—he has an interest in the property into which his money or property can be traced that may be foreclosed to satisfy the lien ahead of general creditors. The lien is valid only to the extent of the value of the money or property taken, although a deficiency judgment may be obtained if the foreclosure sale does not satisfy the lien.

Here, Denise used the proceeds of the sale of the sword to improve her cottage, and she would be unjustly enriched if allowed to retain the value of the sword. As indicated above, Paul's remedy at law is inadequate because Denise is insolvent. Thus, Paul may impose an equitable lien on Denise's cottage to the extent of the value of the sword. Paul is not entitled to recover, however, the increased value of the cottage due to the improvements; he is limited to recovering the value of the sword.

QUESTION 3

You represent Metalco. Six months ago, Metalco signed a one-year contract with Autobody in which Metalco agreed to re-chrome corroded bumpers and exhaust pipes on cars being repaired by Autobody. The contract provided that Metalco would accomplish the work within seven days of receipt of the part. The contract contains a liquidated damages provision which said that Metalco agreed to pay Autobody $5 per day for parts not completed within the seven-day period, up to a maximum of $35 per part.

All went well for four months, and then two months ago Metalco began consistently to fall behind—although they did pay the $5 per day late charge without complaint. Autobody has asserted that the late delivery of the re-chromed parts is causing a problem; late delivery of re-chromed parts means Autobody must store vehicles for several days after they are otherwise repaired. Customer goodwill has suffered, and Autobody asserts that the financial losses exceed $5 per day. Autobody apparently has a more lucrative contract with another repair shop, and is choosing to perform the other contract first.

Autobody has filed an action for preliminary relief, seeking specific performance. The action alleges that Metalco has the capacity to fulfill the contract requirements and is the only available supplier of such services. The action asks that Metalco be required to begin adhering to the repair schedule specified in the agreement.

Metalco has admitted that they often choose to defer Autobody work, because at present they have more work to do than they can get done on time, and they try to spread the burden of delay around to all their customers.

Is Autobody entitled to specific performance? Explain. Include in your answer a discussion and evaluation of the likelihood of success of any defenses and objections to Autobody's action which could be raised by Metalco.

ANSWER TO QUESTION 3

Autobody probably cannot get preliminary relief in its action for specific performance.

The first issue to be resolved here is what preliminary remedy Autobody is seeking. An order for specific performance will not be granted until after a trial on the merits; it cannot be granted as preliminary relief. Autobody can seek, however, a preliminary injunction to prevent injury before the trial can be held.

Where a party wants to preserve the status quo until a full trial on the merits of his action can be held, he may apply to the court for a preliminary injunction. The court will then hold a hearing, and if the moving party can show that he is likely to prevail on the merits and that he will suffer irreparable injury if the preliminary injunction is not granted (*i.e.*, that he will suffer harm before a permanent order is entered), the court will grant the preliminary order, instructing the nonmoving party to do or cease doing whatever is necessary to preserve the status quo. In drastic circumstances, the court may grant such an injunction without notice to the other party and an adversarial hearing (in which case it is called a temporary restraining order or "TRO"), but to obtain a TRO the plaintiff must make a strong showing, in addition to the above, of why notice and an adversarial hearing should not be required.

Here, Autobody probably will not be granted a preliminary order for relief. While it seems that Autobody is suffering irreparable harm (customer goodwill is suffering), it is doubtful that Autobody can succeed on the merits at trial.

Specific performance will be granted only if it can be shown that (i) a contract exists, (ii) all contractual conditions have been fulfilled, (iii) the legal remedy is inadequate, (iv) mutuality of remedy exists, (v) enforcement is feasible, and (vi) no defenses are available to the defendant. A contract certainly exists here, and all contractual conditions can be fulfilled. Mutuality of remedy is not a problem, and no defense appears to be available.

It also seems likely that a court would find that there is no adequate remedy at law. Metalco would likely argue that the liquidated damages clause provides an adequate legal remedy, but this argument will fail. Unless a liquidated damages clause states that it is the exclusive remedy for breach, the courts treat it only as an alternative remedy that does not prevent application of equitable remedies. Moreover, money damages are not an adequate remedy here because the facts state that nobody else does re-chroming work.

It seems unlikely, however, that a court would find that specific performance is feasible, because the contract here is for services. A court generally will not order specific performance of a contract to perform services, both because it would be tantamount to slavery and because of difficulty in supervision. Thus, the action for specific performance will fail, and therefore the request for preliminary relief will also fail.

It should be noted that while the court will not grant specific performance under these facts, if Metalco does not have contracts with its other customers, the court could grant an injunction prohibiting Metalco from working on its other customers' work first, thus enticing Metalco to perform its contractual obligation to Autobody. But if Metalco's other customers have contracts similar to Autobody's contract, it is doubtful that the court would interfere with Metalco's attempt to "spread the burden of delay around to all their customers," as this seems like the fair thing to do, and equitable remedies are discretionary and are granted on the basis of fairness.

QUESTION 4

Larry was the trustee of an inter vivos trust which had been created by Mary naming Nick as the beneficiary. The trust contained $50,000. Unbeknownst to either Mary or Nick, Larry often "borrowed" small portions of the trust money when he ran short of cash, replacing it always within a week's time. You may assume that these "borrowings" were breaches of the fiduciary obligations Larry owed Mary and Nick.

In January 1996, Larry received a very hot tip from his friend Otto that the stock of Petroco would likely go up very fast and that Larry ought to invest as much as he could as quickly as he could. The lure was irresistible. On January 15, Larry "borrowed" $20,000 from the trust and deposited it into his checking account which already contained $10,000. That same day he wrote a check for $20,000 to his broker for 500 shares of Petroco stock for $40 a share, registered in his own name.

By January 25, the check to his broker had cleared and Larry had not replaced the $20,000 he "borrowed" from the trust. On that day, two things happened: 1) Mary and Nick discovered that $20,000 was missing from the trust and that Larry had bought the stock with it; and 2) the hot tip panned out, and the selling price of the stock was now $30,000 and rising.

Two days later, Roger, a judgment creditor with a judgment against Larry in the amount of $50,000, obtained a writ of garnishment and properly served it on the bank holding Larry's checking account. Larry, it turns out, has no other available assets besides the stock and the checking account. Fortunately, he has no other creditors.

1. **Suppose that Mary and Nick seek the actual stock (instead of a money judgment for $20,000) directly from Larry. Can they recover the more-valuable stock itself and, if so, on what basis? Explain.**

2. **Assume now that Mary and Nick were not able to move quickly enough and, during the delay, the stock price plummeted to zero. Since Larry has no assets other than the bank account, that has become their target. Assume that Roger's garnishment proceeding is a proper one and would have captured the bank account in the absence of Mary and Nick's later intervention. If Mary and Nick challenge Roger's rights to the bank account, who will prevail and to what extent? Explain.**

ANSWER TO QUESTION 4

1. Mary and Nick can recover the actual stock under a constructive trust theory.

A constructive trust is a judge-made equitable remedy designed to disgorge unjust enrichment. It is applied where the defendant has title to property that rightfully belongs to the plaintiff and, if the defendant were allowed to keep the property, he would be unjustly enriched. Some courts also require the plaintiff to show that there is no adequate remedy at law. If the remedy is imposed, the defendant is deemed to have been holding the property as a trustee for the plaintiff, and the defendant's sole duty now as trustee is to convey the property back to the plaintiff. Since the property is treated as always having been the plaintiff's property, the plaintiff takes the property free of claims of the defendant's creditors. The trust may be imposed not only on the specific property wrongfully taken from the plaintiff, but also on any property purchased solely with the proceeds of the property wrongfully taken.

All of the elements necessary to impose a constructive trust are present here. The facts state that Larry wrongfully took the $20,000, and he would certainly be unjustly enriched if allowed to keep the money. The main problem here is the tracing issue. The facts say that Larry placed the wrongfully taken $20,000 in a bank account with his own $10,000 and wrote a check from that account to purchase the shares. Thus, all of the stock might be treated as having been purchased with Mary and Nick's $20,000, or as few as half of the shares may be treated as having been purchased with the wrongfully taken money. In deciding how many shares were purchased with the wrongfully taken money, the court will have to impose some presumption (*e.g.*, pro rata; the wrongdoer acted honestly and used all of his own money first; first money in, first money out; last money in, first money out; the wrongdoer acted in the way most beneficial to the plaintiff; etc.). If the court decides that Nick and Mary own fewer than all of the shares, because some of their money was not used to purchase the stock, they may seek to impose an equitable lien on the bank account for whatever money of theirs is left in the account, as discussed below.

2.   If Mary and Nick were not able to move quickly enough, the stock is now worthless, and Larry has no other assets but the bank account, Mary and Nick should seek to impose an equitable lien on the bank account.

An equitable lien is imposed on the defendant's property to secure a debt where a wrongdoer has misappropriated the plaintiff's property under circumstances creating a debt or obligation to repay, the plaintiff's property can be traced to the defendant's property, and the defendant would be unjustly enriched if allowed to keep the property. Some courts require a showing that the legal remedy is inadequate. Unlike a constructive trust, an equitable lien may be imposed on property merely improved with the misappropriated property. When an equitable lien is imposed, the plaintiff is treated as having a lien on the property superior to all other interests except interests of bona fide purchasers.

An equitable lien may be imposed here on the bank account. The facts stipulate Larry wrongfully "borrowed" Mary and Nick's money; thus, Larry has an obligation to return the money. The money can be traced to Larry's bank account (the amount left in the account belonging to Mary and Nick, however, is questionable, as discussed above), and Larry would be unjustly enriched if allowed to keep the money. A judgment creditor is not considered a bona fide purchaser who will cut off equitable rights. Thus, the equitable lien may be imposed, and Mary and Nick will prevail over Roger to the extent that the money in the bank account can be traced to their money.

QUESTION 5

The city of Urban signed a contract six years ago with the Grizzlies, a minor league baseball team. The contract provided that the Grizzlies were to be the principal tenants in the

Urban Stadium for 10 years. The contract also provided that the city was to remodel the stadium (which was also used for other events).

Twenty-four hours ago, the city learned that the Grizzlies were planning to move to Metropolis, in an adjoining state. The attorney for the city appeared, 30 minutes ago, in the judge's chambers and is seeking a temporary restraining order to prevent the Grizzlies from moving any of their equipment out of the city or doing any other act to implement a plan to breach the stadium lease or its obligations to the city until a hearing can be held on a preliminary injunction to block the move. The city attorney, in addition to asserting the city's interests as owner of the Stadium, argued that irreparable harm would result to the vendors and area restaurants whose financial well-being depends on the Grizzlies. The attorney for the city indicated that he had not notified the Grizzlies' counsel of the motion for the TRO because he believed this would merely cause the team to hasten its efforts to depart for Metropolis.

You are the law clerk to the trial judge who is considering the motion. She has asked for your advice. The trial judge has told you that the affidavits seem to indicate that there is a good chance that the Grizzlies' departure would cause substantial financial losses to the community, but that it is not clear to her whether those losses can be considered. In addition, she does not understand how any possible inconvenience to the Grizzlies caused by waiting for the hearing on the preliminary injunction could be a factor in deciding on the TRO, since it is the irreparable harm to the plaintiff which should be the critical factor in considering whether or not to issue the order.

How should the judge rule? Explain.

ANSWER TO QUESTION 5

The judge should grant the temporary restraining order.

A temporary restraining order ("TRO") is an interlocutory injunction imposed to preserve the status quo between the parties until a preliminary hearing can be held. A TRO can be granted ex parte, without notice to the other party, where the moving party can make a strong showing of why notice and an adversarial hearing should not be held. In any case, the moving party must show that irreparable injury will occur before a trial on the merits may be held, and that it is probable that he will succeed on the merits. To succeed on the merits of an action for an injunction, the moving party must show: inadequacy of the legal remedy, a protectable right is about to be infringed, feasibility of enforcement, hardships balance in the movant's favor, and no defenses are available.

Imposition of a TRO would probably be proper here. It is questionable whether the attorney for the city has made a strong showing why notice should not be given to the Grizzlies; he merely asserted a belief that notice would cause the team to hasten their departure. Given the nature of this issue, however (trying to predict what a person might do), and the circumstances, this belief might well be enough because the TRO will be valid only until a hearing on notice can be held.

The city can also show that it is likely to prevail on the merits, since it can show the things necessary for a permanent injunction: the legal remedy would be inadequate because the damages resulting from the Grizzlies' departure would be very difficult to assess, the city has a protectable contract right to have the Grizzlies remain in the city, enforcement could easily be accomplished through a negative injunction prohibiting the Grizzlies' departure, and no defenses appear on the facts.

As far as the balance of hardships goes, it is proper to consider the hardship to local businesses as well as the hardship to the parties in determining whether to grant an injunction. Thus, to answer the judge's query, she can consider the loss to local businesses that will result from the Grizzlies' departure.

Finally, it seems likely that the city can show the necessary irreparable injury, at least when considering the harm to local businesses. The judge's assertion here, however, that only the plaintiff's injury is relevant, is wrong. In deciding whether to grant a TRO, the judge must balance the irreparable harm that the plaintiff will suffer if the injunction is not granted against the harm the defendant will suffer if the injunction is granted.

QUESTION 6

On January 1, 1993, it was a media splash when it hit the newspapers. The new magazine, *Fifty-Something Else*, would fill a media niche somewhere between *Modern Maturity* and *Sports Illustrated*. The concept attracted many writers and reporters with whom the new magazine contracted to develop stories about people in their 50s or above jumping out of airplanes, climbing mountains, wrestling alligators, and the like. Advertising by sports equipment manufacturers, health food suppliers, and upscale travel companies was selling like hotcakes. The magazine's wildly successful efforts to employ writers and to sell advertising were themselves something of a media sensation and were the subject of news stories in widely read newspapers. The stock of Bengay Publishers, the magazine's owner, soared on the stock exchange, and that was news too. The magazine went on the newsstands on January 1, 1994.

It all began to unravel in December 1995 when Gargantuan Media Enterprises, Inc., the owner of a trademark in the name of the old TV show "Thirty Something," sued the magazine for trademark infringement, seeking a preliminary injunction and damages.

Assume that the trademark is valid. Further assume that it is a very close question whether publication of the magazine named *Fifty-Something Else* without permission from Gargantuan could be found to infringe Gargantuan's trademark (differences in the allegedly infringing name and in the publishing media, among other things, could account for the closeness of the infringement question).

1. **Bengay Publishers has asserted that, whatever the validity of Gargantuan's claim on the merits, it is not entitled to a preliminary injunction. How should the court rule? Explain.**

2. **Bengay Publishers has moved to dismiss the lawsuit, asserting that Gargantuan's claim to an injunction is barred by laches. Assume that the statute of limitations for trademark infringement is four years. How should the court rule? Explain.**

ANSWER TO QUESTION 6

1.   The court should probably deny Gargantuan's request for a preliminary injunction. At issue is whether Gargantuan can prove all of the elements necessary to obtain preliminary injunctive relief.

To obtain a preliminary injunction, a plaintiff must show two things: (i) if the injunction is not granted, he will suffer irreparable injury before a trial on the merits can be held; and (ii) there is a substantial likelihood that the plaintiff will succeed on the merits of his claim at trial. Here Gargantuan cannot make either showing.

Gargantuan cannot show a sufficient irreparable harm. Gargantuan will argue that if the injunction is not granted, its trademark will be diluted before a trial on the merits can be held. Since it is difficult to gauge the effect of such dilution, and probably even more difficult to counter the effects of such dilution, there may be some irreparable injury present. However, a strong counterargument might be made that because Gargantuan has not used its trademark for some time (it is from an old television show), in truth, Gargantuan is suffering little or no harm. It is difficult to say which of these two arguments would prevail, and also unnecessary, since Gargantuan clearly cannot show that the harm that it will avoid by the grant of the injunction outweighs the harm that Bengay Publishers ("BP") will suffer.

Equitable remedies are discretionary, and a court will not grant a preliminary injunction unless the harm to be avoided by the injunction greatly outweighs the harm that the injunction may cause the enjoined party. Here, BP will either have to change the name of its magazine or shut down if the preliminary injunction is granted. Either option is a very costly proposition. As discussed above, the only harm that will come from not granting the injunction is the dilution of an unused trademark. Thus, Gargantuan's harm does not outweigh the harm that BP will suffer.

Finally, Gargantuan cannot show that there is a substantial likelihood that it will succeed on the merits of its claim at trial. The facts say that it is a very close question whether there is infringement here. Thus, this requirement is not satisfied.

Since Gargantuan cannot make the required showings, the request for a preliminary injunction should be denied.

2.   BP's motion to dismiss based on laches should be granted. At issue is whether Gargantuan harmed BP by not bringing an action for infringement sooner.

Laches is an equitable defense applicable when a plaintiff in equity has harmed the defendant by waiting too long to bring its claim. The time for laches may be shorter than the applicable statute of limitations for the type of action involved, but the laches period may never be longer. In any case, the plaintiff's delay must be knowing.

BP should prevail in the defense here. Although the statute of limitations for trademark infringement is four years and only about two years have passed since BP allegedly started infringing Gargantuan's trademark, much has happened in the two years. BP's magazine has become "wildly successful." It has become very popular with writers and advertisers over the two-year period and would lose a great deal of recognition if it were forced to stop using its name. Although the facts are not clear on this, it appears that Gargantuan knowingly sat on its rights. Because of *Fifty-Something Else's* success, it was the subject of stories in widely read newspapers and stock reports. Given this, it seems unlikely that Gargantuan just recently heard of the magazine; rather, it seems likely that Gargantuan stood silently by and watched BP build its magazine's reputation so that Gargantuan could pounce at an opportune time. Equity will not allow Gargantuan to do this. Thus, the court should dismiss Gargantuan's injunction claim. However, because the statute of limitations has not run on Gargantuan's claim for damages, that part of the suit should not be dismissed.

QUESTION 7

Save Animals Now ("SAN") is a not-for-profit corporation with limited funding provided through voluntary contributions received from individuals who share SAN's concern for animals which are hunted or raised only to be killed for their fur. For many months, SAN has picketed in front of the Magnificent Minks Fur Salon ("Magnificent Minks"). The picketing has become increasingly boisterous, with the picketers aggressively questioning the incoming customers and shouting "killer" at those who exit with packages. The picketing was having an effect on Magnificent Minks's business and, with the holiday season approaching, Magnificent Minks finally had enough. It therefore brought an action to enjoin the picketing. SAN was served with a copy of the complaint, together with a petition for preliminary injunction, and appeared through its counsel at a brief hearing the following day. Magnificent Minks was granted a preliminary injunction which enjoined SAN and its members from:

> picketing, shouting, or speaking to prospective or actual customers of
> Magnificent Minks within 500 feet of Magnificent Minks's premises.

Magnificent Minks timed its action so that the injunction was entered at the very start of the busiest two shopping weeks of the year. The injunction was properly served on SAN, and individual picketers received actual notice of the injunction.

Believing (correctly) that the injunction was a flagrantly unconstitutional infringement on free speech, SAN considered filing an appeal, but concluded that it would be unable to obtain appellate review of the injunction for at least 10 days. Feeling outflanked by Magnificent Minks's timing, SAN chose instead to ignore the injunction, and its members continued to picket. They were arrested and brought to trial for contempt of court for violating the injunction.

Although the defendants filed a jury demand, the judge conducted a bench trial of the case. At the conclusion of the trial, she found by clear and convincing evidence that SAN and the individual picketing members had violated the injunction. She fined SAN $50,000 and fined the individual picketing members $5,000 each.

SAN and the members have appealed asserting:

1. That the injunction was unconstitutional and, therefore, could form no basis for contempt of court; and

2. That the procedures used for finding contempt were themselves unconstitutional.

Evaluate these claims.

ANSWER TO QUESTION 7

1.   SAN's claim that the injunction was unconstitutional and so could not form a basis for a charge of contempt is incorrect. At issue is whether an enjoined person may disobey an erroneous injunction.

As a general rule, a party who has been enjoined must obey the injunction until it is dissolved. This is true even where it appears that the injunction has been erroneously granted. While special considerations may be involved when deciding whether to grant an injunction involving the freedom of speech, these considerations do not alter the general rule that an injunction must be obeyed. Thus, it does not matter that the preliminary injunction here was unconstitutional; it had to be obeyed. SAN's proper recourse would have been to seek an expedited appeal.

2.   SAN is partially correct and partially incorrect that the procedures used for finding contempt here were unconstitutional. At issue is whether SAN and its members had a right to proof of guilt beyond a reasonable doubt or to a jury trial on the contempt issue.

A court that has issued an injunction may enforce the injunction through its contempt power. The court may impose civil or criminal contempt charges on a recalcitrant party. If the charges are criminal, the alleged contemnor is entitled to all of the protections afforded other criminal defendants, including the right to proof of guilt beyond a reasonable doubt and a jury trial *if* appropriate. If the contempt is civil, no such rights exist. Whether a contempt charge is civil or criminal depends on the goal sought by the court: If the court seeks to punish, the contempt is criminal; if the court seeks to coerce compliance with its order, the contempt is civil.

Here, the court fined SAN $50,000 and the individual members $5,000. The fine was determinate; it could not be lessened by complying with the court's order in the future. Thus, it appears that the fine was imposed as punishment, making the contempt proceedings here criminal, rather than civil, in nature. Thus, SAN and its members are partly correct. The judge found them guilty of contempt using too low a standard of proof—clear and convincing evidence rather than proof beyond a reasonable doubt. However, the defendants are incorrect with regard to the right to a jury trial.

Whether a defendant has a right to a jury trial in a criminal case depends on whether the case involves a serious offense. The Supreme Court has interpreted this to mean a case where imprisonment of more than six months is imposed. A $5,000 fine imposed on an individual has been found not to be sufficient to make the offense serious. Thus, the imposition on SAN members of a $5,000 fine without granting their request for a jury trial was constitutionally sufficient. It is similarly likely that the Court would find the imposition of a $50,000 fine on an organization to be not serious. Thus, SAN's claim with regard to the right to a jury trial is incorrect.

QUESTION 8

Twenty-four months ago, Builder agreed in writing to construct a commercial building on Owner's land. Builder was to complete the construction within 14 months. In addition, the written contract required removal of a foundation of a building previously destroyed by fire.

Builder completed the construction project within the time specified and was paid for that work. However, Builder has not removed the foundation, even though Builder was paid 50% of the fee for that part of the job. Owner believes that one reason Builder has not

removed the foundation is that Builder is broke, and is presently doing only work which will bring in new cash.

Your office represents Owner. Your boss has written a letter to Builder threatening to seek an order of specific performance to have the foundation removed. Builder's reply, prepared without the assistance of an attorney, was largely unresponsive, but did say "I assumed you had changed your mind about the foundation, since I didn't hear from you about it. Anyhow, I don't see how you can talk about suing anyone; I happen to know you still haven't paid my cousin for carpet and furniture you installed in that building—and the money was due six months ago!"

Can Owner obtain specific performance? Explain. Include in your discussion whether it matters that Owner has delayed asking for the work to be completed, that Builder may be insolvent, and that Owner has not yet paid Builder's cousin for furnishings for the building.

ANSWER TO QUESTION 8

Owner cannot obtain specific performance but might be able to get an order prohibiting Builder from working for others before removing the foundation.

Specific performance is an equitable remedy that forces a party to perform his obligations under a contract. It is available when a plaintiff can show that (i) a contract exists, (ii) all contractual conditions have been fulfilled, (iii) the legal remedy is inadequate, (iv) mutuality of remedy exists, (v) enforcement is feasible, and (vi) no defenses are available to the defendant. It is likely that Owner can show all of the necessary elements here. The parties had a contract that required Builder to remove a foundation. Owner has partially paid for the removal and probably is willing to assure his further performance by depositing with the court the balance of the payment. The legal remedy is inadequate because the facts state that Builder is probably insolvent, so money damages would not be available from Builder. Mutuality of remedy is not a problem because, as discussed above, Owner's further performance can be assured by his paying into court the balance he will owe for the work to be performed. However, Builder does have a few possible defenses that merit some further discussion.

First, Owner is seeking to have the court order Builder to perform services. This is not feasible. A court will not grant specific performance in a contract for services because such an order would be tantamount to slavery. In such a case, however, the court will issue an injunction prohibiting the defendant from working for anyone else until the defendant performs for the plaintiff.

Second, Builder's letter raises the unclean hands defense, but that defense is not properly available here. A court of equity will not act where the party seeking equitable relief has acted unfairly in the transaction at hand. This is known as the "unclean hands defense." However, the defense is not available here because the improper conduct must relate to the transaction and parties involved in the current equitable suit. Here, Builder is claiming that Owner cannot sue him because Owner has not paid Builder's cousin on an unrelated contract. Unclean hands in an unrelated transaction is not a defense.

Finally, Builder might raise a laches defense. There is a slim chance that this defense would work, but it seems unlikely. A court will not issue an injunction where the party seeking the injunction has delayed seeking a remedy and the delay has prejudiced the defendant. Here, the facts state that Builder was to complete the contract within 14 months, and 24 months have passed. Builder says that he assumed Owner did not care about the foundation's removal, which is a weak, but plausible, excuse. The facts also indicate Builder is now short on cash. If Builder can show that his cash shortage occurred recently, it could be argued that defendant's position has been prejudiced by Owner's delay (*i.e.*, Builder had sufficient funds to remove the foundation 10 months ago, but does not have sufficient funds now). We do not have the sufficient facts to decide this issue, but it does not seem very plausible. Thus, this defense will probably fail.

QUESTION 9

Everything was set for the Saturday, December 21, 1996, opening in Chicago of *Judicious Pork*, a new animated movie about the barnyard antics of a particularly intelligent pig. It was to be a gala celebration—Producer arranged for limousines to bring honored guests to the theater, for spotlights to be trained into the sky, for receptions following the screening, and for a barrage of advertising to get the movie off on the right foot.

On Wednesday, December 18, Producer was served with a complaint requesting a preliminary injunction to bar the opening of the movie. The underlying claim was one of plagiarism and copyright infringement of Author's earlier-published book, *The Zany Adventures of Bill, a Remarkably Intelligent and Ambitious Pig.* A hearing was scheduled for Thursday, December 19, and both parties attended.

Author furnished a $2,000,000 injunction bond. Because Producer knew Author was extremely wealthy and could afford to pay any later damage award, Producer did not challenge the amount of the bond. After hearing argument on the merits, the court on December 19 preliminarily enjoined the opening of the movie and scheduled the permanent injunction hearing on the underlying infringement claim for February 1997. The court denied Producer's motion to reconsider its decision and dissolve the preliminary injunction.

The preliminary injunction was a disaster for Producer. She was out of pocket $300,000 for the opening night festivities and, because the cancellation came so late, none of that money was refundable. Moreover, the movie missed the all-important Christmas season opening when movie-goers had an appetite for happier movies like *Judicious Pork.* Once the holidays passed, the movie-going public was not only broke, but it was depressed and in need of more violent, get-even movies to elevate its spirits.

At that subsequent February 1997 final hearing on the merits, the court took evidence and concluded that Author did not establish his case for a permanent injunction, finding neither copyright infringement nor plagiarism. It therefore dissolved the preliminary injunction and dismissed Author's case. Producer promptly opened the movie, and it flopped.

At Producer's request, the court scheduled a further hearing to award damages arising from the now-dissolved preliminary injunction or, in the alternative, damages under the bond. That hearing was held in July 1997. Producer proved that the February opening had been a financial disaster and, as a result, the movie lost at least $10 million that it would have earned had it opened as scheduled. Producer has requested the court to enter a judgment in the amount of $10,300,000, the damages she sustained on account of the erroneously entered preliminary injunction or $2,000,000 under the bond.

1. **What relief, if any, should the court award to Producer? Explain.**

2. **Might Producer have been better advised to open the movie as scheduled and later challenge the validity of the preliminary injunction during contempt proceedings? Explain.**

ANSWER TO QUESTION 9

1. The court probably should enter judgment for $10.3 million. At issue is what damages are recoverable when a preliminary injunction is dissolved because it was improvidently granted.

In Illinois and many other states, if a preliminary injunction is improvidently granted, the restrained party has a right to recover damages either by suing on the bond or by suing for damages off the bond. An action on the bond is limited to the amount of the bond, but in an action off the bond, full damages can be recovered.

Here, the facts state that the bond was only $2 million; thus, Producer should not seek recovery from the bond, but instead should sue off the bond for the entire damages proved: $10.3 million. The only stumbling block to recovery would be the speculative nature of the damages—it is very difficult to predict how much a movie would have made because each movie is unique. However, this issue seems to be obviated by the facts, which state that "Producer *proved* . . . the movie lost at least $10 million that it would have earned" in addition to the $300,000 out-of-pocket expenses. Therefore, Producer should be able to recover the entire $10.3 million.

2. Producer would not have been better advised to open the movie and challenge the validity of the preliminary injunction at the contempt proceeding. Once an injunction is issued, a restrained party who knows about the injunction must obey it until it is dissolved. Failure to obey the injunction can result in being held in contempt. Because contempt is an offense against the power of the court, defenses going to the merits of the underlying injunction (*e.g.*, that the injunction should not have been granted) are irrelevant. The only defense is that the court acted without jurisdiction. Contempt is punishable in a number of ways, including fines and imprisonment. Here, Producer's defense goes to the merits of the injunction and not to the court's jurisdiction. Thus, it would not be a defense to a contempt charge. Therefore, if Producer had ignored the preliminary injunction, she would be subject to a fine or imprisonment—very unpleasant alternatives. By obeying the injunction and challenging the merits at trial, she was able to recover millions in damages without the risk of being fined or jailed, clearly the better option.

QUESTION 10

The valuable historical landmark, the Heirloom Building, had just been purchased by Noble Development. In the past, Noble had shown mixed regard for historical preservation. At times, it has restored old buildings to their former grandeur; at other times, it has torn them down with little public notice of its intentions and, at least once, in violation of laws requiring it to get a demolition permit to destroy an historic building. Noble had remained curiously silent about its intentions with respect to the Heirloom Building.

Officious Historical Preservation Consortium wanted to ensure that the Heirloom Building would continue to exist and wanted to get an injunction to prevent the destruction of the Heirloom Building. You may assume that there exist statutes requiring demolition permits for historic buildings.

Before long, Noble signaled its intentions by putting together a consortium for purposes of developing a shopping center on the site after building demolition. Noble acquired option contracts from several prospective lessees, and the project was 80% planned when Officious obtained a preliminary injunction to prevent destruction of the building even with a permit. The court's order enjoined the "demolition, destruction, or disassembly of the Heirloom Building."

Four days after the preliminary injunction was issued, a large fire consumed the Heirloom Building and completely destroyed it. While the Fire Marshal could not find adequate evidence of criminal arson, Officious did its own investigation and found evidence of arson which its investigator could link to Noble. When the local prosecutor declined to prosecute for lack of evidence, Officious moved for civil contempt of the preliminary injunction before the court that issued it. At trial, and over Noble's strident objections, Officious presented its evidence and proved by a preponderance of the evidence that agents of Noble had set the fire and thereby violated the injunction. The court held Noble in civil contempt and ordered it to contribute $1 million to a local historic preservation organization to compensate the victims of its violation of the injunction.

Noble appealed the court's finding of civil contempt and the order to contribute $1 million. How should the appellate court rule? Explain.

ANSWER TO QUESTION 10

The appellate court should set aside both the contempt finding and the fine. The first issue is what standard of proof should be used to impose a fine for violating a preliminary injunction.

Once an injunction is issued by a court, the injunction must be obeyed until it is dissolved or modified. If the injunction is disobeyed, the court may punish the contemptuous conduct by jailing the contemnor, imposing a fine, or both. However, because such sanctions seek to punish past conduct rather than compel compliance with a court order, the proceeding is considered to be criminal in nature. The fact that a proceeding is labeled a "civil contempt proceeding" is unavailing; it is the purpose of the proceeding that determines its nature and not the label of the proceeding. Where a contempt proceeding is criminal in nature, ordinary criminal procedures apply. In criminal cases, guilt must be proved beyond a reasonable doubt. Here, the court ordered Noble not to destroy the Heirloom Building and found, by a preponderance of the evidence, that Noble purposely set fire to the building in order to get around the injunction. The court then imposed a $1 million fine on Noble. Since the purpose of this fine was to punish Noble's past conduct rather than to coerce future compliance, it was criminal in nature. The preponderance standard is too low to impose criminal sanctions. Thus, the contempt holding cannot stand.

The $1 million award to a local historic preservation organization to compensate Noble's victims would be permitted in most states but not in Illinois. At issue is whether damages to victims can be awarded in contempt proceedings.

In most states, a court is allowed to award compensatory damages along with imposing fines and imprisonment in contempt proceedings. However, Illinois views contempt proceedings as an action between the court and the contemnor, and does not allow the court to order compensation to victims in such a proceeding. Instead, Illinois requires the injured party to bring a separate damages action.

QUESTION 11

Barry had a vintage 1936 mahogany speed boat which he used on Lake Michigan every weekend day he was not working at his law offices. He had spent three years repairing and refinishing the all-wood boat. It looked practically new and made Barry into something of a celebrity at the Yacht Club where he kept the boat docked. In its present condition, the boat was worth about $50,000, and it made Barry happy that he was constantly being asked if he would sell. The highest offer he ever received was $49,000. Barry was devastated when the boat was stolen from the Yacht Club on a dark night in July.

It turns out that Curt, another Yacht Club member, had been the thief. Curt, a successful—but erratic—businessman, secretly hated Barry because of his greater success in business, and Curt had been nearly insane with jealousy over the attention Barry got because of the boat. He had planned the theft while watching Barry and his habits for nearly two years. Curt had hired Dave to accompany him to the marina on the fateful night, and the two had untied the boat, hot-wired the engine, and driven off with the boat. They made it all the way to a very small marina in northern Michigan. There, Curt sold the boat to Eddie, a collector of old wood boats, for $100,000. Curt had misrepresented the origin of the boat and, with forged papers, convinced Eddie that Curt was the actual owner the boat.

Curt took the $100,000 and paid Dave the $10,000 he had agreed to for Dave's help. Curt deposited the remaining $90,000 into his bank account. Dave disappeared with his $10,000. Eddie put the boat into his private collection on a secluded lake in northern Michigan where it is unlikely ever to be found.

1.   Exclude the possibility of punitive damages and assume that Curt will have adequate funds to satisfy whatever judgment a court enters. If Barry brings suit against Curt, what are his claims and how much can he recover under them? Explain.

2.   Assume now that Curt has had serious business reversals and is insolvent. His only important asset is his bank account, which currently has $110,000 in it and, at all times since he deposited the boat proceeds, has contained at least $110,000. Fred, a creditor with a $500,000 judgment arising from personal injuries Curt inflicted on him in a barroom brawl, was the first to establish a judicial lien through garnishment on the bank account. Barry has intervened seeking to be paid from the account. What recovery, if any, should Barry have from the bank account? Explain.

ANSWER TO QUESTION 11

1.   Barry should seek to impose an equitable lien on the $90,000 that Curt has left from the sale of the boat and should seek a deficiency judgment for $10,000 to recover the remainder of the

$100,000 that Curt received. At issue is the best remedy to use to recover unjust enrichment against a solvent wrongdoer.

An equitable lien is an equitable charge that can be foreclosed like other liens. It is imposed when a defendant holds title to property that was misappropriated from the plaintiff, or that is traceable to property that was misappropriated from the plaintiff, and the defendant would be unjustly enriched if allowed to keep the property. Some courts also require the plaintiff to show that the remedy at law is inadequate. If the proceeds of the foreclosure sale are insufficient to fully satisfy the plaintiff's claim, the plaintiff can receive a deficiency judgment for the remainder.

Here, Barry's boat was stolen by Curt. Curt then sold the boat for $100,000. Under the circumstances, the $100,000 rightfully belonged to Barry, and Curt would be unjustly enriched if allowed to keep it. Thus, Curt has an equitable obligation to turn over $100,000 to Barry. Curt gave $10,000 of the $100,000 to his accomplice, Dave, and deposited the remaining $90,000 into his bank account, where the money still remains. Because the $90,000 is traceable to the property that was misappropriated from Barry, a court can impose an equitable lien on it. Moreover, because the account contains only $90,000 and the amount by which Curt was unjustly enriched was $100,000, Barry will also be able to obtain a $10,000 deficiency judgment.

Finally, it should also be noted that Barry does not have an adequate remedy at law. Curt converted Barry's boat. The legal remedy for conversion is replevin or damages measured by the fair market value of the chattel at the time and place of conversion. Here, Curt no longer owns the boat, so replevin is not available, and the facts indicate that the fair market value of the boat at the time and place of conversion was about $50,000. Damages of $50,000 would not be an adequate remedy here because Curt sold the boat for $100,000 and so would be unjustly enriched from his wrongdoing if Barry were limited to using the legal remedy.

2.   If Curt's only asset is the bank account in which Fred also has a claim, Barry should seek to impose a constructive trust on the $90,000 in the account that can be traced to the sale of the boat.

A constructive trust is an equitable remedy used by the courts to disgorge unjust enrichment. Like an equitable lien, it is imposed when: (i) a defendant has title to property that can be traced to property that was wrongfully obtained from the plaintiff, (ii) the defendant would be unjustly enriched if allowed to keep the property, and (iii) the plaintiff has no adequate remedy at law. Under a constructive trust, the defendant is treated as holding the property as a trustee of the plaintiff and has the sole duty of conveying the trust property to the plaintiff. Because the property is treated as being held by the trustee only in trust, it is not subject to the claims of the trustee/defendant's creditors. However, no deficiency judgment is available when a constructive trust is imposed.

Here, Curt has title to the $110,000 in his bank account, and as established above, $90,000 of the proceeds from the sale of Barry's boat can be traced to the bank account. That account has not had less than $110,000 in it since the proceeds of the boat sale were deposited there. The court will presume that any withdrawals made since the $90,000 was deposited were of Curt's own money. Moreover, as discussed above, Curt would be unjustly enriched if allowed to keep the $90,000 and Barry has no adequate remedy at law. Therefore, Barry will be allowed to impose a constructive trust on the $90,000 and will be able to recover the trust property free of Fred's lien. However, Barry would have no way to recover the remaining $10,000 of the boat sale price because a deficiency judgment is not available when a constructive trust is imposed (of course, we are using a constructive trust here because Curt is insolvent, so a deficiency judgment would not be helpful anyway). Finally, it should be noted that equitable rights can be cut off by a bona fide purchaser for value ("BFP"), but a judicial lien creditor, such as Fred, would not be treated as a BFP.

QUESTION 12

Archibald, a professional burglar, broke into Zoot's house one afternoon and made off with a great deal of jewelry, silver, and other valuables. One of the items in the take was an old gun hanging on Zoot's wall which had inscribed on it "Pennsylvania Co. 1, 1860." As one might expect, Archibald had an eye for valuables. He believed this to be a Civil War rifle that may have seen action at Gettysburg.

Archibald took the gun to Brower, an antique dealer who knew Archibald well and who often "winked" when Archibald brought him items to buy. The two examined the gun and believed that it was genuine and probably worth about $10,000. Given its source, however, Brower offered Archibald only $1,500 which Archibald gladly took. The joke was on both of them, however, because (it turns out) the gun was a fake worth, at most, $100.

1.   Now that Zoot knows that the gun was a fake, he is not interested in getting it back. Instead, he has elected to pursue a civil money remedy against Archibald. If there are adequate assets available, how can Zoot recover the most from Archibald in a civil suit (exclude the possibility of punitive damages)? Explain.

2.   Brower was not happy about this turn of events and wants to get his money back by seeking an equitable remedy of rescission of the purchase he made from Archibald. Assuming that contract law would otherwise provide substantive grounds under the doctrine of "mutual mistake" for rescinding the contract, can Brower in this case obtain that remedy in equity? Explain.

ANSWER TO QUESTION 12

1.   To maximize his civil recovery, Zoot should seek to have the court impose a constructive trust on the $1,500 Archibald received for the gun that Archibald stole from Zoot. At issue is the best available remedy when a thief steals property and sells it for more than it is actually worth.

A constructive trust is an equitable remedy imposed by the courts to disgorge unjust enrichment. It is applied where the defendant has title to property that rightfully belongs to the plaintiff and, if the defendant were allowed to keep the property, he would be unjustly enriched. Some courts also require the plaintiff to show that there is no adequate remedy at law. If a constructive trust is imposed, the defendant is deemed to hold the property as trustee for the plaintiff, and the defendant's sole duty as trustee is to convey the property to the plaintiff. The trust may be imposed not only on the specific property wrongfully obtained, but also on any proceeds that can be traced to the wrongfully taken property.

All of the elements necessary to impose a constructive trust are present here. Archibald stole the gun and would be unjustly enriched if he were allowed to keep the $1,500 proceeds from the gun's sale. Archibald has title to the money. Moreover, no remedy at law would be adequate because a suit against Archibald for damages for conversion of the gun could be brought only for the fair market value of the gun—about $100, leaving Archibald unjustly enriched in the amount of $1,400. The only real issue involves tracing: The constructive trust may be imposed only if Archibald still has the $1,500 that he received from Brower. If he does, Zoot may recover the $1,500 rather than the gun's $100 value.

2.   It is doubtful that the court would rescind the contract for mutual mistake here. At issue is whether a court will rescind a contract for mutual mistake where the party seeking rescission appears to have known that the goods being sold under the contract were stolen.

Rescission is a remedy that puts an end to a transaction and places the parties in the position they would have been in had the contract not been made. Rescission generally is available where the parties have made a mutual mistake, such as the mistake here—where both parties assumed that the rifle was from the Civil War.

Nevertheless, rescission will not likely be granted here. Rescission is an equitable remedy, and equitable remedies are discretionary. Under the doctrine of unclean hands, a court generally will not grant an equitable remedy to someone who has engaged in wrongful conduct with respect to the transaction in question. Here, Brower engaged in wrongful conduct with respect to his purchase of the gun. The facts state that Brower "knew Archibald well" and often "winked" when Archibald brought in items for Brower to buy. They also indicate that, "knowing its source," Brower offered only $1,500 for a gun that both parties thought was worth about $10,000. These facts lead to the conclusion that Brower knew the gun was stolen. Dealing in stolen merchandise is certainly wrongful conduct, so a court would not likely grant rescission here.

QUESTION 13

Goldman & Keating is an advertising firm located in Ryebrook County, Illinois. From 1992 to 1998, Arthur Halpern served as vice president for creative projects at Goldman & Keating.

On November 9, 1998, Halpern quits his job at Goldman & Keating. On the same date, Halpern accepts a position at Ann Arbor Enterprises, Inc., a diversified manufacturing corporation. Halpern will develop and supervise the advertising strategy at this company. Ann Arbor Enterprises maintains its principal place of business in Ryebrook County, Illinois.

Ann Arbor Enterprises never has been a client of Goldman & Keating. In his new position, Halpern will be responsible solely for the advertising projects of Ann Arbor Enterprises. Halpern will not have any contact with Goldman & Keating clients.

On November 10, 1998, Goldman & Keating files a complaint in the Circuit Court of Ryebrook County, Illinois. The complaint names Arthur Halpern as the only defendant. The complaint filed by Goldman & Keating alleges a single cause of action for breach of contract, a state law claim.

The complaint filed by Goldman & Keating alleges that in 1996, Halpern entered into a five-year employment contract with Goldman & Keating. According to the complaint, the contract included a covenant not to compete. In this covenant, Halpern promised that he would not accept any advertising position in Ryebrook County for one year after leaving

Goldman & Keating. Goldman & Keating alleges that when Halpern took his new job at Ann Arbor Enterprises, Halpern breached the employment contract and the covenant not to compete.

Together with the complaint, on November 10, 1998, Plaintiff Goldman & Keating files a motion for a temporary restraining order. In its motion, Goldman & Keating seeks an order that would prevent Halpern from working at Ann Arbor Enterprises. An affidavit filed in support of the plaintiff's motion for a temporary restraining order provides: "Unless the court prevents Halpern from working at Ann Arbor Enterprises, the already fragile relationship between Defendant Halpern and Plaintiff Goldman & Keating will deteriorate further. Because clients respect Halpern's creative thinking and his understanding of the advertising business, Goldman & Keating will lose about $1 million in advertising revenues if Halpern leaves the firm."

Goldman & Keating seeks a temporary restraining order at an ex parte hearing. Halpern is not represented at the hearing.

Goldman & Keating did not give Halpern any prior notice about the hearing on the plaintiff's motion for a temporary restraining order. When questioned about why Goldman & Keating did not notify Halpern about the hearing, plaintiff's counsel tells the court: "Goldman & Keating is seeking expeditious action that would prevent Halpern from moving to Ann Arbor Enterprises." At the hearing, Goldman & Keating agrees to post an appropriate bond if the court grants the motion for a temporary restraining order.

1. Should the circuit court grant the plaintiff's motion for a temporary restraining order? Explain.

2. For the purpose of this part only, assume that on November 10, 1998, the court denies the plaintiff's motion for a temporary restraining order. Now assume that shortly after the court has denied the motion, Plaintiff Goldman & Keating files a motion for a preliminary injunction.

   On November 13, 1998, the Circuit Court for Ryebrook County holds a hearing on the plaintiff's motion for a preliminary injunction. Both Plaintiff Goldman & Keating and Defendant Arthur Halpern are represented at this hearing. In support of its motion for a preliminary injunction, Plaintiff Goldman & Keating repeats the arguments that the plaintiff made in support of its motion for a temporary restraining order. Goldman & Keating agrees to post an appropriate bond if the court grants the motion for a preliminary injunction.

   Should the court grant the plaintiff's motion for a preliminary injunction? Explain.

ANSWER TO QUESTION 13

1. The circuit court should not grant the motion for a temporary restraining order ("TRO"). At issue is whether the motion can be granted ex parte under the circumstances given here.

A TRO is an emergency order imposed by the court to preserve the status quo until a motion for a preliminary injunction can be heard. Generally, a TRO will be granted only if the moving party can show that he will suffer irreparable injury immediately (*i.e.*, before a hearing for a preliminary injunction can be held) if a TRO is not granted. The party against whom a TRO is sought must be given notice of the hearing and an opportunity to respond unless the moving party makes a strong showing why notice should not be required. Examples of a sufficient showing include the inability to find the defendant in time or the probability that the defendant would hide or dispose of the subject matter of the litigation.

The court should not grant the TRO here. While plaintiff claims that it will suffer irreparable injury if the TRO is not granted—*i.e.*, the fragile relationship between plaintiff and Halpern will deteriorate further if Halpern is allowed to work for Ann Arbor Enterprises ("AAE")—plaintiff has not shown a sufficient reason for granting the motion ex parte. Plaintiff stated that its reason for not notifying defendant is that it wanted to prevent defendant from moving to his new employer. Plaintiff did not indicate that defendant could not be found in a timely manner or that defendant was likely to commit some wrong if given notice of the hearing. Therefore, the motion should be denied.

2.   The circuit court should grant the motion for a preliminary injunction. At issue is whether plaintiff has shown irreparable injury and likelihood of success on the merits of its action.

A preliminary injunction is an interlocutory injunction that is granted to preserve the status quo until a trial on the merits can be held. It will be granted only after a hearing on notice to the defendant. At the hearing, the plaintiff must show that: (i) if the preliminary injunction is not granted, ***irreparable injury will result before a trial can be held***; and (ii) the plaintiff is ***likely to succeed on the merits*** of his claim at trial. Here, plaintiff probably can make both showings.

In determining whether an irreparable injury will result, the court will look to whether money damages can make the plaintiff whole. Where damages are speculative, the legal remedy will be considered inadequate. Here, plaintiff alleged that if it the preliminary injunction is not granted, it will lose clients. Plaintiff's motion estimated that the loss in clients would result in a loss of "about $1 million in revenues." Since the amount stated in the motion was an estimate of lost revenues rather than lost profit and it seems difficult to pinpoint plaintiff's actual damages, a court would likely find that money damages are inadequate here.

Plaintiff can also show that it will likely prevail on the merits of its claim. Plaintiff seeks enforcement of a covenant not to compete. A court will grant specific performance of a covenant not to compete in an employment contract only if: (i) it is ***reasonably necessary to protect a legitimate interest*** of the employer (*e.g.*, the right to unique services); and (ii) it is ***reasonable in its geographic scope and duration***.

Here, the defendant's "creative thinking and his understanding of the advertising business" probably are sufficiently unique to justify enforcement. Moreover, a one-year restriction against working in advertising within the county seems sufficiently narrow in geographic scope and duration. Thus, plaintiff should succeed on the merits of its case.

Halpern could argue that plaintiff has no legitimate interest to protect here because plaintiff sells advertising services to outside companies, and AAE hired Halpern to run its advertising department internally and does not sell advertising to outsiders. Moreover, AAE had never used plaintiff's services. Nevertheless, the noncompete clause prohibits Halpern from accepting ***any*** advertising position in the county for a year, and at the very least, by taking the position with AAE, Halpern has deprived plaintiff of the opportunity to offer Halpern's unique talents to AAE. This seems a sufficient interest to protect.

Note that the court will not enforce the contract by ordering defendant to work for plaintiff, because courts will not grant specific performance of a contract for personal services. Instead, the court will issue an injunction prohibiting defendant from working for anyone in the county other than plaintiff during the term of the contract.

QUESTION 14

Jack has owned Jack's Apple Orchard in Taylorville, Illinois, for over 20 years. Each fall, he and his crew pick the ripe apples from the trees, crate them, and distribute them to Jack's customers across the state.

Zesty Apple Juice, Inc., an Illinois corporation, makes and distributes apple juice, its flagship product. The company supplies apple juice to distributors and retailers across the country. In the past, Zesty Apple Juice, Inc. has purchased apples from many orchards in Illinois.

In June 2001, Zesty Apple Juice, Inc. encounters a fivefold increase in demand for its Zesty Apple Juice. Furthermore, forecasters predict a poor apple harvest during the fall 2001 season and they speculate a 50% increase in the price for apples. Zesty Apple Juice, Inc. knows that it cannot fill all of its orders for Zesty Apple Juice and stay in business without finding an exclusive supply of apples. After careful research, Zesty Apple Juice, Inc. learns that only Jack's Orchard can satisfy the juicemaker's increasing demand for apples at a lower overhead realized by obtaining apples from one exclusive source.

In July 2001, Zesty Apple Juice, Inc. approaches Jack of Jack's Orchard. On July 15, 2001, Jack and Zesty Apple Juice, Inc. enter into a written contract whereby Jack agrees to sell Jack's Orchard to Zesty Apple Juice, Inc. and to transfer title and possession on July 21, 2001, in exchange for monthly payments of $15,000 for 20 years. Zesty Apple Juice, Inc. indicates to Jack that it will execute a mortgage on Jack's Orchard to Jack. The mortgage is never executed.

On July 20, 2001, Jack changes his mind and refuses to transfer title or possession to Zesty Apple Juice, Inc. He and his employees refuse to leave Jack's Orchard and begin to pick apples, crate them, and ship them to rival distributors.

1.   Zesty Apple Juice, Inc. files an action for a preliminary injunction to enjoin Jack and his employees from remaining at Jack's Orchard and removing apples. What result and why?

2.   Zesty Apple Juice, Inc. files an action for specific performance asking the court to order the transfer of title and possession of Jack's Orchard to Zesty Apple Juice, Inc. What result and why?

3.   Assume that the court forces the transfer of title and possession of Jack's Orchard to Zesty Apple Juice, Inc. Six months later, Zesty Apple Juice, Inc. becomes unable to pay Jack $15,000 each month. Does Jack have any recourse in equity? Explain.

ANSWER TO QUESTION 14

1.   The court should grant the motion for a preliminary injunction. At issue is whether Zesty has shown irreparable injury and likelihood of success on the merits of its action.

A preliminary injunction is an interlocutory injunction that is granted to preserve the status quo until a trial on the merits can be held. It will be granted only after a hearing on notice to the defendant. At the hearing, the plaintiff must show that: (i) if the preliminary injunction is not granted, irreparable injury will result before a trial can be held; and (ii) the plaintiff is likely to succeed on the merits of his claim at trial. Here, plaintiff probably can make both showings. Zesty's likelihood of prevailing on the merits is discussed below in part 2., so the discussion here will focus on whether Zesty will suffer irreparable injury before trial.

In determining whether an irreparable injury will result, the court will look to whether money damages can make the plaintiff whole. From the facts, it appears that money damages would be inadequate here. Zesty is seeking to purchase Jack's Orchard because it fears a 50% increase in the price of apples during fall 2001 and has predicted that, as a result, it will not be able to fill customers' orders and stay in business without Jack's Orchard. Thus, Zesty would likely go out of business before a trial on the merits could be held. This constitutes an irreparable injury. Thus, the preliminary injunction should be granted.

2.   Zesty should prevail in its action for specific performance, but only if it first executes the mortgage agreed to by the parties. Specific performance is an equitable remedy that forces a party to perform his obligations under a contract. It is available when a plaintiff can show that (i) a contract exists, (ii) all contractual conditions have been fulfilled, (iii) the legal remedy is inadequate, (iv) mutuality of remedy exists, (v) enforcement is feasible, and (vi) no defenses are available to the defendant. It is likely that Zesty can show all of the necessary elements here. Zesty can show that the parties had a contract that required Jack to give up possession of his orchard to Zesty on July 21 in exchange for $15,000 per month for the next 20 years. Since the contract is for land, money damages are considered inadequate. Mutuality of remedy does not seem to be a problem here nor does feasibility of enforcement, because both parties and the land are within the court's jurisdiction. Neither does Jack seem to have any defenses. There is one slight problem—Zesty has not fulfilled all of its contractual conditions—it has not executed a mortgage in favor of Jack. However, Zesty presumably stands ready, willing, and able to execute the mortgage. The court can require Zesty to execute the mortgage before or contemporaneous to ordering Jack to turn over the deed. Therefore, specific performance should be granted.

3.   If the court forces transfer of the orchard and Zesty subsequently fails to pay, Jack does have a remedy in equity—foreclosure of a grantor's lien.

Because the facts for part 3. do not indicate that Zesty executed a mortgage, presumably there is no mortgage on which Jack can foreclose. Where a seller conveys land to a buyer without obtaining a mortgage to secure payment of the price, equity will imply a lien in favor of the seller called a grantor's lien. If the buyer defaults, the lien may be foreclosed against the property to satisfy the remainder of the purchase price.

QUESTION 15

Kyle Krystopher was a gifted sculptor who did most of his work in bronze. While he occasionally made one-of-a-kind bronzes, most often he would create a mold and make an "edition" of 10 to 12 identical, numbered pieces before he destroyed the form. His work has increased in popularity. One used to be able to pick up a 15-inch-high piece of his work from an edition of 10 for about $500. The same pieces were fetching about $5,000 more recently.

Kyle recently finished an edition of 10 impressionist-style busts of a woman in a soldier's uniform called "Warrior." Her face was obviously fatigued from fighting and conveyed a great pathos about war. Each bust stood about 20 inches high and was numbered. He delivered the entire edition to his agent, Art Possibilities, LLC, for sale to the public.

Linda, an avid art lover, had learned through her underground art network that Kyle had been working on this new piece well before Kyle had finished it. She was a fan of his and wanted to get one of the Warriors. She contacted Art Possibilities and, with lots of cajoling, entered into a written contract to purchase Warrior Number Ten of the 10-unit edition for

$8,000 once the series was completed. The price was as high as it was because the work was not complete yet, and there was the possibility that it would turn out to be Kyle's best work. Linda left a $4,000 deposit with Art Possibilities; the contract provided that the remainder was due, in cash, on delivery of the sculpture.

In June, the work was unveiled at a one-artist show, and it was a tremendous hit. The telling event was the Museum of Modern Art's purchase of Warrior Number One for $20,000 for display in the museum. The value of the remaining nine copies went through the roof; so much so that Art Possibilities opened a bidding process for the other nine. Linda, of course, learned of this and demanded that Art Possibilities perform its contract with her. Art Possibilities told Linda that she could not possibly expect it to sell her Number Ten for $8,000 when the pieces were fetching upwards of $40,000. Linda has now discovered that Art Possibilities has agreed to sell Warrior Number Ten to Michael Mitchellson, a Swiss tycoon, for $45,000.

Linda has retained a lawyer to seek specific performance of the contract to sell Warrior Number Ten to Linda, and to make a motion to preliminarily enjoin the sale to Mitchellson until the specific performance case can be decided.

1. Should the motion for preliminary injunction be granted? Explain.

2. Regardless of how you answered the last question, should the court order specific performance of the contract? Explain.

ANSWER TO QUESTION 15

1. The court should grant the motion for a preliminary injunction to enjoin the sale to Mitchellson. At issue is whether Linda will suffer irreparable harm if the preliminary injunction is not issued.

The purpose of a preliminary injunction is to maintain the status quo between parties until a full trial on the merits can be held. The person requesting a preliminary injunction must show that if the preliminary injunction is not granted, she will suffer irreparable injury before a trial on the merits may be held and that this damage will greatly outweigh any damage that will be caused by granting the preliminary injunction. In addition, the moving party must show that she will likely succeed on the merits. Most states also require that a bond be posted, to cover the enjoined party's damages if it is ultimately decided that the injunction was improvidently granted, but such a bond is discretionary in Illinois.

Linda probably can make the requisite showings here. Since the likelihood of Linda's success at trial is discussed in part 2., below, the discussion here will focus on the irreparable injury element.

Linda will suffer irreparable injury if the preliminary injunction is not granted. In the underlying case, Linda is seeking specific performance of her contract to purchase a particular sculpture (Warrior Number Ten) from Art Possibilities ("AP"). Because she is seeking the sculpture itself rather than money damages, only the sculpture itself can serve as a remedy. If Linda's preliminary injunction is not granted, AP will sell Warrior Number Ten to Michael Mitchellson before Linda's underlying claim is decided. This could leave Linda without a remedy if she ultimately prevails in her underlying case, because AP will already have disposed of Warrior Number Ten (as well as the other nine copies of Warrior). Filing a *lis pendens* probably would not ameliorate this result. The facts indicate that Mitchellson is a Swiss tycoon. If he ships Warrior Number Ten back to Switzerland before Linda's underlying case is decided, the sculpture would be outside the court's jurisdiction and Linda would have trouble recovering it.

Linda's harm greatly outweighs the harm that AP will suffer from grant of the preliminary injunction. If the injunction is granted and AP prevails, it appears that AP can readily sell the sculpture. Moreover, the court could have Linda post a bond for the price difference between the two contracts to cover any possible loss that AP might suffer. Therefore, the court should grant the preliminary injunction.

2.   The court should grant Linda's request for specific performance. The main issues here are whether Linda lacks an adequate remedy at law and whether enforcement of the contract would be unconscionable.

To obtain an order for specific performance, a plaintiff must show that (i) a contract exists, (ii) all contractual conditions have been fulfilled, (iii) the legal remedy is inadequate, (iv) mutuality of remedy exists, (v) enforcement is feasible, and (vi) no defenses are available to the defendant.

Here, there is a contract with definite terms. AP is to sell Warrior Number Ten to Linda for $8,000. Linda has fulfilled the conditions placed on her, having already paid her down payment. Mutuality of remedy can also be assured by requiring Linda to pay the remaining $4,000 of the purchase price into the court. Enforcement is feasible.

Linda also lacks an adequate remedy at law. Ordinarily, specific performance is not available to enforce a contract for the sale of goods because money damages (the legal remedy) usually are sufficient to enable the plaintiff to go out and buy substitute goods. However, money damages will be inadequate if the goods involved are unique or in short supply. Here, the sculpture Linda contracted for is in short supply; only 10 copies were made and the mold for the sculpture has been destroyed. Thus, there is no guarantee that Linda will be able to purchase one later if she is awarded damages. Moreover, the proper amount of damages probably would be speculative. Copies of the sculpture are now selling for $45,000, but the next seller might demand $100,000. It would be unfair to subject Linda to the risks of a wildly fluctuating market. Therefore, Linda lacks an adequate remedy at law.

Finally, AP has no viable defense to Linda's action. AP probably will argue that the contract was unconscionable, because Linda agreed to pay $8,000 for the sculpture and copies of it are now selling for $45,000. This argument will fail, however, because unconscionability is measured at the time the contract was formed and not at the time of performance. At the time the parties made their contract here, the price was more than fair. Similar works were selling for $5,000, and Linda had agreed to pay $8,000 because both parties had speculated that this would be the artist's most popular piece. The fact that the sculpture was even more popular than anticipated is not a defense.

Therefore, Linda should prevail in her action for specific performance.

QUESTION 16

Larry Landowner owned a 10-acre parcel of land on Jefferson Street in McHenry County, Illinois. On December 22, 2001, he met with Diane Developer, a resident of McHenry

County, who wanted to a build a hotel on Jefferson Street. Larry entered into a written contract to sell the 10-acre parcel at 100 Jefferson Street to Diane at a price of $1,000,000.

As part of the agreement, Larry agreed to provide consulting services to Diane for one year regarding the development project because of his specialized and unique knowledge of the terrain on Jefferson Street.

Larry and Diane decided to close on January 15, 2002, and Diane made the first $50,000 payment to Larry by check on December 22, 2001.

The Circuit Court of McHenry County, Illinois, had, two years earlier, ordered Larry to give all proceeds of the sale of 100 Jefferson Street, whenever received, to his first wife, Glenda, as part of Glenda's and Larry's dissolution of marriage agreement. Larry, however, endorsed Diane's check over to his second wife, Wanda, who, aware of that dissolution agreement, used the money to purchase a one-year, $50,000 certificate of deposit in her name at her local bank.

On January 1, 2002, Diane entered into a written contract with Angela, an architect residing in McHenry County, Illinois, to design the hotel that she intended to put up at 100 Jefferson Street in exchange for $25,000, "all money due upon completion of the designs."

On January 15, 2002, Larry and Diane closed the sale. On the day of the closing, Larry told Diane that he had decided to move to San Francisco and could not consult with Diane about the development project.

Diane decided to hold off on the project because she did not have Larry's assistance. She sent Angela a letter stating that she wished to rescind the contract with the architect. Angela sent Diane her uncompleted drawings with a letter stating that she intended to do no further work on the project.

1. Diane files an action for specific performance in the Circuit Court of McHenry County, Illinois, asking the court for an order of specific performance requiring Larry to provide the agreed-upon consulting services to Diane. What result? Explain.

2. Glenda files an action in the Circuit Court of McHenry County, Illinois, seeking an interest in Wanda's certificate of deposit. Does Glenda have any remedy in equity? Explain.

3. Angela contemplates filing an action against Diane asking the court to (i) relieve her of her obligations under the contract that she entered into with Diane; and (ii) order Diane to pay her for the value of her uncompleted drawings. What equitable remedies does Angela have available to her? Explain.

ANSWER TO QUESTION 16

1.   Diane will not be successful in her action for specific performance against Larry. At issue is whether a court will grant specific performance of a contract for services.

Specific performance is an equitable remedy that forces a party to perform his obligations under a contract. It is available when a plaintiff can show that (i) a contract exists, (ii) all contractual conditions have been fulfilled, (iii) the legal remedy is inadequate, (iv) mutuality of remedy exists, (v) enforcement is feasible, and (vi) no defenses are available to the defendant. However, the remedy is discretionary, and even if all of the elements are present, a court will not grant specific performance of a contract to provide services, because forcing someone to perform services is tantamount to slavery, and also it is too difficult for a court to oversee performance of a personal service contract. Thus, even if Diane can show that all of the requirements for specific performance are present here, the court will not grant specific performance because the consulting contract is a personal service contract.

2.   Glenda does have a remedy— constructive trust. At issue are the remedies available against a person who is holding property that rightfully belongs to another.

Where a defendant has title to property that rightfully belongs to the plaintiff, the defendant would be unjustly enriched if allowed to keep the property, and the plaintiff has no adequate remedy at law, a court may impose a constructive trust on the property to force the defendant to turn the property over to the plaintiff. A constructive trust is not limited to the actual property that was wrongfully taken from the plaintiff; it may be imposed on any property to which the defendant has title if the defendant gained title solely with the proceeds of property that was misappropriated from the plaintiff.

Here, Glenda can prove all of the elements required for imposition of a constructive trust on the $50,000 CD: Wanda holds title to the $50,000 CD. She purchased the CD with a $50,000 check that Larry indorsed over to her. The proceeds of the check rightfully belong to Glenda because Larry received the check as proceeds from the sale of the Jefferson Street property and was under a court order to turn over any proceeds from the sale of that property to Glenda. It appears that Wanda would be unjustly enriched if she were allowed to keep the CD because she gave Larry no consideration in exchange for the check. Even if she did give Larry consideration in exchange for the check, she would be unjustly enriched because she knew that Larry was violating the court order by not turning over the proceeds of the sale to Glenda (*i.e.*, Wanda was not a bona fide purchaser who would cut off Glenda's equitable rights). Finally, Glenda has no remedy at law that she can impose against Wanda, and it seems unlikely that Larry has sufficient funds to make a remedy at law against him adequate. Thus, a constructive trust can be imposed on the CD.

3.   Angela may be able to have the contract rescinded and recover in an action for restitution. At issue are the remedies a service provider has after the other party repudiates the contract.

Where a person hires a service provider and then breaches the contract with the service provider after the service provider has partially performed, the service provider may ask the court to rescind the contract (equitable rescission) and restore any benefit that she conferred upon the breaching party (equitable restitution or quasi-contractual relief). Here, Diane hired Angela to design a hotel. After Angela began working on the project, Diane requested that the contract be rescinded. Although the contract provided that Angela was not to be paid until completion of her work, under the circumstances a court will award Angela the value of the drawings she had completed before Diane's request for rescission.

QUESTION 17

The University campus had remained peaceful for most of its recent history, but the new war effort ("war mongering" to quote many students) brought out the peaceniks, much as

the war effort had in the 1960s. Because the University was engaged in government-sponsored research that was useful for defense systems, the University itself was especially a target of protest. There were anti-war protests nearly daily and an occasional blockade of administrator's offices, but never any violence.

A ringleader in the anti-war protest effort was an organization called "ZZ" (pronounced like the last sound in "buzz"). ZZ was successful in organizing students from all parts of the University, including some of the "frat boys" and athletes, and its successes were increasingly a source of anxiety for both the administrators and the government itself. ZZ's particular talent was getting TV coverage, and it did so by getting its protestors to dress up in outlandish costumes that inevitably would attract the media.

The biggest event of all was slated for May 20, when the President of the United States was scheduled to speak at the 4:00 p.m. University commencement. In April, ZZ had announced its intent to peacefully protest during the graduation ceremony and, given the media attention it expected, announced it would protest at some distance from the ceremony to draw attention away from the ceremony.

ZZ was ready to go on May 20 when, at 2:00 p.m., ZZ's leader, Mary Doright, was served with a temporary restraining order which read in its entirety as follows:

> ZZ, all its members and affiliates, and all others operating pursuant to its influence, are hereby ENJOINED from conducting any protest in any location on May 20 including, specifically, the period during which the University commencement will be held.

The order had been obtained ex parte and was signed by a judge with jurisdiction to enter such an order.

1. Aside from the fact that this order violated the First Amendment rights of those affected by it, what other challenges might be made to the order, and how do you think those challenges will be resolved? Explain.

2. John Lawless, a graduating law student, had learned of the temporary restraining order and thought he understood its defects, particularly its First Amendment problems. He dressed himself for the protest and showed up at the appointed time only to be arrested. May the court hold him in contempt for violating the temporary restraining order? Explain.

3. Meredith ("Merry") Sunshine, a free spirit who was not a member of ZZ, had planned to attend the protest and had dressed herself appropriately to the task. Being who she was, she was unaware of any court orders and showed up (with several others like her) at the protest site on schedule. When she did, she was arrested for violating the temporary restraining order. May the court hold her in contempt? Explain.

ANSWER TO QUESTION 17

1. In addition to being challenged for violating the First Amendment rights of those affected by the order, the temporary restraining order ("TRO") can also be challenged on two procedural

grounds. First, under the facts given, there were no grounds to grant a TRO here. Second, even if a TRO were appropriate here, it should not have been granted ex parte.

A TRO is an emergency interlocutory order intended to maintain the status quo until a more in-depth hearing can be held to determine whether a preliminary injunction should be granted. (A preliminary injunction maintains the status quo until the conclusion of a full trial on the merits of the underlying case.) The party seeking a TRO must show two things: (i) that irreparable injury will result if the TRO is not granted, which will heavily outweigh the harm the defendant will suffer if the TRO is granted; and (ii) a likelihood of prevailing on the merits. Neither element can be shown here.

First, no legitimate claim of potential harm can be made. ZZ's protests have always been peaceful and this protest was going to be held at a distance from the event against which it was targeted. University's only purported harm is that ZZ's protest will pull media coverage away from the President's appearance at University's commencement ceremony. However, University has no right to have a ceremony free from competing activities. Moreover, granting the TRO here actually will result in greater harm than good because it will squelch ZZ's First Amendment rights in order to protect University's interest in holding a commencement ceremony free from competing activities. Thus, no irreparable injury could be alleged.

Second, the moving party could not have shown a likelihood of success on the merits of its underlying case. Originally, an injunction could be granted only to protect a property interest, although many states have expanded this to other protectable interests. However, as just discussed, University's interest in a commencement ceremony free from competing activities is not a protectable interest. Moreover, as the facts suggest, the injunction here—prohibiting anyone "operating pursuant to [ZZ's] influence" from protesting "in any location on May 20" is too broad to be constitutional. Thus, the moving party cannot prove the likelihood of succeeding on the merits of the underlying case.

Even if there were grounds for granting a preliminary injunction here, a TRO probably was not appropriate under the facts, and an ex parte TRO was certainly improper. As discussed above, a TRO is appropriate only if there is no time to have a more in-depth hearing on a preliminary injunction. Here, ZZ announced in April that it was going to hold a protest during University's commencement ceremony on May 20. Thus, there was probably time to hold a hearing on whether to grant a preliminary injunction and there was no need to resort to an emergency TRO. However, even if the University found out about ZZ's plans only a few days before May 20, making an emergency TRO appropriate, the TRO should not have been granted ex parte. A TRO can be granted without prior notice to the enjoined party only if the moving party makes a strong showing why notice should not be required, such as that the enjoined party could not be found or there is a strong reason to believe that notice will render the TRO ineffective. No such showing can be made here. Thus, the TRO should not have been granted ex parte.

2.   John Lawless may be held in contempt for failure to obey the TRO even though it was improperly granted and violated his First Amendment rights. Once an injunction is granted, it must be obeyed until it is terminated by the court. Although an injunction cannot bind the whole world, it is binding on the named parties and persons acting in concert with the named parties. There are only two defenses against contempt for violating a TRO: (i) the court lacked jurisdiction to grant the TRO; or (ii) the person charged with contempt did not have notice of what was prohibited. The fact that the injunction was improvidently granted is not a defense. Here, John cannot raise either defense. The facts state that the judge who granted the TRO had jurisdiction to

do so and that John had notice of what was prohibited. Thus, he may be held in contempt for knowingly acting in concert with ZZ to violate the court's order. The fact that the order violated John's First Amendment rights is irrelevant. Rather than disobey the court's order, John should have moved to have the TRO dissolved due to its unconstitutional nature.

3.   The court may not hold Merry in contempt. As discussed above, while an injunction is binding on parties and persons acting in concert with the persons enjoined, one cannot be held in contempt for violating an order unless one had notice of the order at the time it was violated. Here, Merry did not have any notice that her conduct was prohibited. Therefore, she cannot be held in contempt of court for violating the TRO.

QUESTION 18

Urie Fumorsky was a 70-year-old Russian artist who died in December 2001. He worked in many media—he sculpted, painted in oil and watercolor, and made prints. His work was fetching as much as $10,000 for a two-foot by three-foot oil painting during his lifetime, but the prices for his work have gone up astronomically since he died. Before he died, he displayed much of his work in the Eastern Artifacts Gallery in Chicago.

Marilee Mustofski was a wealthy woman of Russian descent who had been an avid Fumorsky fan for many years. In July of 2001, she spotted his very large "Peasant with Gun," a wall-sized painting of an angry Russian farmer, and decided that she "just had to have it." But she did not have the cash to purchase it on the spot. After a little negotiating, she was able to make a contract with Eastern Artifacts (which owned the painting) to buy it for $100,000, delivery in March 2002. This was an attractive deal for Eastern Artifacts. The painting, being so large, was hard to sell and the contract permitted Eastern Artifacts to continue to display the painting, which could be seen from the street and drew customers into the store. The timing, of course, gave Marilee time to assemble the funds to make the purchase.

When Fumorsky died suddenly in December, the value of his work rose sharply. In February 2002, Marilee heard a rumor that Eastern Artifacts may have made arrangements to sell "Peasant with Gun" to the very wealthy John B. Titon from London for the record price of $1 million. When Marilee confronted the gallery, it told her that, under the circumstances, she could not possibly be serious about buying the painting for $100,000. Beyond that, the gallery was unwilling to say anything more about its plans for the painting.

Marilee had made it a point to walk by the gallery every day to confirm that "her" painting was still there. Recently, however, Marilee has learned from a second reliable source that the shipment to Titon in London has been arranged by the gallery and would occur within the month. Given the size of the painting, it must be crated, a process that will take several days from the time the painting is transported from Eastern Artifacts to the shipping depot, and then shipped by sea.

Marilee has hired a lawyer who has drafted a complaint seeking specific performance of her contract and has properly served Eastern Artifacts with process. The lawyer has also drafted a petition for a temporary restraining order ("TRO") forbidding Eastern Artifacts from delivering the painting to anyone. The lawyer is concerned that if she notifies Eastern

Artifacts of her intent to seek a TRO, Eastern Artifacts will ship the painting before a court can act.

1. **Must Eastern Artifacts be given notice that Marilee will seek a TRO? Explain.**

2. **Assume that Marilee obtained a TRO without first giving notice to Eastern Artifacts but, because Marilee and her lawyer were not adequately monitoring the situation, the painting left the United States before her lawyer served the order on Eastern. As a result, Marilee will be put to considerably more expense in recovering the painting, if she can recover it at all. Given that the TRO restricted Eastern's delivering the painting, can Eastern Artifacts be held in civil or criminal contempt for violating the TRO? Explain. Would your answer be different if Eastern Artifacts shipped the painting after receiving a telephone call from Marilee's lawyer describing the order, but before receiving formal service of the order? Explain.**

3. **Assuming that Marilee's contract with the gallery remains valid and the painting remains within the gallery's control, will Marilee be able to obtain specific performance of the contract? Explain.**

ANSWER TO QUESTION 18

1.   Eastern Artifacts ("Eastern") must be given notice that Marilee is seeking a TRO. A TRO is an emergency injunction granted to maintain the status quo until the court can hold a full hearing to determine whether to grant a preliminary injunction until a trial can be held on the merits of a case. The party moving for a TRO must give the party to be restrained notice that a TRO is being sought unless the moving party can make a strong showing why notice should not be required (*e.g.*, the person to be restrained could not be found or there is strong reason to believe that if the person were notified, he would dispose of or hide the subject matter of the litigation). Here, nothing indicates that Eastern cannot be found or that it is likely to quickly hide or dispose of the painting in question. Indeed, the facts indicate that because the painting is "wall sized," it would take several days to crate it for shipment, thus preventing a quick disposal by Eastern. Therefore notice is required.

2.   If Eastern shipped the painting after the TRO was issued but before receiving any notice of the TRO, it could not be held in contempt for violating the TRO. A person cannot be held in contempt for violating a TRO unless the person had notice that the TRO was issued. Given the emergency nature of TROs, the notice does not have to be formal. Thus, if Marilee's attorney had phoned Eastern to advise it of the TRO before it shipped the painting, Eastern could be held liable for criminal or civil contempt.

3.   Assuming that there is a valid contract, Marilee will be able to obtain specific performance. The main issue here is whether Eastern has any viable defenses.

To obtain an order for specific performance, a plaintiff must show that (i) a contract exists, (ii) all contractual conditions have been fulfilled, (iii) the legal remedy is inadequate, (iv) mutuality of remedy exists, (v) enforcement is feasible, and (vi) no defenses are available to the defendant.

Here, there is a contract with definite terms. Marilee is to buy and Eastern is to sell the painting "Peasant with Gun." Although nothing in the facts indicates that Marilee can fulfill her part of the bargain by paying the $100,000 purchase price, presumably she either has the money or can easily obtain it, given that the painting now is worth 10 times the contract price. Marilee also lacks an adequate remedy at law. Ordinarily, specific performance is not available to enforce a contract for the sale of goods, because money damages (the legal remedy) usually are sufficient to enable the plaintiff to go out and buy substitute goods. However, money damages will be inadequate if the goods involved are unique, and here the painting is unique. Mutuality of remedy can be assured by requiring Marilee to pay the purchase price into the court. Enforcement is feasible because the painting is still within the jurisdiction of the court. Finally, Eastern does not appear to have any equitable defenses, although it may have a legal defense—the Statute of Frauds.

Eastern might try raising either of two equitable defenses—laches and unconscionability—but each will fail.

A defense based on laches will not succeed. Laches is an equitable defense similar to the statute of limitations. It cuts off equitable actions if the plaintiff has unreasonably delayed in bringing the action and the delay has caused prejudice to the defendant. Here, it is debatable whether Marilee unreasonably delayed in bringing her specific performance action. She heard a rumor about the sale of the painting in February 2002, but did not bring her action until some time later, when she heard of the sale from a second, reliable source. The first rumor might have been sufficient to put her on notice of the pending sale, because when she confronted the gallery, it told her that under the circumstances she really could not expect it to honor the agreed-upon price, which would make her delay unreasonable. On the other hand, it might have been reason-able to wait until she heard the information from a reliable source, given that the painting re-mained clearly visible at the gallery the whole time. In any case, however, a laches defense will fail because the delay, even if it was unreasonable, did not cause any prejudice to Eastern. It does not appear that Eastern has changed its position in any manner from the time that Marilee first heard the rumor. Therefore laches will not be a good defense.

A defense based on unconscionability will also fail. A court may refuse to order specific perfor-mance if the terms of the contract are unconscionable. Here, the contract price for the painting is only one-tenth of its current market price. However, unconscionability is measured at the time the contract was formed and not at the time of performance. At the time the parties made their contract here, the price was fair. Thus, a defense of unconscionability will fail and the court will grant specific performance.

Eastern might be able to raise the Statute of Frauds as a legal defense. A contract for the sale of goods for $500 or more must be evidenced by a writing that contains the material terms of the contract and is signed by the party sought to be bound. Here, the price of the painting is $100,000, and nothing in the facts indicates whether Eastern signed anything memorializing the deal with Marilee. Absent such a writing, the Statute of Frauds would be a defense.

QUESTION 19

Jones was a wealthy individual whose only daughter, Lydia, had serious problems with budgets. She was constantly spending far more money than she earned at her modest job, and Jones was worried that if he passed his wealth to her directly in his will, it would be

gone within a matter of months. So he devised a trust appointing his friend Kelly to be the trustee. The will bequeathed Jones's fortune in stocks to the trust and directed that Kelly use the trust income and as much principal as Kelly deemed appropriate for the support of Lydia "in the manner in which she is accustomed." Ten years after Jones's death, the principal of the trust was to go directly to Lydia. Jones died, and the trust was established in accordance with the will.

Kelly exercised her discretion as the trust document had directed. But during the 10 years, Lydia's demands—and Kelly's denials—resulted in a very bad relationship between the two. After the 10 years had run, the trust had dissolved, and Lydia had received the principal. Lydia hired an investigator to look into Kelly's handling of the money with an eye to uncovering any type of misbehavior.

The investigator found that five years after Jones's death, Kelly saw "an incredible opportunity" to make a fortune on a hot stock tip. She invested $100,000 of the trust funds for the trust's benefit in a company called Menron, whose stock price was very low but destined to rise. She also "borrowed" another $100,000 from the trust and invested it in Menron for her own benefit. The stock price went up fourfold within a six-month period. In her discretion as trustee, Kelly sold the trust's Menron stock for $400,000 and invested these trust proceeds in a way that kept the trust making money.

She also sold and traded her own Menron stock for cash and securities worth $400,000. Kelly traded $200,000 worth of "her" Menron stock for $200,000 worth of Microhard, a start-up Internet company. She took the remaining value of the Menron stock ($200,000) and invested it in a diverse stock portfolio. Figuring she had more than "covered" the "loan" from the trust to her through her inspired investing in Menron, she never replaced the $100,000 she had "borrowed" from the trust.

By the time the private investigator had uncovered the foregoing, Kelly was having financial difficulties. Kelly's assets include her house (which is fully encumbered with an enforceable mortgage), several thousand dollars in cash, a large portfolio of stocks and bonds, and $65,000 worth of original Microhard stock. It is unclear at this point what her financial situation is—she might be insolvent or she might have ample assets to pay any conceivable claims that might be asserted against her.

1. Assuming Kelly is solvent, what relief should Lydia pursue against Kelly and on what theory or theories? What relief is likely to be awarded if Lydia is successful? Explain.

2. Assume now that Kelly is insolvent and that ordinary creditors will receive no more than 10% of their provable claims. Under these circumstances, what relief should Lydia pursue against Kelly and on what theory or theories? Explain.

ANSWER TO QUESTION 19

1. If Kelly is solvent, Lydia can sue to recover any losses to the trust or profits made by Kelly based on her breach of her duty of loyalty.

Every trustee owes a duty of loyalty to the trust and its beneficiaries, which means that she cannot enter into a transaction in which she is dealing with the trust in her individual capacity. Borrowing funds from the trust breaches this duty, regardless of any intent to repay the money. The beneficiary does not have to show fraud or bad faith, and it is irrelevant that the trustee may have acted in good faith. If the trustee breaches the duty of loyalty, she is liable to the trust estate for: (i) any losses to the trust estate, (ii) any profit that would have accrued to the trust but for her breach, (iii) any profit made by the trustee, and (iv) interest.

Here, Kelly breached her duty of loyalty when she borrowed $100,000 from the trust and invested it in Menron for her own personal benefit. She subsequently sold the stock for cash and securities worth $400,000, thus making a profit of $300,000. Lydia can bring suit to recover that $300,000 profit, the original $100,000 borrowed from the trust, and any profit that the trust would have made absent Kelly's breach, plus any interest.

Note that Lydia has no cause of action with regard to Kelly's investment of $100,000 in Menron for the trust's benefit. Pursuant to the Uniform Prudent Investor Act, a trustee can invest in any type of investment provided she exercises reasonable care, skill, and diligence. There is nothing in the facts to indicate that Kelly acted in an imprudent manner with respect to that investment.

2.   If Kelly is insolvent, Lydia should seek to have a $200,000 equitable lien placed on the Microhard stock and a $200,000 equitable lien placed on Kelly's stock and bond portfolio. At issue are Lydia's equitable remedies.

An equitable lien is an equitable remedy imposed by courts to prevent unjust enrichment when property has been misappropriated from the plaintiff (e.g., through breach of fiduciary duty). The remedy may be imposed on any property that the defendant owns to which the plaintiff's misappropriated property can be traced. An equitable lien is a charge on the defendant's property that may be foreclosed like other liens and is superior to other liens in the same property. Unlike a constructive trust, an equitable lien may be imposed even if the defendant's title was not derived solely from the misappropriated property (e.g., where the defendant commingled misappropriated funds with her own funds or used misappropriated funds to improve property that she already owned). When an equitable lien is imposed, if the proceeds of the sale are less than the amount that was misappropriated, the plaintiff can obtain a deficiency judgment for the amount not repaid. Most courts will impose an equitable lien only if the legal remedy is inadequate, such as when the defendant is insolvent.

Here, equitable liens may be imposed on both the Microhard stock and Kelly's portfolio. Kelly is insolvent and she misappropriated $100,000 from the trust through breach of fiduciary duty, as discussed above. This $100,000 can be traced to Menron stock, which Kelly sold for $400,000. Under the doctrine of tracing, the entire $400,000 rightfully belonged to the trust. Kelly used $200,000 from the sale to purchase Microhard stock now worth $65,000. Therefore, Lydia should seek to have an equitable lien imposed on the Microhard stock and obtain a deficiency judgment for the remaining $135,000 of the $200,000 that was used to purchase the Microhard stock. Kelly commingled the other $200,000 from the sale of Microhard stock with her own funds in her portfolio. Thus, a $200,000 equitable lien may be imposed against the portfolio. Because this portfolio is "large," presumably Lydia will receive her whole $200,000 by foreclosing her lien and will not need to obtain a deficiency judgment regarding this $200,000. Note that an equitable lien may not be imposed against Kelly's house or her cash, because the misappropriated funds cannot be traced to these assets.

QUESTION 20

Sam is a permanent resident of Mesa County, Illinois. Sam owns 10 Illinois gas stations. One of Sam's gas stations is located at 100 Midway Drive in Mesa County.

Prior to 2003, Mesa County residents have speculated that developers plan to construct a new shopping mall, which would include the current site of Sam's Midway Drive gas station. However, no formal announcement about a shopping mall has occurred.

On September 15, 2003, Sam agrees to sell the 100 Midway Drive gas station to Bill. Under the terms of a carefully negotiated written contract, Bill will pay $50,000 for the gas station. In early September 2003, the value of the Midway Drive gas station was assessed at $45,000.

The contract provides that on September 30, 2003, Bill will pay $50,000 to Sam. When Sam receives Bill's payment, Sam will provide Bill with title to the gas station. The contract signed by Bill and Sam includes the following clause: "*Liquidated Damages*. If the seller breaches this contract, the buyer will receive a refund of any deposit, plus $1,000 liquidated damages."

Both Bill and Sam sign the real estate sales contract. Before Sam enters into the September 15 contract, Sam has bought and sold several Illinois gas stations.

On September 22, 2003, the Barnett Development Company announces plans to construct a shopping mall on Midway Drive. The 100 Midway Drive gas station is located near the center of the proposed shopping mall. Also on September 22, Barnett Development states that on December 1, 2003, the company will pay $250,000 to purchase the gas station located at 100 Midway Drive. When Barnett Development builds the shopping mall, the company plans to demolish the gas station.

On September 30, 2003, Bill brings a $50,000 cashier's check to Sam's office. Bill is planning to pay Sam for the gas station.

But on September 30, Sam refuses to accept Bill's check. On September 30, Sam also refuses to sell the Midway Drive gas station to Bill.

Bill subsequently files a suit in the Circuit Court of Mesa County. Bill's complaint names Sam as the only defendant.

The complaint alleges a single cause of action for breach of contract. Bill alleges that Sam breached the September 15 gas station sales contract.

1.   In response to Bill's breach of contract suit, Sam argues that the September 15 gas station contract is unconscionable. Will Sam succeed in arguing that the gas station sales contract is unconscionable? Explain.

2.   For the purpose of this part only, assume that the gas station sales contract was not unconscionable. Further, assume that Sam breached this contract when Sam refused to accept Bill's $50,000 check on September 30.

   Now assume that in Bill's breach of contract suit against Sam, Bill seeks specific performance of the September 15 contract between Bill and Sam. Will the Circuit Court of Mesa County grant Bill's request for specific performance? Explain.

ANSWER TO QUESTION 20

1.   Sam will not succeed in arguing that the September 15 contract is unconscionable. At issue is whether the contract was unfair at the time it was made.

The contract between Sam and Bill is not unconscionable. Unconscionability is an equitable defense to an action for specific performance. A court will not grant specific performance of a contract if the contract was unconscionable at the time it was made. Unconscionability is determined on a case-by-case basis. The basic test is whether, in light of the general commercial background and needs of the particular parties, the contract is so one-sided as to be unconscionable. Unconscionability is often used when one of the parties is in a substantially superior bargaining position (a contract of adhesion) or when enforcement of the contract will result in unfair surprise. Here, however, the parties were not in an unequal bargaining position when the contract was made. Sam was free to sell his land for whatever he thought it was worth. Moreover, there was no unfair surprise here. Sam had sold gas stations before and should have known how the process worked. It also appears that both parties were aware that the gas station property might be part of a proposed shopping mall—the facts say that Mesa County residents had speculated about this possibility before 2003, and Sam appears to have benefited from the speculation because his property had been worth only $45,000 but he was able to get Bill to agree to pay $50,000 for it. The facts also say that the contract was carefully negotiated. In essence, it appears that Bill agreed to pay Sam an extra $5,000 for the possibility that the mall would be built. The subsequent announcement that the mall would in fact be built and that the mall developer was willing to pay $250,000 for the gas station land does not make the contract unconscionable.

2.   The circuit court will grant specific performance here. At issue is whether the liquidated damages clause in the parties' contract makes the legal remedy adequate.

Generally, to obtain an order for specific performance, a plaintiff must show that (i) a contract exists, (ii) all contractual conditions have been fulfilled, (iii) the legal remedy is inadequate, (iv) mutuality of remedy exists, (v) enforcement is feasible, and (vi) no defenses are available to the defendant. All of the requisites are satisfied here. There is a contract with definite terms (Sam is to sell and Bill is to buy the gas station for $50,000). Bill fulfilled his conditions by tendering the $50,000. Mutuality of remedy is present, because a court will grant specific performance to a seller of real property as well as to a buyer. Enforcement is feasible. And there are no apparent defenses available to Sam. The only real issue is whether the remedy at law is adequate.

Generally, the remedy at law will be considered inadequate if the subject matter of the contract is unique. Land is considered unique, so specific performance generally is available when a land sale contract is breached. Moreover, the inclusion of a liquidated damages clause in a land sale contract generally will not change this rule. The general rule is that a liquidated damages clause does not make the legal remedy adequate; the courts treat such a clause only as an alternative remedy. However, if the contract makes it clear that the liquidated damages clause shall be the exclusive remedy in the event of breach (*e.g.*, upon breach, either party's exclusive remedy shall be the payment of $1,000), the remedy at law will be considered adequate. Here, the contract does not make liquidated damages the exclusive remedy. Thus, the legal remedy will be considered inadequate and specific performance will be granted.

QUESTION 21

Mega Insurance Company ("Mega") has embarked on a national effort to educate its residential and commercial policyholders about fire safety in buildings taller than 10 stories.

Mega's efforts are aimed at reducing personal injury claims arising from such fires. As an example to its policyholders, the company will also provide fire-safety training and equipment to all 9,000 employees working in its 60-story headquarters in Chicago.

Commander Bill Frank has been hired by Mega to conduct the training sessions and provide the safety equipment. Commander Frank spent 30 years as a firefighter before retiring 10 years ago to become a fire-safety consultant. Partly because of his assertiveness and marketing savvy, he is considered the nation's foremost fire-safety expert. Also somewhat quirky, at every public appearance Commander Frank carries his beloved steel "hallagan"—a 36-inch, forced-entry device that resembles a crowbar and is used by firefighters across the country. The Commander used the same hallagan throughout his career, and his name and the date he retired are prominently engraved on it.

On June 16, 2004, Mega and Commander Frank entered into a written contract detailing the content of each seminar the Commander would give to Mega's employees. The contract specified that nine identical seminars would be conducted for approximately 1,000 Mega employees at a time. Commander Frank would receive $200,000 for the lectures. Plus, at the conclusion of the final lecture, Commander Frank agreed to surrender to Mega his beloved hallagan—for an additional $10,000. To commemorate its massive training program, Mega planned to display the hallagan in its main lobby.

The weekly lectures began in early September 2004. The contract provided that Commander Frank would be paid the specified $210,000 at the conclusion of the eighth lecture. Accordingly, Commander Frank received full payment on October 26, 2004. To leverage media exposure of its fire-safety initiative, Mega heavily publicized the fact that Commander Frank was personally conducting the sessions.

On July 30, 2004, Mega and Commander Frank entered into a second written contract, this time for the purchase of 10,000 "Take Your Breath Away" ("TYBA") smoke hoods. Each TYBA hood contains a small canister of oxygen and a full-face mask. The hoods provide 30 minutes of breathable air—enough time to permit escape from even the top floor of Mega's headquarters. The hoods were manufactured by a California company and purchased by Commander Frank in March 2004. Mega planned to distribute the hoods to every employee in early November 2004. Pursuant to the contract, Commander Frank delivered 10,000 TYBA hoods to Mega and received $490,000 for them on October 26, 2004.

On October 29, 2004, while Commander Frank was conducting an unrelated fire-safety seminar in Boston, a fire ignited near the 85th floor conference room where he was lecturing. Using his hallagan and brute force, the Commander broke through a locked stairway door and escorted 30 people to safety before firefighters arrived. At an impromptu press conference in front of the still-burning building, the Commander credited his instincts and his trusty hallagan. Fascinated by the Commander's heroics, as well as the irony of a fire starting during a fire-safety seminar, the national media picked up the story. The Commander soon received lucrative offers to appear in movies and even a six-figure offer to purchase his hallagan.

On November 1, 2004, the day before his scheduled final lecture at Mega, Commander Frank advised the company that he would need an additional $50,000 to conduct the lecture and that he was no longer willing to part with his hallagan.

Making matters worse, later that day Mega and Commander Frank were surprised to learn that a California public safety agency issued a recall for all TYBA smoke hoods on May 15, 2004. Once activated, the oxygen canisters created an unacceptable risk of explosion when used near open flames. An automatic reciprocity provision in an Illinois consumer safety statute made use of the hoods illegal in Illinois as of May 15, 2004.

1. Mega seeks to compel Commander Frank to adhere to his agreement to conduct the final lecture in order to avoid the collapse of the company's highly publicized training program. Assess Mega's chances of securing that relief in a court of equity.

2. Mega is unwilling to abandon its plan to display the hallagan as a symbol of the fire-safety training program it conceived and implemented as an example to its policy-holders. Can the company compel Commander Frank to part with the hallagan under the terms of the June 16 contract? Explain.

3. What type of equitable relief is most appropriate for Mega to pursue in conjunction with the TYBA hoods? Assess Mega's chances of succeeding with a claim.

ANSWER TO QUESTION 21

1. Mega will not be able to get a court to order Commander Frank to lecture for the agreed-upon fee. At issue is whether a court will order specific performance of a contract to render services.

Specific performance is an equitable remedy in which the court orders a party to perform as agreed under a contract. To obtain an order for specific performance, a plaintiff must show that (i) a contract exists, (ii) all contractual conditions have been fulfilled, (iii) the legal remedy is inadequate, (iv) mutuality of remedy exists, (v) enforcement is feasible, and (vi) no defenses are available to the defendant. Mega would be able to make such a showing here. There is a contract under which Commander Frank agreed to give lectures in exchange for $200,000. There are no conditions pending from Mega. The legal remedy is inadequate because only Commander Frank—with his unique skills and reputation—can fulfill the contract here; awarding Mega damages would only enable Mega to go out to purchase the services of another person with skills and a reputation different from that of Commander Frank. That will not do because Mega was bargaining for Frank's services specifically. Mutuality of remedy exists in that the court can order Mega to pay the $200,000 fee into court to ensure that Frank is paid after he performs. Enforcement is feasible. Finally, there are no defenses present that would prevent enforcement. Nevertheless, an equity court generally will not order specific performance in a contract for services, both because of supervision problems (how can a court tell if the person performing is performing with adequate skill, care, enthusiasm, etc.?) and because forcing someone to work against his will smacks of slavery. Thus, despite the fact that a prima facie case for specific performance can be made under the facts, specific performance should not be awarded here.

2. Mega can obtain an order compelling Commander Frank to turn over his hallagan as agreed. At issue is whether specific performance will be awarded under a contract for unique goods. Again, to obtain an order for specific performance, a plaintiff must show that (i) a contract exists, (ii) all contractual conditions have been fulfilled, (iii) the legal remedy is inadequate, (iv) mutuality of remedy exists, and (v) there are no defenses available to the defendant. Here, Frank agreed

to turn over his hallagan for $10,000 at the completion of his speaking tour. Mega has not left any of its conditions unfulfilled. The legal remedy here also is inadequate. Damages are the usual legal remedy, and damages would enable Mega to buy a hallagan, but Commander Frank's hallagan is unique. It is special because it is the only hallagan that Frank used throughout his career, making it a collector's item. No other hallagan would have the same mystique. Thus, only that particular hallagan can satisfy the contract. Mutuality of remedy exists in that the courts can order Mega to pay in the $10,000 before it requires Commander Frank to turn over the hallagan. Finally, there are no defenses available to Frank. He will probably argue that it is unconscionable to order him to turn over his hallagan when circumstances have changed and made it much more valuable than when the parties first agreed. However, unconscionability generally is measured at the time the contract was made. When the contract here was made, the agreed-upon $10,000 price was not unconscionable. Thus, Mega should be successful in getting the court to order specific performance of the contract.

3.   Mega should seek to rescind the contract for the TYBA hoods for mutual mistake. Rescission is an equitable remedy that is applied when parties enter into a voidable contract and one of the parties wants to avoid it. A contract can be rescinded for mutual mistake of material fact as long as the mistake existed at the time the contract was made. Here, Mega and Frank entered into a contract on July 30, 2004, under the terms of which Frank delivered 10,000 TYBA smoke hoods to Mega in exchange for $490,000. However, under Illinois law, the sale of such hoods became illegal on May 15, 2004, a few months before the sale here. Thus, both parties were mistaken as to the legality of the sale. Because the legality of the sale is a material fact about which the parties were mistaken, rescission is available.

QUESTION 22

Doctor Elaine Yoon ("Dr. Yoon") is a rising star in the medical world. Thanks to the revolutionary gene-therapy techniques she developed over the past seven years, dozens of patients with Huntington's disease—a hereditary disorder that attacks the brain—have made remarkable recoveries. Dr. Yoon and her cutting-edge procedures have attracted media attention and hold the promise of revolutionizing the treatments for a variety of hereditary diseases.

Frustrated by bureaucratic restrictions at the hospital where she developed her techniques, last year Dr. Yoon left the hospital and opened a small gene-therapy practice in Chicago. She formed a corporation, Chi-Genix, Inc. ("C-G"), issued herself 1,000 shares of its stock, and sold the remaining 3,000 shares on the open market.

In light of the financial freedom that Dr. Yoon expects C-G to afford her, she recently decided to purchase a townhome in Chicago's swanky Gold Coast neighborhood. Dr. Yoon and her real estate broker dealt with the owner's broker, Debra Dartis ("Dartis"). During negotiations over price, Dartis explained that her client, the townhome's owner ("the Owner"), had several offers from other potential buyers fall through when the buyers could not arrange financing for the expensive property. As a result, the Owner would require Dr. Yoon to provide 20% of the purchase price as earnest money to an escrowee who would hold it as a fiduciary from the time the Owner and Dr. Yoon signed a contract until the actual real estate closing (which would happen several weeks later).

Dr. Yoon and the Owner eventually agreed upon a purchase price of $2.5 million—meaning that Dr. Yoon would have to give $500,000 to an escrowee. Because Dr. Yoon was unable to come up with $500,000 in cash, she offered to give the escrowee $100,000 in cash and a document transferring ownership of her 1,000 shares of C-G stock, which were valued at $400,000 at the time.

The Owner agreed to the arrangement and on May 16, 2005, Dr. Yoon and the Owner executed a standard, written contract for the sale of real estate. The real estate contract referred to the cash and stock transfer document collectively as the "Earnest Property." According to paragraph 10 of the contract, Dr. Yoon retained full discretion to cancel the contract if, within 10 calendar days of its signing, she determined, based on the advice of a certified home inspector, that the property was in an unacceptable physical condition. If she elected to cancel based on paragraph 10 (the "Inspection Provision"), Dr. Yoon would be entitled to receive all earnest property back within two calendar days of the cancellation.

As a licensed Illinois real estate broker, Dartis was authorized to act as the escrowee. Dartis and Dr. Yoon executed a separate written contract on May 16, 2005 (the "Escrow Contract"). The Escrow Contract provided that, in exchange for a $100 escrow fee, Dartis would: (1) deposit the $100,000 in an interest-bearing account; (2) place the stock transfer document in a bank safe deposit box; and (3) return all earnest property within two calendar days if Dr. Yoon canceled the real estate contract pursuant to the Inspection Provision. Dr. Yoon paid the $100 fee and Dartis took possession of the Earnest Property on May 16, 2005.

After learning from a certified inspector that the townhome had serious structural defects, Dr. Yoon properly notified the Owner and Dartis on May 20, 2005, that she was cancelling pursuant to the Inspection Provision. After that, Dartis did not return Dr. Yoon's telephone calls or emails.

Then, on June 10, Dr. Yoon learned that Dartis had: (1) used $75,000 of the $100,000 to pay off the mortgage on the home she had owned for 12 years; and (2) used the remaining $25,000 to purchase a set of china and given the set to her daughter as a wedding gift on June 4, 2005.

On June 17, 2005, Dr. Yoon was contacted by a major pharmaceutical company that wanted to purchase the 1,000 shares of C-G stock for $1.2 million. Dr. Yoon was eager to sell the stock for an $800,000 profit, but could do nothing while Dartis held the stock transfer document.

Dr. Yoon is now considering taking legal action against Dartis.

1.   Can Dr. Yoon secure a court order directing Dartis to return the stock transfer document? Assess Dr. Yoon's chances of securing such an order in a court of equity.

2.   What equitable remedy is most appropriate for Dr. Yoon to pursue in connection with the $75,000 Dartis used to pay off the mortgage on her home? Assess Dr. Yoon's chances of success.

3.   What equitable remedy is most appropriate for Dr. Yoon to pursue in connection with the $25,000 Dartis used to purchase the set of china? Assess Dr. Yoon's chances of success.

ANSWER TO QUESTION 22

1.   Dr. Yoon may obtain a court order directing Dartis to return the stock transfer document. At issue is whether Dr. Yoon may obtain an order of specific performance.

Specific performance is an equitable remedy in which the court orders a party to perform as agreed under a contract. To obtain an order for specific performance, a plaintiff must show that (i) a contract exists, (ii) all contractual conditions have been fulfilled, (iii) the legal remedy is inadequate, (iv) mutuality of remedy exists, (v) enforcement is feasible, and (vi) no defenses are available to the defendant. Here, Dartis and Dr. Yoon entered into a contract (the Escrow Contract) that provided, among other things, that in exchange for $100, Dartis would place Dr. Yoon's stock transfer document in a safe deposit box and would return the document if Dr. Yoon properly canceled her contract to purchase Seller's home, which she could do if a certified home inspector determined that the home was in unacceptable physical condition within 10 days of executing the home purchase agreement. Dr. Yoon fulfilled all conditions of the contract because she paid Dartis the $100, had the home inspected, and notified Seller and Dartis on May 20—only four days after she executed the home purchase agreement—that the inspector found serious flaws in the home. The legal remedy (money damages) is inadequate. When Dr. Yoon turned over the stock transfer document, the stock was worth only $400,000, and that would be the amount of her damages at law. However, the stock is now worth $1.2 million. Mutuality of remedy is not an issue here, as the contract is enforceable against both parties. Enforcement is feasible. Finally, Dartis has no apparent defenses. (Note that a constructive trust, which is discussed below, is not an appropriate remedy here because, as escrowee, Dartis does not have title to the stock transfer document, but rather is merely a bailee of the document.)

2.   Dr. Yoon may seek to impose an equitable lien on Dartis's home. At issue is the most appropriate equitable remedy to use when a person uses wrongfully obtained property to improve property that the person already owns.

An equitable lien is an equitable charge on property imposed by the courts to prevent unjust enrichment where a person holds title to property that can be traced to property that was wrongfully obtained from the plaintiff. Most courts also require the plaintiff to show that there is no adequate remedy at law. Once imposed, the lien can be foreclosed and the property sold to satisfy the plaintiff's claim. Such a lien is particularly appropriate where the plaintiff's property was used to improve property already owned by the defendant. Here, Dartis misappropriated $100,000 from Dr. Yoon's escrow account and used $75,000 of the money to pay off her mortgage, which constitutes an improvement in Dartis's equitable interest in her home. Moreover, while the facts are silent on this point, it seems likely that Dartis is insolvent, given the fact that she has taken to converting Dr. Yoon's property in order to pay her mortgage and give her daughter a wedding present. If this is so, the legal remedy would be inadequate. Thus, the most appropriate equitable remedy that Dr. Yoon has concerning the misappropriated $75,000 is an equitable lien.

3.   Dr. Yoon may seek to impose a constructive trust on the china that Dartis gave her daughter as a gift. At issue is the most appropriate equitable remedy to use when a wrongdoer gives the proceeds of wrongfully obtained property as a gift.

A constructive trust is an equitable remedy imposed by the courts to prevent unjust enrichment where a person holds title to property that can be traced to property wrongfully obtained from the plaintiff. It compels the person holding the property to convey it to its rightful owner. Most courts require the plaintiff to show that the legal remedy is inadequate. Here, Dartis misappropriated

$100,000 that she was holding in escrow for Dr. Yoon. Dr. Yoon can trace $25,000 of the misappropriated money to the china held by Dartis's daughter, because Dartis used the misappropriated money to purchase the china that she gave to her daughter. A legal remedy would not be adequate against Dartis (assuming that she is insolvent). Neither would a legal remedy be available against Dartis's daughter, because tracing is not available at law and Dartis's daughter does not hold the property that was misappropriated from Dr. Yoon. Moreover, a constructive trust can be imposed against Dartis's daughter even though she was not the person who wrongfully acquired the property from Dr. Yoon. Although equitable remedies are cut off by a transfer of legal title to a bona fide purchaser (*i.e.*, a "BFP"—one who pays value and takes without notice of the facts), Dartis's daughter is not a BFP of the china; rather she received it as a gift. Thus, Dr. Yoon's most appropriate equitable remedy concerning the misappropriated $25,000 that was used to purchase the china is a constructive trust on the china. Dr. Yoon could instead seek to impose an equitable lien on the china, which requires proof of the same basic elements, but there would be no advantage in imposing an equitable lien here because it is unlikely that a court would allow a deficiency judgment to be obtained against Dartis's daughter, who appears to be an innocent donee.

QUESTION 23

Abracadab Supply is a national distributor of magic supplies throughout the United States. Abracadab has a worldwide network of magic trick inventors who constantly send it their proposed tricks and from whom Abracadab buys its newest sensations. In this way, it manages to develop six to eight new tricks each month.

Abracadab markets these new tricks through the efforts of its "Certified Wizards" (really traveling salesmen/magicians) who visit prospective and established customers and dazzle them with the newest sleights of hand. Abracadab has divided the United States into 30 "districts" for distribution purposes and each district has several of these Certified Wizards who call on customers at intervals of one to two months. The customers are either established magicians or very serious amateurs and they generally regard these calls as entertaining private magic shows (which they are), so the Wizards are almost never turned away. Abracadab has carefully nurtured its customer list over many years; these lists are so good that, on average, a customer will usually buy at least one trick from the itinerant Wizard each time he calls. Illinois, due to its size and population, is its own distribution district.

For several years, Abracadab was the only distributor of sophisticated magic tricks through most of the United States. Its customer and supplier lists were carefully guarded within the Company and its Wizards were required to sign binding agreements not to reveal the customer lists to anyone outside the Company and not to directly solicit Abracadab's customers for three years after discontinuing work for Abracadab. Customers and Wizards alike were also required to sign agreements preserving the "secret" of each trick. Each regarded it in his interest to do so—once the "magic" of a given trick is understood, it no longer has any value to anyone. You may assume that all these agreements are enforceable in Illinois.

All changed with the arrival of Huh?, Inc. on the scene, an Illinois company headed by Allee Chazam, a recent college graduate who regarded herself as a member of the "new generation of magic nuts." Through the Internet, she developed a group of hacker/magicians who supplied her with new tricks—not as high-quality on balance as Abracadab's,

but good enough at least to get some interest from prospective customers. Huh?'s first attempt at selling, through kiosks at local malls, was a flop—most people at malls were simply too busy to stand and watch the attendant do a magic trick. She then tried home shows, having her salespeople hawk the tricks in the same way other vendors sell mops and blenders at those shows. This was even less successful because people who went to home shows were not, typically, in the market for magic tricks.

Nearly out of money and desperate, Huh? next decided to try direct, in-person solicitation. It began by advertising for salespeople with an interest in magic and, out of the applicants, hired five salespeople, three of whom had no experience in selling, and Merlin and Samantha. Merlin and Samantha were, as it turned out, two of Abracadab's former Wizards who had resigned from Abracadab a week earlier.

Abracadab learned of its former Wizards' new employment before Huh? had even finished training them and before they even went into the field. Furious, it promptly brought an action against Merlin and Samantha seeking a preliminary injunction to prevent them from working for Huh? which, according to Abracadab, would result in breaches of their agreements with Abracadab. The Wizards have moved the court to deny the preliminary injunction.

1.   How should the court rule? Explain.

2.   Assume now that the court denied the preliminary injunction without prejudice to Abracadab's reasserting its claims. Perhaps emboldened by the court's decision denying the preliminary injunction, each of the Wizards has visited one or more of Abracadab's customers, attempting to sell them one of Huh?'s tricks. The fact that they made sales in only two cases did not deter Abracadab from filing again for a preliminary injunction to keep them from soliciting any other Abracadab customers. The Wizards have responded this time with the argument that a preliminary injunction should not be granted because Abracadab has an adequate remedy at law. How should the court rule on this assertion? Explain.

3.   Assume now that Abracadab prevailed on the court to enter a preliminary injunction against the Wizards. It reads as follows:

>   Wizards X and Y are hereby preliminarily enjoined from soliciting customers for Huh?, Inc.'s magic tricks anywhere in the state of Illinois pending a full trial on the merits.

The trial will not occur for at least six months.

The Wizards have properly taken an interlocutory appeal from this preliminary injunction. How should the court rule? Explain.

ANSWER TO QUESTION 23

1.   The court should not grant a preliminary injunction to prevent the former Wizards from working for Huh? The issue is whether the court's failure to enjoin the Wizards from working for Huh? will cause irreparable harm to their former employer, Abracadab.

A preliminary injunction preserves the status quo between the parties until a full trial on the merits can be held. The moving party must show that (i) he will likely suffer irreparable harm before the full trial can be held, and (ii) it is probable that he will succeed on the merits of his claim. The court must also weigh the harm that the plaintiff would suffer if the preliminary injunction were not granted against the harm that the defendant would suffer if it were granted. The court will not grant a preliminary injunction if the harm to the defendant substantially outweighs the harm to the plaintiff.

Here, no irreparable harm has been alleged; indeed, nothing in the facts suggests that Merlin and Samantha have done anything to breach their agreement with Abracadab. They agreed to not reveal the customer lists to anyone outside the company, not directly solicit Abracadab's customers for three years after discontinuing work for Abracadab, and not reveal the "secret" of magic tricks learned at Abracadab, and they have not done any of those things. Therefore, the temporary injunction should not be granted.

2. The court should grant the preliminary injunction to prevent the Wizards from soliciting any more of Abracadab's customers. Here, the Wizards violated their binding agreement with Abracadab to not directly solicit Abracadab's customers for three years after discontinuing work for the company. They resigned from Abracadab just one week before they were hired by Huh? and were still in training at their new job, well within the three years called for in the agreement. Moreover, Abracadab had carefully nurtured its customer list over many years, and it resulted in innumerable sales. Loss of exclusive use of the list would result in irreparable financial harm to Abracadab. Arguably, the customer list is a trade secret, *i.e.*, a plan, process, formula, or any other valuable information that is not patented but which gives its possessor a competitive advantage as long as it is kept secret. The takers of this secret (the Wizards) had an express covenant with the owner of the secret to not disclose the secret. Such covenants are always specifically enforceable, because courts of equity consider the legal remedy to be inadequate due to the difficulty of computing damages and the irreparable harm done to the plaintiff. Thus, the plaintiff would prevail at a full trial, and the court will grant the preliminary injunction.

3. The court will strike down the order enjoining the Wizards from soliciting customers for Huh?'s magic tricks anywhere in the state of Illinois pending a full trial on the merits. The issue is whether the order is overbroad. An injunction should not prohibit conduct that is permissible; it should reach only conduct that is prohibited. Here, the Wizards agreed to not solicit Abracadab's customers. However, the order prohibits the Wizards from soliciting anyone in Illinois, and is not limited to those on Abracadab's customer list. Thus, the order is overbroad.

QUESTION 24

Adrian and Bertha, two artists who make tile, began their business very slowly, making ceramic tile more or less as a hobby. When relatives, and then friends, began buying their tiles, they expanded with a larger kiln for firing the tile and, eventually, began hiring employees, engaging an accountant, and even hiring a lawyer to help them create the optimal legal structure for the business. At present, Bertha runs the day-to-day business, called Adrian & Bertha Enterprises ("Adrian & Bertha"). They employ three employees who handle most of the production, from stamping and painting the clay, through firing, and through packaging for shipment. Adrian and Bertha both do design work, visiting a prospective client, helping the client decide on the best kind of tile generally for the job, and

actually designing the embossing or decorating that will go on the tile. In addition, Bertha has come up with a new line of tile that she forges from bronze. This operation she handles almost entirely herself, from the design phase through assembling the tile for packaging (one of the three employees will put the tile into the boxes and ready it for shipment). Adrian & Bertha's product is not for everyone but, in upper-class circles, having an "Adrian & Bertha Tile Bath" is the gold standard.

In January 2002, Adrian & Bertha entered into a contract with George Kent to design and supply tile for the large renovation Kent was making to his master bathroom suite. This was a very large job; it would take Adrian & Bertha at least six months (until the end of June 2002) to complete the design work, manufacture the tile, and have it delivered to Kent. Payment was to be made on delivery of the tile and its acceptance by Kent.

In February 2002, the relationship of the parties had deteriorated because of Kent's continually changing demands. Finally, in the midst of the design phase (but without legal justification), Adrian & Bertha walked off the job, never to return. Kent has brought an action to obtain a court order requiring Adrian & Bertha to return to work and complete the design and manufacturing work for the bathroom. That action is opposed by Adrian & Bertha.

1. Should the court grant the order? Explain.

2. Adrian & Bertha has counterclaimed in this action for $5,000, the reasonable value of the time devoted to the design work that was done before leaving the job. Adrian & Bertha contends that it is entitled to compensation despite the fact that it breached the contract. Identify the likely theory for obtaining relief and give your assessment of whether a court should grant it.

3. Suppose the relationship did not deteriorate in the early stages but, instead, disintegrated after the design and manufacturing work had been completed. The tile has not yet been boxed up but is stacked in Adrian & Bertha's warehouse, but Adrian and Bertha were sufficiently infuriated with Kent that they told him he would get the tile "over our dead bodies." Kent now seeks an order requiring that Adrian & Bertha deliver the tile. Should the court grant the order? Explain.

ANSWER TO QUESTION 24

1. No, the court should not grant Kent's order requiring Adrian & Bertha to return to work and complete the design, manufacture, and delivery of the tiles. At issue is whether a court will grant specific performance of a contract for personal services.

Before a court will order specific performance, the plaintiff must show that: (i) a contract exists; (ii) plaintiff's contractual conditions have been fulfilled; (iii) the legal remedy is inadequate; (iv) mutuality of remedy exists; (v) enforcement is feasible; and (vi) no defenses are available to the defendant. Generally, personal services contracts fail to meet the feasibility requirement because of the difficulty of enforcement and because compelling an individual's work for another would be tantamount to involuntary servitude.

The court will not grant specific performance here because enforcement of the contract is not feasible. The contract at issue here is a personal services contract that calls for Adrian & Bertha to design tiles, manufacture them, and deliver them to Kent. Enforcing Adrian & Bertha's performance would be especially difficult because designing and manufacturing the tiles is an artistic endeavor, and determining whether the tiles conform to the contract would involve some subjectivity. Moreover, the work that still remains, if compelled, would be viewed by the court as involuntary servitude, particularly because it could not be performed by a third party (*see* 3., below). Because enforcement would not be feasible, the court will not grant Kent's request for an order for specific performance of the contract.

2. Adrian & Bertha would seek relief under a theory of restitution or quasi-contract. However, under the facts presented here, the court would not grant such relief to Adrian & Bertha. At issue is whether a party that breaches a contract is entitled to any relief.

Restitution is designed to avoid unjust enrichment of the defendant at the plaintiff's expense. Restitution damages may be awarded to a plaintiff who has failed to render substantial performance, with the damages typically consisting of the value of the benefit conferred on the defendant, minus an offset for damages caused by the plaintiff's breach.

Here, restitution will not be awarded because although Adrian and Bertha had begun to perform under their contract, they walked off the job early, before any tiles were manufactured or delivered to Kent. Consequently, they conferred no benefit on Kent, and Kent was not unjustly enriched by any of the work performed. Therefore, Adrian & Bertha would not be entitled to restitutionary relief.

3. Yes, the court should grant Kent's request for an order requiring Adrian & Bertha to deliver the tile. Again, the main issue is whether the court will grant specific performance of a personal services contract, in this case, when the breaching party has substantially performed.

Here, all of the requirements that must be met before a court will order specific performance (*see* 1., above) have been satisfied. A contract exists and Kent's contractual conditions have been met (*i.e.*, Kent stood ready, willing, and able to pay Adrian & Bertha once the tiles were delivered to him). The legal remedy is inadequate because the tiles at issue are specially designed and unique. Mutuality of remedy exists, and there are no defenses available to the defendant. Moreover, although the order would involve specific performance of a personal services contract, the bulk of Adrian & Bertha's work has already been done, so the problems with enforcement and involuntary servitude discussed in 1., above, would not be present. The only work that remains to be done—boxing up and delivering the tile to Kent—could be easily monitored by the court and enforced. It is the job of one of the three employees to put the tile into the boxes and ready it for shipment, so neither Adrian nor Bertha would be compelled to do these tasks. Thus, the court should grant Kent's order requiring that Adrian & Bertha deliver the tile.

QUESTION 25

Fran and Henry both are permanent residents of Byrd County, Illinois. Fran and Henry live on adjacent parcels of land in Byrd County. Fran and Henry are isolated from other Byrd County residents.

In April 2003, Fran opens a shop, named Fran's Crafts & Gifts. Fran's shop is located next to her Byrd County house. Although Fran sells a variety of gifts, she specializes in scented candles. Fran's Crafts & Gifts becomes a well-known and highly profitable business.

In January 2005, Henry opens a chicken farm on his Byrd County property. Henry starts the farm with 10 chickens. However, Henry hopes eventually to expand his farm to more than 10,000 chickens.

Soon after Henry buys his first chicken, Henry's chicken farm creates a foul odor. The strong smell from the chicken farm is noticeable in the Fran's Crafts & Gifts store. Immediately after Henry starts his chicken farm in January 2005, business at Fran's Craft's & Gifts suffers a noticeable decline.

1.   In December 2006, Fran is contemplating legal action to close Henry's chicken farm. Could Fran succeed in a tort action, alleging that Henry's chicken farm is interfering with the use of her property? Explain.

2.   For the purpose of this part only, assume that Fran files a tort suit against Henry in December 2006. Also, assume that Fran ultimately will succeed in her tort action against Henry. Can Fran obtain a preliminary injunction, requiring that Henry close his chicken farm? Explain.

3.   For the purpose of this part only, assume that in February 2005, Henry asks Fran if she is bothered by the chicken farm. At this time, Henry still has only his original 10 chickens. Fran tells Henry that if he wants to operate a large chicken farm, Fran has "no problem with the idea."

Now assume that in December 2006, Fran first notifies Henry that odor from his chicken farm is hurting her business. At this point, Henry has been operating his chicken farm for more than 18 months.

By December 2006, Henry's chicken farm has grown from his original 10 birds to more than 10,000 chickens. For the first six months of 2007, Henry has committed to supply several local markets with eggs produced on his chicken farm.

Assume that in December 2006, Fran brings a tort action against Henry. The complaint filed by Fran alleges that the chicken farm is interfering with Fran's use of her property. Assume that Fran's suit is not barred by the applicable statute of limitations.

Based on Henry's February 2005 conversation with Fran, does Henry have a defense against Fran's tort suit? Explain.

ANSWER TO QUESTION 25

1.   It is unclear whether Fran would succeed in an action to close Henry's chicken farm. The main issue here is whether Fran can make out a case for nuisance.

A nuisance can be enjoined. A nuisance exists when one person substantially and unreasonably interferes with another person's use or enjoyment of property. To be substantial, the interference must be offensive, inconvenient, or annoying to an average person in the community; it is not sufficient merely to interfere with another's specialized use of her property or that the offensiveness arises from the plaintiff's hypersensitivity. To meet the unreasonableness standard, the severity of the injury inflicted must outweigh the utility of the defendant's conduct.

Here it could be argued that Fran's use is specialized—her business involves scented candles and an offensive odor would interfere with that type of business—and therefore, the chicken farm does not constitute a nuisance. However, the facts state that soon after Henry buys his first chicken, the farm creates a foul (fowl?) odor. Henry started his farm with only 10 chickens. Now, almost two years later, Henry must have many more chickens, so presumably the smell is much worse. Therefore, it seems likely that the odor would be offensive to an average person. Unfortunately, however, there are insufficient facts to determine the unreasonableness of Henry's use of his land. To succeed in her suit, Fran would have to show that her injury outweighed the utility of Henry's farm.

Assuming that the farm does constitute a nuisance, Fran has one more hurdle to clear—the defense of laches, which is discussed below in part 3.

2.   Fran could not obtain a preliminary injunction requiring Henry to close the farm. At issue is whether such an injunction would maintain the status quo.

A preliminary injunction is an interlocutory injunction that can be granted to maintain the status quo between the parties if a party can show likelihood of success on the merits and that she will suffer irreparable injury if the injunction is not granted. Here, a court would not likely grant a preliminary injunction requiring Henry to close his farm. First, such an injunction would not maintain the status quo—Henry is operating the farm now and the injunction would require him to close the farm. Moreover, it is not clear that Fran is suffering any irreparable injury. It appears that her business is still running nearly two years after Henry opened the farm. Any further loss of business that she suffers can be remedied with money damages. The fact that her business operated for two years before Henry opened his chicken farm will provide a basis for assessing damages. Thus, Fran would not likely be able to obtain a preliminary injunction.

3.   Based on Henry's February 2005 conversation with Fran, Henry would have two defenses to Fran's tort suit: laches and estoppel.

Laches is an equitable defense that is available when a person unreasonably delays bringing an action and the delay is prejudicial to the defendant. Here, the facts indicate that Henry started his farm with only 10 chickens in January 2005, and 18 months went by before Fran contemplated bringing an action against Henry. By the time Fran brought her action, Henry's farm grew from 10 chickens to over 10,000 chickens. Moreover, he is contractually obligated to provide eggs to local markets for the next six months. Under these circumstances, Fran's delay in bringing suit was prejudicial, because Henry's operation is much bigger than it was when it first started and he could be held liable in damages for breach of contract if he is forced to shut down his farm. It can also be argued that the delay was unreasonable, as Fran knew that the farm caused a decline in her business immediately after Henry opened the farm. On the other hand, it might be that if the decline was small, Fran wanted to see if things would level out. Or perhaps there has been a gradual decline in business as the number of chickens on the farm increased. Without more facts, it is difficult to make an accurate determination, but it seems likely that a court would find laches here.

A court will apply the estoppel doctrine if a person reasonably relies on a statement relating to present facts, it was intended or foreseeable that the statement would be relied upon, and the person relies on the facts to his detriment. In such a case, the speaker will be barred from denying the truth of the statement. Here, one month after Henry started the chicken farm and while he still had only 10 chickens, Fran told Henry that she had no problem with him opening the farm. It was foreseeable that Henry would rely on such a statement, and he has relied by obtaining over 10,000 chickens. Under these circumstances, Fran would likely be prohibited from now claiming that the farm is "a problem."

QUESTION 1

On the evening of December 19, Carl and Jane Jones were driving north on Oak Street, accompanied by their son Bobo, who was five. As they passed through the intersection of Oak and 12th Street, their SUV was struck by a car driven by Jim Wilson, who was accompanied by his wife, Betty Sue. Jim had failed to notice that he had a red light. Everyone was unharmed except Bobo. Although Bobo was properly restrained, he suffered a broken neck and a broken right arm.

Jim immediately used his cell phone to call for help, and an ambulance and the police were dispatched. After the ambulance arrived, and while waiting for the police to arrive, Carl Jones was walking around the scene. As he went past the Wilson automobile, he heard Betty Sue comment to her husband Jim, "I told you not to have that fifth beer." No blood alcohol testing was performed following the accident. Jim was charged with failing to obey a traffic signal.

A lawsuit was filed on behalf of Bobo against Jim in federal court based on diversity jurisdiction, and the case is now ready for trial. As a part of his defense, Jim Wilson denies any use of alcohol on the evening in question. Under the terms of the pretrial order entered by the court prior to the trial of the case, Betty Sue is listed as a will-call witness and is available to testify at the time of the trial.

Assume jurisdiction is proper in federal court.

1. After establishing the basic facts of how the accident occurred, the plaintiff's attorney calls Bobo, who is six and a half years old at the time of the trial, to testify. The defense objects on the ground that Bobo is incompetent due to his age and injuries. How should the court rule?

2. When Carl Jones is called to testify, he testifies as to the events that occurred immediately prior to and at the time of the impact. Bobo's attorney then asks him to describe the conversation he overheard between Betty Sue and Jim following the accident in regard to the consumption of alcohol. The defense objects on the basis of hearsay. How should the court rule?

3. Although denying liability for the accident, the defendant also takes the position that, if he is liable for causing the accident, the injuries to Bobo were enhanced by a faulty restraint system in the SUV. The defendant proposes to offer testimony from Dr. Smart, presented as an expert in accident reconstruction. Dr. Smart has a Ph.D. in mechanical engineering, but has spent most of his adult life as an aeronautical engineer. In the past two years, he has worked as an accident reconstructionist and has provided testimony by deposition, but this is the first case in which he has been called as a witness at trial. As a part of his testimony, Dr. Smart proposes to utilize measurements of skid marks that were taken by a police officer who investigated the accident but who is unavailable to testify at the time of the trial. Plaintiff objects to the use of the expert based on his lack of qualifications and also objects to any testimony as to the measurement of the skid marks, alleging that the information is hearsay. Should the court allow Dr. Smart to testify?

4. Assume Dr. Smart is allowed to testify. How should the court rule in regard to his use of the skid mark measurements?

5. **After the defense rests, the plaintiff offers as a rebuttal witness the testimony of police sergeant William Brown. Sergeant Brown was the primary investigating officer, but is currently serving in the armed forces and is unavailable. The plaintiff proposes to read the transcript of Brown's prior testimony at the traffic court hearing where the driving charges against Jim were tried one week after the accident occurred. Sergeant Brown testified at length as to his findings at the scene of the accident and his opinions, under oath, at the traffic court hearing. At the time of the traffic court hearing, both parties were present, both parties were represented by counsel, and a court reporter had been retained to record the testimony. The defendant objects to the use of the testimony solely on the basis that it is hearsay. How should the court rule?**

ANSWER TO QUESTION 1

1.   The court should overrule the defendant's objection that Bobo is incompetent to testify due to his age and injuries. At issue is whether a six-year-old can be a competent witness.

The general rule is that every person is competent to be a witness. However, the witness must have personal knowledge of the matter to which he will testify (*i.e.*, the witness must have observed the matter and must have a present recollection of his observation) and must declare that he will testify truthfully. In determining the competency of a child, the court must examine the capacity and intelligence of the particular child.

Here, Bobo is six and a half years old, and as such, he should be able to understand the obligation to testify truthfully. Moreover, so long as Bobo has sufficient recollection of the accident and can relate his recollection at trial, his age and injuries should not bar him from testifying about the accident. Thus, the court should overrule the defendant's objection that Bobo is incompetent to testify at trial.

2.   The court should overrule the defendant's objection to Carl Jones's testimony. The issue is whether the statement is hearsay and if it is, whether it is admissible under an exception to the hearsay rule.

Hearsay is an out-of-court statement offered to prove the truth of the matter asserted. Hearsay generally is inadmissible unless it falls within an exception to the hearsay rule.

Here, the plaintiff seeks to introduce, through Carl Jones's testimony, Betty Sue's statement to Jim that he should not have had that fifth beer. The statement was made out of court and it is being offered to prove the truth of the matter asserted because the plaintiff is attempting to establish that Jim was drunk and that his drunkenness contributed to the accident. Thus, the statement is hearsay. However, the statement may be admitted as an excited utterance. A statement made by a declarant during the stress of excitement is admissible as an exception to the hearsay rule. In this case, the accident was a startling event, and Betty Sue made the statement to Jim shortly after the accident. Not much time could have passed between the accident and Betty Sue's statement to Jim, because the police had not even arrived at the scene at the time Betty Sue made the statement. Therefore, the statement would qualify as an excited utterance and is admissible in evidence.

3.   The court should overrule the plaintiff's objection to Dr. Smart's testifying. The issue is what is required to qualify as an expert witness.

A person may testify as an expert if the person has special knowledge, skill, experience, training, or education sufficient to qualify him as an expert on the subject to which his testimony relates. Consequently, the court has to examine Dr. Smart's qualifications to determine if he can testify as an expert. In this case, Dr. Smart has a Ph.D. in mechanical engineering. Moreover, the defendant offered Dr. Smart as an expert in accident reconstruction, and Dr. Smart has worked as an accident reconstructionist for two years. Therefore, based on Dr. Smart's education and his knowledge and experience as an accident reconstructionist, he should be allowed to testify as an expert witness.

4.   Dr. Smart should be able to use the skid mark measurements in his testimony. An expert's opinion may be based on: (i) facts the expert knows from his own observations; (ii) facts presented in evidence at the trial and submitted to the expert; or (iii) facts not in evidence that were supplied to the expert out of court and which are of a type reasonably relied upon by experts in the field in forming opinions on the subject. Such facts need not even be of a type admissible in evidence. Thus, assuming accident reconstructionists rely on skid mark measurements taken by police officers (which seems very likely), Dr. Smart should be allowed to use the measurements in forming his opinions while testifying.

5.   The court should overrule the defendant's objection to the admission of Sergeant Brown's testimony. The issue here is the former testimony exception to the hearsay rule.

Sergeant Brown's former testimony is clearly hearsay. However, the testimony of a now unavailable witness given under oath at another hearing is admissible in a subsequent trial if there is sufficient similarity of parties and issues so that the opportunity to develop testimony or cross-examination at the prior hearing was meaningful.

Here, Sergeant Brown is now unavailable as a witness because he is serving in the armed forces. Sergeant Brown's prior testimony was given under oath at the traffic court hearing. In addition, the parties were both present at the traffic court hearing; the subject matter of the traffic court hearing and the civil case filed by the plaintiff is the same—it regards Jim's negligent driving; and both parties were represented by counsel at the hearing. Thus, Jim had a meaningful opportunity to cross-examine Sergeant Brown at the prior hearing. Consequently, the court should allow into evidence the transcript of Sergeant Brown's testimony at the traffic court hearing.

QUESTION 2

Three years ago, Mary entered into a five-year contract with Big Burger, Inc. ("BB") to operate a Big Burger restaurant franchise. Two months ago, BB's owner, Howard, terminated Mary's franchise.

Howard claims that Mary's food-handling practices were substandard and that she failed to maintain the basic appearance of the restaurant. If proven, that would constitute a material breach of the contract, entitling BB to terminate the franchise. Mary contends that her franchise has always been clean and well-maintained. She claims Howard terminated her franchise only because he wants his son Junior, an aspiring windsurfer, to run it. Mary has filed suit against BB for breach of contract, and she has requested a jury trial. At trial:

1.   Before any witness is called, Mary's attorney offers a certified copy of the county health department's inspection log listing her franchise as having met food-handling standards in the last three inspections. BB's attorney objects that the log has not been authenticated and that it is hearsay. How should the court rule?

2. **Mary's attorney calls a janitor to testify that he overheard Howard say, "I want Junior off that stupid sailboard and running one of my restaurants." What objection(s) should BB's attorney make and how should the court rule?**

3. **BB's attorney then calls Howard to testify that BB's janitor falsified a time card. What objection(s) should Mary's attorney make and how should the court rule?**

4. **BB's attorney calls Howard to testify that Howard and Ann (the former franchisee) were involved in a bitter personal dispute that ended their business relationship. Ann has already testified, but was not asked about the dispute. What objection(s) should Mary's attorney make and how should the court rule?**

5. **BB's attorney calls Mary's husband to testify that Mary privately told him she had long wanted out of her franchise agreement and had sued BB only to hurt Howard, whom she disliked. What objection(s) should Mary's attorney make and how should the court rule?**

ANSWER TO QUESTION 2

1. *Certified copy of county health inspection log:* The court will likely find the health department inspection log to be admissible. At issue is the admissibility of a certified copy of a government record.

BB's attorney's objection that the log has not been authenticated will be overruled. Under the Federal Rules of Evidence, a certified copy of a public record is self-authenticating. The facts state that the log is a certified copy of the county health department's inspection log. Therefore, it is self-authenticating and the attorney's objection based on authentication should be overruled.

BB's attorney's objection that the log is hearsay will also be overruled. Hearsay is an out-of-court statement offered to prove the truth of the matter asserted. Hearsay is generally inadmissible unless it falls within an exception to the hearsay rule. Here, the log is an out-of-court statement and it is being offered for its truth. However, the log fits into the public records exception. Public records are presumed to be trustworthy because officials are under a duty to record properly that which they do. Here, the log is a public record, and therefore is admissible.

2. *Testimony of janitor regarding Howard's statement:* The court will likely find the janitor's testimony is admissible. At issue is whether this statement constitutes hearsay. As noted above, hearsay is an out-of-court statement offered to prove the truth of the matter asserted. Admissions by parties, however, are treated as nonhearsay under the Federal Rules and are therefore admissible. Here, the statement the janitor wants to testify about was made by Howard, one of the parties. Therefore, it qualifies as an admission of a party-opponent and is admissible.

3. *Howard's testimony about the janitor's time card:* The court will likely exclude the evidence that the janitor falsified his time card. At issue is whether extrinsic proof of bad acts may be used to impeach a witness. A witness's credibility generally can be impeached at trial through cross-examination or through extrinsic evidence (*e.g.*, by testimony about the witness's reputation for truthfulness). However, impeachment through specific acts of misconduct is limited. A witness may be interrogated about specific prior acts of deceit or lying, as long as there is a reasonable basis for believing that the witness may have committed the act. However, extrinsic evidence of the act is not permitted—even if the witness denies having committed the act. Other

witnesses may not be called to testify about the bad act. Here, BB is trying to impeach the janitor's credibility by having Howard testify that the janitor falsified a time card, rather than by asking the janitor about it on cross-examination. This is impermissible, so the evidence will be excluded.

4. ***Howard's testimony about the bitter personal dispute between Ann and Howard:*** The court will likely find that Howard's testimony is inadmissible. At issue is whether extrinsic evidence of a witness's bias can be used to impeach that witness. A witness may be impeached by extrinsic evidence of bias as long as a proper foundation is laid. Such a foundation requires that the witness be asked about the facts that show bias on cross-examination. If the witness denies these facts, the witness can then be impeached by extrinsic evidence of bias. Here, BB wants Howard to testify about the bitter personal dispute between Howard and Ann to show that Ann is biased against Howard, thereby impeaching her credibility. However, Ann was not asked about the facts surrounding the bitter personal dispute on cross-examination. Therefore, it is improper for BB to try to show Ann's bias through extrinsic evidence. Thus, the testimony will be excluded.

5. ***Testimony of Mary's husband about Mary's motive:*** Mary can prevent her husband from testifying as to confidential communications made during their marriage. At issue is whether one spouse can prevent the other from testifying. In any civil or criminal case, a spouse has a privilege to refuse to disclose, and to prevent another from disclosing, a confidential communication made between the spouses while they were husband and wife. Here, the conversation that BB's attorney wants Mary's husband to testify about was private and appears to have been a confidential communication not intended to be disclosed to any other person. Furthermore, the conversation took place while Mary and her husband were married. Therefore, Mary can prevent her spouse from disclosing this information.

QUESTION 3

Alice was riding her bicycle down Main Street. Brent, driving his van, came through the intersection and hit Alice. Alice filed suit against Brent in federal court, alleging that he negligently ran a stop sign, causing her bodily injury. Assume that jurisdiction is proper in federal court.

Applying only the Federal Rules of Evidence, discuss the admissibility of the following evidence offered at trial:

1. **Offered by Alice—Alice's testimony that just after the accident, Brent stepped out of his van and said, "I'm so sorry that I ran that stop sign and hit you."**

2. **Offered by Alice—testimony by Pastor Smith, the pastor at Brent's church, that Brent privately sought counsel from him for depression two years ago.**

3. **Offered by Alice—testimony by Ellen, Brent's former girlfriend, that Brent ran through stop signs without stopping on three other occasions.**

4. **Offered by Brent—a letter written by Ellen to Brent that says, "One of these days, I will get back at you for the heartbreak you caused me."**

5. **Offered by Brent—testimony by Zoe that Alice is known around town for telling "tall tales."**

6. **Offered by Brent—testimony by John that his brother, who witnessed the accident, told him, "Brent stopped at the stop sign and looked both ways before cautiously proceeding into the intersection."**

ANSWER TO QUESTION 3

1. *Brent's statement:* Alice's testimony regarding Brent's statement is admissible. At issue is whether this statement constitutes inadmissible hearsay. Hearsay is a statement, other than one made by the declarant while testifying at the trial, offered in evidence to prove the truth of the matter asserted. Some statements are excluded from the hearsay definition because they are an admission of a party. An admission is a party's own statement offered against him.

Here, Brent is a party. He made the statement and it is offered against him. Therefore, it is not hearsay under the Federal Rules of Evidence and is admissible.

This statement also could come in as an exception to the general hearsay rule. An "excited utterance"—a statement relating to a startling event made while under the stress of excitement from that event—is admissible. A traffic accident is certainly a startling event, and Brent made the statement immediately after the accident. Thus, the statement is likely admissible as an excited utterance.

2. *Pastor's testimony:* Pastor Smith's testimony will likely be excluded. Two issues arise here: privilege and relevance.

The first issue is clergy-penitent privilege. Some states recognize a clergy-penitent privilege that prevents clerics from testifying as to confidential communications made to them in their capacity as spiritual adviser. However, the federal courts do not currently recognize a clergy-penitent privilege. Therefore, Brent cannot claim this privilege to prevent the communication from being admitted. Nevertheless, it will probably be excluded on relevance grounds, as discussed below.

Generally, only relevant evidence is admissible. Relevant evidence is evidence having a tendency to make the existence of any fact that is of consequence to the determination of the action more probable or less probable than it would be without the evidence. However, even relevant evidence may be excluded if its probative value is substantially outweighed by the danger of unfair prejudice, confusion of the issues, or misleading the jury, or by considerations of undue delay or needless presentation of cumulative evidence.

Here, evidence of depression two years ago probably does not have any consequence to the determination of the action. Even if there was some tendency towards relevance, without some evidence of a causal link between the depression and the alleged negligence, the probative value of the pastor's testimony probably is substantially outweighed by the danger of unfair prejudice or misleading the jury. Thus, the evidence should be excluded on relevance grounds.

3. *Ellen's testimony:* Ellen's testimony is inadmissible. At issue is whether evidence of a prior act can be used to prove the character of a person. Evidence of other crimes, wrongs, or acts is not admissible to prove the character of a person in order to show that the person acted in conformity therewith. That Brent previously ran a few stop signs is evidence of "past wrongs or acts." Such evidence cannot be used to prove that on this occasion he also ran a stop sign. Although there are several exceptions to the general rule of exclusion, none applies here. Thus, the testimony is inadmissible.

Alice might argue that this is admissible as "habit" evidence, but such an argument will likely fail. Habit evidence is relevant to prove that the conduct of a person was in conformity with the habit or routine practice. Habit describes one's regular response to a specific set of circumstances. Here, the facts do not demonstrate sufficient frequency or predictability to reach habit. Thus, the evidence is inadmissible.

4. *Ellen's letter:* Ellen's letter is admissible. At issue is whether a letter a witness wrote may be used to impeach that witness. The credibility of a witness may be attacked by evidence that the witness engaged in conduct or made statements showing bias or interest. Here, the letter indicates that Ellen has a grudge against Brent. This is indicative of bias on her part, and may be considered by the finder of fact in assessing her credibility. Thus, the evidence is admissible.

One might argue that the letter is hearsay. However, the letter falls outside the hearsay definition. It is offered to show bias, not to prove "the truth of the matter asserted." Therefore, a hearsay objection would be overruled.

5. *Zoe's testimony:* Zoe's testimony is admissible. At issue is whether a witness may be impeached by another witness testifying about her reputation. The credibility of a witness may be attacked or supported by evidence in the form of opinion or reputation as to the witness's character for truthfulness or untruthfulness. Here, Zoe's testimony apparently comes from general knowledge of Alice's reputation in their community. This testimony goes directly to Alice's untruthfulness. Once it is established that Zoe is familiar with Alice's reputation, this evidence is admissible.

6. *John's testimony:* John's testimony is not admissible. At issue is whether this statement constitutes inadmissible hearsay. As noted under answer 1., above, hearsay is a statement, other than one made by the declarant while testifying at the trial, offered in evidence to prove the truth of the matter asserted. Some statements are excluded from the definition of hearsay, and other statements are admissible because of exceptions to the general rule.

Here, the statement is apparently offered to prove the truth of the matter asserted—that Brent stopped at the stop sign. It was made by a declarant outside of the trial. Therefore, it meets the definition of hearsay and is inadmissible unless otherwise permitted. It does not fit into any of the exclusions (nonhearsay) or exceptions. Thus, the evidence should be excluded.

QUESTION 4

One day last year, while on a cross-country trip, Carl spotted Bob along the side of the highway. Bob was holding a sign indicating that he was seeking a ride west. Bob looked harmless, so Carl decided to offer him a ride. Shortly after Bob joined Carl, the two began talking. It soon became apparent to each man that they were polar opposites on many issues, and their conversation quickly became heated.

A few minutes after the two men began arguing about global warming, Carl had to pull over because of a flat tire. Carl asked Bob to help him change the tire. Bob replied, "There is no help for imbeciles like you," and he stormed off down the road.

After changing the tire, Carl proceeded down the highway. Upon viewing Bob walking on the shoulder, Carl swerved and struck Bob with the right front end of his vehicle and fled the scene.

A police officer soon spotted Bob on the side of the road. Bob was injured, but not seriously. He was able to give the officer a description of Carl and his car, and Carl was quickly located and returned to the scene. Carl admitted to the officer that he had picked up Bob, that they had an argument, and that he was very angry with Bob. This information was subsequently included in the police report.

A few weeks later Bob filed a civil tort battery action against Carl in federal district court, based on diversity jurisdiction. At trial:

1. Bob seeks to introduce a certified copy of Carl's criminal assault conviction that arose from other events two years ago. Carl objects.

2. Bob seeks the introduction of the statement that Carl made to the police and contends that the statement by Carl is not hearsay.

3. Bob further contends that even if the statement is hearsay, it is admissible because it is a:

   (a) Statement of state of mind;

   (b) Business record; or

   (c) Declaration against interest.

How should the court rule on each of the matters raised? Support your answer.

ANSWER TO QUESTION 4

1. The criminal conviction is inadmissible. Evidence of character to prove the conduct of a person in the litigated event is generally not admissible in a civil case. Such evidence is admissible only when a person's character itself is one of the issues in the case. Here, Carl is on trial for battery, so his character is not an issue in the case. Bob likely wants to introduce Carl's prior conviction to show that Carl acted in the same way here. Because this is a civil case and Carl's character is not an issue, the prior conviction is inadmissible.

2. Carl's statement is admissible nonhearsay. Hearsay is an out-of-court statement offered in evidence to prove the truth of the matter asserted. However, under the Federal Rules of Evidence, a statement is not hearsay if it is an admission of a party-opponent. An admission is a statement that amounts to an acknowledgment by one of the parties to an action of one of the relevant facts. A party may offer into evidence against his opponent anything said by the party. Admissions do not have to be against the declarant's interest when made. Thus, Carl's statement is admissible as an admission of a party-opponent. Note that the party making the statement, Carl, can take the stand and explain the statement.

3.(a) If Carl's statement is hearsay, it would not be admissible under the statement of state of mind exception. To fall within this exception, statements must be of a present existing state of mind and must appear to not have been made under suspicious circumstances. Here, Carl's statement was merely an attempt to explain his former conduct rather than one that was evidence of his intent at the time the statement was made. Thus, Carl's statement does not meet the requirements of the state of mind exception.

(b)   If Carl's statement is hearsay, it would not be admissible under the business records exception. The business records exception provides that a writing or record made in the regular course of business as a memorandum or record of any act, transaction, occurrence, or event is admissible as proof of that act, transaction, occurrence, or event.

A police report indicating that an accident occurred, citing the parties involved, and noting other aspects of the accident observable by the investigating officer comes within the exception. However, statements made to the officer by witnesses or parties to the accident are not admissible unless they come within some other hearsay exception. Here, the report contains information supplied to the officer by Carl. Carl does not have a business duty to report accurately. Therefore, his statement does not fall within the business records exception and is inadmissible hearsay.

(c)   If Carl's statement is hearsay, it would not be admissible under the declaration against interest exception. This exception requires that the declarant state facts which are against his pecuniary or proprietary interest at the time they are made, and that the declarant be unavailable at the time of trial. Here, at the time Carl made his statement to the officer, it was against his interest because it would expose him to civil liability. However, Carl is available to testify at trial. For this reason, his statement does not fall within the declaration against interest exception.

QUESTION 5

Carl and Roy were suspected of being drug dealers. Police learned that Carl frequently visited an apartment that was leased to Roy. Police began to observe the apartment and saw Carl there on several occasions. Eventually the police gathered sufficient information to obtain a search warrant for the apartment. Upon entering the apartment the police saw Carl and Roy. Carl's hands were covered with cocaine powder. During the search the police found a large amount of crack cocaine, a set of scales, plastic baggies, and other items associated with the process of changing powdered cocaine into crack cocaine. In addition, a photograph of Carl kneeling behind several stacks of money was found in a back room of the apartment. Carl and Roy were placed under arrest and charged with possession of cocaine with intent to distribute.

Carl admits that he is a drug user, but maintains that he was in the apartment only to purchase drugs from Roy for his own use. Carl claims that his hands were covered with cocaine powder because he was testing the product before purchasing it.

The state attempts to introduce into evidence in its case-in-chief the following: (i) the photograph of Carl found in the back room of the apartment; (ii) Carl's prior conviction from three years ago for felony burglary; and (iii) Carl's offer to testify against Roy in exchange for probation, which was rejected by the prosecutor.

Carl's lawyer objects to the introduction into evidence of (i) the photograph because it is irrelevant and prejudicial; (ii) Carl's prior conviction of burglary; and (iii) Carl's offer to testify against Roy in exchange for probation.

1.   **How will the trial court rule on each of Carl's objections? Explain the basis for each ruling.**

2. **Would the court's ruling change as to any objection if the evidence were offered to impeach Carl's testimony? Explain your answer.**

ANSWER TO QUESTION 5

1.(i)   *The photograph:* The photograph is probably admissible. The issue is whether a photograph of the defendant with large amounts of money is relevant when the defendant is being prosecuted for possession of cocaine with intent to distribute.

Evidence is relevant and therefore admissible if it tends either to establish or disprove the issue in dispute. Carl's lawyer should argue that a photograph of Carl kneeling behind stacks of money has nothing to do with possession of cocaine with the intent to distribute and, therefore, is irrelevant. The state, however, should counter that the picture is relevant for two reasons: First, it tends to disprove Carl's claim that he was in the apartment only to purchase cocaine and suggests a stronger connection between Carl and the apartment (*i.e.,* if Carl was in the apartment only to buy cocaine, how did a picture of him make it into a back room of the apartment?). Second, it tends to prove an intent to distribute, as the picture shows Carl kneeling behind stacks of money, and it is common for drug distributors to possess large sums of money. Thus, an objection that the photograph is irrelevant will likely be overruled by the judge.

Carl's claim that the photograph is prejudicial also will fail. Even relevant evidence may be excluded if its probative value is substantially outweighed by the danger of unfair prejudice. Introducing the photograph into evidence may unfairly prejudice Carl because large amounts of cash often are associated with the drug culture. The balancing of the probative value of the photograph (connecting Carl to the apartment) against its prejudice to the defendant (drug culture association) is done by the trial judge. Although the photograph is unfairly prejudicial, given the connection it creates between Carl and the apartment, the judge will likely overrule this objection. Assuming that the photograph is also properly authenticated, it will likely be admitted into evidence.

(ii)   *Carl's prior conviction:* Carl's prior conviction is not admissible. The issue is whether evidence of another crime is admissible in a criminal trial. The Federal Rules do not allow evidence of other crimes to prove the character of a person in order to show action in conformity therewith. However, evidence of other crimes may be admissible for other purposes, such as proof of motive, opportunity, intent, preparation, common scheme or plan, knowledge, identity, or absence of mistake or accident. Here, none of the exceptions is applicable. Therefore the objection should be sustained by the judge.

(iii) *Carl's offer to testify against Roy:* Carl's offer to testify against Roy is inadmissible. The issue is whether statements made during plea discussions are admissible. Statements made in the course of plea discussions that do not result in a plea of guilty are inadmissible under the Federal Rules. Here, Carl offered to testify against Roy in exchange for probation, which was rejected by the prosecutor. This indicates that the statement was made in connection with plea discussions that did not result in a plea of guilty. Therefore it is not admissible.

2.   The court's ruling on the prior conviction would be different if it were offered to impeach Carl's testimony. The issue is whether a conviction that is inadmissible in the state's case-in-chief may be used to impeach the defendant. For felonies not involving dishonesty (meaning deceit or false statement), a prior conviction will be admitted for purposes of impeachment if the government shows that its probative value as impeachment evidence outweighs its prejudicial effect.

Additionally, the conviction must not be too remote. Under the Federal Rules, a conviction is too remote if more than 10 years have elapsed since the date of the conviction or the date of release from the confinement imposed for the conviction, whichever is later. Here, the conviction falls within the 10-year time limit. The trial judge must weigh the probative value against the prejudicial facts. Based on the facts, the court would probably allow the state to introduce evidence of the conviction.

QUESTION 6

Victor was taken by ambulance to a hospital. Standard hospital practice requires the admitting nurse in the emergency room to record all information provided by a patient about the cause of the patient's illness or injury. Following that practice, the admitting nurse, Nurse, asked Victor: "What happened?" Victor responded: "I was stabbed with a big knife. Dan did it." Nurse immediately wrote Victor's statement in the appropriate place in the hospital record.

One week after his hospital admission, Victor unexpectedly died as a result of the stab wound. Dan was charged with Victor's murder.

When Victor's wife, Wife, heard of Dan's arrest, she was shocked. She told Friend, "When Victor and I were alone together in the hospital, he told me who stabbed him, and it wasn't Dan!" But Wife refused to tell Friend whom Victor had identified as his assailant.

During the trial, in order to prove that Dan stabbed Victor, the prosecutor offered the hospital record made by Nurse that contained Victor's statement that Dan stabbed him. The prosecutor cannot locate Nurse to testify at trial. Defense counsel objected to admission of the hospital record and the statements in it, but the court overruled the objection.

During the presentation of Dan's case, defense counsel suggested that Victor had been attacked by Stepson, Wife's child by a previous marriage. Defense counsel called Wife as a witness and questioned her concerning Victor's statement to her about the identity of his assailant. Wife refused to answer on the basis of the marital privilege. The prosecutor objected to the questions directed to Wife on the grounds that they sought to elicit hearsay. The court sustained both Wife's claim of privilege and the prosecutor's hearsay objection.

1. **Did the trial court err in admitting into evidence the hospital record containing Victor's statement? Explain.**

2. **Did the trial court err in sustaining Wife's claim of privilege? Explain.**

3. **Did the trial court err in sustaining the prosecutor's hearsay objection to Wife's testimony? Explain.**

ANSWER TO QUESTION 6

1. Yes, the court erred in admitting into evidence the hospital record containing Victor's statement. The hospital record and Victor's statement contained within the record constitute "hearsay within

hearsay" and are not admissible. The issue is whether an out-of-court statement is admissible into evidence. Generally, hearsay is an out-of-court statement offered to prove the truth of the matter asserted and is not admissible unless it falls within an exception to the hearsay rule. Hearsay within hearsay is an out-of-court statement that incorporates other hearsay, and is admissible only if *both* the outer hearsay statement and the inner hearsay statement fall within an exception to the hearsay rule. Here, both the hospital record (the outer hearsay) and the statement within it (the inner hearsay) made by Victor must fall within an exception to the hearsay rule in order for the record to be admitted into evidence.

The hospital record is hearsay because it is being offered to prove the truth of the matter asserted—that Victor was stabbed with a knife by Dan. A hospital record is admissible under the business records exception to the hearsay rule if it was: (i) made in the regular course of the business, (ii) the regular course of the business to make the record at the time of the event, and (iii) made by a person whose duty it was to make the record and who had personal knowledge of the event. In this instance, the record was made, pursuant to hospital practice, by the admitting nurse, who had a duty to record all information provided by the patient about the nature and cause of his injury. Thus, the record is properly admissible under the business records exception to the hearsay rule.

The statement within the record also constitutes hearsay because it is being offered to prove the truth of the matter asserted and must fall within an exception to the hearsay rule. Victor made two statements to the nurse—that he was stabbed and that Dan is the person who stabbed him. The first statement ("I was stabbed with a big knife") is a declaration of a past bodily condition. Declarations of past bodily condition are admissible if made to medical personnel to assist in diagnosing or treating a condition. That statement that Victor was stabbed with a big knife is admissible as a declaration of past bodily condition because he made the statement to the admitting nurse and it will be relevant to his diagnosis or treatment. The second statement ("Dan did it") is not admissible. The exception to the hearsay rule allowing declarations of past bodily condition includes any statement of the cause or source of the condition if it is reasonably pertinent to diagnosis or treatment. Although Victor's statement that Dan stabbed him does relate to the cause of his condition, it is inadmissible because it is not pertinent to his treatment.

Although the record itself is admissible under the business records exception to the hearsay rule, it should have been excluded because one of the statements contained within the record fails to satisfy any exception to the hearsay rule.

2.   The court did not err in sustaining Wife's claim of privilege. The issue is whether spouses can refuse to disclose confidential communications with one another. The marital privilege provides that either spouse has a privilege not to testify as to a confidential communication made between spouses during the marriage. The communication must be made in reliance upon the intimacy of the marital relationship, and the privilege survives the marriage. The privilege does not apply, however, if the communication is revealed to a third party. In this case, Victor and Wife were alone together in the hospital room when Victor confided in her the identity of his attacker. The communication was made while they were married and in reliance upon the intimacy of their marriage. The fact that Victor is now dead is irrelevant. Wife did, however, reveal part of the communication to Friend, indicating that Dan did not attack Victor, although she did not reveal the identity of the true attacker. Thus, she can probably claim the privilege with respect to the identity of the true attacker but the court may require that she testify as to the portion of the conversation indicating that Dan did not attack Victor.

3. Yes, the court erred in sustaining the prosecutor's hearsay objection to Wife's testimony. The issue is whether a hearsay declarant can be impeached. Generally, when a hearsay statement is admitted into evidence, the party against whom the statement is offered has the opportunity to impeach the credibility of the declarant by evidence that would be admissible if the declarant had testified as a witness. Here, the court admitted into evidence Victor's hearsay statement that he was stabbed by Dan. The defense should now be given the opportunity to impeach the credibility of Victor by evidence of any inconsistent statements he may have made regarding the identity of his attacker, even if the statement is hearsay. (Note that the statement is admissible only to impeach his credibility, and not as substantive evidence that Stepson was the attacker.) Thus, the court should have overruled the prosecutor's objection.

QUESTION 7

Ray Ramirez ("Ramirez") owns Ray's Roofing, a sole proprietorship. In October of 2006, Ramirez and his crew were replacing the roof on an apartment building in Joliet, Illinois (a city in Will County).

Ramirez had carefully trained his employees to establish wide safety perimeters below their roof projects. The employees did this by installing wooden barricades to prevent pedestrians from entering the area where falling debris could injure them. Tim Onway ("Onway") was responsible for erecting the barricades and completing the company's Daily Safety Summary ("DSS"), which included a list of safety precautions and a computer-generated diagram showing where the barricades were placed. As he always did, Onway completed the DSS at 7:45 a.m. on October 17, 2006, by, in part, checking the box reading "installed as shown" next to the diagram.

At roughly 8 a.m. that day, Anna Boyd ("Boyd") was walking near the project when she was struck by a shingle that had blown off the roof. It hit her in the face, causing significant damage to her left eye. She collapsed and lost consciousness.

Paramedic Frank Field ("Field") was the first medical professional to arrive at the scene, where he found Boyd unresponsive. Field noticed that Boyd was lying outside an incomplete perimeter of barricades, and that other, identical barricades were still stacked on the ground. Field soon overheard Ramirez calmly whisper to Onway—both of whom had rushed down from the roof when the ambulance arrived—"You know perfectly well you're not allowed to set foot on the roof before setting up *all* the barricades. You've really put the company at risk today."

Boyd eventually filed a personal injury action in Will County Circuit Court against Ray Ramirez d/b/a Ray's Roofing. On June 30, 2007, Field sat for a discovery deposition under Illinois Supreme Court Rule 212. In it, he recalled finding Boyd lying outside an incomplete line of barricades. Field also described what he had overheard Ramirez say to Onway. Field later reviewed the deposition transcript and certified its accuracy by signing the certification page.

The case proceeded to trial. Field was a key witness. While testifying on direct examination as a witness for Boyd, Field was asked to describe what Ramirez said to Onway about not going onto the roof until erecting all the barricades. Defense counsel objected on hearsay grounds. The judge overruled the objection and allowed Field to testify about what he had heard.

At a later point during his direct examination, Field testified that he had found Boyd lying *inside* a partially complete barricade. After Field repeated that observation in response to several follow up questions, Boyd's lawyer asked Field to think back to his June 30, 2007, deposition and asked Field whether he recalled testifying then that Boyd was actually lying *outside* the barricade. Defense counsel interposed a hearsay objection, which the judge overruled and allowed the testimony for a limited purpose. Field then testified that he recalled his deposition testimony on the issue, but asserted that he must have been mistaken when testifying at the deposition.

Later, during the defendant's case, Onway testified that he prepared a DSS at the beginning of each work day, and that he prepared the DSS minutes before the accident. Later, he forwarded a copy of the DSS to his office, where it was usually stored in a file. When defense counsel offered the original DSS into evidence, counsel for Boyd objected on hearsay grounds. The judge sustained the objection, preventing the DSS from going into evidence.

(a) Did the judge err in overruling the objection to Field's testimony about the conversation between Ramirez and Onway? Explain.

(b) Did the judge err in overruling the objection to Field's testimony about his statements during the Rule 212 deposition? Explain.

(c) Did the judge err in sustaining the objection to the introduction of the DSS report? Explain.

ANSWER TO QUESTION 7

(a) *Conversation between Ramirez and Onway:* No, the judge did not err in overruling the objection to Field's testimony regarding the statement he overheard. Field can testify regarding the statement made by Ramirez to Onway because it is not hearsay. At issue is whether the statement is hearsay, thus precluding Field's testimony. Hearsay is defined as an out-of-court statement offered to prove the truth of the matter asserted. Here, the statement by Ramirez falls within the traditional definition of hearsay—it is being offered to prove that Onway should not have been on the roof until all the barricades were erected. However, a statement that constitutes an admission by a party-opponent is removed from the definition of hearsay and is admissible. An admission is a statement that amounts to a prior acknowledgment by one of the parties to an action of one of the relevant facts. Here, Ramirez stated that Onway should not have been on the roof until all the barricades were erected. This is an admission by a party and it is relevant in determining whether Onway acted negligently in erecting the barricades. Thus, the statement is admissible and the judge did not err in overruling the objection to Field's testimony.

(b) *Field's deposition statement:* No, the judge did not err in overruling the objection to Field's prior statement. At issue is whether Field's prior statement made during the deposition constitutes hearsay when offered in the subsequent trial. As stated above, hearsay is an out-of-court statement offered to prove the truth of the matter asserted. Here, Field's prior statement falls within the traditional definition of hearsay—it is being offered to prove whether Boyd was lying inside or outside of the barricade. However, a witness's prior inconsistent statement is removed from the definition of hearsay if it was made under oath at a prior proceeding or deposition. The statement is admissible to impeach the witness's credibility and also as substantive evidence. Field's prior inconsistent statement is admissible because it was made under oath during a deposition. Thus, the judge did not err and the statement can be used to impeach Field's credibility and also as substantive evidence.

(c)   ***Introduction of DSS report:*** Yes, the judge erred in sustaining the objection to the admissibility of the DSS report. The issue is whether the DSS report is admissible. Generally, the report constitutes hearsay because it is an out-of-court statement offered to prove the truth of the matter asserted—that the barricades were installed as indicated on the diagram at 7:45 a.m. However, the report is admissible under the business records exception to the hearsay rule. The business records exception provides that any writing or record made as the memorandum or record of any act is admissible in evidence as proof of that act if made in the regular course of business. The record must have been made by someone who had that duty as part of his employment and it must have been made at or near the time of the transaction. Here, completion of the DSS is within the ordinary course of the roofing business and the facts state that Onway completed the DSS "as he always did," indicating that it was his duty to complete the DSS. Additionally, the report was completed immediately after Onway installed the barricades. Thus, the DSS is admissible hearsay pursuant to the business records exception and the judge erred in sustaining the objection to its admissibility.

QUESTION 1

Soon after Herb and Winnie married, Winnie began working as a cook in a local restaurant to support Herb, who had started chiropractic school. Winnie and Herb decided that she would become a surrogate mother to supplement the family income. Herb and Winnie entered into a written agreement with Don, a married man, whose wife Sally had been unable to bear children. The agreement provided that Winnie would 1) be artificially inseminated with Don's semen, 2) bear the child of the resulting pregnancy, 3) relinquish all of her rights to the child, and 4) cooperate in proceedings to terminate her parental rights immediately after the birth of the child. Don agreed to pay Winnie $10,000 and to be responsible for all medical expenses related to the pregnancy and childbirth. Herb consented to Winnie's artificial insemination, agreed not to claim parental rights, and agreed to do whatever was necessary to establish Don as the child's legal father.

Winnie became pregnant as a result of artificial insemination and delivered a baby, Carol, about the time Herb graduated from chiropractic school. By the time the baby arrived, however, Winnie had decided that she would keep Carol. Sally and Don were happy to terminate the contract because Sally had unexpectedly become pregnant. Sally and Don had already paid Winnie's fee and her medical expenses and did not want a refund. However, Herb disagreed with Winnie's desire to keep Carol and reminded her that before they married they had agreed in writing not to have children. Despite Herb's objections, Winnie decided to keep Carol.

Because of their irreconcilable conflict over Carol, Herb and Winnie have agreed to divorce. Winnie, who will have custody of Carol, seeks child support from Herb. She also wants to be compensated for helping put Herb through chiropractic school. Herb and Winnie have virtually no property, and Winnie, who quit school after high school, lacks the skills to get a good job. Herb has a thriving practice as a chiropractor ahead of him.

1.   Is Herb the legal father of Carol? Explain.

2.   Assuming that Herb is the legal father of Carol, is he liable for supporting her? Explain.

3.   Should the court order Herb to compensate Winnie for helping him through school, and, if so, what form should the compensation take? Explain.

ANSWER TO QUESTION 1

1.   Although Herb is not Carol's biological father, he may be her legal father. Whether Herb is Carol's legal father depends on his ability to rebut the presumption that, because Carol is Winnie's child, she is also Herb's child. The presumption that the child of a married woman is the marital child of her husband is rebuttable by clear and convincing evidence in some states, and by a preponderance of the evidence in others. A blood test would show that Herb is not the biological father. Herb would then attempt to use the signed surrogacy agreement (sometimes called a gestational agreement) as evidence that he is also not the legal father, but first he must show that the agreement is valid.

Although the Uniform Status of Children of Assisted Conception Act was promulgated in 1988 and has been incorporated into the Uniform Parentage Act of 2000 (amended in 2002), many states have yet to adopt such legislation, either because they disagree with its content, or because these issues have not yet been presented in their jurisdiction. In states that do not recognize surrogacy agreements, the legal status of children born pursuant to such agreements is uncertain.

In states that recognize and allow surrogacy agreements, if the agreement is not approved by the court before conception, it is unenforceable, the gestational mother is the mother of the resulting child, and the gestational mother's husband (if a party to the agreement) is the father. On the other hand, if the agreement has been approved by the court, upon the birth of a child to the gestational mother, the intended parents must file notice of the birth within 300 days after the assisted reproduction. The court will then issue an order establishing the intended parents as the legal parents of the child. If the intended parents fail to file the required notice, the gestational mother or the appropriate state agency may file notice with the court that a child has been born to the gestational mother within 300 days after assisted reproduction.

In this case, if the state does not recognize and allow gestational agreements, or if this agreement is not approved by the court, Herb will probably not be able to overcome the presumption that he is Carol's legal father. If the gestational agreement is allowed by the state and approved by the court, the intended parents, Don and Sally, should file notice of the birth within 300 days after the assisted reproduction. Since Don and Sally do not want to be Carol's parents, they will not file notice. Although Winnie could file notice, she will not, because she wants to keep Carol.

Herb might argue that Winnie is estopped from claiming he is Carol's legal father because he would not have agreed to the surrogacy contract had he known he might become the father of the resulting child. (After all, Herb indicated his desire to avoid parenthood when he signed the premarital agreement not to have children.) Whether a court would invoke estoppel in these circumstances is speculative at best; however, a court might determine that Herb is Carol's legal father, if only for public policy reasons (to prevent illegitimacy).

2.   Assuming Herb is the legal father of Carol, he is most likely liable for her support. Generally, a child's legal parent is obligated to support the child. Herb may argue that he has no such duty in light of both the surrogacy contract and the premarital agreement, but courts will typically not enforce contracts that adversely affect a child's right to support. [Uniform Premarital Agreement Act §3] If Herb lives in a state that has adopted the 2000 Uniform Parentage Act, he may argue that the Act provides that intended parents under a nonvalidated surrogacy agreement may be held liable for the support of the resulting child, even if the agreement is otherwise unenforceable and the surrogate mother is denominated the mother of the child. However, very few states have adopted the Uniform Parentage Act as revised in 2000, and Herb will probably have to pay for Carol's support.

3.   Winnie is likely to receive some compensation for helping put Herb through chiropractic school. Most jurisdictions that have ruled on the issue have held that professional licenses or degrees are not distributable property—even where the attainment of the degree was made possible through the support of the other spouse—because a degree is not transferable, nor is its long-term value easily determined. However, to prevent harsh results in such cases, courts often hold that a supporting spouse is entitled to reimbursement on an unjust enrichment theory. Supporting spouses may be awarded a larger amount of permanent or temporary spousal support (provided they would otherwise receive spousal support), or the court may award the supporting spouse reimbursement spousal support—an award for a fixed sum which is not modifiable or terminable, and which is available even if the supporting spouse is not otherwise eligible for spousal support. Reimbursement spousal support is calculated on the basis of the amount of the supporting spouse's contribution rather than the value of the professional degree or license.

If Winnie lives in a state where professional licenses and degrees are considered "property," the degree will be subject to valuation and distribution like all other marital property. Although courts sometimes consider the supporting spouse's contributions to the other's education when dividing other marital property, such an approach is unavailable in this situation because Herb and Winnie own very little property. Thus, in such a jurisdiction, the degree would be awarded to Herb, but he would be ordered to pay Winnie her equitable share in a lump sum or in a series of payments.

QUESTION 2

Susan Smith and George Gordon were validly married in State A, where both had been lifelong residents. Three years later, they separated but did not divorce.

A few months later, Susan participated in a marriage ceremony with William Wilkins, another longtime resident of State A. William honestly believed Susan had never been married before. He did not ask any questions on the subject, and Susan did not volunteer any information about her existing marriage to George. The wedding announcement stated that both were taking the surname "Smith-Wilkins." Under that name they maintained joint bank and credit card accounts and rented an apartment together in State A.

Susan and William rented a vacation cabin in State B each summer for the next four years. They generally stayed at the cabin for four months at a time.

Four years after Susan and William's wedding ceremony, while they were still living in State A, Susan received a letter from a friend saying, "Your husband, George, has died from a heart attack." William saw the letter and learned of George's existence. Susan told William about her marriage to George and said, "As far as I'm concerned, nothing has changed between us. Let's just put this behind us and go on with life." William said, "This is pretty hard to take. I'll have to think about it." Although Susan and William continued to live together and to have sexual relations, their relationship became tense and strained. They did not discuss Susan's marriage to George again.

During the next year, Susan and William again rented a cabin in State B for four months. During this stay in State B, Susan and William visited neighbors and bought supplies, as usual. Hiding their marital difficulties, they appeared to be a happily married couple. However, soon after they returned to State A, they separated but did not file for divorce.

Seven months after Susan and William separated, she was killed in a traffic accident. Susan was insured under a group life insurance policy furnished by her employer. The policy provided that if she failed to name a beneficiary, the proceeds would be paid "First to the insured's surviving spouse; or if none, to the insured's surviving children, in equal shares; or if none, to the insured's surviving parent(s); or if none, to the insured's estate." Susan had no children and had not named a beneficiary of the insurance policy.

Susan's parents and William claim the insurance proceeds. Their competing claims are being litigated in State A. Assume that William has no community property interest in the proceeds of the insurance policy and that, if he is not entitled to the insurance money, it will be awarded to Susan's parents.

Common law marriages can be validly formed in State B but not in State A.

To whom should the court award the insurance proceeds? Explain.

ANSWER TO QUESTION 2

The court will most likely award the insurance proceeds to William. At issue is whether Susan and William were married at the time of Susan's death.

To be entitled to the insurance proceeds, William must prove that he was married to Susan when she died. As the facts indicate, Susan was not divorced from her first husband, George, when she married William. Thus, Susan's marriage to William was void.

William could argue that he and Susan created a valid common law marriage during their four-month stay in State B following George's death. (He could also claim that a common law marriage was created earlier, but was only validated after the impediment of Susan's prior marriage was removed by the death of George.) The two parties did in fact meet the basic requirements for the creation of a valid common law marriage: (i) they exchanged consents; (ii) they cohabited; and (iii) they publicly held themselves out as living together as husband and wife by taking a common last name and maintaining joint bank and credit card accounts.

Still, many jurisdictions would be unwilling to recognize the marriage. Although courts that have abolished common law marriage will recognize the common law marriage of a couple who entered into a common law marriage while living in a state that permits such marriages, courts are split as to whether a common law marriage must be recognized when parties who are domiciled in a state that has abolished common law marriage go into another state where such marriages are valid, remain there for a time, then return to their domicile. [Clark, *The Law of Domestic Relations in the United States* §2.4 (2d ed. 1988)] In some jurisdictions, the marriage is upheld on the basis of short visits to the other state, whereas in other jurisdictions, courts will not recognize the marriage due to the domicile state's public policy. Still other courts avoid exclusive reliance on domicile and will make their decision based on factors such as the amount of time the couple spent in the second state. William can emphasize that he and Susan had an established place of abode in State B (*i.e.,* the cabin), where they spent four months each year, and where they established relationships with State B residents who could testify that Susan and William held themselves out as husband and wife. If the State A court recognizes the common law marriage created in State B, William will be entitled to the life insurance proceeds.

William could also argue that the impediment to his initial ceremonial marriage to Susan (*i.e.,* the existence of Susan's living spouse) was removed when George died. Because a void marriage may become merely voidable upon the removal of an impediment, William may claim that his marriage to Susan became valid when he ratified the marriage by continuing to live with her as husband and wife after George's death. That being the case, William would be entitled to the proceeds of Susan's life insurance policy.

QUESTION 3

Fred and Mary were married for 20 years. Until recently they both lived in the home they owned in State X. They have two children, a 15-year-old boy and a two-year-old girl. Eight months ago Fred decided that he no longer wanted to live with Mary. He moved himself and his business permanently to neighboring State Y and took with him $100,000 in cash that he had earned during the course of the marriage. Mary has never been in State Y.

Fred visited the children in State X regularly after he left. He decided, however, that he wanted them to live with him in State Y. Four months ago, over Mary's objections, he took

the children from the marital home in State X and moved them to State Y. Their son, a mature and thoughtful boy, wishes to return to State X to live with his mother because he misses his mother, his friends, and his school. Their daughter seems comfortable with Fred, but she also shows signs of distress that is caused by being separated from her mother.

In State Y Fred filed for divorce, division of property (*i.e.*, the home in State X and the cash and business in State Y), and child custody. Mary did not want a divorce and wanted the children returned to her. Both State X and State Y have adopted the Uniform Child Custody Jurisdiction and Enforcement Act. State Y has a long arm statute allowing it to assert personal jurisdiction to the maximum extent permitted under the federal Due Process Clause. Neither state is a community property state.

1.   If State Y grants Fred a divorce, must State X recognize and enforce it? Explain.

2.   May State Y constitutionally assert jurisdiction to divide the property of Fred and Mary between them? Explain.

3.   Should State Y assert jurisdiction to decide the custody dispute, and, if it does, must State X recognize and enforce the decree? Explain.

4.   What factors should the court consider in determining to whom custody should be awarded, and how important is each factor? Explain.

ANSWER TO QUESTION 3

1.   ***Recognition of the State Y divorce decree by State X:*** State X must recognize and enforce the State Y divorce decree. At issue is the extent to which a state must extend full faith and credit to the ex parte divorce decree of a sister state court.

The general rule is that courts will give full faith and credit to divorce decrees of the courts of sister states if the sister state had proper jurisdiction and the decree is valid in the sister state. The jurisdictional requirement will be satisfied if one of the spouses is domiciled in the state granting the divorce (*e.g.*, in an ex parte divorce). There is a rebuttable presumption that the state granting the divorce is the bona fide domicile of the plaintiff, and the facts here indicate that Fred has indeed established domicile in State Y: He moved both himself and his business to State Y with the intention of remaining there indefinitely. Therefore, State Y had jurisdiction over Fred's divorce, and State X must afford the divorce decree full faith and credit.

2.   ***State Y's assertion of jurisdiction over the marital property:*** The State Y court probably may divide the cash and business which are located in State Y. The State Y court may not, however, assert jurisdiction to divide Fred and Mary's property located in State X, *i.e.*, the marital home. At issue is the right of a court exercising jurisdiction over an ex parte divorce to order the division of marital property which is located either in the state exercising jurisdiction or in a sister state.

Under the doctrine of divisible divorce, an ex parte divorce generally can serve to grant only the divorce. An ex parte divorce decree has no effect on disputes over marital property, unless the property is located within the rendering state. Otherwise, such disputes can be resolved only by a court having personal jurisdiction over both of the parties.

In order for a State Y court to have personal jurisdiction over Mary, either (i) there must be some "minimum contacts" between Mary and State Y, or (ii) Mary must have submitted herself to the jurisdiction of the State Y court. However, the facts indicate that Mary has never been in State Y, and do not indicate any other contacts with State Y. Therefore, the only way State Y may exercise jurisdiction over the marital property is if the property is located within the state. The only such property is the personal property (*i.e.*, the cash and business) that Fred brought with him when he moved to State Y. Therefore, it is only that property that may be the subject of a division decree rendered by a State Y court; the home located in State X is not subject to jurisdiction in State Y.

3.   *State Y's assertion of jurisdiction over the custody dispute:* State Y should not assert jurisdiction to decide the custody dispute. At issue is the right of a court exercising jurisdiction over an ex parte divorce to resolve custody matters. Under the Uniform Child Custody Jurisdiction and Enforcement Act ("UCCJEA"), a state may exercise jurisdiction if it is the *home state* of the child at the time the proceedings began or within six months of the proceedings and a parent still resides in the jurisdiction. A child's home state is the state in which the child lived with a parent (or a person acting as a parent) for at least six consecutive months prior to commencement of the proceeding. Here, State X remains the children's home state since they have only been in State Y for four months and were taken there over their mother's objections. Thus, the court should decline to exercise jurisdiction in favor of State X. Such a decision would best serve the purposes of the UCCJEA by promoting the use of a more convenient forum (in this case, State X, the jurisdiction in which the children and their family have closest connections) and by deterring abductions and unilateral removals of children.

[*Note:* Some states have not adopted the UCCJEA, but follow the Uniform Child Custody Jurisdiction Act ("UCCJA"). Under the UCCJA, a state may exercise jurisdiction if: (i) it was the child's home state at the time the proceedings began, or it was the home state within six months before the commencement of the proceedings and a parent still lives in the state; (ii) asserting jurisdiction is in the child's best interests because the child and at least one party have a significant connection with the state; (iii) the child is physically present in the state and has been abandoned or neglected, or it is necessary to protect the child from abuse; or (iv) no other state has or will assert jurisdiction. In this case, State X would have jurisdiction under the UCCJA as well as under the UCCJEA.]

Whether State X must recognize such a State Y decree: State X does not have to recognize or enforce such a State Y decree regarding custody. At issue is whether a custody order of a court exercising jurisdiction in an ex parte divorce is entitled to full faith and credit when the facts of the case suggest that a parent has wrongfully taken the children from another state.

The federal Parental Kidnapping Prevention Act ("PKPA") requires states to enforce a custody order of another state, but only if the state entering the custody decree had home state jurisdiction. The jurisdictional standards are substantially similar to those in the UCCJEA. Because, as discussed above, State Y would not be the home state under the UCCJEA, it would not be the home state under the PKPA. Therefore, State X is not required to extend full faith and credit to the State Y decree.

4.   *Factors to be considered in determining to whom custody should be awarded:* The standard to be applied in awarding custody is the best interests of the child. Generally, the factors to be considered in making this determination include: the wishes of the parents; the wishes of the child; the interrelationship of the child with his parents, siblings, and others; the child's adjustment to home, school, and community; and the mental and physical health of all individuals involved.

The facts of this case indicate that the 15-year-old son wishes to return to State X to live with his mother. While the preference of a young child is frequently given little weight, the preference of a child over the age of 12 is usually given great weight. Here, the son is 15 years old; he is thoughtful and mature, and is able to articulate his reasons for wishing to return to his mother. As a result, the court is likely to give the son's wishes serious consideration when making the custody determination. Because there is no indication that Mary has pressured the son in any way, and no other facts weigh against giving her custody, the court will probably grant custody of the son to his mother.

The two-year-old daughter seems comfortable with her father; however, she is showing signs of distress due to her separation from her mother. Although some jurisdictions still honor the tender years doctrine, which grants custody of a young child to the mother unless she is proven unfit, the doctrine now has questionable constitutional validity due to its gender-based bias. Instead, many courts are granting custody to the primary caregiver. Here, it is unclear who is the primary caregiver, though it is likely to be Mary since the facts indicate that the children lived with Mary in State X and that Fred took the children from her.

Traditionally, many states would place a child with the parent who was of the same gender as the child. Again, this rule is gender-based and thus of doubtful constitutionality today. Rather than base a decision on this rule, the court is more likely to indicate that because the young girl is showing signs of distress due to separation from her mother, she should be returned to her mother. As previously stated, a child's adjustment and her mental and physical health are important factors when determining custody, and the court will probably give Mary custody of her daughter if it believes this will eliminate the girl's distress.

A decision to give Mary custody of her daughter would be further supported by the fact that Mary will probably be given custody of her son for the reasons stated above, and many courts feel it is best not to split up siblings. The court could find that giving Mary custody of both children would provide them greater support and add stability to their living situation.

Fred could argue that because the children have been with him for the last four months, awarding him custody would best serve the purpose of preserving the children's living situation; however, given the fact that the boy does not wish to stay with his father and the girl is displaying signs of distress, the court is likely to find that the children's best interests are served by granting Mary custody of both of the children.

QUESTION 4

When Husband and Wife divorced in 1990, their final divorce decree provided: (1) Husband would pay Wife $500 per month for 10 years in exchange for Wife's release of any interest she had in Husband's business; (2) Husband would pay Wife an additional $1,000 per month as spousal support; (3) the couple would have joint legal custody of their child, Daughter, age 10, who would reside primarily with Wife; and (4) Husband would pay Wife child support of $400 a month.

Shortly after the divorce, Wife's mother validly transferred title of her apartment building to an irrevocable trust. The trust instrument names Wife as trustee and directs the trustee to use the trust income for the benefit of Daughter until she attains age 21. At that time, the trust is to terminate, and the trustee is to distribute the trust property to Wife. Wife used the trust income to pay for sporting equipment, music lessons, and recreational activities for Daughter.

In 1991, a fire destroyed the apartment building, which Wife, as trustee, had not insured. Wife heard that a developer might be interested in purchasing the vacant land in the future, and she decided to buy the vacant land from the trust for herself at its current fair

market value, hoping to make a large profit in several years. Wife executed and delivered a deed to the land from herself as trustee to herself as an individual.

As trustee, Wife reinvested all of the proceeds from the sale of the land in XYZ stock. XYZ is not a publicly traded stock. Although XYZ stock had historically paid very small cash dividends, the underlying value of the stock seemed likely to increase significantly over time. Wife used the cash dividends for Daughter's sporting equipment, music lessons, and recreational activities.

Manny, Wife's lover, recently moved into the home of Wife and Daughter. Wife and Manny have a marriage-like relationship, but they do not intend to marry. Manny pays Wife rent and contributes half of the cost of groceries and utilities. In all other respects, Manny and Wife keep their finances separate.

1. If Husband properly files a motion to terminate his payments of $500 and $1,000 per month to Wife and to reduce his child support payment of $400 per month on the basis of the fact that Wife is living with Manny, should the court grant his motion? Explain.

2. Has Wife breached any duties as trustee of the trust created by her mother? Explain.

ANSWER TO QUESTION 4

1. *$500/month payment:* Husband will not be able to have the $500/month payment modified. Although the facts do not specifically call this payment a property division, it probably is one because it was ordered in exchange for Wife's relinquishing any interest she had in Husband's business. A court will order cash compensation when dividing property in a case such as this, where a particular asset cannot be easily divided. Property division decrees are not modifiable, and may be reopened only for reasons for which any judgment may be reopened (*e.g.,* fraud).

$1,000/month payment: Husband probably will not be able to terminate this payment altogether, but may be able to have it modified. This obligation is specifically called a spousal support payment (also known as alimony or maintenance) in the facts. The purpose of spousal support is to ensure an adequate income stream for a person whose economic dependency has resulted, at least in part, from the marital relationship. Spousal support is modifiable only when there is a *substantial change in the circumstances* of the parties, either in the recipient's need for the payment or in the payor's ability to pay.

State statutes generally make spousal support specifically terminable upon remarriage; however, only a few states treat cohabitation the same way. Most states instead will consider cohabitation as one factor in determining whether there has been a substantial change in circumstances.

Because Manny is not legally obligated to support Wife, a court will probably find that she has not had such a substantial change in circumstances that Husband should be completely relieved of his obligation. Therefore, unless a statute exists that specifically allows Wife's support to end upon her cohabitation, Husband will not be able to completely terminate the payment obligation. However, he probably will be able to have the payment reduced, in view of the fact that Manny pays Wife's rent and contributes to one-half of the food and utility bills, thereby reducing Wife's need for extra income.

$400/month payment: Husband will not be able to terminate this payment but may be able to have the obligation reduced. The facts specifically call this a child support payment. Both parents

equally share a duty to support their children. Child support payments are modifiable or terminable only if there is a substantial change in circumstances **with regard to the child**, *i.e.,* if there is a change in the **child's** need or in the ability of **both parents** to pay. A court will look at such factors as (i) the parents' employment situation, (ii) the growth of the child, (iii) inflation, (iv) the income of each parent, (v) whether either parent is retired, and (vi) whether either parent has a disabling illness that prevents him from working.

Again, in this case Manny has no legal duty to support Daughter. Thus, she has not had a substantial change in her need for funds as a result of the cohabitation, and the court would probably refuse to order a complete termination of support payments. However, Manny's payment of bills results in Wife's having more disposable income to apply toward Daughter's support, which could justify a reduction in the amount of Husband's payment obligation.

2. Yes, Wife has breached several of her duties as trustee of the trust created by her mother.

Her first breach of duty occurred when she failed to insure the trust property. A trustee has a basic duty to preserve and protect the trust property. Among other things, this duty requires that the trustee exercise reasonable care to secure insurance on trust property. This breach of duty subjects Wife to liability to the trust for the amount of the loss from the fire.

Wife's second breach of duty occurred when she bought the vacant lot from the trust, even though she paid the full market price. A trustee owes a duty of undivided loyalty to the trust and its beneficiaries. Thus, absent court approval or a contrary trust provision, a trustee cannot enter into any transaction in which she is dealing with the trust in her individual capacity. A trustee cannot "wear two hats," and in the same transaction represent both her personal interest and the interests of the trust estate. This duty of loyalty prohibits a trustee from purchasing any property owned by the trust even if she pays full value. Good faith on the trustee's part or benefit to the trust is irrelevant.

Wife's third breach of trust occurred when she purchased the XYZ stock. This purchase breached her duty of due care (prudent investment) and her duty of impartiality.

As part of the trustee's duty to preserve trust property and make it productive, the trustee must invest the trust property in compliance with the "prudent investor rule." Under the Uniform Prudent Investor Act ("UPIA"), a trustee must invest and manage trust assets as a prudent investor would, by considering the purposes, terms, distribution requirements, and other circumstances of the trust. In satisfying this standard, the trustee must exercise reasonable care, skill, and caution. A basic principle of prudent investment is reasonable diversification. Here, Wife invested all of the trust's property in one stock. Since there are no special circumstances justifying this lack of diversification, such as a family business, the investment is improper. The investment is also improper because it favors the remainderman (Wife) over the current income beneficiary (Daughter). As part of the duty of loyalty, the trustee has a duty to deal impartially with all beneficiaries. It is improper to favor one over the other. Here, the investment produces small dividends for the income beneficiary, but should become more valuable over the long term, which favors the remainderman.

QUESTION 5

Four years ago, Father and Mother began living together in Mother's house in a state that does not allow common law marriage. They never married and they never discussed marriage. Father soon took over appointment-making and bookkeeping for Mother's veterinary practice. Mother asked Father to quit touring with his musical group and to stay

home to help her with the practice and care for the home and their pets. "It would make our lives less hectic, and I'll share what I'm making with you," she said. He agreed. Mother did not pay Father a salary for helping her with her veterinary practice or for his house-keeping services.

Twenty months ago, Mother gave birth to Daughter, who is Father's biological child. Mother stayed at home with Daughter for six weeks and then went back to work, leaving Daughter in Father's full-time care.

Ten months ago, Mother told Father that she no longer loved him, and she demanded that he move out. He did so. Within a few weeks Mother married Stepfather, with whom she and Daughter now live. Father made no attempt to see Daughter after he moved out of Mother's house, and he has not paid or offered to pay child support.

Father has learned that a trial court recently entered a decree allowing Stepfather to adopt Daughter. The governing statute provides that notice of adoption proceedings must be given to unmarried fathers only if they have filed a declaration of paternity with the Bureau of Vital Statistics or if, within the six months preceding filing of the motion, they have lived with the child or offered to support the child. Since Father satisfied none of these criteria, he did not receive notice of the adoption proceeding.

1. If Father moves to set aside the adoption of Daughter on the ground that failure to give him notice of the proceeding violates due process, should the court grant the motion? Explain.

2. If the adoption decree is not set aside, may a court order that Father be allowed to visit Daughter over the objections of Mother and Stepfather? Explain.

3. Upon what theories, if any, may Father be entitled to a share of the property that Mother acquired between the time she asked him to quit traveling and stay home and the time he moved out of the house? Explain.

ANSWER TO QUESTION 5

1. No, the court should not grant Father's motion to set aside the adoption of Daughter. The issue is whether the failure to give Father notice of the adoption proceeding violates his right of due process.

Generally, notice to and consent of a child's natural parents to an adoption are required. However, if the parents are unmarried, the father's consent may not be necessary. The type of notice required for the unmarried father of a child who is the subject of an adoption proceeding depends on how actively involved the father has been in that child's life to date. The court will weigh such factors as whether the father lived with the mother and cared for the child, or, if not living with them, visited the child, admitted paternity, or paid child support.

The governing statute requires the father, in order to be entitled to notice, either to file a declaration of paternity or to live with or offer to support the child within the six months preceding the filing of the motion (presumably, the petition for adoption). If filing the declaration were the only manner in which to establish a right to notice, the statute would be unconstitutional; *i.e.*, the father's due process rights would be violated because he would have no reason to believe that he was required to file in order to contest an adoption proceeding. However, the statute also provides a right to notice if the father has lived with, supported, or offered to support the child during the six months prior to the adoption filing. The intent of such a provision is to deny the right to notice to fathers who have abandoned their children. That a biological father has shown an interest in and taken responsibility for a child is more important than the father's genetic link to the child when it comes to determining the father's right to notice or veto power in the adoption of his child. [Lehr v. Robertson, 463 U.S. 248 (1983)]

Father will argue that he did provide support and care for Daughter from the time she was born until she was 10 months old. However, the facts indicate that he made no attempt to visit or pay support to her for the next 10 months, until the present time. This failure to maintain his previous relationship with Daughter would constitute the type of abandonment that the statute seeks to address. Because the statute bases the unmarried father's rights on the level of involvement he has had in the child's life, the statute satisfies due process requirements.

2.   No, a court may not order visitation for Father over the objections of Mother and Stepfather. At issue is a family court's power to grant or deny visitation to a natural parent whose parental rights have been terminated.

In general, the effect of an adoption is to cut off the biological parents' rights and obligations and create a new set of rights and duties between the adoptive parents and the child as if they were biologically related. When the biological parents' rights are terminated, this means that they no longer have the right to visitation.

3.   Father may be entitled to recover a share of Mother's property for the time he stayed home to care for Daughter under contract law. If for some reason the court finds that the contract is invalid, Father may be entitled to an equitable distribution of Mother's property on the bases of constructive trust, resulting trust, or quantum meruit. At issue are the theories under which a court may make a division of property between unmarried cohabitants who later break up.

Contract: The most likely theory under which Father can recover is contract. Contracts between unmarried cohabitants are valid so long as the consideration for the contract is not based solely on sexual relations.

The facts here indicate that there was an agreement for services, with no mention of sexual relations as consideration. Mother's offer was to "share what she was making" with Father if he quit his musical group and helped with the home and her practice, and Father agreed. This might be sufficient to create an enforceable contract, but more likely a court will find it too vague to uphold: There is nothing in the facts to indicate for how long Father was to help with the home and Mother's practice under the contract; neither do the facts give any indication whether Mother's offer to "share" meant a 50/50 split. Thus, it is unlikely the court would enforce an express contract.

Implied contract: In the alternative, Father could argue that he and Mother had an implied contract to share property. The courts can imply a contract based on the conduct of the parties. Here, Father's quitting his job and taking care of the home on mother's suggestion while Mother remained in the marketplace lends credence to the implied contract argument.

Constructive trust: A constructive trust is an equitable remedy imposed by courts when a defendant has obtained title to property through misappropriation (*e.g.*, by fraud, mistake, undue influence, etc.). A constructive trust is used to prevent unjust enrichment if the defendant is allowed to retain the property. If a constructive trust is imposed, the defendant is declared the trustee of the property, and her sole duty is to convey the property to the plaintiff. Some courts require that inadequacy of a legal remedy also be shown.

In this case, Father could argue that Mother induced Father to provide free housekeeping, child care, and bookkeeping services by telling Father that she would "share what she was making" with him and she would be unjustly enriched if she were allowed to keep the property that she obtained by earnings that she promised to share with Father.

Resulting trust: In a similar vein, Father could argue that a court should impose a resulting trust. Father would be declared beneficiary of an implied trust because he is the one who supplied the consideration for a transaction by which Mother acquired property constituting the "res" of the trust. Although such consideration usually is in the form of money, it may also be services. In this case, Mother acquired property that she probably could not have purchased if she had had to employ a nanny, housekeeper, and office manager. Father's contribution of services allowed Mother to obtain the property; therefore, the court should make Father the beneficiary of the resulting trust.

Quantum meruit: Quantum meruit is a doctrine allowing recovery in quasi-contract to prevent unjust enrichment where: the plaintiff has conferred a benefit on the defendant (either property or services); plaintiff has a reasonable expectation of being compensated; benefits were conferred at the express or implied request of defendant; and if defendant is allowed to retain the benefits without compensating plaintiff, defendant will be unjustly enriched. The measure of recovery is usually the benefit received by defendant, but may be the detriment suffered by plaintiff if the benefit is too difficult to quantify.

Here, Father performed housekeeping, child care, and bookkeeping services for Mother (the benefit); Mother gave him the idea that she would share her earnings with him (the expectation); Mother specifically requested that he quit his band (he did not volunteer to do so); and again, Mother probably would not have been able to acquire whatever property she did during the time Father performed these services if she had had to pay someone else to perform them. Therefore, Father should be able to recover the value of the benefit Mother received from Father's assistance.

QUESTION 6

Husband, a freelance writer, and Wife, a successful attorney, divorced amicably after 10 years of marriage. Their separation agreement, which was merged into their divorce decree, gave Husband custody of their child, Son, who is now eight years old. The decree required Wife to (1) pay $800 monthly to Husband for child support until Son reached age 18, (2) set aside $5,000 annually for 10 years to finance Son's college education, and (3) transfer $20,000 annually to Husband during each of the following five years to compensate Husband for his financial contributions toward supporting the family during the marriage while Wife earned her law degree.

One year after the divorce, Wife married New Husband. Two days after they married, Wife executed a valid will leaving her entire estate to New Husband. One year later, she and New Husband had a child, Daughter. Wife died unexpectedly a week after Daughter was born.

In each of the two years immediately following her divorce from Husband, Wife had deposited $5,000 into a savings account in her name alone at Bank. Wife made only one withdrawal from this account, taking out $1,200 just one month before she died.

Although Wife had paid child support to Husband for the two years immediately before her death, she had made only one $20,000 payment to Husband before she died.

Wife owned $500,000 at her death, including the savings account at Bank. New Husband claims Wife's entire estate under her will.

1.   Does Wife's obligation under the divorce decree to support Son survive Wife's death? Explain.

2.   On what theory could Son make a specific claim to the Bank savings account, and would such a claim be likely to succeed? Explain.

3.   Is Wife's estate obligated to pay Husband the unpaid amounts Wife owed him for his financial contributions toward supporting the family while she earned her law degree? Explain.

4.   Do Son and Daughter have any other claims to any share of Wife's estate, and, if so, will they succeed? Explain.

ANSWER TO QUESTION 6

1.   *Survival of Wife's child support obligation to Son:* No, the obligation of Wife to pay $800/month for the support of Son does not survive Wife's death. At issue is when the duty to pay child support terminates.

The general rule is that a child support obligation terminates (i) when the minor reaches the age of majority, (ii) upon the minor's emancipation, or (iii) if there is a termination of parental rights. Jurisdictions differ over whether the duty ends upon the death of the obligor parent. Many state statutes now specifically grant authority to continue payments beyond the obligor's death. Some courts hold that they have authority to continue the obligation even in the absence of a statute. The courts that refuse to enforce support orders beyond the obligor's death do so on the basis that children are not entitled to support from the deceased parent's estate where the marriage did not end in divorce (*i.e.,* children may be disinherited by the parent's will); therefore, they should not be entitled to support just because there was a divorce. In the alternative, some courts hold that the death of the obligor parent is such a change in circumstances that would allow a modification (*i.e.,* termination) of the payor parent's obligation. Nonetheless, the weight of authority still holds that the obligor's child support obligation terminates upon death. Therefore, Wife's obligation to support Son does not survive her death.

2.   *Son's claim on Wife's savings account:* Son may make a claim to the Bank savings account on the ground that the account was back due child support. The issues are whether the divorce decree provisions give Son a claim on Wife's estate, and if so, whether Son is entitled to satisfy his claim from specific assets of the estate.

Although not included in the child support guidelines, postsecondary educational expenses may be awarded by the trial court when determining child support obligations. In this case, the divorce decree required Wife to set aside $5,000 annually for 10 years to finance Son's college education. While the court cannot order posthumous support, the mother's estate would be liable for any back due child support. The bank account would be one source from which the son could satisfy his claim for $10,000 back due child support.

Next, Son must establish that he is entitled to the specific funds that are in Wife's Bank savings account. Although Wife has deposited the amount required by the decree in the account each year, that does not give Son a claim to that specific account. That she withdrew $1,200 from the account indicates that she exerted control over the funds, such that they remained her own, rather than treating them as a required set-aside. Even if Son has a general claim to a share of the estate, he does not appear to be entitled specifically to the contents of the savings account to the detriment of other creditors.

Son may also argue that he is entitled to the money in the bank account because Wife was to pay $5,000 per year for 10 years in trust for him. This argument is not likely to succeed, however, because in order to have a valid trust, the settlor (Wife) must intend to create the trust. From the facts at hand, there is no evidence that Wife had such intent in setting up the bank account. Son may claim that the two $5,000 deposits into the savings account were held by Wife in trust for Son since she made the deposits each year and did not make any other deposits into the account. This argument is not likely to help Son though since Wife withdrew $1,200 one month before her death. Thus, Son is not entitled to the bank account on the theory that Wife created a trust on his behalf.

3. ***Wife's estate's liability to repay Husband's financial contributions:*** Wife's estate is obligated to pay Husband the unpaid amount Wife owed him for his financial contributions toward the support of the family while she earned her law degree. The issue is whether the $20,000 annual payments required by the divorce decree are terminable upon the death of the obligor spouse.

Generally, there are four types of alimony: (i) periodic, which is paid regularly to a spouse to provide for the maintenance and support of a spouse who has neither the resources nor the ability to be self-sustaining; (ii) lump sum, which serves the same purpose as periodic alimony but is paid as a lump sum; (iii) rehabilitative, which consists of regular payments for a limited period of time calculated to enable a spouse to gain skills or education necessary to enter the work force and become self-supporting; and (iv) reimbursement alimony, which is a fixed sum to a spouse who supported the other spouse while the latter obtained a professional license or degree. Most jurisdictions allow periodic, lump sum, and rehabilitative alimony; a growing minority of courts order reimbursement alimony, with or without statutory authority. [Clark, *supra*, at §16.4 n. 97]

The $20,000 annual payments in this case clearly are reimbursement alimony; the facts state that the payments are to serve as compensation for Husband's financial contributions to the family. Reimbursement alimony is neither modifiable nor terminable; thus, Husband has a claim against Wife's estate for $80,000 ($20,000 per year for the remaining four years of the obligation).

4. ***Son and Daughter's claims:*** While a parent does not have to leave anything to her children, most states have an omitted child statute that protects children from **unintentional** disinheritance. In a few states, the omitted child statute applies to existing children as well as afterborns. However, in most states the statute gives protection only to children born or adopted **after** the will is executed. Such a child is entitled to a share of the estate equal in value to that which she would have received had the testator died intestate, **unless:** (i) it appears from the will that it was the intention of the testator to disinherit the child; (ii) at the time the will was executed, the testator had other children and devised substantially all of her estate to the **other parent** of the omitted child; or (iii) the testator provided for the omitted child by a transfer outside of the will with the intent that it was in lieu of a testamentary gift.

Because Wife died leaving a surviving spouse and issue, and because one of those issue (Son) is not issue of the surviving spouse (New Husband), the shares to which the survivors would have been entitled had Wife died intestate are as follows: New Husband, 1/2; Son, 1/4; Daughter, 1/4.

But are Son and Daughter omitted children? Since Son was born *before* Wife executed the will leaving her entire estate to New Husband, under the statute found in most states, Son has no claim as a pretermitted heir. Daughter, on the other hand, was born after the will was executed and was not provided for in the will. Moreover, there is no indication from the facts that Wife intended to disinherit Daughter or that Wife provided for Daughter by a transfer outside of the will. However, Wife did have a child (Son) when she executed the will, and the will did devise substantially all of the estate to the other parent of Daughter, namely, New Husband. Accordingly, neither Son nor Daughter is an omitted child, and neither is entitled to an intestate share of Wife's Estate.

QUESTION 7

Al and Bonnie were graduate students at State University. They rented a house together, and each paid half the rent and utilities. They had separate bedrooms and shared the kitchen, bath, and living room. They usually prepared and ate their evening meals together. They were good friends but not lovers.

Six months ago, Al, who was a foreign student in the United States on a student visa, lost financial support for his research and contemplated quitting school temporarily in order to work. However, he knew that if he quit school he would lose his student visa. He explained his plight to Bonnie and asked if she would go through a marriage ceremony with him but not otherwise change the way they had been living. He believed this would entitle him to remain in the country as the spouse of a United States citizen even though he was not in school. Bonnie agreed on condition that they sign an agreement providing that they would (1) divorce whenever either wanted, (2) be free to come and go and associate with whom they pleased, and (3) not be responsible for each other's school and other debts. Al agreed, and both signed the agreement.

Four months ago, Al and Bonnie obtained a marriage license and participated in a marriage ceremony before a judge at city hall. Thereafter they continued to live as housemates as they had before.

Two weeks ago, Al was seriously injured in an automobile accident. He was brought, unconscious, to Hospital's emergency room, where doctors immediately performed surgery in an attempt to save his life. However, Al died without ever regaining consciousness. The course of treatment the doctors chose was appropriate under the circumstances. At some point, Hospital personnel found a card in Al's wallet that identified Bonnie as his wife and named her as the person to notify in an emergency. They called her, but she arrived at Hospital after he died. At Hospital, she openly grieved for him.

Some time later, Hospital's business office called to ask Bonnie about paying for Al's care, but Bonnie replied that she was "not really Al's wife" and was "not responsible for his debts." Al did not have medical insurance. Hospital has billed Bonnie for the costs of Al's care.

Is Bonnie liable for the payment of Hospital's bill for Al's care? Explain.

ANSWER TO QUESTION 7

Yes. A court will most likely hold Bonnie liable for Al's medical expenses. The first issue to consider is whether Al and Bonnie had a *valid marriage*.

To enter into a valid marriage, the parties: (i) must be of age, (ii) must not be too closely related, (iii) must have consented to the marriage, and (iv) must not be married to anyone else. The only questionable element here is consent. At the time of the marriage, both parties possessed the requisite mental capacity to understand their actions and agree to them. Both parties also entered into the marriage of their own free will. Although Al proposed the marriage to retain a benefit for himself, his actions were neither fraudulent nor coercive and he did not use force to induce Bonnie's decision to enter into the marriage.

However, Bonnie will argue that the marriage was a sham and the parties did not really consent to marry; she and Al married only for a limited purpose, *i.e.*, to provide Al with his United States citizenship. They did not agree to the traditional aspects of marriage, such as economic support, sexual fidelity, and commitment to the relationship. On the other hand, Al and Bonnie did live together, were fond of each other, and shared some household expenses (meals), which a court may view as evidence of their commitment to each other.

Even though there are some potential problems with Al and Bonnie's consent, it is likely that a court would find their marriage valid since they participated in a wedding ceremony at city hall, which fulfills the solemnization requirement, and they satisfied all of the other basic requirements for marriage. Al and Bonnie also represented themselves as spouses to the immigration authorities and, based on their written agreement, they felt that they would need to obtain a divorce in order to terminate their relationship. Based on the above discussion, the court will likely find that Bonnie and Al's marriage is valid.

Having found a valid marriage, the second issue is whether a spouse may be held liable for the other spouse's medical expenses. Generally, one spouse is not liable for the other spouse's debts, but there is an exception for *"necessaries."* Necessaries include food, clothing, and medical care purchased by the other spouse. Under the common law rule regarding necessaries, each party is liable for necessary expenses incurred by the other, including those expenses connected with the final illness of one of the parties. [Cleveland Metropolitan General Hospital v. Olesik, 525 N.E.2d 831 (Ohio App. 1987)] Thus, Al's hospital bills and medical expenses are "necessaries" and a court will hold Bonnie liable for them.

Bonnie will argue, however, that she is not liable for Al's medical bills because of the premarital agreement she and Al signed which specifically relieved them of liability for one another's debts. The court will have to determine whether their antenuptial agreement is enforceable as against the hospital. The general rule is that premarital contracts between spouses are valid if there is consideration, compliance with the Statute of Frauds, voluntariness, and full and fair disclosure by both parties. Entry into marriage is sufficient consideration for an antenuptial agreement and because Al and Bonnie's agreement is in writing, there is no Statute of Frauds issue. Al signed the agreement voluntarily and the facts do not disclose whether either party held back any relevant financial information in drafting the contract. Finally, because the parties to an antenuptial agreement do not deal at arm's length, but out of a relationship of mutual trust and confidence, the court will strictly scrutinize the contract for good faith and a lack of undue influence. Based on the facts presented, the agreement seems to have been signed in good faith and without undue influence.

However, when determining the enforceability of the agreement, the court will also look to the Uniform Premarital Agreement Act ("UPAA"). Under UPAA, parties may not contract with respect to any matter in violation of public policy. In their contract, Bonnie and Al have agreed that they will not be liable for each other's debts. The court will find this provision void as against public policy since spouses may not contract to avoid the very requirements encompassed by a legal marriage. Because the obligation for one spouse to pay for the other's necessary expenses arises by operation of law, parties may not attempt to contract out of such a requirement. The common law requirement for spousal support renders Al and Bonnie's antenuptial agreement insufficient to avoid liability to a third party, such as the hospital. Regardless of their attempted antenuptial agreement, the court will hold that as Al's wife, Bonnie is liable to the hospital for the medical expenses incurred by Al.

QUESTION 8

> NOTE: Applicants answering this question in a community property state should use community property principles. For this purpose, the phrase "marital property" means community property and the phrase "nonmarital property" means separate property.

Harry and Wanda, who have been married for 13 years, have two children. Harry and Wanda are now divorcing. Before marrying, they each earned $25,000 per year as teachers. A year after their wedding, Harry quit teaching to open a television and stereo repair business called Audio-Video Repair ("AVR"). He invested in the business $5,000 that the couple had saved since the wedding and $10,000 that Wanda's father had given the couple as a wedding gift. Wanda continued to work as a teacher. The couple postponed having children and cut back on all expenses. They invested every extra penny in the business.

AVR grew rapidly. Harry decided to incorporate AVR, contributing 52% of the shares to an employee profit-sharing plan and retaining 48% in his name alone. The contribution of shares to the profit-sharing plan was for legitimate business reasons.

At a time when Harry was earning over $150,000 a year, he and Wanda agreed that she would quit her teaching job and have children. Sonny was born the next year, and Debbie was born two years later.

Wanda took care of the house and children and entertained Harry's many business guests. AVR continued to flourish and began to set up franchises in other cities. Harry increasingly devoted himself to the business, so that he had very little time for the children and even less time for Wanda. When Debbie was two years old, Wanda began an affair with a neighbor.

Harry and Wanda have agreed that they will divorce and that the children will live with Wanda. Wanda plans to return to teaching in another two years, when Debbie reaches school age, but she will need to update her teaching credentials and can expect to earn only $35,000 per year. Through AVR, including the franchises, Harry now earns $750,000 a year. AVR is worth $20 million. The parties' only substantial asset besides the AVR stock is the family house, worth $300,000. Harry agrees that it should be awarded to Wanda so that she and the children will have a home.

In the divorce proceeding, Wanda demands a portion of the AVR stock and temporary and permanent spousal support. Harry resists these demands. Wanda also demands child support measured as a percentage of Harry's income. Harry acknowledges his obligation to pay child support but is unwilling to pay the amount Wanda requests.

In this jurisdiction only marital property is subject to division at divorce. Nonmarital property must be awarded to the owner.

1. Are Harry's shares in AVR subject to division? Explain.

2. Will Wanda most likely be awarded permanent spousal support, temporary spousal support, or neither? Explain.

3. What will the court consider in determining the amount of Harry's child support obligation? Explain.

ANSWER TO QUESTION 8

1. Yes. Harry's shares in Audio-Video Repair ("AVR") are subject to division as marital property. In general, all property acquired ***during*** marriage is marital property unless it is acquired through gift, bequest, devise, or descent. Marital property distribution is final and not subject to modification by the court.

One year after they were married, Harry and Wanda pooled their money together in order to open AVR. Harry invested $5,000 from their marital funds into the business as well as a $10,000 wedding gift from Wanda's father. The $5,000 investment is marital property since it comes from joint earnings during the marriage. Although the $10,000 gift from Wanda's father would usually be classified as separate (nonmarital) property, when a gift is given to both parties, courts will look at the donor's intent to determine whether he intended both parties to use the gift. [*See* Hamilton v. Hamilton, 381 So. 2d 517 (La. App. 1979)—wedding shower gifts considered marital property because donor intended joint use] Unless a particular wedding gift is only appropriate for the use of one spouse, wedding gifts should be classified as marital property. [*See* Darwish v. Darwish, 100 Mich. App. 758 (1980)] In this case, Wanda's father probably intended that the couple use the money for joint expenses after the wedding. A court might also note that Harry and Wanda used the money as a joint gift since they invested it in the business, instead of spending it individually. Since there was an intended joint use of the money, the court would likely classify the $10,000 wedding gift as marital property. If the court makes this classification, all of the funds invested into the business ($15,000) will be considered marital funds. The resulting business would then be classified as marital property, subject to equitable distribution by the court.

Any income earned from the business is also subject to distribution as marital property. Even though the AVR stocks are titled in Harry's name alone, they will still be considered marital property since the increase in the value of the stock took place during the marriage. The court will divide the proceeds from the stock equitably between the parties.

In determining how to distribute the funds, the court will look at: (i) the age, education, background, and earning capacity of both parties; (ii) the duration of the marriage; (iii) standard of living during the marriage; (iv) present income of both parties and their employability; (v) source of funds used to purchase the property; (vi) health of the parties; (vii) assets and debts of the parties; (viii) needs of each party; (ix) each party's contribution as a homemaker; and (x) whether the distribution is in lieu of or in addition to alimony. When making the property distribution, the court does not have to divide the stocks equally between the parties. The court would likely consider Wanda's sacrifices at the beginning of the business as well as her decreased earning potential since she chose to stay home with the children while Harry worked.

2.   Wanda will most likely be entitled to temporary spousal support and will not be entitled to a permanent award. The purpose of spousal support is to ensure an adequate income stream for the spouse whose economic dependency has resulted, at least in part, from the marital relationship. Alimony is not based on marital fault; thus Wanda's adulterous affair will not have an effect on her award. The recent trend is to award less alimony than in the past because of the number of couples where both parties have valuable skills for the workforce.

When determining how much support to award, the court considers: (i) the standard of living during the marriage; (ii) the duration of the marriage; (iii) the financial resources of each party, including how marital property was apportioned; (iv) the contribution of each party to the marriage, including homemaking; and (v) the time needed for the payee spouse to secure employment. In addition to looking at these factors, a court may also consider whether a spouse should receive permanent and/or temporary spousal support.

Wanda seeks to receive both permanent and temporary spousal support. Permanent spousal support is awarded to a spouse who has neither the resources nor the ability to be self-sustaining. Wanda may argue that she should be entitled to permanent support since she jeopardized her career for the benefit of the family; however, she has not been out of the teaching field for so long as to make her unemployable. Wanda will need to spend some time updating her teaching credentials, but once she has brushed up her skills, she should be able to secure employment as a teacher. Wanda may argue that her likely salary of $35,000 will not be sufficient for her to be self-sustaining; however, since she will receive a substantial percentage of the stock (as discussed above) and she will also be entitled to the $300,000 marital home, this distribution will significantly add to her financial resources. Since Wanda has substantial resources, in addition to the skills and background to reenter the workforce, it is highly unlikely that a court would award her permanent support.

Wanda has also requested that Harry pay her temporary support. A temporary support award is much more likely in this situation. Wanda will need some time before she reenters the workforce to refresh her skills. Also, since Wanda has planned to stay at home for another two years until Debbie is old enough to attend school, her child care responsibilities could detract from her studies. Based on her situation, it is likely that the court would award temporary support for at least the full two years before Debbie begins school, but possibly longer to account for the time needed to complete her studies. When determining the award, the court will factor in the amount of time it will take Wanda to acquire the necessary skills to reenter the workforce.

3.   When the court calculates how much child support Harry should pay, the court will look primarily to the monetary need of the children and his ability to pay. Most states have adopted specific guidelines to make such a calculation more uniform. State guidelines usually dictate a formula based on the number of children, their ages, any special needs of the children, and the parents' incomes. In this case, however, because the family's income is high, a court will probably stray from the guideline amount to provide for the reasonable expectations of the children. Parents may also be ordered to purchase and maintain medical insurance for their children. Child support is modifiable based on a *substantial* change of circumstances affecting the needs of the children or the ability of the obligor spouse to pay. Other factors considered in modification of a support award are changes in: (i) employment; (ii) growth of the children; (iii) inflation; (iv) retirement; and (v) disabling illness.

QUESTION 9

Anna and Ben were contemplating getting married. Ben had been married before and had gone through an unpleasant divorce in which he felt that he had received unfair financial treatment. Ben told Anna he would not marry her unless she signed a premarital agreement with the following provisions: (1) all property acquired prior to or during the marriage will be held separately; (2) Anna waives all rights to spousal support; (3) if they divorce or separate, custody of any children will be joint and shared; and (4) in the event Anna obtains sole custody, Ben will not be responsible for child support.

Ben's attorney prepared an agreement incorporating these provisions. Ben attached a complete statement of his financial worth to the agreement and gave it to Anna. He recommended to Anna that she show it to her attorney before signing it. Anna's attorney had serious reservations about the document and suggested she refuse to sign it as drafted. However, Anna, who loved Ben and wanted to marry him, signed it anyway without making any changes. Ben and Anna married each other three months after she signed the agreement.

At the time of their marriage, Ben was an investment advisor, with a stock portfolio worth approximately $100,000. Anna was a buyer for a specialty clothing store, making a sizeable salary.

Ben and Anna have now been married for 10 years. Anna worked for the first seven years of the marriage. When the second of their two children was born, she left her job permanently to stay home and care for the children, who are now six and three years of age.

The marriage has broken down, and both Ben and Anna wish to divorce. Ben's annual salary is $150,000 and his portfolio is worth $500,000, in part due to his annually investing part of his salary during the marriage. Anna has no income. Her only asset is a $10,000 Treasury note that she inherited from her aunt.

In the divorce proceedings, Anna requests a property settlement, including a share of Ben's portfolio, as well as spousal support, sole custody of the children, and child support. Ben disagrees and insists that they are bound by the premarital agreement.

How is the court likely to rule on each of Anna's requests? Explain.

ANSWER TO QUESTION 9

The court is likely to grant some, but not all of Anna's requests. As the antenuptial agreement addresses each of her requests, the first issue that must be resolved is whether the agreement is enforceable against Anna. It is likely that the court will find the agreement to be enforceable only in part, and uphold the provision regarding property division, but not the alimony, child custody, and child support provisions.

The Agreement: A valid antenuptial agreement must be in writing, voluntary, and based on full and fair disclosure of each party's financial worth. Entry into the marriage is sufficient consideration for an antenuptial agreement. Here, the agreement appears to meet all of these requirements. First, the agreement was in writing. Next, the court is likely to find that Anna voluntarily consented to the agreement. While it is true that Ben told Anna that he would not marry her unless she signed the agreement, this is probably not enough to establish duress. The wedding was not for three months; thus, Anna had sufficient time to make her decision. In addition, Anna had independent counsel who warned her against signing the agreement. Thus, it is unlikely that the court would find fraud or overreaching. Finally, Ben fully disclosed his financial worth to Anna prior to the execution of the agreement. Therefore, the premarital agreement is probably enforceable. However, even if the agreement is enforceable as a whole, the court must still consider each individual provision to ensure that it is fair and does not violate public policy.

Property Division: The court will probably enforce the property division provision. For a court to enforce a premarital property agreement, the agreement must contain fair and reasonable economic provisions for the claiming spouse. Ben will argue that the agreement is fair because at the time it was made both parties were economically independent. Anna will argue that the provision is unfair and unreasonable as applied. She will note that 10 years have passed since they signed the agreement, and Ben has been able to acquire substantial assets during the marriage, while she stayed at home to care for their children. As unconscionability is generally determined at the time the agreement is formed, the court will probably uphold the property provision and determine that all property acquired prior to or during the marriage is the separate property of its owner. Thus, Anna would likely be denied a property settlement and a share of Ben's portfolio based on the antenuptial agreement.

Spousal Support: The court will not enforce the waiver of spousal support. It is against public policy to enforce this type of provision if to do so would leave a spouse dependent on the state. Although Anna has skills as a buyer with which she could support herself, she currently has no income. Anna gave up her job and sizeable salary to care for their children, and since at least one of the children is still preschool age, it may be that Anna does not wish to return to work at this time. In addition, Anna has no significant assets to rely on. Her only property is the $10,000 Treasury note left to her by her aunt. Therefore, it is likely that Anna would be awarded some form of spousal support.

Child Custody: The court will not enforce the child custody provision. A court is not bound by child custody provisions in antenuptial agreements. Instead, the court will determine issues of child custody and child support based on the best interests of the children. Anna has requested sole custody of the children, while Ben wants joint custody. The court must consider whether joint custody is appropriate, based on factors such as the fitness of both parents, the parents' wishes, the parents' ability to cooperate with each other in sharing custody, the level of involvement of each parent in the children's lives, the geographic proximity of the parents' homes, and the effect a joint custody award would have on the children's psychological development. In addition, the court could also consider the children's preferences, but these children are so young that any preference they would express would probably not be given very much weight.

Child Support: Even if the court were to award sole custody to Anna, Ben would still be responsible for child support. Parents have an equal duty to support their children that they cannot contract away. The amount of the award would be determined by statutory guidelines based on the needs of the children and the parents' incomes.

QUESTION 10

Father and Mother, an unmarried couple, lived together in State X. Three years ago, Mother gave birth to Son. Shortly before Son was born, Father moved out of the house and has never

supported or visited Son. Mother and Son have continued to live in State X. When Son was one year old, Mother decided that raising him alone was more than she could handle emotionally and financially. Mother placed him with the Adoptors, a married couple from State Z. At that time, she signed a document relinquishing her parental rights and consenting to Son's adoption by the Adoptors.

The Adoptors, who were lifelong residents of State Z, picked up Son in State X and immediately returned to State Z with him. They promptly filed a petition to adopt Son in a State Z court. They did not give notice to Father, relying on statutes in State X and State Z that provide that notice of an action to adopt a child born out of wedlock does not have to be given to a putative father if the putative father (i) had actual knowledge of the birth or impending birth of the child and (ii) failed to acknowledge paternity of the child, or to take any legal action to establish his claim to paternity of the child, or to exercise parental rights or duties with regard to the child within the first six months of the child's life. Eighteen months after the adoption petition was filed, the State Z court granted it and entered the final adoption decree.

Seven months after the final adoption decree was entered, Father learned that Mother had placed Son for adoption. In a State Z court, Father moved to set aside the adoption on the grounds that State Z lacked jurisdiction to grant the adoption or, alternatively, that the statute that allowed Son to be adopted without notice to Father violates Father's due process rights.

The adoption statute of limitations in State Z, where the Adoptors reside and which granted the adoption, requires that challenges to adoptions be brought within six months after a decree is entered. The adoption statute of limitations in State X, where Son was born and where Mother and Father have always lived, provides that challenges to adoptions may be brought within one year of the time the decree is entered. Relying on the State Z statute of limitations, the Adoptors moved to dismiss Father's motion as untimely. Father claims that the State X statute of limitations, which has not run, applies.

1. Which statute of limitations applies to Father's cause of action? Explain.

2. Did the court in State Z have jurisdiction to enter the adoption decree? Explain.

3. Did failure to give Father notice of the adoption deny him due process? Explain.

ANSWER TO QUESTION 10

1. State Z's statute of limitations should apply to Father's cause of action. The issue of which state's law to apply depends on whether the statute of limitations is considered substantive or procedural. Generally, courts will apply their own state's procedural laws. Historically, statutes of limitations have been treated as procedural, in which case, the law of the forum, State Z, would apply. The exception to this rule is when the statute conditions a substantive right created by statute, such as in the case of a wrongful death act. This exception does not apply here because Father's claim is based on constitutional law, not on any particular state statute. The modern trend is to treat statutes of limitation as substantive and to apply general choice of law principles. The facts do not indicate which approach to conflicts of law that State Z applies. The general rule

for adoption issues is that the court will apply local law. Thus even under the modern trend, it is likely that State Z's six-month statute of limitations will apply.

2.   The principles of the Uniform Child Custody Jurisdiction and Enforcement Act ("UCCJEA") would apply here. State Z had jurisdiction to enter the adoption decree because it is Son's "home state." A child's home state is the state in which the child lived with a parent (or a person acting as a parent) for at least six consecutive months prior to commencement of the proceeding. Son has been living in State Z with the Adoptors, who are acting as parents, for over two years. Thus under the UCCJEA, State Z had jurisdiction to enter the decree.

Additionally, although not yet adopted by most states, the Uniform Adoption Act provides that a state has jurisdiction in an adoption case if the prospective adoptive parents have lived in the state for at least six consecutive months prior to commencement of the adoption proceedings. State Z would have jurisdiction under this Act as well.

[*Note:* Some states have not adopted the UCCJEA, but follow the Uniform Child Custody Jurisdiction Act ("UCCJA"). Under the UCCJA, a state may exercise jurisdiction if: (i) it was the child's home state at the time the proceedings began, or it was the home state within six months before the commencement of the proceedings and a parent still lives in the state; (ii) asserting jurisdiction is in the child's best interests because the child and at least one party have a significant connection with the state; (iii) the child is physically present in the state and has been abandoned or neglected, or it is necessary to protect the child from abuse; or (iv) no other state has or will assert jurisdiction. In this case, State Z would have jurisdiction under the UCCJA as well as under the UCCJEA.]

3.   Failure to give Father notice of the adoption proceedings did not deny him due process. An unmarried putative father is entitled to notice before the adoption of his child only if he has been involved in the child's life. Here, Father left Mother shortly before Son's birth, and so presumably he was aware of Son's impending birth. Yet, since Son's birth, Father has made no effort to support, or even visit, Son. Furthermore, even if Father had invoked his rights to Son, his rights would continue only if he were willing to assume custody of Son, not merely block Son's adoption by the Adoptors. As it is, Father has made absolutely no effort to establish a parent-child relationship with Son in the three years of Son's life; thus he had no right to notice of the adoption.

QUESTION 11

Alice, a financial consultant, and Ben, an engineer, began living together six years ago in a state that allows common law marriage. Alice and Ben were generally known as a couple, and they adopted Smith as their last name. They never formally married. They do not believe in marriage, a fact that is generally known in their community.

Alice and Ben earned approximately equal salaries during their relationship. They deposited their paychecks into a joint bank account from which they paid all their expenses. They never spent all their salaries, and Alice offered to invest the excess "for our retirement." Ben, who much preferred to tinker in his workshop than to read the newspaper's financial pages, gladly agreed. During the years they lived together, Alice withdrew $50,000 from their joint bank account and invested it in securities titled solely in her name. The investments are now worth $200,000.

Ben recently received a patent in his name on a device that he invented and developed with his own labor while living with Alice. Ben is negotiating with a company interested in

manufacturing the device and believes that rights to the device may eventually be worth several million dollars.

Three months ago, Alice gave birth to a child, Carol. Ben does not deny that he is Carol's biological father. Alice admits that she conceived Carol after she stopped using birth control pills without telling Ben, even though Ben had always made it clear that he did not want children. Ben is so angry at Alice that he has moved out. Ben believes that he should not have to contribute to Carol's support because Alice tricked him into fatherhood.

Ben demands that Alice give him half of the securities that she purchased with their savings. Alice believes that she is entitled to a share of any money Ben makes from his invention.

1.   Is Ben obligated to contribute to Carol's support? Explain.

2.   On what theory or theories might Ben assert a right to a share of the securities and might Alice assert a right to a share in the profits from the invention, and what is the likely result on each theory? Explain.

ANSWER TO QUESTION 11

1.   Yes, Ben is obligated to contribute to Carol's support. Both parents share a duty to support their children. It does not matter whether Ben wanted children or whether he was tricked into fatherhood; he must pay support if the court finds that he is Carol's father.

Any child born during a marriage is presumed to be the child of her mother's husband. However, as discussed in 2., below, Ben and Alice were not married at the time of Carol's birth (there was no valid common law marriage). Thus, Carol is a nonmarital child. Nevertheless, a nonmarital child has the same right to support as a marital child. However, paternity must be established for the duty of support to attach.

Alice may bring a paternity suit against Ben to obtain support for Carol. Evidence that may be introduced in a paternity suit includes: (i) admissions of paternity by the putative father, (ii) medical testimony regarding the probability of paternity based on the time elapsed between sexual relations and the birth of the child, and (iii) blood test results. Proving paternity in this case should be easy. Ben does not deny paternity. Alice and Ben were cohabiting and engaging in sexual relations at the time of Carol's conception. Furthermore, the court could order blood tests, which are likely to prove paternity. Once paternity has been established, Ben will be obligated to support Carol.

2.   The first theory that Alice or Ben could assert is that they had a common law marriage and the items in question are marital property to be divided between them. Common law marriage is an alternative to statutory marriage in some states. Generally speaking, the requirements for a common law marriage are: (i) an exchange of consents between two people, (ii) cohabitation, and (iii) a holding out publicly of living together as husband and wife. If Alice and Ben had a valid common law marriage, either one could file for a divorce and request a division of any marital property. The money in the securities and the patent could be deemed marital property because each was acquired during the marriage by the couple's efforts. However, Alice and Ben's relationship does not meet the three criteria for a common law marriage. While they have cohabited for the past six years in a state that allows common law marriage and they have shared a common

last name and back account, they have made it clear to each other and the community that they are not married. The couple does not believe in marriage, and this is generally known in the community. So obviously there was no exchange of consent to the marriage relationship, nor did they hold themselves out as married. Thus, there was no common law marriage between Alice and Ben, and neither one may recover based on this theory.

The second theory that either Ben or Alice may assert is an implied contract theory. Contracts between unmarried cohabitants are generally valid unless sexual relations constitute the only consideration. Here, either Alice or Ben could argue there was an oral agreement that Alice would do the finances to save for their retirement while Ben would create in his workshop. Each could claim that there was an understanding that they would share their profits. This is a better argument for Ben than for Alice. Ben and Alice explicitly discussed the retirement investments and Alice agreed to invest "for our retirement." Thus, so long as Ben provided consideration, the court could find there was an implied contract.

On the other hand, it would be more difficult for Alice to convince the court that there was any implied contract with regard to Ben's inventions. She would have to argue that she did provide consideration, in that she handled his investments so that he could spend more time working on his inventions. However, this would be admitting that the money in the accounts was for both of them, which is something that she is not likely to want to admit in court.

Ben might assert a right to a share of the securities under the theory of a purchase money resulting trust. Where there is a purchase of property in which one party obtains legal title, but another party supplied the consideration, a court may imply that the party obtaining legal title is trustee and the person paying the consideration is the beneficiary of a resulting trust. Here, Alice used funds from a bank account owned jointly by Alice and Ben and purchased securities which she had titled solely in her name.

There is an exception to the presumption of a resulting trust where the parties are close relatives. In that case, a gift, rather than a resulting trust, is presumed. Alice may try to argue that even though she and Ben were never married, they are married for all intents and purposes and therefore, a gift should be presumed. However, it is doubtful whether this argument will succeed since it is widely known that Alice and Ben do not believe in marriage.

Once Ben proves that he supplied a portion of the consideration to purchase the securities, a resulting trust will be presumed for a pro rata portion of the title. Alice may rebut this presumption by submitting evidence that no trust was intended and that the money used as consideration was a gift, a loan, or in payment of a debt. However, the facts do not appear to support any of these theories. It is likely that a court would find that Alice and Ben are co-tenants in ownership of the securities under the theory of a purchase money resulting trust.

Ben could also assert a right to a share of the securities under the theory of a constructive trust. A constructive trust is a remedy used to prevent unjust enrichment of one person at the expense of another as the result of wrongful conduct, such as a breach of fiduciary duty. Ben could argue that Alice and Ben were in a confidential relationship since Ben relied on Alice to make investment decisions for him and she was, in fact, a financial consultant by trade. Ben may argue that Alice breached her fiduciary duty to him in taking money from their joint account and purchasing securities titled solely in her name. This is also a viable argument by which Ben could claim a right to a share of the securities.

QUESTION 12

Husband and Wife married in State X. Shortly thereafter, they moved to State Y, where they were domiciled for the next 10 years of their marriage. Wife never returned to State X. Recently, however, Husband left Wife and moved to State X, which has a six-week residency requirement for a divorce action. After living continuously for six weeks in State X, Husband filed for divorce in the appropriate state court in State X. Wife was served by registered mail at the couple's home in State Y. Although she received the process, Wife did nothing in response.

The law of State X provides that a plaintiff is presumed to be a domiciliary of State X for divorce purposes upon proof of six weeks' continuous residency in State X at the time of the filing of the divorce action. The long arm statute of State X also provides for service of process on nonresident defendants by registered mail at their last known address. It provides that jurisdiction may be exercised over nonresident defendants in actions for marriage dissolution and for alimony, "to the full extent permitted by the Due Process Clause of the United States Constitution."

The State X court issued a decree granting Husband a divorce and ruling that neither Husband nor Wife was entitled to spousal support. As soon as Wife learned of the decree, she filed her own action for divorce and spousal support in the appropriate state court in State Y, where she was domiciled. Husband was properly served with process in State Y, to which he had returned after receiving the State X divorce.

Consistent with the Due Process and Full Faith and Credit Clauses, may the court in State Y grant the divorce and award spousal support to Wife? Explain.

ANSWER TO QUESTION 12

Divorce decree: The State Y court may not grant the divorce because State X already issued a valid divorce decree which is entitled to full faith and credit in State Y. At issue is the jurisdiction of the State X court over the divorce action.

In general, courts must give full faith and credit to divorce decrees of the courts of sister states if the sister state had proper jurisdiction and the decree is valid in the sister state. For jurisdiction to be proper, one of the parties must be domiciled in State X, the forum. In this case, the law of State X requires that a plaintiff continuously reside in that state for six weeks to be considered a domiciliary for divorce purposes.

The facts state that Husband voluntarily moved to State X and lived there for six weeks continuously. Generally, to have a valid change of domicile, a party must move to the new location with the intent to remain there, regarding it as his home. While Husband appears to have satisfied the domicile requirement, the presumption of domicile is rebuttable. The enforcing court may delve into whether domicile was bona fide, but the attacking party, Wife in this case, bears the burden of proof. Wife would most likely argue that Husband lacked the intent to be domiciled in State X because he returned to State Y immediately after the divorce was granted. Nevertheless, since Husband was a domiciliary *at the time of the suit* per State X's statute, it is doubtful that Wife would be successful in challenging State X's decree. Therefore the divorce granted by State X is valid as an ex parte divorce (one based on the domicile of one spouse without personal jurisdiction over the other). Consequently, State Y must grant full faith and credit to State X's judgment.

State X spousal support: State X may not deny Wife spousal support. At issue is whether the State Y court may award support or property rights to a party subsequent to the earlier decree, which specifically denied such payments. These issues must usually be resolved by a court having ***personal jurisdiction*** over the spouse whose property rights are at issue. In this case, while State X had subject matter jurisdiction over the divorce action because of Husband's residency, it did not have personal jurisdiction over Wife because she was not a resident of State X, she was not physically present in State X at the time of service, and nothing in the facts indicates that Wife has any contacts with State X that could be construed as "minimum contacts" for jurisdictional due process purposes as required by the State X statute and the United States Constitution. In short, although the divorce portion of the judgment is valid, the property portion is not. This is called the "divisible divorce doctrine."

State Y spousal support: State Y may award spousal support to Wife. At issue is whether a court may award support or property rights to a spouse after the divorce decree has been issued. Although it is sufficient that a court have personal jurisdiction over the plaintiff to grant a valid divorce decree, it must also have personal jurisdiction over the defendant spouse where spousal support is to be determined. In this case, Wife was not domiciled in State X, and thus, State X does not have personal jurisdiction over her.

Where a court grants an ex parte divorce, spousal support can be granted subsequent to the divorce decree to the spouse who was not subject to personal jurisdiction. Therefore, Wife will be able to pursue an action for spousal support.

QUESTION 13

Fred, age 12, has a heart ailment that severely limits his physical activity. His parents do not allow him to engage in vigorous sports at school. His doctor predicts that Fred's condition will slowly worsen and that, if he is left untreated, his life expectancy will be reduced by 20 years. Medical experts say that a routine operation can correct his heart defect. However, they have also indicated that it is major surgery, which, with the required anesthetic, is always risky. The hospital stay will be about five days, and recovery from the operation will take six weeks. Although the medical experts believe that postponing the operation until Fred reaches adulthood will result in some permanent loss of function, they also believe that the operation involves slightly less risk if performed on an adult rather than a child.

Fred wants to have the operation performed. He feels left out and different because most of his friends are active in sports. Some kids call him "sicky." The school psychologist has indicated that Fred is withdrawn and unhappy at school and that he is at risk of failing in his school work because of his emotional state.

Fred's parents are opposed to the surgery. While they are concerned about the risks of surgery, an even more compelling reason for their opposition is that their religion does not allow such surgery. They believe that their prayers for Fred are heard and that his illness must be part of a divine plan. Fred's doctor disagrees and wishes to obtain a court order that will allow the operation.

Fred's parents require him to attend weekly religious services with them. Fred, however, has decided that he does not wish to follow their religion but instead wants to convert to the faith of his best friend. When Fred's parents learn that Fred's best friend has been teaching Fred about his religion, they forbid him from attending any religious services other than those of their religion.

1. **Can the surgery proceed with Fred's consent only? Explain.**

2. **Is a court likely to order the surgery over the objection of Fred's parents? Explain.**

3. **Do Fred's parents have the right to direct which religious services Fred will attend? Explain.**

ANSWER TO QUESTION 13

1.   No, the surgery cannot proceed only with Fred's consent. At issue is whether a minor has capacity to consent to a surgical procedure. Children are treated differently from adults under the law because of their immaturity. Generally, parental consent is required before medical treatment can be administered to a person under the legal age of capacity, usually 18. Fred is only 12 years old and there is nothing in the facts that indicates that Fred has been emancipated. Therefore, he is not capable of giving consent to medical treatment. Some states have laws enabling minors to give valid consent to abortions, to obtain birth control, and to consent to treatment for sexually transmitted diseases, but the surgery in this case, to correct Fred's heart ailment, does not fall into one of those categories. Thus, more than Fred's consent alone is required before the surgery can proceed.

2.   No, the court is not likely to order the surgery over the objection of Fred's parents. At issue is whether a court will order nonessential medical treatment over the objections of a child's parents. The constitutional right to privacy gives parents the right to decide issues concerning the care, custody, and control of their children. Parents' decisions on behalf of their child are to be given deference. The court may not override a parent's authority, just because it would have decided an issue differently. A court can override the withholding of parental consent for medical treatment only if withholding treatment would cause irremediable injury to the child. For example, the state could order a lifesaving blood transfusion over the parents' objection. However, that exception does not apply in this case. Here, Fred's life is not in any immediate danger. Although if his ailment is left untreated, his condition will slowly worsen, failure to perform the surgery now does not put Fred's life at risk. In fact, there is even some benefit to delaying the surgery—the medical experts believe that the operation is slightly less risky if performed on an adult rather than a child. Fred's parents have made a decision for their son based on their concerns about the risks of the surgery and their religious beliefs. It is not the place of a judge to second-guess that decision. The court must defer to the wishes of Fred's parents regarding the surgery.

3.   Yes, Fred's parents have the right to direct which religious services Fred will attend. At issue is whether parents have the right to make decisions regarding the religious upbringing of their children. As stated above, parents have a constitutional right to determine issues regarding the care, custody, and control of their children. Children are treated differently than adults under the law; parents are given the right and responsibility to make decisions on their child's behalf. So long as there is no indication that the parents' religious practices are placing the child in harm's way, the child must obey his parents' wishes. Here, there is nothing in the facts that indicates that Fred's parents' religion could seriously harm him; he simply prefers the religion of

his best friend. At this point, the parents' beliefs regarding surgery are not life-threatening to Fred, and there is no indication that refusing to allow him to convert to his friend's religion could put him at risk. Thus, while Fred is still a minor his parents may forbid him from attending any religious service other than their own.

QUESTION 14

Soon after Daughter was born to Father and Mother, Father was killed in an automobile accident. Mother found the economic pressures and time restraints of single parenthood overwhelming, and she began to drink heavily. Mother's friend, Caretaker, a childless widow making a comfortable living, began to help Mother financially and with frequent babysitting.

After a few months, Mother asked Caretaker if she would keep Daughter full time until Mother got her life back together. Caretaker agreed, and for the next four years Daughter lived with Caretaker. Mother, who had a serious alcohol problem and could not keep a job, visited Daughter only twice, and contributed no money towards Daughter's support.

Six months ago, Mother joined Alcoholics Anonymous. Since that time, she has been sober, has found steady work, and has begun visiting Daughter more often. She wants Daughter, now five years old, to come back to live with her and insists that she never intended to relinquish Daughter to Caretaker permanently.

Caretaker, to whom Daughter is closely attached, has refused to return her. She believes that it is in Daughter's best interest to remain with her, because she and Daughter have a stable relationship and Caretaker is the only mother figure Daughter knows. A qualified child psychologist has evaluated Daughter and her relationships with Caretaker and Mother. The psychologist would testify that: (i) Daughter is bonded to Caretaker, who has become Daughter's psychological mother; (ii) Daughter recognizes Mother and is not afraid of her but does not have a child-parent relationship with her; and (iii) if Daughter were separated from Caretaker, she would certainly suffer short-term emotional harm and might suffer permanent emotional damage.

This jurisdiction's adoption statutes provide that a child cannot be adopted without the mother's consent unless the mother has abandoned the child. Caretaker has filed a petition to adopt Daughter, alleging that Mother had abandoned Daughter. In the alternative, Caretaker's petition seeks custody of Daughter. Finally, the petition asks for visitation rights in the event the requests for adoption and custody are denied. Mother opposes Caretaker's petition in all respects.

How should the court rule on Caretaker's petition? Explain.

ANSWER TO QUESTION 14

(a) *Adoption:* Caretaker's petition to adopt Daughter should be granted. At issue is whether Mother's parental rights should be terminated and a new parent-child relationship created between Caretaker and Daughter. Adoption is a two-step process. First, the biological parents' rights must be terminated, and second, a new parent-child relationship must be created between the child and the adoptive parent. Generally the consent of a child's biological parents is required for an adoption. In this case Father is deceased and thus his consent is not required. Although Mother will not consent, in this jurisdiction, her consent is not needed if the court finds that she has abandoned her child. During the last four years, Mother left Daughter with Caretaker and did not contribute to Daughter's financial support. In addition, Mother only visited Daughter twice during those four years. Even though she has now begun to visit Daughter, she still has made no effort to support her financially and thus the court should find that Mother abandoned Daughter and terminate Mother's parental rights. Once Mother's rights have been terminated, the adoption can proceed. Given that Daughter has been living with Caretaker since Daughter was one year old, and a qualified child psychologist would testify that Daughter is bonded to Caretaker, assuming that the court finds Caretaker to be a fit parent, it should grant Caretaker's petition to adopt Daughter.

(b) *Custody:* In the alternative, if the court does not find that Mother abandoned Daughter and thus denies Caretaker's petition for adoption, Caretaker's petition to gain custody of Daughter should also be denied. At issue is when a court will award custody to a third party in a dispute between a biological parent and the third party. In such a situation, the decision does not turn on the child's best interest alone. The court must give great weight to the interests of the natural parent. The prevailing view is that the natural parent has a right to raise her child and, absent voluntary relinquishment, the parent is entitled to custody unless it is shown that the parent is unfit. Only under special circumstances (*e.g.,* when the natural parent has abandoned the child) will custody be awarded to a third party. The most common example is in a situation like the one at issue, where a parent leaves a young child with a third party for a period of years and then later wants to regain custody. Even if the court decides that Mother did not "abandon" Daughter, Caretaker will argue that Mother effectively relinquished custody of Daughter to her when she left Daughter in her care for the last four years, only visited twice, and contributed no money towards Daughter's support. However, Mother will argue that she made it clear to Caretaker that she was leaving Daughter with her only until she "got her life back together," and was not relinquishing custody. Given that Caretaker agreed to the arrangement with that understanding, the court should find that Mother did not voluntarily relinquish Daughter. Since Mother did not voluntarily relinquish Daughter, Caretaker can be awarded custody only if Mother is unfit. This is a judgment call and more facts are needed to make this determination. Although Mother had a serious alcohol problem in the past, she is now sober, has found steady work, and presumably is capable of caring for Daughter. Daughter recognizes Mother and is not afraid of her. Although Daughter will suffer short-term emotional harm and might suffer permanent emotional damage if she is separated from Caretaker, Daughter is still very young and Mother's parental rights will probably outweigh the risk of harm to Daughter. Thus, Caretaker's petition for custody should be denied.

(c) *Visitation:* If the court finds that Mother is fit and denies Caretaker's request for custody of Daughter, it should probably also deny Caretaker's request for visitation. The Supreme Court has held that as long as a parent is fit, that parent's determination as to the appropriateness of third-party visitation must be given "special weight." [Troxel v. Granville, 530 U.S. 57 (2000)] A judge may not override a fit parent's decision regarding third-party visitation merely because she feels a better decision could be made or visitation would be in the best interest of the child. Here Mother opposes Caretaker's petition for visitation. Although it is possible that the court could find that under the circumstances the risk of harm to Daughter outweighs Mother's fundamental right to make decisions concerning her child's care, custody, and control, this is unlikely. Thus, Caretaker's request for visitation rights should be denied.

QUESTION 15

Father and Mother divorced one year ago after a 14-year marriage. At the time of the divorce, Mother and Father lived in State A. They were both 39 years old, each had a college education, and they had two children, aged 10 and 12.

As part of the divorce decree, the court awarded custody of the two children to Mother. The court also ordered Father to pay Mother $2,000 per month in child support. In addition, the court ordered Father to pay Mother $500 per month in spousal support for five years. After their property was divided, they each ended up with $50,000 and a car.

Mother continued living in State A with the children. Mother had been working full-time for $28,000 per year at a daycare center prior to the divorce. Five months after the divorce, she had a heart attack. This forced her to cut back to three-quarter-time work, resulting in a pay reduction to $21,000 per year. Her doctor recommends that she not resume full-time work, because full-time work and caring for the children and the home would be too stressful.

For the first six months after the divorce, Father paid Mother the full amount he owed; but, for the past six months, Father has paid Mother nothing. Three months ago, Father was terminated from his $100,000-per-year job because of company downsizing. He received a lump sum severance payment of $50,000. Father decided to move to State B, in part because he hoped he could avoid paying Mother and in part because the job prospects were better there. He transferred all his bank accounts to State B. Although he has had several interviews and his prospects are good for finding a job comparable to the one he had, he does not yet have another job.

Mother has brought an action in State B court to collect child support and spousal support from Father. She claims that the spousal support obligation should be increased to $1,000 per month because she is in poor health. She also asks that the spousal support be extended for an additional five years.

Father claims that the State A child support order is no longer effective and cannot be enforced because he has moved to State B. In the alternative, he claims that his child support obligation should be reduced from $2,000 to $1,000 per month because of his unemployment. In addition, he asks that this modification be made six months retroactive. Father also opposes any increase in his spousal support obligation.

Both State A and State B are in compliance with federal law concerning the enforcement of child support orders.

1. Is State B required to recognize the State A child support order? Explain.

2. Does the State B court have jurisdiction to modify Father's child support obligation? Explain.

3. Without regard to jurisdictional issues, how should a court rule on Father's requests to modify his child support obligation? Explain.

4. Without regard to jurisdictional issues, how should the State B court rule on Mother's request for an increase in and extension of the spousal support obligations? Explain.

ANSWER TO QUESTION 15

1.   Yes. State B is required to recognize the State A child support order. At issue is when a state must grant full faith and credit to the child support order of a sister state. Generally for full faith and credit to be granted to a judgment, there must have been proper jurisdiction for the judgment, the judgment must have been on the merits, and the judgment must be final. Child support orders do not meet this definition because they are modifiable at any time. However, under the Full Faith and Credit for Child Support Act, full faith and credit must be given to another court's child support order if: (i) the court had jurisdiction over the matter and the parties, and (ii) the parties had reasonable notice and an opportunity to be heard. Here, the child support order was issued as part of a divorce decree in the state in which both Mother and Father resided, and thus which presumably had jurisdiction over them and their marriage. Assuming that the court had proper jurisdiction, and that Father had reasonable notice and an opportunity to be heard at the time the divorce decree was entered, the child support order must be given full faith and credit by State B.

2.   State B probably does not have jurisdiction to modify Father's child support obligation. At issue is when a state may modify the support order of another state. The Uniform Interstate Family Support Act ("UIFSA"), which has been adopted in all 50 states, applies. Under UIFSA, once a state with proper jurisdiction issues a support order, the court of another state is limited to enforcing the original order, unless all the parties no longer reside in the issuing state or the parties agree in writing that the nonissuing court may assert jurisdiction to modify the order. In this case, Mother still resides in the issuing state, State A, so the first exception does not apply. It is a little unclear whether the second exception applies. The facts indicate that Mother has brought an action in State B requesting an increase is *spousal* support, but nothing indicates that she has consented in writing to a modification of the *child* support order. Thus, the State B court probably does not have jurisdiction to modify the child support order. However, an argument might be made that by consenting to modification of one part of the divorce decree, Mother has consented to modification of the other parts, including the child support provision. The success of such an argument is uncertain.

3.   The court should deny Father's request to reduce his child support obligation at this time. Child support is always modifiable based on a substantial change in circumstances affecting the needs of the children or the ability of the parents to pay. Courts will consider various factors, including unemployment. Father was involuntarily terminated from his job, and has not yet found a new one despite his reasonable efforts. The court will probably consider this a substantial change in circumstances. However, at the time he lost his job three months ago, Father received a lump sum severance payment worth half of his yearly salary. Thus he should have no difficulty in paying his child support payments at this time. Furthermore, Father's job prospects are good and he has already had several interviews. Thus the court will likely deny his request to modify his child support obligation, but may reconsider later if Father cannot find new employment.

Even if the court does decide to grant his request to reduce his child support obligation, it will most likely deny his request that the modification be made six months retroactive. Most states hold that past due installments of support cannot be retroactively modified. Thus, it is very unlikely that it will be made retroactive, especially given the fact that Father lost his job only three months ago but has not paid his obligation for the past six months.

4.   State B will most likely grant at least some of Mother's request for an increase in and extension of spousal support. Spousal support can be modified based on a substantial and material change in circumstances affecting the needs of the recipient spouse or the ability to pay of the obligor spouse. Here there is a substantial change in circumstances—Mother had a heart

attack and based on her health cannot resume full-time work while caring for the couple's children. She is likely to have more medical bills while earning only three-fourths of her previous salary. The court is likely to find that this would be sufficient to grant her request for at least some increase in spousal support. However, more facts are needed to determine whether the circumstances warrant a doubling of both the amount of payment and the length of time of the obligation.

In addition, as discussed in part 3., above, Father has also experienced a substantial change in circumstances that may effect his ability to pay—he has lost his job. The court may find that as long as Father is involuntarily unemployed, he is not able to afford the additional payments. Of course, this can be reconsidered when Father finds employment. At that time, given Mother's needs, her request for some increase in spousal support is likely to be granted.

QUESTION 16

Seven months ago, Husband and his wife, Wife, were driving on a highway. Their daughter, Daughter, age 10, was in the backseat. While driving, Husband negligently turned the wheel of the car to the right and hit Frank's car. Frank had parked his car on the shoulder, turned on the emergency flashing lights, and was changing a flat tire. The accident caused Frank's car to hit and kill Frank. Frank's fiancée, Emily, was with Frank, but was not physically injured. However, she witnessed the accident and held Frank in her arms as he died.

Wife was seriously injured in the accident. She was hospitalized for a month with broken bones and internal injuries and is still undergoing physical therapy six months later. Wife and Husband have remained married.

After the accident, Husband took Daughter to the doctor to be examined. Although Daughter was not injured in the accident, the doctor found that she was suffering from an incipient bone disease brought on by calcium deficiency from an imbalanced diet.

Frank and Emily had lived together during their two-year engagement, and Frank died one week before their planned wedding date. Since Frank's death, Emily has suffered from depression because she misses his companionship and intimacy. Consequently, she has been under psychiatric care.

Wife has brought a lawsuit against Husband for his negligence. Emily has also sued Husband for his negligence. Daughter has sued both Husband and Wife for their failure to provide her with a diet richer in calcium.

There is no guest statute in this jurisdiction.

1. **Assuming Wife can prove a prima facie case of negligence, is Husband liable to Wife? Explain.**

2. **Are Husband and Wife liable to Daughter for their failure to provide Daughter with a diet richer in calcium? Explain.**

3. **On what theory or theories arising from her relationship with Frank might Emily reasonably base claims for damages against Husband, and what would be the likely outcome of each claim? Explain.**

ANSWER TO QUESTION 16

1.   Husband is liable to Wife. At issue is husband-wife tort immunity. Under the traditional view, one spouse could not sue another in tort for personal injury. However, most states have abolished interspousal tort immunity. Either spouse may now maintain a tort action against the other. Thus, Husband is liable to Wife for his negligence despite their marriage.

2.   Husband and Wife probably are not liable to Daughter for their failure to provide Daughter with a diet rich in calcium. At issue is parent-child tort immunity. As with husband-wife tort immunity, a majority of states have abolished parent-child tort immunity. However, these states generally grant parents broad discretion in the exercise of parental authority or supervision. How closely parents monitor their child's diet would probably be included in this discretion. Today many, if not most, children in this country do not eat properly balanced diets. It is unlikely that the court would hold all of their parents liable. Thus, even if the court follows the majority rule that abolishes parent-child immunity, it is unlikely that Husband and Wife's actions rise to a level of negligence for which they would be held liable.

3.   Emily could attempt to bring a claim for loss of consortium through a wrongful death action or a claim for negligent infliction of emotional distress, but she will probably be unsuccessful because she was not married to Frank.

In most jurisdictions, either spouse can recover for the loss of the other's consortium or services due to injuries resulting from a defendant's tortious conduct, whether the defendant's conduct was intentional, negligent, or based on strict liability. Here, Frank's death was caused by Husband's negligence, and thus Frank's wife would be entitled to recover for interference with the marital relationship. Her recovery would be through a wrongful death action, which in some states can be brought by the surviving spouse, and in other states by the personal representative of the decedent's estate. However, this claim will not be available to Emily because she was only Frank's fiancée at the time of Frank's death. Their wedding was a week away.

Emily could also try to claim negligent infliction of emotional distress, but this would fail in most states. To succeed in a claim for negligent infliction of emotion distress, a plaintiff must prove that she (i) suffered some physical injury from the distress, and (ii) was in the "target zone" or "zone of danger" at the time of the defendant's negligence. Here, Emily was in the "zone of danger" when Frank was hit because she was with Frank. She witnessed the accident and he died in her arms. However, she did not suffer any physical injury. She was not harmed at the time of the accident, and although since then she has suffered from depression and has been under psychiatric care, emotional distress alone is insufficient in most jurisdictions to satisfy the requirements of negligent infliction of emotional distress.

However, it is important to note that in a substantial minority of jurisdictions, the "zone of danger" standard has been rejected in favor of a foreseeability standard. In these states, recovery is permitted as long as (i) the plaintiff and the person injured by the defendant are closely related; (ii) the plaintiff was present at the scene of the injury; and (iii) the plaintiff personally observed or perceived the event. While some of these jurisdictions also allow recovery for severe emotional distress even in the absence of physical injury, almost all of them require a marital or family relationship for the first element. Thus, Emily will probably not be able to recover because she and Frank were not yet married.

QUESTION 17

Ann and Bert, a married couple, were unable to have biological children because Bert was infertile. They decided to try artificial insemination by an anonymous donor. Their doctor performed the procedure after obtaining written consent from both Ann and Bert. As a result of the artificial insemination, Ann became pregnant.

During the last months of Ann's pregnancy, she and Bert argued constantly, and Ann moved out of the family home into her own apartment. The baby, Daughter, was born while Ann and Bert were living apart. Bert visited Ann and Daughter in the hospital and paid their medical expenses. He tried to convince Ann to reconcile with him, but Ann refused, leaving the hospital with Daughter and returning to her apartment. Bert continued to visit them and contributed to Daughter's support.

Shortly after Daughter's birth, Ann began an affair with Walt. Walt also spent some time with Daughter and grew fond of her. When Daughter was one year old, Ann discovered she was pregnant by Walt. When Walt learned Ann was pregnant, he became very upset and began to abuse Ann verbally and physically. Ann immediately broke off the relationship with Walt. Shortly thereafter, she reconciled with Bert.

Ann, Bert, and Daughter were living together when Ann's baby, Sonny, was born. Walt, Sonny's biological father, contacted Ann, apologized for his past abusive behavior, and requested to see Sonny. He also offered to pay the expenses of Sonny's birth and to contribute to Sonny's support. Ann rejected both his request and his offer.

When Sonny was six months old and Daughter was two years old, Ann was killed in an automobile accident. She left a valid will stating that if she died while her children were minors, she wanted Bert to be named custodian and guardian of both of them.

Walt has sued Bert, seeking to establish himself as Sonny's legal father and requesting custody of both children. Bert claims that he is the legal father of both Daughter and Sonny and wants to maintain physical custody of both children. Under the law of the jurisdiction, both parties have standing to raise these issues.

How should the court rule on Walt's and Bert's claims? Explain.

ANSWER TO QUESTION 17

Daughter: Bert will retain custody of Daughter because he is Daughter's legal father and there is no indication in the facts that he is unfit. The first issue raised regarding Daughter is the paternity of a child born from artificial insemination of a wife by donor sperm during a legal marriage. If Bert and Ann live in a state that applies the Uniform Parentage Act of 2000 (amended in 2002) or the Uniform Status of Children of Assisted Conception Act, the result is clear. Under these Acts, the husband of a woman who bears a child through assisted conception is the child's legal father, unless within two years after learning of the child's birth he commences an action in which it is determined that he did not consent to the assisted conception. That exception clearly does not apply here. Bert consented in writing to the artificial insemination and thus he is Daughter's legal father.

Furthermore, even if Bert and Ann live in a state that has not adopted either the 2000 Uniform Parentage Act or the Uniform Status of Children of Assisted Conception Act, he most likely would still be found to be Daughter's father. For example, in those states that have adopted the 1973 Uniform Parentage Act, a husband is treated as if he were the natural father of a child born as a result of his wife's artificial insemination by donor sperm, provided the insemination was done under the supervision of a licensed physician and the husband consented to the procedure in writing. Again, in this case Bert consented in writing to the artificial insemination and the facts state that a doctor performed the procedure.

Since Bert is Daughter's legal parent, he is entitled to custody of Daughter over Walt. In a dispute between a parent and a nonparent, the courts give great weight to the interests of the parent. Custody does not turn on the child's best interests alone, as it does in disputes between parents. The prevailing view is that a parent has the right to custody over a nonparent, absent voluntary relinquishment, unless it is shown that the parent is unfit. Here, there have been absolutely no facts alleged that Bert is an unfit father. He has not been accused of abuse, neglect, or abandonment of Daughter. In fact, he continued to support Daughter financially and visit with Daughter during his separation from Ann, and he has lived with Daughter for at least the past six months. Ann even indicated in her will that she wanted Bert to have custody of the children. Thus there is no doubt that Bert would be awarded custody of Daughter.

Sonny: Walt will most likely be found to be Sonny's parent and thus presumptively entitled to custody, but given the circumstances, there is a chance that a court will award Bert custody of Sonny. The first issue raised here is who is the legal father of a child born during wedlock as a result of a wife's extramarital affair. Most states presume that a child born during a marriage is the child of the husband, and thus Bert would be Sonny's presumed father. As such, he would be entitled to custody of Sonny for the same reasons he is entitled to custody of Daughter, discussed above.

However, the presumption of a husband's paternity can be rebutted by a preponderance of the evidence in some states, and by clear and convincing evidence in others. Walt will be able to rebut this presumption based on the facts that Bert is infertile and Ann and Bert were living apart when Sonny was conceived. Walt will then have to establish his own paternity, which he can easily do through genetic test results. Next, Walt will have to show that, under the Due Process Clause, he is entitled to his child because he has attempted to take parental responsibility for the child. He can demonstrate this by proving that he has tried to visit Sonny and has offered to contribute to Sonny's financial support. Once Walt has established his own paternity, he will enjoy the presumption that he is entitled to custody.

Bert could try to argue that, because he has been raising Sonny since birth, the presumption should not apply and, instead, the best interests of the child test should be used. However, this argument is weak and likely to fail. Many states have ruled that, when a child has been left with a third party to rear, the biological parent has lost the right to rear that child and the best interests of the child test should be applied. While it is true that Bert has been raising Sonny and Walt has not been in the picture, the problem with Bert's argument here is that Walt has requested to visit Sonny and has offered to pay Sonny's birth expenses and for his support. Ann was the one who rejected Walt's efforts. Walt has not voluntarily abandoned Sonny and therefore it is unlikely that the court will hold this against him.

Bert's best hope for gaining custody of Sonny is to show that Walt is unfit. As discussed above, a parent loses the right to raise his child if he is proven unfit. The facts state that Walt abused Ann verbally and physically during their relationship. This abuse could be used against Walt to demonstrate that he is an unfit custodian for Sonny. More facts are needed to establish whether his behavior rises to the level of unfitness. If Walt is proven unfit, his entitlement to custody as Sonny's legal parent no longer applies, and custody can be determined based on Sonny's best interests. Under this standard, Bert would probably win. Sonny has been living with Bert since birth and is used to that environment, his sister will be residing with Bert, Sonny's mother wanted him to be with Bert, and there is no indication that Bert is anything but a good parent. If the court applies a best interests test to Sonny's custody, Bert will win.

QUESTION 18

Husband and Wife married in State X in 1992 and resided there for the next 10 years. They have three children, ages five, seven, and nine.

In early February 2002, Husband told Wife that he wanted a divorce and was moving to State Z for a new job. He asked Wife to let him take the children. Wife refused. The next day, Husband moved to State Z without the children.

In March 2002, six weeks after arriving in State Z (the minimum period of residence for divorce in State Z), Husband filed an action for divorce. In this action, he also sought primary custody of the three children, asserting that Wife had been violent and abusive toward him throughout their marriage.

Wife was served with the summons and complaint in Husband's action at the family home in State X. Wife, who has never been to State Z, did not answer or appear in Husband's divorce proceeding.

In July 2002, the State Z court granted Husband a default judgment granting Husband a divorce, dividing their property, awarding him primary custody of the three children, and giving Wife "reasonable visitation." Husband served Wife with the judgment.

In August 2002, Wife allowed the children to go to State Z for a two-week visit with Husband, whom they had not seen for nearly five months. This was the children's first time in State Z. At the end of the two-week period, Husband notified Wife that he would not return the children to Wife.

Wife immediately filed an action for divorce, property division, and custody in State X.

Husband appeared in Wife's State X action and contested her claims. He sought enforcement of the State Z judgment awarding him custody. He also argued that Wife's other claims were precluded by Husband's State Z judgment of divorce.

1. **Is the State X court required to enforce the State Z custody decree? Explain.**

2. **Are Wife's claims for divorce and property division precluded by Husband's State Z judgment? Explain.**

ANSWER TO QUESTION 18

1.   No, the State X court is not required to enforce the State Z custody decree. The issue is whether State Z had proper jurisdiction to hear the custody case in the first place. Under the Uniform Child Custody Jurisdiction and Enforcement Act ("UCCJEA"), a state has jurisdiction to hear a child custody case if that state is the child's "home state," *i.e.*, the state in which the child lived with a parent or person acting as a parent since birth or for at least six months prior to the commencement of the custody proceeding. In this case, Husband and Wife's three children had lived in State X their whole lives at the time that Husband filed for custody in State Z. Thus, State X, not State Z, was the children's home state, and State Z did not have jurisdiction over the matter. Husband could try to argue that State Z had jurisdiction under an exception to the home state rule for temporary emergency jurisdiction in the case of abandonment or abuse, but more facts are needed for this argument to be successful. Under the UCCJEA, a court has temporary emergency jurisdiction if it is necessary in an emergency to protect the child because the child or her siblings or a parent is subjected to or threatened with mistreatment or abuse. Although Husband claims that Wife has been violent and abusive toward him throughout their marriage, more facts are needed to establish if this is sufficient to give State Z temporary emergency jurisdiction. Unless this exception can be invoked, State Z did not have proper jurisdiction, and State X is not required to enforce the State Z custody decree.

2.   While Wife's divorce claim is precluded by the previous State Z judgment, her claim for property division is not. At issue is the doctrine of divisible divorce.

Generally, courts must give full faith and credit to divorce decrees of a sister state court if the sister state had proper jurisdiction over the action and the decree is valid in the sister state. For State Z to have had jurisdiction over the divorce, one of the parties must have been domiciled in State Z. The facts state that Husband moved to State Z voluntarily and resided there for the requisite six weeks before filing for divorce from Wife. Husband's domicile probably cannot be challenged because he moved to State Z for a new job—obviously a legitimate reason. Therefore, Husband was a legitimate domiciliary of State Z, rendering the divorce granted by State Z valid as an ex parte divorce (*i.e.,* one based on the domicile of one spouse without having personal jurisdiction over the other). Because the divorce granted by State Z is valid, it is entitled to full faith and credit by State X, and Wife cannot now seek a divorce in State X because the parties are no longer married.

However, under the doctrine of divisible divorce, an ex parte divorce can serve to grant only the divorce. It generally will not affect any property rights or rights to support, which usually must be settled by a court having personal jurisdiction over both of the parties. In this case, the facts indicate that State Z did not have personal jurisdiction over Wife. She has never been to State Z and she did not answer or appear in the divorce proceeding there. Thus, State Z had no jurisdiction to divide the couple's property, and Wife can now make a claim for a property division in State X.

QUESTION 19

NOTE: Applicants answering this question in a community property state should use community property principles. For this purpose, the phrase "marital property" means community property.

On July 1, 1990, Ann and Burt got married in State X, where they have lived all their lives.

At the time of their marriage, Ann and Burt were each 22 years old. Burt had graduated from high school and had been working for one year as a data entry technician, earning $30,000 annually. Ann had graduated from high school and had worked since graduation as a grocery store cashier, earning $27,000 annually. Ann had a trust fund that she acquired when she was 18 years old. The trust fund was worth $200,000, and Burt knew all about it. Neither had any other property or debts. Ann knew that Burt planned to become a lawyer, and Burt knew that Ann intended to be a homemaker.

Three months prior to the marriage, Burt told Ann that he would not marry her unless they signed a premarital agreement. Ann was surprised because Burt had never told her this was a precondition to their marriage. She reluctantly agreed, and they immediately went to the office of Burt's lawyer, Lawyer. Lawyer showed Ann and Burt a draft agreement under which both Ann and Burt would waive all rights to separate and marital property titled solely in the other's name if they divorced. They would also waive any right to claim child support if they divorced.

Lawyer told Ann that by signing the agreement she would be waiving her rights to marital property and child support. Lawyer also told Ann that he represented only Burt, and not her, and that she should retain her own lawyer. Ann decided not to retain her own lawyer because she trusted Burt. Ann read the agreement the next day and expressed no reservations about signing it. Ann and Burt then both signed the agreement.

After the marriage, Burt became a very successful lawyer. Ann became a homemaker and had no out-of-home employment. The value of the property acquired from Burt's earnings during the marriage is $900,000. The value of Ann's trust fund, managed at all times by her father, is now over $800,000. Ann and Burt have two children, currently ages seven and 10.

Ann now sues Burt for divorce in State X. Ann and Burt agree that Ann will have custody of the children. However, the parties cannot agree on the division of property.

Ann seeks property division and child support under the marital dissolution statute. Burt argues that (a) the court should enforce the premarital agreement, and (b) if the court invalidates the premarital agreement, that Ann's trust fund is marital property subject to distribution.

Ann concedes that the premarital agreement was and is substantively fair. Nonetheless, she argues that it is unenforceable (a) because she lacked legal counsel and (b) because it addresses property distribution and child support upon divorce. She also argues (c) that, regardless of the premarital agreement's validity, her trust fund is not subject to division.

1. How should the court rule on Ann and Burt's arguments regarding the premarital agreement? Explain.

2. How should the court rule on Ann and Burt's arguments regarding the trust fund? Explain.

ANSWER TO QUESTION 19

1.　The court should rule that the premarital agreement and the provision regarding property distribution are enforceable, but the court should invalidate the provision regarding child support. To be valid, a premarital agreement must be fair, voluntary, and in writing, and the parties must make a full disclosure as to their assets and debts. As with any contract, it cannot be a product of fraud or duress. Also, because the parties to a premarital agreement are in a relationship of trust, they must act in good faith. The parties may include provisions regarding property division, but they may not waive child support.

Ann's argument that her lack of legal counsel rendered the agreement unenforceable should fail for several reasons. First, Burt's lawyer explained the agreement to Ann and suggested that she retain her own lawyer. Although Ann had money from her trust fund and her job, and could afford to retain an attorney, she chose not to. Next, Ann, like Burt, was a high school graduate and was able to read the contract. She had three months before the wedding to reread the agreement, think about its terms, and obtain legal advice, if necessary. Ann expressed no reservations about signing the agreement, and when the parties signed the agreement, she was the only one with property. Ann was not under duress just because Burt said that he would not marry her unless they signed a premarital agreement. Marriage may be conditioned on the signing of a premarital agreement, and the marriage itself is sufficient consideration to make the agreement enforceable.

Ann's argument that the agreement is unenforceable because it addresses property distribution should also fail, because one of the recognized purposes of premarital agreements is to provide for the disposition of property upon death or divorce. Ann could argue that the court should divide the property, taking into consideration the parties' current circumstances. The agreement was signed many years ago, and since then, Burt has become a successful lawyer, while Ann stayed home to care for the children. However, under the agreement, the parties waived all rights to separate and marital property titled solely in the other's name, and the facts of the case do not say how the property is titled. So, there may still be marital property to which Ann has a right. Also, there is no provision in the agreement that states that the parties waive their rights to spousal support, so the court has the discretion to award Ann spousal support.

The provision regarding child support is unenforceable, because both parents have a duty to support their children, and children's rights to child support cannot be waived. The court will determine the amount of child support based on the parents' income, taking the children's needs into account. Although there is no mention of a severability clause in the agreement, the court should treat the agreement in the same way as other contracts and uphold the property distribution provision even though the child support provision is not enforceable.

2.　The court should rule that the trust fund is Ann's separate property. Property that is acquired by one spouse before marriage remains that spouse's separate property after marriage if nothing has been done to change the characterization of that property. In addition, an increase to the separate property is also separate property if the increase is not due to the contribution of marital funds or the labor of the spouses. Ann acquired the trust fund before the marriage and did not create a gift of it to the marriage, place it in Burt's name, or commingle it with marital property. No marital funds were added to the trust, and Ann's father managed it at all times. Therefore, whether or not the premarital agreement is valid, the trust fund is still Ann's separate property and is not subject to distribution.

QUESTION 20

> **NOTE: Applicants answering this question in a community property state should use community property principles. For this purpose, the phrase "marital property" means community property.**

Harold is the CEO and sole owner of a real estate business that he began about 25 years ago, shortly after he married Wendy. Wendy quit her job when they married and has ever since been a full-time homemaker. Last year, Harold became romantically involved with Carol, an employee of his real estate business. Wendy recently discovered this affair and also learned that Harold had bought expensive gifts for Carol, including a house purchased in Carol's name. Wendy sued Harold for divorce, based on his adultery with Carol.

Wendy would agree that she has never been a good housekeeper. The house was often dirty until the weekly visit by a cleaning company. Meals were often brought in from local restaurants. Wendy spent much of her time tending to the couple's two children, who are now adults, although a live-in nanny helped her until both children entered school. At Harold's request, Wendy occasionally entertained Harold's clients.

Harold has sole title to the real estate business and a private vested pension to which he has contributed since beginning his real estate business. Harold and Wendy have joint title to their family home and a bank account. These assets were acquired with funds Harold earned during the marriage. Wendy has sole title to 1,000 shares of stock that she inherited shortly after she married Harold.

1. Are the real estate business, Harold's pension, the jointly titled family home, the joint bank account, and the stock subject to division at divorce? Explain.

2. What effect, if any, would Harold's affair with Carol and his gifts to her have on any property division? Explain.

3. What arguments regarding property division are available to Harold and Wendy based on Wendy's role as a mother and homemaker? Explain.

ANSWER TO QUESTION 20

1. The real estate business, Harold's pension, the family home, and the joint bank account are marital property subject to division at divorce, but the stock is Wendy's separate property.

Generally, under the equitable division of marital property approach, each spouse takes his separate property, and the court divides the marital property on an equitable, but not necessarily equal, basis. Separate property is any property brought into the marriage, appreciation it has earned (if kept totally separate and not earned through efforts of the other spouse), and property acquired through gift, bequest, devise, or descent. All other property acquired during the marriage is marital property, no matter how the property is titled.

In this case, Harold started the real estate business and began contributing to the pension during the marriage, and the couple purchased the family home and opened the bank account with money Harold earned from the business. Therefore, these assets are marital property, subject to distribution. On the other hand, Wendy inherited the stock. Thus, the stock and any increase in its value due to market conditions is her separate property.

2. Most states do not consider marital fault a factor in the division of property. However, courts do consider a spouse's dissipation of marital assets. Here, Harold misspent marital funds by giving gifts to Carol. Although the affair with Carol by itself will not affect the division of property, Harold's dissipation of assets will be taken into account by the court, and Harold will likely be awarded less of the property than he would otherwise have received.

3. Some of the factors that courts consider when dividing marital property include: the present income of the spouses; their vocational skills, employability, earning capacities, and opportunities to acquire future income; and each party's contribution as a homemaker to the family. Wendy will argue that she has no present income, lacks vocational skills, and will have difficulty finding a job and earning adequate income because she quit her job 25 years ago when the couple married. She will probably claim that she had to forgo pursuing a career so that she could care for the family and that her contribution as a homemaker is an important factor in the division of the property. However, Harold will argue that Wendy's contribution as a homemaker was minimal because she did little cleaning and cooking and had the help of a nanny in caring for the children. The court will consider these arguments along with other factors, such as the parties' ages and the length of the marriage, in making an equitable distribution of the property.

QUESTION 21

Husband and Wife were married for 12 years. The couple had one child, Boy, age seven. Husband and Wife were both devoted parents.

Wife filed for divorce shortly after she learned that Husband and Secretary were having an affair. In the divorce action, Husband and Wife each sought sole custody of Boy.

The court appointed a child custody evaluator. Both parents told the evaluator they were not willing or able to share custody. Boy told the evaluator that he was very upset because his parents were getting a divorce and that he wanted to live with his father. Based upon the child custody evaluator's recommendation, the court awarded Husband sole custody of Boy and gave Wife liberal visitation rights. Neither party appealed this decree. Husband's and Wife's relationship has remained bitter and hostile.

Three months after the custody decree was filed, Secretary moved into Husband's house. Immediately thereafter, Wife filed a petition seeking to modify the custody decree and obtain sole custody of Boy.

At a hearing on Wife's petition, Boy testified, "I miss my mom and I am sad that my parents are divorced." Husband testified that there had been no change in Boy's behavior since Secretary moved into his home and that Boy got along well with Secretary. Wife testified that Boy should not be exposed to his father's nonmarital cohabitation. There was no other testimony. Neither Husband nor Wife sought joint custody.

The court modified the custody decree and awarded Husband and Wife joint custody. Under the modified decree, Boy will reside with each parent for alternating two-week

periods and the parents will share decisionmaking responsibilities. The court held that "this arrangement will give Boy the best of both parents and allow each parent to counter-act any negative influence on Boy by the other parent."

Husband appeals the court's determination.

1.   Did the court err in modifying the custody decree? Explain.

2.   Did the court err in awarding joint custody? Explain.

ANSWER TO QUESTION 21

1.   The court erred in modifying the prior custody decree. The issue is whether Husband's nonmarital cohabitation and Boy's testimony constituted a substantial change in circumstances warranting modification.

It was not proper to modify the custody decree based on Husband's cohabitation with Secretary. Custody orders may be modified based on a substantial change in circumstances affecting the child's well-being. However, to avoid repetitive litigation, most states require a certain amount of time to elapse (*e.g.,* one or two years) since entry of the prior order unless the child's present environment could endanger his physical, mental, moral, or emotional health. The party seeking modification bears the burden of proof.

Here, Wife filed for a change in custody only three months after entry of the original custody decree. Thus, Wife had to prove a substantial change in circumstances and that Boy's welfare is at risk. At the hearing, Wife testified about Husband's nonmarital cohabitation with Secretary. However, in most states, nonmarital cohabitation alone is not a sufficient reason for changing a custody order. There must be some other evidence that the living arrangement and the relation-ships of those in the home have a harmful impact on the child. There was no such evidence here. Indeed, Husband testified that Boy's behavior had not changed since Secretary moved into their home and that Boy and Secretary got along well. No evidence contradicted the testimony. Thus, Wife failed to show that the cohabitation had an adverse effect on Boy.

Neither was it proper for the court to modify the custody decree based on Boy's testimony. When determining whether circumstances justify a change in custody, a court will consider a child's wishes if the child is of sufficient age and maturity to make an intelligent choice regarding custody. The preference of a seven-year-old child like Boy would not ordinarily be given much weight. However, when both parents are found to be equally fit to have custody, a child's prefer-ence is given greater weight.

Here, the evidence showed that Husband and Wife were both devoted to Boy and fit to have custody. In the divorce action, the court awarded Husband custody based on the evaluator's recommendation after Boy said that he wanted to live with his father. At the modification hearing Boy did not say that he wanted to live with his mother, but only that he missed her. In any event, even if Boy had testified that he now wanted to live with his mother, this testimony alone would not constitute a substantial change in circumstances that would justify a change in custody arrangements and another disruption in Boy's life. Stability and predictability are in Boy's best interests, and the custody decree should not have been modified.

2.   The court erred in awarding joint custody. The issue is whether joint custody is appropriate when the parents are hostile toward each other and have not requested joint custody.

The standard to be applied in a custody determination is the best interests of the child. Many courts favor joint custody because it promotes the involvement of both parents in their child's life after the parents divorce. However, joint custody is not appropriate in every situation. If the parents do not want joint custody, they may be reluctant to work together, and some courts do not award joint custody unless the parents agree to it or there is evidence of their ability to cooperate. If the parents are hostile toward one another, it is likely that an attempt to collaborate will only result in more conflict.

Here, the award of joint custody was exceedingly inappropriate. Husband and Wife did not want joint custody, they are bitter and hostile toward each other, and there was no evidence that they could cooperate. It is highly unlikely that they will be able to agree and make decisions together. If they are forced to try to work together, they will probably become even more antagonistic toward each other, and this would certainly not serve Boy's best interests. Furthermore, the prior custody arrangement gave Wife liberal visitation rights while providing stability for Boy. The new custody arrangement would cause instability and would be very difficult on Boy and his parents. Boy would have to make the transition from the home of one parent to the home of the other every two weeks. Moreover, the arrangement does not provide a solution to Wife's concern about Boy's exposure to Husband's nonmarital cohabitation because Boy would be staying with Husband every two weeks.

Therefore, even if a modification of custody had been warranted, the joint custody arrangement would not be appropriate in this case.

QUESTION 22

Harold and Wendy were divorced in State A and awarded joint custody of their two children, John, age five, and Amanda, age three. Under the terms of the divorce decree, both parents were to share in decisions concerning the care, education, religion, medical treatment, and general welfare of the children, but Wendy was awarded primary physical custody, which, in this case, meant that the children would live with her except during alternate weekends and the month of July. Harold was also ordered to pay monthly child support in the amount of $500 per child until each child reached the age of 18.

Two years after the divorce, Wendy was offered a job in State B that would double her salary but necessitate a move to an area of State B located about 100 miles from Harold's home in State A. When Wendy told Harold of her desire to accept the job offer and move to State B, he objected that such a move would prevent him from exercising his visitation rights.

Harold petitioned the State A court to issue an order prohibiting Wendy from relocating with the children. The court found that Wendy's decision to move was motivated by a desire to improve her family's standard of living. It denied Harold's petition. Wendy then moved with the children to State B, where she began her new job, set up a new residence, and registered the child support order.

After Wendy and the children moved to State B, Harold stopped making child support payments. In response, Wendy sought enforcement of the State A support order in a State B court. Wendy also petitioned the State B court to extend Harold's obligation to pay child support until the children reach age 21, as authorized under the law of State B. Under the law of State A, there is no obligation to pay child support for children over the age of 18. She further petitioned the court to modify the State A custody order by eliminating the joint decision-making provision. Harold was personally served when he came to State B to take the children on vacation.

In response to Wendy's petition, Harold claimed that the State B court did not have jurisdiction to enforce or modify any of the State A orders.

1. Was the State A court's decision to allow Wendy to relocate with the children to State B correct? Explain.

2. May the State B court enforce the State A child support order? Explain.

3. May the State B court modify the State A child support order by extending the support obligation to age 21? Explain.

4. May the State B court modify the State A custody decree by eliminating the joint decision-making provision? Explain.

ANSWER TO QUESTION 22

1. The court's decision to allow Wendy to relocate with the children was correct. The issue is whether a custodial parent should be permitted to relocate if the move will interfere with the noncustodial parent's visitation rights. Many courts recognize that in today's mobile society it is unreasonable to deny a custodial parent the right to pursue opportunities that require relocation. These courts allow relocation if it is in the children's best interests, is motivated by a benefit to the family, and is not intended to deprive the noncustodial parent of visitation. In this case, Wendy was motivated by a substantial salary increase, not a desire to frustrate Harold's visitation rights. The children are young enough to adjust to the move, and the facts do not indicate any reason why the move would adversely affect them. Moreover, the move will likely improve the children's quality of life, and Harold can still maintain a relationship with the children through alternate visitation. Therefore, it is proper that Wendy was allowed to relocate.

2. State B may enforce State A's child support order. At issue is whether a state may enforce the child support order of another state if the obligor still resides in the issuing state but the children reside in the nonissuing state. Under the Uniform Interstate Family Support Act ("UIFSA"), which has been adopted in all 50 states, once a state with proper jurisdiction issues a support order, the court of another state with personal jurisdiction over the obligor may enforce the support order by properly registering the order after receiving it from the issuing state. Once the order has been registered in the nonissuing state, it is subject to the same enforcement procedures as if it had been issued in that state. In this case, State B obtained jurisdiction over Harold when he was served while in State B to take the children on vacation. Thus, if State A's support order has been registered in State B, the State B court may enforce State A's support order.

3.   The State B court may not modify the State A child support order by extending the support obligation to age 21. Under UIFSA, the role of the nonissuing state is only to enforce the original order, unless all of the parties no longer reside in the issuing state or the parties agree in writing (or consent in a record) to the nonissuing court's assertion of jurisdiction to modify the order. Here, Harold still resides in the issuing state, State A, and has not consented to jurisdiction in State B. Therefore, State A has continuing, exclusive jurisdiction to modify the order, and State B must apply State A's law regarding termination of child support.

4.   The State B court may not modify the State A custody decree. Under the federal Parental Kidnapping Prevention Act ("PKPA"), states must give full faith and credit to other states' custody determinations, as long as those determinations were made in conformity with the provisions of the PKPA. Furthermore, under the Uniform Child Custody Jurisdiction and Enforcement Act ("UCCJEA"), adopted by the majority of states, the court that made the initial child custody determination has exclusive, continuing jurisdiction over the matter as long as the child, the child's parent, or a person acting as a parent continues to live in the state, or as long as the child has a significant connection with the state and substantial evidence relating to the matter is available in the state. A court must recognize and enforce the child custody determination of a court of another state if that state's court exercised jurisdiction in substantial conformity with the UCCJEA. Thus, because Harold still lives in State A, State B must recognize State A's order and the joint decision-making provision.

QUESTION 23

Husband and Wife married and lived together in State X. While married to Husband, Wife had an affair with Fred and gave birth to Fred's child, Child. Both Husband and Fred knew that Fred was Child's biological father.

After Child's birth, Husband and Wife separated. Wife and Child immediately moved in with Fred and stayed with him for three months. During those three months, Fred supported Wife and Child and told friends and neighbors that Child was his son.

At the end of this three-month period, Wife reconciled with Husband. She and Child left Fred's home and resumed living with Husband. Husband held Child out as his son and supported Child. Although Fred no longer supported Child, he communicated with Child approximately twice a year.

When Child was four years old, Fred filed a petition claiming paternity of Child under the law of State X. State X law provides that "a proceeding brought by an individual, other than the child, to adjudicate the parentage of a child having a presumed father must be commenced not later than two years after the birth of the child." The court dismissed Fred's petition, holding that the two-year statute of limitations barred his action.

Shortly after Fred's paternity claim was dismissed, Husband, Wife, and Child moved to another city in State X, and Fred could not locate them.

Two years later, Wife sued Husband for divorce. In her divorce action, she sought custody of Child and child support. Husband objected to Wife's child support claim on the ground that Fred, Child's biological father, should be required to pay support instead of Husband. A State X court awarded Wife custody of Child and ordered Husband to pay child support.

Shortly after the divorce was final, Fred located Wife and Child. Fred filed a visitation petition under a State X statute permitting "any person to petition for visitation at any time" and authorizing a court to grant visitation whenever "visitation serves the best interests of the child." The trial court granted Fred's petition over Wife's objection, holding, as a matter of law, that "it is always in a child's best interests to know his or her biological parents, regardless of the custodial parent's views about the child's needs."

1. **Did the court violate Fred's substantive due process rights under the U.S. Constitution by dismissing his paternity petition? Explain.**

2. **Did the court properly order Husband to pay child support? Explain.**

3. **Did the court violate Wife's substantive due process rights under the U.S. Constitution by granting Fred visitation? Explain.**

ANSWER TO QUESTION 23

1. The court did not violate Fred's due process rights by dismissing his paternity petition. At issue is whether a biological father's rights are violated if he has only two years to establish paternity.

Substantive due process rights are derived from the Due Process Clause of the Fourteenth Amendment of the Constitution. The Clause guarantees that state and local laws will be reasonable and not arbitrary. Where a law limits a fundamental right, strict scrutiny will be applied and the law will be upheld only if it is necessary to promote a compelling or overriding interest. Parents generally have a fundamental right to make decisions concerning the care, custody, and control of their children. This right can extend to an unwed biological father. However, the Supreme Court has held that an unwed father obtains protection under the Due Process Clause only if he demonstrates a commitment to his parenting responsibilities and participates in child rearing. Here, Fred lived with Child for only three months and had only minimal contact with Child (communicating approximately twice a year) after Wife and Child moved back to live with Husband. Fred never paid child support, nor did he offer to pay child support. Fred could have filed an action to establish his paternity at any time, but he chose to wait four years to do so. Based on these facts, it is doubtful that a court would find that Fred had a significant relationship with Child. Therefore, Fred does not have any substantive due process protection here.

Even if Fred did have a substantial relationship with Child, it is unlikely that the State X court violated his rights by dismissing his petition. Under the common law, the child of a married woman is presumed to be the marital child of her husband, and the Supreme Court has held that the state's interest in protecting the marital family is sufficiently strong to override any interest that an extra-marital father might have in establishing paternity, even if the result is that such a father is completely foreclosed from establishing his paternity. Because the Supreme Court has held that extra-marital father can be completely barred from establishing paternity without a due process violation, surely no violation will be found in State X's requirement that such a father bring suit within two years of the child's birth. Therefore, there was no due process violation here.

2. Yes, Husband was properly ordered to pay child support for Child's benefit. At issue is whether the presumption of legitimacy creates a child support obligation for the presumptive father.

Parents of a child generally have a duty to support the child at least to age 18. As discussed above, Husband will be presumed to be Child's father because Child was born during Husband's marriage to Wife. Under State X's law, Husband had two years to deny paternity. Because he did not bring such an action within two years, he is now barred from challenging paternity under the same statute under which Fred is barred from establishing paternity. Therefore, Husband can be required to pay child support.

It should be noted that the result would be the same even if the State X limitations period does not apply to Husband, because he will be estopped from denying paternity. When a nonparent consents to act as a parent and the child's interests would be harmed by termination of the parental relationship, the nonparent will be estopped from halting his parental responsibilities. Here, Husband knew that Fred was Child's biological father, but he did not challenge the presumption of legitimacy. Instead, he "held Child out as his son and supported Child" after Wife and Child returned to the marital home. Thus, he will be estopped from denying paternity and can be ordered to support Child.

3. The court probably violated Wife's due process rights when it granted visitation to Fred. At issue is whether a fit biological parent's wishes regarding visitation may be overridden by the court.

The standard used in State X to determine whether a third party (*i.e.*, a nonparent) may be granted visitation is whether the visitation will be in the best interests of the child. However, the Supreme Court struck down a similar statute in *Troxel v. Granville*, 530 U.S. 57 (2000). In *Troxel*, the Court held that as long as a parent is fit, that parent's determination as to the appropriateness of third-party visitation must be given special weight. A judge may not override a fit parent's decision merely because he believes that a better decision could have been made or that visitation would be in the best interest of the child. No facts in the question suggest that Wife is anything other than a fit parent. However, the State X court judge gave no weight to Wife's objection to Fred having visitation with Child, holding instead that "it is always in a child's best interests to know his or her biological parents, regardless of the custodial parent's views about the child's needs." The holding is in direct opposition to the guidelines set forth under *Troxel*.

QUESTION 24

Herb petitioned for divorce from Ann after a 20-year marriage. One year later, the court entered a decree of divorce based on irreconcilable differences. The court also awarded Ann a share of the marital property and $1,000 per month in spousal maintenance until her death or remarriage.

After Herb's petition was filed but before the court issued a final decree, Herb married Betty. Betty believed that Herb's divorce was final. After the court issued a final decree, Ann married Charles. Herb then stopped paying spousal maintenance to Ann.

After her marriage to Charles, Ann learned that Charles had misrepresented the value of his stock. Charles said that he owned stock worth "millions." In fact, Charles's stock was worth only $300,000. Ann has filed for annulment of her marriage to Charles. In a separate action, she seeks reinstatement of the spousal maintenance she was awarded in her divorce from Herb.

Betty has petitioned for divorce from Herb. Herb has filed a motion to dismiss the divorce petition on the ground that he and Betty were not lawfully married.

1. **If Ann is granted an annulment of her marriage to Charles, can she obtain reinstatement of the spousal maintenance she was awarded in her divorce from Herb? Explain.**

2. **Can Ann obtain an annulment of her marriage to Charles based on Charles's misrepresentation of his assets? Explain.**

3. **Can Herb obtain dismissal of Betty's divorce petition based on the claim that he and Betty were not lawfully married? Explain.**

ANSWER TO QUESTION 24

1.   Ann is unlikely to receive a reinstatement of her spousal maintenance from Herb. At issue is whether a husband's maintenance obligation that terminated upon his former wife's remarriage can be reinstated if the former wife's new marriage is annulled. Spousal maintenance generally terminates upon the remarriage or cohabitation of the recipient spouse. Here, the terms of the divorce decree specifically dictated that Ann would receive maintenance until her remarriage or death. Therefore, the maintenance properly terminated when Ann married Charles. However, if Ann receives an annulment, her marriage to Charles will be deemed to have never existed—it will be a nullity. Although an annulment legally declares that a marriage never existed, the weight of modern authority does not permit the reinstatement of maintenance based on annulment of the marriage that terminated the obligation. While some courts will permit reinstatement when the equities strongly favor the former recipient, most courts will refuse to revive maintenance payments that were terminated by a later-annulled marriage in order to protect the payor spouse's interest in the certainty of the termination of his obligation. In this case, there are no facts that would justify a reinstatement of Ann's maintenance—Ann married Charles voluntarily and does not suffer from any disability or infirmity that would lead a court to find that reinstatement of maintenance was necessary to balance the equities. Therefore, the court will protect Herb's interest in the finality of the termination of maintenance and deny Ann's request to revive the obligation.

2.   Ann will not be able to annul her marriage to Charles based on his overstatement of his wealth prior to their marriage. At issue is whether an annulment may be obtained based on one spouse's misrepresentation of his assets. Annulment may be sought when a marriage is voidable. A marriage may be voidable based upon fraud if there is a misrepresentation as to the essentials of the marriage. Misrepresentations that are considered to go to the essentials of the marriage include misrepresentations as to the ability or willingness to engage in sexual relations or bear children, misrepresentations as to the paternity of an unborn child, misrepresentations as to the existence of a sexually transmitted disease or drug addiction, and misrepresentations as to the party's religious beliefs. Here, Charles has made a misrepresentation as to his financial condition, specifically, the value of his stock. Such a misrepresentation does not involve the essentials of the marriage. Therefore, Ann is unlikely to be able to obtain an annulment of her marriage to Charles. If she wants to end her marriage based on the value of Charles's stock portfolio, Ann will need to seek a divorce instead.

3.   Herb's motion to dismiss Betty's divorce petition will be denied. At issue is whether a marriage is void if it is contracted after one party has filed a divorce petition in a previous marriage

but before the final decree is entered. In every state, if either party to the marriage has another living spouse, the marriage is bigamous and therefore void. A void marriage is a nullity and no subsequent act can ratify the marriage. However, a void marriage may become merely voidable if the impediment is later removed. If the marriage is then ratified by a continuation of the relationship, it becomes valid. Here, Ann and Herb's marriage did not end until the final decree was entered. Herb married Betty while he was still legally married to Ann. Therefore, Herb and Betty's marriage was bigamous and void as such. However, once the final divorce decree was entered between Ann and Herb, the impediment was removed and Betty and Herb's marriage became merely voidable. Because Betty and Herb's relationship continued after Herb's divorce was final, the relationship was ratified and may be deemed a valid marriage. As such, Herb is not likely to succeed in his motion to dismiss.

QUESTION 25

Ten years ago, Matt Smith, a musician, and Wendy Jones, a business executive, began living together in State A. One year later, they invited 50 friends and relatives to a "ceremony of commitment" at which they publicly vowed to "treat each other as an equal owner of all worldly goods acquired during our life together" and to "forsake all others" until "death do us part." Matt and Wendy did not obtain a marriage license. After the ceremony, Matt and Wendy consistently referred to each other as "my companion." They also opened a joint bank account and rented a house as "Wendy Jones and Matt Smith."

Five years ago, Matt and Wendy moved to State B, where Wendy gave birth to Child. Matt and Wendy thereafter shared child-care responsibilities and spent relatively equal amounts of time with Child.

One year ago, Wendy left Matt and married Steve in State B. After the wedding, Wendy and Child moved to Steve's home, and Wendy began to work part time.

Since her marriage to Steve, Wendy has allowed Matt to visit Child infrequently and only at her home. Matt has tried to give Wendy money for Child's support, but Wendy has refused to take it.

Matt has filed a petition in State B seeking to establish his paternity and obtain joint custody of Child. In a separate State B action, Matt seeks a share of Wendy's property acquired during the time they lived together. Wendy and Steve have filed an adoption petition seeking Child's adoption by Steve. Matt opposes this petition. All of these actions have been consolidated for trial.

Pretrial discovery has established that Matt is Child's biological parent, that Wendy has assets worth $300,000, all obtained from income earned while she lived with Matt, and that Matt has assets worth $1,500. Matt and Wendy each currently earn about $30,000 per year.

A common law marriage can be contracted in State A but not in State B.

1.   May the State B court award Matt a share of Wendy's property? Explain.

2.   May the State B court grant Steve's adoption petition over Matt's opposition? Explain.

ANSWER TO QUESTION 25

1.   The court in State B may award Matt a share of Wendy's property. At issue is whether the parties entered into a valid common law marriage or cohabitation agreement.

Clearly, the State B court has jurisdiction to enter a decree involving Matt and Wendy; both have been living in State B for five years, so the court has jurisdiction over both parties. Thus, the real question here is whether the court has a basis for forcing Wendy to share her property with Matt. Generally, a court may not split a couple's property unless they were married or had a valid cohabitation agreement. Also as a general rule, if a marriage between a man and a woman was valid where entered, it will be recognized in other states as well. Thus, even though State B does not recognize common law marriages, if Matt and Wendy entered into a valid marriage in State A, State B will recognize it.

It is doubtful that the State B court will find that Matt and Wendy entered into a valid common law marriage in State A. The basic requirements to establish a common law marriage are capacity to enter into a marriage, an exchange of consent, cohabitation, and a holding out publicly of living together as husband and wife. Here, nothing in the facts indicates that Matt or Wendy lacked capacity to marry. Moreover, their consent may be found in their commitment ceremony in which each promised to share all worldly possessions and forsake all others until parted by death. These vows are very similar to the traditional vows made during a marriage ceremony. The couple also cohabited after their ceremony for a number of years. The only real question is whether they publicly held each other out as husband and wife.

It is doubtful that the State B court would find a sufficient holding out here. In determining whether there was a sufficient holding out, courts look to conduct such as using a common last name, opening a joint bank account, and telling others in the community that they consider themselves married. Here, Matt and Wendy opened a common bank account and rented a house together, but they continued to use their own names in these joint endeavors. Moreover, they did not hold themselves out as husband and wife, but rather as "companions." Such conduct probably would not be sufficient proof of a common law marriage in a court already predisposed not to recognize common law marriages.

Although the court will not likely find that Matt and Wendy were married, it nonetheless would award Matt a share of Wendy's property based on a cohabitation contract. Contracts between unmarried cohabitants will be enforced if sexual relations are not the only consideration for the contract. Proof of such a contract often is a problem, but here Matt and Wendy agreed in front of 50 people that they would "treat each other as equal owner of all worldly possessions acquired during [their] life together." The court would likely give effect to this contract, as consideration can be found in the mutual promise of each party to share equally what was brought into the relationship, and nothing in the in the agreement even hints that sexual relations was part of the consideration. Thus, the court will likely force Wendy to share with Matt up to half of what she acquired while living with him.

2.   The court may not grant Steve's adoption petition over Matt's objection. At issue is an unwed father's parental rights when he has made an effort to be involved in his child's upbringing.

Again, as a preliminary matter, the court would have jurisdiction to hear the adoption case. A state's courts have jurisdiction over an adoption if the state is the child's home state. A state will be found to be a child's home state if the child has lived in the state for at least six months. Here, Child was born in State A and has lived there for about five years. Thus, a State A court would have jurisdiction over the adoption proceeding.

Generally, a child may not be adopted without consent from both of his biological parents. However, whether consent must be obtained from an unwed father depends on how involved the father was with the child. An unwed father who has never attempted to establish a legal or personal relationship with the child has no rights with respect to an adoption. However, an involved unwed father has a right to block an adoption unless the unwed father is found to be an unfit parent. An unwed father has a due process right to continue his relationship with his child when he demonstrates active involvement with the child, exhibited through conduct such as caring for the child, visiting the child, and/or paying to support the child. Here, Matt lived with Wendy and Child for four years and cared for Child during that time. Although Matt's visitations with Child have been sporadic since Wendy left him, that is because Wendy prevented visitation. This would not be held against Matt. Moreover, Matt has offered Wendy money to help support Child. Again, Wendy's refusal to accept the money will not be held against Matt. Thus, Matt will be found to have had a sufficient relationship with Child to prevent Steve from adopting Child over Matt's objection.

QUESTION 26

Twelve years ago, Husband and Wife married in State A. Their marriage appeared to be happy and stable. However, one year ago, without warning, Husband left Wife and moved to State B, 500 miles away. Husband obtained a new job in State B and rented an apartment there. He has told Wife that he never intends to return to State A.

Last week, Wife was personally served in State A with a copy of Husband's State B divorce petition. The petition requests the State B court to grant a divorce on grounds of a six-month separation and irreconcilable differences. The petition also requests the State B court to award Husband the following assets, all of which are titled solely in Husband's name:

(1)   The marital home in State A, which Husband purchased five years before the marriage. During the marriage, Husband made mortgage payments on the home with his employment income.

(2)   Stock, which Husband inherited from his grandmother during the marriage.

(3)   Bonds, which Husband purchased with his employment income during the marriage.

All of these assets appreciated significantly in value during the marriage. Wife has no assets titled in her name alone or held jointly with Husband.

Wife is determined to fight this divorce. She has never visited State B, knows no one there, and does not believe she should have to defend a divorce action there. At the same time, she wishes to save her marriage. She has called Husband several times urging him to return to State A and enter marriage counseling, but he has refused. Wife is convinced that Husband is going through a "mid-life crisis" and would "return to his senses" with proper counseling and support. She believes she can get him that support and counseling if he returns to State A. Finally, if there must be a divorce, Wife believes that she should receive a share of the assets owned by Husband.

1. Does the State B court have jurisdiction to grant Husband a divorce and award Husband property acquired during the marriage? Explain.

2. Can Wife prevent Husband from obtaining a divorce on the grounds that she does not consent to the divorce and that the marriage might yet be saved? Explain.

3. Without regard to any jurisdictional issues, would Wife, in the event of a divorce, be entitled to a share of any of Husband's assets? Explain.

ANSWER TO QUESTION 26

1. The State B court has jurisdiction to grant a divorce so long as Husband has established a domicile in State B, but it may not issue a binding property division or support order without personal jurisdiction over Wife.

The first issue is whether a state may grant a divorce when it lacks jurisdiction over one spouse. To establish jurisdiction over a divorce action, one of the parties must be a bona fide resident of the jurisdiction where the action is brought. States may set a minimum durational residency requirement, such as 90 days or one year, before the action can be filed. The plaintiff's residence alone may be the basis for a state's granting a divorce, regardless of whether there is personal jurisdiction over the defendant. On these facts, Husband is certainly a bona fide resident of State B. Husband moved to State B over one year ago, has rented an apartment in State B, is employed in State B, and has indicated that he never intends to return to State A. Therefore, a State B court may grant Husband a divorce, even it does not have jurisdiction over Wife.

The next issue is whether a court may divide marital property if it does not have jurisdiction over both spouses. Generally, a court cannot determine property rights or rights to support unless it has jurisdiction over both parties. Thus, in an ex parte divorce (*i.e.*, one where only the plaintiff is before the court), the court can grant the divorce, but cannot award spousal support or divide property. There is a limited exception for marital property located within the state; if the state has sufficient minimum contacts with the defendant and the property, it can adjudicate the parties' rights to that marital property. Here, Wife has no contacts with State B—she has never even visited the state, was served in State A, and has not consented to State B jurisdiction by filing an appearance. State B therefore does not have personal jurisdiction over Wife, and may not award Husband property acquired during the marriage. Note that the exception does not apply here, because State B does not have sufficient contacts with Wife and the assets at issue are not located within the state.

2. Even if she does not consent, Wife will not be able to prevent Husband from obtaining a divorce. At issue is whether both spouses' consent is required for a divorce to be granted. Most states now offer "no-fault" divorces that provide for the dissolution of a marriage without regard to marital fault, generally upon a showing that the marriage is irretrievably broken and that the parties have been living separate and apart for a specified period of time. The fact that one spouse thinks the marriage should be saved and does not agree that it has broken down is generally

insufficient to prevent a divorce judgment if the other spouse believes the marriage cannot be saved and is not interested in continuing the marriage. Here, Wife's efforts will be unsuccessful. The parties have been separated for a year, and Husband is determined to obtain a divorce, making Wife's belief that the marriage can be saved legally irrelevant.

3.   Wife may be entitled to share in a portion of Husband's assets upon divorce. At issue is whether property titled in one spouse's name is subject to division at divorce. As a general rule, the courts have the authority to order an equitable distribution of all marital property, no matter how title is held. All assets acquired during marriage are deemed marital property, unless acquired though gift, bequest, devise, or descent. If property is acquired before the marriage, but paid for after marriage with marital funds, most courts will apportion the property between separate and marital interests in proportion to the contribution of separate and marital funds used to pay for the property. Here, the home was acquired by Husband prior to the marriage, but the mortgage was paid during the marriage with his employment income. The income Husband earned during the marriage is marital income. Therefore, the home will be partially marital property and partially Husband's separate property. The stock was inherited from Husband's grandmother and will remain his separate property, as nothing in the facts indicates that the increase in value during the marriage was due to marital funds or labor. The bonds, however, were acquired during the marriage with marital funds and are deemed marital property. Therefore, Wife is entitled to a share of the bonds and the post-marriage increase in the equity of the house. Husband's stock will remain his separate property, not subject to division upon divorce.

QUESTION 27

Husband and Wife married 11 years ago when both were age 19 and college students. Husband planned to go to medical school and Wife planned to become an accountant. They decided that Wife would defer her educational plans in order to provide support while Husband completed his medical studies. Accordingly, Wife dropped out of college, took a job as a file clerk, and did all of the household chores in order to allow Husband more time to study. This arrangement continued while Husband completed his remaining three years of college, four years of medical school, and a three-year medical residency. Wife expended all of her earnings to support Husband and herself. Husband made minimal financial contributions to the marriage.

Throughout the marriage, Husband was verbally abusive to Wife and occasionally hit her. Husband was always contrite after these incidents and attributed his behavior to stress resulting from his studies.

Three months before Husband completed his medical residency, he and Wife had an argument. During the argument, Husband assaulted Wife and broke her arm. Wife left Husband and filed a petition for divorce.

Husband suggested to Wife that they meet with a divorce mediator, Mediator. Wife agreed to this proposal. Husband and Wife both gave Mediator information about their assets and incomes. Husband indicated that his post-residency salary would be $150,000 per year, listed no assets, and listed school debts totaling $50,000. Wife indicated that her salary was $30,000 per year and listed no assets. Wife also indicated that she intended to return to college in the fall and that her income would then decline.

Last month, Husband and Wife met with Mediator. Mediator did not explain anything about the mediation process or divorce law, nor did she inform Husband and Wife that they could obtain independent legal advice about any agreement reached through mediation. Instead, Mediator asked Husband for a settlement proposal. Husband proposed that each spouse keep his or her personal property and that Husband bear responsibility for his educational loans. Mediator responded, "That sounds like a fair settlement. I'll prepare the paperwork unless Wife objects." Within the view of Mediator and Wife, Husband tightened his fist and gave Wife a menacing look. Wife said, "I have no objection."

After signing the agreement prepared by Mediator, Wife learned that Mediator was an attorney who had represented Husband's family for many years and that Husband had talked to Mediator about the settlement shortly before their meeting.

No divorce judgment has yet been entered.

Wife has petitioned the trial court to set aside the settlement agreement she and Husband had signed and to award her spousal maintenance of $25,000 per year for three years.

1.   On what grounds, if any, could the court set aside the settlement agreement? Explain.

2.   If the settlement agreement is set aside, is Wife entitled to spousal maintenance? Explain.

ANSWER TO QUESTION 27

1.   The court has grounds to set aside the settlement agreement due to Husband's behavior and Mediator's misconduct. At issue is under what circumstances a court may set aside a settlement agreement negotiated by the parties.

When a divorce settlement agreement is challenged prior to the final divorce decree, the court generally has the discretion to reject the agreement, accept the agreement, or accept it with modifications. The determination is made on a case-by-case basis, depending upon the facts presented. A spouse's fraud, duress, or coercive behavior provides a basis for setting aside a settlement agreement that is unconscionable. Here, the marriage had a long history of domestic violence. Husband made threatening gestures to Wife during the mediation. Given the past abuse, Wife was likely afraid to object to the agreement. Under these circumstances, Wife may be said to have signed the agreement under duress. Additionally, both spouses are required to make a full and fair disclosure in order for the agreement to be enforceable. Husband failed to disclose that the mediator had represented Husband's family for many years and that he had previously met with the mediator on his own. A mediator is supposed to be a neutral person, not the representative of one of the parties. Wife may argue that her end of the settlement agreement was procured by fraud, an additional ground for setting aside the settlement agreement.

The settlement agreement could also be set aside due to mediator misconduct. A mediator is required to be impartial, to disclose any potential conflicts of interest, to explain the mediation process, to recognize and control a situation (*e.g.*, domestic violence) that would result in unfairness or prejudice to one of the parties, and may not coerce a party to make a decision. Under these facts, Mediator failed in each of these responsibilities. He did not reveal his relationship with Husband's family and prior meeting with Husband, nor did Mediator screen for domestic violence between Husband and Wife. He additionally failed to explain the mediation process, the law, or the parties' right to independent counsel. Mediator's misconduct gives the trial court another independent basis for setting aside the settlement agreement.

2.   Wife is probably entitled to spousal maintenance if the settlement agreement is set aside. Spousal maintenance is awarded to provide for persons whose economic dependency has resulted from the marital relationship. The court has wide discretion in awarding as much spousal support as is necessary for the maintenance of the party who requests it. Factors to be considered by the court in determining the amount of support include: (i) the standard of living during the marriage; (ii) the duration of the marriage; (iii) the age and physical and emotional condition of both parties; (iv) the financial resources of the parties, including the assets and income of each party; (v) the contribution of each party to the marriage, including services rendered in education and career building of the other party; (vi) the time needed to obtain education or training to enable either party to find appropriate employment; and (vii) the ability of the spouse from whom spousal maintenance is sought to meet his own needs while also paying maintenance.

Here, Wife's economic dependency is a result of the marriage. The parties were married for 11 years, a relatively lengthy marriage. Wife made greatly disproportionate economic and non-economic contributions to the marriage: she deferred her education to put Husband through medical school; she earned nearly all the income and contributed it to the marriage; she did all the household chores so that Husband would be able to study. The parties' financial resources are quite disparate as a result. Husband's salary will soon be five times that of Wife, and his economic prospects are extremely good, while Wife is minimally educated and relatively unskilled—as a result, her economic prospects are poor. This combination of facts would support a spousal maintenance award for Wife. Marital fault is generally not considered in determining spousal support, so Husband's history of domestic violence probably would not factor into the court's decision.

Additionally, because a professional license or degree is generally not distributable property, many jurisdictions will compensate supporting spouses for their contribution during the other spouse's training or education by awarding maintenance on a theory of unjust enrichment, quasi-contract, or reimbursement spousal support. Here, Wife could rely on the fact that the parties agreed that Husband's education would come first, and then Wife's education would follow, in order to recover on a reimbursement theory or in quasi-contract.

Given Husband's anticipated $150,000 salary and Wife's inability to work full time while she returns to college, Wife's request for spousal maintenance of $25,000 per year seems justified under the facts.

QUESTION 28

Husband and Wife married 10 years ago. Shortly thereafter, Husband adopted Wife's two children, Amy, age 6, and Bert, age 9. Neither Amy nor Bert has ever had a relationship with their biological father.

One year ago, Husband and Wife were divorced. The divorce decree provided that:

(1) Husband shall pay Wife $1,000 per month in child support for Amy until Amy is 18 years old;

(2) Husband shall pay child support in the form of college tuition up to $20,000 per year for both Amy and Bert.

Three months ago, Husband stopped making support payments for Amy and college tuition payments for Bert. Husband stopped paying for two reasons:

First, Husband was disinclined to continue supporting Amy and Bert, now ages 16 and 19, respectively. Since the divorce, Husband has quarreled frequently with both children. Bert also disobeyed Husband and joined a rock band that plays at a local bar four nights per week. Since joining the band, Bert's college grades slipped from A's to C's, and he was arrested for driving while intoxicated. Bert has refused Husband's requests that he leave the band and devote more time to study.

Second, Husband, who formerly worked 40 to 60 hours per week, is now working only 10 to 20 hours per week so that he can finish writing a novel. Husband has worked on the novel sporadically over the past few years, but has not had time to complete it. Husband's current income is only 25% of what it was when he was employed full time.

Wife, who works full time at the job she has held since her marriage to Husband, has neither reduced nor increased her income since the divorce. Since Husband stopped paying support, she has been borrowing money to meet the family's expenses.

Wife recently filed a petition to obtain a judgment against Husband for the child-support arrears and Bert's tuition. Husband responded with a petition seeking:

1. A dissolution of his adoption of Amy and Bert on the basis of irreconcilable differences;

2. Downward modification of all of his support obligations, on account of his reduced income, retroactive to the date on which Husband stopped making support and tuition payments; and

3. A declaration that Husband need not pay Bert's college tuition so long as Bert continues to perform in a rock band.

The age of majority in the state is 18. The trial court entered judgment in favor of Wife and denied Husband's petition in all respects.

Did the trial court err? Explain.

ANSWER TO QUESTION 28

1. *Adoption of Amy and Bert:* The trial court did not err in denying Husband's petition seeking a "dissolution" of his adoption of Amy and Bert. At issue is whether an adoption can be undone nearly 10 years after it was finalized. An adoption creates a new and permanent legal relationship between a child and the adoptive parents. While all of the parties to the adoption

must consent, consent cannot be withdrawn after a decree of adoption is entered. Here, Husband has been the legal father to Amy and Bert for a decade and is the only father they have ever known. It is irrelevant that Husband was a stepparent prior to the adoption. He will not be permitted to divorce his children simply because he divorced their mother. Furthermore, "irreconcilable differences" is a ground for divorce and has no legal effect in the context of an adoption. The trial court properly denied Husband's petition for dissolution of adoption.

2. *Modification of support:* The trial court did not err in refusing to modify Husband's past or future support obligations. Child support is modifiable based on a substantial change in circumstances affecting the needs of the children or the ability of the parents to pay. However, most states hold that past-due installments of support cannot be retroactively modified—any modification made by the court will apply only as to future payments. Therefore, Husband's request to modify his support obligation retroactively was properly denied.

As to Husband's future support obligations, the court will consider material changes in (i) employment, (ii) growth of the children, (iii) income, (iv) inflation, (v) retirement, and (vi) disabling illness in deciding whether modification is warranted. Under the facts, Husband has experienced a material change in his employment and income, going from full-time employment of 40 - 60 hours per week to part-time employment of only 10 - 20 hours per week, and his income has been reduced by 75% as a result. Clearly, this is a material change. However, Husband voluntarily reduced his hours in order to have more time to write a novel. Generally, an obligor's self-induced reduction in income cannot be used to obtain a downward modification of support unless it is made in good faith. Given that Husband has been working on this novel "sporadically over the past few years" and that the increase in time devoted to writing comes at the same time as his difficulties with Amy and Bert, it is likely that the trial court did not believe Husband's shift in career focus was in good faith. Therefore, the court did not err in denying Husband's petition for downward modification of future support.

3. *College tuition:* The trial court probably erred by denying Husband's request to make payment of future educational expenses for Bert contingent upon Bert leaving the band. At issue is whether educational support may be made contingent upon compliance with reasonable parental requests. Many courts have ordered continuing child support past the age of 18 if the child remains a full-time student. However, all parents—whether married or divorced—may terminate this additional support to employable children who disobey reasonable parental requests. Husband's demand that Bert leave the band and devote himself to his college course work is reasonable, especially in light of the fact that Bert's involvement in the band has resulted in Bert's grades dropping and a DUI arrest. Because Husband's requests are reasonable and in furtherance of Bert's best interests, the trial court erred in rejecting Husband's petition for modification of his college tuition obligation for Bert.

QUESTION 29

Six years ago, Hal and Wendy were married in State A. Both of them had been previously divorced. Hal, age 40, was a successful businessman earning $200,000 per year. Wendy, age 30, was a struggling songwriter earning $20,000 per year.

Two weeks before their wedding, Hal told Wendy that his lawyer ("Lawyer") had advised him not to marry Wendy unless she signed a premarital agreement. Hal gave Wendy a copy of the agreement Lawyer had proposed and suggested that she review it with Lawyer or another attorney of her own choosing. The agreement specified that in the event of divorce:

1. Each spouse waives all claims to property acquired by the other during the first five years of the marriage;

2. The spouses will share joint physical and legal custody of any children born to them during the marriage.

When Hal gave Wendy the proposed agreement, she burst into tears. Wendy was very angry and hurt, but she did not want to call off the wedding at such a late date. Reluctantly, she agreed to discuss the matter with Lawyer.

Lawyer gave Wendy an accurate list of Hal's assets and a copy of Hal's tax returns for the past three years. Lawyer urged her to consult another attorney. After conferring with her family, but not an attorney, Wendy decided to sign the proposed agreement. The day before their wedding, she and Hal signed the agreement in Lawyer's office in State A.

Four years ago, Hal and Wendy had a child ("Child").

Six months ago, Hal and Wendy moved to State B. Hal's business has continued to prosper. He currently earns $300,000 per year. Since the marriage, Hal has used his business income to acquire assets worth about $500,000. Wendy has continued to write songs. Her current income is $30,000 per year.

Three months ago, after Wendy discovered that Hal was having an affair, she took Child and moved back to State A, where she plans to remain. Since leaving Hal, Wendy has written and recorded several songs about her marriage. Wendy's agent believes that these songs "will hit the top of the charts."

State A has adopted the Uniform Premarital Agreement Act. State B has not. The premarital agreement contains no choice of law provision.

1. Which state's law governs the enforceability of the premarital agreement? Explain.

2. Is the waiver of property rights provision in the premarital agreement enforceable? Explain.

3. Is the child-custody provision in the premarital agreement enforceable? Explain.

4. Are the profits to be derived from Wendy's songs written after she left Hal subject to division at divorce? Explain.

ANSWER TO QUESTION 29

1. State A law will govern the enforceability of the premarital agreement. At issue is whether State A or State B has the most significant relationship to the parties and the transaction. In determining the enforceability of a premarital agreement, either the law of the state with the most significant relationship to the parties and the transaction or the law of the state where the agreement was executed will be applied.

The premarital agreement was entered into in Hal's lawyer's office in State A, and State A law will apply if the court decides to follow the law of the state where the agreement was executed. Under the most significant relationship test of the Second Restatement, the court will look at the specific contacts with each jurisdiction and consider several policy-oriented principles, including the justified expectations of the parties and the interests of the jurisdictions involved. The facts state that Hal and Wendy entered into the premarital agreement in State A, got married in State A, had their child in State A, and lived in State A for almost the entire marriage. Wendy and the child still live in State A and intend to remain in State A. Hal, however, resides in State B and State B was the parties' home state at the time of the separation, albeit only for six months. Considering the contacts that the parties have had with each jurisdiction, as well as State A's interest in contracts that are executed within the state and marriages that are entered into within the state, State A law will likely be applied here.

2.   The waiver of property rights provision of the premarital agreement is probably enforceable. At issue is whether the premarital agreement was voluntarily made and whether Hal sufficiently disclosed his assets to Wendy prior to the agreement.

Under the Uniform Premarital Agreement Act ("UPAA"), adopted in State A, a court determining enforcement of a properly executed premarital agreement considers only two things: voluntariness and unconscionability. A premarital agreement is unenforceable if the party against whom enforcement is sought proves (i) that she did not act voluntarily, or (ii) that the agreement was unconscionable when executed and, before execution, the party was not provided fair disclosure of the other party's finances, did not waive such disclosure in writing, and did not have adequate knowledge of the other party's property or financial obligations.

Here, Wendy will be unable to successfully argue that she did not have adequate knowledge or fair disclosure as to Hal's finances. Hal's accountant provided her with copies of Hal's tax returns for the past three years, along with an accurate list of Hal's assets. These documents are sufficient disclosure to avoid unconscionability. Thus, Wendy must argue that she did not act voluntarily when entering into the premarital agreement. Courts will generally consider an agreement voluntary when it is entered into without fraud, duress, or overreaching. Nothing in the facts indicates the presence of fraud or overreaching. Wendy may attempt to argue duress based upon the presentation of the agreement only two weeks prior to the scheduled wedding, but this argument will likely fail. Wendy had sufficient time to consult with counsel even though she chose not to, was able to discuss the agreement with her family, and had previously been married and divorced, making her familiar with the issues at stake.

A court may choose not to enforce provisions of premarital agreements that would result in a spouse being left a pauper or eligible for public assistance. Here, Wendy's independent income of $30,000 would be sufficient to support her without public assistance. Therefore, under the UPAA, the agreement will be enforced.

3.   The child custody provision of the premarital agreement will not be enforced by the court. The traditional rule is that a premarital agreement cannot bind a court in deciding matters relating to minor children, whether in the nature of custody or support. In all decisions relating to custody of a child, the paramount concern is the best interest of the child. The court may decide that joint custody is, in fact, in the best interests of Child, but will not be bound to do so by the premarital agreement.

4.   The profits from Wendy's songs will likely be subject to division in the divorce action. At issue is whether the song profits are marital property or Wendy's separate property. All property

acquired during the marriage, no matter how title is held, is deemed marital property. Most courts hold that marital property continues to accrue until the final divorce decree is entered, rather than ending upon the date of separation. Because no divorce decree has been entered, Wendy's songs are therefore likely marital property. The property waiver contained in the parties' premarital agreement will not change the characterization of the songs as marital property because the five-year period has passed. Wendy's best argument would be that the songs' value is too uncertain for distribution, given that the songs have not yet been released and her agent's opinion is speculative at best.

QUESTION 1

Daniel was driving a Gasco gasoline truck on an interstate freeway at night when Paul, driver of a minivan, struck the rear end of Daniel's truck, causing a collision and explosion. Paul was severely burned, and Daniel suffered a total memory loss from the accident. Based on physical evidence at the scene of the accident, the cause of the accident appeared to be excessive speed on Paul's part. The only witness to the accident was Wendy, who was driving a Volkswagen behind Paul and Daniel. She stopped after the accident and called the police and paramedics.

Alex, a claims investigator for Gasco's liability insurer, obtained a written statement from Wendy two days after the accident. In Wendy's statement she said that Daniel caused the accident by making an unsafe lane change into Paul's lane. Wendy said that Paul was too close to avoid the accident, although she could not estimate how fast Paul was driving. Alex wrote two comments on Wendy's statement: 1) Wendy is a very credible witness; and 2) her statement is very harmful to Daniel's potential defense. Shortly after making her statement, Wendy disappeared and cannot be found. Alex immediately forwarded Wendy's statement to Lawyer, Gasco's in-house attorney.

Paul sued Daniel and Gasco in a federal district court for personal injury damages based on Daniel's negligent driving of the truck. Paul's suit was properly based upon diversity jurisdiction. Defendants filed an answer specifically denying each allegation of wrongful conduct in Paul's complaint. During discovery, Paul demanded production of Wendy's statement. Defendants claimed that the statement was privileged or otherwise protected from discovery. Paul moved for an order compelling production of the statement. Defendants filed a written response opposing production solely on the ground that the statement was not reliable because it was not under oath. The written response was prepared and signed by Lawyer. Lawyer developed the reliability argument without conducting any research or citing any legal authority.

1.   Should the federal district court judge grant the motion compelling production of Wendy's statement? Explain.

2.   What sanctions, if any, should the federal district court judge impose on Lawyer for making this response? Explain.

ANSWER TO QUESTION 1

The federal district court judge should grant the motion compelling production of Wendy's statement.

1.   The statement is relevant and is not protected by the attorney-client privilege because it was given by a witness, rather than by a client. Thus, the issue is whether the statement is protected as trial preparation material. The work product of lawyers and others made in anticipation of litigation is not discoverable except upon a showing of "substantial need" and "undue hardship" in obtaining the materials by other means. [Fed. R. Civ. P. 26(b)(3)] Alex, the claims investigator for the defendants' liability insurer, is a party representative specifically included under Rule 26(b)(3). The facts do not indicate clearly whether the claims investigator took his statement in preparation

for litigation. Paul may argue that Wendy's statement was not taken in anticipation of litigation because it was taken only two days after the accident. In addition, it is probably in the ordinary course of the insurer's business to take a witness's statement while investigating a claim. However, the court could also find that the statement was taken in anticipation of litigation because Alex immediately sent a copy of the statement to Lawyer, who represents the defendants in the litigation. But even if the court finds that the statement is trial preparation material, the statement must be disclosed if Paul shows "substantial need" and "undue hardship."

The work product of lawyers and others in anticipation of litigation is not discoverable except upon a showing of "substantial need" and "undue hardship" in obtaining the materials by other means. Paul can show substantial need because Wendy was the only witness to the accident; Daniel has suffered a total memory loss; and the evidence is important to Paul's case. Paul can also show undue hardship because he cannot take Wendy's statement since she has disappeared. However, the court must secure against disclosures of mental impressions, conclusions, opinions, or legal theories such as Alex's comments that Wendy is a credible witness and that the statement is damaging to the defense. Thus, the court should order the defendants to produce the statement but with Alex's comments excised.

2. By signing a disclosure or discovery response, an attorney certifies that to the best of his knowledge, information, and belief, formed after a reasonable inquiry, the disclosure is: (i) warranted by existing law or a good faith argument for the extension, modification, or reversal of existing law; (ii) not interposed for any improper purpose, such as to harass, cause unnecessary delay, or needlessly increase the cost of litigation; and (iii) not unreasonable or unduly burdensome or expensive. [Fed. R. Civ. P. 26(g)] The court has discretion to impose sanctions for violating this rule, including payment of reasonable expenses incurred because of the violation. Here, Lawyer failed to cite any legal authority or conduct any research to support his argument. Thus, his argument is not warranted by existing law or a good faith argument for the modification of existing law. Lawyer is subject to sanctions because he signed the response to the motion to compel discovery. The court will likely require Lawyer to pay Paul's reasonable expenses incurred in responding to the paper, including attorneys' fees.

QUESTION 2

Foodco, a food processing company, has its place of incorporation and its principal place of business in State A. Foodco relies extensively on an independent distributor, located in State A, to sell its products to restaurants in State A and State B. In addition, the distributor arranges a monthly shipment of Foodco's sausage to a customer in State C. This sale amounts to less than 5% of Foodco's monthly sales.

Although it obtains most of its supplies from wholesalers in State A, Foodco frequently orders spices from Spiceco, located in adjoining State D, by telephoning Spiceco from State A. For several years, Foodco paid its account by check mailed at the end of each month to Spiceco's office in State D.

For the last three months, Foodco has failed to make payments to suppliers. Its balance with Spiceco has grown to $6,000. After making an unsuccessful demand for payment, Spiceco filed suit against Foodco in a State D trial court. Spiceco attached $5,000 worth of Foodco sausage that had been stored in a warehouse in State D by Foodco's distributor,

pending shipment to the customer in State C. Spiceco then served process on Foodco in State A, informing it of the attachment and of the commencement of the action in State D.

State D statutes permit creditors like Spiceco to institute proceedings by attachment. The statutes permit State D courts 1) to adjudicate claims against nonresidents to the extent of any property located in the state and 2) to assert long arm jurisdiction over nonresident corporations that "transact any business" in the state or fail to perform any contractual obligations with substantial ties to the state. State D courts construe these statutes as authorizing jurisdiction to the full extent permitted by the Due Process Clause of the United States Constitution.

Foodco moved to dismiss the State D action for lack of jurisdiction. In addition to reciting the facts, Foodco supported its motion with an uncontradicted affidavit that no employee of Foodco has ever met with Spiceco in State D.

Should the court grant or deny Foodco's motion to dismiss? Explain.

ANSWER TO QUESTION 2

The court should deny Foodco's motion to dismiss the State D action for lack of jurisdiction. A court's exercise of jurisdiction over out-of-state defendants must meet the constitutional requirements of due process. Mere presence of a person's property within a state is insufficient to confer in personam jurisdiction over an out-of-state defendant. Therefore, Spiceco's seizure of Foodco's sausage in State D alone will not confer in personam jurisdiction. Foodco must have had such minimum contacts with State D that the assertion of jurisdiction does not offend "traditional notions of fair play and substantial justice." [International Shoe v. Washington, 326 U.S. 310 (1945)]

State D's long arm statute provides a basis of jurisdiction over Foodco. The statute allows creditors to assert long arm jurisdiction over nonresident corporations that "transact any business" in the state or fail to perform any contractual obligations with substantial ties to the state. The statute will be construed as authorizing jurisdiction to the full extent permitted by the Due Process Clause. Thus, the court must consider whether Foodco's contacts with State D meet the constitutional standard set forth in *International Shoe*.

Constitutional limitations on in personam jurisdiction over an out-of-state defendant involve two components: notice and nexus. The notice component has been satisfied, since Foodco was properly served. In analyzing the nexus component, the court must determine whether an exercise of jurisdiction offends "traditional notions of fair play and substantial justice." This standard requires both minimum contacts and reasonableness. Under the minimum contacts analysis, the court will balance three considerations: the quantity and nature of the defendant's contacts with the forum, their connection with the cause of action, and the interest of the forum in protecting its citizens. The contacts with the forum cannot be accidental; they must reflect some "purposeful availment" by the defendant of the privilege of transacting business in the forum state and invoking the protection of the forum's laws. In addition, the exercise of jurisdiction must also be reasonable, taking into account the litigants' interests and the state's interests.

Here, Foodco's contacts with State D may be sufficient to meet the minimum contacts standard. The cause of action arises out of Foodco's contacts with the forum: Foodco's failure to pay for spices ordered from Spiceco in State D. Foodco had contacts with Spiceco in State D when it ordered spices by telephoning Spiceco in State D and when it paid its account by mailing checks to State D. These contacts were not isolated incidents, but occurred frequently over the course of several years. The court may find that Foodco purposefully availed itself of the benefits and protections of State D law based on these frequent, long-term contacts. Even though Foodco's affidavit stated that no Foodco employee had ever met with Spiceco in State D, this fact alone will not defeat jurisdiction where other contacts exist. The court may also consider that Foodco's sausage was stored in State D in determining whether minimum contacts exist. It is unclear whether the sausage bears any relation to this litigation, unless Spiceco spices were used to make the sausage. Foodco may argue that the sausage was not stored in State D by Foodco, but rather by Foodco's independent distributor, upon whom Foodco relies to sell its products and to arrange shipment of its sausage. On the other hand, Spiceco may argue that the actions of Foodco's distributor benefited Foodco and should be considered Foodco's contact with State D. Thus, the court may give weight to the fact that Foodco's sausage was stored in State D in determining whether Foodco had sufficient minimum contacts with State D.

If the court finds that Foodco had sufficient minimum contacts with State D, the assertion of jurisdiction over Foodco is also reasonable. State D is a more convenient forum for Spiceco since many of the witnesses are likely to be Spiceco employees who are located in State D. State D also has an interest in providing a forum for resident corporations that are seeking to collect unpaid debts from out-of-state debtors. Thus, Foodco's contacts with State D are probably sufficient to meet the constitutional standard of *International Shoe*. The court should deny Foodco's motion to dismiss for lack of jurisdiction.

QUESTION 3

Hughes Bus Lines, Inc. is a Delaware Corporation, with its principal place of business in Symons County, Illinois. Hughes Bus Lines provides bus service to passengers in Illinois and several other states.

Blue Bus No. 9 is one of the many buses that Hughes Bus Lines operates in Illinois. On September 9, 1992, Blue Bus No. 9 is carrying 60 passengers through Symons County, Illinois. Tim Cave is driving the bus.

On September 9, 1992, Blue Bus No. 9 collides with a passenger car. Jack Scanlon is driving this car. As a result of this accident, 50 of the 60 passengers aboard Blue Bus No. 9 suffer serious injuries.

Alfred Alpha is one of the Hughes Bus Lines passengers injured in the September 9, 1992, accident. Alpha suffered a broken leg in this accident.

In November 1992, Alpha files a suit in the Circuit Court of Symons County, Illinois. Alpha's complaint names Hughes Bus Lines as the only defendant. Alpha's case is assigned to Judge John Morton.

The complaint filed by Alpha alleges a single cause of action for negligence, an Illinois state law claim. According to Alpha's complaint: "Hughes Bus Lines provided bus driver Tim Cave with inadequate training as to the safe operation of a passenger bus. As a result of his inadequate training, Cave did not take appropriate action to avoid the passenger car driven by Jack Scanlon." Alpha seeks $200,000 damages.

In March 1993, a jury trial, *Alpha v. Hughes Bus Lines*, comes to a conclusion. The jury returns a verdict in favor of Defendant Hughes Bus Lines. In response to a special interrogatory given by Judge Morton, the jury explicitly finds: "With respect to the September 9, 1992, accident, Hughes Bus Lines was not negligent." As a result of the jury verdict, Plaintiff Alfred Alpha cannot recover any damages from Defendant Hughes Bus Lines. An appellate court affirms the jury verdict in favor of Hughes Bus Lines.

On September 9, 1992, Bill Beta also was a passenger aboard Blue Bus No. 9. As a result of the September 9, 1992, accident, Beta sustained a serious back injury.

In June 1993, Beta files a suit in the Circuit Court of Symons County, Illinois. Beta's complaint names Hughes Bus Lines as the only defendant. Beta's suit is assigned to Judge Karen Tobiason.

Beta's complaint alleges a single cause of action for negligence, an Illinois state law claim. The negligence allegations that appear in Beta's complaint are identical to the negligence allegations that Plaintiff Alfred Alpha had stated. Beta seeks $500,000 damages.

In response to Beta's complaint, Defendant Hughes Bus Lines files a motion for summary judgment. In this motion, Defendant Hughes Bus Lines relies on the doctrine of collateral estoppel. The summary judgment motion notes that Hughes Bus Lines won the earlier suit brought by Alfred Alpha. Because of this earlier result, Hughes Bus Lines argues that Judge Tobiason must enter a judgment concluding that Hughes Bus Lines was not negligent.

1. Should Judge Tobiason grant the motion for summary judgment filed by Hughes Bus Lines? Explain.

2. For the purpose of this part only, assume that Judge Tobiason denies the motion for summary judgment filed by Defendant Hughes Bus Lines. Plaintiff Bill Beta's case now proceeds to trial. At the conclusion of the trial of *Beta v. Hughes Bus Lines* in November 1993, a jury determines that negligence on the part of Hughes Bus Lines caused the September 9, 1992, accident. The jury awards Beta $300,000 in damages.

    Now assume that on September 9, 1992, Charlie Charles also was a passenger aboard Blue Bus No. 9. As a result of the accident in Symons County, Charles suffered a broken arm.

    In February 1994, Charles files a suit in the Circuit Court of Symons County, Illinois. The complaint filed by Charles names Hughes Bus Lines as the only defendant. The suit filed by Charles is assigned to Judge Beth Silverman.

    The complaint filed by Charles alleges a single cause of action for negligence, an Illinois state law claim. The negligence allegations stated by Charles are identical to the allegations stated by Alpha and Beta in their earlier suits. Charles seeks $100,000 damages. Assume that the suit filed by Charles satisfies the applicable statute of limitations.

    After filing his complaint, Plaintiff Charlie Charles files a timely motion for summary judgment. This motion relies on the result in *Beta v. Hughes Bus Lines* and the doctrine of collateral estoppel. According to Charles, under this doctrine the Symons County court must conclude that negligence by Defendant Hughes Bus Lines caused the September 9, 1992, accident.

    Given the results in *Beta v. Hughes Bus Lines*, should Judge Silverman grant the summary judgment motion filed by Plaintiff Charlie Charles? Explain.

ANSWER TO QUESTION 3

1.   Judge Tobiason should not grant the motion for summary judgment filed by Hughes Bus Lines ("Hughes"). At issue is whether Hughes may rely on the doctrine of collateral estoppel to defeat the plaintiff's cause of action.

Collateral estoppel (issue preclusion) provides that a judgment for a plaintiff or defendant is conclusive in a subsequent action on a different cause of action between the party or his privies as to issues actually litigated and essential to the judgment in the first action. Here, Hughes was the defendant in an earlier action brought by Alfred Alpha. In the first action, Alpha claimed that Hughes negligently provided its driver, Tim Cave, with inadequate training. The negligence allegations that appear in the second action by Bill Beta against Hughes are identical to those in the first action. Although the claim was litigated in the first trial and the jury returned a verdict in favor of Hughes, Hughes may not, however, move for summary judgment on the basis of collateral estoppel because Beta was neither a party nor a privy to a party in the first action and therefore cannot be bound by the judgment. If Judge Tobiason were to grant summary judgment on the basis of collateral estoppel, Beta would be denied the opportunity to be heard on the issue.

2.   Judge Silverman should not grant the summary judgment motion filed by the plaintiff, Charlie Charles. At issue is whether collateral estoppel is available to nonparty plaintiffs.

Traditional "mutuality" rules state that because an earlier judgment cannot be used *against* a person who was not a party, that person is similarly barred from *taking advantage* of the judgment. Although the general rule is that collateral estoppel cannot be used by nonparty plaintiffs, courts have begun to allow nonparty plaintiffs to rely on collateral estoppel if it is fair to the defendant to do so. [Parklane Hosiery Co. v. Shore, 439 U.S. 322 (1979)] In jurisdictions where the mutuality principle has been eroded, a nonparty may rely on a prior judgment only when: (i) the issue decided in the first case was *identical* to that in the second; (ii) there was a final judgment on the *merits*; (iii) the party against whom the judgment is to be used had a *fair opportunity to be heard* on the critical issue; and (iv) the posture of the case is such that it would *not be unfair or inequitable* to a party to apply collateral estoppel.

In this case, Judge Silverman is not likely to grant Charles's motion for summary judgment. Although elements (i) through (iii) may be answered affirmatively, element (iv) is questionable due to the fact that there are conflicting decisions based on the same cause of action (*i.e.,* Alpha was denied recovery, while Beta was awarded $300,000), and more actions may be brought by other victims of the same accident. Allowing collateral estoppel in such a situation could result in an unfair application of the law. As a result, Judge Silverman may determine that collateral estoppel is not available to Charles in this case.

QUESTION 4

See Conflict of Laws Question 6 for Federal Civil Procedure issue.

QUESTION 5

For several years, Employee worked for Boss at Custom Computers in Bordertown, State X. Employee was Boss's sole employee. Together they assembled and sold customized computer hardware and software to local businesses in Bordertown and in surrounding

communities, including Eastville, which is located in State Y. Boss is a citizen of State X. Employee, on the other hand, lives in Eastville and is a citizen of State Y.

On January 1, 1994, Boss fired Employee. On February 1, 1994, Employee opened a new business, Employee's Customized Computers, in Eastville, and began soliciting customers from among the businesses that previously had done business with Boss's firm. Employee won business, in part, by telling Boss's former customers that "I did all the work when I worked for Boss" and that "Boss is a drunken bum who cannot be relied upon."

In late 1994, Boss sued Employee in federal district court in Eastville, alleging that Employee had stolen most of Boss's customers and caused Boss damages of more than $100,000. The complaint alleged that Employee had "maliciously interfered with Boss's contractual relationships with former customers by lying about the extent of Employee's role in Boss's business and by lying about Boss's drinking habits."

A summons and complaint in the action were served on Employee in State Y by a process server who went to Employee's home. Not finding Employee there, the process server slid the summons and complaint under the front door. Employee found the summons upon returning home that evening. State Y's local rules for service of process are identical to Rule 4(e) of the Federal Rules of Civil Procedure.

Both State X and State Y recognize the tort of malicious interference with contractual relations. The law of each state provides that "malice" exists only when one person interferes with another person's contractual relationships either (a) with improper motive—that is, with intent to injure the plaintiff's business for a purpose other than competition or (b) by improper means—that is, by means that are civilly actionable or criminally unlawful.

Employee filed a motion to dismiss the complaint for failure to state a claim upon which relief could be granted. Employee attached to the motion to dismiss an affidavit in which Employee swore "that Employee's efforts to take Boss's customers away were motivated not by malice but by an honest desire to compete and win the business for Employee."

The trial judge accepted Employee's motion and affidavit, treated the motion as a motion for summary judgment, and gave Boss the opportunity to file opposing affidavits. Boss filed a memorandum in opposition to Employee's motion but did not attach any documents or affidavits. The trial judge then denied Employee's motion.

Following denial of the first motion, Employee filed a second motion to dismiss the action, this time on the ground of insufficiency of service of process. The trial judge granted the second motion and dismissed the action for insufficiency of service of process.

Did the trial judge rule correctly on Employee's two motions? Explain.

ANSWER TO QUESTION 5

Employee's First Motion: The trial judge properly treated Employee's first motion as a motion for summary judgment. Moreover, the judge was correct in denying the motion because a genuine issue of material fact exists.

When a court that is considering a motion to dismiss a pleading for failure to state a claim is presented with "matters outside the pleading," which the court chooses not to exclude, the motion must be treated as one for summary judgment and disposed of accordingly. [Fed. R. Civ. P. 12(b)]

Employee attached an affidavit to his first motion and the trial judge considered the affidavit; therefore, the judge properly treated the motion as one for summary judgment.

According to Federal Rule of Civil Procedure 56(c), a motion for summary judgment should be granted only if "the pleadings . . . together with the affidavits . . . show that there is no genuine issue as to any material fact and that the moving party is entitled to a judgment as a matter of law." The court may not decide disputed fact issues on a motion for summary judgment; if there is a disputed fact, the case must go to trial.

In this situation, the judge correctly denied Employee's motion for summary judgment on the malicious interference issue. Under the law in this jurisdiction, malice exists only when one person interferes with another person's contractual relations either (i) with improper motive, or (ii) by improper means. Employee's affidavit indicates that Employee's only motive was to obtain customers for his business. Clearly this motive is not improper, and if improper motive were the sole theory on which malice could be established, Employee's affidavit might have been enough to justify summary judgment in his favor, unless Boss could produce opposing affidavits to support a motive other than business competition.

Unfortunately for Employee, however, malice can also be established by showing that an improper means was used. In the complaint, Boss alleges that Employee lied about the extent of his role in Boss's business and about Boss's drinking habits. If proven, such conduct would establish civilly actionable behavior necessary to establish malice. Since Employee did not produce evidence to (i) contradict these allegations, (ii) prove that the statements were true, or (iii) prove that Employee did not in fact make the statements, the allegations constitute material facts as to which a genuine issue exists. Thus, the trial judge correctly denied Employee's motion for summary judgment.

Employee's Second Motion: Although service of process was improper in this case, the trial judge incorrectly granted the motion to dismiss for insufficiency of service because Employee waived this defense by not raising it in his first motion.

State Y's rules for service of process are identical to Rule 4(e) of the Federal Rules of Civil Procedure. Under that Rule, service of summons and complaint upon an individual may be accomplished only by: (i) delivering a copy to the individual personally, (ii) leaving a copy at the person's house or place of abode with some person of suitable age and discretion residing therein, or (iii) delivering a copy to an agent authorized to receive service of process. Here, Boss's process server slid the summons and complaint under Employee's front door. By failing to leave the summons and complaint with "some person of suitable age and discretion," Boss's process server did not conduct a proper service.

However, when a motion is first made under Rule 12, the Rule provides that certain defenses and objections, including improper service, must be consolidated and raised together. If the defenses or objections are not raised in the first motion, although they could have been and were available at the time of the first filing, the defenses or objections are waived. [Fed. R. Civ. P. 12(b)(5), (g)] In this case, Employee's claim of insufficient service of process was available to Employee at the time he filed his Rule 12 motion. Because he failed to raise the defense in his initial motion, Employee could not raise the defense anytime thereafter. [Fed. R. Civ. P. 12(h)(1)] Hence, the trial judge's decision to grant the second motion was improper.

[*Note:* Credit may also be given to applicants who argue that, because the trial judge treated Employee's first motion as a Rule 56 summary judgment motion, the waiver rule would not apply since the initial motion did not arise under Rule 12(b).]

QUESTION 6

Patient, a resident and domiciliary of State A, traveled to Clinic in State B to receive treatment from Doctor. Due to the negligence of both Doctor and Clinic, Patient's treatment was unsuccessful and Patient was left permanently disabled.

Doctor is a resident and domiciliary of State B. Clinic is owned and operated by Hospitals, Inc. ("Hospitals"), a multistate hospital chain which is incorporated in State B and which has its principal place of business in State B. States A and B are adjoining states, and Patient's home in State A is located just a few miles from Clinic and in the same metropolitan area.

Patient decided to sue Doctor and Hospitals. Patient's lawyer advised Patient to sue Doctor and Hospitals in State Z, a state located about 750 miles from States A and B. State Z was the lawyer's preferred forum because State Z juries are widely known for the generosity of the awards they make in medical malpractice actions, and because Hospitals has recently received bad publicity in State Z for alleged incompetence and substandard care at hospitals it owns in State Z.

Patient sued Doctor and Hospitals for $2 million in state court in State Z. Proper service was made and jurisdiction obtained over Hospitals because Hospitals owns and operates several hospitals in State Z. Jurisdiction was obtained over Doctor when Doctor was properly served with process in State Z while on vacation.

Doctor and Hospitals properly removed the action from state court to the federal district court of State Z, which had jurisdiction over the action because the parties are diverse and the amount in controversy exceeds $75,000. Once in federal district court, Doctor and Hospitals moved to dismiss the action for improper venue. The motion was denied.

Doctor and Hospitals then moved for a transfer of venue from the federal district court of State Z to the federal district court of State B. The federal district court of State Z denied the transfer motion as well, stating that "Patient is entitled to her choice of forum."

Upon entry of the final order denying their motion to transfer, Doctor and Hospitals immediately filed a notice of appeal. Patient responded by filing a motion to dismiss the appeal for lack of a final judgment.

1.   Did the federal district court of State Z correctly deny the motion to dismiss for lack of venue? Explain.

2.   Assuming venue was proper in the federal district court of State Z, should the court have granted the motion to transfer to the federal district court of State B? Explain.

3.   Should defendants' appeal of the order denying transfer be dismissed? Explain.

ANSWER TO QUESTION 6

1.   *Venue:* The federal district court of State Z correctly denied the motion to dismiss for lack of venue. At issue is whether defendants who have properly removed an action to federal district court from a state court in that district may have the case dismissed for lack of venue when venue would not have been proper in the federal district court had the action been filed there originally.

Venue determines the judicial district in which an action may be brought. When an action in federal district court is founded solely on diversity jurisdiction, as is the case in this situation, venue is proper only in (i) a judicial district where any defendant resides, if all defendants reside in the same state, (ii) a judicial district in which a substantial part of the events or omissions giving rise to the claim occurred, or a substantial part of property that is the subject of the action is situated, or (iii) a judicial district in which any defendant is subject to personal jurisdiction at the time the action is commenced, if there is no district in which the action may otherwise be brought. [28 U.S.C. §1391(a)] Pursuant to this rule, a federal district court in State Z would ordinarily not have venue over this case because Doctor and Hospitals do not both reside in State Z; the events giving rise to the action did not occur there; and although both defendants were subject to personal jurisdiction in State Z when the action was commenced, subsection (iii) of the statute is not applicable because the action could have been brought in another jurisdiction, namely, State B, where both defendants had established residence and domicile. However, venue is proper in this instance because the case was removed from state court.

Under 28 U.S.C. section 1441(a), a civil action brought in the state court of which a federal district court has original jurisdiction may be removed by the defendants to the district "embracing the place where such action is pending," provided that, where the jurisdiction of the federal court is based solely on diversity, none of the defendants is a citizen of the state in which the state action was brought. Here, the federal district courts would have original jurisdiction over this action because there is diversity of citizenship between the plaintiff and the defendants, and the amount in controversy exceeds $75,000. As a result, the action may be removed from the state court of State Z to the federal district court for State Z, since that is the place where the action is pending.

The federal courts treat the section 1441(a) removal provision as a venue provision that overrides section 1391(a), thus allowing venue to be proper in cases such as this one, where venue would have been improper had the action originally been filed in the federal district court for State Z. [See Polizzi v. Cowles Magazines, 345 U.S. 663 (1953)] Moreover, an argument may be made that by seeking removal, defendants waive any objection to the venue of the court to which the action is removed. On these bases, venue was proper in the federal district court of State Z, and the court correctly denied the motion to dismiss for lack of venue.

2. *Transfer:* This is a proper case for transfer of venue.

Under 28 U.S.C. section 1404(a), a district court may transfer an action to any other district where the action "might have been brought" even though venue has been properly laid in the court before which the motion to transfer is made. The decision is left to the discretion of the trial judge, who must consider "the convenience of parties and witnesses" and "the interest of justice" when ruling on the motion. Based on these considerations, this action probably should have been transferred from the federal district court of State Z to the federal district court of State B.

As a preliminary matter, it is necessary to determine whether this action could have been originally brought in the federal district court of State B. Under 28 U.S.C. section 1391(a), venue would have been proper in that court because both defendants reside there. Furthermore, Patient could have easily obtained personal jurisdiction over the defendants in State B because both defendants are domiciled and do business there.

Having established that the action could have been brought in the federal district court of State B, the judge should then consider the convenience of the parties and witnesses. Because both Doctor and Hospitals reside in State B and Patient lives just a few miles from State B, State B would seem to be more convenient for all of the parties, particularly since State Z is located 750 miles away. Moreover, the action arose in State B; thus, the forum is likely to be more convenient for potential witnesses.

The interests of justice would also seem to favor transfer to State B because evidence is likely to be more readily available in the state where the action arose. The judge might also find that a suit against Hospitals could be prejudiced by the adverse publicity Hospitals has been receiving in that state for alleged incompetence and substandard care at its State Z facilities.

The State Z court denied the transfer motion, stating that "Patient is entitled to her choice of forum." While a plaintiff's choice of forum deserves respect, this consideration should not be a controlling factor where, as here, the chosen forum has no real connection to the case and considerations of convenience and the interests of justice favor transfer.

Another factor that might justify the State Z district court's refusal to transfer the action is the fact that State Z's choice of law rules will apply to this action even after transfer. The State Z court could claim that because its choice of law rules will apply, the case should remain in a court that has familiarity with State Z law. This argument is not a strong one, however, because due to the fact that State Z has little connection to the case, it is likely that under State Z's choice of law rules, the applicable substantive law that will be used to decide this case will be that of State B, given State B's interest in the litigation. Accordingly, a transfer to the State B court would seem more logical since its medical malpractice law is likely to be applied.

This being the case, it would appear that the convenience of the parties and witnesses and the interests of justice favor transfer; hence, the district court of State Z should have granted the motion to transfer the action to the federal district court of State B.

3.   *Dismissal:* The defendants' appeal of the order denying transfer should be dismissed.

Under the final judgment rule, an appeal from a federal district court decision can generally be taken only after the court has reached a final decision on the case. A final decision is one that disposes of the whole case by rendering final judgment not only as to all the parties, but also as to all causes of action involved. An order denying a motion for transfer of venue is not a final judgment; it is interlocutory and not immediately appealable under 28 U.S.C. section 1291. Thus, an appeal from such an order should be dismissed.

The defendants may attempt to have the order reviewed by a higher court under the collateral order doctrine, which allows immediate appeal of otherwise non-final orders when the order finally decides a matter collateral to the rights underlying the action; the matter is too important to be denied review; and a denial of immediate review may preclude any review whatsoever. However, decisions on transfer are not likely to create such adverse consequences that they are too important to be denied review, particularly since an appellate court may review trial court rulings on transfer after the entry of final judgment in a case, thus eliminating the need for immediate review.

The defendants may also attempt to have the transfer ruling reviewed by a means other than appeal, *i.e.*, by seeking the extraordinary writs of mandamus or prohibition from courts of appeals; however, the likelihood of obtaining such writs is slim in this case since the challenge is based on the allegation that the judge did not properly weigh the factors relevant to the transfer.

The defendants' appeal should be dismissed, but under the circumstances of this case, Doctor and Hospitals may at least attempt to have the order reviewed by a higher court.

QUESTION 7

Artist filed suit in federal district court, properly based on diversity of citizenship, against Gallery for damages in excess of $75,000. Artist alleged that Gallery had breached a contract with Artist to purchase an original painting that Artist was to create specially for Gallery for $85,000. In its answer, Gallery denied the allegations, specifically asserting that Artist failed to deliver the painting when due. Gallery also made a $100,000 counterclaim against Artist for defamation. Artist filed a timely reply denying the counterclaim.

After the discovery deadline had passed, Gallery filed two motions: one for summary judgment against Artist on his claim for breach of contract, and the other for partial summary judgment to establish Artist's liability on Gallery's defamation counterclaim.

Gallery's motion for summary judgment on Artist's claim for breach of contract was supported by an affidavit authenticating a copy of the written contract between Artist and Gallery. Paragraph 4 of the contract provides that Artist shall deliver the painting to Gallery on or before December 31, 1995, and further provides that timely delivery is "of the essence." Paragraph 5 provides that Gallery will pay Artist $85,000 upon delivery of the painting. Paragraph 10 provides that no amendment or alteration of the contract shall be valid unless it is in writing and signed by the parties.

Gallery's motion for summary judgment on Artist's claim for breach of contract was also supported by documents, affidavits, and depositions of witnesses who were competent to testify to the following facts: (1) Artist called Gallery's curator on December 29, 1995, asking for a one-month extension of time to deliver the painting, but Curator denied the request, explaining that Gallery needed the painting by December 31, 1995, to prepare it and the gallery for a major exhibition opening on February 3, 1996; (2) Artist did not deliver the painting on or before December 31, 1995; and (3) Gallery sent and Artist received a letter dated January 29, 1996, canceling the contract because of Artist's failure to make timely delivery of the painting.

In opposition to Gallery's motion for summary judgment on the claim for breach of contract, Artist filed his own affidavit stating that: (1) on December 29, 1995, he called Gallery's curator and asked for a one-month extension of the deadline to deliver the painting, and that Curator said, "Yes, all right;" (2) the painting was 99% finished when he received the January 29, 1996, letter notifying him that Gallery was canceling the contract; (3) Gallery refused to accept the painting when Artist tried to deliver it on January 31, 1996; and (4) the real reason for cancellation was that Gallery had been losing money for several months before it canceled Artist's contract.

Gallery's motion for partial summary judgment on its counterclaim for defamation was supported by five affidavits. Curator's affidavit stated that on February 3, 1996, in the presence of a large number of artists and art patrons, Artist accused Gallery of "stealing" Artist's creative ideas and that after the incident several popular painters told Curator they would never again sell their works to or through Gallery. Four other persons submitted affidavits stating that they personally heard Artist's February 3 accusation that Gallery had "stolen" some of his creative ideas.

In opposition to Gallery's motion for partial summary judgment on its defamation counterclaim, Artist filed his own affidavit stating that he had never said that Gallery had "stolen" any of his creative ideas.

Under the applicable substantive law, a party to a contract may cancel the contract if the other party fails to make timely performance of a material provision; an oral contract, an oral modification, or an oral waiver of a provision of a written contract is not enforceable, and Artist cannot assert an estoppel under these circumstances; and a false accusation made in the hearing of others that someone has "stolen" another's creative ideas renders one liable for the tort of defamation, if proved by clear and convincing evidence, even if special damages have not been alleged and proved.

1.   Should the federal district court grant Gallery's motion for summary judgment on Artist's claim for breach of contract? Explain.

2.   Should the federal district court grant Gallery's motion for partial summary judgment of liability on its counterclaim for defamation? Explain.

ANSWER TO QUESTION 7

1.   The federal district court should grant Gallery's motion for summary judgment on Artist's breach of contract claim.

At issue is whether the Federal Rule of Civil Procedure 56 requirements for obtaining summary judgment have been satisfied. Pursuant to Rule 56(c), summary judgment will be granted only when, after reviewing the pleadings, affidavits, and discovery materials, the court determines that there is no genuine issue of material fact and the moving party is entitled to judgment as a matter of law. The court may not decide disputed issues of fact when ruling on a summary judgment motion.

A defending party may move for summary judgment at any time, provided that he does not delay trial. He may support his motion with affidavits, depositions, pleadings, admissions, and answers to interrogatories. Affidavits must be made on personal knowledge, show that the affiant is competent to testify, and set forth facts that would be admissible in trial.

When a motion for summary judgment is properly supported, the adverse party may not merely rest upon allegations or denials in the pleadings. Rather, he must file a response, supported by affidavits or otherwise, setting forth specific facts which show the existence of issues of material fact that defeat the motion for summary judgment. If supporting affidavits are unavailable to him, he may file an affidavit regarding the reasons why they are unavailable, and the court may deny the motion, order a continuance until affidavits or depositions can be obtained, or make such other order as may be just. If the adverse party does not respond properly, the summary judgment motion, if appropriate, will be granted.

In this problem, Gallery supported its motion for summary judgment in accordance with Rule 56. It attached an affidavit sufficient to prove that a contract was made, imposing on Artist the duty to deliver a painting to Gallery by December 31, 1995, and providing that time was of the essence. The contract also provides that any amendments or alterations to the contract must be made in writing and signed by the parties. Gallery further supported its motion with testimony of competent witnesses setting forth (i) that Gallery orally rejected Artist's request to extend delivery time, (ii) that Artist did not deliver the painting by December 31, and (iii) that after Artist failed to meet the December 31 deadline, Gallery sent Artist a letter purporting to cancel the contract because of Artist's failure to deliver by December 31.

Artist responded to Gallery's motion, supporting it with his own affidavit. He did not contend that other affidavits were unavailable to him, and even if he had, the court would likely find that because the discovery deadline had passed, Artist should have been able to obtain any necessary affidavits.

Artist failed to show the existence of a genuine issue of material fact. Artist did not present any evidence to dispute the existence of the contract or any provision therein, or to dispute that he failed to deliver the painting by December 31. His testimony that prior to December 31, Gallery orally agreed to an extension of time may conflict with Gallery's testimony, but the conflict is immaterial, because (i) the alleged alteration was oral while the written contract expressly provides that the contract can be altered only with a signed writing, and (ii) the law will not enforce an oral waiver of a provision in a written contract. Artist's testimony regarding his ability to deliver the painting after December 31 is also immaterial. The contract provided that time was of the essence, and Artist does not dispute that. Finally, Artist's testimony regarding Gallery's motives is unsubstantiated hearsay, violating the Rule 56 mandate that affidavits set forth only such facts as would be admissible at trial.

Reviewing the record before it, the court should find that there is no genuine issue of material fact on Artist's breach of contract claim, and that Gallery is entitled to judgment as a matter of law. Accordingly, the court should grant Gallery's motion for summary judgment on Artist's breach of contract claim.

2.   The federal district court should deny Gallery's motion for partial summary judgment on its defamation counterclaim.

As above, at issue is whether the Federal Rule of Civil Procedure 56 requirements for obtaining summary judgment have been satisfied. The requirements are set forth in 1., above. Rule 56 provides that summary judgment may be partial as well as complete. For example, summary judgment may be rendered solely on the issue of liability, leaving the issue of damages for trial.

Gallery supported its motion for partial summary judgment with affidavits, pursuant to Rule 56. Gallery's Curator testified that on February 3, 1996, in the presence of many of Gallery's patrons, Artist accused Gallery of stealing Artist's ideas, and that afterward several popular painters told Curator that they would never again use Gallery's services. Four other affiants testified that they heard Artist make his accusation. Artist opposed the motion with his own affidavit, stating that he had never made the accusation.

The primary issue in Gallery's defamation counterclaim is whether Artist made a defamatory accusation in the hearing of others. While Gallery has supported its claim that Artist did make such an accusation in the hearing of others, Artist has put the issue in dispute with his testimony to the contrary. The disputed issue is clearly material to the cause of action. As explained in (a), above, the court cannot decide a factual dispute when ruling on a motion for summary judgment.

Because Artist has shown there to be a genuine issue of material fact, the court should deny Gallery's motion for summary judgment.

QUESTION 8

Ten years ago, a valuable painting by an old master was stolen from Museum, a nonprofit organization incorporated and located in State X. At the time of the theft, the painting was

worth approximately $800,000. Today it is worth several million dollars. Police investigated the theft, but no suspects were identified. Museum made diligent efforts to locate the painting, but it was never recovered.

Two days ago, on Wednesday, Museum Director learned from a friend in the art business that the stolen painting had surfaced in the hands of Collector, a resident and citizen of State Y. Museum Director's friend told him that Collector plans to sell the painting to an art dealer from Germany; that the sale is scheduled to take place tomorrow, on Saturday, at Collector's home in State Y; and that the German dealer has airplane tickets back to Germany shortly after the scheduled sale.

Museum's lawyer prepared a civil action against Collector to recover possession of the painting. This morning (Friday), the verified complaint in that civil action was filed in federal district court in State Y, properly invoking the diversity jurisdiction of the court. Museum simultaneously filed a motion asking the federal district court to restrain Collector's sale of the painting.

Both the verified complaint and the motion allege (among other things) that Museum owns the painting; that it was stolen; that Collector now has possession of it; that the painting is a priceless example of Renaissance artwork; that it was the centerpiece of Museum's collection before its theft; that Museum believes on the basis of reliable information that Collector plans to sell the painting to a foreign purchaser; and that Museum will suffer irreparable injury if the painting is sold and taken out of the country. The motion is also supported by an affidavit, based upon Museum Director's personal knowledge, detailing the difficulty Museum would have in recovering the painting if it left the country.

A separate affidavit by Museum's attorney states that several efforts have been made to locate Collector at his home and office in order to serve process and a copy of the motion, but that those efforts have failed, and that the location of Collector is unknown. Collector is, however, expected to be at his home to consummate the sale of the painting on Saturday morning, and Museum plans to have both the summons and the requested restraining order served on Collector at that time. Museum has filed with its motion a properly secured bond in an amount adequate to reimburse Collector for costs and damages that might result if Collector is wrongfully restrained.

The State Y statute of limitations for a civil action to recover possession of personal property has run. State X has a 15-year statute of limitations for art theft cases, included as part of a law that created a cause of action specifically for recovery of stolen art objects. This statute of limitations has not run.

1.   May the federal district court issue an order restraining the sale of the painting before Collector has been served with process or given notice of the motion to restrain the sale? Explain.

2.   If the court issues a restraining order and it is properly served on Collector (together with copies of the summons and complaint), will the order remain in effect until there can be a trial on the merits of the civil action, or must Museum take further steps to continue the restraint on Collector pending such trial? Explain.

3.   Will the federal district court apply State Y's statute of limitations, thus barring the cause of action created by the law of State X? Explain.

ANSWER TO QUESTION 8

(a)   The federal district court may issue an order restraining the sale of the painting before Collector has been served with process or given notice of the motion to restrain the sale.

Federal Rule of Civil Procedure 65(b) provides that a temporary restraining order can be granted without notice to the other party if it appears from the facts shown by affidavit or verified complaint that immediate and irreparable harm will result before the adverse party can be heard in opposition. The applicant's attorney must also certify to the court in writing the efforts to give notice and the reasons why notice should not be required.

Here, Museum's verified complaint has shown that immediate and irreparable injury will result if the restraining order is not granted: If the restraining order is not granted, the stolen painting, which is unique, will be sold to a collector and almost immediately taken to a foreign country from which retrieval will be difficult. Moreover, Museum's attorney has certified his efforts to notify Collector and has a valid reason for not requiring notice (Collector could not be located). Thus, the district court may issue the temporary restraining order.

(b)   If the court issues the temporary restraining order, it will not remain in effect until the trial on the merits; temporary restraining orders expire at the time fixed by the court, which may not exceed 10 days. To restrain Collector beyond the 10-day period, Museum should move for a preliminary injunction. A preliminary injunction is an order by the court issued to maintain the status quo between the parties until a full trial on the merits may be held. It would thus prohibit Collector from selling the painting. Issuance of a preliminary injunction requires notice to the adverse party. The party moving for the injunction must show that if the injunction is not granted, irreparable injury will result before the trial on the merits is held. The moving party must also show a likelihood of prevailing on the merits.

(c)   It depends—the federal district court may apply State X's statute of limitations because the State X statute pertaining to recovery of stolen art objects conditions a substantive right, but the conclusion may differ if State Y adheres to the modern trend of abandoning the substance/ procedure dichotomy for statutes of limitation.

A federal district court sitting in diversity jurisdiction must apply the conflict of law rules of the state in which it sits. This problem does not specify which choice of law approach the forum, State Y, applies. Statutes of limitations are *usually* treated as procedural, except where a borrowing statute is involved or where the statute of limitations conditions a substantive right (rather than merely barring a remedy). As the facts do not indicate that there is an applicable borrowing statute, the forum court would apply the State Y statute of limitations, which would bar Museum's cause of action.

State X *does have* a statute which creates a special cause of action for the recovery of stolen artwork. This statute also contains its own statute of limitations. If State Y would, under its choice of law principles, choose to apply the State X statute, the State Y court would apply the whole statute, including the ordinarily procedural statute of limitations because it conditions a substantive right. However, the facts do not indicate the choice of law approach used by State Y, so one could, at best, conclude that State Y *may apply* State X's law.

Some states would not engage in the aforementioned traditional analysis. If State Y follows the modern trend, the federal district court would reject the substance/procedure dichotomy as applied to statutes of limitations and treat them like any other substantive choice of law issue. As mentioned above, the facts do not indicate which choice of law approach State Y generally applies. The two major modern trend approaches are the "most significant relationship" approach and the "governmental interest" approach. If the forum uses the "most significant relationship" approach as its general choice of law rule, it will consider the connecting facts and policy-oriented principles to determine which state has the most significant relationship to the case and apply that state's statute of limitations. On these facts, this would be an extraordinarily close call. If the forum uses the "governmental interest" approach, it will apply its own law as long as it has a legitimate interest in the outcome of the litigation. On these facts, given that the art collector in possession of the painting at issue is a State Y domiciliary, State Y clearly has an interest and would apply its own statute.

QUESTION 9

State C has recently enacted an "Unfair Trade Practices Act" ("UTPA"), the key provision of which reads:

> No person shall engage in an unfair method of competition or an unfair
> act or practice in the conduct of any trade or business.

The Act further provides a private right of action for "any individual who suffers an ascertainable monetary loss" as a result of conduct that violates the UTPA.

Acme is an auto liability insurance corporation incorporated under the laws of State A, with its principal place of business in State B. Acme engages in the insurance business in most states in the United States, including State C. Concerned about the size of jury verdicts in personal injury cases tried in State C courts, Acme ran full-page ads in all major newspapers in State C criticizing as grossly excessive the verdicts being returned by State C jurors. In the ads, Acme urged those who were to be jurors in the future to take into account in their deliberations the impact their verdicts would have on their own liability insurance premiums.

Parker is the plaintiff in a major personal injury case soon to be tried in a State C court. Parker, who is not insured by Acme, considers Acme's ad campaign to be a form of "unfair act or practice" in violation of the UTPA. Consequently, Parker has filed an action for $500,000 in damages against Acme in the United States District Court for State C, invoking diversity jurisdiction. At the time this suit was filed, Parker was a citizen of State C. However, one month after the suit was filed, and one week before Acme was served with the summons and complaint, Parker moved his permanent residence to State B, where he now resides.

Acme has simultaneously filed two motions. The first is a motion to dismiss Parker's suit for lack of jurisdiction over the subject matter on the grounds that: (1) Parker, a citizen of State C on the date suit was filed, was not eligible to file a diversity case in a federal court located in the state where Parker was then domiciled; and (2) even if there were diversity jurisdiction at the time the suit was filed, it has been divested by Parker's change of domicile to State B.

Acme's second motion asks the federal district court to stay further proceedings in the case on the ground that it has raised the following defenses: (1) the legislative history of the

UTPA reveals that the private right of action it confers is available only to competitors or customers of the one allegedly violating the Act; (2) Acme's ad campaign is not an "unfair act or practice" within the meaning of the UTPA; and (3) if the UTPA is interpreted to prohibit Acme's ad campaign, the Act violates the free speech provisions of the United States Constitution. Acme argues that the federal district court should postpone deciding these issues because a State C trial court has recently dismissed an action brought under the UTPA because the plaintiff in that action was neither a customer nor a competitor of the defendant in that case. An appeal from that ruling has been accepted by the State C Supreme Court.

1. **How should the federal district court rule on the motion to dismiss for lack of subject matter jurisdiction? Explain.**

2. **How should the federal district court rule on the motion to stay the case? Explain.**

ANSWER TO QUESTION 9

1.   Acme's motion to dismiss Parker's suit for lack of subject matter jurisdiction should be denied on both grounds.

A federal court has diversity jurisdiction over a case if no plaintiff is a citizen of a state in which any defendant is a citizen when the suit is instituted, and the amount in controversy claimed in good faith exceeds $75,000. At the time that the complaint here was filed, Parker was a citizen of the state where he was domiciled (State C), and Acme, a corporation, was a citizen of the state in which it was incorporated (State A), and the state where it had its principal place of business (State B). Furthermore, the amount in controversy is $500,000. Thus there is complete diversity between the parties and the amount in controversy exceeds $75,000 and so diversity jurisdiction may be established in this case.

Acme's motion to dismiss on the ground that Parker was not eligible to file a diversity case in State C because he was domiciled in State C should be denied. No rule prohibits a plaintiff from filing a diversity action in the state in which he is domiciled. Diversity jurisdiction is not affected merely because the plaintiff files suit in the state where he resides. (Note that in its motion Acme is likely confusing subject matter jurisdiction with *removal*, where a *defendant* cannot remove a diversity case to federal court if the case was filed in a state where any defendant resides.)

Acme's second ground for dismissal, that Parker's change of domicile divested the court of diversity jurisdiction, also is unavailing. Diversity jurisdiction was not defeated when Parker moved to State B, where Acme has its principal place of business. Diversity must exist only at the time the action is commenced; it does not have to exist when the cause of action arose, when process is served, or after the suit is filed. If Parker were domiciled in State B when the action was commenced, diversity jurisdiction would not exist, but Parker's moving to State B after filing suit does not destroy diversity jurisdiction. Diversity jurisdiction may be denied if the plaintiff manufactured diversity by claiming a domicile where he did not intend to remain after filing suit. In this case, however, Parker had another suit pending in State C, and there is no suggestion in the facts that Parker was not genuinely domiciled in State C when the complaint was filed. Thus diversity was proper when Parker filed suit, and his subsequent move does not destroy federal diversity jurisdiction.

2.   The court should grant Acme's motion to stay further proceedings. At issue is whether the federal court sitting in diversity should proceed in a case where the state law is unclear and may soon be resolved so as to defeat the entire case or solve certain constitutional issues.

Under the doctrine of abstention, federal courts refrain from deciding a case until a decision has been made by the state's court regarding the clarity or constitutionality of a state law when: (i) the state law is unclear and may be construed erroneously by the federal court; (ii) the law involves predominantly local state factors and the federal court's decision may create unnecessary friction with the state; or (iii) the statute may be construed by the state court in a way that makes the statute constitutional. Other factors may be considered by the federal court in determining whether to refrain from proceeding on a case of this nature and wait for the state's decision.

Under the *Erie* doctrine, a federal court in a diversity case must apply the substantive law of the state in which it is sitting. Here, the federal court will apply State C's substantive law, and the case requires an interpretation of UTPA, which was enacted by State C.

Acme's defenses raise two issues: (i) whether the UTPA is clear in its scope and application, and (ii) whether the UTPA is constitutional. In this case the federal court should abstain from proceeding until the State C Supreme Court issues its ruling. The State C Supreme Court may rule that only the alleged violator's competitors or customers may sue under the act, in which case Parker would lack standing and the case would be dismissed. Also, the State C Supreme Court may interpret the UTPA in a manner that resolves Acme's liability, or that renders the constitutional issue moot. Federal courts generally are reluctant to decide constitutional issues unnecessarily. Thus the federal court should retain jurisdiction, but should stay proceedings until the State C Supreme Court issues its ruling.

QUESTION 10

Passenger was riding as a passenger on a motorcycle operated by Cyclist in State A. She sustained a severe head injury when a westbound car driven by Driver collided with Cyclist's northbound motorcycle at an intersection controlled by stop signs for both roads. The accident left Passenger with permanent amnesia concerning the accident and the events leading to the collision.

Passenger, a citizen of State B, sued Driver, a citizen of State A, in federal district court in State A for $1 million in damages for personal injuries. The federal court properly has diversity jurisdiction.

Passenger's complaint alleged that Driver failed to stop at the stop sign and that Driver's negligent driving was the proximate cause of her injuries. Driver's answer denied that he failed to stop and that there was any negligence on his part. In response to Driver's interrogatories, Passenger stated that her claim of negligence was based on Driver's failure to bring his automobile to a stop before proceeding through the intersection, despite the presence of a plainly visible stop sign regulating westbound traffic. She also stated, on information and belief, that Cyclist's motorcycle had reached the intersection first and was proceeding through it only after coming to a complete stop.

Before either side could take his deposition, Cyclist died of causes not connected with the accident. The only other eyewitness to the collision was Witness, who was traveling in a

westbound truck immediately behind Driver's auto. When Witness's deposition was taken, he testified that he saw Driver come to a complete stop at the intersection, but that Cyclist did not stop. He also stated that the stop sign for westbound traffic was partly obscured by tall weeds, which made it difficult to see until a motorist was quite near the intersection. At her deposition, Passenger testified that, because of the accident-induced amnesia, she had no personal recollection of the events surrounding the collision.

After the close of discovery, Driver moved for summary judgment. Driver supported this motion with: (1) Passenger's answer to the interrogatories; (2) the deposition of Witness; (3) Driver's own affidavit to the effect that the westbound stop sign was difficult to see because of the growth of tall weeds in front of it, but that he had come to a complete stop before entering the intersection, whereas Cyclist did not; and (4) Passenger's deposition testimony regarding her amnesia and lack of personal recollection of the events surrounding the collision.

Passenger opposed the motion for summary judgment. Her opposition papers cited the conflicting facts raised by the allegation in her complaint that Driver failed to stop and Driver's denial of that allegation in his answer. In support of her opposition, Passenger offered (1) an affidavit of the police officer who responded to the accident, stating that the westbound stop sign was not hidden by weeds, but, on the contrary, was plainly visible; and (2) Passenger's own affidavit stating, on information and belief, that Cyclist must have arrived at the intersection first, come to a complete stop, and only then proceeded into the intersection, and that Driver must have entered the intersection without stopping or even slowing down.

Should the trial court grant or deny Driver's motion for summary judgment? Explain.

ANSWER TO QUESTION 10

Defendant's motion for summary judgment should be granted. At issue is whether a genuine issue of material fact is before the court.

A motion for summary judgment should be granted if, based on the pleadings, discovery, and affidavits, there is no genuine issue of material fact and the movant is entitled to judgment as a matter of law. [Fed. R. Civ. P. 56] The motion may be accompanied by affidavits, which must be made on personal knowledge and should state facts with particularity. If a motion for summary judgment is supported by affidavits, the adverse party may not rely on mere allegations, but rather must set forth, in affidavits or otherwise, specific facts showing there is a genuine issue for trial.

In this case, Driver asserted that the westbound stop sign was partially obscured, but that he came to a complete stop at the intersection whereas Cyclist did not stop before entering the intersection. These facts were set forth in the deposition of Witness and in Driver's affidavit. The only specific fact set forth by Passenger in opposition to the motion was that the westbound stop sign was plainly visible. The other allegations made by Passenger were not based on personal knowledge, but only on information and belief.

The allegation in the complaint is that Driver failed to stop before entering the intersection. Driver presented admissible evidence by two witnesses that he did stop at the westbound stop sign. Passenger did not present any admissible evidence that Driver failed to stop. While the issue of whether the stop sign was obscured is in controversy, it is not an issue of material fact, and resolving whether the sign was obscured does not conclusively establish that Driver did or did not stop. Thus there is no genuine issue of material fact before the court, and Driver is entitled to judgment as a matter of law.

QUESTION 11

Husband and Wife, residents of State Y, are owners in joint tenancy of a large tract of land in State Z, which they purchased as an investment several years ago. They recently made an oral agreement to sell the land for $1 million to Developer, a shopping center developer who lives in State Z. The price seemed low to Husband, but he agreed to the sale because Wife told him she was anxious to raise some cash so they could buy a vacation home.

All negotiations concerning the transaction were held at Husband and Wife's home in State Y. Final agreement was reached over dinner after a day of discussions. No written memorandum was made of the oral agreement, but Developer immediately made a $150,000 down payment on the agreed purchase price.

Shortly after the oral agreement was reached, Wife separated from Husband, but she remained domiciled in State Y. Husband later learned from friends that Wife had secretly intended to leave him as soon as the land was sold, that she had privately approached Developer about selling the land before Developer ever contacted Husband and Wife formally, and that Wife had received a separate $250,000 "finder's fee" from Developer for persuading Husband to agree to the sale of the land.

Husband has filed a diversity action against Developer in the federal district court of State Z. The complaint recites the preceding facts and seeks a declaration that the oral agreement for the sale of the land is unenforceable under the State Z Statute of Frauds.

Under State Z's Statute of Frauds, oral agreements for the sale of land are never enforceable. Under State Y law, however, such agreements are enforceable when the purchaser has made a down payment.

In lieu of an answer to the complaint, Developer has filed a Rule 12(b) motion. The motion seeks relief from the complaint on two grounds. First, Developer asks for dismissal of the complaint because of Husband's failure to join Wife in the action. Alternatively, Developer seeks dismissal on the ground that the complaint fails to state a claim on which relief can be granted because the oral contract is enforceable under the law of State Y, where the agreement was made.

1. **What ruling should the court make with respect to the motion to dismiss for failure to join Wife as a party in the action? Explain.**

2. **If the case were not dismissed because of Husband's failure to join Wife, how should the court rule on the motion to dismiss the complaint for failure to state a claim? Explain.**

ANSWER TO QUESTION 11

1.   Developer's motion to dismiss for failure to join Wife as a party should be granted. At issue is whether a complaint should be dismissed when a person necessary for just adjudication is not joined, and joinder would destroy diversity jurisdiction.

Joinder is compulsory when, if a person is not joined, (i) complete relief cannot be given to existing parties in her absence, (ii) disposition of the case in her absence would impair her ability to protect her interest in the controversy, or (iii) her absence would expose existing parties to a substantial risk of double or inconsistent obligations. [Fed. R. Civ. P. 19]

In this case, Wife is necessary for a just adjudication of this action. She is an owner of the land which is the subject of the oral sales agreement, she accepted the down payment with Husband, and she received a separate finder's fee in connection with the agreement to sell. As a party to the contract, a disposition as to the enforceability of the contract without her presence would impair her ability to protect her interests in the contract. Also, Developer could be exposed to further liability if Wife sued later on the same contract. Thus, the joinder of Wife is compulsory.

However, because the joinder of Wife would destroy diversity jurisdiction, the court must determine whether to proceed without her or dismiss the action. The court considers whether: (i) the judgment in her absence would prejudice her or the existing parties; (ii) the prejudice can be reduced by shaping the judgment; (iii) a judgment in the party's absence would be adequate; and (iv) the plaintiff will be deprived of an adequate remedy if the action is dismissed. Courts prefer to dismiss the action if the plaintiff can file his action in an alternative state forum.

Given the circumstances of this case as discussed above, a disposition of the case without Wife would prejudice her interests substantially. Also, Husband can file a state action against Wife and Developer in State Y, as Wife is a resident of State Y, and Developer is probably subject to long arm jurisdiction because the negotiations occurred in State Y. Also, Husband can likely file his action in State Z, as Developer is a resident of State Z, and Wife is likely subject to long arm jurisdiction as the owner of the State Z property that is the subject of the contract dispute, and given the evidence that she initiated a business relationship with Developer in State Z.

Thus, because proceeding without Wife would prejudice her interests, and because Husband can file his action in a state forum, the court should grant the motion to dismiss for failure to join a necessary party.

2.   The court should deny the motion to dismiss for failure to state a claim. At issue is whether the substantive law of State Y or of State Z applies to this action.

Under the *Erie* doctrine, a federal court exercising diversity jurisdiction applies the substantive law of the state in which it is sitting, including that state's conflict of law rules. [Erie Railroad v. Tompkins, 304 U.S. 64 (1938)] Thus, the federal court will apply State Z's conflict of law rules to decide this issue.

The facts do not indicate what approach State Z takes when a conflict of law arises, but under any of the major approaches, State Z would apply its own law, which holds that oral agreements for the sale of land are never enforceable. Therefore, the court should not dismiss the complaint for failure to state a claim.

First Restatement Approach: If State Z follows the vested rights approach of the First Restatement, the first step in determining which state's substantive law applies would be to characterize the area of law at question. In this case the issue is whether an oral agreement for the sale of land is enforceable. Thus, this could be classified as either a contract or a real property issue, but under either classification the result is the same. Under the First Restatement, issues of contract formalities involving real property are governed by the law of the situs, State Z. Likewise, questions involving real property are also governed by the law of the situs. So if State Z follows the First Restatement, it would apply its own law and find the oral contract unenforceable.

Second Restatement Approach: A similar result would occur if the courts of State Z follow the most significant relationship approach of the Second Restatement. Under the Second Restatement, the court must determine which state has the most significant relationship to the issue at hand. Here, it could be argued that State Y has a relationship to the issue because the contract was negotiated there and this is an issue of contract formation. However, the Second Restatement assumes that the state of the situs has the most significant interest in issues of land contracts and will look to that law. Thus, under the Second Restatement Approach, State Z, as the state of the situs, would apply its own substantive law.

Governmental Interest Approach: Under this approach State Z would apply its own law unless requested to consider another state's law by one of the parties. It would then examine its law and that of the other state to see whether both states have an interest in having their own laws applied (*i.e.*, "a true conflict") or whether only one state has an interest in having its law applied (*i.e.,* a "false conflict"). If there is a true conflict, State Z would then reconsider its own policies and, if it still determined that it had a legitimate interest in having its own law applied, it would do so. On the other hand, if the court found a false conflict, it would apply the law of the state with an interest in the issue. In this case, there is true conflict. State Z is interested in the case because the land in question is located in State Z and one of the parties to the contract is a resident of State Z. State Y is also interested because this case involves a contract formed in State Y by two State Y residents. Nevertheless, as State Z has a legitimate interest in having its own law applied, under this approach State Z will apply its own law.

QUESTION 12

Laptop, Inc., a State X corporation, manufactures laptop computers at its principal place of business in State Y. Paul, a resident of State Z, purchased one of Laptop's computers while attending college in State Y. During summer break, Paul took his computer back home with him to State Z, where he has his permanent residence. Shortly after Paul returned home, the computer caught fire while Paul was using it to access Laptop's website. Paul was severely burned in the fire.

The fire was caused by a defective memory chip installed by Laptop during manufacture in State Y. The memory chip was manufactured by Chip, Inc., a company incorporated overseas in Country A.

Laptop sells 50% of its computers in State Y, 25% in State X, and 25% in State Z. It regularly advertises in the State Z market through computer magazines with national circulations. Laptop also maintains a website in State Y where customers can contact it to make purchases and obtain technical help when problems are encountered in the use of its products. The website is accessible to anyone with Internet access anywhere in the world.

Chip sends to Laptop in State Y all of the memory chips it exports to the United States. Laptop installs them in all the computers it manufactures. Chip has sold to Laptop $5

million worth of memory chips per year for the last five years. Chip's income from memory chips sold to Laptop and installed in computers sold in State Z is less than 2% of its total annual income. Although Chip has never advertised in States X, Y, or Z and does not design its products specifically for those markets, Chip knew that its computer chips would be installed in computers sold in States X, Y, and Z.

Paul filed a lawsuit in federal district court in State Z against Laptop and Chip for personal injury damages of $250,000 basing subject matter jurisdiction on diversity of citizenship. Paul alleged both negligence and strict product liability claims against both defendants. Laptop was served with process in State Y, and Chip was served in Country A. The State Z long arm statute authorizes personal jurisdiction over nonresident defendants "on any basis not inconsistent with the United States Constitution."

Both defendants move to dismiss Paul's claims for lack of personal jurisdiction. Alternatively, they move to dismiss and/or transfer venue to the United States District Court in State Y, arguing that venue in the district court in State Z is improper.

1.   Should the court grant Laptop's motion to dismiss Paul's claim for lack of personal jurisdiction? Explain.

2.   Should the court grant Chip's motion to dismiss Paul's claim for lack of personal jurisdiction? Explain.

3.   Should the court grant both defendants' motions to dismiss and/or transfer venue to the district court in State Y? Explain.

ANSWER TO QUESTION 12

1.   The court should deny Laptop's motion to dismiss for lack of personal jurisdiction. At issue is whether the court has personal jurisdiction over Laptop.

Although the case is before a federal district court, the court must determine personal jurisdiction as if it were a State Z court (the state where it sits). When analyzing personal jurisdiction over a nonresident, the court must ensure that its exercise of personal jurisdiction is consistent with the State Z long arm statute and the Due Process Clause of the United States Constitution.

In this case, the State Z long arm statute is an unlimited long arm statute; i.e., it gives its courts power over any person or property over which the state can constitutionally exercise jurisdiction. Thus, State Z's exercise of personal jurisdiction is valid if it is constitutional.

The Due Process Clause requires that: (i) there be minimum contacts between the defendant and the forum state (a nexus) so that the exercise of jurisdiction is fair and reasonable, and (ii) the defendant receive fair and adequate notice of the action.

Analyzing minimum contacts involves a two-part analysis: (i) whether minimum contacts are present, and (ii) whether the exercise of jurisdiction is reasonable. To determine whether minimum contacts exist, the court balances: (i) the quantity and nature of defendant's contacts, (ii) the connection between the contacts and the cause of action, and (iii) the interest of the forum in protecting its citizens. The court must find that through its acts the defendant purposefully availed itself of the benefits and protection of the state's laws. Minimum contacts are found to exist if the defendant engaged in systematic and continuous activity in the state, or if it knew or reasonably should have anticipated that its activities could give rise to the cause of action in the forum state, and that it could be haled into court in that forum.

The court determines the reasonableness of exercising jurisdiction by balancing the interests of the state and the parties involved in the action, *e.g.,* the burden on the defendant in litigating in that forum, the interest of the forum, and, in the case of an international defendant, international interests in subjecting an alien to the United States jurisdiction.

Notice is considered fair and adequate if the defendant was reasonably notified of the pending lawsuit and given an opportunity to appear and be heard.

In this case, the court has personal jurisdiction over Laptop. Minimum contacts exist because Laptop engages in systematic and continuous activity in State Z by regularly advertising in State Z, selling 25% of its computers in State Z, and providing information and technical help via its website which is accessible to State Z residents. The exercise of jurisdiction is reasonable because the burden on Laptop of defending in State Z is minimal, and State Z has an interest in protecting its citizens from dangerous products. Furthermore, notice of the pending lawsuit is adequate because Laptop was served in State Y, where it has its principal place of business, and given an opportunity to appear and be heard. Thus, Laptop's motion should be denied.

2.   The court should grant Chip's motion to dismiss for lack of personal jurisdiction. Using the tests laid out in 1., above, minimum contacts are not present. It is arguable that Chip reasonably should have anticipated that sales of its product in State Z could give rise to a cause of action in State Z, and that it would be haled into a State Z court. However, Chip's income from State Z sales is less than 2% of its annual income, and each year for five years Chip has sent $5 million worth of chips to State Y, not State Z. The defective chip was purchased in State Y and transported to State Z by Paul, not through the stream of commerce. In addition, Chip did nothing to target the State Z market.

Also, the exercise of jurisdiction over Chip would be unreasonable. Although State Z has a strong interest in protecting its citizens from defective products placed into its stream of commerce, the burden on Chip in defending in a foreign jurisdiction would be significant. Thus, the court will probably find its assertion of jurisdiction over Chip unreasonable. Thus, Chip's motion should be granted.

3.   The court should grant the motion to transfer venue to State Y if the court determines that State Z lacks jurisdiction over Chip. If State Z has jurisdiction over Chip, the motion should be denied. At issue is where proper venue lies.

A court is an improper venue if it lacks personal or subject matter jurisdiction in the action. As discussed in 2., above, State Z most likely lacks personal jurisdiction over Chip. Thus, State Z would be an improper venue. However, where the original venue was improper, a court may transfer the case to a proper venue rather than dismiss the action. Thus, if the court determines that State Z lacks personal jurisdiction, the court will transfer venue to a forum where the action might have been brought. The court will have to determine whether State Y would have been a proper venue originally.

Venue is proper, in diversity cases, (i) where any defendant resides, if all defendants reside in the same state, or (ii) where a substantial part of the events giving rise to the claim occurred, or, if no state satisfies (i) or (ii), (iii) where any defendant may be found. For venue purposes, a corporation is deemed to reside in any judicial district where it is subject to personal jurisdiction at the time the action commenced. An alien corporation may be sued in any judicial district.

In this case, part (i) of the venue test is met. Laptop is subject to State Y jurisdiction because it is a citizen of State Y (its principal place of business is in State Y). Thus, Laptop resides in State Y. As an alien corporation, Chip may be sued in any district; therefore, State Y is a proper venue as to Chip. Also, State Y could assert personal jurisdiction over Chip because Chip ships its parts directly to State Y and does $5 million in business there. Furthermore, the computer was manufactured and purchased in State Y, establishing more contacts between the parties and State Y. Thus, State Y is a proper venue under part (i) of the test. (Part (ii) of the test could also be applied because a substantial part of the events giving rise to the claim (*e.g.,* sale of the chips, manufacture of the computer, and sale of the computer) occurred in State Y.) Therefore, State Y is a proper venue where the action could have been brought originally, and if State Z lacks jurisdiction over Chip, the case should be transferred to State Y.

If State Z is found to have personal jurisdiction over Chip, the action should not be transferred because State Z is the more convenient forum. Paul is a resident of State Z, and courts tend to defer to plaintiff's choice of forum if the arguments for transfer are not very strong. Paul was injured in State Z, and if Paul's injuries are very severe, he may be unable to travel at all, which would be a strong argument for keeping venue in State Z. On the other hand, Laptop has its principal place of business in State Y, receives the chips in State Y, and manufactures the computers in State Y; thus, much of the evidence is located in State Y. However, as Laptop does business in State Z, its burden in defending in State Z appears to be minimal and it is likely that the court will find State Z is the more convenient forum.

QUESTION 13

A few years ago, the legislature of State A passed the following statute:

> **The owners of lots fronting on public sidewalk areas between the property line of the lot and the street line shall repair and maintain those areas at their own expense; failure to do so will result in an assessment against the property for the city's cost in making those repairs.**

In the few cases that have arisen under this statute, the trial judges of State A have taken diametrically opposed positions as to its impact on tort cases arising from dangerous conditions in sidewalk areas. Some State A courts have concluded that the statute changes the common law by shifting from the city to the abutting landowner all liability in tort for any injury to a pedestrian caused by a dangerous condition anywhere in the sidewalk area. Other State A trial judges have interpreted the statute merely to obligate abutting landowners either to repair any dangerous condition themselves or to reimburse the city for the cost of doing so, but not to impose on them tort liability for personal injuries. The appellate courts of other states with similar sidewalk-repair statutes also are divided as to its effect. The Supreme Court of State A has yet to rule on a case involving the scope of the statute.

Defendant has long owned and occupied a bungalow on Main Street in the State A city of Suburbia. Main Street is a paved residential street with curbs running the full length of each side. Between Defendant's property line and the street is a "sidewalk area" consisting of a sidewalk, a 10-foot-wide grassy area (called a "parking strip"), and the curbing for the street. This entire area is a "public sidewalk area" within the meaning of the statute quoted above. Suburbia holds title to the street, curbs, parking strip, and sidewalks on Main Street.

Late one winter evening, Plaintiff, at all times a resident and citizen of State B, traveled by taxi to attend a gathering at the home of Defendant's next-door neighbor, Todd. Because two autos were already parked in front of Todd's residence, the taxi driver let Plaintiff out at the curb in front of Defendant's house. After taking a half-dozen steps in the direction of Todd's house, Plaintiff stepped in a leaf-covered six-inch hole in the parking strip area, which caused her to fall and fracture her hip.

Plaintiff sued Defendant for $250,000 in a federal court in State A. The complaint alleged that the hole was located in a part of the parking strip that abutted Defendant's property.

At the week-long jury trial of the case, the testimony was in sharp conflict as to the location of the hole. Some witnesses asserted that it was in front of Defendant's property; others insisted that it was actually in front of Todd's property. Except for this conflict in the testimony, Defendant did not contest Plaintiff's proof of the elements of her case. At the conclusion of all the evidence, Defendant moved for judgment as a matter of law. In support of this motion, Defendant argued that, even if the hole was in an area abutting his lot, the sidewalk-repair statute did not impose upon owners any tort liability for injuries to others from dangerous conditions in the publicly owned parking strip in front of their lots.

The federal district court has taken Defendant's motion under consideration. The court believes that the sounder interpretation of such a "sidewalk-repair" statute would be that it does impose tort liability on abutting owners. However, it also has concluded, from a study of decisions by the State A Supreme Court construing other statutes, that when the issue of the scope of the sidewalk-repair statute eventually reaches that court, it will probably decide that it does not impose tort liability on abutting owners.

1.   Is Defendant entitled to judgment as a matter of law? Explain.

2.   Assuming Defendant is entitled to judgment as a matter of law, should the judge defer ruling for Defendant until after the jury renders its verdict? Explain.

ANSWER TO QUESTION 13

1.   Yes, Defendant is entitled to judgment as a matter of law. At issue is whether the federal court must apply the law that a state supreme court would most likely apply when there is no state precedent.

The *Erie* doctrine requires a federal court sitting in diversity to apply the substantive law of the state in which it is sitting. If the state's highest court has not decided the issue that is before the federal court, the federal court must attempt to determine what decision the highest court of the state would reach if confronted with the issue. Under the *Erie* doctrine, the federal court must apply the likely state interpretation, even if it would hold otherwise.

Judgment as a matter of law is appropriate when a party has been fully heard and there is no legally sufficient evidentiary basis for a reasonable jury to find for that party.

In this case, the federal court has concluded that the State A Supreme Court would probably decide that the statute does not impose tort liability on abutting owners. Thus, even if the hole were abutting Defendant's property, he would not be liable in tort for Plaintiff's injuries under the likely State A interpretation, as the jury could find no set of facts that would entitle Plaintiff to recover from Defendant. Thus, as a matter of law, Defendant is not liable and his motion should be granted.

2.   Although the judge may rule before the jury renders its verdict, the more efficient course of action would be to defer ruling until after the jury's verdict. If the jury determines the location of the hole in favor of Defendant, the issue is moot. If the jury determines the location of the hole in favor of Plaintiff, the defense may renew its motion for judgment as a matter of law, and the judge can then grant the motion.

This procedure is more efficient because after the verdict, if the trial court's ruling on the motion is overturned on appeal, the appellate court may enter judgment in favor of Plaintiff based on the verdict. However, if the motion is ruled upon before the verdict, and is overturned by the appellate court, the appellate court would have to remand the case for a new trial, and the effort and expense of the first trial would be wasted.

QUESTION 14

Adam is a citizen of State A and practices law in State A. He represented a citizen of State A in a criminal prosecution involving drugs and in a related civil forfeiture proceeding, both of which were pending in federal district court in State A. With his client's consent, Adam telephoned Barbara, a citizen of State B practicing law in State B, and reached an agreement that Barbara would become co-counsel in the civil forfeiture case. The client had agreed to pay Adam a contingent fee equal to 50% of the value of any property prevented from being forfeited. Barbara and Adam agreed that Adam would keep the first one-third of any fee resulting from the representation in the civil forfeiture action, and that they would share in the remaining two-thirds in proportion to their respective time spent on the forfeiture matter.

During the next two months, Barbara and Adam talked by telephone on two occasions and exchanged two letters in connection with the civil forfeiture matter. Adam's work on the case was performed entirely in State A, and Barbara's work was performed entirely in State B.

At the end of the two-month period, the government entered into an agreement accepting a guilty plea in the drug action. It also settled the forfeiture claim, agreeing to allow Adam's client to retain property valued at $480,000.

Adam refused to pay Barbara any portion of the $240,000 received as Adam's contingent fee. Barbara subsequently brought a breach of contract action against Adam in federal

district court in State B, claiming $80,000 as her share of the contingent fee. Adam filed a motion to dismiss the action based on lack of jurisdiction over the subject matter or the person. Alternatively, Adam requested a transfer of venue to the federal district court of State A, where he resides and has his place of business. Adam's supporting affidavit stated that the settlement was in no way related to Barbara's efforts, and that Barbara's time spent on the forfeiture matter was less than one-third of the time spent by Adam.

A statute of State B provides:

> **A court may exercise personal jurisdiction over a person, who acts directly or by an agent, as to a cause of action arising from the person's transacting any business in this state.**

How should the court rule on each issue raised by Adam's motion to dismiss and request for transfer of venue? Explain.

ANSWER TO QUESTION 14

The motion to dismiss for lack of subject matter jurisdiction should be denied, the motion to dismiss for lack of personal jurisdiction should probably be denied, and the court will probably deny the motion to transfer venue.

First, the motion to dismiss for lack of subject matter jurisdiction should be denied, as the court has diversity jurisdiction over this case. Diversity jurisdiction is present where the defendant does not reside in the same state as the plaintiff, and the amount in controversy exceeds $75,000. Here, Adam is a citizen of State A, and Barbara is a citizen of State B. Also, Barbara is claiming Adam owes her $80,000. Thus, the elements of diversity jurisdiction are satisfied, and the motion to dismiss on this ground should be denied.

Second, the motion to dismiss for lack of personal jurisdiction should be denied if State B does not require physical presence at the time of the transaction. In a diversity action, a federal court must analyze personal jurisdiction as if it were a court of the state in which it is located.

For a state court to exercise personal jurisdiction over a defendant, there must be a statute granting the court jurisdiction under the circumstances and the grant must be constitutional. Here, the federal court of State B will look to the law of State B in determining whether it has personal jurisdiction over Adam. State B's long arm statute provides that a court has personal jurisdiction over a person who acts directly or by an agent to transact any business in State B, as long as the cause of action arises from that transaction. The statute does not state whether the defendant or his agent must have been physically present in State B. Some courts require that the defendant be physically present in the state at the time of the transaction, but generally courts have taken a broad view, and would find that business conducted by telephone into the state is sufficient to establish a transaction of business and confer personal jurisdiction.

Once jurisdiction is found, the court must determine that the law granting jurisdiction is constitutional. Personal jurisdiction is constitutional if the defendant has engaged in such minimum contacts with the state that it would not offend traditional notions of fair play and substantial justice. The court considers whether the defendant has purposefully availed himself of that state's jurisdiction, and whether the defendant could reasonably anticipate being haled into the state's courts.

In this case, although Adam was never present in State B, Adam telephoned Barbara in State B and entered into the contract over the phone. The court will probably find that asserting jurisdiction over Adam is constitutional. Adam contacted Barbara in State B and entered into a contract with her. He then communicated with her about the case while she was in State B. Thus, Adam could reasonably expect being haled into court in State B in an action based on this contract, and has purposefully availed himself of State B's jurisdiction.

Finally, the court has discretion whether to transfer venue. Venue is proper where any defendant resides, if all defendants reside in the same state, or where a substantial part of the events giving rise to the claim occurred. If it was proper to bring the case in the original court, *i.e.,* subject matter jurisdiction, personal jurisdiction, and venue were proper, the court may transfer venue to another district where the action might have been brought for the convenience of parties and witnesses.

In this case, venue is proper and personal jurisdiction is present in State A because Adam resides in State A. Thus, State A is a proper venue. Venue is also proper in State B, as Barbara was in State B when she entered the agreement and exchanged a total of four phone calls and letters with Adam, and a court is likely to find that this amounts to a substantial part of the events giving rise to the claim. Thus, venue is proper in State B, and the court will transfer venue to State A only if it finds State A is more convenient for the parties and witnesses. However, if there is no clear advantage to transferring venue to State A, the court is likely to honor the plaintiff's choice of forum and deny the motion to transfer venue.

QUESTION 15

Claimant properly invoked the diversity jurisdiction of the federal district court to bring suit to recover damages for the death of Claimant's spouse, Wife. Claimant alleged that Wife died as a result of exposure to asbestos at BrakeCo, an employer that regularly used asbestos in its brakelining operation. The complaint sought damages from all major asbestos manufacturers, including Fiberco, and demanded a jury trial. Controlling law in all relevant jurisdictions would preclude recovery from Fiberco absent specific proof by the plaintiff of exposure to Fiberco asbestos products.

At the final pretrial conference, Fiberco argued that Claimant had failed to produce any evidence through discovery that would tend to establish that Wife had ever been exposed to Fiberco's product. Although the district court refused to grant summary judgment on this issue of exposure, the judge's final pretrial order did schedule the exposure issue as the first issue for trial to the jury (rather than permitting Claimant to put on the case in the order he would prefer). In compliance with the pretrial order, Claimant opened the trial with testimony from a former BrakeCo manager who testified that he often saw Fiberco asbestos packages in the storeroom. The manager admitted on cross-examination, however, that the first time he ever saw Fiberco products in the storeroom was after Wife had ceased working at BrakeCo, even though he was in the storeroom at least once a week throughout the period that Wife worked at BrakeCo.

At the conclusion of this testimony, Claimant's counsel indicated that Claimant had no other evidence to offer on the issue. Fiberco thereupon moved for judgment as a matter of law. The court granted the motion and dismissed the action as to Fiberco.

1.   **Did the district court have the power to require Claimant to present evidence on the exposure issue before proceeding with any other portion of Claimant's case? Explain.**

2.   **Did the court err procedurally in granting the motion for judgment as a matter of law before the close of evidence? Explain.**

3.   **Did the court err substantively in granting the motion for judgment as a matter of law? Explain.**

ANSWER TO QUESTION 15

1.   Yes, the court did have the power to require Claimant to present evidence on the exposure issue first.

A final pretrial conference is held for the purpose of formulating a plan for the trial, including a program for admission of evidence. After the pretrial conference, the court issues an order that controls the subsequent course of events in the case, including issues needing resolution and the order in which they are presented to the jury. This order supersedes the pleadings.

In this case, controlling law required specific proof that Wife had been exposed to Fiberco asbestos products. Thus, the court acted properly and reasonably in requiring proof of exposure before allowing the rest of the case to continue, since without proof of exposure Claimant could not recover.

2.   No, the court did not err procedurally in granting the motion for judgment as a matter of law before the close of evidence.

A party may move for judgment as a matter of law at any time before submission of the case to the jury. The motion may be granted only after the nonmoving party has been fully heard regarding issues and claims, and the court concludes that there is no legally sufficient evidentiary basis for a reasonable jury to conclude in favor of the nonmoving party.

In this case, Claimant's counsel indicated that he had no other evidence to offer on the issue of exposure. Thus, the court did not err procedurally in granting the motion on the issue of exposure.

3.   No, the court did not err substantively in granting the motion for judgment as a matter of law.

A motion for judgment as a matter of law may be granted when the evidence, viewed in the light most favorable to the party against whom the motion is granted, is such that reasonable persons could come to only one conclusion.

In this case, Claimant's only witness on the issue of exposure was unable to establish that Wife was exposed to Fiberco asbestos products. Since Claimant could not recover without specific proof of exposure, the court reasonably concluded that no reasonable jury could find in favor of Claimant. Thus, the motion was properly granted.

QUESTION 16

Victim, a resident of State A, suffered personal injuries in a fall that occurred when she was exiting a tour bus operated by Bus, Inc. ("Bus"), a company incorporated under the laws of State B with its principal place of business in State B. At the time of the injury, Victim and other tour guests were sightseeing in State A.

Victim filed a complaint against Bus in federal district court in State B. The complaint alleged negligence and requested damages in the amount of $100,000 for Victim's medical expenses, lost wages, and pain and suffering. In its answer, Bus denied that it was negligent.

The federal district court in State B requires the initial disclosure provided for by Federal Rule of Civil Procedure 26(a)(1).

After the pleadings closed and the deadline for initial disclosure of documents had passed, the parties engaged in formal discovery for several months. At no time during discovery did either party request or produce the tour ticket or any copy of it.

The federal district judge called a pretrial conference, ordering both counsel and litigants to appear "to discuss further scheduling and the possibility of settlement." No corporate representative of Bus attended the conference. When the judge raised the question of settlement and asked why no representative of Bus had appeared as required by the judge's order, counsel for Bus stated that Bus was unwilling to settle or even discuss settlement and argued that the court lacked authority to require Bus's participation. At that point, the judge held counsel and Bus in contempt for their refusal to participate in settlement discussions.

The final pretrial order, issued after the conference, identified the issues for trial as whether Bus had negligently maintained and operated the tour bus, whether such negligence caused Victim's injuries, and whether Victim's injuries were compensable in damages.

At trial, after the presentation of Victim's case in chief, Bus introduced the stub of the ticket used by Victim, which contained a "Waiver of Liability" clause. When Victim's counsel objected, the court sustained the objection, ruling that the waiver was beyond the scope of the final pretrial order and beyond the scope of the pleadings. Bus's counsel then moved to amend the answer and the pretrial order to include the question of waiver. The judge denied the motion. The jury ultimately returned a general verdict for Victim and awarded Victim full damages. The court entered judgment on the verdict.

Bus has appealed the contempt order on the ground that the trial judge lacked the power to order Bus to participate in settlement discussions. Bus has also appealed the judgment on the grounds that the trial judge erred in not allowing Bus to (i) amend the answer, (ii) amend the pretrial order, and (iii) introduce the waiver into evidence despite not having produced it earlier.

1. Should the contempt order be set aside on the ground urged by Bus? Explain.

2. Should the judgment be reversed on the grounds urged by Bus? Explain.

ANSWER TO QUESTION 16

1.   The contempt order should not be set aside. Under the Federal Rules of Civil Procedure, a court has the power to compel parties to attend a pretrial conference. A party or counsel may be sanctioned for failure to attend a conference or obey an order entered pursuant to a conference. Thus, Bus, Inc. was required to attend the pretrial conference, and it could be held in contempt for failure to attend.

2.   No, the judgment should not be reversed on any of the grounds asserted by Bus, Inc.

(i)   *Amending the Answer:* Generally, a pleading may be amended once before a responsive pleading is served, or if no responsive pleading is required, within 20 days after service of the pleading. Thereafter, a pleading may be amended only by the written consent of the adverse party or by leave of the court upon motion. Leave of the court is "freely given when justice so requires." In this case, the 20-day deadline had passed. Therefore, Bus, Inc. has no right to amend its answer as it is now at the court's discretion. Whether granting leave to amend would be "required by justice" is a question of fact. However, allowing the defendant to amend its answer at this point would defeat the rules of disclosure discussed below. Therefore, the court was correct in refusing to allow Bus, Inc. to amend its answer.

(ii)   *Amending the Pretrial Order:* A pretrial order is issued after the pretrial conference and controls the subsequent course of events in the case, including issues needing resolution and the order in which they are presented to the jury. This order supersedes the pleadings and may be modified "only to prevent manifest injustice." As with amending the answer, the question of whether denying leave to amend the pretrial order would result in manifest injustice is a question of fact. And as with amending the answer, allowing the defendant to amend the pretrial order here would defeat the purpose of pretrial disclosure. Therefore the court was correct in denying Bus, Inc.'s motion.

(iii)   *Introducing the Waiver:* Under Rule 26, at least 30 days before trial, Bus, Inc. had a duty to disclose to other parties and file with the court a list of documents or exhibits it expects to offer or might offer if needed. Additionally, a party must produce all physical material, including documents, relevant to the pending action. The federal rules provide for an automatic sanction against a party who "without substantial justification" fails to disclose information as required under Rule 26, or who fails to supplement or amend discovery responses under Rule 26(e)(1) or (2). Here, Bus, Inc. failed to disclose the waiver during discovery, and nothing in the facts presents an adequate reason for the failure. Therefore, the court properly prohibited introduction of the ticket stub into evidence.

QUESTION 17

Plaintiff, a resident of State X, is a shareholder in Silver, Inc., a State X corporation. Plaintiff purchased 10,000 shares of Silver stock for $20 a share in Silver's initial public offering ("IPO"). Three weeks after the IPO, the value of Silver stock had fallen to $15 a share, and Plaintiff filed an action for securities fraud against Silver in federal district court. The complaint alleged that the registration statement for the IPO filed by Silver with the Securities and Exchange Commission ("SEC") was materially false and misleading, and therefore violated relevant provisions of the Securities Exchange Act of 1934 as well as SEC regulations. Plaintiff sought damages of $50,000 for this violation.

Shortly after Plaintiff's initial filing, the SEC filed a public enforcement lawsuit against Silver, *SEC v. Silver,* in another federal district court. The claim asserted by the SEC, that the registration statement for the IPO contained false and misleading representations, was identical to the claim asserted in the *Plaintiff v. Silver* lawsuit. The SEC lawsuit went to trial very quickly, and Silver vigorously contested the misrepresentation issues in the SEC lawsuit. The SEC won its lawsuit. A declaratory judgment was entered, finding that Silver's registration statement contained false and misleading information and enjoining Silver from making those misrepresentations in the future. That judgment became final, and Silver did not appeal.

Plaintiff then moved for partial summary judgment against Silver based on the judgment in *SEC v. Silver.* Plaintiff argued that the *SEC v. Silver* judgment conclusively determined the issue whether the information contained in the registration statement was false and misleading. Silver opposed the motion on the ground that it had the right to litigate this issue against Plaintiff because Plaintiff had not been a party to the *SEC v. Silver* lawsuit.

The district court judge denied Plaintiff's motion for partial summary judgment on the ground that Plaintiff, a nonparty to the *SEC v. Silver* action, could not rely upon the judgment in that case to preclude Silver from relitigating issues that were central to Plaintiff's claim. Plaintiff filed an appeal from this decision, although Plaintiff's case against Silver is still going forward in the district court.

Silver has moved to dismiss Plaintiff's appeal on the following grounds: (a) that the district court's denial of Plaintiff's judgment was not a final judgment subject to review; (b) that the collateral order exception is inapplicable; and (c) mandamus does not lie.

1. Did the district court properly refuse to give preclusive effect to the *SEC v. Silver* judgment when it denied Plaintiff's motion for partial summary judgment? Explain.

2. How should the appellate court rule on each of the grounds asserted in Silver's motion to dismiss the appeal? Explain.

ANSWER TO QUESTION 17

1.   The district court improperly refused to give preclusive effect to the *SEC v. Silver* judgment when it denied Plaintiff's motion for partial summary judgment. At issue is whether a person who was not a party to a prior action in which a judgment was rendered can use the judgment in a subsequent action against a party from the prior action (*i.e.,* whether a nonparty can use collateral estoppel as a sword).

Collateral estoppel would apply here. Under the traditional mutuality rule, because an earlier judgment cannot be used *against* a person who was not party, that person is similarly barred from *taking advantage* of the judgment. However, the federal courts recognize an exception to the traditional mutuality rule. In federal courts, a nonparty may rely on a prior judgment if (i) the issue decided in the first case was *identical* to that in the second; (ii) there was a final judgment on the *merits*; (iii) the party against whom the judgment is to be used had a *fair opportunity to be heard* on the critical issue; and (iv) the posture of the case is such that it would *not be unfair or inequitable* to a party to apply collateral estoppel.

In this case, all conditions are met. The judgment obtained by the SEC was final, and Silver did not appeal. The issue, whether the registration statement contained false and misleading statements, is the same. Furthermore, Silver had the opportunity to, and in fact did, vigorously contest the merits. Finally, given that the issues are the same, that it had the means and opportunity to contest the issue in the SEC action, and that *SEC v. Silver* was filed after *Plaintiff v. Silver* (Silver would have had to know that Plaintiff would try to use the SEC judgment as collateral estoppel), it would not be unfair or inequitable to give preclusive effect to the judgment in *SEC v. Silver*. For these reasons, the district court's decision is wrong.

2.(a)   The appellate court should grant Silver's motion to dismiss the appeal.

At issue is whether the denial of Plaintiff's motion for partial summary judgment is a final order. As a general rule, only final orders are appealable; interlocutory orders are not. A final order is one that disposes of an entire case by rendering final judgment as to all parties and all causes of action. There are several exceptions to the general rule (*e.g.,* orders related to injunctions, to the appointment of a receiver or related to receiverships, to admiralty, to patent infringement, and to property possession), but the decision to deny Plaintiff's use of the judgment in *SEC v. Silver* for its preclusive effect is not one of them. Thus, the order is not appealable.

(b)   The appeal also does not fall under the "collateral order rule." If a claim or issue is separable from and collateral to the main suit, and it is a claim that is too important to require deferring appellate review, it may be classified as a judgment in a separate ("collateral") proceeding and thus be appealable. For example, if the court denies a governmental agency's claims of immunity, the issue would be appealable under the collateral order rule. Otherwise, the governmental agency would be forced to litigate a claim for which it may have immunity, thus the agency's immunity would be effectively negated. However, no such significant claim exists in the instant case. Plaintiff will merely be required to relitigate the issue of whether Silver's statement contains false and misleading statements. Furthermore, the judge's order may be reviewed on appeal, if Plaintiff loses and an appeal becomes necessary. Therefore, the order is not appealable under the collateral order rule.

(c)   Finally, the extraordinary writ of mandamus should not be available to Plaintiff. To have a writ of mandamus issued, Plaintiff must show that (i) he has no other adequate means, such as direct appeal, to obtain the relief desired and (ii) the trial court's action constitutes a serious abuse of power that must be immediately corrected. Neither element can be met. First, Plaintiff could have requested the trial judge to reconsider his prior ruling and can directly appeal the ruling if he loses the case. Second, it is doubtful that the trial court's error in denying the motion for partial summary judgment constitutes a serious abuse of power, given that the judge has discretion to weigh several factors when deciding whether to apply collateral estoppel. For these reasons, the writ should not issue.

QUESTION 18

Teacher lived in State A, where he taught in the public schools for eight years. Toward the end of his eighth year, Teacher was offered a lucrative teaching position in State B. Teacher decided to accept the offer and to move to State B. Teacher notified his school principal that he was leaving and put his State A home up for sale.

The day he sold his house, Teacher packed his belongings, rented a truck from Rentco, a State C corporation with its principal place of business in State A, and began the long drive

to State B. While speeding on a State A highway toward State B, Teacher came upon a slow-moving car and applied the brakes in an effort to avoid an accident. The brakes failed, and Teacher rear-ended the slow-moving car. Passenger, a citizen of State A who was riding in the slower car, suffered severe back and neck injuries in the collision. After the State A police prepared a report of the accident, Teacher continued on to State B. Shortly after he arrived there, he purchased a home and began his new job.

Nine months after the accident, Passenger filed suit against Teacher in the United States District Court for the District of State A, alleging that Teacher's negligence caused Passenger serious personal injury. Passenger's complaint sought damages in excess of $100,000.

Teacher timely moved to dismiss the complaint on the grounds that the court lacked subject matter jurisdiction and that venue was improper. While the motion to dismiss was pending, Teacher filed a third-party complaint against Rentco, seeking indemnification and claiming that the accident occurred because the brakes on the rental truck were defective. Before Teacher's motion could be heard, Passenger amended her complaint to state a claim directly against Rentco for negligence.

1. How should the federal district court rule on Teacher's motion to dismiss for lack of subject matter jurisdiction? Explain.

2. How should the federal district court rule on Teacher's motion to dismiss for improper venue? Explain.

3. If the district court were to deny Teacher's motion to dismiss on both grounds, would it have subject matter jurisdiction over Passenger's direct claim against Rentco? Explain.

ANSWER TO QUESTION 18

1. At issue is whether the United States District Court for State A should grant Teacher's motion to dismiss based on the lack of subject matter jurisdiction. A federal court has subject matter jurisdiction in two types of cases—(i) when a federal question is presented or (ii) when the requirements of diversity jurisdiction are met. Because the case is a run-of-the-mill auto accident, no federal question has been presented, making diversity jurisdiction the only permissible basis for subject matter jurisdiction.

For diversity jurisdiction to be proper, the amount in controversy must exceed $75,000, and complete diversity between each plaintiff and each defendant must exist. For the amount in controversy, the plaintiff must make a good faith allegation that her damages exceed $75,000. Given that the facts of the question state that Passenger was "severely" injured (and therefore will probably recover for her pain and suffering), it is likely that Passenger's allegation that her damages exceed $100,000 would be deemed to have been made in good faith.

In addition to the amount in controversy, complete diversity must exist between the plaintiffs and the defendants. A person's citizenship is determined by his domicile—the place where he intends to live—*at the time the suit is commenced*. The facts state that Passenger is a citizen of State A, and that Teacher, as a result of his finding a new home and a new job in State B before the suit was filed, is a citizen of State B. Therefore, given that the suit is between a citizen of state A and a citizen of State B, and that the amount in controversy is more than $75,000, diversity jurisdiction exists and the motion to dismiss should be denied.

2.   Venue is proper in the United States District Court for State A. At issue is whether Passenger filed suit in the proper district court. In diversity cases, venue is proper in the district in which (i) any defendant resides, if all defendants reside in the same state or (ii) a substantial part of the events that prompted plaintiff to file suit took place. If there is no district that satisfies (i) or (ii), the plaintiff may file in the district in which (iii) a substantial part of the property that is the subject of the lawsuit is situated; or (iv) any defendant is subject to personal jurisdiction, provided that the action is not based solely on diversity. Because the accident occurred in State A, venue is proper in the district court for State A.

3.   If the court were to deny Teacher's motion to dismiss, it would not have subject matter jurisdiction over Passenger's direct claim against Rentco. At issue is whether there must be an independent basis for subject matter jurisdiction—either diversity or a federal question—for a direct claim against a new defendant added by amendment. Under federal law, when additional parties are joined, an independent basis for jurisdiction must exist, unless the supplemental jurisdiction statute would enable the court to exercise jurisdiction. As discussed above, this case here does not involve a federal question. Also as discussed above, the required amount in controversy should not pose a problem. However, Passenger is a citizen of State A, and Rentco, a corporation, is a citizen of State A (its principal place of business) and State C (its place of incorporation); thus, complete diversity is lacking. The supplemental jurisdiction statute allows the court to entertain certain actions, such as ***third-party*** claims and when a party seeks to intervene as a defendant as a matter of right, provided the new claim arose out of the same transaction or occurrence as the underlying claim. Here, however, the supplemental jurisdiction statute does not apply—Passenger is seeking to amend her complaint to add a new defendant, not a third-party defendant. Furthermore, as stated above, the court must determine on its own that it has jurisdiction to hear a case. Thus, because Passenger and Rentco are citizens of the same state, the court would not have jurisdiction to hear the direct claim, and it would have to dismiss the claim even if Rentco never raises the issue.

QUESTION 19

Seller manufactures vending machines at a facility located in State A, where Seller is incorporated and has its principal place of business. Buyer, a German company with its principal place of business in Munich, Germany, contracted to purchase 1,000 vending machines from Seller for a total price of $500,000.

The contract was carefully negotiated during lengthy discussions held in Germany. Early in the negotiations, each side insisted that the contract should be governed by its own law and that disputes should be resolved in its own courts. In the end, however, the parties agreed on contract clauses that provided: (i) "the substantive rights and remedies of the parties to this contract shall be governed by the Commercial Code of State N"; (ii) "any and all litigation brought concerning this contract shall be brought in the state or federal courts of State N"; and (iii) "Seller and Buyer hereby consent to venue, jurisdiction, and service of process by courts in State N." Apart from these clauses, there is no connection between

State N and the parties or the transaction. State N is located on the eastern seaboard of the United States. The parties chose State N because it has convenient air links to Germany and a widely respected judiciary that is regarded as expert in commercial law matters.

Seller shipped the vending machines to Germany, but Buyer refused the shipment after discovering that the goods had been seriously damaged during the ocean voyage and arrived in Germany in a worthless condition. Seller then sued Buyer in federal district court in State A, properly invoking the court's subject matter jurisdiction and seeking recovery of the $500,000 contract price on the ground that the risk of damage to the goods during transport was on Buyer throughout the ocean voyage.

In responding to Seller's complaint, Buyer moved to transfer the case to the federal district court in State N, pursuant to 28 U.S.C. section 1404(a) and the forum-selection clause in the contract. Seller resisted Buyer's transfer request on the grounds that (i) State A was a more convenient forum for Seller, and (ii) the forum-selection clause was unenforceable under State A law, which declares such clauses to be "void as a matter of public policy."

While the transfer motion was pending, Seller delivered a notice of deposition to Buyer, demanding that Buyer's chief executive officer appear for a deposition. Buyer responded by asking the court for a protective order on the ground that its "officers, directors, and managing agents" are all in Germany and are therefore beyond the subpoena power or other authority of the court.

Assume that there are no applicable international law principles or treaties.

1.   Should the federal district court in State A transfer the action to State N? Explain.

2.   Irrespective of how the court rules on the transfer motion, should Buyer's request for a protective order be granted? Explain.

ANSWER TO QUESTION 19

1.   The federal district court in State A should uphold the forum selection clause and transfer the action to State N. At issue is the validity of the forum selection clause in light of State A's public policy position, and whether State A is a more convenient forum for the action.

Seller argues that the forum selection clause should be invalidated because it is "void as a matter of public policy" in State A. However, venue in federal courts is considered a procedural matter and is determined by federal law (28 U.S.C. section 1404). Furthermore, federal case law also holds that the presence of a forum selection clause in a contract—by which the parties have specified a particular forum as the appropriate place for litigation—is only a factor to be considered, along with the convenience of the parties and the interests of justice. Thus, the only relevant inquiry becomes whether State A is a more convenient forum than State N.

Generally, courts allow contracting parties to expressly incorporate a foreign state's law into their contract, and even allow them to designate the law of a state with which there are no contacts with the parties or the transaction. However, several exceptions to the general rule exist, where such a provision will not be upheld. Specifically, a forum selection clause will not be upheld where: (i) there is no reasonable basis for the parties' choice because the chosen state bears no substantial relationship to the parties or the transaction; (ii) there was no "true consent" to the choice (*e.g.*, as in an adhesion contract); and (iii) the law of the chosen state would be contrary to a fundamental public policy of a state that has a materially greater interest than the chosen state in determining the particular issue. The existence of any one of these exceptions will result in the invalidation of the forum selection clause. None are present here.

In this case, Seller first argues that State A is a more convenient forum than State N. However, the facts tell us that after much deliberation, State N was selected as the forum because of its "convenient" air links to Germany and because of its "widely respected judiciary," which reportedly possesses expertise in commercial law. These reasons are clearly valid and it was reasonable for the parties to choose State N, regardless of State N's lack of additional contacts with Buyer, Seller, or the actual contract at issue. It is also safe to assume that Seller knew at the time of contract negotiations where State N was located, and Seller nevertheless agreed to State N. Furthermore, both Buyer and Seller appear to be well-established corporations well-versed in negotiating the terms of a contract. Indeed, the facts clearly state that the contract was "carefully negotiated during lengthy discussions." Thus, there is nothing here to indicate a lack of true consent by either party. Therefore, while State A may indeed be a more convenient forum for Seller, this is not enough to overcome the fact that Seller went into this agreement fully aware of the details of each forum and was well-informed when it agreed to State N, and that State N may be a more convenient forum for Buyer.

2.   The court could issue a protective order limiting the manner in which the deposition is taken, but it should not issue a blanket protective order that would prohibit any deposition from the company's officers on the ground that its officers all reside in Germany.

At issue is whether a party may take the deposition of a representative of a foreign corporation that has voluntarily submitted to the jurisdiction of a United States court. A party may take the deposition of another party on notice to all involved parties (as has occurred here), regardless of whether a subpoena has been issued. Buyer is a party/defendant in the suit and is subject to the rules of the court. The fact that its officers do not reside within the United States is irrelevant as to whether any deposition may take place.

However, Rule 30 provides that a court may order that a deposition be taken "by telephone or some other remote electronic means." Given the distance that some of the corporate officers may be required to travel, a protective order limiting depositions to telephonic or another remote means may be appropriate. Relevant to this discussion would be what Seller hopes to discover by an in-person deposition of Buyer's CEO, because the court should weigh the cost/benefits of an in-person deposition. Absent a compelling reason for an in-person deposition, the court should grant a protective order limiting the deposition to a deposition by telephone or other remote electronic means. Therefore, while a blanket order of protection may be inappropriate, some sort of limited order of protection may be appropriate.

QUESTION 20

Acme Corporation, a citizen of State X, manufactures widgets. Acme widgets are distributed to retailers throughout the United States by Widgets, Inc., a citizen of State Y. Plaintiff, a

citizen of State Y, purchased an Acme widget from a retailer in her hometown. Shortly after purchasing the widget, Plaintiff was seriously injured when the widget overheated and exploded.

Plaintiff sued Acme in the federal district court located in State Y, properly invoking the court's diversity jurisdiction. Plaintiff sought $100,000 in damages on two state-law tort theories: (1) failure to warn and (2) sale of a dangerously defective product.

Under the applicable state law, a manufacturer's duty to warn is fully discharged if a proper warning is affixed to the product *at the point of delivery to its distributor.* A distributor's duty is fully discharged if the warning is affixed *at the point of delivery to the retailer.* State law further provides that both manufacturers and distributors may be held separately and strictly liable for selling a "dangerously defective" product, even if they have given adequate warning of the risks. Plaintiff's complaint alleged both that Acme had failed to affix a warning label to the product and that Acme's widgets had a dangerous propensity to over-heat.

After extensive discovery, Acme filed a motion for summary judgment on the failure to warn claim. It attached to its motion the supporting affidavits of employees of both Acme and Widgets attesting that a proper warning label had been affixed to the widget both at the time of delivery to Widgets and at the time of distribution to the retailer who sold the widget to Plaintiff. While conceding that the warning label usually provided with the product did give adequate notice of the danger of overheating and explosion under certain circumstances, Plaintiff nevertheless contested the motion for summary judgment with her own affidavit, in which she stated that there had been no warning label affixed to her widget when she purchased it from her local retailer.

The federal court granted Acme's motion for summary judgment on the failure to warn claim and entered judgment on that claim against Plaintiff. No appeal was taken. Soon afterward, Acme and Plaintiff settled the dangerous defect claim for an undisclosed amount.

Shortly after the conclusion of the federal litigation, Plaintiff filed suit in the state court of State Y, asserting against Widgets, Inc. the same two claims she had asserted against Acme in federal court: failure to warn and sale of a dangerously defective product. Widgets answered and then moved to dismiss on grounds of claim and issue preclusion.

1. In Plaintiff's suit against Acme, did the federal court properly grant Acme's motion for summary judgment on the failure to warn claim? Explain.

2. Should the State Y state court give preclusive effect to the federal court judgment and dismiss Plaintiff's claims against Widgets? Explain.

ANSWER TO QUESTION 20

1.   At issue is whether the court properly granted Acme's motion for summary judgment with regard to Plaintiff's suit based on a failure-to-warn theory in a products liability case. In general,

a summary judgment must be granted if, from the pleadings, affidavits, and discovery materials, it appears that there is no genuine issue of material fact and the moving party is entitled to judgment as a matter of law. If the moving party submits an affidavit in support of the motion for summary judgment, the nonmoving party must counter that affidavit with his own. In the present case, Acme submitted affidavits from employees of both Acme (the manufacturer) and Widgets, Inc. (the distributor) stating that the widget had a proper warning attached when the widget was delivered to Widgets, and Plaintiff submitted an affidavit stating that the widget had no warning attached when she bought the widget from the retailer. It is important to note that, under state law, Acme's liability is discharged if a proper warning label was affixed when Acme delivered the widgets to Widgets, Inc. Thus, although Plaintiff submitted her own affidavit in response to the motion for summary judgment, it did not address the relevant issue under state law—whether a proper warning was affixed when Acme delivered the widget to Widgets, its distributor. Therefore, there was no genuine issue of material fact, and Acme was entitled to a judgment as a matter of law. As a result, the federal court's ruling was proper.

2.   At issue is whether the state court should give preclusive effect (of either the claim or issue variety) to the federal court's rulings in *Plaintiff v. Acme*. First, Widgets is attempting to assert that Plaintiff's claim is barred by the disposition of the claims in *Plaintiff v. Acme*. For claim preclusion to apply, there must have been a valid, final judgment on the merits, **both** parties must be the same (or be in privity with a party in the prior suit), and the new action must involve the same cause of action, meaning that all claims must arise out of the same transaction or occurrence. Here, although the decision in *Plaintiff v. Acme* is a final judgment on the merits and the cause of action arose from the same transaction or occurrence, the parties are not the same, as Acme was being sued in the first case while Widgets is being sued in the second case. Thus, application of claim preclusion would be inappropriate.

Next, Widgets is also claiming that the federal court has already ruled in *Plaintiff v. Acme* that a proper warning had been affixed to the widget. For issue preclusion to apply, the issues in both actions must be the same, there must have been a final judgment as to that issue, the party against whom collateral estoppel is asserted must have had a fair opportunity to be heard on the matter, and the posture of the case must be such that it would not be unfair or inequitable to apply collateral estoppel. In *Plaintiff v. Widgets*, it is the first element that is lacking. In *Plaintiff v. Acme*, the issue was whether a proper warning had been affixed when Acme delivered the widget to Widgets, the distributor. In *Plaintiff v. Widgets*, the issue is whether a proper warning had been affixed when Widgets delivered the widget to the retailer. Therefore, an affidavit (or discovery) will have to be obtained from the retailer. If the retailer states that the warning was affixed, Widgets will be able to make a motion for summary judgment, much like Acme did in the first case, because under state law a distributor's duty is discharged if a warning label was affixed when the product was delivered to the retailer. If the retailer states that the warning was not affixed, Plaintiff will be able to survive any motion for summary judgment, as there would be a genuine issue of material fact for the jury to decide. However, because the issues are not the same, use of issue preclusion would be inappropriate.

QUESTION 21

Farmer brought a class action lawsuit in federal district court in State A, alleging that the defendant, Truckco, marketed a line of pickup trucks with defective shock absorbers.

Farmer's complaint identified the members of the class as 100,000 individuals nationwide who had bought the trucks from 1995-2000 and suffered losses as a result of the defective shock absorbers. The alleged losses ranged from the $250 cost of replacing the shock absorbers to serious personal injuries suffered in accidents alleged to have been caused by the defective shock absorbers. The only claim personal to Farmer was the $250 replacement cost claim. Farmer properly asserted that federal jurisdiction was based on a breach of warranty claim under a recently enacted federal automobile safety statute.

Farmer moved to certify the class. Opposing this motion, Truckco submitted court papers from lawsuits brought by individual owners who claimed to have suffered a wide variety of personal injuries as a result of accidents said to have resulted from the failure of the defective shock absorbers during the years in question. Truckco also noted that Farmer had previously filed (and still has pending) a class action against Truckco in a state court in State Z. In the State Z case, which was premised on state-law warranty claims, Farmer sought relief similar to the relief sought in the federal action and asked to represent the same class of plaintiffs. Finally, Truckco pointed out that Farmer's lawyer in both actions was a recent bar admittee who had not previously handled class action litigation.

In addition to arguing against certification of the class, Truckco asked the federal district court to abstain from adjudicating the class action in light of the pendency of the state court class action.

The federal district court first denied Truckco's motion for abstention. The court then denied Farmer's motion for class certification, finding that class certification was "inappropriate under the circumstances."

1. Was the court's ruling on Truckco's motion for abstention correct? Explain.

2. Was the court's ruling on Farmer's motion for class certification appropriate? Explain.

ANSWER TO QUESTION 21

1. The federal district court's decision not to abstain from ruling on the class action in light of the pendency of the similar state court class action was correct. At issue is whether a federal court must abstain from deciding a question that could affect a similar state court proceeding. Generally, a federal court can retain jurisdiction over a case, but abstain from ruling on the question, when a challenge to the constitutionality of a state statute is at issue. In the instant case, Truckco is not challenging the constitutionality of a state statute; in fact, the claim is based on a recently enacted federal law. Thus, there is no reason for the federal court to abstain from ruling on the case, and the federal court did not err in failing to abstain from ruling on the class action.

2. The federal district court's ruling that class certification was inappropriate under the circumstances was correct. At issue is whether Farmer met all of the prerequisites for class certification under Rule 23. Under Rule 23, there are five requirements for class certification: (i) the class must be so numerous that joinder of all members is impracticable; (ii) the class must have common questions of law or fact; (iii) the named party's interest must be typical of the class; (iv) the

named party's representative must be able to ensure fair and adequate representation of the absent class members; and (v) the action must be one of the types listed under Rule 23(b)—there must be a risk of inconsistent results such that trial of each plaintiff's claim individually would establish inconsistent standards of conduct for the defendant or a risk that trial of one of the plaintiff's claims could impair the rights of all of the plaintiffs; a defendant must have acted or refused to act on grounds applicable to the whole class and injunctive or declaratory relief would be appropriate to the whole class; or the common questions of law or fact predominate over all of the individual claims and a class action is the superior method of adjudication. Given that there are 100,000 individuals within the class, the "numerosity" requirement has probably been met. Furthermore, because the actions are based primarily on the new federal automobile safety statute and on whether Truckco violated this statute, common questions of law and fact exist. However, it is questionable whether Farmer can meet parts (iii) and (iv). The facts state that the claims range in value from $250 (the replacement cost of the shock absorber) to an amount appropriate for a serious personal injury, and that Farmer's claim is for the lowest amount. There is no breakdown as to the number of claimants with personal injury claims, but those claims would have to include complex testimony from expert witnesses regarding that class member's injuries and possible testimony regarding causation and contributory negligence. Thus, because of the differing evidence required for the personal injury claims, Farmer's claim probably should not be considered "typical" of the class. Furthermore, the fact that Farmer's claim may be relatively small may hinder his ability to fairly and adequately represent the class (part (iv)). Because his claim is small, he may be more likely to settle the class action than would a representative who suffered greater injury. It should also be noted that his counsel does not have experience with class actions, another factor to consider when deciding whether the named plaintiff can adequately represent the class. Additionally, although it is unclear if there is a risk of inconsistent results or of the setting of inconsistent standards, the final requirement—that the action must fall into one of the Rule 23(b) categories—probably could not be met because injunctive or declaratory relief would not be appropriate and the questions related to the breach of warranty claim would not predominate over the individual personal injury claims. In any case, because Farmer cannot show that his claim is "typical" of the class or that he can adequately represent the class, the case should not proceed as a class action.

QUESTION 22

Motorist was driving his automobile in the northbound lane on a highway in State X. Exceeding the posted maximum speed limit by 10 miles per hour, Motorist was gaining on a slow-moving U.S. Army truck convoy traveling in the same lane. At the same time, a motorcycle, driven by Husband with Wife as a passenger, was approaching the convoy from the opposite direction. Husband was operating the motorcycle at the posted speed limit and was traveling in the proper (southbound) lane.

The soldier driving the last truck in the convoy was feeling drowsy because he had not slept the night before. Suddenly, realizing that he had driven his truck far too close to the Army truck just ahead of him, he slammed on his brakes. Motorist, who had nearly overtaken the convoy, reacted to the sight of the truck's brake lights by frantically swerving his automobile into the southbound lane, where he sideswiped Husband's motorcycle. Husband was thrown to the pavement and seriously injured. Wife, however, miraculously avoided physical injury.

At the time of the accident, Husband and Wife were citizens of State Y, but a few months later they moved permanently to State X. Motorist was at all times a citizen of State X.

Shortly after moving to State X, Husband and Wife filed an action in the United States District Court for the District of State X seeking to recover for the injuries they suffered as a result of the accident. In the action, Husband claimed $50,000 in damages for his injuries, and Wife claimed $5,000 for her loss of Husband's consortium. They named as defendants both the United States of America and Motorist. Their claims against the United States are based on the Federal Tort Claims Act, which provides that federal district courts have exclusive jurisdiction over tort claims against the United States government. Their claims against Motorist are based on the tort law of State X, where the accident occurred.

1. **Can Husband and Wife, as plaintiffs, join their respective personal injury and loss-of-consortium claims in a single action in the district court? Explain.**

2. **Can Husband and Wife join their respective claims against the United States and Motorist, as defendants, in a single action in the district court? Explain.**

3. **Does the district court have subject matter jurisdiction over the state law claims of Husband and Wife against Motorist? Explain.**

ANSWER TO QUESTION 22

1.   Husband and Wife may join their respective personal injury and loss-of-consortium claims in a single action in the district court. At issue is whether Husband and Wife may join personal injury and loss-of-consortium claims as plaintiffs in a single action. Ignoring the subject matter issue for the moment, the rule is that parties may be permissively joined as plaintiffs whenever (i) some claim is made by each plaintiff and against each defendant relating to and arising out of the same series of occurrences or transactions; and (ii) there is question of fact or law common to all the parties. Thus, claims may be joined when at least one of the claims arises out of a transaction in which all of the parties were involved. Here, Husband was injured when Motorist swerved into his lane due to the army truck's sudden slowdown. Wife's loss-of-consortium claim is factually based on Husband's injury. Thus, Husband and Wife may be joined as plaintiffs because their claims, by necessity, arise from the same accident/transaction and share common issues of the army truck driver's negligence and Motorist's negligence. Furthermore, given that all claims arise from the same accident/transaction, joinder of the loss-of-consortium and personal injury claims is proper. (Note that the court would have discretion to sever the claims.)

2.   Husband and Wife may join their respective claims against the United States and Motorist, as defendants, in a single action in the district court. At issue is whether the United States and Motorist may be joined as defendants in a single action. Again, the rule is that parties may be permissively joined as defendants whenever (i) some claim is made against each defendant relating to and arising out of the same series of occurrences or transactions; and (ii) there is a question of fact or law common to all parties. As stated above, the claims against the United States and Motorist necessarily involve the same series of occurrences or transactions—it was the army truck's sudden slowdown that caused Motorist to swerve into Husband's lane. Furthermore, the common question of law or fact is the respective degrees of negligence assigned to each defendant. Thus, the United States and Motorist may be joined as defendants in the same action.

3.   The district court has subject matter jurisdiction over all claims, in that it has federal question jurisdiction over claims asserted against the United States and supplemental (pendent) jurisdiction over claims asserted against Motorist. At issue is whether the district court has federal question jurisdiction, diversity of citizenship jurisdiction, or supplemental jurisdiction over the claims before it. A district court has federal question jurisdiction when the claim arises under federal law. As to the claims against the United States based on the Federal Tort Claims Act, the court would have federal question jurisdiction, because Husband and Wife are asserting rights based on federal statutory law.

However, the claims against Motorist are based solely on state law. As a result, Husband and Wife must invoke either diversity of citizenship or supplemental jurisdiction to have their claims against Motorist heard in federal court. Diversity of citizenship requires an amount in controversy of more than $75,000 and that all plaintiffs be of diverse citizenship from all defendants. Here, diversity of citizenship does not exist, because Husband, Wife, and Motorist are all citizens of State X. (Citizenship is determined at the time suit is filed; thus, Husband's and Wife's move from State Y to State X before the suit was filed makes them citizens of State X.) Furthermore, the claims total only $55,000, falling short of the $75,000 amount in controversy requirement. Thus, diversity of citizenship jurisdiction does not exist.

Therefore, in order to successfully maintain their claims in federal court, Husband and Wife must invoke supplemental (pendent) jurisdiction. In a case based on a federal question, the federal court has discretion to exercise supplemental (pendent) jurisdiction over claims based on state law if the two claims derive from common facts and are such that the plaintiff would be expected to try all of them in one proceeding. Here, the accident resulted from a series of events that have a cause-and-effect relationship, in that the actions of the army truck driver caused Motorist to swerve, which in turn caused the accident and Husband's injuries and Wife's claim for loss-of-consortium. Thus, the claims derive from a common nucleus of fact. Additionally, actions against joint tortfeasors are usually tried together. As a result, the court has supplemental (pendent) jurisdiction over Motorist. (Note that the exercise of jurisdiction is discretionary with the court when, for example, the case presents a novel issue of state law. None of the discretionary bases for refusing jurisdiction appear here.)

Because the district court has federal question jurisdiction over the claims asserted against the United States and supplemental (pendent) jurisdiction over the state law claims, it has subject matter jurisdiction over all of the claims here.

QUESTION 23

Plaintiff, a domiciliary of State X, was severely injured in a car accident in State X. Tortfeasor, the uninsured owner and driver of the other vehicle involved in the accident, was also a citizen of State X. Before any litigation regarding the accident began, Tortfeasor died of a heart attack.

Following Tortfeasor's death, Plaintiff commenced an action against Executor, the legal representative of Tortfeasor's estate. Executor is a citizen of State Y. Plaintiff sued Executor in the federal district court of State Y. The complaint, which alleged that Tortfeasor's negligence caused the accident and Plaintiff's injuries, sought damages in excess of $500,000.

Executor answered the complaint, denying the allegations of negligence but admitting the court's subject matter jurisdiction. A year later, however, after extensive discovery, Executor moved to dismiss the complaint for lack of subject matter jurisdiction. After the submission of briefs and oral argument on the jurisdictional issue, the federal court denied Executor's motion to dismiss, ruling that "jurisdiction exists and, in any event, the motion was untimely." A trial was held and the jury rendered a verdict in Plaintiff's favor for $80,000.

The federal court entered judgment on the verdict. No appeal was taken.

When Executor declined to pay the judgment, Plaintiff commenced suit in a state court in State X to enforce the federal judgment. In the state suit, Executor challenged the validity of the judgment, claiming that the federal district court of State Y lacked subject matter jurisdiction.

1.   Did the federal district court of State Y err in denying Executor's motion to dismiss for lack of subject matter jurisdiction? Explain.

2.   Should the state court in State X enforce the federal judgment? Explain.

ANSWER TO QUESTION 23

1.   The federal district court erred in denying Executor's motion to dismiss for lack of subject matter jurisdiction. At issue is whether diversity of citizenship exists in a case against an executor when the plaintiff shares citizenship with the decedent but not with the executor. (Note that Plaintiff's claim of damages in excess of $500,000 easily satisfies the amount in controversy requirement of $75,000 for diversity jurisdiction and that no federal question has been presented.) To determine whether diversity of citizenship exists, the court must look at the citizenship of the decedent, not the citizenship of the executor, because a legal representative is deemed to be a citizen only of the same state as the decedent. Thus, although diversity exists between Executor, a citizen of State Y, and Plaintiff, a citizen of State X, diversity of citizenship does not exist because the deceased Tortfeasor was also a citizen of State X. As a result, the court erred in failing to dismiss the suit for lack of diversity jurisdiction.

The court also erred in stating that the motion to dismiss for lack of subject matter jurisdiction was not timely filed. At issue in this case is when a motion to dismiss for lack of subject matter jurisdiction must be made. Generally, the lack of subject matter jurisdiction may be raised at any time in the litigation, even on appeal. Here, Executor raised the issue at the trial court level before the trial took place. Thus, Executor raised this issue in a timely manner. However, because Executor failed to appeal, that judgment became valid, final, and on the merits (*see* below).

2.   The state court in State X should enforce the judgment of the federal court. At issue is whether a judgment issued by a federal court without subject matter jurisdiction is entitled to full faith and credit in a state court. Generally, there are three requirements for full faith and credit: (i) there must be proper jurisdiction; (ii) the judgment must have been on the merits; and (iii) the judgment must be final. (Note that full faith and credit applies to state courts and federal court alike; *i.e.*, each must give full faith and credit to the others' judgments if the requirements for full faith and credit have been met.) Here, given that the judgment was on the merits because it determined the rights and liabilities of the parties, and that the judgment was final because it found liability on the part of Tortfeasor and awarded $80,000 to Plaintiff, only requirement (i)

remains an issue. Ordinarily, a judgment issued by the court without subject matter jurisdiction is void. However, an exception exists when the party contesting jurisdiction appears and litigates the issue in the trial court, but loses. In that case, the findings of the court regarding its jurisdiction, even if in error, become binding and conclusive in later litigation. That is the case here—Executor brought the matter to the attention of the trial court, and he had a full and fair opportunity to litigate the issue at the trial court level. Executor also failed to appeal the judgment in federal court. Thus, under the principles of res judicata, the state court in State X should enforce the judgment of the federal district court in State Y. (*Note:* Because the lack of subject matter jurisdiction was clear, a strong argument could be made that the court in State X should not give full faith and credit to the judgment.)

QUESTION 24

Buyer and Seller were both citizens of State X, where they attended State University. Just before they graduated, Buyer purchased Seller's car for $2,500. At the time, Seller told Buyer that the car was "in good working order" and that it was a "safe, reliable little car." Seller knew, however, that a local mechanic's inspection of the car had revealed that its brakes were so worn that they presented a significant safety hazard and required immediate replacement. Instead of informing Buyer of the danger, Seller showed Buyer the mechanic's bill and told him that the car "has just been checked out."

After graduation, Buyer decided to move permanently to Big City in State Y. Buyer decided to use the car he bought from Seller for the move. He believed that in a few round-trips he could transport all of his belongings to his new apartment in Big City. On his way back to his State X apartment after his first trip to his new apartment in Big City, Buyer was seriously injured in a one-car accident on a highway in State X. Friend, a citizen of State X and a passenger in Buyer's car, was the only witness to the accident. He and Buyer will testify that the accident happened when the brakes failed as Buyer attempted to negotiate a curve in the highway.

After weeks of hospitalization in State X, Buyer settled permanently in his apartment in Big City in State Y. Having discovered Seller's deceit, Buyer sued Seller in the U.S. District Court for the District of State X, seeking to recover $500,000 under State X tort law for his injuries and lost wages. In addition, Buyer claimed Seller's misrepresentations constituted a breach of warranty under State X contract law and sought recovery of the $2,500 paid for the car.

One week after the suit was filed, Seller also decided to relocate from State X to Big City, taking a job there and assuming State Y citizenship.

Seller has filed a motion to dismiss Buyer's two claims for lack of subject matter jurisdiction. Seller has also moved for a change of venue to the U.S. District Court for the District of State Y.

1. **Should the court dismiss Buyer's tort claim, Buyer's contract claim, or both for lack of subject matter jurisdiction? Explain.**

2. **How should the court rule on Seller's motion for a change of venue? Explain.**

ANSWER TO QUESTION 24

1. The court should not dismiss either claim for lack of subject matter jurisdiction. At issue is whether the requirements for diversity of citizenship jurisdiction have been satisfied. For a court to have subject matter jurisdiction under diversity of citizenship, two requirements must be satisfied: (i) the amount in controversy must be greater than $75,000; and (ii) all plaintiffs must be of diverse citizenship from all defendants.

As to the amount in controversy requirement, the issue is whether the $2,500 contract claim may be heard in federal court even though it is for less than $75,000. Under federal law, claims by a single plaintiff against a single defendant may be aggregated to satisfy the amount in controversy requirement. In the instant case, Buyer alleges that he incurred damages of $2,500 when Seller breached a contract warranty and damages of $500,000 for a tort that Seller committed against him. Thus, for purposes of diversity jurisdiction, the amount in controversy here is $502,500, well above the minimum threshold.

As to the diversity of citizenship requirement, the issue is when the citizenship of a party is determined. Under federal law, a party is a citizen of the state in which he resides at the time the suit is filed. The facts state that Buyer "settled permanently" in State Y before filing suit; thus, he is a citizen of State Y. The facts also state that Seller relocated from State X to State Y one week *after* suit was filed. Thus, because he was a citizen of State X when suit was filed, he is a citizen of State X for diversity purposes. As a result, the suit is by a citizen of State Y (Buyer) against a citizen of State X (Seller), and the complete diversity of citizenship requirement was satisfied.

Given that the requirements of diversity of citizenship have been satisfied, the court has subject matter jurisdiction over the case, and the motion to dismiss either claim should be denied.

2. The court should deny Seller's motion for change of venue. The main issues here are whether the U.S. District Court for the District of State X is a proper venue and whether Seller may have venue transferred based on inconvenience.

For a civil action in federal court, venue is proper (i) in a judicial district in which any defendant resides, if all defendants reside in the same state; (ii) in a judicial district in which a substantial part of the events of the lawsuit occurred or in which a substantial part of the property that is the subject matter of the lawsuit is situated; or (iii) if neither (i) or (ii) can be satisfied, venue is proper in a district in which any defendant is subject to personal jurisdiction at the time the action is commenced (diversity cases) or in a judicial district in which any defendant may be found (cases not based on diversity). Thus, given that a substantial part of the events involved here occurred in State X (*e.g.*, the accident occurred in State X and the contract was formed in State X), and that Seller was a resident of State X when suit was filed, venue is proper in State X.

However, Seller may also contend that the district court in State X is an inconvenient forum. If venue was properly laid in the action, venue may be transferred to another more convenient forum in which the action might have been brought. In the instant case, venue is proper only in State X, given that State X is the state in which Seller resided when suit was brought and in which a substantial part of the events of the lawsuit took place. Furthermore, it is unlikely that State Y would be a more convenient forum for the parties *and witnesses*. The facts state that the only witness to the accident, Friend, was a citizen of State X. Furthermore, the hospital in which Buyer was treated is also located in State X. The district court in State X presumably would be more convenient for Friend and the employees of the hospital. Furthermore, given that Buyer intended to make two trips from State X to State Y during his move, it is also likely that State X and State Y are in close proximity to one another. Thus, the inconvenience to Seller in litigating in State X is probably not significant enough to outweigh Buyer's right to choose the forum. For all of these reasons, a motion to transfer venue based on inconvenience should be denied.

QUESTION 25

Drugco, a State B corporation with its principal place of business in State B, employs sales representatives and assigns them to work in exclusive geographical areas. The Drugco sales representatives provide pharmacists in their areas with product literature, pricing information, and highly confidential sheets (known as "chem sheets") listing the chemical composition of each drug. The chem sheets ensure that the pharmacists understand how each Drugco drug interacts with other commonly prescribed drugs.

Drugco hired Claire, a resident of State A, under an employment agreement that contained a "noncompete" clause barring her, for one year following the termination of her employment with Drugco, from soliciting any pharmacists in her territory (defined as Elm, Maple, and Cherry counties of State A) or from engaging in any other activity competitive with Drugco's business within her territory. The agreement also included a trade-secrets clause that required Claire to return to Drugco all pricing information and chem sheets in her possession upon termination of her employment.

The laws of State A and State B provide that: (1) chemical formulas and drug pricing information are trade secrets and (2) noncompete clauses in employment agreements are valid so long as they are reasonable in duration and geographical scope.

Claire was an excellent sales representative for Drugco, and she quickly developed strong working relationships with the pharmacists in her territory. Eighteen months after she began working for Drugco, Claire tendered her resignation to Drugco and the next day began working for Medico, a competing pharmaceuticals firm. Claire, who had retained a number of Drugco chem sheets, was contacting the same pharmacists in the same geographical area that she had covered for Drugco. Moreover, she was selling Medico products that were in direct competition with Drugco products.

Drugco has properly invoked diversity jurisdiction and has sued Claire in federal district court in State A for breach of contract.

Drugco seeks to enforce the noncompete clause in Claire's employment contract and to bar her from soliciting the pharmacists with whom she developed relationships while working for Drugco. Drugco fears that it may take more than a year to litigate the case to final judgment and wants to bar Claire from soliciting these pharmacists *now*. Drugco also wants to compel Claire to return immediately all Drugco chem sheets and pricing information within her possession.

What provisional remedies might Drugco seek to enforce the noncompete and trade-secrets clauses immediately and during the pendency of the lawsuit, and what is the likelihood that the court will grant each such remedy? Explain.

ANSWER TO QUESTION 25

Noncompete Clause: To enforce the noncompete clause, Drugco should seek a temporary restraining order ("TRO") or preliminary injunction. Such orders are derived from equity and are available in the federal courts pursuant to Federal Rule of Civil Procedure 65. The main issue is whether Drugco can show immediate and irreparable injury that will outweigh the harm that Claire would suffer if the court issues the TRO or injunction.

A TRO is granted by a court to prevent irreparable injury before a preliminary injunction hearing can be held. The person requesting a TRO must show that if the TRO is not granted now, it will suffer irreparable injury before a trial on the merits can be held and that this injury greatly outweighs any harm that will be caused to the restrained party or the public if it turns out that the TRO was improvidently granted. In addition, the moving party must show that it will likely succeed on the merits of its underlying case. The moving party will also be required to post a bond to protect the restrained party against possible harm if the TRO is improvidently granted. Notice to the adverse party is generally required unless the moving party can show that it reasonably attempted to give the other party notice and/or strong reasons why notice should not be required in this case. A TRO cannot be effective for more than 10 days from its issuance.

A preliminary injunction is similar to a TRO; its issuance requires proof of the same elements. However, a preliminary injunction cannot be issued ex parte—a full hearing on notice must be held—and a preliminary injunction remains in effect throughout the pendency of the litigation until dissolved by the court.

In the instant case, Drugco can show that irreparable injury will result if the noncompete clause is not enforced before a hearing for a preliminary injunction can be held. If Claire is not restrained, she will be able to contact her former customers in her old territory, use the chem sheets and confidential pricing information that she has, and steal customers from Drugco. The potential permanent loss of customers would be difficult to value, making Drugco's harm irreparable. Moreover, this potential harm greatly outweighs any harm that the injunction would cause Claire if it turns out to be improvidently granted, because the noncompete clause is of limited scope— Claire will still be able to solicit sales from pharmacists in her old territory for noncompeting drugs, or she could still market her new firm's products in counties outside of her original sales territory. Additionally, no apparent harm would come to the public from issuance of the TRO here. Finally, Drugco is likely to succeed on the merits of its underlying case. The laws of State A and State B enforce noncompete clauses that are reasonable in scope and duration. Here, the noncompete clause is for only one year and applies only to a specific geographic area—Claire's sales territory with Drugco—which encompasses only three counties in State A. Thus, the scope of the noncompete clause seems reasonable. Therefore, Drugco will probably be successful in obtaining a TRO enforcing the noncompete clause against Claire. For the same reasons, the court would probably issue a preliminary injunction enforcing the noncompete clause after a full hearing.

Return of the Chem Sheets and Pricing Information: Drugco can seek a TRO or preliminary injunction to obtain the return of the chem sheets and pricing information as well as to restrain Claire from violating the noncompete clause. At issue is whether a court may issue a mandatory injunction.

TROs and preliminary injunctions are not limited to restraining a party's action; a court may also issue a TRO or preliminary injunction ordering a party to perform an act (a "mandatory" injunction). The same factors that were discussed above regarding the noncompete clause would be examined. The chem sheets are highly confidential and contain the composition of each drug. If Claire is allowed to reveal this information, Drugco's secret formulas will be out, and it would be nearly impossible to get the genie back in the bottle once it was out. The same is true for the pricing information—it too is confidential, and revealing Drugco's secret pricing information to a competitor would put Drugco at a permanent disadvantage. Forcing Claire to return the information would not cause any apparent harm to her or the public. Finally, because state law recognizes trade secrets, it seems likely that Drugco would prevail on the merits of its underlying case. Therefore, the court would likely grant Drugco a TRO and/or preliminary injunction ordering Claire to return the chem sheets and pricing information.

QUESTION 26

Defendant is a political commentator and freelance journalist who moved from his home state of State A to State B approximately three years ago. Defendant has told his family and friends that he still considers State A "home" and intends to return "someday," but that "I'm happy in State B for now." Defendant votes, pays taxes, and owns property only in State B.

Defendant publishes an online newsletter called "Nothing But the Truth" that is accessible over the Internet from his website, *www.NBT.com*. Viewers can access *www.NBT.com* and download articles, but they cannot post their messages through the site. The central computer that people access when they view the website is located in State B.

The political commentary and journalism posted on the *www.NBT.com* website focus almost exclusively on people and events in State A—Defendant's old stomping grounds and the region where he is best known as a political reporter. Indeed, Defendant's website receives so many hits from people in State A that most of the advertisers on the website are State A firms seeking to attract customers who live in State A.

Plaintiff is a resident and domiciliary of State A who previously worked as a high-level State A government employee. In a recent story posted on his website, Defendant reported on rumors he had heard concerning Plaintiff's alleged acceptance of kickbacks for the award of State A contracts.

Shortly after Defendant published this story on his website, Plaintiff was dismissed from employment with State A. Plaintiff maintains that the allegations contained in Defendant's article about Plaintiff are patently false. Plaintiff contacted Defendant shortly after the initial publication, asking Defendant to retract the story. Defendant refused and insisted that he was protected by the First Amendment of the United States Constitution, even if the story was false, so long as he had not acted maliciously.

Plaintiff has filed a lawsuit against Defendant in the United States District Court for the District of State A. Her complaint alleges that the story published on Defendant's website defamed Plaintiff under applicable state law. In addition, the complaint asserts that the First Amendment does not shield Defendant from the defamation claim under these circumstances. The complaint alleges facts establishing damages for Plaintiff in the amount of $200,000. Convinced that Defendant acted maliciously, Plaintiff also seeks punitive damages in the amount of $1,000,000. The complaint alleges that jurisdiction is proper on both federal question and diversity grounds.

The State A long arm statute provides that the courts of State A may exercise jurisdiction over absent defendants to the "full extent permitted by the Due Process Clause of the United States Constitution."

In lieu of an answer to the complaint, Defendant has filed a motion to dismiss for lack of subject matter and personal jurisdiction.

1. **On what basis, if any, would a federal district court have subject matter jurisdiction over the lawsuit by Plaintiff against Defendant? Explain.**

2. **Would the United States District Court for the District of State A have personal jurisdiction over Defendant? Explain.**

ANSWER TO QUESTION 26

1.   The federal court here can exercise diversity jurisdiction, but not federal question jurisdiction. Two main issues are presented: whether a federal defense can give rise to federal question jurisdiction and whether the court should look at a party's actions or stated intent in determining in which state the party is domiciled for diversity purposes.

Generally, there are two main bases for federal court subject matter jurisdiction: federal question jurisdiction and diversity jurisdiction. A court will have federal question jurisdiction if the plaintiff's case presents a question of federal law. In determining whether a federal question is presented, the federal courts follow the well-pleaded complaint rule—the federal question must appear as part of the plaintiff's cause of action as set out in a well-pleaded complaint. Federal defenses—whether set out in the defendant's answer or in the plaintiff's complaint in anticipation of the defendant's answer—are irrelevant. Diversity jurisdiction exists where there is diversity of citizenship between the plaintiff and defendant and the amount in controversy exceeds $75,000.

Here, there is no federal question. Plaintiff's claim presents nothing more than a state law defamation claim. Plaintiff's assertion in her complaint that Defendant's website is not protected by the First Amendment, and Defendant's answer claiming First Amendment protection do nothing to change the nature of Plaintiff's claim—the First Amendment presents only a possible federal defense and is not part of a well-pleaded complaint for defamation. Thus, there is no federal question jurisdiction here.

The court may exercise diversity jurisdiction under the facts. The $75,000 amount in controversy requirement is satisfied, given that Plaintiff, apparently in good faith, is seeking $200,000 for compensatory damages and $1 million in punitive damages. There also is diversity of citizenship between the parties. Generally, a person is considered to be a citizen of the state in which he is domiciled—the place in which he is physically present with the intent to remain there (*i.e.,* no *present* intent to go elsewhere). The facts indicate that Plaintiff is a citizen of State A and that Defendant, while professing a desire to "someday" return to State A, owns real property, has registered to vote, and pays taxes in State B. Such facts indicate his *present* intent to remain in State B despite the vague intent to return to State A someday. Thus, for diversity purposes, Defendant is a citizen of State B. As a result, the complete diversity requirement has been satisfied, given that the action is by a citizen of State A against a citizen of State B. Coupled with the satisfaction of the amount in controversy requirement, this provides the federal court with subject matter jurisdiction based on diversity of citizenship jurisdiction.

2.   The court has personal jurisdiction over Defendant. At issue is to what extent commercial Internet activity subjects a defendant to personal jurisdiction in a particular forum.

For a *federal* court to have personal jurisdiction over a defendant, the exercise of such jurisdiction must be both constitutional and authorized by a *state* statute, given that a federal court analyzes personal jurisdiction as if it were a state court sitting in the jurisdiction.

Here, the "statutorily authorized" prong is rather simple to analyze, given that State A's long arm statute extends as far as the Constitution allows. In other words, if the exercise of personal jurisdiction over a defendant is constitutional, it falls under the long arm statute, making the constitutionality of the exercise of personal jurisdiction the only relevant inquiry.

For the exercise of jurisdiction over a particular defendant to be constitutionally permissible, the defendant either must be a citizen of that state or have sufficient contacts with the forum such that the exercise of personal jurisdiction over him would be fair and reasonable. If the defendant is a citizen of the state, or if the defendant is conducting substantial business within the jurisdiction such that the business should be considered to be a citizen of the state (*i.e.,* "doing business"), the court would have general jurisdiction over the defendant (*i.e.,* jurisdiction over all claims against the defendant). If the contacts are more isolated, the court would have specific jurisdiction over the defendant (*i.e.,* jurisdiction over a specific cause of action, and the cause of action must arise from the defendant's in-state conduct).

As discussed in 1., above, it is likely that Defendant would be considered to be a citizen of State B. Thus, State A may exercise jurisdiction over Defendant only if he has sufficient minimum contacts with State A and the cause of action asserted arises from those contacts. Although it is debatable whether the maintenance of a passive website (*i.e.,* one that requires no user input) would subject a defendant to personal jurisdiction in all states in which the website could be viewed, here Defendant has other contacts within State A that would make the exercise of personal jurisdiction over him fair and reasonable. Defendant maintained a website that targeted readers in State A with content that probably would interest only readers in State A and derived revenue from advertising space sold to businesses in State A. This active targeting of State A readers plus the generation of revenue from State A, should have led Defendant to reasonably anticipate being haled into a State A court. Note also that State A would have a strong interest in providing a forum for one of its citizens who was possibly defamed by Internet articles that targeted the state. Plus, the cause of action (defamation based on an Internet article) arises from the contact with the state (the maintenance of an Internet site that targets State A readers). Thus, it appears that a State A court (and thus a federal court sitting in State A) has personal jurisdiction over Defendant.

However, if the court were to decide that Defendant is a citizen of State A, a State A court would have personal jurisdiction over him for any cause of action (*i.e.,* general jurisdiction) based on that status. (A state court has general jurisdiction over its residents, and, as stated above, a federal court analyzes jurisdiction as if it were a state court sitting in the jurisdiction.) Of course, the *federal* court would then lack *subject matter* jurisdiction because diversity would not exist, but a *state* court in State A presumably would have both subject matter jurisdiction and personal jurisdiction.

QUESTION 27

Pat, a State A resident, was driving in State B when her car was struck by a truck driven by Driver. A sign on the truck's door read "Smith Brothers Transport Co." The police accident

report correctly listed Driver's name and license number, but mistakenly identified the truck's owner as Smith Brothers Trucking Company, Inc., instead of the correct owner, Smith Brothers Transport Company, Inc. Smith Brothers Trucking and Smith Brothers Transport are both owned and operated by Robert and William Smith. The two companies share office space. The Smith brothers are careful, however, to maintain the two corporations as separate and distinct legal entities, following all legal requirements to avoid any alter ego problems. Both companies are incorporated in and have their principal places of business in State B. Both companies identify Robert Smith as agent for service of process.

Two days before the deadline for filing suit under the applicable statute of limitations, Pat filed a proper diversity action in federal court in State B, alleging damages exceeding $75,000 against both Driver and Smith Brothers Trucking (the incorrect defendant). The summons and complaint were promptly served on Robert Smith, as agent for Smith Brothers Trucking.

Five days after filing the complaint and before any responsive pleading had been served, Pat's attorney realized that she had incorrectly named Smith Brothers Trucking as defendant. She promptly amended her complaint to name Smith Brothers Transport as defendant and served that amended complaint and an amended summons on Robert Smith, as agent for Smith Brothers Transport.

Two days later, Smith Brothers Transport moved to dismiss the amended complaint on the ground that the applicable statute of limitations had run before the amended complaint was filed. The court denied this motion and refused Smith Brothers Transport's request for certification of the matter as appropriate for an immediate appeal.

Following the filing of responsive pleadings, the judge directed the attorneys for all parties to appear before her for a pretrial conference to discuss the possibility of settlement. The attorneys for Pat and Smith Brothers Transport appeared, but the attorney for defendant Driver did not appear. Instead, Driver's attorney left a message for the judge, stating that he would not appear because Driver was not prepared to engage in settlement discussions.

The judge noted Driver's attorney's nonappearance and conducted the pretrial conference between the attorneys representing Pat and Smith Brothers Transport. The judge also ordered Driver's attorney to appear before her to explain why she should not impose sanctions on Driver for his attorney's nonattendance at the pretrial conference. Driver's attorney appeared and argued that he did not attend the pretrial conference because his client had no intention of negotiating a settlement and had directed him (the attorney) not to "waste my money" by attending. The judge, angry at this apparent disregard of her authority, ordered that Driver's answer be stricken and that a post-answer default judgment be entered against Driver.

1. Did the trial court err in refusing to dismiss the amended complaint against Smith Brothers Transport? Explain.

2. May Smith Brothers Transport immediately appeal the denial of its motion to dismiss? Explain.

3. Did the trial court err in striking Driver's answer and ordering the entry of a default judgment as a sanction for the failure of Driver's attorney to participate in a pretrial conference? Explain.

ANSWER TO QUESTION 27

1.   The trial court did not err in refusing to dismiss the amended complaint against Smith Brothers Transport based on the fact that the statute of limitations had expired before the amended complaint was filed. At issue is whether an amendment changing the defendant relates back to the filing of the original complaint.

Under Federal Rule 15(c), an amended complaint changing the party or the name of the party against whom a claim is asserted relates back to the date the original complaint was filed if the *amendment concerns the same conduct, transaction, or occurrence* as the original complaint and if, *within 120 days* (the time period for service of process), the party to be brought in by amendment has received *such notice of the action that she will not be prejudiced in maintaining her defense on the merits* and that she knew or should have known that, *but for a mistake concerning the proper party's identity, the action would have been brought against her.*

All of these requirements are satisfied in the instant case. The amendment does not allege new misconduct on the part of the defendant; rather, it merely changes the defendant's name from Smith Brothers Trucking to Smith Brothers Transport. Furthermore, Smith Brothers shares common owners and the agent for service of process (who also co-owns the companies). Smith Brothers was served with a copy of the original complaint within the period authorized for service of process. Additionally, given the fact that the amendment occurred only five days after the statute of limitations expired, and before Smith Brothers filed an answer, no prejudice to Smith Brothers could possibly exist—discovery has not yet even started. Finally, Smith Brothers, at the very least, should have been aware that the accident involved Smith Brothers Transport, and not Smith Brothers Trucking. Driver was Smith Brothers Transport's employee, and (one would hope) there should not be many accidents involving Driver, and mistakes concerning identity must be fairly common due to the common ownership and similar names.

Given that all the requirements of Rule 15(c) have been satisfied, the court properly denied the motion to dismiss based on the running of the statute of limitations.

2.   Smith Brothers Transport may not immediately appeal the denial of its motion to dismiss. At issue is whether a denial of a motion to dismiss based on the statute of limitations is a final order that may be immediately appealed, or whether such denial falls within the exception to a final order rule.

Generally, only a final order—an order that disposes of the entire case on the merits—may be appealed. In the instant case, the denial of a motion to dismiss is not a final order, given that the case continues on the merits. Some interlocutory orders may be appealed as of right (*e.g.,* an order relating to an injunction), but the denial of a motion to dismiss based on the statute of limitations is not among them. The trial court may also certify, as a discretionary matter, an appeal when there is a controlling question of law over which there is substantial ground for difference of opinion. However, the trial court refused to certify the issue, thus making the "discretionary appeal" path inapplicable. As a result, because the order is not final, and because no interlocutory appeal appears to be applicable, Smith Brothers Transport may not immediately appeal the denial of its motion to dismiss.

3.   The trial court probably erred in striking Driver's answer and ordering the entry of a default judgment as a sanction for the failure of Driver's attorney to participate in the pretrial conference. At issue is whether the trial judge may permissibly strike pleadings and enter a default judgment based on the party's failure to attend a pretrial conference.

Under federal law, a judge may hold scheduling conferences, and the judge may inquire into the possibility of settlement. For failure to attend the conference, a judge may impose a range of sanctions—including holding the party in contempt, the striking of pleadings, and prohibiting the introduction of evidence—against a party who fails to attend a pretrial conference. The imposition of a sanction should bear some relationship to the violation, and, on appeal, the decision to impose sanctions will be reviewed on an "abuse of discretion" standard. In the instant case, it does not appear that Driver's attorney's nonattendance was willful, in that he called the judge beforehand and explained that his client was not prepared to discuss settlement. Furthermore, at such an early stage, the entry of a default judgment appears to be a drastic remedy. Holding Driver in contempt, along with a possible monetary fine, might be the better means of getting across the point to Driver that it would not be a "waste of money" to have his attorney attend a mandatory pretrial conference. Thus, it appears that the judge in this case abused his discretion by imposing the drastic remedy of striking the answer and entering a default against Driver.

QUESTION 28

Transit Authority, Inc. ("Transit Authority") operates a bus system in Big City. Last month, a Transit Authority bus collided with a passenger car driven by Tourist. The accident occurred when Tourist suddenly veered into the bus operator's lane at a major intersection. The bus operator was unable to stop the bus in time to avoid the collision, and Tourist was injured. Immediately after the accident occurred, the bus operator telephoned his supervisor to report the accident. Then, following Transit Authority's standard procedures, the bus operator completed an "Operator's Report of Accident" form. The completed form included the date, time, and place of the accident, the road conditions, the names of witnesses, a brief description of how the accident occurred, and a description of the personal injuries and property damage caused by the accident.

When a Transit Authority supervisor arrived 20 minutes after the accident occurred, she took a statement from the bus operator and recorded that statement on a "Supervisor's Investigative Report" form. Then she interviewed Tourist and recorded Tourist's statement on the "Supervisor's Investigative Report" form. The supervisor noted all witnesses' names, addresses, and telephone numbers in her report. She took photographs of the accident scene, including the position of each vehicle. Finally, she drew a diagram of the scene on the last page of the "Supervisor's Investigative Report" form.

Tourist has filed a personal injury action against Transit Authority in federal court, properly invoking the court's diversity jurisdiction. Tourist alleges that the bus operator, Transit Authority's employee, was driving negligently. She further alleges personal injury and property damage in a total amount exceeding $200,000. Transit Authority has filed an answer denying the claim of negligence and asserting contributory negligence.

Tourist served two requests for production of documents on Transit Authority. One request was for "any and all accident reports, diagrams, photographs, and any other documents which relate in any way to the collision between the bus and the car." A second request was for the bus operator's "entire personnel file that is maintained by Transit Authority, including disciplinary actions, safety records, and driving records." Transit Authority has refused to produce the accident reports that the operator and the supervisor created on the grounds that the reports were "prepared in anticipation of litigation." In addition, Transit Authority refuses to produce the bus operator's personnel file because the information that it contains "is not relevant."

Tourist has made a motion to compel production of the accident reports and the bus operator's "entire personnel file."

Should Tourist's motion be granted in whole or in part? Explain.

ANSWER TO QUESTION 28

Tourist's motion should be granted in part. At issue is the discoverability of personnel records and accident reports compiled by a potential party.

Generally, discovery may be had of any matter not privileged that is relevant to the claim or defense of any party, including the identity of persons having knowledge of relevant facts. On a showing of good cause, the court may order disclosure of information that is relevant to the subject matter (not necessarily the claim or defense) of the lawsuit. However, work product of lawyers and others prepared in anticipation of litigation is discoverable only on a showing of substantial need and to avoid undue hardship in obtaining the material from other sources.

In the instant case, the "Supervisor's Investigative Report" clearly relates to the defenses of the Transit Authority because it will relate to the relative negligence of each potential party. Additionally, although the report was prepared immediately after the accident, it probably was not prepared "in anticipation of litigation" because no case had been filed at the time, nor is there any indication that litigation was threatened or that any impressions or trial strategy of the Authority's attorney was involved in making the report. Furthermore, even if it were somehow possible to conclude that the report is work product, Tourist might still be entitled to it based on substantial need, given that the photographs and interviews were taken shortly after the accident. It would be impossible to get those "fresh" items from other sources, as such items made so closely after the accident simply could not be re-created.

However, the bus driver's personnel file presents a somewhat different problem. As above, any parts of the personnel file that contain information that relates to Tourist's claim or Transit Authority's defenses must be disclosed. On a showing of good cause, the court could order disclosure of any information (*e.g.*, driver's safety record) that is relevant to the subject matter of the current litigation. Notwithstanding, the personnel file could (and probably does) contain information about the driver that is completely irrelevant to the pending case. The court probably will have to make an in camera inspection of the file and redact out any information that is irrelevant to the current litigation.

Thus, given that the "Supervisor's Investigative Report" should be completely disclosed to Tourist and that driver's personnel file may contain some relevant information that must be disclosed, Tourist's motion should be granted in part.

QUESTION 29

Al is a citizen and domiciliary of State A. While Al was visiting his parents in State B, he was involved in an automobile accident. Al's sports car was demolished in the accident, but he was miraculously unhurt. He returned to his home in State A shortly after the accident. Bert, a citizen and domiciliary of State B who was the driver of the other automobile involved in the accident, was not so lucky. Bert was seriously injured in the accident and was hospitalized for several weeks.

Shortly after Bert's release from the hospital, Al sued him in the federal district court for State B. Al's complaint properly invoked the court's diversity jurisdiction, alleged that the collision had been caused by Bert's negligence, and sought $90,000 in damages (the value of Al's demolished sports car).

Bert, who was uninsured and unemployed, failed to answer Al's complaint and did not defend the action, despite having been properly served and having received notice of the action. The court entered a default judgment against Bert for $90,000. The judgment was not paid, and Al took no steps to enforce it.

One year after the accident, Al died at his home in State A. His estate is being administered by Executor, who is a citizen of State B.

Bert recently filed a timely lawsuit against Executor, as administrator of Al's estate. The lawsuit, filed in state court in State B, alleges that Al's reckless driving was the cause of the accident and that Bert is permanently disabled by the injuries he suffered in the accident. Bert is seeking $3 million in damages from Al's estate.

Executor filed a timely notice of removal of the state action with the federal district court in State B. She then served the notice on Bert and filed a copy with the State B state court. She also arranged for copies of all records and proceedings in the state court action to be filed with the clerk of the federal district court in State B. Executor then filed a timely motion with the federal district court to dismiss Bert's case with prejudice on the ground that it was barred by the prior default judgment awarded to Al in his earlier suit against Bert.

Bert has filed a timely motion with the federal court asking it to remand the action to state court on the ground that the requirements for removal are not met on these facts. Alternatively, in the event the federal court retains the action, Bert has asked it to deny Executor's motion to dismiss.

1.   Was removal of Bert's claim to federal district court appropriate? Explain.

2.   If the federal court retains the action, should it grant Executor's motion to dismiss Bert's suit? Explain.

ANSWER TO QUESTION 29

1.   The removal of Bert's claim to the federal district court was proper. At issue is whether there is diversity of citizenship jurisdiction. Generally, a defendant in a state court action may remove an action that originally could have been brought by the plaintiff in federal court; provided that, for cases seeking removal based on diversity of citizenship, the defendant is not a citizen of the forum state. In the instant case, Bert could have brought the action in federal court under diversity of citizenship jurisdiction, which requires an amount in controversy of more than $75,000 and complete diversity of citizenship (no plaintiff may share state citizenship with any defendant). For diversity purposes, an executor is deemed to be a citizen of the decedent's former citizenship. In the instant action, Bert, a citizen of State B, is suing Executor, deemed to be a citizen of State A, for a claim for $3 million in a court of State B. Thus, the requirements for diversity of citizenship are present, and the "home state" restriction on removal does not apply. As a result, the removal of Bert's claim to federal district court was proper.

2. If the federal court retains the action, Executor's motion to dismiss Bert's suit would be granted. At issue is whether Bert's claim is barred by the compulsory counterclaim rule. In determining whether a subsequent action is barred by a compulsory counterclaim rule, the court will look to the law of the rendering state (*i.e.,* the preclusive effect of a judgment is determined by state law). Ordinarily, a state will not give a judgment more preclusive effect than a rendering state would. Under the compulsory counterclaim rule, if a potential counterclaim arises out the same transaction or occurrence as the plaintiff's claim, it is compulsory and must be pleaded or it will be barred. If State B follows such a rule, Bert obviously would have been required to plead the claim in the initial action. Even states that do not follow the compulsory counterclaim rule (*i.e.,* all counterclaims are permissive) generally prohibit a party from asserting a claim when the successful assertion of that claim would have the effect of rendering a prior judgment moot. In the instant action, if Bert were to successfully prosecute his case, it would have the effect of rendering the default judgment obtained by Al (now deceased) moot by re-determining liability and potentially subjecting Al's Executor to much greater monetary liability. Furthermore, the default judgment is a valid, final judgment on the merits. Given that the court in State B had personal jurisdiction over Bert (because he was a citizen of State B) and that he was properly served with process and had notice of the action, no grounds for vacating the default appear. The judgment thus should be considered a valid judgment. As it concluded the prior litigation, it is also final. Thus, no grounds appear for vacating the default, and it should be given preclusive effect. As a result of his failure to prosecute his claim in the first action, Bert will be barred from asserting the claim in the subsequent action, and Executor's motion to dismiss Bert's suit should be granted.

QUESTION 30

Plaintiff worked for Corporation. In her fifth year of employment, Plaintiff complained that she had been passed over for promotion to a management position in favor of a less experienced male colleague. Shortly after voicing her discontent, Plaintiff was fired. Plaintiff sued Corporation in federal district court alleging that she was fired because of sex discrimination in violation of federal law. Corporation filed an answer denying the material allegations of the complaint and alleging that Plaintiff was fired for inadequate work performance.

During voir dire, the court asked each prospective juror whether he or she had ever been a party to an employment discrimination lawsuit. None of the prospective jurors answered in the affirmative.

At trial, Plaintiff offered evidence to support her claim that she had been fired for discriminatory reasons. Her evidence included testimony by a former co-worker relating a conversation the co-worker had had with Plaintiff's supervisor. In the conversation, the supervisor reportedly said that women were ill-suited for managerial positions and that men did not like taking orders from women.

At the close of Plaintiff's evidence, Corporation moved for judgment as a matter of law ("JMOL"). The court denied the motion. Corporation then submitted its own evidence. The evidence consisted primarily of Plaintiff's employment records and testimony by Plaintiff's supervisor, who testified that Plaintiff's work had been rated unsatisfactory several times in the past.

At the close of all the evidence, neither party made further motions. After instructions from the court, the case was submitted to the jury. The jury deliberated for several hours and then returned a verdict for Plaintiff. The jury specifically found that Plaintiff had been passed over for promotion and fired as the result of sex discrimination and that she was entitled to backpay and reinstatement.

Two days after the entry of judgment, Corporation learned for the first time that the jury foreperson had previously filed and lost two employment discrimination lawsuits and that, upon learning she was part of the jury pool in this case, had said to a friend, "I'm going to get on that jury and stick it to Corporation. Somebody needs to teach these companies not to discriminate."

Eight days after the entry of judgment, Corporation moved for a post-judgment JMOL or, in the alternative, for a new trial. Corporation made two arguments. First, Corporation claimed that the evidence it presented at trial regarding the reasons for Plaintiff's termination was more persuasive and more credible than Plaintiff's evidence. Second, Corporation claimed that a new trial is required because of the jury foreperson's failure to disclose during voir dire her prior involvement in employment discrimination lawsuits.

The trial judge believes that Corporation's evidence at trial was more credible and persuasive than Plaintiff's. The trial judge also believes that Corporation's information about the jury foreperson's prior experiences and her statements to her friend is credible and suggestive of possible juror bias.

1. Was Corporation's motion for a post-judgment JMOL procedurally proper? Explain.

2. Without regard to its procedural propriety, should the trial court grant Corporation's motion for a post-judgment JMOL? Explain.

3. Should the trial court grant Corporation's motion for a new trial on the ground that Corporation's evidence was more persuasive and credible than Plaintiff's evidence? Explain.

4. Should the trial court grant Corporation's motion for a new trial because of the jury foreperson's conduct? Explain.

ANSWER TO QUESTION 30

1. The Corporation's motion for a renewed motion for judgment as a matter of law ("JMOL") was not procedurally proper, in that it raised new grounds in the motion. At issue is the motion's timeliness and whether new grounds may be raised in a post-verdict motion. Under the federal rules, the requirement that a motion for a judgment as a matter of law be made at the close of all the evidence has been eliminated, so long as the motion was made at some point during the trial. A party also is limited to the grounds raised in the initial JMOL. (In other words, a party is unable to "renew" an objection that was not raised in the initial motion, as there would be no objection to renew.) The party also must make the renewed motion for JMOL within 10 days of the judgment. In the instant case, this means that the post-judgment JMOL arguably was timely made, in that some JMOL motion was made during the trial and Corporation is still within the

10-day window. However, the facts also indicate that the basis for the Corporation's motion was that its evidence was more persuasive and more credible than that of the plaintiff. Obviously, given that the Corporation moved for a JMOL at the close of the *plaintiff's* case, the defendant had not yet presented any evidence. Thus, the post-verdict motion for JMOL raised new grounds—Corporation could not have argued at the close of the plaintiff's case that its evidence was more persuasive, because it had not presented that evidence yet. As a result, it would be procedurally improper to consider that argument after the verdict is reached, as Corporation attempted to "renew" a motion that was never presented to the court in the first place.

2.   Even if the motion was procedurally proper, the court probably should not grant Corporation's motion for JMOL. At issue is under what circumstance a court may overturn a jury verdict, given that Corporation's motion is based on its belief that its evidence is more persuasive and credible than Plaintiff's evidence. To grant a motion for JMOL or a renewed motion for JMOL, the court must find that a reasonable jury would not have a legally sufficient basis to find for the party on the issue. The court must view the evidence in a light most favorable to the nonmoving party and without considering the credibility of witnesses. The facts indicate that Plaintiff called a witness who heard Plaintiff's supervisor say that women were unsuited for management work. The facts also imply that Plaintiff submitted other evidence. Given the high hurdle that must be reached before taking a case from the jury, this evidence likely would be sufficient to defeat a motion or renewed motion for JMOL. As a result, even if the motion were procedurally proper, it should not be granted for the substantive grounds as described above. (*Note:* The juror misconduct would not be a reason to grant judgment in favor of the losing party; rather, a new trial would be the appropriate remedy, as discussed below.)

3.   The court should not grant a motion for a new trial on the ground that Corporation's evidence was more persuasive and credible than Plaintiff's evidence. At issue is when a new trial may be granted. Generally, a new trial may be granted because of some serious error that occurred during the trial (*e.g.,* an error in the admission of evidence, error in instructing the jury, the verdict is excessive, etc.). In theory, a new trial could be granted if the jury's verdict is a clear miscarriage of justice, but the judge may not replace the jury verdict with the verdict he would have reached. On the evidence of the case, it is not clear that a miscarriage of justice has resulted from the jury's verdict. Plaintiff must have presented some substantial evidence, because the judge refused to grant a motion for JMOL at the close of Plaintiff's case. As a result, the jury's verdict should not be overturned lightly, at least not because the judge believes the jury misweighed the evidence. Therefore, the court should not grant a motion for a new trial on the ground that Corporation's evidence was more persuasive and credible than Plaintiff's evidence.

4.   The court should grant the Corporation's motion for a new trial because of the jury foreperson's misconduct, both for failing to disclose her participation in two prior discrimination lawsuits and for having a bias against corporations. At issue is whether alleged juror bias and nondisclosure of information are grounds for a new trial. The rule for granting new trials based on juror bias or misconduct is essentially the same as described in 3., above. In the instant case, the jury foreperson failed to inform the court that she had previously filed and lost two employment discrimination lawsuits. This factor alone, without any other showing of actual bias, probably would have been sufficient to have her disqualified for cause. (It is unlikely that she could have put aside her two losses when hearing the same type of case without prejudging the matter.) The fact that she made statements to the effect that she was out to get Corporation further buttresses this position, in that her failure to disclose may have been outright lying rather than a mere oversight, which shows her unfair bias against Corporation. She also was the jury foreperson, giving her the position to

possibly influence the jury to an even greater degree. Given this taint, the jury's verdict may have been unfairly compromised, thus entitling Corporation to a new trial.

QUESTION 31

Guest, a citizen of State A, ate oysters at Ron's Restaurant in State B. Guest paid for the meal with a $50 check. Ron's Restaurant is owned and operated by Ron, a citizen of State B.

After eating the oysters at Ron's Restaurant, Guest ate an ice cream sundae at the ice cream shop next door, which is owned and operated by CreamCorp, a State B corporation with its principal place of business in State B.

An hour later, Guest became ill and went to a hospital emergency room. Guest had to be admitted to the hospital for several days of tests, treatment, and observation. Ultimately, the doctors concluded that Guest was suffering from a severe case of food poisoning. Guest's hospital bills exceeded $75,000.

Guest stopped payment on the $50 check to Ron's Restaurant before the check cleared and has not otherwise paid for the meal.

Guest sued Ron (doing business as Ron's Restaurant) in the federal district court for the District of State B. Guest's complaint alleged that the oysters she ate at Ron's Restaurant caused her food poisoning. Guest further alleged that her damages exceed $75,000, exclusive of costs and interest.

Ron doubts that the oysters were contaminated because no other patrons suffered an adverse reaction to the oysters served that day. Ron believes that Guest became ill because the ice cream served at CreamCorp's shop was made with unpasteurized milk. Thus, Ron has moved to compel the joinder of CreamCorp as an additional defendant in the lawsuit so that, if the jury concludes Guest became sick from the ice cream, it can render a verdict against CreamCorp and not Ron. Ron has also added to his answer a claim against Guest for the unpaid $50.

Guest objects to the joinder of CreamCorp. Guest has also moved to strike Ron's claim for the unpaid $50 from Ron's answer.

1. Should the court order the joinder of CreamCorp as an additional defendant? Explain.

2. Do the Federal Rules of Civil Procedure permit Ron to join his claim against Guest for the unpaid $50 to Guest's lawsuit against Ron? Explain.

3. If the Federal Rules of Civil Procedure permit Ron to join his claim against Guest for the unpaid $50, will the court have subject matter jurisdiction to hear that claim? Explain.

ANSWER TO QUESTION 31

1. The court should not order the joinder of CreamCorp as an additional party defendant. At

issue is whether CreamCorp must be joined as a defendant. The determination of whether a party must be joined is a three-step process: (i) whether the party *should* be joined; (ii) if the party should be joined, whether it is *feasible to join* the party; and (iii) if the party should be joined and joinder is feasible, whether the party *must* be joined.

As the first step, the court must determine if the party *should* (not must) be joined. Such a party is sometimes called a necessary party. A party should be joined if: (i) complete relief cannot be given to the existing parties in his absence; (ii) the disposition in the party's absence may impair the absent party's ability to protect her interest in the controversy; or (iii) the party's absence would expose existing parties to a substantial risk of double or inconsistent obligations. In the instant case, none of these three prongs are met. If the court or jury determines that Ron was the cause of Guest's illness, it will be solely liable to Guest, and Guest will be precluded from claiming that CreamCorp was the cause of his injury in a subsequent suit. If the court or jury determines Ron was not the cause of Guest's illness, Guest will have to seek recovery from CreamCorp; this will require Guest to prove CreamCorp's negligence. CreamCorp, not having had the opportunity to be heard on the matter, will not be precluded from relitigating any issues in the subsequent suit. Even if the court or jury somehow determines that Ron's and CreamCorp were somehow jointly responsible for Guest's illness, Guest may seek full recovery for either of the joint tortfeasors. For these reasons, complete relief may be given without CreamCorp's presence, and the disposition of the action will not negatively affect CreamCorp in any subsequent litigation. Thus, CreamCorp is not a necessary party, and joinder should not be ordered.

Given the determination that CreamCorp is not a necessary party, it is unnecessary to consider the next two steps: (ii) if the party *should* be joined, the court next must determine if it is *feasible to join* the party (*e.g.,* determine if the joinder of the party would destroy venue or jurisdiction), and (iii) if the party should be joined and his presence would be feasible, the court lastly must decide whether the party *must* be joined (*i.e.,* whether the court must dismiss the action or whether it can proceed without the absent party, looking at such factors as the prejudice to both the present and absent parties, whether judgment can be shaped to avoid such prejudice, whether the judgment will be adequate without the absent party, and whether the plaintiff will be deprived of an adequate remedy if the action were to be dismissed (*e.g.,* no other forum is available to hear the case)). If the court determines that it must dismiss the action, the absent party is sometimes called a necessary and indispensable party.

2.   Ron is permitted to join his claim against Guest for the unpaid $50 restaurant bill. At issue is whether a defendant may join a counterclaim he has against the plaintiff in the pending litigation. Under the federal rules, a defendant may assert any counterclaims he may have even if there is no relationship between it and the plaintiff's claim. Such a counterclaim is permissive. If the counterclaim arises out of the same transaction or occurrence as the plaintiff's claim, it is a compulsory counterclaim and *must* be pleaded or it is barred. In the instant case, the nonpayment of the restaurant tab will probably be viewed as a compulsory counterclaim, given that nonpayment likely was the result of Guest's illness. (Guest probably did not pay the bill because he became sick.) However, even if the claim is considered to be permissive, Ron may still join the claim as a permissive counterclaim. Thus, Ron is permitted to join his claim against Guest to the pending litigation, most likely as a compulsory counterclaim (but definitely as a permissive counterclaim).

3.   The court has subject matter jurisdiction over Ron's $50 claim. At issue is whether the court has diversity, federal question, or supplemental jurisdiction over the claim. Diversity of citizenship jurisdiction requires complete diversity of citizenship (*i.e.,* no single plaintiff may be of the

same state citizenship as any defendant) and an amount in controversy of more than $75,000. In the instant case, the facts state that Ron is a citizen of State B and Guest is a citizen of State A; thus, complete diversity exists. However, the $50 claim falls well below the $75,000 amount in controversy requirement. As a result, diversity of citizenship jurisdiction does not exist. Furthermore, no federal question appears to have been raised in the complaint, so federal question jurisdiction does not exist for the claim. However, a federal court has supplemental jurisdiction over claims that arise from the same nucleus of common fact. By definition, a compulsory counterclaim meets this definition. (If Ron is *required* to bring the claim, there must be supplemental jurisdiction for the claim.) As stated above, both claims arise from the meal that Ron served Guest; as such, they arise from the same nucleus of common fact. Thus, the court has supplemental jurisdiction over the claim.

QUESTION 1

Mark Hudson owns and operates Hudson Jewelers, Inc. Hudson Jewelers is an Illinois corporation, with its only place of business in Kaufman County, Illinois. Hudson Jewelers sells jewelry to retail customers.

Helen Tabb works as a sales representative for Precious Metals Wholesalers, Inc. Precious Metals Wholesalers is a Delaware corporation, with its principal place of business in Kaufman County, Illinois. Among other things, Precious Metals Wholesalers sells jewelry on a wholesale basis to a number of jewelry merchants.

On February 3, 1992, Helen Tabb visits Hudson Jewelers. Mark Hudson and Tabb discuss possible purchases by Hudson Jewelers from Precious Metals Wholesalers.

At the end of this February 1992 meeting, Hudson is convinced that he has entered into an oral contract with Precious Metals Wholesalers. Under this oral contract, Precious Metals Wholesalers would sell 200 gold necklaces to Hudson Jewelers. When Precious Metals Wholesalers delivered the necklaces, Hudson Jewelers would pay $50 per necklace. Precious Metals Wholesalers would deliver the necklaces by April 6, 1992.

On May 4, 1992, Hudson Jewelers has not received any gold necklaces from Precious Metals Wholesalers. On May 4, Mark Hudson phones Helen Tabb. During this phone conversation, Tabb asserts that Precious Metals Wholesalers did not enter into any contract with Mark Hudson or Hudson Jewelers.

On June 8, 1992, Mark Hudson files a suit in the Circuit Court of Kaufman County. Hudson's complaint names Precious Metals Wholesalers as the only defendant. Attorney Jack Eth represents Hudson in Hudson's suit against Precious Metals Wholesalers. The case is assigned to Judge Ellen Malone.

Hudson's complaint states a single cause of action, under the heading "Count I." According to Count I of the complaint: "Precious Metals Wholesalers did not deliver on an understanding reached by Hudson and Tabb on February 3, 1992." Hudson seeks $10,000 damages.

1.   In June 1992, Precious Metals Wholesalers files a timely motion to dismiss Hudson's complaint. According to the motion to dismiss, Count I of Hudson's complaint does not meet Illinois pleading standards. The motion to dismiss asserts: "In Count I, Hudson attempts to recover damages for a breach of contract. However, Count I nowhere uses the term 'breach of contract.' Instead, Hudson contends that Precious Metals Wholesalers 'did not deliver on an understanding.' Because Hudson has not described his breach of contract suit with the correct terminology, Hudson's complaint does not satisfy Illinois pleading requirements."

Should Judge Malone grant the motion to dismiss filed by Precious Metals Wholesalers? Explain.

2.   For the purpose of this part only, assume that Judge Malone denies the motion to dismiss filed by Precious Metals Wholesalers. In February 1993, discovery in *Hudson v. Precious Metals Wholesalers* has concluded.

On March 5, 1993, Precious Metals Wholesalers files a motion for summary judgment. An affidavit signed by Helen Tabb accompanies this motion. In her affidavit, Tabb states: "I never agreed to any contract with Hudson Jewelers."

Together with her affidavit, Tabb includes a copy of an orders worksheet. The orders worksheet is signed by Tabb, and is dated February 28, 1992. The orders worksheet records oral and written contracts that Tabb negotiated for Precious Metals Wholesalers in February 1992. No contract between Precious Metals Wholesalers and Hudson Jewelers appears on the orders worksheet.

In March 1993, Hudson Jewelers files papers in opposition to the defendant's motion for summary judgment. These opposition papers include a single affidavit. The affidavit is signed by Brad Rychner.

Rychner works as a sales associate at the Hudson Jewelers store in Kaufman County. In his affidavit, Rychner states: "On February 3, 1992, I overheard Mark Hudson and Helen Tabb agree to an oral contract. Under this agreement, Precious Metals Wholesalers would sell 200 gold necklaces to Hudson Jewelers, for a price of $50 per necklace."

Should Judge Malone grant the motion for summary judgment filed by Precious Metals Wholesalers? Explain.

ANSWER TO QUESTION 1

1. Under Illinois law, pleadings are to be liberally construed with a view to doing substantial justice between the parties. No pleading is bad in substance if it contains such information as reasonably informs the opposite party of the nature of the claim or defense that he is called upon to meet. Where any pleading is insufficient in substance or form, the court may order a fuller or more particular statement and, where the issues are insufficiently defined, a new pleading. Here, Hudson's statement is sufficient to inform Precious Metals that the nature of the claim is breach of contract. The court should not dismiss the complaint, but may order Hudson to file a more particular statement.

2. The court should not grant Precious Metals's motion for summary judgment. Summary judgment may be entered where the pleadings, information obtained by discovery, and any affidavits show that there is no genuine issue as to any material fact and the moving party is entitled to judgment as a matter of law. Affidavits in support of a motion for summary judgment must be made on the personal knowledge of the affiant and must state facts with particularity. Here, there is controverted evidence on material issues. Helen Tabb's affidavit states that she never agreed to any contract, and her supporting documentation shows that there were no written or oral contracts in February 1992. However, Brad Rychner's affidavit states that he overheard Hudson and Tabb agree to an oral contract on February 3, 1992. Thus, there is a genuine issue of material fact; the court should deny Precious Metals's motion for summary judgment.

QUESTION 2

[*Editor's Note:* **Portions of this question and answer dealing with the special appearance rules have been deleted due to changes in the law. For this question, assume that defendant**

Dan McKenna has waived any personal jurisdiction issue.] Phillips Freight, Inc., is an Illinois corporation. Phillips Freight sells trucking services to firms located throughout the midwestern United States.

White Insurance, Inc., provides liability insurance for Phillips Freight trucks. White Insurance is an Illinois corporation, with its principal place of business in Pagano County, Illinois. Under the insurance policy, in any single accident involving a Phillips Freight truck, White Insurance may be liable for a maximum amount of $500,000.

On March 6, 1994, a Phillips Freight truck becomes involved in an accident. The accident occurs in Cahill, Missouri. Cahill is located near the Missouri-Illinois border.

In the March 6, 1994, accident, drivers of three different cars collide with the Phillips Freight truck. These three drivers are Jennifer Booth, Lisa Winter, and Dan McKenna. Both Booth and Winter are permanent residents of Illinois. McKenna is a permanent resident of Missouri. Booth, Winter, and McKenna all suffer serious injuries in this accident.

In June 1994, White Insurance files an interpleader complaint in the Circuit Court of Pagano County, Illinois. The complaint names Booth, Winter, and McKenna as defendants. As of June 1994, neither Booth, Winter, nor McKenna has filed a suit against either Phillips Freight or White Insurance.

The interpleader complaint filed by White Insurance includes the following allegations: "White Insurance believes that the Phillips Freight driver did not commit any act of negligence on March 6, 1994. However, this court might conclude that Phillips Freight is liable to Booth, Winter, and/or McKenna. Should the court find that Phillips Freight is liable, White Insurance asks the court to determine the extent of the liability of White Insurance to each driver on the Phillips Freight insurance policy." White Insurance delivers a $500,000 bond to the clerk of the Pagano County Circuit Court.

Defendant Jennifer Booth files a timely motion to dismiss the interpleader action brought by White Insurance. Booth raises two arguments in support of her motion to dismiss. First, Booth asserts that White Insurance cannot maintain the interpleader action while denying that Phillips Freight is liable. Second, Booth argues that White Insurance cannot bring an interpleader action until each of the defendants has obtained a judgment in separate suits against Phillips Freight.

Should the Pagano County Circuit Court grant Booth's motion to dismiss? Explain.

ANSWER TO QUESTION 2

The court should deny Booth's motion to dismiss. Interpleader permits a party to join persons whose claims against him may subject him to multiple liability and require the joined parties to litigate between themselves the right to a single fund. The purpose of interpleader is to prevent double or multiple liability based on inconsistent judgments in separate lawsuits. The Illinois interpleader statute permits interpleader even if the plaintiff denies any liability. Thus, Booth's motion to dismiss will not be granted on the ground that White Insurance denies that Phillips, its insured, is liable. In addition, Booth's motion will not be granted on the ground that White

Insurance cannot bring an interpleader action until each defendant has obtained a judgment in separate suits against Phillips because the purpose of interpleader is to avoid multiple liability that may arise from inconsistent judgments in separate lawsuits. Thus, the court should deny Booth's motion to dismiss.

QUESTION 3

True Stories, Inc., is a Colorado corporation, with its principal place of business in Denver, Colorado. True Stories publishes *The World News*, a weekly sensationalistic newspaper. Among other things, *The World News* includes stories that claim to describe extraterrestrial life forms, ghosts, and strange diseases.

True Stories, Inc., sells *The World News* in 20 states, including Illinois. However, True Stories owns no real property in Illinois, maintains no Illinois offices, and does not employ any Illinois residents.

In Illinois, independent newsstand owners sell *The World News*. Each time a newspaper is sold, the newsstand owner receives a 10¢ commission. True Stories, Inc., earns about 10% of its annual revenues from Illinois sales of *The World News*.

On May 3, 1994, *The World News* prints a story, titled "The Fattest Woman in the World." The newspaper story describes Maureen Shields of Saunders County, Illinois. According to this story, Shields weighs more than 500 pounds. The story states that Shields "usually eats five steaks for dinner." The story also asserts that Shields will "devour any food in sight." The story includes a blurry photo of a very overweight woman. The May 3, 1994, issue of *The World News* is sold throughout the United States. This issue is sold in Saunders County, Illinois, and at other Illinois newsstands.

In fact, a woman named Maureen Shields lives in Saunders County, Illinois. Shields weighs about 135 pounds. She is perhaps 10 pounds overweight. However, Shields bears no resemblance to the woman described in *The World News* story.

As a result of the story appearing in the May 3 issue of *The World News*, Shields suffers severe emotional anguish. Shields becomes particularly distraught when friends and business acquaintances in Saunders County, Illinois, ask Shields if she is the woman described in *The World News* story dated May 3, 1994.

In August 1994, Shields files a suit in the Circuit Court of Saunders County. The complaint filed by Shields names True Stories, Inc., as the only defendant.

The complaint filed by Shields alleges a single cause of action for libel, an Illinois state law claim. According to her complaint: "Defendant True Stories published its inaccurate and misleading article about Maureen Shields with malice, and without regard for the truth. This story has damaged Shields's reputation. Because of the story, Shields has been subject to public ridicule." Shields seeks $45,000 in compensatory damages.

Kurt Darmenan is the vice president for operations of Defendant True Stories, Inc. Darmenan is a permanent resident of Denver, Colorado. In August 1994, messenger Mary Ann Velez provides Darmenan with personal service of a summons and the complaint filed by Shields.

As of August 1994, Velez is 20 years old. Darmenan receives the service at the True Stories headquarters in Denver, Colorado.

1. **Has True Stories, Inc., received proper service of process? Explain.**

2. **For the purpose of this part only, assume that True Stories, Inc., has received proper service of process. May the Saunders County Circuit Court exercise personal jurisdiction over True Stories, Inc.? Explain.**

ANSWER TO QUESTION 3

1.   True Stories, Inc., did receive proper service of process. At issue is whether Darmenan, an employee of the defendant, was properly served with process. Service of process is the act by which personal jurisdiction over the defendant is obtained. Illinois law provides for service on corporations by service on a registered agent of the corporation or any officer or agent of the corporation. Service on nonresident defendants outside Illinois is performed in the same manner as service in Illinois and has the same force and effect on nonresidents who fall within the long arm statute (*see* 2., below). Darmenan, as vice president for operations of True Stories, Inc., is an officer of the defendant qualified to receive service on behalf of the defendant. Furthermore, section 2-208(b) of the long arm statute provides that service of process may be made on an out-of-state defendant by any nonparty who is over 18 years old without any special appointment by the court. Thus, even though Velez was not appointed by the court, service of process by him was proper here. Given that service was made by an authorized person on a person qualified to receive process, True Stories has received proper service of process.

2.   The Saunders County Circuit Court may exercise personal jurisdiction over True Stories, Inc. At issue is whether the Illinois court has personal jurisdiction over the out-of-state defendant. Personal jurisdiction is the power of a court over a defendant's person and property. A court has this power if state law grants it and if the law is constitutional. Illinois courts may exercise personal jurisdiction to the maximum extent permitted by the United States Constitution. A defendant may be subject to two kinds of personal jurisdiction: (i) general jurisdiction gives the court power over the defendant as to any cause of action; and (ii) specific jurisdiction gives the court power only over causes of action related to the defendant's activities in the state.

Here, specific jurisdiction is available under the Illinois long arm statute. This statute lists 14 specific acts that give rise to personal jurisdiction over the defendant as well as a catch-all provision that permits jurisdiction on any other basis as long as it meets constitutional requirements. The constitutional standard is minimum contacts: the defendant must have engaged in such minimum contacts with Illinois that an exercise of jurisdiction would not offend traditional notions of fair play and substantial justice. The defendant must have availed himself of the benefits and protections of Illinois law such that he should reasonably anticipate being haled into Illinois courts. One of the bases for personal jurisdiction over a nonresident under the long arm statute is the commission of a tortious act in Illinois. Illinois courts have construed the phrase "tortious act" liberally. It does not matter where the tortious act was committed, as long as the injury occurs in Illinois. Thus, since Shields's claim alleges the commission of a tortious act, *i.e.,* libel, that arose from the sale of *The World News* newspaper in Illinois, and the injury occurred in Illinois, the requirements for specific jurisdiction under the long arm statute have been met. In addition, minimum contacts are satisfied because True Stories, Inc., could reasonably anticipate being sued in Illinois regarding the article about Shields, an Illinois resident, particularly since True Stories, Inc., sold many of its newspapers in Illinois.

QUESTION 4

Karen Probert and Daniel Grad are permanent residents of Jersey County, Illinois. In March 1995, Probert filed a complaint in the Circuit Court of Jersey County, Illinois. Probert's complaint named Grad as the only defendant.

The entire text of Probert's complaint read as follows:

IN THE CIRCUIT COURT
JERSEY COUNTY, ILLINOIS

KAREN PROBERT Plaintiff,	}	
	}	
v.	}	**No. 95-L-15**
	}	
DANIEL GRAD Defendant.	}	

COMPLAINT
The court has jurisdiction to hear this suit.

COUNT I
Daniel Grad promised to purchase a house owned by Karen Probert. Daniel Grad did not live up to his promise. Karen Probert suffered $75,000 damages.

Wherefore, Plaintiff Karen Probert prays for judgment against Defendant Daniel Grad in the amount of $75,000 and costs.

COUNT II
In his dealings with Karen Probert, Daniel Grad committed acts of fraud. Karen Probert suffered $75,000 damages.

Wherefore, Plaintiff Karen Probert prays for judgment against Defendant Daniel Grad in the amount of $75,000 and costs.

---

1. Does Count I of Karen Probert's complaint meet Illinois pleading requirements? Explain.

2. Does Count II of Karen Probert's complaint meet Illinois pleading requirements? Explain.

ANSWER TO QUESTION 4

1.   Count I of Plaintiff Karen Probert's complaint will probably meet Illinois pleading requirements. At issue is what information must be included in a complaint to fulfill Illinois pleading requirements.

Illinois is a hybrid pleading state. Unlike the federal courts, which require pure notice pleading (*i.e.*, the inclusion of enough information to give a party sufficient notice of a claim or defense), Illinois courts require a complaint to contain facts constituting a cause of action. Illinois courts will, however, construe complaints liberally in order to see that justice is served. In addition to requiring such "fact pleading," Illinois courts also require that a party include a specific prayer for relief.

In Count I of her complaint, Probert set out facts relevant to a breach of contract suit as well as a prayer for relief (*i.e.*, $75,000). Although she did not specifically state that the suit is one for breach of contract, Illinois courts may infer that that is the plaintiff's intention from the facts given. Moreover, because the "facts" standard is so difficult to administer, courts will allow some facts necessary to establish the elements of the action to be inferred from other facts and language in the complaint. In this case, the court is likely to find that the elements necessary for a breach of contract action have either been expressly stated or may be reasonably inferred and determine that Probert's first count is sufficient to meet Illinois pleading requirements.

2.   Count II of Probert's complaint is less likely to meet Illinois pleading requirements. Although Probert indicated the general nature of her claim (*i.e.*, fraud) and included a prayer for relief (again in the amount of $75,000), she failed to supply enough facts from which a court could either directly or impliedly find the elements necessary for a fraud action. The facts supporting a charge of fraud or conspiracy must be specially alleged in Illinois, and clearly, Probert has not done so in her second count. As a result, a court is likely to find that Count II is an insufficient pleading.

In short, Probert properly separated the two causes of action into two counts because each could stand alone if properly pled. Probert's first count is likely to meet Illinois pleading requirements, while the second count will not.

QUESTION 5

Chris Findley resides at 250 Norris Road in Swift County, Illinois. As of August 7, 1988, Findley will have been married for 10 years to his wife, Kelly Torres.

As an anniversary present for his wife, Findley decides to build an in-ground swimming pool at the couple's 250 Norris Road home. Findley and Torres plan to unveil the swimming pool at an August 7, 1988, party. The party would celebrate the couple's 10-year anniversary.

On June 8, 1988, Findley hires Jack McClellan to construct the in-ground swimming pool at 250 Norris Road. In a written contract executed on June 8, McClellan promises "to construct a 150 foot by 24 foot in-ground heated swimming pool." When McClellan has completed work on the swimming pool, Findley will pay $10,000 to McClellan. On June 8,

Findley gives McClellan a $1,000 deposit. In a separate oral promise made on June 8, 1988, McClellan states: "I will complete work on the pool by August 1, 1988."

On June 10 and June 11, 1988, McClellan digs a deep hole in Findley's backyard. But after June 11, McClellan does not return to Findley's property.

Findley leaves repeated and increasingly concerned phone messages on McClellan's answering machine. Findley finally talks with McClellan on July 8, 1988. In this conversation, McClellan tells Findley: "I've landed better paying work. Find someone else to build your pool." McClellan never returns Findley's $1,000 deposit.

On July 10, 1988, Findley hires Armstrong Pool, Inc., to build Findley's swimming pool. Charles Armstrong owns Armstrong Pool, Inc. When Armstrong agrees to build Findley's swimming pool, Armstrong tells Findley that the pool cannot be completed by August 7, 1988. Because the pool will remain under construction on August 7, 1988, Findley's house will not provide an attractive setting suitable for Findley's anniversary party.

Also, Charles Armstrong accurately observes that on June 10 and June 11, McClellan actually had damaged Findley's property. To repair this damage, Armstrong must undertake expensive landscaping work. As a result, Findley must pay Armstrong Pool, Inc., $15,000 to repair Findley's property and to construct the swimming pool.

On May 17, 1993, Chris Findley files a suit in the Circuit Court of Swift County, Illinois. Findley's complaint names Jack McClellan as the only defendant. Findley's case is assigned to Judge Robert Speidel.

Findley's complaint states a single cause of action for breach of contract, an Illinois state law claim. The complaint alleges: "On June 8, 1988, Jack McClellan agreed to build an in-ground swimming pool at Plaintiff Findley's 250 Norris Road residence. When he failed to build the swimming pool, McClellan breached this contract." Findley seeks $7,000 compensatory damages.

Plaintiff Findley wishes to present his breach of contract case at a bench trial, with Judge Speidel making all of the findings of fact and conclusions of law. Chris Findley does not demand a jury trial in his complaint, or in any other document.

McClellan files a timely answer to Findley's complaint. The first page of McClellan's answer includes the following caption: "Defendant Jack McClellan Demands a Jury Trial." This filing is accompanied by payment of the appropriate jury fee. Plaintiff Findley opposes McClellan's request for a jury trial.

1.   Should a jury hear Plaintiff Findley's suit? Explain.

2.   On August 16, 1993, Plaintiff Findley files a motion to amend his complaint. Findley's amendment would state a single cause of action for fraud, an Illinois common law claim. Defendant McClellan opposes Findley's motion to amend.

     Findley's proposed fraud action would allege: "On June 8, 1988, McClellan stated that he would complete work on Findley's in-ground pool by August 1, 1988. When he made this statement, McClellan did not actually intend to build the pool. Instead, McClellan intended to defraud Findley." Assume that a five-year statute of limitations governs common law fraud in Illinois.

     Is Findley's fraud action barred by the five-year statute of limitations? Explain.

ANSWER TO QUESTION 5

1. A jury should hear Plaintiff Findley's suit. At issue is whether a defendant in a breach of contract suit is entitled to request a jury trial in his answer to the plaintiff's complaint when the plaintiff has not requested a jury.

The right to a jury trial in civil cases is determined by the Illinois Constitution and Illinois statutes. Whether there is a constitutional right to a jury trial in a particular case is determined by whether the dominant issue in the case presented is legal or equitable; issues of law may be tried before a jury, while an equitable case will be determined by the court without a jury. The plaintiff in this case is seeking damages for an alleged breach of contract. As this is a legal issue, the case may be heard by a jury, provided a jury has been properly demanded.

A defendant must demand a jury not later than the filing of his answer or his right to a jury will be waived. [Code §2-1105] Here, Defendant McClellan included his jury demand in the text of his answer. He accompanied the request with the appropriate jury fee. Hence, Defendant McClellan is entitled to a jury trial. The fact that Plaintiff Findley does not want the issue tried before a jury will not affect Defendant McClellan's right to a jury trial in this situation.

2. Plaintiff Findley's fraud action is not barred by the five-year statute of limitations for common law fraud. At issue is whether an action is barred by the statute of limitations when the action is introduced as an amendment to change a cause of action that was originally set forth in a timely filed complaint.

The Illinois Code of Civil Procedure, section 2-616(a), allows a party to amend a complaint by changing the complaint's cause of action at any time before final judgment. Pursuant to this rule, Plaintiff Findley is allowed to change his previous action for breach of contract to an action for fraud. More significant, however, is the fact that under the Code, the new cause of action will not be barred by lapse of time under any statute or contract prescribing or limiting the time within which an action may be brought if: (i) the time prescribed or limited had not expired when the original pleading was filed, and (ii) the cause of action asserted in the amended pleading grew out of the same transaction or occurrence set forth in the original pleading. [Code §2-616(b)] Here, Plaintiff Findley filed his original action in a timely manner. Moreover, his amended cause of action arose out of the same transaction or occurrence as the first cause of action, *i.e.*, Defendant McClellan's promise to build the pool. In the breach of contract action, Plaintiff Findley alleged that the promise was breached by Defendant McClellan's failure to build the pool, whereas in the fraud action, Plaintiff Findley alleged that at the time Defendant McClellan made the promise, he did not actually intend to carry it out. Because both actions involved Defendant McClellan's promise to build the pool, Plaintiff Findley's amended cause of action is not barred by the statute of limitations. The fact that the original pleading did not allege certain elements of the new cause of action is irrelevant; the amendment to the pleading will be held to relate back to the date of the original filing.

QUESTION 6

Pat Weine, Tim Shute, and Herbert Perez are permanent residents of Elk County, Illinois. Weine, Shute, and Perez are neighbors who live on Halpert Avenue in Elk County.

On December 13, 1995, Halpert Avenue freezes and becomes very slippery. On December 13, Weine, Shute, and Perez are involved in a three-car accident. The three autos driven by Weine, Shute, and Perez collide at the same moment in time.

In January 1996, Weine files a suit in the circuit court of Elk County, Illinois. Weine's complaint names Tim Shute as the only defendant. Weine's case is assigned to Judge Pamela Whittaker.

Weine's complaint states a single cause of action for negligence, an Illinois state law claim. According to the complaint: "Shute's negligent operation of his auto caused Weine to suffer property damage and personal injuries." Weine seeks $200,000 damages. Assume that Shute receives proper service of Weine's complaint.

Now assume that in February 1996, defendant Tim Shute files a timely motion to dismiss. According to this motion: "Herbert Perez drove a car that was involved in the December 13, 1995, auto accident. The negligent conduct of Perez was in whole or in part the cause of the accident, making Perez a necessary and indispensable party to any suit arising from this auto accident. Because Weine's complaint does not name Perez as a defendant, this court must dismiss Weine's suit."

1.   Should Judge Whittaker grant the motion to dismiss filed by defendant Tim Shute? Explain.

2.   For the purpose of this part only, assume that defendant Tim Shute does not file a motion to dismiss Weine's action. Instead, Shute responds to this suit with an answer. In addition, Shute files a timely third-party complaint. Shute's action names Herbert Perez as the only defendant. Assume that Perez receives proper service of Shute's third-party complaint.

Shute's third-party complaint does not seek damages arising out of the December 13, 1995, auto accident. Instead, Shute's third-party complaint states a single cause of action for trespass, an Illinois state law claim. According to the third-party complaint: "Without obtaining Shute's permission, during 1995 Perez regularly would trespass across Shute's property to fish in a lake located behind the property. During these trips, Perez would trample Shute's garden of prize-winning tulips." Shute seeks a permanent injunction that would prevent any future trespass by Perez, as well as $10,000 damages.

May Shute maintain his third-party complaint against Perez? Explain.

ANSWER TO QUESTION 6

1.   Judge Whittaker should not grant Shute's motion to dismiss.

The issues in this problem are whether Perez was a necessary and indispensable party to the action and should be joined, and if so, whether his nonjoinder is grounds for dismissal.

In general, a party is necessary and indispensable if he must be joined for the complete determination of any cause of action involved. [Code §2-406] Failure to join a necessary party is not grounds for dismissal until reasonable time has been given for joinder, which may be permitted at any time. [Code §2-407] Unless a party is necessary and indispensable, joinder is permissive.

In this problem, Perez is not a necessary and indispensable party. Weine's complaint asserts negligence against Shute, and Weine can recover against Shute regardless of whether Perez was also negligent. Shute can always seek contribution or indemnification from Perez in this lawsuit or in a future suit. Accordingly, joinder of Perez would be permissive—not mandatory. Failure to make a permissive joinder is never grounds for dismissal. Accordingly, Judge Whittaker should not grant Shute's motion to dismiss.

2.   Shute may not maintain his third-party complaint against Perez.

Within the time for filing his answer (or later by leave of court), a defendant may file a third-party complaint bringing into the lawsuit as a third-party defendant any person not a party to the action who is or may be liable to the original defendant for all or part of the plaintiff's claim against him. [Code §2-406] The purpose of third-party practice is to permit the determination of the rights and liabilities of all parties connected with a transaction or occurrence before a single tribunal and upon the same evidence, thereby avoiding multiplicity of actions.

In this problem, Shute has not plead that Perez is or may be liable for all or part of Weine's action against Shute. Shute has merely asserted against Perez a wholly separate cause of action which involves a separate occurrence and entirely different evidence. Permitting Shute to bring this claim would unduly complicate the plaintiff's lawsuit and would not serve the purpose of avoiding multiple suits. Under these facts, Shute may not maintain his third-party complaint.

QUESTION 7

Singleton Publishing, Inc. is a Delaware corporation with its principal place of business in Hartman County, Illinois. Singleton sells college and graduate school textbooks. Singleton operates a printing facility in Hartman County.

At the company's printing plant, Singleton employs about 250 "production workers." Singleton maintains a personnel file for each production worker, which includes the employee's home address and telephone number.

Singleton employees typically work 40 hours each week. Singleton pays a production worker for each hour worked. Production workers frequently will work "overtime" hours, in addition to the standard 40-hour work week.

Each worker has signed an almost identical employment contract with Singleton. The hourly wage is the only term that varies in the contracts signed by different workers. Singleton workers with the most seniority and the highest skill levels earn the highest wage rates.

Christopher Saunders is a production worker at the Singleton plant in Hartman County. In February 1996, Saunders, by his attorney, files a class action complaint against Singleton in the circuit court of Hartman County. The complaint is assigned to Judge Janet Parrish.

The complaint states a single cause of action for breach of contract, an Illinois state law claim, and seeks compensatory damages. Singleton receives proper service of the complaint. According to the complaint:

> In its contracts, Singleton promises that each production worker will receive five times his standard salary for each "overtime" hour worked beyond the standard 40-hour work week. But during 1995, Singleton paid employees who worked overtime at straight time rates. In other words, a Singleton production worker who earned $10 per hour continued to make only $10 per hour for any overtime hours worked.

Plaintiff Saunders files a timely motion for class certification. Saunders seeks to certify a class of the 250 Singleton production employees who worked some overtime hours during 1995.

Singleton opposes the motion for class certification. In its opposition papers, the defendant states: "Singleton production employees worked very different amounts of overtime in 1995. If Saunders succeeds on his breach of contract theory, Singleton will owe damages to individual employees ranging from less than $30 to about $15,000." Saunders does not dispute the defendant's argument that if Judge Parrish grants class certification, members of the plaintiff class would assert widely varying damage claims.

If Judge Parrish grants class certification, Saunders will serve as the representative plaintiff for the class. Saunders graduated from a high school in Hartman County. While some members of the plaintiff class have graduated with college degrees, Saunders never has enrolled in a college course.

Singleton acknowledges that Saunders is a responsible and capable worker. Saunders is familiar with and understands the complaint. If Judge Parrish grants the motion for class certification, Saunders will devote significant time to the class action.

1.   Should Judge Parrish grant the motion for class certification? Explain.

2.   For the purpose of this part only, assume that in April 1996, Judge Parrish grants Saunders's motion for class certification. Saunders now proposes that he notify potential class members of the suit against Singleton solely by purchasing one-half page advertisements in the *Hartman County Register*, a local newspaper. The advertisements would inform Singleton workers of procedures for opting out of the action and of the consequences of failure to opt out. Under this plan, the advertisements would appear in the newspaper on four consecutive Sundays.

      Should Judge Parrish approve the notice plan proposed by Christopher Saunders? Explain.

ANSWER TO QUESTION 7

1.   Judge Parrish should grant Saunders's motion for class certification.

In Illinois courts, a class action may be maintained, and a party may sue as a representative of the class, only if all of the following requirements are met: (i) the class is so numerous that joinder of all members is impracticable; (ii) there are questions of law or fact common to the class and these questions predominate over questions only affecting individual members; (iii) the representative will fairly and adequately protect the interests of the class; and (iv) a class action is an appropriate (though not necessarily superior) method for the fair and efficient adjudication of the controversy. [Code §§2-801 - 2-806] The court determines by order whether the class action may be maintained.

In Saunders's action, all four of these requirements have been met: (i) Although there is no specific number beyond which a class is so numerous that joinder is impracticable, 250 is certain to be a large enough number to satisfy the first requirement. (ii) There are questions of law or fact common to the class, primarily whether each production worker signed substantially identical contracts promising overtime pay, production workers frequently work overtime, and production workers have not been compensated for overtime in accordance with the contract. Although the amount of damages may differ as to each member of the class, the common questions predominate in this action, because damages are of the same type and can be easily calculated (*i.e.,* monetary damages measured at five-times each worker's standard salary for overtime hours worked). (iii) Saunders will fairly and adequately protect the interests of the class. Saunders is himself a production worker at Singleton, so he is clearly interested in the outcome of the suit. He has demonstrated his willingness to protect the interests of the class by retaining an attorney, filing in a timely fashion, and properly serving notice to Singleton. Singleton itself has acknowledged that Saunders is responsible and capable. Furthermore, Saunders is familiar with and understands the complaint, and is willing to devote significant time to the class action. Clearly, Saunders is a person who will protect the interests of the class. (iv) Although there are other methods for adjudicating such a controversy, a class action is an appropriate method for the fair and efficient adjudication of the controversy. Considering that there are 250 people who may be able to recover damages under the same facts, other methods, including joinder or facing numerous individual suits, would be unnecessarily time consuming. The fact that all members of the class work at the same facility and can therefore easily become familiar with or involved in the action adds to the fairness and efficiency of adjudicating this action as a class action.

Because all of the requirements for bringing a class action are satisfied, Judge Parrish should grant the motion for class certification.

2.   Judge Parrish probably should approve Saunders's notice plan.

In Illinois, the court, in its discretion, may order such notice as it deems necessary to protect the interests of the class and the parties. Saunders's plan proposes notice on four consecutive Sundays in the newspaper of the county in which all 250 members of the class work. The notice would be in the form of a conspicuous one-half page ad, and would notify Singleton workers of the suit, the procedures for opting out, and the consequences of failing to opt out. Provided that most of the workers live in the county and the newspaper is widely read throughout the county, the proposed notice should be adequate. The notice will be read by a good number of the class members, and will surely be further communicated by word of mouth. Ideally, some form of notice would be distributed or displayed at the place of work, but this may be difficult because the place of work is the defendant. Individual notice to all 250 members would be costly and impracticable.

Because the interests of the class and the parties should be adequately protected by the notice proposed by Saunders, Judge Parrish probably should approve the notice plan.

QUESTION 8

Lake Hazem is located in Dale County, Illinois. According to legend and rumor, Lake Hazem is the home of the "Hazem monster." The monster reportedly is a large aquatic reptile, similar to extinct dinosaurs.

Rideout, Inc. is an Illinois corporation, with its principal place of business in Dale County, Illinois. Rideout, Inc. owns and operates the Rideout Inn. This hotel is located on a hill overlooking the shores of Lake Hazem in Dale County, Illinois.

Visitors hoping to spot the Hazem monster frequently stay at the Rideout Inn. The inn is the only business owned and operated by Rideout, Inc.

On November 11, 1994, 50 guests are lodged at the Rideout Inn. On the night of November 11, a heavy thunderstorm moves into Dale County.

During the storm, the ground slides out from under the Rideout Inn. One section of the hotel collapses. About 25 guests sustain injuries in this accident. According to a subsequent investigation, the foundation of the Rideout Inn was not constructed properly.

1.   Ken Mepthum is one of the Rideout Inn guests injured in the November 11, 1994, accident. Mepthum suffers a fractured spine. Mepthum is a permanent resident of Sosa County, Illinois.

   In January 1995, Mepthum files a suit in the circuit court of Sosa County. Mepthum's complaint names Rideout, Inc. as the only defendant.

   Mepthum's complaint alleges a single cause of action for negligence, a state law claim. According to the complaint: "Rideout, Inc. failed to exercise due care when the company built and maintained the foundation of the Rideout Inn. The corporation's negligence caused the November 11, 1994, accident." Mepthum seeks $1 million compensatory damages and $1 million punitive damages.

   Is the Sosa County Circuit Court a proper venue for Mepthum's suit? Explain.

2.   For the purpose of this part only, assume that Mepthum filed his negligence action in the circuit court of Dale County. In November 1995, Mepthum's action against Rideout, Inc. proceeds to trial.

   Rideout, Inc. vigorously defends against Mepthum's suit. Nonetheless, at the conclusion of the trial of Mepthum's case, a jury determines that Defendant Rideout was negligent in building and maintaining the foundation of the Rideout Inn. The jury awards Mepthum $500,000 compensatory damages, and $500,000 punitive damages. This judgment against Rideout, Inc. is affirmed on appeal.

   On November 11, 1994, Percy Hermitt also was a guest at the Rideout Inn. Hermitt suffered a broken arm in this accident.

   In January 1996, Hermitt files a suit in the circuit court of Dale County. Hermitt's complaint names Rideout, Inc. as the only defendant. Hermitt's action is assigned to Judge Robert Jayne.

   Hermitt's complaint alleges a single cause of action for negligence, a state law claim. Hermitt's negligence allegations are identical to the allegations stated in Mepthum's complaint. Hermitt seeks $100,000 compensatory damages.

   Now assume that Hermitt files a timely motion for summary judgment. According to this motion, the judgment entered against Rideout, Inc. in Mepthum's suit establishes as a matter of law that negligence by Defendant Rideout, Inc. caused the November 11,

1994, accident where Hermitt sustained his injuries. Hermitt's summary judgment motion asserts that Defendant Rideout, Inc. is liable to Plaintiff Hermitt.

Should Judge Jayne grant Hermitt's motion for summary judgment? Explain.

ANSWER TO QUESTION 8

1.   Sosa County is not a proper venue for this action. At issue is whether venue is proper in the county where the plaintiff resides when a defendant resides in Illinois.

Venue in Illinois is proper in (i) the county where a defendant resides, or (ii) the place where the occurrence which is the subject of the suit occurred. For purposes of venue, an Illinois corporation is deemed to reside in a county where it has an office or where it does business.

In this case Rideout has its office and does business only in Dale County. Also, the accident occurred in Dale County. Thus, venue is proper in Dale County, and not Sosa County. If no defendant resided in Illinois, venue would then be proper in any county.

2.   The court should grant Hermitt's motion for summary judgment on the issue of liability, but should allow Rideout to defend on the issue of damages. At issue is whether a prior judgment may be used as a "sword" by a stranger to the prior judgment against the same defendant. Summary judgment is appropriate when there is no genuine issue of material fact, and the moving party is entitled to judgment as a matter of law.

Collateral estoppel precludes a party and his privies from litigating the same issue which had been litigated in a prior suit and which was essential to the judgment in that prior suit. Collateral estoppel may sometimes be used as a "sword" by a stranger to the first suit, *i.e.,* a person not a party in the prior suit may use a judgment from that suit to establish the defendant's liability in her own suit. Although courts generally do not allow a prior judgment to be used in a subsequent lawsuit, the courts will allow it if: (i) the issue in the first case is identical to the issue in the second case; (ii) the final judgment in the first case was on the merits; (iii) the defendant had a full and fair opportunity to be heard on the critical issues in the first case; and (iv) it is not unfair to the defendant to follow the judgment from the first case.

In this case the issue of Rideout's negligence is identical to Mepthum's allegations, the final judgment was reached after the case was tried and appealed on its merits, and Rideout had the opportunity to vigorously defend itself in the first suit. Although fairness to Rideout in applying the first judgment is less certain, given the other factors the court would likely find that it was fair to enforce the judgment of liability on Rideout in the second case. Thus the court should grant Hermitt's motion on the issue of Rideout's negligence.

The court should not, however, grant the motion as to damages. The issue of compensatory damages should be tried to the jury. Hermitt's injuries are less severe than those of Mepthum, and Rideout should be given the opportunity to defend itself on the issue of damages.

QUESTION 9

Barco, Inc. is a Spanish corporation with its principal place of business in Madrid, Spain. Among other things, Barco manufactures propellers used in boat motors.

Rutherford, Inc. buys all of the propellers manufactured by Barco. Rutherford, Inc. is a British corporation, with its principal place of business in London, England. Rutherford sells parts for motors. Barco gives Rutherford no instructions about where Rutherford should sell the Barco propellers.

In 1995, most of Barco's propellers were installed in European boats. However, American boats use about 10% of the propellers manufactured by Barco. About 1% of Barco's propellers are installed in Illinois boats.

Barco officers are aware that some boats in the United States use Barco propellers. However, Barco maintains no United States offices and does not employ anyone working in the United States. Barco does not advertise its propellers in the United States. The company does not make any effort to sell Barco products in the United States. Further, Barco officers are not aware that any Barco propellers are used in Illinois.

Nygard Aquatics, Inc. is a Delaware corporation with its principal place of business in Toledo, Ohio. Nygard Aquatics manufactures and sells recreational boats.

Nygard Aquatics does not employ any Illinois residents and maintains no offices in Illinois. In 1995, Nygard Aquatics sold about 40% of its boats in Illinois. Nygard Aquatics officers are aware of the volume of the corporation's Illinois sales.

However, Nygard Aquatics frequently advertises its boats on Illinois television stations. Each month, Nygard Aquatics salesmen attempt to convince a number of Illinois boat dealers that they should purchase Nygard Aquatics boats. In addition, Nygard Aquatics displays its boats at the annual Illinois Sports and Boat Show. One week each February, the Sports and Boat Show is held in a Chicago, Illinois convention center.

Jerry Jacobs is a permanent resident of Salmon, Illinois. Jacobs owns a Nygard Aquatics boat. The boat motor contains a propeller manufactured by Barco, Inc. Jacobs purchased the boat in Illinois.

In June 1995, Jacobs is operating his boat on Mudcat Lake in Illinois. After turning the boat engine on, Jacobs checks the engine. While Jacobs is leaning over the engine, the Barco propeller detaches from the engine, flies out of the water, and strikes Jacobs on the head. Jacobs sustains serious injuries in this accident.

In August 1995, Jacobs files a suit in the circuit court of Neagle County, Illinois. The complaint filed by Jacobs names two defendants: Nygard Aquatics, Inc. and Barco, Inc. Assume that both defendants receive proper service of the complaint.

The complaint filed by Jacobs states a single cause of action for strict liability, a state tort law claim. According to the complaint: "When Barco made the propeller installed on the motor of Jacobs's boat, the company used defective steel. Proper testing by either Barco, Inc. or Nygard Aquatics, Inc. would have revealed this defect."

1. May the Neagle County Circuit Court exercise personal jurisdiction over Nygard Aquatics, Inc.? Explain.

2. May the Neagle County Circuit Court exercise personal jurisdiction over Barco, Inc.? Explain.

ANSWER TO QUESTION 9

1.   The Neagle County court may exercise personal jurisdiction over Nygard. At issue is whether such minimum contacts between Illinois and Nygard exist so that it is reasonable to require Nygard to litigate in Illinois.

To have personal jurisdiction over a corporation, the court must satisfy the personal jurisdiction requirements of Illinois, and the exercise of personal jurisdiction must be constitutional.

To satisfy due process, the court must find that there is a nexus between the state and the corporation, *i.e.*, that such minimum contacts exist so as not to offend traditional notions of fair play and substantial justice. The court must find that it is reasonable to require the corporation to litigate in Illinois. Also, the court must provide notice to the parties of the pendency of the action.

Illinois has four bases of personal jurisdiction: (i) consent; (ii) physical presence at the time of service; (iii) doing business in Illinois; and (iv) domicile or residence.

The court should find that Nygard was doing business in Illinois and that minimum contacts between Nygard and Illinois exist. Nygard sold 40% of its boats in Illinois in 1995, which would constitute regular, ongoing activity. Nygard was aware of this volume as well. In addition, Nygard advertised, marketed, and displayed its boats in Illinois. Given these factors, it would be fair and reasonable to require Nygard to litigate in Illinois, as minimum contacts between Nygard and Illinois exist.

2.   Illinois, however, cannot exercise personal jurisdiction over Barco unless Barco consents to personal jurisdiction or was present in Illinois when served. Applying the same test, Barco cannot be found to be doing business in Illinois, and the court will not find that enough minimum contacts exist to make it reasonable to require Barco to litigate in Illinois. Barco has no office or agent in Illinois, does not advertise or market its product in Illinois, is not aware that its propellers are used or sold in Illinois, and does not sell to Nygard, but to Rutherford, a British corporation. Although 1% of its propellers are sold in Illinois without its knowledge, this is not sufficient to establish minimum contacts so as not to offend traditional notions of fair play and substantial justice.

QUESTION 10

Amy Trout owns and operates Trout's Tropical Fish Emporium, Inc. Trout's Tropical Fish Emporium sells freshwater tropical fish and saltwater tropical fish for display in aquariums. Trout's Tropical Fish Emporium is an Illinois corporation, which maintains its only store and place of business in Salmon County, Illinois.

On May 15, 1994, Don Herring is shopping at Trout's Tropical Fish Emporium. While in the store, Herring slips and falls. Herring tears a ligament in his right knee. In order to repair Herring's injured knee, doctors must perform surgery on Herring.

On February 21, 1995, Herring files a suit in the circuit court of Salmon County. Herring's complaint names Trout's Tropical Fish Emporium as the only defendant. Herring's case is assigned to Judge Marilyn Pike.

Herring's complaint alleges a single cause of action for negligence, an Illinois state law claim. According to the complaint: "Herring sustained his injury because he slipped on a wet floor at Trout's Tropical Fish Emporium. By allowing the floor to collect water, Trout's Tropical Fish Emporium breached a duty of due care that the company owed to its customers." Herring seeks $50,000 compensatory damages.

1.   In March 1996, defendant Trout's Tropical Fish Emporium files a timely motion for summary judgment. According to the motion, a jury could not conclude that Trout's Tropical Fish Emporium was negligent on May 15, 1994, because the defendant had exercised reasonable care. The sole support for this motion is an affidavit filed by Amy Trout, who operates the tropical fish store.

In her affidavit, Trout writes: "On May 15, 1994, I was working at Trout's Tropical Fish Emporium. When I worked at the store, I always checked the floor for wet spots every 30 minutes. If I found any water on the floor, I immediately would mop and dry the wet area of the floor. On May 15, 1994, the floor was not wet."

In timely papers filed in opposition to the defendant's motion for summary judgment, the plaintiff relies entirely on an affidavit submitted by Don Herring. In this affidavit, Herring writes: "I hurt my knee when my foot suddenly slid on the floor of Trout's Tropical Fish Emporium. I fell to the floor. When I rolled over after hurting my knee, my shirt was covered with water from the floor of the tropical fish shop."

Should Judge Pike grant the motion for summary judgment filed by defendant Trout's Tropical Fish Emporium? Explain.

2.   For the purpose of this part only, assume that on May 14, 1996, Judge Pike denies the motion for summary judgment. After denying the motion, Judge Pike schedules a status conference for June 3, 1996. Judge Pike's clerk mails a notice of this conference to counsel for both parties.

Carl Bass represents plaintiff Don Herring. Bass maintains a one-attorney practice in Salmon County. In May 1996, Bass had moved his law office from 700 Marlin Avenue to 5 Muskie Lane. Bass had asked the United States Post Office to forward all of his mail from his old office to his new office. However, the notice of the June 3 status conference does not reach Bass at his new office.

When Bass does not appear at the June 3, 1996, status conference, Judge Marilyn Pike reschedules the status conference for June 10, 1996. In her notice describing the June 10 conference, Judge Pike informs Bass that if no plaintiff representative appears on June 10, Judge Pike will dismiss plaintiff Don Herring's case for want of prosecution.

The notice of the June 10 conference reaches the new office that Carl Bass had opened in May 1996. But when the letter arrives at the office, Bass is recovering from surgery at Pollack Memorial Hospital. On June 5, 1996, Bass required an immediate operation to remove his appendix. For this reason, Bass does not receive Judge Pike's notice until after June 10.

On June 10, no attorney representing plaintiff Don Herring appears at the status conference before Judge Marilyn Pike. Judge Pike enters a judgment on June 10, which dismisses the suit brought by Herring against Trout's Tropical Fish Emporium for want of prosecution.

On July 20, 1996, plaintiff Don Herring files a petition to vacate Judge Pike's June 10, 1996, judgment. Defendant Trout's Tropical Fish Emporium opposes the petition.

Should Judge Pike grant plaintiff Herring's petition to vacate the judgment dismissing his suit? Explain.

ANSWER TO QUESTION 10

1.   Defendant's motion for summary judgment should be denied. At issue is whether a genuine issue of material fact is before the court.

A motion for summary judgment should be granted if, based on the pleadings, discovery, and affidavits, there is no genuine issue of material fact and the movant is entitled to judgment as a matter of law. The motion may be accompanied by affidavits, which must be made on personal knowledge and should state facts with particularity.

In this case, defendant's motion is supported by an affidavit by Amy Trout, which states on personal knowledge that the defendant was not negligent and that it did not allow water to accumulate on the floor. Plaintiff's response is supported by plaintiff's affidavit, and alleges that there was water on defendant's floor which caused plaintiff to fall and become injured.

Since the issue in the case is defendant's negligence, and both affidavits contest the facts upon which the negligence claim is based, there clearly is a genuine issue of material fact in this case, and defendant's motion for summary judgment should be denied.

2.   Plaintiff's petition should be granted. At issue is whether plaintiff is entitled to equitable relief from a default judgment.

The court properly entered a judgment of default for want of prosecution when plaintiff failed to appear at two status conferences after the court had sent notice to the parties. A default judgment may be set aside on motion filed within 30 days of the final default order. However, plaintiff failed to file a motion to set aside the order within 30 days, and may seek equitable relief only.

A party may seek equitable relief from a judgment if he presents to the court facts which, if known to the court at the time of the judgment, would have prevented the court from such judgment. The party must show that under the circumstances the judgment was unfair. This remedy is not available to relieve a party from mere negligence or delinquency of the party or his counsel.

The party must seek relief through a petition supported by an affidavit, filed after 30 days but no more than two years from the date of the final order. The petition must show the grounds for the excusable neglect on its face and due diligence of the party.

In this case attorney Bass missed the first notice due to a failure of the post office to forward his mail. Assuming he was not obligated to notify the court of his new address, his failure to appear should be excused because he had never received notice. The second notice for the June 10 conference was not received until after June 10 because of Bass's emergency surgery. His second absence is excusable because the court would not have entered a default judgment against the plaintiff if it had known of Bass's illness. Assuming that the petition was supported by an affidavit, that no one was available at Bass's office to receive notice and appear on his behalf, and that

Bass exercised due diligence in filing the petition, the court should grant plaintiff's petition in the interests of justice.

QUESTION 11

Max Kimel is a permanent resident of Megan County, Michigan. On the night of April 3, 1995, Kimel is driving along Route 10 in his pickup truck. Route 10 is an unpaved road in Megan County. At one point, Route 10 crosses railroad tracks.

When he crosses the railroad tracks, an oncoming railroad train strikes Kimel and his truck. As a result of this accident, Kimel suffers serious injuries.

Montgomery and West Railroad, Inc. ("Railroad"), operates the train that hit Kimel. Railroad is a Delaware corporation, with its principal place of business in Minneapolis, Minnesota. Railroad maintains permanent regional offices in Megan County, Michigan, and Smith County, Illinois.

Because drivers rarely use Route 10, Megan County has not installed warning lights or a crossing guard where the unpaved road crosses Railroad's tracks. Max Kimel contends that just before his April 3, 1995, accident, Kimel had no notice that a train was approaching. Although the accident occurred at night, Kimel asserts that Railroad's train had not illuminated any of its exterior lights. Also, according to Kimel, Railroad's train did not sound a horn before approaching the intersection with Route 10. In defending this suit, Railroad will argue that Kimel easily could have seen the approaching train from Route 10.

On July 6, 1995, Kimel files a complaint in the circuit court of Smith County, Illinois. Kimel's complaint names Railroad as the only defendant. Kimel's suit is assigned to Judge Beth Biagas. The Smith County Circuit Court possesses personal jurisdiction over defendant Railroad. Also, assume that Smith County is a proper venue for Kimel's suit.

Kimel's complaint alleges a single cause of action for negligence. According to the complaint: "On April 3, 1995, employees operating Railroad's train failed to exercise reasonable care as the train approached the intersection with Route 10 in Megan County, Michigan. As a result of this negligence, the train collided with a pickup truck driven by Max Kimel." Both plaintiff Kimel and defendant Railroad agree that Michigan law governs Kimel's negligence action. Kimel seeks $1 million damages.

At a trial of Kimel's suit, plaintiff Kimel and defendant Railroad each primarily would rely on the testimony of two witnesses. Kimel will testify in support of his case. Kimel's attorney also plans to call Dr. Lisa Feigin as a witness. After the April 3 accident, Dr. Feigin treated Kimel at Goldman Memorial Hospital. The hospital is located in Megan County, Michigan. Dr. Feigin is a permanent resident of Megan County.

Defendant Railroad plans to call Eleanor Malone as a witness. On April 3, 1995, Malone was driving the train that hit Kimel's truck. Malone will testify that she used reasonable care in approaching the intersection of Railroad's tracks and Route 10.

Keith Diamond also will testify on behalf of Railroad. Diamond is a manager of Railroad's regional office in Megan County. Diamond is familiar with train routes passing through Megan County. Diamond will testify that from Route 10, Kimel should have seen the approaching train. Both Malone and Diamond are permanent residents of Megan County, Michigan.

The average civil case filed in the Circuit Court of Smith County, Illinois, is resolved in 18 months. The average case filed in the Megan County, Michigan, state courts is resolved in 17 months.

Now assume that defendant Railroad files a timely motion to dismiss based on the doctrine of forum non conveniens. According to this motion, the Michigan state courts located in Megan County would provide a more convenient forum for plaintiff Kimel's suit than the circuit court of Smith County. Both plaintiff Kimel and defendant Railroad agree that the Michigan state courts would possess subject matter jurisdiction over Kimel's suit and personal jurisdiction over defendant Railroad.

Should Judge Biagas grant the motion to dismiss? Explain.

ANSWER TO QUESTION 11

Defendant's motion to dismiss for forum non conveniens should be granted. At issue is whether another forum is more convenient to the parties.

A motion to dismiss for forum non conveniens is granted when a case is properly filed in one forum, but another forum is more convenient for the parties. Although Illinois courts generally favor the plaintiff's choice of forum, the courts will grant the motion if the balance of factors favors trying the case in another forum. Also, the courts will usually grant the motion if the parties have no relationship with Illinois or property in Illinois.

The factors which the court considers include: the plaintiff's interest in Illinois; inconvenience to the defendant in trying the case in Illinois; public interest of Illinois citizens in the case; which forum has greater access to the evidence; enforceability of a judgment by Illinois courts; which forum's laws apply; and congestion in the court systems.

In this case, the plaintiff is a resident of Megan County, Michigan, and the defendant has permanent offices in Megan County. The accident occurred in Megan County, and the four key witnesses all reside in Megan County. Michigan law will be applied to this case as well. Also, the Megan County court system is slightly less congested than in the Smith County courts. Given all these factors, it is clear that it will be more convenient for all the parties to try the case in Megan County and that the parties have little or no relationship to Illinois. Thus the motion to dismiss should be granted.

The motion is granted with two conditions, however. First, if the plaintiff files his case within six months in another forum, the defendant must accept service of process. Second, if the plaintiff files his case within six months, and the statute of limitations in the other forum has expired, the defendant must waive the statute of limitations defense.

QUESTION 12

George O'Leary is a permanent resident of Willard County, Illinois. On January 13, 1997, O'Leary is involved in a three-car accident. O'Leary suffers serious injuries in this accident.

Sarah Flynn and Martin Gershon are the other drivers involved in the January 1997 accident. Like O'Leary, Flynn and Gershon are permanent residents of Willard County.

On March 3, 1997, O'Leary files a suit in the Circuit Court of Willard County. O'Leary's complaint names "Sarah Flint" as the only defendant. The case is assigned to Judge Karen Torres.

O'Leary's complaint states a single cause of action for negligence, an Illinois state law claim. The complaint alleges that the defendant failed to exercise reasonable care, and that the defendant's actions caused the accident where O'Leary sustained his injuries. O'Leary seeks $100,000 compensatory damages.

1.   Now assume that defendant Sarah Flynn files a motion to dismiss O'Leary's complaint. Flynn was properly served with a summons and a copy of O'Leary's complaint. But throughout his complaint, O'Leary inaccurately identifies defendant Sarah Flynn as "Sarah Flint." Flynn argues that, as a result of this error, O'Leary's complaint does not meet Illinois pleading requirements.

Should Judge Karen Torres dismiss George O'Leary's complaint, because O'Leary has not satisfied Illinois pleading requirements? Explain.

2.   For the purpose of this part only, assume that the motion filed by defendant Sarah Flynn states an alternative argument for dismissing O'Leary's complaint. Flynn notes that in his complaint, O'Leary has not named Martin Gershon as a defendant. Gershon was the third driver involved in the January 1997 accident that included O'Leary and Flynn.

Flynn argues that Gershon is a necessary and indispensable party to the case filed by O'Leary, because "through his negligent conduct, Gershon was at least in part responsible for the January 13 accident." Flynn concludes that the Illinois court must dismiss O'Leary's complaint, because O'Leary has failed to name Martin Gershon as a defendant.

Should Judge Karen Torres dismiss George O'Leary's complaint, because O'Leary has not named Martin Gershon as a defendant? Explain.

ANSWER TO QUESTION 12

1.   Judge Torres should not dismiss the complaint based on failure to satisfy the pleading requirements of Illinois. Generally, a plaintiff may correct a "misnomer" of a party at any time. [Code §2-401(a), (b)] A "misnomer" occurs when the plaintiff intends to sue and serve the correct party in a correct capacity, but somehow incorrectly names that defendant in the complaint or summons—a typographical error is a "classic" example. Note that a "misnomer" is not the same situation as when the plaintiff intends to sue a party against whom he has no cause of action, but somehow serves the correct defendant with process—intending to sue a corporation that is in fact an individual doing business as a sole proprietor, and then serving the individual, is a "classic" example. Here, there is clearly a misnomer. The plaintiff intended to sue Sarah Flynn in her capacity as an individual, although he incorrectly named Flynn as "Flint." Thus, the plaintiff should be allowed to amend the complaint to read "Flynn" rather than "Flint," and the motion to dismiss should be denied.

2.   Judge Torres should not dismiss O'Leary's complaint. At issue is whether the failure to name all persons potentially liable as defendants defeats a cause of action. O'Leary may join Gershon as a new party by order of the court, or Flynn may file a third-party complaint against Gershon.

Joinder is mandatory if a person is necessary and indispensable to the cause of action and must be joined to satisfy due process, *e.g.,* when the determination of a case would affect the person's rights in property, and due process dictates that the person be given an opportunity to represent his interests. However, joinder is permissive if the person is alleged to be liable to one or more parties because of the same occurrence which is the subject of the suit. [Code §2-405(a)] Because Gershon's interests are not directly affected by a determination of the suit against Flynn, joinder of Gershon is permissive. If O'Leary moves to join Gershon as a defendant, the court will likely grant his motion in the interests of efficiency. Even if Gershon were a necessary and indispensable party, Judge Torres may not dismiss O'Leary's complaint for nonjoinder without giving him a reasonable opportunity to add Gershon as a new party. [Code §2-407]

Flynn may file a third-party complaint against Gershon, alleging that Gershon is liable to her for all or part of O'Leary's claim against her. [Code §2-406] A third-party complaint may be filed as a matter of right within the time for answering the complaint, or by leave of court if the time for answering has passed. [Code §2-406(b)] The court is likely to allow a third-party complaint if it will permit the determination of the rights and liabilities of all the parties connected with a transaction or occurrence before a single tribunal on the same evidence, thereby avoiding a multiplicity of actions. If Flynn files a third-party complaint, O'Leary may amend his complaint to assert claims against Gershon.

In this case, Gershon may be partially liable to the other parties in the accident, so it would be most efficient to make him a party to the action, either by permissive joinder or as a third-party defendant. However, failure to name Gershon in the complaint is not a ground to dismiss the complaint.

QUESTION 13

Barbara Lochmiller and Erica Scanlon are permanent residents of Calvin County, Illinois. On January 11, 1992, Lochmiller and Scanlon attend a party at Lochmiller's second-floor apartment in Calvin County.

During the January 11 party, Lochmiller and Scanlon lean against a railing on the landing outside of Lochmiller's apartment. The railing breaks. Lochmiller and Scanlon fall down a stairway in the apartment building.

In this accident, Lochmiller suffers a broken left knee. As a result of her fall, Scanlon sustains several cuts and bruises.

Berexa Metals, Inc. manufactured the broken stairway railing. Berexa Metals is an Illinois corporation, with its principal place of business in Rizza County, Illinois.

On December 27, 1992, Lochmiller and Scanlon file a single complaint with the Circuit Court of Rizza County, Illinois. The complaint names Berexa Metals as the only defendant. The case filed by Lochmiller and Scanlon is assigned to Judge Sharon Herilla.

In their complaint, Lochmiller and Scanlon allege a single cause of action for strict liability, an Illinois state law claim. According to the complaint: "Berexa Metals relied on an unreasonably dangerous design when the company constructed the stairway railing that was used outside of plaintiff Barbara Lochmiller's apartment."

1.   In response to the complaint filed by Lochmiller and Scanlon, defendant Berexa Metals, Inc. submits a timely motion to dismiss. In its motion, Berexa Metals asserts that Lochmiller and Scanlon cannot file a single complaint. According to Berexa Metals, Lochmiller and Scanlon could pursue their claims against the company only in two independent suits.

      Should Judge Herilla grant the motion to dismiss filed by Berexa Metals? Explain.

2.   For the purpose of this part only, assume that Judge Herilla denies the motion to dismiss filed by Berexa Metals.

      Now assume that on November 2, 1994, Lochmiller moves to amend the complaint that she has filed together with Scanlon. Lochmiller alleges that on August 7, 1991, she was involved in a Calvin County auto accident. Lochmiller's auto was hit by a truck. Lochmiller suffered a back injury in this auto accident.

      Coincidentally, defendant Berexa Metals, Inc. owned the truck that hit Lochmiller. In her motion to amend, Lochmiller seeks to add a negligence action to the December 27, 1992, complaint filed by Lochmiller and Scanlon.

      Berexa Metals is the only defendant named in Lochmiller's negligence action. Lochmiller alleges that the August 1991 auto accident "was caused by negligence on the part of the Berexa Metals employee who was driving the company's truck." Lochmiller seeks to recover compensatory damages for her injuries in the auto accident.

      Should Judge Sharon Herilla grant Lochmiller's motion to amend? Explain.

ANSWER TO QUESTION 13

1.   Judge Herilla should not grant the motion to dismiss. At issue is whether plaintiffs may join their causes of action against a defendant when the causes of action arise from the same transaction or occurrence.

Two or more plaintiffs may join their causes of action when separate trials would be essentially the same other than on the issue of damages. [Code §2-404] Two conditions must be satisfied: (i) the right to relief of each plaintiff must arise out of the same event; and (ii) separate actions brought by the plaintiffs would raise common questions of law or fact.

In this case, the injuries suffered by Lochmiller and Scanlon resulted from the same accident in which the railing manufactured by the defendant broke. The claim is based on strict liability, and two separate trials would be virtually identical except on the issue of damages. Thus, Lochmiller and Scanlon may join as plaintiffs against the defendant.

2.   Judge Herilla should not grant Lochmiller's motion to amend. The issue is when a plaintiff may amend her complaint to add an additional cause of action after the statute of limitations has run for the additional claim.

Illinois courts allow great latitude in amending pleadings. [Code §2-616(a)] Amendments to the pleadings may be made anytime prior to final judgment on just and reasonable terms. [Code §2-616(c)] A claim barred by the statute of limitations still may be added to the original complaint if it relates back to the original complaint. [Code §2-616(b)] In order to amend after the statute of limitations has run, two conditions must be met: (i) the original pleading was filed on time; and (ii) the added claim arose from the same transaction or occurrence.

In this case, the original complaint was timely filed, and Lochmiller's additional claim is barred by the two-year statute of limitations. Because her second claim arose from a different accident, it does not relate back to the original pleading. Lochmiller's claim arising from the 1991 car accident is therefore barred, and the motion to amend should be denied.

QUESTION 14

Carl Reuter is a permanent resident of Pole County, Illinois. In July 1997, Reuter files a complaint in the Circuit Court of Baker County, Illinois.

Reuter's complaint names Tavarez Homes, Inc. as the only defendant. Tavarez Homes is an Illinois corporation, with its principal place of business in Baker County, Illinois.

Reuter's complaint states a single cause of action. The complaint alleges that when defendant Tavarez Homes constructed a house for plaintiff Reuter at 30 Hamilton Street the defendant breached the implied warranty of habitability, a state law claim. Reuter's complaint alleges: "When plaintiff Carl Reuter moved into the house at 30 Hamilton Street constructed by defendant Tavarez Homes the plumbing in the house did not function. Reuter found that he could not bring any running water into the house." Plaintiff Carl Reuter seeks $50,000 compensatory damages.

1.   **In July 1997, defendant Tavarez Homes files a timely answer to plaintiff Reuter's complaint. Together with this answer, Tavarez Homes files a third-party complaint against Darwin Copper, Inc. Darwin Copper is a Delaware corporation, with its principal place of business in Baker County, Illinois.**

The third-party complaint filed by Tavarez Homes states a single cause of action for breach of contract, an Illinois state law claim. The third-party complaint alleges: "Darwin Copper sold copper pipe to Tavarez Homes, pursuant to a written sales contract. Tavarez Homes planned to install the copper pipe in a house at 30 Hamilton Street, which Tavarez Homes was building for Carl Reuter. However, the pipe provided by Darwin Copper was defective and did not conform to specifications in the sales contract." Tavarez Homes alleges that as a result of this breach of contract, "Darwin Copper is liable to Tavarez Homes for any damages that Tavarez Homes must pay to plaintiff Carl Reuter."

In response to the third-party complaint filed by Tavarez Homes, Darwin Copper files a motion to dismiss. This motion asserts that Tavarez Homes cannot maintain its breach of contract action against Darwin Copper as a third-party complaint. The

motion concludes that if Tavarez Homes wishes to sue Darwin Copper for a breach of contract, Tavarez Homes must initiate a new case.

Should the court grant the motion to dismiss filed by Darwin Copper? Explain.

2. In September 1997, Tavarez Homes, Inc. files a suit against Carl Reuter in the Circuit Court of Pole County, Illinois.

The complaint filed by Tavarez Homes alleges a single cause of action for breach of contract, an Illinois state law claim. The complaint alleges: "Tavarez Homes constructed a house for Carl Reuter at 30 Hamilton Street. Under the contract between Reuter and Tavarez Homes, as of July 1, 1997, Reuter owed Tavarez Homes $100,000. Reuter has not yet made this $100,000 payment." Tavarez Homes seeks $100,000 compensatory damages.

In response to the Pole County suit filed by plaintiff Tavarez Homes, defendant Carl Reuter files a motion for summary judgment. In this motion, Reuter asserts that Tavarez Homes should have brought its breach of contract action as a compulsory counterclaim to Reuter's July 1997 suit against Tavarez Homes, filed in Baker County. Reuter's motion concludes that Tavarez Homes may raise the breach of contract action only as a counterclaim in Reuter's earlier suit, and that Tavarez Homes cannot maintain its Pole County suit.

Should the court grant the motion for summary judgment filed by defendant Carl Reuter? Explain.

ANSWER TO QUESTION 14

1. Darwin Copper's motion to dismiss should be denied. At issue is whether a defendant may file a third-party complaint against a nonparty who may be liable to the defendant in the pending action.

A defendant may bring a third-party complaint against any person not a party to the original action who is or may be liable to the defendant for all or part of the plaintiff's claim. The third-party complaint may be filed as a matter of right within the time for answering the complaint. [Code §2-406(b)] The purpose of the third-party complaint is to avoid multiplicity of actions and to determine the rights and liabilities of all parties connected with a transaction or occurrence on the same evidence before a single tribunal.

In this case, the original complaint against Tavarez Homes, Inc. ("Tavarez") alleges that the house built for Carl Reuter ("Reuter") had no functioning plumbing. Tavarez's third-party complaint against Darwin Copper, Inc. ("Darwin") alleges that the pipe installed in Reuter's house was provided to Tavarez by Darwin, and that Darwin failed to meet the specifications in the sales contract with Tavarez. Thus, both the complaint and the third-party complaint arise from the issue of liability for the malfunctioning plumbing in Reuter's house. Since Darwin provided to Tavarez the pipe for Reuter's house, Darwin may be liable to Tavarez for part or all of any judgment Reuter may collect from Tavarez. Trying Tavarez's case against Darwin in a separate action would be inefficient as it would involve much of the same evidence as Reuter's case against Tavarez. Also, Tavarez filed its third-party complaint within the time for answering Reuter's complaint.

Therefore, since Darwin may be liable for part or all of the judgment against Tavarez and the third-party complaint was timely filed, Darwin's motion to dismiss should be denied.

2.   The court should deny Reuter's motion for summary judgment. At issue is whether the plaintiff is entitled to judgment as a matter of law when a defendant chooses to file a separate action against the plaintiff rather than a counterclaim in the original action between the same parties.

A motion for summary judgment should be granted when, based on the pleadings, discovery, affidavits, and testimony, there is no genuine issue of material fact and the moving party is entitled to judgment as a matter of law.

In this case, Reuter does not present any factual or legal evidence in support of his motion. His only argument is that Tavarez must bring its cause of action as a compulsory counterclaim, and that it may not file a separate suit. However, Illinois does not recognize the distinction between compulsory and permissive counterclaims. [Code §2-608] All counterclaims in Illinois are permissive, so a defendant is not required to raise a counterclaim, even if it arises from the same transaction or occurrence which is alleged in the original complaint. Thus, although the two lawsuits arise out of the same contract for the construction of Reuter's house, Tavarez is entitled to bring a separate breach of contract action against Reuter.

Therefore, because Illinois does not recognize compulsory counterclaims, Reuter failed to establish that he is entitled to judgment as a matter of law based on the evidence presented, and the motion for summary judgment should be denied.

QUESTION 15

In February 1998, Theresa Kramish is a 19-year-old college freshman. Kramish is attending Northeastern Illinois University in Cohen County, Illinois.

Kramish owns a 1995 Phoenix auto. Phipps, Inc. manufactured this auto. Phipps is a Delaware corporation, with its principal place of business in Peoria, Illinois.

On February 10, 1998, the steering system failed in Kramish's Phoenix auto. Unable to steer the car, Kramish crashed into a concrete highway embankment in Cohen County, Illinois. Kramish suffered serious injuries in this accident.

At her attorney's request, Kramish has maintained a diary concerning her symptoms, medical treatment, and expenses incurred. Kramish had never suffered serious injuries prior to this accident, and her only prior medical treatment was for an eating disorder when she was 10 years old. The medical records pertaining to the prior treatment are in Kramish's possession.

On April 27, 1998, Kramish files suit in the Circuit Court of Cohen County, Illinois. In her complaint, Kramish names Phipps, Inc. as the only defendant.

The complaint filed by Kramish states a single cause of action for strict liability, a state law claim. According to the complaint, Phipps used an unreasonably dangerous design for the steering mechanism in the 1995 Phoenix auto owned by Kramish. The complaint seeks $250,000 in compensatory damages.

During discovery, plaintiff Theresa Kramish serves a set of interrogatories and a set of document requests on defendant Phipps, Inc. Plaintiff's Interrogatory 10 provides:

> 10. Identify any persons who have knowledge of how defendant designed the steering mechanism in the 1995 Phoenix auto.

Plaintiff's Document Request 5 asks Defendant Phipps, Inc. to produce:

> 5. All memoranda prepared by attorneys representing defendant that researched or evaluated the Illinois law governing design defect cases, and that were written in response to the complaint filed by plaintiff.

Also during discovery, defendant Phipps, Inc. serves a set of document requests on plaintiff Theresa Kramish for production of the following:

> (A) All documents pertaining to plaintiff's injury, including diaries, journals and memoranda referring to treatment;

> (B) All medical records in plaintiff's possession pertaining to plaintiff's medical or psychological treatment for the alleged injuries; and

> (C) All medical records in plaintiff's possession disclosing any medical or psychological treatment that plaintiff received before the accident.

1. Must defendant Phipps, Inc. answer Interrogatory 10? Explain.

2. Must defendant Phipps, Inc. produce the documents requested in Document Request 5? Explain.

3. Must plaintiff Theresa Kramish produce the documents described at (A), (B), and (C)? Explain.

ANSWER TO QUESTION 15

1. Yes, Phipps, Inc. ("Phipps") must answer Interrogatory 10. At issue is whether a party must disclose a list of persons having knowledge of facts relevant to the case.

A party may obtain full disclosure of the identity and location of persons having knowledge of facts relevant to the case. [Ill. S. Ct. R. 201(b)(1)] In this case, Theresa Kramish ("Kramish") is requesting the identity of persons who have knowledge of how the defendant designed the steering mechanism of the car she was driving in the accident. Because the design of the steering mechanism is relevant to the case, Phipps must identify the persons with knowledge of how it was designed.

2.	No, Phipps is not required to produce the documents requested in Document Request 5. At issue is whether research by a party's attorneys in response to a complaint is privileged attorney work product.

In Illinois, material prepared by or for a party in preparation for trial is freely discoverable. However, work product that contains the theories, mental impressions, or litigation plans of a party's attorney is privileged and not discoverable. [Ill. S. Ct. R. 201(b)(2)]

In this case, memoranda evaluating and researching the law written in response to the plaintiff's complaint will very likely contain the opinions, theories, and strategies of Phipps's counsel. Thus, Phipps may claim the work product privilege.

3.(a)	Yes, Kramish must produce all documents pertaining to her injury, including her own diaries, journals, and memoranda prepared at the request of her attorney. At issue is whether a party who has claimed an injury in her complaint must produce documents relating to that injury.

A party may request from any other party the production of any document that is not privileged and is relevant to the subject matter of the action. [Ill. S. Ct. R. 214] In this case, Kramish is alleging personal injury in her complaint and is seeking damages in relation to the accident. Although she kept the diary at the direction of her attorney, it does not contain her attorney's thoughts or strategies in relation to the litigation, so under Illinois law it is not privileged work product. [Ill. S. Ct. R. 201(b)(2)] Thus, Kramish's diary of her symptoms and treatment is relevant and not privileged, and she must produce it to the defense.

(b)	Yes, Kramish must produce the medical records relating to her injuries and treatment. At issue is whether a party who has claimed an injury in her complaint must produce medical records relating to that injury.

As in part (a), a party must produce any document that is relevant to the litigation and not privileged. [Ill. S. Ct. R. 214] In this case, the records are relevant because Kramish is alleging personal injury. When a party alleges personal injury in a complaint, she is deemed to waive any medical privilege between herself and her health care provider. [Code §2-1003] Thus, the medical records are relevant, in her possession, and not privileged, and she must produce them.

(c)	Kramish probably will have to disclose the records of her prior physical and psychological treatment. At issue is whether records of prior illnesses or injuries are discoverable in a lawsuit alleging personal injury.

Kramish may object that the request is overbroad or irrelevant. However, in Illinois a party may obtain full disclosure of any documents relevant to the subject matter of the pending action or calculated to lead to the discovery of relevant documents. [Ill. S. Ct. R. 201(b)(1), 214] Also, discovery is not limited to information that would be admissible in evidence at trial. In this case, Kramish's prior medical records are arguably relevant to her current injuries or to the cause of the accident, and thus Kramish probably will have to disclose any prior medical records in her possession.

QUESTION 16

Frank Slater is a permanent resident of Kane County, Illinois. From 1991 until July 8, 1996, Robert Garcia employs Slater as a store manager. Garcia owns and operates Red

Rooster Convenience Stores. These stores are located throughout Illinois. Slater manages a Red Rooster store in Kane County.

On July 8, 1996, Garcia meets with Slater. At this meeting, Garcia tells Slater that Slater's employment at the Red Rooster store is terminated.

On April 16, 1997, Slater files a suit in the Circuit Court of Kane County. Slater's complaint names Robert Garcia as the only defendant.

Slater's complaint states a single cause of action for breach of contract. The complaint alleges that when Garcia fired Slater, Garcia breached an employment contract that Slater had entered into with Garcia. Slater seeks compensatory damages.

1.   On June 3, 1997, Slater moves to amend his complaint. Slater's amendment alleges a second cause of action, stating a claim for libel. When Slater makes this motion to amend, discovery recently has begun in his suit against Garcia.

   The cause of action that Slater seeks to add by amendment alleges: "Between July 8, 1996 and July 30, 1996, Garcia made misrepresentations about Slater's job performance to other convenience store operators in Kane County. Garcia made these false statements of fact intentionally and with malice. Garcia's misrepresentations prevented Slater from obtaining another position in the convenience store industry."

   Under Illinois law, a one-year statute of limitations governs libel actions.

   Should the court grant Slater's motion to amend? Explain.

2.   Now assume that Slater first filed his motion to amend the complaint on September 8, 1997, instead of June 3, 1997. The motion to amend would add the libel action described in Part 1. of this problem.

   Should the court grant Slater's motion to amend? Explain.

ANSWER TO QUESTION 16

1.   Slater's motion to amend should be granted. At issue is whether a complaint may be amended to add a new cause of action.

Illinois gives great latitude in allowing amendments to pleadings at any time before final judgment, including amendments to add new causes of action. [Code §2-616(a)] In this case, the amendment is within the statute of limitations period. Thus, the motion should be granted.

2.   Slater's motion to amend should be denied. At issue is whether the amendment relates back to the original complaint. Whether the court will grant a motion to amend is within the court's discretion.

Since the motion was filed after the statute of limitations had run, the amendment is barred unless it relates back to the date of the filing of the original complaint. An amendment relates back to the original pleading if (i) the original pleading was timely filed and (ii) the added claim arises from the same transaction or occurrence as the original pleading. [Code §2-616(b)] The rationale is that the opposing party is not prejudiced by the lapse of time because he had notice of what evidence needed to be preserved before the statute of limitations had run.

In this case, the original complaint was timely filed, but the amendment does not arise from the same transaction or occurrence as the original pleading. The amendment does not relate back as it is a libel action involving a period of time after the discharge, and Garcia will be prejudiced because discovery commenced three months earlier. Although both actions involve the facts surrounding Slater's discharge and job performance, a court is likely to find the amendment is not part of the same transaction. Thus, the motion should be denied.

QUESTION 17

Assume that in December 1998, Plaintiff Beth Fure files the following complaint in the Circuit Court of Wexford County, Illinois.

Beth Fure,	
Plaintiff	**No. 98-9705**
-v-	**Judge Saunders**
House of Curran, Inc.,	**Jury Trial Demanded**
Defendant.	

Common Law Fraud

1.   **The court has jurisdiction to hear this case.**

2.   **Plaintiff Beth Fure ("Fure") is a permanent resident of Westmoreland County, Pennsylvania. Until two years prior to the events alleged herein, plaintiff resided in Wexford County, Illinois, where her father and sister maintain a law office.**

3.   **Defendant House of Curran, Inc. ("House of Curran"), is a Delaware corporation, with its principal place of business in Pittsburgh, Pennsylvania. House of Curran purchases and resells valuable art work and antiques.**

4.   **Defendant House of Curran maintains 10 permanent offices in Illinois, including an office in Wexford County. Defendant House of Curran also maintains offices in 37 other states and the District of Columbia. One of the defendant's offices is located in the City of Latrobe in Westmoreland County, Pennsylvania.**

5.   On September 24, 1998, a representative from the Latrobe, Pennsylvania office of Defendant House of Curran visited Plaintiff Beth Fure at her home. The representative was responding to a phone call from Fure. In this call, Fure had asked House of Curran to look at "an old painting she had found in her garage."

6.   On September 24, 1998, the House of Curran representative convinced Fure to sell the painting to the House of Curran for $50. The representative obtained the painting through various acts of deception.

7.   The painting sold by Fure actually was a lost original work, painted by the artist, Vincent van Gogh.

8.   In November 1998, the House of Curran sold Fure's van Gogh painting for $500,000.

9.   Defendant House of Curran obtained the van Gogh painting from Fure through acts of deception amounting to common law fraud.

10.   Fure seeks $500,000 compensatory damages, $500,000 punitive damages, and such other relief as this court finds to be just.

Respectfully submitted,

/s/ Tracy Brostoff
Tracy Brostoff
Attorney for Plaintiff Beth Fure

Assume that you represent Defendant House of Curran, Inc. Also, assume Pennsylvania law will apply to the common law fraud action and that Plaintiff Beth Fure could have filed her suit in a Pennsylvania state court.

You plan to file a motion to dismiss in response to Beth Fure's complaint. What arguments should you raise in the motion to dismiss? Explain.

ANSWER TO QUESTION 17

House of Curran may move to dismiss the complaint on two grounds: failure to state a claim and forum non conveniens.

House of Curran may move to dismiss the complaint for failure to state a claim. At issue is whether the complaint meets the fact pleading requirements in Illinois. Although Pennsylvania substantive law will apply, the court will apply Illinois procedural law.

Illinois is a "fact pleading" state, which means the plaintiff must plead the specific facts upon which a claim is based, and may not simply give the defendant notice of the incident out of which the claim arose. In addition, when the charge is for fraud, as in this case, particularized pleading of the facts is specially required.

In this case the complaint contains conclusions of law and general statements of the fraudulent transaction without giving detailed facts supporting the charge of fraud. Paragraph 6 states defendant "convinced" plaintiff to sell the painting "through various acts of deception." Paragraph 9 claims defendant engaged in "acts of deception amounting to common law fraud." These are general statements of the allegation and conclusions of law, and thus the complaint fails to state a claim under Illinois's fact pleading requirements.

Also, House of Curran may move to dismiss for forum non conveniens. At issue is whether Wexford County is the most convenient forum.

A forum non conveniens dismissal is granted when venue and jurisdiction in the original court are proper, but a more convenient forum in another state is available to the parties. When the defendant is a corporation or a registered foreign corporation, venue is proper in any county in which it has an office or is doing business. Thus, Wexford County is a proper venue because defendant has a permanent office in Wexford County. Also, assuming service was proper, the Illinois court has personal jurisdiction over the defendant because it does business in Illinois (10 permanent offices), and thus is deemed to consent to suit in Illinois. Therefore, Wexford County is a proper venue, and the issue is whether it is the most convenient venue.

Although Illinois courts favor the plaintiff's choice of forum, a court will balance factors to determine whether another forum is more convenient to the parties. These factors include: (i) the plaintiff's interest in staying in Illinois, (ii) the inconvenience to the defendant, and (iii) the public's interest in keeping the case in Illinois (*e.g.*, which court has greater access to the evidence, which forum can more easily enforce a judgment, and which forum's law applies).

In this case, Pennsylvania law applies, both parties are citizens of Pennsylvania, the alleged fraud occurred in Pennsylvania, the evidence and witnesses are in Pennsylvania, and the Pennsylvania court will be able to enforce a judgment more easily than the Illinois court. Although the plaintiff has an interest in keeping the case in Illinois because her family's law practice is there, her interest will not outweigh the other factors listed above. Thus, Pennsylvania is the more convenient forum. Specifically, Westmoreland County would be a proper and more convenient venue as the defendant maintains an office in Westmoreland County.

If the motion to dismiss for forum non conveniens is granted, plaintiff may file her suit in Pennsylvania within six months, and defendant must accept service of process.

Thus, defendant should move to dismiss based on failure to state a claim and forum non conveniens.

QUESTION 18

Harold Black and Bruce White each maintain a separate law office in the city of Indigo in Vermillion County, Illinois. Both the offices of Black and White are located in a two-story building at 175 Golden Way in Indigo. Black owns the second floor of the building. White owns the first floor of the building.

In two identical contracts dated February 4, 1998, Sharon Greene agrees to purchase the building at 175 Golden Way from Black and White. Once she has purchased the building at 175 Golden Way, Greene plans to renovate the building and sell condominium units in the building.

Greene agrees to purchase the second floor of 175 Golden Way from Harold Black for $75,000. In a contract identical to her agreement with Black, Greene agrees to purchase the first floor of 175 Golden Way from Bruce White for $75,000.

Cindy Brown is a Vermillion County real estate agent. Pursuant to the two contracts with Black and White, on February 4, 1998, Sharon Greene gives Cindy Brown two checks for $2,500. According to the contracts, Brown will hold $5,000 of Greene's money in escrow until the sale of the 175 Golden Way building has been completed.

Under the terms of the contracts with Black and White, Sharon Greene is obligated to pay the full amount owed to each seller by April 30, 1998. If Greene fails to pay the outstanding purchase price to Black and White, the contracts require that the $5,000 held in escrow will be forfeited to Black and White.

On April 30, 1998, Sharon Greene does not pay the contract price to Black and White. In a letter dated May 1, 1998, Greene promises that she will pay the purchase price to each of the sellers "in the immediate future."

On May 8, 1998, Harold Black and Bruce White commence a suit in the Circuit Court of Vermillion County. The suit names Cindy Brown as the only defendant.

The complaint filed by Black and White alleges a single cause of action for breach of contract, a state law claim. Black and White base their breach of contract action on Greene's failure to pay the purchase price for the 175 Golden Way building by April 30, 1998. In their suit, Black and White each seek to recover $2,500 of the $5,000 held in escrow by Cindy Brown.

1.   Defendant Cindy Brown files a motion to dismiss the suit commenced by Black and White. According to this motion, Black and White cannot join together as plaintiffs in a single suit. Instead, Black and White must commence individual breach of contract actions.

   Should the trial court grant the motion to dismiss filed by Cindy Brown? Explain.

2.   For the purpose of this part, assume that Defendant Cindy Brown raises a second argument in her motion to dismiss. Brown asserts that Sharon Greene is a necessary and indispensable party to the action filed by Black and White. Because the plaintiffs have not named Greene as a defendant, Brown argues that the court must dismiss the breach of contract action.

   Should the court grant the motion to dismiss on the basis that Sharon Greene is a necessary and indispensable party to the breach of contract suit filed by Black and White? Explain.

ANSWER TO QUESTION 18

1.   The motion to dismiss should be denied. At issue is whether joinder of the plaintiffs was proper.

Joinder of plaintiffs is allowed when separate trials would be almost complete duplicates, except on the issue of damages. Two conditions must be satisfied: (i) the right to relief of each plaintiff must arise out of the same transaction or series of transactions, and (ii) separate actions would raise common questions of law or fact. However, joinder is not permitted when multiple plaintiffs have dealt with a defendant at separate times, even if the separate transactions are part of a repeated pattern of conduct.

In this case, Black and White's claim for relief arises out of the two sales contracts. Each contract was for one-half of a building, each was signed on the same day and for the same amount, and identical amounts of money were put into the same escrow account pending completion of the sale. Also, Greene wrote only one letter to Black and White after the deadline for payment passed. Thus, Black and White's claim for relief arises out of the same series of transactions, and Black and White dealt with Greene at the same time.

Furthermore, if Black and White were to bring separate causes of actions, the issues of law and fact would be the same, and the trials would be duplicates of each other. Thus, the motion to dismiss should be denied.

2.   The motion to dismiss should be denied, and the plaintiffs should be given a reasonable opportunity to add Greene as a defendant. At issue is whether Greene is a necessary and indispensable party.

A party is necessary and indispensable if the determination of the case will necessarily affect her interest or right in property. In this case, Greene signed the contracts providing for a $5,000 forfeiture and subsequently breached them. Greene then sent a letter to the plaintiffs regarding her failure to pay on time, and promising to pay in the immediate future. Finally, Greene put the $5,000 into escrow pending completion of the sale. If the case is resolved without Greene, she will lose her right in the $5,000 in escrow. Also, a determination of the plaintiffs' right to the money requires a finding as to whether Greene breached the contracts; thus she would lose her interest in the sales contracts as well. Therefore, Greene is a necessary party to the action.

However, Illinois courts will not dismiss a case for nonjoinder of a necessary party until a reasonable opportunity to add the necessary party has been given. Thus, the court should deny the motion to dismiss, and should give Black and White a reasonable opportunity to join Greene as a defendant.

QUESTION 19

At 7 p.m. on September 5, 1998, Alvin Stitz, a state EPA inspector who resides in Madison County, Illinois, finished a day-long inspection at Medi-Tech, Inc.'s facility in Franklin County, Illinois. Alvin was loading medical research equipment when he felt a slight scratch on his left hand. He looked down and saw a tiny pinprick tear through the palm of the single-layer glove he was wearing. Ordinarily this would not be a big deal, but Alvin knew that the equipment which he was handling contained highly radioactive waste.

Alvin quickly walked over to Tom Jones, a Medi-Tech supervisor, and showed him the tear. Tom had been working in the industry for 15 years. He worked for a competing firm in Madison County, Illinois, for five years before joining Medi-Tech. He then spent three years at Medi-Tech's headquarters in Macon County, Illinois, and seven at its downstate facility

in Williamson County, Illinois, near Tom's home in the same county. With his experience, Tom was aware of the serious implications of this mishap.

Tom immediately called 911 and had an ambulance take Alvin to Tucker Regional Medical Center in Jackson County, Illinois. Emergency Room Doctor Francis Benedict, who lives in St. Clair County, Illinois, began treating Alvin for his radiation exposure by 8 p.m. However, Doctor Benedict was finishing a 48-hour duty shift, and his fatigue caused him to make serious mistakes in his treatment of Alvin, including not calling in a specialist in a timely manner. Doctor Luke Dysinger, a specialist in radiation exposure, was jogging a five-mile course near his home in Jackson County, Illinois, when Alvin arrived at the hospital. However, Doctor Dysinger was not paged until four hours after Alvin got to the hospital.

Alvin was permanently injured by his radiation exposure and has received all of his subsequent medical care in St. Clair County, Illinois. He intends to file a complaint in which he sues four defendants: Medi-Tech, Inc. and Tom Jones for their negligence in failing to warn of the equipment's sharp edge; Tucker Regional Medical Center for medical malpractice stemming from its policy requiring 48-hour work shifts; and Doctor Benedict for medical malpractice.

1.   In which counties is venue proper? Explain.

2.   For purposes of this part only, assume the case was filed in St. Clair County. The defendants have filed a timely motion to transfer to Macon County based on forum non conveniens. How should the court rule? Explain.

ANSWER TO QUESTION 19

1.   Venue is proper in Franklin, Macon, Williamson, Jackson, and St. Clair Counties. At issue is where venue is proper.

Venue is proper in the county of residence of any defendant, or in the county where the event giving rise to the cause of action occurred. A corporation is a resident of any county in which it has an office or is doing business.

In this case, Medi-Tech, Inc. is a resident of Franklin County (facility), Macon County (headquarters), and Williamson County (facility). Jones is a resident of Williamson County, the Medical Center "resides" in Jackson County, and Benedict resides in St. Clair County. Also, the accident occurred in Franklin County. Thus, venue is proper in any of these five counties.

2.   The court should deny the motion to transfer for forum non conveniens. At issue is whether the case should be transferred to a forum more convenient to the parties.

A forum non conveniens motion is granted in the court's discretion if another proper venue is more convenient to the parties and witnesses. The original venue must be proper for a court to transfer jurisdiction.

Courts generally prefer to keep a case in the venue chosen by the plaintiff. In fact, courts generally will grant a motion only if the proper venue chosen by the plaintiff is grossly inconvenient. However, courts will allow a case to be transferred to another venue if consideration of the following factors strongly favors the moving defendant: the plaintiff's interests in the current venue, inconvenience to the defendants, and public interest, including access to proof and availability of witnesses.

In this case, Alvin has a strong interest in St. Clair County, which is a proper venue. All of Alvin's subsequent medical care has been in St. Clair County. The facts are not clear as to how extensive Alvin's injuries are, but as his treatments are in St. Clair County it appears St. Clair County is the most convenient venue for Alvin. Balanced against Alvin's interests are those of the defendants. The defendants' inconvenience in litigating in St. Clair appears to be minimal. Benedict lives there, and the other three defendants are not likely far from St. Clair County, since from the facts all of the defendants appear to live and work in the same general area. Also, since the counties appear to be close, the venue should not present a problem regarding availability of witnesses and evidence.

Macon county does not seem to be a better venue, as it is only a proper venue as Medi-Tech's headquarters, and was not the place where the injury occurred or the machine in question was located.

Alvin chose St. Clair County and has an interest in remaining there, and the defendants' interests in moving to Macon County do not grossly outweigh Alvin's interests. Thus, the motion should be denied.

QUESTION 20

Billy Pilgrim is a permanent resident of Rosewater County, Illinois. Billy Pilgrim owns a bookstore in Rosewater County, where he sells rare books.

In September 1999, Pilgrim enters into a written contract with Paul Lazaro. Lazaro is a permanent resident of Ilium County, Wisconsin. Lazaro regularly visits bookstores in Rosewater County, Illinois, where he sells books.

In the September 1999 contract, Pilgrim agrees to purchase 10 books from Lazaro. The books are written by legendary science fiction writer Kilgore Trout. Lazaro's books are particularly valuable because Trout has signed these limited edition books.

Pilgrim agrees to pay $500 for each of the 10 books sold by Lazaro. Pilgrim and Lazaro negotiate and execute the book sale contract at Pilgrim's bookstore in Rosewater County. One paragraph of the contract provides: "Illinois law shall apply to any dispute arising out of this agreement."

In November 1999, Pilgrim discovers that the books sold by Lazaro are not limited edition novels signed by Kilgore Trout. Instead, Lazaro has sold Pilgrim standard copies of books by Trout. The author's signature is forged inside each of the books. The books purchased by Pilgrim are each worth about $10.

In November 1999, Billy Pilgrim files a complaint in the Circuit Court of Rosewater County, Illinois. Pilgrim's complaint names Paul Lazaro as the only defendant.

Pilgrim's complaint states a single cause of action for breach of warranty, an Illinois state law claim. Pilgrim seeks $5,000 damages.

1. **May the Rosewater County Circuit Court exercise personal jurisdiction over Defendant Paul Lazaro? Explain.**

2. **Is Rosewater County a proper venue for the suit filed by Billy Pilgrim? Explain.**

ANSWER TO QUESTION 20

1.   The Rosewater County Circuit Court may exercise personal jurisdiction over Lazaro.

An Illinois court may assert personal jurisdiction if (i) Illinois law grants personal jurisdiction over the defendant, and (ii) the law is constitutional.

In Illinois, there are two forms of personal jurisdiction: general and specific. General jurisdiction gives the court jurisdiction over the defendant as to any cause of action. Specific jurisdiction gives the court jurisdiction over the defendant only as to the particular cause of action which arose from the defendant's conduct.

General jurisdiction is found if the defendant: (i) gives express or implied consent to jurisdiction; (ii) is present in Illinois when served with process; (iii) is domiciled in Illinois; or (iv) is doing business in Illinois. A defendant can give express consent by agreeing in a contract that disputes will be litigated in an Illinois court. Doing business is defined as regular, systematic, ongoing, continuous business in the state.

Specific jurisdiction is found if the defendant's conduct is one of the 14 acts enumerated in the Illinois long arm statute, and the conduct is the basis for the cause of action. Among the acts listed, the long arm statute confers specific jurisdiction over a defendant if the cause of action arises out of a transaction of business conducted by the defendant in Illinois.

Once general or specific jurisdiction is found, the court must determine that the law granting jurisdiction is constitutional. Personal jurisdiction is constitutional if the defendant has engaged in such minimum contacts that it would not offend traditional notions of fair play and substantial justice. The court considers whether the defendant has purposefully availed himself of Illinois jurisdiction, and whether the defendant could reasonably anticipate being haled into Illinois courts.

In this case, the court has general jurisdiction over Lazaro. Lazaro regularly visits bookstores in Rosewater County to sell books, and this regular, ongoing activity constitutes doing business in Illinois. Furthermore, although a choice of law provision would by itself be insufficient to confer jurisdiction over a defendant, it would be another factor to consider in the minimum contacts analysis; here, the choice of law favors jurisdiction in Illinois. Thus, the court has general jurisdiction under the doing business or consent categories of jurisdiction.

The court also has specific jurisdiction because the contract was negotiated and entered into in Rosewater County, Illinois, and the cause of action arises from breach of this contract. Thus, the court has specific jurisdiction under the Illinois long arm statute because Lazaro transacted business in Illinois, and the cause of action arose from this transaction.

Also, the court will find that asserting jurisdiction over Lazaro is constitutional. Lazaro regularly visits Rosewater County to sell books, agreed to the contract term that Illinois law would apply to any dispute, and negotiated and executed the contract in Rosewater County. Thus, Lazaro could reasonably expect being haled into court in Illinois, and has purposefully availed himself to Illinois jurisdiction.

Therefore, the court has personal jurisdiction over Lazaro.

2.   Rosewater County is a proper venue.

In Illinois, venue is proper in the county where the defendant resides, or the county in which the transaction or some part of it occurred out of which the cause of action arose. However, if no defendant is a resident of Illinois, the action may be tried in any county.

Lazaro, the only defendant, is a resident of Ilium County, Wisconsin. Thus, no defendant resides in Illinois, and venue is proper in any county, including Rosewater County.

QUESTION 21

Jack Gatewood is a permanent resident of the city of Sheridan, Illinois. Sheridan is located in LaSalle County, Illinois. Gatewood owns Noyes Hill Gardens, an apartment building located in Sheridan.

Until about 1995, Noyes Hill Gardens was a well-known mansion and landmark. In recent years, the building has decayed. Today, tenants rent only a few rooms in the building. These apartments do not comply with the City of Sheridan housing code.

Most of the apartments in the building are vacant. The building has become a breeding ground for rats and cockroaches.

On April 8, 1999, the Sheridan City Council decides that city workers will demolish the building by no later than June 30, 1999. In response to this decision, on April 15, 1999, Gatewood files a complaint in the Circuit Court of LaSalle County. Attorney Eric Jensen represents Gatewood. Jensen signs Gatewood's complaint.

Gatewood's complaint names the City of Sheridan as the only defendant. The complaint alleges: "The City of Sheridan decided to demolish the Noyes Hill Gardens apartment building without giving Gatewood notice or an opportunity to participate in a hearing. The City's decision violated Gatewood's constitutional rights." Gatewood seeks damages and an injunction, which would prohibit the City from demolishing the building.

1.   **Matt Swanson is a permanent resident of Foster, Illinois. Swanson's residence is located about five miles from the Noyes Hill Gardens building and Sheridan, Illinois.**

      In May 1999, Swanson files a petition to intervene as a plaintiff in the suit initiated by Gatewood against the City of Sheridan. Swanson's petition provides: "The Noyes Hill Gardens building is a structure with tremendous value as a work of architecture and as a landmark. I drive by the building at least once every six months, because I enjoy seeing this work of architecture. If Noyes Hill Gardens is demolished, citizens living in our region will suffer an irreparable historical and aesthetic loss." Based on these assertions, Swanson seeks to intervene in Gatewood's suit as a matter of right.

May Swanson intervene as a matter of right in the suit filed by Gatewood? Explain.

2. **For the purpose of this part only, assume that in June 1999, the City of Sheridan files a motion for sanctions against Eric Jensen. According to the motion, in January 1999 the Sheridan City Council held a public hearing on the fate of the Noyes Hill Gardens apartment building.**

    The motion asserts that Gatewood testified at the January public hearing. In January 1999, Gatewood also gave Council members a memorandum which explained why Gatewood opposed the demolition of Noyes Hill Gardens. The City's motion concludes: "The factual allegations appearing in Gatewood's complaint are not accurate."

    As an exhibit to the motion for sanctions, the City attaches public records. The records include a transcript of Gatewood's testimony at the January 1999 City Council hearing.

    In opposing the sanctions motion, Eric Jensen acknowledges that Gatewood's complaint contained inaccurate allegations. In particular, Jensen erred in alleging that the City of Sheridan did not provide Gatewood with an opportunity for a hearing before the City Council decided to demolish the Noyes Hill Gardens apartment building.

    However, Jensen's papers in opposition to the motion assert: "When Jensen made inaccurate allegations in Gatewood's complaint, Jensen relied on Gatewood's representations. Gatewood maintained that he did not receive prior notice or an opportunity for a hearing before the City of Sheridan decided to demolish Gatewood's building. This court cannot order that Jensen must pay sanctions because Jensen relied on the representations of his client."

    Should the court grant the City of Sheridan's motion for sanctions against Eric Jensen? Explain.

ANSWER TO QUESTION 21

1. Swanson will not be permitted to intervene as of right.

Intervention as of right is permitted where (i) a statute confers the right; (ii) a person may be bound by a judgment and his interest is inadequately represented by existing parties; or (iii) a person will be adversely affected by the court's disposition of property. This third avenue to intervene has been interpreted to mean a person must have a legal right to protect; the interest must be of a pecuniary or proprietary nature, and aesthetic interests are not sufficient.

In this case, Swanson's "interest" is the pleasure of seeing the building two times a year as he drives by. His aesthetic and historical interest in the building does not amount to a pecuniary or property interest, and he will not be permitted to intervene.

2. The court should grant the motion for sanctions against Jensen.

Illinois Supreme Court Rule 137 states in part that the signature of an attorney constitutes a certificate that he has read the pleading, and that, to the best of his knowledge, information, and belief formed after a reasonable inquiry, it is well grounded in fact. An attorney is subject to sanctions for violation of this rule.

In this case, Jensen signed the complaint relying only on Gatewood's representations. This does not constitute a reasonable inquiry. A brief investigation of the case likely would have revealed the public records of the City Council hearing. Thus, the motion for sanctions should be granted.

QUESTION 22

Mike McCain and Earl Yokoo are permanent residents of Hancock County, Illinois. In May 2000, McCain files a complaint in the Circuit Court of Hancock County. McCain's complaint names Yokoo as the only defendant.

The entire text of Mike McCain's complaint reads as follows:

COMPLAINT

1. **The court has jurisdiction to hear this suit.**

2. **Earl Yokoo promised to hire Mike McCain to manage a sporting goods store in Hancock County. Yokoo promised to pay McCain an annual salary of $35,000.**

3. **Yokoo went back on his word and hired someone else. When McCain was not hired by Yokoo, McCain lost the $35,000 annual salary that Yokoo had promised to pay McCain.**

1. **Assume that in response to this complaint, Defendant Earl Yokoo files a motion to dismiss. According to this motion, the complaint filed by McCain does not meet Illinois pleading requirements.**

   Should the court grant the motion to dismiss filed by Earl Yokoo? Explain.

2. **For the purpose of this part only, assume that Defendant Earl Yokoo does not file a motion to dismiss. Instead, Yokoo files a timely answer. The entire text of Yokoo's answer provides: "Earl Yokoo denies each of Mike McCain's allegations."**

   Has Defendant Earl Yokoo filed an adequate answer? Explain.

3. **For the purpose of this part only, assume that in his answer, Defendant Earl Yokoo seeks to recover damages from Leonard James. The complaint filed by McCain did not name James as a party.**

   Yokoo's answer to McCain's complaint provides in part: "In October 1999, James negligently hit a golf ball through the back window of Yokoo's house, located at 5 Fair Way in Hancock County. The golf ball destroyed a valuable glass chandelier hanging in Yokoo's dining room."

   Should the court allow Earl Yokoo to maintain his negligence action against Leonard James? Explain.

ANSWER TO QUESTION 22

1.   The motion to dismiss should be denied. In Illinois, a complaint must contain a plain and concise statement of the pleader's cause of action. The complaint is liberally construed by the court, and it is acceptable if it contains enough information to reasonably inform the opposing party of the nature of the claim. Illinois is a fact pleading state, which means that the facts upon which the cause of action is based must be pleaded.

In this case, the complaint will probably be found to have sufficient facts to inform Yokoo of the nature of McCain's claim. Thus, the motion should be denied.

2.   Yokoo has not filed an adequate answer. In Illinois, every allegation of the complaint must be specifically admitted or denied in an answer. General denials are not permitted in Illinois. Also, every factual allegation, other than damages, that is not specifically denied is deemed admitted.

In this case, Yokoo filed a general answer denying McCain's allegations. This is not sufficient in Illinois, and thus the answer is not adequate.

3.   The court should not allow Yokoo to maintain his negligence action against James. Yokoo may not join James as a defendant because James has no interest in the controversy and is in no way liable for the breach of contract action brought by McCain. Yokoo may not bring a third-party complaint against James because he is not alleging that James may be liable to him on McCain's breach of contract action. The court has no cause to include James on the basis of judicial economy or efficiency.

Yokoo may file a separate complaint against James, but he should not be allowed to maintain the negligence action in connection with McCain's breach of contract suit.

QUESTION 23

Star Agency ("Star"), an Illinois corporation, is a talent agency whose offices are in Chicago. Ego Films ("Ego"), a Delaware corporation not licensed to do business in Illinois, is a small independent film company whose principal place of business is Hollywood, California. Star specializes in the placement of actors within the film industry. Star is paid a fee if an actor referred by Star is hired. In early 1999, an Ego producer contacted Star, requesting assistance in finding an actor for a supporting role in a new Ego film project.

Star sent Ego the names and resumes of several actors, one of whom was J. Barrymore. Star's accompanying letter stated: "As you know from our previous correspondence, these actors are being submitted to you upon the understanding that, if they are employed, our fee will be paid by Ego Films and will be 20% of the actor's salary. Also, a fee will be due from Ego Films as to any actor you hire within two years of our submission or referral of the actor to you. Please sign the enclosed copy of this agreement and return." A representative of Ego Films signed the agreement in Hollywood and delivered it to a Star representative who just happened to be in southern California on business. An Ego producer subsequently met with Barrymore in Chicago and offered Barrymore the supporting role in the new film. Barrymore rejected the offer.

Several months later, Ego contacted the Big Apple Agency ("Apple"), a New York City talent agency, and related that Ego was seeking a lead actor for the new Ego film. Apple submitted the names of a number of actors, including that of Barrymore. After another interview with Barrymore, this time in Hollywood, Ego offered Barrymore the leading role, and Barrymore accepted.

Barrymore began working for Ego Films in December 1999, and Ego paid Apple a commission. Star later became aware of Ego's hiring of Barrymore. Star demanded a commission fee, representing 20% of Barrymore's salary. When Ego refused to pay the commission to Star, Star filed an action for breach of contract against Ego in the Circuit Court of Cook County, Illinois. Process was served on Ego's president, Mr. Big, when he was attending a week-long film festival in Chicago.

Ego Films transacted no business at the Chicago film festival. Ego does not have an office or employees in Illinois, nor does it have an Illinois telephone number. Its films are advertised in Illinois, but only as the product of, and under the name of, major film studios that buy the distribution rights to Ego's films. These major studios also solely control the distribution of Ego films in Illinois theaters. The Illinois advertisers and film distributors receive no direct payments from Ego Films.

Ego filed a motion seeking dismissal of the suit on the grounds that the Circuit Court of Cook County did not have in personam jurisdiction over it under either the Illinois long arm statute or on any other basis.

How should the court rule on Ego's motion? Explain.

ANSWER TO QUESTION 23

Ego's motion to dismiss should be denied. Illinois may exercise personal jurisdiction over a corporation when Illinois law grants such power, and that Illinois law is constitutional.

First, Illinois may not exercise general jurisdiction over Ego. Ego did not consent to jurisdiction because it filed a timely motion to dismiss for lack of personal jurisdiction, and it was not doing business in Illinois. Although the president was personally served in Chicago, service on an agent of an unregistered foreign corporation that is not doing business in Illinois is insufficient to establish personal jurisdiction over that corporation. Thus, Illinois cannot assert general jurisdiction over Ego.

However, Illinois may assert specific jurisdiction over Ego under the Illinois long arm statute. Ego was transacting business in Illinois, and Star's cause of action arises out of Ego's transaction of business. First, Ego contacted Star in Illinois and solicited its assistance in finding an actor. Ego also entered into a contract with Star, an Illinois corporation. Finally, Ego sent an agent to meet with Barrymore in Chicago in relation to the contract. These actions constitute the transaction of business in Illinois, and thus Illinois may assert specific jurisdiction over Ego in relation to Star's cause of action.

Furthermore, the exercise of jurisdiction over Ego is constitutional. Ego engaged in sufficient minimum contacts with Illinois that the exercise of jurisdiction does not offend traditional notions of fair play and substantial justice. The exercise of jurisdiction is reasonable, as Illinois has an interest in the action since it involves an Illinois corporation. Also, it is not unreasonable to require Ego to defend in Illinois, since it solicited an Illinois corporation and is able to send agents to Illinois with little burden. Finally, Ego received sufficient notice to apprise it of the pendency of the action when Star served Ego's president in Chicago.

Thus, Illinois may assert specific jurisdiction under the long arm statute, and the assertion of jurisdiction is constitutional. Ego's motion should therefore be denied.

QUESTION 24

Hank Angstrom is a permanent resident of Livingston County, Illinois. On October 12, 2000, Angstrom is involved in a serious auto accident while driving on a highway in Livingston County. A car driven by Carl Stavros hits Angstrom's auto. Angstrom suffers serious injuries in the accident.

Janet Springer and her son Nick Springer witness the October 12 accident. Janet and Nick are permanent residents of Livingston County, Illinois. Angstrom is treated for his injuries by Dr. Al Buchanan at Verity Memorial Hospital in Livingston County. Angstrom spends several days at Verity Memorial Hospital.

Carl Stavros is a permanent resident of Penn County, Pennsylvania. When he became involved in the October 12 auto accident, Stravros was driving from Pennsylvania to visit friends in Iowa. Prior to October 12, Stavros never had entered Illinois.

Carl Stavros is not hurt in his accident with Angstrom. After the accident on October 12, Stavros cancels his trip to Iowa.

On October 13, 2000, Stavros flies from Livingston County to his home in Pennsylvania.

In December 2000, Hank Angstrom files a suit in the Circuit Court of Livingston County, Illinois. Angstrom's complaint names Carl Stavros as the only defendant.

Angstrom's complaint states a single cause of action for negligence, a state law claim. According to the complaint: "By failing to exercise reasonable care, Carl Stavros caused the October 12, 2000, auto accident with Hank Angstrom." Assume that Illinois law will apply to Angstrom's negligence action.

Angstrom's complaint seeks $100,000 compensatory damages. Carl Stavros receives proper service of the complaint at his home in Pennsylvania.

1. In response to Angstrom's complaint, Stavros files a motion to dismiss. According to this motion, the Livingston County Circuit Court cannot exercise personal jurisdiction over Carl Stavros.

   Should the Livingston County Circuit Court grant the motion to dismiss? Explain.

2. For the purpose of this part only, assume that the Livingston County Circuit Court possesses personal jurisdiction over Carl Stavros. However, now assume that the motion to dismiss filed by Carl Stavros raises a second argument for dismissing Hank Angstrom's suit.

According to Stavros, the Livingston County Circuit Court should dismiss Angstrom's complaint under the doctrine of forum non conveniens. Stavros argues that a Pennsylvania state court in Penn County would provide a more appropriate forum for Angstrom's suit than the Livingston County Circuit Court. In response to the motion filed by Stavros, Angstrom concedes that a state court located in Penn County, Pennsylvania, would possess subject matter jurisdiction over Angstrom's suit against Stavros.

Should the Livingston County Circuit Court dismiss Angstrom's suit, based on the doctrine of forum non conveniens? Explain.

ANSWER TO QUESTION 24

1.   The Livingston County Circuit Court should not grant Stavros's motion to dismiss. At issue is whether the Illinois courts may exercise personal jurisdiction over the out-of-state defendant, Stavros.

Generally, Illinois courts have personal jurisdiction if Illinois law grants power over the defendant's person or property and if the Illinois law is constitutional. Illinois law provides for two types of personal jurisdiction: general jurisdiction and specific jurisdiction. General jurisdiction gives courts power to hear any case against the defendant and generally arises from service of process in Illinois or Illinois residency. Specific jurisdiction gives the court power only over causes of action related to the defendant's activities in the state. Specific jurisdiction is granted under the Illinois long arm statute, which lists 14 acts that give rise to specific jurisdiction, as well as a catch-all provision that permits jurisdiction on any other constitutional basis.

The constitutional requirement is minimum contacts: At a minimum, the defendant must have had contact with Illinois such that requiring him to defend an action in Illinois would not offend traditional notions of fair play and substantial justice. The defendant must have availed himself of the benefits and protections of Illinois law such that he should reasonably anticipate being haled into an Illinois court. Furthermore, it must be reasonable to require the defendant to defend the action in Illinois.

While Stavros is not subject to general jurisdiction in Illinois because he is not a resident and was not served in Illinois, he is subject to specific jurisdiction under the Illinois long arm statute. One provision of the long arm statute grants Illinois courts specific jurisdiction over persons who commit a tort within Illinois. Here, Stavros allegedly committed a tort—negligent driving— which caused the damages in question. Exercise of jurisdiction here also is constitutional because by driving through Illinois, Stavros was taking advantage of the protections of Illinois law, and he should reasonably anticipate that he could, therefore, be haled into court in Illinois if he violated any state law while in Illinois. Thus, jurisdiction exists, and Stavros's motion should be denied.

2.   The court should not dismiss the suit on the basis of forum non conveniens. Illinois courts are reluctant to rule against the plaintiff's choice of forum unless the balance of factors strongly favors the moving defendant. The factors considered by the court on this issue are: (i) the plaintiff's interest or convenience in staying in Illinois; (ii) the inconvenience to the defendant; and (iii) the public's interest in keeping the case in Illinois.

In this case, the plaintiff's interest in staying in Illinois is extremely strong. Not only is the plaintiff an Illinois resident, but (i) the two witnesses to the accident are Illinois residents, and (ii) any medical records regarding Angstrom's treatment would come from the Illinois hospital where he was treated. Granted, it would be inconvenient for Stavros to return to Illinois to defend the suit; however, his inconvenience is outweighed by Angstrom's interest in remaining in Illinois. Finally, as stated already, the public's interest in keeping the case in Illinois is demonstrated by the fact that all necessary witnesses and possible evidence are located in Illinois. Therefore, the court should not dismiss the suit.

QUESTION 25

Mark Breed works as a software engineer. In January 1999, Breed purchases a personal computer from E-Boxes, Inc. E-Boxes is an Illinois corporation, with its principal place of business in the City of Chicago, Cook County, Illinois. E-Boxes sells computers and related equipment over the Internet.

In December 1999, Breed's personal computer crashes. Breed determines that the computer has suffered irreparable damage. When the computer crashes, Breed loses a number of irreplaceable software programs. Breed had written and stored these programs on the hard drive of his computer. After December 1999, Breed cannot retrieve any programs from the computer's hard drive.

The January 2000 suit. In January 2000, Breed files a suit in the Circuit Court of Cook County, Illinois. Breed's complaint names E-Boxes as the only defendant.

Breed's complaint states a single cause of action based on products liability, a state law claim. According to the complaint, Breed's computer contained a design defect, which could destroy the hard drive of the computer at any time. Breed seeks $100,000 compensatory damages.

In July 2000, Breed's case against E-Boxes goes to trial. At the trial, E-Boxes introduces extensive evidence that Plaintiff Mark Breed destroyed his computer as a result of his own negligent tinkering. In July 2000, a jury trial concludes with a verdict for Defendant E-Boxes in the products liability action. Breed does not appeal from this verdict.

The October 2000 suit. In October 2000, Mark Breed files a second suit against E-Boxes, Inc. Breed files his new suit in the Circuit Court of Cook County, Illinois. As in his January 2000 action, Breed seeks to recover damages that he sustained when his E-Boxes computer crashed in December 1999.

However, Breed's Cook County suit alleges a new cause of action. Breed's complaint now alleges a cause of action for breach of warranty, rather than products liability. According to the complaint, the computer sold by E-Boxes "was not fit for the ordinary uses of a computer." Breed's new complaint alleges that the hard drive of the computer was defective and could cause the computer to crash at any time.

1. E-Boxes files a motion to dismiss. May Mark Breed maintain his October 2000 breach of warranty action against E-Boxes? Explain.

2. **Recall that Mark Breed's first suit against E-Boxes, Inc. concluded in July 2000 with a verdict for defendant E-Boxes. In September 2000, Kathy Minton files a suit against E-Boxes in the Circuit Court of Cook County, Illinois.**

   Like Mark Breed, Kathy Minton purchased a personal computer from E-Boxes. Like Breed, Minton's computer crashed a few months after she had purchased the computer. Minton and Breed never have met and do not know each other.

   In her September 2000 complaint, Minton alleges a single cause of action for products liability, an Illinois state law claim. The products liability allegations in Minton's complaint are identical to the allegations in Breed's first complaint, filed in January 2000.

   In response to Minton's complaint, Defendant E-Boxes, Inc. files a motion for summary judgment. In this motion, E-Boxes relies on the doctrine of collateral estoppel. E-Boxes notes that after a jury trial of Mark Breed's first suit in July 2000, the jury found in favor of E-Boxes. Because of this earlier result, E-Boxes argues that Kathy Minton cannot now prevail in her products liability action.

   Should the Cook County Circuit Court grant the motion of summary judgment filed by E-Boxes, Inc.? Explain.

ANSWER TO QUESTION 25

1.   Breed should not be able to maintain his October 2000 breach of warranty action against E-Boxes because the action is barred by res judicata. Once a final judgment on the merits has been rendered on a particular cause of action, res judicata bars the claimant from asserting the same cause of action in a later lawsuit. For res judicata to apply, it must be shown: (i) that the earlier judgment is final and on the merits; and (ii) that the same cause of action (or claim) is involved in the later lawsuit. Courts typically hold that any claim arising from the same transaction or occurrence is the same cause of action.

In this case, Breed's October action arose out of the same occurrence as his January action—his computer crashing in December 1999. Furthermore, the facts state that the jury returned a verdict for E-Boxes, which was a final judgment on the merits. Therefore, even though Breed's October suit is alleging breach of warranty rather than a product defect, the suit is still arising out of the same occurrence and is barred.

2.   No. The court should not grant E-Boxes's motion for summary judgment. At issue is whether a genuine issue of material fact remains that would make the granting of summary judgment improper.

A motion for summary judgment should be granted if, based on the pleadings, discovery, and affidavits, there is no genuine issue of material fact and the movant is entitled to judgment as a matter of law. Collateral estoppel precludes a party and his privies from litigating the same issue which had been litigated in a prior suit and which was essential to the judgment in that prior suit. A court will allow a prior judgment to be used in a subsequent lawsuit if: (i) the issue in the first case is identical to the issue in the second case; (ii) the final judgment in the first case was on the merits; (iii) the defendant had a full and fair opportunity to be heard on the critical issues in the first case; and (iv) it is not unfair to the defendant to follow the judgment from the first case.

In this case, it is reasonable to conclude that E-Boxes is alleging that the facts of Kathy Minton's case are identical to Mark Breed's and that those facts and issues were resolved in the first suit, which was decided in E-Boxes's favor. However, it is not clear how the issue of E-Boxes's negligence was decided in Breed's case. While like Minton, Breed alleged that the E-Boxes computer had a design defect, in the Breed case, E-Boxes alleged that Breed's own negligence caused the computer to crash. The jury returned a verdict for E-Boxes, but we do not know if that is because the jury found that the E-Boxes computer was properly designed or because Breed was negligent. Moreover, Breed's negligence is not at issue in Minton's case, so we have a different set of facts for the court to examine. Therefore, collateral estoppel would not apply and summary judgment in Kathy Minton's case would be improper.

QUESTION 26

Robert Garcia is a permanent resident of Cook County, Illinois. During the first week of August 2000, Garcia is vacationing in Yellowstone National Park, located in Wyoming.

On August 3, 2000, Garcia is injured in a two-car accident. The accident occurs in Yellowstone National Park.

A rental car driven by Erich Schmidt hits Garcia's auto. Schmidt is a German businessman. Like Garcia, Schmidt is vacationing in Yellowstone National Park. Schmidt is a permanent resident of Bonn, Germany.

On October 5, 2000, Garcia files a suit in the Circuit Court of Cook County, Illinois. Garcia names Erich Schmidt as the only defendant.

Garcia's complaint alleges a single cause of action for negligence, a state law claim. According to the compliant, Erich Schmidt's failure to exercise reasonable care caused the August 3, 2000, accident in Yellowstone National Park. Garcia alleges $100,000 damages.

On October 9, 2000, Erich Schmidt is served with a copy of Garcia's complaint at O'Hare Airport in Cook County, Illinois. When Schmidt receives this service, Schmidt is traveling from Germany to Buenos Aires, Argentina, on a business trip. Schmidt spends about three hours at O'Hare Airport, as he waits to board a connecting flight that will depart for Argentina.

Each year, Schmidt stops at O'Hare Airport and changes planes on about six different days. Schmidt never spends more than six hours at the airport. With the exception of these stops at O'Hare Airport, Schmidt has no connection with Illinois.

1. **In response to Plaintiff Robert Garcia's complaint, Defendant Erich Schmidt argues that the Illinois courts cannot exercise personal jurisdiction over Schmidt.**

    For the purpose of this part only, assume that Defendant Erich Schmidt does not waive any personal jurisdiction objections. May the Illinois courts exercise personal jurisdiction over Schmidt? Explain.

2. **For the purpose of this part only, assume that the attorney representing Defendant Erich Schmidt first responds to Robert Garcia's complaint with an answer. The answer**

does not mention a personal jurisdiction defense. Ten days later, defense counsel files a second document, titled: Motion to Dismiss Plaintiff Erich Schmidt's Complaint for Lack of Personal Jurisdiction.

Has Defendant Erich Schmidt waived any objections to personal jurisdiction? Explain.

ANSWER TO QUESTION 26

1.   A court in Illinois may exercise personal jurisdiction over Erich Schmidt.

A court in Illinois may assert personal jurisdiction if (i) Illinois law grants personal jurisdiction over the defendant, and (ii) the law is constitutional. In Illinois, there are two forms of personal jurisdiction: general and specific. General jurisdiction provides the court jurisdiction over the defendant as to any cause of action. Specific jurisdiction provides the court jurisdiction over the defendant only as to the particular cause of action which arose from the defendant's conduct.

General jurisdiction exists when the defendant: (i) gives express or implied consent to jurisdiction; (ii) is present in Illinois when served with process; (iii) is domiciled in Illinois; or (iv) is doing business in Illinois. Obviously, only the second rule is relevant here. The only exceptions to the rule that a court has jurisdiction over a defendant served in Illinois are when: (i) a plaintiff entices a defendant into Illinois; or (ii) the defendant has immunity from process while in Illinois. Neither of these exceptions are relevant here—Mr. Schmidt was voluntarily in Illinois changing planes on personal business. Because Mr. Schmidt was present in Illinois at the time of service, even though his presence was transitory, a court in Illinois would have general jurisdiction over Mr. Schmidt. And, it is well established that exercise of jurisdiction based on physical presence in a state at time of service is constitutional. Therefore, an Illinois court may exercise personal jurisdiction over Mr. Schmidt.

2.   Defendant Erich Schmidt has waived his objections to personal jurisdiction. In Illinois, to object to the exercise of personal jurisdiction by a court, a defendant must object before filing a responsive pleading or a motion (other than a motion for an extension of time). Because Mr. Schmidt filed an answer, which is considered a responsive pleading, before bringing his motion to dismiss based on a lack of personal jurisdiction, he has waived that objection.

QUESTION 27

Andrew and Beth commute to work each day on Friendly Bus Lines. One day during their morning commute, the bus, driven by Driver, swerves off the road and hits a tree. Andrew and Beth both lose consciousness momentarily and sustain life-threatening injuries.

Andrew files a complaint against Driver and Friendly Bus Lines in the Circuit Court of Kendall County, Illinois. The one-count complaint for negligence, an Illinois state law claim, names Driver and Friendly Bus Lines as defendants. Andrew seeks $100,000 in damages. Andrew requests a jury trial.

After Andrew presents his case-in-chief to the jury, the attorneys for Friendly Bus Lines and Driver both move for a directed verdict. The court grants the motion of Friendly Bus

Lines because Andrew fails to present a prima facie case of negligence against Friendly Bus Lines. However, the court denies Driver's motion, and the case proceeds against Driver. The jury awards Andrew $25,000 against Driver on his one count of negligence. Andrew believes that he could have received a greater verdict had he hired a more competent medical expert.

At the conclusion of the first suit, Andrew and Beth file a second complaint against Driver and Friendly Bus Lines in the Circuit Court of LaSalle County, Illinois. The one-count complaint for negligence, an Illinois state law claim, names Driver and Friendly Bus Lines as defendants. They each seek $100,000 in damages. Andrew hires a new medical expert for the LaSalle County trial.

1.   Driver and Friendly Bus Lines ask the Circuit Court of LaSalle County to dismiss Andrew's claim from the action in light of the Kendall County judgment. What result? Explain.

2.   Beth asks the Circuit Court of LaSalle County to make a pre-trial finding that Driver acted negligently in light of the jury verdict in the Kenall County action. What result? Explain.

3.   Friendly Bus Lines asks the Circuit Court of LaSalle County to dismiss Beth's complaint against Friendly Bus Lines in light of the ruling on Friendly Bus Lines's motion for directed verdict in the Kendall County action. What result? Explain.

ANSWER TO QUESTION 27

1.   The Circuit Court of LaSalle County should dismiss Andrew's claim based on res judicata.

The issues are whether the cause of action Andrew has against defendant Driver merged with the judgment in Kendall County and whether the directed verdict obtained by Friendly Bus Lines in the Kendall County litigation bars Andrew's subsequent suit in LaSalle County. (The concepts are collectively known as "res judicata.")

Before the merger and bar rules apply, it must be shown that the earlier judgment is final and on the merits, and that the same cause of action is involved in the later suit.

As to Andrew's suit against defendant Driver, all three elements are easily met. Andrew was awarded a verdict of $25,000. An award made after a full trial is "final," and Andrew's only recourse is an appeal (if any). It is also "on the merits," because a jury could not have awarded any damages to Andrew without finding Driver negligent. Finally, both suits are one-count complaints based on negligence and arise out of the same transaction or occurrence; therefore, both suits arise out of the same cause of action. Without the merger doctrine, an unsuccessful plaintiff could relitigate a cause of action until he receives the verdict he desires, as Andrew is attempting to do here.

As to Andrew's suit against Friendly Bus Lines, all three elements are again met. A directed verdict is considered final. Given that Andrew had the opportunity to present all his evidence in Kendall County, there is also no doubt that the judgment was on the merits. Both suits against Friendly arise out of the same transaction or occurrence and are, therefore, the same cause of action.

Because res judicata applies to both of Andrew's actions, both causes of action should be dismissed.

2.   The Circuit Court of LaSalle County should make a pretrial finding that Driver acted negligently. At issue is whether collateral estoppel is available to a person who was not a party to the prior proceeding on which the claim of collateral estoppel is based.

Traditional mutuality rules provide that because an earlier judgment cannot be used against a person who was not a party to the earlier proceeding, that person is similarly barred from taking advantage of the judgment. However, courts have begun to allow nonparty plaintiffs to rely on collateral estoppel if it is fair to the defendant to do so. In jurisdictions where the mutuality principle has been eroded, a nonparty may rely on a prior judgment when: (i) the issue decided in the first case is identical to that in the second; (ii) there was a final judgment on the merits; (iii) the party against whom the judgment is to be used had a fair opportunity to be heard on the critical issue; and (iv) the posture of the case is such that it would not be unfair or inequitable to a party to apply collateral estoppel.

In the instant case, the court could apply collateral estoppel to prevent Driver from contesting his negligence. Absent any facts that Beth was somehow comparatively or contributorily negligent, Driver's negligence is the same in both cases. Additionally, the LaSalle County judgment against Driver was final (assuming the time for Driver's appeal has expired) and on the merits. Furthermore, Driver had the opportunity and same incentive to litigate the negligence issue in LaSalle County, and therefore it would not be inequitable to apply collateral estoppel against him in subsequent civil suits. Thus, the Circuit Court should allow Beth to use collateral estoppel against Driver.

3.   The Circuit Court of LaSalle County should not dismiss Beth's complaint against Friendly Bus Lines in light of the ruling in *Andrew's* action against Friendly Bus Lines. At issue is whether Friendly Bus Lines may rely on the doctrine of collateral estoppel to defeat Beth's action.

Collateral estoppel (issue preclusion) provides that a judgment for a plaintiff or defendant is conclusive in a subsequent action on a different cause of action between the party or his privies as to issues actually litigated and essential to the judgment in the first action. Here, Friendly Bus Lines claims that the directed verdict it obtained in Andrew's case (because of Andrew's failure to present a prima facie case) should prevent Beth from pursuing her claim. Although it could be argued that the issue was actually litigated (albeit incompetently) and essential to the judgment in the first case, it cannot be used in the second case against Beth because she was neither a party nor a privy to a party in the first action and she did not have the opportunity to be heard on any issue in the first action.

QUESTION 28

Bob owns Bob's Bakery in Kendall County, Illinois. On June 6, 2000, Bob hired Jack to work at Bob's Bakery full-time as a baker. Jack started working for Bob the next day. After six months, on December 6, 2000, Bob fired Jack.

Jack then learned about a job opening at Patty's Pastries. Jack applied and interviewed with Patty, the owner. Patty called Jack three days after the interview to tell Jack that she could not hire him because of his reputation as a "lazy and dishonest baker" that she learned about from another bakery owner.

On December 18, 2000, Jack filed a two-count unverified complaint in the Circuit Court of Kendall County, Illinois, against Bob for slander and breach of contract. Jack made one allegation in the complaint as to the breach of contract count. He alleged: "Bob breached an oral 11-month employment contract with Jack. Bob owes Jack $12,500 in additional compensation."

Bob answered the slander count and filed a motion to strike the breach of contract count on the ground that Jack failed to plead a legally sufficient claim. The court denied Bob's motion and ordered the parties to proceed with discovery on both counts.

At the close of discovery, Bob filed a motion for partial summary judgment on the breach of contract count. Bob stated in his motion that the court should find for him because no employment contract between him and Jack existed. He attached a signed and notarized affidavit stating that when he hired Jack on June 6, 2000, he told him, "We shall take the job one day at a time. There is no need to bind either of us." He swore that Jack answered, "I agree. I do not want any commitment." Jack responded that he intended to introduce evidence of an oral contract through testimony at trial. He did not attach any supporting document to his response. The court granted partial summary judgment in favor of Bob.

The court held a jury trial on the slander count. To prevail, Jack had the burden to prove his one disputed contention that Bob, and not someone else, described Jack as a "lazy and dishonest baker" to Patty. Jack called himself as his only witness at trial. Jack offered no testimony linking Bob to Patty's information about Jack. For the defense, Bob testified that he never talked to Patty about Jack. Patty, the other defense witness, agreed and testified that she learned of Jack's alleged reputation from her friend Dan of Dan's Donuts, where Jack worked as an intern while attending cooking school. The jury found for Jack and awarded him $50,000 in damages. The next day, Bob filed a motion for judgment notwithstanding the verdict.

1.   Did the court err in denying Bob's motion to strike the breach of contract count? Explain.

2.   Did the court err in granting Bob's motion for partial summary judgment? Explain.

3.   How should the court rule on the motion for judgment notwithstanding the verdict? Explain.

ANSWER TO QUESTION 28

1.   The court erred in denying Bob's motion to strike the breach of contract count. At issue is whether Jack's two-sentence count is sufficient to withstand a motion to strike.

In ruling on a motion to strike, the question for the court is whether the pleader has set forth any facts that would support relief. Illinois has not adopted "notice pleading"—in Illinois, a party must allege facts on which a cause of action could be based. Although all well-pleaded facts are taken as true, legal conclusions are not. If the pleader relies on conclusions (or facts that show he is not entitled to relief), the motion should be granted. However, pleadings also must be liberally construed to do substantial justice between the parties, and some facts may be inferred from other language in the complaint.

To properly plead a breach of contract, a plaintiff must plead facts indicating (i) the existence of a contract (that there was an offer, acceptance, and consideration), (ii) that the plaintiff has performed all contractual conditions under the contract, (iii) that a breach occurred, and (iv) the existence of damages. Jack did not plead any such facts; he merely alleged that "Bob breached an oral 11-month employment contract with Jack. Bob owes Jack $12,500 in additional compensation."

Using the term "breach" without any supporting facts is a conclusion, and the court should have disregarded any conclusions contained in the complaint. Additionally, Jack did not plead any facts indicating how the breach occurred, or any facts indicating that Jack performed his part of the contract. Thus, the motion to strike should have been granted, because Jack has failed to plead a prima facie case. (Note that Jack did include a proper prayer for relief as required under Illinois law, and that the pleadings did not have to be verified.)

2.   The court did not err in granting Bob's motion for partial summary judgment on the breach of contract count.

The question is whether there is genuine issue as to any material fact, such that the moving party is entitled to judgment as a matter of law. In ruling on the motion, the court will consider any pleadings on file, admissions on file, discovery, and affidavits, and the court may take oral or written testimony. If a pleading is controverted by an affidavit, the opposing party may not rest on pleadings to survive a motion for summary judgment—he must submit his own affidavit or point to some other competent evidence (*e.g.,* deposition testimony) that would indicate a material fact is at issue.

In the instant case, given that Bob submitted an affidavit stating that there was no guarantee of employment, Jack was required to submit an affidavit or to point to some other competent evidence to show that a valid contract did exist, and he failed to do so. Therefore, the court should have found, as it did, that there was no genuine issue of any material fact, and that Bob was entitled to partial judgment as a matter of law.

Thus, the court did not err when it granted Bob's motion for partial summary judgment.

3.   The court should grant the motion for judgment notwithstanding the verdict. At issue is the standard for granting or denying a motion notwithstanding the verdict.

In Illinois, a motion for judgment notwithstanding the verdict should be granted if all the evidence, when viewed in a light most favorable to the nonmoving party, so overwhelmingly favors the moving party that no contrary verdict for the nonmoving party could ever stand. Note that in Illinois, a party is not required to move for a directed verdict at the close of the case to preserve a later motion for judgment notwithstanding the verdict.

In the instant case, Jack, who as the plaintiff has the burden to prove that Bob slandered him, has not presented any evidence linking Bob to the statement that Jack was a "lazy and dishonest baker." The judgment against Bob could be overturned on this fact alone. Furthermore, Bob and Patty both testified that they never talked to one another about Jack, and Patty further testified that she learned of Jack's laziness through Dan, another of Jack's former employers. Viewing the evidence—no testimony presented by Jack that Bob slandered him and testimony presented by Bob that someone else may have slandered Jack—in a light most favorable to Jack, no jury could possibly find that Bob slandered Jack. Even if the jury did not believe that Bob and Patty were credible witnesses, it still should have found for Bob, given Jack's failure to present any evidence linking Bob to the slander.

Therefore, the court should grant Bob's request for a judgment notwithstanding the verdict.

QUESTION 29

Lucky Cereal Co. is an Illinois corporation with its principal place of business in Chicago, Illinois. Lucky Cereal Co. distributes Berry Bits, Crispy Crunch, and Tangy Tarts cereals to all 50 states. Throughout 2001, Lucky Cereal Co. advertised a promotion on the sides of its cereal boxes. In exchange for five proofs of purchase from any one kind of the company's cereal, Lucky Cereal Co. offered to send the customer a matchbox car valued at $6.00. However, it ran out of matchbox cars in March 2001, leaving 75,000 unhappy customers who had complied with the promotion. Lucky Cereal Co. stored the names and addresses of the 75,000 customers in a database in the event that it ordered more matchbox cars.

Arthur is a resident of Chicago, Illinois. In June of 2001, he had accumulated five proofs of purchase of Berry Bits cereal. He sent in the proofs of purchase to Lucky Cereal Co. but never received a matchbox car. Bob, Arthur's brother, and Calvin, Arthur's brother-in-law, both did not receive matchbox cars after returning five proofs of purchase of Crispy Crunch and Tangy Tarts cereal, respectively.

On November 18, 2001, Arthur, Bob, and Calvin filed a complaint for breach of contract in the Circuit Court of Cook County, Illinois, against Lucky Cereal Co.

On December 17, 2001, Arthur, Bob, and Calvin filed a motion for certification of a class defined as "them and all others similarly situated nationwide who returned five proofs of purchase of Berry Bits, Crispy Crunch, or Tangy Tarts cereal in 2001 and did not receive a matchbox car." They did not research contract law in all 50 states, but knew that the law varied only slightly from one state to the next. Lucky Cereal Co. objected on two grounds: (1) there are different questions of fact and law precluding class certification; and (2) the court does not have personal jurisdiction over the out-of-state plaintiffs who have no contacts with Illinois and thus cannot certify a nationwide class. The court certified a nationwide class over Lucky Cereal Co.'s objections.

The trial court then held a hearing to determine what constituted proper notice to the nationwide class members. Lucky Cereal Co. asked the court to require Arthur, Bob, and Calvin to provide individual notice to each of the class members. At the end of the hearing, the trial court instead ordered that Arthur, Bob, and Calvin publish notices in the major newspapers in all 50 states.

Upset with the ruling, Lucky Cereal Co.'s lawyer stormed out of the courtroom and filed a notice of appeal with the Illinois appellate court. It asked the appellate court to order the trial court to require Arthur, Bob, and Calvin to give individual notice to each class member. The appellate court refused to consider the appeal on the ground that it lacked jurisdiction.

1.   Did the trial court err in certifying the nationwide class over Lucky Cereal Co.'s two objections? Explain.

2.   Did the trial court err in the notice that it required Arthur, Bob, and Calvin to give to class members? Explain.

3.   Did the appellate court err in finding that it lacked jurisdiction over the appeal? Explain.

ANSWER TO QUESTION 29

1.   The trial court did not err in certifying the nationwide class over Lucky Cereal Co.'s two objections. At issue is whether an Illinois court may certify a nationwide class action when some of the class members are not residents of Illinois, and the extent to which the claims of the class members may have different facts and different law applied to each case.

Generally, to certify a class for a class action lawsuit in Illinois, the court must find that: (i) the class is so numerous that joinder of all plaintiffs is impracticable; (ii) common questions of law or fact predominate over any issues affecting only individual class members; (iii) the representative will fairly and adequately protect the interests of the class; and (iv) a class action lawsuit is an appropriate (not necessarily superior) method for a fair adjudication of the controversy.

Lucky Cereal Co. objected to class certification on two grounds: (i) that there are different questions of fact and law that preclude class certification, and (ii) that the court did not have personal jurisdiction of out-of-state plaintiffs who did not have any contacts with Illinois. Both objections are without merit.

As to the first objection, Lucky Cereal Co. is incorrect in stating that the different questions of fact or law preclude class action certification—the real question is whether the common questions *predominate* over the individual question. In the instant case, the slight variations in state law should not bar certification of the class action, because common questions of fact (given the great similarity of the individual causes of action) predominate over individual questions, and common questions of law will probably arise notwithstanding some slight variations of state law. The claims of all class members do not have to be *exactly* the same—the common questions must predominate over the individual claims. Additionally, Illinois allows classes to be broken down into subclasses. Thus, out-of-state plaintiffs could be broken down into subclasses, enabling the court to easily apply different states' laws (assuming Illinois law would not apply to the entire case).

Ordinarily, plaintiffs consent to jurisdiction by filing a lawsuit. However, this general rule is not applicable here—the plaintiffs are not voluntarily filing suit; rather, they are having a suit filed for them by the class representative. As to the second objection, the minimum contacts test of *International Shoe* does not apply to *plaintiffs* of class action lawsuits. Although procedural due process—notice and an opportunity to be heard or object (discussed below)—must be satisfied, the fact that some members of the class are not residents of Illinois and do not have minimum contacts with Illinois would not prevent a class action lawsuit. Therefore, the trial court did not err in certifying the nationwide class.

2.   The trial court did err in the notice it required. At issue is whether a trial court may allow class representatives to give the other class members notice by publication when the addresses of the class members are available.

Plaintiffs in a class action lawsuit must be afforded procedural due process—that is, notice and an opportunity to be heard. Notice must be of a type that, considering all of the circumstances, provides actual notice and an opportunity to be heard or to object to the class action by opting out. Lucky Cereal Co. has maintained a list of 75,000 customers who sent in the required box tops but did not receive a matchbox car. Given that *all* potential plaintiffs are easily identifiable and that the cost of a mailing to these individuals would probably be slight in comparison with the potential claim ($0.34 plus other mailing expenses vs. $6.00 per matchbox car), notification by first class mail should have been made, in addition to notice by publication. Lucky Cereal has standing to raise the due process claim of the class members because it has an interest in ensuring that each member's claim is resolved, one way or another, through the class action.

Thus, the court erred in not requiring Arthur, Bob, and Calvin to give other potential class members individual notice, plus notice by publication for those members who for one reason or another could not be contacted.

3.   The appellate court did not err in finding that it lacked jurisdiction over the appeal. At issue is whether the appellate court has jurisdiction over an appeal claiming that notice to absent class members was not sufficient. In Illinois, generally only final orders (and some orders by rule) are appealable. The appellant also may request that the trial court certify the issue as one involving a question of law with substantial grounds for difference of opinion, with an additional finding by the court that an immediate appeal from the order would materially advance the ultimate termination of the litigation. Here, however, there is no indication that Lucky requested the certificate or that the trial court issued one. Furthermore, although the certification of a class is an appealable order under Illinois Supreme Court Rule 306, the order here deals with notice to the class, not certification. Thus, the appellate court lacked jurisdiction over the appeal.

QUESTION 30

Harry Homeowner has resided in Grundy County, Illinois, since 1990. In January 2001, he decided that he wanted to build a new home on a lot that he had bought adjacent to his then current home. He entered into a contract with Bob, doing business as Bob's Builders, for Bob to design and build the new home by October 1, 2001, in exchange for $80,000. Bob operated his business out of his home in Grundy County, Illinois.

Harry made a $10,000 down payment to Bob, and Bob began to design and build Harry's new home. Bob subcontracted with his nephew Ralph Roofer for Ralph to put on the roof of Harry's house. Ralph has resided in Omaha, Nebraska, all his life and visited Illinois only for three weeks in October 2001, when he stayed with his uncle Bob and installed the roof of Harry's house.

Bob finished the job on November 15, 2001, and Harry moved into his new home at the end of November. Harry refused to pay Bob the $70,000 balance due on the home because Bob finished building the home late.

During the evening of December 17, 2001, Grundy County received its first snowfall of the season, and a part of the roof on Harry's new home collapsed. It turned out that Ralph negligently had failed to seal the roof.

Bob filed a one-count complaint in the Circuit Court of Grundy County, Illinois, against Harry for breach of contract to recover the $70,000 due on the home. After a bench trial on the merits, the court entered judgment for Bob in the amount of $70,000. Harry did not allege any affirmative defenses or file any counterclaims in that action.

Three days after the court entered judgment, Harry initiated a one-count complaint against Bob in the Circuit Court of Grundy County, Illinois, for breach of warranty. Bob filed a motion to dismiss the complaint on the grounds that (i) Harry did not plead the cause of action as a counterclaim in the prior action and (ii) res judicata. The court denied Bob's motion on both counts.

Bob subsequently filed a third-party complaint against his nephew Ralph for negligence, alleging that Ralph was liable to Bob to the extent of Bob's liability to Harry. Bob properly served Ralph in Omaha. Ralph filed a motion to dismiss alleging that (i) Bob improperly joined him as a party to the litigation; and (ii) the court lacked personal jurisdiction over Ralph.

1.   Did the court err in denying Bob's motion? Explain as to both grounds.

2.   How should the court rule on Ralph's motion? Explain as to both grounds.

ANSWER TO QUESTION 30

1.   The court erred in denying Bob's motion. At issue is whether Harry's warranty claim was a compulsory counterclaim or barred by res judicata.

Harry's warranty claim should not be viewed as a compulsory counterclaim. In many jurisdictions, a compulsory counterclaim is generally defined as a claim that must be asserted in the pending action because it arises from the same transactions or occurrences at issue in the pending action, and, if a compulsory counterclaim is not asserted in the pending action, it is lost. On the other hand, a permissive counterclaim is generally defined as a claim that need not be brought in the pending action because it does not arise out of the same transaction or occurrence. However, Illinois does not draw a distinction between permissive and compulsory counterclaims—all are permissive. Because Harry's counterclaim is permissive, it need not have been brought in the initial action. Thus, Harry's lawsuit should not be dismissed on this basis.

However, the doctrine of res judicata should prevent Harry's suit. For res judicata to apply, the earlier judgment must (i) be final, (ii) be on the merits, and (iii) involve the same cause of action as the present suit. Additionally, for res judicata to bar a defendant from bringing a potential counterclaim as a separate action in a later suit, it must be shown that a successful prosecution of the second action would nullify the initial judgment or would impair the rights established in the second action. In the instant case, it is the third requirement of res judicata that is in question. Originally, Bob sued Harry for breach of contract based on Harry's failure to pay. Now, Harry is suing Bob based on breach of warranty because of a defect in the roof. However, an Illinois court would use a "transactional" test to determine whether Harry's claim should be barred by res judicata. That is, if the current and former claims arise from a single group of operative facts, the current claim will be barred. Factors to be considered include whether (i) the facts occurred within a short period; (ii) the facts have a common origin; (iii) the facts would be more conveniently tried together; and (iv) a joint trial of all facts would conform to the parties' expectations or common business practices. Here, both cases arise out of the building of Harry's home. The breach of contract (Bob's case) also matured within one month of Harry's breach of warranty claim. Finally, since both cases involved a potential payment relating to the same house, the two claims would have been more conveniently tried together, and the judgment in the initial case would be impaired if Harry were to be successful in the second case. Thus, Harry's claim should be barred by res judicata.

2.   The court should deny Ralph's motion to dismiss based on improper joinder and the lack of personal jurisdiction over Ralph, who is a citizen of Nebraska.

Within the time for filing an answer (or later with leave of court), a defendant may file a third-party complaint against another party if that party may be liable to the original defendant for all or part of the plaintiff's claim against him. [Code §2-406] The purpose of third-party practice is to permit a court to determine the rights and liabilities of all the parties connected with a transaction or occurrence in a single action, thereby avoiding multiplicity of actions.

In the underlying case, Harry is suing Bob based on breach of warranty. The defect that caused the breach of warranty was Ralph's failure to properly seal the roof, which is the subject of Bob's third-party complaint based on negligence. Thus, both claims arise from the same set of facts, and it would be inefficient to try the claims separately, given that much of the evidence would be the same. Therefore, assuming the third-party complaint was filed timely (or with leave of the court), Ralph's motion to dismiss based on improper joinder should be denied.

Furthermore, Ralph's contention that the court lacks personal jurisdiction over him is without merit. To be valid, the exercise of jurisdiction must be authorized by law and constitutionally permissible. Illinois has four traditional common law bases of personal jurisdiction—(i) consent, (ii) physical presence at the time of service, (iii) the "doing business" standard for foreign corporations and individuals (that is more than one isolated transaction), and (iv) domicile or residence in Illinois. Additionally, jurisdiction over the person may be asserted on the basis of the Illinois long arm statute.

Given that Ralph's conduct/status does not fall within the traditional common law bases, the question is whether the Illinois long arm statute authorizes a court to exercise jurisdiction over a person who commits a tort in Illinois if the lawsuit is related to the tort. The negligence alleged in Bob's third-party complaint—the failure to properly seal the roof—occurred in Illinois. Thus, in this case, jurisdiction is authorized by the long arm statute. It should also be noted that the Illinois long arm statute authorizes personal jurisdiction over a defendant who has made or performed a contract or promise substantially connected with Illinois. In the present case, the contract involved the construction of a home (real property) located within Illinois boundaries. Therefore, the contract is undoubtedly "substantially connected" with Illinois, and personal jurisdiction would have been authorized by the long arm statute if the third party complaint were based on a contract theory. However, given that the third-party complaint is instead based on negligence, the commission of a tort portion of the long arm statute should be used as the basis for jurisdiction.

The only question then is whether the exercise of jurisdiction would be constitutional. The exercise of personal jurisdiction would be constitutional if the defendant has engaged in such minimum contacts that the exercise of jurisdiction over the defendant would not offend the traditional notions of fair play and substantial justice. A court would consider whether the defendant has purposefully availed himself of Illinois jurisdiction, and whether the defendant could have reasonably anticipated being haled into an Illinois court. Here, Ralph contracted to build a roof for a house located in Illinois in exchange for money. By entering into Illinois for business purposes, Ralph purposefully availed himself of rights, privileges, and protection under Illinois law. Furthermore, one should reasonably expect that, when he performs services on a fixed piece of property within a state, he might be haled into a court of that state for defects in workmanship. Given that Ralph purposefully availed himself of Illinois jurisdiction, and that Ralph should have reasonably anticipated being sued in Illinois under the given facts, the exercise of jurisdiction in this case would be constitutional.

QUESTION 31

Roberta resides in Will County, Illinois. On the evening of June 1, 2001, Roberta and her next-door neighbor Theresa decided to go bowling at Penny's Pins, a bowling alley owned by Penny in Will County, Illinois. They drove to Penny's Pins and then rented and changed into their bowling shoes, picked out their bowling balls, and walked to their assigned lane. Unfortunately, as Roberta stepped up to the lane to bowl for the first time, she slipped on water that had been spilled; she fell and hurt her back.

Roberta hired Alice Attorney to represent her. Alice immediately filed a one-count complaint on Roberta's behalf against Penny for negligence in the Circuit Court of Will County, Illinois. Alice also called Theresa and took Theresa's statement by telephone in which Theresa recounted what she remembered about Roberta's fall, including names of witnesses, the type of spill, and the nature of Roberta's injuries. Alice taped the statement, without interrupting Theresa, and Alice's secretary transcribed the statement.

Penny hired Larry Lawyer to defend her. Immediately after Penny received Roberta's complaint, she sent a copy of the bowling alley's operating manual to Larry, which included a section about how often Penny's employees should check the lanes for spills. Next to that section, Penny had made a notation, before the accident, that she saw "room for improvement."

Penny filed an answer, and the parties began discovery. The parties served document requests on each other. In response to Penny's document requests, Roberta answered that her attorney had the transcript of Theresa's statement but Alice and Roberta refused to produce it because the statement was protected by the attorney-client privilege and work product doctrine. They also objected to producing it on the ground that it would be deemed irrelevant at trial because Alice did not intend to call Theresa as a witness.

In response to Roberta's document requests, Penny stated that her attorney had a copy of the bowling alley's operating manual (with comments). However, Larry and Penny refused to produce it, because they claimed that it was protected by the attorney-client privilege and work product doctrine.

Penny served a set of interrogatories on Theresa. Theresa threw them into the wastebasket without looking at them.

The attorneys for the parties attempted to resolve their discovery disputes informally, but they were unable to do so.

1. **Larry Lawyer files a motion to compel Roberta and Alice to produce the transcript of Theresa's statement in Alice's possession over Roberta's objections. What result and why?**

2. **Alice Attorney files a motion to compel Penny and Larry to produce the copy of Penny's operating manual in Larry's possession over Penny's objections. What result and why?**

3. **Larry Lawyer files a motion to compel Theresa to answer the interrogatories served upon her. What result and why?**

ANSWER TO QUESTION 31

1.   The court should compel Roberta and Alice to produce the transcript of Theresa's statement. At issue is whether the transcript of Theresa's statement is (i) "undiscoverable" work product, (ii) covered by the attorney-client privilege, or (iii) irrelevant because Alice does not intend to call Theresa as a witness.

In Illinois, work product—material prepared by or for a party in preparation for trial—is freely discoverable unless disclosure would reveal the attorney's theories, mental impressions, or litigation strategy. Although Theresa made the taped statement during a phone call with Alice (Roberta's attorney), it was done without interruption by Alice. Because of Alice's lack of participation in eliciting facts from Theresa, disclosure could not reveal any of Alice's theories, impressions, or trial strategy.

Furthermore, the statement would not be covered by the attorney-client privilege. Attorney-client privilege covers communications between a client and her attorney. Here, the "client" part of the "attorney-client" privilege is missing because Theresa is only a witness in the case. Thus, there is no attorney-client privilege.

Finally, the fact that Alice does not intend to call Theresa as a witness is irrelevant. In Illinois, full disclosure of relevant matter is required, including the "identity and location of persons having knowledge of relevant facts." [Ill. S. Ct. R. 201(b)(1)] Thus, the depth of discovery is broad—it extends to any matter related to the lawsuit, and it is not limited to information that would be admissible in evidence at trial. Given the fact-based nature of Theresa's statement, it clearly relates and is relevant to the lawsuit.

Because the statement is not protected by the work product doctrine or attorney-client privilege, and because it is relevant for purposes of discovery, the court should compel Roberta and Alice to produce the transcript of Theresa's statement.

2.   The court should compel Penny and Larry to produce a copy of Penny's operating manual that is currently in Larry's possession. At issue is whether the attorney-client privilege or work product doctrine would allow Penny and Larry to refuse to produce the document.

In the instant case, the attorney-client privilege would not prevent disclosure. As stated previously, the attorney-client privilege covers communications between a client and her attorney. Here, before the accident and before consulting with her attorney, Penny made a notation in the manual that she saw "room for improvement." Thus, the "attorney" part of the "attorney-client" privilege is missing, and the manual cannot be withheld on this basis.

Furthermore, the work product doctrine does not prevent disclosure. In Illinois, the work product doctrine would prevent disclosure of material prepared for trial only if disclosure would reveal the attorney's theories, mental impressions, or trial strategy. None of these elements is present with regard to the operating manual. First, the manual was not prepared in preparation for trial; thus, the doctrine is not even applicable because the manual is not "work product." Second, even if the manual were somehow considered work product, disclosure would not reveal any of Larry's theories, mental impressions, or trial strategy.

Because neither the attorney-client privilege nor the work product doctrine prevents disclosure, the motion to compel should be granted.

3.   The court should not compel Theresa to answer the interrogatories. Interrogatories may only be served on parties in the case. [Ill. S. Ct. R. 213(a)] Theresa is a witness in the case, not a party. Thus, she cannot be compelled to answer the interrogatories, and the motion to compel should be denied. The proper procedure would have been either to serve Theresa with a subpoena to compel her appearance at a deposition, then ask the questions contained in the interrogatories during the deposition, or to properly notice and have taken a deposition on written questions.

QUESTION 32

Julie is the sole proprietor of Julie's Jewelers, a company that buys and sells diamonds out of Julie's home in Winnebago County, Illinois. At the beginning of 2002, Harry, who also resides in Winnebago County, inherited a wedding band from his grandfather. The band had stones that looked like diamonds. Harry was unemployed, so he brought the ring to Julie to sell it to her and told her of his suspicion that the stones were not real. Julie looked at the ring and said, "Yeah, the stones are fake, but I will give you the $200 that the ring is worth." Harry accepted the offer, gave Julie the ring, and received his $200. Two weeks later, Harry bumped into his sister, Sally Sister, who said, "Oh, I forgot to tell you, Grandpa wanted you to know that the ring he left you was worth $20,000."

Harry called Julie, but Julie refused to return the ring. Harry filed a two-count complaint in the Circuit Court of Winnebago County, Illinois, against Julie and Julie's Jewelers for fraud and negligent misrepresentation. Harry alleged in count one (fraud) that Julie knew the worth of the ring when she bought it and purposefully misled him. In count two (negligent misrepresentation), he alleged that Julie did not know the value of the ring when she bought it but failed to exercise due care in appraising and representing to him the value of the ring.

Rather than answer the complaint, Julie filed a motion to dismiss on the ground that Harry's two counts contained conflicting factual allegations regarding whether Julie knew the value of the ring when she bought it from Harry. The court denied the motion.

Julie then answered the complaint, and the parties proceeded with discovery. During discovery, the court ordered Julie to make the ring readily available to Harry for inspection, which she did. Julie's lawyer, Larry Lawyer, hired Alice Appraiser to appraise the ring, though Larry never intended for Alice to testify at trial. Harry subpoenaed Alice for a deposition to ask her solely about her appraisal, and Julie moved to quash the subpoena on the ground that the information Harry sought was privileged. The court granted the motion.

The parties proceeded to trial, without a jury. Harry presented his case but offered no evidence to establish that the ring was worth more than $200 (*i.e.*, that Julie made a misstatement of fact in representing to Harry the value of the ring)—a critical element of both counts on which he had the burden of proof. The court did not let Harry or Sally Sister testify to the value of the ring because they had no first-hand knowledge of its worth. Harry called no other witnesses. At the close of Harry's case, Julie moved the court to enter judgment in her favor over Harry's objection that the court should await Julie's case so he could challenge her credibility. The court granted the motion and dismissed the case.

1. **Did the court err in not granting Julie's motion to dismiss? Explain.**

2. **Did the court err in quashing the subpoena for Alice Appraiser's deposition? Explain.**

3. **Did the court err procedurally in granting Julie's motion for judgment in her favor at the close of Harry's case? Explain.**

4. **Did the court err substantively in granting Julie's motion for judgment in her favor at the close of Harry's case? Explain.**

ANSWER TO QUESTION 32

1.   The court did not err in denying Julie's motion to dismiss. At issue is whether a plaintiff may plead factually inconsistent causes of action. Generally, when a plaintiff does not know which of two or more statements of fact is true, he may plead them alternatively in the same or separate counts regardless of their consistency or inconsistency. Thus, if Harry truly did not know whether Julie knowingly or negligently misrepresented the value of the ring, he may plead separate causes of action based on fraud and negligent misrepresentation. Therefore, the court was correct in not granting Julie's motion to dismiss.

2.   The court did not err in quashing the subpoena for Alice Appraiser's deposition. At issue is when a party may depose his opponent's consulting expert. In Illinois, a consulting expert— defined as a person who is specially employed to assist with the litigation but who will not be called as a witness—is discoverable only on a showing of exceptional circumstances under which it is impracticable for a party seeking discovery to obtain facts or opinions of the same matter by other means. In the instant case, it is reasonable to assume that Harry could easily hire his own jewelry appraiser. Thus, the court did not err in quashing the subpoena for Alice Appraiser's deposition.

3.   The court did not procedurally err in granting Julie's motion for judgment at the close of Harry's case. At issue is when a court may direct a verdict. Illinois law provides that a party may move for a judgment (directed verdict), at the close of the evidence and before the case is submitted to the jury. Here, Harry has objected due to the fact that Julie has yet to put on her case. That objection is without merit. Harry had the burden of proof in the case and had an opportunity to meet that burden. As discussed below, he failed to meet that burden, and Julie need do nothing to prevail. Although the credibility of witnesses is for the jury to decide, Julie's credibility is not at issue. (Harry failed to call her as a witness, and she need not testify on her own behalf.) Thus, a directed verdict would be appropriate when Harry closed his case, and the court did not procedurally err in granting the motion.

4.   The court did not substantively err in granting the motion for judgment. At issue is under what circumstances a directed verdict may be granted. Generally, a directed verdict may be granted when the evidence, viewed in a light most favorable to the nonmoving party, so overwhelmingly favors the moving party that no contrary verdict could, on the evidence presented, possibly stand. Here, Harry—who has the burden of proof in the case—presented no evidence as to the ring's true value. Thus, based on the evidence, no jury could possibly find that Julie intentionally or negligently misrepresented the value of the ring, as the true value of the ring was never established. Therefore, the court did not substantively err in granting the motion for judgment.

QUESTION 33

Peachy Properties, Inc. ("Peachy Properties") leases apartment units to residential tenants at five properties located in Will County, Illinois. In late December 2001, Rachel Renter signed a lease with Peachy Properties to rent a unit in one of the company's buildings from January 1, 2002, through December 31, 2002.

Rachel moved into the unit, and at some time in the middle of February 2002, Steve Superintendent, the building superintendent and a Peachy Properties employee, remarked to her, "You know this place is loaded with asbestos." Steve Superintendent, a lifelong resident of Illinois, had been the superintendent of Rachel's building for the past 17 years.

Rachel thought Steve was joking, so she ignored the remark. Meanwhile, in August 2002, Izzy Inspector, the county's building inspector, found traces of asbestos in Rachel's unit during a routine inspection. The county ordered all tenants to vacate the building, and the building has been vacant since. Steve Superintendent retired to Florida three days after the county shut down the building.

Rachel made an appointment with her doctor, who told her that asbestos exposure causes an increased risk of lung cancer. Upon advice of a lawyer, Rachel filed a one-count complaint for negligence against Peachy Properties and Steve Superintendent in the Circuit Court of Will County, Illinois, for failing to exercise due care in maintaining her former building. Service of process on both defendants was proper. Peachy Properties answered the complaint, and Steve Superintendent filed a motion to dismiss the complaint for lack of personal jurisdiction. The court granted Steve Superintendent's motion.

The parties then proceeded with discovery and some pretrial motions. Before the final pretrial conference, Peachy Properties filed a motion to bifurcate the liability and damage phases of the trial to prevent the testimony on the health consequences of asbestos exposure from prejudicing the jury on liability. Rachel objected, and the court denied the motion.

At the pretrial conference, the court informed the parties of its new way of conducting voir dire. The court told the parties that to speed up voir dire, the interrogation of prospective jurors would be done solely by the court. The court also said that it would not permit challenges of prospective jurors by the parties' attorneys.

The court is rethinking its decision and seeks your advice.

1. **Did the court err in refusing to bifurcate the trial? Explain.**

2. **Did the court err in granting Steve Superintendent's motion to dismiss for lack of personal jurisdiction? Explain.**

3. **Can the court deny the attorneys the opportunity to interrogate prospective jurors? Explain.**

4. **Can the court deny the attorneys the ability to exercise challenges of prospective jurors? Explain.**

ANSWER TO QUESTION 33

1.   The court did not err in refusing to bifurcate a trial. At issue is whether a trial court must sever issues of liability and damages when there is a potential that the jury will become unduly swayed to find the defendant liable because of the extent of the plaintiff's injuries. Unlike federal practice, in Illinois there is no authority for a trial judge to sever the issues of liability and damages. In fact, in Illinois state courts, a trial judge may ***not*** sever the issues of liability and damages over the objection of a party. Therefore, the trial court did not err in refusing to bifurcate the trial, as it was prohibited from doing so over Rachel's objection.

2.   The court erred in granting Steve Superintendent's motion to dismiss on the basis of a lack of personal jurisdiction. At issue is whether an Illinois court has jurisdiction over a person who commits a tort within Illinois while a domiciliary of Illinois, but who subsequently moves to another state.

An Illinois court may assert personal jurisdiction when such jurisdiction is authorized by statute and constitutional. Note that there are two forms of personal jurisdiction: general and specific. General jurisdiction refers to jurisdiction over a defendant for all causes of action, and it is proper when (i) a defendant consents to it, (ii) a defendant is in Illinois when served with process, or (iii) a defendant is domiciled or "doing business" in Illinois. Specific jurisdiction provides the court with jurisdiction over a particular defendant only for causes of action arising from the defendant's conduct in the forum. Here, although the court could no longer exercise general jurisdiction over Steve because he is no longer domiciled in Illinois, the long arm statute of Illinois provides for specific jurisdiction over nonresidents who commit torts within Illinois. Steve is alleged to have committed a tort within Illinois. Thus, even though Steve is (now) a domiciliary of Florida, the court is authorized by the long arm statute to exercise jurisdiction over him.

As stated, once the court finds that jurisdiction is authorized by statute, it must determine that the law granting jurisdiction is constitutional. Personal jurisdiction is constitutional when the defendant has engaged in such minimum contacts that it would not offend the traditional notions of fair play and substantial justice. The court considers whether the defendant has purposefully availed himself of Illinois, and whether the defendant could reasonably anticipate being haled into an Illinois court. Here, Steve is alleged to have committed a tort while a resident of Illinois, and the cause of action arises from that tort. Furthermore, Steve reached out to Illinois by residing in Illinois and by making money in Illinois, and he had to have reasonably anticipated being haled into an Illinois court based on his conduct that occurred within Illinois. Given these factors, the exercise of personal jurisdiction over Steve would have been constitutional.

Therefore, given that the court had both a statutory basis to exercise jurisdiction, and such exercise would have been constitutional, the court erred in granting the motion to dismiss based on personal jurisdiction.

3.　The court abused its discretion by denying the parties an opportunity to interrogate the prospective jurors. At issue is whether the court must allow the parties the opportunity to interrogate potential jurors. Under Illinois Supreme Court Rule 234, the court is given broad discretion in managing voir dire. The court may limit further questioning of the jury and require the parties to submit any questions to it before the questions are put to the potential juror(s). The court may also prohibit direct examination by the parties (by requiring parties to submit questions to the court, with the court reading the question to the prospective juror), and the court may also prohibit the party from asking questions the court deems improper. However, this discretion is not limitless; any refusal to allow the parties to interrogate potential jurors would be reviewed by an appellate court under an "abuse of discretion" standard, taking into consideration whether the party was afforded an opportunity to probe for potential juror bias. In the present case, it is not clear if the court is merely requiring the parties to submit questions to it to read to the prospective jurors, or if the court is not allowing the parties to submit any questions whatsoever. If the former, the judge clearly would not be abusing his discretion—the rule expressly condones such a procedure. If the latter, it is far more likely that an appellate court would find an abuse of discretion. The appellate court would consider such factors as the length and scope of the court's initial questioning, the specific questions the parties desire to ask, the nature and complexity of the case, and whether potential juror bias was effectively probed. Given that the parties in the present case would not be afforded *any* opportunity to probe for juror bias, a per se prohibition of further questioning would most likely be an abuse of discretion. The court should at least allow the parties to submit questions before refusing to put them to the prospective jurors. Therefore, I would advise the court to allow the parties some opportunity to interrogate the prospective jurors (but note that the court may require the parties to submit the questions to it beforehand, and it may refuse to allow any question it deems improper).

4.　The court may not deny the attorneys the ability to exercise challenges of prospective jurors. At issue is whether a party has the right to peremptory challenges and challenges for cause. First, the Illinois Constitution provides for the right to a jury trial. Implicit within this provision is the right to an impartial jury. A challenge for cause is the primary method for ensuring that an impartial juror is selected, and any denial of a challenge for cause will be reviewed on an "abuse of discretion" standard. By not even hearing the challenge for cause, the court is very likely abusing its discretion and denying the party his right to an impartial jury. Second, Illinois Code of Civil Procedure section 2-1106 provides that each side is entitled to a certain number of peremptory challenges (depending on the number of parties). The court is not free to change this statutory provision. Therefore, the court must allow each party its statutory share of peremptory challenges and any number of challenges for cause to ensure that an impartial jury is seated.

QUESTION 34

James Jalopy resides in McHenry County, Illinois. He often drinks at Sam's Sports Bar, a sole proprietorship in Kane County, Illinois. One night in late 2002, after drinking at Sam's, James went joyriding in his jalopy through the streets of Chicago, which is located in Cook County, Illinois.

As he drove through the streets, James ran a red light and hit Peter Pedestrian. Peter, who lives in Chicago, sustained broken bones, fractures, and bruises. There were two witnesses to Sam serving James alcohol earlier that evening, one who lives in Kane County and one who lives in DuPage County, Illinois. There were two witnesses to the accident, one who resides in Cook County and the other who resides in McHenry County. Peter Pedestrian received immediate medical attention from the Chicago Police and Fire Departments and at a local hospital in Cook County, Illinois.

Peter filed a two-count complaint against James Jalopy and Sam (as owner of Sam's Sports Bar) in the Circuit Court of Cook County, Illinois, seeking $40,000 in damages. Peter made a jury demand. In count one (recklessness), he alleged that James Jalopy drove recklessly through the streets of Chicago and, in doing so, hit and injured Peter. In count two (Illinois Dram Shop Act), Peter alleged that Sam caused Peter's injuries by serving James alcohol, despite knowing that he would be driving when he left the bar.

The Cook County Sheriff's Office served a copy of the summons and complaint on one of Sam's bartenders, who happened to be alone at the bar when the officer arrived. The sheriff's office could not effectuate service on James despite three attempts to do so. When Peter's lawyer learned that the sheriff's office had failed on its third try, she decided that she had waited long enough and immediately had her 27-year-old paralegal serve the complaint and summons on James personally. The paralegal was successful in doing so.

James and Sam each made appearances for the sole purpose of moving to dismiss the complaint for improper service of process, and the court denied both motions. James and Sam then answered the complaint, and with his answer, Sam filed a motion to transfer the case to either Kane or McHenry County on the ground that Cook County was a forum non conveniens because neither defendant resided there. The court denied that motion as well.

Pursuant to Supreme Court Rules and applicable rules of the Circuit Court of Cook County, the court ordered arbitration. The arbitrators ruled 2-1 in Peter's favor on both counts, assessing damages of $30,000 against Sam and $5,000 against James.

1.   Did the court err in denying James's motion to dismiss for improper service of process? Explain.

2.   Did the court err in denying Sam's motion to dismiss for improper service of process? Explain.

3.   Did the court err in denying Sam's motion to transfer? Explain.

4.   Does Sam have the ability to reject the decision of the arbitrators and, if so, can Sam call the dissenting arbitrator who ruled in his favor as a witness at trial? Explain.

ANSWER TO QUESTION 34

1.   The court erred in denying James's motion to dismiss for improper service. At issue is who may properly serve process in Illinois. In Illinois, in addition to the county sheriff, any person who is older than 18 years, not a party to the action, **and** appointed by the court may serve process. The plaintiff's attorney (and the attorney's employees by extension) are not considered

parties. In the present case, the problem is not that the paralegal was too young or was an employee of Peter's attorney. Rather, the facts state that Peter's attorney "immediately" had her paralegal serve process; thus, it appears that the paralegal was not appointed by the court. Therefore, the court erred in denying the motion to dismiss for improper service.

2.   The court probably erred in denying Sam's motion to dismiss for improper service of process. At issue is who may properly accept service of process for an individual defendant. In Illinois, to serve an individual, the plaintiff must have the defendant (i) served personally or (ii) served by leaving a copy of the complaint at his "usual place of abode" with a person residing there, provided that the person actually served is older than 13. Here, service was made on a bartender at Sam's place. Thus, Sam was not served personally, and effective "abode service" was not accomplished because the complaint was not left at Sam's house with someone of suitable age living there. Thus, the court erred in denying the motion.

3.   The court did not err in denying Sam's motion to transfer based on forum non conveniens. At issue is whether the fact that no defendant resides in the county of venue is grounds to transfer an action to another county based on forum non conveniens. In Illinois, forum non conveniens is a discretionary means by which a trial judge may transfer a case to another county when maintenance of the suit in the present county would be *grossly* inconvenient to the parties or witnesses. In the instant case, Sam claims that Cook County is an inconvenient forum for both defendants. Although no defendant resides in Cook County, both are residents of Illinois, and all are located within commuting distance of Chicago. After all, James (defendant one) found it convenient enough to drive while intoxicated from the bar owned by Sam (defendant two) to Chicago, resulting in the accident in question. Because maintenance of the suit in Cook County would not be grossly inconvenient, the judge did not err in denying Sam's motion to transfer based on forum non conveniens.

4.   Sam may reject the arbitration award, but he may not call the dissenting arbitrator as a witness. The issues are whether a party has the right to reject an arbitration award and what effect arbitration proceedings have on a case. In Illinois, by supreme court rule, a party may reject an arbitration award by serving a written notice of rejection on all other parties and filing it with the court. Assuming Sam follows this procedure, he may reject the award. Once a party rejects an arbitration award, the case proceeds to trial, but the party may not use the arbitration proceedings as evidence. Thus, although Sam may reject the award, he cannot call the dissenting arbitrator as a witness.

QUESTION 35

Toothy Toothpaste Corp. ("Toothy") has its principal place of business in Kankakee County, Illinois. Starting in June 2002, Toothy manufactured, marketed, and distributed the Toothy Whitener, a new toothpaste that Toothy claimed would whiten teeth in 10 days. Toothy marketed and sold the product through the end of 2002, but recalled the product in January 2003 because thousands of consumers who had used the Toothy Whitener had developed yellow stains on their teeth.

Jack, a resident of Kankakee County, Illinois, was one of those consumers. In February 2003, he inherited a one-count complaint for negligent misrepresentation against Toothy in the Circuit Court of the 21st Judicial Circuit, Kankakee County, Illinois ("*Toothy I*"). He

brought the action "on behalf of himself and all others similarly situated who had yellow stains on their teeth after using the Toothy Whitener between July 2002 and December 2002."

In April 2003, Jack moved for class certification, but the court denied class certification. Jack, skeptical about proceeding solely on his own behalf, asked the Illinois Appellate Court to review the order denying class certification. The Illinois Appellate Court assumed jurisdiction over the appeal and ordered the trial court to certify the class.

The trial court certified the class, and Jack then gave proper notice to all class members. Lisa, a resident of New York, New York, who had spent over $20,000 in dental bills after using the Toothy Whitener in September 2002, properly opted out of the class.

The court bifurcated the liability and damage phases of the trial. At the end of the liability phase, the jury found Toothy liable for negligent misrepresentation, and the court entered judgment for plaintiffs on liability. The parties then proposed a damages settlement to the court and provided notice of the proposed settlement to all class members, including to Monica, a resident of San Francisco, California, who had incurred $12,000 in dental bills to repair her teeth cosmetically after she had used the Toothy Whitener. Monica had not opted out of the class. Under the formula specified in the settlement proposal, Monica would have received $100.

Monica filed an objection to the proposed settlement with the court. She received a hearing on her objection, but the court approved the settlement anyway.

Monica received her $100 check in the mail, tore it up, and filed a one-count complaint against Toothy for negligent misrepresentation in the Circuit Court of the 21st Judicial Circuit, Kankakee County, Illinois ("*Toothy II*") to recover the full amount of her dental expenses. Toothy moved to dismiss the complaint on the ground that *Toothy I* barred the claim.

Lisa, who opted out of the class, filed a one-count complaint against Toothy for negligent misrepresentation in the Circuit Court of the 21st Judicial Circuit, Kankakee County, Illinois ("*Toothy III*"). She moved for partial summary judgment on the issue of liability on the ground that Toothy was bound by the judgment for the plaintiffs on liability in *Toothy I*.

1.   Did the appellate court have the authority in *Toothy I* to review the order of the trial court denying class certification? Explain.

2.   How should the court rule on Toothy's motion to dismiss in *Toothy II*? Explain.

3.   How should the court rule on Lisa's motion for partial summary judgment in *Toothy III*? Explain.

ANSWER TO QUESTION 35

1.   The appellate court had the authority in *Toothy I* to review the order of the trial court denying class certification. At issue is whether an order denying class certification may be appealed. In Illinois, only final orders are appealable, with certain exceptions. One exception is the grant or

denial of class certification. [Ill. S. Ct. R. 306] Thus, the appellate court had the authority to review the order relating to class certification.

2.   The court should grant Toothy's motion to dismiss in *Toothy II*. At issue is the res judicata effect given to a class action settlement against those plaintiffs who fail to opt out after being given an opportunity to do so. Any prior judgment (class action or not) is given res judicata effect if it is final and on the merits, and if it involves the same cause of action as the current suit. Additionally, a judgment in a class action is binding on all class members except those who have been properly excluded or who have properly requested exclusion. The judgment/settlement in *Toothy I* is entitled to res judicata effect, given that it finally disposed of all claims in *Toothy I*, that it was on the merits (in that Toothy admitted liability and paid claims according to a formula), and that it involved the same cause of action (the yellowing of Monica's teeth). Additionally, Monica received proper notice of the class action but failed to opt out of the class. Thus, she is bound by the settlement. Therefore, the court should grant Toothy's motion to dismiss *Toothy II* as being barred by res judicata.

3.   The court should grant Lisa's motion for partial summary judgment on liability in *Toothy III*. At issue is whether Toothy can be collaterally estopped from denying liability for Lisa's dental injuries by virtue of the judgment of *Toothy I*, in which it was held liable for negligent misrepresentation. In Illinois, a party may be collaterally estopped from litigating an issue when (i) the issue in the first case is identical to the issue presented in the second case; (ii) there was a final judgment on the merits in the first case; (iii) the party against whom collateral estoppel is to be applied was a party or in privity with a party in the first case; and (iv) the application of collateral estoppel is not fundamentally unfair to the party being estopped. Note that Illinois does not require mutuality of parties. All four factors are met. The first judgment found Toothy liable based on negligent misrepresentation, the same theory under which Lisa is asserting her claim. The judgment in *Toothy I* is also a final judgment on the merits, in that the first judgment disposed of all claims and specifically found Toothy liable under a negligent misrepresentation theory. Additionally, Toothy was obviously a party to the first case. Finally, the application of collateral estoppel would not be fundamentally unfair, given that both actions are civil actions with the same burden of proof, and that Toothy had every incentive to fully litigate the issue in *Toothy I*, as it had to know that there would be other lawsuits to follow if it lost. Thus, the court should grant Lisa's motion for partial summary judgment in *Toothy III*, given that Toothy should be collaterally estopped from litigating its liability based on negligent misrepresentation.

QUESTION 36

Sal's Shopping Emporium, Inc., is an Illinois corporation that manages large suburban shopping malls in two neighboring Illinois counties, Clark County and Crawford County. Sal, the 100% shareholder of the corporation, has his office connected to Crawford Crossings, the shopping mall in Crawford County. Sal's loyal employee of 20 years, Ellen Employee, has an office connected to Clark Crossings, the shopping mall in Clark County, and has primary responsibility for supervising that mall.

Carla Consumer is a resident of Crawford County, Illinois, and one night in February 2003, went to Crawford Crossings to shop. She parked her new 2003 Buick Skylark in the Crawford Crossings parking lot, where she left it for about an hour while she shopped in three stores at Crawford Crossings. When she returned to her car, she found it vandalized;

there was over $5,000 in damage to the body of the car, the tires were flattened, and her customized compact disc player was missing from the car. She recalled that her friend, Frank Friend, had a similar experience in the Crawford Crossings parking lot that past January. Frank also resides in Crawford County, Illinois.

Carla Consumer filed a one-count complaint for negligence against Sal's Shopping Emporium, Inc., in the Circuit Court of Clark County, Illinois, alleging that the corporation failed to exercise reasonable care in providing parking lot security at Crawford Crossings. Sal filed a motion to dismiss the complaint for improper venue, and, in the alternative, moved the court to transfer the case based on the doctrine of intrastate forum non conveniens, to Crawford County, Illinois. The court denied both motions.

After Sal answered the complaint and both parties engaged in discovery, Sal's Shopping Emporium, Inc., filed a motion for summary judgment. Sal attached a sworn affidavit to his motion from his security director, also a resident of Crawford County, Illinois, who attested that he had personally installed the lighting in the Crawford Crossings parking lot, that the lot was well lit, that he was personally on duty the night that Carla's car was vandalized and that despite his vigilance he did not see any wrongdoing. Carla's attorney responded to the motion with two sworn affidavits. One affidavit, signed by Carla Consumer, included a list of all reported crimes over the past year in the Crawford Crossings parking lot that the attorney gathered from the police blotter of the local paper. In another affidavit, signed by Carla's expert, the expert wrote, "In my opinion, Crawford Crossings did not meet the standard of care for maintaining the security of its parking lot." Sal filed a motion to strike the affidavits. Carla Consumer's attorney, worried about the success of her case, filed a motion for voluntary dismissal of Carla Consumer's complaint. The court denied that motion, granted Sal's motion to strike, and entered summary judgment in favor of Sal's Shopping Emporium, Inc.

1. Did the court err in denying the motion of Sal's Shopping Emporium, Inc., to dismiss the complaint for improper venue and, if not, did the court err in denying the motion to transfer the case to Crawford County, Illinois? Explain.

2. Did the court err when it denied Carla Consumer's motion for voluntary dismissal? Explain.

3. Did the court err in granting the motion of Sal's Shopping Emporium, Inc., to strike the two affidavits submitted by Carla Consumer's attorney? Explain.

ANSWER TO QUESTION 36

1. The court did not err in denying Sal's Shopping Emporium's motion to dismiss the complaint for improper venue. At issue is the place of proper venue for corporations and the appropriate remedy for improper venue. In Illinois, venue is proper in the county in which the transaction, or some part it, occurred. Additionally, for a corporation, venue is proper in any county in which it has an office or is doing business. If suit is brought in an improper venue, the court should transfer the case to a county of proper venue. Here, the complaint arises out of events taking place in Crawford County, and Sal's Shopping Emporium has offices and is doing business in both Crawford County and Clark County. Thus, venue would be proper in either Crawford

County or Clark County. Furthermore, a dismissal of Carla's case would not have been the appropriate remedy. Rather, had venue been improper, the appropriate remedy would have been transfer of the case to a county of proper venue.

However, the court probably erred in refusing to transfer the case based on the inconvenience of the chosen forum, although this decision is unlikely to be overturned on appeal. In Illinois, a court may transfer a case from a proper, but inconvenient, Illinois forum to another proper forum. Great deference is given to the plaintiff's choice of venue, and consideration is also given to the source of and access to proof, court dockets, and the cost and burden to the parties and their attorneys. In the instant case, virtually all persons associated with the case reside in Crawford County. The alleged negligence giving rise to the case occurred in Crawford County; Sal's Shopping Emporium's main office is in Crawford County; and most potential witnesses (Frank Friend and Sal's security director) are residents of Crawford County. The facts do not state in which county Carla's expert resides, but an out-of-county expert probably would not bar transfer of the case because expert witnesses are probably accustomed to traveling for court dates. Assuming that transfer to Crawford County would not materially increase the burden or cost to Carla, the court probably erred in denying the motion to transfer venue due to the inconvenience of Clark County. That said, the trial court's decision is unlikely to be overturned on appeal—the combination of the deference given to a trial court's ruling ("abuse of discretion" standard) and the deference given to a plaintiff's choice of venue would probably preclude a successful appeal.

2. The court did not err in denying Carla's motion for a voluntary dismissal. At issue is when a plaintiff may seek a voluntary dismissal. In Illinois, a plaintiff may dismiss her action without prejudice before trial or before a hearing on the merits is held; if the trial has begun or if a hearing has been held, the plaintiff may voluntarily dismiss only on stipulation with the defendant or on motion supported by affidavit. Even then, the court may rule on potentially dispositive motions that have already been filed. In the instant case, the court had already ruled on a motion to dismiss; thus, Carla could only voluntarily dismiss with leave of court supported by affidavit. She did not follow this procedure, and the court could have denied the motion for this reason. Furthermore, because Sal's Shopping Emporium filed a motion—the motion for summary judgment—that could finally dispose of the case before Carla moved for a voluntary dismissal, the court could hear and decide the motion for summary judgment first. Thus, the court did not err in denying Carla's motion for a voluntary dismissal.

3. The court did not err in striking the affidavits submitted by Carla's attorney. At issue are the requirements for an affidavit in Illinois. In Illinois, an affidavit in support of a motion for summary judgment must be made on personal knowledge of the affiant and must state facts with particularity. In the instant case, Carla signed an affidavit in which she provided all of the reported crimes in Sal's Shopping Emporium's parking lot over the past year as gathered by her attorney from the local paper. Carla's expert's affidavit merely states that, in his opinion, Crawford Crossings did not meet the standard of care for maintaining the security of its parking lot. Because Carla did not personally compile the crime statistics, the affidavit fails because it was not based on personal knowledge. Additionally, the affidavit by Carla's expert merely states a conclusion without any supporting facts. Thus, that affidavit fails to state facts with particularity. Therefore, the court did not err in striking both affidavits.

QUESTION 37

On January 3, 2003, in McHenry County, Illinois, Tara Trucker, driving her Ford Ranger, and Dana Driver, driving a Honda Civic, had a car accident. They each reached a four-way

stop sign at the same time, Dana Driver going east and Tara Trucker going north. They both stopped at the stop sign, but their vehicles collided when they entered the intersection. Dana Driver alleges that she had the right-of-way because she reached the four-way stop sign first. Tara Trucker alleges that Dana Driver was intoxicated and talking on her cellular telephone at the time of the accident, and that she had already entered the intersection before Dana did.

Dana Driver filed a one-count complaint for negligence against Tara Trucker in the Circuit Court of McHenry County, Illinois. Tara Trucker answered the complaint, and both parties engaged in discovery.

On June 15, 2003, Tara Trucker served on Dana's lawyer, Alice Attorney, requests for admissions of facts pursuant to Illinois Supreme Court Rule 216, including requests to admit that Dana had been intoxicated and talking on a cellular telephone at the time of the accident. On July 10, 2003, Alice Attorney filed an answer to the requests, denying the matters for which admissions were requested. Only Alice Attorney signed the answer, and she served a copy of the answer on Tara Trucker. Tara Trucker filed a motion to strike the answer, and the court granted the motion on August 15, 2003. Neither Alice Attorney nor her client, Dana Driver, ever filed a further answer to the requests for admissions of facts.

Two months later, Tara Trucker filed for summary judgment on the basis of facts that were deemed admitted by Dana Driver's failure to answer Tara Trucker's requests for admissions. The parties briefed the motion for summary judgment, and, before the hearing, Alice Attorney filed a motion to bar the use of the alleged admitted facts. The court denied Alice Attorney's motion. Before the court could rule on Tara Trucker's motion for summary judgment, Alice Attorney asked the court to certify the legal issue raised in her motion for appeal to the Appellate Court of Illinois. She feared that she would lose the case if the appellate court did not hear her appeal. The court refused, and Alice Attorney filed a notice of appeal with the Appellate Court of Illinois anyway, seeking a reversal of the adverse ruling on Dana Driver's motion to bar the use of the alleged admitted facts. The trial court decided to defer ruling on Tara Trucker's motion for summary judgment until the appellate court decided whether to take jurisdiction of the appeal.

1.   Did the trial court err in granting Tara Trucker's motion to strike on August 15, 2003? Explain.

2.   Did the trial court err in denying Alice Attorney's motion to bar the use of the alleged admitted facts? Explain.

3.   Did the trial court err in not granting Alice Attorney's leave to appeal the denial of her motion to bar the use of the alleged admitted facts? Explain.

4.   Should the Appellate Court of Illinois assume jurisdiction over Dana Driver's appeal? Explain.

ANSWER TO QUESTION 37

1.   The trial court did not err in granting Tara Trucker's motion to strike the response to the requests for admissions filed by Alice Attorney. At issue is whether the response to requests for

admissions must be signed by the party. In Illinois, the denial of facts alleged in requests for admissions must be made under oath by the party. In the instant case, Dana Driver did not deny the facts under oath, as the facts state that only Alice Attorney signed the document. Thus, the trial court did not err in granting Tara Trucker's motion to strike the response to the requests for admissions.

2.   The trial court did not err in denying Alice Attorney's motion to bar the use of the alleged admitted facts. At issue is the effect of a failure to respond to requests for admissions. In Illinois, if a party fails within 28 days to deny all facts under oath contained within requests for admissions, those facts are deemed admitted. (Under Rule 183, the court may extend the deadline for good cause, but no good cause appears on the given facts.) In the instant case, the court struck Dana Driver's original response to the requests for admissions of facts, and Dana Driver failed to file another response to the requests. As a result, the facts—that Dana was talking on her cellphone and that Dana was intoxicated at the time of the accident—are deemed admitted.

3.   The trial court did not err in not granting Alice Attorney's leave to appeal the denial of her motion to bar the use of the alleged admitted facts. At issue is when a decision by the court may be appealed. In Illinois, the general rule is that only final orders may be appealed. An exception to the general rule exists when the court finds that (i) the order involves a question of law as to which there is a substantial ground for difference of opinion; and (ii) an immediate appeal from the order would materially advance the ultimate termination of the litigation. In the instant case, the court has not yet ruled on the motion for summary judgment, so there is no final order. Additionally, the order in question—whether the trial court improperly struck Dana's original response to the request for the admission of facts and whether the defendant may rely, for purposes of seeking a summary judgment, on facts not denied in a request for admissions—does not appear to present a novel question of law. Furthermore, the issues probably could proceed to the appellate court via the "normal" appellate channels once the trial court rules on the motion for summary judgment. If the trial court grants the motion for summary judgment, the resulting order could be appealed as a "final order," as it would most likely terminate the litigation in Tara Trucker's favor. As a result, an immediate appeal would not materially advance the ultimate termination of the litigation. Therefore, the trial court did not err in denying Alice Attorney's leave to appeal the denial of her motion to bar the use of the alleged admitted facts.

4.   The appellate court should not assume jurisdiction over Dana Driver's appeal. At issue is an appellate court's jurisdiction to hear an appeal. As stated above, only a final order may be appealed, with certain exceptions by rule (*e.g.*, an interlocutory appeal as described above and some circuit court orders such as an order granting a new trial). The trial court has not yet issued a final order, and none of the exceptions applies. Thus, the appellate court should not assume jurisdiction over Dana Driver's appeal.

QUESTION 38

Lucky, a resident of St. Louis, Missouri, is the sole proprietor of Lucky's Limousines, a limousine company that transports clients to and from Lambert-St. Louis International Airport. While Lucky's Limousines only advertises in Missouri, the company fulfills, on average, a few requests each year to transport clients to and from Illinois. Lucky himself has never been to Illinois, and he has no idea how his Illinois customers hear about Lucky's Limousines.

On January 3, 2002, Lucky's Limousines sent Donald Driver, a new driver with the company, to pick up a client in Jackson County, Illinois. When he reached Jackson County, Donald Driver looked down at his notes to find the address of his client. While he was looking down, his limousine hit and seriously injured Paula Pedestrian. Donald Driver sped away from the scene. Donald Driver, a resident of St. Louis, Missouri, had not been in Illinois before the incident, and has not been in Illinois since.

On December 15, 2003, within the two-year statute of limitations, Paula Pedestrian, a resident of Jackson County, Illinois, filed a one-count complaint in the Circuit Court of Jackson County, Illinois, against Lucky and Lucky's Limousines, alleging that Lucky was vicariously liable for Donald Driver's negligence because Donald Driver caused the injuries to Paula Pedestrian while acting within the scope of his employment for Lucky's Limousines. To serve Lucky, Paula Pedestrian's attorney sent Lucky a copy of the complaint and summons to his residence in St. Louis by registered mail.

On January 16, 2004, outside the two-year statute of limitations, Paula Pedestrian filed a motion to amend her complaint to add a second count of negligence against Lucky and Lucky's Limousines. She alleged that Lucky was negligent in hiring and supervising Donald Driver because Lucky knew that Donald Driver had been in seven accidents in the year prior to being hired by Lucky's Limousines.

Lucky filed a motion to dismiss the complaint for (i) lack of personal jurisdiction and (ii) improper service of process. The court denied both motions. The parties then briefed Paula Pedestrian's motion to amend her complaint, and the court denied that motion as well, on the ground that Paula Pedestrian's second count was barred by the statute of limitations.

1. Did the court err in denying Lucky's motion to dismiss the complaint for lack of personal jurisdiction? Explain.

2. Did the court err in denying Lucky's motion to dismiss the complaint for improper service of process? Explain.

3. Did the court err in denying Paula Pedestrian's motion to amend her complaint? Explain.

ANSWER TO QUESTION 38

1.   The court would not have erred in denying Lucky's motion to dismiss based on the allegation that the court did not have personal jurisdiction over Lucky, had Lucky been served in an authorized manner (*see* 2., below). At issue is whether jurisdiction over Lucky was authorized by an Illinois statute and whether Lucky had sufficient minimum contacts with Illinois.

The Illinois long arm statute authorizes "specific" jurisdiction (*i.e.*, jurisdiction over actions arising from the defendant's act) over defendants who commit certain acts in Illinois. One of those acts is the commission of a tort within Illinois. Here, Lucky's employee, Donald Driver, committed a tort within Illinois by allegedly hitting Paula Pedestrian with one of Lucky's limos. Lucky may be held vicariously liable for the acts of his employees, even for acts committed out of state. Thus, given that Lucky's conduct falls under the long arm statute, jurisdiction over Lucky is authorized by statute.

After finding that jurisdiction over a particular defendant is authorized by statute, the next inquiry is whether the exercise of such jurisdiction is constitutional, *i.e.*, whether the defendant has such contacts with the forum state such that the exercise of jurisdiction over him is fair and reasonable. If the court were exercising "general" jurisdiction (*i.e.*, jurisdiction over Lucky for all causes of action), substantial contacts with Illinois would have been required. However, the court here is asserting "specific" jurisdiction over Lucky. In such situations, the close contact between the in-state act (here, the commission of a negligent act) and the lawsuit provides the necessary minimum contact with the jurisdiction.

Furthermore, the Illinois long arm statute generally requires in-hand service, which clearly satisfies the requirement that service be reasonably calculated to give the defendant actual notice. (Unfortunately, plaintiff failed to use this method, and that fact will deprive the court of jurisdiction. *See* below.)

However, but for the lack of proper service, the court did not err in denying Lucky's motion to dismiss based on the lack of jurisdiction over him.

2.   The court erred in denying Lucky's motion to dismiss based on the allegation that he was improperly served. At issue are the authorized methods of service in Illinois. Under the Illinois long arm statute, service must be made in the same manner as service within the state, with the exception that court appointment is not needed to have a person over 18 serve the defendant. In Illinois, service on a sole proprietorship is perfected by in-hand service on an agent of the business. Here, Paula served Lucky by certified mail, which is not authorized by statute. In an Illinois state court, the only time service by mail is authorized is when it is used as part of a request to waive service of process. Given that Paula did not use an authorized method of service of process, the court erred in denying Lucky's motion to dismiss based on improper service of process.

3.   The court did not err in denying Paula Pedestrian's motion to amend her complaint to add a new claim against Lucky. At issue is whether a plaintiff may amend her complaint to add a new claim after the statute of limitations for that claim has run. In Illinois, a plaintiff may amend her complaint to add a new claim after the statute of limitations has run if (i) the original pleading was filed on time; and (ii) the added claim arose from the same transaction or occurrence as that of the original pleading. Here, although the original pleading was filed on time, the new claim does not relate to the old claim. The new claim is for the negligent hiring of Donald Driver, which arose from a transaction or occurrence distinct from the accident that gave rise to Paula's original claim. Thus, given that the new claim did not arise out of the same transaction or occurrence as the original claim, the court did not err in denying Paula Pedestrian's motion to amend her complaint.

QUESTION 39

Greg Grocer resides in Kendall County, Illinois, and is the sole proprietor of a grocery store within the county. In June 2002, he entered into an employment contract with Calvin Clerk, in which Calvin agreed to work 40 hours per week in Greg's grocery store.

By March 2003, the relationship between Greg Grocer and Calvin Clerk soured, and Greg terminated Calvin. Calvin Clerk filed a one-count complaint in the Circuit Court of Kendall County, Illinois, against Greg Grocer alleging breach of a written employment contract.

Greg Grocer answered the complaint, and pled, as an affirmative defense, "The Statute of Frauds bars Calvin Clerk's claim."

Calvin Clerk moved to strike Greg Grocer's affirmative defense on the ground that it was inadequately pleaded. The court granted the motion, and Greg Grocer never replead his affirmative defense.

Next, Calvin Clerk filed a motion to amend his complaint, to which he attached an amended complaint that included a second count for negligence against Greg Grocer. Calvin Clerk alleged that Greg Grocer was negligent in parking his car at the grocery store in November 2003, crashing his car into Calvin Clerk's parked car and causing damage to Calvin Clerk's car. Greg Grocer opposed Calvin Clerk's motion to amend his complaint on the ground that the second count of the complaint was unrelated to the first count. The court granted Calvin Clerk's motion to amend his complaint.

Near the close of discovery, Greg Grocer filed a motion for partial summary judgment on the breach of contract claim. To the motion, he attached an affidavit in which he attested that he never had entered into any employment contract with Calvin Clerk and that Calvin Clerk had been an employee at will. In Calvin Clerk's response to the motion, he wrote that summary judgment was inappropriate because there was a factual dispute as to whether he had a written employment contract with Greg Grocer. He then wrote that he would testify as to the existence of the written contract at trial. The court granted Greg Grocer's motion for partial summary judgment.

The court then scheduled a settlement conference. The court, after listening to Calvin Clerk's and Greg Grocer's positions on the negligence claim, recommended to the parties that they settle Calvin Clerk's negligence claim for $750. The parties followed the court's recommendation.

1.   Did the trial court err in granting Calvin Clerk's motion to strike Greg Grocer's affirmative defense? Explain.

2.   Did the trial court err in granting Calvin Clerk's motion to amend his complaint? Explain.

3.   Did the trial court err in granting Greg Grocer's motion for partial summary judgment? Explain.

4.   Did the trial court abuse its authority in recommending to Calvin Clerk and Greg Grocer how they should settle Calvin Clerk's negligence claim? Explain.

ANSWER TO QUESTION 39

1.   The court did not err in granting Calvin Clerk's motion to strike Greg Grocer's affirmative defense. At issue is whether the sentence "The Statute of Frauds bars Calvin Clerk's claim" is a sufficient pleading to establish an affirmative defense. In Illinois, although pleadings are to be construed liberally to do substantial justice between the parties, fact pleading is still used. To set up an affirmative defense, Greg must use facts showing that the Statute of Frauds applies in this

case. His statement is a mere legal conclusion and fails to allege any supporting facts. Thus, the court did not err in granting Calvin Clerk's motion to strike Greg Grocer's affirmative defense.

2.   The court did not err in granting Calvin Clerk's motion to amend his complaint despite Greg Grocer's objection that the claims are not related. At issue is whether, in Illinois, a plaintiff may join separate and distinct causes of action in a single action. In Illinois, a plaintiff may join any number of causes of action he wishes to assert against a defendant in a single action, although the court certainly has the discretion to order separate trials. Here, Calvin Clerk is asserting a breach of contract claim and a negligence claim against Greg Grocer, which is proper under the rules of procedure for Illinois. Thus, the court did not err in granting Calvin Clerk's motion to amend his complaint to add an unrelated negligence claim.

3.   The court did not err in granting Greg Grocer's motion for partial summary judgment. At issue is whether a party, when confronted with a motion for summary judgment that is supported by affidavits, can rest on responses that basically repeat pleading allegations, or whether he must submit his own affidavit or similar evidence showing that there is a material issue of genuine fact for a jury to decide. In Illinois, when confronted with a motion for summary judgment that is supported by an affidavit, the opposing party must submit his own affidavit or similar evidence (a copy of the contract would have sufficed) to show that there is a genuine issue of material fact for the jury to decide. Here, Calvin Clerk failed to do this. Rather, he basically attempted to rely on pleading allegations and the statement that he would testify to its existence at trial. That is not sufficient to survive a motion for summary judgment. Thus, the court did not err in granting Greg Grocer's motion for partial summary judgment.

4.   The court did not abuse its authority in recommending a settlement amount to the parties for Calvin Clerk's negligence claim. At issue is the pretrial role of the court in controlling litigation, and whether the judge abused his discretion in suggesting a settlement. In Illinois, the court has the express authority to hold pretrial conferences to explore the possibility of settlement and any other matters that may aid in the disposition of the case. Here, the court suggested a settlement of the case for $750. The parties were free to refuse to settle for this amount, or for any amount. Thus, the court's suggestion should be seen as exploring the possibility of settlement, as expressly authorized by Illinois law. Therefore, the court did not abuse its authority in recommending to the parties how they should settle Calvin Clerk's negligence claim.

QUESTION 40

Larry's Life Insurance Co. is a licensed insurance company located in Cook County, Illinois. In 2001, Paul Parent took out a $1 million life insurance policy and named as the beneficiaries "all of my children." He bought the policy from a life insurance sales representative in Grundy County, Illinois. Unfortunately, Paul Parent died in June 2003 in Grundy County.

Paul Parent had two biological children, a stepchild, and a foster child. The biological children, Claire and Abigail, live in Kankakee County, Illinois. Michael, the stepchild, lives in New York, and came to Illinois about once a year before Paul Parent's death to visit his stepfather. Ronald, the foster child, lives in Jackson County, Illinois, and he, who was 37 at the time of Paul Parent's death, had not seen Paul Parent since the age of 18.

Claire and Abigail filed a claim with Larry's Life Insurance Co. for the $1 million. They did not want Michael or Ronald to share in the money, but did alert Larry's Life Insurance Co. to Michael's and Ronald's potential claims.

Larry's Life Insurance Co. filed a complaint in the Circuit Court of Cook County, Illinois, against Claire, Abigail, and Michael, in which it asked the court to determine how it should distribute the $1 million. Michael consented to the jurisdiction of the court, but filed a motion to dismiss or transfer the complaint for improper venue, and to dismiss the complaint for failure to state a claim upon which relief could be granted. The court denied the motion on both grounds.

Michael then filed a motion asking the court to direct Larry's Life Insurance Co. to add Ronald as a defendant in the case. The court granted the motion. Larry's Life Insurance Co. amended its complaint to add Ronald as a defendant and then served Ronald with a complaint and summons. Two days prior to receiving the complaint and summons, Ronald had filed a separate action against Larry's Life Insurance Co. in the Circuit Court of Cook County, Illinois. Larry's Life Insurance Co. filed a motion to consolidate that case with the prior action brought by Larry's Life Insurance Co.

1. Did the court rule correctly on Michael's motion to dismiss or transfer the complaint for improper venue? Explain.

2. Did the court rule correctly on Michael's motion to dismiss the complaint for failure to state a claim upon which relief could be granted? Explain.

3. Did the court rule correctly on Michael's motion asking the court to direct Larry's Life Insurance Co. to add Ronald as a party to the case? Explain.

4. How should the court rule on Larry's Life Insurance Co.'s motion to consolidate? Explain.

ANSWER TO QUESTION 40

1. The court did not correctly rule on Michael's motion to dismiss or transfer the complaint for improper venue. At issue is whether venue was properly laid in Cook County, which is the county in which the plaintiff, Larry's Life Insurance Co., is located. In Illinois, venue is usually proper in either the county of the residence of any defendant who was joined in good faith or the county in which the transaction, or some part of it, took place. If *all* defendants are nonresidents, the case may be heard in any county. In the instant case, two defendants, Claire and Abigail, are residents of Kankakee County, and the policy was purchased in Grundy County. Thus, venue was proper either in Kankakee County or Grundy County. Given that the case was brought in Cook County, the court should have granted Michael's motion to transfer the case to a place of proper venue.

2. The court correctly ruled on Michael's motion to dismiss the complaint for failure to state a claim on which relief could be granted. At issue is whether a potential defendant may bring suit in order to have its potential liability judicially determined. In Illinois, any party may join persons whose claims against him (arising out of the same or related subject matter) may otherwise

subject him to multiple liability and require the joined parties to interplead, *i.e.*, to litigate between themselves the right to a single fund or item of personal property. Here, Larry's Life Insurance Co. is certainly liable to someone for the amount of the insurance policy ($1 million). The only question is to whom it is liable—*i.e.*, whether the beneficiary designation of "all of my children" includes stepchildren and foster children. Thus, Larry's Life Insurance Co. may properly interplead all potential claimants—Claire, Abigail, Michael, and Ronald—in order to have the phrase "all of my children" interpreted by a court of law, thereby avoiding the possibility that Larry's would be required to pay more than $1 million. As a result, the court properly denied Michael's motion to dismiss for failure to state a cause of action.

3.   The court correctly ruled on Michael's motion that requested the court to direct Larry's Life Insurance Co. to add Ronald as a party to the case. At issue is whether the court may properly join a person who has an interest in the case as a defendant. In Illinois, joinder of defendants is always permissive. That said, a person may be joined as a defendant when he (i) is alleged to have an interest in the action; (ii) must be joined for a complete determination of the issue; or (iii) is alleged to be jointly, severally, or alternatively liable to the plaintiff. Here, although it is unlikely that a foster child would be included in the phrase "all of my children," Ronald arguably has an interest in the proceeds of the insurance policy (so much so that he has filed his own lawsuit against Larry's Life Insurance Co.). Thus, the court correctly ruled that Ronald should be joined to the action as a defendant.

4.   The court should grant Larry's Life Insurance Co.'s motion to consolidate the present case with Ronald's case. At issue is whether an Illinois court may consolidate cases pending before it. In Illinois, actions pending in the same court may be consolidated as an aid to convenience whenever it can be done without prejudice to a substantial right. Here, consolidation of the cases would aid the court in determining who has the rights to the insurance proceeds; in fact, the purpose of the interpleader action would be subverted if Ronald were allowed to maintain his own action. Ronald will still have the opportunity to litigate his right to the insurance proceeds before the court; as such, none of his rights are being violated. Therefore, the court should order that the cases be consolidated.

QUESTION 41

On April 7, 2001, while Mary was patiently waiting for a light to turn green, Harry Holder, driving way too fast for conditions that day, rear-ended her sharply. Mary said that at the scene Harry identified himself as Horatio Holder, who was the actual owner of the car. Horatio is Harry's brother.

Harry denied this and claimed that Mary must have misunderstood. Harry said he mentioned his brother's name to Mary at the scene, either in reference to being the owner or insurer of the car.

Deputy Ranger, who responded to the scene, prepared the accident report, which indicated that the driver was Harry and the owner was Horatio. Mary claimed she never received a copy of the report, even though Deputy Ranger said he told her one would be mailed to her. Harry received a copy at the scene.

On March 31, 2003, about one week before the expiration of the applicable statute of limitations, Mary filed a personal injury complaint, naming Horatio Holder as the defendant.

She alleged that the driver of the car committed several violations in violation of his duty of care to her.

About one week later, on April 8, 2003, Horatio was served with summons and the complaint by substitute service on his mother. At the time, he and Harry were living with her. When Horatio got home, his mother showed him the papers. He, in turn, showed them to Harry when Harry returned home from work. Harry thought he dodged the proverbial bullet since his name was not on any of the documents.

On May 2, 2003, Mary filed a motion for leave to amend her complaint. The amended complaint named Harry as the defendant, and alleged that the driver of the car was negligent, caused an accident on April 7, 2001, and proximately caused her injuries, and was essentially the same in all other respects.

1.   Should the court grant Mary's motion? Explain.

2.   For purposes of this part only, assume that the court allowed Mary's motion and that defendant Harry Holder filed a motion to dismiss on the basis of the statute of limitations. How should the court rule? Explain.

ANSWER TO QUESTION 41

1.   The court should allow Mary to amend her complaint. Ignoring for the moment whether the statute of limitations has run on the claim, the issue here is under what circumstances a party may amend her pleadings. In Illinois, amendments of pleadings are liberally allowed (and can even be amended at trial), subject to any just and reasonable terms the court may decide to impose as a condition to granting leave to amend. Here, given the fact that the case is still early in litigation, there is no reason not to allow Mary to amend her complaint to correct a pleading error (discussed below). As a result, Mary should be allowed to amend her complaint to change the named defendant from "Horatio Holder" to "Harry Holder."

2.   The court should deny the motion based on the allegation that the statute of limitations has expired. At issue is whether the amended complaint "relates back" to the date the original complaint was filed. Under the Illinois Code, an amended complaint relates back if: (i) the original complaint was *filed within the statute of limitations period*; (ii) the defendant, *within the time that the action might have been brought plus a reasonable time for service of process,* received notice of the action such that he would not be prejudiced in maintaining his defense; and the defendant *should have known that, but for a mistake concerning identity, the action would have been brought against him*; and (iii) the amended action *grew out of the same transaction or occurrence* as the original complaint.

The first prong is easily satisfied—the facts specifically state that the complaint was filed one week before the statute of limitations expired. The second prong is also satisfied—the facts state that Horatio showed Harry the summons and complaint on the same day they were served on Horatio. This occurred one week after the statute of limitations had expired. Allowing a plaintiff one week to serve the defendant is reasonable, and there are no facts indicating that Mary was not diligent in serving process on Horatio. Thus, Harry had notice of the suit within the statute of limitations period *plus a reasonable time for service of process*, even though he was not formally served with process. The facts state that Harry believed "he dodged the proverbial bullet since his name was not on any of the documents"; this shows that Harry knew that, but for Mary's mistake, the action would have been brought against him. Finally, the third prong is satisfied because the amended action obviously grew out of the same accident.

Given that the requirements of the statute have been satisfied, the complaint relates back to the date that the original complaint was filed. As a result, the motion to dismiss on the basis that the statute of limitations has expired should be denied.

[*Editor's note:* This question was derived verbatim from *Fassero v. Turigliatto*, 349 Ill. App. 3d 368 (2004)]

QUESTION 42

On April 7, 2005, Mr. Ning Lan ("Lan"), a resident of Minneapolis, Minnesota, had a planned, six-hour layover at O'Hare Airport while returning to Minneapolis from a vacation in Miami, Florida. While at O'Hare, Lan approached Illinois resident Sarah Vale ("Vale") in an airport bar and told her a heartbreaking tale.

Posing as "Dr. John Tanaka," Lan told Vale he was en route from Miami to Minneapolis to attend his mother's funeral, but that his mobile phone, wallet, money, and credit cards had been stolen from his carry-on bag 20 minutes before in an O'Hare bathroom. Doing his best to appear panicked and desperate, Lan advised Vale that although he still had his airplane ticket to Minneapolis, he needed cash to take a taxi from the Minneapolis airport to his mother's funeral—which he asserted was set to begin just one hour after his scheduled arrival in Minneapolis. Falling for the ruse, Vale gave the man she knew as Dr. John Tanaka $100 in exchange for the doctor's promise to reimburse her by mail. As his final act during their conversation, Lan secretly removed Vale's expensive palmtop computer from her purse and tucked it into his pocket. After Vale gave Lan her home address, Lan quickly boarded his flight to Minneapolis.

A few minutes later, an off-duty police officer approached Vale and advised her that he had seen Lan steal her palmtop computer. With the help of the officer and the airline on which Lan had departed, Vale learned Lan's true identity and home address in Minneapolis. The following week, a Minneapolis private investigator hired by Vale easily determined that Lan's story about the funeral was false—Lan's mother was alive and well in Pittsburgh.

Three weeks after the incident at O'Hare, Lan, a/k/a Dr. John Tanaka, was properly served in Minneapolis with an Illinois state court complaint filed by Vale alleging conversion and fraudulent misrepresentation counts. The entire fraudulent misrepresentation count read as follows:

> Defendant: (1) made false statements of material fact to the Plaintiff; (2) knew or believed the statements to be false; and (3) intended to induce the Plaintiff to act. The Plaintiff acted in reliance on the truth of these false statements. As a result of her reliance, the Plaintiff has been damaged in the amount of $100.

The first thing Lan's attorney filed was a motion to dismiss the complaint for lack of personal jurisdiction. The judge denied the motion.

Next, Lan's attorney filed a motion under section 2-615 of the Illinois Code of Civil Procedure asking the court to dismiss the fraudulent misrepresentation count for failure properly to allege that cause of action. The judge denied that motion, too.

Later, pursuant to Supreme Court Rule 216, Vale's attorney served Lan with the following requests to admit:

> (1)   Admit that on April 7, 2005, you spoke in person with the Plaintiff at O'Hare Airport.

> (2)   Admit that on April 7, 2005, you told the Plaintiff your name was "Dr. John Tanaka."

> (3)   Admit that your actions on April 7, 2005, constituted fraudulent misrepresentation.

Lan's attorney filed a motion to strike the requests to admit as improper. The judge denied the motion and ordered Lan to respond to the requests within 28 days of the denial of the motion, or run the risk that the matters inquired about would be automatically admitted, pursuant to Rule 216.

1.   Did the judge err in denying Lan's motion to dismiss for lack of personal jurisdiction? Explain.

2.   Did the judge err in denying Lan's motion to dismiss the fraudulent misrepresentation count? Explain.

3.   Did the judge err in denying Lan's motion to strike the request to admit? Explain.

ANSWER TO QUESTION 42

1.   The court did not err in denying Lan's motion to dismiss for lack of personal jurisdiction. At issue is whether an Illinois court has personal jurisdiction over a defendant who commits a tort in Illinois.

A court in Illinois may assert personal jurisdiction over a defendant if (i) Illinois law grants personal jurisdiction over the defendant and (ii) the law is constitutional. Illinois's long arm statute both extends as far as due process allows and specifically authorizes an Illinois court to exercise personal jurisdiction over a defendant who commits a tort in Illinois. In either case, the claim against the defendant must be related to the long arm act. Here, Lan is being sued in tort for defrauding Vale out of $100 and for converting her palmtop computer, both of which occurred in Illinois and form the basis of Vale's lawsuit. As a result, the "authorized by statute" portion of the analysis is easily satisfied.

After finding that jurisdiction over a particular defendant is authorized by statute, the next inquiry is whether the exercise of such jurisdiction is constitutional, *i.e.,* whether the defendant has sufficient contacts with the forum state such that the exercise of jurisdiction over him is fair and reasonable. If the court were exercising "general" jurisdiction—jurisdiction over Lan for all causes of action—substantial contacts with Illinois would be required. However, where the court is asserting "specific" jurisdiction—jurisdiction over a defendant for one case that is based on the defendant's commission of an act falling under the long arm statute—substantial contacts are not required. Instead, the close contact between the in-state act (here, the act of fraud and the conversion) and the lawsuit provides the necessary minimum contacts with the jurisdiction. Thus, despite the fact that Lan has no other contacts with Illinois other than his acts at the airport, the exercise of jurisdiction over him is constitutional under the Due Process Clause. As a result, the court did not err in denying Lan's motion to dismiss for lack of personal jurisdiction.

2.   The court erred in denying Lan's motion to dismiss the fraudulent misrepresentation claim. At issue is the degree of specificity a plaintiff must have in her pleadings in order to survive a motion to dismiss.

Illinois, unlike the federal courts, requires a party to plead facts supporting his claim. Facts are those statements that are neither so particularized as to be irrelevant or verbose, nor so generalized as to simply be the elements of a particular cause of action. Furthermore, claims of fraud must be pleaded with specificity. Here, Vale has merely alleged that the defendant "made false statements of material fact" without alleging what those statements were. Such a pleading is not sufficient; rather, Vale should have included, to the degree possible, the exact statement that Lan used, and should have included the fact that Lan was using a false identity. (It is even debatable whether the complaint here would be sufficient in a notice pleading jurisdiction to put Lan on notice of the conduct alleged to be fraudulent.)

Thus, Vale has not properly set out a case of fraud against Lan. As a result, the court erred in denying Lan's motion to dismiss.

3.   The court partly erred in denying Lan's motion to strike the requests to admit. At issue is whether a party may request his opponent to admit a fact that he would ordinarily have the burden of proving at trial and whether the request may require the other party to admit a legal conclusion.

Generally, any party may serve on any other party a written request for admission as to the truth or genuineness of any matter or document described in the request. A request to admit a legal conclusion or irrelevant facts will be stricken on motion. The fact that a party's admission of facts may leave no issues for trial is irrelevant, as a party may request another party to admit "ultimate facts."

In the instant case, the first two requests to admit were proper, and the court did not err in denying the motion to strike. However, the third request to "Admit that your actions . . . constituted fraudulent misrepresentation" presents a closer question. First, the request requires the defendant to draw a legal conclusion as to what constitutes "fraudulent misrepresentation." Second, the request lacks any degree of specificity, in that the term "actions" is somewhat ambiguous. A better request might have included a request for Lan to admit that his representation that he was Dr. Tanaka, that he needed $100 for cab fare, that he was flying to his mother's funeral in Minneapolis, etc., were false. Thus, given that the third request requires Lan to draw a legal conclusion and that the request is framed too broadly, the court erred in not striking the third request to admit.

QUESTION 43

Allison's Autos, Inc., an Illinois corporation, is an antique automobile dealership located in Winnebago County, Illinois.

Carl Collector, an enthusiastic collector of antique cars, is a resident of Winnebago County. In late 2003, he went to Allison's Autos, Inc. because he was interested in purchasing a 1971 Ford Mustang that Allison had advertised in the newspaper. Carl test-drove the car, and then asked Allison about the engine. Allison told Carl, "The engine runs like new. You will be able to drive this car for decades." Carl trusted Allison because he had purchased antique cars from her in the past, so he gave her a $1,000 down payment, signed a promissory note for the balance due on the car, and drove the Ford Mustang off of the lot.

Three days later, the car stalled in Carl's driveway. He had it towed to Michelle Mechanic, who advised Carl that the Ford Mustang needed a new engine. Allison would not take the car back, so Carl Collector sued Allison's Autos, Inc. in the Circuit Court of Winnebago County, Illinois, for fraud. In his only count, he alleged that "Allison's Autos, Inc. had sold him the car fraudulently in representing to him that the engine ran like new."

Allison's Autos, Inc. moved to dismiss the complaint on the ground that Carl Collector did not plead fraud with specificity. The court granted the motion to dismiss without prejudice, and gave Carl Collector 60 days to amend his complaint. Within 60 days, Carl Collector moved both to voluntarily dismiss his fraud count and to amend his complaint to allege that Allison's Autos, Inc. breached an express warranty to Carl. With his amended complaint, Carl Collector filed a motion with the court for a substitution of judge as of right. The court granted Carl Collector's motion to voluntarily dismiss his fraud count and to amend his complaint, but denied his motion for a substitution of judge.

Allison's Autos, Inc. won the case on a motion for summary judgment, in which the court concluded that Allison's Autos, Inc. did not make any express warranty to Carl. The court entered a final order. Allison's Autos, Inc. then proceeded to file a one-count complaint in the Circuit Court of Winnebago County, Illinois, against Carl Collector for nonpayment of his promissory note. Carl Collector counterclaimed, alleging that Allison's Autos, Inc. engaged in fraud in "telling him that the engine of the Ford Mustang ran like new." To his counterclaim, he attached a letter from the previous owner of the Ford Mustang detailing to Allison the poor condition of the engine. Allison's Autos, Inc. filed a motion to dismiss Carl Collector's counterclaim on the ground that it was barred by the prior action, and Carl Collector filed a motion to dismiss Allison's Autos, Inc.'s complaint on the ground that it was barred by the prior action.

1.   Did the trial court rule correctly (in the first action) on Carl Collector's motion to voluntarily dismiss the fraud count in his complaint? Explain.

2.   Did the trial court judge rule correctly (in the first action) on Carl Collector's motion for a substitution of judge? Explain.

3.   How should the court rule (in the second action) on Carl Collector's motion to dismiss Allison's Autos, Inc.'s complaint? Explain.

4.   How should the court rule (in the second action) on Allison's Autos, Inc.'s motion to dismiss Carl Collector's counterclaim? Explain.

ANSWER TO QUESTION 43

1.   The court did not err in allowing Carl to voluntarily dismiss his fraud complaint. At issue is whether a claimant has an absolute right to voluntarily dismiss his complaint when the court has

ruled on a motion to dismiss, but also has granted the claimant leave to amend. In Illinois, before trial or hearing, a claimant has an absolute right to voluntarily dismiss his claim without prejudice if he notifies every party who has appeared and pays costs. After the trial or a hearing on the merits has begun, a claimant may voluntarily dismiss, upon payment of costs, only with the stipulation of the adverse party or on motion supported by an affidavit. In the context of voluntary dismissals, a "hearing" generally is the equitable equivalent of a trial; *i.e.,* a trial or a hearing involves a determination of the rights of the parties. In the instant case, no substantive issue has been presented before the court. Thus, Carl still has the absolute right to voluntarily dismiss the action. As a result, the court did not err in allowing Carl to voluntarily dismiss his fraud complaint.

2. The court did not err in denying Carl's motion for substitution of judges. At issue is whether a party has a right for substitution of a judge if the judge has already made a substantive ruling in the case. In Illinois, each party has a right to move for a substitution of a judge as a matter of right one time, provided that the judge has not yet ruled on a substantive issue. (A party would also have a right to substitution of judges when the judge has an interest in the litigation; here, there are no facts to support such a claim.) In the instant case, the judge had already ruled on a motion to dismiss. Thus, given that Carl's motion for substitution of judges was not timely, the court did not err in denying Carl's motion.

3. The court should deny Carl's motion to dismiss Allison's Autos, Inc.'s complaint. At issue is the doctrine of res judicata. In many jurisdictions, if a claim or counterclaim arises from the same transaction or occurrence at issue in the pending action, it is compulsory, and if a compulsory counterclaim is not asserted in the pending action, it is lost, regardless of the judgment in the case. However, in Illinois, all counterclaims are considered to be permissive and are not lost just because they are related to a pending claim. Thus, res judicata will not bar a counterclaim based on the facts of the case.

Notwithstanding the foregoing rule, a party might lose his cause of action based on collateral estoppel because a key fact needed to prove an element of his prima facie case could have been determined adversely in the prior litigation (technically, though, the claim would not be "barred" as Carl claims; rather, the claim would be susceptible to a motion for summary judgment). In the instant case, Allison's Autos claim is based on Carl's nonpayment of the note on the car. No facts were determined with regard to the note in the prior litigation. Thus, collateral estoppel does not apply here either. As a result, the court should deny Carl's motion to dismiss Allison's Autos, Inc.'s complaint.

4. The court should grant Allison's Autos, Inc.'s motion to dismiss Carl's counterclaim. At issue is whether res judicata applies to bar Carl's claim against Allison's Autos, Inc. based on a fraudulent misrepresentation that the engine was sound. Res judicata applies when (i) the earlier judgment is final; (ii) the earlier judgment is on the merits; and (iii) the same cause of action is involved in the later lawsuit. Here, the court had granted Allison's Autos, Inc.'s motion for summary judgment in the first case, finding that it had not made an express warranty to Carl about the car's engine. That judgment was final, and obviously on the merits, as it had terminated the litigation in the case. Furthermore, a court will apply a "transactional" test to determine if the second case involves the same cause of action for res judicata purposes. Factors to be considered are whether: (i) the facts of the two cases occurred within a short time frame; (ii) the facts have a common origin; (iii) the facts would be more conveniently tried together; and (iv) a joint trial of all facts would conform to the parties' expectations or common business practices. Here, one would have expected Carl to bring all claims relating to the statement that the car's engine was

sound in one action, whether the claim eventually was based on an express warranty or fraudulent misrepresentation. Thus, a claim based on an express warranty (that the car's engine was sound) and a claim based on a fraudulent misrepresentation (that the statement that the car's engine was sound was falsely made) should have been brought in one action. As a result, res judicata applies, and the court should dismiss Carl's counterclaim.

QUESTION 44

Homer is a permanent resident of Sangamon County, Illinois. On July 15, 2005, in Shelby County, Pennsylvania, Homer suffered serious injuries in an automobile accident. A car driven by Robert, a permanent resident of Shelby County, Pennsylvania, hit Homer's car in a head-on collision. When Robert's car hit Homer's auto, Robert was driving 20 miles per hour over the speed limit.

Robert was driving a Phoenix Automobile, manufactured by Belchfire Motor Company, Inc. Belchfire Motor Company is a Delaware corporation, with its principal place of business in Dearborn, Michigan. Belchfire Motor Company sells cars throughout the United States.

After the accident with Homer, tests on Robert's car revealed a problem in the brake system. Specifically, the brake pad on one of the front brakes in Robert's car was defective.

The brake pad was manufactured by the China Vehicle Corporation ("China Vehicle"). China Vehicle is a Chinese corporation, with its principal place of business in Shanghai, China. China Vehicle has no offices in the United States, owns no real property in the United States, and has no employees who live in the United States. China Vehicle also does no advertising in the United States. China Vehicle officers are aware that American cars often contain brake pads manufactured by China Vehicle.

Delhi Brake Systems, Inc. ("Delhi Brake Systems") buys all of the brake pads manufactured by China Vehicle. Delhi Brake Systems is an Indian corporation, with its principal place of business in Bombay, India. Delhi Brake Systems builds brake systems for a number of auto manufacturers located throughout the world. Delhi Brake Systems builds many of the brake systems for cars manufactured by the Belchfire Motor Company.

The brake system in Robert's Phoenix Automobile was manufactured by Delhi Brake Systems. The defective brake pad was manufactured by China Vehicle.

In October 2005, Homer filed a suit in the Circuit Court of Sangamon County, Illinois. Homer's complaint names two defendants: 1. Robert; and 2. China Vehicle. Assume that both defendants received proper service of process.

Delhi Brake Systems and Belchfire Motor Company both entered into settlement agreements with Homer. Delhi Brake Systems and Belchfire Motor Company are named in Homer's complaint.

Homer's complaint alleges that misconduct by defendants Robert and China Vehicle resulted in Homer's injuries. With respect to Robert, Homer's complaint alleges a single cause of action for negligence, a state law tort claim. According to Homer's complaint, Robert's speeding and failure to exercise reasonable care resulted in the July 15, 2005, auto accident and Homer's injuries.

With respect to China Vehicle, Homer's complaint alleges a single cause of action for strict liability, a state law tort claim. According to the complaint, China Vehicle manufactured a defective brake pad, which eventually found its way into Robert's car.

Robert never has visited Illinois. Robert's Uncle Abraham resided in Sangamon County, Illinois. In 2000, Abraham died. In his will, Abraham left his coin collection worth $500 to Robert.

Abraham kept the coin collection in a safe deposit box at a bank in Sangamon County, Illinois. Since Abraham died, Robert has not taken possession of his coin collection, which remains in the Sangamon County safe deposit box. The coin collection is Robert's only connection with Illinois.

In 2004, a significant number of Illinois auto accidents resulted from brake system failures. As a result, an Illinois consumer advocacy group surveyed the type of brake system components found in Illinois autos. According to an estimate in this survey, China Vehicle had manufactured the brake pads in about 20% of the automobiles in Illinois. China Vehicle officers are aware of these Illinois survey results.

1.   May the Sangamon County Circuit Court exercise personal jurisdiction over Robert? Explain.

2.   May the Sangamon County Circuit Court exercise personal jurisdiction over China Vehicle? Explain.

ANSWER TO QUESTION 44

1.   The Sangamon County Circuit Court may not exercise personal jurisdiction over Robert. At issue is whether the ownership of personal property within a state subjects the owner to personal jurisdiction within that state for a cause of action unrelated to the property. (This type of jurisdiction is known as quasi in rem—type II.) Generally, for the exercise of personal jurisdiction to be permissible, it must be both authorized by statute and constitutional. In the instant case, neither prong is met. The accident, and thus any tort, was in Pennsylvania by a citizen of Pennsylvania. Thus, no specific provision of the Illinois long arm statute would apply, and the court would be required to rely on the catch-all provision, which extends personal jurisdiction to the constitutional limits, to assert personal jurisdiction over Robert. The Supreme Court has ruled that the minimum contacts test of *International Shoe v. Washington*, 326 U.S. 310 (1945), applies to such quasi in rem actions. Accordingly, the defendant must have sufficient minimum contacts with the forum such that the exercise of personal jurisdiction over him would be fair and reasonable. In the instant case, the only contact that Robert has with Illinois is the ownership of the $500 coin collection. (In fact, Robert has never even set foot in Illinois.) It is also unlikely that Robert anticipated being haled into an Illinois court for any and all causes of action, nor has he committed any purposeful act to subject himself to personal jurisdiction in Illinois. Thus, it would not be fair for an Illinois court to subject Robert to personal jurisdiction based on the ownership of personal property in the state. As a result, this sole contact is not a sufficient minimum contact for an Illinois court to assert personal jurisdiction over Robert, and the court would not have a statutorily authorized basis to assert jurisdiction.

2.   The Sangamon County Circuit Court probably would not have personal jurisdiction over China Vehicle, although the case is not as clear as that of Robert. At issue is whether a corporation that puts a product in the stream of commerce may be haled into a forum wherever that product winds up, so long as the defendant realized that a significant portion of its product wound up in that forum. As stated above, personal jurisdiction must be both authorized by statute and constitutional.

As with Robert's case, the court would have to rely on the catch-all provision in order to satisfy the "statutorily authorized" prong. First, China Vehicle does not "do business" in Illinois for purposes of general jurisdiction, as it maintains no offices or factories in Illinois, nor does it solicit or transact any business in Illinois. The facts state that the brake pads were manufactured in China, incorporated into a braking system in India, and thereafter probably incorporated into a Belchfire car in Michigan (Belchfire's principal place of business). Furthermore, the allegation is that the brake pad on Robert's car was defective; given that the facts state that Robert never set foot in Illinois, he obviously did not buy the Belchfire car in Illinois. Thus, there appears to be no connection to Illinois, and, as in 1., above, no specific provision of the long arm statute applies, and the court would again have to rely on the catch-all provision (*i.e.,* jurisdiction to the constitutional limits) for jurisdiction, as above.

Under *International Shoe, supra,* the defendant must have such minimum contacts with the forum such that the exercise of personal jurisdiction would be fair and reasonable. The defendant's contacts cannot be accidental—there must be some evidence that the defendant purposefully availed himself to the benefits and protections of the forum state. In *Asahi v. Superior Court*, 480 U.S. 102 (1987), the Supreme Court split as to what constitutes "purposeful availment" in stream of commerce cases. Four justices opined that knowledge that its product is winding up in a particular forum constitutes purposeful availment, while four other justices required an additional step on the part of the defendant. The Court has also held that in deciding the jurisdictional issue, a court may consider the state interest in protecting its citizens, providing its citizens with a judicial forum, and the interstate judicial system's interest in obtaining the most efficient resolution of controversies.

In the instant case, China Vehicle only knows that 20% of its brake pads find their way to Illinois—the facts do not indicate that it has done some other purposeful act to capture the Illinois market. Furthermore, there appears to be no Illinois act involved in the case—as stated in the "doing business" analysis above, the accident occurred in Pennsylvania, the brake pad was manufactured in China, incorporated into a braking system in India, which was thereafter incorporated into a Belchfire car in Michigan. Additionally, although an Illinois court would have an interest in protecting Illinois consumers, and although China Vehicle knows 20% of its brake pads wind up in Illinois, it was not one of those 20% that caused the accident. Additionally, had the accident occurred in Illinois, not only would the connection to Illinois have been strengthened, but Homer could also argue that state interest in protecting consumers in support of jurisdiction. However, that "state interest" argument is not very strong under these facts because of the lack of any connection to Illinois, and it is unlikely that this factor alone would be sufficient to support jurisdiction. Furthermore, it is unclear from the facts whether the brake pad failure was an isolated occurrence (which would further lessen the state interest) or part of a pattern. Additionally, judicial economy does not support jurisdiction under these facts because Robert, as explained above, will have to be sued in Pennsylvania. Furthermore, for specific jurisdiction (jurisdiction over the cause of action only) under the long arm statute to be proper, the cause of action asserted in the lawsuit must be related to the state contact, and here the cause of action technically does not arise from China Vehicle's Illinois activity. As a result, it seems that an

Illinois court would not have personal jurisdiction over China Vehicle, and thus, like the case with Robert, the Illinois long arm statute would not apply.

QUESTION 45

Sergeant Lou Kramer works for the Madison County Sheriff. In July 2005, Sergeant Kramer receives an anonymous telephone tip. According to the tipster, one of the residents at 250 Houston Street in Madison County is selling cocaine. The tipster states that a large quantity of cocaine is located in one of the first floor condominiums at 250 Houston Street.

Only two condominiums are located on the first floor of 250 Houston Street. Steve McCoy owns one of the first floor condominiums, and Mary Ruskin owns the other.

On July 20, 2005, Sergeant Kramer conducts a search of the condominiums owned by McCoy and Ruskin. Kramer does not obtain a warrant before he searches the two condominiums.

Sergeant Kramer does not find cocaine or any other controlled substances in either McCoy's condominium or Ruskin's condominium. During his July 20 search, Kramer damages personal property located in both condominiums, including valuable antiques owned by McCoy.

Later on July 20, Steve McCoy learns that Sergeant Kramer has searched McCoy's residence. On July 21, McCoy contacts Paul Fallow, a reporter for the Madison County Daily Herald newspaper. On July 22, the newspaper publishes a story about Sergeant Kramer's unsuccessful search. In the story, McCoy describes Kramer as "a hooligan and a thug."

On September 25, 2005, Steve McCoy and Mary Ruskin file a single complaint in the Circuit Court of Madison County. The complaint names Sergeant Lou Kramer as the only defendant.

The complaint states a single cause of action, alleging a violation of the Fourth Amendment to the United States Constitution. According to the complaint, Sergeant Kramer violated the Fourth Amendment when he searched the plaintiffs' condominiums without a warrant. Assume that the Madison County Circuit Court possesses subject matter jurisdiction over this suit.

Steve McCoy and Mary Ruskin alleged that during the search, Sergeant Kramer damaged personal property in each condominium. McCoy seeks $20,000 damages. Ruskin seeks $5,000 damages.

1. Defendant Lou Kramer files a timely motion to dismiss the suit commenced by McCoy and Ruskin. According to Kramer, McCoy and Ruskin cannot join together in a single suit. Instead, McCoy and Ruskin must commence individual Fourth Amendment actions.

   Should the circuit court judge grant the motion to dismiss filed by Defendant Lou Kramer? Explain.

2. For the purpose of this question and question 3., assume that the circuit court denies the motion to dismiss filed by Defendant Lou Kramer. Now assume that on November 3, 2005, McCoy and Ruskin file a motion to amend their complaint. At this time, the suit filed by McCoy and Ruskin is in the initial stages of discovery.

   The plaintiffs' amendment seeks to add a second cause of action for trespass, an Illinois state law claim. According to the amendment, on July 20, 2005, Lou Kramer unlawfully entered the condominiums owned by McCoy and Ruskin without the owners' permission. Defendant Kramer opposes the amendment.

   Should the Madison County Circuit Court allow McCoy and Ruskin to amend their complaint? Explain.

3. Now assume that on December 5, 2005, Lou Kramer files a suit in the Madison County Circuit Court. Kramer's complaint names Steve McCoy as the only defendant.

   Kramer's complaint states a single cause of action for defamation, an Illinois state law claim. The complaint alleges: "When Steve McCoy described Lou Kramer as a hooligan and a thug, McCoy made malicious statements that damaged Kramer's reputation." Kramer seeks $10,000 compensatory damages.

   In response to plaintiff Lou Kramer's suit, Defendant Steve McCoy files a timely motion for summary judgment. In this motion, McCoy asserts that Kramer should have filed his defamation action as a counterclaim to the September 25 Fourth Amendment suit initiated by McCoy. The summary judgment motion concludes that Kramer cannot maintain his defamation action as a separate suit.

   Should the trial judge grant the motion for summary judgment filed by Defendant Steve McCoy? Explain.

ANSWER TO QUESTION 45

1. The court should deny Kramer's motion to dismiss. At issue is whether two plaintiffs may join together as plaintiffs in a single suit. Two or more plaintiffs may join to bring a single cause of action whenever: (i) the right to relief of each arises out of the same transaction or series of transactions, whether their rights are joint, several, or in the alternative; and (ii) separate actions would have raised a common question of law or fact. Joinder is not permitted for multiple plaintiffs who have dealt with the defendant at separate times or on whom fraud has been perpetrated separately, even though the separate transactions appear to be part of a repeated pattern of conduct by the defendant. In the instant case, Sergeant Kramer conducted warrantless searches of separate condominiums owned by McCoy and Ruskin, but the searches were conducted on the same day and were based on a single anonymous telephone tip. McCoy and Ruskin each claims damages based on this Fourth Amendment violation. Thus, McCoy's and Ruskin's right to relief arises out of the same transaction—the failure of Kramer to secure a warrant. Furthermore, McCoy's case and Ruskin's case raise a common question of law or fact—to what extent may Kramer have relied on the tip to conduct a search? As a result, McCoy and Ruskin should be allowed to join in a single suit, and Kramer's motion to dismiss on that basis should be denied.

2. The motion by McCoy and Ruskin to amend their complaint to add a cause of action for trespass should be granted. At issue is when a party may be granted leave to amend his pleading. In Illinois, leave to amend a pleading is freely granted. In the instant case, the original cause of action accrued on July 20, 2005, and the facts state that the case is in the initial phase of discovery. Plaintiffs filed their lawsuit on September 25, 2005. Now, on November 3, 2005, less than four months after the cause of action accrued and less than two months after the original suit was filed, plaintiffs are seeking to amend their case to add a cause of action based on the same transaction (the illegal searches of their condominiums). Because of the short period of time involved, the statute of limitations has not expired (whether the applicable limitation is five years under the catch-all provision, five years for damage to property, or two years for personal injury actions). McCoy and Ruskin could file a separate suit based on trespass. As a result, Kramer suffers no prejudice in allowing the amendment—the cause of action is still within the original statute of limitations and discovery has just begun. Given no prejudice to Kramer, leave to amend should be granted.

3. McCoy's motion for summary judgment based on the contention that the claim should have been pleaded as a counterclaim in the original action should be denied. At issue is whether, in Illinois, counterclaims are lost if they are not pleaded in the original action. In Illinois, all counterclaims are considered to be permissive. That said, res judicata may bar the counterclaim as a separate cause of action if it is deemed to be the "same cause of action," in other words, if the causes of action arise from a single set of operative facts. Here, there is no such problem, given that the claim based on the warrantless search arises from different facts than the claim based on defamation for statements that McCoy made to the reporter about Kramer being "a hooligan and a thug." The claims have very little to do with each other. (In fact, a court conceivably could find that Kramer violated McCoy's Fourth Amendment rights, but that such a violation was an isolated occurrence, thus potentially making McCoy's statements defaming.) Thus, Kramer was not required to plead his counterclaim based on defamation in the original suit, and McCoy's motion for summary judgment should be denied.

QUESTION 46

Larry Lessor leased space for a restaurant in Union County, Illinois, to Rock Island Restaurant from January 1, 2001, to December 31, 2006. Rock Island Restaurant operated its business and paid the monthly rent on time each month through February 28, 2006. On March 1, 2006, Rock Island Restaurant closed down its operations, abandoned the space, and stopped paying rent to Larry Lessor.

When Larry Lessor inspected the premises in March, he found that Rock Island Restaurant had damaged the kitchen fixtures that Larry Lessor owned, and, in doing so, Rock Island Restaurant violated the parties' written lease. The written lease between Larry Lessor and Rock Island Restaurant made no reference to whether either party could recover attorneys' fees if the other party defaulted.

Larry Lessor brought a two-count complaint against Rock Island Restaurant in the Circuit Court of Union County, Illinois, for $45,000. In Count I, Larry Lessor alleged breach of contract and sued for the rent that Rock Island Restaurant owed between March 1, 2006, and December 31, 2006. In Count II, Larry Lessor also alleged breach of contract and sued for the damage to its kitchen fixtures. Larry Lessor sought a bench trial.

Rock Island Restaurant answered the complaint and the parties exchanged their initial disclosures mandated by Illinois law. Rock Island Restaurant did not list Brad Baker as a potential witness and never disclosed his name to Larry Lessor. Mr. Baker was going to testify how he tried unsuccessfully on May 15, 2006, to rent from Larry Lessor the space vacated by Rock Island Restaurant to help prove Rock Island Restaurant's theory that Larry Lessor failed to mitigate damages. After the parties exchanged disclosures, Rock Island Restaurant made a jury demand. Larry Lessor objected to the jury demand as untimely.

Three months before trial, Larry Lessor disclosed to Rock Island Restaurant that he intended for Edward Expert to testify at trial about the damage to Larry Lessor's kitchen fixtures. However, Larry Lessor refused to make Edward Expert available for a deposition. Rock Island Restaurant filed a motion to compel Edward Expert's deposition, but Rock Island Restaurant refused to take the deposition on the days that the court ordered Larry Lessor to make Edward Expert available for deposition.

Larry Lessor presented his case at trial and had Edward Expert testify on his behalf. Rock Island Restaurant made no objection to Edward Expert's testimony. When Rock Island Restaurant called Brad Baker to testify in its defense, the court barred Brad Baker from testifying. The court entered judgment in favor of Larry Lessor.

1.   Did the court err in striking Rock Island Restaurant's jury demand as untimely? Explain.

2.   Did the court err in barring Brad Baker from testifying? Explain.

3.   If Larry Lessor files a petition for attorneys' fees, should the court grant that petition? Explain.

4.   If Rock Island Restaurant appeals the judgment, should it be able to argue before the appellate court, as a matter of procedure, that the trial court erred in allowing Edward Expert to testify? Explain.

ANSWER TO QUESTION 46

1.   The court did not err in striking Rock Island Restaurant's jury demand as untimely. At issue is when a jury demand must be made in order for it to be deemed timely. In Illinois, if a defendant in a civil case desires a trial by jury, he must file a jury demand before he files his answer. In the instant case, the facts indicate that Rock Island Restaurant filed its answer before it attempted to demand a jury. Thus, it appears that Rock Island was late in filing its request for a jury trial. As a result, the court did not err in striking Rock Island's jury demand.

2.   The court did not err in barring Brad Baker from testifying. At issue is whether a witness may be precluded from testifying when the party fails to disclose the existence of the witness under the "limited and simplified" discovery process. Under Illinois Supreme Court Rule 222, when the amount of damages sought by the plaintiff is less than $50,000, a "limited and simplified" discovery process sometimes applies. When that process applies, the parties must make certain initial disclosures, including the factual basis for the claim or defense, and the names and addresses of trial witnesses and other persons with knowledge of the events. The penalty for

failure to disclose is the possible exclusion of the evidence, unless the court finds good cause for allowing the evidence. In the instant case, Rock Island Restaurant failed to disclose the existence of Brad Baker in violation of the rule, and there are no facts to indicate good cause. Thus, the court did not err in barring Brad Baker from testifying.

3.   The court should not grant Larry Lessor's petition for attorneys' fees. At issue is whether a party is entitled to recover attorneys' fees on a breach of lease claim when the lease is silent about such recovery. Generally, a party must bear his own litigation expenses, including attorneys' fees, unless a contract or statute allows for recovery of attorneys' fees. In the instant case, the lease was silent as to recovery of attorneys' fees, and no statute for such recovery exists. Thus, the court should not grant Larry Lessor's petition for attorneys' fees.

4.   On appeal, Rock Island Restaurant should not be able to argue that the trial court erred in allowing Edward Expert to testify. At issue is whether a party may waive objections to witness testimony at trial. In most states, if a party fails to object at trial to the introduction of evidence, he waives any objection on appeal. Here, Rock Island failed to object when Edward Expert began to testify. Thus, Rock Island waived any objection on appeal, and it should not be able to argue, on appeal, that the trial court erred in allowing Edward Expert to testify.

QUESTION 47

Adventureland, Inc. is an Illinois corporation, with its principal place of business in Ferris County, Illinois. Adventureland operates an amusement park in Ferris County.

The Giant Dipper is a popular roller coaster ride at the Adventureland park. In October 2001, one of the cars on the Giant Dipper runs off of the roller coaster tracks. Seventeen people are injured seriously in this accident. After the accident, an investigation determines that the wheels on the roller coaster car were defective.

Far Eastern Steel is a Japanese corporation, with its principal place of business in Osaka, Japan. After resales by several middlemen, wheels manufactured by Far Eastern Steel eventually found their way onto the Adventureland Giant Dipper roller coaster car. Adventureland does not have any direct contact with Far Eastern Steel.

Paul is one of the Adventureland customers injured in the October 2001 roller coaster accident. In November 2001, Paul files a suit in the Circuit Court of Ferris County, Illinois. Paul's complaint names two defendants: 1. Adventureland; and 2. Far Eastern Steel.

Paul's complaint states a single cause of action for products liability, an Illinois state law claim. The complaint alleges that the wheels on the Adventureland roller coaster car were a defective product. Paul seeks $1 million damages.

Shortly after Paul files his complaint, Far Eastern Steel files a motion to dismiss. According to the motion, the Illinois courts cannot exercise personal jurisdiction over Far Eastern Steel.

After hearing Paul's argument in opposition to the motion to dismiss, the Ferris County Circuit Court grants the motion. In a written opinion issued in December 2001, the court concludes that the Illinois courts cannot exercise personal jurisdiction over Far Eastern Steel. Paul does not appeal from this decision.

In March 2002, Paul's case proceeds to trial, with Adventureland as the only remaining defendant. At the conclusion of the trial, a jury determines that the wheels on the Adventureland roller coaster were defective. The jury awards Paul $500,000. Defendant Adventureland does not appeal from this verdict.

1. In April 2002, Paul files a new suit in the Circuit Court of Bumper County, Illinois. Like his earlier Ferris County suit, Paul's complaint alleges a single cause of action for products liability. The complaint alleges that the wheels on the Giant Dipper roller coaster car were a defective product.

    Paul's new complaint names Far Eastern Steel as the only defendant. The complaint alleges that the Illinois courts in fact possess personal jurisdiction over Far Eastern Steel. Paul now argues that Far Eastern Steel solicits business in Illinois. In his earlier Ferris County suit, Paul did not argue that Far Eastern Steel solicited business in Illinois.

    Assuming that Paul is able to prove the allegations in his complaint, may Paul maintain his Bumper County suit against Far Eastern Steel? Explain.

2. Now assume that in May 2002, Brenda files a suit in the Circuit Court of Bumper County, Illinois. Like Paul, Brenda is an Adventureland customer who suffered serious injuries in the October 2001 roller coaster accident.

    Brenda's complaint names Adventureland as the only defendant. The complaint states a single cause of action for products liability, an Illinois state law claim. Brenda's products liability action is identical to the Ferris County suit filed by Paul in November 2001.

    Shortly after filing her complaint, Plaintiff Brenda files a timely motion for summary judgment. The motion relies on the judgment entered in Paul's Ferris County suit against Adventureland. According to Brenda's summary judgment motion, the judgment entered against Adventureland establishes as a matter of law that the wheels on the Giant Dipper roller coaster car were a defective product.

    Should the Bumper County Circuit Court grant the plaintiff's motion for summary judgment filed by Brenda? Explain.

ANSWER TO QUESTION 47

1. Paul may not maintain his Bumper County suit against Far Eastern Steel.

There are two issues to resolve: (i) whether the prior determination that a defendant does not have minimum contacts with the state is entitled to preclusive effect; and (ii) whether the additional fact that a defendant solicited business in state would provide a court with personal jurisdiction over the defendant.

First, Paul would not be prevented from litigating the personal jurisdiction issues again because the issues in the two cases are not identical. For collateral estoppel to apply, it must be shown that: (i) the issue in the first case is *identical* to that in the second; (ii) there was *a final judgment on the merits*; (iii) the party *against whom* collateral estoppel is to be applied was *a party or in privity with a party in the first case*; and (iv) the application of collateral estoppel would *not be fundamentally unfair* to the party being estopped. In the instant case, the issues would not be the same, in that the court never determined whether Far Eastern solicited business in Illinois such that it would be amenable to jurisdiction within Illinois, either based on the fact that the additional contact would satisfy the minimum contacts standard or on the fact that it was doing business in Illinois. (It should also be noted that the judgment in the prior case is not on the merits for res judicata purposes, in that it did not decide any material issues in the case such to preclude litigation of the case in another jurisdiction.)

However, even assuming that Paul is not barred from relitigating the issue, the fact that Far Eastern Steel solicited business probably would not provide the necessary minimum contacts with Illinois or jurisdiction over Far Eastern Steel based on a "doing business" theory. First, without any other facts supporting personal jurisdiction over Far Eastern Steel, it is unlikely that the fact that Far Eastern Steel solicited business in Illinois would push the balance over to a finding that Far Eastern Steel has sufficient minimum contacts with Illinois. Furthermore, mere solicitation also would not be sufficient for a finding that Far Eastern "does business" within Illinois. The "doing business" theory of personal jurisdiction requires a greater amount of contact with Illinois—*i.e.*, the contacts with Illinois need to be of such a degree to justify a finding that the defendant is effectively present in Illinois for all potential cases against it. Thus, although the facts are silent on what Far Eastern's other Illinois contacts are, or how the steel it supplied to the amusement park wound up in Illinois, if there are not sufficient minimum contacts to justify exercising personal jurisdiction based on an isolated transaction with Illinois, it is unlikely that Far Eastern would be "doing business" in Illinois. In short, mere solicitation, without more, is insufficient for a finding that Far Eastern Steel is "doing business" in Illinois. Thus, it is unlikely that Paul will be able to maintain his Bumper suit against Far Eastern Steel.

2. The court should grant partial summary judgment in favor of Brenda. At issue is whether a nonparty may take advantage of collateral estoppel. Traditionally, since a judgment would not bind a nonparty, the nonparty could not use a prior judgment in a pending case as collateral estoppel or res judicata. However, Illinois does not adhere to the traditional mutuality rule. As stated above, for collateral estoppel to apply, it must be shown that: (i) the issue in the first case is identical to that in the second; (ii) there was a final judgment on the merits; (iii) the party against whom collateral estoppel is to be applied was a party or in privity with a party in the first case; and (iv) the application of collateral estoppel would not be fundamentally unfair to the party being estopped. In the instant case, all four requirements can be met. First, the issue— whether the wheels on the Giant Dipper roller coaster car were a defective product—is identical, given that both plaintiffs were injured in the same accident. Next, Paul's judgment appears to be final, and Adventureland was a party to the prior litigation, thus satisfying the second and third elements. Finally, there are no facts indicating that it would be unfair to apply the judgment against Adventureland. Due to the fact that Paul was seeking $1 million in damages, Adventureland had every incentive to fully and effectively litigate the issue in the first case. Thus, Adventureland should be collaterally estopped from contesting the defective nature of the brakes, and partial summary judgment on that issue should be granted.

QUESTION 48

Gold Coast Investors, Inc., is an Illinois corporation, with its principal place of business in Kettle County, Illinois. Gold Coast Investors regularly purchases 30-minute television segments on local Illinois television stations. Gold Cost Investors uses these segments to air programs that advertise Gold Coast Investors's products.

In fall 2005, one of the products advertised by Gold Coast Investors was a four-hour DVD disk titled *Real Estate Secrets*. The *Real Estate Secrets* DVD costs $39. According to Gold Coast Investors, the DVD provides real estate novices "with all of the information that anyone needs to get rich investing in real estate."

Unfortunately, every *Real Estate Secrets* DVD that Gold Coast shipped contained a defect. The DVDs will not play in most DVD machines.

In February 2006, Plaintiff Patricia Carpenter files a class action complaint in the Circuit Court of Kettle County. In September 2005, Carpenter had purchased the *Real Estate Secrets* DVD. Carpenter alleges that the *Real Estate Secrets* DVD would not play in Carpenter's DVD machine.

Carpenter's complaint states a single cause of action for breach of warranty, a state law claim. According to the complaint, when Gold Coast Investors sold defective copies of the *Real Estate Secrets* DVD, the company breached an implied warranty of merchantability.

Members of the plaintiff class will include about 10,000 Illinois residents who purchased the *Real Estate Secrets* DVD. Gold Coast Investors has maintained a customer list. The list includes the address of anyone who purchased a *Real Estate Secrets* DVD.

Each member of the plaintiff class only will seek to recover the $39 cost of the *Real Estate Secrets* DVD. None of the class members will seek to recover consequential damages.

Patricia Carpenter is a retired elementary school teacher. Carpenter earned her under-graduate degree from a respected Illinois college. Carpenter understands the class action complaint. Carpenter is willing to devote substantial time to the class action.

Attorney Michelle Wood represents Patricia Carpenter. Wood also seeks to represent the plaintiff class. Wood has represented three successful plaintiff classes in prior class action suits. In March 2006, Wood files a motion for class certification.

Neither Carpenter nor Wood has sufficient funds to pay the cost of mailing individual letters to the 10,000 potential class members who reside in Illinois. Accordingly, Wood proposes that potential class members receive notice of the class action through an adver-tisement published in *The Illinois Real Estate Journal*. This weekly trade magazine is widely read in the real estate industry.

Under Wood's proposed notice plan, Wood would purchase a one-half page advertisement in *The Illinois Real Estate Journal,* for four consecutive weeks. The advertisement would describe Carpenter's class action. The advertisement would include a form. By cutting out this form and mailing it to Wood's office and the court clerk, potential class members could opt out of Carpenter's class action.

1.   **Is the notice plan proposed by Michelle Wood adequate? Explain.**

2.   **For the purpose of this part only, assume that Wood proposes an adequate notice plan. Should the Kettle County circuit court grant the motion for class certification filed by plaintiff Patricia Carpenter? Explain.**

ANSWER TO QUESTION 48

1.   The notice plan proposed by attorney Michelle Wood is not adequate. At issue is whether notice by publication is sufficient to inform potential class members of the pending class action.

In Illinois, the type of notice to potential class members is left to the sound discretion of the trial court, taking into consideration the cost and potential effectiveness of the notice. The notice also must be reasonably calculated, under the circumstances, to give actual notice of the proceeding. Additionally, although individual notice is not always required, it should be given when the names and addresses of potential class members are readily available.

In the instant case, publication notice in a specialty magazine for real estate probably does not have a high probability of providing actual notice to the potential class action plaintiffs because it is unlikely that the average purchaser of the DVD was a real estate professional (as shown by the fact that the class representative was a retired schoolteacher). Furthermore, the names and addresses of the potential plaintiffs were known; thus, notice by mail should be required.

2.   The class action should be certified. The primary issue here is whether the class representative will fairly and adequately protect the interests of the class.

In Illinois, a lawsuit may be maintained as a class action if: (i) the class is so numerous that joinder of all members is impracticable; (ii) there are questions of law or fact common to the class and these questions predominate over all other questions in the case; (iii) the class representative will fairly and adequately protect the interests of the class; and (iv) a class action is an appropriate method of trying the case.

Here, there are 10,000 potential plaintiffs, making joinder of all plaintiffs virtually impossible. Thus, the numerosity requirement has been met. Next, given that the facts state that none of the class members will be seeking consequential damages, the main question in this case will be whether the DVDs were defective. As a result, a common question of fact would predominate over the litigation. The third requirement poses a closer question. Given that Carpenter is a retired school teacher and that no conflicts with other class members are revealed by the facts, she apparently has the experience, education, and time necessary to fairly and adequately represent the class. Additionally, attorney Wood has successfully represented class action plaintiffs. However, a question could be raised about their financial capability to represent the class, given that they apparently could not afford to provide mail notice to their co-plaintiffs. Assuming they are financially capable of representing the class, there are no other facts to indicate that Carpenter could not fairly and adequately represent the class. Finally, given the small value for the potential claims, it would be financially unwise for each class member to sue for an individual claim—court costs would likely be larger than any potential award. Accordingly, a class action would be an appropriate method for trying the case. For these reasons, the class action should be certified.

QUESTION 49

Raymond Demitrius ("Demitrius") runs a modestly successful business, Demitrius Debris Collection, Inc. ("DDC"), based in Valparaiso, Indiana (about 50 miles southeast of Chicago). DDC's 15 trucks and two cranes collect and haul storm debris, construction waste, and other garbage from commercial and residential properties to landfills in Indiana. Mostly because DDC only advertises in Indiana publications, the company's crews have made just five working trips to Illinois during the last 10 years. Demitrius and his wife, however, often travel to Chicago to visit friends or attend sporting events.

Jack Jacobs ("Jacobs") and his brother own and manage several small apartment buildings in Joliet, Illinois (about 40 miles south of Chicago). An Illinois partnership that Jacobs and his brother created and control, Milbank Partners, actually holds title to the properties. Milbank Partners operates from an office in Joliet—the county seat of Will County.

In May of 2006, several days after a ferocious storm hit the Chicago region, Demitrius got a call from his old friend, Jacobs. Calling from his office in Joliet, Jacobs was desperate to find a company with the capacity to remove two large trees that had fallen during the storm and were blocking the entrance of one of the buildings owned by Milbank Partners. Demitrius dispatched DDC's largest crane and agreed to charge Milbank Partners a flat $500 fee.

Jacobs met the workers at the building. After providing the DDC crane operator with blueprints of the building and a recent technical survey of the building's foundation and basement, Jacobs departed to handle other matters. Minutes later, when the crane moved too close to the building, its weight breached the foundation and caused part of the building to collapse—seriously injuring one of the tenants, Jill Haley ("Haley").

Haley timely filed a personal injury action against DDC and Milbank Partners in the Circuit Court of Will County. The lawsuit alleged negligence in the supervision and execution of the debris-removal project and sought damages in excess of $50,000.

DDC's registered agent was properly served with the complaint and summons at the company's office in Valparaiso, Indiana. Jacobs was served with the complaint and summons at his home in Chicago (located in Cook County). His brother was not served.

The first thing DDC's attorney filed was a motion to dismiss the complaint for lack of personal jurisdiction. The judge denied the motion.

Milbank Partners filed a motion to dismiss the complaint for improper service. The judge denied that motion too.

Later, pursuant to Illinois Supreme Court Rule 216, Haley's attorney served DDC with 15 requests to admit, one of which asked DDC to admit that the blueprints and technical survey that its crane operator received from Jacobs clearly indicated the maximum weight loads that could safely be applied to the areas within 15 feet of the building's foundation and basement. DDC still had the materials that Jacobs had given the crane operator. Demitrius instructed DDC's lawyer to respond by asserting that DDC "had insufficient knowledge to admit or deny," which the lawyer did.

1. Did the judge err in denying DDC's motion to dismiss for lack of personal jurisdiction? Explain.

2. **Did the judge err in denying the motion to dismiss filed by Milbank Partners? Explain.**

3. **Was DDC's response to the request to admit proper? Explain.**

4. **Could Haley have properly filed her lawsuit in Chicago instead of Joliet? Explain.**

ANSWER TO QUESTION 49

1.   No, the judge did not err in denying DDC's motion to dismiss for lack of personal jurisdiction. At issue is whether an Illinois court has long arm jurisdiction over DDC. As is the case in all states, the exercise of personal jurisdiction over a particular defendant must be ***authorized by statute*** and ***constitutional***.

Pursuant to Illinois's long arm statute, an Illinois court will have personal jurisdiction over a nonresident that performs enumerated acts within the state, including, among other things, committing a tort within the state. In the instant case, DDC may have committed a tort in Joliet when it (allegedly) failed to properly read the blueprints and technical survey to determine the maximum load-bearing capacity of the foundation. This fits the "commission of a tort" prong of the long arm statute; obviously then, the "statutorily authorized" prong is satisfied.

To be constitutional, the defendant must have such minimum contacts with the jurisdiction that the exercise of personal jurisdiction over him would be fair and reasonable. In assessing whether the defendant had sufficient minimum contacts, the court will consider whether the defendant purposefully availed himself of the benefits and protections of state law, whether the defendant could have reasonably anticipated that his activities within the state could make him amenable to a lawsuit within the state, and whether the exercise of jurisdiction within the state would offend the traditional notions of fair play and substantial justice. In the instant case, DDC voluntarily contracted with Millbanks Partners to perform work within Illinois. By doing so, it invoked the benefits and protections of Illinois state law. Furthermore, DDC should have reasonably anticipated that performing construction-type work in Illinois might lead to an injury and a lawsuit in Illinois. Finally, even though DDC does not have continuous contacts within Illinois, it would be fair and reasonable to try a case in Illinois when the case is based on an act performed in Illinois, the injury occurred in Illinois, and the plaintiff is from Illinois. For these reasons, the "constitutional" prong is satisfied.

As a result, given that the exercise of personal jurisdiction would be both authorized by the Illinois long arm statute and constitutionally permissible, the judge did not err in denying DDC's motion to dismiss based on an alleged lack of personal jurisdiction.

2.   No, the judge did not err in denying Milbank Partners's motion to dismiss based on improper service of process. At issue is the proper method for service of process on an Illinois partnership. In Illinois, a partnership sued in the firm's name may be served by personally serving one of the partners. Here, John Jacobs, a partner in Milbank Partners, was personally served at his home in Chicago. Thus, service of process was proper. Accordingly, the judge did not err in denying Milbank Partners's motion to dismiss.

3.   No, DDC's response to Haley's request to admit, in which it stated that it "had insufficient knowledge to admit or deny," was improper. At issue is whether a party may state that it does not have sufficient knowledge to answer the request without performing any research or looking at

any of its internal documents. Generally, a party may not state that it has insufficient knowledge of the topic to admit or deny when the party could gain that knowledge (*e.g.,* by looking at documents within its possession or by interviewing employees). In the instant case, DDC still had the blueprints and technical survey in its possession. Thus, it probably could determine whether the documents specified the maximum weight loads that could safely be applied to areas within 15 feet of the building's foundation and basement. As a result, its answer that it has insufficient knowledge to admit or deny is improper.

4.   Suit against the Milbank Partners could have been properly filed in Chicago (Cook County). At issue is the place of proper venue for a suit against a partnership in the firm's name. In Illinois, venue is proper in the county in which any defendant resides or in which the transaction (or some part of it) occurred. A partnership sued in the firm's name is deemed to reside in any county in which any partner resides, in which the partnership has an office, or in which the partnership was doing business. Here, the facts state that Jack Jacobs was served at his home in Chicago. Thus, given that Jack Jacobs resides in Chicago, venue in Cook County would be proper.

QUESTION 50

Builder Bob and Homeowner Harry are friends who both live in Winnebago County, Illinois. Harry wanted to collect baseball cards as a hobby. Bob wanted to sell his baseball card collection. In October 2006, Bob sold and delivered his baseball card collection to Harry for a negotiated price of $20,000. Bob told Harry that Harry could pay him when Harry had some extra money.

In February 2007, Homeowner Harry contracted with Builder Bob for Bob to build Harry a new home in Winnebago County, with a May 2007 completion date. One of Bob's employees, Roofer Ralph, worked on the roof of Harry's new home. Roofer Ralph liked to keep records of what he did, so he did not make the same mistake twice. So he took some notes documenting some cracks he noticed in the roofing work that he did for Harry.

Homeowner Harry's home was completed in May 2007, and Harry paid Builder Bob the full contract price for the home. Harry had not been living in the house for more than two weeks when rain began coming through the roof, causing more than $50,000 in damages. Builder Bob refused to fix the roof.

Homeowner Harry sued Builder Bob for breach of the implied warranty of habitability in the Circuit Court of Winnebago County, Illinois. Bob counterclaimed against Harry for breach of contract in the amount of $20,000, to recover the purchase price of the baseball card collection he had previously delivered to Harry.

Homeowner Harry moved to strike Builder Bob's counterclaim because it was unrelated to Harry's claim for breach of the implied warranty of habitability. The court denied the motion.

Builder Bob hired Lawyer Larry. Larry interviewed Roofer Ralph about what he knew about Homeowner Harry's home and titled the document "Interview with Roofer Ralph." Ralph also gave his personal notes to Larry that he kept while working on the construction project.

After interviewing various witnesses, Lawyer Larry composed a document titled "Case Theories." He noted how he intended to argue at trial that the extreme rainfall in May and not shoddy workmanship caused the damage to Homeowner Harry's home.

1. **Was the court correct in denying Homeowner Harry's motion to strike Builder Bob's counterclaim? Explain.**

2. **Are Roofer Ralph's notes protected by the attorney-client privilege? Explain.**

3. **Are Lawyer Larry's documents titled, (a) "Interview with Roofer Ralph," or (b) "Case Theories" protected by the work product doctrine? Explain.**

ANSWER TO QUESTION 50

1.   The court was correct in denying Homeowner Harry's motion to strike Builder Bob's counterclaim. At issue is whether a defendant may assert an unrelated counterclaim against a plaintiff. In Illinois, a counterclaim need not be related to the plaintiff's claim in order for it to be brought in the current case. Thus, there is no prohibition against a joint trial of Builder Bob's counterclaim for breach of contract for the baseball card transaction with Homeowner Harry's claim for breach of the warranty of habitability regarding the building of the home. Although the court retains discretion to order separate trials if a joint trial would result in unnecessary complication of issues, unnecessary embarrassment to one of the parties, or undue delay, it apparently chose not to do so in this case. As a result, the motion to strike was properly denied.

2.   Roofer Ralph's notes are not protected by attorney-client privilege. At issue is whether statements by an employee are protected by the attorney-client privilege, and whether material created prior to the formation of any attorney-client relationship may be protected by the attorney-client privilege. In Illinois, communications between a party or his agent and his attorney regarding a case are privileged. However, a party cannot prevent the disclosure of otherwise discoverable information by turning the information over to his attorney. In the instant case, although Builder Bob, not Roofer Ralph, hired Larry Lawyer for legal representation, Ralph was Bob's employee and, thus, his agent. As a result, any communication between Ralph and Larry potentially falls under the attorney-client privilege. However, Ralph would have made his notes prior to any possible attorney-client relationship, and the notes, being relevant to the current litigation, ordinarily would be discoverable during the course of the litigation. Ralph may not immunize the notes from discovery by turning them over to Larry. As a result, although an attorney-client relationship exists for the purposes of the litigation, the notes are not protected by the attorney-client privilege.

3.   The document titled "Case Theories" is certainly protected by the work product doctrine, and, although a somewhat closer call, the document titled "Interview with Roofer Ralph" also should be so protected. At issue is when material prepared by the attorney should be disclosed during the discovery process. In Illinois, material that is prepared by or for a party in anticipation of trial is protected under the work product doctrine. Protected work product is subject to discovery only if it does not contain or disclose the theories, mental impressions, or litigation plans of the party's attorney. Material that would disclose the mental impressions of the lawyer is then discoverable only on a showing that it would be impossible to secure similar information from other sources. In the instant case, the "Case Theories" document, as the name implies, would disclose the mental impression and trial strategy of Larry Lawyer. Homeowner Harry can secure

the information by interviewing the witnesses and reviewing the evidence from which Larry derived his "Case Theories." Thus, the document is not discoverable. Although a slightly closer call, the document titled "Interview with Roofer Ralph" also should be protected. In contrast to a verbatim statement by a witness, the back-and-forth of an interview session, and the exact questions asked by Larry might disclose the legal theories on which Larry intends to rely. (Larry would be required to make the document available for an in camera inspection to ensure that is the case.) Additionally, given that Roofer Ralph is still available to testify and give interviews, there can be no claim of impossibility of securing the information from other sources. Thus, that document should also be protected.

QUESTION 51

Smith Soda, Inc. is an Illinois corporation, with its principal place of business in Tin County, Illinois. Smith Soda makes cans and distributes a variety of flavored drinks.

Cobra Cola is one of the best selling products marketed by Smith Soda. Cobra Cola is an "energy drink," containing large amounts of sugar and caffeine.

Peg is a permanent resident of Tin County, Illinois. On May 1, 2005, Peg buys a can of Cobra Cola from a vending machine in Tin County. When Peg attempts to open the can of soda, the can explodes. Metal pieces from the can cut Peg's face, arms, and stomach. Peg suffers serious injuries in this accident.

On June 1, 2005, Peg files a complaint in the Circuit Court of Tin County. Peg's complaint names Smith Soda as the only defendant.

In her complaint, Peg alleges a single cause of action for strict liability, an Illinois state law claim. According to the complaint: "Smith Soda relied on an unreasonably dangerous design when the company developed its can for Cobra Cola. As a result of this design defect, cans of Cobra Cola sometimes explode when opened." Peg seeks $1 million in compensatory damages.

1. Now assume on July 15, 2005, Peg moves to amend her complaint. At this time, Peg's case is in the initial stages of discovery.

    In her amendment, Peg seeks to add a cause of action for breach of warranty to Peg's complaint against Smith Soda. The new cause of action would provide: "The can of Cobra Cola purchased by Peg was not fit for ordinary purposes. By selling this can of cola, Smith Soda breached the implied warranty of merchantability." Assume that Peg's proposed amendment satisfies the applicable Illinois statute of limitations.

    Should the Tin County Circuit Court grant Peg's motion to amend her complaint? Explain.

2. For the purpose of this part, assume that Peg did not file a motion to amend her complaint on July 15, 2005. Instead, assume that Peg first moves to amend her complaint on September 4, 2007. In her September 2007 motion, Peg seeks to add a cause of action for negligence. This new cause of action would allege: "Smith Soda failed to exercise reasonable care in designing and producing Cobra Cola cans."

As of September 4, 2007, Peg's case against Smith Soda has not yet proceeded to trial. Defendant Smith Soda opposes Peg's motion to amend.

Assume that a two-year Illinois statute of limitations governs the negligence action filed by Peg. Further assume that this statute of limitations began to run on May 1, 2005, when the exploding soda can injured Peg.

Should the Tin County Circuit Court grant Peg's September 2007 motion to amend her complaint? Explain.

ANSWER TO QUESTION 51

1. The Tin County Circuit Court should allow Peg to amend her complaint. At issue is whether, in Illinois, a party may amend her complaint once it has been filed. In Illinois, motions to amend pleadings are to be liberally granted. Given this great latitude, the Tin County Circuit Court should allow Peg to amend her complaint, especially considering that the statute of limitations has not yet run. (Peg would be able to voluntarily dismiss her complaint and refile the complaint with both causes of action if she were not allowed to amend her complaint.)

2. The Tin County Circuit Court should allow Peg to amend her complaint even if the statute of limitations had expired at the time of the motion. At issue is whether, in Illinois, a party may amend her complaint to assert a new claim if the statute of limitations has expired for that claim. In Illinois, a plaintiff may amend her complaint to assert a new claim after the statute of limitations has expired if: (i) the original complaint was timely filed; and (ii) the claim asserted in the amended complaint arose from the same transaction or occurrence as the claim asserted in the original complaint.

Here, both requirements are satisfied. Peg was injured, and the claim accrued, on May 1, 2005. Peg filed her original complaint a month later on June 1, 2005, well within the statute of limitations period. Furthermore, both claims arise from the same transaction or occurrence. The original complaint asserts a claim based on strict liability based on the design of the soda can. The amended complaint seeks to add an additional claim based on the negligent design of the soda can. Given that both claims generally relate to how the can was designed and that both claims seek compensation for the exploding soda can, the cause of action asserted in the amended complaint arises from the same transaction or occurrence as the cause of action asserted in the original complaint. As a result, the Tin County Circuit Court should allow Peg to amend her complaint to assert a claim based on the negligent design of the soda can.

QUESTION 52

Backside Chiropractic, Inc. ("Backside") runs a chiropractic clinic at its principal place of business in Chesterfield, Missouri. The three shareholders of Backside are chiropractors Abel, Beth, and Carla. They all perform spinal adjustments out of Backside's office in Chesterfield.

In July 2007, Backside designed a web site, backside.com, to try to attract new customers to its clinic. The web site listed clinic hours, chiropractors, procedures, and fees, as well as

general information about the practice of chiropractic medicine. Additionally, Abel, Beth, and Carla had a page on the web site with their clinic forms that new patients had to complete. New patients had the option of printing forms, completing them, and bringing them to their first visit. Patients nationwide could access the web site.

In addition, Backside occasionally sent post cards to potential customers to increase business. They usually targeted customers in the Chesterfield area of Missouri but, for the first time in October 2007, sent 500 postcards to residents of Illinois who lived near the Missouri border. They did not have much success with that mailing so, after that, decided to focus their advertising efforts on Chesterfield.

Paula Patient is a resident of East St. Louis, Illinois, which is in St. Clair County. In November 2007, her friend, who lives in Chesterfield, Missouri, recommended that Paula receive treatment at Backside for her back pain. Paula was not familiar with Backside's web site and had not received a postcard. She called Backside and made an appointment. At her first appointment, she completed the new patient forms, and Abel evaluated her and adjusted her spine.

Paula Patient had increased back pain after her visit to Backside. She visited an attorney and decided to sue Backside for malpractice. She filed a complaint in the Circuit Court of St. Clair County, Illinois. The clerk issued the summons, and the attorney mailed the complaint and summons to Beth, one of the Backside shareholders and chiropractors. Backside was not served in any other way.

Backside answered the complaint and served the answer on Paula Patient's attorney. Ten days later, Backside filed a motion to dismiss the complaint for lack of personal jurisdiction and improper service of process. The court has yet to rule on the motion.

1. Does the Circuit Court of St. Clair County, Illinois have personal jurisdiction over Backside Chiropractic, Inc.? Explain.

2. Was service of process on Backside Chiropractic, Inc. proper? Explain.

3. Is Backside Chiropractic, Inc.'s motion for lack of personal jurisdiction and improper service of process timely? Explain.

ANSWER TO QUESTION 52

1. The Circuit Court of St. Clair County does have personal jurisdiction over Backside Chiropractic ("Backside"). The issues are whether an Illinois court has general jurisdiction (*i.e.,* jurisdiction over all causes of action) or specific jurisdiction (*i.e.,* jurisdiction under the long arm statute for an act committed in Illinois) over Backside and whether the motion was timely made.

General jurisdiction: Illinois authorizes an Illinois court to exercise personal jurisdiction, for all causes of action, over a defendant who conducts business in Illinois. Mere solicitation of orders that must be accepted out of state is insufficient to be "doing business"; there must be some further activity by the defendant within Illinois. Examples of the further activity include processing complaints, granting credit, and servicing and taking back goods. In the instant case, Backside sent 500 postcards into Illinois and it maintains a web site that can be accessed in Illinois.

This activity is insufficient activity to be "doing business" in Illinois. The postcards required Illinois residents to travel to Missouri for treatment, and thus fall under the mere solicitation rule. Arguably, the maintenance of a mostly passive web site might be "further activity" in Illinois to enable the court to exercise personal jurisdiction under a "doing business" theory. However, the web site in question is passive in nature and thus should be viewed as no more than general advertising not directed at Illinois. Furthermore, the only thing the web site allows a patient to do is print out forms, regardless of the patient's home state. (Presumably, the forms could be printed and filled out in Illinois.) The patient must take the form to his first appointment in Missouri for processing. Such activity does not rise to the examples listed above, and does not represent the kind of systematic and continuous activity contemplated by the statute. Thus, Backside is not doing business in Illinois.

Specific jurisdiction: Alternatively, an Illinois court could have long arm jurisdiction over a nonresident who commits certain acts within Illinois. Illinois's long arm statute provides specific bases for exercising personal jurisdiction and has a catchall provision that authorizes the court to exercise jurisdiction as far as constitutionally permissible. Among the specific listed bases are transacting business in Illinois and the commission of a tort in Illinois (which has been interpreted to include the commission of an out-of-state act that causes injury in Illinois). Additionally, the cause of action must arise out of the defendant's Illinois contacts. First, the "transaction of business" provision would not apply because Paula's cause of action did not arise out of any business Backside may have transacted in Illinois. As for the "commission of a tort" provision, Paula received treatment at Backside's Missouri office and presumably was first injured by Backside in Missouri (although Paula may have some more severe manifestations of the injury in Illinois). Thus, the tort and Paula's injury occurred in Missouri, making the "commission of a tort" provision inapplicable. The question then becomes whether the catchall provision applies— in other words, whether it is constitutionally permissible to exercise personal jurisdiction over an out-of-state defendant who causes an out-of-state injury that may manifest itself in Illinois. Under these facts, it is not. To be constitutional, the defendant must have such minimum contacts with the state such that the exercise of personal jurisdiction would be fair and reasonable, and notice must be provided. In the instant case, the only contacts that Backside has with Illinois are the postcard mailing, the maintenance of a web site, and the fact that it treated an Illinois resident in Missouri. None of these contacts make it foreseeable that Backside could be sued in Illinois. As a result, the "minimum contacts" test cannot be satisfied, and the catchall provision would not provide a basis for exercising personal jurisdiction over Backside.

Nevertheless, the motion was not timely made; therefore Backside waived the objection to personal jurisdiction. (*See* 3., below.) As a result, an Illinois court would have personal jurisdiction over Backside.

2.   The service of process on Backside was not proper. At issue is whether service by mail is authorized in Illinois. Illinois authorizes service on an out-of-state defendant in a like manner as service within Illinois by any person over 18 (appointment by the court is not necessary). In Illinois, a corporation is served by leaving a copy of the process on the registered agent or any officer or agent of the corporation. "Agent" is defined broadly; what is important is whether the duties of the person served would make it likely that she would know to forward the process to a proper person. Here, the facts indicate that the complaint was mailed to Beth, a Backside shareholder and one of its chiropractors. Although Beth is a proper party to be served, because her duties as a chiropractor would make her an agent of Backside, mailing is not an authorized method of service in Illinois. Thus, the service of process was not proper.

3.   Backside's motion for lack of personal jurisdiction and improper service was not timely. At issue is when a party waives objections to personal jurisdiction or the sufficiency of service of process. In Illinois, a party must object to personal jurisdiction or the sufficiency of service of process prior to filing any pleading or motion other than a motion for an extension of time to answer or appear. If the party files a responsive pleading or motion (other than for an extension of time) before a motion challenging personal jurisdiction, that party is deemed to have waived all personal jurisdiction objections. Here, Backside filed and served an answer before objecting to personal jurisdiction or service of process. Thus, the objection as to personal jurisdiction is waived, and the motion was not timely.

QUESTION 1

Wendy was a waitress in a tavern owned and operated by Tim. One of her duties was to clean the tables at the end of the evening. One night she discovered three "Instant Winner" lottery tickets on one of the tables. The tickets invited purchasers to scratch an opaque coating off the tickets; if three matching dollar figures were revealed, the person turning the card in received the designated amount. Two of the three tickets were worthless. The figures on the third, however, were incompletely revealed. When Wendy scratched the covering from the rest of the card, she discovered that the ticket was a $1,000 winner.

Who is entitled to the $1,000? Give reasons.

ANSWER TO QUESTION 1

Wendy is probably entitled to the $1,000.

In determining who has title to found property, the property must first be characterized as lost, mislaid, or abandoned. Property is lost if the owner accidentally and involuntarily parted with possession and does not know where to find it. Property is mislaid when, judging from the place it is found, it can reasonably be determined that it was intentionally placed there and then forgotten. Property is abandoned if the owner has voluntarily relinquished all ownership without reference to any particular person or purpose, with the intent of giving up both title and possession.

Because the lottery ticket was apparently intentionally placed on the table, it would not be characterized as lost. The evidence best supports a conclusion that it was abandoned: The owner believed the partially scratched ticket was a loser like the other two and left all three to be disposed of by the waitress when she cleaned the table. A less plausible argument might be made that the owner was interrupted or for some other reason decided to wait until later to finish scratching the ticket, and then forgot to pick it up. If this argument is successful, the ticket would be characterized as mislaid.

If the ticket is characterized as abandoned, Wendy becomes the owner as against both the original owner and Tim. Title to abandoned chattels is acquired by (i) actual or constructive control or dominion over the thing and (ii) intent to assert ownership of it. Wendy has met these requirements. Tim has not met them; even if his ownership of the premises were considered constructive dominion over the tickets, he still would not meet the intent requirement.

In the less likely event that the ticket is characterized as mislaid, the original owner, should he be found, may claim it. The finder would be held to be under a duty to use reasonable means to find the owner. If the original owner cannot be located, Tim, as owner of the place where the mislaid property was found, would achieve the right of possession as against all but the true owner. He would acquire title after a sufficient time passes for the ticket to be deemed abandoned, or until the statute of limitations has run.

QUESTION 2

Pat handed her best friend, Ann, a box containing coins intended as a gift to her nephew, Nick. Pat said, "I'll tell Nick to pick up the box at your office." The next day, a young man

who called himself Nick arrived at Ann's office and claimed the coins. (He was not, in fact, Nick, but rather a con man who had overheard the conversation between Pat and Ann.)

The next day, Pat called Ann and said, "I've changed my mind about the gift. Don't give the coins to Nick." Ann said it was too late—she had already delivered the coins to Nick. Pat knew something was wrong since she had spoken to Nick on the phone about the coins, but later in the same conversation, after an argument, she had repudiated the gift.

Pat is furious about the loss of the coins and blames Ann for delivering the coins to the con man. She wants to sue Ann. You have learned that Nick has already told Ann that he has no interest in making any claim against her.

Discuss Ann's possible defenses in a suit by Pat and whether Ann would prevail. Give reasons.

ANSWER TO QUESTION 2

Ann has two possible defenses, neither of which will be successful.

First, Ann may argue that Pat had made a completed gift of the coins to Nick, and therefore no longer has any claim to them. A valid gift inter vivos requires (i) donative intent, (ii) delivery, and (iii) acceptance. Pat clearly had donative intent, and acceptance will be presumed where a gift is beneficial to the donee, so it is delivery that is at issue. Where delivery is made through an agent, the time at which a gift becomes effective depends on whose agent is used. If a gift is made through an agent of the donee, it is effective when delivered to the agent; if made through an agent of the donor, it is effective when the agent delivers it to the donee. Here, Ann appears to be Pat's agent, since she is Pat's best friend and apparently does not even know Nick on sight. Therefore, the gift would have been effective when Ann delivered the coins to Nick; it was not effective at the time Pat delivered the coins to Ann. Because no completed gift was made, Pat continued to have an interest in the coins, and Ann may not defend by asserting otherwise.

Ann's second defense will be that as a gratuitous bailee she owed only a slight duty of care toward the bailed property and that she met this standard. A bailment is created when one party transfers possession of personal property to another for the accomplishment of a particular purpose. There is no transfer of title, and the bailee must treat the property in accordance with the terms of the bailment. Under the facts of this question, Pat created a bailment when she delivered the box of coins to Ann so that Ann could redeliver them to Nick.

As a general rule, a bailee is not an insurer of bailed property, but must exercise due care to protect and preserve it. The specific degree of care required varies with the type of bailment. The traditional rule is that where, as here, the bailment is for the sole benefit of the bailor, only slight care is required, and liability will rest only upon gross negligence. Under the modern trend, bailments are not strictly classified according to whom they benefit, and the court will consider whether the bailee has exercised due care under the circumstances. Ann will argue that she exercised the proper degree of care with respect to the coins, and that her misdelivery to the con man was a reasonable mistake.

Ann's argument will not succeed, however, because the above general rule regarding a bailee's duty of care does not apply in misdelivery situations. Where a bailee redelivers bailed goods to the wrong person, the bailee is held absolutely liable, no matter how reasonable the mistake. Liability is thus not based on negligence at all, so the concept of degree or duty of care is not relevant. (A narrow exception, not applicable here, is made where the person falsely claiming the goods supplies an indispensable instrument, such as a claim check.) Because liability in this situation is absolute and not based on negligence, Ann cannot prevail by claiming that she exercised an appropriate degree of care.

Because neither of her defenses will prevail, Ann will be held liable for the loss of the coins.

QUESTION 3

Auto Dealership, for advertising purposes, loaned two new cars to Service Club for use in the Small Town Centennial Parade, which was being sponsored and organized by Service Club. The cars were parked for two days in a vacant lot next to the parade route. The morning of the parade there was a severe storm. There was damaging hail and a tornado warning (but no tornado). The parade organizers scurried for shelter. After the storm it was discovered that one of the cars had been seriously damaged by hail, and that the other had disappeared.

Auto Dealership's investigation has failed to discover anything about the circumstances surrounding the disappearance of the missing car. Auto Dealership's manager suspects the keys had been left in the ignition, though no one will admit as much. The president of Service Club has returned one set of keys, but the manager thinks he gave the Service Club president two sets. As to the hail damage, Auto Dealership's manager believes the car should have been moved to a garage when weather forecasts indicated the likelihood of an approaching hailstorm; many town residents quickly garaged their cars, or tried to get them under some kind of shelter. Manager has admitted that Auto Dealership does not always attempt to move the cars on its lot to shelter, even when such shelter is available for some (though not all) of the cars on its lot.

Will Auto Dealership recover from Service Club:

1. The value of the missing car? Give reasons.

2. The damage to the other car? Give reasons.

ANSWER TO QUESTION 3

1. Auto Dealership will probably recover the value of the missing car.

At issue are a bailee's duty of care with respect to bailed goods and the burden of proof in litigation following a bailee's failure to return bailed property according to the terms of the bailment.

A bailment is created when one party (the bailor) transfers custody of personal property to another who intends to control it as a bailee. A bailment arose when Auto Dealership lent Service Club the two cars for use in the parade.

4. PERSONAL PROPERTY

A bailee must exercise due care with respect to the bailed goods. The degree of negligence upon which liability will rest varies with the type of bailment; *i.e.,* for whose benefit the bailment was entered. Where, as here, the bailment was for mutual benefit (Auto Dealership benefited from the advertising and Service Club benefited from use of the cars), ordinary due care is required. The modern trend is away from classification on the basis of who benefits, toward a rule requiring ordinary care under all circumstances.

Where the bailor shows that it has delivered property to the bailee and the bailee has failed to return it or has returned it in damaged condition, the bailor has made out a prima facie case for recovery, and the burden is on the bailee to explain why the property was lost or damaged. The reason for this rule is that the bailee has in its possession the means of ascertaining the cause of the loss or damage.

Because the car was delivered to Service Club and not returned, a prima facie case exists. It is up to Service Club to explain that the loss occurred despite its due care. Service Club is apparently unable to do this, so it will be held liable.

2.   Auto Dealership is also likely to recover for the hail damage to the other car, but it is a close question.

Again, the burden of proof is on the bailee (Service Club) to prove that the loss was caused despite its due care. On these facts, evidence as to the appropriate standard of care is found in the fact that there was some advance warning of the storm and that many town residents garaged their cars. (That Auto Dealership sometimes did not move its cars is not helpful to Service Club, since whether Auto Dealership itself always exercised due care is not at issue.) In arguing that it exercised due care, Service Club will point out the unreliability of hailstorm forecasts, the fact that some residents did not bother to garage their cars, and the likely difficulty of finding shelter on short notice for the cars.

Because Service Club apparently took no action at all to protect the cars, the court is most likely to find that it has not met its burden of proving that it exercised due care.

QUESTION 4

Pat left her portable television set at Dave's repair shop to have a new picture tube installed. Next to the counter, Dave had placed a 12-inch square sign which read, "Not responsible for items not picked up within 30 days after repairs are completed."

Pat was out of town for two months, and when she returned to town she went to Dave's to pick up her television set. Dave could not find the set. Dave's practice was to move equipment to an unlocked storeroom 40 days after repairs had been finished since his work area could not accommodate the unrepaired, unrepairable, and repaired-but-not-paid-for equipment that accumulated over time.

Pat is furious. She has consulted you about her rights. She told you that in the first place she did not see the "Not responsible . . ." sign, and, furthermore, that she heard one of Dave's employees tell Dave while they were looking for the set that he was pretty sure someone had picked up the set, having described it and related a story about the loss of the claim ticket in a canoeing accident.

Advise Pat. Give reasons.

ANSWER TO QUESTION 4

Pat can probably recover the value of the television set from Dave's repair shop. At issue is the liability of a bailee for failure to redeliver bailed property. A bailment was created when Pat, the bailor, left her television set with Dave, the bailee, who took custody of it with the intent to serve as a bailee.

Upon termination of the bailment, the bailee is under a duty to redeliver the bailed item to the bailor. This duty is absolute; liability for misdelivery is not based on the bailee's negligence. An exception to this general rule exists where the bailee, without notice, misdelivers the property to someone holding an indispensable instrument such as a claim check. This exception does not apply on these facts because the conversation Pat overheard suggests that the person who picked up the set did not have the claim check and convinced Dave's employee to deliver the set without it. Even if the exception should potentially apply, the bailee would still be liable on a negligence theory given these facts. Since this is a mutual bailment, the governing standard would be that of reasonable care/ordinary care.

A bailee may by contract limit his liability for loss of bailed goods. Dave attempted to do this by posting the sign disclaiming responsibility for items left more than 30 days. Given the "30-day" aspect, this clause should be construed as a limitation on liability, not a complete exculpation. Such signs are held to be ineffective unless the bailee can prove that the bailor read the notice or, because of its size and location, should have read it. Pat claims she did not see the sign in Dave's shop. Whether she should have seen it is a question of fact, but the court would probably find that the sign was not so obvious as to have become a part of the bailment agreement between Dave and Pat.

Pat may thus recover the value of the television set from Dave.

QUESTION 5

Dora was hospitalized in anticipation of a complicated heart operation. Without the operation she would die. There was a 30% chance that the operation would prove successful and she would recover, and a 70% chance that the operation would prove fruitless.

Dora was visited by her niece, Laura, with whom she had always had a cordial, but not close, relationship. While her niece was at her bedside, Dora took an emerald pin from a small box, handed it to Laura and said, "I would like you to have this. Wear it, or sell it if you need to—but remember me. My chances aren't so good, I understand." Laura hugged Dora, and said, "I'm sure the operation will be a success. You're a strong person. I'll see you again soon." Laura put the pin on her sweater and left. Dora's son, Paul, was present during the conversation.

Dora's operation was a success. On three occasions Laura visited Dora in the hospital during Dora's recuperation, but neither Dora nor Laura said anything about the pin. Two months later Dora was killed in a car accident. Her son and sole heir, Paul, has sued Laura for the return of the emerald pin, which is worth $10,000.

Discuss the arguments which will be made by Laura and Paul, and indicate who should prevail. Give reasons.

ANSWER TO QUESTION 5

Laura will argue that the emerald pin was an unconditional gift inter vivos to her from Dora. Paul will argue that the pin was a gift causa mortis that should have been returned to Dora after the successful heart operation. Laura will prevail.

A valid gift inter vivos requires three elements: donative intent, delivery, and acceptance. All three were present when Dora transferred possession of the pin to Laura. Dora's statement that she would like Laura to have the pin reveals donative intent. Dora handed the pin to Laura, who put it on and left, indicating delivery and acceptance.

A gift causa mortis has an additional requirement—that the gift have been made in contemplation of death. The donor must be realistically confronted with imminent death, and not merely be abstractly fearing death at some time in the future. Dora's upcoming heart operation, which had only a 30% chance of success, qualifies as a sufficiently imminent cause of death, and this will be the basis of Paul's argument that the pin was a gift causa mortis.

Paul's argument that the pin was given as a gift causa mortis will not succeed, however, because although Dora was confronted with imminent death, she apparently intended the gift to be unconditional. Dora began her conversation with Laura by saying she wanted Laura to have the pin, and she gave Laura permission to sell it. Dora's reference to her present health appears to have been an incidental remark; she did not condition the making of the gift on her likely imminent death. Although not conclusive, further evidence of the unconditional nature of the gift is found in Dora's failure to ask for return of the pin during any of Laura's three visits after the operation. In short, the court should find that although Dora had reason to contemplate death, this contemplation was not a significant factor in the making of the gift.

In the event the court finds that the gift was a gift causa mortis, Paul will prevail, since a gift causa mortis is revoked by operation of law upon the donor's recovery from the illness that placed her in contemplation of death. Thus, Dora's gift would have been revoked when she recovered from the heart operation, and her subsequent death in the car accident would be irrelevant.

QUESTION 6

Paul owned a home next to a county park. In November 1989, he noticed a small motorcycle—equipped as a "dirt bike"—leaning against a shelter in the park. It had no license plate. It was still there in December, and he covered it with a plastic tarp to protect it from the elements. In March 1990, Paul moved the motorcycle to his garage, where he disassembled, cleaned, and reassembled the engine. He began to ride the motorcycle, but continued to park it next to the shelter where he had found it.

In June of 1992, Paul injured his ankle, which prevented him from riding the motorcycle. He left the motorcycle in the park as he had in the past. On January 10, 1993, Paul discovered Don loading the motorcycle onto a pickup truck. After a short discussion, Don admitted that he was not the original owner, but claimed that he had as much right to the motorcycle as Paul.

Paul and Don have come to you and asked that you award the motorcycle to one of them, according to the strength of their respective legal claims.

Decision? Explain.

ANSWER TO QUESTION 6

Paul is entitled to the motorcycle. The evidence best supports a finding that the motorcycle was abandoned when Paul found it, that he became its owner, and that he never relinquished ownership of it.

Property is abandoned when the owner gives up possession with the intent to relinquish title. It is not known why the motorcycle was left in the park initially, but in the absence of better information, a reasonable interpretation of the facts is that the owner abandoned it there. This view is supported by the length of time the motorcycle was left unattended in the park and the absence of a license plate. If this turns out not to be true—if, for example, the motorcycle was stolen and left in the park by a thief—Paul's rights will be subject to the rights of the true owner.

Title to abandoned property is acquired when the new owner takes possession with the intent to acquire title. Paul probably first accomplished the requisite possession when he began protecting the motorcycle with a tarp; he certainly possessed the motorcycle when he moved it to his garage and repaired it. There might be some question as to whether Paul had the requisite intent to assert ownership, since after each use he returned the motorcycle to the place where he found it. This is probably best viewed as a precautionary safeguarding of the original owner's rights in case the motorcycle was not truly abandoned. Paul appears to have considered the motorcycle as his own, with the possible single exception of the original owner.

Don will argue that Paul himself then abandoned the motorcycle after he injured his ankle. Paul's leaving the motorcycle in the park does not itself amount to abandonment, since intent must be shown. Paul's objection to Don's loading of the motorcycle onto his truck indicates that intent to abandon was never present. Paul still considered the motorcycle his, although the facts suggest that he would have relinquished it to the original owner if asked.

Because Paul acquired title to abandoned property and did not then himself abandon the property, it continues to belong to him.

QUESTION 1

ABC Corporation owned an office building. On January 1, ABC leased the building to Dentist. The written lease was for a term of five years and required monthly rental payments. The lease required Dentist to procure, pay the premiums on, and maintain during the term of the lease, a fire insurance policy for the full insurable value of the building, payable to ABC. The lease also provided that should the building be rendered untenantable by fire, the lease would not be terminated and ABC would be obligated to rebuild the building with the insurance proceeds. Dentist never obtained the insurance policy.

Dentist operated his business in the building until September 1, during which time he paid his monthly rent as required by the lease. On September 1, Dentist retired and assigned the remainder of the lease to his son ("Son"), who had recently been licensed as a dentist. The assignment was in writing. The lease between ABC and Dentist did not contain any provisions regarding assignment of the lease or subletting. Son received a copy of the lease but did not bother to read it.

On September 10, a fire of unknown origin caused extensive damage to the building. A sprinkler system, installed by ABC as required by the local fire code, worked but caused extensive water damage to Son's office. The local fire marshal prohibited anyone from occupying the building until needed repairs were made.

Shortly after the fire, ABC repaired the building at its expense, and the local fire marshal approved it for occupancy on December 31. Son had discontinued paying rent while the building was being repaired and refused to return to the building when the repairs were completed, having found a new location during the interim.

You are counsel for ABC Corporation. On what bases would you suggest the corporation file suit, against whom, and what are possible defenses that would be raised?

ANSWER TO QUESTION 1

I would advise ABC to file suit against both Dentist and Son for breach of the lease—both for failure to pay rent and for failure to maintain fire insurance on the property. The main issue here is whether the covenants to pay rent and maintain fire insurance run with the land.

A lease is a contract containing the promises (covenants) of the parties. A lease covenant binds not only the parties who agreed to it (*i.e.,* those in privity of contract), but also assignees of the parties if: (i) they are in privity of estate, and (ii) the covenant is one that runs with the land. An assignee will be considered to be in privity of estate if he takes the entire remaining estate of his assignor. A covenant will be considered to run with the land if the parties so intend and both the benefit and burden of the covenant touch and concern the land (*i.e.,* directly affect the party in use or enjoyment of the land). A covenant to pay rent is considered to run with the land. A covenant to maintain fire insurance will also be considered to run with the land if the lease requires the landlord to use insurance proceeds for rebuilding.

If one party breaches a covenant contained in a lease, the other party can recover damages. Here, the lease between Dentist and ABC required Dentist to make monthly rental payments for five years and to maintain fire insurance on the premises. Dentist failed to maintain fire insurance and stopped paying rent when he retired. Thus, the lease covenants clearly have been breached. As a result, ABC may be able to recover damages, depending on whether Dentist and Son have any valid defenses.

Here, Dentist might argue that he is not liable for the covenants because he assigned his interest in the leased premises to Son. Absent an express restriction in the lease, a tenant may freely assign his leasehold interest. However, this does not help Dentist. A lease covenant remains binding on the parties who made it even after assignment, because the parties are in privity of contract. Thus, Dentist remained liable on the lease covenants both to pay rent and to maintain insurance even after he assigned the lease to Son.

Son may argue that he is not liable on the covenants because he is not in privity of contract with ABC. However, this argument will fail because Son is bound through the doctrine of privity of estate. Here, there is privity of estate between ABC and Son because Dentist assigned the remainder of his estate to Son. Moreover, as established above, the covenant to pay rent is considered to run with the land, and the covenant to maintain fire insurance here will be considered to run with the land because the lease provides that ABC must use the proceeds to rebuild the building. Thus, Son is bound on the covenants through privity of estate.

Son may also argue that he should not be liable for either covenant because he did not read the lease and was unaware of the requirements that it contained. However, this argument will not prevail. Parties who sign contracts are expected to have read them and are bound by their terms.

Dentist and Son may argue that they were relieved of their obligation to pay rent under the doctrine of constructive eviction. However, this defense will fail. Under the doctrine, if the landlord does an act or fails to provide some service that he has a legal duty to provide and thereby makes the property uninhabitable, the tenant may terminate the lease and cease paying rent. Here, after the fire it was impossible to operate a business in the building due to the fire and water damage. Indeed, the fire marshal prohibited anyone from occupying the building before it was repaired. Nevertheless, this defense will fail because constructive eviction is a defense only when the *landlord* interferes with the tenant's use and enjoyment of the premises. Here, the interference was not caused by the landlord, but rather by a fire of unknown origin. Thus, a constructive eviction defense will not succeed.

Dentist and Son might also argue that the interference that constitutes constructive eviction was caused by water damage from the sprinkler system rather than by the fire. The lease only provides that it will not be terminated if the building is rendered untenantable by fire. Moreover, the sprinkler system was installed by ABC and thus the constructive eviction was "caused" by the landlord. However, this argument probably will also fail, as the water damage is a result of the fire.

Therefore, Dentist and Son do not have any valid defenses, and ABC is entitled to damages for breach of the lease covenants.

QUESTION 2

Ten years ago, Al and Bev married and purchased a ranch, taking title as tenants by the entirety. From the start, their marriage suffered from the poor financial decisions they made. They separated two years ago and were ultimately divorced last month.

A separation agreement provided that Al was to convey his interest in the ranch to Bev. Bev in turn wishes to sell the ranch, and Charles is interested in purchasing it. Charles contacted Second National Mortgage Company for a loan, and the mortgage company has retained you to do a title search of the property.

The land records reveal the following:

1.   The deed for the property is in the name of Al and Bev.

2.   There is a judgment against Al in favor of ABC Credit Card Company in the amount of $3,000. It was entered during his marriage to Bev.

3.   There is a judgment against Al and Bev jointly and severally in favor of XYZ Bank in the amount of $2,500.

4.   There is a right of way in favor of the next door neighbor, Jones, across the rear of the property to provide additional access to Jones's garage. It was written nine years ago and states: "Al and Bev grant to Jones the right of ingress and egress across the rear 10 feet of our property to provide access to his garage." Eight years ago, Jones moved his garage to the other side of his property and surrounded his property with a fence.

5.   Finally, EZ Furniture has filed suit against Bev for $21,000 for furniture purchased while she and Al were separated but before they were divorced. Trial is set for next month.

A statute of the jurisdiction in which the ranch is located provides: "Any judgment properly filed shall, for 10 years from filing, be a lien on the real property then owned or subsequently acquired by any person against whom the judgment is rendered." A second statute provides: "No conveyance of an interest in land shall be good against any subsequent purchaser for value without notice, who shall first record." The jurisdiction follows the majority with respect to concurrent ownership.

What must be done regarding each of the enumerated facts in order for Second National Mortgage Company to have a first lien on the home?

ANSWER TO QUESTION 2

This is a race-notice jurisdiction, which protects a bona fide purchaser for value without notice who records first. Because Second National Mortgage Company ("SNMC") has actual notice of the recorded judgment liens and easement (by virtue of the title search), SNMC will have to take the appropriate actions to eliminate these encumbrances in order to have a first lien, as discussed below.

1.   The first thing that must be done in order for SNMC to have a valid first mortgage on the property is that Al must convey his interest in the property to Bev. At issue is whether a creditor of one co-tenant can have a lien on the other co-tenant's interest. Divorce severs a tenancy by the entirety and in most states converts it into a tenancy in common. A tenant in common can convey his property interest and, thus, is free to mortgage his property (because a mortgage is considered the conveyance of an interest in land). However, a conveyance by one co-tenant does not affect the interest of the other co-tenant. Here, Al and Bev took title to their home as tenants by the

entirety, but they became tenants in common upon their divorce. Although under the parties' separation agreement Al was to convey his interest in the home to Bev, he has not yet done so. Therefore, in order to have a first lien over all of the property, SNMC must ensure that it acquires Al's interest in the property as well as Bev's interest. This can be done by having Al convey his interest in the property to Bev, as required by the divorce decree, before SNMC takes its mortgage.

2.   To have priority over ABC, SNMC will have to ensure that ABC is paid and a release of judgment is filed. At issue is whether a creditor can attach one spouse's tenancy by the entirety interest. In most states, the judgment lien against Al could not attach to the ranch when Al and Bev were still married—because when property is held in tenancy by the entirety, the general rule is that neither spouse alone can sever the tenancy by conveying his interest. However, as discussed above, in most states, property held in tenancy by the entirety converts to tenancy in common property upon divorce. Thus, once Al and Bev divorced, the tenancy by the entirety was severed and ABC's $3,000 lien attached to Al's interest in the property. Thus, SNMC must ensure that ABC is paid and files a release of lien in order for SNMC to have a first priority lien.

3.   Likewise, SNMC must ensure that the $2,500 judgment held by XYZ is paid. At issue is whether a creditor can attach both spouses' tenancy by the entirety interest. In most states, although neither spouse alone can encumber the property by transferring his interest, both spouses acting together can transfer their interest. Thus, the XYZ judgment, which was filed against Al and Bev jointly when they were married, attached to the property and remained so even after the divorce. SNMC must also pay this lien and obtain a release in order to have a first priority lien.

4.   SNMC need not do anything regarding Jones's right of way. At issue is whether the easement was terminated. An express easement is an interest in land and may be terminated when an easement owner demonstrates by physical action an intent to permanently abandon the easement. Here, Jones moved the garage and built a fence around his entire property, which made use of the right of way impossible. Therefore, because the easement has been terminated by abandonment, the right of way is no longer an encumbrance.

5.   Similarly, SNMC need not do anything regarding the EZ lawsuit. At issue is whether a lawsuit constitutes an encumbrance on property. In this jurisdiction, judgment liens have priority only when they are recorded before the mortgage. Here, the suit filed by EZ has not yet been reduced to a judgment. Therefore, so long as SNMC records its mortgage prior to entry of a final judgment in favor of EZ, it will have priority over EZ's $21,000 claim.

QUESTION 3

On June 1, Owens contracted to sell his residence to Byer for $100,000 cash with a deposit of $10,000. The contract provided that the seller would convey "good and marketable title, free and clear of all liens and encumbrances." A closing of title was to take place "on or before September 1," at the office of Byer's attorney. On August 20, Byer told Owens that he would need until September 8 to raise the necessary funds. Owens replied that he had to close title on September 1, in accordance with the contract, because he needed the proceeds to purchase another home that same day.

On August 28, Byer for the first time examined a copy of Owens's recorded deed. Byer noted that the land was described as follows:

> The parcel known as Homeacre, beginning at the large boulder located
> at the Northwest corner of the property, then East along Main Street to
> the edge of Babbling Brook, then South along Babbling Brook to the oak
> tree, then West to the maple tree, then North to the point of beginning,
> consisting of 4.3 acres.

In fact, "Homeacre" consists of 3.9 acres, and the description using the boulder, Babbling Brook, and the two trees yields 4.1 acres. Moreover, a title search revealed the following:

1. The property is subject to a mortgage, held by National Bank, in the amount of $50,000.

2. Ten years ago, a zoning law was passed that prohibits the erection of any additional structures on the property.

That same day, Byer notified Owens that the deed raised certain questions in his mind, especially because he wanted to build a storage shed in the back yard. Owens replied by merely renewing his demand that Byer close title no later than September 1 or risk forfeiture of his deposit. Byer has consulted you to represent his interests.

1. Will Byer breach the contract if he does not tender payment until September 8?

2. How many acres will the deed convey?

3. Does Byer have a cause of action against Owens for unmarketable title?

ANSWER TO QUESTION 3

1. Byer will not breach the contract if he does not tender payment until September 8. At issue is whether the closing must take place by the date specified in the contract.

Generally, a contract for the sale of land is enforceable after the date specified in the contract if performance is tendered within a reasonable time. However, if the contract states that "time is of the essence," breach occurs if performance is not offered by the specified date. Here, the contract states that the closing is to take place "on or before September 1," but the facts do not indicate that "time is of the essence." Thus, Byer may tender payment within a reasonable time after September 1. Although Byer will not be able to acquire the necessary funds until September 8, a court is likely to determine that eight days is a reasonable period. Therefore, Byer will not be in breach of the contract if he offers payment on September 8.

2. The deed will convey 4.1 acres. At issue is which description in the deed controls.

One of the requirements of a valid deed is that it must contain a sufficient description of the property. A sufficient description is one that provides a good lead as to the identity of the property. Extrinsic evidence may be admitted to clear up an ambiguity in the description, but such evidence will not be admitted if the description is clear. However, if there is a mistake or inconsistency in the description, the parties' intent as to the land to be conveyed can be ascertained through the use of certain rules of construction. According to these rules, the various methods of describing property are arranged in a hierarchy, with the first (highest and most reliable) one prevailing over the next, and so on: natural monuments, artificial monuments, courses, distances, name, and quantity.

Here, the property is described by three different methods: First, it is described by name as "Homeacre." The second description is based on natural monuments, specifically a large boulder, river, and trees. Finally, the property is described by an exact quantity of 4.3 acres. Because each method yields a different acreage, the rules of construction will be applied to determine how much property the parties intended to convey. Of the three methods, the description based on natural monuments prevails. Thus, the deed will convey 4.1 acres.

3.   Byer does not yet have a cause of action against Owens for unmarketable title. At issue is when the implied warranty of marketable title may be breached.

Implied in every contract for the sale of land is a warranty that *at closing* the seller will provide marketable title. Marketable title is title reasonably free from doubt, *i.e.,* title that a reasonably prudent buyer would be willing to accept because there is no reasonable probability that it will subject him to a lawsuit. Title may be rendered unmarketable, *e.g.,* by defects in the chain of title, mortgages, liens, covenants, or easements. However, a mortgage is not an encumbrance if the seller pays it off before closing or at closing with the proceeds of the sale. Zoning laws do not affect the marketability of title; existing zoning violations, however, do render title unmarketable.

Here, there is a $50,000 mortgage on the property. However, Byer cannot yet claim that it renders title unmarketable because Owens has until the date of closing to pay off the mortgage, and he can even satisfy it with the sale proceeds. Moreover, the zoning law does not render title unmarketable. Although Byer will not be able to build a shed on the property, there are no existing zoning violations evident in the facts. Therefore, Byer currently does not have a viable claim that title is unmarketable.

QUESTION 4

Three years ago, Developer developed an attractive 30-lot subdivision and sold 28 of the lots within a 10-month period. In each of the 28 duly recorded deeds there appeared this language: "Premises restricted to single-family residential use; grantor agrees that all of grantor's retained lots are similarly restricted."

Two years ago, the property bordering the eastern edge of the subdivision underwent commercial development. Due to the increase in noise and traffic, Developer did not succeed in selling Lots 19 and 20, contiguous lots on the eastern side of the subdivision. Last month, Bill approached Developer and offered to buy Lots 19 and 20 as a site for a strip mall. Seeing an opportunity to rid himself of the remaining lots, Developer sold and conveyed Lots 19 and 20 to Bill by a deed that did not mention any restrictions.

Recently, all 28 owners of single-family homes in the subdivision have sued Bill to enjoin the building of anything but single-family homes on Lots 19 and 20. Bill admits that the restriction in the deeds to the other lots, if applicable, would prevent his plans. But he resists the injunction on the grounds that he bought Lots 19 and 20 without knowledge of the restriction and, alternatively, that the neighborhood has so changed that Lots 19 and 20 are unsuitable for single-family homes.

1.   **Are Lots 19 and 20 subject to the single-family residential restriction? Why or why not?**

2.   **Assuming that the 28 homeowners can enforce the single-family restriction on Lots 19 and 20, will Bill's defense that the change in the neighborhood has made the lots unsuitable for single-family homes be successful? Why or why not?**

ANSWER TO QUESTION 4

1.   Lots 19 and 20 are subject to the single-family residential restriction. At issue is whether a subdivision lot may be bound by a restriction that is not contained in the deed.

A covenant is a promise to do or not to do something on the land. Covenants may be character-ized as either real covenants or equitable servitudes. If a party is suing for breach of the promise and wants money damages, he must show that the covenant qualifies as a real covenant. A real covenant runs with the land *at law*, which means that subsequent owners of the land may enforce or be burdened by the covenant if certain requirements are met. However, if the party seeks an injunction or specific performance of the promise, he must show that the covenant qualifies as an equitable servitude, which is enforceable *in equity*. In all states, a real covenant must be in writing. Many states also require a writing for an equitable servitude, but the majority of states will imply a reciprocal negative servitude from a developer's common scheme for a residential subdivision.

In the case of a residential subdivision, most courts will imply "reciprocal negative servitudes" on lots that do not contain the written promises in their deeds if: (i) a developer has a common scheme calling for the development of all of the lots in the same character, and (ii) the owners of the lots and their successors have notice of the covenants. The common scheme must exist at the time the developer sells the first burdened lot. The notice may be actual, record, or inquiry. The owner or successor has actual notice if he actually knows about the covenant. If the covenant is in the owner or successor's deed or chain of title, he has record notice by operation of law. Inquiry notice is notice that the owner or successor would have because of the visible character of the subdivision (*e.g.,* all of the other properties are single-family homes).

Here, the homeowners are seeking equitable relief (an injunction) against Bill. Thus, because the language of the covenant is not included in Bill's deed, the homeowners must show that the covenant qualifies as a reciprocal negative servitude. First, Developer had a common scheme regarding the subdivision lots because when he conveyed 28 of the 30 lots, he included the covenant within their deeds along with the language "grantor agrees that all of grantor's retained lots [Lots 19 and 20] are similarly restricted." This common scheme existed when the first lot was sold. Moreover, Bill even admits that the restriction would apply to his lots if he had notice of the covenant at the time of purchase. Second, Bill had inquiry notice of the covenant because of the uniform single-family home character of the other lots in the subdivision.

2.   Bill's defense that the change in the neighborhood has made Lots 19 and 20 unsuitable for single-family homes will not be successful. At issue is whether changed conditions that affect the border lots in a subdivision are sufficient to prevent enforcement of the covenant against those lots.

If the neighborhood has so significantly changed since the time the servitude was created, such that it would be inequitable to enforce the restriction, injunctive relief will not be granted. However, change that affects only the border subdivision lots is insufficient to prevent enforcement of the covenant against those lots. Here, the commercial development bordering the subdivision appears to have rendered Lots 19 and 20 unsuitable for single-family use, as they remained unsold for some time. However, there is no evidence that any other subdivision lot was affected by the commercial development such that the purposes of the single-family restrictions could no longer be achieved for any owner. Therefore, Bill's defense will likely fail.

QUESTION 5

Paul and Jamie are married and live in the city with their one-year-old daughter, Matty. Paul is terminally ill. Paul's Uncle Sal owns a house in the country and thinks it would be best for Paul and his family to live there. To the dismay of his own children, Uncle Sal conveys the house and property as follows:

> **To Paul for life, then to Jamie for so long as she remains single. If Jamie takes but remarries, then to Matty and her heirs when Matty is at least 18 years old.**

Applying common law, except for the Rule in Shelley's Case, fully identify the present or future interests of the following grantees. (Do not discuss the rights or liabilities arising from such interests.)

1. Paul;

2. Jamie;

3. Matty;

4. Uncle Sal.

ANSWER TO QUESTION 5

1. *Paul:* Paul has a life estate. At issue is the type of estate created by the conveyance "To Paul for life."

A life estate is a present possessory estate measured by the life or lives of one or more persons. The "measuring life" can be (i) the grantee's life, or (ii) the life of someone other than the life tenant (*i.e.*, a life estate pur autre vie). When the measuring life ends, the estate either reverts to the grantor or passes to the remaindermen. Here, Uncle Sal conveyed to Paul an estate measured by Paul's life. Therefore, Paul has a life estate.

2. *Jamie:* Jamie has a vested remainder subject to divestment. At issue is the type of estate created by the conveyance "then to Jamie for so long as she remains single. If Jamie takes but remarries, then to Matty."

A remainder is a future interest that is capable of becoming possessory on the natural termination of the preceding estate. Remainders usually follow life estates. Here, Jamie's interest follows Paul's life estate. The life estate will naturally expire upon Paul's death, at which time Jamie's interest could become possessory. Therefore, Jamie's interest is a remainder.

Remainders may be "vested" or "contingent." Vested remainders are created in an ascertained person and are not subject to any condition precedent. Contingent remainders are either created in an unascertained person or are subject to a condition precedent. Here, there is no express condition (*e.g.*, "then to Jamie if she . . .") attached to Jamie's gift. Therefore, she has a vested remainder.

Vested remainders may be indefeasibly vested, vested subject to open, or vested subject to divestment. A remainder is indefeasibly vested when it is certain to become possessory on termination of the prior estates and is not subject to being defeated, divested, or diminished in size. A vested remainder subject to open is an interest in a class of persons, where at least one member is qualified to take possession but more persons can become class members. A vested remainder is subject to divestment when a condition subsequent could divest the interest. Here, there is a condition subsequent—Jamie's remarrying—in the terms of the conveyance. Jamie's interest will be divested if she remarries. Thus, Jamie has a valid vested remainder subject to divestment.

Note that the conveyance does not contain an invalid restraint on marriage. The language "to Jamie for so long as she remains single," indicates intent to provide Jamie with support until she marries and receives support from the new spouse, rather than to penalize Jamie for getting married.

3. *Matty:* Matty has an executory interest that may be springing or shifting. At issue is the type of estate created by the conveyance, "If Jamie takes but remarries, then to Matty and her heirs when Matty is at least 18 years old."

A future interest that does not qualify as a remainder is an executory interest. There are two types of executory interests: springing and shifting. Shifting executory interests cut short a previous estate by divesting the grantee of her interest, while springing executory interests spring out of and divest the grantor's interests. Here, Matty will have a shifting executory interest if she is 18 when Jamie remarries, because the interest will cut short Jamie's (the grantee's) estate. If Matty is not 18 when Jamie remarries, Matty's executory interest will be springing because it will spring out of the interest of Uncle Sal and his estate (*see* below) when Matty turns 18.

Executory interests are subject to the Rule Against Perpetuities. The Rule Against Perpetuities provides that no interest is good unless it must vest, if at all, not later than 21 years after some life in being at the creation of the interest ("measuring life"). Because the Rule focuses on what might happen, if there is any possibility that an interest will vest too remotely, the interest is void. The Rule applies only to contingent remainders and executory interests. The only possible persons who can be measuring lives are those who can affect the vesting of interests. Here, Jamie is the measuring life because Matty will take only if Jamie remarries. Matty's gift is certain to vest or fail within Jamie's lifetime (because Jamie can get married only while she is alive) and so does not violate the Rule. Therefore, Matty's executory interest is valid.

4. *Uncle Sal:* Uncle Sal and his heirs have a possibility of reverter. At issue is whether the grantor retained an interest in the property he conveyed.

If the grantor retains an interest in the property he conveys, it must be a reversion, right of entry, or possibility of reverter. If the grantor fails to give away his entire estate in the conveyance, his interest is a reversion, because the property will revert back to the grantor when the lesser estate ends. A right of entry exists when the grantor expressly retains the right to cut short the estate he conveyed. A possibility of reverter arises when the grantor carves out for himself a determinable estate, which means that the property "possibly" may revert back to the grantor if an estate ends.

Here, the property may revert back to Uncle Sal if Jamie takes and remarries when Matty is not yet 18. Thus, Uncle Sal's retained interest is a possibility of a reverter, not a reversion, because it is only possible that his interest will become possessory (whereas with a reversion the interest is certain to become possessory).

QUESTION 6

Owen owned vacant land (Whiteacre) in State B located 500 yards from a lake and bordered by vacant land owned by others. Owen, who lived 50 miles from Whiteacre, used Whiteacre for cutting firewood and for parking his car when he used the lake.

Twenty years ago, Owen delivered to Abe a deed that read in its entirety:

> Owen hereby conveys to the grantee by a general warranty deed that parcel of vacant land in State B known as Whiteacre.

Owen signed the deed immediately below the quoted language and his signature was notarized. The deed was never recorded.

For the next 11 years, Abe seasonally planted vegetables on Whiteacre, cut timber on it, parked vehicles there when he and his family used the nearby lake for recreation, and gave permission to friends to park their cars and recreational vehicles there. He also paid the real property taxes due on the land, although the tax bills were actually sent to Owen because title had not been registered in Abe's name on the assessor's books. Abe did not build any structure on Whiteacre, fence it, or post no-trespassing signs.

Nine years ago, Abe moved to State C. Since that time, he has neither used Whiteacre nor given others permission to use Whiteacre, and to all outward appearances the land has appeared unoccupied.

Last year, Owen died intestate, leaving his daughter Doris as his sole heir. After Owen's death, Doris conveyed Whiteacre by a valid deed to Buyer, who paid fair market value for Whiteacre. Neither Doris nor Buyer knew of the Owen-to-Abe deed. Both Doris and Buyer believed that Owen was the owner of Whiteacre at the time of his death. Buyer promptly and properly recorded the deed from Doris and immediately went into possession of Whiteacre.

Last month Abe returned to State B. When he discovered Buyer in possession of Whiteacre, he sued Buyer for possession.

State B has enacted the following statutes:

1. Actions to recover possession of real property shall be brought within 10 years after the cause of action accrues.

2.   No conveyance or mortgage of real property shall be good against subsequent purchasers for value and without notice unless the same be recorded according to law.

Who is entitled to possession of Whiteacre? Explain.

ANSWER TO QUESTION 6

Abe is entitled to possession of Whiteacre. The first issue is whether Abe acquired title to Whiteacre by deed from Owen. To be valid, a deed must (i) be in writing, (ii) sufficiently describe the land, (iii) identify the grantor and grantee, (iv) evidence an intention to convey the land, and (v) be signed by the grantor. The parties may be identified by name or by describing them in some other way (*e.g.*, "to my eldest daughter," "to the trustee of my irrevocable trust"). If the deed is delivered with the identity of the grantee left blank, some courts presume that the person taking delivery has authority to fill in the name of the grantee, and if he does so, the deed is valid.

Here, the Owen-to-Abe deed is in writing, describes Whiteacre, identifies Owen as the grantor, shows a present intent to convey ("hereby conveys"), and is signed by Owen. However, it does not identify the grantee by name or otherwise. Moreover, nothing in the facts indicates that Abe wrote in his name after accepting the deed from Owen. Thus, the deed is invalid and Owen did not effectively convey title to Whiteacre to Abe.

The next issue is whether Abe acquired title to Whiteacre by adverse possession. To establish title by adverse possession, the possession must be (i) actual and exclusive, (ii) open and notorious, (iii) adverse and under a claim of right (hostile), and (iv) continuous throughout the statutory period. Exclusive possession generally means not sharing possession with the true owner or the general public. Possession is open and notorious when it is such as the usual owner would make of the land and is sufficient to put the true owner on notice of the fact of possession. Possession is hostile when it is without the owner's consent; it does not matter whether the possessor believes he is on his own land or knows he is trespassing on someone else's land. Continuous possession is possession that the average owner would make of the property under the circumstances. The statutory period is the limitations period for an ejectment action; in State B, the limitations period is 10 years. In most states, payment of property taxes is not required to establish title by adverse possession but is good evidence of a claim of right.

Here, Abe's possession of Whiteacre was clearly actual and exclusive, as he did not share possession with Owen or the general public (Abe's "friends" do not constitute the general public). His possession was open and notorious, as he planted vegetables, cut timber, and parked vehicles there when using the nearby lake for recreation—similar uses to which Owen made of the property. Thus, it does not matter that Abe did not build structures on Whiteacre, fence it, or post no-trespassing signs. Although Abe believed he was on his own land, his state of mind is irrelevant. Because he did not enter Whiteacre with Owen's permission (the deed was void), Abe's possession was hostile. He possessed the property for 11 years, one year beyond that required by the statute of limitations. Finally, Abe paid the property taxes, although in most states this is not necessary to establish an adverse possession claim. Thus, Abe has a strong claim that he acquired title to Whiteacre by adverse possession.

The final issue is whether Buyer's title to Whiteacre is superior to Abe's title. State B's recording act is a notice statute. Under a notice statute, a subsequent bona fide purchaser ("BFP") prevails regardless of whether he records at all. A BFP is a purchaser who takes for valuable consideration and without notice of a prior claim at the time of the conveyance. There are three types of notice: Actual notice is what the purchaser actually knows. Record notice is notice that the law imputes to the purchaser, which means that if there is a prior deed on record, the purchaser cannot be a BFP. Inquiry notice is notice that the purchaser would have by inquiring into the property (*e.g.*, by visiting it to determine who is occupying the land).

Here, Buyer purchased Whiteacre for valuable consideration, namely fair market value. It is irrelevant that she obtained title from a donee (Doris). Moreover, Buyer seemingly took without notice of a prior claim. She had no actual knowledge that Abe had a potential claim to the property. Because Abe moved to State C and has neither used Whiteacre nor permitted others to use Whiteacre, Buyer did not have inquiry notice, as inquiry would have revealed that Whiteacre was unoccupied. Finally, Buyer did not have record notice of the void Owen-to-Abe deed because the deed was not recorded. However, the recording acts do not protect a subsequent purchaser against interests that arise by *operation of law* (*e.g.*, implied easements, title by adverse possession), because there is no instrument to record in order to perfect such interests. Instead, subsequent purchasers take subject to those interests. Thus, Abe's title to Whiteacre, acquired by adverse possession, is superior to Buyer's title.

QUESTION 7

Two years ago, Landlord and Tenant entered into a five-year oral lease of an office at $800 per month, payable on the first day of each month. The lease was silent regarding Tenant's right to assign or sublet the office.

Three weeks ago, Tenant called Landlord, gave two weeks' notice of lease termination and said that she planned to move out of state permanently.

Tenant told Landlord that Friend had agreed to take over the office space for the balance of the five-year lease. Landlord said that he would not accept Friend as a new tenant even though she was financially capable of paying the rent and that he would hold Tenant to the lease agreement for the balance of the five-year term.

Two weeks ago, Tenant vacated the office.

One week ago, on the day the next month's rent payment was due, Friend sent Landlord a check for $800, which Landlord refuses to cash. Landlord insists that Tenant is liable for the $800 rent. Tenant has not paid the $800 monthly rent. Landlord has sued Tenant to recover the $800 rent that she has not paid.

1. What type of tenancy did the oral lease agreement between Landlord and Tenant create? Explain.

2. Did Tenant properly terminate the tenancy? Explain.

3. Is Landlord entitled to collect $800 from Tenant? Explain.

ANSWER TO QUESTION 7

1.   Tenant had a periodic month-to-month tenancy. At issue is whether Tenant's possession and Landlord's acceptance of rent created a periodic tenancy by operation of law.

In most states, the Statute of Frauds requires that a lease creating a tenancy for more than one year be in writing. When a tenant goes into possession under an oral lease, a tenancy at will is usually created. A tenancy at will is an estate in land that is terminable at the will of either the landlord or the tenant. However, the payment of rent will usually convert a tenancy at will into a periodic tenancy. The period of the tenancy coincides with the period for which the rent is paid.

Here, Tenant took possession of the office under an oral lease, which would usually create a tenancy at will. However, Landlord accepted monthly rent payments from Tenant for nearly two years. Thus, a periodic tenancy was created, with the period being from month to month.

2.   Tenant did not properly terminate the lease. At issue is the notice required to terminate a month-to-month tenancy.

A periodic tenancy is automatically renewed, from period to period, until proper notice of termination is given by either party. Although governed by statute in many states, generally a full period's notice in advance of the period in question is required. Thus, for a month-to-month tenancy, one month's notice is required. The notice generally must be in writing and be delivered.

Here, Tenant gave Landlord only a two-week notice instead of the requisite one-month notice. Moreover, Tenant's notice was oral (a phone call) rather than in writing. Thus, the notice was improper and did not terminate the tenancy as of the beginning of the next month.

3.   Landlord is not entitled to collect $800 from Tenant. At issue is whether Tenant's assignment of the lease to Friend was effective.

Absent an express restriction in the lease, a tenant may freely transfer her leasehold interest, in whole or in part. If she makes a complete transfer of the entire remaining term, she has made an assignment. The assignee and the landlord are in privity of estate, and each is liable to the other on all covenants in the lease that run with the land. Because the covenant to pay rent runs with the land, an assignee owes the rent directly to the landlord for the time she is in privity of estate. After assignment, the original tenant is no longer in privity of estate with the landlord, but can still be held liable on her original contractual obligations (*e.g.*, rent) on privity of contract grounds.

Here, the facts do not indicate that the lease prohibited assignment without Landlord's consent. Thus, Tenant's transfer of the balance of the five-year lease to Friend was a valid assignment, and Friend became liable for rent on privity of estate grounds. Because Friend timely paid the next month's $800 rent, Tenant is not liable for any additional rent.

QUESTION 1

On May 1, Bisco entered into a financing arrangement with Lender. As part of the deal, Lender loaned Bisco $150,000 and Bisco properly executed a security agreement granting Lender a security interest in all of Bisco's inventory and equipment and after-acquired inventory and equipment. Lender properly perfected the security interest by filing a financing statement in the appropriate government office on May 3.

On June 1, Bisco and Carton Inc. signed a written agreement for Bisco to purchase 200,000 cardboard boxes suitable for packing its baked goods. Carton had over one million of these boxes in its inventory. The price of the boxes, which were to be delivered on June 17, was $5,000. Payment was due seven days after delivery.

Because of an industry-wide labor dispute on June 5, a general shortage of boxes developed. On June 10, Carton learned that the market value of 200,000 boxes of the kind ordered by Bisco had risen to $20,000. Carton also knew that Bisco would be unable to obtain a sufficient number of boxes elsewhere in time for its busy summer season. Carton's manager telephoned the owner of Bisco and told him that Carton would not deliver the boxes on June 17 unless Bisco agreed to pay $20,000 for them. Bisco protested and asked Carton to "live up to the contract." When Carton reiterated that Carton would not deliver the boxes unless Bisco agreed to the price increase, Bisco reluctantly stated, "O.K., I guess I've got no choice." The next day, Bisco signed a "modification agreement," which was identical to the original contract except that the price of the boxes was $20,000 instead of $5,000.

On June 17, Carton delivered the boxes to Bisco from Carton's inventory. On June 20, Carton received a check from Bisco for $20,000, which Carton's bank returned to Carton five days later marked "insufficient funds." On the same day, Carton learned that Bisco had, in fact, been insolvent since June 17.

On June 26, Carton demanded that Bisco return the boxes, but Lender had already repossessed them from Bisco. Bisco had failed to make an installment payment to Lender on June 18, an event of default under Bisco's security agreement with Lender.

1.   Was the modification agreement signed by Bisco enforceable? Explain.

2.   If Lender had not already repossessed the boxes, would Carton have had any right to recover them from Bisco? Explain.

3.   What rights, if any, does Carton have to recover the boxes as against Lender? Explain.

(Do not discuss bankruptcy law.)

ANSWER TO QUESTION 1

1.   The modification agreement signed by Bisco is probably not enforceable. At issue is the enforceability of a modification agreement created when the seller, knowing that the contracted goods have become difficult to obtain, refuses to deliver the goods as contracted unless the buyer agrees to pay a higher price.

2. SALES

Under the common law preexisting duty rule, a contract modification generally is not enforceable unless it is supported by new consideration. Accordingly, Bisco's promise to pay $20,000 would not be enforceable under the preexisting duty rule, since Carton was already obligated to deliver the boxes for $5,000.

Although Article 2 does not follow the common law rule, an Article 2 analysis is not likely to change the above result. Under Article 2, contract modifications sought in good faith are binding without consideration. However, modifications that are extorted from a party in bad faith are **unenforceable**. In this case, Carton's threat to not deliver the boxes unless Bisco paid four times the contracted price most likely constitutes a modification sought in bad faith, particularly in light of the fact that Bisco had no reasonable alternative but to pay the increased price to obtain the boxes necessary for its business operations. Thus, the modification agreement need not be honored.

Carton may allege that the original contract was discharged by operation of law under the doctrine of commercial impracticability by arguing that an unanticipated event (an industry-wide labor dispute) caused a substantial increase in the market price and that no reasonable seller would sell the product at a price four times below the market price. However, such an event is not typically considered sufficient to excuse performance. Generally, a seller assumes the risk of the occurrence of such an event and must continue to perform, especially in a case such as this one, where the seller has ample goods in its inventory and performance would not require it to incur any additional cost.

In the unlikely event that Carton convinces a court that it acted in good faith, the modification agreement would be enforceable because it satisfies all necessary contractual requirements, including the Statute of Frauds.

2.   Carton could have reclaimed the boxes from Bisco if Lender had not already repossessed them, even if the modification agreement was unenforceable. Under the U.C.C., an unpaid seller who discovers that the buyer has received goods on credit while insolvent may reclaim the goods upon demand made within 10 days after receipt of the goods. Here, Bisco received the boxes on June 17, at which time Bisco was insolvent. Carton's bank returned the check for insufficient funds on June 25, only eight days after delivery of the boxes. Carton was able to demand return of the goods within the 10-day time period; thus, Carton could have reclaimed the goods if they were in Bisco's possession. The result would be the same whether Carton was to receive $5,000 or $20,000 for the boxes.

[*Note: Students may also receive credit if they conclude that under U.C.C. section 2-702(3), Carton's rights were immediately subject to Lender's rights because Lender had a valid security interest in the boxes. Under this analysis, Carton could not recover the boxes even if Lender had not yet repossessed them.*]

3.   Carton does not have any right to recover the boxes as against Lender. At issue is whether the holder of a perfected security interest in inventory and equipment has rights superior to a seller of the collateral during the 10 days after the collateral is delivered to the buyer on credit when the buyer is insolvent.

As discussed above, an unpaid seller who discovers that the buyer has received goods on credit while insolvent has a general right to reclaim the goods within 10 days after they are received by the buyer. However, the general right of reclamation is cut off by a buyer in the ordinary course of business or other good faith purchaser.

Lender has a perfected security interest in the boxes at issue here—by virtue of the after-acquired property clause—and so constitutes a good faith purchaser of them.

The holder of a perfected security interest has a right to repossess the collateral securing an obligation owed to the secured party when, as here, the obligation is in default. Lender has a perfected security interest in the boxes because the security interest attached to the boxes (since there was a written security agreement that included as collateral all after-acquired equipment and inventory, Lender gave value for the security interest—the $150,000 loan—and Bisco had rights in the boxes) and the security interest was property perfected in the appropriate office. Thus, Lender had a right to repossess the boxes.

Moreover, as a taker of the boxes, Lender constitutes a purchaser, since the U.C.C. provides that purchasers include persons who take by pledge, lien, or "any other voluntary transaction creating an interest in property." Lender took in good faith, since nothing in the facts gives rise to an inference of bad faith. Thus, Lender's rights in the boxes are superior to Carton's rights.

QUESTION 2

On May 1, 1995, Sarah agreed to sell her ultra-lightweight canoe to Bill for $2,000. Bill agreed to pick up the canoe on July 1, 1995, and to pay Sarah by certified check. They embodied their agreement in a written document most of which they copied from a book they found in the public library. It provided that, "No modification or amendment to this agreement is effective unless it is in writing and signed by both parties to the contract" and "Both parties agree that this is the entire agreement between the parties, and that there are no terms other than those set forth above."

On May 15, Bill called and said he had learned that Sarah's canoe was really not worth $2,000, and he felt he shouldn't have to pay that much. Sarah said she was sorry he felt that way, but a deal was a deal. She did say she would include the paddles and a life-vest, worth about $200.

On July 1, Bill arrived with a certified check. He complained about the price again, and when Sarah appeared unsympathetic, Bill got angry and said he didn't want the canoe, and if Sarah wanted her money she would have to sue him.

Sarah's lawyer has demanded the $2,000 Sarah says Bill owes her. You have agreed to represent Bill. Bill said that a friend in the canoe business (whom he should have talked to before) would testify that the canoe is worth $1,700, and the paddles and vest are worth about $200. You have talked to Sarah's lawyer who has said he thinks Bill should just pay up, and that the May 15 phone call is irrelevant under the parol evidence rule and the no modification provision, plus there was no consideration.

1.   **What is the extent, if any, of Bill's liability? Explain.**

2.   **What is the effect of the May 15 phone call in light of the issues raised by Sarah's lawyer? Explain.**

ANSWER TO QUESTION 2

1.   Bill probably is liable only for the difference between the contract price and the market value of the canoe (or its resale price if Sarah chooses to resell). At issue is a seller's remedies when a buyer breaches a contract to purchase goods. Because the contract here involves the sale of goods (*i.e.*, things moveable), Article 2 of the Uniform Commercial Code ("U.C.C.") governs.

Bill's refusal to purchase the canoe constitutes a breach of contract. The agreement between Bill and Sarah appears to be a valid contract, since the parties agreed to the sale and there was consideration on both sides (Sarah promised to sell and Bill promised to buy), and no defense to formation or enforceability appears to be present (while the contract was within the Statute of Frauds because it involved the sale of goods for $500 or more, the parties made a sufficient writing, which, presumably, was signed by both parties). Thus, Bill's refusal to buy the canoe constitutes a breach.

When a buyer breaches a contract for the sale and purchase of goods, the U.C.C. provides that the seller is entitled to incidental damages plus the difference between the contract price and the market value of the goods (or the resale price if the seller resells the goods). If these damages are not sufficient to put the seller in as good a position as performance would have, lost profits can be recovered, and if the goods cannot be resold, an action for the price is possible.

Here, damages based on the difference between the contract price and the market value of the canoe (or its resale price) seems to be the most appropriate remedy. An action for the price is not appropriate, since nothing in the facts indicates that the goods cannot be resold (there apparently is a market for used canoes). Neither is an action for lost profits appropriate, because damages can put Sarah in as good a position as performance would have. Thus, Bill is liable only for the difference between the contract price ($2,000) and the market value ($1,700 according to Bill's friend).

2.   The phone call had no effect on the contract due to the no modification clause. The parol evidence rule and the lack of consideration are irrelevant.

The U.C.C. provides that an agreement excluding modification except by a signed writing is enforceable, although a party can waive such a condition, and the waiver will be binding if the other party relies on it. Here, the contract clearly says that it cannot be modified except by a signed writing. It could be argued that Sarah waived the writing requirement, but because Bill did not change his position in reliance on Sarah's statements, the waiver is not binding. Thus, Bill cannot enforce the promise to include the paddles and the life jacket (which would have lowered Sarah's damages because their $200 market value would have been added to the market value of the goods—making the goods' market value $1,900), and so Sarah's damages remain at $300.

Note that the parol evidence rule is irrelevant under the facts, because the rule merely prohibits introduction into evidence prior or contemporaneous statements that seek to vary the terms of a fully integrated contract (*i.e.,* one that appears to embody the whole agreement between the parties), and the modification sought to be introduced here was made subsequent to the contract. Neither is lack of consideration relevant, because under the U.C.C., parties to a contract for the sale of goods can modify the contract in good faith without consideration. The modification here was sought in good faith because Bill honestly believed he was being overcharged.

QUESTION 3

Distributor signed a contract to purchase 1,000 copies of a new board game entitled *Marooned* from Maker (the company manufacturing the game). Delivery was to occur within 30 days. The form contract, provided by Maker, simply identified the game by name and did not specify its component parts. Maker had provided a sample of the game to Distributor; the sample had contained a board made from 1/4" pressed fibre-board. Twenty-five days later, when the cartons containing the games arrived on Distributor's loading dock, one of the cartons was opened by a warehouse supervisor to verify that it contained the *Marooned* games and that the individual boxes were not crushed or otherwise damaged. The warehouse supervisor then marked "accepted by customer" on the invoice presented by the driver who had delivered the cartons. Two weeks later, the sales manager of Distributor was examining one of the games and discovered that the board was made of 3/16" fibre-board. The sales manager believed that this gave the board a less "luxurious" feel, and became concerned that it might affect the game's marketability.

Your firm represents Distributor. The sales manager has called you and asked what, if anything, she can do. She is considering returning the games to Maker if she is entitled to do so. Does Distributor have a claim for breach of the agreement with Maker that gives it the right to return the shipment to Maker? Explain. You need not address any damages claims that Distributor might have.

ANSWER TO QUESTION 3

Distributor may be able to return the board games to Maker. The issues presented are whether Distributor accepted the games, and whether Distributor may return the nonconforming goods if there was an acceptance.

The perfect tender rule provides that if the goods or the tender of delivery fail in any respect to conform to the contract, the buyer may reject the contract, accept the contract, or accept part and reject part of the contract. Here, Maker provided a model of the game that became the basis of the bargain. Distributor contracted to purchase games identical to the model; *i.e.*, games with boards made of 1/4" pressed fibre-board. By providing boards made of 3/16" pressed fibre-board, Maker failed to conform to the specifications of the model; thus, Maker delivered nonconforming goods. (*Note*: Courts may also consider this a breach of an express warranty.)

Generally, a buyer may reject nonconforming goods within a reasonable time after delivery or tender and before acceptance, provided the buyer seasonably notifies the seller of his intent to reject the goods. The seller may then "cure" by giving the buyer reasonable notice and making a new tender of conforming goods within the time originally provided for performance (and in many cases, beyond the original contract time if the seller reasonably believed the tender would be acceptable). In this situation, however, Distributor had already expressly accepted the goods, as demonstrated by the warehouse supervisor's notation on the invoice.

Distributor could argue that the warehouse supervisor did not "accept" the goods in the strict legal sense of the word, nor did he closely inspect the goods, but instead only checked to see that the proper games were enclosed and that the individual boxes were not damaged. In the unlikely event that a court finds that the supervisor's notation merely indicated that Distributor received the shipment and that actual inspection was not made until two weeks later, when the sales manager discovered the boards were made of 3/16" pressed fibre-board, the court may allow Distributor to reject the goods. As previously noted, however, Maker would be given a reasonable opportunity to cure; thus, in the case of rejection, Distributor would not be able to return the games unless Maker failed to cure.

In reality, however, the court is more likely to find that Distributor accepted the board games. Once the buyer has made a technical "acceptance" of the goods, the buyer's power to reject the goods is terminated, and the buyer is obligated to pay the seller the contract price less any damages due to the seller's breach, unless the buyer is entitled to revocation of the contract. A buyer may revoke his acceptance of goods if the defect materially impairs their value to the buyer and (i) the buyer accepted them on the reasonable belief that the defect would be cured and it has not been; or (ii) the buyer accepted the goods because of the difficulty of discovering defects or because of the seller's assurance that the goods conformed to the contract. Here, Distributor may argue that the thickness of the boards was difficult to discover, but would greatly affect the game's marketability because, as the sales manager put it, the board felt less "luxurious"; thus, people would be less inclined to buy the game. If the court accepts Distributor's argument, it is likely to find proper revocation because the buyer revoked within a reasonable time after discovering the defects and the goods were not changed in any way after acceptance.

A proper revocation of acceptance has the effect of a rejection; thus, Distributor could return the games to Maker.

QUESTION 4

As part of a plan to open a restaurant, Buyer contacted SignCo, a business which specialized in making large outdoor neon signs. After Buyer and the sales manager of SignCo had discussed a custom design for Buyer and the price, Buyer called the sales manager and authorized the manufacture of the sign for a price of $18,000.

SignCo began manufacture of the sign, and had spent $8,000, when Buyer called and said financing for the construction of the restaurant had become more expensive than was "feasible," and that he would not be able to go forward with making the contract to buy the sign. Buyer has refused to pay SignCo anything, asserting that he was not obligated to pay since the financing had not proven feasible and there was nothing in writing. SignCo expected to spend $6,000 more to finish the sign. SignCo stopped work, and sold the part of the sign which had been completed to a scrap dealer for $750.

How much, if any, is SignCo entitled to recover? Explain.

ANSWER TO QUESTION 4

SignCo can recover the difference between the $18,000 contract price and the $750 resale price, plus incidental damages, minus $6,000 in expenses saved.

The first issue is whether there is an enforceable contract. As a general rule, the Statute of Frauds provides that a contract for the sale of goods for $500 or more is not enforceable unless there is some writing signed by the party to be charged or his agent. However, one exception to this rule arises when the goods are to be specially manufactured for the buyer and are not suitable for sale to others in the ordinary course of business *and* the seller has, under circumstances that reasonably indicate that the goods are for the buyer, made substantial beginnings in their manufacture before notice of repudiation is received.

In this problem, SignCo and Buyer orally agreed that SignCo would manufacture a sign for Buyer for which Buyer would pay SignCo $18,000. Ordinarily, such a contract would have to be in writing and signed by the party to be charged to be enforceable. However, this particular agreement falls under the "specially manufactured goods" exception to the Statute of Frauds. Pursuant to the agreement, SignCo's duty was to make a custom-designed neon sign for Buyer's new restaurant. Presumably, this custom-made sign was not one which SignCo could sell to another customer in the ordinary course of business. SignCo had made substantial beginnings in the manufacture of the sign and had already spent $8,000 of the $14,000 it would cost to make the sign by the time Buyer called and repudiated the contract. Under these circumstances, the contract is enforceable even though there is no writing.

Having established that there is an enforceable contract, the next issue is whether Buyer was discharged from the contract by his failure to obtain adequate financing. Buyer argues that he is not obligated to pay SignCo because he has failed to obtain adequate financing for the restaurant. This argument will fail because obtaining adequate financing for the restaurant was not made a condition to the contract for the neon sign. An argument that the failure to obtain adequate financing constituted a failure of a presupposed condition, entitling Buyer to a discharge, would also fail. First, to obtain a discharge under this rule, *both* parties must have assumed that a circumstance would not occur. Here, nothing in the facts indicates that Buyer discussed any financing issue with SignCo, and thus, it is unlikely that SignCo assumed that Buyer's obtaining adequate financing was a condition of the contract. Second, increased costs are rarely a sufficient reason for discharge, unless they change the nature of the contract. Here, the increased costs of constructing the restaurant, at best, indirectly affect the ability to pay for a sign for the restaurant and do not change the nature of the contract. For these reasons and because no other cause for discharge is apparent from the facts, Buyer was not discharged from performance of his contractual duty to pay.

Because there was an enforceable contract from which Buyer was not discharged and Buyer breached the contract by refusing to pay, SignCo is entitled to recover damages. Thus, the final issue is what damages SignCo may recover.

When a buyer repudiates a contract, a seller is entitled to incidental damages plus either the difference between the contract price and the market price or the difference between the contract price and the resale price of the particular goods. Here, there is presumably no market for the custom-designed neon sign, so SignCo will have to use the second measure of damages.

The nonbreaching party in a breach of contract situation has a duty to mitigate damages. In a contract to manufacture goods where the buyer breaches, the duty to mitigate damages includes the seller's duty not to continue to manufacture unless completion would decrease damages. In SignCo's case, a completed sign would not decrease damages, because it would have no more resale value than the partially completed sign. SignCo had the duty to resell through a public or private good faith, commercially reasonable sale. Although it would have been impossible for

SignCo to sell the sign in the ordinary course of business, SignCo demonstrated its good faith by selling the completed portion of the sign for $750 to a scrap dealer. SignCo has clearly met its obligation to mitigate damages.

In addition to recovering the contract price minus the resale price, SignCo may recover any incidental damages it may have incurred due to the breach. The incidental damages may include costs of storing, shipping, and reselling the sign. Any expenses which SignCo saved as a consequence of the breach, on the other hand, must be subtracted from SignCo's recovery. In this case, SignCo saved $6,000 in expenses as a result of the breach.

Accordingly, SignCo is entitled to damages in the amount of the difference between the $18,000 contract price and the $750 resale price, plus incidental damages, minus $6,000 in expenses saved.

QUESTION 5

James bought a used car from Kreative Karl's Used Cars for a total price of $1,000 cash which was what the car was worth in perfect condition. The sales contract was lengthy and on the back was printed Paragraph 24 which read as follows:

> **24. Accompanying the transfer of title from the party of the first part of the party of the second part is no affirmation, promise, endorsement, assertion, or declaration relating to any feature, trait, characteristic, attribute, or quality of any good/service supplied by the party of the first part to the party of the second part and the party of the first part hereby absolutely, unequivocally, unconditionally, and definitely disaffirms any such express or implied affirmation, promise, endorsement, assertion, or declaration which might have been made by any individual, person, human being, or anyone else to anyone.**

A day after it was delivered, James discovered that the car had been delivered with a cracked block which would cost more than $1,500 to repair. As scrap the car is worth $100. James is considering a lawsuit.

1. **Discuss the effect of Paragraph 24. Will it bar James's claim(s)? Explain.**

2. **Assume that James can avoid the effect of Paragraph 24. What are James's damages if he prevails on liability in a lawsuit against Kreative Karl's? Explain.**

ANSWER TO QUESTION 5

1. Paragraph 24 probably has no effect on the sale contract between James and Kreative. At issue is the effect of an inconspicuous written disclaimer of any and all affirmations in a contract for the sale of goods. Because the contract is for a car and cars constitute goods (*i.e.,* all things movable) under Article 2 of the Uniform Commercial Code, Article 2 will govern.

Article 2 includes a number of rules regarding disclaimers of warranties. As to express warranties, which arise from any affirmation of fact or promise, description of the goods, model, or sample, Article 2 provides that a negation of an express warranty is inoperative to the extent that such construction is unreasonable. Generally, it would be unreasonable to allow someone to make an express warranty and then to disclaim that warranty. Thus, the attempted disclaimer here of any and every type of promise or affirmation made with regard to the car sold probably is without effect. At the very least, the disclaimer would be ineffective to disclaim the basic obligation to deliver an automobile, and an automobile with a blown engine, it could be argued, does not meet the basic obligation of delivering an automobile.

Paragraph 24 would also be ineffective to disclaim the warranty of merchantability. Whenever goods are sold by a merchant (*i.e.*, one who regularly deals in goods of the kind sold) an implied warranty arises that the goods shall be merchantable, which, among other things, means that the goods shall be fit for their ordinary purpose. The warranty applies even in the sale of used goods. The warranty can be disclaimed by a conspicuous written disclaimer that mentions the warranty of merchantability. Here, Kreative is a car merchant since it regularly sells cars. Paragraph 24 is not conspicuous since nothing indicates that it is in special type or otherwise stands out in the contract, and the paragraph does not specifically mention the warranty of merchantability. Thus, the paragraph is not sufficient to disclaim this warranty.

Paragraph 24 also is insufficient to disclaim the implied warranty of fitness for particular purpose if such a warranty was made. Whenever a buyer informs a seller of particular purposes for the goods to be purchased and relies on the seller to provide suitable goods for those needs, an implied warranty arises that the goods provided shall be fit for those purposes. This warranty can be disclaimed by a conspicuous written disclaimer; fitness for particular purpose need not be mentioned in the disclaimer. Here, it is not clear that any warranty of fitness was made, since nothing in the facts indicates that James relied on Kreative to choose a car suitable for any particular purpose. If such a warranty were made, paragraph 24 would be insufficient to disclaim the warranty because the paragraph is not conspicuous.

2.   It is hard to put an exact dollar amount on James's damages from the facts given, but they appear to be around $900. At issue is the appropriate measure of damages for breach of warranty.

Article 2 provides that the basic measure of damages appropriate when a buyer has accepted goods that breach a warranty is the difference between the value of the goods as delivered and the value the goods would have had if they had conformed to the contract, plus incidental and consequential damages. Here, we are told that the car is worth $100 as scrap and the car would have been worth $1,000 had it been in perfect condition. Thus, the apparent damages are $900 plus James's consequential and incidental damages (*e.g.*, the costs of having a mechanic look at it to determine that the engine block was cracked, loss of use, etc.). However, it could be argued that nothing in the contract indicated that the car was "in perfect condition," so James might recover something less.

QUESTION 6

Elgin Electronics sells new and used stereos and computer systems and services electronics equipment as well. Glenda's computer crashed, and she brought it to Elgin to be repaired. Elgin said it would charge her $25 for an estimate on repairs, gave her a signed receipt for

the computer, and pushed the computer through an opening in the wall to the "back room" where repair people worked on the electronics gear.

Unbeknownst to Glenda, Elgin Electronics was having serious financial trouble and was being hounded by very aggressive creditors. Its short-term (and very short-sighted) solution to its financial problems was to sell repaired computers and stereos as "reconditioned" merchandise. Thus, after Elgin repaired Glenda's computer (worth $1,200 repaired), Elgin sold the computer to Harry, its accountant, as a reconditioned computer for the "bargain basement" price of $400. Harry paid for the computer by deducting $400 from the accounting bill he sent to Elgin.

When Glenda called Elgin to get her estimate, she got an answering machine reporting that Elgin had filed a bankruptcy petition and that further information could be obtained from the bankruptcy court. Glenda learned that Elgin's financial problems were very deep: in bankruptcy, Glenda and the other creditors like her will get nothing.

Glenda has located Harry and has now asserted a claim to the computer or $1,200 against Harry. Analyze her claim.

ANSWER TO QUESTION 6

Glenda may recover the computer or its value from Harry in a replevin action. The issue is whether Harry has obtained title to the computer as a buyer in the ordinary course of business.

Article 2 of the U.C.C. applies in this case because it involves a sale of goods. Generally, a buyer acquires all title that the seller had. In this case, Elgin did not have title to the computer when it sold the computer to Harry because Glenda had entrusted the computer to Elgin solely for repairs. However, the U.C.C. provides that when an owner entrusts her property to a merchant who deals in goods of that kind, the merchant has the power to transfer all rights in that property to a buyer in the ordinary course of business. A buyer in the ordinary course of business is a person who buys the item in good faith and without notice of the ownership rights of a third party. If the buyer obtains the property in the ordinary course of business, the former owner has no remedy against the buyer, only against the merchant.

In this case Harry is not a buyer in the ordinary course of business. Although he took the computer in exchange for partial satisfaction of the accounting debt, the U.C.C. provides that "buying" may not include a transfer in total or partial satisfaction of a money debt. Furthermore, while Harry's knowledge of the circumstances is unclear from the fact pattern, it is arguable that as Elgin's accountant, the circumstances surrounding the sale of the computer would put Harry on notice that a third person held title to the computer.

Thus Harry is not a buyer in the ordinary course of business and did not acquire title to the computer from Elgin. Glenda may seek to recover the computer or its value in a replevin action.

QUESTION 7

See Secured Transaction Question 9 for Sales issues.

SALES 11.

QUESTION 8

Dealer owns and operates an antique store. On January 4, Bank loaned $250,000 to Dealer to finance Dealer's business operations. In connection with the loan, Dealer signed a security agreement that granted Bank a security interest in Dealer's "inventory" and assigned Dealer's "accounts and chattel paper" to Bank. The agreement covered "any and all obligations owed by Dealer to Bank including future advances." Later that day, Bank properly filed a financing statement reflecting its security interest.

On May 1, Thief stole a 17th-century cedar chest from Owner. Thief then sold it to Dealer. Dealer did not know the chest had been stolen. On June 1, Dealer sold the cedar chest to Purchaser, an interior designer, for $50,000. Purchaser bought the cedar chest for resale to a client.

Purchaser made a $10,000 down payment and signed an installment sales contract for the remainder of the purchase price, plus interest, to be paid monthly over 12 months. The installment sales contract granted to Dealer a security interest in the cedar chest and provided that all payments were to be made directly to Dealer. Purchaser subsequently made the payments due on July 1, August 1, and September 1 by sending checks to Dealer.

On September 1, Dealer failed to make a payment due on its loan from Bank. Bank immediately declared Dealer in default, as it was permitted to do under the loan and security agreements between the parties. Bank also sent a letter to Purchaser informing Purchaser of Dealer's default, advising Purchaser of Bank's security interest, and directing Purchaser to make all further payments on the installment sales contract directly to Bank. Purchaser contacted Dealer, who admitted that he was in default and that Bank had a security interest. However, Dealer told Purchaser, "Don't worry. I will pay Bank my September payment soon. Things will be straightened out. You should continue to send your monthly payments directly to me. Bank has no right to collect from you in any event. Our arrangement is between us."

On September 20, Purchaser was served with papers in a replevin action brought by Owner to recover the cedar chest. According to the complaint in the replevin action, the cedar chest had been stolen from Owner, and the bill of sale and other documents presented to Purchaser by Dealer as proof of Dealer's ownership were forgeries. Purchaser immediately answered the replevin action with a pleading alleging (i) that as a good faith purchaser for value, Purchaser's claim was superior to Owner's and (ii) that any right of Owner to recover the cedar chest should be conditioned on Owner's reimbursing Purchaser for amounts paid to Dealer.

1. Who should prevail in Owner's replevin action to recover the cedar chest? Explain.

2. Assuming Purchaser prevails in the replevin action, should future payments on the installment sales contract be made to Dealer or to Bank? Explain.

3. Assuming Purchaser loses in the replevin action, does Purchaser continue to be liable for the payments on the installment sales contract either to Dealer or Bank? Explain.

ANSWER TO QUESTION 8

1. Owner should prevail in her replevin action to recover the cedar chest and she does not need

to reimburse Purchaser for the amounts paid to Dealer. Under Article 2 of the Uniform Commercial Code ("U.C.C."), a purchaser of goods can only acquire the title that "his transferor had or had power to transfer." As a result, a thief, who does not acquire title to goods when he steals them, is unable to transfer title to a purchaser, even if the purchaser buys in good faith and for value. In this case, Thief stole the cedar chest from Owner and sold it to Dealer, who then sold it to Purchaser. Thief did not acquire title or the power to transfer title to the cedar chest when he stole it, so he was unable to transfer title to Dealer, and Dealer was unable to transfer title to Purchaser for the same reason. Therefore, Owner, as the only party with a claim of title to the cedar chest, should be able to recover the cedar chest without reimbursing Purchaser for the payments Purchaser made.

2.   Assuming that Purchaser prevails in the replevin action, future payments on the installment contract should be made to Bank, rather than Dealer. Under Article 9 of the U.C.C., if a debtor defaults on a loan secured by an assignment of nongoods collateral, such as accounts or chattel paper, the creditor is entitled to notify the account debtor (*i.e.,* the party owing the debtor money on the underlying account or chattel paper) to make payment to the creditor, rather than to the debtor. Upon notification, the account debtor must pay the creditor rather than the debtor, even if the debtor was already making collections on the collateral. In this case, the facts are unclear about the nature of the installment sales contract, but it is probably either an account (*i.e.,* a right to payment not evidenced by an instrument) or chattel paper (*i.e.,* writings evidencing both a monetary obligation and a security interest in specific goods). Since Dealer defaulted on the loan secured by an assignment of the accounts or chattel paper, Bank (the creditor) was entitled to notify Purchaser (the account debtor) to pay it rather than Dealer (the debtor), and Purchaser must comply. Dealer's assertion that he, rather than Bank, has the right to collect on the installment sales contract does not affect Bank's right to receive the payments.

3.   Assuming that Purchaser loses in the replevin action, Purchaser is not liable to Dealer or Bank for the remainder of the installment payments. In every sale of goods, the seller makes an implied warranty of good title to the buyer, unless the warranty is properly disclaimed. In this case, Dealer did not attempt to disclaim the warranty of title, and he breached the warranty when he sold the cedar chest to Purchaser without having title to it. Purchaser can recover the loss resulting from the breach, which in this case would be the value of the cedar chest. Therefore, Purchaser has a defense against Dealer if Dealer attempts to recover the remaining payments for the installment sales contract. Purchaser also has this defense against Bank because an assignee of accounts, chattel paper, or general intangibles is also subject to defenses arising out of the contract between the account debtor and the assignor, unless the account debtor agreed not to assert such defenses against an assignee. Because the facts do not indicate that Purchaser did not make such an agreement with Dealer, Purchaser can use its contract defense against Bank and will not be obligated to pay Bank.

QUESTION 9

See Commercial Paper Question 17 for Sales issues.

QUESTION 10

See Secured Transactions Question 18 for Sales issues.

QUESTION 11

Ted Tailor makes and sells custom-tailored shirts and suits. Ted schedules fittings by appointment and only makes made-to-measure clothing that matches the specifications and measurements of his customers.

In October 2007, after making an appointment, Sam came into Ted Tailor's tailor shop in Springfield, Illinois, to order a two-piece suit. Sam, who is six feet, seven inches tall, told Ted that he could wear only custom-made suits because his left arm is shorter than his right arm and his left leg is shorter than his right leg.

Sam chose a suit with a three-button jacket and pants with pleats among the styles that Ted Tailor offered. Sam chose a very fine blue wool fabric among Ted's array of fabrics. Then Ted proceeded to take Sam's measurements.

Ted Tailor quoted a price of $800. Sam agreed to that price, gave Ted a deposit of $100, and Ted and Sam agreed that Sam could pick up the suit on November 15, 2007.

On November, 8, 2007, Ted Tailor called Sam to tell him that his suit was ready. Sam came into Ted's shop that same day to pick up his suit and was dismayed to find that his pants did not have pleats. Ted apologized, told Sam that he would alter the pants to include pleats, and that Sam could pick up the suit, as ordered, the next day. Sam stormed out of Ted's shop and told Ted he did not want the suit because Ted "breached the contract." Ted never heard from Sam again.

Ted Tailor altered the pants to Sam's suit to include pleats. The suit then conformed to Sam's order in every way. On November, 9, 2007, Ted called Sam to tell him that the suit was ready. Sam never came in to pick up the suit and never paid Ted the balance due. Ted tried calling Sam repeatedly and then finally gave up in the middle of February 2008.

By February 2008, Ted Tailor no longer had space to store the suit. He had no customers with similar measurements to Sam and he could not reuse the fabric in Sam's suit. Ted Tailor realized that the most he could get for the suit was $50 if he sold the suit to a used fabric store. So that is what Ted did.

Assume for both questions that Ted Tailor and Sam had a valid contract under Illinois law.

(a) Ted Tailor wants to know if he did, in fact, breach his contract with Sam. What do you tell Ted Tailor and why?

(b) Assume, for this question only, that Sam wrongfully rejected the suit that Ted Tailor made for him. How much, if anything, can Ted Tailor recover from Sam? Explain.

ANSWER TO QUESTION 11

(a) I would tell Ted Tailor that he did not breach the contract. Although he did not make a perfect tender, delivery had not yet come due and he was permitted to "cure" before performance was due to avoid a breach, which he did.

In a single delivery contract, the buyer can reject goods for any "defect" in the goods or tender. The seller must make a "perfect tender." A material breach is not required. Where the buyer has rejected goods because of a defect, the seller may, within the time originally provided for performance, "cure" by giving reasonable notice of his intention to do so and making a new tender of conforming goods that the buyer must then accept.

Here, the pants that were part of the custom-made suit that Ted tendered to Sam did not conform to the precise specifications for making the suit because they did not have pleats. Thus, it was not a perfect tender and Sam had the right to reject the suit. However, the suit was tendered to Sam on November 8, seven days before performance was due on November 15. After Sam rejected the suit, Ted told Sam that he would alter the pants to include pleats and in fact did so. The suit, as altered, was ready to be picked up on November 9, which was still six days before the date that performance was due. Thus, Ted did not breach the contract because he cured the defect within the proper time period, making Sam obligated to accept the suit.

I would also tell Ted that he has a breach of contract claim against Sam for Sam's refusal to accept the suit after the nonconformity was cured within the proper time frame. Sam might try to defend against such a claim based on the Statute of Frauds, which requires a writing evidencing the agreement and signed by the party to be charged in the case of a sale of goods valued at $500 or more (and there was no writing here). However, he would not be successful because of an exception for specially manufactured goods not suitable for sale to others by the seller in the ordinary course of business. Here, the suit was custom-made to Sam's unique measurements and Ted, in fact, could not resell the suit after Sam refused to accept it.

(b)   When the seller repudiates or refuses to accept goods, the seller is entitled to recover either (i) the difference between the contract price and the market price, or (ii) the difference between the contract price and the resale price of the particular goods, plus incidental damages (*i.e.,* the costs of storing, shipping, returning, and reselling the goods, which are incurred as a result of the buyer's breach). If the seller chooses as his measure of damages the difference between the contract price and the resale price, he must act in good faith, and the sale (either private or by auction) must be commercially reasonable. In the case of a private sale, the breaching buyer must be given reasonable notice of intention to resell. Also, under the U.C.C. the seller has the right to force goods on a buyer who has not accepted them if the seller is unable to resell the goods to others at a reasonable price.

In this case, the suit had virtually no market value because Ted had no customers with similar measurements to Sam. The resale value was $50, indicated by the amount of money Ted received when he sold the suit to a used fabric store. Thus, Ted's damages would be the contract price ($800) minus the resale price ($50), or $750, plus incidental damages associated with the storage and sale of the suit. However, Ted should have exercised his right to compel specific performance and forced the sale of the suit upon Sam for the $800 contract price or, alternatively, given Sam reasonable notice of his intention to resell the suit, and his failure to do so could mean that he would not be entitled to damages for the breach.

QUESTION 1

Mary Ann Fonda operates Fonda Diners, Inc. Fonda Diners maintains a number of restaurants in Youngstown County, Illinois. All of the Fonda Diners restaurants, as well as the company's chief executive office, are located in Youngstown County. Mary Ann Fonda has furnished these restaurants to resemble diners common in the 1950s.

On January 7, 1993, Fonda Diners obtained a $10,000 loan from Primero Financial Services. In consideration for this loan, on January 7, 1993, Fonda Diners executed a written security agreement. The agreement gave Primero Financial Services "a security interest in all equipment owned by Fonda Diners, Inc., including equipment acquired after January 7, 1993." The security agreement also provided that Primero Financial Services may make additional future advances to Fonda Diners.

Also on January 7, 1993, Fonda Diners and Primero Financial Services executed a financing statement. The financing statement included the same description of collateral as the security agreement. The financing statement contained only one error. The financing statement referred to the debtor as "Fonda Restaurants, Inc." rather than "Fonda Diners, Inc." Primero Financial Services filed this financing statement at the appropriate office.

On July 16, 1993, Fonda Diners purchased a jukebox from Messina's Music Shoppe, Inc. Also on July 16, Fonda Diners took possession of the jukebox.

Fonda Diners bought the jukebox on an installment payment contract. Under this contract, Messina's Music Shoppe retained a security interest in the jukebox.

On August 16, 1993, Messina's Music Shoppe filed an effective financing statement at the appropriate office. The financing statement recorded the security interest in the jukebox retained by Messina's Music Shoppe.

1. Assume that on August 1, 1994, Fonda Diners defaults on both the loan made by Primero Financial Services, and also on the installment sales contract executed by Messina's Music Shoppe. Does Primero Financial Services or Messina's Music Shoppe have priority to the jukebox purchased by Fonda Diners? Explain.

2. Now assume that on October 1, 1993, Primero Financial Services advanced an additional $5,000 to Fonda Diners. Primero Financial Services made this advance pursuant to the security agreement executed by Primero Financial Services and Fonda Diners on January 7, 1993.

Does Primero Financial Services have priority over Messina's Music Shoppe with respect to the $5,000 advance made on October 1, 1993? Explain.

ANSWER TO QUESTION 1

1. Primero Financial Services ("PFS") will have priority in the jukebox over Messina's Music Shoppe ("MMS"). Because the questions here involve secured transactions, Article 9 of the Uniform Commercial Code will govern.

2. SECURED TRANSACTIONS

Article 9 contains a number of rules on priority of security interests. The rule that governs here, as will be explained below, is that as between two perfected security interests in the same collateral, the first to be filed or perfected has priority. Here, PFS filed its security interest on January 7, 1993, and MMS filed on August 16, 1993. Thus, PFS has priority as long as it has a perfected security interest in the jukebox.

Both PFS and MMS have perfected security interests in the jukebox. To have a perfected security interest in collateral it is first necessary for the security interest to attach. A security interest will attach if (i) the secured party and the debtor agree to create a security interest (as evidenced by an authenticated security agreement or by the secured party's taking possession or control of the collateral), (ii) the secured party gives value for the security interest, and (iii) the debtor has rights in the collateral.

Here, PFS's security interest in the jukebox attached on July 16, the day Fonda Diners took possession of the jukebox because: (i) the parties made a written security agreement that was presumably authenticated (*i.e.,* signed) by Fonda Diners (the January 7, 1993, agreement gave PFS a security interest in all of Fonda Diners's equipment, including after-acquired equipment, and the jukebox constitutes equipment since it is used in Fonda Diners's business); (ii) the secured party (PFS) gave value for the security interest ($10,000); and the debtor gained rights in the collateral (ownership), at the latest, on the day it was delivered (July 16).

MMS also had a security interest in the jukebox, assuming that the installment contract through which Fonda Diners purchased the jukebox fulfilled the requirements for an authenticated security agreement.

Both parties also perfected their security interests. There are a number of ways to perfect a security interest in equipment. Both parties here perfected by filing a financing statement in a proper place (according to the facts). These financing statements needed to be authorized by the debtor in an authenticated record, and this was accomplished automatically when Fonda Diners authenticated the security agreements. The fact that the financing statement filed by PFS called Fonda Diners "Fonda Restaurants" probably will not invalidate PFS's filing because a filing that contains an error that is not seriously misleading will be effective. Note that MMS's security interest was not automatically perfected. Article 9 provides that a purchase money security interest ("PMSI"—*i.e.*, a security interest retained by the seller of goods on credit to secure the purchase price) in consumer goods (*i.e.*, goods used for personal, family, or household purposes) is automatically perfected without filing, but the collateral here is equipment, not consumer goods.

When two parties have perfected security interests in the same collateral, Article 9 provides that the first party to file or perfect its security interest has priority. Here, PFS filed on January 7 and its security interest in the jukebox became perfected as soon as the debtor (Fonda Diners) gained rights in the collateral. MMS filed, and its interest in the jukebox became perfected, on August 16, 1993, long after PFS filed.

Note that MMS does not have superpriority over PFS by virtue of a PMSI. Article 9 provides that the holder of a PMSI in equipment has priority over even prior perfected security interests in the same collateral if the PMSI is perfected by filing within 20 days after the debtor receives possession of the collateral. Here, MMS did not file until a month after the debtor got possession of the jukebox.

2. PFS has priority in the jukebox. At issue is the effect of a future advance clause.

A secured party who contemplates making future loans to the debtor is allowed to provide in a security agreement that the security interest covers not only current obligations that the debtor owes the secured party, but also obligations arising from future advances. The security interest with respect to the future advances has the same priority as the other obligations secured. Thus, because, as discussed above, PFS has priority in the jukebox with respect to the original $10,000 debt, it has priority under the future advance clause with respect to the extra $5,000 as well.

QUESTION 2

See Sales Question 1 for Secured Transactions issue.

QUESTION 3

Acme needed money to finance its manufacturing operations. Brenda agreed to lend Acme $100,000 if Acme would grant Brenda a security interest in Acme's primary production machine. At that time, the machine was unencumbered by any other security interests.

After agreeing to Brenda's terms, Acme delivered to Brenda a properly executed $100,000 negotiable note payable to the order of Brenda. Immediately upon disbursing the loan funds to Acme, Brenda filed a properly executed financing statement in the appropriate U.C.C. public filing office. She neglected, however, to obtain a written security agreement from Acme.

Two months later, through no fault of Brenda's, Cathy stole the Acme note from Brenda's safe, forged Brenda's signature on the back of the note, and sold the note to Dan, who took the instrument for value, in good faith, and without notice of the theft. Brenda learned that Dan now held the note. Brenda also heard that last week Acme had borrowed $50,000 from Edward and that Edward also had taken a security interest in Acme's primary production machine.

After hearing about Edward's loan and security interest, Brenda realized that she had never obtained a signed security agreement from Acme granting her an interest in the machine. Upon discovering this oversight, Brenda got Acme to sign such an agreement. By then, however, Edward had already loaned the $50,000 to Acme, had received Acme's signature on a security agreement, and had properly filed a financing statement covering Acme's machine.

1. Does Brenda's security interest in Acme's machine take priority over Edward's interest? Explain.

2. As between Dan and Brenda, who has superior rights to the note? Explain.

3. If Brenda's rights are superior to Dan's, on what theories, if any, under the U.C.C., may Dan recover against Cathy? Explain.

ANSWER TO QUESTION 3

1. Brenda's security interest in Acme's machine has priority over Edward's interest. At issue is the priority of two perfected security interests in the same collateral. Since the transaction involves security interests in personal property, Article 9 of the Uniform Commercial Code ("U.C.C.") governs.

Brenda's security interest in Acme's machine has priority over Edward's interest. Article 9 provides that when there are two perfected security interests in the same collateral, the interest that was either *filed or perfected first* has priority. Here, both Brenda and Edward have perfected security interests in Acme's production machine. A security interest can be perfected by filing a financing statement describing the collateral that is authorized by the debtor in an authenticated record. Brenda perfected by filing a financing statement that was automatically authorized by Acme when it later signed a security agreement (the later authorization ratified the financing statement from the moment of filing). While she filed the statement immediately after disbursing funds to Acme—the debtor—she did not complete perfection at that time, because a security interest cannot be perfected before it attaches to the collateral, and Brenda's security interest did not attach to Acme's machine until she obtained a signed security agreement from Acme (a security interest cannot attach until: (i) the parties agree to create a security interest, as evidenced by either (a) a security agreement authenticated (*e.g.,* signed) by the debtor that describes the collateral—a signed financing statement generally is insufficient for this purpose because financing statements usually do not purport to create security interests—or (b) the secured party's taking possession or control of the collateral pursuant to the agreement, (ii) the secured party gives value for the collateral—here, the loan proceeds—and (iii) the debtor has rights in the collateral—here, Acme's ownership interest in its machine). Edward also perfected by filing a financing statement that was automatically authorized by Acme when it signed Edward's security agreement, but according to the facts, he completed perfection before Brenda, since he loaned Acme money, obtained Acme's signature on a security agreement, and filed a financing statement covering the machine before Brenda completed perfection by obtaining Acme's signature on a security agreement. Nevertheless, Brenda will prevail, because the rule is that the first to *file* or perfect has priority, and Brenda filed before Edward filed or perfected.

2. Brenda's interest in the note is superior to Dan's interest. At issue is who has the right to enforce a stolen note payable to order when the payee's signature has been forged. Because a note is a negotiable instrument, U.C.C. Article 3 governs.

Article 3 provides that the following people have a right to enforce a negotiable instrument: the holder, a nonholder who has the rights of a holder (such as a person who obtained the note through subrogation), and a person not in possession of the instrument but who is entitled to enforce it (such as a person from whom an instrument was stolen). Dan is neither a holder, a nonholder with rights of a holder, nor a person not in possession with a right to enforce. A person becomes the holder of an instrument through proper negotiation. What is required for proper negotiation depends on whether the instrument is bearer paper or order paper (*i.e.*, paper payable to an identified person). Bearer paper is negotiated by mere transfer of possession. Negotiation of order paper requires delivery of possession plus the genuine indorsement of any identified person(s) (or an authorized agent for such person(s)) to whom the instrument is payable. Forgery of an identified payee's signature at any time breaks the chain of title, and no person taking possession after the break can become a holder. Here, when the note was drawn, it was payable to an identified person—Brenda. Brenda did not sign the note; rather, the note was stolen and Brenda's signature was forged by Cathy. The forgery breaks the chain of title; Dan therefore did not become the holder of the note by Cathy's subsequent transfer of it to him, despite Dan's taking the note for value, in good faith, and without notice of the theft. Neither does anything in the facts indicate that Dan is the subrogee of a holder (since Cathy stole the note and forged Brenda's signature, Cathy cannot be a holder).

Brenda, on the other hand, is a person not in possession who has a right to enforce the note. The note was drawn to Brenda and she did not transfer possession of it; rather, it was stolen from her. The Code gives such a person a right to enforce the stolen instrument. Thus, Brenda has a right to enforce the note and Dan does not.

3.   Dan may recover against Cathy on a breach of warranty theory. At issue is what remedy is available to a person to whom a forger transferred a negotiable note.

U.C.C. Article 3 imposes a number of warranties on a transferor of negotiable instruments, including warranties that the transferor is entitled to enforce the instrument, that all signatures on the instrument are genuine, and that no defenses of any party are good against the transferor. Cathy breached all three of these warranties by forging Brenda's signature.

QUESTION 4

In 1993, Debtor, a retail seller of power boats, established a line of credit with Bank. In order to secure the loan, Debtor signed a security agreement granting Bank a security interest in its "inventory of boats, now existing and hereafter acquired." Bank promptly and properly filed a financing statement, which described the collateral as "inventory." Bank made periodic advances to Debtor in an amount up to 75% of the value of Debtor's inventory.

Recently Debtor's business slackened, and it needed an additional source of financing. Debtor approached Finance Company and asked for a loan. Finance loaned money to Debtor on January 2, 1995. As collateral for the loan, Debtor transferred to Finance all of Debtor's then existing chattel paper, all of which had been generated by sales of Debtor's inventory prior to January 2. Debtor has not transferred to Finance any chattel paper generated from several boat sales that occurred after January 2, 1995.

In mid-January, Debtor sold a large boat to Purchaser for recreational use by Purchaser's family. Purchaser signed a contract (chattel paper) promising to pay the purchase price in monthly installments over the next three years and granting Debtor a security interest in the boat.

On March 1, 1995, Debtor defaulted on its loans to Bank and Finance.

1.   After Debtor's default, what rights do Bank and Finance have with respect to chattel paper generated from the sales of Debtor's inventory? Explain.

2.   After Debtor's default, what rights do Bank and Finance have with respect to Purchaser's boat? Explain.

ANSWER TO QUESTION 4

1. Finance Company ("Finance") has a right to all of the chattel paper in its possession, and Bank has a right to the other chattel paper. At issue are conflicting security interests in chattel paper proceeds.

Generally, a perfected security interest has priority over an unperfected security interest. For a security interest to be perfected, it must be attached to the collateral. Attachment requires an agreement creating the security interest, the secured party's giving value for the interest, and the debtor's having rights in the collateral. The agreement must be evidenced either by an authenticated security agreement or by the secured party's taking possession or control of the collateral. If a security interest has attached, it may be perfected in a variety of ways. Two methods are relevant here: filing and possession. A security interest may be perfected by filing, in an appropriate place, a financing statement describing the collateral that is authorized by the debtor in an authenticated record. A security interest may also be perfected by the secured party's taking possession of the collateral.

Here, both Bank and Finance have security interests in Debtor's chattel paper. Finance attached a security interest to the chattel paper arising from sales prior to January 2 by taking possession of the chattel paper. It gave value (the loan), and Debtor had an interest in the chattel paper. Moreover, taking possession of the chattel paper was a sufficient method to perfect the interest.

Bank also has a perfected security interest in Debtor's chattel paper. Bank's security interest attached to the chattel paper, even though Bank's written security agreement describes as collateral only Debtor's "inventory of boats," because as a general rule, a security interest continues in collateral and its proceeds. "Proceeds" are whatever is received in exchange for collateral on its disposition. Here, when Debtor sold the boats, it received chattel paper. Thus, the chattel paper is proceeds of the inventory.

Bank's interest in the chattel paper is also perfected. The Code provides that if a security interest is perfected, a security interest in proceeds of the collateral will be perfected for 20 days, but then will become unperfected except under certain circumstances. Bank's security interest in the boats was perfected since the facts indicate that Bank filed a financing statement in the proper place. Debtor automatically authorized the financing statement when he signed the security agreement. Moreover, Bank's security interest in the proceeds continued beyond the 20-day period because one of the exceptions applies. The Code provides that perfection will extend beyond the 20-day period if a filed financing statement covers the original collateral, the proceeds are collateral in which a security interest may be perfected in the same office where the financing statement for the original collateral is filed, and the proceeds are not purchased with cash proceeds of the collateral. [U.C.C. §9-315] Here, a filed financing statement covers the original collateral, and a security interest in chattel paper may be perfected by filing in the same place that would be proper for filing a security interest in inventory (generally, with the secretary of state). Also, the chattel paper was not purchased with cash proceeds of the original collateral.

Thus, the dispute is between persons having perfected security interests in the same collateral. Ordinarily, the rule for determining priority between conflicting perfected security interests is the first to file or perfect rule (*i.e.*, the first security interest that is filed or perfected has priority), but that rule does not apply here. Instead, the Code has a special rule that applies: a purchaser of chattel paper who gives new value and takes possession in the ordinary course of his business has priority over a security interest in the chattel paper which is claimed merely as proceeds of inventory. [U.C.C. §9-330] This rule applies here. A person like Finance, who takes a security interest, is treated as a purchaser. Finance gave new value (the loan), and took the chattel paper in the ordinary course of its business. Finally, Bank's security interest in the chattel paper is claimed merely as proceeds of inventory. Thus, Finance has priority in the chattel paper in its possession and Bank has priority in any other chattel paper.

2.   Despite Debtor's default, neither Finance nor Bank has a right to take the boat sold to Purchaser. At issue are the rights of a person who buys ordinary course of business inventory that is serving as collateral.

Finance has no interest in the boat sold to Purchaser because Finance's only security interest was in the chattel paper that it took. Finance never had a security interest in Debtor's inventory, and it does not have the chattel paper generated from the sale of the boat to Purchaser, so Finance simply has no interest in the boat.

Bank's only interest in the boat would arise if Purchaser defaults (because Bank holds the chattel paper on the boat). Purchaser took the boat free of the Bank's security interest in Debtor's inventory, because a buyer of goods from a seller engaged in the business of selling goods generally takes free of a nonpossessory perfected security interest created by his seller if the buyer buys the goods in the ordinary course of the seller's business. Purchaser purchased the boat from Debtor in the ordinary course of Debtor's business. Thus, Purchaser took free of the security created by his seller (Debtor). However, Purchaser did not take free of the security interest that he himself created (*i.e.*, the security interest that Purchaser gave Debtor to secure the purchase price of the boat), and having taken the chattel paper, Bank now has a security interest in the boat for its purchase price. If Purchaser stops making payments, Bank can foreclose on this security interest.

QUESTION 5

On September 10, 1995, Bank loaned $400,000 to PartsCo, a wholesale supplier of automobile parts to retail auto parts stores. The loan was evidenced by a duly executed promissory note and a security agreement that granted Bank a security interest in all of PartsCo's "now existing and hereafter acquired inventory." Also on September 10, 1995, Bank filed a U.C.C. financing statement in the proper places in the state.

Bank had previously searched the official U.C.C. financing statement records on September 6, 1995, and found a financing statement filed on November 1, 1992, naming PartsCo as debtor, identifying Finance as the secured party, and describing the collateral as PartsCo's "existing and after-acquired inventory." Neither the underlying security agreement nor the financing statement mentioned future advances. When Bank asked PartsCo about this financing statement, PartsCo's president truthfully replied, "We paid that off in 1994."

On November 15, 1995, Finance offered to reestablish its lending relationship with PartsCo, which needed additional funds. Finance loaned PartsCo $200,000. PartsCo signed another security agreement providing that the $200,000 loan was secured by PartsCo's now existing and hereafter acquired inventory. Also on November 15, 1995, a proper financing statement was executed by PartsCo and filed by Finance in the proper places in the state.

PartsCo is in default on both loans, owing Bank $300,000 and Finance $175,000. Bank has begun judicial proceedings to foreclose on PartsCo's inventory (worth approximately

$150,000), as well as $50,000 in uncollected accounts receivable that arose from sales of PartsCo's inventory and $30,000 in a special "compensating balance" deposit account set up at the request of Bank and in which PartsCo has deposited only the proceeds of inventory sales. Both the accounts receivable and the $30,000 deposit account were generated by sales made after January 1, 1996.

1.   As between Bank and Finance, which one has superior rights in PartsCo's unsold inventory? Explain.

2.   As between Bank and Finance, which one has superior rights in the proceeds of the sale of PartsCo's inventory? Explain.

3.   In light of the fact that Bank has commenced judicial foreclosure proceedings, what should Finance do to best protect its interests, and how should the proceeds of a foreclosure sale be distributed as between Bank and Finance? Explain.

ANSWER TO QUESTION 5

1.   As between Bank and Finance, Finance has a superior right to PartsCo's inventory. At issue is the priority of two conflicting security interests in the same collateral.

When two secured parties have perfected security interests in the same collateral, Article 9 of the Uniform Commercial Code, which governs security interests in personal property, provides that the first party to file or to perfect will have priority in the collateral.

Both Bank and Finance have perfected security interests in PartsCo's inventory. A security interest may be perfected in collateral only if the security interest has attached to the collateral. Attachment requires three things: (i) an agreement to create the security interest, evidenced by an authenticated security agreement or the secured party's taking possession or control of the collateral; (ii) the secured party must give value for the security interest; and (iii) the debtor must have rights in the collateral. Here, both Bank and Finance obtained security agreements authenticated (*i.e.,* signed) by PartsCo granting each a security interest in PartsCo's inventory. Each secured party gave value (Bank gave $400,000 and Finance gave $200,000). Finally, PartsCo had rights (ownership) in its inventory.

Both secured parties properly perfected their security interests. A security interest can be perfected by filing, in the proper place, a financing statement that is authorized by the debtor in an authenticated record. In this case, PartsCo authorized Bank's and Finance's financing statements automatically when the security agreements were signed. In addition, the facts here say that Bank and Finance filed financing statements in the proper places to perfect. Bank's security interest became effective as soon as it filed on September 10. Finance's security interest did not become perfected until November 15. This is because the first security agreement between Finance and PartsCo did not cover future advances; thus, Finance had to obtain a new security agreement from PartsCo in order to attach a security interest on PartsCo's inventory with regard to the later loan. This security interest became perfected as soon as it attached, because the original filing by Finance was still effective (financing statements are effective for five years); the second filing by Finance was unnecessary.

Since Finance filed in 1992 and Bank did not file or perfect until September 10, 1995, Finance has priority in the inventory under the first to file or perfect rule.

2.   As between Bank and Finance, Finance also has superior rights in the proceeds of the sale of PartsCo's inventory.

As a general rule, a party with a perfected security interest in collateral will have a perfected security interest in the proceeds of that collateral on its disposition, and that perfected security interest will relate back to the date of perfection of the security interest in the original collateral. The security interest in the proceeds becomes unperfected after 20 days except in several common circumstances. One circumstance is where the proceeds are identifiable cash proceeds, such as the cash that is in the deposit account that contains only proceeds of the sale of the inventory. Another exception applies where the security interest in the proceeds could be perfected by filing a financing statement in the same office in which the financing statement was filed to perfect the security interest in the original collateral. A financing statement in accounts receivable can be filed in the same place as a financing statement covering inventory (centrally). Thus, Finance's security interests in the deposit account and the accounts receivable both relate back to the 1992 filing and have priority over Bank's security interests.

3.   As the secured party with highest priority, Finance should intervene in the judicial foreclosure proceeding to best protect its interests. The first $175,000 netted (*i.e.*, after paying expenses) from the sale of the collateral (*i.e.*, the inventory, accounts, and deposit account) should be distributed to Finance to satisfy the entire secured debt owed by PartsCo to Finance. Any remaining net proceeds should be distributed to Bank to satisfy part of the $300,000 debt PartsCo owes to Bank.

QUESTION 6

Debtor manufactures widgets. On May 3, 1996, Lender loaned Debtor $100,000 for general operating expenses. That same day, Lender filed a valid financing statement signed by Debtor, in the proper U.C.C. filing offices. The financing statement covered all widget machines owned by Debtor, "including after-acquired widget machines." On that date, May 3, Debtor owned just one widget machine, Machine No. 1, which was worth $50,000. No security agreement was signed at that time.

On May 13, 1996, a second lender, Bank, loaned Debtor an additional $100,000 for general operating expenses. On the same day, Debtor signed a valid security agreement that granted Bank a security interest in "all widget machines, now owned or hereafter acquired by Debtor." Debtor also signed a valid financing statement which covered all widget machines owned by Debtor, "including after-acquired widget machines." That day, Bank filed the financing statement in the proper U.C.C. filing offices. At that point, Debtor still owned just one widget machine, Machine No. 1.

On May 16, 1996, a third lender, CreditCo, loaned Debtor an additional $50,000 to purchase a second widget machine, Machine No. 2. On that day, Debtor signed a valid security agreement that granted CreditCo a security interest in Machine No. 2. Debtor used the proceeds of CreditCo's loan to purchase Machine No. 2 for $50,000 on the next day, May 17. Debtor, however, did not receive possession of Machine No. 2 until May 28. On May 31,

CreditCo filed a valid financing statement that covered Machine No. 2, signed by Debtor, in the proper U.C.C. filing offices.

Meanwhile, on May 29, 1996, Lender discovered that it had forgotten to have Debtor sign a security agreement for the May 3 loan. Later that day, May 29, Lender got Debtor to sign a security agreement in which Debtor granted to Lender a security interest in all of Debtor's widget machines, "including after-acquired widget machines." On that date, May 29, Debtor owned both widget machines, Machine No. 1 and Machine No. 2, each of which was worth $50,000.

Debtor subsequently defaulted on all three loans. Shortly after the default, but before any of Debtor's creditors took steps to repossess the widget machines, Debtor sold Machine No. 2 to WidgetCo, another widget manufacturer, for $25,000. WidgetCo purchased the machine in good faith and had no actual knowledge that Machine No. 2 was covered by a security interest.

1. **As between Lender and Bank, whose security interest has first priority as to Machine No. 1? Explain.**

2. **As among Lender, Bank, and CreditCo, whose security interest has first priority as to Machine No. 2? Explain.**

3. **Can the secured party with priority recover Machine No. 2 from the purchaser, WidgetCo? Explain.**

ANSWER TO QUESTION 6

1.   As between Lender and Bank, Lender has priority in Machine No. 1. At issue is the priority between two perfected security interests in the same collateral.

Article 9 of the Uniform Commercial Code governs security interests and provides rules for priority of security interests. The basic priority rule for competing security interests where both are perfected is that the first interest for which a financing statement is filed or the first interest to be perfected, whichever is first, has priority.

Here, both Lender and Bank have perfected security interests. A security interest may be perfected by filing in the appropriate office a financing statement describing the collateral that is authorized by the debtor in an authenticated record. Here, Lender filed a financing statement on May 3, and Bank filed a financing statement on May 13. Debtor's signature on the financing statements authorized the filings. However, filing is not all that is necessary for perfection; the security interest must also attach to the collateral. A security interest will attach to collateral when all of the following occur: (i) the debtor has authenticated a security agreement describing the collateral and granting a security interest in the collateral; (ii) the debtor has rights in the collateral; and (iii) the secured party gives value in exchange for the security interest. Debtor clearly had rights in the machine here, since it owns the machine, and Lender and Bank each gave value in exchange for their security interests ($100,000 loans). Thus, Lender's security interest attached on May 29, when occurred the last event necessary for attachment (getting debtor to sign a written security agreement), and that is when Lender's security interest became perfected. Bank's security interest attached on May 13, the date Bank accomplished all steps necessary for attachment of its security agreement, and became perfected on that same date since that is the day it filed its financing statement. Thus, both Lender and Bank have perfected security interests in Machine No. 1.

Since both Lender and Bank have perfected security interests in the same collateral and Lender filed before Bank filed or perfected, Lender has priority in Machine No. 1. It does not matter that Bank's security interest was perfected first, because under the rule mentioned above for competing perfected security interests, priority goes to the first to file or perfect, whichever occurs first.

2. CreditCo has first priority in Machine No. 2. At issue is whether CreditCo has the super-priority of a purchase money security interest ("PMSI").

As discussed above, the general rule for priority when there are competing perfected security interests in the same collateral is the first to file or perfect rule. Here, Lender has a perfected security interest in Machine No. 2 since Lender's security interest and financing statement included an after-acquired property clause granting Lender a security interest in any widget machines that Debtor may acquire in the future. This is permissible under Article 9, and a security interest in after-acquired property has the same priority as the security interest in the original collateral. Bank similarly reserved a security interest in after-acquired widget machines and has a perfected security interest in Machine No. 2. Nevertheless, CreditCo has first priority in Machine No. 2 because Article 9 provides that a PMSI in noninventory collateral will have priority over other perfected security interests in the same collateral as long as the security interest is perfected within 20 days after the debtor receives possession of the collateral.

CreditCo has a PMSI in Machine No. 2 and its security interest was perfected within 20 days after Debtor received possession of the machine. A PMSI arises where a creditor advances funds which are used by the debtor to purchase the collateral. Here, CreditCo gave Debtor $50,000 to purchase Machine No. 2 and Debtor used the money to purchase that machine. Moreover, CreditCo's security interest attached to the machine since CreditCo gave value (the $50,000 loan), Debtor has an interest in the machine (it owns the machine), and Debtor signed a security agreement granting CreditCo a security interest in the machine. CreditCo also perfected its security interest by filing an authorized financing statement in the appropriate filing office on May 31. Since the filing took place just three days after Debtor received possession of the machine, CreditCo qualifies for the PMSI superpriority and has first priority in Machine No. 2.

3. The secured party with priority can recover Machine No. 2 from WidgetCo. At issue is whether a buyer of goods outside the ordinary course of business takes the goods subject to a perfected security interest in the goods.

As a general rule, a perfected security interest in collateral is not defeated by a sale of the collateral to a third party; the third party takes the collateral subject to the perfected security interest and the secured party will have the right to recover the collateral from the third-party purchaser on the debtor's default. This is true even if the third party purchased the collateral in good faith and without actual knowledge of the perfected security interest because perfection is deemed to provide sufficient constructive notice of the security interest. An exception to this rule applies if the buyer buys the goods in the regular course of business (*i.e.,* from someone in the business of selling goods of the kind), but here nothing in the facts indicates that the sale by Debtor was in the regular course of business. Thus, the exception does not apply.

QUESTION 7

See Commercial Paper Question 6 for Secured Transactions issue.

QUESTION 8

Debtor publishes a newspaper. On May 3, Lender loaned Debtor $100,000 for general operating expenses. On May 4, Debtor signed a security agreement, which stated in full:

> Debtor hereby grants Lender a security interest in Debtor's equipment to secure repayment of the $100,000 loan made by Lender to Debtor on May 3.

Also on May 4, Lender filed a valid financing statement, signed by Debtor, in the proper U.C.C. filing offices.

On May 13, a second lender, Bank, also loaned Debtor $100,000 for general operating expenses. In conjunction with that loan, Debtor signed a standard form security agreement provided by Bank giving Bank a security interest in:

> All Debtor's equipment now owned or hereafter acquired to secure repayment of all debts of whatever nature owed by Debtor to Bank, including all loans and future advances.

Bank failed to file a financing statement covering this transaction. At the time of both of these loans, Debtor owned a single printing press, Press No. 1.

On June 1, Debtor borrowed $50,000 from a third lender, CreditCo, for the specific purpose of purchasing a second printing press, Press No. 2. In conjunction with that loan, CreditCo had Debtor sign on that same day a valid security agreement that granted CreditCo a security interest in Press No. 2. Debtor used the proceeds of CreditCo's loan to purchase Press No. 2 for $50,000. Debtor took possession of Press No. 2 on June 2. No financing statement was filed in connection with this transaction.

Debtor made regular payments on its obligations to Lender and Bank. By July 15, Debtor had completely paid off its original debts to both Lender and Bank.

On August 1, however, Debtor borrowed an additional $50,000 from Lender and an additional $100,000 from Bank. No new security agreements or financing statements were generated in connection with these new loans.

It is now September 15. Debtor owes $50,000 each to Lender and CreditCo and $100,000 to Bank. Debtor is in default on all three loans, and Debtor's creditors are seeking to foreclose on Press No. 1 and Press No. 2. The presses are each worth $50,000.

1. As between Lender and Bank, which has the superior claim to Press No. 1? Explain.

2. As among Lender, Bank, and CreditCo, which has the superior claim to Press No. 2? Explain.

ANSWER TO QUESTION 8

1.   As between Lender and Bank, Bank has a superior claim to Press No. 1. At issue are the rights of secured creditors. Since a secured transaction is involved, Article 9 of the Uniform Commercial Code ("U.C.C.") applies.

Article 9 provides a secured creditor with an unperfected security interest with rights in collateral as against a debtor, while an unsecured creditor has no rights in any specific property of a debtor. Here, Bank has a security interest in Press No. 1, while Lender is unsecured.

Lender is an unsecured creditor because any security interest it may have had in Press No. 1 expired. A creditor has a security interest in collateral only to the extent the debtor grants him a security interest. Here, Debtor gave Lender an authenticated security agreement on May 4, granting Lender a security interest in Press No. 1 until repayment of the $100,000, May 1 loan. That loan was repaid by July 15; thus, any security interest that Lender had in the press by virtue of the May 4 security agreement expired by July 15. The security interest could not be revived merely by the fact that Lender made a later loan to Debtor.

Bank, on the other hand, has a security interest in Press No. 1. A creditor will have a security interest in collateral to the extent the security interest is attached. A security interest will attach to collateral if the debtor has given the creditor an authenticated security agreement granting a security interest in the collateral, the creditor has given value for the security interest, and the debtor has rights in the collateral. Here, Bank's security interest in Press No. 1 attached. On May 13, Debtor gave Bank a written security agreement granting Bank a security interest in Debtor's "equipment" (which includes the press, since it is used in Debtor's business) for all debts between the parties, including future advances. Such future advance clauses are permitted by Article 9. Thus, the agreement did not become extinguished when the May 13 loan was repaid and is effective to create a security interest in the press to secure the August 1 loan. The other requirements for attachment are also present: Bank gave value (the loan), and Debtor had an interest in the collateral—it owned the press. Bank's security interest was not perfected, since bank failed to file a financing statement, but its claim to Press No. 1 is nevertheless superior to Lender's claim, because, as discussed above, an unperfected security interest gives the secured creditor rights in the collateral whereas an unsecured creditor, such as Lender, has no rights in specific property of the debtor.

2.   As among Lender, Bank, and CreditCo, CreditCo has the superior claim to Press No. 2.

Lender has no security interest in Press No. 2 for much the same reason that it has no security interest in Press No. 1: There is no security agreement granting Lender a security interest in Press No. 2.

Bank has an unperfected security interest in Press No. 2 by virtue of the May 13 security agreement. That agreement granted Bank a security interest in all of Debtor's current equipment and also in all equipment Debtor acquired in the future. Such after-acquired property clauses are valid under Article 9. Bank's security interest attached to Press No. 2 when the last of the three conditions necessary for attachment, discussed above, occurred. The last event to occur was the Bank's giving value. The security agreement was made on May 13, and Debtor had an interest in the collateral from the time it took possession of the press on June 2. Bank had given value much earlier (the May 4 loan), but that security interest expired when the original loan was repaid on July 15, and a new security interest did not attach to the collateral until August 1, when Bank made the additional $100,000 loan. Again, Bank did nothing to perfect its security interest, and so Bank's security interest is unperfected.

CreditCo also has an unperfected security interest in Press No. 2. CreditCo's security interest attached to Press No. 2 on June 2: Debtor signed a security agreement granting CreditCo a security interest in the press on June 1, and on that same day CreditCo gave value (the money for the press itself). On June 2, Debtor gained rights in the press when Debtor took possession of it. Thus, CreditCo's interest attached on June 2. CreditCo's security interest is also a purchase money security interest ("PMSI") since CreditCo loaned Debtor the money that Debtor used to purchase the collateral. However, the PMSI is unperfected because CreditCo did not file a financing statement, and PMSIs in equipment are not automatically perfected.

CreditCo's interest in Press No. 2 is superior to Bank's interest because Article 9 provides that when there is a conflict between two unperfected security interests, the first to attach has priority. Here, as discussed above, CreditCo's interest attached on June 2, and Bank's interest attached on August 1. Thus, CreditCo's interest is superior.

QUESTION 9

Builder constructs and manages large condominium developments. In January, Builder began work on a 240-unit complex of luxury condominiums known as the "Eden Project." Builder borrowed $6 million from Bank to finance this project and granted Bank a construction mortgage on the "land and any improvements thereon" constituting the Eden Project. Bank recorded the mortgage in the proper real estate recording office. The mortgage document recited that the mortgage secured funds loaned "for acquisition of the land and for construction of improvements on the land."

In March, Builder contacted Seller, an appliance manufacturer, about supplying built-in dishwashers and ranges, and freestanding clothes washers and dryers for the Eden Project. After preliminary negotiations, Builder sent Seller a Purchase Order for the necessary numbers and types of appliances at a total price of $300,000. The Purchase Order also provided that: "Goods are sold to Builder on 120-day credit without interest. Builder hereby grants Seller an unconditional security interest in any and all goods delivered under this contract to secure payment of all amounts owing pursuant to this contract." Builder signed the Purchase Order.

Seller responded to the Purchase Order by sending Builder an "Order Acknowledgment." The Order Acknowledgment recited the quantity and price information that appeared on the Purchase Order and indicated that payment should be made "on credit, per Builder's Purchase Order, subject to the terms and conditions on the reverse of this Acknowledgment." The back of the Order Acknowledgment contained several preprinted terms, including one term which read as follows: "In addition to the purchase price, the buyer shall pay the seller the amount of all shipping and handling charges." Builder's Purchase Order did not mention shipping and handling.

In April, Seller shipped the appliances. Builder installed the appliances in the condominium units in May. On August 1, Seller sent Builder a bill for $315,000, of which $300,000 was for the appliances and $15,000 was for shipping and handling.

It is November, and Builder is unable to pay its bills. It has not paid Seller and is far behind on its payments to Bank.

Seller wishes to repossess the appliances sold to Builder and remove them from the condominium project.

1. **Is Builder liable to Seller for the shipping and handling charges? Explain.**

2. **Does Seller have the right to repossess any or all of the appliances? Explain.**

ANSWER TO QUESTION 9

1.   Builder will not be liable to Seller for the extra charges because Seller's acceptance probably materially modified the terms of Builder's offer by adding shipping and handling charges.

This question concerns the U.C.C. Article 2 "Battle of the Forms" provision. [U.C.C. §2-207] Unlike the common law of contracts, which requires the terms of an acceptance to mirror those of an offer in order for a contract to be formed, Article 2 states that an acceptance will be sufficient to form a contract even if it includes additional or different terms. In this case, Builder's Purchase Order was the offer and Seller's Order Acknowledgment was the acceptance. Seller's notation that shipping and handling charges would be included in the contract price was an additional term not stated in the offer. However, under Article 2, the acceptance creates a contract in spite of the additional term.

The additional term should not be included in the contract. Between merchants, additional terms in the acceptance will become part of the contract unless the acceptance materially alters the terms of the offer, the offer expressly limits acceptance to the terms of the offer, or the offeror objects to the acceptance within a reasonable time. Article 2 defines merchants as those dealing in goods of the kind or those holding themselves out as having knowledge or skill peculiar to the practices or goods involved in the transaction. Seller, an appliance manufacturer, is a merchant because Seller regularly deals in the manufacture and sale of appliances. Builder is a merchant because, as a real estate developer, he holds himself out as having knowledge peculiar to appliances and other equipment being installed in his developments. The addition of shipping and handling charges probably materially modifies the contract because it substantially increases Builder's obligation to Seller by changing the contract price from $300,000 to $315,000 (a 5% increase in price). However, if the addition of shipping and handling charges is a normal practice in such sales contracts and should have been expected according to the usage of trade, the new term will not be considered material and Builder will be bound to pay the extra charges.

2.   Seller will not be able to repossess any appliances that have become fixtures, but will be able to repossess any other appliances. At issue is the priority between an unperfected security interest and a construction mortgage. Because the question involves a security interest in goods, Article 9 of the U.C.C. governs.

Seller will not be able to repossess any of the appliances that have become fixtures. Bank had a construction mortgage since it loaned Builder $6 million to construct the condominiums and recorded a mortgage covering the "land and any improvements thereon." Article 9 provides that a construction mortgage has priority over any security interest in a fixture to be installed during construction if the mortgage was recorded before the goods became fixtures. A fixture is personal property so attached to real property that it becomes part of the real property. The dishwashers and ranges will probably qualify as fixtures because they are "built-in." Thus, Bank's mortgage, which was recorded before the appliances became fixtures, will have priority over any security interest Seller might have in the built-in appliances. However, Bank's mortgage will not extend to any appliances that are not built-in, such as the "freestanding clothes washers and dryers."

Seller will be able to repossess the appliances that have not become fixtures because Seller's security interest has attached. Under Article 9, a party whose security interest has attached to collateral can repossess the collateral on the buyer's default, assuming there are no other creditors with a superior interest in the collateral. A security interest attaches when: (i) the debtor grants the creditor a security interest in the collateral, evidenced by the creditor's taking possession or control of the collateral or by a security agreement describing the collateral that is authenticated by the debtor; (ii) the debtor has rights in the collateral; and (iii) the secured party gives value. All three requirements were met here: Builder's purchase order can qualify as an authenticated security agreement because it granted Seller a security interest, it described the appliances, and it was signed by Builder. Seller did not alter this term in its acceptance, so the term became part of the parties' contract. Builder obtained rights in the collateral when they were delivered to Builder. Finally, Seller gave value—the appliances. Seller took no steps to perfect its security interest, and its security interest is not of the type that would be automatically perfected since Builder did not purchase the appliances for Builder's own household uses. Nevertheless, perfection is irrelevant as between the secured party and the debtor, and as discussed above, would not have given Seller priority over Bank in the appliances that have become fixtures. Thus, Seller has a right to repossess the freestanding appliances, but not the built-in appliances.

QUESTION 10

On April 1, Debtor bought a used car from Smith Motors for his personal use. Debtor financed the sale with Smith Motors. The cash price was $16,500, and the credit service charge (total interest payments for the life of the loan) was $4,000. Debtor made a $500 down payment and agreed to pay the remaining $20,000 in 24 monthly payments. At the time of the purchase, Debtor executed a sales contract and granted a security interest in the car to Smith Motors. Smith Motors properly perfected that security interest.

After making only one monthly payment, Debtor defaulted on the contract. Following a peaceful repossession, Smith Motors decided to sell the car at auction on August 15. At that time, the unpaid balance of principal and accrued interest was $17,000. Smith Motors contacted a few dealers but did not advertise the auction.

On August 12, Smith Motors mailed notice of the August 15 auction by regular mail to Debtor at his home address. The notice arrived on August 14, one day before the auction. On August 15, the car was sold at auction for $10,000, which was well below the car's market value of $14,000. The only bidder at the auction was a dealer who specialized in repossessed vehicles.

Smith Motors has sued Debtor for the deficiency of $7,000 between the unpaid contract price and the amount for which the car was sold.

1. **On what theories and in what amounts may Debtor recover damages from Smith Motors under the Uniform Commercial Code? Explain.**

2. **Is Debtor liable to Smith Motors for any part of the $7,000 deficiency? Explain.**

ANSWER TO QUESTION 10

1.   Debtor should be able to recover at least 10% of the cash price of the car ($1,650), plus the amount of interest that would have been paid throughout the life of the loan ($4,000). At issue is whether Smith Motors sold Debtor's car in a commercially reasonable manner.

Article 9 of the Uniform Commercial Code ("U.C.C.") governs the repossession of a defaulting debtor's personal property. Article 9 requires secured parties to act in a commercially reasonable manner when repossessing and selling collateral. For a sale to be valid, the method, manner, time, place, and terms of the sale must be commercially reasonable. [U.C.C. §§9-610, 9-627] The mere fact that a creditor could have obtained a better price from a sale at a different time or in a different manner is not sufficient by itself to establish that the sale was not commercially reasonable. However, the court will take into consideration the fact that Smith Motors sold the car for $4,000 less than its market value, which is far below a reasonable sale price. Furthermore, Smith Motors did not properly advertise the auction and only contacted a few dealers about the auction. As a result, there was only one bid for the car by a dealer specializing in repossessed vehicles. Had Smith Motors attempted to advertise the auction, it likely would have found a buyer willing to pay a price closer to the market price. As a result, Smith Motors's sale of the car was not commercially reasonable and the sale is invalid.

In addition, according to Article 9, a creditor may sell by auction the collateral it repossesses from a debtor, but the creditor must give the debtor authenticated notice of the time and place of sale, unless the collateral is perishable, threatens to decline speedily in value, or is of a type customarily sold in a recognized market. The notice must be sent within a reasonable time before the sale. In this case, Debtor's repossessed car is not perishable, it will not rapidly decline in value, and it is not customarily sold in a recognized market. Although Smith Motors notified Debtor that it was selling Debtor's car by public auction, Debtor did not receive the notice within a reasonable time before the sale. Smith Motors mailed the notice by ordinary mail only three days before the auction, and Debtor did not receive the notice until one day before the auction. As a result, Debtor might not have had time to participate in the auction and attempt to redeem his car if he wished to do so. Therefore, Smith Motors failed to give the required reasonable notice to Debtor.

Because Smith Motors did not act in a commercially reasonable manner or give proper notice of the sale, Debtor may recover damages. According to Article 9, if the collateral is consumer goods, the debtor is entitled to a minimum of 10% of the cash price of the goods plus an amount equal to all the interest charges to be paid over the life of the loan. [U.C.C. §9-625] Here, the car is a consumer good because Debtor bought it for his personal use. Ten percent of the $16,500 cash price of the car is $1,650. The total interest to be paid over the life of the loan was $4,000. Therefore, Debtor should seek at least $5,650 in damages from Smith Motors.

2.   It is unclear whether Debtor is liable for any of the $7,000 deficiency, but Debtor should at least be able to set off the deficiency with any damages he is awarded against Smith Motors.

The U.C.C. does not state whether a creditor may claim a deficiency if it fails to follow the Article 9 foreclosure rules in a consumer transaction. Courts generally take one of three approaches: (i) they presume that the value of the collateral equals the amount of the debt unless the secured party proves otherwise; (ii) they deny the secured party a deficiency regardless of whether she can prove that the collateral is worth less than the debt; or (iii) they allow the secured party to recover the deficiency minus any actual damages that the debtor can prove.

In this case, which involves a consumer transaction, Smith Motors violated the Code foreclosure rules as detailed above. Thus, depending on which approach a court may take, Smith Motors may be absolutely barred from recovering a deficiency, there may be a rebuttable presumption that the value of the collateral equals the amount of the debt, or Debtor would be allowed to set off against the deficiency the damages he is awarded for Smith Motors's failure to comply with the Code foreclosure requirements.

QUESTION 11

Jane wanted to purchase a computer for home use and for her young children to use for school work and entertainment. On January 15, Jane went to Dealer, a retail store specializing in computers, and told a salesperson of her family's needs. She was shown a computer that she was told would suffice. She agreed to buy the computer and told Dealer that she would have to borrow the money to pay for it. Dealer agreed to finance the sale and gave Jane $3,000 in credit to buy the computer. Jane took delivery and signed a security agreement that described the computer and granted Dealer a security interest in it. Dealer did not file a financing statement.

Immediately after purchasing the computer from Dealer, Jane changed her mind about how she would use it. Jane had just begun work as an independent consultant, so she took the computer to her office and began using it for business purposes. She did not inform Dealer of this change of use.

On May 1, Jane borrowed $25,000 from Bank as operating capital for her business. She executed a security agreement granting Bank a security interest in her office machinery, including the computer. Also on May 1, Bank filed a valid financing statement in all proper public offices.

Jane defaulted on the loans to both Dealer and Bank. On December 1, Dealer peacefully repossessed the computer. Both Dealer and Bank claim a security interest in the computer.

As between Dealer and Bank, whose security interest takes priority? Explain.

ANSWER TO QUESTION 11

Dealer's security interest in the computer probably has priority over Bank's security interest. At issue is the priority of two conflicting security interests in the same collateral. Article 9 of the Uniform Commercial Code ("U.C.C.") governs security interests and provides rules for their priority.

Both Dealer and Bank had attached security interests in the computer. Attachment gives the creditor rights against the debtor in the collateral. To attach a security interest: (i) either the debtor must authenticate a security agreement granting the creditor a security interest in collateral that describes the collateral or the creditor must take possession or control of the collateral, (ii) the creditor must give value, and (iii) the debtor must have rights in the collateral. [U.C.C. §9-203] In this case, Dealer's security interest attached on January 15 when Jane signed a security agreement describing the computer, Dealer gave Jane the computer, and Jane obtained rights in the computer (*i.e.,* ownership). Bank's security interest attached as of May 1 when Jane signed a security agreement describing the computer, Bank loaned Jane $25,000, and Jane owned the computer.

To obtain rights against another claimant to a debtor's collateral, a secured party must also perfect its security interest. A creditor can perfect its security interest by: (i) filing, in the proper public office, a financing statement that is authorized by the debtor in an authenticated record, or (ii) by taking possession. [U.C.C. §§9-310, 9-501, 9-509]

According to the facts given, Bank perfected its security interest by filing a "valid financing statement in all proper public offices" on May 1.

Although Dealer did not file, a purchase money security interest ("PMSI") in consumer goods is automatically perfected upon attachment. A PMSI is created when a creditor advances credit or provides the funds needed to make a purchase possible and takes a security interest in the goods purchased. [U.C.C. §9-107] In this case, Dealer has a PMSI because it sold the computer to Jane on credit and retained a security interest in the computer. Consumer goods are goods that are used or bought for use primarily for personal, family, or household purposes. [U.C.C. §9-109] Jane originally intended to use the computer for such purposes. However, she changed her mind and used the computer for her business instead. Goods that are not consumer goods, inventory, or farm products are equipment. Generally, goods used primarily in a business are equipment under this definition. [U.C.C. §9-102] However, under the original use test, a debtor's original intended use of collateral governs the collateral's classification. Here, the computer is classified as a consumer good under the original use test because Jane originally intended to use the computer as a consumer good and she told Dealer she was using it as a consumer good. Therefore, Dealer's PMSI was automatically perfected on January 15 under this test.

However, if a court does not follow the original use test and instead finds that the debtor's final use of the collateral determines the collateral's classification, the collateral would be classified as equipment because Jane used the computer in her business until it was repossessed. In this scenario, Dealer's security interest was perfected by possession when Dealer repossessed the computer on December 1.

The first secured party to file or perfect has priority. [U.C.C. §9-324] Assuming the computer will be classified as a consumer good, Dealer was the first secured party to file or perfect when its security interest was automatically perfected on January 15, so Dealer's security interest in the computer has priority over Bank's security interest, which was filed and perfected on May 1. However, if a court determines that the computer is equipment, Bank would have priority because Bank filed and perfected on May 1 before Dealer perfected on December 1.

QUESTION 12

See Sales Question 8 for Secured Transactions issue.

QUESTION 13

Arcade, Inc. is in the business of selling pinball machines. Arcade needed funds to buy furniture for its showroom. On February 1, Arcade borrowed $10,000 from Bank and

signed a valid financing statement, which stated that it covered all of Arcade's "inventory now owned or hereafter acquired." Bank neglected to obtain a signed security agreement from Arcade but properly filed the financing statement in the correct locations on February 12.

On June 1, Arcade borrowed $40,000 for working capital from Finance and signed a valid security agreement granting to Finance a security interest in its "inventory now owned or hereafter acquired." Also on June 1, Arcade signed financing statements, which properly described the collateral. On June 5, Finance filed proper financing statements in the correct locations.

On July 1, Bank realized that it had failed to obtain a security agreement from Arcade. On that date and at Bank's request, Arcade signed a valid security agreement, properly describing the collateral as "inventory now owned or hereafter acquired."

On August 20, Arcade purchased three pinball machines from Supplier on credit. The three machines were set aside in Supplier's warehouse and tagged "Sold to Arcade." Supplier took a security interest in the three pinball machines to secure payment of the purchase price. Also on August 20, Arcade signed both a valid security agreement covering the three pinball machines and valid financing statements. Supplier filed the financing statements in the correct locations on August 21 and sent proper notice of its security interest to Bank and Finance, both of whom received and read the notice by August 25. Arcade took possession of the machines on August 31 and placed them in its showroom for sale to customers.

On October 1, Oscar purchased a pinball machine from Arcade. This machine was one of the three machines that Arcade had purchased from Supplier. Oscar had no actual knowledge of any of the security interests held by Arcade's creditors.

Arcade defaulted on its loans to Bank and Finance, and failed to pay Supplier. At the time of the default, Arcade's inventory consisted only of the two remaining pinball machines that had been previously purchased from Supplier. Bank, Finance, and Supplier are all claiming security interests in the two remaining pinball machines, as well as in the pinball machine purchased by Oscar.

1.   What is the order of priority among Bank, Finance, and Supplier in their respective claims to a security interest in the two remaining pinball machines left in Arcade's inventory? Explain.

2.   Can Bank, Finance, or Supplier successfully enforce a security interest in the pinball machine purchased by Oscar? Explain.

ANSWER TO QUESTION 13

1.   Supplier has first priority in Arcade's two remaining pinball machines, followed by Bank, and then Finance. The issue is whether a seller of inventory on credit can take priority over earlier perfected security interests.

Creditors gain priority by attaching and perfecting their security interests. A creditor attaches his security interest if: (i) the debtor authenticates (*e.g.,* signs) a security agreement granting the creditor an interest in collateral, (ii) the debtor has rights in the collateral, and (iii) the creditor gives value. Bank attached a security interest in Arcade's inventory on July 1 when Arcade signed a security agreement granting Bank a security interest in "inventory now owned or hereafter acquired." Bank already had given value ($10,000) on February 1. Arcade also had rights in the inventory it owned. Because Bank's security agreement covered inventory acquired in the future as well as inventory then owned by Arcade, Bank's security interest also attached to inventory purchased in the future by Arcade as soon as Arcade acquired rights in it. Finance's security interest attached to Arcade's inventory on June 1, when: (i) Arcade signed a security agreement granting Finance a security interest in "inventory now owned or hereafter acquired," (ii) Finance gave Arcade value ($40,000), and (iii) Arcade had rights in the inventory. Finance's security interest in inventory purchased in the future by Arcade attached as soon as Arcade acquired rights in it. Finally, Supplier's security interest probably attached to the three pinball machines it sold to Arcade on either August 20 or August 31. On August 20, Arcade signed a security agreement granting Supplier a security interest in the three pinball machines being sold, Supplier gave value by promising to sell the pinball machines in return for Arcade's promise to pay, and Arcade likely acquired rights in the collateral when it identified the three pinball machines to the sales contract by segregating them and tagging them "Sold to Arcade." Even if Arcade did not acquire rights in the collateral on August 20 when the pinball machines were identified, Arcade definitely acquired rights in the collateral on August 31 when the pinball machines were delivered.

A security interest is perfected if there has been attachment and if a financing statement covering the collateral has been properly filed. Bank, Finance, and Supplier perfected their security interests in the three pinball machines on either August 20 or August 31, when Arcade acquired rights in the machines. (*See* above.) Bank filed on February 12, Finance filed on June 5, and Supplier filed on August 21.

The general rule of priority is that between two or more perfected creditors, the first party to file a financing statement or perfect prevails. Here, Bank filed first on February 12, so Bank has priority under this rule even though it and the other parties did not perfect until August 20 or 31. Finance filed next on June 5. Finally, Supplier filed on August 21. However, there is an exception to the general rule for purchase money security interests ("PMSIs") in inventory. A PMSI in inventory has "superpriority" over other security interests in the same inventory, regardless of the time of filing or perfection, if: (i) the security interest is perfected at the time the debtor gets possession of the inventory, and (ii) other creditors with perfected security interests in the inventory receive authenticated notice of the PMSI before the debtor receives possession of the inventory. This rule applies here because the pinball machines were inventory (*i.e.,* goods held for sale or lease) and Supplier's security interest was a PMSI (*i.e.,* Supplier sold the pinball machines to Arcade on credit and retained a security interest in them). Therefore, under the rule, Supplier's PMSI in the three machines has superpriority over the security interests of Bank and Finance because (i) Supplier perfected its security interest by no later than August 31, the date on which the pinball machines were delivered, and (ii) Bank and Finance received notice on August 25, which was before the August 31 delivery date.

As a result, Supplier's PMSI has first priority under the PMSI in inventory exception. Bank and Finance have second and third priority, respectively, under the "first-to-file-or-perfect" rule.

2.   Neither Bank, Finance, nor Supplier can successfully enforce its security interest in the pinball machine purchased by Oscar, because Oscar is a buyer in the ordinary course of business ("BIOC").

A BIOC is a buyer who buys goods in the ordinary course from a seller engaged in the business of selling goods of the kind purchased. A BIOC takes collateral free of any security interests in the collateral that were created by the seller, unless the buyer knows that the sale violates a security agreement. Oscar is a BIOC because he bought the machine in the ordinary course from Arcade, which is "in the business of selling pinball machines." Oscar also had no knowledge that the sale was in violation of any security interests. In fact, he even did not have actual knowledge that the security interests existed. Therefore, Oscar took the pinball machine free of the perfected security interests of Bank, Finance, and Supplier, all of which were created by the seller, Arcade.

QUESTION 14

On January 2, Bank loaned Debtor $5,000 and took a security interest in Debtor's "equipment now owned or hereafter acquired." On that date, Debtor signed a valid security agreement and financing statement that properly described the collateral. The security agreement contained a proper future advance clause. On January 3, Bank filed the financing statement in the correct locations.

On February 1, Seller sold a $10,000 computer to Debtor on credit for use in Debtor's business. To secure payment of the purchase price, Seller took a security interest in the computer. Also on February 1, Debtor signed a valid security agreement and financing statement for Seller that properly described the collateral. Seller, however, did not file the financing statement. Debtor received possession of the computer on February 12 and began using it in her business on that same day.

On February 14, the sheriff lawfully seized the computer pursuant to a writ of execution obtained by Larry, a judgment creditor of Debtor, and sent notice of the levy to Bank. Bank received the notice on February 16. On February 17, Bank advanced Debtor $12,000.

On February 20, Seller learned of Larry's levy. That same day, Seller filed in the correct locations the financing statement it had received from Debtor on February 1.

On March 1, Debtor defaulted on her obligation to Bank and on her obligation to Seller.

1. **As between Bank and Seller, which has the superior security interest in the computer? Explain.**

2. **As between Seller and Larry, which has a superior interest in the computer? Explain.**

3. **Is Bank's security interest in the computer as collateral for the $12,000 advance superior to Larry's claim? Explain.**

ANSWER TO QUESTION 14

1. As between Bank and Seller, Seller has priority in the computer. At issue is the priority between two conflicting perfected security interests in the same collateral. Because this question involves the law of secured transactions, Uniform Commercial Code ("U.C.C.") Article 9 governs.

A creditor can gain priority over other creditors by attaching and perfecting a security interest in the collateral. A security interest becomes attached when (i) the parties enter into a security agreement evidenced either by a record authenticated by the debtor that describes the collateral or by the creditor's possession or control of the collateral; (ii) the creditor gives value; and (iii) the debtor acquires rights in the collateral. One way a security interest can become perfected is if the creditor attaches its security interest and properly files a financing statement describing the collateral.

In this case, both Bank and Seller attached and perfected their security interests in the computer. Bank's security interest in the computer attached no later than February 12, when Debtor received possession of the computer. All of the requirements for attachment were fulfilled when (i) Debtor signed a security agreement covering "equipment now owned or hereafter acquired" (the computer was equipment because it was used for business purposes, and the "hereafter acquired" clause extends the coverage of the security agreement to the later acquired computer); (ii) Bank gave value ($5,000); and (iii) Debtor acquired rights in the computer (no later than the date of Debtor's possession of the computer). Bank perfected by properly filing a financing statement. Bank filed the financing statement on January 3, and it became perfected by February 12, when all of the requirements for attachment were fulfilled. Seller also attached its security interest no later than February 12, when Debtor received possession of the computer. Seller's security interest attached because (i) Debtor signed a security agreement covering the computer; (ii) Seller gave value (the computer); and (iii) Debtor acquired rights in the computer (no later than the date of Debtor's possession of the computer). Seller's security interest was perfected when Seller, which had already attached its security interest, properly filed a financing statement on February 20.

If two creditors have perfected security interests in collateral, the general rule is that the first creditor to file or perfect has priority. Under this rule, Bank would have priority because it filed before Seller filed or perfected. However, if a creditor has a purchase money security interest ("PMSI") in equipment, the creditor has superpriority over all other creditors in the same equipment if the creditor perfects within 20 days after the debtor receives possession of the equipment. In this case, Seller had a PMSI in the computer because it sold the computer to Debtor on credit and took a security interest in the computer. Because Seller perfected by filing on February 20, which is within 20 days of February 12, when Debtor received the computer, Seller meets the requirements of the PMSI superpriority rule and thus has priority over Bank in the computer.

2. As between Seller and Larry, Seller has a superior interest in the computer. At issue is the priority in collateral between a secured creditor and a lien creditor.

Generally, if a security interest in collateral is unperfected at the time a lien creditor's lien on the same collateral arises, the lien creditor has priority. Here, Larry would have priority because Larry became a lien creditor on February 14, when the sheriff seized the computer, but Seller did not perfect until February 20 (*see* 1., above). However, in a conflict between a creditor with a PMSI in collateral and a lien creditor, if the PMSI creditor attaches its security interest before the lien arises, the PMSI creditor will prevail if it files within 20 days after the debtor receives the collateral. In this case, as discussed in 1., above, Seller attached a PMSI in the computer by February 12 and filed within 20 days after Debtor received the computer. Larry's lien arose on February 14, when the sheriff seized the computer. Therefore, because Seller attached before Larry's lien arose and filed within 20 days after Debtor received the computer, Seller prevails.

3.   Bank's security interest in the computer as collateral for the $12,000 advance is superior to Larry's claim. At issue is the priority between a lien creditor and a perfected secured creditor that makes a future advance after the lien creditor levies on the collateral.

Generally, a prior perfected security interest in collateral has priority over a lien creditor's interest in the same collateral. However, there is an exception for future advances: If a creditor with a prior perfected security interest makes a future advance more than 45 days after the lien arises, the lien creditor will have priority in the future advance unless the future advance was made (i) without knowledge of the lien, or (ii) pursuant to a commitment made without knowledge of the lien. Here, Bank made its advance three days after the lien arose, which is within the 45-day time limit. Therefore, Bank's prior perfected security interest in the computer as collateral for its $12,000 future advance has priority over Larry's interest in the computer.

QUESTION 15

Debtor bought a motor home from Uptown RV Sales on credit. Debtor signed a security agreement granting Uptown a security interest in the motor home. Two years later, Debtor lost her job and then defaulted on her loan by failing to make several monthly payments. Without sending any notice of default to Debtor, Uptown dispatched Ernest, one of its employees, to take possession of the motor home.

Ernest located the motor home parked on a public street. When he opened the door with a duplicate key, he found Debtor inside and told her that he was there to repossess the motor home. Debtor began yelling at him, "Get out of my home or I'll throw you out! This is the only place I have to live, and, anyway, you don't have any right to take my clothes and other stuff." Ernest departed without the motor home.

Two weeks later, the owner of Uptown sent Ernest back, this time to post a coupon on the windshield of the motor home fictitiously advertising a free steak dinner at the grand opening of a local restaurant on Friday evening. Debtor fell for the ploy. She went to the restaurant on Friday evening, parked the motor home in the lot at the rear of the restaurant, and went inside to see about her free dinner. She had left the door to the motor home unlocked.

Ernest, who had followed Debtor, waited for Debtor to get inside the restaurant, entered the motor home through the unlocked door, "hot-wired" the engine, and drove the motor home back to Uptown's garage. Debtor came out of the restaurant to find her motor home was gone.

Uptown's owner had arranged with a uniformed deputy sheriff to stand by in case it became necessary to keep the peace. The deputy sheriff observed the events from her patrol car parked some distance away but did not otherwise assist in the repossession.

1.   Did Uptown have the right to repossess the motor home without sending notice of default to Debtor and without judicial process? Explain.

2.   What arguments might Debtor reasonably make, based on the facts, that Uptown failed to carry out the repossession in a lawful manner? Explain.

ANSWER TO QUESTION 15

1. Uptown can repossess Debtor's motor home without judicial process and without giving Debtor notice of default as long as Uptown does not breach the peace during repossession. The issue is whether a secured party must use judicial process or give a debtor notice of default before repossessing collateral. Because a secured transaction is involved, this answer is governed by Article 9 of the Uniform Commercial Code ("U.C.C.").

Upon a debtor's default on the security agreement, a secured party has the right to take possession of the collateral by self-help without judicial process if she can do so without a breach of the peace. [U.C.C. §9-609] In this case, the facts state that Debtor defaulted on the loan by missing several monthly payments. As a result, Uptown is allowed to repossess the motor home without judicial process as long as there is no breach of the peace during repossession. Furthermore, Uptown did not need to give Debtor notice of default before repossession because the U.C.C. does not require such notice to be given.

2. Debtor can make several reasonable arguments that Uptown failed to carry out the repossession in a lawful manner. At issue is whether Uptown breached the peace when it repossessed Debtor's mobile home. As stated above, a secured party may take possession by self-help without judicial process only if she can do so without a breach of the peace. The U.C.C. does not define "breach of the peace," so its meaning is determined by case law.

First, Debtor can argue that any repossession performed over protest of the debtor constitutes a breach of the peace, even if no violence or significant disturbance actually occurs. In this case, even though Ernest repossessed the motor home when no one was present, Debtor had protested against Ernest's repossession during an earlier visit, shouting, "Get out of my home or I'll throw you out!" Therefore, Debtor can argue that the earlier threat constitutes a protest to any subsequent repossession, so there was a breach of the peace. However, Uptown could respond that the earlier protest of Debtor does not prevent future attempts at repossession, and thus there was no breach of the peace.

Debtor also can argue that Ernest's use of trickery (*i.e.,* the coupon) to lure Debtor out of the mobile home is a breach of the peace. Courts have ruled both ways on this issue, but Debtor can argue that Ernest's prior attempt at repossession failed because of Debtor's threats, and Ernest's use of trickery to prevent Debtor from protesting repossession in the future is a breach of the peace.

In addition, Debtor can assert that Ernest's unauthorized entry and hot-wiring of the mobile home constitutes a breach of the peace. Courts have found that breaking and entering a residence is a breach of the peace. In this case, Debtor can argue that the mobile home is more of a residence than a vehicle. The fact that Debtor's "clothes and stuff" were located inside the mobile home supports this argument. On the other hand, Uptown can counter that the mobile home was more of a vehicle than a residence, and some courts have allowed repossessing creditors to hot-wire vehicles.

Finally, Debtor could argue that Uptown's use of a deputy sheriff constituted a breach of the peace. A threat of force can constitute a breach of peace, and bringing along a presumably armed sheriff could constitute a threat of force. However, Uptown can respond that the deputy remained in her patrol car, so Debtor had no knowledge of her presence and she did not facilitate the repossession, and thus the use of a deputy was not a breach of the peace.

QUESTION 16

Debtor, the sole proprietor of a small restaurant, borrowed $20,000 from Bank. The loan was used to purchase kitchen equipment for Debtor's business, including a stove unit, a large refrigerator, two freezers, and a commercial microwave oven. Debtor signed a promissory note and a security agreement granting Bank a security interest in the items purchased. The security agreement contained clauses (1) waiving Debtor's right of redemption should default occur, and (2) providing that, if Debtor failed to make any regular installment payment, "the entire unpaid obligation due from Debtor to Bank shall, without further notice, immediately become due and payable." Bank properly perfected its security interest in the collateral.

Debtor missed four monthly installment payments. When Debtor was approximately $1,600 in arrears, Bank's representative drove a large truck to the alley behind the restaurant. Bank's representative was accompanied by two movers. The time was 11:10 p.m., shortly after the restaurant's closing time. Bank's representative pounded loudly on the locked back door, which was opened by one of the restaurant's employees. "We're here to repossess the kitchen equipment," stated Bank's representative. "Well, my boss isn't here, and I don't think I should let you in," replied the employee. Without further discussion, Bank's representative and the two movers walked right past the employee and began moving the kitchen equipment out to the truck. At first, the employee objected loudly, but soon he shrugged and watched quietly as they removed the equipment.

The next day, Debtor went to Bank and offered to pay the $1,600 arrearage in monthly payments. Bank refused the tender, reminding Debtor the entire balance was now due. When Debtor then offered to pay the entire balance due, including Bank's repossession expenses, Bank told Debtor that it would not allow him to redeem because he had waived his right of redemption. Thereafter, Bank sent Debtor a notice of public sale and then duly held the sale, the terms of which were commercially reasonable. Bank now has threatened to sue Debtor for a deficiency judgment of $4,000, the difference between Debtor's unpaid loan obligation and what Bank recovered in the sale.

Debtor has had to close the restaurant because the kitchen equipment was repossessed.

What are Debtor's rights, remedies, and liabilities under the Uniform Commercial Code? Explain.

ANSWER TO QUESTION 16

Debtor can sue Bank for all of the damages that were caused by the repossession and probably is not liable for any deficiency. At issue is whether Bank's repossession of debtor's equipment was proper under Uniform Commercial Code Article 9, which governs secured transactions.

Generally if a debtor defaults on a secured transaction, the creditor has a right to repossess the collateral on which it has attached a security interest. A security interest attaches to collateral when: (i) the debtor agrees to give the creditor a security interest in it, as evidenced by an authenticated security agreement; (ii) the creditor gives value for the security interest; and (iii) the debtor has rights in the collateral. All three conditions were met here: Debtor agreed to give Bank a security interest in the specific items of restaurant equipment, as evidenced by the written and signed security agreement; Bank gave Debtor value for the security interest (the equipment); and Debtor had ownership rights in the equipment once it was delivered. Moreover Debtor has defaulted on its obligation to Bank. Therefore Bank has a right to repossess the equipment. However, Article 9 also provides that a secured party will be liable to the debtor for any damage caused by a failure to follow any of the rules provided by Article 9, and will be prohibited from collecting any deficiency if any Article 9 rules regarding the debtor's default are broken unless the secured party can show that the breach did not cause the deficiency. Here Bank has failed to follow several Article 9 rules.

Article 9 provides that a secured party can use self-help to repossess collateral after there has been a default; the creditor need not seek an order from a court in order to repossess. However, a secured party can use self-help to repossess collateral only if it can do so without a breach of the peace. A repossession over a debtor's protest constitutes a breach of the peace. Here there probably was a breach of the peace, although this is a close call. Bank's representative announced that he intended to repossess the kitchen equipment, and a restaurant employee objected. However, other than objecting orally and loudly a few times, the employee did nothing more. It is unclear whether this protest is sufficient to constitute a breach of the peace, but it likely does.

Debtor's waiver of redemption also was improper under Article 9. Article 9 provides that a secured party has a right to redeem collateral after a default. This right can be waived but only after there has been a default. Here the security agreement included a waiver of the right to redeem. Because that waiver was obtained long before there was any default, it is invalid. Thus Bank's refusal to allow Debtor to redeem the collateral was improper. It should be noted, however, that there was nothing wrong with Bank including a clause accelerating all payments in the event of a default, and consequently there was nothing wrong with Bank's refusal to allow Debtor to redeem the collateral merely by offering to pay the four installment payments that were missed. However, once Debtor offered to pay the entire amount due on the loan plus repossession expenses, Bank had to allow Debtor to redeem the collateral, and its failure to do so violates Article 9.

Because Bank violated several Article 9 rules, it will be liable to Debtor for any damages caused by its breach, including the damages that have resulted from Debtor's closing his business. Moreover, it will not be allowed to obtain a deficiency judgment against Debtor unless it can prove that the deficiency did not result from its breach. Because the facts indicate that the default sale was commercially reasonable, Bank may be able to make such a showing. Moreover, Bank may argue that Debtor had a duty to mitigate damages and breached this duty by not bidding at the sale. The facts indicate that Debtor had enough money to pay off the entire indebtedness before the sale. If Debtor had bid that amount at the sale, there would have been no deficiency and Debtor's damages for being out of business would have been greatly reduced, because Debtor would have been out of business only temporarily.

QUESTION 17

PC is a professional law corporation formed by Ted and Teresa. In 2002, PC obtained a $100,000 line of credit from First Bank, and PC authenticated a security agreement that granted First Bank a security interest in "all of PC's equipment, now owned or hereafter acquired."

Although PC did not specifically authorize it, First Bank promptly filed a financing statement in the appropriate state offices. The financing statement, which PC had not signed,

recited erroneously that First Bank had a security interest in "all of PC's equipment, inventory, and accounts receivable." PC knew that First Bank had filed a financing statement but was unaware that the financing statement covered collateral not mentioned in the security agreement.

In 2003, PC entered into contracts to provide legal services to a number of municipalities, one of which was the city of Eden. To perform these contracts, PC decided to expand its operation by hiring an additional attorney, adding office staff, and increasing its office space. When First Bank refused to increase PC's line of credit to finance the expansion, PC approached Second Bank about obtaining a separate business expansion loan.

Second Bank agreed to loan PC $100,000, provided that the loan was secured by a first security interest in PC's accounts receivable. However, the arrangement fell through when Second Bank discovered that First Bank had already filed a financing statement covering PC's accounts receivable. First Bank ignored repeated requests from PC to terminate or amend the financing statement, and Second Bank was unwilling to make a loan until First Bank's filing was changed. As a result, PC was not able to secure financing from Second Bank.

Because of its inability to secure this financing, PC was unable to hire additional staff and could not adequately perform the contracts. After PC's attorneys failed to attend two important city council meetings because they were occupied with other duties, the city of Eden terminated its contract with PC, a contract that PC had expected to generate $250,000 in revenue over two years.

Also in 2003, Luke, a former employee of PC's, sued PC and won a judgment for $50,000. Luke immediately obtained a judicial lien against all of PC's assets, including its equipment and accounts receivable.

1. As between Luke and First Bank, who has the superior claim to PC's equipment? Explain.

2. As between Luke and First Bank, who has the superior claim to PC's accounts receivable? Explain.

3. What claims, if any, does PC have against First Bank under the Uniform Commercial Code? Explain.

ANSWER TO QUESTION 17

1.   Between Luke and First Bank, First Bank has the superior claim to PC's equipment. Luke is a lien creditor by virtue of his obtaining a lien on the collateral through judicial attachment. A lien creditor will prevail over the holder of a security interest in collateral if the lien creditor becomes such before the security interest is perfected. [U.C.C. §9-317] Luke obtained his judicial lien against PC in 2003. Thus, he will prevail against First Bank unless First Bank perfected a security interest in PC's equipment before 2003, the time Luke obtained his judicial lien. Here, First Bank perfected its security interest in 2002. A security interest in equipment may be perfected by filing a financing statement. For a financing statement to be effective, the debtor must

authorize it in an authenticated (*i.e.*, non-oral) record. The debtor authorizes the financing statement if he authenticates the financing statement or authenticates a security agreement covering the same collateral as the financing statement. Here, PC authenticated a security agreement granting a security interest in the equipment when it obtained the line of credit. However, perfection of a security interest cannot be completed until it has attached. There are three requisites for attachment of a security interest: (i) the parties must have an agreement that the security interest attach; (ii) value must be given by the secured party; and (iii) the debtor must have rights in the collateral. [U.C.C. §9-203(b)] Under the facts presented here, all of these factors have taken place. Because Luke did not become a lien creditor until after First Bank attached and perfected its security interest in PC's equipment, First Bank will have priority over Luke in the equipment.

2.   Between Luke and First Bank, Luke has the superior claim to PC's accounts receivable. As discussed above, Luke is a lien creditor who will prevail over the holder of a security interest in the same collateral if he became a lien creditor before a conflicting security interest was perfected. [U.C.C. §9-317] While First Bank holds a prior perfected security interest with regard to PC's equipment, the bank does not have a perfected security interest in PC's accounts receivable because it did not attach a security interest to the accounts receivable. A secured party may not perfect a security interest in property to which the security interest has not attached. Here First Bank did not attach a security interest to the accounts receivable because there was no agreement between the parties giving First Bank a security interest in the accounts receivable. Thus, Luke has the superior claim to PC's accounts receivable.

3.   PC may pursue a claim against First Bank for damages under the U.C.C. Pursuant to Article 9 of the U.C.C., an entity is liable for damages in the amount of any loss caused by a failure to comply with any of Article 9's rules, including losses resulting from the debtor's inability to obtain alternative financing. [U.C.C. §9-625(b)] Because of First Bank's erroneous financing statement, and subsequent failure to correct or terminate the financing statement, PC was unable to obtain alternative financing. As a direct result of its inability to obtain financing, PC lost a contract that was expected to generate $250,000 in revenues. Therefore, PC can recover any damages caused by this lost revenue, plus any other losses associated with its inability to secure financing from Second Bank.

QUESTION 18

Seller is in the business of selling new and used road construction equipment. On January 15, Buyer, a road builder, entered into a written purchase agreement with Seller for the sale of a used excavator for $100,000. The purchase agreement provided that Seller would add certain attachments to the excavator. The cost of the attachments was included in the purchase price. Buyer and Seller agreed that the specially equipped excavator would be ready for Buyer by April 5, in time for the start of the road construction season.

When Buyer signed the contract, Buyer gave Seller a $25,000 down payment. The remaining $75,000 was to be paid as follows: $25,000 on March 1; $25,000 on April 1; and $25,000 on May 1.

On January 20, Seller borrowed $1 million from Finance Co. to finance Seller's business operations. Finance Co. obtained a properly perfected security interest specifically assigning to Finance Co. all payments from Seller's accounts receivable and chattel paper.

On February 20, Seller failed to make a payment due on its loan from Finance Co. Finance Co. declared Seller in default. However, it informed Seller that it would not require immediate repayment of the full amount of the loan, but would instead begin collecting payments on all of Seller's outstanding accounts and chattel paper directly from the account debtors.

Finance Co. properly notified Buyer that Seller had assigned to Finance Co. the right to receive payment under the purchase agreement and that Buyer should make all future payments on the purchase agreement directly to Finance Co. However, Seller told Buyer to disregard Finance Co.'s notification and to continue to make payments directly to Seller. Buyer then sent its March and April payments directly to Seller.

On April 5, Buyer went to pick up the excavator from Seller. Buyer discovered that Seller had not equipped the excavator with any of the attachments required by their purchase agreement. Buyer informed Seller that it would take the excavator, despite its nonconformity with the contract, but that it would find and add the necessary attachments itself and would withhold from its final payment the cost of making the goods conform to the contract. Seller stated that it expected full payment but allowed Buyer to take the excavator.

On May 5, Finance Co. demanded that Buyer immediately pay Finance Co. $75,000, the full amount of the March, April, and May payments under the purchase agreement. Buyer refused, asserting that it made the March and April payments to Seller and that no remaining payment was due because the cost of bringing the excavator up to contract specifications exceeded $30,000, substantially more than the amount of the May payment.

How much, if anything, does Buyer owe Finance Co.? Explain.

ANSWER TO QUESTION 18

Buyer will owe Finance Co. $45,000. At issue is whether Buyer owes Finance for the March and April payments, and whether Buyer may offset its obligation to Finance Co. by subtracting damages for Seller's breach of contract.

Buyer will owe Finance Co. for the March and April payments that it made to Seller. At issue is whether Buyer was obligated to make the payments to Finance Co. after it was notified of the assignments. Under these facts, Finance Co. has a properly perfected security agreement that assigned to it all of Seller's accounts receivable and chattel paper. The payments to be made by Buyer for the construction equipment are among the accounts receivable. The holder of a security interest in accounts receivable may notify an account debtor to pay the secured party directly. Therefore, Finance Co. had the right to demand payment from Buyer directly after Seller defaulted. Once notified, an account debtor has an obligation to pay the secured party. Because Buyer received proper notification that its payments should be made to Finance Co., Buyer can discharge its obligation *only* by paying Finance Co.—the payments made to Seller will not suffice. It is no defense that Seller told Buyer to disregard the notice from Finance Co. Therefore, Buyer is still obligated to pay Finance Co. the $50,000 it already paid to Seller, plus the final payment.

Buyer, however, may not be obligated to make the final payment to Finance Co. At issue is whether Buyer may deduct damages from the amount remaining to be paid under the contract.

When a buyer accepts nonconforming goods from a seller, the buyer may seek damages for the nonconforming goods. Here, the excavator was received without the attachments specifically required by the purchase agreement. Therefore, the excavator is a nonconforming good. Buyer may offset its damages from the price owed to Seller, so long as proper notice is given. Buyer provided such notice at the time it picked up the excavator, stating that it would take the excavator in spite of the deficiencies, add the necessary attachments itself, and withhold the cost of doing so from its final payment. Thus, Buyer is entitled to deduct damages from the final $25,000 owed to Seller.

The deduction that Buyer is entitled to from Seller remains available even though Seller has assigned the contract to Finance Co. An assignee cannot be assigned greater rights than the assignor possessed. Therefore, the assignee takes the contract subject to any valid defenses that the assignor was subject to prior to the assignment. Here, Finance Co. will be subject to the set-off that Buyer is entitled to deduct from the final payment to be made to Seller. As discussed above, the deduction from the outstanding payment is justified as damages for breach of contract by the nonconforming excavator.

Buyer is required to pay Finance Co. $75,000 under the assigned contract. However, because Finance Co. is also subject to defenses Buyer has against Seller, Buyer may deduct the approximately $30,000 that it spent to bring the excavator up to contract specifications. After the damages are deducted, Buyer must pay Finance Co. roughly $45,000.

QUESTION 19

Bill operated a restaurant in a building he owned. On March 1, he purchased a large oven on credit for $8,000 from Sal's Appliance Barn. On that same day, the oven was set aside in Sal's warehouse and marked with a tag reading, "Sold to Bill." Also on March 1, Bill signed a security agreement that gave Sal's a security interest in the oven to secure the unpaid purchase price of the oven.

On March 14, the oven was delivered and bolted permanently into a specially built niche in the kitchen in Bill's restaurant, thus becoming a fixture under local real estate law.

On March 26, the local sheriff came to the restaurant and announced that he was there to execute a levy to satisfy a $3,000 judgment against Bill in favor of Local Bank. The sheriff saw the new oven in the restaurant's kitchen and announced that he was levying on the oven. He then physically disabled the oven by handcuffing it shut and placed a notice-of-levy sticker on it, which qualified as a valid levy under state law.

On March 28, after learning from Bill about what happened with the sheriff and the oven, Sal's filed its financing statement in the secretary of state's office but not in the local real estate records office. Sal's financing statement properly described the oven.

On March 29, Bill obtained a $10,000 loan from Finance Company and gave Finance Company a mortgage on his building to secure repayment of the loan. On the same day, Finance Company properly perfected a valid lien against the restaurant building and accompanying fixtures by filing in the local real estate records office designated by state law.

1. As between Sal's and Local Bank, who has priority as to the oven? Explain.

2. As between Sal's and Finance Company, who has priority as to the oven? Explain.

ANSWER TO QUESTION 19

1. Between Sal's and Local Bank, Sal's will have priority as to the oven. At issue is whether a judicial lien creditor will take priority over a purchase money security interest ("PMSI"). A judicial lien creditor (*i.e.*, a person who has acquired a lien on the collateral through judicial attachment, levy, or the like) prevails over the holder of a security interest in collateral if the lien creditor becomes such before the security interest is perfected. However, an exception to the rule exists. A secured party who attaches a PMSI on the debtor's collateral before a judicial lien creditor acquires an interest in the collateral will have priority over the judicial lien creditor if the secured party files within 20 days after the debtor receives the collateral. Here, Local Bank is a judicial lien creditor by virtue of the levy. Sal's has a PMSI in the oven because it sold the oven to Bill on credit and reserved a security interest. Local Bank acquired judicial lien creditor status on March 26, when it had the sheriff levy the oven. Sal's filed its financing statement on March 28.

The question of who takes priority will turn upon when Sal's PMSI attached, thereby determining whether Sal's filed its financing statement within the 20-day grace period. A security interest becomes attached when (i) the parties enter into a security agreement evidenced either by a record authenticated by the debtor that describes the collateral or by the creditor's possession or control of the collateral; (ii) the creditor gives value; and (iii) the debtor acquires rights in the collateral. Here, the security interest attached on March 1. All of the requirements for attachment were fulfilled: (i) Bill signed a security agreement; (ii) Sal's gave value (the oven); and (iii) Bill acquired rights in the oven when he received the right to obtain possession of the collateral. Although the oven was not delivered to Bill until March 14, Bill had the right to obtain possession of the oven on March 1 when it was marked "Sold to Bill." Therefore, Sal's PMSI in the oven attached on March 1, long before Local Bank acquired its interest in the oven on March 26. The oven was delivered March 14, and Sal's filed its financing statement on March 28, within 20 days of Bill receiving the collateral. Therefore, Sal's PMSI will take priority over Local Bank's levy.

2. Between Sal's and Finance Company, Finance Company will have priority as to the oven. At issue is the priority between the holder of a PMSI in a fixture and a holder of an interest in the real property to which the fixture is attached. Sal's has a PMSI in the oven, as discussed above. The facts state that the oven is a fixture, *i.e.*, a good that is so attached to real property that an interest in the good arises under real property law. Generally, in a contest between a holder of a security interest in a fixture and a holder of an interest in the real property to which the fixture is attached, the first party to file a fixture filing or record its real property interest prevails. A "fixture filing" is accomplished by filing a financing statement in the office where a mortgage on real property would be recorded. In addition to the standard requirements for a financing statement, a fixture filing financing statement must contain a description of the real property to which the fixture is attached.

Under these facts, Sal's did not make a fixture filing. Sal's filed a financing statement in the secretary of state's office, but failed to file in the real estate records office. Also, it does not appear that the financing statement described the real property to which the oven is attached, as the facts state that it properly described the oven only. Finance Co., however, did file in the local real estate records office. It is safe to assume that the "properly perfected valid lien" filed by Finance Co. included a description of the real property, as mortgages customarily include such information. Because Sal's did not make a proper fixture filing, Finance Company will have priority based upon its properly filed March 29 lien.

QUESTION 20

On August 1, 2003, Builder, a construction company, borrowed $2 million from Lender to finance the purchase of a heavy-duty construction crane. Shareholder, a very wealthy shareholder of Builder, personally guaranteed the loan. Builder signed an agreement granting Lender a security interest in the new crane to secure the loan. However, Lender neglected to file a financing statement reflecting its security interest.

Due to severe cash flow problems, Builder stopped making scheduled loan payments four months ago, leaving a balance of $1.5 million on the loan.

In response to Builder's failure to make the scheduled loan payments, Lender hired a repossession service to recover the crane. Employees of the repossession service visited Builder's unprotected job site and, without notice to Builder, took the crane away. This occurred on Sunday, June 5, 2005, when no one from Builder was present and thus no dispute erupted.

On June 7, 2005, Lender mailed a notice to Builder announcing that Lender was going to sell the crane at an auction on June 21, 2005. Lender did not send separate notice of the auction to Shareholder. On the announced auction date, Lender sold the crane to Dealer, the highest bidder at the auction, for $1 million. Shareholder knew about the auction but did not bid at it. It can be proved that if Shareholder had bid, the bid would have been $1.2 million.

Builder asserts that: (a) Lender's actions amounted to a conversion of the crane because Lender's security interest was not perfected, and (b) Lender handled the repossession and sale improperly. Builder sues Lender for $1.7 million, which Builder says is the fair market value of the crane.

Lender counterclaims for the $500,000 deficiency, which it says is still owed by Builder on the loan after taking into account the proceeds received by Lender from the sale of the crane.

1. Did Lender have the right to repossess and sell the crane? Explain.

2. Did Lender's handling of the repossession, foreclosure, and sale comply with all legal requirements, and is Lender entitled to recover the $500,000 deficiency from Builder? Explain.

ANSWER TO QUESTION 20

1. Lender did have the right to repossess and sell the crane. At issue are the rights of the holder

of a security interest in collateral. Because this question involves the rights of a secured creditor, Article 9 of the Uniform Commercial Code will govern.

The holder of a security interest in collateral has a right to use self-help to repossess the collateral and sell it to satisfy the secured obligation if the debtor defaults and the repossession does not involve a breach of the peace. Here, Lender had a security interest in the crane, Builder probably was in default of the secured obligation, and the repossession did not involve a breach of the peace.

To attach a security interest to collateral, the parties must agree to create a security interest. The agreement must reasonably identify the collateral and be evidenced by: (i) a record authenticated by the debtor; (ii) the creditor's taking possession of the collateral; or (iii) in certain cases, the creditor's being given control over the collateral. The secured party must also give value in exchange for the security interest, and the debtor must have rights in the collateral. Here, all of the requirements were satisfied: Builder signed a security agreement granting Lender a security interest in the crane in exchange for Lender's giving Builder money to buy the crane, and after purchasing the crane, Builder had an ownership interest in it. The fact that Lender did not perfect its security interest by filing a financing statement is irrelevant here. Rights between a secured party and a debtor are established by attachment of the security interest; filing a financing statement (a method of perfection) is relevant only to establish the secured party's rights against third parties who might also have an interest in the collateral.

Builder probably also defaulted on the secured obligation. Article 9 does not specify what constitutes a default, leaving the definition to the parties' agreement. However, most agreements provide that the failure to make a scheduled payment constitutes a default.

Finally, the repossession here was done without a breach of the peace. The facts state that the crane was repossessed from an unprotected work site while no one was around. Thus, Lender had a security interest in the crane, Builder had defaulted on the secured obligation, and the repossession was peaceful. Therefore, Lender had a right to repossess and sell the collateral.

2. Lender's handling of the repossession, foreclosure, and sale did not comply with all requirements of Article 9 and as a result Lender probably will not be able to recover the $500,000 deficiency that it seeks.

After a secured creditor repossesses collateral, he has a right to sell the collateral at a public or private (*i.e.*, auction) sale. However, reasonable notice authenticated by the creditor must be given to the debtor and any surety on the obligation. The notice must describe the debtor, the secured party, the collateral, and the method of sale; explain the debtor's right to an accounting; and state the time and place of any public sale. In nonconsumer cases (*i.e.*, cases not involving goods for personal or household use) notice will be deemed reasonable if it was given at least 10 days before the sale. Moreover all aspects of the sale must be commercially reasonable.

Here, we are dealing with a nonconsumer case (the crane is a piece of construction equipment). The notice appears to have been proper in all respects, in that it announced that Lender was going to sell the crane at an auction on June 21, 14 days after the notice was mailed. Moreover, nothing in the facts indicates that the sale was other than commercially reasonable. However, notice of the sale was sent only to Builder and was not sent to Shareholder, who personally guaranteed the loan and who, therefore, was a surety on the loan and entitled to notice. It does not matter that Shareholder actually found out about the sale; Article 9 clearly requires notice authenticated by the secured party.

When a secured creditor fails to comply with all of Article 9's foreclosure requirements, a rebuttable presumption arises that the value of the collateral was equal to the value of the loan; *i.e.*, that if the sale had been conducted properly, it would have generated enough money to pay off the debt in its entirety. Thus, the secured creditor cannot recover any deficiency unless it can rebut the presumption. It is unclear whether Lender will be able to rebut the presumption here. On the one hand, it can argue that if Shareholder had been given notice, the crane still would have sold for only $1 million because Shareholder knew about the sale and did not bid. However, we do not know why Shareholder did not bid. It could be that he received notice too late to raise the needed money. In that case, Lender's deficiency would be reduced by $200,000, because the facts state that if Shareholder had bid, the bid would have been $1.2 million—$200,000 more than the winning bid.

QUESTION 21

Specialty Audio, Inc. ("Specialty") manufactures high-quality stereo speakers worth about $2,000 each. Because its business is fairly small, Specialty has no showroom or sales staff of its own.

Specialty entered into a consignment arrangement with Giant Electronics Store ("Giant"). Pursuant to the written consignment agreement, Specialty delivers speakers to Giant, and Giant displays those speakers on its showroom floor and sells them on behalf of Specialty. When a customer buys a pair of speakers, Giant keeps a commission as compensation for Giant's effort and pays the rest of the customer's purchase price to Specialty. At any given time, Giant has about two dozen pairs of Specialty's speakers on hand.

Specialty holds title to the speakers until they are sold. However, as far as any third party can discern, the speakers are part of Giant's own inventory. There is no indication that Specialty is the owner of the speakers. Moreover, Giant does not generally engage in the sale of goods for others and is not known by its creditors to do so.

After establishing the consignment relationship with Specialty, Giant borrowed $1 million from Bank to open new stores. As security for its obligation to repay the money, Giant granted Bank a security interest in "all inventory, whether now owned or hereafter acquired." Bank properly perfected its security interest by filing a financing statement in the appropriate state office.

Giant defaulted on its loan from Bank. Bank peaceably repossessed all of Giant's goods, including all the Specialty speakers Giant had on display and, after providing proper notice, sold everything at a commercially reasonable sale.

1. Did Bank have the right to repossess and sell the Specialty speakers even though, under the consignment agreement, they belonged to Specialty and not to Giant? Explain.

2. What rights, if any, does Specialty have against Bank to recover the proceeds from the sale of the speakers? Explain.

3. What action might Specialty have taken to protect its interest in the speakers more completely? Explain.

ANSWER TO QUESTION 21

1.   Bank had the right to repossess and sell the Specialty speakers even though, under the consignment agreement, they belonged to Specialty ("consignor") and not to Giant ("consignee"). The issue is whether Giant's apparent ownership of the speakers gave Bank the right to take the speakers from Giant to satisfy Giant's debt to Bank.

Where: (i) consigned goods are worth a total of $1,000 or more; (ii) the consignor did not use the goods for personal, family, or household purposes; (iii) the consignee is a person who deals in goods of that kind under a name other than the consignor's; (iv) the consignee is not an auctioneer; and (v) the consignee is not generally known by his creditors to be substantially engaged in selling the goods of others, the consignor's interest in the consigned goods is treated like a purchase money security interest ("PMSI") in inventory vis-à-vis other creditors of the consignee, and the consignee is treated like the owner of the goods.

Here, the consigned speakers were worth $2,000; Specialty did not use the speakers for personal, family, or household purposes; Giant deals in the same kind of goods (electronics) under a different name than Specialty; Giant is not an auctioneer; and Giant does not generally engage in the sale of goods for others and is not known by its creditors to do so. Thus, as to Giant's other creditors, Specialty had only an unperfected security interest in the speakers, and Giant is treated like the owner of the speakers. Because Bank perfected a security interest in all of Giant's inventory, including after-acquired inventory, and the speakers are treated as part of Giant's inventory, Bank had a right to repossess the speakers upon Giant's default despite the consignment agreement between Giant and Specialty.

2.   Specialty has no rights against Bank to recover the proceeds from the sale of the speakers. The issue is whether Specialty properly protected its interest in the speakers as against its consignee's creditors so as to have first right to the proceeds of the speakers upon their sale.

A perfected security interest has priority over an unperfected security interest. Moreover, when a secured creditor repossesses collateral, interests junior to the repossessing secured creditor's interest are wiped out. Here, the facts state that Bank properly perfected its security interest in Giant's inventory, which included the speakers. Specialty, on the other hand, took no steps to perfect the security interest that, as discussed above, it is deemed to have had in the speakers. Thus, Specialty's interest in the speakers was wiped out when Bank repossessed them.

3.   To protect its interest in the speakers, Specialty needed to file a financing statement and give Bank notice of its security interest in the speakers before delivering them to Giant. At issue is how to obtain superpriority for a PMSI in inventory.

A PMSI in inventory will have priority over even prior-perfected security interests in the same collateral if: (i) the PMSI is perfected at the time the debtor obtains possession of the inventory (i.e., the PMSI holder must have filed a financing statement covering the inventory before delivering it to the debtor); and (ii) the PMSI holder gives notice to each creditor with a conflicting interest in the same collateral before delivering the collateral to the debtor. Thus, if Specialty had filed a financing statement covering the speakers and had given Bank notice that it was retaining a security interest in the speakers before delivering them to Giant, it would have had priority in the speakers over Bank upon Giant's default.

QUESTION 22

Joe purchased a boat for use by his family from Dealer. Dealer extended credit for the purchase and retained a security interest in the boat as collateral for payment of the balance due. Joe failed to make a number of the payments, and, on May 1, Dealer peacefully repossessed the boat as Dealer was entitled to do under the U.C.C.

On May 3, Dealer mailed Joe a letter that stated the following: the balance due on the boat was $10,000; Dealer had credited Joe with $7,500, Dealer's good faith estimate of the boat's value, leaving a deficiency balance due of $2,500; Dealer had disposed of the boat by purchasing it for use as a rental boat in Dealer's marina; and Dealer had saved Joe money by disposing of the boat in this way because, if Dealer had publicized the availability of the boat for sale to third parties, Joe would have to pay the additional cost of the publicity. The letter also demanded that Joe pay the $2,500 deficiency.

This letter was the only communication between Dealer and Joe after the peaceful repossession of the boat.

Used boats are typically sold through privately negotiated sales or in occasional dealer auctions. There is no recognized market on which they are customarily sold. Moreover, used boats are not subject to standardized price quotations. Quoted pricing is widely variable, with used boats of the same age and model being subject to different prices depending on their condition and features. Sale prices are also heavily influenced by the negotiating skills of the parties to the transaction. Nonetheless, the $7,500 value that Dealer placed on Joe's boat was in the middle of the range of prices for which used boats of that age and model have sold in the area over the past year.

1. Did Dealer properly dispose of the collateral under the U.C.C.? Explain.

2. On these facts, what are Joe's rights, remedies, and obligations under the U.C.C.? Explain.

ANSWER TO QUESTION 22

1. Dealer did not properly dispose of the collateral. The issue is whether Dealer's means of disposal—purchase of the boat for use as a rental in Dealer's marina—complied with U.C.C. requirements for repossessed property.

After default, the secured party may sell, lease, or license repossessed collateral by either public sale (auction) or private sale. In either case, all aspects of the sale must be commercially reasonable. The secured party must give the debtor and any sureties on the debt reasonable notice of the sale in writing, unless the debtor or surety, after default, waives the right to notice of the sale. However, notice need not be given if the collateral is perishable or threatens to decline rapidly in value or is of a kind ordinarily sold in a recognized market. Notice must be sent within a reasonable time before the sale.

Generally, the secured party may purchase the collateral at a public sale, or at a private sale if the collateral is of a type customarily sold in a recognized market or is of a type on which there are widely distributed price quotations.

Here, the sale was improper on two grounds: First, Dealer had no right to purchase the boat at a private sale because the collateral was not of a type customarily sold in a recognized market and was not subject to widely distributed price quotations. Second, Joe was not given reasonable notice before the sale—here, Dealer sent Joe a letter notifying him of the disposition of the boat *after* the sale. For both of these reasons, Dealer did not properly dispose of the collateral under the U.C.C.

2.   Joe may recover actual damages or statutory damages, and may not be liable for paying any deficiency. In the alternative, Joe could ask a court to void the "sale" and redeem the boat from Dealer. At issue is what remedies are available to Joe, the debtor, following an improper sale of collateral repossessed from him by the secured party.

A secured party is liable for actual damages caused by the failure to comply with U.C.C. requirements regarding the sale of repossessed collateral. When the secured party violates the U.C.C. default rules with respect to collateral that is a consumer good, the debtor is entitled under the Code to either actual damages or, at a minimum, 10% of the cash price of the goods plus an amount equal to all of the interest charges to be paid over the life of the loan. Actual damages usually are measured by the difference between the price obtained for the collateral and the price the collateral would have fetched at a proper sale. Because the facts tell us that despite Code violations, the $7,500 price was an average price for the boat, Joe should seek his statutory damages, which are available because the boat here is consumer goods, as it was bought for family use.

When the Code's foreclosure rules are not followed, the secured party may also lose the right to a deficiency judgment. A court will generally follow one of three approaches when the collateral is a consumer good: (i) the rebuttable presumption rule, which states that the value of the collateral is presumed to equal the amount of the debt unless the secured party proves otherwise; (ii) the absolute bar rule, which denies the secured party a deficiency regardless of whether the secured party can prove that the collateral is worth less than the debt; or (iii) the setoff rule, which allows the secured party to recover the deficiency minus any actual damages that the debtor can prove. Thus, whether Joe may be liable for any deficiency depends on which approach the court follows.

Alternatively, Joe could seek to redeem the boat. After default and repossession, a debtor may redeem the collateral by paying off the secured obligation along with reasonable expenses incurred by the secured party in relation to the repossession. However, this right is cut off by the sale of the collateral. Here, there was no real sale of the boat to a third party; Dealer "sold" the boat to itself, and the boat is still in Dealer's possession. Because this "sale" was improper and the boat is not in the hands of a bona fide purchaser, Joe could probably ask the court to void the private sale to Dealer and redeem the boat, if he so desired.

QUESTION 23

Nine months ago, Feagle Construction Company, Inc. ("Feagle"), which does business under the trade name of On Top Roofing, obtained a $150,000 loan from National Bank. To secure the loan, Feagle assigned to National Bank "all rights to payment owed to Feagle Construction Company, Inc., by Hotel Corporation for the roofing construction project on its Broadway Street Hotel." The Broadway Street Hotel roofing project was by far the largest of Feagle's 15 roofing projects and represented its largest account receivable.

National Bank promptly filed a financing statement with this same collateral description, using the trade name of On Top Roofing for the debtor. The financing statement was filed in the appropriate location and indexed only in the name of On Top Roofing.

Three months after these events, Feagle needed additional monies. It approached State Bank for a loan of $100,000. State Bank conducted a search of the filing office's records for financing statements relating to "Feagle Construction Company, Inc.," but its search did not retrieve National Bank's financing statement. Accordingly, State Bank granted the $100,000 loan and obtained a written agreement from Feagle granting State Bank a security interest in "all of Feagle Construction Company, Inc.'s, accounts, whether now owned or hereafter acquired." State Bank filed a financing statement in the appropriate location in the name of "Feagle Construction Company, Inc.," as debtor.

Another six months later, mounting financial stress forced Feagle to default on its loans to both National Bank and State Bank. Feagle has about $75,000 worth of outstanding accounts receivable. In particular, Hotel Corporation still owes Feagle $50,000 for the hotel roofing project. In addition, Feagle is owed about $25,000 on a total of 10 other roofing projects it has recently completed. Both National Bank and State Bank are seeking to recover some of what Feagle owes them by collecting from Hotel Corporation the amount it still owes Feagle.

Does National Bank or State Bank have first priority in the money owed to Feagle by Hotel Corporation? Explain.

ANSWER TO QUESTION 23

State Bank has first priority in the money owed to Feagle by Hotel Corporation because its security interest in the money (*i.e.*, the collateral) was properly perfected while National Bank's security interest in the money was not.

The issue is which creditor—National Bank or State Bank—first perfected its security interest in the collateral and, thus, has priority in the interest.

Generally, a perfected security interest prevails over an unperfected security interest in the same collateral. In the case of conflicting perfected security interests, the party that files or perfects first has priority. The Uniform Commercial Code ("U.C.C.") provides for perfection by simple "notice" filing for all kinds of collateral except deposit accounts and money. For collateral other than real estate, a financing statement is filed centrally with the secretary of state. This financing statement must contain: (i) the name and mailing address of the debtor, (ii) the name and address of the secured party, and (iii) an indication of the collateral covered by the financing statement. The financing statement must not contain any seriously misleading errors. If the debtor is a registered organization (*e.g.*, a corporation), the debtor's name will be considered seriously misleading and, thus, the filing will not be effective, if it does not match the name under which the debtor was organized. Also, use of the debtor's trade name will invalidate the filing. However, an incorrect name will not be treated as seriously misleading under a "safe harbor" provision if the financing statement would be discovered in a filing office search under the debtor's correct name.

Additionally, perfection may occur automatically, without filing, in the case of a security interest in a small-scale assignment of an account or payment intangible. This rule applies to an assignment of accounts or payment intangibles that does not alone, or in conjunction with other assignments to the same assignee, transfer a significant part of the assignor's outstanding accounts or payments intangibles to the creditor.

Here, the collateral at issue is an account because it involves a right to payment for goods and services, namely, money owed to Feagle for its work on a roofing construction project on Hotel Corporation's Broadway Street Hotel. Typically, perfection of a security interest in such collateral would be achieved through filing. In this case, National Bank filed a financing statement for its security interest three months before State Bank filed a financing statement for the same collateral. However, National Benk's filing was invalid because, rather than filing the financing statement using the debtor's proper name (*i.e.*, the name under which it was incorporated—Feagle Construction Company, Inc.), National Bank filed the financing statement using Feagle's trade name, On Top Roofing, and the financing statement was indexed only in the name of On Top Roofing. When State Bank searched the filing office's records for financing statements relating to Feagle Construction Company, Inc., the search did not reveal National Bank's financing statement. Thus, the error made in listing the debtor's name was seriously misleading and the mistake could not be forgiven under the safe harbor provision. Consequently, National Bank's filing of the financing statement was not effective and National Bank's interest remained unperfected.

State Bank, on the other hand, did file a proper financing statement because it named Feagle Construction Company, Inc. as debtor, identified the collateral as "all Feagle Construction Company, Inc.'s accounts, whether now owned or hereafter acquired," and filed the financing statement in the appropriate location. Therefore, even though State Bank filed its financing statement *after* National Bank filed its statement, State Bank properly perfected while National Bank did not.

Also, there was probably no automatic perfection of National Bank's assigned security interest in the payment that Hotel Corporation owed to the debtor, Feagle Construction Company, Inc., so National Bank would not have priority over State Bank on that basis. Although the Hotel Corporation account was a single account, the facts indicate that that receivable was by far the largest of Feagle's 15 roofing projects and was its single largest receivable. Thus, in all likelihood, a court would find that the transfer was a significant part of Feagle's outstanding accounts and, therefore, there was no automatic perfection of National Bank's security interest. So, because State Bank properly perfected its security interest by filing and National Bank did not, and National Bank's security interest was not automatically perfected, State Bank has priority over National Bank with respect to the collateral at issue.

QUESTION 24

On October 1, Dart Corporation ("DC"), a State A corporation, borrowed $300,000 from State Bank, a State A bank. On behalf of DC, DC's president signed a written security agreement giving State Bank a security interest in DC's State Bank checking account (a demand account) to secure its obligation to repay the loan. State Bank did not file a financing statement reflecting that interest.

On December 1, First Bank, another State A bank, agreed to loan $60,000 to DC. DC's president, on behalf of DC, signed a written security agreement granting First Bank a

security interest in all of DC's "office equipment and deposit accounts." First Bank immediately advanced $60,000 to DC and filed a financing statement reflecting its interest.

First Bank's financing statement was filed in the correct filing office in State A and listed the collateral as "office equipment and deposit accounts." It correctly identified First Bank as the secured party, and it correctly gave the address of the debtor as "123 Smith Street, City, State A." However, First Bank's financing statement incorrectly listed the name of the debtor as "Dart Incorporated," rather than "Dart Corporation," the correct name of the company as reflected on its certificate of incorporation and other public records. Despite this error, a search under the name "Dart Corporation" using the State A filing office's standard search logic would turn up the financing statement listing "Dart Incorporated" as the debtor.

Shortly after receiving the loan from First Bank, DC defaulted on the obligations it owed to State Bank and First Bank.

On December 23, State Bank obtained a judgment against DC in connection with its unpaid $300,000 loan.

On January 3 of the following year, a State A sheriff levied on DC's office equipment on behalf of State Bank.

1. As between First Bank and State Bank, which has a superior claim to DC's checking account at State Bank? Explain.

2. As between First Bank and State Bank, which has a superior claim to DC's office equipment? Explain.

ANSWER TO QUESTION 24

1. State Bank has a superior claim over First Bank to debtor DC's checking account at State Bank. The issue is which creditor has priority over a deposit account: the bank that has failed to file a financing statement but is the bank where the deposit account is maintained, or the bank that has filed a financing statement covering the account.

A security agreement for a nonconsumer deposit account is evidenced by control. The bank in which the nonconsumer deposit account is maintained automatically has control over a deposit account. Other means of gaining control over a nonconsumer deposit account are: (i) putting the deposit account in the secured party's name; or (ii) agreeing in an authenticated record with the debtor and the bank in which the deposit account is maintained that the bank will comply with the secured party's orders regarding the deposit account without the debtor's consent. A security interest may be perfected by filing as to all kinds of collateral *except deposit accounts* and money. Generally, a perfected security interest prevails over an unperfected security interest.

The facts state that the account in question is a demand account, which under Article 9 is a "deposit account." Moreover, it is a *nonconsumer* deposit account because it is for a corporation's use, and not for personal use. Both State Bank and First Bank have enforceable security interests in the account because (i) DC's president signed a security agreement granting each bank an interest in the account; (ii) DC has rights in the account; and (iii) each bank extended value to DC by giving DC a loan.

Although First Bank filed a financing statement covering the deposit account, First Bank's interest is not perfected because it did not have control over the account. First Bank was not the bank where the account was maintained, the deposit account was not in its name, and there was no authenticated record between First Bank and the bank in which the account is maintained (State Bank) stating that the latter will comply with First Bank's orders regarding the deposit account without the debtor's consent. Because none of the requirements for control were met by First Bank, its security interest in the deposit account is unperfected.

State Bank, on the other hand, does have a perfected security interest in the deposit account, even though it did not file a financing statement, because State Bank is the bank that maintains the account. Therefore, State Bank has control over the account. As between an unperfected secured creditor (First Bank) and a perfected secured creditor (State Bank), the perfected secured creditor has the superior claim.

2.   First Bank has a superior claim over State Bank to DC's office equipment. The issues are whether the filing of a financing statement is valid where there is an error in the debtor's name on the statement and, if so, who prevails when there are competing security interests held by a perfected secured creditor and a judgment lien creditor.

For a financing statement to be effective, it must contain three pieces of information: (i) the name and mailing address of the debtor; (ii) the name and mailing address of the secured party; and (iii) an indication of the collateral covered by the financing statement. Minor errors in the debtor's name will not render the financing statement ineffective, unless those errors make the financing statement "seriously misleading." If the debtor is a registered organization (*e.g.,* a corporation, limited partnership, or limited liability company), the debtor's name is seriously misleading if it does not match the name under which the debtor was organized. Use of the debtor's trade name is also insufficient. However, under a "safe harbor" provision, the incorrect name is not seriously misleading if the financial statement would be discovered in a filing office search under the debtor's correct name, using the filing office's standard search logic, if any.

Here, First Bank filed a financing statement covering DC's office equipment. First Bank incorrectly listed the name of the debtor as "Dart Incorporated," rather than "Dart Corporation," the correct name of the company as reflected on its certificate of incorporation and other public records. The facts state that despite this error, a search under the name "Dart Corporation" using the state filing office's standard search logic would turn up the financing statement with the erroneous name. Thus, under the safe harbor provision, the name would not be seriously misleading. Because the filing was proper in all other respects, the perfection of First Bank's security interest by filing is valid.

As for the question of priority of interests between First Bank and State Bank, a prior perfected security interest in collateral trumps a judicial lien. In this case, First Bank perfected its security interest in the office equipment by filing December 1. State Bank became a judgment lien creditor when the sheriff levied on the office equipment on State Bank's behalf on January 3 of the following year. Thus, First Bank has a prior perfected security interest in the office equipment.

Because First Bank's financing statement with respect to the office equipment was properly filed, and the statement was filed more than a month before State Bank became a judgment lien creditor on the same collateral, First Bank has priority over State Bank in DC's office equipment.

QUESTION 25

Debtor sells and delivers medical supplies to hospitals. It owns a fleet of 40 trucks that it uses to make deliveries. Debtor has a state-issued certificate of title for each truck. The state has a statute that provides: "All security interests in a motor vehicle must be noted on the vehicle's certificate of title as a condition for perfection."

On June 1, Bank made a $100,000 loan to Debtor. In order to secure the loan, Debtor signed a valid security agreement granting Bank a security interest in "all Debtor's inventory and equipment, whether now owned or hereafter acquired." Bank did not note its security interest on the certificates of title issued for the trucks. However, Bank immediately filed an appropriate financing statement in the proper state office that listed its collateral as "all Debtor's inventory and equipment, whether now owned or hereafter acquired."

On July 1, Finance Company loaned $75,000 to Debtor. On that same day, Debtor signed a valid security agreement granting Finance Company a security interest in 25 of Debtor's "delivery trucks" and "any accessories now or hereafter installed." Each truck was identified individually and by its vehicle identification number. Although Finance Company never filed a financing statement, its security interest was noted on the certificate of title for each truck.

On August 1, Debtor entered into a contract with Global Inc. to buy 40 global positioning system units ("GPS units") to be installed on all 40 delivery trucks (including the 25 trucks covered by Finance Company's security agreement). GPS units are bolted on the dashboard of a vehicle and hooked up directly to the battery for power, but they otherwise operate independently of the vehicle.

The GPS units cost $50,000. Debtor made a down payment of $10,000 and signed an agreement to pay the remaining $40,000, plus interest, in equal monthly installments over a two-year period. To secure the amount owed on the contract, Debtor signed a security agreement giving Global a security interest in "the GPS units to be installed on Debtor's delivery trucks."

On August 2, Global properly filed a financing statement covering the GPS units. The GPS units were delivered to Debtor on August 10, and Debtor installed them on its delivery trucks shortly thereafter.

On October 1, Debtor defaulted on its obligations to Bank, Finance Company, and Global. Bank has repossessed all 40 of Debtor's trucks, and it is now negotiating with Finance Company and Global about their respective claims to the trucks and the 40 GPS units installed in them.

1. Which of Bank or Finance Company has the superior claim to the 25 delivery trucks claimed by Finance Company? Explain.

2. Which of Global or Finance Company has the superior claim to the GPS units installed in the 25 delivery trucks claimed by Finance Company? Explain.

3. Which of Bank or Global has the superior claim to the remaining 15 GPS units? Explain.

ANSWER TO QUESTION 25

1.   Finance Company has a superior claim over Bank as to the 25 delivery trucks in which it has a security interest because its interest is perfected and Bank's interest is not. The issue is whether a security interest in a motor vehicle is perfected absent a notation on the vehicle's certificate of title, where a state statute calls for perfection of a security interest in a motor vehicle by such notation.

Debtor's fleet of delivery trucks is "equipment" for purposes of Article 9. Goods that are not consumer goods, farm products, or inventory are equipment. Bank had a security interest in the delivery trucks (*i.e.,* the equipment). However, the delivery trucks are subject to a state statute that provides for perfection of a security interest in motor vehicles by notation of the security interest on the certificate of title. Filing a financing statement is not effective to perfect a security interest in property subject to such a statute. Thus, Bank did not perfect a security interest in Debtor's delivery trucks by filing a financing statement. Finance Company, on the other hand, did perfect its interest in the 25 trucks by complying with the statute and noting its interest on the certificates of title. Thus, Finance Company's perfected security interest in the 25 trucks prevails over Bank's unperfected interest.

2.   Finance Company has a superior claim over Global as to the GPS units installed in the 25 delivery trucks. The issue is whether a security interest in goods continues after the goods have been attached to other goods in which another creditor has a security interest.

When goods are physically united with other goods in such a manner that the identity of the original goods is not lost, the goods become accessions. A security interest in goods that is created and perfected before the goods become accessions continues after the goods become accessions. Thus, Global's security interest in the GPS units, which was properly perfected on August 2, continued when the units were attached to Debtor's trucks some eight days later. But when the collateral of one creditor becomes united with the collateral of another creditor, each creditor's collateral is an "accession" to the other creditor's collateral, and the two items of collateral together are regarded as "the whole." Whether either creditor's security interest applies to "the whole," or applies only to its original collateral, turns on the description of the collateral in that creditor's security agreement. In this case, Global's security interest in the GPS units does not cover "the whole" (*i.e.,* delivery trucks with GPS units installed). On the other hand, Finance Company's described security interest in the specifically identified delivery trucks expressly includes all installed accessories and therefore covers the GPS units.

The priority rules governing accessions are normally the same as the rules for other collateral. However, Article 9 makes an exception when, as here, there is an applicable certificate-of-title statute. The security interest in the whole, when perfected in compliance with the requirements of the certificate-of-title statute, has priority over the security interest in the accession. Thus, Finance Company's claim, which was perfected by notation on the trucks' certificate of title, has priority over Global's security interest in the GPS units installed in the trucks claimed by Finance Company. The policy rationale for preferring Finance Company in these circumstances is to enable a secured party to rely upon a certificate of title without having to check the U.C.C. files to determine whether any components of the collateral may be encumbered.

3.   Global has a superior claim over Bank as to the remaining 15 GPS units. The issue is whether a properly perfected purchase money security interest ("PMSI") will prevail over an earlier perfected security interest in the same equipment.

Bank's perfected security interest covers inventory and equipment, including after-acquired equipment and inventory. The GPS units are equipment because they are not inventory, farm products, or consumer goods. The after-acquired collateral clause in Bank's security agreement is valid, and Bank's priority dates back to the time it filed its financing statement covering equipment, even though its interest in the GPS units did not attach or become perfected until Debtor acquired rights in the units. Thus, Bank has a perfected security interest in the GPS units.

Global, however, has a PMSI in the GPS units. A security interest in goods is a PMSI if the collateral secures a purchase money obligation incurred with respect to that collateral. A PMSI arises when (i) a creditor sells the goods to the debtor on credit, retaining a security interest in the goods for all or part of the purchase price; or (ii) a creditor advances funds that are used by the debtor to purchase the goods. Here, Debtor purchased the GPS units from Global, and Global took a security interest in the units. Global's interest in the GPS units secures a purchase money obligation—the $40,000 debt to Global that Debtor incurred "as all or part of the price of the collateral." Hence, the security interest is a PMSI. Global promptly filed a financing statement and its interest was perfected as soon as Debtor obtained possession of the GPS units.

A PMSI in equipment that is perfected when the debtor takes possession of the collateral prevails over a conflicting perfected interest in the same equipment, even if the conflicting interest is earlier in time. Therefore, even though Bank's priority dates to June 1, its interest is nonetheless subordinate to Global's later-in-time PMSI.

QUESTION 1

Dennis, a 10-year-old, saw his 11-year-old neighbor, Margaret, ahead of him on the sidewalk. He called out, threatening to throw an apple at her. Margaret became furious, and when Dennis turned his back to pick up an apple, Margaret threw an apple at him. The apple missed Dennis, who then decided to point an empty squirt gun at Margaret. Dennis knew that the squirt gun was unloaded, but he wanted to scare Margaret. Margaret saw Dennis pointing the squirt gun at her. "A little water isn't going to scare me," she yelled to him. Dennis pulled the trigger and then shouted, "See, it wasn't even loaded."

The next day, Margaret wanted to make up with Dennis and offered him some lemonade, but Dennis had an unexpected allergic reaction to the lemonade and was rushed to the hospital, where he recovered.

**1.	What rights does Margaret have against Dennis? Explain.**

**2.	What rights does Dennis have against Margaret? Explain.**

ANSWER TO QUESTION 1

1.	***Margaret's rights against Dennis:*** Margaret may be able to recover against Dennis for assault by means of the squirt gun.

The issue is whether Dennis's act of threatening Margaret with the squirt gun placed Margaret in apprehension of imminent harmful or offensive contact. An assault is an affirmative act by the defendant with the intent to place the plaintiff in apprehension of an imminent harmful or offensive contact to his person and that actually causes the plaintiff apprehension. Children of the ages of Dennis and Margaret are deemed to be capable of forming the intent for assault and other intentional torts; in fact, in the well-known case of *Garrett v. Dailey,* a five-year-old boy was held potentially liable for battery. The plaintiff need not be placed in fear of the contact; an apprehension of contact that is offensive (*i.e.,* not consented to) is sufficient. Furthermore, the apparent ability to inflict the contact is all that is needed; the fact that it could not be carried out is irrelevant.

Here, while Margaret claimed (probably truthfully) that she was not afraid of the squirt gun, she was put in apprehension of imminent offensive contact, namely the squirts of water. And the fact that Dennis knew that the squirt gun was unloaded does not affect his liability, because Margaret apparently was not aware of that fact; hence, Dennis had the apparent ability to inflict the contact. Dennis's actions also show that he intended to cause Margaret to believe that she was going to get squirted, thus satisfying the intent requirement and completing the prima facie case for assault.

Regarding Dennis's earlier conduct, he is probably not liable for assault for threatening to throw an apple at Margaret. The issue is whether Dennis's threats created apprehension of imminent contact. The act requirement is generally not satisfied by words alone—there usually has to be some volitional movement of the body for there to be a reasonable apprehension of imminent contact. Here, Dennis's mere verbal threat, apparently without any other action, would fail to satisfy that requirement. In the absence of additional facts, Dennis would not be liable for assault for his threat to throw an apple.

Nor is Dennis liable for intentional infliction of emotional distress. The issue is whether his conduct rises to the level of outrageous conduct required for this tort. Intentional infliction of emotional distress requires that the defendant act in an extreme and outrageous manner with the intent to cause extreme emotional distress (or recklessness as to the effect of the act) and that the victim actually suffers extreme emotional distress. Here, it is questionable whether in any setting threatening to throw an apple or pointing a water pistol at someone, as Dennis did, could be characterized as extreme and outrageous, but in the context of children playing it would be even less likely to be characterized this way. Current societal standards would probably not label this relatively brief interaction among children of almost equal age to be outrageous. Moreover, there is no evidence that Margaret suffered the requisite extreme mental distress from the allegedly outrageous conduct of Dennis. Consequently, this element of the tort remains unsatisfied as well.

2.   ***Dennis's rights against Margaret:*** Dennis will not be able to recover against Margaret for any tort.

It is unlikely that Margaret will be liable for assault for throwing the apple at Dennis. The issue again is whether the conduct here created an apprehension of imminent contact. Because Dennis apparently did not see the apple thrown at him, he probably did not suffer the requisite apprehension of imminent harmful or offensive contact. However, if Dennis was otherwise aware of Margaret throwing the apple (such as by hearing it being thrown or seeing it out of the corner of his eye), Margaret would be liable for assault because she had the requisite intent. Under the doctrine of transferred intent, the intent to inflict a battery satisfies the intent requirement for assault, and here Margaret did have the intent to commit a battery. Because there is no evidence of apprehension on Dennis's part, however, Margaret is not liable for assault.

Margaret is not liable for battery for serving Dennis lemonade. The issue is whether Margaret had the intent for battery. A battery occurs when the defendant commits an affirmative act against the plaintiff with the intent to bring about a harmful or offensive contact and that actually causes such a contact. Here, Margaret has committed an act by giving Dennis the lemonade and the act caused Dennis harmful or offensive contact (the allergic reaction), but the required intent is lacking. There is no indication that Margaret knew that Dennis would have that reaction; rather, the facts indicate that she wanted to make up with Dennis by offering him the lemonade. Thus, she did not have the intent to cause harmful or offensive contact.

Margaret is also not liable for intentional infliction of mental distress. As with Dennis, the issue is whether Margaret's conduct rises to the level of outrageous conduct required for this tort. Here, it is doubtful whether throwing an apple at someone, as Margaret did, could be characterized as extreme and outrageous in the context of children interacting. Nor is there is evidence that Dennis suffered the requisite extreme mental distress from the allegedly outrageous conduct of Margaret. Consequently, this element of the tort remains unsatisfied as well.

QUESTION 2

Agency, licensed with the state, provides in-home care to ill or elderly patients. Agency states in its promotional literature that all of its employees undergo a thorough background check. In fact, due to the expense of such investigation and a high rate of turnover among employees, Agency actually makes no attempt to discover whether applicants for employment have a criminal record.

Jane applied for work at Agency and supplied a resume for review. The resume indicated a five-year gap in Jane's employment history. The application form inquired as to whether the applicant had ever been convicted of a crime. Jane left that part of the application blank. However, Agency needed someone right away and did not press for any explanation of the discrepancy. The lengthy period of unemployment was in fact due to Jane's incarceration for burglary and aggravated sexual battery. Jane was a registered sex offender and was listed on the state's Bureau of Investigation's web page. A few days after Jane became employed, Agency received a written notification from the state's Department of Corrections that stated Jane's sex offender status. An office clerk at Agency simply put the notice in Jane's file without reading it or reporting its contents to management.

Agency sent Jane to work in the home of Mary, who was elderly and in poor health. Jane almost immediately began stealing valuable items from Mary's home and pawned them for cash. When Mary and her son noticed items missing from the house, they contacted Agency. Agency's owner told Mary that it was not possible that Jane was responsible because there had been a careful background check and Jane had never been in any legal trouble.

Jane eventually assaulted Mary, stole her checkbook and credit cards, and went on a spending spree. When this was discovered, Mary sued Agency.

What are Mary's rights against Agency? Discuss.

ANSWER TO QUESTION 2

Mary can recover against Agency for its negligent hiring and retention of Jane, and for intentional misrepresentation. The issues at trial will be whether an employer is directly liable for the intentional tortious conduct of its employee and whether an employer is liable for intentional misrepresentations regarding its employee.

An employer may be liable to victims of tortious conduct committed by employees either under vicarious liability principles or due to the employer's own negligence in hiring, supervising, or retaining the employee. To find liability under vicarious liability (respondeat superior), a plaintiff must show that the tortious conduct by the employee was committed within the scope of the employment relationship. Intentional torts by employees will be deemed to be outside the scope of employment unless (i) force is authorized in the employment, (ii) friction is generated by the employment, or (iii) the employee is furthering the business of the employer.

To find liability under negligent hiring, supervision, or retention of an employee, a plaintiff must establish the elements of a negligence cause of action: (i) the employer owed a duty of care to the plaintiff, (ii) the employer breached that duty, (iii) the breach was the actual and proximate cause of the harm, and (iv) the plaintiff suffered damages as a result.

Here, Jane's intentional torts were not authorized, were not the result of friction, and were not furthering Agency's business. They were outside the scope of the employment relationship, so Agency will not be vicariously liable for those torts.

However, the facts clearly establish a breach of Agency's duty that it owed directly to Mary. Agency owed its homebound customers, such as Mary, a duty of care in the hiring, supervision, and retention of employees that it sent into their homes.

Agency failed to conduct a background check on Jane, failed to investigate a five-year gap in her employment history, failed to take action when its employee received notice of Jane's sex offender status, and failed to investigate Jane after Agency's owner received complaints about missing items in Mary's house.

Agency's conduct was an actual cause of the harm subsequently inflicted on Mary by Jane, because it would not have occurred but for Agency's failure to take action. The conduct was also a proximate cause of the harm, because Mary's intentional tortious conduct was not only foreseeable but also the precise type of employee conduct that Agency had a duty to try to prevent through careful hiring and supervision. Mary suffered physical and monetary damages, for which Agency can be found liable.

Agency may also be liable to Mary for intentional misrepresentation (fraud). The following elements must be shown: (i) misrepresentation made by the defendant, (ii) scienter, (iii) an intent to induce plaintiff's reliance on the misrepresentation, (iv) causation, (v) justifiable reliance, and (vi) damages.

Here, Agency's promotional literature and its owner's statements about Jane constituted misrepresentations made with knowledge that they were false. The misrepresentations in its promotional literature were made to induce customers such as Mary to use Agency's services, and its owner's misrepresentations were made to induce Mary to keep using Jane's services. Mary likely can show that the misrepresentations were a substantial factor in causing her to hire Agency and to retain Jane, and Mary was justified in relying on these factual representations. Therefore, Mary can recover all of her actual pecuniary loss as a result of her reliance on the misrepresentations.

QUESTION 3

Don, as a subscriber, received a printed credit report from Credit Co. ("Credit") stating that Paula, an employee of Don, had over the past year written three checks that were returned for insufficient funds. This statement was incorrect, because Credit had confused Paula with another person of the same name.

Thereafter, Don called Paula into his office and told her that he was firing her. When Paula asked why she was being fired, Don replied, "Because you write bad checks." Paula strenuously denied ever writing bad checks, but Don refused to reconsider his decision.

Paula then sought employment with another employer. This prospective employer called Don and asked why she had been let go, and Don relayed the statement he had received from Credit. The prospective employer then declined to hire Paula.

1. **What rights does Paula have against Credit? Explain.**

2. **What rights does Paula have against Don? Explain.**

ANSWER TO QUESTION 3

1. ***Paula v. Credit:*** Paula may have a claim of defamation against Credit, but will probably not be successful because Credit can defend that it had a qualified privilege to issue the report. The

issues are whether Credit, by way of its inaccurate credit statement, defamed Paula and whether it was privileged to make its statement.

A defamation case is established if there is a publication to a third person of a statement understood as defamatory of the plaintiff that causes damage to the plaintiff's reputation. The type of damage the plaintiff must prove depends on whether the defamation constitutes libel or slander. Libel is the written or printed publication of defamatory language wherein the plaintiff does not need to prove special damages and general damages are presumed. Slander is spoken defamation wherein the plaintiff must prove special (*i.e.*, pecuniary) damages unless the defamation falls within a slander per se category.

When the defamation involves a public figure and a matter of public concern, the plaintiff must prove, in addition to the common law elements, the falsity of the statements as well as malice (knowledge of falsity or reckless disregard of truth) on the part of the defendant. When the defamation involves a private person but a matter of public concern, the plaintiff must prove at least negligence and actual injury, in addition to falsity and the common law elements.

Here, Paula does not appear to be a public figure, and a credit report by a credit reporting agency to a subscriber has been held to be speech solely in the private interest of the speaker and his audience rather than speech on a matter of public concern. [*See* Dun & Bradstreet, Inc. v. Greenmoss Builders, Inc.] Even if it were a matter of public concern, it appears that Credit may have acted negligently by mixing up the names and Paula certainly suffered actual injury from the false statement because she lost her job.

The common law elements for defamation are present here. Credit submitted a printed statement to Don incorrectly stating that Paula had bounced three checks, and its statement led to Paula's losing her job. The statement was damaging to Paula's reputation, establishing the common law elements of defamation by libel, for which damages usually will be presumed.

Paula can also establish the elements of defamation against Credit for Don's repetition of the statement to the prospective employer, because republication by another party was reasonably foreseeable. The repetition is deemed to be libel, even though it was oral, because the original statement was libel.

In any case, however, Credit can claim that it has a common law qualified (also called "conditional") privilege to report information that the recipient has a legitimate interest in obtaining. Such a privilege exists when the potential speaker needs to be encouraged to speak; *i.e.*, needs protection from the strict liability that might otherwise inhibit the potential speaker from speaking. A qualified privilege, unlike an absolute privilege, can be lost through bad faith or abuse, shown through a lack of an honest belief in the truth of the statement, malice in the publication, or excessive publication. Here, while the facts do not indicate whether Don had a legitimate interest in obtaining Paula's credit rating, Don was Credit's customer and Paula's employer, not an intermeddler. Thus, Credit probably had a qualified privilege to report to Don, its subscriber. Here, Credit does not appear to have abused its qualified privilege. There is no indication that Credit lacked belief in the truth of its statement, that it acted with malice, or that it published the statement excessively. While Credit may have been negligent, that does not suffice to negate the privilege. Thus, while Paula may file a defamation claim, she probably will not succeed due to Credit's valid defense.

Paula may also file a claim against Credit for a "false light" invasion of her right to privacy, but is again unlikely to succeed. The issues are whether Credit's inaccurate report was published to a reasonable number of third persons and whether Paula will be permitted to bring such an action.

Invasion of privacy based on false light requires publication by the defendant that places the plaintiff in a false light that would be highly offensive to a reasonable person, causation, and damages for injury to reputation, emotional distress, and/or pecuniary harm. For the plaintiff to suffer damages from a "false light" publication, there must be dissemination to a reasonable number of persons, *i.e.*, "publicity." Additionally, if the false light would affect the plaintiff's reputation in the community and an action for defamation might also lie, many states prevent a plaintiff from escaping the restrictions of defamation law simply by calling the action one for privacy, and some states do not recognize the tort at all because of its close relation to defamation.

Here, Credit informed Don through printed publication that Paula had bounced three checks, which she had not actually done. Such misinformation would be highly offensive to a reasonable person, and it caused her to lose her job as well as a prospective job. However, Credit only published the information to one person, Don, and it was only republished to one additional person by Don. That is not likely to suffice as dissemination to a reasonable number of persons for purposes of this tort. Also, in states allowing for this tort, Paula probably will be unable to succeed because she can bring a defamation action and would not be permitted to circumvent Credit's qualified privilege defense for defamation simply by filing a false light claim. Thus, while Paula may file a false light claim, she is unlikely to succeed.

2. ***Paula v. Don:*** Paula can bring a defamation action against Don, but her chance of prevailing is doubtful. The issue is whether Don can claim a qualified privilege for the statement he made to the prospective employer.

As discussed above, the statement from Credit that Don repeated was defamatory. One who repeats a defamatory statement will be held liable on the same general basis as a primary publisher, even if the republisher states the source or makes it clear that he does not believe the defamation. However, the same qualified privileges apply to the republisher, including the privilege to report information that the recipient has a legitimate interest in obtaining. Where no relationship exists between the provider and the recipient, the privilege applies if the defamation was made in response to a request for the information by the recipient, rather than volunteered by the provider. As noted previously, the privilege can be lost due to, among other things, a lack of an honest belief in the truth of the statement.

Here, Don repeated Credit's defamatory statement to the prospective employer. Even though he may have identified the source of the statement, and even if he also relayed Paula's denial (although not indicated by the facts), he still has made a defamatory statement. Although Don had no relationship with the prospective employer, he can claim a qualified privilege because he provided the information in response to a request by the prospective employer. Paula would argue that the privilege is unavailable because he could not have honestly believed the truth of the statement after her strenuous denials, but nothing in the facts suggests that Don doubted the accuracy of Credit's report. Hence, while Paula may pursue a defamation claim against Don, she does not have a strong chance of prevailing.

QUESTION 4

Jane Walker, in a hurry to get to the bank before it closed, stepped into the street in the middle of the block and did not notice a bicycle messenger bearing down on her. Wayne Duke, who did not know Jane, was walking in the other direction on the sidewalk and saw

the bike approaching. He immediately reached out and yanked Jane back onto the sidewalk. Jane tripped on the curb and landed hard on her knee, cutting it open and causing it to bleed profusely. Wayne immediately called 911 from his cell phone and gave her first aid.

Paramedics arrived and Jane was transported to the county hospital. She received prompt treatment for her wound, including stitches, in the emergency room of the hospital. However, because a surgical instrument used in her treatment had been negligently sterilized and because she had been taking medicine that weakened her immune system, her wound became infected and painful. She had to return to the hospital for several days and required lengthy medical treatment to recover.

Jane has engaged your law firm to represent her. Assume that the hospital and its employees are immune from liability.

What are Jane's rights against Wayne? Explain.

ANSWER TO QUESTION 4

Jane may bring a battery action and a negligence action against Wayne. If the trier of fact determines that Wayne acted unreasonably by using excessive force, Jane will be able to recover from him most, if not all, of her damages for the harm she suffered from this incident.

Battery
To establish battery, the plaintiff must prove the following elements: (i) an act by the defendant that brings about a harmful or offensive contact to the plaintiff's person; (ii) intent on the part of the defendant to bring about harmful or offensive contact to the plaintiff's person; and (iii) causation. The defendant need not intend the injury; all that is necessary is that the defendant intend to bring about a harmful or offensive contact. The defendant is liable not only when he directly causes harmful or offensive contact, but also when he sets in motion a force that brings about the harmful or offensive contact.

Here, Wayne intentionally yanked Jane back onto the sidewalk, which caused her to trip and land on her knee, injuring it. This satisfies the act and causation elements of battery. However, the requisite intent may be absent here. Wayne clearly did not intend to cause a harmful contact to Jane—he was attempting to prevent harm to her by pulling her away from the bicycle bearing down on her. Whether he intended to cause an offensive contact is a closer question. Offensive contact is contact that offends a reasonable person's sense of personal dignity; however, contact will not be deemed offensive if the plaintiff has either expressly or impliedly consented to it. Whether the defense of implied consent applies here will need to be determined by the trier of fact, as discussed below.

A defendant is not liable for an otherwise tortious act if the plaintiff consented to the defendant's act. In addition to express consent, consent may be inferred as a matter of usage and custom (*e.g.*, minor bumping in a crowd) or implied by law (*e.g.*, in an emergency situation where there is no opportunity to obtain the plaintiff's consent), on the theory that a reasonable person would consent to such contact. However, the defendant may be liable if he exceeds the scope of the consent implied by the occasion, such as by using unreasonable force.

Here, Wayne could argue that consent should be implied because he had to act immediately to prevent Jane from getting hit, and there was no time to get her consent. Jane would argue that she would not have consented to the force that Wayne used, which exceeded the degree of force that was reasonable under the circumstances, and that Wayne at least should have been prepared to keep her from falling when he yanked her back. If the trier of fact determines that Wayne acted reasonably, Jane will be deemed to have impliedly consented to his contact and he will not be liable for battery. If Wayne is determined to have exceeded the scope of any implied consent, he will have intentionally committed an offensive contact and be liable for battery.

If Wayne is liable for battery, Jane's recovery would include both economic and noneconomic damages, including damages from the subsequent negligence of the hospital.

Negligence

To establish a prima facie case for negligence, the plaintiff must prove (i) the existence of a duty on the defendant's part to conform to a specific standard of conduct for the protection of the plaintiff against unreasonable risk of injury, (ii) a breach of that duty by the defendant, (iii) that the breach of duty was the actual and proximate cause of the plaintiff's injury, and (iv) damage to the plaintiff's person or property.

While a general duty of care is imposed on all human activity, the general rule is that no legal duty is imposed on any person to affirmatively act for the benefit of others. However, one who gratuitously acts for the benefit of another, although under no duty to do so in the first instance, is then under a duty to act as a prudent and reasonable person. The existence of an emergency will be one of the factors taken into account when evaluating whether the defendant acted reasonably.

Here, although Wayne was under no duty to protect Jane, a stranger, from the possible collision, once he undertook to do so by pulling her back, he owed her a duty to do so with care under the exigent circumstances. If the trier of fact determines that he acted as a reasonable person exercising ordinary care when he grabbed Jane, he will not be liable for negligence. If the trier of fact determines that he used less care than a person of reasonable prudence would have used, such as by using excessive force or failing to warn or catch Jane, he will have breached his duty to Jane.

Proof of actual cause typically requires the plaintiff to show that he would not have been injured but for the defendant's act, while proximate cause imposes limits on the defendant's liability for unforeseeable or unusual occurrences or consequences following the defendant's act. In an indirect cause case, an intervening force comes into motion after the time of the defendant's negligent act and combines with it to cause the injury to the plaintiff. If the defendant's negligence created a foreseeable risk that an intervening force would contribute to the plaintiff's harm, the defendant is liable for the harm caused. Furthermore, the fact that the extent or severity of the harm was not foreseeable does not relieve the defendant of liability; *i.e.*, the tortfeasor takes his victim as he finds him.

QUESTION 5

Motorist was driving a new car on a highway when he noticed that the car's turn signals were not working. Believing that this was unsafe, Motorist pulled over to the side of the road to see if he could get the signals to work. While Motorist was in his car, parked at the side of the road, a vehicle operated by Napper collided with Motorist's car, injuring Motorist.

Motorist's injuries required a lengthy period of treatment and convalescence. Later, Motorist became depressed because his injuries prevented him from pursuing activities he had previously enjoyed. This depression led Motorist to commit suicide.

The turn signals on Motorist's car did not work because a wire had become disconnected. The connections used were typical of those used by manufacturers of new cars at the time the car was produced. Their failure rate was very low. Recently, however, better wiring systems have been invented that reduce the risks of disconnection by about 80%. Using the newer systems would add about $10 to the cost of a typical automobile.

Napper had fallen asleep at the wheel just before the collision. He had fallen asleep because he had been driving for 19 consecutive hours in an effort to reach a certain city in time for an important business appointment.

1. What rights does Motorist's estate have against Napper? Discuss.

2. What rights does Motorist's estate have against the car manufacturer? Discuss.

ANSWER TO QUESTION 5

1. *Motorist's estate v. Napper:* Napper is likely to be liable for Motorist's injuries and death.

A prima facie case for negligence requires (i) the existence of a duty to conform to a specific standard of conduct in order to protect the plaintiff against an unreasonable risk of injury; (ii) breach of that duty by the defendant; (iii) the breach of duty constituted the actual and proximate cause of the plaintiff's injury; and (iv) damage to the plaintiff's person or property. Each person owes a duty to behave as a reasonable person would under the same or similar circumstances. Hence, a duty is owed to anyone to whom a reasonable person would have foreseen a risk of harm under the circumstances.

Here, there is no real issue regarding Napper's duty and breach. Napper owed a duty to anyone who might be on or near the road to drive carefully. He breached that duty by driving for 19 consecutive hours, because driving for such a long period without a break makes falling asleep at the wheel likely; a reasonable, prudent person would not have set up a situation in which he was likely to fall asleep at the wheel.

Neither is there much of an issue as to whether Napper's act was the actual cause of Motorist's injuries. An act will be considered an actual cause (cause in fact) of an injury if, but for the defendant's act, the injury would not have occurred. Here, but for Napper's falling asleep at the wheel, Motorist would not have been injured, would not have become depressed by the limitations on activities caused by his injuries, and would not have committed suicide.

It is questionable whether Napper's act will be considered the proximate cause of Motorist's suicide. An act will be considered the proximate cause of an injury if the injury was a foreseeable consequence of the act. This is really a policy determination; the court determines whether it would be unfair to hold the defendant legally responsible for the plaintiff's injury. Such questions can be split into a few categories: a foreseeable result can occur in an unforeseeable manner; a foreseeable plaintiff can receive unexpected ("unforeseeable") injuries; or an unforeseeable plaintiff can receive the type of injuries that were the foreseeable result of the plaintiff's act. Such cases can also be categorized by whether an outside force intervened between the defendant's negligent act and the plaintiff's injury. If an outside force did not intervene, the case is said to be a direct cause case; if an outside force did intervene, the case is said to be an indirect cause case. Generally, in both direct and indirect cause cases, a defendant will be found liable if the resulting injury was foreseeable, although there are a few exceptions.

Here, there is no problem establishing proximate cause for Motorist's initial injuries from the collision with Napper; Napper's falling asleep at the wheel and hitting Motorist's car was the direct cause of Motorist's physical injuries and there were no intervening causes. Napper may not successfully argue that the faulty turn signals were an intervening cause, because contributing factors that are already in operation when the defendant acts are not intervening. Further, proximate cause is also present for Motorist's depression that resulted from his injuries, because such a reaction is a foreseeable result of serious physical injuries. However, Motorist's suicide may be treated differently. Unless the decedent was driven insane and the suicide was the product of his insanity, the act of suicide is generally considered to be an independent, superseding cause that cuts off the defendant's liability, even though it was prompted by depression from the decedent's injuries.

The final element, damages, is present here. A plaintiff in a negligence action is to be compensated for all his damage (past, present, and future), including medical expenses, lost earnings, pain and suffering, impaired future earning capacity, and property damage. Survival statutes preserve the right to recover these damages after the death of the victim. Hence, Motorist's estate can recover damages for Motorist's medical expenses, pain and suffering, and depression prior to his death. (Note also that if the court were to find that Napper's negligence was a proximate cause of Motorist's suicide, Motorist's survivors might have a wrongful death action against Napper for their own pecuniary loss.)

Lastly, there is no evidence that Motorist acted unreasonably when he parked at the side of the road, thus precluding any contributory negligence defense.

2. ***Motorist's estate v. the car manufacturer:*** The car manufacturer is not likely to be liable for Motorist's injuries. The two main issues are whether Motorist's car was defectively designed and whether the faulty turn signals would be considered the proximate cause of Motorist's injuries.

Because the car manufacturer is a commercial supplier of the product that allegedly was defective, Motorist's estate may bring a strict liability action against the manufacturer. A strict liability action based on supplying a defective product requires proof of duty, breach, actual and proximate cause, and damages. The duty is owed by any commercial supplier of a product. Breach of duty requires proof that the product sold was in a defective condition unreasonably dangerous to users. In a case of defective design, the prevailing "feasible alternative" test provides that the product is defective if the defendant could have removed the danger without serious adverse impact on the product's utility or price.

Here, the car manufacturer had a duty to design and build cars that were not in a defective condition unreasonably dangerous to users. The question is whether producing cars with wire connectors that had a very low failure rate breached that duty. Motorist's estate would argue that the duty was breached because, subsequent to his car's manufacture, better connectors have been invented that add only $10 to the cost of a typical automobile. However, whether an alternative design was feasible is determined in light of the conditions that existed at the time the product was designed and built. The fact that improvements in the state of the art occur after a product is manufactured is not proof that the product was defectively designed in the context of knowledge and technology available at the time of manufacture. The car manufacturer will argue that the turn signals were not defective because at the time of manufacture there was no feasible alternative to the wiring that was used. While the safer wiring systems would have cost only $10, the facts indicate that they had not been invented at the time the car was manufactured.

Even assuming that the car was defectively designed and breach of duty is established, causation would still be an issue. While, as discussed above, the faulty turn signals would be considered a "but for" cause of Motorist's injuries, it is questionable whether they would be considered a proximate cause. The foreseeable risk introduced by defective design of a car's turn signals is that a collision will take place when the operator of the car turns or changes lanes and another driver who has no warning of that movement drives his vehicle into the turning or lane-changing vehicle. Here, Motorist's injuries were the result of Motorist parking his car on the side of the road to investigate why his turn signal was not working, and Napper's falling asleep at the wheel was an intervening cause. On the other hand, Motorist's estate would argue that parking on the side of the road was a foreseeable response to the turn signal problem, and being struck by a negligent driver is a foreseeable intervening cause. Ultimately the trier of fact would need to decide the proximate cause issue.

QUESTION 6

See Constitutional Law Question 6 for Torts issues.

QUESTION 7

Last month, Paul attended a fund-raising lunch at Library, where he purchased and ate a chicken salad sandwich. Later that day, he became severely ill and was diagnosed with food poisoning. As a result of the food poisoning, Paul developed a permanent digestive disorder.

Several other people also became sick after eating at the lunch, and the Health Department determined that the chicken salad was contaminated with salmonella bacteria. According to the Health Department, raw chicken often contains salmonella bacteria. Although the risk of salmonella contamination cannot be eliminated, proper preparation and cooking can ensure that the chicken is safe for eating. The chicken must be thoroughly cooked, and all utensils or surfaces that come in contact with raw chicken must be thoroughly cleaned with hot water and soap before further use.

The Reading Club had initiated and planned the Library's first and only fund-raising lunch. Ann, Bill, and Chuck independently volunteered to make the chicken salad. Each made a separate batch of salad, using their own recipes and working individually at their own homes. Another volunteer combined the three batches of salad at Library, and a Library employee sold sandwiches at the lunch. All lunch profits went to Library.

Ann, Bill, and Chuck each purchased their chicken from Supermarket. The chicken was contained in packages labeled with a prominent warning describing the risk of salmonella contamination and the precautions necessary to avoid that risk.

A Health Department spokesperson has said that "Someone who made the chicken salad did not take proper precautions." Ann, Bill, and Chuck all claim they took the proper precautions.

Paul has consulted an attorney about bringing a tort action against: (1) Library, (2) Supermarket, and (3) Ann, Bill, and Chuck. If Paul can prove only the facts outlined above:

1.   Can Library be found liable to Paul under a strict liability theory? Explain.

2.   Can Supermarket be found liable to Paul under a strict liability theory? Explain.

3.   Can Ann, Bill, and Chuck be found liable to Paul under either a strict liability or negligence theory? Explain.

ANSWER TO QUESTION 7

1.   Library cannot be found liable to Paul under a strict liability theory.

Products liability is the only strict liability theory that Paul could raise here. The prima facie case requires (i) a strict duty owed by a commercial supplier, (ii) breach of that duty by supplying a defective product unreasonably dangerous to users, (iii) actual and proximate cause, and (iv) damages. While Paul can argue that Library supplied a dangerously defective product that caused him injury, he cannot show that Library owed him a strict duty as a commercial supplier. The defendant must be a commercial supplier of the product in question to impose strict liability. A casual seller will not be strictly liable. Here, Library was selling the sandwiches for a one-time-only fundraising lunch; hence, it was a casual seller of the defective chicken salad rather than a commercial supplier, and will not be strictly liable to Paul.

2.   Supermarket probably will not be strictly liable to Paul.

Applying the products liability elements discussed above, Supermarket is a commercial supplier that owes a strict duty not to supply a product that is in a defective condition unreasonably dangerous to users. However, the test for whether a food product is dangerously defective is the same as for a manufacturing defect: the product must be dangerous beyond the expectation of a reasonable consumer. Here, raw chicken often contains salmonella bacteria, which realistically cannot be eliminated prior to purchase. The chicken was sold in packages labeled with a prominent warning describing the risk of salmonella contamination and the precautions necessary to avoid those risks. Hence, a court is likely to find that a reasonable consumer is aware of the danger and knows that it can be eliminated through proper preparation and thorough cooking, and that therefore the chicken sold by Supermarket was not dangerous beyond the expectation of the ordinary consumer.

In the event that the court finds that selling the contaminated chicken *is* a breach of Supermarket's duty, Paul can establish actual and proximate cause and damages to complete his prima facie case. Supermarket might raise a proximate cause argument that the failure of one of the volunteers to properly prepare the chicken is a superseding cause that cuts off its liability. However, a court is likely to characterize the improper preparation as ordinary foreseeable negligence that would not cut off Supermarket's strict liability to Paul.

3.   Ann, Bill, and Chuck ("the volunteers") are not likely to be found liable to Paul under either a strict liability theory or a negligence theory.

The volunteers are not strictly liable to Paul because they are not commercial suppliers of the sandwiches under the product liability rules discussed above.

The volunteer who improperly cooked the chicken is liable for negligence, but Paul is unlikely to prove his case. The elements of the prima facie case for negligence are (i) a duty owed to the plaintiff, (ii) breach of that duty, (iii) actual and proximate cause, and (iv) damages. Here, the volunteers owed a duty of care to anyone consuming the chicken salad. Based on the Health Department findings, at least one of them breached that duty by improperly preparing or cooking the chicken. That breach of duty caused Paul to suffer food poisoning and permanent digestive injuries. However, Paul probably cannot establish his case against any volunteer because he cannot show which of them breached the duty of care.

Res ipsa loquitur does not apply because more than one person supplied the chicken salad. The res ipsa loquitur doctrine enables a plaintiff to establish breach of duty just from the fact that an injury occurred that would not ordinarily occur unless someone was negligent. However, the plaintiff must establish evidence connecting a particular defendant with the negligence to support a finding of liability against that defendant. When more than one person was in control of the instrumentality that caused the injury, such as here, res ipsa loquitur generally may not be used. The doctrine sometimes has been applied to multiple parties involved in a joint venture, but that does not apply in this case. Each person volunteered independently to make the chicken salad, and each of them worked individually with their own recipes in their own homes, and another person combined the three batches of chicken salad.

Nor can Paul shift his burden to prove actual cause onto the volunteers to prove that they did *not* cause the injury. The alternative causes approach of *Summers v. Tice* applies when two or more persons have been negligent but it cannot be determined which one caused the plaintiff's injury. The court will shift the burden of proof to each of the negligent defendants to show that his negligence was not the actual cause of the injury. Here, however, there is no evidence that all of the volunteers were negligent, so they will not be required to prove that they did not cause Paul's injury.

Hence, it is unlikely that Paul will be able to establish a prima facie case of negligence against any of the volunteers.

QUESTION 1

Testator transferred property to Trustee to hold in a testamentary spendthrift trust according to the following terms and provisions:

> To pay to, or apply toward the benefit of, Daughter (1) whatever income is necessary to provide for her support and (2) so much of the principal of the trust as Trustee deems advisable in its absolute and unreviewable discretion to provide for Daughter's comfort and happiness. Upon Daughter's death, the trust principal is distributable to Testator's brothers and sisters.

Because of her profound physical and mental disabilities, Daughter resides at Comfort Acres, a long-term care facility, which provides her with all of her support. Daughter must reside at Comfort Acres or a similar facility for the rest of her life.

For the last 15 years, Trustee has paid Comfort Acres $25,000 annually from the trust income to support Daughter. Recently, however, even though the investments were prudent, the trust income has declined to $40,000 annually. In addition, Comfort Acres has advised Trustee that its annual charges will increase to $45,000. Trustee has advised Comfort Acres and Guardian, Daughter's legal guardian, that it will not pay more than $35,000 from the trust income toward Comfort Acres's annual charge. Trustee takes this position for three reasons. First, because Daughter has a life expectancy of approximately 30 years, it is concerned that the trust property will be exhausted by periodic invasions of the principal before she dies. Second, Trustee is concerned over the substantial increase in Comfort Acres's charges which appear out of line with charges Trustee will pay next year from other trusts on behalf of similarly situated beneficiaries who are confined to nursing homes. Third, it is also concerned about its potential liability to Testator's brothers and sisters who are the remaindermen of the trust.

Guardian, on the other hand, believes that Trustee must pay the entire Comfort Acres bill from the income and principal of the trust. Guardian also has told Trustee that if it does not make the full payment to Comfort Acres, Guardian will commence a judicial proceeding to terminate the trust.

1. Can Guardian compel Trustee to distribute trust income in payment of Comfort Acres' annual charge? Explain.

2. Can Guardian compel Trustee to distribute any of the trust principal in payment of Comfort Acres' annual charge? Explain.

3. Can a court revoke the trust upon the unilateral application of Guardian? Explain.

ANSWER TO QUESTION 1

1.   Guardian can probably compel Trustee to distribute trust income in payment of the Comfort Acres's annual charge.

This is a combination support trust and discretionary trust, with the income component set up as a support trust and the principal component set up as a discretionary trust. A support trust is one in which the trustee is **required** to pay or apply so much of the trust as is necessary for the support of the beneficiary. The trustee does not have discretion to refuse to pay bills necessary for the beneficiary's support. Since this trust clearly states that Trustee is to pay "whatever income is necessary to provide for [Daughter's] support," Trustee must pay Comfort Acres, which is supplying Daughter's support, the $40,000 income to apply to its $45,000 bill. Trustee's only possible argument for paying less is that the $45,000 is not a "necessary" expense. Trustee can put forth a good argument based on the large size of the cost increase, the fact that the charge is out of line with similar nursing homes, and the fact that the charge is more than the total income. Thus, Trustee's argument would be that the money is not needed for Daughter's support since she could be supported in a similar facility for a more reasonable sum. Other factors, however, may enter into Guardian's decision to keep Daughter at Comfort Acres (Daughter's long-term relationships with staff, etc.). As long as Daughter remains at Comfort Acres, Trustee will be obligated to pay Comfort Acres for Daughter's support up to the total amount of the income of the trust.

2. Guardian most likely cannot compel Trustee to distribute any of the trust principal in payment of the Comfort Acres' charge.

The principal here is held in a discretionary trust. In a discretionary trust, the trustee is given discretion whether to apply or withhold payment of trust property to the beneficiary. This discretion actually limits the rights of the beneficiary to the amounts the trustee decides to give her. The beneficiary cannot interfere with the exercise of the trustee's discretion unless the trustee abuses her power. What constitutes abuse depends on the extent of discretion conferred on the trustee. Generally, a court will not interfere unless the trustee has acted in bad faith or dishonestly.

In this case, Trustee is given "absolute and unreviewable discretion" to invade the principal for Daughter's comfort and happiness. While a court is more likely to interfere when, as here, the discretionary trust is a support trust, the absolute and **unreviewable** discretion conferred upon the trustee makes court interference unlikely. Moreover, there is no evidence that Trustee abused his power in refusing to invade the corpus of the trust. All three reasons put forth by Trustee for his refusal comport with his fiduciary duties as trustee. Trustee's concern that the trust not be exhausted during Daughter's lifetime and that Comfort Acres' fees are excessive reflects his duty to preserve trust property and make it productive. Trustee has a duty to Daughter to make sure the trust produces income for her support. If the trust is prematurely depleted by excessive charges from Comfort Acres, there will be no income for Daughter's support. Trustee's concern about preserving the trust corpus for the remaindermen is consistent with his duty of loyalty. The trustee's duty of loyalty extends to all beneficiaries equally. Trustee has a duty to Daughter to see that the trust produces income, but Trustee also has a duty to Testator's brothers and sisters to insure that the trust corpus is not depleted. Thus, Trustee did not abuse his discretion in refusing to invade the trust corpus, and Guardian cannot compel him to do so.

3. A court cannot revoke the trust upon the unilateral application of Guardian.

Most jurisdictions permit termination of a trust by its beneficiaries only if all of the beneficiaries consent and the modification will not interfere with a material purpose of the trust. In this case, in addition to Guardian (who represents one beneficiary, Daughter), Testator's brothers and sisters, who are also beneficiaries under the trust, would have to consent to the termination. The first problem is that Testator's brothers and sisters may not all be in being or capable of consent. If Testator's parents are still living, there is always the possibility of an unborn or unascertained sibling. Most states do not permit a guardian to consent to the termination of a trust on behalf of unborn beneficiaries.

Even assuming the brothers and sisters could and would consent, the court would not terminate this trust because to do so would interfere with a material purpose of the trust. The presence of a spendthrift provision precludes termination of a trust because it shows the settlor's purpose and manifests his lack of confidence in the judgment and management ability of the beneficiary. If the settlor were to join in the request for termination, the material purpose will be waived. Here, there is a spendthrift provision and the settlor is dead (this was a testamentary trust) and thus unable to join in the request. Thus, the trust cannot be terminated by the beneficiaries.

A court can terminate a trust prior to the time fixed in the instrument if the trust purposes are accomplished early or the trust purposes become illegal or impossible to carry out. Neither is the case here.

Note that termination of the trust does not seem the appropriate remedy that Guardian should be seeking. Rather, Guardian should be asking the court for relief from the strict interpretation of the trust's terms; *i.e.*, to direct the trustee to deviate from the trust's terms because of changed circumstances. While a court generally cannot, under the doctrine of changed circumstances, change the beneficial rights of the beneficiaries, a court may strain to find an implied power of invasion of the corpus in the trust instrument, particularly if, as here, it can find that support of the income beneficiary was the primary purpose of the trust.

QUESTION 2

Settlor executed a trust instrument entitled "Settlor's Trust" naming Trustee-1 as trustee. Settlor's Trust includes the following terms:

(1)   **All income is payable to Beneficiary for life.**

(2)   **Upon Beneficiary's death, the trust principal is distributable, outright or in further trust, among such of Beneficiary's issue as Beneficiary appoints by Beneficiary's last will but, if Beneficiary fails effectively to exercise the power, the trust property is distributable to Default Taker upon Beneficiary's death.**

(3)   **In order to exercise the power, Beneficiary must make a specific reference to the power of appointment and to the instrument creating the power.**

(4)   **No interest of any individual is assignable or reachable by the individual's creditors.**

When Settlor's Trust was created, Beneficiary had no issue. However, three years later, Beneficiary had a son, Child. During Beneficiary's lifetime, Default Taker signed a deed conveying all of her right, title, and interest in the trust to Assignee.

Beneficiary died last year, leaving a valid will drafted by Beneficiary's attorney. In their discussions leading to the preparation of this will, Beneficiary told the attorney to merge Beneficiary's personal assets and the assets of Settlor's Trust. The last paragraph of Beneficiary's will provides:

> **All the rest, residue, and remainder of my estate, including any property over which I have a power of appointment, I give, devise, bequeath, and appoint to Trustee-2 to hold in further trust to pay the income to Child for life, remainder to such of Child's issue as attain the age of twenty-five.**

Six months ago, the executor of Beneficiary's estate funded this testamentary trust. Trustee-2 then contacted Trustee-1 requesting that the assets of Settlor's Trust also be distributed to Trustee-2 to hold in trust under the terms of Beneficiary's will. Trustee-1 then brought a declaratory judgment action seeking judicial instructions regarding the respective rights of Child, Child's issue, Default Taker, and Assignee in the assets of Settlor's Trust.

1. **Was the language of the last paragraph of Beneficiary's will sufficient to exercise Beneficiary's power of appointment in light of the requirements set forth in Settlor's Trust? Explain.**

2. **If the language of Beneficiary's will was sufficient to exercise Beneficiary's power of appointment, what interests in the principal, if any, were created as a result of that exercise in Child, Child's issue, Default Taker, and Assignee? Explain.**

3. **If the language of Beneficiary's will was not sufficient to exercise Beneficiary's power of appointment, what interests, if any, would Child, Child's issue, Default Taker, and Assignee have in the principal? Explain.**

ANSWER TO QUESTION 2

1. No, the language of the last paragraph of Beneficiary's will is not sufficient to exercise the power of appointment in light of the requirements set forth in Settlor's Trust.

Settlor's Trust created a special testamentary power of appointment with Beneficiary, as donee and Beneficiary's issue as the objects of the power. The trust also included the requirement that Beneficiary's will must make a specific reference to the power and to the instrument creating that power (Settlor's Trust) in order to exercise the power. A residuary clause, by itself, is not sufficient to exercise a power. However, a residuary clause coupled with a blanket exercise clause (*e.g.*, I devise the residue of my estate, ***including any property over which I have a power of appointment . . .***), is generally sufficient to exercise a power of appointment. The only time that such a clause is not sufficient is when, as here, the donor has specified that the appointment must be made by an instrument that specifically refers to the power. In this case, Settlor called for not only a specific reference to the power, but also a specific reference to the Settlor's Trust. Since Beneficiary's will made no such references, the power of appointment was not effectively exercised, and the corpus of the trust passes to Default Taker as the taker in default of appointment. Note that an argument can be made, particularly in jurisdictions that follow the Uniform Probate

Code, that the donee's intent to exercise should control. The usual reason for requiring a specific reference to exercise the power is to avoid exercising it inadvertently. Thus, if extrinsic evidence were to show that Beneficiary intended to exercise the power created by the Settlor's Trust by using the blanket clause (*e.g.*, if it was the only power of appointment Beneficiary had and he inserted the clause after he became the donee of the power), it could be argued that the language in Beneficiary's will should suffice to exercise the power. This is the position taken by the Uniform Probate Code. If the court is persuaded by this argument and assuming that the gifts are otherwise valid, Child would have the income interest for life and Child's issue who attain age 25 would take the remainder.

2. If the language of Beneficiary's will was sufficient to exercise the power, Child has a life estate, Child's issue have nothing, Default Taker or Assignee (*see* below) has a vested remainder.

Under the common law Rule Against Perpetuities, an interest is void if there is any possibility that it may vest more than 21 years after some life in being at the creation of the interest. Here, Beneficiary was granted a special testamentary power of appointment. Under the common law Rule Against Perpetuities, the perpetuities period for an interest created by the exercise of a special or testamentary power begins to run from the ***creation of the power***. In this case, that means that the perpetuities period begins to run from the creation of Settlor's Trust. The interests created by the exercise of the power are thus read back into the instrument creating the power for purposes of determining their validity. Here it is as though Settlor made the following grant: "To Beneficiary for life, then to Child for life, remainder to such of Child's issue as attain the age of 25." Child's life estate is valid because it will vest, if at all, on the death of Beneficiary, who is a life in being. The interest of Child's issue, however, is not valid because it is a contingent interest that might vest beyond the perpetuities period. Child was not even a life in being at the time Settlor's Trust was created and so could not be a measuring life (although even if he were a measuring life, the gift to issue would still violate the Rule). An interest that violates the Rule is stricken, but the rest of the interests created by the instrument are given effect. Thus, Beneficiary's exercise of the power is incomplete in that it effectively grants only a life estate to Child.

Since Settlor's Trust specified Default Taker as the taker in default of appointment, Default Taker will take the remainder interest. Default Taker was in being at the creation of Settlor's Trust; thus, there is no perpetuities problem with respect to his interest. There is however, the issue of his assignment of his interest to Assignee. Settlor's Trust is a spendthrift trust, which means that it provides that each beneficiary is prohibited from transferring his interest voluntarily and that his creditors cannot reach that interest to satisfy their claims. Spendthrift trusts are valid. Default Taker, as a beneficiary of Settlor's Trust, was subject to the spendthrift restriction contained therein, and his assignment of his interest to Assignee violated that restriction. If in contravention of a valid spendthrift provision a beneficiary attempts to assign his trust interest, the assignee cannot enforce the assignment over the beneficiary's later objection; *i.e.*, the purported assignment is revocable. The transfer is not void; as long as it has not been retracted, it operates as authorization for the trustee to transfer the assets to the assignee. Thus, if Default Taker does not revoke his assignment to Assignee, Trustee-2 may pay the principal of the trust to Assignee on Child's death. If Default Taker objects to this distribution at any time prior to the payment, Trustee-2 must give the assets to Default Taker. (In that circumstance, Assignee could pursue a claim against Default Taker for restitution.)

Note that the interests of Child's issue might be valid under perpetuities reform doctrines or statutes, such as wait-and-see, cy pres, or the Statutory Rule Against Perpetuities. Under the wait-and-see approach, interests that in fact vest within the period of a life in being plus 21 years are valid. Thus, any of Child's issue that reach age 25 within 21 years of the death of a measuring life (probably Beneficiary's) plus 21 years would be entitled to the trust property. Similarly, the cy pres doctrine would reform Beneficiary's trust to come within the confines of the perpetuities period. The Uniform Statutory Rule Against Perpetuities also takes a wait-and-see approach, but includes an alternate perpetuities period of 90 years. Thus, under the Uniform Rule, any of Child's issue who reach age 25 within 90 years of the creation of Settlor's Trust will be entitled to the corpus of the trust.

3. If the language of Beneficiary's will is not sufficient to exercise Beneficiary's power of appointment, Child would take nothing, Child's issue would take nothing, and either Default Taker or Assignee would take the corpus of the trust.

If a donee fails to effectively exercise his power of appointment, persons designated as takers in default of appointment take the property. Here, Default Taker was designated by Settlor as the taker in default of appointment. As discussed above, Default Taker assigned his interest despite a valid spendthrift clause. Thus, he can revoke the assignment and require the trustee to pay the corpus to him on Beneficiary's death. If he does not revoke the assignment, Trustee-1 may pay Assignee the corpus of Settlor's Trust.

QUESTION 3

See Wills Question 5 for Trusts issue.

QUESTION 4

See Family Law Question 4 for Trusts issue.

QUESTION 5

In 1980, Smith, a graduate of Education College, created the Smith Trust, naming himself as Trustee. Under the terms of the Smith Trust, all income was to be used to "provide four-year full scholarships for deserving children of Smith Corporation employees to attend Education College." The Smith Trust also provided that "if, for any reason, Education College should cease operations as a four-year college, the trust shall terminate and the trust property shall revert to Smith." Smith reserved the power to revoke and amend this trust. Smith Corporation employs 15,000 people.

In 1994, Testator, also a graduate of Education College, and a resident of Smalltown, executed a will leaving $300,000 to Testator's child, Able. Testator's will also provided:

> My child, Able, has been well provided for, and I do not want to discourage him from becoming a useful and productive citizen by leaving him more. For that reason, and because I have seen firsthand the tremendous benefits that Education College provides to people of diverse backgrounds, I give my residuary estate to the Trustee of the Smith Trust, as the same is amended from time to time, to be held and disposed of as part of the principal of the Smith Trust.

In 1995, Smith amended the terms of the Smith Trust to limit scholarships to "Presbyterian children of Smith Corporation employees," rather than "deserving children of Smith Corporation employees."

Three months later, Smith died intestate survived by only one child, Harry. Bank became successor trustee of the Smith Trust.

On September 1, 1996, Education College closed permanently because of a lack of resources.

One month later, Testator died leaving an estate of $2 million. Able was Testator's only heir.

Harry claims that the Smith Trust terminated upon the closing of Education College and that Harry is entitled to the property Smith transferred to this trust.

Able claims that Testator's residuary bequest to the Trustee of the Smith Trust fails and that Able is entitled to this bequest. As successor trustee, Bank claims that the Smith Trust is entitled to Testator's residuary estate in accordance with the terms of Testator's will. The Smalltown Civic Corporation, a local nonprofit corporation that annually awards $5,000 scholarships to high ranking Smalltown High School graduates, also claims that it is entitled to Testator's residuary estate. It proposes to use the income from the bequest to award additional scholarships to high school graduates of diverse backgrounds.

1.   Is Harry entitled to the property Smith transferred to the Smith Trust? Explain.

2.   To whom should Testator's estate be distributed? Explain.

ANSWER TO QUESTION 5

1.   Harry is entitled to the property Smith transferred to the Smith Trust because Education College closed and Smith did not have a general charitable intent which would allow application of the cy pres doctrine. Thus, the trust res would revert to Smith's estate, per the terms of the trust agreement, and Harry would take as Smith's only heir. The issues presented are whether: (i) Smith Trust is a charitable trust, (ii) Smith Trust failed as a result of the closing of Education College, and (iii) the cy pres doctrine should be applied.

Smith Trust is a charitable trust. Charitable trusts are trusts intended to benefit society. They must be limited to purposes that are considered charitable, such as the advancement of education. A purpose that limits the benefits of a trust to a particular class of the public may be charitable but the class may not be so narrowly defined that it designates only a few individuals upon whom the settlor wishes to confer private benefits. In this case, Smith Trust is a charitable trust because its purpose is the advancement of education, to be achieved by establishing a scholarship program. The benefits of the trust are limited to a particular class of people—as amended, it applied to Presbyterian children of Smith Corporation employees. This class is probably sufficiently broad because Smith Corporation has 15,000 employees and it is likely that a vast number of them would have children that qualified for a Smith Trust scholarship.

Smith Trust failed as a result of the closing of Education College. A trust can terminate on its own terms, such as when the settlor has specified that the trust would end on the happening of a certain event. In this case, Smith expressly provided in the trust instrument that "if, for any reason, Education College should cease operations as a four-year college, the trust shall terminate and the trust property shall revert to Smith." Since Education College ceased to operate as a college altogether, the trust fails on its terms and the res should revert to Smith's estate, with Harry taking as Smith's only heir.

However, this being a charitable trust, one must consider the cy pres doctrine. The cy pres doctrine applies when a specific charitable purpose indicated by the settlor is no longer possible or practical, and the settlor manifested a general charitable intent. In such a case, the court can direct that the trust property be applied to another charitable purpose as close as possible to the original one, rather than permit the trust to fail. Here, Smith does not appear to have a general charitable intent; his intent was very specific—he intended to benefit particular children, namely Presbyterian children of Smith Corporation employees, and only if they attended a particular institution—Education College. Furthermore, Smith's express provision that the trust was to terminate if Education College ceased to operate should preclude application of the cy pres doctrine. Thus, the cy pres doctrine would not apply and Harry will take.

2.   Testator's estate should probably be distributed to the Smalltown Civic Corporation because Testator had a general charitable intent which would allow application of the cy pres doctrine. The issues presented are whether: (i) Testator can validly fund a trust created by someone else, (ii) the devise lapsed because the Smith Trust terminated, and (iii) the cy pres doctrine should be applied.

Testator validly funded the trust created by Smith. A will may validly devise property to a pre-existing trust created either by the testator or another person, even though the trust may be amendable or revocable. Unless the will provides otherwise, the trust will be administered according to the provisions in the trust instrument and will include any amendments made before or after the testator's death. Thus, Testator could validly devise property to fund the Smith Trust, a trust already in existence at the time Testator made the disposition.

Although Testator validly devised property to the Smith Trust, the devise lapsed because the trust failed. If a trust fails before a testator dies, the devise lapses (*i.e.*, it fails for want of a beneficiary). Here, Testator died in 1997; Education College had already closed in 1996, causing Smith Trust to terminate (as discussed above). Thus, Testator's devise lapses.

However, Testator's devise would be saved by the cy pres doctrine. As discussed above, cy pres operates when the charitable purpose indicated by the settlor is no longer possible, and the settlor manifested a general charitable intent. In this case, Testator arguably did have a general charitable intent—supporting the higher education of people from diverse backgrounds. Furthermore, Testator indicated that he wanted his son, Able, to receive only $300,000. If the devise to the trust—Testator's residuary estate—fails, the residue would be disposed of according to the laws of intestacy. This would frustrate Testator's wishes, because Able, as Testator's sole heir, would take Testator's entire estate.

Testator's residuary estate should be given to the Smalltown Civic Corporation. Where a settlor has a general charitable intent, the court should apply the trust property to another charitable purpose that would most closely approximate the general objectives sought by the settlor. Here, Testator's objective was supporting the higher education of people from diverse backgrounds. It is likely that the court would award the property to the Smalltown Civic Corporation, a local nonprofit corporation that already awards scholarships to high ranking high school graduates and promises to use Testator's funds to award more scholarships to high school graduates of diverse backgrounds.

QUESTION 6

Decedent recently died, owning a bank account at First Bank registered in the name of "Decedent in trust for Grandchild." At her death, the balance in this account was $15,000. Decedent had made all the deposits into this account.

Decedent was also a co-owner of an account at Second Bank, registered in the name of "Decedent and Son, as joint tenants with right of survivorship." Only Decedent had made deposits into this account. It had a balance of $20,000 at her death. Decedent had opened this account three years before she died, near the time that she sold the family home and moved into Son's home rather than a nursing home. At the time Decedent opened this account, the Second Bank bank officer told her that "a joint account is an ideal way to let Son draw on the account in case you need to reach the money you have put into it."

Three weeks before she died, Decedent typed a letter to Friend, who lived in another state. The letter said: "I haven't been feeling well lately. I give you my diamond ring to remember me by. It's yours, but Son would be upset if he learned I had given it to you, and so I'll hold on to it for you. When I die, bring this letter to him and get it." Decedent signed and immediately mailed the letter to Friend, who received it the next day. The ring, which was found among Decedent's personal effects, was valued at $5,000.

Decedent died indebted and with only the foregoing assets. Her creditors claim that the two bank accounts and the ring must be used to satisfy their claims against her estate.

Are the two bank accounts and diamond ring available for payment of the creditors' claims? Explain.

ANSWER TO QUESTION 6

The first bank account, "Decedent in trust for Grandchild," is available for payment of the creditors' claims. The second bank account, "Decedent and Son, as joint tenants with right of survivorship," may be available for payment of the creditors' claims, depending on the approach followed by the state. The ring is not available for the payment of the creditors' claims.

The "Decedent in trust for Grandchild" account: This bank account can be reached by Decedent's creditors under the rules applicable to Totten trust accounts. At issue is whether a decedent's creditors can reach the assets of the decedent's bank account held "in trust" for another.

When, as here, a person deposits money in her own bank account "in trust" for another person, a "Totten trust" is created. In a Totten trust, the depositor remains the owner of all funds on deposit during her lifetime and can withdraw them, or revoke the trust entirely, at any time. The transfer to the trust is not completed until the depositor's death; *i.e.*, it is not until the depositor's death that the sum remaining on deposit belongs to the designated beneficiary. Since the depositor has complete control over the deposits during her lifetime, she is treated as the owner insofar as her creditors are concerned. Her creditors can reach the deposits while she is living and can reach them as part of her estate on death. Thus, by designating herself trustee of her bank account for the benefit of Grandchild, Decedent created a Totten trust and her creditors can reach the money in the trust to satisfy their claims against Decedent's estate.

The "Decedent and Son, as joint tenants with right of survivorship" account: Decedent's creditors can reach this bank account in states following the Uniform Probate Code ("U.P.C."), but probably not in other jurisdictions. At issue is whether a decedent's creditors can reach the assets in a bank account held in joint tenancy with right of survivorship.

Generally, if money is deposited into a bank account in the names of two persons "with right of survivorship" and one joint tenant dies, the survivor has the right to all the money in the account, even as against claims of the depositor's creditors. However, under the U.P.C., if a decedent's probate estate is insufficient to pay the claims of creditors, the creditors can reach the funds in the joint account that were deposited by the decedent. Here, the facts indicate that Decedent's estate is insufficient to pay her creditor's claims and that she deposited all of the money in the joint account. Thus, in states following the U.P.C., the creditors of Decedent's estate can access these funds.

In states not following the U.P.C., it is arguable, but not likely, that the same result would be reached. Even though the "right of survivorship" language seems unambiguous, many states permit third parties to bring in extrinsic evidence to show that the deceased depositor did not really intend a gift to the survivor, but rather set up the account as a convenience for paying the depositor's bills. Here, the creditors could bring in the bank officer's explanation to Decedent that the "joint account is an ideal way to let Son draw on the account. . . ." On the other hand, since the joint tenant here was Decedent's son and Decedent was living with him rather than going to a nursing home, it seems just as likely that Decedent would want Son to have any money still in the account when she died. On balance, there does not seem to be enough evidence to uphold the argument that a gift was not intended, so the "survivorship" language should stand and the creditors will not be able to reach this bank account.

The ring: The creditors cannot reach the ring to satisfy their claims. At issue is whether Decedent made a valid inter vivos gift of the ring.

Decedent's letter to Friend cannot be considered a will or codicil because it was not witnessed by two witnesses. This would be the result even in states that recognize holographic (handwritten, signed, but unwitnessed) wills, because the letter was typewritten. Moreover, the letter purported to have a present operative effect: "I [now] give you my diamond ring." An instrument that has any operative effect during the maker's lifetime cannot be a will.

However, Decedent made a valid inter vivos gift of the ring. A gift inter vivos requires three elements: donative intent, delivery, and acceptance. The donor must have the present mental capacity and must intend to make an effective gift of her property. If the donor intends to pass the property to the donee at some future date, the requisite intent is not present and there can be no gift inter vivos. However, the donee may evidence a present intent to make a gift and vest the donee with title, yet reserve the right of possession until some future date. It appears that Decedent did just that—Decedent had the present intention to make a gift of the ring to Friend, but she retained possession of it until a date in the future (some time after she died).

Delivery of a gift can be either actual, constructive, or symbolic. Most courts will allow symbolic delivery (the delivery of a written document evidencing the gift) if the subject matter of the gift cannot be actually delivered. To be sufficient, the writing should manifest the donor's intent, describe the subject matter of the gift, be signed by the donor, and be delivered. Here, symbolic delivery was appropriate because Friend lived in a different state, Decedent was not feeling well, and Decedent delivered a writing to Friend that fulfilled the above requirements—Decedent mailed Friend a signed letter that stated she intended to give Friend her diamond ring.

Acceptance of a gift, when beneficial to the donee, is presumed. However, a donee may refuse to accept a gift by affirmative act. Here, the gift is beneficial to Friend in that it has both market value ($5,000 according to the facts) and sentimental value (it is a gift from a friend), so it is presumed that she accepted the gift. Furthermore, it does not appear that Friend did anything to indicate that she was refusing to accept that gift. Thus, there was acceptance of the gift of the ring and all three elements for a valid gift inter vivos were met. Therefore, the ring was not part of Decedent's estate when she died and so her creditors cannot reach it.

Creditors of Decedent's estate may argue that the gift was not valid because it was a failed attempt at a gift causa mortis. A gift causa mortis is a gift given in contemplation of death. There are four requirements for a gift causa mortis: donative intent, delivery, acceptance, and anticipation of death. The donative intent and acceptance requirements are the same as required for a gift inter vivos. However, the delivery requirement is more stringent. A significant number of states hold that a gift causa mortis cannot be accomplished by symbolic delivery, the kind of delivery that Decedent used to give the ring to Friend. If Decedent intended to make a gift causa mortis of the ring in such a state, the gift would be invalid. The gift would also be an invalid gift causa mortis because the gift must be given in contemplation of imminent death. It is unclear, on the facts, whether Decedent wrote the letter in contemplation of imminent death or whether she was experiencing some general misgivings about the state of her overall health ("I haven't been feeling well lately . . . ."). If Decedent was indeed intending to make a gift causa mortis, the gift would not be valid and the ring would be available for payment of the creditors' claims.

It also should be noted that many states have "exempt property set-aside" statutes, which protect items of tangible personal property in a decedent's estate (up to a specific dollar limit) against creditors' claims. While the particular state's statutes must be consulted, it may be that the ring qualifies as exempt property.

QUESTION 7

Testator owned 50% of the stock of the ABC Corporation. Testator's sister, Sister, owned the other 50% of the stock.

Testator died in 1994. Under the terms of his testamentary trust, funded solely with his ABC stock, all income was payable to Testator's wife, Wife, for her life. Upon Wife's death the trust principal was payable to Child, who was the child of Testator from a prior marriage. Sister was named trustee of this trust.

In 1995, Sister, as trustee, attempted to sell the trust's ABC stock. The best offer she received was from Buyer, who offered her $80,000 for the stock. Buyer also offered Sister $400,000 if Sister would sell Buyer both the trust's ABC stock and Sister's own 50% share of the outstanding ABC stock. Sister declined this offer, preferring to retain her stock in ABC. After three more months, during which time no other offer materialized, Sister bought the ABC stock from the trust for $100,000. This represented a 25% premium over Buyer's offer.

Sister then invested the entire $100,000 held in the trust in 1,000 shares of Lo-Tech, Inc., a publicly traded company, which had a long record of paying steady and high dividends. At a time when other suitable trust investments were yielding a return of 5% per year, Lo-Tech

paid a cash dividend of $8 per share on shares selling for $100 each. Just before Sister bought Lo-Tech stock for the trust, Lo-Tech hit hard times. Nonetheless, it announced that it would continue to pay its usual high dividends, even if share prices would decline as a result. Lo-Tech did so until 1997, and Sister paid all cash dividends to Wife.

In 1997, as Lo-Tech's business continued to slide, Lo-Tech substituted a stock dividend (one tenth of a share for every share owned) for its previous cash dividend. Thereafter, Sister paid all stock dividends to Wife.

In 1998, Sister sold the trust's 1,000 shares of Lo-Tech because of her concerns about Lo-Tech's financial health. She realized only $50,000 as a result of the company's financial slide. Sister invested the $50,000 in a low-risk mutual fund.

Wife has just died.

What fiduciary duties owed to Child did Sister violate and, as to each:

1.   What amount of damages may Child recover; and

2.   What other remedies, if any, are available to Child? Explain.

ANSWER TO QUESTION 7

Sister violated her duty of loyalty owed to Child. A trustee has a duty of loyalty, which requires the trustee to administer the trust property according to the interest of the beneficiaries alone. This duty prohibits the trustee from placing herself in a position in which a conflict of interest may arise. Absent court approval or contrary trust provision, a trustee cannot enter into any transaction in which she is dealing with the trust in her individual capacity. Here, since Sister did not obtain court approval, her purchase of ABC stock from the trust violated her duty of loyalty. Even though Sister paid a 25% premium over Buyer's previous offer, she still breached her fiduciary duty by purchasing the stock.

1.   Child has several remedies: Child can either set aside the transaction, recover the profit made by the trustee (reduced by the losses arising out of the same transaction), or affirm the transaction. It is not clear what amount of damages Child may recover for this breach. The facts show that Sister was offered $400,000 for both her stock and the trust's stock in ABC Corporation. If, after purchasing the trust's stock, Sister proceeded to sell all the ABC stock to Buyer for $400,000, Child could probably recover $100,000 in damages because this represents half the amount offered by Buyer, $200,000, minus the amount Sister paid the trust, $100,000.

2.   If Child elects to set aside the transaction, she will seek to have a constructive trust imposed on the shares of ABC Corporation. A constructive trust is an equitable remedy imposed by a court to prevent unjust enrichment of one person at the expense of another resulting from wrongful conduct. The constructive trustee's sole duty is to convey the property to the person who would have owned it but for the wrongful conduct, permitting the wronged party to receive the very property of which she was deprived. A constructive trust may arise from a breach of a fiduciary duty. Here, Sister breached her duty of loyalty to Child. Therefore, if Sister has not sold the ABC stock to Buyer, Child may recover the shares from Sister under a constructive trust. If

she has sold the shares, Child may recover whatever Sister now has in her possession that is traceable to the proceeds of the sale.

Sister also violated her duty to preserve trust property and make it productive. A trustee has a basic duty to preserve and protect the trust corpus. From this basic duty, there is implied the duty to make the trust property productive, which includes the duty to invest. Under the Uniform Prudent Investor Act ("UPIA"), the trustee must invest and manage trust assets as would a prudent person, taking into account the purposes, terms, distribution requirements, and other circumstances of the trust. In satisfying this standard, the trustee must exercise reasonable care, skill, and caution in making investment decisions. The prudence of each decision is evaluated in the context of the entire trust portfolio and as part of an overall investment strategy rather than on an individual basis. Although historically trustees invested with the goal of generating income for the trust, under the UPIA a prudent investor seeks overall return, not merely income. Other key factors in determining whether an investment is prudent include general economic conditions, the expected total return from income and appreciation of capital, and needs for liquidity.

Investment in Lo-Tech, Inc. was not a prudent investment. Even though Lo-Tech was a publicly traded company which paid regular dividends above market rate, just before Sister purchased Lo-Tech, the company hit hard times and announced that it would continue to pay high dividends even if the share prices would decline as a result. This means Sister knew that even though Wife would enjoy steady income from the stock, the trust corpus would suffer because the value of the stock was probably going to decline. Moreover, even if Lo-Tech was an appropriate investment, it certainly was not prudent for Sister to have invested the entire $100,000 in Lo-Tech stock. She should have diversified the investments so that any decline in the stock value would be offset. Sister is liable to the trust estate for losses resulting from the breach and for any profit that would have accrued to the trust but for the breach. Child may not be able to recover the entire $50,000 loss from Sister because Sister may have been entitled to invest some portion of the trust corpus in Lo-Tech stock. Therefore, Child can recover some percentage of the $50,000 plus interest from the time of breach. In addition, Child can seek to have Sister removed from office.

Sister misallocated dividends when she distributed stock dividends to the income beneficiary under the trust. Cash dividends are treated as income, but dividends payable in the stock of the declaring corporation are allocable to trust principal. Therefore, while it was proper for Sister to pay all cash dividends to Wife, Sister should have paid all stock dividends to Child, not Wife. Child can probably recover damages from the Trustee for this breach, or she may seek to impose a constructive trust on the stock dividends against Wife's estate. It is not clear what amount of damages Child may recover, but it would be based on the value of the stock dividends distributed to Wife. Since Lo-Tech paid stock dividends in 1997 and 1998, at the rate of one-tenth of a share for every share owned, Child could recover the value of 100 shares when Lo-Tech made the 1997 stock dividend distribution and the value of 110 shares when Lo-Tech made the 1998 distribution. In the alternative, Child could seek to have a constructive trust imposed on the 210 shares now held in Wife's estate.

QUESTION 8

Testator bequeathed her residuary estate "to Trustee, as trustee," on the following terms:

> I direct Trustee to distribute the income from the trust to my son, Adam, until he reaches the age of 30. In addition, I authorize Trustee to invade

the principal of the trust if, in its absolute discretion, it deems it necessary to provide for Adam's education. At Adam's 30th birthday, I direct Trustee to terminate the trust and to distribute the trust principal equally between my two children, Adam and Betsy.

When Testator executed her will, her estate was large enough so that her residuary estate would have been valued at $800,000. However, business reverses during the two years between execution of the will and Testator's death reduced the value of the residuary estate to $300,000.

Testator died last year survived by her husband, Husband, by their son, Adam, and by Betsy, Testator's daughter from a prior marriage.

Adam is currently 23 years old, has no assets other than the interest in the trust, and has just entered dental school.

Husband has an annual income of $80,000 and assets of $400,000. Last month, Husband loaned Adam $25,000 to pay tuition at dental school.

The trust income is currently $18,000 per year, which Adam uses to pay for rent and food. Adam now asks Trustee to invade the trust principal to permit Adam to purchase a $50,000 automobile and to repay the $25,000 tuition loan from Husband.

1. Should Trustee invade the trust principal to enable Adam to purchase the automobile? Explain.

2. Can Trustee refuse to invade the trust principal to enable Adam to repay the loan he received from Husband? Explain.

3. If Trustee distributes trust principal to Adam to enable him to purchase the automobile, what are the rights and liabilities of Trustee, Adam, and Betsy? Explain.

ANSWER TO QUESTION 8

1. No, Trustee should not invade the trust principal to enable Adam to purchase the automobile because the trust does not expressly permit such a distribution and, therefore, the distribution would be a breach of trust.

A trustee can properly exercise only such powers as are expressly or impliedly conferred by the terms of the trust or by statute or court order, or those powers necessary or appropriate to carry out the purposes of the trust, if not forbidden by the terms of the trust. Here, the trust terms clearly state Trustee's powers: to pay Adam the income from the trust until he reaches age 30, and then to distribute the principal to Adam and Betsy. Trustee can invade the principal only for Adam's education. Under the terms of the trust, Trustee has no other power to invade.

Adam may argue that he needs the car for transportation to and from school. However, while there may be merit to this argument, Adam obviously does not need such an expensive car for this purpose. Therefore, Trustee should not invade the principal to enable Adam to buy the car.

Adam could also argue that since he will eventually receive the trust principal, Trustee could invade the principal now. However, this would be inconsistent with the express terms of the trust, which limit invasion only for educational expenses. Also, it would jeopardize the interests of the other beneficiary, Betsy, and Trustee owes a duty to protect her interests. For these reasons, Trustee should not invade the principal.

There is no basis for modification of the trust. Most jurisdictions permit a beneficiary to modify or terminate a trust only if all beneficiaries consent and if the modification or termination will not interfere with a material purpose of the trust. If Adam were the sole beneficiary of the trust, a court might authorize Trustee to invade the principal to permit Adam to purchase the car. Here, Adam is not the sole beneficiary and there is no indication that Betsy would agree to modify the trust to allow Trustee to invade the principal for a non-education-related expense, especially because the trust corpus is only $300,000 and Adam is asking for $50,000.

2.   Trustee likely can refuse to invade the trust principal to enable Adam to repay the loan he received from Husband to pay his tuition for dental school. When a testator confers discretion on a trustee to make or withhold distributions, a court will not compel the trustee to exercise that discretion unless the trustee's refusal constitutes an abuse of discretion.

Testator provided a standard by which Trustee's conduct was to be judged. Trustee was to invade the principal as necessary in its *absolute discretion* to provide for Adam's education. Trustee may argue that in declining to invade the principal to repay the loan, it acted reasonably since Adam's educational expenses were met by the loan from his father, and because there was another beneficiary who ultimately would be entitled to share in the trust principal.

On the other hand, Adam may argue that Trustee's refusal to invade the principal to repay the loan is an abuse of discretion. Adam may argue that Testator intended for Adam to receive distributions from the trust for all of his educational expenses, regardless of other possible sources of support.

In conclusion, the facts do not warrant a conclusion that Trustee would be abusing its discretion by refusing to repay the loan for Adam's tuition.

3.   If Trustee wrongfully invades the principal to pay Adam to allow him to purchase the car, Betsy can seek to have Trustee surcharged for breach of trust. When a trustee distributes property in breach of the trust terms, the trustee is liable for the resulting loss to the trust and other beneficiaries. Thus, if Trustee invades the corpus to enable Adam to purchase the $50,000 car, this will violate the specific terms of the trust (*see* 2., above). Also, such action will substantially reduce the principal amount Betsy would receive upon the trust's termination and would constitute a breach of trust. Thus, Trustee will be liable for the loss.

A trustee who overpays a beneficiary may try to recover the overpayment. Thus, Trustee could attempt to recover the money from Adam. If that is not possible, Trustee could subject Adam's interest in the principal to a charge of overpayment. In any event, Trustee is liable if Betsy is not made whole.

Betsy may also seek to have Trustee removed from office. However, that remedy is usually used where the trustee benefits from the breach, which did not occur here.

While ordinarily a beneficiary cannot bring an action against a third party (in this case, Adam), Betsy can sue Adam directly since it could be argued that Adam participated in the breach of trust. Betsy may seek to have a constructive trust imposed upon the funds, requiring Adam to return the funds to the trust. A constructive trust is a remedy to prevent unjust enrichment of one person at the expense of another as the result of wrongful conduct. Even if Adam has already used the trust funds to purchase the car, Betsy may be able to trace the assets and have the car sold to recover the funds.

QUESTION 9

Grantor was wealthy, childless, and unmarried. Grantor created a revocable living trust and transferred assets to Trustee. The trust instrument directed Trustee "to pay the trust income to Grantor for life and, upon her death, to pay the trust income to Grantor's brother, Brother, for his life and, upon his death, to distribute the trust principal to Cousin's children who attain age 21."

Grantor died several years later without having modified or revoked the trust. Grantor was survived by Brother and Cousin.

When Grantor created the trust, Cousin was married to Wife and had a young child, Adam, from that marriage. Shortly after Grantor's death, Cousin and Wife had another child, Ellen. Later, Cousin and Wife divorced, and Cousin married Second Wife. Cousin adopted Second Wife's child, Doris, a minor. Doris presently lives with Cousin and Second Wife.

Brother has recently died, survived by Cousin; Cousin's child, Adam, age 22; and Ellen and Doris, both of whom are under the age of 21.

1. **Does the trust violate the common law Rule Against Perpetuities? Explain.**

2. **Assuming that the trust does not violate the common law Rule Against Perpetuities, are Adam, Ellen, and Doris entitled to a share of the trust principal and when, if at all, would each be entitled to possession of that share? Explain.**

ANSWER TO QUESTION 9

1.   The trust does not violate the Rule Against Perpetuities. Under the Rule Against Perpetuities, an interest is void if there is any possibility that it may vest more than 21 years after some life in being at the creation of the interest. For revocable trusts, the Rule Against Perpetuities period begins to run on the date of the settlor's death. In the instant case, Brother's interest vests upon Grantor's death. Thus, his interest is valid. To determine whether the interests of Adam, Ellen, and Doris are valid, Cousin's life is used as the measuring life, as his is the life connected with the vesting of their interests. The gift to Cousin's children does not violate the Rule because their interests will either vest or fail when Cousin dies or within 21 years thereafter. Thus, the trust does not violate the Rule Against Perpetuities.

2.   Adam takes a share of the trust principal, and Ellen and Doris will each take a share unless they die before attaining age 21. The issues are whether Cousin's children are members of the class and when the class closes for distribution.

In general, a gift to a person's children includes that person's children from all marriages, as well as adopted children. Thus, Adam, Ellen, and Doris are all included in the class. To determine when membership of a class closes, courts apply the rule of convenience. Under the rule of convenience, when there is a gift to a class conditioned upon the members attaining a certain age, the class closes when (i) the preceding estate, if any, terminates, and (ii) the first class member reaches the specified age. That class member's minimum share should be determined and distributed to him at that time. Here, the gift to Cousin's children is conditioned upon their reaching the age of 21. Thus, the class closes when Brother's preceding estate terminates *and* when one of Cousin's children reaches the age of 21. Since Brother's estate terminated when he died and Adam is 22 years old, the class is closed and any children subsequently born to, or adopted by, Cousin will not share in the gift. Adam can demand distribution of his minimum share (one-third). Since the gift of principal was "to Cousin's children who attain age 21," the gift was contingent on reaching that age. Thus, Ellen and Doris will receive their shares only when and if they reach the age of 21. But if, for example, Ellen attains age 21 but Doris dies before reaching that age, Adam's share will increase to one-half and Ellen will take the other one-half.

QUESTION 10

In 1998, Grantor created an irrevocable inter vivos trust naming Bank as trustee. The trust directed the trustee to pay the income to Grantor's child, Son, for life. The instrument further provided that upon Son's death, the trust principal should be distributed in equal shares to Son's surviving children. The trust instrument did not authorize the trustee to invade the trust principal for the benefit of Son.

At the time the trust was created, Son was divorced and was in some financial difficulties. Accordingly, Grantor included the following clause in the trust instrument:

> The interest of any trust beneficiary, whether in the income or principal of the trust, shall not be capable of assignment, anticipation, or seizure by legal process. In particular, none of the trust income shall be used to satisfy any claim against any beneficiary for unpaid alimony or child support.

The trust principal consisted of 500 shares of XYZ Corporation common stock.

Prior to 1996, Son's former spouse, Wife, had obtained a judgment against him for $10,000 for unpaid alimony. In 1997, Creditor had obtained a judgment against Son for $20,000 for money it lent to Son to finance Son's failed business venture. Wife and Creditor seek to enforce their respective judgments against Son's interest in the trust.

In 2000, XYZ Corporation, which typically distributed dividends in cash, paid the trustee a stock dividend of one-tenth of a share of stock for each share the trust owned.

1.   Can Creditor compel Bank to pay its claim against Son from either the trust's income or principal? Explain.

2.   Can Wife compel Bank to pay her claim for unpaid alimony from either the trust's income or principal? Explain.

3. **Can Son be compelled to pay the claims of Wife or Creditor from the trust income that is actually distributed to him from the trust? Explain.**

4. **Should Bank distribute the stock dividend to Son as income or retain the dividend as part of the trust principal? Explain.**

ANSWER TO QUESTION 10

Grantor has created a spendthrift trust in favor of Son. A spendthrift trust is one in which the beneficiary is unable voluntarily or involuntarily to transfer his interest in the trust. He cannot sell or give away his rights to future income or capital, and his creditors are unable to collect or attach such rights. A spendthrift trust is usually created to provide a fund for the maintenance of the beneficiary which will be free from creditors' claims.

1. Creditor cannot compel Bank to pay its claim against Son from either the trust's principal or income. It should first be noted that Son has no interest in the trust's principal—the terms of the trust give Son an interest only in the trust income—so Creditor cannot compel Bank to invade the principal. Generally, a beneficiary's creditors cannot reach the beneficiary's interest in a spend-thrift trust. However, an exception is made for certain types of claims, such as the claims of dependents, the government, and persons supplying necessities. Here, Creditor cannot reach Son's future interests in the trust income because Creditor does not fall into the special class of creditors exempted from the general rule (*e.g.*, it is not a supplier of necessities). Rather, Creditor's claim derives from Son's inability to repay a $20,000 loan due to a failed business venture. Thus, Creditor cannot compel Bank to pay its claim from Son's interest in the trust.

2. Wife can compel Bank to pay her alimony claim against Son from the trust income. As discussed above, a beneficiary's creditors normally cannot reach the beneficiary's interest in a spendthrift trust. However, there are exceptions for certain classes of creditors. Here, Wife falls into the special class of creditors exempted from the general rule—she is a dependent to whom alimony payments are owed. A divorced wife can usually reach her ex-husband's interest to satisfy a claim for alimony. Note, however, that Wife can only compel payment from the trust income because Son has no interest in the principal (*see* above).

3. Son can be compelled to pay the claims of both Wife and Creditor from the trust income that is actually distributed to him. Although creditors cannot reach the beneficiary's income interest in the trust by garnishment or attachment, neither the spendthrift clause nor any other provision applies to the income *after* it has been distributed to the beneficiary. Here, Wife and Creditor may seek payment from any trust income that has already been paid to Son.

4. Bank should retain the stock dividend as part of the trust principal. Generally, cash dividends are allocated to income and stock dividends declared and paid by the corporation are allocated to principal. Here, although XYZ Corporation typically distributed dividends in cash, which would be allocated to income, it paid the trustee a stock dividend, which is allocated to principal.

QUESTION 11

Harry, a widower, and Wanda, residents of State A, decided to marry. Prior to the wedding ceremony, they signed a prenuptial agreement in which Wanda waived her right to receive

alimony in the event of a divorce. The agreement further stated that "in consideration of this waiver, Harry shall establish an inter vivos trust of the first $1 million he inherits from his mother, with himself as trustee to pay the income to Wanda for life." They agreed that Harry was free to designate any person to take the trust property at Wanda's death.

Three years later, Harry's mother died, leaving her substantial estate to him. In addition to Harry, her only surviving relatives were Charles, who is Harry's child from his first marriage, and Mary and Pat, Harry's two nieces.

Two months after his mother died, Harry orally declared himself trustee of $1 million. In making this oral declaration, Harry stated: "I will pay all trust income to my wife, Wanda, for her life and, when she dies, if I don't have any issue who survive me, then I or my successor should distribute the trust principal to my surviving nieces and nephews." Harry did not state who would succeed him as the trustee if he died prior to the termination of trust.

Harry died two months ago at his home in State A. Until his death, he faithfully paid the trust income to Wanda. Harry was survived by Wanda and by Charles, Mary, and Pat. One month after Harry died, Wanda, who had recently inherited substantial property from her father, disclaimed her income interest in the trust property.

Under the laws of State A, Wanda's disclaimer of her interest in the trust property is valid. In addition, under the intestacy laws of State A, any property distributable as part of Harry's probate estate passes one-third to Wanda and two-thirds to Charles.

1. Was Harry's promise in the prenuptial agreement to create a trust in the future for Wanda legally enforceable? Explain.

2. Was the trust Harry later created for Wanda validly created? Explain.

3. Assuming the trust for Wanda was validly created, did the trust terminate at Harry's death because there was then no trustee? Explain.

4. Assuming the trust for Wanda was validly created, what is the effect of her valid disclaimer, and should the trust principal be immediately distributed and, if so, to whom? Explain.

ANSWER TO QUESTION 11

1. Harry's promise to create a trust in the future was legally enforceable. The issue is whether a waiver of future alimony is sufficient consideration to create an enforceable promise. When a settlor promises to create a trust in the future and the promise is supported by valid consideration, the trust can arise in the future, when the property is acquired, without any further manifestation of intent. In the present case, Harry promised to create a trust for Wanda in consideration for her waiver to receive alimony in the event of a divorce. This promise was incorporated in the prenuptial agreement and Wanda's waiver constituted valid consideration for Harry's promise to create the trust. Thus, Harry's promise to create the trust for Wanda was legally enforceable.

2.   Harry created a valid inter vivos trust. The issue is whether trusts of tangible personal property must be in writing. To create a valid trust, there must be intent by the grantor, trust property, one or more beneficiaries, and a trustee. A person can create a trust by declaring himself trustee for another. Although trusts must generally be in writing, most states do not require a writing for a trust of personal property. In this case, Harry's intent to create the trust was clear from his oral declaration. His inheritance was the property of the trust, and Wanda was the designated beneficiary. Although Harry was the creator of the trust, he was also the trustee. Since the trust property was tangible personal property, no writing was required to satisfy the Statute of Frauds. Thus, Harry created a valid trust benefiting Wanda.

3.   The trust did not terminate on Harry's death. The issue is whether a trust terminates on the death of the trustee. The general rule is that once a trust is established it will not fail merely because of the trustee's death. The court will appoint a successor trustee to carry out the testator's intention if he intended the trust to continue beyond the death of the trustee. In the present case, Harry made it clear that he intended the trust to continue for Wanda's life. Further, in creating the trust he specifically mentioned a successor trustee, again indicating that the trust was to continue after his death. Thus, the trust for Wanda will continue without interruption, and the court will appoint a new trustee to carry out Harry's intentions.

4.   The beneficiary of the trust principal is contingent on whether Harry made an implied gift to his issue. If he did, the trust principal will be distributed to Charles. If he did not, the trust principal will be distributed between Wanda and Charles, according to their respective intestate shares. The issue is how trust property is distributed when the trust terms do not clearly indicate the settlor's intent. A valid disclaimer has the effect of treating the beneficiary as having predeceased the settlor and any remainder interest following the renounced life interest is accelerated if appropriate to do so. When Wanda disclaimed her interest in the trust, she was treated as having predeceased Harry and the remainder was accelerated. However, the terms of the trust specify that the remainder should be distributed to Harry's nieces and nephews *only if* Harry does not have any surviving issue when Wanda dies. Charles, Harry's son from his first marriage, was alive when Wanda disclaimed her interest in the trust. Thus, the remainder of the principal to Harry's nieces and nephews failed. Unfortunately, the terms of the trust do not provide directions for distribution of the principal in this event. The court can either: (i) imply a gift of the principal to Charles by assuming that Harry intended, but inadvertently omitted, the gift if he had issue who survived Wanda, or (ii) hold that Harry did not make a complete disposition of the trust principal, in which case the principal reverts to Harry's estate and will be distributed to his intestate heirs. If a gift is implied to Charles, he will receive the entire principal. However, if the court holds that there was an incomplete disposition of the principal, Wanda will receive her intestate share as Harry's surviving spouse (typically one-half or one-third) and Charles will receive the remainder. Note that Wanda will receive a share because she only disclaimed her interest in the trust, not in Harry's intestate estate.

QUESTION 12

On February 5, 1999, Testator created a revocable inter vivos trust. This trust was validly executed. Bank was designated trustee of the revocable trust.

Under the terms of the trust, Testator retained all income for life. The trust then provided in Article II that "upon my death the principal shall be held in further trust with the income payable to my wife, Wanda, for life, remainder to my children."

Contemporaneous with the creation of the revocable trust, Testator validly executed a will devising Testator's entire probate estate to the trustee of the revocable trust to be disposed of as part of that trust. The will further provided that, if the trust was revoked prior to Testator's death, Testator's entire estate should pass to Wanda.

On March 1, 2000, Testator sent a validly executed trust amendment to Bank revoking Article II of the revocable trust and substituting for it a new Article II. This new article stated that "upon my death the principal shall be held in further trust with the income payable to my wife, Wanda, for the immediate two years after my death, and, at the end of the two-year period, the trust principal shall be distributed to my surviving children."

In March 2001, Testator and Wanda were divorced.

In March 2002, Testator died, leaving a probate estate of $100,000. The revocable trust had not been funded prior to Testator's death. Testator was survived by Wanda and by their three children, Adam, Ben, and Carrie.

Two months later, both Wanda and Adam died in an automobile accident. Under Wanda's probated will, her entire estate passed to a charitable institution, Hope, and under Adam's probated will, his entire estate passed to University. Ben and Carrie are alive. They each have one child who also survived Testator. Adam never had any children.

1.   Which instruments control the disposition of the property included in Testator's probate estate? Explain.

2.   Upon Testator's death, what interest, if any, did Wanda have under the revocable trust? Explain.

3.   Assuming that Wanda had an interest under the trust, what rights, if any, do Hope and University have under the revocable trust upon the deaths of Wanda and Adam? Explain.

ANSWER TO QUESTION 12

1.   *Instruments governing disposition of Testator's property:* The disposition of Testator's property is governed by both his will and the trust instrument as amended on March 1, 2000. The issue is whether the disposition of a testator's property is governed by the terms of his will or trust. To create a valid pour-over gift from a will to a revocable trust, the trust must be in existence or must be executed at the time of the will's execution. Here, the trust and the will were executed contemporaneously. Additionally, pour-over gifts are valid even if the trust is unfunded during the testator's lifetime and even if the trust is amended prior to the testator's death, both of which occurred in this case. Thus, the disposition of Testator's property is governed by both the will and trust—the validly executed will created a pour-over gift into the validly executed trust.

2.   *Wanda's interest in revocable trust:* Upon Testator's death, Wanda was entitled to the trust income for two years. The issue is whether a spouse's interest in a trust is revoked upon divorce.

By operation of law, any bequests to Wanda under Testator's **will** would be revoked upon the couple's divorce. However, there is no rule revoking the beneficiary designation of a former spouse under a **trust**. Wanda remained the beneficiary of the trust income as stated in the amendment to the trust.

3. ***Hope's and University's rights:*** Hope will receive Wanda's remaining income interest but University will not receive anything as Adam will not be alive when the principal is distributed. The issue is whether devisees of the beneficiaries can succeed to the beneficiaries' interests in a trust. Interests in a trust are freely devisable and descendible; thus, Wanda and Adam were free to devise their respective interests in the trust to whomever they chose. As such, Hope will succeed to Wanda's interest. However, there was a condition of survival attached to Adam's interest. Specifically, the trust states, "at the end of [Wanda's] two-year period, the trust principal shall be distributed to my surviving children." Because Adam will not be alive at the expiration of the two-year period, he has no interest in the trust that can be devised to University.

QUESTION 13

Decedent died one year ago. Decedent's duly probated will created a $1 million trust. Trustee was the trustee of this trust. The trust provides that:

> **Trust income shall be payable annually to my son Adam for 10 years. Adam's interest shall be free from control, debts, liabilities, and assignments by Adam and shall not be subject to execution or process for the enforcement of judgments or claims of any sort against Adam. After 10 years, I direct that the income be paid for five years to Charity, a charitable organization. After this five-year period, the trust will terminate and the principal shall be paid to my daughter Beth.**

Decedent was survived by Adam and Beth. Adam had a history of lavish spending, which Decedent deplored. Beth was very careful in her financial dealings.

Three months ago, Susan, Adam's former spouse, gave Trustee a copy of a judgment for alimony she had obtained against Adam and proof that Adam had failed to pay her the required $5,000. Susan demanded that Trustee pay her $5,000, which was less than the trust's annual income.

Two months ago, Beth gave Trustee a copy of a tort judgment that John had obtained against Beth. She then requested that Trustee pay John $10,000, the amount of that judgment, from the trust principal.

Last month, Adam, Beth, and Charity commenced an appropriate judicial action to terminate the trust and have the trust assets distributed to them. Trustee has filed appropriate objections in this action.

1. **Is Susan entitled to be paid $5,000 from the trust income? Explain.**

2. **Can Trustee properly pay John $10,000 from the trust principal? Explain.**

3. **Should the court terminate the trust and distribute the trust assets to Adam, Beth, and Charity? Explain.**

ANSWER TO QUESTION 13

Susan's alimony judgment: Susan might be able to have the alimony judgment satisfied out of Adam's income interest in the trust. The issue is whether a spendthrift provision can be enforced against a former spouse seeking satisfaction of an alimony judgment.

Generally, a spendthrift provision prohibits the voluntary or involuntary transfer of the beneficiary's interest in the trust. In other words, the beneficiary cannot assign his interest to another, and the interest is free from the claims of creditors. However, some states do not enforce a spendthrift provision against certain types of creditors, such as dependents of the beneficiary.

Here, the language of Decedent's trust contains a spendthrift provision in regard to Adam's income interest—Adam cannot transfer his interest and it cannot be reached by his creditors. However, depending on the jurisdiction, the spendthrift provision might not apply to Susan. Susan is considered Adam's dependent because he owes her alimony payments. Therefore, her alimony judgment might be satisfied from Adam's income interest in the trust.

John's judgment against Beth: John is not entitled to have his judgment against Beth satisfied out of the trust principal. The issue is whether a creditor can reach a beneficiary's future interest in a trust.

In the absence of a spendthrift provision, a creditor can reach a beneficiary's interest in a trust. However, the creditor is entitled only to the beneficiary's interest in the trust. In this case, there is no spendthrift provision on Beth's interest; however, she has no present interest in the trust principal that can be reached by John. Rather, she merely holds a future interest in the principal, which will vest after the expiration of Adam's and Charity's income interests. Therefore, John cannot seek satisfaction of his judgment out of the trust principal.

Termination of trust by beneficiaries: The court should not terminate the trust and distribute the assets to the beneficiaries. The issue is whether termination of a trust is appropriate when it interferes with a material purpose of the trust.

Termination of a trust is usually permitted if all the beneficiaries consent to termination and the termination does not interfere with a material purpose of the trust. An example of a "material purpose" of the trust includes the desire to protect a beneficiary from his own improvidence. Here, the beneficiaries clearly consent to terminate the trust. However, to do so would interfere with one of Testator's clearly delineated purposes of the trust. Specifically, Testator wanted Adam's interest to be distributed on a yearly basis, with Adam having no right to transfer or otherwise alienate his interest, due to his poor money management. To terminate the trust and give Adam an early distribution of the income would clearly interfere with Testator's express purpose—to protect Adam from carelessly spending such a large sum of money. Therefore, the court should not terminate the trust and distribute the assets to the beneficiaries.

QUESTION 14

Testator, a widower, died one year ago at the age of 86 survived by his only two children, Angela and Brian (ages 40 and 45), 12 grandchildren (ranging in age from 17 to 27), and six great-grandchildren (ranging in age from 2 to 7). Testator's will bequeathed his entire estate to his "great-grandchildren living when my will is probated." Testator's will was probated two months after Testator died.

Before he died, Testator created a revocable trust with Friend as trustee. Friend was a long-time confidante of Testator and his family, with intimate knowledge of all of their financial and personal affairs. The trust provided that upon Testator's death the trust income could be paid to and among Testator's issue in such shares as Friend determined, with any unpaid income to be accumulated. It also provided that upon the death of Angela and Brian, the trust would terminate, and the corpus would be distributed to Testator's then living issue.

The trust contained no provisions relating to its administration. Because Friend was not very experienced in the administration of trusts and particularly in selecting appropriate trust investments, she interviewed a number of possible bank trust officers to assist her in administering the trust. Then she contracted with Bank, an institution wholly unfamiliar with Testator's family, to make all determinations regarding the distribution of trust income and how the trust's assets should be prudently invested.

Bank immediately sold all of the trust assets and reinvested all of the proceeds in XYZ Corporation, a telecommunications company whose shares are publicly traded. Bank paid $60 per share for this stock. Today, however, each share is worth only $21. The loss in value is due to the general decline in the telecommunications industry and not to any inherent weaknesses in XYZ.

Twice, after contracting with Bank, Friend called Bank to see how things were going. On these two occasions Friend was advised that "all is well." Friend never made further inquiries.

The common law Rule Against Perpetuities, as modified by the wait-and-see doctrine, applies in this jurisdiction.

1. To whom should Testator's probate estate be distributed? Explain.

2. What fiduciary duties, if any, did Friend breach with respect to the trust? Explain.

ANSWER TO QUESTION 14

1. Testator's probate estate should be distributed to his six great-grandchildren under the terms of his will. The issue is whether the class gift violates the Rule Against Perpetuities. Under the common law Rule Against Perpetuities, a gift must vest or fail within 21 years after a life in being. However, under the modified "wait and see" approach to the Rule, the validity of events is judged by actual events as they happen—the goal is to wait out the common law perpetuities period before declaring the interest void.

Here, Testator's will devises a gift to his great-grandchildren as a class. Therefore, the class must close within the perpetuities period for the gift to be valid. Under the rule of convenience, when a will makes a class gift but postpones the time for possession and enjoyment of the gift, the class closes at the time fixed for distribution. Testator's will directed that the great-grandchildren were to receive the gift when his will was probated. Therefore, the class would close at that time. Under the common law Rule Against Perpetuities, the gift would fail because it is possible that Testator's will would not be probated within 21 years after his death. However, under the "wait and see" approach, the gift to the great-grandchildren is saved because the class closed, and their interest actually vested, two months after his death when his will was probated, which is within the perpetuities period. Thus, the six great-grandchildren are entitled to Testator's estate and there is no violation of the Rule Against Perpetuities.

2.   Friend has breached several duties under the Uniform Prudent Investor Act ("UPIA"). The issue is whether Friend acted prudently in delegating the trust's administration to Bank. Generally, the UPIA requires that a trustee exercise reasonable care, skill, and caution in investing and managing trust assets. The trustee can invest in any kind of investment, but must diversify the investments of the trust absent special circumstances. If the trustee has limited expertise, she can delegate investment and management duties. However, to avoid liability for the agent's actions, the trustee must exercise reasonable care, skill, and caution in selecting an agent, establishing the scope and terms of the delegation, and periodically reviewing the agent's actions to monitor the agent's performance.

Here, Friend had reason to delegate the trust's administration due to her limited experience in trust administration and investments. However, she failed to act as a prudent trustee in selecting Bank as agent, establishing the scope and terms of the delegation, and monitoring Bank's actions. Specifically, the facts state that Friend selected Bank as the agent despite the fact that Bank was not familiar with Testator's family, and gave Bank full discretion with respect to income distribution and investment of the trust assets. Additionally, Friend failed to periodically monitor Bank's actions. To the contrary, she contacted Bank only twice and did not make any inquiries into the status of the trust assets after being told that "all is well." As a result of Friend's breach, Bank reinvested all of the trust assets in XYZ Corporation, failing to diversify the investments and resulting in a loss to the trust. Therefore, Friend failed to act as a prudent trustee under the UPIA and will be subject to liability.

QUESTION 15

Five years ago, Settlor created an irrevocable trust (the "Settlor Trust"). The trust provided that Trustee should pay annually "all of the trust income to my son Zack for life, with Zack to use such income to send Zack's children to college." The trust instrument further provided that, upon Zack's death, Trustee should "distribute the trust corpus in equal shares to Zack's children, issue of any deceased child to take his or her parent's share."

When Settlor Trust was created, Zack was married to Spouse. Zack and Spouse had three living children, Abel, age 23; Brian, age 19; and Carrie, age 15. Abel had one living child, Grandchild. Neither Brian, a college student, nor Carrie, a high-school student, was married or had children.

Two years later, Zack and Spouse had another child, Debbie. Following Debbie's birth, Zack stopped paying Brian's college expenses and told Carrie that he would not pay her future college expenses.

Trustee distributed last year's trust income to Zack. Shortly thereafter, Abel, Carrie, and Zack were all killed in an automobile accident. None of them had a will. Zack had not spent any of last year's income distribution. Zack was survived by Spouse, Brian, Debbie, and Grandchild.

Under state law, Abel and Carrie are deemed to have predeceased Zack. State law also provides that an intestate's estate passes to the intestate's spouse and children in equal

shares or, if there is no surviving spouse or children, to the intestate's parents in equal shares or, if there is no surviving parent, to the intestate's siblings.

1.   **Can Brian impress a trust upon the income distributed to Zack from Settlor Trust to pay for Brian's college education? Explain.**

2.   **To whom, and in what shares, should the principal of Settlor Trust be distributed? Explain.**

ANSWER TO QUESTION 15

1.   Brian can probably impress a trust upon the income distributed to Zack from Settlor's Trust to pay for his college education. At issue is whether the language in the trust instrument creates an enforceable trust.

One of the required characteristics of an enforceable trust is the settlor's intent to create a trust. Most courts hold that language merely expressing the settlor's hope, wish, or desire that the trust property be used for a certain purpose does not create a valid trust. In this case, the language in the trust instrument seems to be clear, expressing Settlor's intent that the income be used to send Zack's children to college. Moreover, common precatory terms (*e.g.*, hope, wish, desire) are not used. Therefore, a court is likely to hold that a valid trust was created, and Brian can impose a trust on the income distributed to Zack before Zack died.

Alternatively, the language could be interpreted as precatory because Zack's interest in the income continues for life even if he no longer has children in college. In that case, if the trust is not enforceable, Brian could not impose a trust on the income.

2.   Debbie, Grandchild, Brian, and Spouse should each take 1/4 of the principal. At issue is how to determine the takers under a class gift.

Debbie takes a share because she qualifies as a class member. Settlor created a class gift in the trust principal to "Zack's children." In determining class membership, courts apply a rule of construction known as the rule of convenience. This rule applies in the absence of a contrary expression of intent by the settlor. The rule of convenience provides that a class remains open until some member of the class can call for distribution of the class gift. When possession and enjoyment are postponed, as where the gift follows a life estate, the class remains open until the time fixed for distribution (*e.g.*, death of the life tenant). In this case, because the gift to Zack's children is postponed, the class does not close until Zack's death. Therefore, Debbie, who was born after the trust's creation but before Zack's death, is a class member and is entitled to a share of the principal.

Whether Grandchild takes a share depends on Settlor's intent. By the terms of the trust, Settlor expressed his intent that should any of Zack's children predecease Zack, that child's issue should take her parent's share. Therefore, Abel's share passes to Grandchild. Brian also has a right to an equal share because he was alive at the trust's creation and clearly falls within the class.

Carrie's share passes to her mother, Spouse, through intestacy. In general, future interests can pass at death by will or intestacy unless the interest is subject to a condition of survival. At common law, a remainder interest to children is not impliedly conditioned on survival. (The

Uniform Probate Code ("UPC"), however, does imply a condition of survival on such interests.) In this case, because Carrie predeceased Zack, her share would pass to her only heir, Spouse, through intestacy according to state law. (Under the UPC, Carrie's share would fail and pass to the surviving members of the class, Debbie, Grandchild, and Brian.)

QUESTION 16

Two years ago, Testator died. By her duly probated will, Testator created two separate trusts naming First Bank as the trustee of each trust.

1. **Testator left $100,000 to Friends' Trust and directed First Bank "to distribute the income annually among my friends in equal shares. At the end of 10 years, this trust shall terminate and the trust corpus shall be added to the principal of Residuary Trust created under this will."**

2. **Testator left $500,000 to Residuary Trust and directed First Bank "to pay the income to Carrie for life and to distribute the principal, during Carrie's life or upon her death, to any or all of Carrie's issue as she appoints by deed or will and, in the absence of such appointment, to my alma mater, University, upon Carrie's death."**

Last week, First Bank received two instruments in the mail. The first was a letter from George seeking a distribution of income from Friends' Trust and correctly claiming that he was a close friend of Testator.

The second was a deed labeled "Appointment" from Carrie directing First Bank to hold the $500,000 Residuary Trust in a new trust and to distribute income to Carrie's son, John, during his life. This deed further provided that upon John's death, First Bank should distribute the trust principal to Charity, a charitable organization, instead of to University as directed by Testator in her will.

1. **Can First Bank distribute income from Friends' Trust to George? Explain.**

2. **Did Carrie validly appoint an interest in Residuary Trust to her son, John? Explain.**

3. **In light of Carrie's deed of appointment, what, if any, are the interests of Charity and University in the new trust? Explain.**

ANSWER TO QUESTION 16

1. First Bank should not distribute income from Friends' Trust to George. The issue is whether Friends' Trust is invalid for failure to have "definite beneficiaries."

In order to create a valid trust, there must be a *settlor* who, *intending* to create a trust for a valid *trust purpose*, *delivers* the *trust property* to the *trustee* to hold for the benefit of one or more *beneficiaries.* Because a trust cannot exist without someone to enforce it, definite beneficiaries are necessary to the validity of a trust. Although the beneficiaries need not be identified at the time a trust is created, they must be susceptible of identification by the time their interests are to come into enjoyment. The trust beneficiaries may be a class, provided that the class is *sufficiently definite.* The settlor can even allow the trustee in its discretion to select the members as long as the class is *reasonably definite.* If the class is too broad, however, the trust may be invalid for lack of definite beneficiaries.

Here, Friends' Trust has a settlor with intent (Testator), a valid trust purpose (to distribute income among Testator's friends annually for 10 years), delivery of trust property ($100,000), and a trustee (First Bank). The question is whether there is a definite beneficiary. Friends' Trust is purportedly for the benefit of a class, Testator's friends. "Friends," however, does not sufficiently define who are the beneficiaries. Moreover, there are no facts to suggest that First Bank had the authority to determine who are Testator's friends. Thus, the trust fails for lack of a definite beneficiary, and George is not entitled to any distributions from the trust.

2.   Carrie validly appointed an interest in Residuary Trust to her son, John. The issue is whether the donee of a special power of appointment exercisable in favor of the donee's issue can exercise the power by appointing only a life estate to a permissible object of the power.

A power of appointment is an authority created in a donee enabling the donee to designate, within the limits prescribed by the donor of the power, the objects (*i.e.,* persons) who shall take certain property and the manner in which they shall take it. A general power of appointment is exercisable in favor of the donee, her estate, her creditors, or the creditors of her estate. A special power of appointment, on the other hand, is exercisable in favor of a specified class of persons *not* including the donee, her estate, her creditors, or the creditors of her estate.

Here, Testator gave Carrie a special power of appointment because the permissible objects of the power are "Carrie's issue." Carrie's exercise of the power in favor of her son, John, is thus permissible. Moreover, because a donee can designate the manner in which an object takes the property, giving John a life estate was also proper. However, appointing the remainder interest to Charity was impermissible (*see* below).

3.   Charity has no interest in the new trust, and University has a remainder interest in the new trust. The issue is whether the donee of a special power of appointment exercisable in favor of the donee's issue can exercise the power by appointing an interest in the property to a charitable organization and, if not, who succeeds to the impermissibly appointed interest.

As explained above, Carrie had a special power of appointment to designate her "issue" as the objects of the power. Charity, a charitable organization, does not fall into the permissible class. Thus, designating Charity as the remainderman was improper. The issue becomes who succeeds to the remainder interest.

If a donee fails to exercise her power of appointment, the appointive property passes to the "takers in default of appointment" (*i.e.,* the persons designated by the donor to take the property in such a situation). Here, because Charity was not a permissible object, Carrie failed to exercise her power of appointment with respect to the remainder interest in the new trust. Thus, the interest passes to the person (or entity) designated to take the property when the donee fails to exercise her power. According to the terms of Residuary Trust, the taker in default of appointment is University. Thus, University holds the remainder interest in the new trust.

QUESTION 17

Seven years ago, Settlor announced at a dinner party:

> I am hereby creating the Settlor's Family Trust and naming myself as trustee. In about three years, I expect to sell some stock and to fund this trust with the sale proceeds. I reserve the power to pay to myself trust income and principal for my support at any time. When I die, all remaining trust assets are to be distributed to my daughter, Dawn. Neither my creditors nor Dawn's creditors can reach the trust assets to satisfy their claims, and neither of us is free to sell or otherwise transfer our respective trust interests. Please join me in a toast as I sign this cocktail napkin on which I have written the terms of the trust.

Five years ago, Settlor's sister-in-law, In-Law, executed a will leaving her entire $300,000 estate to the Settlor's Family Trust.

Four years ago, Settlor sold some stock and deposited the $100,000 sale proceeds into an account at First Bank in the name of "Settlor, as Trustee of the Settlor's Family Trust."

Two months ago, In-Law died. Had In-Law died intestate, her estate would have passed to her brother Bill. Both Settlor, as trustee of the Settlor's Family Trust, and Bill claim In-Law's estate.

One month ago, Victim obtained a $75,000 tort judgment against Settlor because of injuries sustained as a result of Settlor's negligence. Victim immediately sought to collect that judgment from the First Bank account, notwithstanding Settlor's claims that this account was beyond the reach of his judgment creditors. Before this dispute could be resolved, Settlor died.

1. **Was the Settlor's Family Trust validly created? Explain.**

2. **Who is entitled to In-Law's estate? Explain.**

3. **Can Victim reach the assets of the First Bank account to satisfy Victim's claim against Settlor? Explain.**

ANSWER TO QUESTION 17

1. The Settlor's Family Trust was not validly created seven years ago, but became valid four years ago when Settlor deposited the stock sale proceeds into a First Bank account in the name of Settlor, as trustee. At issue is whether the trust was properly funded.

To create a valid trust, there must be a *settlor* who, *intending* to create a trust for a valid *trust purpose*, *delivers* the *trust property* to the *trustee* to hold for the benefit of one or more *beneficiaries*. If there are no trust assets when the trust instrument is executed (*i.e.*, the settlor promises gratuitously to create a trust in the future), a trust arises in the future only if, when the assets come into existence, the settlor manifests anew an intention to create the trust. This remanifestation is not required, however, if the promise is supported by valid consideration.

Here, the Settlor's Family Trust has a settlor (Settlor) with intent (memorialized on the napkin), a valid trust purpose (to provide Settlor with support during his lifetime), a trustee (Settlor), and definite beneficiaries (Settlor and Dawn). The question is whether the trust has sufficient assets. When the trust instrument was executed seven years ago, Settlor "expected" to fund the trust with sale proceeds that did not yet exist. Thus, the trust will fail for lack of trust property. Neither can it be argued that there was a valid contract to create a trust in the future because there was no valid consideration. Thus, Settlor's gratuitous promise was unenforceable at that time. However, three years later when Settlor sold the stock and deposited the $100,000 proceeds into an account at First Bank, the trust became valid because Settlor remanifested an intention to create the trust by opening the account "as Trustee of the Settlor's Family Trust." Thus, although the trust was not valid at the time of execution of the trust instrument, it became valid after the deposit into the First Bank account.

[*Note:* Merger of title, which results in termination of a trust where the sole trustee is also the sole beneficiary, does not apply here because although Settlor is the settlor, trustee, and beneficiary, there is a second beneficiary—Dawn.]

2.   Settlor, as trustee of the Settlor's Family Trust, is entitled to In-Law's estate. At issue is whether In-Law's will created a valid pour-over gift to the trust.

To create a valid pour-over gift from a will to a revocable trust, the trust must be in existence or must be executed at the time of the will's execution. Here, the trust instrument was executed two years before the will. Additionally, pour-over gifts are valid even if the trust is unfunded during the testator's lifetime, which is the case here, and even if the trust is amended prior to the testator's death. Thus, In-Law's validly executed will created a pour-over gift to the validly executed trust, and Bill has no valid claim to In-Law's estate.

3.   Victim can reach the assets of the First Bank account to satisfy Victim's claim against Settlor. At issue is whether the trust assets are shielded from the claims of Settlor's creditors by the spendthrift provision.

A spendthrift trust is one in which the beneficiary is unable voluntarily or involuntarily to transfer his interest in the trust. He cannot sell or give away his rights to future income or capital, and his creditors generally are unable to collect or attach such rights. However, an exception is made when the settlor is a beneficiary of the trust and attempts to protect his own retained interests from his creditors by the inclusion of a spendthrift provision. In that event, the settlor-beneficiary's creditors can reach his right to the income just as if the spendthrift restriction did not exist. Here, Settlor is the settlor and also a beneficiary of the trust. Thus, the spendthrift provision is invalid as to Settlor, and Victim can reach the First Bank account assets to satisfy the tort judgment.

QUESTION 18

Testator died three years ago. His duly probated will provided that:

> **1.   I give $100,000 to Trustee to hold in trust and to distribute the trust income equally among those persons who are my friends at my death. After 10 years, the trust shall terminate and the trust property shall be distributed equally between my son, Sam, and the fine arts program at State University. In no event shall this trust terminate earlier than 10 years after my death.**

> **2.   I give the rest of my estate to my daughter, Donna.**

Both Sam and Donna survived Testator.

Walter and Janice, two neighbors of Testator, correctly claim they were good friends of Testator at the time of his death and demand that Trustee pay the income from the $100,000 trust to them. Claimant, who has a tort judgment against Sam, demands that "Trustee immediately pay Claimant $25,000 from the trust to satisfy the judgment.

Two years after Testator died, State University closed as a result of a state budget crunch and the legislature's determination that the programs at State University, including its fine arts program, were largely duplicative of the programs at State Polytech, the other public university in the state.

1. **To whom should the income from the $100,000 trust be distributed? Explain.**

2. **Should Trustee immediately pay $25,000 from the trust to Claimant? Explain.**

3. **To whom should Trustee pay the trust principal at the end of the 10-year period? Explain.**

ANSWER TO QUESTION 18

1.   The income from the $100,000 trust should be distributed to Donna. At issue is whether the income portion of the trust fails for lack of definite beneficiaries.

In order to create a valid trust, there must be a *settlor* who, *intending* to create a trust for a valid *trust purpose*, *delivers* the *trust property* to the *trustee* to hold for the benefit of one or more *beneficiaries*. Because a trust cannot exist without someone to enforce it, definite beneficiaries are necessary to the validity of a trust. Although the beneficiaries need not be identified at the time a trust is created, they must be susceptible of identification by the time their interests are to come into enjoyment. The trust beneficiaries may be a class, provided that the class is sufficiently definite. The settlor can even allow the trustee in its discretion to select the members as long as the class is *reasonably definite*. If the class is too broad, however, the trust (or a portion thereof) may be invalid for lack of definite beneficiaries.

Here, the trust has a settlor with intent (Testator), a valid trust purpose (to distribute income among Testator's friends for 10 years), delivery of trust property ($100,000), and a trustee (Trustee). The question is whether there is a definite beneficiary. The trust is purportedly for the benefit of a class, Testator's friends. Although the facts state that Walter and Janice were Testator's good friends, the income is to be distributed equally among *all* of Testator's friends. "Friends," however, does not sufficiently define who are all of the beneficiaries. Moreover, there are no facts to suggest that Trustee had the authority to determine who are Testator's friends. Thus, the income portion of the trust fails for lack of a definite beneficiary, and Walter and Janice are not entitled to any income distributions from the trust.

When a portion of a trust fails for lack of a beneficiary, a resulting trust in favor of the settlor or the settlor's successors in interest is presumed. Here, because Testator is dead, the income should be distributed under Testator's will to the residuary beneficiary, Donna.

2.   Trustee should not immediately pay $25,000 from the trust to Claimant. At issue is whether a remainder beneficiary's judgment creditor has a right to immediate payment from the trust.

Except as otherwise provided by statute or as validly restricted by the terms of the trust instrument (*e.g.*, a spendthrift provision), the interest of an insolvent trust beneficiary can generally be reached in appropriate proceedings to satisfy the claims of his creditors. However, the creditor reaches only the *interest* of the beneficiary and not the trust property itself.

Here, the trust does not contain a spendthrift provision so Claimant may reach Sam's interest in the trust principal. However, Sam is not entitled to any trust principal until the trust terminates, which by the express terms of the trust will not occur until 10 years after Testator's death. Thus, Claimant is not entitled to an immediate $25,000 payment from the trust. Note that upon the trust's termination, if the judgment remains outstanding and Sam's interest is at least $25,000, Trustee may be required to pay the money directly to Claimant rather than to Sam.

3.   At the end of the 10-year period, Trustee should pay one-half of the trust principal to Sam, subject to the rights of Claimant, and the other one-half to State Polytech. At issue is whether the cy pres doctrine should be applied.

The cy pres doctrine applies when a specific charitable purpose indicated by the settlor is no longer possible or practical, and the settlor manifested a general charitable intent. In such a case, the court can direct that the trust property be applied to another charitable purpose as close as possible to the original one, rather than permit the trust to fail and become a resulting trust.

Here, by the express terms of the trust, Sam is entitled to one-half of the trust principal at the end of 10 years (subject to Claimaint's claim as discussed in 2., above). State University would be entitled to the other one-half of the trust principal except that the university no longer exists. However, Testator arguably had a general charitable intent—supporting the fine arts program at a state university. The legislature has already determined that the fine arts program at State Polytech, the other state university, is "largely duplicative" of the program at State University. Thus, the court likely would apply the cy pres doctrine and award the property to State Polytech.

Alternatively, if the court did not apply the cy pres doctrine, the gift to State University would fail and likely pass under a resulting trust to Donna as discussed in 1., above.

QUESTION 19

Settlor, age 60, consulted an attorney, Attorney, about the creation of a trust. Settlor gave Attorney a memorandum containing the following information about his family:

Family Members	Relationship	Age
1. Wife	Spouse	48
2. Son	Child	21
3. Daughter 1	Child	16
4. Daughter 2	Child	10
5. Grandchild	Grandchild (Son's child)	1

Settlor also outlined his goals in creating the trust:

1. I want to fully control trust assets and enjoy all trust income until I die.

2. After I die, I want trust assets used to ensure that Wife is comfortably provided for. I also want Wife to be able to use trust assets to reward, in her will, whichever children have been most helpful to her. I don't want Wife to be a trustee; she doesn't have the financial background.

3. After Wife dies, I want my children to get the remaining trust assets. But, of course, if Son dies before Wife, I'd want his share to go to Grandchild.

4. I'm planning to fund the trust with cash and stocks. I may want to add some other assets later, but I'm not sure.

Based on the information provided by Settlor, Attorney drafted the following trust instrument:

SETTLOR TRUST AGREEMENT

1. I appoint Bank as trustee of the Settlor Trust.

2. I direct Bank to hold all assets listed on Schedule A in trust, and I direct Bank to dispose of these assets as follows:

    a. Bank shall pay all trust income to Settlor during Settlor's lifetime.

    b. After Settlor's death, Bank shall pay trust income and principal to Wife in such amounts as Bank, in its sole discretion, deems appropriate.

    c. After Wife's death, Bank shall distribute all remaining trust assets equally among Settlor's surviving children, share and share alike.

3. Bank accepts and agrees to faithfully carry out the terms of this trust.

    [Signatures, dates, and acknowledgments are omitted]

    SCHEDULE A

    12,000 Shares of XYZ Corporation, common stock
    $150,000 (cash)

How would you revise the Settlor Trust Agreement to more fully meet Settlor's stated goals? Explain.

ANSWER TO QUESTION 19

Retain full control of trust assets and income; add trust assets in future: Settlor should be appointed trustee of the Settlor Trust and expressly reserve the right to revoke the trust. At issue is how a settlor can retain full control of the trust assets and income during his lifetime and the right to make future additions to the trust.

A trustee holds legal title to specific property under a fiduciary duty to manage, invest, safeguard, and administer the trust assets and income for the benefit of designated beneficiaries, who hold equitable title. Here, because Settlor wishes to retain full control of the trust assets, he should be appointed trustee. Although a trust will not fail for lack of a trustee (*e.g.*, when Settlor dies), Settlor could name Bank as successor trustee to ensure that Wife is not appointed ("I don't want Wife to be a trustee"). *Note:* Merger of title, which results in termination of a trust where the sole trustee is also the sole beneficiary, does not apply here because although Settlor would be the settlor, trustee, and beneficiary, there are other beneficiaries—Wife and Settlor's issue.

Additional control could be retained by expressly reserving the power to revoke the trust. In those states that have adopt the Uniform Trust Code, an inter vivos trust is revocable unless it is expressly made irrevocable, but the majority of states provide that an inter vivos trust is irrevocable unless the instrument expressly provides otherwise. Thus, the trust instrument should expressly state that it is revocable. Because the power to revoke includes the power to amend, Settlor will also be able to withdraw or add trust assets in the future.

Another method Settlor could use to add assets to the trust is by including a pour-over provision in his will. A pour-over gift is a testamentary gift to a trust created during the testator's lifetime, with the testamentary assets to be administered and distributed as part of that trust. To create a valid pour-over gift, the trust must be in existence or must be executed at the time of the will's execution. Additionally, pour-over gifts are valid even if the trust is amended prior to the testator's death.

Ensure that Wife is comfortably provided for: An ascertainable standard should be attached to Wife's interest. At issue is how a settlor can ensure that a beneficiary is comfortably provided for after his death.

With respect to Wife, the current Settlor Trust is a discretionary trust. In a discretionary trust, the trustee is given discretion whether to apply or withhold payments of income or principal to a beneficiary. This discretion actually limits the rights of the beneficiary to the amounts the trustee decides to give her. The beneficiary cannot interfere with the exercise of the trustee's discretion unless the trustee abuses his power. On the other hand, a support trust is one where the trustee is ***required*** to pay or apply so much of the income or principal as is necessary for the beneficiary's support. Here, a discretionary trust does not accomplish Settlor's goal to ensure that Wife is "comfortably provided for" because the trustee could decide not to pay trust property to Wife, and Wife could not compel the trustee to pay in the absence of an abuse of discretion. However, if the trust were limited by an ascertainable standard—*e.g.*, "trustee shall pay trust income and principal to Wife as is necessary to comfortably provide for her support"—Wife could compel distributions.

Allow Wife to allocate trust assets in her will: Wife should be given a special testamentary power of appointment. At issue is how a settlor can give a beneficiary the power to allocate trust assets in her will in favor of his issue.

A power of appointment is an authority created in a donee enabling the donee to designate, within the limits prescribed by the donor of the power, the persons who shall take certain property and the manner in which they shall take it. A general power of appointment is exercisable in favor of the donee, her estate, her creditors, or the creditors of her estate. A special power of appointment, on the other hand, is exercisable in favor of a specified class of persons that does *not* include the donee, her estate, her creditors, or the creditors of her estate. A presently exercisable power is exercisable by the donee during her lifetime. A testamentary power is one that is exercisable only by the donee's will. Here, because Settlor wishes to limit the class of objects to his children and issue of deceased children (*see* below) and for the power to be exercisable only by Wife's will, a special testamentary power of appointment would more fully meet his goal.

Ensure that issue of deceased children take parent's share: The trust should expressly provide that in the event any child predeceases the income beneficiary, that child's share shall be paid to his issue. At issue is how a settlor can ensure that the share of any deceased child passes to the child's issue.

The current Settlor Trust provides that after Wife's death the remaining trust assets are to be distributed "among Settlor's surviving children, share and share alike." Where a remainder interest is conditioned on a beneficiary's surviving the settlor and the beneficiary does not meet the condition, his interest fails. Nearly all states have anti-lapse statutes that operate to save a gift to a predeceasing beneficiary if the beneficiary was in a specified degree of relationship to the *testator* and left surviving descendants. Because in most states the anti-lapse statute applies only to testamentary gifts, it is not applicable here. In this case, Settlor's probable goal is for the remaining trust assets to pass to his surviving children and *issue* of deceased children (because, *e.g.*, Grandchild could have a child, Great-Grandchild, and both Son and Grandchild could predecease Wife). Thus, the trust instrument should expressly provide that issue of deceased children take their parent's share.

Note: Because Wife will be given a special testamentary power of appointment in the revised Settlor Trust, Settlor's surviving children and issue of deceased children will be the takers in default of appointment (*i.e.*, the persons designated to take the property if the donee fails to effectively exercise her power of appointment).

QUESTION 20

Six years ago, Settlor created a valid inter vivos irrevocable trust. Settlor funded the trust with publicly traded securities, named Friend as sole trustee, and directed Friend, as trustee, to distribute all trust income to James, whom Settlor had been supporting for several years. Settlor also gave James the right to withdraw up to 5% of the trust's principal annually during the first 10 years of the trust's existence.

Four years ago, Friend sold all of the trust's publicly traded securities and reinvested 45% of the proceeds in the preferred stock of A Corp., 45% of the proceeds in the preferred stock of B Corp., and 10% of the proceeds in different publicly traded securities. Both A Corp. and B Corp. were closely held companies that were newly organized and cash poor. Their preferred stocks were not publicly traded and were subject to valid restraints on alienation that effectively made them nontransferable by the trustee for the next 10 years. Furthermore, although both preferred stocks guaranteed an annual 5% dividend, these dividends were not payable until after the 10-year restraint-on-alienation period had expired.

At the time Friend invested in the preferred stocks of A Corp. and B Corp., both companies were developing competing technologies to make ballpoint pens that also function as cell phones. Neither company had yet developed working prototypes of the proposed product.

Friend honestly believed that the preferred stocks represented a safe investment that would produce returns in excess of those available from any other investment. Friend did not individually own any preferred stock of A Corp. or B Corp. However, Friend did individually own 70% of the common stock of A Corp., but had no interest in B Corp.

Despite Friend's confidence, the A Corp. and B Corp. investments have proven disastrous. Since the preferred stocks were purchased, neither company has succeeded in producing a marketable product or making a profit. Both are now near bankruptcy. Moreover, because the stocks have not paid dividends and cannot be sold, James's income from the trust has declined precipitously. Furthermore, because of the valid restraints on alienation, Friend has truthfully told James that any withdrawal requests cannot be honored.

Friend has consulted your law firm, concerned that he may have breached one or more of his fiduciary duties. Explain to Friend which duties, if any, he may have breached in carrying out his responsibilities.

ANSWER TO QUESTION 20

Friend has breached several duties under the Uniform Prudent Investor Act ("UPIA"). At issue are the duties of a trustee regarding investment of trust assets.

Duty of loyalty: Under the UPIA, a trustee must act exclusively for the beneficiary when investing and managing trust assets, or he is acting imprudently. Absent court approval or a contrary trust provision, a trustee breaches this duty when he enters into any transaction in which he is dealing with the trust in his individual capacity (self-dealing). A transaction in which the trustee invests trust assets in a corporation of which the trustee is a principal shareholder is considered self-dealing. [*Note:* Under the Uniform Trust Code, followed in many states, such a transaction is *presumed* to be a violation of the trustee's duty of loyalty.]

Here, Friend invested 45% of the trust assets in A Corp., in which he individually owns 70% of the common stock. Thus, Friend has breached the duty of loyalty.

Duty to invest prudently: Under the UPIA, a trustee must invest and manage trust assets as a prudent investor would. No particular type of investment is inherently imprudent, because a trustee may invest in *any* type of investment consistent with the standards of the Act. These standards require the trustee to consider the following circumstances (among others) in making investment decisions: (i) general economic conditions; (ii) the role that each investment plays within the overall trust portfolio; (iii) the expected total return from income and the appreciation of capital; and (iv) needs for liquidity, regularity of income, and preservation or appreciation of capital. Compliance with the UPIA is determined in light of the facts and circumstances existing at the time of the trustee's decision or action.

Here, the majority (90%) of the trust portfolio consists of investments in two newly organized and cash-poor companies. Because the companies have failed to develop working prototypes of their proposed products, there is no guarantee that their products will succeed and produce any profits. Moreover, they are competing products, so it is likely that one of them will eventually fail. Finally, investment in A Corp. and B Corp. has reduced the liquidity of the trust due to the 10-year restraint on alienation. As Friend knew these facts at the time he made the investments, they will likely be considered imprudent. Thus, Friend breached the duty to invest prudently.

Duty to diversify: Under the UPIA, a trustee must diversify the investments of the trust unless he reasonably determines that, because of special circumstances, the purposes of the trust are better served without diversification.

Here, Friend invested the majority (90%) of the trust's assets in one narrow and untested segment of the market—ballpoint pens that also function as cell phones. Nothing in the facts indicates that special circumstances (*e.g.*, Settlor owned one of the corporations) warranted nondiversification. Thus, Friend has breached the duty to diversify.

Duty of care: Under the UPIA, a trustee must invest and manage trust assets as a prudent investor would, taking into account the purposes, terms, and distribution requirements of the trust. To satisfy this objective standard of prudence, the trustee must exercise reasonable care, skill, and caution.

Here, the trust provides that James, the beneficiary, is to receive all of the income and has the power to annually withdraw up to 5% of the trust's principal. Moreover, Settlor had been supporting James for several years, indicating that James is likely relying on a steady stream of income from the trust. However, because 90% of the trust's assets are subject to a 10-year restraint on alienation, which also prevents the companies from paying the annual 5% dividends, James's right to both income and principal is significantly impaired. Thus, Friend has breached the duty of care.

QUESTION 21

Ten years ago, Wife created a valid trust ("Wife's Trust") and named Bank as trustee. The trust instrument directed Bank to: (1) pay all trust income to Wife during her lifetime; (2) upon Wife's death, pay all trust income to Niece during Niece's lifetime; and (3) upon Niece's death, distribute the trust principal to Niece's "then-living issue."

Article Five of Wife's Trust provided as follows:

> Wife may revoke or amend this trust at any time prior to her death by a written instrument delivered to Bank.

Contemporaneously with the creation of Wife's Trust, Wife and her husband, Husband, executed separate wills. Each will devised the respective testator's entire probate estate to Bank "to hold as part of the principal of Wife's Trust, which was created simultaneously with the execution of my will."

Five years ago, Wife delivered to Bank a written instrument titled "Amendment to Wife's Trust." In this instrument, Wife directed Bank to distribute the trust principal to Niece's "children age 21 years or older who are living when Wife's Trust terminates."

Four months ago, Wife, Husband, and Niece were involved in an automobile accident. Wife was pronounced dead in the ambulance. Husband died three days later, and Niece died seven days later. Wife, who had previously transferred all of her assets to Wife's Trust, had no probate estate. Husband's probate estate was worth $300,000.

Niece had two children: Son, now age 20, and Daughter, who died one year ago at the age of 28. Daughter had one child (Grandchild), now age 4.

1.   Does the Amendment to Wife's Trust apply to the assets distributable to that trust from Husband's probate estate? Explain.

2.   Is Son entitled to a share of the assets of Wife's Trust given the language of the Amendment to Wife's Trust? Explain.

3.   Is Grandchild entitled to a share of the assets of Wife's Trust given the language of the Amendment to Wife's Trust? Explain.

ANSWER TO QUESTION 21

1.   The amendment to Wife's Trust applies to the assets distributable to that trust from Husband's probate estate. At issue is whether Husband can pour over the assets of his probate estate into a revocable trust he did not create.

Under the Uniform Testamentary Additions to Trusts Act, a pour-over gift from a will to an inter vivos trust is valid if the trust was executed prior to or contemporaneously with the will. A pour-over gift is valid even though the inter vivos trust is amendable and revocable. The gift is to the trust as it exists at the testator's death, including amendments to the trust made after the will was executed. There is no requirement that the trust and will be executed by the same person.

Here, Wife's Trust is a revocable inter vivos trust because it was created during Wife's lifetime and provides that it may be revoked or amended. Because the trust was created simultaneously with the execution of Husband's will, a valid pour-over gift was created. Thus, Wife's Trust, as amended, will govern the disposition of Husband's estate.

2.   Son may be entitled to a share of the assets of Wife's Trust when he reaches age 21. At issue is how a court will construe the amendment to Wife's Trust.

Courts will construe the words of a trust to effect the settlor's intent. Here, the language of the amendment to Wife's Trust is subject to two interpretations. According to the original terms of the trust, the trust terminates upon Niece's death because that is when the principal is to be distributed. Based upon a strict reading of the amendment, only Niece's children who are age 21 or older and living at her death are entitled to the trust principal. Because Son was only 20 years old at the time of Niece's death, he would not be entitled to a share of the assets of Wife's Trust.

However, an argument can be made that Wife did not intend this strict interpretation. When she executed the amendment to the trust, only Daughter satisfied the age requirement; Son was only 15. As nothing in the facts indicates any reason why Wife would want to exclude Son as a beneficiary of the trust, her purpose may have been to keep the principal out of Son's hands until he reached a more mature age. Wife's use of the language "when Wife's Trust terminates" versus the original "upon Niece's death" might also indicate that Wife misunderstood when the trust terminated. Thus, under this broader interpretation, Son will take a share of the assets of Wife's Trust if he reaches age 21.

3.   Grandchild likely is not entitled to a share of the assets of Wife's Trust. At issue is whether Grandchild succeeds to Daughter's interest.

Although a gift to a decedent's "issue" includes all lineal descendants (*e.g.*, children, grandchildren), a gift to a decedent's "children" includes only the decedent's immediate offspring. Here, the principal was to be distributed to Niece's "children" who survived the trust's termination. Thus, Grandchild would not be entitled to a share of the assets of Wife's Trust.

However, nearly all states have anti-lapse statutes that operate to save a gift to a predeceased beneficiary if the beneficiary was in a certain degree of relationship with the decedent and left surviving descendants. As most states' anti-lapse statutes apply only to testamentary gifts and do not apply if there is a contrary provision in the instrument (*i.e.*, the gift is contingent on the beneficiary's surviving the decedent), Grandchild would not be entitled to Daughter's share of the trust as a substituted taker. However, in some states and under the Uniform Probate Code, the anti-lapse statute also applies to revocable inter vivos trusts and is not affected by words of survivorship. In these states, if the trust creates a class gift and a class member dies before the event upon which the interest becomes possessory occurs, her descendants succeed to the interest. Thus, in these states Grandchild would succeed to Daughter's interest.

QUESTION 1

Ted and Martha were married in 1985. Their marriage ended in divorce in 1990. In 1991, Ted married Helen, and they had a child, Clarissa, born in 1993. Ted died on January 4, 1995. Martha, Helen, and Clarissa are all alive.

After Ted's death, Martha offered for probate a one-page document clearly written in Ted's handwriting, which reads as follows:

> November 12, 1988
>
> This is my will, and I want it clear that I leave everything I own except my hunting cabin to my wife, Martha. The cabin goes to my brother Jim.
>
> Ted

The document was signed, directly under Ted's signature, by Jim and by Ted's friend, Fred. Both Jim and Fred will testify that they signed the document at Ted's request while they were on a hunting trip at the cabin in north-central Illinois.

Ted's probate estate (after taxes and administration expenses) consists of the hunting cabin, valued at $40,000, and liquid assets valued at $160,000. How should Ted's probate estate be distributed? Explain.

ANSWER TO QUESTION 1

Ted's estate should be distributed one-half to Helen and one-half to Clarissa. Martha and Jim take nothing.

To create a valid will in Illinois, the testator must be 18 years old, be of sound mind, and have the intent that a particular instrument operate as his will. It seems clear that Ted satisfied all three of these requirements when he executed the 1988 document.

Further, an Illinois will must be in writing, signed by the testator, and attested by two witnesses in the testator's presence. The first issue is whether "Ted" constitutes a signature. It does. Any mark affixed by the testator with the intent that it operate as the testator's signature satisfies the signature requirement.

The 1988 document was witnessed by two attesting witnesses, Jim and Fred. However, since Jim was a beneficiary under the will, he is an interested witness. This does not impact the validity of the will. The fact that a will makes a gift to an attesting witness never results in denial of probate of the will, but the witness-beneficiary may lose his legacy under the purging statute. The statute eliminates the problem by purging the witness's legacy, thereby making him a disinterested witness. Here, Jim will lose his gift of the cabin under the will. He would be able to keep it if there were two other disinterested witnesses (there are not), or if he would have been entitled to the amount of the bequest had Ted died intestate (he would not be entitled to anything had Ted died intestate). Since Jim and Fred signed the will at Ted's request while all three were on a hunting trip, we can probably safely assume that Jim and Fred signed in Ted's presence.

Jim may try to argue that the 1988 document, which was entirely in Ted's handwriting, constitutes a valid holographic will, making Jim's attestation unnecessary. In states that recognize holographic wills, a will entirely in the testator's handwriting and signed by the testator, but not witnessed by attesting witnesses, is valid. In such a state, Jim's argument would be valid, and he could probably take the cabin. Illinois, however, does not recognize holographic wills. All Illinois wills must be witnessed regardless of whether they are in the testator's handwriting.

The 1988 will was thus valid with Jim's gift of the cabin purged. In 1990, however, Ted and Martha's divorce revoked the gift to Martha by operation of law. If a testator is divorced after making a will, all gifts to the former spouse are revoked, and the will takes effect as though the former spouse had predeceased the testator. Since the 1988 will left everything to Martha, all of the estate will pass as though Martha predeceased Ted; *i.e.,* the entire estate will pass by intestacy.

Under the Illinois intestacy statute, if a decedent dies survived by a spouse and by descendants, the surviving spouse takes one-half of the decedent's real and personal property, and the descendants take the other one-half. Here, Ted is survived by a spouse, Helen, and one descendant, Clarissa. Thus, Helen takes one-half ($100,000) and Clarissa takes one-half ($100,000).

QUESTION 2

Five years ago, Harry married Wilma. Wilma had a child from her prior marriage, Dorothy, who was 14. Although Harry did not adopt Dorothy, he raised her as if she were his biological child. Harry had a son from a prior marriage, Steve. Wilma and Steve never got along.

Three months ago, Harry properly executed a will leaving (1) $10,000 to Steve, (2) $50,000 to Dorothy, and (3) the rest of his estate (valued at $700,000) to Wilma. This will, prepared under the supervision of Harry's longtime attorney, also provided that "if any person shall contest any provision of this will, such person shall forfeit any right to claim any share of my estate." During the 35 years prior to his death at age 62, Harry had been a successful commercial banker with a reputation within the community for being "fair but very hardnosed."

Harry died unexpectedly in an automobile accident while on his way to a meeting with a client to close a $5 million deal. Five minutes before the accident, he had dropped Wilma off at their stockbroker's office to "sign off" on changes in their jointly held stock portfolio. They had argued strenuously about these changes, but Harry had prevailed.

In many ways, Steve was the exact opposite of Harry. During Harry and Wilma's marriage, Steve had been unsuccessful in holding any job for longer than four months. He often asked Harry for money, which Harry thought Steve spent too lavishly. Harry often complained that Steve "refused to settle down."

Steve, who is now 24 years old, seeks to invalidate the will and claim an intestate share of his father's estate. Steve says that for the three years immediately preceding Harry's death, Harry appeared mildly distracted and occasionally forgetful. Steve also claims that Wilma was "constantly carping" to Harry about Steve. He also says that Wilma (1) refused to be in the family home when Steve came to visit, (2) on at least one occasion hid a letter Steve had written to Harry while Steve was on vacation in Europe, and (3) many times refused to let Steve talk to Harry on the telephone, falsely claiming Harry was not home. Steve also claims that Wilma always insisted that Harry attend every school function in which Dorothy participated, praised Dorothy's schoolwork to Harry, and denigrated Steve to Harry whenever possible.

1. **On what grounds might Steve seek to invalidate Harry's will, and is Steve likely to be successful? Explain.**

2. **If Steve is not successful in contesting Harry's will, what amount, if any, will Steve receive from Harry's estate? Explain.**

ANSWER TO QUESTION 2

1. Steve could seek to invalidate Harry's will on the grounds of lack of capacity, undue influence, and fraud.

The only evidence that Steve can offer that Harry lacked testamentary capacity is that Harry was mildly distracted and occasionally forgetful in the three years preceding his death. This will not be sufficient to sustain a will contest. The standard for capacity to make a will is quite low. One may have capacity to make a will even though one lacks capacity to make a contract. The law presumes that every person is of sound mind unless the contrary is shown. The burden of proof is on the will contestant to show that, at the time he executed the will, the testator did not have sufficient capacity to understand the nature of his act (that he was writing a will), know the nature and character of his property, know the objects of his bounty, and make a disposition of property according to a plan formed in his own mind. All of the facts presented seem to cut against Steve's position. The will itself, the no-contest clause, and the preparation of the will seem clear that Harry knew he was executing a will. The fact that Harry was arguing with Wilma about changes in their stock portfolio seems to indicate that he was aware of the nature and character of his property. He left something to each of the natural objects of his bounty (Steve, Dorothy, and Wilma), so it would seem he was aware of who they are. There is no indication that the dispositive plan came from anyone's mind other than Harry's. Finally, at the time of his death, Harry was on his way to close a $5 million deal, which indicates he was still capable of complex business transactions.

Steve may also attempt to argue that Wilma exerted undue influence over Harry. A will may be denied probate if it is shown that it was the product of undue influence exerted upon the testator. Undue influence is mental coercion that prevents the testator from exercising his free will and produces a will or a gift therein that reflects the will, not of the testator, but of the party exerting the influence.

The burden of proving undue influence is on the will contestant, who must show that: specific acts of influence were exerted, the effect of the influence was to overpower the mind and free will of the testator, and the product of the influence was the will or gift that would not have been made but for the influence. Steve will point to Harry's mildly distracted state, Wilma's constant carping, and Wilma's attempts to manipulate Harry's behavior. Steve will most likely fail in his undue influence argument, however, because he cannot overcome the second prong of the test.

Even if influence was exerted, it was not enough to overpower Harry's free will. As evidence of that fact, Wilma can point to the argument she and Harry had concerning their stock portfolio, in which Harry prevailed over Wilma. This does not sound like a man who has capitulated his free will to another. Steve cannot shift the burden back to Wilma by claiming that she and Harry were in a confidential relationship, because the presumption of undue influence that arises when a bequest is made to one in a confidential relationship does not apply to spouses.

Finally, Steve will argue that Wilma's attempts to influence Harry amounted to fraud in the inducement. Where the execution of the will or the inclusion therein of a particular gift is the result of fraud, the will or the gift is invalid. To show fraud sufficient to invalidate a will, the will contestant must show that (i) someone made a false representation of material fact, knowing it to be false; (ii) the representation was made for the purpose of inducing the testator to write a will in a particular way; and (iii) the testator reasonably believed and relied on the statement in making the will. While it too will likely fail, this is Steve's strongest argument.

Hiding Steve's letter, refusing to let Steve speak to Harry by phone while falsely claiming Harry was not at home, and denigrating Steve to Harry whenever possible could amount to a knowingly false representation of a material fact. It would probably not be terribly difficult to prove that Wilma's actions were based at least partly on a desire to manipulate Harry's disposition of his property. The biggest problem would be to show that Harry relied on these actions and statements when he made his will. He seemed to express disappointment that Steve had not settled down as the reason for the small bequest. He did not mention problems between Steve and Wilma, or that Steve seldom called or wrote letters. The fact that Wilma encouraged Harry's relationship with Dorothy has no effect on this analysis other than to show Wilma's motive. Thus, it seems unlikely that Steve will be able to show that it was Wilma's actions that induced Harry to make the small bequest to Steve and leave the rest to Wilma and Dorothy.

2.   If Steve is not successful in contesting Harry's will, he will receive nothing from Harry's estate.

A clause in a will providing that a beneficiary will forfeit his interest in the estate if he contests the will is valid and enforceable in Illinois. Some states will not give effect to the forfeiture clause if the contestant has challenged the will with good faith and probable cause, but Illinois does not recognize this exception.

QUESTION 3

Testator was a successful businesswoman and had acquired a considerable personal fortune. When Testator executed her will, she was married to Husband. Husband had a child from a prior marriage, Child. Testator had great affection for Child.

Testator's properly executed will made the following dispositions: "First, I give my diamond ring to Friend. Second, I give $10,000 to Child. Third, I give the rest of my estate to Husband."

Ten years after Testator executed this will, she and Husband divorced and entered into a property settlement agreement. Thereafter, Testator lost all contact with Child.

Three years after the divorce, Testator suffered a severe stroke. A conservator was appointed to manage Testator's property. The conservator sold Testator's diamond ring for $50,000 and put the proceeds in a savings account to pay Testator's living expenses.

Testator died three months after her stroke. She was survived by Husband (from whom she was divorced), Child, Friend, and three grandnieces, Alice, Barbara, and Carol. The three grandnieces were the grandchildren of Testator's brother, Barry, who had predeceased Testator. Barry had two children, Donna and Ed, both of whom also predeceased Testator. Alice was Donna's child, and Barbara and Carol were Ed's children. Testator's relatives are shown on the following family tree:

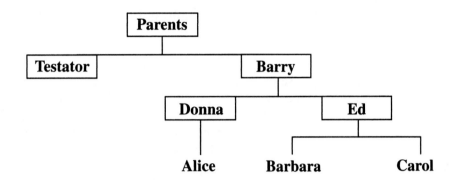

Testator had no other surviving relatives. Testator never revised her will after her divorce. At the time of her death, her $600,000 estate included the $50,000 savings account consisting entirely of the proceeds from the sale of her diamond ring.

How should Testator's estate be distributed? Explain.

ANSWER TO QUESTION 3

Testator's estate should be distributed as follows: $50,000 to Friend, $10,000 to Child, $270,000 to Alice, and $135,000 each to Barbara and Carol. Note that in most jurisdictions, Alice, Barbara and Carol would split the $540,000 equally.

Generally, when specifically bequeathed property is not owned by the testator at death, the bequest is adeemed (it fails). Here, the ring bequeathed to Friend is no longer in Testator's estate at the time of her death. Under the identity theory applied in most states, the ademption doctrine is an objective test that does not take into account the testator's probable intent. If the property is not in the estate at the testator's death, it is adeemed, and the reason it is not in the estate is immaterial. Illinois courts, however, have tempered the ademption doctrine by requiring some act of the testator from which it can be inferred that she wanted the gift revoked. Given this requirement, if a guardian or conservator is appointed for the testator after the will is executed and the bequeathed property is sold by the guardian, the beneficiary is entitled to the sale proceeds to the extent they have not been expended for the testator's care. In this case, a conservator was appointed for Testator after the will was executed, the ring was sold by the conservator, and the entire amount of the sale proceeds remain. Thus, since there was no act on the part of Testator from which it could be inferred that she intended to revoke the gift to Friend, Friend is entitled to the $50,000 proceeds from the sale of the ring.

Husband takes nothing from Testator's estate, but Child is entitled to the $10,000 bequeathed to her. Testator's divorce from Husband does not affect Child's bequest, and Testator has not validly revoked the gift. Without revocation, a bequest in a validly executed will remains in full force regardless of the subsequent relationship of the parties.

If a testator is divorced after making a will, all gifts to the former spouse are revoked, and the will takes effect as though the former spouse predeceased the testator. Thus, the provision leaving the residue of Testator's estate to Husband is revoked by operation of law, and the residue will pass under the law of intestacy (*see* below). Child takes her $10,000 bequest because Testator's divorce from Husband revokes only gifts to Husband, not gifts to anyone else. Without a valid revocation, a bequest in a validly executed will remains in full force regardless of the subsequent relationship of the parties. Since Testator did not revoke Child's gift, Child is entitled to $10,000.

The rest of Testator's estate will pass under the intestacy statute of her state. In most states, if a decedent is not survived by a spouse or descendants, her intestate property passes to her parents and/or siblings (and children of deceased siblings per stirpes). Here, Testator's parents and brother have predeceased her. In most states, that would mean that the three grandnieces would split the residue of Testator's estate evenly (a per capita with representation distribution). The property is divided at the first generational level at which there are living takers. Here, that would be the level of the grandnieces, and they would each take one-third of the $540,000 residue. Some states follow a per capita at each generational level type of distribution that would also result in an equal split among the grandnieces. Illinois, however, adheres to a strict per stirpes method of distribution. Under this method, the stirpital shares are always determined at the first generational level (the child level) regardless of whether there are living takers. Since Barry had two children, Donna and Ed, there are two stirpital shares. One goes to Alice, and the other is split between Barbara and Carol.

In conclusion, Testator's estate will be distributed $50,000 to Friend, $10,000 to Child, $270,000 to Alice, and $135,000 each to Barbara and Carol.

QUESTION 4

Tim executed a valid will in 1993 with the following dispositive provisions:

> **(1) I give my pickup truck to my nephew Alexander.**
> **(2) I give my house at 241 Landfill Road to my nephews Bertram and Charley, share and share alike.**
> **(3) I give all the money in my checking account at the Fourth Street State Bank to my niece Debra.**
> **(4) I give $100,000 to my nephew Ernest.**
> **(5) I give $100,000 to my niece Florence.**
> **(6) All the rest, residue, and remainder of my estate I give to my sister, Grace.**

In May of 1994, Tim sold his house at 241 Landfill Road and purchased a new house at 386 New Mine Lane with the proceeds. In June of 1994, Tim traded in his 1984 Ford pickup (which he owned when he executed his will in 1993) on the purchase of a new Dodge pickup, for which he otherwise paid cash. In July of 1994, Tim transferred the funds in his Fourth Street State Bank checking account to a savings account in the same bank. In January of 1995, Tim's niece Florence died, survived by her husband, Herbert, and her two children, Isabelle and Jersey.

Tim died on May 28, 1995. The assets available for distribution after payment of all taxes and expenses of administration are:

House at 386 New Mine Lane	**$65,000**
Dodge pickup	**12,000**
Fourth Street State Bank savings account	**15,000**
Checking account at another bank	**7,000**

How are these assets distributed? Explain.

ANSWER TO QUESTION 4

Tim's assets will be distributed as follows: Alexander will take the Dodge pickup; Bertram and Charley will take nothing; Debra will take the $15,000 savings account at Fourth Street State Bank; Ernest will take the house on New Mine Lane (or its proceeds) and the checking account; and Grace, Herbert, Isabelle, and Jersey will take nothing.

Alexander will take the Dodge pickup truck under the first clause of Tim's will. The will states "my pickup truck," and Tim owned a pickup truck that was in his estate at his death; thus, Alexander will take the Dodge pickup truck. The fact that Tim owned a Ford pickup truck at the time he executed his will does not affect this outcome. A will takes effect and "speaks" at the time of the testator's death. Thus, the will operates on facts as they exist at the time of the testator's death. The circumstances at the time the will was executed are relevant in determining the testator's intent if that is in issue, but here the disposition in the will is clear. If the will clearly specifies a particular disposition, it must be carried out, and extrinsic evidence of a contrary intent of the testator is not permitted. Here, Tim's will clearly states that Alexander is to receive Tim's pickup. Tim has a pickup in his estate; thus, it passes to Alexander. Note that although Tim's purchase of the Dodge pickup had the effect of changing Tim's will as to the identity of the gift, under the "facts of independent significance doctrine," Tim is deemed to have a lifetime motive and purpose in buying the new pickup. Thus, testamentary formalities are not required, and the Dodge pickup is substituted for the Ford.

Bertram and Charley take nothing because the house at 241 Landfill Road was not in Tim's estate at his death. When specifically bequeathed property is not owned by the testator at death, the bequest is adeemed (*i.e.*, it fails). A specific devise is a gift of specifically described property that can be satisfied only by the receipt of the particular property described. The bequest to Bertram and Charley could be satisfied only with the house on Landfill Road; since Tim no longer owned the house on Landfill Road, the gift fails. Note that specific devisees, such as Bertram and Charley, have no interest in the sale proceeds of the specifically devised property. Bertram and Charley, therefore, have no interest in the New Mine Lane property.

Debra will probably take the $15,000 in the Fourth Street State Bank savings account. As applied to the facts at Tim's death, the bequest to Debra of "all the money in my checking account at Fourth Street State Bank" is ambiguous because Tim has a checking account at a different bank and a savings account at Fourth Street. This is a latent ambiguity, which means that the language of the will is clear, but a misdescription results when the language is applied to the facts. In Illinois, extrinsic evidence is admissible to cure all ambiguities. Testimony regarding the testator's surrounding circumstances at the time of the execution is permitted, although the testator's own declarations are not. In this case, at the time of execution, the funds that are currently in the savings account were in the checking account. Thus, assuming extrinsic evidence does not show a contrary intention, the court would probably find that Tim intended Debra to take those funds. Note that the bequest to Debra is a specific bequest (it did not state a dollar amount), but was not adeemed because changing accounts is generally construed as merely a change in form.

Ernest will take the remainder of Tim's estate, and Florence's estate and her descendants will take nothing. Ernest and Florence were given general legacies of $100,000 each. A general legacy is a bequest of a dollar amount that is payable out of the general assets of the estate without a claim on any particular source of payment. The doctrine of ademption does not apply to general legacies.

Florence's estate takes nothing because her bequest lapsed. When a beneficiary dies during the testator's lifetime, the gift lapses (it fails). The lapsed gift passes as part of the residue. Illinois has an anti-lapse statute that operates to save the gift if the predeceasing beneficiary was a descendant of the testator and left descendants who survived the testator. Here, Florence left descendants who survived Tim, but Florence, Tim's niece, was not Tim's descendant. Thus, the anti-lapse statute does not apply, and the $100,000 bequest to Florence lapses. Many states have broader anti-lapse statutes that apply whenever the predeceasing beneficiary is related in any way to the testator. In those states, Isabelle and Jersey would have been substituted for Florence and taken the legacy. Note that under no circumstance would Herbert have taken the legacy. An anti-lapse statute does not save the gift for the beneficiary's estate, but rather substitutes the beneficiary's descendants as takers.

Since Tim's estate is not sufficient to pay the $100,000 legacy to Ernest, Ernest will take the house or its proceeds (worth $65,000) and the checking account (worth $7,000); the remaining $28,000 of his legacy is abated. When the assets owned by the testator at death are not sufficient to pay all of his debts and satisfy all of the specific, demonstrative, and general legacies of his will, the assets abate in the following order: residuary estate, general legacies, and then specific bequests. There is no residue; so Grace takes nothing.

QUESTION 5

Wife and Husband were married in 1988. They had two children, Anna and Barbara, born in 1989 and 1991. In 1992, Wife validly executed a will which provided:

> I leave Husband $100,000 and hope and expect that he will continue to provide for my mother Mattie, as I have done for many years. I leave the rest of my estate to Husband. I name Husband executor of my estate. I intentionally disinherit any person not named in this will.

In February 1995, Wife filed for divorce from Husband. In August 1995, the trial court entered a decree that granted Wife a divorce, divided the property of Wife and Husband, and ordered Husband to pay child support. The economic terms of the decree became effective immediately, but the portion of the decree that actually ended the marriage between Wife and Husband was not to become final until November 1995.

Wife was killed in an automobile accident in September 1995, two months before the divorce decree was to become final. She was survived by Husband, her children Anna and

Barbara, and her mother Mattie. For 10 years before her death, Wife had sent Mattie, who was disabled, $400 per month.

Under the law of intestate succession in this jurisdiction, a decedent's surviving spouse is entitled to one-half of the estate if the decedent is survived by children; decedent's children are entitled to one-half of the estate if there is a surviving spouse and to the entire estate if there is no surviving spouse.

1.   Is Husband barred from taking under Wife's will? Explain.

2.   Assuming Husband is not barred from taking under Wife's will, to whom should Wife's estate be distributed? Explain.

ANSWER TO QUESTION 5

1.   Husband will probably not be barred from taking under Wife's will. At issue is whether the initial decree of divorce with the property settlement is sufficient to revoke Wife's will provisions in favor of Husband by operation of law.

In Illinois and nearly all states, if a testator is divorced after making a will, all gifts to the former spouse and all appointments of the spouse as executor or trustee under the will are revoked, and the will takes effect as though the former spouse had predeceased the testator. However, this rule generally applies only to final decrees of divorce. Anything short of a *final* decree of divorce generally does not revoke provisions in favor of a spouse, regardless of how close the couple is to the final decree. Thus, the fact that all of the economic provisions of the divorce had been decided and became effective before Wife's death will not prevent Husband from taking under Wife's will. Note, however, that the Uniform Probate Code ("UPC") takes a different view. In a UPC jurisdiction, Husband would be barred from taking under Wife's will, even without a final decree of divorce. The UPC provides that a complete property settlement entered into after or in anticipation of a separation or divorce operates as a disclaimer of the spouse's elective share, family protections, intestate share, and provisions under a will that was executed before the property settlement. [U.P.C. §2-207]

2.   Husband will take the entire estate, but will hold $100,000 as trustee of a trust for the benefit of Mattie. The issues are whether the language regarding the $100,000 created a trust and whether Anna and Barbara are entitled to take anything.

Usually, a settlor clearly directs the trustee to carry out the intended terms of a trust, but difficulties arise when the transferor merely expresses a hope, wish, or suggestion that the property be used for a certain purpose. A direction such as the one used in this case with respect to the $100,000 bequest to Husband that "[I] hope and expect that he will continue to provide for my mother Mattie . . ." is precatory language. Most courts today infer from such language that no trust was intended and that the transferor merely wanted her desires known so that the transferee could comply if he so wished. The inference against the creation of a trust may be overcome, however, if: (i) the directions are not vague, but definite and precise; (ii) the directions are addressed by a decedent to his executor or administrator; (iii) failure to impose the trust results in an unnatural disposition by the testator; or (iv) extrinsic evidence shows that the transferor had been supporting the alleged beneficiary prior to executing the instrument, and the beneficiary would not have sufficient means of support without the trust.

In this case, the facts support overcoming the inference on three of the four possible grounds. Wife's directions are fairly precise in that there is a stated dollar amount to be used for her mother's support, with the direction to provide for her "as I have done," knowing that Husband must be aware of the amount of monthly support Wife has been sending. Wife's directions are addressed to the executor of her estate, Husband. Finally, extrinsic evidence would show that Wife had been supporting Mattie for seven years prior to the execution of her will and likely would show that Mattie needs the income to have sufficient means. The fact that Husband is to take the remainder of the estate is another strong indication that Wife intended to create a trust. Since Husband was taking the entire estate, there would be no other reason to segregate $100,000 from the rest of the estate. Thus, the court will almost certainly find that Wife's will created an enforceable trust for the benefit of her mother, Mattie.

If the court finds that no trust was created, the $100,000 would pass to Husband under the residuary clause in Wife's will. Anna and Barbara would take nothing because Wife's will effectively disposes of all of Wife's estate and thus nothing passes by intestacy to Wife's heirs. (Note that Wife's language of disinheritance would have no effect on property passing under the intestacy laws. The only way to disinherit intestate heirs is by disposing of all of the property by will.)

In summary, Husband will take title to the entire estate and will be appointed executor, and Mattie has a beneficial interest in a $100,000 trust to be administered by Husband as trustee. Anna and Barbara will take nothing.

QUESTION 6

Following extensive conversations and negotiations, Husband and Wife agreed to the terms of reciprocal wills under which each left his or her entire estate to the survivor and the survivor left the survivor's entire estate one-half to Husband's family and one-half to Wife's family. Each of their wills, dated September 10, 1994, was properly executed. Each will contained the following clause: "This will and the will of my spouse each were executed after extensive conversations and negotiations."

On May 10, 1995, Husband wrote a valid holographic will that reads:

> **Notwithstanding the provisions of my will dated September 10, 1994, I leave $50,000 to Wife; my stamp collection, which is located in my safe deposit box, to those friends of mine listed on a sheet of paper that is attached to the cover of the collection; and the balance of my estate to Sister.**

Husband placed the May instrument in a desk drawer in his home office. Wife inadvertently discovered the instrument and confronted Husband about it. In the course of a heated argument, Husband told Wife he had changed his will because he did not like her family. One month later, Husband had a fatal heart attack.

Husband's estate consists only of $400,000 in cash and the stamp collection. Wife, Sister, and Friend, whose name is the only name that appears on a sheet of paper attached to the cover of Husband's stamp collection in his safe deposit box, dispute how the estate should be distributed.

Under state law, holographic wills are valid.

How should Husband's estate be distributed? Explain.

ANSWER TO QUESTION 6

Husband's estate should be distributed as follows: One-half of the entire estate ($400,000 + the value of the stamp collection) to Wife, the stamp collection and the remainder of the estate to Sister. The issues presented are whether Wife and Husband had valid, enforceable contractual wills; whether the list regarding the stamp collection is incorporated by reference into the holographic will; and whether Wife should take her elective share.

Husband and Wife might have had contractual wills; nevertheless, husband's subsequent holographic will is effective. If wills are contractual, the contract is that the survivor shall not revoke the will after the death of the first to die. However, courts imply a term that the parties are free to rescind the contract while both are still alive by giving notice to the other party. Contractual wills are recognized in Illinois if the contract is proven by clear and convincing evidence. A court will look to the will itself, as well as to extrinsic evidence, to determine whether such clear and convincing evidence exists.

Here, Husband and Wife had written mutual reciprocal wills (*i.e.,* separate wills containing similar dispositive provisions). This alone does not give rise to a presumption that the wills were contractual. However, the reciprocal provisions coupled with the language indicating that the wills each were executed after negotiations with the other spouse might be sufficient evidence that the wills were contractual. Nevertheless, even if there is sufficient evidence to find contractual wills, Husband's effective holographic will—which Wife found while both parties were alive—was sufficient both to give Wife notice of Husband's intent to rescind and to revoke the first will (*see* discussion below). Thus, if a contractual will was made, it was rescinded and Wife's only remedy with regard to the rescinded contract is to change her own will.

The valid holographic will of 1995 revoked the 1994 will in its entirety. If a second testamentary instrument does not expressly revoke a prior will, the instruments are read together to the extent possible. However, the second instrument revokes the first to the extent of any inconsistent provisions. Here, although it did not expressly state that it was revoking the 1994 will, the 1995 will disposed of Husband's entire estate and was thus entirely inconsistent with the 1994 will. Since the 1994 will is revoked and the 1995 will is valid, the next issue is whether the provision regarding the stamp collection is valid and enforceable. (Note that Illinois does not recognize holographic wills. The question, however, stated that the answer was to assume that holographic wills are valid.)

In most states, an extrinsic document may be incorporated into a will by reference, so that it is considered part of the will, if: (i) the document is in existence at the time the will is executed, (ii) the will itself refers to the document incorporated as being in existence at the time the will was executed, and (iii) the language of the will sufficiently describes the writing, making the writing identifiable. In this case, it is not clear whether the list naming Friend as the recipient of the stamp collection was in existence at the time Husband executed the 1995 will. The will did not refer to the document as if it was definitively in existence; describing a document as being "attached to the cover" may or may not be interpreted as meaning that the document already existed. Furthermore, Husband's use of the word "friends" in the will is problematic because only one name, Friend, appeared on the document attached to the stamp collection. This could indicate that Husband wrote the will, thought about to whom he wanted the collection to go, came up with only one name, and then wrote the document that was found attached to the stamp collection. It simply is not clear. Thus, it is unlikely that the writing naming Friend as the beneficiary of the stamp collection will be found to be incorporated by reference. Note that the doctrine of acts of independent significance is of no help in saving the gift to Friend because the list appears to have no nontestamentary purpose. The stamp collection will pass to the residue of the estate, and thus, to Sister.

Nearly all states have an elective share statute, which gives a surviving spouse the election to take a statutory share of the decedent's estate in lieu of taking under the will. In Illinois, the statutory share is one-half of the probate estate if the decedent is not survived by issue and one-third if the decedent is survived by issue. Nothing in the facts suggests that Husband has any descendants; thus, Wife would be entitled to a statutory share of one-half of Husband's net estate. Husband's probate estate is $400,000, plus the value of the stamp collection. Clearly, it would be in Wife's best interest to take her statutory elective share rather than the $50,000 bequest in the will. Sister's gift of the remainder interest will abate accordingly.

QUESTION 7

See Family Law Question 6 for Wills issue.

QUESTION 8

Jim began work with Ajax Corporation in 1989, at which time he filed papers naming his father, Fred, as beneficiary on his employer-provided life insurance policy. Jim executed a valid will on May 9, 1993, containing the following dispositive provisions:

    (a) I give my car to my friend, George.

    (b) All the rest of my estate I give to my brother, Barton.

After executing the 1993 will, Jim met Megan, whom he married on June 10, 1995. Their daughter, Lindsey, was born on October 15, 1996. Jim died on January 2, 1997, without ever having revoked his 1993 will. The property in which he held interests at his death consisted of the following (computed after payment of taxes and administration expenses):

(a) A 1996 Honda automobile, titled in Jim's name alone, valued at $10,000.

(b) Bank accounts in Jim's name alone, with a final balance of $50,000.

(c) His employer-provided life insurance policy proceeds, in the sum of $50,000.

Jim is survived by his wife, Megan, his daughter, Lindsey, his parents, and his brother, Barton. How are these assets distributed at Jim's death? Explain.

ANSWER TO QUESTION 8

Father will take the $50,000 in life insurance as the named beneficiary on the policy. Of the remaining property (a $10,000 car and $50,000 in cash), one-third ($20,000) will pass to Megan if she timely files for an elective share, one-half ($30,000) will pass to Lindsey as a pretermitted child, and the rest ($10,000) will pass to Barton under the residuary clause of Jim's will.

The $50,000 life insurance proceeds: The life insurance proceeds will be distributed to Jim's father, Fred, as the beneficiary designated on the policy. Payment of life insurance proceeds is governed by the terms of the insurance contract; the proceeds go to the named beneficiary as a valid nonprobate transfer that is not affected by the insured's will. Also, Jim's subsequent marriage and birth of a child had no effect on the beneficiary designation. Since Jim did not change the policy beneficiary after his marriage or after Lindsey was born, Fred takes the insurance proceeds.

The 1996 Honda automobile: The Honda passes with the residuary estate. Under the acts of independent significance doctrine, the bequest of the Honda was valid even though Jim wrote the will in 1993 and acquired the Honda in 1996. In effect, this was a bequest of "the car that I own at my death." However, George apparently predeceased the testator in this case because he is not among the persons named as having survived Jim. The Illinois anti-lapse statute does not apply to save the gift because George was merely a friend; he was not a descendant of the testator. Therefore, the bequest of the Honda lapses, and falls into the residuary estate.

The $50,000 bank accounts: The $50,000 in Jim's bank accounts is also part of the residuary estate. Disposition of a bank account depends on the manner in which it is held. Jim held the account in his name alone; no survivorship provision applied to the account, and no other terms of the account directed how the account should be disposed of on Jim's death. The property is thus part of Jim's general estate, subject to his will and any statutory rights of Megan and Lindsey.

Megan: Megan married Jim after Jim executed his will. Unlike some states, Illinois does not have a "pretermitted spouse" statute. In Illinois, marriage following the execution of a will has no effect on the will. However, Megan is entitled to an elective share of Jim's estate (a "right of renunciation") if she files notice of election within seven months after the admission of Jim's will to probate. In this case, Megan's elective share will be one-third of Jim's net estate, or $20,000, because Jim was survived by a descendant (Lindsey). Unlike many states, which apply the elective share fraction to the "augmented estate" (which includes certain nonprobate transfers as well as the probate estate), the Illinois elective share applies only to the net probate estate—here, property worth $60,000.

Lindsey: Lindsey was born after Jim executed his will. Unlike marriage, birth or adoption of a child after a will's execution has an effect on the will. Under the Illinois pretermitted child statute, a child born after the will is executed takes a portion of the estate equal to the amount the child would have received had the testator died intestate ***unless*** (i) provision is made for the child in the will or (ii) it appears from the will that the testator intended to disinherit the child. Here, no provision was made for Lindsey in the will and the will contains no provision that purports to disinherit or exclude her. Accordingly, Lindsey takes an amount equal to her intestate share. Because Jim was survived by a wife and a child, if Jim had died intestate, Lindsey's intestate share would be one-half of the net probate estate, or property worth $30,000.

Barton: Barton will take the remainder of the probate estate as the residuary beneficiary in Jim's will. However, Megan will take property worth $20,000 as her elective share, and Lindscy as a pretermitted child will take property worth $30,000, so only $10,000 passes to Barton.

QUESTION 9

See Trusts Question 5 for Wills issue.

QUESTION 10

Husband's valid will provides:

> **I, Husband, leave my entire estate to Wife, or, if she predeceases me, I leave my entire estate in equal shares to my son, Son, and my daughter, Daughter.**

Wife's valid will bequeaths her entire estate to Husband. It does not provide for an alternate gift if Husband predeceases her.

Husband and Wife recently died in a fire in their home. The fire was set by Son in his second-floor bedroom at 2:00 a.m. Wife's body was found in her nightclothes in the second-floor bedroom she shared with Husband. Husband's body was found in his nightclothes at the base of the stairs on the first floor of their home with his head facing the front door, his feet toward the upstairs landing, and red marks on his stomach indicating that he had been crawling down the stairs when he had been overcome by smoke.

Husband and Wife were survived by Son and Daughter and by Son's daughter, Granddaughter.

Son claims the fire was set inadvertently when a cigarette he was smoking in bed dropped to the mattress, causing it to ignite. The fire marshal has found traces of a combustible substance on the premises, suggesting the possibility that the fire may have been set intentionally. The local prosecutors, however, have declined to seek an indictment because, although the available evidence indicates that it is more likely than not Son intentionally set the fire, the evidence is insufficient to support a criminal conviction.

The intestate succession statute of this jurisdiction provides that a decedent's surviving spouse is his or her sole heir. If there is no surviving spouse, the decedent's issue take the estate per stirpes. This jurisdiction also has enacted the Uniform Simultaneous Death Act.

1. To whom should Husband's estate be distributed? Explain.

2. To whom should Wife's estate be distributed? Explain.

ANSWER TO QUESTION 10

1. Husband's estate passes according to his will, one-half to Daughter and one-half to Son, unless Son is barred from inheriting. If Son is barred from inheriting, Granddaughter would take Son's one-half under the Illinois anti-lapse statute.

The issues are whether: (i) Wife predeceased Husband, (ii) Son would be barred from taking a portion of Husband's estate, and (iii) Granddaughter would take Son's share of Husband's estate if Son is barred from taking.

It is likely that the fact finder would conclude that Wife predeceased Husband under the Uniform Simultaneous Death Act. The Uniform Simultaneous Death Act provides that when the title to property or its devolution depends on priority of death and there is no sufficient evidence that the persons have died otherwise than simultaneously, the property of each person is disposed of as if he had survived; *i.e.*, the property passes as though the beneficiary or heir predeceased the other decedent.

In this case, the fact finder would likely conclude that Wife predeceased Husband. From the facts, it appears that the fire started on the second floor of the home while both Husband and Wife were asleep (owing to the time of the fire and the fact that both were found in their night-clothes). While Husband was able to get out of bed and crawl down the stairs to the first floor, Wife was overcome while still in the bedroom. One could also probably assume that due to the nature of the marital relationship, Husband would not have left Wife upstairs if she was still alive. Thus, there is sufficient evidence that Husband and Wife did not die simultaneously but rather that Husband survived Wife by a short time. Husband's estate would pass one-half to Son and one-half to Daughter, per the alternative disposition in his will; however, Son may be barred from taking if he is a "slayer."

Under the Illinois Probate Code, one who intentionally and unjustifiably causes the death of a decedent forfeits any interest in the decedent's estate. The property passes as though the killer predeceased the decedent. A conviction of murder in any degree is conclusive proof for a probate proceeding. However, in the absence of a murder conviction, any competent court may make a determination of guilt. (Note, however, that the civil trial cannot take place before a final determination is made in a criminal trial or, if there is no criminal trial, one year after the date of death.) In this case, although Son was not convicted of murder (or even tried), a court could find that Son killed Husband based on the fire marshal's evidence. If the court so finds, Son would be barred from taking from Husband's estate. The estate would be distributed as if Son predeceased Husband—one-half to Daughter and one-half would lapse unless the anti-lapse statute applies.

Here, Granddaughter takes Son's share under the Illinois anti-lapse statute. Normally, if a will beneficiary dies (or is treated as having died) during the testator's lifetime, the gift lapses. However, Illinois has an anti-lapse statute that saves a gift if the predeceasing beneficiary was a descendant of the testator. The beneficiary's descendant takes by substitution. Here, Son is treated as having predeceased the testator, but he has a living descendant, Granddaughter, who would take Son's share by substitution.

2.   Wife's estate passes to Husband, according to her will. As discussed above, Husband survived Wife and the Uniform Simultaneous Death Act does not apply. Therefore, Wife's estate would pass to Husband under her will; then Husband's estate would be distributed as discussed in 1., above.

QUESTION 11

Theresa purchased a cottage just outside the town of North Lake, Illinois, on May 5, 1995, for $60,000. She financed the purchase, in part, with a mortgage loan from First State Bank, in the amount of $31,000.

On October 15, 1995, Theresa executed a valid will containing the following provisions:

      (A) I direct that my executor pay all my just debts.

      (B) I give my cottage near North Lake to my nephew, Ned.

      (C) I give my shares of stock in Acme Corporation to my friend, Freida, if she survives me.

      (D) I give the residue of my estate to my mother, Mona, and my sister, Sarah, share and share alike.

Mona died on November 20, 1995 (Theresa's father had died in 1985). Theresa and her friend Freida died simultaneously on December 20, 1995, in an automobile accident while driving to the North Lake cottage. Theresa is survived by her nephew, Ned, and her two sisters, Sarah and Patricia. Freida, who died intestate, is survived by her son, Sam, who is her sole heir.

Theresa's estate (after taxes and administration expenses) consists of the cottage near North Lake, 100 shares of Acme Corporation common stock, and cash accounts at local banks totaling $60,000. The balance remaining due on the mortgage is $30,000.

How will the assets in Theresa's estate be distributed? Explain.

ANSWER TO QUESTION 11

Theresa's assets will be divided as follows: Ned takes the cottage near North Lake, subject to the $30,000 mortgage, and Sarah takes the $60,000 in the cash accounts and the 100 shares of common stock in Acme Corporation.

Cottage near North Lake, Illinois: At issue is whether Nephew Ned takes the cottage near North Lake subject to the $30,000 mortgage or whether the cottage passes to Ned free of the mortgage. Contrary to the common law, by statute Illinois has abolished the exoneration of liens doctrine. Liens on specifically bequeathed property, such as the cottage in North Lake, are ***not exonerated*** unless the will specifically directs exoneration. Under the statute, a general statement in the will calling for the payment of the testator's debts is not considered an expression of intent that any liens on property be exonerated. In this case, Theresa's will devises the cottage to Ned; however, it does not address what is to be done about the mortgage. The general statement directing the executor to "pay all my just debts" is not enough to show that Theresa intended the lien to be exonerated. Thus, Ned takes the cottage encumbered by a $30,000 mortgage.

100 shares of Acme Corporation common stock: The devise of "my shares of stock in Acme Corporation" lapses because Freida is treated as having predeceased Theresa. At issue is whether Freida survived Theresa, which would allow Freida to take the Acme stock left to her in Theresa's will. Illinois has adopted the Uniform Simultaneous Death Act, which states that when devolution of property depends on priority of death and there is no sufficient evidence that the persons have died otherwise than simultaneously, the property of each person is distributed as if she has survived. According to the facts, Theresa and Freida died simultaneously in an automobile accident. Since there is no evidence that the deaths were anything but simultaneous, Freida will be treated as if she predeceased Theresa and the devise of the stock lapses and falls into the residuary estate. (Note that the Illinois anti-lapse statute would not apply even if Freida were a descendant because the will shows a contrary intention—*i.e.,* Theresa wanted Freida to take only if she survived Theresa.)

$60,000 in cash accounts: The $60,000 and Theresa's 100 shares of Acme Corporation stock in the residuary estate will be distributed to Sarah. Sarah takes the entire residuary estate because Mona, the other residuary beneficiary, predeceased Theresa. Theresa's will gave the residue of her estate to her mother, Mona, and her sister, Sarah, "share and share alike." Because Mona predeceased Theresa, the issues are whether: (i) the Illinois anti-lapse statute operates to save the devise to Mona, and (ii) Sarah, the surviving residuary beneficiary, takes the share of the deceased residuary beneficiary, Mona.

Mona's share of the residuary estate ($30,000 + 50 shares of Acme stock) will not be saved by the Illinois anti-lapse statute. The Illinois statute applies only if the predeceasing beneficiary was a descendant of the testator. In this case, since Mona is Theresa's mother and not one of Theresa's descendants, the gift will lapse.

As to whether Sarah takes Mona's share of the residue, Illinois does not follow the common law "no residue of a residue" rule which provides that a lapsed residuary gift "falls out of the will" and passes by intestacy. Instead, Illinois law provides that the residuary beneficiaries who survive the testator take the deceased beneficiary's share of the residuary estate in proportion to their interests in the residue. Under this rule, Sarah, as the sole surviving residuary beneficiary, takes Mona's share of the residuary estate (in addition to her own). Thus, Sarah takes the entire $60,000, plus the 100 shares of Acme Corporation stock that fell into the residuary as a result of the failed devise to Freida.

QUESTION 12

Child was the biological daughter of Dad and Mom. When Child was an infant, Husband and Wife legally adopted her in State A with the consent of Dad and Mom. All the parties then lived in State A.

Three years after Child was adopted, Husband died. Thereafter, Wife married New Husband. At the time of this marriage, Child was four years old. Five years later, New Husband died intestate, domiciled in State A. He was survived by Wife, Child, and his closest blood relative, Uncle. Although New Husband never adopted Child, Child resided with Wife and New Husband until New Husband's death. New Husband raised Child and treated Child in all respects as if she were his biological child.

After New Husband's death, Wife moved to State B and established her domicile there. She died intestate in State B, survived by Child and by Grandmother, Wife's closest living blood relative. At the time of Wife's death, she owned property in State B and a summer vacation home in State A.

Grandmother, who was a domiciliary of State B, had a close relationship with Wife and Child. One week after Wife died, Grandmother died testate. Her valid will, executed two years earlier, bequeathed her entire estate to Wife, or "if Wife predeceases me, to such of Wife's children who survive me."

The laws of intestate succession in States A and B provide that one-half of an intestate decedent's property is distributable to the decedent's spouse and the other half to the decedent's issue per stirpes, or absent such issue, to the decedent's ancestors or, if none, to the decedent's collateral blood relatives.

The law of State A provides that an adopted child cannot inherit from the biological parents but can inherit from the adopting parents as if the adopted child were a biological child of the adopting parents.

The law of State B provides that an adopted child cannot inherit from an adopting parent who died intestate. However, State B law concerning the construction of wills provides, "If an adopting parent leaves a testamentary class gift to his or her children, adopted children are included in the class gift."

There are no other governing state statutes.

1.   Is Child entitled to inherit from New Husband's estate? Explain.

2.   Is Child entitled to inherit from Wife's estate? Explain.

3.   Is Child entitled to inherit from Grandmother's estate? Explain.

ANSWER TO QUESTION 12

1.   Child is probably not entitled to inherit from New Husband's estate. At issue is whether a stepchild who was raised and treated in all respects as a biological child is entitled to a share of her stepparent's intestate estate.

Generally, stepchildren have no inheritance rights because there is no legal relationship between the stepchild and stepparent. However, the doctrine of *equitable adoption* or adoption by estoppel (recognized by about one-half of the states) allows a child who has been treated in all respects as if she were adopted, to inherit from the parent-like figure. When considering an equitable adoption situation, courts are usually hesitant to find an equitable adoption unless the "parent" has made an express oral or written promise to adopt the child. [*See* Clark, *Law of Domestic Relations in the United States*, at §20.9] If State A recognizes equitable adoptions and Child can demonstrate the required factors, she may be able to inherit New Husband's estate. Since the facts do not mention an agreement by New Husband to adopt Child, nor do the facts discuss whether State A recognizes equitable adoption, it is unlikely that Child will inherit from his estate.

2.   Child will inherit Wife's vacation home in State A directly from Wife. Although Child is not entitled to inherit Wife's real or personal property in State B because State B law provides that an adopted child cannot inherit from an adopting parent who dies intestate, Child will probably take the State B property via Grandmother—the property will pass to Grandmother by intestacy, and then to Child under Grandmother's will (*see* 3., below). At issue is which state's law will govern the disposition of Wife's property.

Devolution of real property on intestacy is governed by the law of the state where the property is located (lex situs). Here, the facts state that there is real property in State A (a vacation home) and there may be real property in State B (the facts refer only to "property in State B"). State A law allows an adopted child to inherit from an adopting parent as if she were a biological child of the adopting parent. Thus, Child would inherit the vacation home in State A. In contrast, State B does not allow an adopted child to inherit from an adopting parent who dies intestate. Thus, any real property in State B would not pass to Child. Instead it would pass to Wife's closest living blood relative, Grandmother.

Devolution of personal property on intestacy is governed by the decedent's domicile at the date of death. In this case, Wife probably had personal property in State B, the state in which she was domiciled. However, according to State B law, an adopted child may not inherit from an adopting parent who dies intestate. Thus, Child would not inherit any of Wife's personal property in State B because she is an adopted child. Any such property would pass to Wife's closest living blood relative, Grandmother.

3.   Child will probably take under Grandmother's will since the court must give the testator's intent full effect if there is ambiguity as to the disposition of the will.

Since Grandmother's domicile at death was State B, State B law will determine whether Child takes under her will. A State B statute provides that "if an adopting parent leaves a testamentary class gift to his or her children, adopted children are included in the class gift." Based on this statute, a child could share in the testamentary gift of an adoptive *parent*, but it is unclear how the statute treats a class gift from a *grandparent*. Since the statute does not mention grandchildren, Child cannot argue that she takes under the will based solely on the statutory language.

However, when analyzing the will, the court will look to Grandmother's intent at the time she made the will. Since Grandmother had a close relationship with Wife and Child, it is likely that she intended her property to go to Wife or Child. From the facts presented, it appears that Grandmother treated Child as her own grandchild. Even though Grandmother was not a party to the adoption, it is likely that a court would extend the statutory treatment of adoptive parents to grandparents in this situation. From a public policy standpoint, Child would have a strong argument as to her inclusion in the class gift since the state statute already includes adoptive children in class gifts. Thus, based on this reasoning, Child will probably inherit from Grandmother's estate.

QUESTION 13

On January 2, 1995, Testator died testate in a nursing care facility called Nursing Home, Inc. Testator's will, signed on December 28, 1994, when she was mentally competent, makes two bequests: (1) a bequest of $100,000 to "my heirs at law" and (2) a bequest of "my residuary estate to Nursing Home, where I shall be resident at my death." President, who is both a director and the president of Nursing Home, was named executor. Testator's will was drafted by Lawyer, a shareholder of Nursing Home, who also serves as Nursing Home's attorney. Testator's only heir is her cousin, Charles, who last saw Testator nearly a decade ago.

Throughout the 1980s, Testator's health declined. During the 1980s, while still living on her own, Testator became close friends with President. He visited her apartment many times and arranged for employees of Nursing Home to moonlight as nurses in her apartment. In

1992, Testator's physical condition deteriorated so significantly that she needed full-time care. President helped Testator make arrangements for admission to Nursing Home. While Testator was living at Nursing Home, a number of "estate planning seminars" were presented there by Lawyer, and a pamphlet titled "Will Information Guide" was distributed to the residents. The pamphlet, written by President, had extensive provisions regarding Nursing Home's need for charitable gifts and the proper method of including bequests to Nursing Home in a will.

On the evening of December 28, 1994, after attending an estate planning seminar given by Lawyer, Testator said she wanted to write her will. Testator, Lawyer, and President immediately went into President's office, where Lawyer drafted the will in full accord with Testator's instructions and with President present. Two visiting friends of Testator were also present in the room when the will was signed. They will testify that after Testator declared the document to be her will and asked them to sign as witnesses, she attempted to sign the will. However, because of a chronic tremor, Testator's hand shook so badly that she was unable to hold the pen despite repeated attempts. In frustration, she finally asked President if he would write her name for her on the will, which President did. Immediately thereafter, the two friends signed the will as witnesses.

After the will was executed, Lawyer gave the will to Testator. She later placed it in her night table drawer for safekeeping.

After Testator's death, a nurse found the will in the night table. She gave it to President. When he read the will he saw that the bequest of $100,000 to Testator's heirs at law had been crossed out with a straight black line made by a felt-tip marking pen.

President petitions for the probate of Testator's will. In the petition, President alleges that the entire estate should pass to Nursing Home because the will was validly executed and the bequest to Charles had been revoked.

1.   On what grounds might Charles contest the will, and how likely is he to succeed on each ground? Explain.

2.   If the will is probated, is Charles entitled to the $100,000 bequest? Explain.

ANSWER TO QUESTION 13

1.   Charles might argue that the will was not duly executed with the formalities required under Illinois law and thus should be denied probate. He may further argue that the will should be denied probate because Nursing Home exerted undue influence. Charles will not likely prevail on the first argument but may prevail on a contest alleging undue influence.

To be valid in Illinois, a will must be in writing, be signed by the testator, and be attested by two credible witnesses who signed in the testator's presence. Charles might argue that the signature on the will is not Testator's, since it was actually President who wrote Testator's name. However, this argument will fail. Recognizing that a testator may be physically unable to sign, Illinois law allows a testator's signature to be made by another in the testator's presence (scope of vision) and at the testator's direction. Here, because of a chronic tremor, Testator asked President to sign, which he did in her presence. Hence, Testator's signature is valid. The will was also witnessed by visiting friends who were present when the will was signed and who signed in Testator's presence. Thus, the will was duly executed.

Duly executed wills may be contested on a number of grounds, including undue influence. To prove undue influence, the will contestant must show that specific acts of influence were exerted on the testator that had the effect of overpowering the testator's mind and free agency such that the will would not have been executed but for the influence. However, a presumption of undue influence will arise if the contestant can show that: (i) the will gives a substantial benefit to a party who stood in a confidential relationship with the testator; (ii) the testator was in a dependent situation in which the party was in a dominant role; (iii) the testator reposed trust and confidence in the party; and (iv) the party was instrumental in preparing or procuring the will.

Charles can successfully raise the presumption here. First, the will left the residue of Testator's estate—presumably a substantial amount—to Nursing Home. This gift indirectly benefited Nursing Home's president and a stockholder, Lawyer, each of whom had a confidential relationship with Testator. Testator had relied on President's help in procuring care since before she was a resident at Nursing Home, and Lawyer drafted Testator's will, making him Testator's fiduciary by law. In addition, as a resident of Nursing Home, Testator was in a dependent relationship in which President was in a dominant role since Testator depended on President for her care. Testator was also undoubtedly dependent on Nursing Home to give her sound estate planning advice. Furthermore, since Testator and President were close friends, Testator must have trusted him and had confidence in him to act in her best interests. Lastly, Lawyer and President were both instrumental in preparing and procuring the will. Testator directed that her will be drafted after reading President's pamphlet urging gifts to Nursing Home and attending Lawyer's estate planning seminar at Nursing Home. The will was even prepared in President's office by Lawyer. Thus, the facts raise the presumption of undue influence.

The effect of the presumption is to shift the burden of proof to the beneficiary. The presumption can be rebutted only by clear and convincing evidence. Nursing Home may attempt to rebut the presumption by showing that Nursing Home would have been given the same amount or more absent these circumstances because Testator had lived there for the last few years of her life, Testator had not been in close contact with her family, and Testator and President were friends. In addition, Nursing Home may attempt to establish that the witnesses who saw all the dealings between Testator and President and Lawyer saw no evidence of undue influence. However, there is probably not sufficient evidence to rebut the presumption of undue influence.

In sum, while there is no direct evidence that Testator's free agency was overcome by President, Charles may be able to establish a presumption that undue influence was exerted on Testator.

2.   If the will is probated, Charles will be entitled to the $100,000 bequest. At issue is the effect of the line drawn through the gift to Charles.

While most states permit partial revocation by physical act of the Testator, Illinois does not. The only way to partially revoke a will in Illinois is to execute a codicil to the will. A mark of cancellation such as the one in Testator's will is disregarded. If the $100,000 bequest had been crossed out before execution, then the cross out would be given effect, and the gift would pass as part of the residuary clause to Nursing Home. Since Testator did not execute a codicil and since the facts do not reveal that Testator crossed out this provision before executing the will, the marks will be disregarded and Charles is entitled to the bequest.

QUESTION 14

Testator's validly executed will dated September 1, 1996, reads as follows:

I, Testator, being of sound and disposing mind, give:

1.   All of my tangible personal property to Sister.

2. $1,000 to Uncle, to be paid from my bank account at Bank.

3. $5,000 to Friend.

4.   100 shares of ABC common stock to Brother.

5.   The residue of my estate to Charity, a charitable organization.

At Testator's death, Testator's estate was valued at $50,000. This included tangibles valued at $1,000, Testator's bank account at Bank with a balance of $750, and 100 shares of ABC common stock valued at $20,000. ABC is a closely held corporation. Testator bought the 100 shares in December 1995. The balance of Testator's estate was held in publicly traded securities.

Testator died in an automobile accident resulting from Testator's negligence. The other party in that accident filed a claim against Testator's estate in the amount of $28,000. This claim was duly allowed by the court having jurisdiction over the estate, and $28,000 of the publicly traded securities were liquidated to pay the claim. There are no other debts, expenses, or taxes for Testator's estate.

Sister, Uncle, Friend, and Brother survived Testator. Uncle timely disclaimed any interest in the $1,000 bequest. Uncle's child, Son, also survived Testator.

How should Testator's estate remaining after the payment of the $28,000 claim be distributed among Sister, Uncle, Friend, Brother, Charity, and Son? Explain.

ANSWER TO QUESTION 14

Testator's estate should be distributed as follows: Sister gets all tangible personal property; Brother gets 100 shares of ABC common stock; Friend gets $1,000; and Uncle, Charity, and Son get nothing.

After paying the $28,000 claim out of the liquidated publicly traded securities, there will only be $22,000 in assets in Testator's estate. Since there are $22,000 in specific bequests and $5,000 in general bequests, there are insufficient assets in the estate to satisfy all of the bequests in Testator's will. Therefore, certain gifts must be reduced. Under the Illinois Probate Act, absent a contrary provision in the will, the estate will abate in the following order: (i) the residuary estate; (ii) general legacies, which abate pro rata; and (iii) specific devises and bequests. Therefore, Testator's estate should be distributed as follows:

Sister: Sister should receive all of the tangible personal property in Testator's estate, which is valued at $1,000. This is a specific bequest, and since there are sufficient assets, it does not abate.

Brother: Brother will receive 100 shares of ABC common stock. Ascertaining whether Testator intended a specific bequest of stock depends on what issue the court is deciding. Courts usually construe a gift of "100 shares of ABC common stock" as a general bequest for purposes of ademption. In contrast, such a bequest is treated as a specific bequest where there has been an increase in the number of shares. At issue here is whether the gift to Brother should abate. Since the gift to Brother identifies particular property capable of being identified, it is likely a specific bequest and should not abate. Therefore, Brother is entitled to all 100 shares of ABC common stock.

Uncle: The gift to Uncle is a demonstrative gift because it specifies the source of the gift—the bank account. Demonstrative gifts are treated as specific bequests for purposes of abatement, but to the extent the source of funds is insufficient, such gifts are treated as general bequests and are subject to abatement. Thus, the $750 contained in Testator's bank account will be treated as a specific bequest and the remaining $250 will be treated as a general bequest.

Nevertheless, Uncle will receive nothing under Testator's will since he timely disclaimed his interest in the $1,000 bequest. A beneficiary may disclaim any interest that passes to him from the decedent's estate. Such an interest passes as though the disclaiming party predeceased the decedent. Since Uncle does not fall within the purview of the anti-lapse statute (*see* discussion of Son below), the bank account contents will fall into the residuary.

Friend: The gift of $5,000 to Friend is a general bequest. After satisfying the specific bequests, there will only be $1,000 worth of assets in Testator's estate. Therefore, according to the Illinois abatement scheme, since this is a general bequest, she will receive $1,000 from the residuary.

Charity: Charity will receive nothing. Since there are not adequate assets to satisfy all bequests, the residuary estate is the first to abate, and consequently, there will be no property in the residuary estate.

Son: Son is not entitled to the bequest to Uncle. Since Uncle properly disclaimed his interest in the bequest, the gift is treated as if Uncle predeceased Testator. Almost all states have anti-lapse statutes that operate to save the gift if the predeceasing beneficiary was in a specified degree of relationship to the testator and left descendants who survived the testator. In Illinois, the anti-lapse statute applies only when the predeceasing beneficiary is a descendant of the testator. Since Uncle is not Testator's descendant, the gift to Uncle lapses and falls into the residuary estate, and Son gets nothing.

QUESTION 15

Tom and Wanda were married and had a child, Anna. After Wanda died, Tom had a non-marital relationship with Nancy, who had a child, Bill, from a prior marriage. At the time the relationship between Tom and Nancy began, Anna was 12 and Bill was 17. Three years after the relationship between Tom and Nancy began, they had a child, Chris. Shortly thereafter Nancy was killed in an automobile accident. Tom continued to raise all three children as his own but took no steps to adopt Bill. Although he acknowledged he was Chris's father, he took no steps to establish his paternity judicially.

During the 20 years following Nancy's death, the relationship between Tom and Anna soured, but Tom's relationships with Bill and Chris blossomed. Eventually, Tom came to

have little to do with Anna. Last year, things came to a head. At Thanksgiving dinner, Tom handed each of the children a check in the amount of $50,000. Each check was accompanied by a personal handwritten note signed by Tom. The note to Anna read: "You have been a constant disappointment to me over these years. Take this but expect no more from me." The notes to Bill and Chris, which were identical, read: "You have been a wonderful child to me. Use this gift well. I love you very much."

Four months ago, Anna died survived by her son, Danny. One month later, Tom died intestate leaving a probate estate of $250,000. Tom was survived by Bill, Chris, and Danny.

A state statute provides that property descends to issue if the intestate has no surviving spouse. It defines "children" as children born during marriage, adopted children, and children born out of wedlock, provided paternity is established judicially or is otherwise recognized by the father. State law prohibits holographic wills.

How should Tom's estate be distributed? Explain.

ANSWER TO QUESTION 15

Tom's estate should be distributed one-half to Chris and one-half to Danny. Bill will receive nothing.

In every state, an intestate's estate is distributable to the intestate's surviving descendants when the intestate dies without a spouse, as Tom did. Tom died intestate with one surviving child, Chris, and one surviving grandchild, Danny.

Bill, Tom's stepchild, has no inheritance rights. The fact that Tom appeared to have treated Bill as his own child is of no consequence; there is no legal relationship between Tom and Bill since Tom did not adopt Bill. Furthermore, Bill does not fit the statutory definition of a child of Tom set forth in the facts. Therefore, Bill receives nothing from Tom's probate estate.

Chris is a child of Tom under the statute set forth in the facts. The statute defines "children" to include nonmarital children provided that paternity is "recognized by the father." Here, the facts state that Tom acknowledged that he was Chris's father and he indicated as much in the note given with the $50,000 (although he wrote the same to Bill, who was not his child). Thus, Chris will inherit as Tom's child.

It could be argued that the note accompanying the gift to Anna renders the gift to her an advancement and therefore, reduces Anna's share of Tom's estate. In Illinois and most states, no gift is considered an advancement of an intestate share unless it is made to the donor's descendant and is declared an advancement in a writing by the donor or acknowledged as an advancement by the donee. Although Tom's writing did not expressly state an intention to have the gift treated as an advancement, it evidences an intent to limit the amount Anna would receive from Tom in the future. Thus, it could be argued that the note evidenced an advancement.

This answer assumes that, even if an advancement to Anna is found, it will not have the effect of reducing the shares of her issue, and so Danny's share will not be reduced by the $50,000 given to Anna.

If the note to Anna is interpreted as stating that Anna will never receive anything more from Tom, these words of apparent disinheritance are ineffective since Tom died intestate. Tom could alter the statutory scheme of distribution only by writing a will. Even if he had done so, it is not likely that Anna's issue would be disinherited unless Tom expressly stated that he intended to disinherit Anna's issue or he had executed a will disposing of all of his property to others, leaving nothing for Anna's issue.

The lifetime gifts to Bill and Chris are not advancements. The notes to Bill and Chris refer to the $50,000 as gifts. Further, there is no language suggesting that Tom intended the gifts to be treated as advancements.

Under the method of distribution prescribed by the Illinois intestacy statute, the decedent's issue take their shares per stirpes. Under this method of distribution, the property is divided into equal shares at the first generational level regardless of whether there are any living takers. Each living person at the level takes a share, and the share of each deceased person at that level passes to his issue by right of representation. Therefore, since Tom had two children, Anna and Chris, his estate would be divided into two shares, with Chris taking a one-half share, and the other one-half share passing by right of representation to Anna's child, Danny.

QUESTION 16

Banks was a 70-year-old bachelor. His closest living relatives were his two nieces. Banks had long been a patron of the arts and of the Opera Society. On January 15, 1997, Banks executed a will bequeathing $100,000 to each of his nieces and leaving his residuary estate to the Banks Foundation for Opera, a private foundation that he planned to establish when he retired. He hoped that in gratitude for his generosity the Opera Society would name the new opera house after him.

A year later, Banks learned that he had a terminal disease. He told his nieces he would leave them his entire estate if they would take care of him. They agreed to do so, and, in February 1998, Banks moved in with his two nieces and asked his attorney to draft a new will bequeathing them all his property and expressly revoking his January 15, 1997, will.

Shortly before Banks was to execute the new will, the president of the Opera Society told Banks that the Board had agreed to name the building in his honor if they received a substantial bequest from him. Banks then decided to execute the new will using his two nieces as the only witnesses, believing this would render the will invalid. A day later, Banks signed the new will and, at his request, the nieces witnessed it. It was dated February 10, 1998. Banks placed this will inside an envelope, wrote in ink on the outside of the envelope, "Not to be opened until my death," and initialed the writing.

Banks died without having created the Banks Foundation for Opera. The February 10, 1998 will was found in the envelope with the following unsigned note in Banks's handwriting on the back of the last page of the will: "Ignore this will. I never intended to give my whole estate to my nieces. I signed it only to trick them into caring for me. Long live the Banks Opera House!"

1. For what reasons, if any, could the February 10, 1998, will be denied probate as Banks's last will? Explain.

2. **If the will of January 15, 1997, is probated, on what theory or theories, other than fraud, may the nieces assert a claim against the estate of their uncle for their care of him? Explain.**

3. **If the will of January 15, 1997, is probated, on what theory, if any, might the Opera Society assert a claim to the residuary estate? Explain.**

ANSWER TO QUESTION 16

1. The February 10, 1998, will may be denied probate as Banks's last will for several reasons.

First, it could be argued that the 1998 will was not executed with the requisite testamentary intent. For a will to be valid, the testator must intend that the particular instrument operate as his will. The use of language such as "This is my last will" raises a presumption of testamentary intent, but the presumption is rebuttable. Here, the writing on the back of the 1998 will will be introduced as evidence that Banks did not intend for the instrument to operate as his will. From the writing on the back of Banks's will, it is clear that Banks did not intend for his nieces to inherit his entire estate and that he wrote the will only to induce them to take care of him. Therefore, on these grounds, Banks's 1998 will will likely be denied probate.

In addition, it may be argued that the 1998 will was revoked by Banks. A will may be effectively revoked by operation of law, by a subsequently written instrument, or by physical act. Here, Banks wrote "Ignore this will . . ." on the back of the last page of his 1998 will. It may be asserted that this writing revoked the will. To revoke a will by written instrument, there must be a present intent to revoke, and the instrument must be executed with the same formalities as are required for the execution of a will. Here, Banks obviously intended to revoke the will. However, the writing on the back of the will was not executed with testamentary formalities. There were no witnesses and it was not signed by the testator. (Note that Illinois does not recognize holographic wills, *i.e.*, wills written entirely in the testator's handwriting and signed by the testator, but not witnessed. In states that recognize holographic wills, a valid holographic will may revoke a typewritten, attested will. However, this writing does not qualify as a valid holographic will, even though it was in Banks's handwriting, because it was not signed by him.)

It could further be argued that the 1998 will was revoked by physical act. A will can be revoked by burning, canceling, tearing, or obliterating it with the intent to revoke. Generally, the act must be shown to have had an actual effect on the will or its language. Here, by writing "Ignore this will" on the back of the last page of his will, Banks did not accomplish a revocation by physical act because no portion of the will was canceled or obliterated. Therefore, the argument that the 1998 will was revoked will fail.

Banks's belief that the 1998 will was invalid because it was witnessed by Banks's two nieces who are beneficiaries under the will is incorrect. While at common law, if one of the two necessary, attesting witnesses was a beneficiary, the will could not be probated, this is no longer the rule. In Illinois, the fact that the will makes a gift to an attesting witness never results in denial of probate of the will. The only effect is that the witness-beneficiary may lose her legacy. The will is valid, but the gift to the witness-beneficiary is void. If the beneficiary would have been entitled to a share of the estate if the will were not probated, she is entitled to the lesser of the bequest in the will or the share of the estate she would have taken if the will were not probated. (Note that some states have repealed their "interested witness" statutes altogether. In these states, the fact that a witness is also a beneficiary has no effect on the will whatsoever.) Thus, Banks's 1998 will will not be denied probate on these grounds.

2.   Banks's nieces may assert a claim against his estate on the theory that Banks and his nieces had a contract in which he promised to leave them his entire estate in return for them taking care of him. In such a case, contracts law, not wills law, controls.

In Illinois, a contract to make a will, if supported by valid and adequate consideration, is enforceable in equity. Services rendered to family members, without clear and convincing evidence of a contract, are presumed to be gratuitous and do not constitute sufficient consideration to establish a contract. Banks's statement to his nieces that he would leave them his entire estate if they would take care of him is not sufficient evidence that a contract existed. Banks's nieces should introduce the 1998 will (even though under this fact pattern it will not be probated), in which Banks left his entire estate to his nieces, as evidence of the contract to support their claim. Banks's nieces may be able to successfully claim that Banks died in breach of contract. They can seek damages equaling the value of the property promised, which in this case would be the value of Banks's entire estate.

3.   If the 1997 will is probated, the Opera Society may assert a claim to the residuary estate under the theory of cy pres. The doctrine of cy pres is used to further the testator's intent and ensure that a charitable gift does not fail if the specific charitable purpose indicated by the settlor is accomplished or becomes impractical. If the settlor had a general charitable intent, the court will direct that the trust property be applied to another charitable purpose as close as possible to the original one, rather then permit the trust to fail and become a resulting trust. Application of the cy pres doctrine is not limited to charitable trusts. It also applies to outright bequests to charities where, as here, the named charity is not in existence at the testator's death.

In his 1997 will, Banks left his residuary estate to the Banks Foundation for Opera, a private foundation that he planned to establish when he retired, but he died without having created the foundation. Therefore, if the doctrine of cy pres is not applied, the gift will fail and become a resulting trust in favor of Banks's heirs (his two nieces). The Society will argue that cy pres should be applied and that the residuary estate should be used to fund a trust in favor of the Opera Society. The Society will argue that Banks had a general charitable intent to benefit the art of opera and this intent would be furthered by applying cy pres so that Banks's residuary estate benefits the Opera Society.

QUESTION 17

Testator, a domiciliary of State A, died on February 1, 1998, leaving a net estate valued at $100,000. Testator was survived by three children, Andy, Billy, and Cory, and one grandchild, Gary, who is Cory's only child. The following documents were found in Testator's safe deposit box:

1.   **At the top, there was an envelope containing Testator's canceled check dated February 1, 1990, made payable to Charity Y in the amount of $15,000. Attached to this check were copies of other canceled checks to Charity Y paid over the previous 15 years and a copy of a note from Testator to Charity Y dated February 1, 1990, stating: "Enclosed**

is my check in the amount of $15,000. 1 know you will use this as you have all of my prior gifts to carry out the important work of your organization. I hope I'll be in a position to do more for you in the future. Your work is very important to me."

2.　Underneath the first envelope was a second envelope containing a one-page typewritten will dated September 10, 1989, leaving all of Testator's estate to Andy and Billy. Testator had duly executed this will. However, the phrase "VOID—May 18, 1993" was written in large print across the entire face of the will, and on the back of the will the following words appeared: "Revoked, because I really prefer my March 2, 1983, will."

3.　Underneath the second envelope was Testator's duly executed one-page typewritten will dated March 2, 1983. In this will, Testator bequeathed "$50,000 to Cory, $10,000 to Charity Y, and the residue of the estate to Andy and Billy."

On October 30, 1998, Cory filed a properly acknowledged document with the appropriate persons, renouncing all rights Cory had under Testator's two wills.

State A does not permit holographic wills. Under State A law, (1) an intestate's heirs are the intestate's surviving children, and (2) the issue of any child who predeceases the intestate take the deceased child's share.

1.　Under what theory could the March 2, 1983, will be probated, and to whom would the estate be distributed under that will? Explain.

2.　Under what theory could the September 10, 1989, will be probated, and to whom would the estate be distributed under that will? Explain.

ANSWER TO QUESTION 17

1.　The 1983 will cannot be probated in Illinois. The issue is whether the 1983 will can be probated even though it was revoked when the 1989 will was executed under the doctrine of revocation by inconsistency.

Illinois does not permit revival of a revoked will unless it is (i) reexecuted with the proper testamentary formalities or acknowledged by the testator, or (ii) republished by a validly executed codicil. Here, the will cannot be probated because it was not reexecuted, acknowledged, or republished by a properly executed codicil. The notation on the back of the 1989 will is not a valid codicil because it was not properly witnessed and Illinois does not recognize holographic instruments. Thus, the 1983 will may not be probated.

Assuming that the 1983 will can be probated, it must be determined who will share in Testator's estate. The issues are whether the check to Charity Y was in satisfaction of its gift in the will and whether Cory properly disclaimed his interest.

Charity Y: The check to Charity Y was not in satisfaction of the gift in Testator's will. Illinois does not have a statute on gifts in satisfaction; however, it is likely to apply the common law rule. Under the common law, an inter vivos gift made subsequent to a will's execution is generally deemed to be in satisfaction of the gift in the will if the testator so intended. However, a gift to someone ***unrelated*** to the testator is presumptively ***not*** in satisfaction of the legacy. In this case, there is nothing indicating Testator's intent that the check to Charity Y was to be in satisfaction of the gift in the will. Indeed, Testator's letter indicated a desire to bestow more gifts on Charity Y in the future. Also, Charity Y was an unrelated party. Thus, Charity Y is entitled to the $10,000 gift made in the 1983 will.

Cory: Cory's interest passes to his son, Gary. Illinois law does not set a time limit for filing a disclaimer. Once disclaimed, the interest passes as though the disclaiming party predeceased the decedent. If Cory had predeceased Testator, the gift to Cory would have gone to his son Gary under the Illinois anti-lapse statute. The Illinois anti-lapse statute provides that a gift to a descendant of the testator who predeceases the testator does not lapse, but rather goes to the descendants of the predeceased descendant who survive the testator, unless there is a contrary provision in the will. The facts indicate that Cory properly filed his disclaimer. Thus, he is treated as having predeceased Testator, and the anti-lapse statute is applied to determine the substitute taker. Here, the predeceasing beneficiary, Cory, was Testator's descendant and left surviving issue, Gary. Also, there were no contrary provisions in Testator's will. Thus, under the anti-lapse statute, Gary receives Cory's share.

Andy and Billy: Andy and Billy will each receive $20,000 as residuary legatees. A residuary legatee takes whatever is left after the general and specific legacies made under a will are distributed. Here, Testator's net estate is valued at $100,000. After making the $10,000 gift to Charity Y and the $50,000 gift to Cory, $40,000 remains to be divided equally between Andy and Billy— $20,000 each.

2.   The 1989 will may be able to be probated under the doctrine of dependent relative revocation ("DRR"), but this is doubtful. At issue is whether the 1989 will or intestate distribution comes closer to effectuating Testator's intent.

DRR allows a court to disregard the revocation of a will when it appears that the testator revoked the will because of a mistake of law and the belief that another disposition of his property was effective. However, a court will not apply DRR if intestate distribution would come closer to effectuating what the testator was trying to accomplish by revoking the will.

Here, Testator revoked his 1989 will under the belief that his 1983 will would become effective. If Testator was mistaken and the 1983 will did not become effective, DRR could be applied. However, applying DRR would not come as close to effectuating Testator's intent to go back to the distribution scheme under the 1983 will as would intestate distribution. The 1983 will left a $50,000 gift to Testator's son Cory, $10,000 to Testator's favorite charity, and the rest of his estate ($40,000) to his two other sons. If revocation of the 1989 will is disregarded, that will will be effective. The 1989 will leaves everything to Testator's sons Andy and Billy ($50,000 each), but nothing to Testator's son Cory or to the charity. On the other hand, all three sons would take an equal gift under intestacy, because under the laws of intestacy, if a testator dies leaving descendants but no spouse, the testator's property passes to his surviving descendants per capita with representation. In other words, the property is divided into equal shares at the first generational level at which there are living takers. Thus, Andy, Billy, and Cory would receive one-third each. This seems closer to effectuating Testator's intent than would a distribution under the 1989 will. Therefore, a court would probably not apply DRR and instead would allow Testator's estate to pass through intestacy.

Note that the facts say that Cory only disclaimed his interest under Testator's two wills. He did not disclaim any interest under intestacy. If he had disclaimed under intestacy, Cory would be deemed to have predeceased Testator and his one-third share would pass to his son Gary under the intestacy statute.

QUESTION 18

Testator's last will included the following four dispositive provisions:

1. I leave my family portrait painted by Painter to my sister, Susan.

2. I leave $100,000 each to my child Leslie, my child Doris, and my wife, Wendy.

3. I leave $40,000 to my brother, Ben, and direct that my stamp collection be sold to satisfy this bequest.

4. I leave the balance of my estate to the trustees of my alma mater, University.

Testator's will was signed by Testator and witnessed by Testator's brother, Ben, and by Testator's accountant, Aaron.

Two years after the will was executed, Testator and Wendy divorced. As a result of their property settlement agreement incident to that divorce, Testator transferred $200,000 to Wendy. That agreement imposed no further obligations on Testator.

Testator never remarried. Three years after the divorce, Testator died a domiciliary of State A. He was survived by Leslie and Doris, his only heirs, and the other individual devisees named in his will. Testator's estate consisted of the family portrait valued at $2,000, the stamp collection valued at $20,000, and $110,000 on deposit at a local bank.

State A law provides that a will must be signed by the testator and witnessed by two witnesses.

How should Testator's estate of $132,000 be distributed? Explain.

ANSWER TO QUESTION 18

Is the will valid? In State A (as in Illinois), a will must be attested by two competent witnesses. At common law, an attesting witness who was also a beneficiary under the will (*i.e.*, an interested witness) was not a competent witness, and if one of the two required witnesses was a beneficiary, the will was denied probate. However, in most states today, statutes have changed the common law rule: The will is valid, although the interested beneficiary may lose his gift. Thus, this will is valid despite having Ben as a witness. (For a discussion of Ben's share, *see* below.)

Does Testator and Wendy's divorce revoke the gift to Wendy? Assuming State A has a statute like that in Illinois, divorce following execution of a will revokes all gifts and appointments in favor of the former spouse. The rest of the will remains valid and is read as though the ex-spouse predeceased the testator. Here, Testator and Wendy divorced two years after the will's execution. Thus, the $100,000 legacy to Wendy is revoked and falls into the residuary estate.

How will the estate be distributed? Abatement is the process of reducing testamentary gifts when estate assets are insufficient to satisfy all bequests and devises. The testator may set out an order of abatement in his will, but if he does not, an estate generally abates in the following order: (i) property passing by intestacy; (ii) the residuary estate; (iii) general legacies, which abate pro rata;

and (iv) specific devises and bequests. For abatement purposes, a demonstrative legacy is treated as a specific legacy up to the value of the particular asset, and as a general legacy as to the rest.

Susan: Since specific gifts are satisfied first, Susan receives the portrait, valued at $2,000.

Ben: As mentioned above, Ben is an interested witness. In most states, an interested witness's gift under the will is eliminated ("purged"). Exceptions are made if (i) the interested witness is a supernumerary witness (*i.e.*, an "extra" witness, leaving a sufficient number of disinterested witnesses to attest)—not the case here—or (ii) the interested witness would have taken under intestacy or an earlier will—again not the case here, because a brother will not take as an heir when the decedent's children survive, and there is no mention of an earlier will. Thus, Ben's gift is eliminated.

The Uniform Probate Code ("UPC") and statutes in several non-UPC states have abolished the interested witness rule, and a bequest to an interested witness is not purged. Therefore, if State A has adopted the UPC, Ben would be entitled to his gift. Because the gift to Ben was a demonstrative legacy (*i.e.,* gift of a general amount to be funded from a specific source), Ben would receive $20,000 from the sale of the stamp collection. The other $20,000 would be treated as a general legacy and would abate (*see* below).

Leslie and Doris: In most states, Leslie and Doris will equally share $130,000 because Ben's interested witness status purges his gift. If State A is a UPC state, Ben will be paid $20,000 for the stamp collection and the remaining $110,000 will be divided between Leslie, Doris, and Ben in proportion to their gifts under the will.

University: Since the residuary estate is exhausted after satisfying the specific and general gifts, University receives nothing.

QUESTION 19

On May 18, 1997, Testator duly executed a typewritten will in the presence of three witnesses.

The will contained only the following three paragraphs:

> 1.   **I give my watch to my brother, Ben.**
>
> 2.   **I give my dining room table to my sister, Sarah.**
>
> 3.   **I give the balance of my tangible personal property to the person named in a letter I signed and dated May 17, 1997, which I have placed in the desk in my home.**

Testator died on January 2, 2000, a domiciliary of State A. The foregoing will was found in the desk in Testator's home. However, in paragraph 2. of the will, the phrase "dining room table" had been scratched out and immediately above it the word "automobile" was typed. And, on the back of the will, the following language appeared in Testator's handwriting: "I don't want Ben to have my watch. I want it to go to my first cousin, Chris." No signatures appeared on the back of the will beneath this writing.

The letter referred to in paragraph 3. of the will was found in the desk, and named Nicole, the daughter of Sarah, as the beneficiary.

Testator's only surviving blood relatives are Ben, Sarah, Chris, and Nicole. In addition to the watch, dining room table, and automobile, Testator left a $10,000 bank account.

State A permits wills to be completely or partially revoked by the execution of a subsequent will or codicil, by physical act, or by cancellation, when accompanied by an intent to revoke. State A law also provides that "unsigned holographic wills or codicils are valid."

To whom should Testator's estate be distributed? Explain.

ANSWER TO QUESTION 19

Testator's estate is distributed as follows: Chris receives the watch, Nicole receives the automobile and dining room table, and Sarah and Ben share the bank account.

Watch: The watch belongs to Chris. The issue is whether the clause devising the watch to Ben in the original will was validly revoked by the execution of the holographic codicil on the back of the will. A holographic instrument is an unattested instrument that is entirely in the testator's handwriting. Normally, holographic instruments are not valid unless they are signed by the testator. However, State A permits unsigned holographic instruments. Holographic instruments may revoke or modify typewritten, attested wills. The writing on the back of the original will is a valid holographic instrument because it is entirely in Testator's handwriting. The fact that it was not signed by Testator is irrelevant since State A does not require holographic instruments to be signed. The codicil revoked the bequest of the watch to Ben and instead bequeathed it to Chris. Thus, Chris is entitled to the watch. (Note that Illinois does not recognize holographic instruments. Thus, if Illinois law were to apply, the holographic codicil would be invalid and the watch would belong to Ben.)

Dining room table: The dining room table falls into the residuary estate and belongs to Nicole. The issues are whether Testator (i) properly revoked the bequest of the dining room table to Sarah, and (ii) effectively bequeathed the automobile to Sarah.

A partial revocation occurs when a testator cancels only a portion of the will with the intent to do so. State A permits partial revocations by cancellation. Here, Testator scratched out the phrase "dining room table" in his will, but did not touch any other portions of the will. Moreover, Testator attempted to simply change the bequest to Sarah from a dining room table to an automobile. Thus, it is clear that he intended to revoke only the provision bequeathing the dining room table to Sarah, and not the remainder of the will. Because partial revocations are valid in State A, Testator validly revoked the bequest of the dining room table to Sarah. (In Illinois, however, partial revocations by physical act are not permitted and the deletion is disregarded. If Testator's will was probated in Illinois, the revocation of the clause bequeathing the dining room table would be disregarded.)

Testator attempted to bequeath the automobile to Sarah after the will was executed. In Illinois and most states, any alteration made after the will is executed is ineffective to change the will unless the will is properly reexecuted. Only the words present when the will was executed constitute the decedent's will, and any subsequent writings are unattested words. The result is that the will is given effect as originally written. In the present case, Testator attempted to change the devise to Sarah by crossing out the words "dining room table" and substituting the word "automobile," but failed to properly reexecute the will after making the alteration. Thus, "automobile" is an unattested word and the alteration is ineffective. Further, the addition of the word "automobile" is not a valid holographic codicil because it was not in Testator's handwriting—it was typewritten. Thus, the will is read as originally written, minus the bequest of the dining room table to Sarah that Testator revoked. (Under Illinois law, Sarah is still entitled to receive the dining room table.)

If the revocation of the bequest of the dining room table is effective, Sarah should argue that the doctrine of Dependent Relative Revocation ("DRR") applies. Under DRR, a court may disregard a revocation if it determines that the revocation was premised on a mistake of law and would not have occurred but for the testator's mistaken belief that another disposition was valid. If the other disposition is ineffective, the revocation accompanying the attempted disposition fails and the will remains in force. For DRR to apply, the disposition that results from disregarding the revocation must come closer to effectuating what the testator tried but failed to do than would an intestate distribution. Here, Testator believed that the disposition of the automobile to Sarah would be effective, and revoked the bequest of the dining room table based on that mistaken belief. However, DRR does not save the bequest under these circumstances because it would not come closer to what Testator tried but failed to do than would an intestate distribution. For whatever reason, Testator decided that he did not want to leave the dining room table to Sarah. Testator's intent was merely to provide a gift to Sarah from his estate. This can be accomplished through intestate distribution, under which she will share in his bank account, as discussed below.

Tangible personal property: The dining room table and automobile belong to Nicole. The issue is whether the letter found in Testator's desk can be incorporated by reference into the will. An extrinsic document that is not present when the will was executed may be incorporated into the will by reference. To be incorporated (i) the document must be in existence at the time the will is executed, (ii) the will must refer to the document as being in existence, and (iii) the will must sufficiently describe the document to permit its identification. In the present case, Testator's will unequivocally refers to a document dated May 17, 1997, illustrating that it was in existence when the will was executed. The will also identifies the document as the one that Testator placed in his desk at home, which is where the letter was subsequently found. That letter, which names Nicole as the beneficiary of the balance of Testator's tangible personal property, is validly incorporated into Testator's will. When Testator died, the balance of his tangible personal property, including the dining room table and automobile, passed to Nicole. (Note that in Illinois Nicole receives only the automobile, since the revocation of the bequest of the dining room table to Sarah was ineffective.)

Bank account: The bank account is distributed to Sarah and Ben in equal shares. Because paragraph 3. referred to tangible personal property, it did not dispose of the bank account, which was intangible personal property. The will does not contain a residuary clause, and therefore the will does not govern disposition of the bank account. When a testator's will fails to dispose of all of his property, partial intestacy results, and the undisposed of property passes to the testator's heirs through intestate succession. If a decedent is not survived by a spouse or descendants, his property is distributed in the following order: (i) to his parents, (ii) to the descendants of his parents, (iii) to his grandparents, (iv) to more remote ancestors, and (v) to the county. Here, Testator was not survived by a spouse, children, or parents. Thus, his closest living relatives are his siblings, Sarah and Ben, who succeed to the bank account in equal shares.

QUESTION 20

Testator duly executed a will dated March 1, 1998. Among other things, the will stated:

1. I direct that all of my just debts and expenses be paid by my executor.

2. I give my family home to my daughter, Daughter.

3. I give my 24-carat gold watch to my son, Son.

4. I give the rest of my estate, including any property over which I may have a power of appointment, to Trustee to hold in trust for the primary benefit of Son and Daughter, with the remainder to their children.

Testator was the income beneficiary of two separate testamentary trusts, one created by Testator's mother, Mary, the other by Testator's father, Frank.

Testator had a special testamentary power of appointment exercisable in favor of Testator's issue over the testamentary trust created by Mary. Mary's will provided that Testator could exercise the power only by a specific reference to the power of appointment created by Mary's will.

Testator had a general testamentary power of appointment over the testamentary trust created by Frank.

Both Mary and Frank died in 1990. They were survived by Testator, Son, and Daughter.

At Testator's death in October 2001, Testator owned (a) the family home on which Testator was personally liable for a $50,000 mortgage, (b) an insurance policy that specifically insured Testator's 24-carat gold watch, which had been stolen from Testator five days before Testator died, and (c) a portfolio of stocks and bonds. Testator owned no other assets.

Bank was appointed executor of the estate. Trustee was named trustee of the trust created in paragraph 4 of Testator's will. Bank collected the value of the stolen watch from the insurance company.

1. Did Testator effectively exercise the two powers of appointment he had at the time of his death? Explain.

2. Should the $50,000 mortgage on Testator's home be paid out of the assets of Testator's residuary estate? Explain.

3. Should the insurance proceeds for the stolen watch be distributed to Son, as legatee of the watch, or to Trustee? Explain.

ANSWER TO QUESTION 20

1.(a) *Mary's power of appointment:* Testator did not properly exercise the power of appointment granted by Mary. The issue is whether a testamentary power of appointment is validly exercised by a general statement when the donor requires that the power be specifically referred to. A special testamentary power of appointment is one that is exercisable only by the donee's will and is in favor of a specified class of persons. A testamentary power of appointment is properly exercised by the donee's validly executed will. If the donor specifies that the power must be exercised by specifically referring to the power, the direction must be complied with—the power cannot be exercised by implication or by a blanket statement. Here, the terms of Mary's power of appointment specified that it could be exercised only by specifically referring to the power of appointment created in Mary's will. Although Testator properly exercised the power by his will and in favor of the class specified by Mary—his issue—he did not specifically refer to the power created in Mary's will. Instead, he attempted to exercise the power by a blanket statement in his residuary clause. Therefore, Testator did not properly exercise the power of appointment in Mary's will.

(b) ***Frank's power of appointment:*** Testator properly exercised the power of appointment granted by Frank. The issue is whether a testamentary power of appointment is validly exercised by a blanket statement. A general testamentary power of appointment is one that is exercisable only by the donee's will and is in favor of the donee, his estate, his creditors, or the creditors of his estate. A blanket exercise of a power of appointment is valid provided the donor's will does not require that the exercise specifically refer to the power of appointment. Thus, a devise stating, "all the rest, residue, and remainder of my property, including any property over which I may have a power of appointment," will be given effect. Testator properly executed Frank's power of appointment by a blanket statement in his residuary clause. A residuary clause, by itself, is generally insufficient to exercise a power of appointment. However, the residuary clause in Testator's will specifically mentioned the power of appointment ("including any power over which I may have a power of appointment") and thus was a valid exercise of the power of appointment granted by Frank.

2.   Daughter is not entitled to have the mortgage on the home paid out of the residuary estate. The issue is whether the beneficiary of specifically devised property is entitled to have any liens on the property exonerated. Although the common law permits exoneration of liens on specifically bequeathed property, Illinois has abolished the exoneration of liens doctrine. Thus, liens on specifically bequeathed property are not exonerated unless there is a specific direction to do so in the testator's will. Further, a general direction in the testator's will to pay all debts is not sufficient to justify exoneration of the lien. In this case, Testator's will merely directs that all of his "just debts and expenses be paid." This direction is not sufficient to allow exoneration of the mortgage out of his residuary estate. Thus, Daughter takes the family home subject to the mortgage.

3.   Son is entitled to the insurance proceeds from the stolen watch. The issue is whether the beneficiary of specifically devised property is entitled to insurance proceeds when the subject of the devise is no longer in the testator's estate at death. Generally, if specifically bequeathed property is not in the testator's estate when he dies, the gift adeems (*i.e.*, it fails). However, the Illinois courts provide that if the property is damaged or destroyed under circumstances in which the testator could not have ***intended*** an ademption, the beneficiary is entitled to any casualty insurance proceeds resulting from the loss. Here, Testator's watch was stolen only five days before he died and the insurance proceeds were collected by Bank. There is no indication that Testator intended the ademption and Son should receive the proceeds.

QUESTION 21

On February 10, 2000, Testator signed her last will, which was witnessed by two witnesses—

Testator's nephew, Nephew, and Testator's next-door neighbor. Testator died on May 10, 2000, after a brief hospitalization.

During the six months before she died, Testator experienced frequent episodes of forgetfulness. For example, Testator often missed appointments with her physicians and her bank trust officer. Testator had also become increasingly forgetful about matters of personal hygiene. On the other hand, throughout that six-month period, Testator maintained all of her financial records and visited in person and by telephone with each of her 20 living relatives, all of whom she easily recognized and identified. On April 3, she contacted her broker to advise him to sell her shares in Able Corporation because she had lost complete faith in the corporation's management following the release of its poor quarterly earnings report.

Testator's will bequeathed $100,000 to Nephew and the residue of her estate to Charity, a charitable organization with which Testator had been associated for more than 35 years. Nephew had no knowledge of the $100,000 bequest until after Testator died. She left no bequest to her three nieces, who are Nephew's three sisters. None of Testator's other living relatives was as closely related to her as Nephew and her three nieces.

Contemporaneous with the execution of her last will, Testator signed a durable health care power of attorney designating Nephew as her agent to make all health care decisions for her in the event she could no longer make them for herself. Nephew and Testator's next-door neighbor also witnessed this document.

One week before she died, Testator was admitted into a local hospital following a massive stroke causing severe brain damage. The following day, she lapsed into a coma and was connected to a life-support system. Four days later, Testator's physician advised Nephew that there was nothing medical science could do for Testator. After considering this advice, Nephew directed the physician to remove Testator from all life-support systems. The following day, Testator was removed from the life-support system and she died. She left an estate in excess of $1 million.

Testator's three nieces argue that Testator's durable health care power was not valid and that as a result Nephew should be liable in wrongful death for causing Testator's death because Nephew directed Testator's physician to withdraw Testator's life-support systems. Furthermore, they claim that either Testator's will is invalid or that, at minimum, the bequest to Nephew should be forfeited.

1.   Is Nephew liable in wrongful death for causing Testator's death? Explain.

2.   Is Testator's will invalid because of incapacity? Explain.

3.   Assuming Testator's will is valid, is the bequest to Nephew valid? Explain.

ANSWER TO QUESTION 21

1.   *Nephew's liability for testator's death:* Nephew is not liable for Testator's death. At issue is the liability of a durable power of attorney for decisions regarding the testator's life. A durable health-care power becomes effective when the principal (Testator) becomes incapacitated. The

power extends to all health-care decisions regarding the principal. In Illinois, an agent under a durable health-care power has authority to make any health-care decisions on behalf of the principal that the principal could have made for herself if she had capacity. The agent must act in the principal's best interest if no powers are specified in the instrument and is not subject to liability, as long as he acts in good faith.

Here, the durable health-care power became effective when Testator lapsed into a coma and became incapacitated. At that point, Nephew had the power to make any decisions regarding Testator's care providing they are in her best interest. After Testator's doctors informed Nephew that there was nothing that could be done for Testator, Nephew considered the advice and made the decision to discontinue life support. Nephew clearly acted in good faith in doing so and was not motivated by the bequest to him in the will because he was unaware of it until Testator's death. Therefore, Nephew is not subject to any liability for Testator's death.

2.   *Validity of Testator's will:* Testator's will is valid. The issue is whether a testator's lapses in memory indicate lack of testamentary capacity. In Illinois, a testator is presumed to be of sound mind unless proven otherwise. Testamentary capacity is measured at the time of the will's execution and exists if the testator (i) understood the nature of her act, (ii) knew the nature of her property, (iii) knew the objects of her bounty, and (iv) disposed of her property in accordance with her own desires. Mere evidence that the testator is old or in poor health is insufficient to establish lack of testamentary capacity.

In this case, the fact that Testator was forgetful during the months preceding the will's execution is not enough to prove incapacity, particularly because her episodes of forgetfulness were during a time when she maintained all her financial records, recognized and communicated with all her relatives, and was able to make coherent decisions regarding the sale of her stock. Testator understood that she was executing a will and knew the nature of her property. Further, the fact that she kept in touch with her relatives illustrates that she knew the objects of her bounty, and there is no evidence that the bequests in the will were procured by fraud or duress. Therefore, Testator's will is valid.

3.   *Bequest to Nephew:* The bequest to Nephew is valid. At issue is whether an attesting witness can take a gift under a will. Generally, an interested witness will lose a gift under the will unless one of two exceptions applies: (i) the witness was a supernumerary witness, or (ii) he would have taken a part of the estate if the will was not probated ("whichever is least" rule). In Illinois, a will must be witnessed by at least two witnesses. Here, there were only two witnesses to the will, so Nephew is not a supernumerary witness. Nevertheless, Nephew will take under the will because the other exception applies. In Illinois, under the "whichever is least" rule, Nephew is entitled to the lesser of the gift in the will or an intestate share because he would have been an intestate heir if the will had been denied probate. Under the Illinois intestacy statutes, if a testator is not survived by a spouse, descendants, or parents, the estate passes to descendants of the decedent's parents (*e.g.,* nephews and nieces). The facts state that Nephew and his three sisters were the most closely related to Testator; thus, they would be the only intestate heirs. Nephew will take the $100,000 bequest under the will because it is less than his intestate share, which would have been $250,000 ($1 million estate divided between Nephew and his three sisters).

QUESTION 22

Testator was an 80-year-old mentally alert widow. Testator retained Lawyer to prepare her

will naming Charity, a charitable organization, as the sole beneficiary of her estate. One week later, Testator received a photocopy of a proposed will that Lawyer had prepared for her.

A few days later, on October 1, 1998, Lawyer called Testator to inquire whether the proposed will conformed with her wishes. When Testator responded that it did, Lawyer suggested that Testator make an appointment to come to his office so that she could execute the original, which was in his possession. Testator responded that, because of her arthritic condition, it would not be convenient for her to do so, and she told him, "Just go ahead and sign the will for me." Lawyer said, "OK."

Later that day, Lawyer inserted "October 1, 1998" as the date of execution on the original will and signed Testator's name on the will in front of three secretaries who acted as witnesses. The secretaries then signed their names in the spaces provided on the will. All of them saw Lawyer sign Testator's name, and each of them saw the others sign their own names. Lawyer then called Testator and told her the will had been signed and witnessed. Testator replied, "Good, now it's done. Please keep the will for me."

A year later, Testator decided that she wanted to change the will to give her diamond ring to her niece, Nora. Deciding to make the change herself, she asked a friend to type up a document, which was identified as "a codicil to my existing last will." This document was then validly executed and stated, "I leave my diamond ring to my niece, Nora. In all other respects I hereby affirm my existing last will, executed on October 1, 1998."

A year later, Testator had a falling out with Nora. Remembering that she had devised her diamond ring to Nora, she gave the ring to another niece, Betty, as a gift. Testator died a few months later. Her closest surviving relatives were her two nieces, Nora and Betty. At the time of her death, her only asset was a parcel of real estate known as "Blackacre."

Who is entitled to Blackacre and to the diamond ring? Explain.

ANSWER TO QUESTION 22

Charity is entitled to Blackacre and Betty is entitled to the diamond ring. The issues are whether (i) the 1998 instrument was a validly executed will; (ii) the later codicil incorporated by reference the 1998 instrument; and (iii) the gift of the diamond ring to Nora was adeemed.

The 1998 instrument is not a valid will because it was not signed by Testator or by another in her presence. For a will to be validly executed, it must be signed by the testator. However, Illinois permits the testator's signature to be made by another person provided it is made at the testator's direction and in her presence. Here, Testator expressly authorized Lawyer to sign the will for her; however, Lawyer did not do so in Testator's presence. Therefore, the instrument is not a valid will and cannot stand on its own.

However, the 1998 instrument was validly incorporated by reference into the later codicil. Incorporation by reference allows an extrinsic document (here, the 1998 instrument) to be considered a part of the will even if it was not present when the will was executed. In Illinois, an extrinsic document can be incorporated by reference if: (i) the document was in existence at the time the will was executed, (ii) the will refers to the document as being in existence, and (iii) the language of the will reasonably identifies the document. The 1998 instrument, which was not present when the codicil was executed because it was in Lawyer's possession, can be incorporated into the codicil because all three elements are satisfied. First, the instrument was in existence as it was drafted a year prior to the codicil. Second, the codicil refers to the 1998 instrument as being in existence—the language of the codicil refers to "my existing last will" and specifies that it was executed on October 1, 1998. Third, the language of the codicil unambiguously identifies the instrument as the will executed "on October 1, 1998." Therefore, the 1998 instrument can be incorporated into the later codicil and be given effect even though it was not validly executed.

The gift of the diamond ring to Nora was adeemed when Testator gave it to Betty. A specific devise adeems (*i.e.*, it fails) when it is not owned by the testator at death. Here, Testator no longer owned the diamond ring on her death because she gave it to Betty during her lifetime. As a result, the testamentary gift of the ring to Nora fails and Nora takes nothing.

In conclusion, Charity receives Blackacre under the terms of the 1998 instrument that was incorporated into the later codicil, and Betty keeps the lifetime gift of the diamond ring.

QUESTION 23

In 1988, Testator duly executed a will devising Blackacre to Adam, $100,000 to Carrie, and the residue of her estate to Doris. However, in 1992, Testator telephoned her lawyer, Lawyer, who had possession of the 1988 will, and asked her to destroy it because Testator had changed her mind. Lawyer agreed. Immediately after hanging up the phone, Lawyer found the will, shredded it, and threw it away.

In 1996, Testator signed and dated a wholly handwritten document that stated: "I devise Blackacre to Earl and $2,500,000 to my good friend, Fred."

Testator died in 2002, a domiciliary of State A. She was survived by Greg, age 30, who was her child and only heir. Adam, Carrie, Doris, Earl, and Fred also survived Testator. There was no surviving spouse. Testator's net probate estate (after taxes, debts, and expenses) consisted of $5,000,000, plus Blackacre.

The 1996 document, together with an unexecuted copy of the 1988 will, the original of which Lawyer had shredded, were found among Testator's valuable papers. Both documents were offered for probate.

Under State A law, holographic wills are valid.

1. **Which documents, if any, govern the distribution of Testator's estate? Explain.**

2. **What are the respective shares, if any, in Testator's estate of each of the following: Adam, Carrie, Doris, Earl, Fred, and Greg? Explain.**

ANSWER TO QUESTION 23

1. *Validity of wills:* Both documents can be admitted to probate and will govern the distribution

of Testator's estate. The first issue is whether Testator validly revoked the 1988 will. Testator failed to validly revoke the 1988 will. In Illinois, a will can be revoked by a physical act (*e.g.*, burning, tearing, obliterating) if the act is accompanied by a present intent to revoke the will. The act of revocation can be performed by someone other than the testator if the revocation is at the testator's direction and in her presence. Here, Lawyer's attempt to revoke Testator's will by physical act was invalid because although the act was done with Testator's permission, it was not done in her presence. Additionally, the 1988 will was not revoked when Testator executed the 1996 will because the 1996 will did not contain a clause expressly revoking the 1988 will. Therefore, the 1988 will was not validly revoked and was still valid at Testator's death.

The second issue is whether the 1996 will is valid. Testator's 1996 will can be probated as a valid holographic will. A holographic will is validly executed if it is entirely in the testator's handwriting and signed by the testator. Here, the 1996 will was wholly in Testator's handwriting and was signed by her; therefore, it is valid. (Note that Illinois does not recognize holographic wills, although State A does.)

In conclusion, the 1988 and 1996 wills are both valid and both instruments will govern the distribution of Testator's estate.

2. ***Distribution of estate:*** Testator's estate will be distributed as follows: Carrie will receive $100,000, Earl will receive Blackacre, Fred will receive $2.5 million, and Doris will receive the residue. Adam and Greg will not share in Testator's estate.

The first issue is distribution of Testator's estate in light of the two wills. When a testator has validly executed two wills (as Testator did here), both wills are admissible to probate, and the later will revokes the prior will to the extent of any inconsistencies. Here, the 1996 will controls any inconsistencies between the two wills. In reading the provisions of the two wills, the only inconsistency is the devise of Blackacre—the 1988 will devises it to Adam, and the 1996 will devises it to Earl. Since the 1996 will is the most recent, it controls the inconsistency (*i.e.*, it revokes the earlier devise of Blackacre to Adam), and Blackacre therefore belongs to Earl; Adam takes nothing. The remaining provisions provide that Carrie receives $100,000, Fred receives $2.5 million, and Doris receives the residue (or $2.4 million).

The second issue is whether Greg, Testator's son, is a pretermitted child because Testator did not provide for him in either will. Greg does not take as a pretermitted child. In general, a child is pretermitted if he is born or adopted after execution of the will. Here, Greg is 30 years old and therefore he was alive when both wills were executed. Thus, he does not qualify as a pretermitted child and does not partake in Testator's estate.

QUESTION 24

In 1995, Testator, age 85, executed a will in the presence of two witnesses. Immediately before signing the document, Testator's attorney asked Testator if she declared the instrument to be her will. Testator responded: "You bet it is. I want Charity to have everything. My family has enough." Then the attorney had Testator sign the document on the line provided for her signature. The two witnesses signed immediately below Testator's signature without any further direction or comment from Testator.

When Testator executed this will, she was suffering from cancer and her medications made it very difficult for her to remember facts. For example, when she executed her will she knew, correctly, that her estate was worth $500,000 and that she had previously made large gifts to her child and some of her grandchildren. However, she could neither remember the name of her stockbroker nor recount the names of her stocks under her stockbroker's management. Also, she had no difficulty correctly naming her child and all of her grand-children, but she could not recall that she had a great-grandchild. She also knew she owned both a home and a condominium but could not recall the precise street address for either residence.

Testator died in 2002 survived by her only child, Mary, and by three grandchildren and one great-grandchild, all of whom are descendants of Mary. Testator's will, which devised her entire estate to Charity, was timely offered for probate by Bank, the executor named in the will. Mary and one of her children, Grandchild, have initiated a timely contest of the will.

Governing state law provides that a will is properly executed if the testator signs the will in the presence of two witnesses after having (a) declared the instrument to be her will and (b) requested the witnesses to act in such capacity.

1.   Do Mary and Grandchild each have standing to contest Testator's will? Explain.

2.   On what theory or theories, other than undue influence, might a person with standing contest Testator's will; what defenses might Bank, as executor, assert; and what is the likely outcome? Explain.

ANSWER TO QUESTION 24

1.   Mary has standing to contest the will but Grandchild does not. The issue is who qualifies as an interested party in a will contest. In Illinois, only an interested party has standing to contest a will. An interested party is anyone who would be adversely affected by the will's admission to probate, *e.g.*, intestate heirs and legatees under an earlier will. Here, if Testator had died intestate, her only heir would be her daughter Mary, because in Illinois if a Testator is not survived by a spouse, her entire estate passes to her descendants per stirpes. Because Mary is alive, Grandchild would not be considered an intestate heir, and because there is no prior will naming her as lega-tee, she has no standing to contest the will.

2.   The will can be contested on grounds of improper execution and lack of testamentary capacity. However, Bank is likely to prevail in its defenses so the will should be admitted to probate. The issue is on what grounds a will contest can be based under these facts.

Improper execution: The will contestants can argue that the will is invalid because it was im-properly executed. A will is improperly executed if it does not meet the state's requirements for due execution. Here, the state requires that a will be: (i) signed by the testator, (ii) in the presence of two witnesses, after the testator (iii) declares the instrument to be her will and (iv) requests the witnesses to act in such capacity. Here, Testator signed the will before two witnesses and de-clared the instrument to be her will in response to the attorney's question as to whether she declared it to be her will. However, the facts state that the witnesses signed without any direction to do so from Testator, implying that she did not meet the fourth requirement. However, Bank can argue that Testator did in fact ask the witnesses to sign in such capacity because they were present at the will's execution and knew that they were to sign the will. Therefore, this requirement is probably met and this argument will fail.

Lack of testamentary capacity: The will contestants can allege that Testator lacked testamentary capacity at the time the will was executed. To establish lack of testamentary capacity, the will contestants must establish that at the time the will was executed the testator did not: (i) understand the nature of her act, (ii) know the nature and character of her property, (iii) know the objects of her bounty, and (iv) dispose of her property according to her own plan. Here, whether Testator had the required testamentary capacity when she executed her will is questionable. It is clear that Testator understood that she was executing her will and appears to have disposed of her property according to her own wishes ("I want Charity to have everything"). However, the contestants will argue that she did not know the nature and character of her property or the objects of her bounty. Specifically, the facts indicate that due to her cancer medication she had trouble remembering certain facts, particularly the name of her stockbroker, the names of the stocks he managed, and that she had a great-grandchild. Additionally, she was unable to remember the addresses for her home and condominium. However, Bank can counter that although she may not have been able to recall all facts, she nevertheless had an idea of what she owned and to whom she was related. Testator was in fact aware of the value of her estate and that she owned stocks, a home, and a condominium. The fact that she did not remember the names of the stocks or her addresses is not sufficient to establish lack of testamentary capacity under these facts. Therefore, this argument will also fail and the will should be admitted to probate.

QUESTION 25

Decedent and his only child, Clara, died as the result of an accident when Clara's car was struck from the rear by a truck. Clara was driving and Decedent was riding in the back seat directly behind her. The emergency medical team that arrived at the accident scene found no evidence that either of them was alive. The emergency room physician examined their bodies as they were being removed from the ambulance. She first pronounced Decedent dead and then pronounced Clara dead.

Clara was survived by her spouse, Son-in-Law, who was named as the sole beneficiary of her estate under her duly probated will. Clara had no descendants.

Decedent died intestate leaving an estate of approximately $300,000. Decedent left no surviving spouse. Decedent's parents had predeceased him by many years. Decedent's closest surviving relatives are:

1.   A brother, Brother;

2.   A half-sister, Half-Sister, who is related to Decedent through a common mother;

3.   An adopted sister, Adopted-Sister, who was adopted by Decedent's parents; and

4.   His paternal grandfather, Gramps.

Three years before Decedent died, he gave Brother a check for $90,000 to enable Brother to buy a new home.

Among Son-in-Law, Brother, Half-Sister, Adopted-Sister, and Gramps, who will share in Decedent's estate, and what is the value of the share each will receive? Explain.

ANSWER TO QUESTION 25

Brother, Half-Sister, and Adopted-Sister will each take an equal share of Decedent's estate; Son-in-law and Gramps will take nothing.

When a decedent dies without a will, his estate is distributed through the laws of intestacy. Here, decedent had no will, so the intestacy statutes will apply.

Son-in-Law will not take any of Decedent's estate. At issue is whether Clara survived Decedent. Under the Illinois intestacy statute, when a decedent dies without a spouse, his children take his entire estate if they survive him. Here, Decedent died without a spouse and his only child, Clara, died in the same accident in which he died. The facts do not state whether Clara survived Decedent. The emergency medical team at the scene found no evidence that either was alive when they arrived. Decedent was officially declared dead first by the emergency room doctor, but that does not mean that he actually died first. Nothing else in the facts indicates the order of death, so we will assume that the two died simultaneously. When, as here, title to property depends on the order of death and there is no sufficient evidence that the persons have died otherwise than simultaneously, the property of each person will be distributed as if he survived (the Uniform Simultaneous Death Act rule). Thus, here, Decedent will be treated as having survived Clara. Because Clara is treated as predeceasing her father, Clara's estate would not take anything from Decedent's estate. Therefore, none of Decedent's estate would pass to Son-in-Law through Clara's will. (If evidence had shown that Clara died anytime after her father, she would inherit Decedent's estate, and then it would pass by will to Son-in-Law.)

Brother, Half-Sister, and Adopted-Sister will share equally in Decedent's estate. At issue is who inherits a decedent's estate when there is no surviving spouse or issue. Under the Illinois intestacy statute, if a decedent dies without spouse or issue, his estate passes equally to his surviving parents and siblings. Here, Decedent was survived by three siblings: Brother, Half-Sister, and Adopted-Sister. Siblings of the half-blood and adopted siblings are each treated like siblings of the whole blood, so Brother, Half-Sister, and Adopted-Sister each will share equally in Decedent's estate. Although Gramps also survived Decedent, he takes nothing under the statute because there are siblings alive to take.

The last issue to address is whether the $90,000 that Decedent gave to Brother three years ago constitutes an advancement on his inheritance, which would be included in Decedent's estate (effectively increasing the estate to around $390,000) and treated as already having been paid to Brother. At common law, whenever a parent gave his child a substantial gift, it was treated as an advancement, under the presumption that the parent would want to treat all of his children equally. However, Illinois and most other states have abandoned the common law rule and treat a substantial lifetime gift as an advancement only if it is made to a descendant and the donor or donee acknowledged in writing that the gift was an advancement. Brother is not a descendant of Decedent and there is no written acknowledgment here. Thus, the $90,000 will not be treated as an advancement—it will not be added into decedent's estate and will not be deducted from Brother's share of the estate. As a result, Brother, Half-Sister, and Adopted-Sister each will take about $100,000.

QUESTION 26

In 1991, Testator validly executed a typewritten will. Its dispositive provision provided that:

1.   I give $10,000 to Cousin.

2.   I give Blackacre, my family home, to Sister.

3.   I give the residue of my estate to University, my alma mater.

Three months after executing this will, Testator, desiring to increase the bequest to Cousin, scratched out Item 1 in its entirety and immediately above it wrote in by hand: *"I give $100,000 to Cousin."* This handwritten $100,000 bequest was not witnessed.

In 1994, Testator sold Blackacre, the family home, and reinvested the entire sales proceeds in Whiteacre, which became Testator's new family home.

In 1994, one month after buying Whiteacre and following a heated argument with Cousin, Testator validly executed two copies of a new typewritten will that left his entire estate to University. Testator then put both executed copies of the 1994 will in his safe deposit box, where the 1991 will was also located.

In 1999, Testator and Cousin reconciled. Immediately thereafter, Testator went to the safe deposit box and removed one of the executed copies of the 1994 will. In the course of reviewing it, Testator had second thoughts about leaving nothing to Cousin. However, rather than executing a new will, he tore up that copy of the 1994 will in the presence of his neighbor and stated: "I feel better now. Cousin is taken care of."

Last year, Testator, a domiciliary of State A, died leaving a substantial estate, including Whiteacre. Both the 1991 will with the handwritten changes and the remaining executed copy of the 1994 will were found in Testator's safe deposit box.

Both Cousin and Sister survived Testator. Under State A intestacy law, Sister would be Testator's only heir. State A also has a statute providing: "The revocation of a will that revoked an earlier will revives the earlier will in the absence of a contrary intention." State A does not permit holographic wills.

What, if anything, are Cousin and Sister entitled to receive from Testator's estate? Explain.

ANSWER TO QUESTION 26

Under the 1991 will, Cousin is entitled to $10,000, Sister is not entitled to anything, and University is entitled to the residue of Testator's estate, including Whiteacre.

The first issue is whether Testator left a valid will. A will may be revoked or altered by a subsequently written will. If the later will does not expressly revoke the earlier will, the two instruments are read together, and the later will revokes the earlier will to the extent of any inconsistent provisions. In this case, it is not clear whether Testator's 1994 will expressly revoked his 1991 will. However, the 1994 will was wholly inconsistent with the 1991 will in that it left his entire estate to University. Therefore, the 1994 will revoked the 1991 will.

In 1999, Testator also revoked his 1994 will. A will may be revoked by performing an act (*e.g.*, burning, tearing, or canceling) upon it with the intent to revoke. An act of revocation on an executed copy of a will revokes all other executed copies. In this case, Testator tore up an executed copy of his 1991 will. This act effectively revoked the other copy of the 1994 will. Therefore, it appears that both wills were validly revoked.

In Illinois and most states, a will, once revoked, is not revived unless it is reexecuted or republished by codicil. However, State A holds that "revocation of a will that revoked an earlier will revives the earlier will in the absence of a contrary intention." In this case, there is no evidence of Testator's contrary intent. In fact, Testator expressed his satisfaction that Cousin would be "taken care of" after he tore up a copy of his 1994 will, implying that he thought the 1991 will would be effective. Therefore, the 1991 will is revived and should be probated.

The next issue is whether Testator's handwritten changes to his 1991 will are valid. Most states permit partial, as well as total, revocation by physical act. In Illinois, however, a will cannot be partially revoked by physical act; the deletion is disregarded. In this case, if State A law is similar to Illinois law, Testator's deletion will be disregarded and Cousin will be entitled to $10,000.

Even if State A follows the majority rule, in which case the $10,000 bequest to Cousin was validly revoked, the bequest could be saved by the doctrine of dependent relative revocation ("DRR"). Under this doctrine, a court may disregard a revocation if (i) it determines that the act of revocation was premised on a mistaken belief that another disposition of the property was valid, and (ii) the disposition that results from disregarding the revocation comes closer to what the testator tried (but failed) to do than would an intestate distribution. In this case, it seems clear that Testator would not have canceled the $10,000 bequest except for the belief that the $100,000 bequest was valid. Due to the fact that State A does not recognize holographic (handwritten) wills, the $100,000 bequest is invalid. Because Testator was attempting to increase Cousin's gift, application of DRR would come closer to Testator's intent than would an intestate distribution, which would leave Cousin with nothing because, according to the facts, Cousin is not an heir of Testator. Therefore, Cousin is entitled to $10,000.

The next issue is whether Sister has a claim to Whiteacre. Under the doctrine of ademption, when specifically bequeathed property is not in the testator's estate at death (*e.g.*, it was destroyed, lost, or sold), the bequest is adeemed; *i.e.*, it fails. A specific bequest is a gift of particularly designated property. In this case, ademption applies because Testator did not own Blackacre at his death. Sister could argue that Testator intended to bequeath her his "family home," and that she is therefore entitled to Whiteacre, which was Testator's family home at his death. Generally, the testator's intent is irrelevant and ademption is based solely on whether the particularly designated property was part of the testator's estate at his death. Illinois courts have tempered this doctrine by requiring some act by the testator from which his intent to revoke the gift may be inferred. Under either approach, Sister's argument would fail because Testator sold Blackacre before his death and failed to change his will. Therefore, Sister has no claim to Whiteacre and is not entitled to any part of Testator's estate.

QUESTION 27

Ten years ago, Testator purchased an insurance policy on his life from Insurer. The policy provided that Insurer would pay the proceeds only to the person named on a beneficiary

form filed with Insurer. Testator filed such a form with Insurer, naming his son Sam as the sole beneficiary.

A year later, Testator, concerned about his failing physical health, opened Account #1 at Bank in the name of "Testator and Sam" as joint tenants with right of survivorship, not as tenants in common. Testator thereafter gave Sam checks that would enable him to withdraw funds from Account #1. Testator was the only person who deposited funds into Account #1, and he received all statements relating to it.

Five years ago, Testator duly executed a will containing the following dispositive clauses:

1. I give the proceeds of my Insurer life insurance policy to my daughter, Doris.

2. I give Account #1 at Bank to my daughter, Doris.

3. I give the balance of my estate to the children of my son Sam, to be divided equally among them.

Three months ago, Testator died and his will was duly probated. Testator was survived by Sam, Doris, and one of Sam's three children. Two of Sam's children predeceased Testator. One of the predeceased children, Ann, died seven years ago, and the other, Bill, died two years ago. Ann had a child who survived Testator, and Bill had a child who survived Testator.

Testator was a domiciliary of State A. State A law provides that, "if a beneficiary who is a descendant of the testator predeceases the testator, the beneficiary's surviving issue take the share the deceased beneficiary would have taken had the beneficiary survived."

To whom should the life insurance proceeds, Account #1, and the balance of Testator's estate be distributed? Explain.

ANSWER TO QUESTION 27

Life insurance proceeds: The life insurance proceeds should be distributed to Sam. The issue is whether an insured can change a life insurance beneficiary designation by will.

A will can only dispose of property owned by the decedent at death. Nonprobate assets, which are interests that pass at death other than by will or intestacy, cannot be disposed of by will. Life insurance proceeds are nonprobate assets that are payable to the beneficiary designated by the insured in his contract with the life insurance company. Because payment of the proceeds is governed by this contract, the beneficiary can be changed only by complying with the terms of the policy governing beneficiary designations. Here, Sam is the sole beneficiary named in Testator's life insurance policy with Insurer. Moreover, the policy provides that the proceeds will be paid "only to the person named on a beneficiary form filed with Insurer." Thus, the will provision changing the beneficiary of the policy to Doris is ineffective and Sam takes the insurance proceeds.

Account #1: Account #1 should probably be distributed to Sam. The issue is whether a joint tenant who contributed all of the funds deposited in a joint tenancy bank account retains the right to bequeath the account to an individual who is not the surviving joint tenant.

In Illinois, the deposit of money in a bank account naming two persons as joint tenants with right of survivorship gives the survivor of the joint account the absolute right to all of the money; the account *cannot* be bequeathed by will. Here, Testator's attempt to bequeath the account by will to Doris is invalid. Thus, Sam, as the surviving joint tenant, is entitled to Account #1.

Balance of Testator's estate: The balance of Testator's estate should be distributed one-third each to Sam's surviving child, Ann's child, and Bill's child. The issue is whether State A's anti-lapse statute applies to class members who predecease the testator or die before the execution of the will.

Generally, if a will beneficiary dies during the testator's lifetime, the gift to him lapses (*i.e.,* it fails). However, State A has an anti-lapse statute that operates to save the gift if the deceased beneficiary (i) was a descendant of the testator, (ii) left issue who survived the testator, and (iii) would have taken a share of the testator's estate had the beneficiary survived. In Illinois, the anti-lapse statute also applies to void gifts—although a gift is generally void if made to a beneficiary who was dead at the time of the will's execution, the gift may be saved if the deceased beneficiary falls within the scope of the state's anti-lapse statute. Moreover, if the will makes a gift to a class of beneficiaries and a class member dies during the testator's lifetime, the surviving class members take unless the deceased beneficiary falls within the scope of the state's anti-lapse statute, in which case his issue take by substitution.

Here, Testator's will makes a class gift to "the children of my son, Sam." Because one of Sam's children survived Testator, that child will take a share of the balance of the estate. Sam's other two children, Ann and Bill, predeceased the testator so their gifts lapse. Although Ann's gift was void because she died before the execution of the will, her child will take because Ann falls within the scope of State A's anti-lapse statute: Ann (i) was a descendant of Testator, (ii) left a child who survived Testator, and (iii) would have taken a share of Testator's estate had she survived. Bill also falls within the scope of the anti-lapse statute so Bill's child is entitled to a share of the balance of the estate. Because the will provides that the shares should be "divided equally among them," Sam's surviving child, Ann's child, and Bill's child will each take a one-third share of the balance of Testator's estate.

QUESTION 28

Dorothy had three children, Abel, Brandon, and Carrie. Abel had two children, Grandchild 1 and Grandchild 2; Brandon had three children, Grandchild 3, Grandchild 4, and Grandchild 5; and Carrie had one child, Grandchild 6.

Following the deaths of all three of her children, Dorothy was judicially appointed the guardian of all six grandchildren. Dorothy raised all of the grandchildren in her home and loved them all equally.

Five years ago, Dorothy gave $60,000 to Grandchild 6 to help Grandchild 6 buy a new home. The only statement Dorothy ever made regarding this payment was a contemporaneous statement to Grandchild 6: "This is for you because I love you." Dorothy made no other transfers to her grandchildren.

One year ago, Dorothy executed a valid will providing: "I give my entire estate to my heirs, said heirs to take the same shares thereof that they would have taken had I died intestate."

Three months ago, Dorothy was visiting Grandchild 1's home. While Dorothy was working in the front yard, Grandchild 1 backed a car out of the garage and, inadvertently, albeit negligently, struck Dorothy. Dorothy later died from the injuries.

Dorothy's only survivors are all six grandchildren and one great-grandchild, who is a child of Grandchild 1. Dorothy left a probate estate of $120,000.

To whom should Dorothy's $120,000 probate estate be distributed, and what is the amount of each person's share? Explain.

ANSWER TO QUESTION 28

Dorothy's probate estate should be distributed one-sixth each to Grandchildren 1 and 2; one-ninth each to Grandchildren 3, 4, and 5; and one-third to Grandchild 6; Dorothy's great-grandchild will take nothing.

Advancement: The first issue is whether the $60,000 lifetime gift to Grandchild 6 constitutes an advancement on Grandchild 6's inheritance, which would be included in Dorothy's estate (effectively increasing the estate to $180,000) and treated as already having been paid to Grandchild 6.

At common law, whenever a parent gave his child a substantial gift, it was treated as an advancement, under the presumption that the parent would want to treat all of his children equally. However, Illinois and most states have abandoned the common law rule and treat a substantial lifetime gift made to any heir as an advancement only if the donor or donee acknowledged *in writing* that the gift was an advancement. Here, there is no written acknowledgment, only a contemporaneous statement that the gift was made out of Dorothy's love for Grandchild 6. Thus, the $60,000 will not be treated as an advancement—it will not be added into Dorothy's estate and will not be deducted from Grandchild 6's share of the estate.

Slayer statute: The second issue is whether Grandchild 1 forfeited any interest in Dorothy's estate by negligently causing Dorothy's death.

In Illinois, a person who *intentionally and unjustifiably* causes the death of another forfeits any property, benefit, or other interest that passes by reason of that death, whether as heir, legatee, beneficiary, or in any other capacity. The property, benefit, or other interest passes as if the person causing the death predeceased the decedent. A conviction of murder in any degree is conclusive proof of the killing. Here, the facts state that Grandchild 1 acted inadvertently and negligently in causing Dorothy's death. Thus, Grandchild 1 would not be barred by Illinois's slayer statute from sharing in Dorothy's estate.

Amount of shares: Assuming that both Grandchild 1 and Grandchild 6 are entitled to share in Dorothy's estate, Grandchildren 1 and 2 will each take a one-sixth share; Grandchildren 3, 4, and 5 will each take a one-ninth share; and Grandchild 6 will take a one-third share.

Generally, a decedent's probate estate is distributed according to the provisions of her will. Here, however, Dorothy directed that her estate be distributed according to the laws of intestacy. Illinois provides for a *strict per stirpes* distribution, under which the stirpital shares are always divided at the first generational level, regardless of whether there are any living takers at that level. Each living child takes a share, and the share of each deceased child who left descendants passes to his descendants. Here, Dorothy's estate would initially be divided into three equal shares, but because all three of Dorothy's children predeceased her, the one-third shares pass by representation to the grandchildren. Thus, the one-third share that Abel would have inherited had he survived Dorothy passes by representation to his children, Grandchild 1 and Grandchild 2 (one-sixth each); Brandon's one-third share passes in equal shares to Grandchild 3, Grandchild 4, and Grandchild 5 (one-ninth each); and Carrie's one-third share passes to Grandchild 6.

QUESTION 29

In 1995, Husband and Wife duly executed a joint will that provided in relevant part:

> Each of us agrees that, when one of us dies, all of our property shall be distributed to the survivor. Furthermore, upon the death of the survivor we agree that: (1) $1,000 shall be distributed to the person who is then the pastor of the First Avenue Church; (2) $1,000 shall be distributed to the person named in a memorandum that the survivor shall leave in our safe deposit box at the Main Street Bank; and (3) at the survivor's death, the remainder of the survivor's property, however acquired, shall be distributed to our child, Child.

When this joint will was executed, George was the pastor of the First Avenue Church.

In 2000, Husband died. His estate of $150,000 was distributed to Wife pursuant to the joint will.

In 2001, Wife inherited $200,000 from her sister.

In 2002, Wife duly executed a new will providing in relevant part:

> Upon my death I give: (1) $1,000 to the person who is then the pastor of the First Avenue Church; (2) $1,000 to the person named in a memorandum to be left in my safe deposit box; (3) $100,000 to my child, Child; and (4) the balance of my estate to my boyfriend, John, who has provided me with loving companionship since my late husband died.

In late 2003, Wife died leaving an estate valued at $400,000. A memorandum, dated February 2, 2003, and signed by Wife, was found in Wife's safe deposit box directing that $1,000 be distributed to her friend, Robin. Wife was survived by John, Robin, Child, George, and Ted, who had been appointed pastor of the First Avenue Church one week before Wife died. Wife's 2002 will was duly admitted to probate.

To whom should Wife's estate be distributed? Explain.

ANSWER TO QUESTION 29

Wife's estate should be distributed as follows: $1,000 to Ted and the residue to Child.

Contractual will: The first issue is whether the 1995 joint will is contractual. If a will is contractual, the contract is that the survivor shall not revoke the will after the death of the first to die. Contractual wills are recognized in Illinois if the contract is proven by clear and convincing evidence. A court will look to the will itself, as well as to extrinsic evidence, to determine whether such clear and convincing evidence exists.

Here, Husband and Wife had a joint will (*i.e.*, the will of two or more persons executed on the same piece of paper). This alone does not give rise to a presumption that the wills were contractual. However, Illinois courts have recognized five common characteristics of contractual wills: (i) the will is labeled "joint and mutual"; (ii) the will makes reciprocal provisions (*i.e.*, leaves entire estate to the other); (iii) the will disposes of all of the testators' property; (iv) the will makes a uniform disposition upon the death of the survivor; and (v) plural possessive pronouns are used throughout the will. If all or most of these factors are present, the court is likely to rule that the will is contractual. On the other hand, if most of the factors are absent, the court is likely to rule that the surviving party is free to revoke the will and execute a new will.

Here, there is no evidence that the 1995 joint will was labeled "joint and mutual." However, the will leaves the entire estate of the first to die to the survivor, disposes of all of Husband and Wife's property, contains a common dispositive scheme ($1,000 each to pastor and person named in memorandum, residuary to Child), and contains plural possessive pronouns ("we" and "our") throughout. Moreover, language in the will—"[e]ach of us agrees that," "we agree that"—indicates that there is an agreement to dispose of the property in a certain way. Thus, a court would likely determine that the joint will is contractual. Although either party may revoke a contractual will during the joint testators' lifetimes (with notice), the contract becomes irrevocable upon the first party's death. Here, the 1995 contract became irrevocable in 2000 when Husband died. Consequently, Wife breached the contract by executing a new will two years later. Wife may argue that she did not breach the contract with respect to the $200,000 she inherited from her sister after Husband's death. However, the contract was that the survivor distribute on her death "the remainder of [her] property, ***however acquired.***"

Wife's breach of contract does not, however, invalidate her 2002 will, which must be probated because it was Wife's last will and it was validly executed. However, the beneficiaries of the 1995 joint will can now bring an action to impress a constructive trust against the beneficiaries of the 2002 will because execution of the second will was in breach of Wife's contract with Husband. The sole duty of the constructive trustees (*i.e.*, the beneficiaries of the 2002 will) is to convey the property to the contract beneficiaries. Thus, Child, and not John, is entitled to the remainder.

$1,000 bequest to pastor: The next issue is the validity of the $1,000 bequest to "the pastor of the First Avenue Church." Under the acts of independent significance doctrine, the fact that the identification of a beneficiary will be determined by some future unattested act does not invalidate the gift as long as the act has some lifetime significance other than providing for the testamentary gift. Here, the identity of "the pastor of the First Avenue Church" has significance apart from the $1,000 bequest because the church is unlikely to select a pastor simply based on the fact that the one chosen will receive $1,000 from Husband and Wife's estate. Thus, the doctrine applies and Ted, the current pastor of the First Avenue Church, takes the $1,000.

Moreover, a will takes effect only upon the death of the testator. Thus, a will "speaks at the time of death," and operates upon circumstances and properties as they exist at the time of the testator's death. Here, Ted is the only person who fits the description "the pastor of the First Avenue Church" at Wife's death. Therefore, under either the acts of independent significance doctrine or the general rule of construction of a will, Ted, and not George, takes the $1,000.

Memorandum: The final issue is whether the provision regarding the $1,000 bequest "to the person named in a memorandum" is valid and enforceable. In Illinois, an extrinsic document may be incorporated into a will by reference so that it is considered part of the will if: (i) the document was in existence at the time the will was executed; (ii) the will refers to the document as being in existence; and (iii) the language of the will reasonably identifies the document. Here, it is clear that the memorandum dated February 2, 2003, naming Robin as the recipient of the $1,000 bequest was *not* in existence at the time either the 1995 will or the 2002 will was executed. Thus, the memorandum cannot be incorporated by reference.

Note that the doctrine of acts of independent significance is of no help in saving the gift to Robin because the memorandum appears to have no nontestamentary purpose. Thus, the $1,000 bequest fails and passes to the residuary estate, and thus to Child.

QUESTION 30

In 2000, Testator executed a valid will. The will provided:

1. I give my 100 shares of stock in XYZ Company to Brother.

2. I give $3,000 to Sister.

3. I give $5,000 to Uncle.

4. I give $10,000 to Cousin.

5. I give the residue of my estate to my alma mater, Polytech.

In 2001, XYZ Company issued its annual dividend in stock. For each 100 shares held, the dividend was six shares of XYZ stock.

In 2002, Testator gave $5,000 to Uncle on Uncle's birthday.

In 2005, Testator died, survived by Brother, Sister, Uncle, and Cousin. Testator's estate consists of the following assets: 106 shares of XYZ Company stock (worth $1 per share) and $9,000. Sister made a valid disclaimer of her interest in Testator's estate.

How should Testator's estate be distributed? Explain.

ANSWER TO QUESTION 30

Testator's estate should be distributed as follows: 100 shares of XYZ Company ("XYZ") stock to Brother, $3,000 plus two shares of XYZ stock to Uncle, and $6,000 plus four shares of XYZ stock to Cousin; Sister and Polytech take nothing.

Stock dividends: The first issue is whether Brother is entitled to the additional shares produced by a stock dividend issued before Testator's death. Illinois follows the common law rule, under which a specific bequest of stock (*e.g., my* 100 shares) includes any additional shares produced by a stock split, but does not include shares produced by a stock dividend. Thus, Brother is entitled only to 100 shares of XYZ stock; the other six shares fall into the residuary as undisposed-of property.

Disclaimer: The second issue is the effect of Sister's disclaimer. A beneficiary may disclaim an interest that otherwise would pass to her from the decedent's estate. Such an interest passes as though the disclaimant predeceased the decedent. Nearly all states have anti-lapse statutes that operate to save the gift if the predeceasing beneficiary was in a specified degree of relationship to the testator and left descendants who survived the testator. In Illinois, the anti-lapse statute applies only when the predeceasing beneficiary is a descendant of the testator. Here, Sister validly disclaimed her interest in Testator's estate. However, because Sister is not Testator's descendant, the anti-lapse statute does not apply and her gift lapses (*i.e.,* fails) and falls into the residuary.

Satisfaction: The next issue is whether the $5,000 lifetime gift to Uncle satisfies his bequest. In Illinois, a lifetime gift to a child is presumptively in satisfaction of the prior legacy. By contrast, a lifetime gift to anyone other than a child does not trigger the presumption of satisfaction; the gift will be deemed in satisfaction of the legacy only if the testator intended the gift to be in satisfaction. Here, Uncle is not Testator's child and thus the presumption of satisfaction does not apply. Moreover, there is no evidence that Testator intended the birthday gift to be in satisfaction of Uncle's bequest. Thus, Uncle's bequest was not satisfied.

Abatement: The final issue is how the remaining $9,000 plus six shares of stock should be distributed. Abatement is the process of reducing testamentary gifts where estate assets are insufficient to satisfy all legacies and devises. The testator may set out an order of abatement in her will, but if she does not, in Illinois assets abate in the following order: (i) the residuary estate, (ii) general legacies, and (iii) specific devises. Within each category, legacies and devises abate pro rata, with no distinction between real and personal property in that category. Here, there are insufficient assets in the estate to satisfy all of the bequests in Testator's will. As discussed above, Brother should receive 100 shares of stock, which is a specific bequest and does not abate. The gifts of $5,000 to Uncle and $10,000 to Cousin are general bequests and abate pro rata (1:2 ratio). Thus, Uncle is entitled to $3,000 and Cousin is entitled to $6,000. The additional six shares of stock will be distributed in a like manner in payment of the general legacies: two to Uncle and four to Cousin. Because the residuary estate is exhausted after satisfying the specific and general gifts, Polytech receives nothing.

QUESTION 31

Six years ago, Testator retired from his work as a business executive. Testator continued to serve as a trustee of several nonprofit organizations and manage all of his own financial affairs. He maintained these activities until his death.

Five years ago, Testator hired a housekeeper, Harriet.

Four years ago, Harriet began to ask Testator to provide for her in his will. She also began to interfere with Testator's relationship with his daughter, Doris. When Doris called,

Harriet sometimes falsely told her that Testator was sleeping and could not talk on the phone. When Doris came to visit Testator, Harriet often stayed in the room to overhear their conversations. Harriet also made critical remarks about Doris to Testator and told him that Doris should visit him more regularly.

On a number of occasions, Harriet threatened to quit if Testator did not provide for her in his will. These threats made Testator fearful, particularly during the last year of his life when his declining health made him increasingly dependent on Harriet.

Six months ago, Harriet again threatened to quit if Testator did not provide for her in his will and told Testator that he should see her attorney. Testator told Harriet: "Stop bugging me. I'll see my own attorney."

Three months ago, Testator executed a will in accordance with the applicable statute of wills. The will was drafted by Testator's attorney pursuant to Testator's handwritten instructions.

The will specified as follows:

"I leave my estate in equal shares to my housekeeper, Harriet, and my daughter, Doris."

This is the only will Testator ever executed.

Testator recently died at age 78. Testator left a substantial estate.

Both Harriet and Doris survived Testator. Testator was also survived by a son (Sam), a grandchild (Ella), who was the child of Doris, and a grandchild (Fred), who was the child of Testator's son, Bob. Both Testator's spouse and Bob predeceased Testator. Testator and Sam had been estranged for several years prior to the time of Testator's death.

1. Is the will invalid in whole or in part? Explain.

2. Assuming the will is invalid in whole, to whom and in what shares should Testator's estate be distributed? Explain.

3. Assuming the will is invalid in part, to whom and in what shares should Testator's estate be distributed? Explain.

ANSWER TO QUESTION 31

1. The will is invalid, but whether it is wholly or partially invalid is unclear.

The first issue is whether the will is a product of undue influence. A will (or a gift in a will) is invalid if it is obtained through the exercise of undue influence. To establish undue influence, the contestants, who have the burden of proof, must establish that: (i) influence was exerted on the testator, (ii) the effect of the influence was to overpower the mind and free will of the testator, and (iii) the product of the influence was a will that would not have been executed but for the influence. A presumption of undue influence arises when: (i) the will gives a substantial benefit to a party who stood in a fiduciary or confidential relationship with the testator, (ii) the testator was in a dependent situation in which the party was in a dominant role, (iii) the testator reposed trust and confidence in the party, and (iv) the party was instrumental in preparing or procuring the will. Once these elements appear, the burden shifts to the proponent of the will to prove by clear and convincing evidence that it was not induced by her undue influence.

Here, although Harriet was Testator's housekeeper and he became "increasingly dependent on" her, it is unclear whether this amounts to a confidential relationship. Also, Harriet probably did not "procure" the will because Testator had his own attorney draft it. Thus, the contestants will likely bear the burden of establishing undue influence. They will argue that Harriet exerted influence over Testator by criticizing and limiting his contacts with his daughter, Doris. More-over, although Testator continued to serve as a trustee and manage his own financial affairs, Harriet's threats of quitting to an increasingly dependent Testator overpowered his mind and free will in that he became "fearful." This fear led to Testator's finally bequeathing one-half of his estate to Harriet. Thus, the contestants would likely be successful in challenging the will on grounds of undue influence.

The second issue is whether the will is wholly or partially invalid. The part of a will that is affected by undue influence is stricken, and the remainder of the will is allowed to stand if doing so does not defeat the testator's intent or destroy the testamentary scheme.

Here, it is unclear whether the entire will or only the bequest to Harriet was procured by undue influence. First, Testator had lived 78 years of his life without having executed a will; thus, he might not have executed a will in the absence of Harriet's undue influence, instead letting his estate pass by intestacy (see 2., infra). Second, although Sam might have been excluded from Testator's will due to their estranged relationship, the facts do not indicate there were problems with Bob's or either grandchild's relationship with Testator; thus, he might have bequeathed shares to them in the absence of Harriet's undue influence. Therefore, whether the court will invalidate the entire will or only the bequest to Harriet is unclear.

2.   If the will is wholly invalid, Testator's estate should be distributed in equal shares to Doris, Sam, and Fred. At issue is the distribution of a testator's estate when his will is denied probate.

Intestate succession is the statutory method of distributing assets that are not disposed of by will. If a decedent's will is denied probate (e.g., due to a successful will contest), his entire estate passes by intestacy. If there is no surviving spouse, the entire estate passes to the decedent's children and descendants of deceased children. In Illinois, the descendants take per stirpes; i.e., the property is divided into equal shares at the first generational level (regardless of whether there are any living takers), with the shares of each deceased child who left descendants passing to his descendants.

Here, if the will is wholly invalid, Testator's entire estate passes by intestacy. As Testator's spouse predeceased him, his entire estate passes to his descendants. Because Testator had three children, two of which survived him, his estate will be split into three equal shares. Doris and Sam will each take their share, and the share of Testator's deceased son Bob will pass to Bob's child, Fred. Ella takes nothing even though she is Testator's descendant because her mother, Doris, is alive to inherit.

3.   If the will is partially invalid, Testator's estate should be distributed all to Doris. At issue is the distribution of a lapsed residuary gift.

At common law, if a testator's residuary estate (*i.e.*, the portion of the estate that has not otherwise been particularly devised or bequeathed) is bequeathed to two or more beneficiaries and one of the beneficiaries' shares lapses (*i.e.*, fails), that share does not pass to the remaining beneficiaries, but instead "falls out of the will" and passes by intestacy. However, Illinois has replaced this rule by statute, under which the lapsed share passes to the other residuary beneficiaries in proportion to their interests in the residue.

Here, if only the bequest to Harriet is invalid, Doris still takes one-half of Testator's estate under his will. Harriet's one-half lapsed share will pass to the remaining beneficiary under the will, Doris, who would take the entire estate.

QUESTION 32

Tom Testator, age 37, lived in Jackson County, Illinois. Tom was divorced from his ex-wife, Elaine, and had two children, a son, Sam and a daughter, Diane.

In November 2006, he had Larry Lawyer draft a will for him. In the will, Tom Testator bequeathed (1) his home at 123 College Street to his nephew Neil; (2) all of his personal property, except his stamp collection and his baseball card collection, to his niece Nancy; (3) his stamp collection to his friend Frank; and (4) his baseball card collection to his brother Bob. His children had not talked to him in years so he did not want to leave anything to them.

Of sound mind and memory, Tom Testator signed the will and had it duly executed. The two witnesses to Tom's signature were his friend Frank and Larry Lawyer's assistant, Alice. They signed the will as well.

In April 2007, Tom Testator got into a fight with his brother Bob. Tom decided that his brother should no longer receive the baseball card collection. He used a black marker to cross out his brother's name in the will though he told no one and showed no one.

In November 2007, Tom Testator decided to sell his house at 123 College Street. He entered into a contract with Barbara Buyer. Barbara agreed to buy the house at 123 College Street for $200,000 with a closing date of January 15, 2008.

On December 31, 2007, Tom Testator died of a heart attack. Tom had no debts upon his death. His only assets were his house at 123 College Street, his stamp collection, and his baseball card collection. He was survived by Alice, Barbara Buyer, Bob, Diane, Elaine, Frank, Nancy, Neil, and Sam.

On January 15, 2008, Tom Testator's executor transferred the deed to 123 College Street to Barbara Buyer. Barbara Buyer wrote the estate a check for $200,000, which the executor is holding subject to your advice.

Assume the costs and expenses of probate are negligible.

1. Who should receive the $200,000 from Barbara Buyer? Explain.

2. Who should receive Tom Testator's stamp collection? Explain.

3. Who should receive Tom Testator's baseball card collection? Explain.

ANSWER TO QUESTION 32

1.   Neil should receive the $200,000 from Barbara Buyer ("Buyer"). The issue is whether a specific devisee is entitled to the proceeds left unpaid at the testator's death from the sale of specifically bequeathed property during the testator's lifetime.

Generally, if specifically bequeathed property is not owned by the testator at death, the gift adeems (*i.e.*, it fails). The doctrine of equitable conversion provides that when a seller enters into a specifically enforceable contract for the sale of real property, in equity the seller no longer owns real property (the land), but instead owns personal property (the right to the sale proceeds). Thus, if a testator enters into a contract for the sale of specifically bequeathed property and the contract is still executory (*i.e.*, has not been fully performed) at his death, ademption applies because the testator did not own the real property at his death. The purchaser would take the property and the sale proceeds would pass to the beneficiaries of the testator's personal property rather than to the specific devisee. However, an Illinois statute overturns application of equitable conversion in this situation. Instead, the specific devisee takes the testator's rights under the contract—*i.e.*, the right to the sale proceeds.

Here, Tom Testator ("Testator") specifically bequeathed his house at 123 College Street to Neil, and thereafter entered into a contract for its sale to Buyer. Because the closing had not yet taken place at the time of Testator's death, the contract remained executory. Under the Illinois statute, Neil takes Testator's rights under the contract. Thus, Neil takes the $200,000 from Buyer.

2.   Sam and Diane should receive Testator's stamp collection. The issue is whether an attesting witness can take a gift under a will.

In Illinois, a will must be witnessed by at least two witnesses. The fact that the will makes a gift to an attesting witness never results in denial of the will to probate. However, the bequest to the attesting witness is void unless: (i) the will was also witnessed by two disinterested witnesses (*i.e.*, the interested witness is "supernumerary"); or (ii) the beneficiary would have been entitled to a share of the estate if the will were not probated, in which case he takes the lesser of the bequest in the will or the share of the estate he would have taken if the will were not established. Here, there were only two witnesses to the will (Frank and Alice), so Frank is not a supernumerary witness. Moreover, Frank would not have shared in the estate if the will had been denied probate because he is not Testator's heir and there is no earlier will. Thus, Frank's gift is void.

Because there is no alternate distribution of Testator's stamp collection—Nancy was bequeathed all of Testator's personal property "except his stamp collection"—the gift lapses and passes as part of the residue. Testator's will, however, does not dispose of the residue and thus there is a partial intestacy. In Illinois, if the decedent leaves no surviving spouse, the entire intestate estate passes to the decedent's descendants, per stirpes. Here, Testator is survived by his *ex*-wife Elaine and two children, Sam and Diane. Thus, even though Testator did not want to leave anything to his children, Sam and Diane take equal shares of his stamp collection.

3.   Bob should receive Testator's baseball card collection. The issue is whether crossing out a beneficiary's name in a will effectively revokes the gift to that beneficiary.

A will can be revoked by physical act by burning, canceling, tearing, or obliterating it with the intent to revoke it. Most states permit partial revocations by a physical act of the testator, as by crossing out one clause in the will. However, in Illinois a will cannot be partially revoked by physical act; the deletion is disregarded. The only way that a will can be partially revoked in Illinois is by executing a codicil to the will.

Here, Testator intended to revoke the gift to Bob by crossing out Bob's name in the will with a black marker. However, the attempted partial revocation is ineffective in Illinois. Thus, Bob is entitled to the baseball card collection.